THE PHOENIX RETURNS

Aquarius Dawns ∞ Liberation Begins

By: Kristina Gale-Kumar

Cardinal Enterprises
Hawaii

This book may be purchased at your local bookstore or you may order it directly from Cardinal Enterprises at a cost of $10.95 plus $1.75 for postage (sea mail) or $3.75 for postage (air mail). Send check or money order to Cardinal Enterprises, P.O. Box 1363, Hilo, Hawaii 96721.

Published by Cardinal Enterprises, P.O. Box 1363, Hilo, Hawaii 96720.

ISBN 0-9611204-0-1

TABLE OF CONTENTS

DEDICATION

Dedicated to the ever-living Saint Dadaji (Sri Dilip Kumar Roy) and the ever-loving Ma (Smt. Indira Devi), and all other seekers of the Divine.

"To bring God down to the world on Earth we came
To change the earthly life to Life Divine...
A mutual debt binds man to the Supreme:
His nature we must put on as He put ours;
We are children of God and must be even as He:
His human portion, we must grow Divine.
Our life is a paradox with God for key...

"Nature shall live to manifest secret God,
The Spirit shall take up the human play,
This earthly life become the Life Divine...

"Oh, surely one day He shall come to our cry,
One day He shall create our life anew
And utter the magic formula of Peace
And bring perfection to the scheme of things.

"One day He shall descend to life and Earth...
And bring the Truth that sets the Spirit free,
The job that is the baptism of the soul,
The strength that is the outstretched arm of Love..."

—Sri Aurobindo

THE LEGEND OF THE PHOENIX BIRD AND THE END TIMES: A NEW BEGINNING

Phoenix: The World Book Encyclopedia and the American Heritage Dictionary explain "Phoenix" as follows:

> 1) According to Egyptian and Greek mythology, a bird representing the sun (Son?) that consumed itself by fire after living many, many years (hundreds according to some, thousands according to others), and then rose renewed from its ashes; a symbol of immortality and spiritual rebirth.
>
> 2) A person or thing of unsurpassed excellence or beauty; a paragon—model or **pattern** of excellence and perfection of a kind; a peerless example.[1]

Edgar Cayce—perhaps America's greatest psychic—on the meaning of the words: **Jesus** and **Christ**:

> "Jesus is the man—the activity, the mind, the relationships that He bore to others...
>
> "Ye are made strong-in body, in mind, in soul and purpose-by that power in Christ [by being God Incarnate]. The POWER, then, is in the Christ [God]. The PATTERN is in Jesus [the man]."[2]

What does the Phoenix bird have to do with Jesus Christ? As with the Phoenix, so with Jesus: He too rose from His own ashes in the tomb and overcame death, thereby becoming humankind's symbol of immortality and spiritual rebirth.

The Phoenix is the perfect symbol of our times, the End Times; a time when the world is consuming itself with the fires of hatred, war, divisiveness, discord, and strife, both figuratively and literally through nuclear proliferation and chemicalization. But take heart, for the Christ—"the divine manifestation of God who comes in the flesh to destroy incarnate error,"[3] what Eastern philosophy calls an Avatar—is coming again soon and will raise up from the ashes of this polluted, scorched, and beleaguered planet, a New World of Light, Love, Peace, Harmony and Unity.

What does this mean for us? Precisely this: we must prepare ourselves for this time of Tribulation/Purification by following the **Pattern** of excellence and perfection we see in the original

Phoenix—Jesus—"the highest human (physical) concept of the divine idea."[4]

This is the Golden Lining of the End Times—what the Hindus call the Kali Age, the Age of Chaos: no matter what wrongs we may have done, what sins we may have committed in thought, word or deed in the past, if we will truly repent and turn to the Lord and follow His example of Love, Compassion, Sharing, Caring, Giving and Forgiving, not only will our physical and material lives be improved, but we will also save our souls, and like the Phoenix, we will be reborn from the ashes of ignorance into the Light of Spiritual Truth and dwell in the ocean of God's Bliss.

As the Lord in Revelations states: "Behold, I make all things new."[5] So let us look forward to this New Beginning, for nothing and no one can keep the Sun (Son) from rising again and rejuvenating the world with His Light!

INTRODUCTION

GOD (G for Generating Principle—O for Organizing Principle—D for Destroying Principle)[1] is coming again soon! The purpose of this book is: 1-to announce the Good News of the imminent return of our Lord, 2-to show the "Oneness" of all religions, 3-to ring in the Age of Aquarius and the spreading of the Christ or Aquarian Consciousness, 4-to prove that the "End Times" and a New Beginning are upon us, and 5-to help people prepare for the above.

Today many people are already aware that we are living in the Last Days, those days just prior to our Lord's return and the ushering in of a New Era of Spirituality, of Peace, of Love, of Truth, of Brotherhood and Sisterhood for all humankind. If you are a Christian, you are awaiting the Second Coming of Christ; if a Jew—the Messiah; a Moslem—the Mahdi; a Buddhist—the Maitreya Buddha; a Hindu—Lord Kalki; an American Indian—the return of both the Pale Prophet or Lost White Brother **AND** the White Buffalo Cow Woman.

No matter which religion one studies, they all say the same thing: the Lord is coming soon! When one studies the prophecies of all the major religions of the world, one sees that all these prophecies are the same, and that almost all of them have been fulfilled, as this book will show. An example of a prophecy common to all major religions is that bizarre weather changes, increased earthquake activity, ecological disasters stemming from chemical pollutions, and social, political, and economic chaos bringing the world to the brink of catastrophe will immediately precede the Lord's coming. **But the proof of the imminent coming of the Lord is based not only on religious prophecies, but also on scientific, astrological, astronomical, political, historical, and current events,** all of which have been researched, explored and tied together in this book.

Further, it is not just the physical presence of our Lord on Earth that we are awaiting; we are also awaiting the birth of what has been called the "Christ Consciousness" or "Aquarian Consciousness" within us all, the unfolding of the Divine Spirit within and its manifestation without. For without this unfolding, without the birth of this new, greater, Divine Consciousness, mankind is doomed!

ix

As Sri Aurobindo, one of the greatest spiritual masters, explains:

> "Without an inner change man can no longer cope with the gigantic development of the outer life...If humanity is to survive, a radical transformation of human nature is indispensable...An evolution of consciousness is the central motive of terrestrial (earthly) existence...**A change of consciousness is the major fact of the next evolutionary transformation**...To be wholly...conscious of oneself and of all the truth of one's being is what is implied by the perfect emergence of the individual consciousness, and it is **that** towards which evolution tends. **All being is one,** and to be fully conscious means to be integrated with the consciousness of all..."[2]—or, in other words, to be One with All and, therefore, One with the Lord!

What do we mean by "the Oneness" of all religions? We mean just this: that God is One, no matter what different names one may give to Him, and that all religions spring from the same Source—the One God. Just as H_2O is called "water" in English, "aqua" in Spanish, "eau" in French, "pani" in Hindi, "jal" in Bengali, etc., the words are different but the substance is the same.

The religions of the world are like the spokes of a wheel, all leading to the same center—the One God. Whether you call this One God Christ, Jehovah, Allah, Om, Buddha, Krishna, The Great Spirit, or just Primal Energy makes no difference. They are all just different names for the same Source from which everything springs. Or as Mahatma Gandhi, the great spiritual/political leader of the Indian nation, once said, "Religions are different roads converging upon the same point. What does it matter that we take different roads so long as we reach the same goal?...The Bible is as much a book of religion with me as the *Gita* and the *Koran*."[3]

In English we have perhaps unwittingly used the Hindu word for God—**Om**—to describe God: **Om**-nipresent, **Om**-niscient, and **Om**-nipotent. Omnipresent means the presence of Om or God everywhere, or always-present; Omniscient means the knowledge of Om or God, or all-knowing; Omnipotent means the power of Om or God, or all-powerful. "Om" comes from Sanskrit, which is the oldest written language known to man and predates even Latin. The Latin word "Omni" means "All," indicating God, since God is All or Everything.

Throughout this book we will further explore and expand upon the similarities of the teachings and truths contained in the world's major religions, our purpose being to create more harmony, unity, and understanding between peoples of different religions, and to clear away a lot of confusion, misunderstanding, and misconceptions which people of differing faiths have about each other. Organized religion, instead of being the great uniter of mankind and the world, has often been the great divider of mankind and the world. To quote Sri Aurobindo:

> "This would not have been so if religion were the true and sufficient guide of the whole of human life...True religion is spiritual religion, it is a seeking after God, the opening of the deepest life of the soul to the **indwelling** Godhead, the eternal Omnipresence."[4]

As Lord Jesus Christ said, "The Kingdom of Heaven is within you."[5] Sri Aurobindo continues:

> "In spirituality, then, restored to its true sense, we must seek for the directing light and the harmonizing law ...Spirituality is something else than intellectuality; its appearance is the sign that a Power greater than the mind is striving to emerge in its turn...Spirituality is a progressive awakening to the inner reality of our being, to a spirit, self, soul which is other than our mind, life, and body. It is an inner aspiration to know, to enter into contact and union with the greater Reality beyond, which also pervades the universe and dwells in us, and, as a result of that aspiration, that contact and that union, a turning, a conversion, a birth into a new being..."[6]—or, in other words, to become a Gnostic Being, "Gnostic" meaning knowledge of God through direct, personal spiritual experience.

As Lord Jesus said, "Lest one be **born again** one cannot enter the Kingdom of God...[7] Repent! For the Kingdom of God is at hand!"[8] The Biblical word "repent" is translated from the Greek word "metanoia." The original New Testament was, according to Rev. C.F. Potter, written in Koine, which was a mixture of various languages of the region, mostly Greek, and was later translated into pure Greek.[9] "Metanoia" or "repent" means a complete change of mind, a total **turning** around and going in the opposite direction, or to "revolute," change everything, and with this changing or conversion, one is **"born again."** Isn't it interesting that the above words of Christ so closely parallel those of Sri Aurobindo, the great Indian master? This book will contain many more such parallels.

We stand on the threshold of a New Age, the Age of Aquarius, the Age of Enlightenment. Come! Join us! As St. Paul said:

"As God's partners we beg you not to toss aside this marvelous message of God's great kindness. For God says, 'Your cry came to me at a favourable time, when the doors of welcome were wide open. I helped you on a day when salvation was being offered.' Behold, **NOW** is the acceptable time; behold, **NOW** is the day of salvation!"[10]

★★★★★★★★★★★★ 1984 UPDATE ★★★★★★★★★★★★

In Revelations God reveals that at the time of the end of this Age of Chaos, the Divine Mother (or God as the Mother) would come to Earth for a period of 1260 days, would have 12 stars around her head and would be pursued by the "Red Dragon." (REV. 12) The above was prophesied 2000 years ago.

On June 24, 1981, on a mountainside behind the village of Medugorje, Yugoslavia, the Divine Mother started appearing to six children—four girls and two boys ages 10 to 17. According to eyewitnesses, which include Turks, Moslems, Communists and believers alike, miracles have accompanied these apparitions. For example, on August 2, 1981, " ... the people saw the sun begin to spin and move towards them as the earth began to darken ... "[1]—the exact same sign or miracle the Holy Mother gave on October 13, 1917 in Fatima, Portugal. Other miracles include 1) a blazing fire seen on the mountainside, yet when police rushed up, no sign of anything burning or burnt was found; 2) the word "MIR" or "PEACE" written across the sky in letters of light; and 3) a brilliant light appearing around a huge cement cross erected on the mountain peak—a light so brilliant that the cross was seen spinning in rainbows of light.[2]

Alarmed by the massive spiritual conversions these events have initiated, the communist authorities or "Red Dragon" have fenced off the mountain with barbed wire and have arrested people including the parish priest and the 6 children who, despite being severely threatened, refused to deny the Mother's appearances and, thus, were eventually released. Since then, the people have been forced to worship inside St. James parish where the Divine Mother, who calls Herself "The Queen of Peace" and who, according to the children, wears a crown of 12 stars, has been appearing to them daily for the past three years.

The Mother has told the children that, due to man's sin, the world is on the brink of a major catastrophe. The "chastisement" cannot be avoided, but its days

(continued on page 448)

xii

PART I

Prophetic Links

LORD BUDDHA - Circa 563 B.C. / LORD JESUS - Circa 7 B.C.

"Foolish to think that truth is in untruth, equally foolish that untruth is in truth—truth is always truth, untruth always untruth...Only suffering for the evil man—suffering now, suffering later, suffering in this world and the next. Happiness for the good man—happiness now, happiness later, happiness in this world and the next...

"Right views will be the torch to light his way. Right aspirations will be his guide. Right speech will be his dwelling-place on the road. His gait will be straight, for it is right behavior. His refreshments will be the right way of earning his livelihood. Right efforts will be his steps: right thoughts his breath; and right contemplation will give him the peace that follows in his footprints."

—Lord Buddha

"Blessed are those who mourn, for they shall be comforted. Blessed are the meek, for they shall inherit the earth. Blessed are those who hunger and thirst for righteousness, for they shall be satisfied. Blessed are the merciful, for they shall obtain mercy. Blessed are the pure in heart, for they shall see God. Blessed are the peacemakers, for they shall be called the children of God. Blessed are those who are persecuted for righteousness' sake, for theirs is the kingdom of heaven...

"Ask, and it will be given to you; seek, and you will find; knock, and the door shall be opened to you. For every one who asks receives, and he who seeks finds, and to him who knocks it will be opened...For there is nothing hid, except to be made manifest; nor is anything secret, except to come to light."

—Lord Jesus Christ

Chapter 1

WHY TODAY?

> "There are two states for man—the state in this world, and the state in the next; there is also a third state...intermediate between these two, which can be likened to a dream...while in the intermediate state, he foresees both the evils and the blessings that will yet come to him, as these are determined by his conduct (or karma), good or bad, upon the earth..."[1]

From the *Upanishads,* part of the *Vedas*—Hinduism's **and** humankind's oldest Scriptures

"It was such a beautiful day, I just had to go to the beach. So I jumped into the car for the ten minute drive, but I never made it...By the time I saw the other car coming, it was too late to do anything about it, **but pray.** I heard the sounds of brakes screeching and metal crunching, and then everything went black.

"The next thing I remember is feeling myself being drawn through this dark tunnel at incredible speed, kind of like I was falling down this deep well, and as I fell, all my cares and troubles seemed to melt away. There was no pain at all; just a feeling of warmth, of peace and calm and solitude. As I was falling, I could hear this beautiful music all around me, like bells tinkling or choirs humming. It was as if my being or soul was pulsating or vibrating with this music.

"At the end of this tunnel was this beautiful bright light. It was small at first, but got bigger and brighter as I moved toward it. I was drawn to it, like a magnet. Suddenly this white light was all around me, enveloping me, surrounding me with warmth and love. But it was more than just light; it was a **Being,** a Divine Presence with a definite personality. While in Its presence I felt totally accepted, loved and secure.

"Then the Being asked me a question: What had I done with my life to show Him, and was I ready to die? **Suddenly, I saw a panoramic view of my whole life**—all the things I had ever thought or said or done were there in full color—like a cinema show, but more real. It was as if the Being was helping me to judge myself and my life.

"Then it was as if nine-tenths of my brain was opened up and I was

1

privileged to see, hear and understand all knowledge; for a second, all the secrets of the ages and Universe, the meaning of Creation and life and death and its endless cycles were revealed to me.

"Next the Being showed me this beautiful place—it was like Heaven—with light and music everywhere. It was like a beautiful countryside or forest, and I was part of it with other people, too. No words can describe the beauty of this place or the love and warmth I felt being there.

"The Being asked me if I wanted to stay and I said, "Yes!" I never wanted to leave this place or His presence. But then He said to me that I couldn't stay here yet; that I still had a mission to accomplish, things to do for Him, and that if I really loved Him, I would go back and finish these deeds for Him.

"Suddenly, I was back in that tunnel and everything went black again. When I next awoke, I realized that my soul was once again in the prison of the body. I cried off and on for the next few weeks because I had to live in this world after seeing that one. But I knew what I now must do: 1) **LOVE** everyone the way He had loved me—totally and unconditionally—and help all in whatever ways I can, and 2) **LEARN** more about Him, His Creation and His ways; gain wisdom and spiritual knowledge and put it to work to help others and His Creation.

"I no longer fear death because I know what to expect, and He'll be there to greet me. But I have no wish to die immediately either; I still have work to do for Him, and the next time I go, I want to go with no regrets!"[2]

A glimpse of HEAVEN?

★★★★★★★★★★★★★★★★★★★★★★★

"I really had loved that job, what with all its prestige and privileges. But now all that had changed. I had been fired because I had shown up at work drunk once too often. How could I explain things to my wife, my kids? What would my friends think of me, now that I was no longer the big wheeler-dealer, but a drunken bum without a job! I decided that I just couldn't face them—any of them. I decided not to try; I decided to end it all, right now. That last drink gave me the "courage" I needed.

"I stumbled out of the bar and into my car, and drove off down the highway toward the cliff. As I reached the cliff, I veered to the right and the car, with me in it, went sailing off into space. I felt the crash shake my whole body, and pain shot through my head, and I blacked out.

"The next thing I knew I was out of my body and trapped in some kind of awful limbo state. It was horrible! Everything from which I had been trying to escape—the loss of my job, the embarrassment, the drinking—all of it kept going on and on, again and again. It was like some kind of rerun. Every time I would go through the whole sequence of events, I would think, "Boy, I'm glad that's over!," and then it would start all over again, and I knew that I would be in this horrible place, this pathetic state of existence, for a long time—maybe forever!

"I immediately saw the mistake I had made and wished I hadn't done it, but now there was nothing I could do about it because I couldn't get out of this place and back into my body. All of my problems were still with me, but in even greater intensity! It was like I couldn't think of anything else **BUT** my problems! I was confused and perplexed and felt like my brain had been "dulled." I was depressed and couldn't figure out what to do or where to go; it was hopeless; there seemed to be no way out!

"Then these ugly beings came toward me and dragged me deeper into this place. I felt like I was being tormented and bitten by snakes—the snakes of my passions were striking back at me!* The beings forced me to go with them and I suddenly found myself in a bar, watching other human beings drink. As they were drinking, these "demons"—I don't know what other word to use—tried to possess their bodies! I tried to tell the people in the bar to stop—stop what they were doing so that they wouldn't end up like me, but they couldn't hear me.

"Next these beings dragged me to a fiery pit—all bubbling and smoking. They forced me to look into it and there I saw the consequences of what I had done. My wife and kids were grieving for me, and then they were being thrown out of our house because they had no money to pay the mortgage.

"I screamed and cried to be forgiven for what I had done, and the Lord, in His great Mercy, heard my cry. Suddenly I found myself

---

* Black Elk, the great holy man of the Oglala Sioux, "emphasized that this event should not only be taken as an event in time, but also as an eternal truth. 'Any man,' he said, 'who is attached to the senses and to the things of this world, is one who lives in ignorance and is being consumed by snakes which represent his own passions.'"[3]

back in my body—in a great deal of pain, but back in my body. God had given me a second chance!'"⁴

A glimpse of HELL?

★ ★

What you have just read are composites taken from actual, factual life-after-death experiences. The events of the first narrative—a glimpse of a heavenly afterlife—were taken from true accounts of individuals who had "died" either through accidents or through natural causes, and who later came back to physical life, their souls being reunited with their bodies. The majority of these individuals were not great saints or overly spiritual; they were, on the whole, ordinary persons who were basically good and loving, but not perfect or God-Realized. They had made plenty of mistakes in their lives, as have we all. And yet, their experiences in the afterlife were very pleasant, if not heavenly, and in general profoundly affected the individual's outlook on the meaning of life, love and God in a very positive way.

The events of the second narrative—a glimpse of a hellish afterlife—were taken from actual accounts of individuals who had either tried to commit suicide or had lived rather self-destructive, egotistical, and hateful lives; and who were given a second chance at life in order to change their ways. They too were, in general, greatly affected by their death experiences, and in many, if not most cases, did change the way they had been living; specifically, they became more loving and caring, and more mindful of others' needs. They recognized that they had been living against God's Law of Love and had been viewed as "rebels" against God on "the other side."

Why should we be concerned about these experiences? We should be **very** concerned because, according to several prophecies, within the next twenty years, as many as 90% of us living today may be "dead" and, therefore, experiencing one or the other of these "afterlives"! And, as we have seen, the choice really is ours as to which place or "world" we will go—Heaven or Hell! If we are loving and mindful of keeping God's Laws, Heaven awaits us! If we are hateful and destructive, constantly breaking God's Laws and destroying His Creation, Hell awaits us!

But what prophecies are we talking about, and why should these prophecies be fulfilled now? We are talking about the prophecies concerning the End Times; the End of this Age—what the Hindus call the Kali Age, the Age of Chaos. We are talking about the end of this **system of things**—of ego, lies, hatred, violence and destruction; the end of man's system and manmade laws, to be replaced by God's system and God's laws of Love, Peace, Balance, Unity and Truth.

But throughout the ages, "doomsday" prophets have been announcing "the end of this world or age" (the original Greek word in the Bible is **aion,** meaning "age.") Why should we believe that "the end," (which is not really the end, but a New Beginning) should take place now? To what facts can one point to **prove** that we are in the End Times?

The following prophecies have come from different sources and different parts of the world. Though they were made hundreds and thousands of years ago, they could not have been fulfilled prior to the last few decades. Their fulfillment proves that these are the End Times!

Hopi Indian Prophecy

The Hopi Indian Prophecies, which date back at least 2000 years, are drawn on a rock in Black Mesa, near the "Four Corners Area" of the Southwest, U.S.A. They predict a time of great destruction. The Hopi would know that this time had come and that the great Tribulation/Purification was very near when "a gourd of ashes" would be invented. This weapon would be so powerful that, if dropped from the sky, it would be capable of boiling the oceans and burning the land so badly that nothing would be able to grow for many years.

The discovery of this weapon was to trigger the release of certain Indian teachings to the general public; teachings meant to warn the world that a final calamity could bring an end to all life on the planet if the people of the world did not wake up and change their ways, **AND** force their leaders to change their direction toward planetary annihilation. This weapon—the gourd of ashes—is, of course, the atomic bomb whose mushroom-shaped cloud also resembles an American Indian gourd.

Jesus Christ

When asked by His disciples as to what would be the signs of the end of this Age, Jesus mentioned wars, earthquakes, famines,

5

epidemics, false prophets, and religious persecutions. Then, as to the last signs, He said:

> "And there will be signs in (the) sun and moon and stars...men fainting with fear and with foreboding of what is coming on the world; **for the powers of the heavens will be shaken.**"[5]

In this context, the word "heavens" means "celestial powers,"[6] or powers of creation. The original Greek word for "heavens" is "Ourania," which is also the root word for **"uranium."** Rewritten, the passage reads: "and the powers of **uranium** shall be shaken." Uranium is shaken to produce atomic power. So the discovery of atomic power was predicted by Jesus almost 2000 years ago and was to be viewed as a sign of the end of this age!

Reading further: "then will appear the sign of the Son of man in heaven...and they will see the Son of man coming on the clouds of heaven with power and great glory..."[7]

Is it merely a coincidence that the first successful atomic or nuclear fusion test was code-named "**Baby Jesus,**" and that the first successful atomic or nuclear blast was called "**The Trinity**"? Or was it fulfillment of Biblical prophecy? It is interesting to note that after witnessing the first atomic explosion, Professor J. Robert Oppenheimer, the "father" of the first atomic weapon, who later repudiated the use of atomic/nuclear weapons, despairingly quoted the Bhagavat Gita, a Hindu scripture, saying, "I have become Death; the destroyer of worlds!"

Certainly the discovery and subsequent use of the atomic bomb on Hiroshima and Nagasaki and the death of tens of thousands **did** fulfill both Christian and American Indian prophecies concerning the signs of the end of this age.

> "For then there will be great tribulation, such as has not been from the beginning of the world until now, no, and never will be. And if those days had not been shortened, **no living thing would be left alive...**"[8]

Never before has man had the power to destroy every living thing on the Earth. But, as both Jesus and the Hopis foresaw, he does now!

> "Now when these things begin to take place, look up and raise your heads, because your redemption is drawing

6

Near the Hypocenter   Nagasaki

Everything burnable burnt. Agonizing death swiftly overtook those trying to
flee, their bodies lying there. August 10, 1945, about noon.

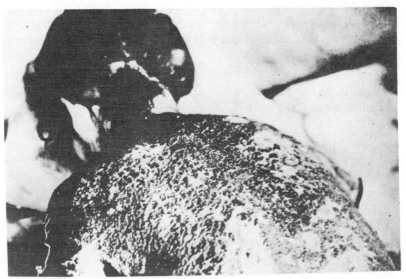

Both photos reprinted with permission from No More Hiroshimas, Japan.

Burns on the Back   Hiroshima

Immobilized with severe burns: Slightest body movement caused excruciating
pain. So they died. Relief Station at Ninoshima. August 7, 1945.

near...Truly, I say to you, **this generation** will not pass away till all has taken place."[9]

Which generation? The generation that saw the discovery and use of atomic/nuclear power. How long is a generation? In the Bible, a generation is usually around forty years. The first atomic experiments were conducted during 1944 to 1945. Perhaps George Orwell's date of 1984 was more prophetic than even **he** realized!

Michel de Nostradamus (1503-1566)

Michel de Nostradamus was a French physician and prophet whose incredibly accurate predictions have astounded the world for over four centuries. He believed that his gift of prophecy came from God and carefully cultivated it through prayer and meditation. He foresaw both the French and American Revolutions over **200 years before their occurrence,** even stating that the American Revolution would precede the French by 15 years, America's birth date being 1776 and France's being 1791. He foresaw the assassinations of both Abraham Lincoln and John F. Kennedy, as well as naming certain important individuals of history, such as Louis Pasteur and Spain's Franco, **300 and 400 years before these people were even born.**

Nostradamus also predicted the Russian Revolution and both World Wars I and II almost **400 years beforehand.** In one quatrain, Nostradamus foretold the horrors that would befall the peoples of two cities by the sea—hunger, plague, and homelessness—due to mass destruction of their cities by a newly-invented, horrendous weapon. Both Nagasaki and Hiroshima are on the sea and the people there surely did experience the horrors of hunger, homelessness, and plague—the plague of nuclear or atomic fallout which produces lesions on the skin that greatly resemble those produced by the bubonic plagues of Nostradmus' time, of which he was very familiar, being a physician. Remember, Nostradamus predicted this **400 years before it happened!**

In several quatrains, Nostradamus helps to further narrow down the timing of the Great Tribulation and Purification that immediately precedes the New Age. He speaks of a troubled period of intense chemical pollution that is to come right before the Great Cleansing; a period of chemicalization similar to the one we have been going through during the last two decades.

8

Remember Love Canal? Toxic chemicals that had been dumped years ago began to resurface, contaminating an entire residential community, calling the American public's attention to the severe problem of chemical pollution that is plaguing America. Remember Three Mile Island? The nation's most serious nuclear accident occurred there, raising fears of a "meltdown," which could have led to an explosion that could have devastated the entire state of Pennsylvania with radiation, again calling the American public's attention to the serious question of the safety of nuclear power technology.

He further states that after the Great Seventh Number is completed, a large-scale sacrifice will occur, "not far from the age of the great millennium, when the dead will come out of their graves."[10] The Great Seventh Number which is not far from the great millennium would seem to mean that after the end of the 1970's—a time not far from the great millennium of the year 2000—a large group of people will make a great sacrifice—a "Hecatomb, at the time of the Games."[11]

In ancient Greece, a hecatomb was a large-scale public offering and sacrifice to the gods. It is interesting to note that it was also in Greece that the first Olympic Games were played. Could he be referring to the large-scale public sacrifice made by the athletes around the world who boycotted the Olympic Games held in Russia in 1980 as a protest to the Soviet invasion of Afghanistan? After all, for many of the athletes it was a once-in-a-lifetime opportunity to participate in the Olympics. They gave up that opportunity in the name of Peace.

And it was not only the athletes who made a sacrifice; governments and businesses around the world sacrificed millions of dollars that could have been reaped from the sales of various goods and services in connection with the Olympic Games—the airlines, the media, the hotels, and merchants selling Olympic momentos are just a few examples.

What of the last part of the prophecy? Could he be referring to the Great Rapture and call to Judgement that Jesus referred to when He said, "For the hour is coming when all who are in the tombs will hear His voice and come forth, those who have done good, to the resurrection of life, and those who have done evil, to the resurrection of judgement!"[12] But the Rapture and great Judgement have not taken place yet en masse. The next Olympic Games are in 1984, again after the end of the '70's and not far from the great millennium of 2000 A.D. Strange that that date—

1984—keeps coming up, isn't it?

There are many other prophets—from the East as well as the West, both ancient and modern-day—who have made prophecies about our times. To those of us who already believe in prophecy, several questions present themselves; questions that will be answered in the following chapters of this book. For example: What are the prophecies and who made them? What further signs did the prophets give us to look for with regards to the End Times? Why do we have to go through this period of intense tribulation and change at all? What changes can we make in our own lives to help smooth our transition into the New Age? What can we do to help others face and weather these turbulent times? Which teachers should we learn from and trust so that we do not fall prey to the false prophets of whom Jesus spoke? And, finally, if we change and help others with their own changes, can the world not avoid the horrendous upheavals that have been predicted and enter the New Age on a more harmonious note?

For those sceptics who still have doubts about the validity of prophecy, may we remind them that it is not only religious fanatics and wild-eyed, toga-wearing, Einstein-looking "weirdos" who are announcing the end of an era or age. As we will show, scientists, academicians, physicians, and leaders and politicians around the world are echoing their words and cries of concern about our future, due to the pressing problems we face regarding over-population, dwindling food supplies, nuclear proliferation, escalating violence, chemical pollution, deforestation and other ecological disasters due to man's interference with the Balance of Nature which will and already have begun to adversely affect our weather, our environment, and our future in general.

But if there are still doubts, the best way to erase those doubts is to demonstrate the accuracy of past prophecies. The best way to do this is to examine certain events in history that have been verified by secular (nonreligious) and scientific sources, and see what prophecies had been made about these events prior to their occurrence. This will prove that the spirit of prophecy **is** the spirit of Truth, and that the prophets were accurate in their predictions. And if they were accurate in the past, perhaps we had better look closely at what they say about our present and immediate future, for it is these very same prophets who have foreseen the events that **we all** will soon be experiencing! We'll start with examples taken from what in the West is probably the most famous book of prophecies—the Bible.

Chapter 2

BIBLICAL PROPHECIES FULFILLED

The Bible contains not only the teachings of God, but also contains a chronicle of the trials, tribulations and travels of the Hebrew people—the 12 tribes of Israel—and is filled with prophecies about the past, present and future, including prophecies concerning Europe and the United States of America, whose peoples are the descendants of the Ten Lost Tribes of Israel!

In the year 925 B.C., these 12 tribes separated into two sovereign and distinct nations. Ten settled in what is now Northern Israel or Palestine and were called the House of Israel. The other two, the tribes of Judah and Benjamin, along with the Levites or priests, settled in and around Jerusalem and Southern Israel and came to be known as the House of Judah.

The Ten Lost Tribes of Israel

Over the years the House of Israel started to abandon its Hebrew laws and God, and lived more and more like its Gentile neighbors, the Syrians, who did not recognize the One, Supreme, all-pervading Lord, but were instead idol worshippers who mistakenly attributed human and worldly weaknesses such as lust, greed, anger, etc., to their various gods, rather than Divine qualities of Love, Truth, and Peace. One of the Bible's greatest prophets—Isaiah—observed this trend and predicted the disasters that would befall the Israelites for turning away from God. He foresaw the destruction of the House of Israel by the Assyrians (encompassing approximately modern-day Iraq), and that all its people would be captured and taken away as slaves. Furthermore, he prophesied that the Israelites would lose their identity and would no longer be a people; that they would lose their culture, their history, their religion, their language, and their heritage, and would no longer inhabit the lands of their forefathers.

As time went by, friction grew between the Israelites and the Jews until the Israelites actually made an alliance with Syria against their own brothers—the Jews—and threatened invasion of Jerusalem. This threat came to naught, however, because Syria and the House of Israel were themselves invaded and conquered

11

HISTORIC MAP OF THE MIDDLE EAST

(Insert: Close-up of Ancient Palestine)

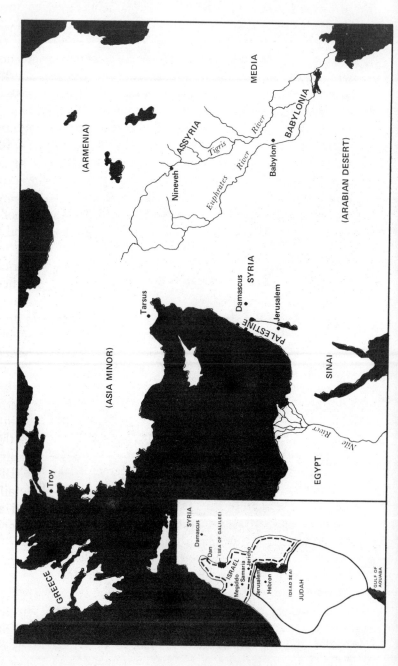

by the Assyrians (Iraq) in the year 722 B.C., **some 40 years after the prophet Isaiah had predicted.** The Israelites were captured and taken away as slaves, never to return to the land of their ancestors. These are the peoples that are commonly referred to as the Ten Lost Tribes of Israel. Many theologians and historians now believe that the peoples of Europe and the United States are descendants of these tribes. They make this claim on the basis of trade routes, names of towns, etc., and other historical data.

For example, the peoples of Ireland are said to be descendants of the tribe of Dan, while the ancestors of the peoples of Great Britain are said to have been from the tribe of Ephraim—one-half of the House of Joseph. The other half of Joseph's House is said to be the peoples of America—descendants from the tribe of Manasseh, Ephraim's brother and Joseph's second son. Proof of our past connections with the 12 tribes of Israel can be found on the coats of arms of both Great Britain and the United States. The British arms contain the Harp of David, and the American "arms" have the Star of David. If you look above the eagle's head on a dollar bill, you can see the six-pointed "Mogen David" formed by the placement of the 13 stars! So the prophecies of the future about the tribes of Israel concern not only the Jews and those living in Israel today, **but us in the Western world, too![1]**

The prophets of the Bible, such as Isaiah, Jeremiah and Ezekiel, foresaw great events in history, some being fulfilled in their own lifetime, such as Isaiah's and the fall of the Israelites, and others happening hundreds or thousands of years after their deaths. Many of the prophecies had double and triple meanings with fulfillment coming immediately after the prediction as well as hundreds or thousands of years later. In many cases their detailed descriptions of the events and the time periods involved are absolutely uncanny. An example of this would be the prophecies concerning the fall of the House of Judah to Babylon.

The Fall of Judah

After the House of Israel was destroyed and its people enslaved by the Assyrians (Iraq), the House of Judah feared for its own existence, as it too had forgotten much of God's teachings and laws. The King of Judah sought military alliances with Egypt and

Babylon to thwart Assyria's aggressions. The prophet Isaiah warned against such alliances, saying that Egypt itself would have to pay tribute to Assyria, and that Babylon would turn on Jerusalem, destroy her and enslave her people. "Seek God's protection; not man's!" Isaiah admonished the King.

Again Isaiah's visions were shown to be true. Egypt was subjugated to Assyria (Iraq) and had to pay tribute in order to exist. Jerusalem was Assyria's next target and its mighty forces surrounded Jerusalem's city walls. The night before the Assyrian forces were to invade Jerusalem, they fell victim to a strange plague which killed all of them, but did not harm the Jews! **God's protection prevailed; not man's!**

Over a century later, the House of Judah again began to stray from God's righteousness and Moses' laws. The officials and kings had become corrupt and the people in general had forgotten the Path to Truth and Light as set forth by Moses. History was about to repeat itself, as it always does when man forgets or fails to learn from it.

Isaiah's warnings regarding Babylon were echoed by other prophets who warned that Jerusalem and its great temple would be destroyed, and that the land would be ruined and left desolate for a period of 70 years. They warned that the whole nation of Judah, including its ruling class, would have to serve the Babylonians. The King of Jerusalem, they said, would never see Babylon as he would be killed and his body left unburied, and that no more kings from the House of David would rule in Jerusalem again until the coming of the Messiah.

In the year 607 B.C., Babylon did indeed turn on Judah and destroy Jerusalem and its great temple, **just as predicted by Isaiah over 100 years before.** The land was laid waste and desolate, and all the people, including the ruling class, were taken off to Babylon as slaves, **as predicted.** The King of Jerusalem did not see Babylon as his eyes were gouged out before he was killed, his body being left unburied outside the city walls, **as predicted.**

In the year 537 B.C., King Cyrus allowed the Jews to return to Jerusalem and rebuild their temple, **70 years after its destruction, exactly as predicted by the prophet Jeremiah.** Though the Jews were allowed to return to Jerusalem, no king from the royal house of David has sat on Jerusalem's throne to this day, **as predicted by the prophet Ezekiel!**

The Fall of Babylon

Isaiah also made several predictions about Babylon. For example, he foretold that Babylon would fall in a single day **200 years before it happened.** Not only did he predict who her conquerors would be—the Medes and Persians, peoples who were of no significance and little threat to Babylon in Isaiah's time—but he also named the commander of the Medo-Persian forces—Cyrus. Further, he explained the strategy that Cyrus would use—all of Babylon's waters would dry up—and that the city gates would be left open.

Jeremiah gave more prophetic glimpses of Babylon's fall, stating that she would fall during a drunken festival, that there would be little fighting, that the king would be slain in his own palace, and that Babylon would be left desolate and uninhabited except by animals for generations to come.

Babylon remained the world's "greatest," or rather strongest empire until the year 539 B.C. when it did fall in **one night** to the Medes and Persians, **just as Isaiah had predicted over 200 years earlier.** The commander of the Medo-Persian forces was named Cyrus, **as predicted.** Babylon was a network of canals and moats. Cyrus' strategy was to build trenches and redirect the water so that his soldiers could walk up the dried river canals right into the city, **as had been predicted.** The invasion came during a drunken festival, **as predicted,** and the gates of the city had been left wide open, **as predicted.** There was little fighting and the King was slain in his own palace. Babylon was left desolate and uninhabited except by animals, **as predicted,** and the Medo-Persians were the new "rulers" of the world.

The Amazing Prophet Daniel

One of the greatest prophets in history was Daniel, who lived in Babylon during the height of its power as well as the time of its destruction. One night King Nebuchadnezzar of Babylon had a dream that so frightened him that he forgot it! He was greatly agitated by this as he felt that the dream was of great importance. He called together his soothsayers (so called because they **say** things to **soothe** the King!), "wisemen," and prophets, and demanded they help him recall the dream, and then interpret it. Of course, they could not, and the enraged King sent out an edict to have all wisemen, soothsayers, prophets, etc., including Daniel, put to death. Upon hearing the edict, Daniel begged the King to give him 24 hours to pray to God to reveal the King's dream to him. The King agreed.

Twenty-four hours later Daniel did reveal the dream and its interpretation! The King had seen a monstrous beast come out of the water. The beast represented the kingdoms of man, the political empires that were to rule the earth down through history. The beast had a head of gold, representing Babylon itself. Its chest and arms were of silver, representing the Medo-Persian Empire. Its belly and thighs were of copper, representing Greece, and its legs were of iron, representing the Roman Empire. Its feet were part iron and part clay and represent the political governments of today, which are basically split between the Industrialized, mainly Western nations that have grown out of the old Roman Empire of iron, and the undeveloped or underdeveloped Third World countries that are still tied to the clay soil.

To check the accuracy of Daniel's prophecies all one need do is open any encyclopedia. Babylon's reign as "THE" World Power started approximately 626 B.C. and ended 539 B.C., the night Cyrus and his Medo-Persian forces invaded Babylon. Daniel was alive and present in the palace that night. It seems Babylon's King Belshazzar (who was Nebuchadnezzar's grandson) was entertaining his guests in his palace and was using the wine chalices that the Hebrews had used in their temple as wine cups—a great sacrilege. As he had invited guests from outside the immediate city limits, he had ordered the city gates left open. He and his friends got more and more drunk until, suddenly, **a disembodied hand appeared in front of them and wrote on the opposite wall, "Mene, Mene, Tekel, and Parsin."** Needless to say the King and his drunken court were astounded and terrified. The King called his soothsayers to translate the words, but none could until the old Hebrew prophet Daniel appeared. Daniel could indeed "read the writing on the wall," this being the incident which spawned that phrase! He told the King that his kingdom had become corrupt and that he and it had been weighed in God's great balance scales, and been found wanting. His kingdom, therefore, would fall and be divided between the Medes and Persians that very night. And, lo and behold, as per Daniel's prophecy, the kingdom and the King fell that very night!

The Medes and Persians, represented by the silver chest and **two** arms, as it was a dual world power, reigned jointly from that

16

THE DISEMBODIED HAND

fateful night of 539 B.C. until 333 B.C., when they in turn were overthrown by Alexander the Great of Greece, represented by the copper belly and thighs, as Daniel had predicted **over 200 years earlier.** Daniel even had some prophetic dreams of his own about this change of world dominion where he foresaw not only Alexander's conquests and rapid rise to glory, but also Alexander's death at the height of his career—at age 33— and the subsequent division of the Greek Empire among his four top generals. His dream included glimpses of the next world power—the iron rule of Rome—that was represented by the beast's iron legs of Nebuchadnezzar's dream-beast.

Greece's world rule ended around 146 B.C. when the Roman Empire swallowed it up along with the remnants of all the previous world empires. Rome's Empire was more extensive than any of the previous world empires, covering England and Germany to the North, Ethiopia to the South, Spain to the West, and the Arabian Sea and beyond to the East. It was indeed different from its predecessors, as Daniel had seen. Its geographic size was matched only by its brutality and savagery. It truly was an "Iron Empire," interested in power and lacking even the glitter of copper that the Greeks had had. It, too, was divided in half, East and West, in later years, as the two iron legs suggest, around the Fifth Century A.D., and was later divided even further into various nation-states.

This brings us to the beast's feet and toes partly of iron and partly of clay, which represent the world's political situation today. We truly are a world divided along the lines of iron—the industrialized, mainly Western nations which have grown out of the old Roman Empire—and clay—the mainly agricultural underdeveloped Third World nations whose people are materially or economically poor, or what Americans would call "dirt poor," and whose only source of income is generally the natural resources and raw materials that come from the clay earth.

Further, the clay on the feet of Nebuchadnezzar's dream-beast was cracking and breaking up, unable to stick onto or mix with the iron feet, which is a very prophetic picture of the Third World nations today. They are literally cracking up and breaking apart socially, politically, and economically from the pressures of trying to live in this unnatural, ironized, industrialized world. Revolutions and political assassinations are commonplace due to social unrest because of the disparity between the poor and the ruling rich, the "haves" and the "have-nots." Plus, many if not most of the Third World nations are in such desperate economic shape with huge debts owed to the world's banks that they cannot even pay the interest on their loans much less the loans themselves! Mexico, Brazil, Venezuela, Argentina, Chile, and Bolivia are just a few examples, not to mention the desperate plight of several African and Asian nations.

So what does Daniel's interpretation of Nebuchadnezzar's dream foretell of our own immediate future? Nebuchadnezzar saw **a stone cut out, not by human hands, hit the beast on its feet of clay and iron.** The beast came crashing down and was ground to dust, which was blown away by the wind so that no trace of the beast was left. The stone became a mountain and filled the entire earth. **The stone represents the Kingdom of God which is to come and destroy the political beast, and then fill the earth with Peace.**

This part of Nebuchadnezzar's dream will be discussed more thoroughly in later chapters. Also discussed will be Daniel's vision of the Last Days and the last political beast which is supposed to be "different from all the rest"—the Antichrist!

18

THE BEAST

19

Chapter 3

THE BIRTH, LIFE, AND DEATH OF THE MESSIAH

One figure dominates the prophecies of the Old Testament of the Bible more than any other; that figure is the Messiah. There are over 300 prophecies concerning His birth, life, and death, some of which were made in 1000 B.C., most of which were fulfilled by Jesus of Nazareth almost 2000 years ago. The remainder are to be fulfilled in **this** generation: today!

Below are some of the prophecies about the Messiah which have already been fulfilled through the life of Jesus of Nazareth:

1- He was to be a descendant of Abraham (Genesis 12·1-3, approximately 1270 B.C.);

2- He was to be from the House of Judah (Genesis 49·10, approx. 1270 B.C.);

3- He was to be a descendant of King David after David's descendants had stopped ruling Judah (I Chronicles 17·11-13, approx. 1000 B.C., Isaiah 11, approx. 740 B.C.);

4- He was to be born in Bethlehem (Micah 5·2, approx. 715 B.C.);

5- He would heal the lame, give sight to the blind, hearing to the deaf, cleanse the lepers, and raise the dead (Isaiah 35·4-6, approx. 740 B.C.);

6- He would ride into Jerusalem on a colt or donkey (Zechariah 9·9, approx. 520 B.C.);

7- He would be betrayed by one of His own followers for 30 pieces of silver and that the money would be used for a Potter's field (poorman's burial site) after being thrown down in the Temple (Zech. 11·12, 13, approx. 520 B.C.);

8- He would be rejected and handed over to the Gentiles for punishment and execution (Isaiah 52 & 53, approx. 740 B.C.);

9- He would not defend Himself at His trial (Isaiah 52 & 53, approx. 740 B.C.);

10- He would be flogged and His face beaten so badly that He would be hard to recognize (Isaiah 52·7, 53, approx. 740 B.C.);

11- He would be pierced (Zech. 10, 12, approx. 520 B.C.);

12- He would die with criminals and be buried in a rich man's tomb (Isaiah 52 & 53, approx. 740 B.C.)

All of the above prophecies and many more were fulfilled by the birth, life, and death of Jesus of Nazareth, even to His burial in the tomb of Joseph of Arimathea, a rich merchant, Pharisee, and follower of Jesus Christ. Some of the prophecies are astounding because of the accuracy of their detail and the time-span between the date of the prediction and their subsequent fulfillment. An example of this is recorded in Psalm 22 which relates the vision King David had **over 1000 years before Jesus' crucifixion.** King David saw that heavy perspiration would pour forth (from hanging all day in the sun), that His bones would be out of joint (the ligaments stretch and the bones pop out—excruciatingly painful!), that He would have intense thirst, that His feet and hands would be pierced, and that the "Dogs" would part His garments and cast lots for them. During Christ's lifetime, the term "Dogs" was used by the Jews when referring to the Roman soldiers, peoples of whom King David knew nothing!

Another astounding fact is that the use of crucifixion as a form of execution was unknown in King David's time. It was first introduced by the Romans about 200 years before Christ—**800 years after King David had his remarkably accurate vision!** So we can see that time is no barrier to those with the gift of prophecy![1]

Jesus Himself foretold that He would be betrayed by one of His own followers, that He would be rejected by the high priests and elders of the church, handed over to the Gentiles who would scourge, mock and crucify Him, and that after three days, He would rise again. He also foretold the persecution of His followers and that some of them would be brought before kings and governors, as St. Paul and others were. He also foretold, as had Daniel before Him, the destruction of Jerusalem and its mighty temple ("Truly, I say to you, there will not be left here one stone upon another, that will not be thrown down." Matthew 24·2),[2] the slaughter of many Jews by the Romans and the enslaving and scattering of the remainder to all nations until the end of the Gentiles' time. He even said that it would happen to the same generation that would witness His crucifixion and Resurrection, this being an example of a prophecy with a double meaning. ("Truly, I say to you, **this generation** will not pass away till all these things take place." Matthew 24·34)[3]

21

The total destruction of Jerusalem and its mighty temple in 70 A.D. by Titus and his Roman forces was indeed experienced by that same generation that had witnessed Jesus Christ's crucifixion and Resurrection some thirty to forty years earlier. Over 1 million Jews were slaughtered during the following 3½ years of terror, so many that there was no wood to be found for fires as most of the available wood had been used to build crosses to crucify them! The people were starved by the Romans prior to Jerusalem's destruction; crime and corruption reigned supreme; brother turned against brother and father against son—**all exactly as Jesus had predicted.**

Christians became the scapegoats for all the region's troubles and great persecutions followed. When, at last, the Roman legions surrounded the city, those who remembered the warning signs Jesus had given over thirty years earlier did escape into the hills and were saved ["But when you see the desolating sacrilege set up where it ought not to be (i.e., the Roman armies standing in the temple square—a great sacrilege!)...then flee to the mountains."][4] Those who did not, experienced such tribulation as had never been seen before in the land of Judea: torture, rape, crucifixion, and enslavement, finally culminating in the last futile stand of the Hebrew Zealots on the top of Masada. Here the Zealots committed mass suicide rather than face the hell that the Romans had waiting for them.

All of the above concerning Jerusalem's destruction is a matter of historical fact. But what proof is there that Jesus of Nazareth actually existed; that He was beaten, flogged, crucified, and finally pierced by a lance? And, more importantly, what tangible evidence is there that the Resurrection actually took place? They say, "Seeing is believing," so the best proof is what is called by scientists and theologians alike the oldest known photograph in the world—the Holy Shroud of Turin—believed by many to be the actual burial shroud of Jesus Christ!

The Enigma that is the Shroud of Turin

The Shroud is a white linen cloth approximately 14'3" long by 3'7" wide, and has the shadowy but definite full-length back and front image of a man who bears all the markings of a Roman style crucifixion. Scientists call it the oldest known photograph because the image on the Shroud is a photographic negative. The

Shroud was first photographed in 1898 by Secundo Pia. As he examined his first glass-plate negative, he was amazed to see, not a confusing photographic negative, but a clear **positive** image! But how could that be? Who could have produced a photographic negative, which the Shroud is, hundreds of years before the invention of photography? And why? How did the image get on the cloth? And, more importantly, is the man pictured on the Shroud really Jesus of Nazareth?

Over the last few years, teams of scientists have been doing a battery of tests on the Shroud to try and solve its mysteries. The overwhelming conclusion of the scientists who have been privileged to see and work on the Shroud is that it is **not** a forgery or fake. To quote Ernest H. Brooks II, scientist and president of the Brooks Institute, a research and educational institute, "We are convinced that what we have found is not a forgery."[5] According to a UPI release, one scientist, Donald J. Lynn of the Jet Propulsion Laboratory in Pasadena, California, who is an expert in computer enhancement for NASA projects, said he felt the existence of the research project itself was Divinely inspired. "God set us up," Lynn said in explaining how all the scientists from different fields and different parts of the world got together for the project.[6] Said Barrie Schwortz, a photographer with the project, "It's an enigma. We can't figure out how this image came to be, but the person that we see here fits only one person known to history—Jesus Christ."[7]

Robert Bucklin, a professor and clinical pathologist at the University of Southern California who has researched the Shroud for over thirty years says:

> "The markings on this image are so clear and so medically accurate that the pathological facts which they reflect concerning the suffering and death of the man depicted here are in my opinion beyond dispute...If I were asked in a court of law to stake my professional reputation on the validity of the Shroud of Turin, I would answer very positively and firmly that it's the burial cloth of Christ and that it is Jesus whose figure appears on the Shroud...It's not a matter of faith to me, it's just a matter of common sense. Knowing what we know, who else could this have happened to?"[8]

And German professor Werner Bulst agrees: "Despite decades of effort, the opponents of the cloth have not succeeded in proving a single violation of the laws of physiology and anatomy in the image of the Shroud."[9]

The image and bloodstains on the Shroud correspond exactly to the descriptions given in the Gospels of the crucifixion of Jesus Christ: that He was a Jew (the image shows a man with the long Jewish side-locks that distinguished Jews from Gentiles, as well as the loose knot of hair at the nape of the neck which was typical Jewish fashion at that time); that He was beaten (the face of the image is greatly swollen); that He was flogged or scourged (there are, according to New Scotland Yard, as many as 120 scourge marks, probably caused by a Roman whip called the flagrum, whose leather thongs were tipped with bits of lead or bone, which tore out pieces of the flesh each time the whip was applied—Romans were never whipped with a flagrum, only Jews); that He was mocked by the Gentiles as the King of the Jews (bloodstains around the head correspond exactly to the cuts a cap-like crown of thorns would have inflicted); that He had to carry His own cross, and that He fell several times on His way to Calvary (there are bruises and bloodstains marking the shoulders and knees of the image); that He was crucified (nail wounds and corresponding bloodstains are seen in the feet and wrists, the Greek word for hand being "cheir," which includes the wrist and forearm); that not a bone of His would be broken to fulfill prophecy (it was common practice to break the legs of those crucified to speed up death as it could take as long as 48 hours for one to die on a cross; Jesus is said to have died in 6 hours; the legs on the Shroud image were not broken); that He was pierced by a spear or lance to make sure He was dead (there is blood and serum on the side and trickling around the back of the image from a side-wound that obviously pierced the heart); that He was laid on a linen burial shroud (the fabric of the Shroud has traces of cotton of a Middle Eastern variety as well as pollen fossils that, according to Swiss criminologist Dr. Max Frei, could only have come from plants that grew exclusively in the Palestine region at the time of Christ; the weave, which is a herring-bone twill, is a pattern found in fabrics from the Middle East dating from 100 to 300 A.D. and corresponds with the "richman's burial" that Christ was supposed to have had, as plain weave was much more commonly used for grave clothes); that He was hastily buried as the Sabbath was about to begin (hence the bloodstains from an unwashed body); and that His body was annointed with aloe and spices (there are

24

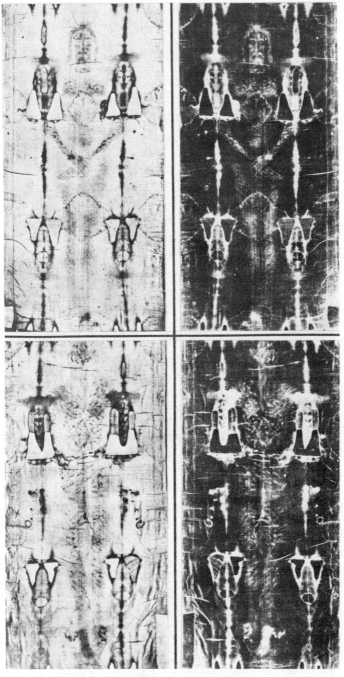

Full-Length View of The Holy Shroud

25

traces of an ointment made from an aloe plant that grows only on an island off the coast of South Yemen, but as time was short, the annointing of the body was not completed, and would have to be finished after the Sabbath; thus setting the stage for Mary's encounter with the Risen Lord on the Third Day!)

There's more! In ancient Palestine, it was a custom to place coins on the eyes of the dead. Surely Joseph of Arimathea, being a wealthy man, would have done so for Jesus. On both eyes of the image on the Shroud, scientists have discovered the imprints of two Pontius Pilate coins minted in 29 A.D. and used around Palestine until 70 A.D. Magnifications of the coin covering the right eye are especially convincing as to place of origin and date of minting for two reasons, according to Professor Alan D. Whanger of Duke University. First, the coin contains an astrologer's augur or lituus—a curved staff like a shepherd's crook. Whanger says that only Pontius Pilate used the lituus on coins. Second, the coin contains the lettering "Tiberius Caesar" around the margin with a rare misspelling in Greek of the name Caesar, using a "C" instead of a "K." Critics at first doubted the validity of the finding, but on November 20, 1981, UPI reported that Rev. Francis L. Filas, a professor of theology at Chicago's Loyola University, had discovered a second coin with the same rare misspelling found on the Shroud image's right eye. To quote Rev. Filas:

> "Imprints of a misspelled Pontius Pilate coin now in existence are the same as imprints of an apparent coin on the right eye of the crucified man's figure on the Shroud...This discovery proves the authenticity, the place of origin, and the approximate dating of the Shroud of Turin beyond reasonable doubt...The unexpected discovery of a second Pontius Pilate coin with the same rare misspelling...closes the door on objections...Every reasonable objection has now been met by the finding of an independent second coin. One wonders how the evidence for the Shroud could be added to any more."[10]

Questions and Answers

But how did the image get there? The overwhelming majority of scientists who have worked on the Shroud have ruled out the possibility of it being an elaborate painting or photograph as 1-

there is no evidence of paint or pigment or brush strokes of any kind on the fabric itself, and 2-the Shroud's image is three-dimensional whereas a painting or photograph would be only two-dimensional.

As to the first point, a fire in 1532 which endangered the Shroud had heat sufficient to char the fabric and would have altered the color of the image had it been painted, but the image is not altered at all and is uniform throughout, even next to the burned areas. Also, water used to put out the fire stained the cloth, but again, did not alter the image which would have been the case if it had been painted on.

As to the second point, two scientists from the U.S. Air Force have proven that the image is three-dimensional, meaning that the image varies in direct proportion to how far that part of the body was from the cloth, the darkest portions being closest to the sheet, and the lightest farthest away. Photographs and paintings have only two dimensions. This three-dimensional aspect also proves that the image could not have been formed as a result of time and direct contact with body oils, sweat, or spices, the so-called "vaporgraph" theory, as it would again have had only two dimensions and not nearly as many details in the face where a cloth would not have touched.

Ray Rogers, a chemist of the Los Alamos National Scientific Laboratory, summed it up, "Nearly all of us now believe that the Shroud is not a painting. Except for a small amount of iron oxide, we found no pigment. And we do not think that either liquid or vapor could have produced the image we see."[11]

The theory that the image was scorched onto the fabric by draping it over a hot etched plate or statue has also been ruled out because of the great details that are on the Shroud image.

However, scientists believe that some sort of scorching mechanism seems to be the most logical explanation for the Shroud's image. Many believe that the Shroud's image not only proves that Jesus of Nazareth existed, but that it also proves the Resurrection of Jesus. They believe that the image was scorched onto the fabric at the moment of Christ's Resurrection, when the body dissolved in a blaze of light.

But is there any scientific proof to substantiate this theory, i.e., that the Resurrection of Jesus actually took place and caused the Shroud's image? In the past, some have argued that Jesus did not die on the cross at all, but fell into a coma-like swoon and was later revived in the cool of the tomb. This theory, however, has been proven false by the image on the Shroud. First, according to scientists, the effects of rigor mortis on the body of the man in the Shroud are unmistakable. Second, the blood and serum separations that appear on parts of the Shroud only occur after death. Third, there are no signs whatsoever of decomposition or decay of the body before the image was transferred onto the Shroud. Decomposition usually sets in within 24 to 48 hours after rigor mortis. The image on the Shroud, however, shows no signs of body relaxation and there is no evidence of decomposition on the cloth itself.

So the body must have been encased within the Shroud for less than 48 hours. If the body had simply been removed, as had been suggested, there would have been some evidence, such as smeared bloodstains or damage to the cloth itself. But no smears exist and the cloth is undamaged. So how did the image get there?

Scientists believe that some sort of radiant energy similar to a pulsed laser beam was employed. Theoretically, a pulsed laser beam can cause the dematerialization of even a human body. In explaining the Shroud image, John H. Heller of the New England Institute said, "It is as if every pore and each hair of the body contained a micro-miniature laser."[12]

Laboratory experiments have used pulsed laser beams to produce coherent bursts of light that can record a three-dimensional picture of a human body on celluloid film, which is similar to linen cloth in that both come from celluloid—all happening literally in the twinkling of an eye! This three-dimensional picture would be an actual recording of the invisible light-wave data of the human body.

But there were no manmade laser beams or laboratories at the time of Christ's Resurrection; obviously the source of the burst of coherent radiant light or energy that left the Shroud's image was other than manmade—it was Divine!

According to Janet Bock, author of *The Jesus Mystery:*

"The closest known approximations to the Shroud images were discovered by a Dr. Volkringer at the French Academy of Sciences. He found that leaves accidentally left between the pages of a book for over 100 years had formed a highly detailed negative image on the paper several pages away...some form of life energy had radiated from the leaves, through the adjoining pages, and formed the image."[13]

She goes on to explain that similar life energy may have radiated from Jesus' body to form the image on the Shroud,"...the difference being that the leaves radiated at a low intensity for a hundred years...," while Jesus' body radiated at a very high intensity for a brief time in the tomb—the time of the Resurrection and the dissolution of Jesus' material body into pure Spirit, Energy, or Light.[14] As Jesus said, "I am the Light."

Bock explains that further scientific confirmation of life energies radiating from living things, whether they are human, plant, or animal, have come through the discovery of Kirlian photography. Scientists have used this technique to photograph the auras of energy or light that surround living things, such as a leaf, and have even shown that this aura or light-energy pattern that surrounds the physical body remains even when a portion of that body has been cut away. Bock continues:

> "Christian saints and angels, as well as Jesus Himself, have traditionally been portrayed with a golden circle of light around the head. Is it possible these halos represent an unseen aura projected by the godly, an emanation once seen by men and portrayed in art that is too subtle for our eyes?
>
> "What the Bible calls 'the single eye,' and Eastern philosophy calls 'the third eye,' enables some individuals to perceive the auras of people around them. What they reportedly see is that the aura of light around an ordinary man extends some two to three feet from the body, while the aura of a saint extends twenty or thirty feet, giving it an intensity at the body surface of over ten times that of a man whose consciousness is blocked by ego, illness, and other human limitations."[15]

So the aura or energy pattern that surrounds a person increases in direct proportion to how much one thinks about God. Science has confirmed this by using Kirlian photography to photograph an Indian yogi before and during meditation. The photographs show that the aura or energy pattern around the hands of the yogi increased dramatically while the yogi was meditating as compared to when he was just resting.

Kirlian Photo of Tomato Leaf

Leaf cut away above line.
NOTE: Aura remains whole

Since Jesus was the Son of God, or what Eastern religions call an avatar—God in man's form—the life-force or energy from His body would have been very great. As Bock says, "For some, this theory goes a long way toward explaining the body images left on the burial shroud. It also explains why no other shroud images have been found in the centuries following the death of Jesus."[16]

30

Kirlian Photo of Faith-Healer's Hands

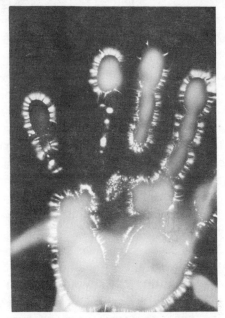

ABOVE: before healing

BELOW: during healing — note expanded and directed aura patterns.

31

Chapter 4

GOD IS "ABOVE" THE PHYSICAL

Two other aspects of the Shroud's image should be noted. First, all who have seen the Shroud, including the scientists, have remarked on how the image's face is "hauntingly serene" in death. It's as if the crucified man of the Shroud had experienced no pain. But how would that be possible? Crucifixion was so horrendously painful, as described before, that even the Romans outlawed it as a form of punishment in the Fourth Century A.D. One would think that the image's face would have reflected some of that torturous pain, and yet, it reflects peace and calm. Is it possible then that Jesus felt no pain, even on the cross?

The standard Bible accounts of Jesus' crucifixion seem to indicate that He suffered greatly, but there are other accounts of the crucifixion that indicate that Jesus was "above" the pain. One such account is found in the *Lost Gospel According to Peter;* a gospel that, at one time in the early Christian Church, was held in as high esteem as Matthew's and Mark's, and even higher than those of Luke and John, but was later rejected by the organized Church for inclusion into the standardized Bible. The Gospel is considered absolutely authentic, as are many other gospels and epistles that have been left out of the Bible because they did not suit the purposes of the organizers of the early Christian Church. It, as well as the others, were "lost" to the lay reader for almost 1500 years until 1926, when they were finally translated from their original language into English and made available to the general public.

In this gospel, Peter describes the crucifixion scene in much the same manner as the orthodox gospels except for the following: "And they brought two malefactors, and they crucified the Lord between them. But He held His peace, **as though having no pain.**"[1]

The Gnostic Gospels

Other accounts of the Lord's crucifixion are even more explicit as to the Lord's lack of pain or of being literally "above" the pain. These accounts can be found in the Gnostic Gospels which are a collection of manuscripts found in a cave near Nag Hammadi, Egypt, in 1945. Most people have heard of the Dead Sea Scrolls discovered in 1947 near Jericho, between Israel and Jordan. This set of manuscripts dates back to Christ's time or even earlier and has been linked to the Essenes, a Jewish sect of which John the Baptist and Jesus of Nazareth were said to have been members. They were hidden in caves for safekeeping during the Roman persecutions of the Jews. These scrolls describe the society, customs, and religious ceremonies of the region at the time of Christ, but nowhere in the scrolls is Jesus of Nazareth mentioned by name.

The Gnostic Gospels, on the other hand, are filled with Jesus' name and the names of His followers. Some of the Gospels and/or traditions contained in them may even be older than the gospels of the New Testament (c. 60-110 A.D.), according to Professor Helmut Koester of Harvard University, possibly dating as far back as 50 to 100 A.D., which is as early or earlier than Mark, Matthew, Luke and John, the four gospels which make up most of the New Testament.[2]

The Gnostics were a Christian Coptic sect dating back to Christ's time whose emphasis was on knowledge (gnosis) of the Lord through **personal spiritual experience,** as opposed to rituals, ceremonies, and book knowledge. Interestingly enough, those who have had death experiences recount that, after Love, the acquisition of knowledge of God was stressed the most: knowledge, not in a technical sense, but in an ethical or spiritual sense, put into practice in a morally correct way; knowledge of the basic cause of things, of basic universal principles; deeper knowledge as it relates to the soul; knowledge acquired through **direct personal spiritual experience and application,** what one woman called Wisdom.[3]

Not surprisingly, most of the Gnostic Gospels concern themselves with this kind of knowledge, and one of them is even entitled *Sophia,* the Greek word for **wisdom!** So both the Gnostic Christians and those who have had death experiences stress that we must acquire not knowledge of rituals, dogmas, or ceremonies, but wisdom—knowledge—gnosis—of the basic cause of all things; in other words, knowledge of God, of His Universe, of His Laws of Karma as exemplified by the Balance of Nature.

The Gnostics, too, were persecuted, which is why their teachings were hidden away, however not by the Romans—but by the orthodox Christian Church who labeled the Gnostics as heretics! It seems that the followers of the early Christian Church began to split into two groups, the Gnostics and the Orthodox, towards the beginning of the Second Century. By the middle of that century the orthodox group had denounced the Gnostics as "blasphemers" and sought to ban their teachings. By the Fourth Century, the orthodox church had merged its power with that of the state and used that power to destroy the Gnostics and their teachings. The persecutees of Rome had become the persecutors of "fellow Christians." Gnostic books were banned and possession of them became a criminal offense, punishable by imprisonment and even death. The books themselves were condemned as "perverse" and, as Pope Leo the Great (c. 447 A.D.) said, "...should not only be forbidden, but entirely destroyed and burned with fire!'";[4] hence the clay pots and caves in Egypt to save them from those fires.

Even today few people have heard of these gospels even though they were discovered almost 40 years ago. Due to political, religious, and academic infighting, the gospels were not available to the general public until the late '70's, when the first complete edition in English was published in the U.S.

In these gospels, then, we see quite a different version of the Lord's crucifixion. To quote from *The Apocalypse of Peter:*

> "...I saw Him apparently being seized by them. And I said, 'What am I seeing, O Lord? Is it really you whom they take? And are they hammering the feet and hands of another? Who is this one **above** the cross, who is glad and laughing?' The Savior said to me, 'He whom you saw being glad and laughing above the cross is the Living Jesus. But He into whose hands and feet they are driving the nails is His fleshly part, which is the substitute. They put to shame that which remained in His likeness. And look at Him, and (look at) me!' "[5]

In the *Second Treatise of the Great Seth,* Christ says:

> "...it was another...who drank the gall and the vinegar; it was not I. They struck me with the reed; it was another, Simon, who bore the cross on his shoulder. It was another upon whom they placed the crown of thorns. But I was rejoicing in the height over...their error...And I was laughing at their ignorance."[6]

And again, in *The Acts of John,* after showing His disciples a sacred dance, Jesus says:

"You who dance, consider what I do, for yours is this passion of Man which I am to suffer. For you could by no means have understood what you suffer unless to you as **Logos** (The Word, The Sacred Name made flesh) I had been sent by the Father...

"Learn how to suffer and you shall be able not to suffer."[7]

And, later, while John is in a cave during the crucifixion, Jesus says to him in a vision:

"John, for the people below...I am being crucified and pierced with lances...and given vinegar and gall to drink. But to you I am speaking, and listen to what I speak...

"I have suffered none of the things which they will say of me; even that suffering which I showed to you and to the rest in my dance, I will that it be called a mystery."[8]

So we see two radically different views of the crucifixion, both of which are supported by the evidence of the Shroud. For, after seeing it, who can deny that the body of Jesus was beaten, scourged, crowned with thorns, impaled by nails and speared in the side? But, at the same time, who can deny that look of serenity and peace that emanates from His face!

Beyond Pain

Is there any scientific or documented evidence to support the idea that Jesus could have endured the crucifixion without experiencing pain? During the 1960's, at least one Buddhist monk had a unique way of protesting the Vietnam War. The monk doused himself with gasoline, sat down in the middle of a busy street in Saigon, and proceeded to light a match to himself. He immediately became engulfed in flames while television cameramen and photographers caught the spectacle on film. By the time the flames were out, all that was left of the monk's body was ashes. The most amazing part is that the monk never uttered a word, never gave out a cry the whole time his body was burning. On the contrary, his face was incredibly serene and peaceful to the end.

More recently scientists have been baffled by Shamans (priests) from Java, Indonesia, who can walk on broken glass and rub it on their faces without being cut, and can sandwich themselves front and back with huge thorns long and sharp enough to kill a man, without being punctured; or the Kurdish howling dervishes who communicate with God through pain and, through faith, can bite swords, poke needles through their bodies, "eat" fire, and stab their eyes with knives—all without any blood, burns or pain; or Indian yogis who can sit on beds of nails, walk over hot coals, and even withstand the direct weight of an elephant on their chest without being crushed or suffering any adverse effects at all. One Hindu sect being studied by scientists deep in the jungles of Sri Lanka (Ceylon) can suspend themselves in midair from as many as twenty steel hooks thrust through their skin for up to 12 hours at a time without experiencing any pain! These monks, from the holy Hindu shrine of Katargama, recently performed their incredible feat for doctors in medical college laboratories. The doctors stated that the monks did not bleed at all, and that there was no tetanus or any other form of infection afterwards. The monks spoke in a normal fashion while hanging, and throughout the experiment, the faces of the monks were described as "serene."

One more example may help to explain how such things are possible. Sri Ramana Maharshi of India was one of the greatest saints of this century. Toward the end of his life, a cancerous lesion developed on his arm and had to be cut out. The doctor who performed the surgery (whom one of the authors has met) relates that it was done without any anesthesia of any kind. While the doctor was cutting away, Sri Ramana, who was sitting calmly and exhibiting no signs of pain, said to him, "You think you are hurting me, but it is only the body that suffers."

What did the Indian yogi mean when he said "only the body suffers"? He meant that those who are absorbed in the Bliss of the Lord are above the body, and therefore, do not feel bodily pleasure and pain. They reside in the Spirit of God, and therefore, no bodily ailment can truly touch them. When one is continually absorbed in the Lord's Bliss, then one goes beyond the dualities of pain and pleasure and is no longer affected by them. One is "above" the pain, as Jesus was "above" the pain of His crucifixion.

When asked for the spiritual meaning behind the crucifixion,

36

Sri Ramana explained that the physical body of Jesus represented man's ego and attachments to this ephemeral world; attachment to this doomed system of things and to the pain and pleasure that that attachment brings. The body was nailed to the cross of Truth; the Truth that the body is temporary and will die, and with its death comes liberation and freedom from this world and all its sorrows; the Truth that it is the Spirit alone that is eternal and therefore above the dualities of pain and pleasure, life and death. Similarly, one must strive to kill one's ego, so that the spirit of Truth may be liberated, freed, and allowed to grow and flourish. If one ceases to identify with one's body and ego and, instead, strives more and more to identify with one's inner Self, Soul, or Spirit, then one will transcend the limitations of the body/ego consciousness and will dwell in Bliss and Union with the Lord. One must kill the ego and stop thinking in terms of "I" and "mine," and must, instead, start to recognize that the One Great Spirit of the Lord pervades all and dwells equally in all.

So we see that there is documented scientific evidence to support the theory that Jesus could have endured the crucifixion without experiencing pain; hence, that serene face on the Shroud.

Chapter 5

THE MISSING LINK

The last aspect of the Shroud that should be noted, and probably its most important and intriguing, is the shape of the most prominent bloodstain on the forehead of the image's face. That bloodstain bears a striking resemblance to the Hindu or Sanskrit word for God—Om, written ॐ ! But what is the Hindu word for God doing on the forehead of the Christian Messiah? Does it mean that Jesus of Nazareth was somehow linked to India? And, if so, how? Is there a possibility that Jesus went to India, and, if so, when?

The answer seems to lie in what are called "the lost years" of Jesus—those years covering age 12 to 30 about which the Bible is absolutely silent. The orthodox Christian view of those years is that Jesus spent His time in Nazareth, as an apprentice to His father Joseph, the carpenter. But if this is so, why was Jesus not married by age 30, as the Jewish custom was to marry very young, even at age 13? Also, records indicate that Jesus was absent at the time of His father's death, which is said to have occurred around Jesus' 20th year. And finally, according to the Bible itself, John the Baptist did not recognize Jesus at first ("I myself did not know him...").[1] It should be remembered that John and Jesus were cousins, and their families lived fairly close to one another. If Jesus had spent all of His life in Nazareth, why, then, did John, his own cousin, not recognize Him? So, where was He all those years?

Many believe that Jesus was indeed in India during most of those "lost years," and there are accounts to support their beliefs. Such accounts can be found in a book called *The Aquarian Gospel of Jesus The Christ,* by Levi. This book covers the birth, childhood and education of Jesus' mother Mary, of John the Baptist, and of Jesus Himself. It also covers those so-called "lost years" during which Jesus traveled through India, Tibet, Persia, Assyria, Greece, and Egypt, with most of those 18 years being spent in India. Here Jesus is said to have met Brahmin priests who introduced Him to the great Hindu scriptures—the *Vedas* and *Upanishads,* humankind's earliest spiritual scriptures. It is said that He mastered these teachings, as well as healing techniques using prayer, water, earth, air and the laying on of hands.

38

The Face on the Holy Shroud of Turin
(A Photographic Negative Image)

INSERT: Image as it Appears
on the Shroud.

After mastering the greater part of Hinduism, Jesus is said to have traveled to North India, Nepal, and then on to Tibet, where the Buddhist priests welcomed Him with open arms. He quickly learned the Pali language, in which Lord Buddha's teachings were written, and mastered them as well. Here He is said to have taught the Word of God and healed many people. He then traveled through the Kashmir mountains and valleys into Western India (Pakistan), and on into Persia, where He met three Magian priests with whom He meditated in silence for seven days.[2] Many people feel that the three Wisemen from the East of whom the Bible speaks came from Persia, while others feel they came from India and that the initial reason for Jesus' trip to India was to return their visit. In any case, while in Persia, Jesus taught and healed many, and then traveled on to Assyria, Greece, and Egypt, teaching and healing wherever He went.

While in Egypt, it is written that Jesus reaffirmed the way to Truth by engaging in and passing the seven final tests of Brotherhood—Sincerity, Justice, Faith, Philanthropy, Heroism, Love Divine, and three days and nights in the Tomb of the Dead—to reveal Himself as the **Christ, Logos,** the **Living Word of God.**[3] From Egypt, Jesus the Christ is said to have gone to Galilee to meet John the Baptist, and thus, having gone full circle, began His ministry in His native land among His own countrymen.

The rest of the *Aquarian Gospel* closely follows the accounts of the orthodox New Testament with regard to Jesus' ministry in Israel, His betrayal and trial, execution and Resurrection.

Cayce Sees and Agrees

Other accounts of Jesus' "lost years" have come through the clairvoyant readings of Edgar Cayce, America's greatest modern-day psychic and prophet. Cayce gave more than 14,500 readings, many of which had to do with physical ailments that traditional medicine could not cure. Cayce's unorthodox therapies and treatments worked, which helped give further credence to his other readings dealing with past, present, and future events. (Many of Cayce's treatments are being successfully used today by several physicians.)

Cayce is credited with foretelling, in 1919, the second rise of Germany within two decades; in 1925, the crash of the stock market that occurred four years later; and in 1939, the entry of the U.S. into World War II and the date of the Allies' victory in 1945.[4]

He also gave amazingly accurate accounts as to past events, such as the destruction and sinking of Atlantis, part of which Cayce said would be rediscovered near the Bahamas. In 1968, divers found a massive stone wall (perhaps the sea wall that surrounded the island of Atlantis?) at the bottom of the ocean off the coast of the Bahamas, and in 1974, archaeological researchers did indeed discover part of an island—part of old Atlantis—off the coast of one of the Bimini Islands in the Bahamas—**exactly where Cayce had predicted decades earlier!**

So we can see that Edgar Cayce had an incredible gift of prophecy that he believed came from God, as he was a devout Christian. Over a period of several years, Cayce had many visions of Jesus and His early life and education. Regarding those years of training, Cayce said:

> "The periods of study in Palestine were only at the time of His sojourn in the temple, or in Jerusalem during those periods when He was quoted by Luke as being among the rabbis or teachers. His studies in Persia, India, and Egypt covered much greater periods...
>
> "[In India:] Those cleansings of the body related to preparation for strength in the physical, as well as in the mental man."[5]

Yogic Cleansings

To what cleansings was Cayce referring? In the ancient science of Yoga as practiced in India one seeks to cleanse the body and mind of its impurities through fastings, exercises, austerities—what the Indians call "askesis"—and meditation. One must rid the body of the toxins or poisons that have accumulated within it, strengthen it through certain stretching exercises and positions called "asanas," and eat pure, uncontaminated foods that are easily digested and cause no bodily discomfort. This way the body becomes an aid to meditation rather than an obstacle. If one's body is constantly aching or calling attention to itself, it becomes very difficult for the mind to concentrate or meditate. If, however, one's body is healthy and strong and free of discomforts, it becomes much easier to forget about **it** and start concentrating on **God.**

"The first signs of progress on the path of yoga are health, a sense of physical lightness, clearness of complexion, a beautiful voice, an agreeable odor of the person, and freedom from craving."[6] *(Upanishads)*

This does not mean that one needs to cleanse the body before one starts to practice meditation, or that if one's body is ill that one should not think about God—not at all! Thinking or praying to God and meditating on Him will help speed up the healing process. When one's mind is cleansed through the practice of meditation, one's body becomes free of stress and, therefore, disease as most diseases are brought on by stress and wrong living habits. The body can then manifest its power or energy more easily. For the body is usually a reflection of the state of one's mind: if the mind is at ease and free of stress, so will be the body.

Medical science is beginning to recognize this truth: i.e., that it is the mind that controls or should control the body and not the other way around. This truth has been demonstrated again and again by what physicians call "the placebo effect," which refers to the positive physical improvements in a patient's condition after his taking a placebo—a pill that has absolutely no medical value. The patient **believes** that the pill will help him and, therefore, improves even though the pill may be made of nothing but ordinary flour!

There have also been accounts of remarkable cures of what had been considered terminally-ill cancer patients who were taught a technique called "visual imagery," which is actually a form of meditation. The patient actively uses his mind in a positive way to visualize the destruction of cancer cells in his own body. In some cases, these "incurably ill" people have rid themselves of the cancer in their bodies in a matter of a few weeks! It is simply a case of believing the old adage: mind over matter!

The Process of Meditation

Cleansing of the mind is achieved through a twofold process. First, one must become an observer to one's own thoughts throughout the day. One must strive to root out negative/ego-oriented thoughts of greed, anger, lust and hatred, and start replacing these with positive/God-oriented thoughts of truth, peace, love, and compassion. As one cleanses one's thoughts, one is able to control one's ego more and more, and one's actions are cleansed as a natural consequence of this practice, since the mind does control the body.

The second aspect of cleansing the mind consists of concentrating on God in whatever form one wishes—Christ, Buddha, Allah, Jehovah, Om or just Pure Light. By continually practicing this form of concentration, one eventually loses the sense of "I" and "mine" and, effacing his individual ego, merges into the Bliss of the Lord.

Chanting of the Lord's Name helps to set up a positive vibration, conducive to mergence with the Lord. What chanting and meditating actually do is synchronize the electrical activity of both hemispheres of the brain. This, in turn, helps to release hormones in the brain called endorphines, which have been likened to natural opiates by scientists. This is why one feels blissful, peaceful and pain-free during meditation.

Meditation also helps to release the great amount of energy that is stored at the bottom of the spine. This ball of energy, which is called "kundalini," has been likened to a serpent coiled at the base of the spinal column. As one continues to meditate, this energy rises up through a very narrow channel in the spinal column—a channel whose purpose had eluded scientists for years, but which was well-known for aeons by yogis and mystics. It is the same channel, on a physical plane, of which Jesus spoke when He said that the gateway and/or road to heaven was very narrow.[7]

As the kundalini rises it activates seven centers of energy, or "chakras." These chakras are (from lowest to highest or in order of ascendancy): Elimination, Reproduction, Power, Divine Love, Creativity, Awareness, and Union with the Lord. When the kundalini rises to the sixth chakra, located midway between the eyebrows and commonly referred to as the Third Eye, it activates the psychic organ in the brain—the pineal gland. Alcohol has a very detrimental effect on this gland, as well as on the delicate fibers of the other chakras. It actually atrophies or shrivels it up, and brain cells, like teeth, **do not regenerate!** This is the reason why mystics around the world, including the American Indians, have been so adamantly against the use of alcohol.

Autopsies conducted on various individuals reveal that in those who drank, the gland was completely atrophied or shriveled up; in those who had begun to cleanse physically by abstaining from

THE SEVEN CHAKRAS
(FROM LOWEST TO HIGHEST)

Elimination, Reproduction, Power, Divine Love, Creativity, Awareness, Union: Described as the thousand petalled lotus, represented in artwork by the beaded pattern on Lord Buddha's head.

44

alcohol and other detrimental chemicals, and eating organic health-enhancing foods, the gland was filled with a grainy, sand-like substance; in those who had dedicated their lives to spiritual pursuits and meditation, the gland was filled with a clear fluid. Jesus said that one must have **a clear eye** if one is to see!

Though brain cells do not usually regenerate, it should be remembered that **God can do anything.** An example of this was illustrated by a recent UPI release which stated that an 110-year-old woman who had been toothless for at least half a century had suddenly grown a sparkling new set of teeth![8] So what won't God do for one who truly turns to Him!

One of India's greatest saints, so great that he heard Lord Krishna's flute constantly during the last years of his life, was the world-renowned mystic and musician, Sri Dilip Kumar Roy. Dada-ji, as he was affectionately called by his disciples, was also a prolific writer and master of approximately seventeen languages, including English, German, French, Italian, and Sanskrit. In his translation of the *Bhagavad Gita,* translated directly from the original Sanskrit, Lord Krishna explains the practice of meditation as follows:

> "By the discipline of mental concentration, meditating ever one-pointedly on the Supreme Divine, one can attain to Him...
>
> "The devotee who does this, concentrating steadfastly all his life-force midway between the eyebrows with all the resolution and strength of Yoga, shall attain the Goal of the Supreme Divine...
>
> "Closing all the senses' doors and the mind withdrawn in the heart, the life-force taken up out of its restless movement into the head, the intellect rapt in the utterance of the Om (Jesus, Allah, etc.) and remembering me...he attains...the highest Goal."[9]

As Dadaji's daughter-disciple Smt. Indira Devi, a guru in her own right, explains:

> "Meditation is not **done,** it just **happens.** It is complete relaxation, the act of **being** and not trying to **become** anything.
>
> "Meditation is not breathing exercises, rigid postures or attempting to silence the mind and in the process making oneself that much more tense. Neither is it a mathematical process

or a scientific achievement that can be won in the laboratories. Meditation is a contract with the Beloved, your real Self. It is the completeness of being alone with oneself, a state of Grace in which one spontaneously opens one's heart to the Light. See how the sunflower opens its petals to the sun—effortlessly, yet so definitely."[10]

This does not mean that breath control, good posture, etc., can not be used as aids in **preparation** to meditation. After all, the Holy Spirit or Spirit of God has often been associated with breath, as in the phrase "the Breath of Life." Furthermore, taking a few deep breaths **prior** to actually meditating can help one to relax one's self and to focus the mind on the Light. But as Smt. Indira Devi, affectionately known as "Ma" by her disciples, points out, one must not become preoccupied with one's breathing as the point of **true** meditation is to forget the physical, not to get into it even more by being uncomfortably stiff and rigid in posture or counting and holding one's breath!

If one wishes to learn meditation through music, one has only to listen to the Moody Blues' song, "One Step Into the Light," on their album *Octave*. The practice of meditation as well as its fruits have been discussed at length in India's oldest and most important holy scriptures—the *Vedas*. Each of the four *Vedas* is divided into two parts: work and knowledge, the former being instructions regarding rites, ceremonies, rules of conduct, etc., and the latter, called the *Upanishads*, being concerned with knowledge of God—"the highest aspect of religious Truth."[11]

The *Upanishads* are the work of saints and sages who reported insights and truths which came to them in thought or vision. In other words, the *Upanishads* are the result of **Gnosis**— knowledge gained through **personal spiritual experience**, and are thus strikingly similar, and in many cases identical to the writings of Gnostic Christians such as Mary Magdalene, St. Thomas, and St. John, as would have to be the case since the authors of both sets of scriptures were in direct communion with the Lord, the only difference being the *Upanishads* were written thousands of years before the Christian Gnostic Gospels!

In the *Upanishads*, then, we find the following passages regarding preparation for, the actual process and fruits of meditation:

"Retire to a solitary place, such as a mountain cave or any

46

sacred spot (such as an area in the house set aside for prayer). The place must be protected from the wind and rain, and it must have a smooth, clean floor, free from pebbles and dust. It must not be damp, and it must be free from disturbing noises. It must be pleasing to the eye and quieting to the mind. Seated there, practice meditation and other spiritual exercises...

"Sit upright, holding the chest, throat, and head erect. Turn the senses and mind inward to the lotus of the heart (10 fingers above the navel—at the Heart Chakra). Meditate on Brahman (God) with the help of the syllable OM (humankind's oldest known word for God, coming from the ancient Sanskrit language). Cross the fearful currents of the ocean of worldliness by means of the raft of Brahman (God)—the sacred syllable OM.

"With **earnest effort** hold the senses in check. Controlling the breath, regulate the vital activities. As a charioteer holds back his restive horses, so does a persevering aspirant hold back his mind...

"As you practice meditation, you may see in vision forms resembling snow, crystal, wind, smoke, fire, lightning, fireflies, the sun, the moon. These are signs that you are on your way to the revelation of Brahman (God).

"As you become absorbed in meditation, you will realize that the Self is separate from the body and for this reason will not be affected by disease, old age, or death...By meditating on Him, by identifying oneself with Him, one ceases to be ignorant.

"Know God, and all fetters will be loosed. Ignorance will vanish. Birth, death, and rebirth will be no more. Meditate upon Him and transcend physical consciousness. Thus you will reach union with the Lord of the universe...Meditate, and you will realize that mind, matter and Maya (the power that unites mind and matter) are but three aspects of Brahman (God), the one reality.

"Fire, though present in the firesticks, is not perceived until one stick is rubbed against another...Let your body be the stick that is rubbed, the sacred syllable OM the stick that is rubbed against it. Thus shall you realize God, who is hidden within the body as fire is hidden within the wood...

"Let a man meditate upon Brahman (God) as support, and

he will be supported. Let him meditate upon Brahman as greatness, and he will be great. Let him meditate upon Brahman as mind, and he will be endowed with intellectual power. Let him meditate upon Brahman as adoration, and he will be adored. Let him worship Brahman as Brahman, and he will become Brahman..."[12]—or, in other words, realize God and become One with Him.

Few people can remain at the heights of Bliss one eventually experiences during meditation all of the time, but because one has seen these higher realms of reality and knows that they exist, one cannot forget them. The idea is to persevere, continually striving to repeat these blissful experiences until they become permanent. This is, after all, a process of transformation—a transformation from a low, ego-oriented, half-conscious or half-awake individual to a high, God-oriented, fully conscious, fully awake and aware instrument of the Lord—and the process may take a long time. **DO NOT BE DISCOURAGED!** Cultivate patience and forebearance; seek to bring the Light down to you as you simultaneously rise to meet it. Call upon the Lord for aid—**He will not fail you! For God's delay does not mean denial!**

And when you begin to experience new sensations of Bliss, Lightness, and Oneness, give into them; merge into them; do not withdraw from them out of fear of the unknown, for fear comes from ignorance, and what is really afraid is the ego losing its control over you as you grow closer to God by acquiring new knowledge of Him from **personal spiritual experience. Trust, Love and have Full Faith in God, and Let Him Guide You!**

Baptism and Yoga

One other aspect of cleansing should be mentioned. John the Baptist prepared people for the coming of the Lord by immersing them in water. John learned from the Essenes, who in turn got their teachings from Buddhist monks, who were sent out as missionaries by the great Indian Emperor Asoka about 250 B.C.[13] Lord Buddha came from India where bathing is not only a physical act of cleansing, but also a symbolic act of cleansing the mind and heart of evil thoughts and propensities. This ancient practice can be observed even today in several cities in India, like Haridwar and Benares. So the Christian rite of Baptism has its origin in India!

One more note of interest: the word "Yoga" means "Union," indicating the union of the purified individualized soul with the Lord—the All-Soul. Jesus used to say, "Take my **yoke** upon you and learn of me, for my **yoke** is easy."[14] Both "yoga" and "yoke" come from the same Greek word—"Zeugos." Rewritten, the sentence becomes, "Take my **yoga** upon you and learn of me, for my **yoga** is easy." Could it be that Jesus is admonishing His followers to follow Him by practicing His yoga, the same yoga that has been practiced by yogis since time immemorial in India as the Path to Oneness with the Lord? Another link to India?

Chapter 6

THE LEGEND OF SAINT ISSA (JESUS)

Both Cayce's and Levi's accounts of the travels of Jesus were a result of visions that each man received. From where did these visions come? Cayce and Levi explain that they got their visions from what the Hebrews call "The Book of God's Remembrance," or the Akashic Records, "Akasha" being a Sanskrit word meaning "Primary substance," or the Spirit of God, as the origin of all things is God.

But are there any other accounts of Jesus' travels that do not rely on visions? And if Jesus did travel through these countries, wouldn't there be folk legends or accounts of His visits, or at least references to Him somewhere in those countries? The answer to both questions is an emphatic "YES!"

The oldest reference to Jesus can be found in a set of Hindu scriptures called *The Shrimad Bhagavatam,* which has been described as "the fruit of the Vedas and Upanishads" and "the embodiment of the Lord Himself" in this age—the Kali Age, the Age of Chaos, or End Times. *The Shrimad Bhagavatam* is similar to the Judeo-Christian Bible in that it recounts the lives of great saints and sages as well as the teachings of the Lord Himself throughout the ages. It accurately chronicles historical events such as the creation of the universe and this world, and the Great Flood that covered the earth, the only difference being that this account of the flood is at least 1000 years older than the account of Noah found in the Bible!

It also contains a section remarkably similar to the lines of kings and rulers found in Daniel of the Old Testament. Of course the kings and the duration of their rule mentioned here refers to India, but it is every bit as accurate, historically, as is Daniel's with regards to Middle Eastern rulers.

The birth and life of the Lord as Sri Krishna is recounted as well as the prophecies and predictions that preceded His coming at that time. Also prophesied is the birth of the Lord as the Buddha, including the area in which the Lord would be born: "When Kali (the age of chaos) sets in, He (the Lord) will be born in Magadha (North Bihar, India) as Buddha...with a view to deluding the enemies of God."[1] Lord Buddha was indeed born in 563 B.C. in ancient Kapilavatthu, which lay in North Bihar, India.

There are other prophecies concerning the Lord's incarnation during the Kali Age. It states that the Lord would come again and that this time He would be followed mostly by the poor and fishermen, and that these devotees would be the ones who would initially spread the words of Truth:

> "People in that age (the age of Kali and the time of Christ's coming) turn out to be greedy, immoral and merciless, enter into hostility without cause and are unlucky and extremely covetous. (Pretty accurate description of the rulers at that time!) The Sudras (lower classes or poor laborers), **fishermen,** and the like take the lead."[2]

It should be remembered that most of the early followers of Jesus were the poor or lower classes of society. They flocked around Him for He gave them hope of a brighter future. It should also be remembered that Jesus' closest disciples were mostly fishermen, including Simon Peter, Andrew, James, and John, among others.

Throughout the *Shrimad Bhagavatam* the word "Isa" is found. "Isa" means "God" or "Lord of Created Beings." It is interesting to note that the Moslems, who believe Jesus was a great prophet, call Him "Isa." Coincidence?

The Buddha, too, foretold of the future incarnation of God on Earth. When He was about to leave this physical plane, His disciple tearfully said to Him, "Who shall teach us when thou art gone?" And Lord Buddha replied:

> "I am not the first Buddha (enlightened one—avatar—Son of God) who came upon earth, nor shall I be the last. In due time another Buddha will arise in the world, a Holy One, a supremely enlightened One, endowed with wisdom in conduct, auspicious, knowing the universe, an incomparable leader of men, a master of angels and mortals. He will reveal to you the same eternal truths which I have taught you. He will preach His religion, glorious in its origin, glorious at the climax, and glorious at the goal, in the spirit and in the letter. He will proclaim a religious life, wholly perfect and pure; such as I now proclaim."[3]

The disciple asked, "How shall we know Him?"

And the Buddha said, "He will be known as Metteyya, which means 'He whose name is kindness.' "[4]

Was He talking about Jesus? Well, it is interesting that Jesus has been described as the embodiment of compassion, kindness, and Divine Love. In artwork He is frequently shown pointing to His Sacred Heart—the symbol of kindness and Divine Love. This, coupled with the fact that His followers were to be fishermen, certainly gives weight to the idea that Lord Buddha was referring to Jesus.

And, according to the *Aquarian Gospel,* after hearing Jesus speak, the Buddhist priests themselves recognized Jesus as being "The Holy One," the reincarnation of the Lord whose advent had been prophesied by Lord Buddha almost 600 years earlier!

> "Now, Vidyapati, wisest of the Indian sages, chief of (the Buddhist) temple...heard the Hebrew prophet, and he said,
>
> " 'You priests...hear me speak: We stand today upon a crest of time. Six times ago (six centuries ago) a master soul (Lord Buddha) was born who gave a glory Light to man, and now a master sage stands here in (the) temple...
>
> " 'This Hebrew prophet is the rising star of wisdom, deified. He brings us a knowledge of the secret things of God; and all the world will hear His words, will heed His words, and glorify His name. You priests of (the) temple, stay! be still and listen when He speaks; He is the Living Oracle of God.'
>
> "And all the priests gave thanks, and praised the Buddha of Enlightenment (Jesus)."[5]

The Legend

There's more...

The most explicit account of Jesus' travels throughout India and other lands is found in a Buddhist manuscript called *The Legend of Saint Issa* (Issa=Isa=Jesus), which dates back to the First Century A.D., making it at least as old, if not older than the accounts of the New Testament, and in which Issa, or Jesus, is described as being the one "...whom the Buddha had elected to spread His holy word..."[6]

The first Westerner to hear about the manuscript was a Russian explorer named Nicolas Notovitch. Notovitch had traveled extensively throughout India, Afghanistan, and Tibet in the late 1800's and heard about the legend and the manuscript during his travels. He decided to check out the legend and journeyed to a Buddhist monastery called Himis in Leh, Ledak, formerly part of Tibet, now the northernmost part of India. The original manuscript was written in the ancient Pali language, and had been brought to Tibet from India.

The legend of Saint Issa closely paralleled the life of Jesus, including His torture and execution by crucifixion, but also covered those "lost years" of Jesus about which the Bible is silent. Convinced of the authenticity of the manuscript, Notovitch wrote a book on his travels and the legend of St. Issa which included a translation of the original manuscript.

Thirty-five years later, in 1922, Swami Abhedananda, a follower of one of the greatest saints to have lived on Earth—Sri Ramakrishna—also traveled to Himis to see the manuscript for himself. He, too, was convinced of its authenticity and wrote about it in his book called *Kashmiri O Tibbetti.*[7]

The legend of St. Issa opens with these words:

"The earth trembled and the heavens wept, because of the great crime committed in the land of Israel.

"For there was tortured and murdered the great and just Issa, in whom was manifest the soul of the Universe;

"Which had incarnated in a simple mortal, to benefit men and destroy the evil spirit in them;

"To lead back to peace, love and happiness, man, degraded by his sins, and recall him to the one and indivisible Creator whose mercy is infinite..."[8]

The legend goes on to give accounts brought by merchants from Israel on what had happened. It follows the people of Israel through their troubles, first with the Pharoahs of Egypt and their subsequent deliverance by Mossa (Moses), and then by the Pagans from the land of Romeles (Rome). It explains that the hardships that the Israelites suffered were due to their own sins in forgetting the laws of God and cleaving, instead, to sensual pleasures and the laws of mortal men. Because of their sufferings the people again began to remember and pray to the One and only

God to hear them, forgive them, and deliver them from their distress. He did! The legend continues:

"At that time the moment had come for the compassionate Judge to re-incarnate in a human form;

"And the eternal Spirit, resting in a state of complete inaction and supreme bliss, awakened and separated from the eternal Being for an undetermined period,

"So that, in human form, He might teach man to identify himself with the Divinity and attain to eternal felicity;

"And to show, by His example, how man can attain moral purity and free his soul from the domination of the physical senses, so that it may achieve the perfection necessary for it to enter the Kingdom of Heaven, which is immutable and where bliss eternal reigns.

"Soon after, a marvelous child was born in the land of Israel. God Himself spoke, through the mouth of this child, of the miseries of the body and the grandeur of the soul...

"The divine child, to whom the name Issa was given, commenced in His tender years, to talk of the only and indivisible God, exhorting the strayed souls to repent and purify themselves from the sins of which they had become guilty.

"People came from all parts to hear Him, and marveled at the discourses which came from His infantile mouth; and all Israel agreed that the Spirit of the Eternal dwelt in this child."[9]

The legend goes on to say that Issa or Jesus left His parents' home at age 13 and traveled toward India, "with the object of perfecting Himself in the Knowledge of the word of God and the study of the laws of the great Buddhas (enlightened ones)."[10] He settled in India, "...the country beloved by God,"[11] and spent six years in Jaggannath, in Radjugriha, in Benares, and in other holy cities, first studying and later teaching and expounding upon the *Vedas*—Hinduism's and the world's oldest holy scriptures—to all members of society.

Here, as in Israel, Jesus aroused the anger of certain orthodox Brahmin priests who had twisted God's teachings about the caste system by saying that all men were not equal in God's eyes and that some, the Sudras or members of the "lowest" caste, were unworthy even to hear the Lord's words, much less read them.

Jesus denounced this false doctrine of inequality and warned the priests to beware of perverting the purpose behind God's Great Plan. He admonished them to return to the Truth and to re-examine God's teachings regarding the caste system.

So, before going further, we will do just that; i.e., examine the origin, purpose, and function of the caste system in society in order to clear up any misconceptions and misunderstandings about it and the equality of all people. We will also examine the universal Truths that are found in unadulterated scriptures of all of the major religions of the world, as confirmed by Jesus in His travels throughout India, Tibet, Persia, Greece, Egypt, and Palestine. We will also compare the various prophecies of the major religions so as to prove beyond the shadow of a doubt that these are the End Times!

PART II

Follow Your Own
True Nature

MOTHER NATURE - (White Buffalo Cow Woman)
LORD KRISHNA - Circa 2500 B.C. / GURU NANAK - Circa 1500 A.D.

56

Chapter 1

FOLLOW YOUR OWN NATURE

So, then, what exactly is the caste system? What is its origin and what was its true function in society? In the *Gita,* the Lord as Krishna explains:

> "I classed men into four castes and assigned different functions to them in accordance with their different temperaments and karma (past actions)... The works assigned to Brahmins (priests), Ksatriyas (warriors), Vaisyas (farmers, merchants, etc.) and Sudras (laborers) are graded in accordance with the qualities born of their inner nature.
>
> "Serenity, self-mastery, purity, spirituality, forebearance, wisdom, askesis and ingenuousness— all these are known as the Brahmin's natural attributes.
>
> "Heroism, prowess, steadiness, skillfulness, large-heartedness, in battle dauntlessness, administrative ability— all these are a Ksatriya's natural attributes.
>
> "Trade, commerce, agriculture and tending cattle are a Vaisya's natural duty, even as serving men through work is a Sudra's duty."[1]

In other words, it was a recognition of the different natural talents and abilities of each individual. Sri Aurobindo, the Master Yogi, explains that:

> "There are thus four kinds of works, the work of religious ministration, letters, learning and knowledge; the work of government, politics, administration and war; the work of production, wealth-making and exchange; the work of hired labour and service. An endeavour was made to found and establish the whole arrangement of society on the partition of these four functions among four clearly marked classes. The system was not peculiar to India, but was with certain differences the dominating feature of a stage of social evolution in other ancient or mediaeval societies. The four functions are still inherent in the life of all normal communities, but the clear divisions no longer exist anywhere."[2]

Even today one can't help but notice that there are basically four types of works in the world that loosely parallel those outlined above. And it is in following one's own nature and developing one's innate talents that true happiness in one's work is usually found. Not all have the gift of drawing; not all have a "green thumb" for growing things; nor do we all have computer-like brains for numbers and science; nor do we all feel drawn to studying philosophy or religion. But everyone is blessed with certain talents, and it behooves each one of us to discover what are **our** natural attributes and to nurture them, help them to grow and flourish. For we all have a place in God's Master Plan, and it is in discovering our place or role in that Divine Plan that true peace, harmony and happiness can be found.

Lord Jesus explains this idea with the parable of the talents where He compares talents to money. In the parable, the master calls three servants and gives each a number of talents or sums of money according to their individual abilities. The ones receiving five and two talents respectively quickly double their number through hard work and ingenuity. But the one receiving only a single talent does nothing; he does not even try to use it or expand it in any way.

When the master returns, he is greatly pleased with the first two servants who have wisely used their talents and increased their size and value. "Well done, good and faithful servants," says the master. "You have been faithful over a little, I will set you over much; enter into the joy of your master."[3]

But to the servant who did not even try to be a good steward, who refused to even use the talent given him, the master said angrily, "You wicked and slothful servant!... You ought to have invested my money with the bankers, and at my coming I should have received what was my own with interest."[4]

He took away the servant's single talent and gave it to him who had the most talents, for he had used what God had given him wisely, saying, "The man who uses well what he is given shall be given more, and he shall have abundance. But from the man who is unfaithful, even what little responsibility he has shall be taken from him. And throw the useless servant out into outer darkness..."[5]

In the *Gita*, Lord Krishna, too, admonishes us to discover our true selves, our true nature, and follow it. Thus He says:

"Everyone acts impelled by his own Nature: even the illuminate is no exception. How then can inhibition avail

58

in life?...

" 'Tis wiser to follow a line of evolution consonant with one's nature even when 'tis imperfect than to tread to perfection a path alien to one's native temperament."[6]

And again, He states:

"A man attains salvation when he cleaves to his own vocation. Let me explain to you how he achieves this when he does his duty. The One who pervades the universe and is the origin of the compulsive urge to action—when Him men worship with their works, assigned by Him as their duty they attain perfection.

"Better is an action prompted by your nature—even if it is not done well—than the one well done when 'tis another person's duty, but not your own. You incur no sin when you do your duty that suits your temperament.

"None must disown a work hailed by his nature, even when 'tis defective. For all work is dogged by defects even as fire by smoke."[7]

So it is in going against one's nature, one's natural inclinations that one incurs sin! Why? For two reasons, the first one being that God put all of us here for a purpose, that purpose being to serve Him in the way that He has ordained. Thus, when one follows one's nature and develops one's innate attributes and God-given talents, no matter what the field, one is fulfilling his or her purpose, playing his or her role in God's Great Cosmic Play.

To paraphrase Shakespeare, "All the world's a stage, and we are but players on that stage." Not everyone can be the leading man or lady, but the play can not go on without the stage hands, the lighting crews, the costume-makers, and the ticket-takers! All are equally essential and important to the overall production.

In India, the various castes are said to correspond to various parts of the body of the Lord depending on their functions. The priests and holy people are said to correspond with the Lord's head as learning, speaking and teaching are their main functions; the warriors and politicians are said to be from the Lord's arms and hands as they are His instruments of direction and protection; the shepherds and farmers are from the Lord's belly area as their works usually involve foodstuffs, etc., and the laborers are from the Lord's feet as it is upon their labour that the rest of society stands. The idea is that all members of society, regardless of their function and work, are from the Lord and are part of the Lord; therefore, they are all essentially equal as how can one part of God be superior to another part of God?

St. Paul compares the various members of society and God's "church" to various parts of our own body. He also says that all members of God's family or church (which means all humankind) are part of the body of the One God. A hand cannot see, but an eye cannot hold things; a foot cannot talk, but a mouth cannot walk. But when put together, the body is whole; and when each part performs its function well, the whole body benefits and works in harmony:

> "Now God gives us many kinds of special abilities, but it is the same Holy Spirit who is the source of them all. There are different kinds of service to God, but it is the same Lord we are serving. There are many ways in which God works in our lives, but it is the same God who does the work in and through all of us...
>
> "The Holy Spirit displays God's power through each of us as a means of helping the entire church...It is the same and only Holy Spirit who gives all these gifts and powers, deciding which each one of us should have...Each of us is a part of the one body of Christ...The Holy Spirit has fitted us all together into one body...He has made many parts, but still there is only one body...This makes for happiness among the parts, so that the parts have the same care for each other that they do for themselves. If one part suffers, all the parts suffer with it, and if one part is honored, all the parts are glad...
>
> **"All of you together are the one body of Christ and each one of you is a separate and necessary part of it."**[8]

Isn't it interesting that both the Christians and Hindus use the same illustration of the body of the One Lord to explain this idea of equality? In essence, what St. Paul and the Hindu scriptures are saying is that all human beings are equal in God's eyes as every human being is a part of the One God. Therefore, no caste, class, race, sex, religion, nationality, etc., can be viewed as superior or inferior to another for how can one part of God be superior/inferior to another part of God? For, as the Old Testament points out: "Have we not all one father?"[9]

60

The caste system, then, was meant as a logical division of labours based on one's natural attributes. However, the castes were not meant to be in watertight compartments. For example, if an individual were born into a farmer's household and yet his/her natural abilities and propensities lay in another area, such as politics or religion, he/she should have the right to freely follow his or her nature and do the work that suits his or her temperament. To deny a person this free mobility would be interfering with God's plan for that individual.

One of the main lessons that people who have had death experiences say they learned on "the other side" was that it was not only wrong to kill one's self, as that would be like throwing God's gift of life back in His face, but that it was also wrong to kill anyone else, as that would be interfering with God's plan and purpose for that person. In the same way, to deny someone the right to follow his/her nature and pursue the type of work that God has ordained for him/her is to, again, interfere with His plan and purpose for that individual.

As the *Legend of St. Issa* points out, Jesus or Issa was adamant about the equality and equal opportunity of all to perceive God and achieve union with Him:

> "He declaimed strongly against man's arrogating himself the authority to deprive his fellow-beings of their human and spiritual rights. 'Verily,' He said, 'God has made no difference between His children, who are all alike dear to Him...
>
> "One law has been given to man to guide him in his actions:
>
> " 'Fear the Lord, thy God; bend thy knees only before Him and bring to Him only the offerings which come from thy earnings...
>
> " '...be humble and humiliate not your fellow-man. Help the poor, support the weak, do evil to none, covet not that which ye have not and which belongs to others...
>
> " 'He who has recovered his primitive purity shall die with his transgressions forgiven and have the right to contemplate the majesty of God.' "[10]

In the *Aquarian Gospel,* Jesus reiterates this Truth of the Oneness of the Human Family, whose only Father is the One God:

"My Father-God, who was and is and evermore shall be...Who in the boundlessness of love has made all men to equal be. The white, the black, the yellow, and the red can look up in thy face and say, Our Father-God...

"The Holy One has said that all His children shall be free; and every soul is child of God. The sudras shall be as free as priest; the farmers shall walk hand in hand with king, for all the world will own the brotherhood of man.

"O men, arise! Be conscious of your powers, for he who wills need not remain a slave. Just live as you would have your brother live; unfold each day as does the flower; for earth is yours, and heaven is yours, and God will bring you to your own."[11]

Chapter 2

WOMEN AND GOD

This incident of Jesus' with the orthodox Brahmin priests reminds one of the fact that many of Jesus' disciples and followers in Israel or Palestine were women, who were considered "unworthy" by the orthodox Jewish priests to enter into the Inner Temple of the synagogues. Women were viewed as existing solely for the service of men and were definitely second class citizens, if not third or fourth class! Jesus decried this inequality and the double standard of justice meted out to women, as in the case of the adultress ("He among you who is without sin, let him cast the first stone.")

Jesus made no distinction between men and women when it came to His followers, and it is perhaps for this reason that Jesus showed Himself first to a woman—Mary Magdalene—upon His Resurrection.

In the *Legend of St. Issa,* Jesus or Issa is even more explicit about women and the way men should treat them. During a discourse He gave in Israel or Palestine, the following incident is recounted:

"...an old woman who had approached the group, to better hear Issa, was pushed aside by (a man), who placed himself before her.

"Then said Issa: 'It is not good for a son to push away his mother, that he may occupy the place which belongs to her. Who so doth not respect his mother—the most sacred being after his God—is unworthy of the name of son.

" 'Hearken to what I say to you: Respect woman; for in her we see the mother of the universe, and all the truth of divine creation is to come through her.

" 'She is the fount of everything good and beautiful, as she is also the germ of life and death. Upon her man depends in all his existence, for she is his moral and natural support in his labors.

" 'In pain and suffering she brings you forth; in the sweat of her brow she watches over your growth, and until her death you cause her great anxieties. Bless her and adore her, for she is your only friend and support on earth.

63

" 'Respect her; defend her. In so doing you will gain for yourself her love; you will find favor before God, and for her sake many sins will be remitted to you.

" 'Love your wives and respect them, for they will be the mothers of tomorrow and later the grandmothers of a whole nation.

" 'Be submissive to the wife; her love ennobles man, softens his hardened heart, tames the wild beast in him and changes it to a lamb.

" 'Wife and mother are the priceless treasures which God has given to you. They are the most beautiful ornaments of the universe, and from them will be born all who will inhabit the world.

" 'Even as the Lord of Hosts separated the light from the darkness, and the dry land from the waters, so does woman possess the divine gift calling forth out of man's evil nature all the good that is in him.

" 'Therefore I say to you, after God, to woman must belong your best thoughts, for she is the divine temple where you will most easily obtain perfect happiness.

" 'Draw from this temple your moral force. There you will forget your sorrows and your failures, and recover the love necessary to aid your fellow-men.

" 'Suffer her not to be humiliated, for by humiliating her you humiliate yourselves, and lose the sentiment of love, without which nothing can exist here on earth.

" 'Protect your wife, that she may protect you—you and all your household. All that you do for your mothers, your wives, for a widow, or for any other woman in distress, you will do for your God.' "[1]

The Role of Women in Spiritual Life

Clearly Jesus did not view women as inferior to men. On the contrary, He stressed that it was the feminine aspects of love and compassion that men themselves must cultivate if they are to realize the highest spiritual truths. As Marilyn Ferguson points out in her thought-provoking book, *The Aquarian Conspiracy,* even scientists are recognizing the need to place greater emphasis on stimulating the right hemisphere of the brain, which is the side that is associated with what we have traditionally considered feminine qualities—love and nurturance, cooperation and compassion, patience and tolerance, intuition and creativity. Scientists say that we need to activate this right hemisphere in order to perceive other levels of consciousness and spiritual realizations. They point out that the left hemisphere of the brain—the analytical side that controls logic, reason, etc., (qualities that have been traditionally associated with men)—cannot initiate these spiritual experiences; it can only interpret and catalogue them.

Not only is it necessary for us to cultivate these qualities of love, compassion, and tolerance on a personal level in order to experience higher realms of consciousness; we must cultivate them on an international level so that we do not end up destroying ourselves and the world with us! Lou Harris, the famous pollster, is quoted by Ferguson as remarking that, "women are far ahead of men in pushing for basic human qualities; they are more dedicated to peace and opposed to war, more concerned about child abuse, deeply moved by...'the pall of violence' " that surrounds us all everyday.[2]

What is happening today with the women's movement and the influence it has brought is a necessary righting of the balance between the yin and the yang—the feminine and masculine aspects of the Universe. Further, it is a necessary step toward the realization of the New Era that is dawning upon us. As Patricia Mische, author of *Women and Power* points out: " 'The values that have been labeled feminine—compassion, cooperation and patience—are very badly needed in giving birth to and nurturing a new era in human history.' "[3]

Ferguson quotes one psychologist as saying: " 'Perhaps the women's movement is part of an evolutionary process that will keep us from going the way of the dinosaur and the dodo!' "[4] And Mahatma Gandhi, the great Indian spiritual/political leader, known as the Father of the Indian Nation, once said, " 'If **satya graha** ("soul force" or "truth force") is to be the mode of the future, then the future belongs to women,' "[5] and "To call women the weaker sex is a libel; it is man's injustice to women."[6]

Women are beginning to call for a new vision of our future politically, economically, and spiritually: a vision of mutual cooperation, not competition; of trust and love, not suspicion and hate. Examples can be seen worldwide as women become more visible and begin to gain a new sense of awareness and confidence in themselves and in their ability to perform the various roles assigned to them in God's Cosmic Play: as wives and mothers, scientists and teachers, social activists and politicians, and above all, as **spiritual leaders calling for Peace in the world.** The first anti-nuclear protest ever held in Russia was led by Scandinavian women, who were joined by thousands of Russian women and some men as they marched from city to city. This is just one example of the rising tide of feminine influence that is sweeping across the world and will, hopefully, transform it and our future positively.

Our Mother is Coming

Indeed, it is no coincidence that women have begun to be more vocal nationally and internationally; it is instead fulfillment of prophecy. The American Indians are awaiting the return of, not only God in a masculine form, but God in a feminine form—the return of the White Buffalo Cow Woman. According to Indian tradition, this feminine form of God incarnated ages ago and brought the Word of Truth, as well as the Sacred Pipe—the Peace Pipe— to the Indian people. She promised that She would return at the end of this Age to help usher in the New World of Peace.

The Buddhists, too, are awaiting God in Her feminine form. An incident related by Marilyn Ferguson during a recent seminar in Hawaii illustrates this point well. Ms. Ferguson said that there is a beautiful statue of a woman at the Hyatt Regency Hotel on Maui. Every time she took a picture of this statue the picture showed a blue aura or light next to the statue. Finally she asked the concierge of the Hotel the name of the statue. The concierge replied that the statue itself is a replica of an Eighth Century Buddhist statue—"The Buddha of the Future." The story is that because of the harsh times we have gone through in the past, the spiritual teachers had to be men with both feet on the ground. But there would come a gentler time when the spirit of the Buddha would be female.

Signs in the Heavens

The stars in the heavens seem to be verifying the fulfillment of these prophecies, i.e., that the feminine aspect of God is to make Her appearance on Earth and Her influence felt throughout the world. In 1981, a rare triple conjunction of the planets Jupiter and Saturn took place in the only purely feminine sign of the twelve signs of the zodiac—Virgo, representing the Virgin or the Mother. This is the same conjunction that took place around the time of Christ's birth, and which has been theorized by astrologers, astronomers, historians, and theologians as being the famous Star of Bethlehem of which the Bible speaks. The experts point out that the Magi were highly knowledgeable about astronomy and astrology, and that they understood the meaning of this rare conjunction; i.e., that a great Saviour or Messiah was to be born. They explain that though the stars do not **control** earthly life, they do influence and **reflect** events taking place on earth.

This rare conjunction took place in Pisces around Christ's birth, Pisces being the sign of the zodiac representing the Son and corresponding on the earth to the country of Palestine, and placed exactly opposite Virgo, representing the Virgin or the Mother, on the zodiac! Isn't it interesting that Jesus, the Son, was born of Mary, the Virgin Mother! This rare conjunction also took place at the time of the Buddha's birth—563 B.C., and again forty years later at the time of His "Enlightenment." Coincidence?

God the Mother

Another proof of the rising influence of the feminine aspect of God has come through the visions that various Christians have had during this century. Most of these visions involved, **not** God as the Father, but **God as the Holy Mother,** as with the visions of the Holy Mother at Lourdes (France), Fatima (Portugal), and elsewhere, including a vision of the Mother seen by Catholicism's newest canonized saint—Maximilian Kolbe, a Polish priest and victim of Hitler's notorious concentration camp—Auschwitz.

Maximilian's vision came to him one day while praying in church when he was still just a boy. He had a vision of the Holy Mother holding two crowns, one red and one white. She told him that the white crown meant that he would remain pure and that the red crown meant that he would be a martyr. Both aspects of the vision came true as Maximilian remained pure in heart and became a Franciscan priest devoted to the Mother. Years later he volunteered to starve to death in place of another man in Auschwitz death-camp. The man whose life he saved had been one of the ten prisoners chosen by the Nazis to starve to death as a

67

reprisal against the whole camp for the escape of one prisoner. The man had a wife and children, so Kolbe volunteered to take his place in the underground "hunger bunker" instead. After two weeks, Kolbe was still alive, so the Nazis injected him with a lethal drug. Thus, the second half of the vision was fulfilled, and Kolbe's sacrifice helped to stimulate courage and brotherly love among the rest of the prisoners at Auschwitz.[7]

The other visions of the Mother mentioned here have also been accepted as true occurrences, and have been accompanied by miraculous healings and signs in the sky, such as the appearance of the sun falling in Fatima, which was witnessed and verified by tens of thousands of individuals. In fact, one of the main reasons given by the Holy Mother at Fatima as to why She had made Her appearance at that time was that God wanted the world to begin worshipping the feminine aspect of the universe, as exemplified by the Holy Mother. In this way, the world would begin to recognize the equality of both sexes and, hopefully, start allowing the feminine qualities of Love, Peace, Compassion, and Tolerance to come forth from within, thus keeping the world from consuming itself in the fires of hatred and violence.

It is not just certain Twentieth Century Christians that have begun to visualize and worship God as the Mother; the Gnostic Christians, too, worshipped the feminine aspect of God as the Creator and Seed of all life in the cosmos. Their teachings abound with feminine references to various aspects of the Godhead. Further, most Gnostics followed Jesus' lead of equality of the sexes, allowing women equal right and opportunity to teach, read and lead in their group discussions and meetings. As a matter of fact, Mary Magdalene was recognized as the leader of the Gnostic Christians as Peter was recognized as the spokesman for the orthodox Christians. In many of the Gnostic Gospels, Mary is praised as "Jesus' most intimate companion, the symbol of divine wisdom,"[8] and "...a woman who knew the All (God)."[9]

This sometimes led to a bit of conflict due to male chauvinism on Peter's part. In one gospel called *Pistis Sophia* ("Faith Wisdom"), "Peter complains that Mary is dominating the conversation with Jesus and displacing the rightful (?!) priority of Peter and his brother apostles. He urges Jesus to silence her and is quickly rebuked. Later, however, Mary admits to Jesus that she..." finds it difficult to speak freely in front of Peter as he has difficulty accepting teaching or advice from a woman, whereupon, "Jesus replies that whoever the Spirit inspires is divinely ordained to speak, whether man or woman."[10]

Furthermore, Elaine Pagels, the author of *The Gnostic Gospels,* points out that many of the letters and teachings that have been attributed to St. Paul were, in fact, never written by Paul! Since the Bible has been translated about 1600 times, there have been ample opportunities to tamper with, delete and add to it; a fact that has been admitted to by theologians for centuries. These pseudo-Pauline letters, as she calls them, often have to do with church organization, rituals, dogmas, and doctrines. It is here that we see Paul's so-called "disdain" for women where he says that women have to be subservient to men, that they have no right to speak, much less teach in the church. These teachings could not have come from Paul as, first, the style of writing is totally unlike Paul's; second, in several instances Paul directs certain male seekers to go to certain Christian women, such as Priscilla, for further instruction as these women were highly knowledgeable about God, and third and most important, St. Paul was a **Gnostic;** he had visions of God, which is why he became a Christian at all (i.e., his vision of God on the road to Damascus which led to his conversion). In these visions, Paul saw the Oneness of all things in God, and even said, "In Christ, there is neither male or female." So neither sex could be viewed as superior or inferior to the other as **we all** are ultimately part of the One God!

The Gnostics also taught that God created **not** Adam, the man, first and Eve, the woman, second, but human beings of both sexes simultaneously. Indeed, the literal translation of the *Book of Genesis* in our own Bible quite plainly states that God created " 'adham," the Hebrew word for "human being," NOT " 'ish" or "Zakar," the Hebrew for "male human being." There is even a question as to whether Eve was the first woman because of the references made to a woman named "Lilith" in many creation legends. In these legends, Lilith, the predecessor to Eve, demanded to be viewed as Adam's equal, and was therefore exiled from the Garden of Eden by Adam. Enter Eve and the apple, and soon, Adam himself was thrown out of Eden! Was it really Eve's fault, or simply Adam's own karma rebounding on him?[11]

Furthermore, the Hebrew word used for God in Genesis is "Elohim." This word has been translated as "God" or "He," but its roots are of both masculine and feminine origin, "Eloh"—the feminine singular for "goddess," and the masculine plural ending "im." Perhaps this was Moses' way of intimating the many-sided, all-encompassing aspects of God; i.e., that God is both masculine and feminine, singular and plural and One and above all of these categories and distinctions![12]

The Dual Nature of the Godhead

Gnostic references to the feminine aspects and the masculine/feminine dual nature of the Godhead are quite plentiful throughout their teachings. One example of this, which echoes scientists' explanations of the dual aspects of the human brain— the masculine side being the organizer and categorizer and the feminine side being the creator and initiator—is found in the *Great Announcement*, which explains the origin of the universe as follows:

> "From the power of Silence appeared 'a great power, the Mind of the Universe, which manages all things, and is a male...the other...a great Intelligence...is a female which produces all things'...these powers, joined in union, 'are discovered to be duality...This is Mind in Intelligence, and these are separable from one another, and yet are one, found in a state of duality.' This means...that 'there is in everyone (divine power) existing in a latent condition...This is one power divided above and below; generating itself, being the mother of itself, father of itself, sister of itself, spouse of itself, daughter of itself, son of itself—mother, father, unity, being a source of the entire circle of existence.' "[13]

In the *Aprocryphon of John,* we again read about the dual nature of the Godhead. John relates a mystical vision he has of the Trinity after the crucifixion:

> "The (heavens were opened and the whole) creation (which is) under heaven shone and (the world) was shaken. (And I was afraid, and...I) saw in the light...a likeness with multiple forms... and the likeness had three forms...He said to me, 'John, Jo(h)n, why do you doubt, and why are you afraid?...I am the one who (is with you) forever. I (am the Father); I am the Mother; I am the Son.' "[14]

In the *Secret Book,* we find the Hebrew term "ruah," a feminine word, used for "spirit." The Book goes on to describe this divine Mother-Spirit:

> "(She is)...the image of the invisible, virginal, perfect spirit...She became the Mother of everything, for She existed before them all, the Mother-Father..."[15]

In the *Gospel to the Hebrews,* Jesus also speaks of "my Mother, the Spirit,"[16] adding that whosoever becomes a true believer in God gains both father and mother for the Spirit (ruah) is "Mother of many."[17]

So perhaps it is not just the arrival of a physical female incarnation of God that the stars foretell; perhaps they also foretell the necessary unfolding of the Mother-Spirit within us all; the birth of the Christ-Consciousness in each and every heart and the realization of our Mother/Father within as well as without; for as Sri Aurobindo has said, "A change of consciousness is the major fact of the next evolutionary transformation."[18]

Steps to God

It was not only the Gnostic Christians who worshipped God as the Mother; religions around the world have recognized and praised not only our heavenly Father, but also God as the Divine Mother and Creator of all life. Indeed, it is the total lack of feminine references to God that sets apart orthodox Judaism, orthodox Christianity, and orthodox Islam from the rest of the world's religions, whether they be Egyptian or Greek, Babilonian or early Roman, African, North American, or Indian.

In India, the feminine aspect of God has been worshipped in various forms by both men and women since time immemorial. An example of this type of worship was illustrated through the life of possibly India's greatest saint—Sri Ramakrishna. Sri Ramakrishna (1836-1886) worshipped and realized God in Her feminine form as the Mother—Kali. His closeness to God was so great, especially in Her feminine form, that he could invoke Her to appear physically, even in front of others.

One such occasion took place in order to prove to Sri Ramakrishna's closest disciple—Swami Vivekananda—that God is the Mother, too. Swami Vivekananda suffered from the same "ego illness" as did St. Peter—male chauvinism—and refused to believe that God could also come in a feminine form. Since seeing is believing, Sri Ramakrishna invoked God to show Herself physically to Vivekananda in order to put his masculine doubts to rest. She did indeed appear at Ramakrishna's request, and Vivekananda swore he would never again doubt the divinity of the Mother!

As a matter of fact, years later Vivekananda himself taught that one must realize God as the Mother if one is to reach the highest spiritual heights. He lists the five stages in the Path of Divine Love of God as follows:

"(1) Man is fearful and needs help.
(2) He sees God as Father.
(3) He sees God as Mother. (And it is only from this stage that real love begins, for only then does it become intimate and fearless.)
(4) He loves for the sake of love—beyond all other qualities and beyond good and evil. [Or the distinctions of Mother and Father, or any other dualities.]
(5) He realizes love in Divine union, Unity."[19]

It is interesting to note that those who have had death experiences relate that when the physical body is dropped, so are all societal "masks." In other words, all distinctions of class, caste, race, nationality, or sex—all worldly dualities—disappear; there is no longer any identification with the body, and, therefore, these worldly categories no longer exist or have meaning. It should also be mentioned here that these death experiences cut across all cultural and religious lines; in other words, they are the same regardless of the race, creed, color, sex, or nationality of the person who "died." Both North Americans and Asian Indians have reported the same basic elements of the death experience.

Similarly, though the Being of Light had a definite personality, as well as a great sense of humor, It was not seen to have any particular sex either. Though many identified It with various religious names depending on the individual's religious background, the Being Itself never gave Its name or any other label. It was beyond these dualities; It was instead, Divine Love—pure love for the sake of love without any limitations or conditions!

Three Aspects of the Godhead Realized

Sri Ramakrishna was brought to the ocean of God's Bliss often through Love of God as the Mother. But he also experienced and realized God in His masculine form: as Allah, the Islamic God, and as Christ. In both cases, Ramakrishna threw himself into the teachings of each religion. In the case of Islam, he repeated the name of Allah and even wore the robes of a Mussulman. Eventually, he had a visual materialization of the Islamic ideal—the Prophet. Ramakrishna merged with him and, was once again, though by a different river, brought back to the ocean of God's Bliss.

His experience with Christ happened seven years later occurring soon after the Bible was first read to him. To quote Romain Rolland's beautiful biography, *The Life of Sri Ramakrishna:*

"One day when he (Ramakrishna) was sitting in the room of a friend, a rich Hindu, he saw on the wall a picture representing the Madonna and Child. The figures became alive...the holy visions came close to him and entered into him so that his whole being was impregnated with them...the inflowing...covered his entire soul, breaking down all barriers...The spirit of the Hindu was changed. He had no room for anything but Christ. For several days he was filled by Christian thought and Christian love...Then one afternoon in the grove of Dakshineswar (Ramakrishna's temple) he saw coming towards him a person with beautiful large eyes, a serene regard and a fair skin. Although he did not know who it was, he succumbed to the charm of his unknown guest. He drew near and a voice sang in the depths of Ramakrishna's soul:

" 'Behold the Christ, who shed His heart's blood for the redemption of the world, who suffered a sea of anguish for love of men. It is He, the master Yogi, who is in eternal union with God. It is Jesus, Love incarnate...'

"The Son of Man embraced the seer of India, the Son of the Mother, and absorbed him into Himself. Ramakrishna was lost in ecstasy. Once again he realized union with Brahman (God). Then gradually he came down to earth, but from that time he believed in the Divinity of Jesus Christ, the Incarnate God...In his...room amongst his Divine pictures was one of the Christ, and he burnt incense before it morning and evening. Later it came to pass that Indian Christians recognized in him a direct manifestation of the Christ and went into ecstasy before him...But, for him, Christ was not the only Incarnation. Buddha and Krishna were others...,"[20] which brings us to the question of Avatars.

Chapter 3

THE QUESTION OF AVATARS

What is an avatar? What is His purpose? Has there only been one avatar—Jesus Christ? And how does one recognize an avatar?

Simply stated, an avatar is God in human form; It is what the West calls the Son of God, the Messiah, the Savior, the Christ. An avatar comes directly from the Spirit of God; He/She goes through no evolutionary changes as do we; He/She is unaffected by karma; an avatar is of pure virgin spirit.

What is His purpose? The *Legend of St. Issa* summarizes the answer to this question beautifully when describing the advent of Jesus Christ:

> "At that time the moment had come for the compassionate Judge to **re-incarnate** in a human form;
>
> "And the eternal Spirit, resting in a state of complete inaction and supreme bliss, awakened and separated from the eternal Being, for an undetermined period,
>
> "**So that, in human form, He might teach man to identify himself with the Divinity and attain to eternal felicity;**
>
> "**And to show, by His example, how man can attain moral purity and free his soul from the domination of the physical senses, so that it may achieve the perfection necessary for it to enter the Kingdom of Heaven, which is immutable and where bliss eternal reigns.**"[1]

In other words, an avatar comes to show us the way back **H-OM-E** to Him, as **He**, the **Om**, is what E.T. called, **"Home!"**

Has there only been one avatar—Jesus Christ? This is the question that has caused more suffering, destruction, brutality and war "in the name of God" than any other question man has ever asked. But were these wars fought for God and, therefore, Love and Truth? Or were they fought for power, greed, the suppression of Truth, and the confusion of the One God?

Notice that in the *Legend of St. Issa,* it says that the Lord is about to "re-incarnate" in human form. This naturally presupposes that God had incarnated in human form before. In the East as in the West, Jesus is recognized as an avatar, or the Son of God,

74

and is seen as the Way, the Light, and the embodiment of Truth. But there is one great and vital difference, to quote Swami Paramananda:

> "Orthodox Christianity exalts Christ to the exclusion of all other divine manifestations, while the Eastern soul receives Him as the Cosmic Light, blending its harmony with both past and present (avatars or other divine manifestations that have come before and after Jesus). Whichever concept we hold will have a marked influence upon our life and destiny. For the one (which says Jesus is the only Son of God) invariably works for the destruction of what is not its own, and the other for the preservation and assimilation of what may not seem at first sight to be its own. The one holds to the dogmatic Christ, the creed-bound Christ of organization and institution; the other looks to that Christ who is the soul of Divinity, who cannot be partitioned off any more than we can partition off the infinite sky."[2]

For how can one limit God, who is limitless? Can we determine that God can only come in one form—a carpenter's son called Jesus, in one place—the Middle East, at one time in human history, and even on one planet? Of course not; to do that would be naive. For God, who is eternal, omnipresent and all-pervasive, can and has come in different manifestations in different parts of the world at different points in time.

How can we ever use an exclusive word like "only" when dealing with the Lord, who is all-inclusive? Even in the Christian creeds the word "catholic" is used—"catholic" meaning "universal" and "all-inclusive."

God comes down in different forms or manifestations, to different parts of the world, to different societies in the way that He will be best recognized, accepted and understood. Thus, we see the Lord clothing Himself in whatever outward appearance will most easily blend in with the surrounding culture, whether that be as Jesus, the Buddha, Krishna, or whoever.

As Sathya Sai Baba, a great yogi living today, said, "To elevate man, to raise the level of his consciousness, God has to incarnate as Man. He has to speak to them in their own style and languages, He has to teach them the methods that they can adopt and practise."[3]

Among many people in the West, there is a misconception

about people in India worshipping several different Gods, whereas, in fact, unlike the Syrians, mentioned in Part I, Chapter II, the Indians are worshipping the One God in His different manifestations, including Jesus. People there recognize that God is limitless, and by dedicating their temples to His numberless aspects and attributes, they worship Him in the form that they are most comfortable.

As Janet Bock explains:

> "Just as each of us may be someone's child, someone else's spouse, brother or sister, employer or friend, but not six different people, so the fact that God is perceived as the embodiment of righteousness in one manifestation, as the overcomer of obstacles in another, and as the source of learning, strength, or wealth in still others, means that the One God is all pervading. It does not mean each is a separate God mutually exclusive of all the others."[4]

Further, people in India often adorn their temples with statues, images, or pictures of the various aspects of God. Often, Westerners have misunderstood the purpose of these statues, thinking that the Hindus actually worship the stone "idol" itself. This, of course, is absurd! The statue, image or "idol" is but a way of focusing one's attention on God; it is a reminder of God's Eternal Presence. Just as we keep photographs of our loved ones in our offices and homes so that we may glance at them from time to time and be reminded of the love we feel for them, so, too, the Indians have statues and pictures of God in His various forms so as to remind them of Him and of the love they bear for Him. We know that our photographs are not really the flesh and blood person; they only represent them. So it is with the Asian Indians and their "idols" of God.

After all, how can it be wrong to be reminded of God all of the time? And if it was wrong, why would Jesus Christ have left His own image on His burial shroud? Was it not meant to be a reminder of Him and of the suffering He bore because of the love He has for us? It should be remembered that there are pictures and statues of Jesus Christ in Christian churches, too. So what is the difference? The only difference is that the Christian churches recognize only one manifestation of God, while the Hindus recognize them all!

76

The *Shrimad Bhagavatam* explains that the Lord comes from age to age according to the needs of the age, and is worshipped by human beings belonging to the different yugas or ages with a name and in a form appropriate to the age, which is why the avatars have different faces, names, etc., but always teach the same Eternal Truths. The different avatars or forms of God can be compared to water in its various forms. The outer form of water changes in accordance to its environment. Thus, we see water change to snow, ice, sleet, hail, fog, mist and rain as the environmental factors affecting its outer form change. But its basic components are the same—it is still water. Just so the outer forms of God change in accordance with the environmental/societal setting into which He has come. But His basic component is the same—He is still God! To deny the Divinity of Krishna or the Buddha or any other avatar is like saying that the basic component of water is not H_2O! The basic components of all avatars are Truth and Love—They are all the embodiment of Truth and Love. They are all **Logos, the Living Word of God made flesh,** which is why that bloodstain on Jesus' forehead is in the shape of the Om— ॐ: to demonstrate beyond the shadow of a doubt that Jesus Christ was indeed God Incarnate, and to show the unity of God in all His various forms.

But if one is still unconvinced as to the Divinity of other avatars, such as the Buddha or Lord Krishna, the best way to remove those doubts is to examine the lives and teachings of the other avatars and compare them with those of Jesus Christ, thereby answering the last question: how does one recognize an avatar?

Recognition

In comparing the life stories of the various avatars, we see some striking parallels. First and foremost, the world situation in each case was perilous and true spirituality had been lost. The rulers were generally harsh and brutal, and the priests had become stuck in the mire of dogma and doctrine. Instead of simplifying God to the people, they complicated Him, thus making it harder for people to understand and know Him, instead of easier. To sum it up, it was again a situation of a greed and power trip by the priests and ruling classes over the people. It is due to these above conditions, to right the wrong and show the way back to Truth and Love, that the Lord incarnates in our world. As Lord Krishna explains in the *Bhagavad Gita:*

"Whenever (dharma) righteousness declines and there is an uprise of iniquity, I (the Lord) loose myself forth into birth in the world. For the protection of the holy men, the chastisement of the wicked and the enthroning of dharma (righteousness) I am born from age to age."[5]

In at least two cases, that of Lord Krishna (c. 2500 B.C.) and of Lord Jesus, the kings Kamsa and Herod were so evil that they ordered all the infants put to death because there were prophecies about the "Deliverer" or "Messiah" being born at that time. These prophecies included signs in the heavens, and, again, in at least two cases, that of Lord Buddha and Lord Jesus, those signs were interpreted to be the triple conjunctions of the planets Jupiter and Saturn that took place in 563 B.C.—the date of Lord Buddha's birth—and again at the time of Christ's birth.

In each case, the Lord was born into a family of righteous and pious people who had tread the path of Truth and Love in spite of the pressures of the world. The Lord's birth was always accompanied by celestial music, and in at least two cases, those of Lord Krishna and Lord Jesus, the first visitors to the newborn Lord were shepherds bearing gifts. In each case, the prophets of the era recognized the Divinity of the newborn child in words similar to those of Simeon and the prophetess Anna in the case of Jesus.

In every case, the Lord demonstrated incredible knowledge of the One and Indivisible God as a child, continually stressing the grandeur of the spirit, the nothingness of the body, and the necessity for repentance and a return to Truth. Examples of this knowledge can be seen in the lives of all the avatars. In the case of Lord Jesus, who can forget His discourses as a boy of 12 in the Synagogue in Jerusalem—discourses so beautiful and enlightening that the priests and elders gathered round in great crowds to hear Him. In the case of Guru Nanak (an incarnation of the Lord who came approximately 500 years ago to India and the Middle East, and was followed and worshipped by Hindus and Muslims alike), He spoke so eloquently of the Lord that His own tutor recognized Him as an avatar—an incarnation of God. In a discussion with His tutor, Guru Nanak said:

"All learning is vain, except to know Him and to serve Him...to love Him is the end of knowledge and to forget Him is to forget the truth, even though one may carry a cartload of

78

books...This creation is His and He is everywhere...His love pervades all things...When we act against the law of love, we chain ourselves to the wheel of cause and effect (Karma)."[6]

When asked by His tutor if knowledge can burn up our seeds of Karma, Guru Nanak replied:

> "Yes, with realization (direct personal spiritual experience—gnosis), but not with book knowledge. He alone is learned who knows Him. As letters are symbols of speech, so various forms are manifestations of God. He is the Enjoyer of all sense-objects. He is within and without all beings. He who knows God is all and in all and consequently loses all sense of otherness, he alone escapes from the prison of I-AM-NESS. In selfhood (egoism) is bondage; in losing the self (ego), is freedom."[7]

Guru Nanak said these words when He was just 9 years old!

Miracles

The Lord as a child performed many miracles. Most of Jesus' childhood miracles have been taken out of the Bible, but can be found in other books, including one mentioned earlier called *The Lost Books of the Bible.* Many of these miracles had to do with healings and the transformation of matter.

In several cases, the Lord, through His example, stressed the need for solitude and silence, which is why all of the avatars spent so much time in the forest. All were tested by the temptations of life—lust, power, greed—as with Jesus' forty days in the wilderness, but all came through the tests without a single fault. Lord Buddha's words to Mara, the temptress (what Westerners would call the Devil) are strikingly similar to Jesus' during His forty-day fast. When tempted by Mara with food during His own fast, Lord Buddha said: "O thou friend of the indolent, thou wicked one; for what purpose hast thou come? Let the flesh waste away, if but the mind becomes more tranquil and attention more steadfast (so that it may better concentrate on the Lord)."[8]

Jesus said: "Man shall not live by bread alone, but by every word that proceeds from the mouth of God."[9]

Guru Nanak, too, was tested by the passions of evil, but said in response:

> "What does it matter if I become a king, and command mighty armies, and occupy a golden throne, and like the wind my commands encompass the earth?...If I exercise supernatural powers and can create wealth at a gesture, can appear and disappear at will and thus win popular respect, these delude fools only who have not Him in their hearts."[10]

Jesus Christ rose from the dead and was resurrected after three days. As with Jesus, so with Guru Nanak: He, too, was resurrected from the dead after three days. He had walked into a lake in front of many people and completely disappeared into it. His family and others searched for His body in vain. Three days later, He reappeared with a luminous glow around Him and pronounced the first principle of His faith:

> "There is but one God, Truth is His Name. Maker of all things, free of fear and hate, timeless, birthless, self-existent, known by the grace of the Guru (Spiritual Teacher or Guide). Meditate on the True Name...
>
> "He who has arranged this play of the Universe, this material world, in various forms and hues, He shall never pass away. He enjoys the sight of His own artistry, to His own Eternal Glory. He is the All-powerful, subject to no other command. He is the Lord of lords, the King of kings, all live under His will...
>
> "You are all wisdom, omniscient, deeper than the oceans...You are everywhere, wherever I look, there You are. Separated from you, like a fish I die...All acts are performed in His presence. He sees all...
>
> "You are near, You are far, You are All in All, You see, You hear, You create this Universe; what pleases You, **that** is the only right action."[11]

Also, like Jesus, Guru Nanak and Lord Krishna disappeared from this earth without leaving any physical body behind. This is an example of the inborn, natural powers of an avatar. It is said that an avatar is recognized by His or Her actions, and that He/She possesses 16 siddhis or Divine powers. An avatar has control over the five functions of the body (speaking, eating, reproduction, elimination, and motion), over the five senses (taste, touch, smell, sight, and hearing), and over the five elements of Nature (earth, air, water, fire, and ether). Yogis, too, can attain one or several of these powers or qualities—kalas—but only an avatar possesses them all, including the last and most important one—omniscience, or all-knowledge of the past, present, and future.

These powers or qualities are natural and normal to an avatar and are used in a spontaneous manner; they are not the result of time and discipline, as is the case with ordinary human beings. An avatar is born with these powers; this is why the avatars are able to perform miracles as children. All of the miracles that each avatar performs are a result of their **inborn, natural** yogic powers.

Power Over the Elements, Matter and the Body

These powers included control over the elements, as explained before. An example of this power was illustrated by Jesus when he calmed the raging storm at sea that threatened to swamp His disciples' boat. Guru Nanak, too, demonstrated His control over the elements in an amusing incident. The Guru was travelling to Mecca, one of the holiest Muslim cities, when He met a group of Muslims who joined Him in His journey:

> "After a few days of travelling together one asked Him what His religion was. 'I belong to the religion of those who follow the path of God,' replied Nanak.
> "They pressed Him to confess that He was a Muslim but He refused to do so. This greatly troubled them. They were not sure whether they were right in having along a man who was an infidel. The Guru saw this and disappeared with his two attendants. They noticed that **a cloud that had protected them from the scorching rays of the sun also disappeared with Him.**"[12]

The group of Muslims thought that the Guru would never make it through the desert alone, and were astounded to find Him in Mecca when they arrived. Further, he had been there several days! Convinced that He had to be a great soul, they "begged Him to forgive them for their suspicions about Him."[13]

Lord Krishna, too, demonstrated incredible mastery over the

elements in several incidents, such as calming the sea, quieting the wind, controlling the lightning, etc. For example, a whirlwind of such hurricane force that heavy objects were being flung in the air like feathers, and one could not see anything due to the dust in the air, was calmed by Lord Krishna when He was a one-year-old child! On two occasions, He saved the inhabitants and animals of a village from fierce fires with His breath, "possessed as he was by unlimited energy."[14] *(Shrimad Bhagavatam)*

All of the avatars were Love and Compassion Incarnate and, therefore, felt sympathy for those who were ill of body, mind, or spirit. They cured these afflictions regardless of the race, color, creed, sex or nationality of the sufferer by teaching the Truth to those in spiritual darkness, casting out "demons" (actually the ego gone "mad") from those suffering mentally, and healing the limbs and wounds of those suffering physically. All of them gave sight to the physically blind, hearing to the deaf, cleansed the lepers, mended broken bones, and even restored severed limbs.

All of them raised people, and in at least two cases animals, from the dead in accounts that are almost identical to those given about Lord Jesus, except that some of them took place hundreds or thousands of years before Jesus was even born! For example, Lord Krishna not only raised one child from the dead as did Jesus with Jairus' daughter; He raised at least a dozen or so young cowherds AND their cows, who had died from drinking poisoned water, simply by looking at them!

Guru Nanak, too, raised the dead, including an elephant. In explaining why He was able to do this, Guru Nanak said, "It is only He who can reanimate the dead. There is no other but God. His will be done."[15]

As mentioned earlier, these miracles often included the transformation of matter into other forms and/or the materialization or dematerialization of matter. An example of this is illustrated by the feeding of the 5000, where Jesus transformed five loaves and two fishes into enough food to feed all, and fill several baskets with leftovers. He performed the same miracle on another occasion for 4000 with seven loaves and a few small fishes. Another example was His causing so many fish to appear in the nets of His fishermen-disciples that the nets almost burst!

Guru Nanak, too, transformed matter on several occasions. Once, the cows that the young Guru was looking after went into a neighbor's field and ate up everything growing there. Naturally, the neighbor was very annoyed and ran to the village chief to complain. But when he and the chief returned, they found the neighbor's field lush and green, with a more beautiful crop than before! Later, in His last job as a householder, Guru Nanak was in charge of the King's granaries. He always gave grain to anyone who asked in accordance with their need, and yet the granaries were always full!

Further, to illustrate the all-pervasive quality of the One God, the following incident about Guru Nanak is recounted: The Guru was scolded by a priest for sleeping with His feet toward the Kaaba, the "house of God" in Mecca, whereupon the Guru told the priest, " 'Turn my feet towards the place where God does not dwell.' " So the priest tried, "but whichever direction they turned His feet the Kaaba turned with them!"[16] Guru Nanak explained that if one is a true believer in God then one would find that there is no place where the house of God does not exist!

Lord Krishna transformed matter all through His life. There are several accounts where the enemies of the Lord tried to kill Him with arrows, but each time the arrow got close to Him, it would become a flower lei or garland, and land around His neck! Lord Krishna also transformed matter into food or simply caused food to appear and disappear like Lord Jesus.

Appearing and Disappearing

Just about all of the avatars have also made themselves appear and disappear, and/or taken on new appearances or different forms in front of their followers. The White Buffalo Cow Woman was so-named because She was able to turn Herself from a beautiful woman into a buffalo calf of various colors in front of Her devotees' eyes! Lord Krishna could disappear and appear at will, and appear in two different forms simultaneously. He also could physically reproduce identical forms simultaneously, like one who is standing in a three-way mirror. One such occasion occurred during the Rasa Dance of the Gopis or cow-herdesses, when the Lord "introduced Himself in so many identical forms between every two gopis."[17] *(Shrimad Bhagavatam)*

Further, on one occasion the description of Lord Krishna's appearance in front of Arjuna, His closest disciple, is strikingly similar to the description given in the New Testament of Lord Jesus' transformation where the Lord is surrounded by a brilliant light that penetrates through and radiates from His entire Being.

Guru Nanak, too, appeared and disappeared on occasion. He performed this miracle once to deflate the egos of some occult-yogis who had acquired certain siddhis or powers, and were showing them off in an attempt to impress the Guru:

> " 'You see my disciple sitting in front of you, watch him,' said Bhartari (the head yogi). 'He will rise up to the skies and become invisible in a moment. If you have any power, bring him back to earth.'
>
> "The disciple in a moment flew upward, and was soon out of sight. Bhartari turned to the Guru, and said, 'Find him.'
>
> " 'Hide and seek is a game for children. Wait and see.' As Nanak said this, His two sandals flew up and in a short while the disciple descended, the sandals beating him down. (The yogis) couldn't stop the beating. The disciple fell at the Guru's feet.
>
> "Then all of a sudden the Guru disappeared and Bhartari himself went in search of Him. After a long time he returned. 'I have searched the earth and the water and the high heavens,' he said, 'but I cannot find Guru Nanak.' Just as he said this he found the Guru seated where He was before.
>
> " 'Where did You hide Yourself?' inquired Bhartari full of astonishment.
>
> " 'I was with you all the time,' said the Guru. 'The body dissolved itself into its elements and the soul into the All-Soul.'
>
> "The Sidhas (yogis with powers) were overwhelmed with awe and sat spell-bound."[18]

There were other occasions where Guru Nanak would be visible to some and totally invisible to others. In one incident, a very learned Pandit (scriptural teacher) who had acquired certain sidhis or powers tried to impress the Guru by arriving to meet Him on a flying carpet. But when he arrived, he found that he could not see the Guru although a large crowd could. When asked by the Pandit where the Guru was, the crowd replied that He was right in front of him: "The Pandit was not only annoyed but felt humiliated as his carpet refused to fly back to his place. He had no option but to walk back..."[19]

Later, when he asked someone why he could not see the Guru when everyone else could, he was told that: " It was your pride that darkened your vision. If you go on foot without pride or power, you will benefit by the sight of Him...,"[20] which the Pandit did do the next day. Guru Nanak then explained to him:

" 'Is there any darkness denser than pride? Because you could fly you thought you were almost a superman...'

" 'Forgive me, teacher,' said the Pandit. 'I have read sacred books and acquired superphysical powers. I must confess I have found no peace. Tell me how I can touch the feet of the Lord.'

" 'Knowledge which partakes of the darkness of the ego is of little avail,' said the Guru. 'You have followed men of much learning, but you have not grasped the truth that is within you. You have sought Him in things which are a mere reflection of reality. You are lost in the wilderness of knowledge. Words only acquire a meaning when you realize the truth of which they are the symbols...

" 'Another man's wife, another man's property, covetousness, evil desire, search of sense objects, bad temper, backbiting, lustfulness and wrath—He who rids himself of these will find in himself the Infinite, the Unknowable. This hidden nectar only he discovers who receives the jewel of the Guru's Word and makes it his life breath...In the dawn of true wisdom—buddhi—fed by the light of God's Name, in the company of saints, devoted to the Guru, the Guru, the Giver, bestows the sacred Name. Treasuring it, the disciple is absorbed in Him. He alone obtains the sacred Word who earns the grace of the Lord. This body is the temple of the Lord. In the heart is His Light. Says Nanak, let the Word of the Guru enter the heart and by the grace of God effect everlasting union.'

"The Pandit bowed and said, 'I have now learned the truth, to seek within and not outside, to get rid of the evil passions, to seek the favor of the Lord and remain absorbed in the Guru's Word.' "[21]

Lord Jesus, too, appeared and disappeared at will, even **before** His crucifixion and Resurrection. As a matter of fact, His body was so finely attuned to the spirit, that it seemed to have no substance to it whatever at times. An account of this is found in one of the most famous Gnostic Gospels: *The Acts of John.* In this gospel, John relates certain strange incidents which suggest that Jesus was far from an ordinary physical human being, and that even His body was not always your ordinary body:

> " 'I will tell you another glory, brethren; sometimes when I meant to touch Him I encountered a material, solid body; but at other times again when I felt Him, His substance was immaterial and incorporeal...as if it did not exist at all.' "[22]

Jesus said: "That which is born of the flesh is flesh, and that which is born of the spirit is spirit."[23]

It should be remembered that this incident took place **before** Jesus' crucifixion. Even after His "death" and Resurrection, Jesus was able to materialize and dematerialize into a human body at will, such as that witnessed by two of His disciples on the road to Emmaus, and again in order to convince "doubting" Thomas that He truly did exist and was not just a ghost or apparition. He had such control over matter that He was able to eat food and produce a solid body **after** His death, and yet able to create an etheric, or body without substance **before** His death!

Further, like Lord Krishna, Jesus, too, had the ability to appear in different forms simultaneously. The following incident happened before His death and is found in the Gnostic Gospel *The Acts of John:*

> The Acts tells how James once saw Him standing on the shore in the form of a child, but when he pointed him out to John,
>
> "I (John) said, 'Which child?' And he answered me, 'The one who is beckoning to us.' And I said, 'This is because of the long watch we have kept at sea. You are not seeing straight, brother James. Do you not see the man standing there who is handsome, fair and cheerful looking?' But he said to me, 'I do not see that man, my brother.' "
>
> Going ashore to investigate, they became even more confused. According to John,
>
> "He appeared to me again as rather bald-(headed) but with a thick flowing beard, but to James as a young man

86

whose beard was just beginning...I tried to see Him as He was...But He sometimes appeared to me as a small man with no good looks, and then again as looking up to heaven.''[24]

This incident testifies to the Truth that the Lord is seen by different people in different ways. It does not mean that there are different Gods; it's just that people perceive Him in different ways, and therefore worship Him in the form of their own perception.

Lord Krishna echoes this Truth in the *Gita* when He says, "In whatever form a devotee may choose to worship me, I bless and sustain his faith so it may stay unwavering on his way.''[25]

For, as we have been told not only by the saints and avatars, but also by those who have had death experiences, it is not the **form** that is permanent or important; it is the **spirit** of Love **inside** the form that is permanent and important. This is why Jesus allowed His body to be crucified: to show that the body is temporary and, therefore, one must not get attached to it. Instead one must seek out and attach oneself to that which is permanent—the soul or spirit within, the aura or light that is seen around the physical body in Kirlian photography which is unaffected by physical pain or death, and remains perfect even after the body is cut away or dropped.

Walking on Water—A Question of Faith

Walking on water seems to be a universal example of the Lord's great powers. Just about every avatar seems to have done it at one time or another, including Jesus, Guru Nanak, Lord Krishna, and Lord Buddha. For example, the Buddha crossed a river on foot instead of accepting invitations by those with boats so as not to offend anyone, and in order to drive home the Truth that "the rafts of asceticism (self-mortification) and the gaudy gondolas of religious ceremonies were not staunch enough to weather the storms of Samsara (worldliness), while the Tathagata (the Perfect One—the Buddha) can walk dry-shod over the ocean of worldliness.''[26]

Not only did the Lord Himself walk on water; He also helped His disciples walk on water, too, provided they had enough Faith to do so. When Jesus was walking out to His disciples' boat on the lake, Peter walked on the water to greet Him. When Peter began to doubt, he started to sink. Jesus saved him, saying, "O man of little faith, why did you doubt?"[27]

A follower of Lord Buddha's displayed the kind of faith Jesus was talking about. This follower's desire to hear Lord Buddha's words was so great that he was able to walk over a river without sinking. When he reached the other side, his astonished neighbors asked him how he did it, He replied:

> " 'I lived in ignorance until I heard the voice of the Buddha. As I was anxious to hear the doctrine of salvation, I crossed the river and I walked over its troubled waters because I had faith. Faith, nothing else, enabled me to do so, and now I am here in the bliss of the Master's presence.' "[28]

Another example of a disciple's great faith was demonstrated by Hanuman, a loving devotee of Sri Rama (an incarnation of the Lord who came to India hundreds of years prior to Sri Krishna). Sri Rama and His entourage needed to cross the ocean from South India to the island of Sri Lanka (or Ceylon) off India's southern tip. Hanuman wrote the Lord's Name on rocks and threw them into the water. The rocks floated and formed a bridge for Hanuman, Sri Rama and His group to walk on!

Guru Nanak gives the reason why the above worked so well. When He wished to see a true seeker of God in Sri Lanka, He, too, needed to cross that same part of the ocean from South India to Sri Lanka. When asked how He would do it, He replied: "If the Sacred Name has the power to enable all men to cross the ocean of death, the Name can take you across this small span of water!"[29] Whereupon, Guru Nanak walked onto the surface of the water followed by His disciples and crossed over to Sri Lanka completely dry!

Faith, then, is the cornerstone around which we must build our spiritual foundation: faith in God, and faith in the power of His Holy Name. For with the power of His Name, one can literally move mountains. An example of this was illustrated by Lord Krishna who lifted Mount Govardhana with one hand "even as a child would pull out a mushroom."[30] *(Shrimad Bhagavatam)*

If there are doubts about the reality of this incident, all one need do is read Jesus Christ's words in the Bible with regard to faith: "Truly, I say to you, if you have faith and never doubt...you (shall be able to) say to this mountain, 'Be taken up and cast into the sea,' it will be done. And whatever you ask in prayer, you will receive, **if you have faith.**"[31]

And again Jesus said: "For truly, I say to you, if you have faith as a grain of mustard seed, you will say to this mountain, 'Move hence to yonder place,' and it will move; and nothing will be impossible to you."[32]

The Pale Prophet

Jesus Himself seems to have literally moved a mountain, too, but not in Palestine or even India; He moved it during His travels through the Americas after His Resurrection!

Just about all of the Native American Indians have legends about a Pale Prophet or Lost White Brother who came to them thousands of years ago and brought with Him the Teachings of the Great Spirit. He taught them to love one another and often used examples from Nature to illustrate His lessons. He performed incredible miracles, one of which was to raise a huge stone in Monument Valley—actually it was half a cliff that had fallen down off a mountain. Other miracles included controlling the elements, miraculous healings, and even raising the dead.

The people loved Him and flocked to Him, but the priests were afraid of Him because He represented a threat to their power. He is always pictured as having a beard, longish hair, a fair complexion, blue-green eyes, wearing sandals and a long white toga with His symbol—the cross—embroidered around the edges. His sign of greeting was His hand raised in Peace, which is why the American Indians greeted, and still greet people in like manner. His hands, too, had the mark of the cross on them.

He had the people build pyramid-style temples, and told them to smoke the Peace Pipe in His memory. He brought them seeds for several different plants, including the mescal plant, and foretold what the future held for the American Indians and their beloved land, including the arrival of the white man whom He called "those who conquer," which is known in Spanish as "conquistadors," who did indeed arrive 1500 years after His prophecy! (These prophecies will be discussed in greater detail later.)

He admonished the people to never touch the white man's whiskey, which He called "Devil-Water"; a description echoed by the saint Sri D. K. Roy or Dadaji almost 2000 years later who, in a letter to the authors, wrote that alcohol was "one of the most demonic influences in the world." The Pale Prophet said that this Devil-Water or alcohol unsettled one's reason, loosened one's tongue, and caused one to act foolishly.

The current information on alcohol has more than justified Jesus' warnings about it. Physicians are now warning that alcohol kills brain cells, including the pineal gland, which cannot be regenerated; has a toxic or poisonous effect on the lungs and heart, causing irreversible damage to the heart muscle; degenerates liver tissue, even in so-called social drinkers; causes inflammation of the pancreas; impairs the functioning of the endocrine gland; causes premature senility, including sexual dysfunction; causes red blood cells to clump together, thereby slowing circulation and depriving every tissue and organ in the body of vital oxygen; lowers the body's resistance to disease and infection; creates "drunken cells" that form brittle bones; causes inflammation of the nerves; as well as being linked to all kinds of cancers. It also causes fetal alcohol syndrome in human fetuses, even in babies whose mothers may only have had a few drinks during the entire pregnancy period, leaving babies mentally and/or physically impaired. It also produces an abnormal gene that is passed on to offspring, leaving the offspring more susceptible to various illnesses and alcoholism itself. A positive example for children must be set by the parents. Today, "one out of every 10 parents in the U.S. has a drinking problem that forces their children to withdraw into a secret world...(and) for every alcoholic parent, 4 or 5 other family members are directly affected."[33] Hence, we must help our children by first helping ourselves and setting the right examples for them.

At one time, the Pale Prophet relayed to the people His background. He said that He was born across the sea to the East:

> "in a land where all men were bearded...He was born of a virgin on a night when a bright star came out of the heavens...the heavens opened and down came winged beings singing chants of exquisite beauty...He spoke of (His country's) houses, their cattle, their clothes and customs, their ships and temples, their metal-clad armies."[34]

He spoke further of His life there: of healing and teaching, of how the people loved Him, but the priests hated Him, again because He threatened their power. He spoke of His trial, His prison stay where He was lashed and beaten, of His execution-cross which He had to carry Himself, of His crucifixion AND of His Resurrection!

He was called different names by different peoples because, as He explained it, names were of little meaning or value; it was the Truths that He taught that were important. So He allowed each tribe to name Him whatever they wanted. Thus the peoples called Him the Fish God (remember that the fish was the symbol of the early Christians!), the Lord of the Wind and Water—Hurukan, from which we get our modern term "hurricane," the Plumed Serpent or Quetzal-Coatl—Quetzal being the sacred bird of the Toltecs, Mayans, and Aztecs, representing the wind or air (hence, the Spirit), being brilliantly colored with long tail feathers, nesting in trees that are in their last stages of decay, and, today, an endangered species, and "tl" meaning "Lord," Kate-Zahl, Kane, the Pale One, the Healer, or just the Prophet. However, when pressed by some of His native followers to tell them what His name was in His Homeland to the East, He answered: "Chee-Zoos, God of the Dawn Light," and said that the name that His countrymen used for God was "Great Yeh-ho-vah."[35]

Skeptics may not believe the American Indian legends, saying that the Indians simply "borrowed" the character of Jesus after hearing of Him from Christian missionaries. But this cannot be so as these legends date back almost 2000 years. And, Jesus Himself said that He had other flocks to tend:

> "I am the Good Shepherd...I have other sheep, which are not of this fold: I must bring them also, and they will heed my voice. So there shall be one flock, one shepherd."[36]

These—the American Indians—are the other sheep of whom Jesus spoke. Further, there are accounts that when the Spanish Conquistadors were butchering their way into Colulua, a sacred city of the Indians, they came upon a Great Pyramid Temple—the Temple of Quetzal-Coatl, whose base is greater than Egypt's Cheops. Quetzal-Coatl had foretold the arrival of these bearded white men, who would wear metal-tipped boots and carry iron rods that made loud noises and could kill men from a great distance. He had also foretold the desecration of His mighty temple by these forces, even to the fighting that would take place on the tiers or steps to the top of the temple.

Indeed, in the bloodiest battle of all Meshico (Mexico), the Spanish did slaughter their way up the temple's steps, but stopped in their tracks when they reached the top. The reason? At the top of the temple there was a life-size statue of a Christ-like man worked in pale marble in a flowing robe standing with outstretched arms (Jesus' Resurrection pose) to greet them![37]

What's more, there are newly discovered artifacts with the sign of the cross through the hand—the sign of the Pale Prophet—from archeological "digs" of native American spiro mounds that have been carbon-dated to the First Century, A.D. Other artifacts include pieces of parchment, now held in Harvard, which have quotations from the Old Testament written in Archaic Hebrew! One recorder of Indian legends—a man called Hubert H. Bancroft—writes that his father once found a stone pictograph of the white-robed teacher. It showed His hair, beard and toga, and "above His head, in Ancient Hebrew were the words of the Ten Commandments."[38] (The reader is urged to see *He Walked The Americas,* by L. Taylor Hansen, who spent over 25 years of her life verifying these legends, seeking out the tribal holy men, going through the ancient artifacts with the Prophet's symbol on them, and tracing the steps of His travels through the Americas.)

Chapter 4

THE QUESTION OF WHY

Jesus, as the Pale Prophet, promised the American Indians that He would return again at the end of this age. But what is the significance of Jesus' travels to the Americas, and why did He travel to the East, as has now been proven through the *Legend of St. Issa* and other writings? To quote Paramahansa Yogananda in answer:

> "God made Jesus Christ an Oriental in order to bring East and West together. Christ came to awaken the Divine Consciousness of brotherhood in the East and the West. It is true that Christ lived in India during most of the eighteen unaccounted-for years of His life, studying with India's great masters. That doesn't take away from his divinity and uniqueness. It shows the unity and brotherhood of all saints and avatars."[1]

Jesus Christ was unique as are all avatars. They are unique as is each snow-flake; no two are exactly alike and yet they are united in that they come from the same source and are made of the same substance. They are unique and yet united in the Truth of the Fatherhood/Motherhood of God and the brotherhood/sisterhood of humanity. They all stem from the One God, who has numberless manifestations, but is One—One in Spirit, One in Love, One in Truth. For as Sri Aurobindo has said, "Unity does not imply uniformity!"[2]

The religions of the world have been compared to three blindfolded men who were taken to different parts of an elephant and asked to guess what it was. The first man took hold of its trunk and declared it to be a large snake. The second felt its leg and declared it to be a tree. The third felt its tail and declared it was a whip. It wasn't until they took off their blindfolds that they were able to see the entire elephant. Then they realized that each had been accurate in his description of the part of the elephant he had touched, but none had correctly guessed the real nature of the whole animal.

Similarly, we must take off our blindfolds of prejudice and ignorance and see the overall nature of the Lord, because, as the

American Indians believe, no one religion contains all the Truth; each one is but an attempt to understand the Nature of God and is, in reality, just a different path leading to the same Goal—the One Great Spirit who pervades all and is within and without all, and is beyond all worldly dualities, all distinctions, all physical attributes; the eternal Being—Sat-chit-ananda, Being-Consciousness-Bliss, where Love Eternal reigns supreme.

It is to the Realization of and Union with this Eternal Being—God without attributes, the Great Spirit behind all creation—that all avatars and true prophets are leading us. The example given by the life of Sri Ramakrishna and his realizations of the Lord through three different paths proves that God is One, but that there are several paths to Him. The only difference in Ramakrishna's experiences is that he entered into union with the Lord through three different doors: Hinduism's Mother, Islam's Prophet, and Christianity's Jesus. It was through merging with these manifested forms of the Lord that Ramakrishna realized and achieved union with the unmanifested Lord, the Great Spirit, the Being of Light of whom those who have had death experiences speak.

Further, the teachings of all of God's Messengers are so similar that if one did not know whose teachings one were reading, it would be difficult to guess correctly who said what! For example, Elaine Pagels relates that the teachings of the Christian Gnostic Gospels are so similar to those of the East:

> "the identity of the divine with the human, the concern with illusion and enlightenment, the founder who is presented not (just) as Lord, but (also) as spiritual guide—(that) some scholars have suggested that if the names were changed, the 'living Buddha' appropriately could say what the *Gospel of Thomas* attributes to the living Jesus."[3]

True and False Prophets

Baha'u'llah (1817-1892), who lived in Persia or Iran and is believed by those of the Baha'i faith (an offshoot of Islam) to have been an avatar or incarnation of the Lord, and was, at the very least, one of humankind's greatest spiritual masters, explained that **all** those who spread God's Truths are reflections of the Supreme Being. He states that in God, in His Grace:

94

"hath caused those luminous Gems of Holiness to appear out of the realm of the spirit...and be made manifest unto all men, that they may impart unto the world the mysteries of the unchangeable Being, and tell of the subtleties of His imperishable Essence.

"These sanctified Mirrors...are, one and all, the Exponents on earth of Him Who is the Central Orb of the universe, its Essence and ultimate Purpose...They are the Treasures of Divine knowledge, and the Repositories of celestial wisdom. Through them is transmitted a grace that is infinite, and by them is revealed the Light that can never fade...

"It is clear and evident...that all the Prophets are the Temples and the Cause of God...all abiding in the same tabernacle, soaring in the same heaven,...uttering the same speech, and proclaiming the same Faith...

"...the works and acts of each and every one of these Manifestations of God...are all ordained by God, and are a reflection of His Will and Purpose. Whoso maketh the slightest possible difference between their persons, their words, their messages, their acts and manners, hath indeed disbelieved in God, hath repudiated His signs, and betrayed the Cause of His Messengers."[4]

Why? Because the Truth that underlies all the teachings of all True Prophets and Avatars is the Unity of the One God and the brotherhood/sisterhood of all humankind. Those who fail to recognize this Truth and who repudiate the Oneness of these teachings drive a wedge between the religions of the world and thereby divide mankind instead of uniting it.

As Baha'u'llah explains: "Leaders of religion in every age hindered their people from attaining the shores of eternal salvation...Some for the lust of leadership (power and greed), others through want of knowledge and understanding..."[5]

Because of their own ignorance, and sometimes due to malice of forethought, religious leaders have confused and complicated God so much that the people have had no concept of what He truly is or how to attain Him. In several cases, these religious leaders have not even allowed the people to pray to the Lord in their own native tongue. For example, until recently almost all of the Catholic services and prayers were said in Latin, a language that

95

was understood centuries ago, but which very few people understand today. The same is true of orthodox Hinduism where most of the prayers and chants are in Sanskrit, again, a language understood long ago, but which is today unfamiliar to most except for a handful of scholars and theologians.

Even in certain Christian Protestant religions, the services are held in such archaic English that the phrases and words used have either lost and/or changed their meanings altogether. An example of this would be the phrase "simple-minded" which is used today to describe one who may not have all his mental marbles, but which in the past meant to think in an uncomplicated way, i.e., a clear-thinker. The connotation of the term "meek" has also changed; today, it gives the picture of one who is weak, almost crouching in the corner out of fear, whereas in the past it meant one who freely submits to God's Will and follows His laws humbly, and has, therefore, the greatest strength because he or she is obeying the Lord, not bowing to the pressures of the world and manmade laws. For from obedience to the Lord comes strength of resolve.

Ridiculous Ceremonies and Silly Superstitions

Throughout the history of religion, priests have used ridiculous ceremonies and silly superstitions to further complicate God, cloud the Truth, and confuse people. Every true prophet or teacher of God has bewailed these false practices. Jesus Himself cried out against the priests who "strain out a gnat and swallow a camel," clinging to the letter of the law and violating the heart of the law, calling them blind guides "because you shut the kingdom of heaven against men; for you neither enter yourselves, nor allow those who would enter to go in."[6] Then He compared them to whitewashed tombs that are all clean and shiny without, but filled with corruption and hypocrisy within.

Jesus warned His followers against Pharisaism, saying that:

"...they preach, but do not practice. They bind heavy burdens, hard to bear, and lay them on men's shoulders; but they themselves will not move them with their finger. They do all their deeds to be seen by men;...and they love the place of honor at feasts and the best seats in the synagogues, and salutations in the market places, and being called rabbi by men...Whoever exalts himself will be humbled, and whoever humbles himself will be exalted."[7]

When the Pharisees chastised Jesus for healing a cripple on the Sabbath—the day of rest—Jesus replied: "What man of you, if he has one sheep and it falls into a pit on the sabbath will not lay hold of it and lift it out?...So it is lawful to do good on the sabbath."[8]

The Lord as Guru Nanak gives some hilarious responses to certain orthodox ceremonies He observed. When He had reached a certain age, he was to be invested with a "sacred thread," thereby showing His status as being part of a particular caste, and of having a "spiritual inheritance." The ceremony was attended by a great crowd of family members and friends, and a huge feast had been prepared for the occasion, including some roasted goats, as His family was of a caste that was "permitted" to eat meat! Guru Nanak said to the priest performing the ceremony, and to the crowd attending:

> "What strange ceremony is this? The Brahmin (priest) spins a thread out of cotton and twists it into shape. When it decays, a new one takes its place. If the thread had any virtue it would not decay or break. They kill goats without mercy and prepare a feast and guests clamour for more and more.
>
> "My elders, worthy of all respect, is it not strange that he who performs the ceremony and claims to foretell the future charges a fee for the performance? He places no control on his senses nor protects his beard from the spit of greed. He puts no restraint on his eyes or tongue, on his hands and feet. In all actions, he is unrestrained and yet he puts a twisted thread round the neck of another. See this strange phenomenon—the man with a blind mind claims to be enlightened. I will not wear this thread. It is no more sacred than the cotton from which it is made."[9]

When asked what kind of a sacred thread He would wear, Guru Nanak replied:

> "Out of the cotton of compassion spin the thread of contentment, tie the knots of continence, give it the twist of truth. Make such a sacred thread for the mind, such a thread

once worn will never break nor get soiled, burnt or lost. The Man who wears such a thread is blessed.

"You buy a thread for pennies and seated in a plastered square put it around the neck of others. Claiming an inheritance of holiness your thread helps neither here nor hereafter. The wearer dies and leaves it behind."[10]

On another occasion, Guru Nanak demonstrated the ridiculousness of a ceremony for the "departed," and that there are no "quick-fixes" for salvation. He came upon a group of orthodox priests who had claimed that if one made an offering of food to his ancestors and God at a particular place on the river, he would secure absolution for his ancestors. As the Guru watched the stone-faced priests conducting their prolonged ceremonies, He burst out laughing and said:

"Don't you see how ridiculous your ceremonies are? Those who have left this body, do they need food, do they need the glow of a lamp to see where neither the sun nor the moon shed their light?...

"Brimful with the oil of suffering is the lamp of life. Kindle the flame of the Name. The flame of the Sacred Name will consume the oil of sufferings, and the Lord Himself will be seen...The Brahmin makes rolls, offers them to ancestors and to God, but eats them himself!"[11]

Whereupon the priests said that the meanings of the scriptures were beyond the bounds of human understanding. Guru Nanak retorted:

"You follow the scriptures when it suits you. You follow what is convenient and profitable but you shun the call for sacrifice. Do your scriptures recommend indulgence in lust and greed? If you are learned in the scriptures, tell me, what is truth? Point out the difference between the path of darkness and the path of light. You are not only untrue to yourselves, but you mislead others. You prevent people from taking the right path by showing easy methods of salvation. All such acts are sinful. How can you help those who are gone when your own actions are not free from sin?...

"You read and you recite but you rarely realize Truth. Mere lip service is of little avail. You never grasp even the

98

real importance of the words you read. Then you perform endless ceremonies to secure enjoyment and greatness and feed the fire of desire, thus sowing fresh seeds of Karma, but you make no attempt to be one with Him, by serving His creation. Every selfish action forges fetters and binds the soul to the cycle of birth and death. The recitation of Mantras, the repetition of the Sacred Name impelled by whirlwinds of desire is of no use in the wilderness of the world. As long as passion, attachment, hate and pride preside, the reading of the scriptures and telling the rosary are of no avail. It is like clinging to a carcass which is without life.

"Worshipping a stone God, displaying a rosary of sacred beads, is like watering barren soil. Why waste life in empty formalities and plaster the body from without when it is crumbling from within? Fill the mind with charitable thoughts, make a raft of the Sacred Name, become bountiful and cross the ocean of life."[12]

Prayer: Not Where, But How

All true prophets have also emphasized that since God is everywhere, it is not **where** one prays but **HOW** one prays that is important. The prayer must be sincere and from the heart; it must not be done for show or for the admiration of others. Jesus said that one should not go to the temples and wailing walls or give alms in public, for the admiration of others is the only reward one will get:

"Beware of practicing your piety before men in order to be seen by them...when you give alms, sound no trumpet before you, as the hypocrites do in the synagogues and in the streets, that they may be praised by men. Truly, I say to you, they have their reward...(Rather, give) your alms...in secret, and your Father who sees in secret will reward you.

"And when you pray, you must not be like the hypocrites, for they love to stand and pray in the synagogues and at the street corners, that they may be seen by men...they have their reward. But when you pray, go into your room and shut the door and pray to your Father in secret; and your Father who sees in secret will reward you."[13]

99

And, again, Jesus or St. Issa said:

"Enter into your temple, into your heart; illuminate it with good thoughts, with patience and the unshakeable faith which you owe to your Father.

"And your sacred vessels! they are your hands and your eyes. Look to do that which is agreeable to God, for in doing good to your fellowmen, you perform a ceremony that embellishes the temple wherein abideth Him who has created you...

"Therefore, I say unto you,...perform not ceremonies which separate you from your Father and bind you to the priests, from whom heaven has turned away. For it is they who have led you away from the true God, and by superstitions and cruelty perverted the spirit and made you blind to the knowledge of the truth..."[14]

This does not mean that all priests or religious leaders are bad, or that going to a church, temple or synagogue is wrong, or that all ceremonies are of no value. Not at all. However, it must be remembered that the bowing and kneeling done in ceremonies in religious structures must be but the outward signs of the humbleness and humility of the spirit or heart within to the Lord who is within and without all. When we forget the meanings behind the ceremonies and perform them only in a mechanical way, with no true spirit of love and repentance, then all this outward show is meaningless and of no value. What we must remember is, as Guru Nanak said, "God is in every heart and every heart is His temple."[15]

Know Them by Their Fruits

Further, it is true that organized religion has often misled humanity and put forth ridiculous doctrines and meaningless rituals, spinning a web of confusion and fear, thereby clouding and perverting the word of God, in order to maintain control and power over the people. As Sri Aurobindo explains:

"Very often the accredited (organized) religions have opposed progress and sided with the forces of obscurity and oppression...If religion has failed, it is because it has confused the essential with the adventitious (those things which lie **outside** the essential heart of true religion; the dogmas, doctrines,

100

rituals and ceremonies that have been accumulated by organized religion almost accidentally for the sake of convenience). True religion is spiritual religion, it is a seeking after God (who dwells within each of us)...Dogmas, cults, moral codes are aids and props; they may be offered to man but not imposed on him."[16]

What **is** essential is to seek the Truth of the One God, to learn of His laws and to serve His Creation. But in order to learn and understand more about the Lord, most of us do need a guide or spiritual teacher. The problem is to distinguish between the good teachers and the bad teachers, the true prophets and the false. How does one make this distinction? Jesus Christ gave us the answer: "You will know them by their fruits."[17]

In other words, one must look to the actions, the fruits of those who would be teachers or guides. Those who preach the Oneness of God and the brotherhood/sisterhood of humanity, who, like the American Indians, "respect all worship of Him by others...(and) show respect to such things as are held sacred by others,"[18] who bring peace and unity to the world by sowing the seeds of love and compassion, patience and tolerance, and who practice what they preach by helping all in need, regardless of race, color, creed, sex, nationality, etc.: they are blessed and are true prophets—the Peacemakers—whose guidance we must seek in our spiritual quest.

Conversely, those who preach that "their way" is the only way, who sow the seeds of hatred and violence, division and disharmony, who point out the differences rather than the similarities between us all, and even those who may preach love, but who practice hate, who fail to serve all equally or give to those in need: know them to be the false prophets of whom Jesus warned, the wolves in sheep's clothing, the dividers of humanity and the disrupters of the natural flow of Oneness, Unity and Harmony. These are the ones that deny that God is the only real force in the world, who do not believe the Truth that God is the God of **Good only** and that the only evil that exists is that which lies in the hearts of those who would turn God's children away from the Path of Truth and Unity. These are the ones who stubbornly refuse to recognize the Truth that has been expounded by all of God's prophets and incarnations: the Truth that God is One, but has come time and time again to the earth in the forms of avatars and saints,

101

prophets and rishis in order to show man the way back to Truth and Light, Unity and Oneness with all Creation.

Recently on the island of Oahu, Hawaii, there was a beautiful example of interfaith unity during the dedication ceremony of a newly-constructed Buddhist temple. Leaders from several faiths, including the Jewish, Muslim, Catholic, and Protestant religions, joined together to dedicate this Buddhist Temple of Peace. One of the Christian pastors there compared the different faiths to the strings of a musical instrument, each having a distinct sound and character, but still harmonizing with all the others. The Jewish rabbi attending said the following concerning world peace and the unity of all faiths and humanity as a whole:

> "Here, on this high elevation, a structure dedicated to world peace has flowered. Perhaps our best response would be just to gaze at it in perfect silence, to meditate on its meaning, and after a while, to look at each other with a smile of recognition, a smile of love, a smile of hope...
>
> "Unless we go forth from here to build a temple of peace in our own hearts, this beautiful Pagoda of Dae-Won-Sa Temple will not be dedicated. If we go forth from here so furious about the exclusive rightness of our own religion that we become irreligiously religious, then we are as guilty of disturbing world peace as are those who dangle the weapons of war in front of those whom they consider to be their enemies."[19]

As Guru Nanak explains:

> "Only he has a right to call himself religious, who lives in the light of God's word brought to earth by prophets of all religions. To me all religions are His...Ignorance is the cause of all religious conflicts. People talk and yet fail to realize religion. There is no difference between Hindu and Muslim (Christian or Jew, Buddhist or Baha'i). (All) are from the same mold. Only the veil of ignorance separates them...Ignorance has its roots in the ego, it does not see Him in all things..."[20]

When asked which is the best name of God, Guru Nanak replied: "By whatever name we remember Him it is the best...,"[21] whatever that Name may be—Jehovah, Om, Krishna, Christ,

Buddha, Allah, Great Spirit, or whatever. What matters is that one think of Him ceaselessly—not just one hour out of one day out of the week—and to repeat His Name, whichever name one wishes, in One's heart, thereby lighting the Lamp of Love within and letting its luminous glow fill our entire being with Light: Light that shines forth to touch and warm, illuminate and comfort all with whom we come in contact, that we may be children of Peace and Lovers of God and serve Him in all we think, do and say.

Further, we must learn more about Him and His ways by seeking out the spiritual truths that are in all Holy Scriptures. As the *Shrimad Bhagavatam* says: "Like the bee collecting honey from many flowers a discriminating person should gather the essence from all scriptures, great or small."[22]

Thus, let us see what other Truths and words of guidance have been brought to us over the ages by all of God's representatives throughout the world. For, as the Buddha said:

"No matter whose the teachings, my friend, if you are sure of this—These doctrines conduce to serenity, not passion; freedom, not bondage;...thrift, not greed; calm, not restlessness; solitude, not noisy company; energy, not sloth; performance of good, not delight in evil—that is the Dhamma (Teaching), that is the Discipline, that is the Master's Way."[23]

Chapter 5

THE PATHS TO GOD

Several spiritual teachings and truths from different faiths have already been discussed and compared in earlier chapters of this book, such as past prophecies that have been fulfilled, yogic cleansings, how to meditate, the caste system and the equality of all human beings, the role of women in spiritual life and the New Age, the dual aspect of the Godhead, the question of avatars, their lives and miracles, and how to recognize true and false prophets. This section will describe in more detail the different paths one may follow to attain God-Realization, the synthesis of these paths, and the nature of God's Great Spirit that pervades all.

There are basically three roads to Union with the Lord as described by all of God's representatives: 1- the Way of Knowledge or Gnosis, 2- the Way of Love or Devotion, and 3- the Way of Works or Karma. When these three paths are followed simultaneously, they have a profound effect upon one's spiritual growth, greatly accelerating the process of spiritual transformation. The three paths are described below.

The Path of Knowledge

The path of knowledge has already been discussed to a large degree earlier in this book. The knowledge of which God's Chosen have spoken, including those who have had death experiences, is knowledge of God, of His Creation, and of His Laws of Karma and of the Balance of Nature. In the *Gita,* Lord Krishna explains what type of knowledge we must seek to acquire:

> "Disowning of conceit and violence, forgiveness, serving the master, purity, ingenuousness, steadfastness, self-control, humility, indifference to the objects of sense, a perception of this earthly life's deep limitations—a pointless cycle of birth, disease and sorrow, petering out in death— non-attachment to the home and family, looking with an equal eye on pleasure and pain, unwavering devotion to me, the Lord, turning to solitude far from the din of crowds, deep aspiration for the lore of the soul and a seeking of spiritual Truth; all this is the authentic knowledge—and what is at

variance with it is ignorance."[1]

This, then, is true knowledge, which must be acquired, as Lord Krishna points out, **through direct, personal, spiritual experience: gnosis,** and not simply through books and mere memorization. This does not mean that one should not read spiritual books, especially books which have been written by those who have had gnostic experiences themselves, such as the Upanishads, the Gnostic Gospels, and the writings of all of the great masters, saints, and yogis East and West, such as Sri Aurobindo, Sri D.K. Roy, St. Francis, St. Paul, Sri Ramakrishna, Sri Ramana Maharshi, Swami Vivekananda, etc. One should also read unadulterated scriptures of the Lord's direct teachings through His descents as avatars. Books can act as important tutors or guides helping prepare one for a gnostic experience, or as confirmations and explanations of such experiences, thereby simplifying God and helping one to understand what one is experiencing, or as signposts pointing the way toward higher realizations and truths.

But somewhere along the way one must start **experiencing** these revelations and truths, thereby not relying solely on books for knowledge, because for all their value, books are, in themselves, limited as they are but a third-hand rendering of the Eternal Truths of which yogis and those who have had death experiences say no words can adequately describe, as they are beyond explanation in ordinary human languages or terminology: truths that must be seen, heard and **felt** within one's heart and soul, if these truths are to become a living Reality for us and the new basis of our life's journey.

How does one promote these experiences? Various external methods have been used, including biofeedback, hypnosis, rebirthing, rolfing, isolation (samadhi) tanks, etc. However, all of the above rely on some form of external stimulus, apparatus or control to promote the experience. If one is to have these experiences on a more regular basis, one must look to the ancient science of Yoga for instruction and guidance.

Yoga implies Union with the Lord through **discipline:** discipline of one's thoughts, of one's emotions, of one's actions; discipline and control over one's ego and all ego-oriented activities whether of a vital (physical or bodily), mental, or emotional nature. With this discipline, one roots out the cravings that besiege our lower nature, for as the Buddha points out:

"Craving is like a creeper, it strangles the fool...When craving, like poison, takes hold of a man, his sorrows increase like wild grass. When this terrible craving, fierce to subdue, is subdued, sorrows slip off like drops on a lotus leaf...Root out craving...Weeds are the poison of fields and passion, hate, folly and desire the poison(s) of man...Cut off the five: egoism, doubt, false holiness, lust and hatred. Destroy these five fetters, and you will have crossed the stream of life."[2]

In other words, one must control one's vital self—eating, sleeping, procreating, eliminating, etc.; one's mind—rooting out negative thoughts of greed, lust, power, guilt, doubt, etc., replacing them with positive thoughts of God, truth, caring, sharing, tolerance, etc.; and one's emotions—rooting out anger, violence, hatred, jealousy, envy, and other negative emotions, replacing them with love, compassion, faith, humility, and all other positive emotions that help evoke devotion to the Lord.

The internal methods of meditation on and chanting of the Lord's Name as described earlier in the book help one to control one's thoughts and cleanse the mind, which in turn helps to promote these spiritual experiences without resorting to external aids. This does not mean that the use of external aids can not be helpful initially, but ultimately one has to drop all artificial crutches on the road to spiritual development and eventual God-Realization.

When one controls one's thoughts through these internal methods, one comes closer and closer to the Goal. The Buddha says:

"We are what we think, having become what we thought. Like the wheel that follows the cart-pulling ox, sorrow follows an evil thought. And joy follows a pure thought, like a shadow faithfully tailing a man...Clear thinking leads to Nirvana (Samadhi, Bliss, Mystical Union with the Lord), a confused mind is a place of death. Clear thinkers do not die, the confused ones have never lived...Clear thinking, right action, discipline and restraint make an island for the wise man, an island safe from floods."[3]

As one begins to gain knowledge of God through reading the right books, disciplining one's senses, practicing meditation, etc., one begins to realize and experience the Oneness of All Creation;

one begins to tap into the Universal Consciousness and All-Pervading Spirit of God; one sees that we are all but a tiny part of the Whole of the Eternal Being. As a result, the desire to meet and merge into this Eternal Being grows, with love and bhakti or devotion to the Lord increasing correspondingly, which brings us to the next and most important path to God-Realization: The Path of Love.

The Path of Love and Devotion

God is Love. His Creation is a result of His Eternal Love. Though there may be technically as many paths to the Lord as there are beings in the universe, in reality there is, as Smt. Indira Devi has pointed out, but One Path to God-Realization, and that is the Path of Love.

St. Dadaji (Sri D.K. Roy) lists nine stages on the Path of Love as follows: "1- faith, 2- consorting with holy men, 3- spiritual self-discipline or askesis, 4- overcoming obstacles that come in the way, 5- determination to follow His lead of light, 6- finding an incipient pleasure in plodding on, 7- the pleasure deepening into joy, (or) savouring what seemed dry for years, 8- devotion or bhakti, and 9- prem or devotion ripening into ecstatic God-love."[4]

The type of faith to which Dadaji is referring is that which "knows that there is a Sun denied by the evidence of dusk and clouds";[5] faith that there is a Creator, Healer and Sustainer; "faith that is there lying latent in every soul,"[6] but which must first be awakened. This awakening can only be achieved by seeking "the help and blessings of the illuminates who live in the light,"[7] who must be approached with an attitude of humility, "for only an attitude of humility can make an aspiring intellect receptive to the light of knowledge or spiritual wisdom."[8] (Dadaji)

With this spiritual wisdom comes the recognition of the Primary Importance of Love in the Path toward God-Realization. All of God's Messengers have reiterated this message, i.e., that God is Love and our path to Him lies in Loving Him and His Creation. St. Paul describes what love is and holds it in the highest esteem, above all other spiritual qualities:

"If I have prophetic powers; and understand all mysteries and all knowledge, and if I have all faith, so as to remove

107

mountains, but have not love, I am nothing. If I give away all I have, and if I deliver my body to be burned, but have not love, I gain nothing.

"Love is patient and kind; love is not jealous or boastful; it is not arrogant or rude. Love does not insist on its own way; it is not irritable or resentful; it does not rejoice at wrong, but rejoices in the right. Love bears all things, believes all things, hopes all things, endures all things.

"Love never ends; as for prophecies, they will pass away; as for tongues, they will cease; as for knowledge, it will pass away. For our knowledge is imperfect and our prophecy is imperfect; but when the perfect comes, the imperfect will pass away...So faith, hope, love abide, these three; **but the greatest of these is Love.**"[9]

Guru Nanak, too, speaks of love as the highest spiritual Truth, saying: "...to love Him is the end of knowledge and to forget Him is to forget the truth, even though one may carry a cartload of books."[10]

This is not to say that the paths of love and knowledge are exclusive of one another; on the contrary, as Sri Aurobindo has pointed out, the two paths compliment one another: "Love fulfilled does not exclude knowledge, but itself brings knowledge; and the completer the knowledge, the richer the possibility of love."[11] And again he says: "...when the God-lover is also the God-knower, the lover becomes oneself with the Beloved."[12] Sri Ramana Maharshi once told Sri D.K. Roy or Dadaji that "he regarded bhakti as jnana-mata, that is, love is the mother of knowledge."[13] Further, Dadaji points out that in the *Gita,* Lord Krishna maintains that:

"...the ultimate Goal (of God-Realization) can be attained best and quickest through love guided by knowledge...(for) at the summit of mystic love, bhakti and jnana (love and knowledge) merge into each other and shine almost like two facets of the same Realization. A great Yogi has said: 'He who says he knows but does not love does not know and he who says he loves but does not know does not love.' "[14]

Love of God

There are two aspects to the Path of Love, and thus two ways in which our love must express itself. The first way is to Love God above all else. He must be our Goal above all other goals. As Dadaji states:

"Krishna tells us time and again that only when you offer your heart to the Lord of your heart or emulate the great (saints and sages) can you feel truly freed from the ego's cage against whose bars your bird-soul beats its bleeding wings...(and thus) learn to experience the peace of blue freedom—nirvana...(attainable only) through the miracle power of love..."[15], blue touched with gold being the color of the highest chakra, the crown chakra, the door to Union.

Lord Krishna explains this concept of Love in the *Gita* as follows:

"The Supreme in whom abide all sentient creatures and who is Omniprevalent, can be attained by single-minded love alone...

"Among the ones who turn to me stand out the illuminates who worship me (God) alone; I am their hearts' beloved, as they are mine. Noble indeed they all are, but I cherish Him as my heart's beloved whose soul is linked with mine and who is havened in me alone, in devotion, hailing me as the highest Goal...

"The great-souled who dwell in the divine nature knowing me as the eternal source of the world, worship me with a single-minded love, and, pledged to me, bow before me in devotion, singing of me day after resonant day...

"Not through a mastery of Vedic lore, askesis, benefactions or sacrifice can one behold what I have unveiled to you: only by a dint of the soul's one-pointed love can you know and see and enter into my essence...

"I am the primal origin of all; from me stem all, the wise who know this Truth worship me as such in love's pure ecstasy, their minds and hearts centered in me, they dwell in flawless joy on this one blessed theme, day after day delighting one another. To such dedicated souls who live to love me one-pointedly, at one with me—I grant the mind of light so

109

they may come home to me."[16]

With this mind of light one begins to perceive the true nature of God: that He is all Love and all Forgiveness. False prophets of the past and present have injected fear into the minds and hearts of those who would seek a closer relationship with Him; they have not been "honest brokers" because they have not wanted to lose their control over the general public. By portraying God as severe and unforgiving, they have perverted the view one should have toward God. One **should** be in **awe** of Him and of His magnificence, but one should ultimately view Him as the Source of All Love.

As the famous American author, Ellen G. White explains in her beautiful book *Steps to Christ:* "It was to remove this dark shadow (of fear), by revealing to the world the infinite love of God, that Jesus came to live among men..."—which is one of the reasons that all of the avatars have come to the earth.[17]

But God has a dual nature: as a manifested being, which is what avatars are, and as an unmanifested being or the Great Spirit, from which comes all manifested beings, including the avatars. In the *Gita,* Lord Krishna further explains the Nature of God, who and what He is, and what His Great Spirit is and does:

"I'm the father, mother, sponsor and grandsire of the world, the goal of knowledge, the pure Om, the triple Vedas...I am the Goal, the upholder of all, their Lord and refuge, friend and ultimate abode, the fount and basis of the universe, the divine ground, the imperishable seed. I shed heat, I draw water from the earth and then send it back once more as the rain, I am immortality as well as death. I am, friend, at once Being and non-Being...

"My unmanifested Being pervades this Universe. All creatures reside in me...Behold my mystery divine: my Spirit, the origin of all, sustaining all that is on earth...As the vast, ubiquitous, untrammelled air abides in the sky—even so, know this that every creature does abide in me...

"Intellect, knowledge, truth, self-mastery, tranquillity and freedom from illusions, non-violence,...birth and death, penury, affluence and equality,...contentment, charity, forgiveness, askesis...All of these states of being derive from me...

"I preside in the hearts of all: I am the beginning, middle and end of all that is. I am Vishnu among the Vedic gods and among the lights I am the radiant sun. Lastly, I am the ultimate seed of all creatures in cosmos: naught that is immobile or mobile, friend, can ever exist without me. There is no end to my supernal powers. All I have told you is but a brief resume of my multitudinous glory.

"Wherever you find an effloressence of grace, opulence, grandeur or power that thrills the heart—know: it all derives from a gleam of my sun-splendor. But I need hardly elaborate it to you in detail: suffice it that **this universe is upheld by but a fraction of my Self.**"[18]

This Great Spirit, the unmanifested Lord, God without attributes and beyond all worldly names and labels, is that which pervades all and sustains all. It is the light we see surrounding the physical body in Kirlian photography. It is unaffected by gross physical imperfections, always remaining whole, luminous and perfect regardless of what happens to its physical "shell" or "scab." It is the Being of Light and the aura of Light seen everywhere of which those who have had death experiences speak, and from which radiated warmth and unconditional love.

It was this unconditional love that most affected those people as they were reviewing their own lives. They came to realize that it was this kind of love that we all must demonstrate to one another, which brings us to the second way in which we must express our love for God: by loving one another.

Love Thy Neighbor as Thyself

The history of mankind is marred with terrible violence precisely because we have failed to see in each other, our brother. Baha'u'llah describes the world's situation thus:

"The world is engaged in war and struggle, and mankind is in the utmost conflict and danger. The darkness of unfaithfulness has enshrouded the earth...The prominent men become commanders and boast of bloodshed, and glory in destruction...In all regions friendship and uprightness are denounced and reconciliation and regard for truth are despised."[19]

111

Jesus Christ stressed this need to love one another throughout His travels East and West, both before and after His Resurrection. When told by one of the elders that the "heart of the Law" was to love the Lord, our God, with all our mind, heart, soul and strength, Jesus proclaimed that there was a second commandment equally great and important: "You shall love your neighbor as yourself!"[20] On these two commandments hang all the Laws and the Prophets. Further, when Jesus was chastised by some orthodox Jews for helping a Roman centurian by curing his servant—the Jews claiming that they were "the chosen people" of God and that a "pagan" was not worthy of such concern from God or Jesus—Jesus retorted that everyone was invited to His Father's table—rich or poor, slave or free, Jew or "pagan": "I tell you, many will come from East and West and sit at the table with Abraham, Isaac and Jacob in the Kingdom of Heaven..."[21]

While in Oklahoma among the American Indians, Jesus reiterated this truth: "Do not kill or injure your neighbor, for it is not he that you injure; you injure yourself...Do not wrong or hate your neighbor; for it is not he that you wrong: you wrong yourself. Rather love him, for the Great Spirit loves him, even as He loves you."[22]

As said before, this Great Spirit pervades all and is within all. Therefore, all Creation, all Life is Divine. Sathya Sai Baba has pointed out that during the Last Supper, Jesus said that the bread was His body and that the "fruit of the vine" (the literal translation) was His blood:

> "He meant that all beings alive with flesh and blood are to be treated as He Himself and no distinction should be made as friend or foe, we or they. Every body is His body...every drop of blood flowing in the veins of every living being is His- ...That is to say, every man and woman is Divine and has to be revered as such."[23]

Thus, when we injure another we are injuring a part of God, and if we truly love the Lord, we would never do such a thing. Further, when we injure another, we injure ourselves because, as the *Vedas* point out: "Thou art that." In other words, we are a part of that Great Spirit that pervades all, so by hurting others, we are really hurting an extension of our own selves.

Those who have had death experiences have said that the Being of Light was most interested in their ability to love one another, and to demonstrate this love in their actions throughout their lives:

"...the kind of love that has nothing to do with downgrading people. Could I love people, even when I knew them really well, even their faults...Love was it. And He meant the kind of love that makes me want to know if my neighbor is fed and clothed and makes me want to help him, if he is not."[24]

Guru Nanak explains that it is through serving others that we serve Him, the Lord, reiterating Jesus' words that whatever good things we do for others, in reality, we are doing for Him:

"He is pleased when in others we see the face of a brother and extend the help which we wish others to extend to us. The more this feeling of fellowship grows, the nearer we draw to God. There is no other way but this, **that we learn to love one another and thus find the secret of loving God...**Most people profess to love others, but they only love themselves; a few love those who love them, but **a true disciple of the Guru must love all, even those who hate him...**a follower of the Guru must serve friends and foes alike, knowing that it is only thus he can serve God."[25]

Jesus Christ said:

"Love your enemies, do good to those who hate you, bless those who curse you, pray for those who abuse you. To him who strikes you on one cheek, offer the other also; and from him who takes away your cloak do not withhold your coat as well. Give to everyone who begs from you; and of him who takes away your goods do not ask them again. And as you wish that men would do to you, do so to them...and your reward will be great, and you will be sons of the Most High; for He is kind to the ungrateful and the selfish. Be merciful, even as your Father is merciful.

"Judge not, and you will not be judged; condemn not, and you will not be condemned; forgive, and you will be forgiven; give, and it will be given to you...For the measure you give will be the measure you get back...first take the log out of your own eye, and then you will see clearly to take out the

113

speck that is in your brother's eye."[26]

As Guru Nanak explained to a physician: "You cannot act as a physician unless you can first remove your own disease (which is the sickness of the soul—the ego)—the pain that disturbs your peace. Then you may treat others and call yourself a physician."[27] And, again, as an ancient American Indian prayer puts it: "Great Spirit—Grant that I may not criticize my neighbor until I have walked a mile in his moccasins." For the Lord has said that we must not only love one another, but forgive each others' debts as He has forgiven ours. As St Paul said:

> "Since you have been chosen by God who has given you this new kind of life, and because of His deep love and concern for you, you should practice tender hearted mercy and kindness to others. Don't worry about making a good impression on them but be ready to suffer quietly and patiently. Be gentle and ready to forgive, never hold grudges. Remember, the Lord forgave you, so you must forgive others. And above all these put on love, which binds everything together in perfect harmony."[28]

Thus, it is by loving and helping others including our enemies that we draw closer to God and the Realization of His New World of Love. Jonathan Schell, the author of the best seller *The Fate of the Earth* concludes that dismantling the world's nuclear arsenals is only the first necessary step we must take on the road to Peace, because even without the weapons, we will still be "cursed" with the knowledge of how to rebuild them. It is only a change of attitude towards our "enemies" that will insure permanent peace; we truly must recognize in him our own selves and put into practice the teaching of love and nonviolence that all of God's Messengers have given us:

> "Do not to others what ye do not wish done to yourself: and wish for others too what ye desire and long for, for yourself. This is the whole of righteousness, heed it well...With kindness conquer rage; with goodness malice; with generosity defeat all meanness; with the straight truth defeat lies and deceit."[29]

—Hinduism's Mahabharata

> "That which is good for all and anyone, for whomsoever—

114

that is good for me...What I hold good for self, I should for all. Only Law Universal is true law."[30]
—Zoroaster of Persia, c. 600 B.C.

"Do not to others as you would not like done to yourself...Recompense injury with justice, and return good for good."[31]
—Confucius of China, c. 550 B.C.

"What is hateful to thee, do not unto thy fellowman; this is the whole Law. The rest is but commentary."[32]
—Hillel, the Elder, a sage of Judaism

"Conquer yourself, not others. Discipline yourself, learn restraint...Do as you would want done to you...No malice, no injury, disciplined eating and behaving, high thinking and simple living—this is the teaching of the enlightened ones[33]...Let a man overcome evil by good; let him overcome the greedy by generosity, and a liar by the truth[34]...There is only one eternal law: **Hate never destroys hate; only love does**...Let us live happily, hating none though others hate. Let us live without hate among those who hate...Let us live diseaseless among the diseased...Let us live without grief among those who grieve."[35]
—The Buddha, c. 563 B.C.

"To the good I would be good. To the not-good I would also be good in order to make them good. Recompense injury with kindness...Of all noble qualities, loving compassion is the noblest."[36]
—Laotze, founder of Taoism, c. 600 B.C.

"They who actually love even those that do not love them in return are compassionate and loving too like one's parents. There is blameless virtue as well as goodwill operating here!"[37]
—Lord Krishna, c. 2500 B.C.

"It is an absolute mercy and a complete bounty, the illumination of the world, fellowship and harmony, love and union; nay, rather, mercifulness and oneness, the elimination of discord and the unity of whosoever are on earth in the utmost of freedom and dignity. The Blessed Beauty said: 'All

115

are the fruits of one tree and the leaves of one branch'...They must purify their sight... and must always be thinking of doing good to someone, of love, consideration, affection and assistance to somebody. They must see no enemy and count no one as an ill wisher. They must consider everyone on the earth as a friend; regard the stranger as an intimate, and the alien as a companion...These are the commands of the Blessed Beauty, these are the counsels of the Greatest Name...The herald of peace, reformation, love and reconciliation is the Religion of the Blessed Beauty..."[38]

—Baha'u'llah, of Persia, c. 1800's A.D.

"Love is a rare herb that makes a friend even out of a sworn enemy and this herb grows out of nonviolence."[39]

—Mahatma Ghandi (1869-1948)

"If thine enemy be hungry, give him bread; if he be thirsty, give him water; so shalt thou heap coals of fire upon his head; and so the Lord shall award thee; for thy enemy will feel ashamed of his hostile feeling, and his head, his face, will 'burn' with shame, and he will give up enmity and become thy friend, and that will be thy great reward."[40]

—Proverbs, Old Testament

Thus by continually showering love and good deeds on all, including our "enemies," ignoring all societal labels and distinctions, we make for ourselves friends everywhere, thereby helping to build for ourselves a world of kindness and love, tolerance and understanding, compassion and peace. Hence, when we leave our bodies behind, as we all must do in the end, we can review our lives without regret, knowing that we have loved and cared for Him in all His diverse forms and manifestations, which are our fellow-creatures and inhabitants of His Universe. As Guru Nanak explains:

"Man exalts or lowers himself by His own acts...Do not worry about distinction of caste (or class or creed or race or sex or nationality, etc., for in truth, these labels have no meaning once the body is gone, as those who have had death experiences have attested). Realize that His light is in All; there is no caste (class, race, sex, creed, nationality, etc.) on the other side!"[41]

Chapter 6

GOD'S HOLY NAME

While on the "other side," the Being of Light will be there to greet us with His Light surrounding and pervading all. But this Light is the second form of the Eternal Being; Its first form is that of **sound.** Those who have had death experiences have all stated that as they felt themselves being drawn out of their body through the dark tunnel, and **before** they saw the white light, they heard a sound, variously described as a buzzing, or bells tinkling or a humming. This humming is the Lord's first form—Sound.

Science has shown that sound has the power to destroy, as exemplified through a glass shattering when certain high-pitched notes are played or sung, or windows breaking due to the sonic boom produced by certain jet-planes flying overhead. But sound also has the power to **create,** as all holy scriptures have stated:

> "In the beginning the Lord of the Universe alone existed. With Him the word (Om) was the second, and the world is verily the Supreme Brahman (God)."[1] —The Vedas

> "In the beginning was the Word, and the Word was with God, and the Word was God (Om)."[2] —New Testament

Guru Nanak explains the power of the Word, the Lord's Sacred Name, to reabsorb and recreate:

> " 'The whole universe flowed from sound, the sound formed itself into the sacred Name. The sacred Name is the first manifestation of the unmanifest (the Great Spirit), in it all that is has its beginning. It is the one word that leads the manifest to the unmanifest'—(which is why those who have had death experiences have heard that humming sound.)

> "The Pir (spiritual teacher of a certain rank) asked, 'Can you prove the power of the Word to reabsorb and recreate?'

> "The Guru smiled and said, 'Calm yourself,' and with these words He put His hand on the head of the Pir and uttered the divine Word, and in an instant the Pir was reduced to ashes. Again the Guru looked at the ashes and uttered the Word and the Pir appeared sitting in his place saying, 'La-Ilaha-Illa-**Allah.**' "[3]

117

On another occasion, Guru Nanak again demonstrated the power of the Lord's Sacred Name: "He said, 'La' and as He uttered the Word, the whole creation disappeared. Then He uttered 'Allah' (God) and the creation came into existence again. 'Know,' said the Guru, 'that the Word brought the Universe into existence and the Word can gather it back again...Meditate on the Word Om.' "[4]

Vibrations originate from sound. Sound waves or vibrations are a form of energy. Isn't it interesting that scientists use the term "ohms" (pronounced $\overline{O}M$) with which to measure the output of electrical energy? Further, scientists have pointed out that human beings are unable to hear certain pitches or tones of sounds, although these sounds are perceived by other animals. We also are unable to see certain light frequencies, such as X ray and ultraviolet, although again certain animals are able to perceive these light wave frequencies. What we see as dark space in the cosmos is, in fact, filled with energy and light. It is from sound vibrations that all light and life come, and our Goal in life is to become One with the Original Word of God, to be in tune with what the Moody Blues have called the "Lost Chord"—Om.

According to certain spiritual scriptures, including the *Aquarian Gospel of Jesus the Christ* and Hinduism's *Shrimad Bhagavatam,* all manifested life is a result of sound vibrations. Initially, all life was in a pure spiritual or ethereal form, vibrating at a very high rate of speed. As this vibration began to slow down, the ethers began to coagulate into coarser and coarser forms, eventually becoming flesh. Thus our spirits became incased in bodies of flesh.

This concept can be compared to a child's toy—the spinning top. When the top is spinning its fastest, it remains in one place and is perfectly balanced. But as soon as the spinning is disturbed and, hence, slowed down, the top starts to wobble from side to side and eventually falls over.

Again, the concept can be compared to various stages of H_2O (water) molecules. Scientists have proven that all matter—even seemingly solid forms of matter—are actually in a continual state of flux, with molecules and atoms continuously moving, even though we may not be able to see the movement with the naked eye. When H_2O or water molecules vibrate or move at their highest frequency, the water becomes a gas—water vapor in the air which makes up the clouds in the sky. As these molecules cool

118

and slow down, they coagulate and become water again in the forms of rain, snow, etc., depending on their vibratory level. In its lowest vibrational level, the H_2O molecules move very slowly and solidify even more to form ice—a seemingly unmoving, solid substance.

This process is reversed when we leave our bodies, either through physical death of the body, or through meditation on the Lord's Name. Our soul or being starts to vibrate at a higher and higher speed until it reaches its perfect Balance in the presence of the Lord. This is why those who have had death experiences say that they seemed to be moving at an incredible speed—the speed of light—and that their soul or being seemed to pulsate or vibrate with the humming sound they heard; they were experiencing the Truth of what Guru Nanak said, i.e., that it is through the Eternal Sound of the Lord's Sacred Name that the manifested being—a living, physical person—is brought back to the unmanifest—the Being of Light, the Great Spirit, our Lord God.

This is why it is so important to continually meditate on His Name (whichever one we wish to use), especially when one is about to die. For then we are assured of going to the highest vibrational level and of being in the presence of the Lord. For, as Lord Jesus taught in His most famous prayer: "Our Father, who art in heaven, **Hallowed be thy Name...**"[5] or Holy is Thy Name. As all of God's Messengers have said, we must make His Name our Life's Breath; thus on the winds of His Sacred Name our souls, like kites, will soar higher and higher until, as Guru Nanak said, "in the innermost recess of the brain the spirit buzzes like a bee,"[6] filled with the nectar of the Word.

From the sound of the Word, the Lord's Sacred Name, comes **LOGOS**—the Living Word of God made flesh, the Avatars, the Messiahs, the Sons of God, the Proclaimers of Truth whose forms may vary, but whose message is the same: Love the Lord our God, and Love one another and His Creation. This message has been revealed time and time again, throughout the ages, by avatars, saints and prophets alike. The point is not to get hung up on **Who** said it, but to **put into practice what they all have said.** The *Upanishads* explain it thus:

> "Cows are of many colours, but milk is of one color, white; so the proclaimers who proclaim the Truth use many varying forms to put it in, but yet the Truth enclosed in all is One."[7]

THE LORD'S WHEEL

INDICATING THE DIFFERENT
NAMES AND INCARNATIONS
OF THE ONE GOD.

As Jesus Christ explained: "I came not to destroy the law or the prophets but to fulfill them."[8]

And as the Prophet Mohammed states in the Holy *Koran* of the Islamic faith:

> "This that I am now uttering unto you, the Holy *Quran*— it is to be found within the ancient Seers' writings too; for Teachers have been sent to every race. Of human beings no community is left without a warner and a guide. And aught of difference we do not make—for disagreement there is none 'twixt them—between these Prophets. All that have been sent have been so sent but One Truth to proclaim—'I verily the I All-One, am God; there is no other God than I, (the Self, the Universal all-pervading Self), and I alone should be adored by all.' "[9]

Constantine and the Perversion of Truth

So, then, from where did this idea of Jesus being the **only** Son of God or avatar, and Christianity being the only path to God come? What was the real motivation behind this teaching and who was to benefit from its perpetuation?

The answer is that it was the same old story of greed and lust for power—an unholy marriage between unspiritual false prophets who twisted and perverted God's word, and merciless warriors/ rulers (politicians) who used their power to cloud the Truth and rape the people of their just due. In short, it was a merging of the power of the organized church with that of the state, which was instituted by King Constantine in the early part of the Fourth Century, A.D. when he declared Christianity to be the official religion of Rome. In doing so, he ensured that the dictates of the state would be heeded by the general populace. For now the people not only had threats of bodily harm and imprisonment if they refused to follow state laws, but also the threat of "eternal damnation" for going against the "Church of God!"

It was Constantine, then, who first exempted the organized church from property taxes. It was also Constantine who convened the First Council of Christian Bishops at Nicaea. He did so because of the split that had arisen between the orthodox Christians and the Gnostics, as mentioned earlier. This division within the early Christian Church threatened its unity and, therefore, its use by Constantine as a political tool for controlling the Empire. It is interesting to note that Pope Silvester I as well as most of the Western Bishops did not attend. Therefore, the results of the Council were not supported by the Church as a whole.

It was at this council that the concept of the Trinity was endorsed, and that Jesus of Nazareth was declared "the **only** Son of God," as is found in the Nicaean Creed today. But the original Greek word meant not "only," but "unique," which makes a big difference in the light of other religious figures of history, such as the Buddha, Krishna, etc. The solution to this problem, i.e., that history and many writings about Jesus and His early years conflicted with Constantine's new creed, was an Imperial edict that ordered Gnostic teachings banned, their books burned and imprisonment or death for anyone going against Constantine and his new creed.

This ban included all references to those years that Jesus spent abroad as any knowledge of His travels and reaffirmations of the teachings of other religious figures, such as the Buddha or Krishna, might jeopardize the concept of Jesus being the **only** Son of God. This, in turn, might threaten the power of the organized Christian Church as being the only door to salvation. In order to insure that no records of Gnostic teachings or of Jesus' travels were found, Christian armies burned the great library of Alexandria in 389 A.D., which housed the most complete collection of ancient manuscripts, records, etc., at that time, thereby destroying forever vital links to our past.

As Janet Bock explains:

> "As it became apparent to us that the question of the lost years was central to the entire belief structure of the church, we had to consider the possibility that the official canonized nature of Jesus as perceived and perpetuated by the Church had come about as the result of political expediency on the part of an emperor trying to keep his dominions under control."[10]

But what is the real significance of those lost years of Jesus? The significance lies in the difference between the words "only" versus "unique" Son of God. If we perceive Jesus as the only Son of God, then Christianity alone is based on the Truth and all other religions must be viewed as false. If, however, we recognize the basic Truth that underlies all religions, then we must admit the possibility of there being more than one Son of God, more than one Savior, more than one avatar, or God-in-man's-form, and, therefore, more than one path to the Lord.

Once, during a discussion with half-a-dozen Indian children, one of the authors was asked by one of the children, "Why don't Christians accept Krishna? We accept Christ." The answer is that we in the West have been ignorant: ignorant of the Truth that all religions in the end lead to the same Goal—the One God. We are ignorant because we lack the knowledge of this Truth: knowledge that was once available to all, but has since been literally burned up in men's fiery passion for power, as we have seen.

From this fiery passion came a manmade world of intolerance, hatred, divisiveness and ego: a world too brutal to even consider the concept of God as the Mother. God was only the Father, and a strict, stern, unforgiving, jealous Father at that: a Father that Jesus Himself would have had difficulty recognizing. For He saw and spoke of God as the source of all love, peace, harmony, forgiveness, tolerance, and compassion—qualities that our man-made world has considered "weak" and "effeminate."

What is needed today is the recognition and introduction of women and their feminine qualities into the mainstream of life, both worldly and religious. We need to strike a proper balance between the masculine and feminine aspects within ourselves and realize this balance in daily living. This balance has often been exemplified in the East when God has come down to earth with His feminine counterpart in order to set the right example for both sexes to follow: Rama and Sita, Krishna and Radha are just a couple of examples. In this way one sees the different aspects of both sexes demonstrated perfectly: the male's being fatherly protection, guidance and strength, reasoning and logic, etc., and the female's being motherly love and nurturance, patience and tolerance, compassion and peacefulness. Further, one sees demonstrated the cooperation, not competition that should exist between man and woman, complimenting, not complicating each others' lives.

Even today many of India's great saints, sages, and gurus are of both sexes, sometimes living together in a cooperative community. Often a male yogi will have a woman as his closest companion, confidant and devotee. Examples of this would be Sri D. K. Roy and his daughter-disciple Smt. Indira Devi, Sri Aurobindo Ghose and his French companion—the Mother, and Sri Ramakrishna and his wife Sri Sarada Devi.

The Question of Marriage

This brings us to the question of marriage and the spiritual life—do the two mix? First we must recognize the difference between **love** and **lust** in a relationship. In order for a marriage to be meaningful, truly happy and lasting, it must not be based predominantly on impermanent things such as physical beauty, etc. For physical beauty fades and sexual enjoyments grow stale over the years, if not months! Rather, a good marriage must be based on spiritual values and have God as the Goal. For only He is permanent and everlasting.

Further, how can a marriage be happy without Truth and Love, which are Divine qualities? Since both partners are part of the One God, and therefore equal, a happy marriage must also have equality as one of its foundation stones. As Mahatma Gandhi said, "The wife is not the husband's bondslave but his companion and his help-mate and an equal partner in all his joys and sorrows—as free as the husband to choose her own path."[11] This means that the spouses must not compete, but cooperate; not complicate, but compliment each other. When disagreements arise, solve them with honesty and love, not ego and hate. In the *Gita*, Lord Krishna tells us that we must beware of lust and anger as they stem from the ego and, thus, darken the light of the soul. In answer to the question of what compels man to continue to do what in his heart he knows is sinful, Lord Krishna says:

> "They are lust and anger...They are unappeasable and deadly—mark them as your eternal foes...the senses, mind and intellect of a man are the time-old haunts of this relentless lust which veils his knowledge to delude his soul. Therefore you ought to control first your senses and do to death this fiendish foe which stands in the way of wisdom and discrimination.
>
> "The senses are commendable; the mind is greater than the senses; greater still is intelligence and the greatest of all is He. Thus, knowing Him, the Divine, who is beyond the intelligence—you must subdue your mind, and by your soul's own light slay once for all this redoubtable and elusive enemy—lust."[12]

Or, as Mahatma Gandhi once said:

> "If I preach against the modern artificial life of sensual

124

enjoyment, and ask men and women to go back to the simple life epitomized in the charkha (spinning wheel), I do so because I know that without an intelligent return to simplicity, there is no escape from our descent to a state lower than brutality."[13]

St. Paul has said:

"(It is) the hour for you to wake from sleep, for our salvation is closer than when we first believed; the night is far gone, the day is at hand. Let us cast off deeds of darkness and put on the armour of light. Let us live honorably as in the daylight: not in carousing and drunkenness, not in sexual excess and lust, not in quarrelling and jealousy. Rather put on the Lord Jesus Christ and make no provision for the desires of the flesh."[14]

It is essential that both partners help each other in their spiritual evolution, and thus marriage can become an aid to reaching the Lord instead of an obstacle. Through patience, love and understanding, each partner can help the other by-pass the road-blocks on the path to the Lord and God-Realization. For, in truth, where does the love that the spouses feel for one another come from but from Him, as He is the source of all Love. For that matter, the love we feel for and receive from any other person is coming from that part of the Divine that is within each of us, and thus, all love we receive and give stems, in the ultimate analysis, from Him. As the *Upanishads* point out:

"It is not for the sake of the husband, my beloved, that the husband is dear, but for the sake of the Self (the Lord that is within the husband). It is not for the sake of the wife, my beloved, that the wife is dear, but for the sake of the Self (the Lord that is within the wife and within each of us.)"[15]

Of course, for some, the pull to the divine life is so strong that they leave all worldly life, including their families. But this is not the path for most people. Further, it should be pointed out that one must not use God as an excuse to neglect one's worldly duties and reponsibilities, whether to one's family or business associates. The great sage-messiah Sri Ramakrishna illustrated this point with the following example. A man came to him and asked if he could stay with him. Sri Ramakrishna said:

"I came to know that he had left his wife and children with

his father-in-law. He has a whole brood of them! So I took him to task. Just fancy! He is the father of so many children! Will people from the neighborhood feed them and bring them up? He isn't even ashamed that someone else is feeding his wife and children...I scolded him very hard and asked him to look for a job. Then he was willing to leave here."[16]

When asked how one should live in the world, Sri Ramakrishna said:

"Do all your duties, but keep your mind on God. Live with all—with wife and children, father and mother—and serve them. Treat them as if they were very dear to you, but know in your heart of hearts that they do not belong to you."[17]

When Sri Ramakrishna himself had a compelling urge to enter spiritual life, he first consulted his wife and told her he was willing to stay and fulfill his worldly obligations if that was her wish. But she refused to be an obstacle in his spiritual quest. Instead, she encouraged him towards the Godly path and became his constant companion and first disciple:

"At the end of his spiritual practice he literally worshipped his wife as the embodiment of the Divine Mother. After his passing away the Holy Mother became the spiritual guide not only of large numbers of householders, but also of many monastic members of the Ramakrishna Order."[18] *(Gospel of Sri Ramakrishna)*

This idea that one must first put one's own worldly/family life in order before entering spiritual life was again demonstrated by the Lord as Guru Nanak. He lived the life of a householder for three years, His purpose being to show that the household was a training area or "school" where love for one's self was changed into love for others, and in order to demonstrate the necessity of earning an honest living as a prerequisite to godliness. When He was preparing to leave His home and family so that he could continue doing His and our Father's work and help others to follow the Path of Truth, His brother-in-law asked Him if renouncing the world and, therefore, family life was the way to spiritual enlightenment. Guru Nanak replied:

"No, my brother...Haven't I lived the life of a householder? No, I am not going to become a monk, but show the way every householder can follow to attain

126

liberation...

"It is not by shirking our duty that we become saints, but by daily performance of that which is ordained. We learn the beginning of self-denial by denying ourselves for the sake of our family, by active sympathy with suffering, and forebearance for all."[19]

His wife, recognizing the necessity and importance of her husband's mission, gave Him her love and told Him to go and help the world as it was aflame with the fires of ego and hatred.

The term "family" is not limited to worldly families, but also extends to spiritual "families," made up of individuals who are not related to each other through blood, but through their common love of and aspiration for the Lord. Living in cooperative situations, these spiritual aspirants learn the same lessons of love and compassion, sacrifice and self-denial for the sake of their spiritual "family," as do the members of a worldly family.

When asked why people leave their homes in search of God, Guru Nanak answered:

"There are true seekers and selfish escapists, but my way lies in living in the world and rising step by step steadily and surely, by purification of the mind by daily conflict with the force that darkens the light of the soul. This is only possible if we do our day-to-day duties with the Name of God on our lips, so that all our actions are performed in the service of Him who is the Lord of all that exists...Remember, renunciation of outward things does not make for inner righteousness. Words are meaningless till translated into action."[20]

And again, the Lord as Guru Nanak stated:

"It is not necessary to dress as a beggar or to leave home. The one thing necessary is to remove the impurities of the mind, and fill the heart with longing to receive His Grace. Just as the true desire of a woman, her faith and devotion, draws the beloved to her, so does a devotee draw the Lord by his true-hearted consecration to His service...

"He who is sinless, even though leading the life of a householder, whose spirit is awake, the thirst of whose mind is quenched with the nectar of the Name, the Guru shows him how to serve the True One and realize Him..."[21] — which brings us to the last Path to the Lord: the Path of Action or Works; the Path of Karma.

Chapter 7

THE PATH OF WORKS OR KARMA

This path has been described as the Path of Will or Action, where one dedicates all one's works and actions to the Lord. It is a natural outgrowth of the path of love. For when one loves God with all one's heart, then one is willing to surrender all one has to Him. Surrendering to the will of the Lord is the greatest display of faith and trust in Him, and love for Him, that we can make. Only after we have surrendered ourselves in Love to Him, is it possible for us to become perfect instruments of His Will.

When we dedicate all our actions and works to Him we gradually become aware of His Presence within us, His Voice and Lead of Light, helping us to merge our will into His Will, helping us efface our ego and all egoistic reasons for our actions, the impetus for our works becoming a desire to serve Him and His Creation, rather than self-gratification of our own petty desires, or a search for the world's vain glories. Thus, in doing our best and dedicating all our actions to Him, we come closer to God and inevitably do a better job.

Lord Krishna explains it thus:

"Whatever you offer me in simple love—a leaf, fruit, flower or even a drop of water—I accept in love as your heart's dedication. Whatever you do enjoy or sacrifice, whatever you give away in charity, whatever askesis you undertake—all offer to me in complete surrender. For only then shall you shake off the bondage of works with their good or evil consequences and through renunciation of all attachment, achieving liberation, shall commune with me and, finally repose in me."[1]

Again, the Lord states:

"The devotee who lives and works for me, forever emancipated from all attachments, and who bears ill-will to none—attains me...

"I promptly save from the death-bound ocean of life those who dedicate all their works to me and with an unfaltering ardour meditate and worship me with their hearts affianced to me.

"Center your mind on me alone and let your intellect abide

in me—thereafter you shall ever in my Self dwell, rest assured. But if, my friend, you fail to rivet your thoughts on me, then seek to win me by the practice of concentration and mental discipline. If, however, you cannot discipline your mind, then do your works all for my sake (whose one and only aim is service to me) for, doing all your works for me alone, you shall attain the ultimate self-fulfillment. If you fail to achieve even this, then havened in me, and renouncing the fruits of all your actions, practice the Yoga, master of your self."[2]

What does the Lord mean when He says to renounce all attachments and the fruits of all our actions? Does He mean that we must give up all that we have: our wealth, our homes, our families, our jobs, etc., and live as hermits in the woods? Of course not; as already explained, this is not necessary for most, although it is the right path for some. We must remember His words—**follow your own nature.** For some, this does mean giving up "worldly life," i.e., family, business, wealth, etc., and living in a monastery or seeking a life of solitude in the woods. But this way of life does not appeal to the majority of people, nor was it meant for all.

The Question of Wealth

The life of Lord Buddha illustrates this point beautifully. Lord Buddha had been born a royal prince. He had wealth and luxury beyond belief, including at least seven palaces. It was His nature to leave this wealth and worldly life and seek spiritual enlightenment in the woods. He first went the route of a poor ascetic, but recognizing that this was as much an extreme and perversion of the Natural Law as is hoarding wealth, He turned instead to the Middle Path, the Path of Moderation.

After attaining enlightenment, the Buddha was approached by a wealthy man who wished to be His disciple. The following discourse took place:

The wealthy man said: "My life is full of work, and having acquired great wealth, I am surrounded with cares. Yet I enjoy my work, and apply myself to it with all diligence. Many people are in my employ and depend upon the success of my enterprises.

"Now, I have heard thy disciples praise the bliss of the

129

hermit and denounce the unrest of the world. 'The Holy One,' they say, 'has given up his kingdom and his inheritance, and has found the path of righteousness, thus setting an example to all of the world how to attain Nirvana.'

"My heart yearns to do what is right and to be a blessing unto my fellows. Let me then ask thee, Must I give up my wealth, my home, and my business enterprises, and, like thyself, go into homelessness in order to attain the bliss of a religious life?"

And the Buddha replied: "The bliss of a religious life is attainable to everyone who walks in the noble eightfold path. He that cleaves to wealth had better cast it away than allow his heart to be poisoned by it; but he who does not cleave to wealth, and possessing riches, uses them rightly, will be a blessing unto his fellows.

"**It is not life and wealth and power that enslave men, but the cleaving to life and wealth and power.**

"The bhikku (disciple) who retires from the world in order to lead a life of leisure will have no gain, for a life of indolence is an abomination, and lack of energy is to be despised.

"The Dharma of the Tathagata (Teaching or Path of the Buddha) does not require a man to go into homelessness or to resign the world, **unless he feels called upon to do so;** but (it does) require every man to free himself from the illusion of self, to cleanse his heart, to give up his thirst for pleasure and lead a life of righteousness.

"And whatever men do, whether they remain in the world as artisans, merchants, and officers of the king, or retire from the world and devote themselves to a life of religious meditation, let them put their whole heart into their task; let them be diligent and energetic, and, if they are like the lotus, which, although it grows in the water, yet remains untouched by the water, if they struggle in life without cherishing envy or hatred, if they live in the world not a life of self (ego) but a life of truth, then surely joy, peace, and bliss will dwell in their minds."[3]

Whereupon the wealthy man donated a garden in which a temple would be erected for the use of the Buddha and His disciples or brotherhood. Seeing that the gift was made purely from a sense of unselfish charity and **NOT** in order to receive fame or praise, the Buddha accepted the offer with these words:

> "The charitable man is loved by all; his friendship is prized highly; in death his heart is at rest and full of joy, for he suffers not from repentance; he receives the opening flower of his reward and the fruit that ripens from it.
>
> "Hard it is to understand: By giving away our food, we get more strength, by bestowing clothing on others, we gain more beauty; by donating abodes of purity and truth, we acquire great treasures...
>
> "Loving and compassionate he gives with reverence and banishes all hatred, envy and anger. The charitable man has found the path of salvation. He is like the man who plants a sapling, securing thereby the shade, the flowers, and the fruit in future years. Even so is the result of charity; even so is the joy of him who helps those that are in need of assistance; even so is the great Nirvana (Bliss of the Lord).
>
> "We reach the immortal path only by continuous acts of kindliness and we perfect our soul by compassion and charity."[4]

Or, as Lord Jesus said, "Purity is best demonstrated by generosity."[5]

So, then, it is not wealth, but the cleaving or attachment to it, choosing it over God, that is wrong. Baha'u'llah reiterates this truth, i.e., that it is all right for one to enjoy earthly things so long as nothing comes between you and God:

> "Should a man wish to adorn himself with the ornaments of the earth, to wear its apparels, or partake of the benefits it can bestow, no harm can befall him, **if he alloweth nothing whatever to intervene between him and God,** for God hath ordained every good thing, whether created in the heavens or in the earth, for such of His servants as truly believe in Him. Eat ye, O people, of the good things which God hath allowed you, and deprive not yourselves from His wondrous bounties. Render thanks and praise unto Him, and be of them that are truly thankful."[6]

Why, then, did Jesus say that: "It is easier for a camel to go through the eye of a needle than for a rich man to enter the kingdom of God"?[7] He said this because wealth can be a burden that can hinder us from thinking about God. If one cleaves to it and does not share it with those in need; if all of one's time is spent thinking about it, how to safe guard it, etc., then it truly **is** a burden, just as not having enough money can be an equally oppressive burden. For then all our time is taken up thinking of ways to **get** it, how to survive, etc., etc.

Sai Baba, a great yogi living today, once compared money to a pair of shoes. He explained that too little of it is like a pair of shoes that are too small—they pinch the feet and cause discomfort, while too much of it is like a pair of shoes that are too large—they become a burden and an obstacle to walking![8]

Again emphasizing the Middle Path, Lord Buddha said:

> "Avoid these two extremes...Which two? On the one hand, low, vulgar, ignoble, and useless indulgence in passion and luxury; and on the other, painful, ignoble and useless practice of self-torture and mortification. Take the Middle Path advised by the Buddha, for it leads to insight and peace, wisdom and enlightenment, and to Nirvana (Mystical Union with the Lord.)"[9]

It should be pointed out that Jesus, too, had wealthy disciples. Who can forget that it was a wealthy merchant—Joseph of Arimathea—who asked Pilate for Jesus' body, and then, tenderly and gently wrapped it in the shroud and laid it in his own tomb! And don't forget Barnabas, St. Paul's faithful companion in his early travels around the Mediterranean. It was the personal fortune of Barnabas that helped to keep Simon Peter and the early Christian Church fed and alive!

Then what did Jesus mean when He said: "And everyone who has left houses or brothers or sisters or father or mother or spouses or children or lands for my name's sake and for the sake of my gospel, will receive a hundred-fold, in this time and in the age to come eternal life"?[10] He meant that we must give up the **attachment** to these things and not allow them to become obstacles on the Path to Truth. For it is the attachment, the cleaving to objects that is the real hindrance or fetter in our spiritual growth.

Giving up Attachments

Before He left for spiritual life, the Buddha was married and had a son. He named His son "Rahula," which in Sanskrit means "obstacle." It was necessary for the Buddha to leave His wife and child in order to attain enlightenment and fulfill His destiny, just as it was necessary for Jesus to leave His family, Mary and Joseph, when He was still a boy in order to seek out the Truth and fulfill His mission as the Messiah. And yet, in both cases, the sacrifices made were returned a hundred-fold in later life. In the case of the Buddha, His son grew up and became one of His closest disciples, and His wife, as well as His mother and father, became His first "lay" disciples. In the case of Jesus, His mother Mary was His constant support, companion, and disciple after He returned to the land of Palestine.

Another illustration of "giving up" and receiving manifold more can be seen in the lives of two of India's present-day yogis: Sri Dilip Kumar Roy and Smt. Indira Devi. Dadaji came from a very wealthy family, as did his daughter-disciple Smt. Indira Devi. Both of them gave up their wealth and families in order to enter monastic life. In the case of Indira Devi, that meant not only parents and brothers and a sister, but also a husband and two sons. The pull of spiritual life was too strong to deny; it was in their natures to follow the call of the Lord away from "worldly life" into spiritual life.

But though both gave up all they had—giving vast sums of money, etc., to the poor and needy—they themselves were never in want for anything. On the contrary, they lived in comfort their entire lives, (and Ma still does, though Dadaji has passed on to the Lord's abode), and in the case of Indira Devi, received manifold "children" in the form of disciples and devotees, including her sister's family, her own two sons and even her husband, all of whom became disciples of Dadaji.

In essence, what Dadaji and Ma did was to follow exactly what Jesus Christ admonished His own disciples to do:

> "If you would be perfect, go, sell what you possess and give to the poor, and you will have treasure in heaven: and come, follow me...
>
> "Therefore I tell you, do not be anxious about your life, what you shall eat, nor about your body, what you shall put on. For life is more than food, and the body more than clothing. Consider the ravens: they neither sow nor reap, they have neither storehouse nor barn, and yet God feeds them...
>
> "And which of you by being anxious can add a cubit to his

span of life? If then you are not able to do as small a thing as that, why are you anxious about the rest? Consider the lilies (of the field), how they grow; they neither toil nor spin; yet I tell you, even Solomon in all his glory was not arrayed like one of these. But If God so clothes the grass which is alive in the field today and tomorrow is thrown into the oven, how much more will He clothe you, O ye of little faith! And do not seek what you are to eat and what you are to drink, nor be of anxious mind. For all the nations of the world seek these things; and your Father knows that you need them. **Instead, seek His Kingdom, and these things shall be yours as well.**

"Fear not, little flock, for it is your Father's good pleasure to give you the kingdom. Sell your possessions, and give alms; provide yourself with purses that do not grow old, with a treasure in the heavens that does not fail, where no thief approaches and no moth destroys. **For where your treasure is, there will your heart be also.**"[11]

So what we need to do is give up this idea that we lose anything when we go to the Lord or become His devotees. On the contrary, we gain everything when we go to Him and do all our works for Him because He is everything! Not only that; when we go to the Lord, He guarantees that all of our needs in all areas will be taken care of, as Jesus said. Further, He promises to safeguard those things which we have already acquired—both in a spiritual and physical sense. Lord Krishna gives us His pledge as follows: "To those who worship me (God), meditating on my utter Self, and who are in constant touch with me—I grant the boons they have not won and security in all that they have garnered."[12]

What we need to give up is our **attachment** to things, our ego and the sense of "I" and "mine," and instead recognize that everything is, in the final analysis, the Lord's anyway. Everything we have, everything we "own," even our bodies are not really our own possessions, as those who have had death experiences have attested—they are all "on loan," as it were, from the Lord, and it is therefore His right to recall these things at any time. What we must do, especially if we have been blessed with wealth, property, etc., is to act as stewards of the Lord's gifts, protecting them, using them, and distributing them in the proper spiritual ways. As St. Paul wrote:

"The Scriptures say: 'The godly man gives generously to

134

the poor. His good deeds will be an honor to him forever.'

"For God, who gives seed to the farmer to plant, and...crops to harvest and eat, will give you more and more seed to plant and will make it grow so that you can give away more...fruit from your harvest.

"Yes, God will give you much so that you can give away much,...So, two good things happen as a result of your gifts—those in need are helped, and they overflow with thanks to God."[13]

As Baha'u'llah explains it: "They who are possessed of riches, however, must have the utmost regard for the poor, for great is the honor destined by God for those poor who are steadfast in patience."[14]

In other words, we must be acutely aware of the needs of the poor and help them whenever we can. For the poor who cling to their faith in God find special favor in God's eyes as they love Him **not** because of what He has given them, but for the sake of Love alone. Thus, those who have been blessed with riches, etc., and perform Good Works by helping others, especially the poor and downtrodden, also gain special favor in God's eyes. For as Lord Jesus said:

"Come, blessed of my Father, into the kingdom prepared for you from the foundation of the world. For I was hungry and you fed me...thirsty and you gave me water...a stranger and you invited me into your homes; naked and you clothed me; sick and in prison, and you visited me..."[15]

And the righteous will ask when did they do this for Him? The Lord answers, **"When you did it to the least of my brothers you were doing it to me!"**[16] For God is in everyone, and by serving others, we are serving Him. And to those who would not do the above, i.e., help those in need, regardless of race, sex, creed, nationality, color, etc., the Lord declared that they be sent away from His presence, "but the righteous into everlasting life!"[17]

Guru Nanak reiterated this Truth of the Way of Works by saying:

"He who earns and gives away knows something of the Way (in Chinese, the **Tao**). He who does not appropriate everything to himself, but gives and induces others to give in

135

the Name of God is blessed. He who shares his bread with others knows the law of living...Righteous aspirations gradually gather the treasures of Truth."[18]

These treasures of Truth include the knowledge that we are all a part of Him, the One God, but that He has given us all different talents and abilities with which to serve Him and His Creation. Thus we are all united by the Spirit of the One God which pervades and envelopes us all, and yet we are all unique individuals with different attributes and propensities. As Sri Aurobindo explains: "The law of the Supermind (the Universal Consciousness) is unity fulfilled in diversity; **unity does not imply uniformity.**"[19] Thus when we follow our own nature, dedicating all we are and have to Him, we become a part of a great Cosmic Orchestra whose diverse instruments Unite to create a beautiful Universal Harmony.

Right Profession

However, it is essential and vital that one understand that following one's nature does not mean doing the wrong things, but the right things. Thus, the scientists of Nazi Germany who were following their nature in being scientists incurred horrendous sin because their science was used for cruel, inhuman, and unspiritual things—like experimenting with and torturing prisoners in concentration camps—as do scientists today who use animals for experiments in cruel and inhumane ways. This is why those who have had death experiences stated that all knowledge must be used in a morally correct way, with an eye to the consequences of our actions on others and on the Lord's Creation as a whole.

To better understand this point, one needs to learn what the Lord as the Buddha taught. The following is what the Buddha called the Eight-fold Path:

> "Right views, right intentions, right speech, right action, right profession, right effort, right watchfulness, and right concentration. This is the Middle Path, which leads to insight, peace, wisdom, enlightenment, and Nirvana (Bliss, the Rapture of the Lord)."[20]

Those who have had death experiences have stated that their experiences caused them to re-evalute their lives in many different aspects, including the type of work they were doing. Many stated a desire to do more "meaningful" work, such as helping people cope with life physically, mentally, and/or emotionally. Others came to the realization that their present jobs were actually detrimental to others and/or the environment or God's Creation, and were, therefore, actually working **against** God's Goals of Peace, Unity and Purity. As a consequence, these individuals felt compelled to change their jobs for the better. Thus, they followed their **true nature** and began to use their God-given talents for good and spiritual purposes, as should we all.

So rejoice in **your** talents and thank God for them. Do not try to be something for which you were never destined. Seek, instead, to enhance and expand upon those gifts God has given you, whether they lie in music and the arts, agriculture or carpentry, science or math, family life or business, politics or religion. Seek to do God's Will through your works; seek to play your role as best as you can, not seeking the role of another. For if you abandon your job and do that of another, your own job for which you have been created will stand undone.

Chapter 8

KARMA

Earlier in the book, it was mentioned that there were two reasons that one incurred sin when one went against one's true nature. It was also stated that there were two reasons for one's placement into a particular caste, class or circumstance. The first reason for both of the above has been explored, i.e., that each individual has been born on Earth to perform a certain function in God's Great Master Plan. Further, He has provided everyone with certain talents and abilities which are to be used to fulfill one's ordained mission here on Earth.

The second reason one incurs sin when one goes against one's nature is also the second criterion the Lord mentioned regarding one's placement into a particular class, caste, or circumstance. It is also the second reason one should dedicate one's works to the Lord, the first one being because we love Him, and that second reason is one's Karma.

The word "Karma" has been used often in this book, but what exactly do we mean by that term? Further, what exactly is the Law of Karma and how does it work? The Lord as Jesus Christ defined it the best when He said: **"As you sow, so shall you reap."**

That very definition was also given by the Lord as the Buddha, Sri Krishna, Guru Nanak, and just about every other Messenger from God. If we do good deeds, then good will come back to us, and likewise for evil deeds. One's Karma can be compared to throwing a boomerang. No matter how far one may throw it, in the end it will come right back to us.

In schools in the United States, children are taught the Golden Rule, which, by the way, was taught by the Buddha over 2000 years before there was a United States! It says: "Do unto others as you would have others do unto you." Science has recognized this truth, too. It is called Newton's Law of Physics, which says: "For every action there is an equal and opposite reaction." When Newton's Law is coupled with the Golden Rule, we see the logic behind doing good and heeding the Law of Karma: "Do unto others as you would have them do unto you **because** for every action there is an equal and opposite reaction."

In other words, what we think, do or say will come back to either haunt or help us. So it behooves us not to forget this vital part of

God's Law of Balance, lest we get hit on the head by our own boomeranging actions, having forgotten their consequences!

Thus, when we experience pain or sorrow, it is due to something that we ourselves have done in the past or present and is, therefore, our **own** fault, **not God's!** People often ask why God has caused this or that calamity to visit them, or why God has allowed something horrible to happen to them. But it is not God who has caused the calamity; it is our own Godless actions that have caused it. So let's stop blaming and cursing God for our troubles because He is not the source of them; our own wrong actions are the source!

Refusing to recognize this Truth, i.e., the Law of Karma, and blaming God for problems that we ourselves have created is like one who, refusing to recognize the Law of Gravity, spits upward toward Heaven and then blames God for letting the spittle come back down on his face! The Buddha has explained the Law of Karma beautifully in the following:

> "Like dust flung at the wind which the wind flings back, evil recoils on the fool who harms the innocent...Diamond breaks diamond, evil crushes the evildoer...the foolish man sows his own (seeds of) destruction by mocking the wise, the noble, and the virtuous."[1]

The karmic effects of our good deeds and right actions, too, come back to us. So the more right things we do, the more love we give, the more love and good things we will receive. As Jesus Christ said, "Give and it shall be given to you...For the measure you give is the measure you will get back!"[2]

But who takes account of all of our actions, right and wrong? They are recorded by God and kept in the Akashic Records, what Christians call the Book of Life and the Hebrews call the Book of God's Remembrance, mentioned earlier. Edgar Cayce, the great American prophet who had the ability to tap into these records at will, likened them to an etheric television screen, (pointing out that T.V. and radio waves have always existed; man only **discovered** them—he did not create them), and saying that these records have existed since the beginning of Creation. In explaining the Law of Karma, Cayce said: "...it is true that man brings order out of chaos by his compliance with Divine Law. Or by his disregard of the laws of Divine influence, man brings chaos and destructive forces into his experience."[3]

Thus, our willingness to respect or disregard God's Divine Laws of Love and Balance determines our fate. Our actions, then, right and wrong, are recorded on this etheric "film" for us to see when our physical bodies die, as has been verified by those who have had death experiences. Just about all of these people have stated that after leaving their bodies and meeting the Being of Light, they were shown a three-dimensional review, like a cinema show but more real, of everything they had thought, said or did in their lives up to the point of their physical death. They mentioned that they were also able to **feel** the same emotions that they had felt when the events had occurred in the past. This is why many of them expressed a desire to come back to physical life on Earth as they felt that they had not given enough **love** to others while living.

Dr. Elisabeth Kubler-Ross, who has worked with terminally ill patients for over twenty years, has said that life after life is not a theory; it is a fact:

> "Death is graduation from the school of life...At the moment of death there is never any fear, pain, panic or anxiety. You never die alone. Those loved ones that have died before you will be there. Your guardian angel, who is with you from the moment you are born to guide you, direct you, impinge on you and protect you, is there. You are surrounded with total, total unconditional love at the moment of death.
>
> "When we leave our physical body we are like a butterfly coming out of a cocoon. We are fully aware of the moment of shedding our physical body and at that moment we are very, very viable."[4]

According to Kubler-Ross, our being or soul finds itself in a new "body" that is perfect, without the handicaps, limitations or imperfections of the physical body. Then, our soul or being approaches the Being of Light or God. Kubler-Ross continues:

> "Once you have been in the closeness of the Light your only desire is to stay near and not be sent back to physical life and you can never, never be afraid of death again...in the presence of that Light you are asked to review and evaluate your entire existence. Every thought, every deed, every word you have spoken will be evaluated and you will simultaneously

140

know the consequences of your life and whether you have learned your lessons or not."[5]

She goes on to explain that the reason most people fear dying is that they feel that they have missed a great opportunity and/or misused or abused the gift of life. And for those who have missed the Goal of Life—God-Realization—and/or who have not learned the lessons of living and loving, they are right; they have missed an incredible opportunity: the opportunity of spiritual liberation and God-Realization that each individual is given when he or she incarnates into a physical body. But God is All-Merciful and because of this, He gives us another opportunity to learn our lessons and reach the Goal every time we are reborn, which brings up the question of reincarnation.

Karma and Reincarnation

Dr. Kubler-Ross has stated that every human being is given the opportunity and potential of attaining the Goal of Life in a single lifetime:

> "All of us can do this, but very, very few do. Your potential (for reaching the Goal) is predetermined (by God), but your choices determine your life. The result of your life is literally nothing else but the consequences of the result of your choices. Whether you take a lower choice or a higher choice...
>
> "The transition we call death is only complete when you shed the psychic body (the body we receive after we drop our physical one) and become that energy form that is immortal and which is really you."[6]

In other words, it is only when we merge our individual being or soul into God, the All-Soul, and realize Him that our soul's journey is complete and the Goal finally won. Until then, we must reincarnate again and again until all of life's lessons have been learned and our souls have finally been purified of all sin. As Kubler-Ross explains, "Until you learn all your lessons you return again and again to physical being."[7]

The environment and circumstances of your present life were predetermined by the lessons one needed to learn due to one's karma or actions of the past. For example, if one needed to learn humility, one may be born a beggar in Calcutta. But the real you, your soul, that part of you which God first created, is always the same. As Kubler-Ross explains, "You are always you. Your body is a temporary temple for your soul and it is this soul which re-enters another body."[8]

Dr. Kubler-Ross' findings have been verified again and again by other medical and/or scientific professionals, such as Dr. Raymond Moody, author of *Life After Life* and *Reflections on Life After Life*. Other professionals believe that past-life experiences may well account for present-day problems, including the problem of autism, where an individual does not respond to the outside world, the belief being that some traumatic event of the past has caused the present inability to communicate with the outside world. Psychologist Edith Fiore has used hypnosis to regress her patients to past lives in order to discover the reasons behind a particular problem, phobia or allergy. She says that she now believes in reincarnation because of her work and gives some examples:

> "I believe the material stemming from regression (hypnosis) is valid because of the inevitable link with a present life problem. A realtor suffering from insomnia recalls a previous life as a gun slinger always afraid of surprise attack. An obese man becomes so because he once starved to death on a becalmed sailing vessel. An executive's career and family life are stunted by a fear of heights stemming from a previous existence as a repairman who fell from a Gothic cathedral."[9]

Ms. Fiore says that her belief in reincarnation represents a 180° shift in her previous attitude toward it, having been raised a strict traditional Protestant and becoming an agnostic in college. She says that the vivid physical and physiological changes that have occurred in her patients when they have been relaying their past-life experiences have convinced her that they were not acting or making it up:

> "A patient may be sitting back completely comfortable and relaxed describing a scene from the past and then suddenly she'll cry out in fear. The color will drain from her face and her whole body will be convulsed with terror. Obviously this isn't acting. How could I doubt that kind of evidence?"[10]

Another example of the success of this type of therapy includes the case of a white woman who was regressed to a past life as a black woman in the South after Reconstruction. This black woman hated her life as a sharecropper so much that it carried over to her present life and manifested itself as a severe allergy to any fresh vegetable. After the past-life regression session, the white woman's allergies completely disappeared!

Other professionals have become convinced or at least intrigued by the possibility of reincarnation because of numerous accounts of individuals consciously remembering their past lives. Dr. Ian Stevenson, a University of Virginia parapsychologist, has investigated over 1600 cases of apparent reincarnation firsthand. Examples include:

1) a Brazilian woman who predicted she would be reborn as her best friend's daughter—a daughter who was born 10 months after the woman's death and who, at the age of 2½, began to describe her previous life, making 120 statements about her previous existence which were verified;

2) an Alaskan Indian who predicted he would be reborn as his niece's son, and that the new son would bear birth marks in the exact places where he had scars—a son who was born 18 months after the old man's death, bearing the scars of the woman's late uncle, who, at 13 months, declared that his name was that of the late uncle, and who, at the ages of 2 and 3, recognized the late uncle's stepdaughter, son and widow;

3) twin boys in India who, at the age of 3, recalled their previous lives as twins in another Indian village who had been murdered and even named a suspect in the murder case and who, upon being taken to the other village, were able to recognize and correctly identify friends and relatives of the murdered twins; and

4) a 2-year-old boy in Sri Lanka (Ceylon) who recalled his past life as his father's brother, including the fact that he had been hanged for having murdered his own wife with a Malay knife—details that the father had told no one, even the boy's mother.[11]

All of this scientific/medical research into death, dying and reincarnation has reconfirmed what Eastern religions have taught for ages: i.e., that the Goal of Life is God-Realization, and that until we merge our being into the Eternal Being, we must reincarnate again and again on different levels and in different circumstances according to our past actions, or Karma. As Lord Krishna explains it so beautifully in the *Bhagavad Gita:*

"Never was there a time when you or I...were non-existent. Nor shall ever come a time when any of us will cease to exist. As the soul fares ever on through childhood, youth and old age, when a person breathes his last, It journeys on to assume another body: so no true sage is ever deceived by death...

"Only the material forms, assumed by the Soul, which is fathomless and eternal, comes to an end...Neither he who thinks he can kill the Soul, nor he who thinks It is killed knows the truth: for It can neither kill nor ever be killed...Unborn, immutable, eternal, ageless, the Soul is not slain when the body's slain...

"Even as a man discards his worn-out robe for a new one, so a worn-out body is left by the Soul for a new one after death...One is unmanifest at the beginning, manifest in the middle and becomes unmanifest in the end once more. So what is there so tragic about this law of life?"[12]

Reiterating Lord Jesus' words that in His Father's house are many mansions, Lord Krishna goes on to explain that after physical death, our soul goes on to other realms of existence depending on the state of one's mind at the moment of death: "When a man in his last hour, his body leaves, **whatever state of being he meditates on, in full absorption that state he'll attain.**"[13]

This is why those who have been hateful and egoed-out in one way or another have often gone to frightful states of existence! Thus, it is so important for us to think of Him all the time, but especially at the moment of death. As Lord Krishna explains: "Those who worship the gods wend to the gods, who worship the ancestors repair to them, who worship the elemental spirits go to their abode and my own priests come to me."[14]

The above quote explains why most people see their loved ones when they die; the reason is that they feel closest and the most love for them, and, therefore, they are greeted by them "on the other side." However, for those who have gone beyond worldly attachments to family members, etc., and have seen beyond the dualities of the world, having recognized that He is the source of all love, including the love they receive from friends and family, and recognizing this, have decided to try for the Whole instead of just a few parts of the Whole, another possibility and destination arises for them at the moment of death: they come Home to Him and Merge into Him. They have transcended the world and what are called the modes or methods of action of Nature, through attachment to which our ego binds our soul to the earth and bodily existence. Lord Krishna explains:

"When one transcends the modes he passes on beyond the ambit of mortal destiny of birth and death, old age and pain, and wins the eternal bliss of immortality...

"Who worships me (the Lord) with an unfaltering love transcends the modes forever and becomes eligible for union with God. For I am the Divine Ground, the foundation of eternal dharma (righteousness) and immortal life and bliss...

"So at all times remember me...(Do your duty urged by your innate nature.) When your mind and intellect are poised in me, to me alone you shall come, rest assured...In his last hour, when the aspirant leaves for the great Beyond, he must think only of Him who is subtler than the subtle and whose color is resplendent like the sun. The devotee who does this, concentrating steadfastly all his life-force midway between the eyebrows with all the resolution and strength of Yoga, shall attain the Goal of the Supreme Divine...

"Who are one-pointed and in their hearts remember me constantly, attain me easily, and those great souls who have realized me once and so won the highest status are never reborn in this ephemeral world, the house of sorrow. From the high world of God all creatures are reborn again and again. But those who have attained me reach the point of no return...

"Those who have no faith in this gospel of mine shall not attain me and must time and time again tread the track of this death-bound universe."[15]

What about those of us who, though we love God and have tried to do good in our lives, slip up? What happens then? Lord Krishna's closest disciple, Arjuna, asked this same question of the Lord, and the Lord's answer to that question has been like a great beacon of hope to all spiritual aspirants, a light that has illuminated the darkness caused by the ego in the form of doubt and fear:

145

Arjuna: "He who cannot control himself and though he has faith slips up inadvertently, failing to win his goal, how does he fare (straying from his path thus, on a sudden impulse?) And if and when he strays from the Godward path, shall he miss both this life and the life eternal as a stray and way-lost cloud dissolves on high? Thou must dispel once and for all my doubt which none else, Lord, is competent to achieve."

Lord Krishna: "My friend, **here or hereafter none who is a true aspirant ever can come to grief.** Having dwelt in the world of the virtuous for many, many years, he's born once more in the house of the affluent and pure of heart. Or else he's born in an authentic yogi's family—but very rare is such a birth.

"There he recaptures the predilection of his past birth (namely, the hunger for the life spiritual) and thereafter, once again, he aspires for the deliverance of his soul, feeling impelled by the urge of his former birth as though irresistibly...the yogi who strives assiduously and is purged after many lives of his sins, attains at long last to the highest goal of life..."[16]—which is God-Realization or Union with the Lord.

And, again, the Lord in the *Shrimad Bhagavatam* states: "If a beloved devotee who has forsaken all other attachments and sought shelter in the soles of the feet of the Lord incurs any sin for any reason...the Supreme Lord...enshrined in his heart, washes off all that sin."[17]

The Lord then describes the different natures of the two types of human beings that are born on the earth: those of Divine nature and those of demonic nature. He also foretells the fate of demonic individuals, having already told the fate of the virtuous. Further, He enjoins us to be guided by the truths found in unadulterated scriptures whenever we are in doubt as to what is right or wrong, and to follow their lead when we act:

"A man born with the divine nature is fearless, simple and pure, a votary of the Yoga of knowledge, generous, master of self (the ego), a student of the scriptures. He practices hard

146

askesis* and offers sacrifices. He is ingenuous, truthful, free from anger, tranquil in mind, serene, unmarred by malice, gentle, forgiving, peaceful, strong, not fractious, greedy, haughty or hypersensitive.

"A man born with demonic nature is conceited, arrogant, choleric and harsh. The divine endowments lead to liberation and demonic proclivities will lead to bondage..."

"Those who are born with a demonic nature...know not truth, purity or right conduct. They proclaim that this is a dark godless world of falsehood, based on no moral law, where all the creatures are conceived in lust or born in copulation. With this outlook these perverts do wrong actions, lost souls of little understanding, they come as enemies of the world to destroy all.

"With insatiable pride and full of deceit, arrogant, drunk with pride and self-importance; they run blindly after what is despicable and all the ends they foster are unclean. Plagued by numberless cares which cannot come to an end except at death, they hold that life's summum bonum is sensual enjoyment...Helpless puppets of anger and lust...striv(ing) by dishonest means to go on hoarding wealth...

"In the cycles of life and death these evil-doers and malignant creatures I (the Lord) cast time again back into the wombs of degraded beings; so these lost souls, reborn to demon darkness, birth after birth come not back home to me, but roll down into hell inexorably."[18] *(Bhagavad Gita)*

The Lord states that there are three gates to perdition or hell— the death of the soul: the gates of lust, of wrath and of greed, and warns us to beware of these. When one successfully by-passes these three, then one enters the Righteous Path which will lead to the liberation of one's soul from bondage.

But what if one, who, having led a rather unspiritual life, realizes his or her mistake and, truly repentant, turns to God. Will the Lord still show His Mercy or is one condemned for all time? Lord Krishna's answer to this question sprouts seeds of hope of

* "Worship of God and gurus, sages, (true) priests (Brahmins), ingeniousness, nonviolence, cleanliness and sexual purity—all this is known as the askesis of the body. The utterance of words which give no offense, words which are good, to speak the truth that heals but does not hurt and regular study of the sacred books—all this is known as the askesis of the speech. The practice of serene simplicity, gentleness, silence, purity of thought and self-control—is the askesis of the mind."[19]

deliverance in the hearts of all, even the most wicked among us:

> **"Even if a sinner of sinners turns to me (the Lord) he should be accounted righteous—because he has entered on the Homeward Path.** Aye, he shall swiftly be transformed into a saint and achieve eternal peace. **I pledge my word: my devotee shall never come to grief.**
>
> "Born to a dismal and unstable world you turn to me; focus your mind on me; become my loyal devotee and priest, bow down and dedicate your utter self to me alone and you'll come home to me."[20]

Could we have a more heartening reassurance of the Lord's Mercy and Forgiveness? And, again, Ezekiel of the Old Testament reiterates God's Pledge of Mercy and Forgiveness for all who truly turn to Him, regardless of their past sins. The prophet Ezekiel quotes the Lord as saying:

> "And you, son of man, say to the House of Israel, Thus have you said: 'Our transgressions and our sins are upon us, and we waste away because of them; how then can we live?' Say to them, As I live, says the Lord God, I have no pleasure in the death of the wicked, but that the wicked turn from his way and live; **turn back, turn back from your evil ways; for why will you die, O House of Israel?** (Remember, whenever the Bible speaks of the House of Israel, it is referring to the peoples of Great Britain, Western Europe and the United States of America, as explained before in the opening chapters of this book! For Ezekiel lived almost 150 to 200 years after the fall of the House of Israel to Assyria and the scattering of its tribes to the West; yet the Lord admonished him to be the watchtower for this House, knowing that his warnings would be read and understood in the distant future!)
>
> "...Again, though I say to the wicked, 'You shall surely die,' yet **if he turns from his sin and does what is lawful and right, if the wicked restores the pledge, gives back what he has taken by robbery,** and walks in the statutes of life, committing no iniquity; he shall surely live, he shall not die. **None of the sins that he has committed shall be remembered against him;** he has done what is lawful and right, he

shall surely live.

"Yet your people say, 'The way of the Lord is not just'; when it is their own way that is not just. **When the righteous turns from his righteousness, and commits iniquity, he shall die for it. And when the wicked turns from his wickedness, and does what is lawful and right, he shall live by it.** Yet you say, 'The way of the Lord is not just.' O House of Israel, **I will judge each of you according to his ways.**"[21]

As further confirmation of the above, the *Shrimad Bhagavatam* restates the Lord's pledge that **whosoever turneth to Him shall be accounted righteous and will have all his evil deeds of the past forgiven, no matter how horrendous they may have been. This is the Golden Lining of this age**—the Kali Age, the Age of Chaos: through sheer devotion to Him, the Lord, all one's past deeds are forgiven, all the seeds of one's karma are burned up in the fire of devotion to the Supreme:

> "Those men who constantly perpetrate sinful deeds, who are ever addicted to immoral practices, who take to evil ways, who are consumed by the fire of anger, and who are wicked and full of passion are purified in Kaliyuga (simply by turning to Him and devoting oneself to Him)...Even those who are devoid of truthfulness, who revile their parents, who are restless due to thirst for pleasures, who do not follow the duties (prescibed by the Lord)...who are hypocrites, who are jealous of the achievements of others, who take delight in destruction of life become holy...in Kaliyuga (by turning to Him). Those who commit the five great sins (which are listed as **drinking alcohol**—reiterating the American Indians' adamant stand against consumption of alcohol, killing a Brahmin or holy person, stealing gold or property, having intercourse with the spouse of one's preceptor or teacher, and treachery), who are ever engaged in practicing deception and chicanery, who are cruel and merciless like demons, who have grown fat with the money of Brahmins (holy people), who commit adultery, are all purified in Kaliyuga (by turning to the Lord and becoming His devotee)...
>
> "The fools who are ever obstinately engaged in committing sins by thought, word and deed, who are parasites, whose mind is impure and whose heart is wicked, they all attain purity (by turning to Him)..."[22]

The Lord is always as good as His word. Take Mary Magdalene as an example. She had been a prostitute, revelling in the flesh and consorting with the lowest of the low, and yet, her true-hearted repentance was received with joy by Lord Jesus. Not only did He forgive her, He showed Himself to her first upon His Resurrection, and she went on to become a great spiritual light to other followers of Christ.

Or take the case of Matthew or Levi, and his brother James, the tax collectors. People in their profession were not even allowed in the synagogues because they bled their own people of their hard-earned money, stealing a good amount for themselves and turning the remainder over to the very people who occupied their homeland—the Romans. When Matthew and James showed the least bit of interest in His Teachings, Jesus went out of His way to help show them the Light and bring them back into God's fold, saying: "There will be more joy in heaven over one sinner who repents than over ninety-nine righteous persons who need no repentance."[23]

Or look at the example of St. Paul; he had actually overseen the stoning-execution of one of Christ's disciples—Stephen. In fact, he was on his way to Damascus to round up other followers of Christ in order to bring them to Jerusalem for punishment when Lord Jesus appeared to him as a bright light. Paul was told by the Lord that he was to be His instrument to spread the Gospel, and thus, a sinner of sinners became a great saint!

Jesus' parable of the prodigal son illustrates the joy of God over the return of any sinner to His fold. The son had squandered all his father had given him on riotous living and then suffered the karmic effects of his foolishness when a great famine came and he was left with no food and no money to buy any. Realizing his mistake, the son set off for home to beg his father's forgiveness. When his father saw him coming, he ran to him, embraced him and kissed him, even though the son protested, saying that he was no longer worthy to be called his father's son. But the father persisted, showering love and goods on his returned son and throwing a huge feast in his honor because he was so delighted to see his son again: "For this my son was dead, and is alive again; he was lost, and is found!"[24]

The elder son heard of his younger brother's return and was upset by the royal reception his father was giving him, saying that he (the elder son) had never disobeyed the father and yet the father had never given him such a feast or party. His father explained: "Son, you are always with me, and all that is mine is yours. But it is fitting to be merry and glad, for this your brother was dead, and is alive; he was lost, and is found!"[25]

The **one key** to all of this Divine Grace and Forgiveness that the Lord poured out onto those former sinners was that **they turned to Him;** they repented their past and turned toward God, as must we all if we are ever to reach our Home which lies in His Heart. When we turn to Him, we must devote all of our works to Him. In doing so, we burn up the seeds of our karma and purify ourselves. As we've seen, all our actions—right and wrong—are recorded and tallied. As we devote ourselves and our works to the Lord, doing more and more good and righteous deeds, we help to erase the marks on the negative side of that karmic tally-sheet and add marks to the positive side. Lord Krishna explains it thus:

> "Who does the work he is missioned to do, not craving the fruits of his action is the authentic illuminate and not the one who, averse to action, lights not the sacred fire. What people call renunciation is, in essence, disciplined activity; for none can be a yogi who has not disowned all selfish purpose once for all.
>
> "Dispassionate action is the means whereby an aspirant climbs up to the heights of Yoga, and serenity the means which keeps him poised on the Yoga's summit once he has attained it...
>
> "In the Yoga of action (works) nothing you undertake can ever be vain, nor obstacles prevail. **For even an iota of righteousness, friend, shall deliver you from cosmic fear...**
>
> "The wise who merge their intellect in Him, renouncing the fruit of all their actions on earth, are freed forever from the bondage of birth and attain the ultimate and sorrowless state."[26]

Thus we see that by dedicating ourselves and all our actions to Him, continually doing good deeds and heeding the Law of Karma, we help to burn up the negative consequences of our acts and, hopefully, win the Goal of Union within this very lifetime. But, even if we do not reach that Goal in this life, the Lord, in His Mercy, gives us another chance in our next lifetime. Further, because

151

we have aspired for the Light in our present life, we are born into an environment that is even more conducive to spiritual growth in our next one, and thus our soul, in its new body, continues its upward climb from where it left off in the old until the summit is reached.

Chapter 9

EVOLUTION AND CREATION

Reincarnation, then, is the next evolutionary step of the soul, which brings up the question of evolution; what exactly is it? Since human beings are imperfect, the process from imperfection to the perfection that is God is called evolution. Sri Aurobindo explains that: "The evolutionary working of Nature has a double process: an evolution of forms, an evolution of the soul."[1]

Science has proven the evolution of forms or of physical bodies through the unearthing of various ancient fossils. These fossils have shown us that the physical form of a plant and/or animal changes over time in order to better adapt to its environment. Even today there are reminders of the evolution of man's present form from that of his primate past. Recently, Dr. Fred Ledley wrote a report in the *New England Journal of Medicine* about the birth of a human baby with a tail, calling it a reminder of human evolution from the apes. The baby was born normal in every other way except for a two-inch, skin-covered tail. He pointed out in his report that tails occur on about one out of 100,000 infants, adding that, in fact, all human beings start out life with a tail that is virtually identical to those of other species. As the human fetus grows, however, the tail usually regresses.[2]

There is nothing contradictory in the processes of creation and evolution because one does not exclude the other; on the contrary, the two compliment each other. The Bible itself reiterates the two processes and confirms what both theologians and scientists have stated. In the opening of the *Book of Genesis,* the processes of both are described as follows:

First there was darkness and a void. Then the Spirit or Breath of God moved across the void and brought forth light (what scientists call the "Big Bang" of the Cosmos—the Creative Force of the Lord), and He separated the darkness from the light, then the heavens from the physical earth, and the waters from the dry lands. Then He brought forth vegetation of various kinds in the sea and on the earth, and then the living creatures—**first of the water,** as scientific evolutionists have verified, and then of the air and earth. Lastly, He brought forth man—a relatively late arrival on the earth, again, as verified by scientists.

Thus we see that the Bible confirms the theory of evolution.

153

Trouble comes when one tries to say that the process of evolution is without direction. This, of course, is ridiculous for the Guiding Hand of God can be seen throughout Creation. Even the word we use for the universe—Cosmos—attests to the Divine Plan, as "cosmos" means "order." So, as Sri Aurobido has pointed out so beautifully:

> "The cosmos is no accident in Time; there is meaning in each play of Chance, there is freedom in each face of Fate...This world was not built with random bricks of chance, a blind god is not destiny's architect; a conscious power has drawn the plan of life, there is a meaning in each curve and line."[3]

We may not understand the meaning behind each curve and line, but that does not mean that there isn't one! More trouble comes when people misunderstand the Bible when it says that God created the world in six days. They confuse six human days, with only 24 hours in each, with six days of God. The *Gita* explains that: "Those who know that a day as well as a night of Brahma (God, the Creator) lasts a thousand ages (yugas); are the authentic knowers of day and night."[4]

One yuga or age is said to last over 1,742,000 human years, so 1000 times that figure certainly gives you a lot of time! Even St. Peter says that, "With the Lord one day is a thousand years, and a thousand years as one day."[5] Thus, it is easy to see that both the theologians and the evolutionists are correct: i.e., God **did** create the world and the cosmos in six days, but six of **His** days, not ours, which translates into millions and billions of human years—plenty of time for the process from creation to evolution to take place!

The soul, too, evolves from the darkness and ignorance of the ego to the light and awareness of the awakened, liberated, Aquarian consciousness. For if we were already perfect, we would not make mistakes, and just by looking at the shape the world is in today, we can see that we've made **lots** of them! God has given us a free will to choose between right and wrong, good and bad, and the right to choose to heed and follow His Laws of Balance and Karma, or ignore them and suffer the consequences, which is what is happening right now.

Reincarnation, then, is the method God has chosen to help our souls evolve spiritually. Our soul will continue to reincarnate into physical bodies until we have reached Him and merged our souls into Him. As Sri Aurobindo has pointed out, this evolution of the soul or consciousness is the primary motivation behind earthly or physical existence, the evolution of the physical form being of secondary importance, being merely a vehicle for the evolution of the soul:

> "The nature of the next step (in the evolution of the soul) is indicated by the deep aspirations awakening in the human race...Man's urge towards spirituality is an undeniable indication of the inner drive of the Spirit within towards emergence, its insistence towards the next step of its manifestation...
>
> "A change of consciousness is the major fact of the next evolutionary transformation, and the consciousness itself, by its own mutation, will impose and effect any necessary mutation of the body (Mind over Matter!)...Matter (the physical body, etc.) will reveal itself as an instrument of the manifestation of Spirit...The body will become a faithful and capable instrument, perfectly responsive to the Spirit... Health, strength, duration, bodily happiness and ease, liberation from suffering are a part of the physical perfection which the gnostic (spiritually conscious) evolution is called upon to realize...
>
> "New powers of consciousness and new faculties (which we today would call miraculous) will develop in the gnostic (perfectly spiritualized) being who will use them in a natural, normal and spontaneous way both for knowledge and action...The life of gnostic beings might fitly be characterized as a superhuman or divine life...
>
> "There is no reason to suppose that this transformation is impossible on earth. In fact, it would give the truest meaning to earthly existence."[6]

What's more, this transformation has **already been completed** and realized by certain individuals in the past and present. What is needed today is for this spiritual transformation, this revolution and evolution of consciousness to happen **en masse, in toto,** within each and every human being on earth.

Only with a change of consciousness can we hope to weather the violent storms that lie ahead. The tribulations that we are already experiencing, and which will intensify, are part of the purification of the earth, due to the negative effects of man's karma. The more people that change for the better within, the less need for violent and destructive change without. The more who change and reach for the Light, the more the blows of the tribulation will be cushioned. Thus we must all strive for that Light by following the three Paths described earlier—Knowledge (Gnosis) of God, Love of God and His Creation (which includes our fellow humans), and Works dedicated to God—thereby realizing the Divine Life on Earth.

Reincarnation, Evolution and Christianity

As we have seen, science has proven what religions—both East and West—have taught for ages, i.e., that evolution and reincarnation as a consequence of one's karma are not mere theories but facts. The teaching of reincarnation can be found in all of the Eastern philosophies and religions, and most of those of the West, too, including the Egyptian Mystery Religions, Persian Mithraism and Zoroasterianism, and Alexandrian Neoplatonic theology (the teachings of Plato). Why, then, is the fact of reincarnation not taught in most Christian churches?

In truth, the early Christians **did** believe in reincarnation, as Swami Kriyananda, the American disciple of Paramahansa Yogananda, points out:

> "In fact, one gets the impression that other things were taken out of the Bible, too. You know, the early Christians used to believe in reincarnation, the Jews believed in it, the orthodox Jews still believe in it. And Origen, one of the greatest theologians, second to Saint Augustine even, so great was he, said that he got the teaching of reincarnation from apostolic times. This teaching wasn't taken out of Christian doctrine until 553 A.D. at the Second Council of Constantinople. They found recently that Pope Vigilius who was present in Constantinople, boycotted that council...They banned Origen for political reasons and, at the same time, took out all his teachings, including that of reincarnation. But we do find little glimpses and hints in the Bible about reincarnation..."[7]

One example of this is seen after Jesus' transfiguration, where He became radiant like the sun and was shown speaking with

Moses and Elijah, and where a voice from heaven was heard to say: "This is my beloved Son, with whom I am well pleased; listen to him."[8] Whereupon Jesus told His disciples to tell no one of the vision until after He, the Messiah, had been Resurrected. Confused, the disciples asked Him why the scribes always said that Elijah had to come again before the Messiah would come. Jesus answered them, saying:

> " 'Elijah does come, and he is to restore all things; but **I tell you that Elijah has already come,** and they did not know him, but did to him whatever they pleased. So also the Son of Man will suffer at their hands.' Then the disciples understood that **He was speaking to them of John the Baptist.**"[9]

Speaking to the multitudes, Jesus reiterated this truth, i.e., that John the Baptist was Elijah reincarnated:

> "This is he (John) of whom it is written, 'Behold, I send my Messenger before thy face, who shall prepare thy way before thee.' Truly, I say to you, among those born of women there has risen no one greater than **John the Baptist**...and if you are willing to accept it, **he is Elijah** who is to come. He who has ears to hear, let him hear."[10]

In two more examples, Jesus illustrated both the teachings of karma and that of reincarnation. In one case, Jesus took pity on a man who had been paralyzed for over thirty-eight years—virtually the man's entire life—and healed him, saying, "See, you are well! **Sin no more, that nothing worse befalls you.**"[11] Jesus was referring to the sins of the man in his previous life.

In the other case, Jesus was walking by a man who had been blind since birth and was asked by His disciples, "Who sinned, this man or his parents, that he was born blind?"

Jesus answered, "It was not that this man sinned, or his parents." He indicated that due to the sinful deeds that this man committed in a previous life he was now fulfilling God's Law of Karma through reincarnation, and hence was born blind, "that the works of God might be made manifest in him..."[12] whereupon Jesus proceeded to heal him as well.

So then, why was the teaching of reincarnation taken out of the Bible? To quote Swami Kriyananda in answer:

> "So we get the impression that the Bible was tampered with for the usual reason, which is institutional (organized) religion. When they try to institutionalize religion they also

bring out the more convenient things that will support their church dogmas, and that is what...Yogananda indicated that they did do with the Bible. That there were many high and deep teachings there that are not available except through the lives of great saints who lived those teachings and realized them in their own lives."[13]

In other words, the organized church that had become one with the state did not want anyone to realize that we have more than one chance or more than one way to reach God. If we believe that we have only one life, and further, if we believe that there is only one door to salvation—namely Jesus—naturally we will go to the organization that bears His name and pay whatever the price in order to "buy" our way into heaven. This assures that institution of continued monetary support, and assures the state that its laws will be followed as they are backed by "God's Church."

Thus, the church/state union is able to ban and burn all teachings that do not agree and/or support "their" view of things. Hence, true knowledge of God is perverted, clouded and obscured, causing confusion among the people as to what are right works and what are wrong. Due to this confusion, the church/state union is able to get people to do things that are otherwise obviously not in harmony with God's True Plan of Peace, Unity and Brotherhood, such as fighting in the Crusades or so-called "Holy-Wars," where killing one's brother is justified in the name of God. That is the blasphemy: using the name of God to justify killing one's brother. But during these times, he is not called "brother," but "pagan," "heathen," "alien," "non-believer," "heretic," or other dehumanizing and senseless terms.

Those who encourage this "brainwashing" forget that they will have to face the consequences of their evil deeds. Those who would turn the minds of the young away from brotherhood, love and therefore God, toward hatred, division and evil deeds would do well to remember Jesus' words about the consequences of such Godless acts: "Whoever causes one of these little ones who believe in me (and therefore His teaching of Love) to sin (by teaching them to hate), it would be better for him to have a great millstone fastened round his neck and to be drowned in the depth of the sea!"[14]

This does not mean that one should not defend righteousness, or try to stop atrocities and atrocious leaders like Hitler from perpetrating their evil deeds. But the key word here is "defense," which negates any idea of "pre-emptive strikes," for that is offensive action, not defensive! This also does not justify terrorism, either by individuals or by governments, such as governments who imprison, torture and/or kill their political dissidents, or who support such governments who do such evil things.

Again, Lord Buddha's words explain it all: **"Hate never conquers hate; only love does!"** God's Teaching is one of Tolerance and Love, and from this Love springs True Knowledge and the desire to surrender one's will, one's actions and one's entire being to Him. Therefore, above all else, we must Love: Love Him, Love His Creation and Love our neighbor. As Sri Aurobindo, the master yogi, puts it:

> "An entire Godlove and adoration extends to a love, of the world and all its forms and powers and creatures—in all the Divine is seen, is found, is adored, is served or is felt in oneness. Add to knowledge and works this crown of the eternal triune delight, admit this love, learn this worship: make it one spirit with works and knowledge. That is the apex of the perfection.
>
> "This Yoga of love will give you a highest potential force for spiritual largeness and unity and freedom. But it must be a love which is one with God-knowledge. There is a devotion which seeks God in suffering for consolation, succour and deliverance; there is a devotion which seeks Him for His gifts, for divine aid and protection and as a fountain of the satisfaction of desire; there is a devotion that, still ignorant, turns to Him for light and knowledge...But when the God-lover is also the God-knower, the lover becomes oneself with the Beloved...Develop in yourself this God-engrossed love; the heart spiritualized and lifted beyond the limitations of its lower nature will reveal to you most intimately the secrets of God's immeasurable being, bring into you the whole touch and influx and glory of His divine powers and open to you the mysteries of an eternal rapture...
>
> "This love that is knowledge, this love that can be the deep heart of your action, will be your most effective force for an utter consecration and complete perfection. An integral union of the individual's being with the Divine Being is the condition of a perfect spiritual life. Turn then altogether

towards the Divine; make one with Him by knowledge, love and works all your nature. Turn utterly towards Him and give up ungrudgingly into His hands your mind and your heart and your will, all your consciousness and even your very senses and body. Let your consciousness be sovereignly moulded by Him into a flawless mould of His divine consciousness. Let your heart become a lucid or flaming heart of the Divine. Let your will be an impeccable action of His will. Let your very senses and body be the rapturous sensation and body of the Divine. Adore and sacrifice to Him with all you are; remember Him in every thought and feeling, every impulsion and act. Persevere until all these things are wholly His and He has taken up even in most common and outward things as in the inmost sacred chamber of your spirit His constant transmuting Presence."[15]

PART III

Karma
And
The End Times

THE COMING OF THE LORD

Chapter 1

KARMA AND THE BALANCE OF NATURE

In the last chapters of Part II we discussed the paths to the Lord, and the concept of Karma with particular emphasis on the karmic effects we reap in our dealings with other human beings. In Part III we will deal with the question of the End Times, the reasons for it, and preparations to be made for the New Age.

The tribulations of the End Times are actually the consequences of Man's Karma in his dealings with the Earth as a living organism and a part of God's Creation. It must be understood that karma involves **all** of our actions—good or bad—in **all** circumstances and under **all** conditions and with respect to **all** parts of the Lord's Creation. Thus, the karmic effects or the reactions to our own actions that we receive involve not just our dealings with people in general, but also extend to our use or abuse of **all of God's Creation.** The manner in which we use or abuse the natural resources with which the world has been blessed determines the type of karmic effect we will receive. When we use these resources wisely, with an eye to keeping the balance and maintaining the harmony of the natural order of things, we will be blessed in return.

But when we ignore God's Great Design of Life—the Balance of Nature—and go against the natural order of things, abusing instead of using, wasting instead of conserving, polluting instead of beautifying, then we condemn ourselves to experiencing the negative or adverse reactions that are sure to follow such godless actions.

What exactly is the Balance of Nature? It is an order—cosmos—of natural cycles which the Lord Himself has set into motion and which man dare not interrupt lest he bring down the whole cosmos on his head! One may learn of God's Balance by observing its functioning in Nature. As the Lord as Sri Krishna says in the *Gita:* "Under my aegis (guidance, protection, sponsorship) Nature, *Prakrti,* gives birth to all things, moving and unmoving. For this reason the world evolves in cycles."[1]

To us these cycles may seem to be confusing and contradictory, but if we look behind these seeming contradictions, we may perceive the perfection and harmony from which these cycles stem—the One God, who is beyond the dualities of pain and pleasure, birth and death, good and evil, positive and negative.

162

It is in observing these cycles, then—these apparent contradictions—that we may better understand the workings of God's Great Law of Karma, as exemplified through the Balance of Nature.

As Sri Aurobindo explains in his marvelous revelation *Savitri:*

> "Our Destiny is written in double terms:
> Through Nature's contraries we draw near God...
> All contraries are aspects of God's face;
> The many are the innumerable One...
> Impenetrable, a mystery recondite
> Is the vast plan of which we are a part;
> Its harmonies are discords to our view,
> Because we know not the great theme they serve...
> The cosmos is no accident in Time;
> There is meaning in each play of Chance,
> There is a freedom in each face of Fate...
> This world was not built with random bricks of chance,
> A blind god is not destiny's architect;
> A conscious power has drawn the plan of life,
> There is a meaning in each curve and line."[2]

So it is in observing and understanding Nature that we may better understand God and His Divine Laws. Why? Because Nature and God are one and the same. Nature is God's outer manifestation; through Nature we can begin to see and hear and feel God's love for us all. For where else is God's perfection and care for all creatures more apparent than in the untainted purity and beauty of Nature? And where else are God's lessons of sharing and caring, loving and living better exemplified than through the lives of His creatures who live according to His laws!

As Ellen G. White has written in her book *Steps to Christ:*

> "Nature and revelation alike testify of God's love...'God is love' is written upon every opening bud, upon every spire of springing grass...all testify to the tender, fatherly care of our God and to His desire to make His children happy...
>
> "Many are the ways in which God is seeking to make Himself known to us and bring us into communion with Him. Nature speaks to our senses without ceasing. The open heart will be impressed with the love and glory of God as revealed

through the works of His hands. The listening ear can hear and understand the communications of God through the things of Nature. The green fields, the lofty trees, the buds and flowers, the passing cloud, the falling rain, the babbling brook, the glories of the heavens, speak to our hearts, and invite us to become acquainted with Him who made them all...No one can fully appreciate the significance of hill and vale, river and sea, who does not look upon them as an expression of God's love to man."[3]

Sri Aurobindo explains that through Nature we may be privileged to see and hear our Lord through His outer manifestations:

"His laughter of beauty breaks out in green trees,
His moments of beauty triumph in a flower;
The blue sea's chant, the rivulet's wandering voice
Are murmurs falling from the Eternal's harp.
This world is God fulfilled in outwardnesss...
To meet Him crowded plains of brilliant calm,
Mountains and violet valleys of the Blest,
Deep glens of joy and crooning waterfalls
And woods of quivering purple solitude..."[4]

Solitude and Silence—these are two vital things that all great masters have said one must have if one is to realize God. For without these two essentials, one is constantly distracted by the world, away from Him, and thus it is difficult to reach the Goal. This silence must begin with one's own self. For how can we learn to silence our minds if we don't first learn to silence our mouths! Leo Buscaglia, author of the best seller *Living, Loving and Learning,* once said that he firmly believes that God only speaks in whispers. So we must be silent sometimes or else we will never be able to hear what He is saying to us! And He is speaking continually to our hearts; we just have to stop talking ourselves and start listening to Him.

Baha'u'llah is even more adamant about the need for one to be silent. He states that a seeker of God:

"...must wash away from the tablet of his heart every trace of pride and vain-glory, must cling unto patience and resignation, **observe silence and refrain from idle talk. For the tongue is a smouldering fire, and excess of speech a**

164

deadly poison...He should treasure the companionship of those that have renounced the world, and regard avoidance of boastful and worldly people a precious benefit."[5]

Or, as Lord Buddha put it:

"If you have a friend sober, pure, and wise, let nothing hold you back—find delight and instruction in his company...

"If you find no better or equal on life's road, go alone! Loneliness is better than friendship of a fool."[6]

In other words, if one fails to find spiritual people with whom to communicate and share life's journey, it is better to make that journey alone than to compromise one's own spiritual growth by consorting with boistrous, foolish and egoistic people who scoff at spiritual endeavors and drain the true spiritual aspirant of his/her energy and purpose.

Although some have been able to achieve God-Realization without resorting to the peace of the forests, most find it an extremely difficult thing to do. Even the Lord as Jesus went to the woods when he felt the need to commune with the Spirit in solutide and have a respite from the clamouring of the crowds that always gathered round Him in the villages and cities. For in the woods, one is constantly reminded of God's Love and Perfection. Our senses are not jarred by artificial distractions of man. Thus the Lord as the Buddha said:

"Holy is the forest.
Holy is the place where the senses are at peace,
Where the saint finds refuge and simple delight."[7]

It is in Nature that we may learn God's most important lessons. As Ellen White explains:

"God would have His children appreciate His works and delight in the simple, quiet beauty with which He has adorned our earthly home. He is the lover of the beautiful...He would have us cultivate purity and simplicity, the quiet graces of the flowers.

"If we will but listen, God's created works will teach us precious lessons of obedience and trust...The things of Nature obey the Creator's will."[8]

As Sai Baba has pointed out: "Birds and beasts need no Divine Incarnation as birds or beasts to guide them for they have no

165

inclination to stray away from their path. Man alone forgets or ignores the goal of life..."[9]—which is God-Realization.

Guru and God

Nature, then, is the Guide that God has given us to teach us the Truths of His Love and to bring us back to His heart. For it is true that one is closer to God's heart in beautiful Nature than anywhere else on Earth!

This guidance is essential if we are to get through the maze of distractions and illusions that surround us and keep us from union with the Beloved Lord. It is therefore an absolute necessity to have a Guide, a Guru to help us pierce the veil that separates us from God.

To most, the idea of a Guru conjures up visions of ascetic men wrapped in loin cloths or yellow robes sitting cross-legged in meditation. To be sure, many **Sat Gurus** (True Teachers) do fit that description. But a Guru need not be so garbed; in fact, he need not be human at all.

This question of the necessity of a Guru and the form(s) He may take was once discussed between Sri D.K. Roy (Dadaji) and the great Indian master, Sri Ramana Maharshi. It was often said that Sri Ramana had never had a Guru, but Sri Ramana said that this was not so, that it depended on what one calls a Guru. He said that the Guru is absolutely necessary, but that it did not have to be in human form. His Guru was the mountain—Arunachala—upon which he lived; therefore, Nature had been his Guide back to God:

> "What is a Guru? Guru is God or the Self. First a man prays to God to fulfill his desires, then a time comes when he does not pray for the fulfillment of a desire but for God Himself. So God appears to him in some form or other, human or non-human, to guide him as a Guru in answer to his prayer."[10]

For most, this does mean a human Guide or Guru as most need to verbalize and have things explained to them in a human language, although God's perfections are seen easiest and clearest in Nature. Even Lord Jesus often gave examples in Nature to explain things. He used the parables of the lilies of the fields and the swallows to illustrate Faith, Trust, and Love.

Perhaps the peoples that have been recognized in the West as

MOTHER NATURE

being the most intimately linked to and guided by Nature are the American Indians. The lifestyle of the American Indians was one in tune with Nature and Her cycles. Their religious ceremonies and even their religious artifacts, including the Peace Pipe, were all intricately linked to Nature as God's outer manifestation and as their Guide to pure, spiritual living. The pipe itself was made in such a way as to represent the various aspects of Nature. When the Lord as the White Buffalo Cow Woman gave the Indians the sacred pipe, She told them:

"The Earth is your Grandmother and Mother, and She is sacred. Every step that is taken upon Her should be as a prayer...All these peoples (of Nature), and all the things of the universe, are joined to you who smoke the pipe—all send their voices to Wakan-Tanka, the Great Spirit. When you pray with this pipe, you pray for and with everything...

"Every dawn as it comes is a holy event, and every day is holy, for the light comes from your Father...and also you must always remember that the two-leggeds and all the other (creatures) who stand upon this earth are sacred and should be treated as such...Behold this pipe! Always remember how sacred it is, and treat it as such, for it will take you to the end."[11]

Whereupon She said that the Indian peoples would live for as long as these spiritual ceremonies were known and the pipe was used. "But as soon as the sacred pipe is forgotten, the people will be without a center and they will perish."[12] In other words, as soon as the people forgot their links to Nature/God, they would be without guidance, and therefore perish.

Various mixtures of barks and herbs were used with the sacred pipe, including cannabis and peyote. They were viewed as spiritual aids for enlightenment and guidance to reach God, and were used **only** for that purpose. There were basically three times when the American Indians would seek to use plants like peyote and psilocybine mushrooms: 1- when one had a serious illness and one wished to find out how much of the illness was due to mental versus physical reasons, 2- when one had reached a crisis or turning point in one's life, and 3- when one felt a need to commune with God.

This last reason was the most important reason for the use of any psycho-active or psychedelic agent. As a matter of fact,

Richard Evans Schultes (Director of the Harvard Botanical Museum) and Dr. Albert Hofmann (the Director of the Pharmaceutical-Chemical Research Laboratories of Sandoz in Switzerland-now retired) theorize in their book *Plants of the Gods* that it was the ingestion of such psycho-active plants that first caused man to conceive of God and other realms of reality:

"The amazing effects of these mind-altering plants are frequently inexplicable and indeed uncanny.

"Little wonder, then, that they have long played an important role in the religious rites of early civilizations and are still held in veneration and awe as sacred elements by certain peoples...How could man in primitive societies better contact the spirit world than through the use of plants with psychic effects enabling the partaker to communicate with supernatural realms? What more direct method than to permit man to free himself from the prosaic confines of this mundane existence and to enable him to enter temporarily the fascinating worlds of indescribably ethereal wonder opened to him...

"...all aboriginal societies have considered—and still do—that these plants are the gifts of the gods, if not the gods themselves...

"There are many examples...of plants that are sacred and even revered as gods. Soma, (an) ancient god...of India may be the most outstanding example. Most hallucinogens are holy mediators between man and the supernatural, but Soma was deified. So holy was Soma that it has been suggested that even the idea of deity may have arisen from experiences with its unearthly effects...

"Of the more than 1000 holy hymns in the Rig-Veda, 120 are devoted exclusively to Soma, and references to this vegetal sacrament run through many of the other hymns."[13]

Dr. Hofmann and Professor Schultes compare the use of psychedelic plants as holy sacraments to the Christians' use of the host and wine, the plants being given such names as "divine flesh" and "vine of the soul,"[14] the word "psychedelic" itself meaning literally "clear mind" or "vision of the soul."[15] In the *Shrimad Bhagavatam*, Lord Krishna is described as wearing earrings made out of the seeds of the hemp or cannabis plant.[16]

Schultes and Hofmann point out that many cultures consider cannabis not only a sacred plant, but also a valuable medicinal herb for such ailments as glaucoma, nausea, depression, vomiting, epilepsy, muscle spasms, asthma, bronchitis, dandruff, leprosy, malaria, constipation, venereal disease, whooping cough, earaches, and tuberculosis, and as an agent for the relief of pain due to headaches, backaches, migraines, rheumatism, etc., and as a tranquilizer, antibiotic, antitussive, appetite stimulant, and topical anesthetic.* They also state that, according to Hindu tradition, cannabis is the holy plant of Lord Shiva, the destroyer of ignorance. The Tibetans as well are said to consider the plant sacred:

> "A Mahayana Buddhist tradition maintains that during the six steps of asceticism leading to His enlightenment, Buddha lived on one Hemp seed a day. He is often depicted with 'Soma leaves' in His begging bowl and the mysterious god...Soma has occasionally been identified with Hemp. In Tantric Buddhism of the Himalayas of Tibet, Cannabis plays a very significant role in the meditative ritual used to facilitate deep meditation and heighten awareness."[17]

Today, the American Indians as well as others still use these plants for mystical experiences and for personal or direct communication with God, the plants being viewed as divine messengers "enabling the individual to communicate with God without the medium of a priest...(the plants being) an earthly representative of God..."[18] In fact, Indians believe that these plants were given to them directly by God in the form of the Pale Prophet. As one native American Indian is quoted as explaining to an anthropologist:

> "God told the Delawares (Indians) to do good even before he sent Christ to the whites who killed Him...God made Peyote. It is His power. It is the power of Jesus. Jesus came afterwards on this earth, after Peyote...God (through Peyote) told the Delawares the same things that Jesus told the whites."
>
> "The white man goes into his church house and talks **about** Jesus; the Indian goes into his teepee and talks **to** Jesus."[19]

The use of these agents in Western society and their connection with the New Age Consciousness has been examined by Marilyn Ferguson in *The Aquarian Conspiracy:* "For many people in many

---

* Presently, approximately 32 states in the U.S. have legalized the medicinal use of cannabis for diseases such as glaucoma, cancer, etc.

cultures, psychedelic drugs have offered a beginning trail if seldom a fully transformative path."[20]

In other words, they have been viewed as a key to open the door, but are not the Goal in and of themselves. She goes on to say that, "(Aldous) Huxley believed that the long-predicted religious revival in the U.S. would start with"[21] the use of these psycho-active agents. He stated that:

> " 'Although these new mind-changers may start by being something of an embarrassment, they will tend in the long run to deepen the spiritual life of the communities...From being an activity concerned mainly with symbols, religion will be transformed into an activity concerned mainly with experience and intuition—an everyday mysticism...'
>
> "He (Huxley) said that he himself had been electrified by understanding fully, under the influence of mescaline, the radical meaning of the phrase **God is Love.** One of the Aquarian Conspirators said, 'After many years in intellectual, left-brain pursuit of 'reality', I learned from LSD about alternative realities—and suddenly all bibles made sense.' Others (who answered her questionnaire on psychedelics) have said that they seemed to experience the nature of matter, the unity of all things, life as a splendid game we are playing (what Hindus call the Divine Lila or God's Great Cosmic Play), a story we are telling."[22]

Ferguson states that Psychiatrist Stanislav Grof sees Nature's Aids or psychedelics as catalysts or amplifiers to the mind, helping one to realize and experience other realms of consciousness and planes of existence of which all but a chosen few are unaware in "normal," everyday life. But she states that not all who have taken LSD or other psychedelics have had such mystical, spiritual experiences:

> "Compelling mystical experiences are by no means universal among psychedelics users. These are dependent on many factors: dosage, prior experiences, introspectiveness, willingness to explore states of consciousness, prior interest in spirituality, expectations, and an appropriate environment. Casual recreational use often results in little more than sensory alterations and a 'high.' "[23]

The American Indians and other ancient societies believe that the differences between the experiences of those who have taken these agents for recreational use versus those who have taken them for spiritual use or as a means to seek out spiritual truths is the difference between use and abuse. Rolling Thunder, a great present-day Indian healer and spiritual leader who has astounding siddhis or spiritual powers, including great healing powers and the powers of materialization and control over the elements, reiterates this difference between use and abuse:

" 'Some of these people interested in ecology want to protect the earth, and yet they will cram anything into their mouths just for tripping or freaking out—even using some of our sacred agents. Some of these things (like cannabis, mushrooms, and peyote) I call helpers, and they are very good if they are taken very, very seriously, but they have to be used in the right way; otherwise they'll be useless and harmful, and most people don't know about these things. All these things have to be understood...

" '(The Peyote Tea Ceremony) is a purification ceremony. like most of our ceremonies. It's not used to get high or for foolishness. It's used in a way that we want to cleanse our systems and our minds, so we can put ourselves on a higher plane of life...'

"...all traditional Indians considered the use of peyote for 'spacing out'...a gross misuse of the agent and a misuse of the mind. Both the agent and the mind are sacred...The meaningful use of drugs requires a state of mind that can be acquired only through practice and purification, and a great deal of careful preparation...Rolling Thunder said he knew that there were a couple of groups of white people now who are using peyote right, 'but the great majority of them aren't using peyote right at all, and they might be punished for it. I've seen some of the results of punishment. It's terrible when it kicks back on you. But peyote is good. I've seen it used for many good purposes when it is used right.' "[24]*

The reason Rolling Thunder and others have stressed that "spacing out" on drugs is not the way to go is that: 1- one can literally "burn out" from abusing them, and 2- one defeats the

---

* Rolling Thunder is a member of the Native American Church, the only group of people in the U.S. that are currently allowed to use these substances for spiritual/religious purposes.

whole purpose of taking the Nature's Aid in the first place. St. Rolling Thunder explains that the purpose of the aid is to help one to concentrate, to achieve and maintain that one-pointedness of mind that is absolutely necessary in order to realize and understand true spiritual experiences. Just about all true spiritual teachers and guides—East and West—have stressed the importance of this one-pointedness of mind, the ability to control one's attention and focus it on one's chosen Ideal:

> "There can be no healing, no meditation, no meaningful spiritual experience (much less Union with the Lord) without that highest of disciplines (one-pointedness of mind)—particularly if drugs are to be used and not be dangerously distracting or defeating."[25]

Dr. Raymond Moody points out in his book *Life after Life* that man has used psycho-active compounds throughout the ages as a means of achieving enlightenment. He points to the American Indians and their use of peyote as just one example of this, saying that the aid "is ingested in order to attain religious visions and enlightenment."[26] He states that similar groups round the world have used psychedelics for the same reason:

> "The belief (being) that the drug they employ provides a means of passage into other dimensions of reality...it could be hypothesized that drug use would be only one pathway among many leading to the achievement of enlightenment and to the discovery of other realms of existence. The experience of dying could, then, be another such pathway, and all this would help to account for the resemblance of drug-induced experiences...to near-death experiences..."[27] —and to meditative experiences, too.

Various other methods have been used to open these doors to other dimensions of reality and reach the Goal of Union with the Lord. Marilyn Ferguson points out that the visions one receives through the ingestion of certain psychedelics are just a glimpse of the Ultimate Reality. The Goal in life is to make those glimpses **permanent,** to transform our everyday, mundane existence into the vibrant, vivid, spontaneous Divine Life here on Earth. But if one is to maintain this vision on a permanent basis, one must seek other, more "controlled" methods in order to make the transformation complete.

Thus, other techniques of transformation or psychotechnologies, as she calls them, must be explored and employed. As we mentioned before, rolfing, running, isolation tanks, biofeedback, etc., are some of these more "controlled" methods. But the best and surest method, the one which needs no outside controller or apparatus is, again, meditation as taught by the Yogic Masters. Through continual practice of meditation one gains the inner vision of the Supreme Reality. As one becomes more and more proficient, this Inner Reality becomes the Outer Reality, too. In other words, one sees the Lord within and without. As the *Upanishads* explain it:

"What is within us is also without. What is without is also within. He who sees a difference between the two goes evermore from death to death. By the purified mind alone is the indivisible Brahman (God) to be attained...

"Thus Brahman (God the Creator) is all in all. He is action, knowledge, goodness supreme. To know Him, hidden in the lotus of the heart, is to untie the knot of ignorance...With mind illumined by the power of meditation, the wise know Him, the blissful, the immortal. The knot of the heart, which is ignorance, is loosed, all doubts are dissolved, all evil effects of deeds are destroyed, when He who is both personal and impersonal is realized...

"The Lord is the one life shining forth from every creature. Seeing Him present in all, the wise man is humble...he serves the Lord in all...such are the true knowers of Brahman (God the Creator)...

"The immortal Self is the sun shining in the sky, He is the breeze blowing in space, He is the fire burning on the altar, He is the guest dwelling in the house; He is in all (beings)...He is in the ether, He is wherever there is truth; He is the fish that is born in water, He is the plant that grows in the soil, He is the river that gushes from the mountain—He, the changeless reality, the illimitable!...

"He is one...of one form, He makes of Himself many forms. To him who sees the Self revealed in his heart belongs eternal bliss—to none else, to none else!...He is the one light that gives light to all. He shining, everything shines...

"The secret of immortality is to be found in purification

of the heart, in meditation, in realization of the identity of the Self (God) within and Brahman (God the Creator) without. For immortality is simply Union with God."[28]

Thus, through meditation and purification of our mind, heart and actions we can begin to realize the Ultimate Reality—the Divine Life on Earth: to see the Divine within our very own Self and to see His Majesty revealed through the Beauty, Purity and Simplicity of Nature. So let us see what we can learn from the Lord in Nature, for as Sri Aurobindo says:

"His failure is not failure whom God leads;
And how shall the end be vain when God is Guide?"[29]

Chapter 2

THE BALANCE IN ACTION

In areas where man has not intruded or where man has not upset the Balance of Nature/God, but instead lived in harmony, such as the African Pygmies, the American Indians, or the villagers in some of the mountainous regions of Asia, we may observe the natural cycles of birth and death, predator and prey which have gone on since time immemorial, and under which the Natural World has flourished in abundance. In these cycles we see that each species, whether plant or animal, plays a part, a vital role in God's Balance. With respect to the cycle of predator and prey, the predator seeks out only the old, the sick or deformed, or the excess of the young as food. All animals are given certain natural defenses that keep them from the predator unless there is a defect in those defenses. By culling out those defective individuals, the predator insures that the healthiest and best of the species, which naturally have the healthiest genes, are left to propagate, thereby controlling its population and insuring the future survival of the species as a whole. Without predatory controls, those with defects might propagate and pass on defective genes to their offspring, thereby weakening the species and ultimately threatening its survival.

Often we impose our so-called "moral" judgements on events in Nature, cursing the predator and feeling sorry for the prey. In truth, to die at the jaws of a predator is a quicker and less painful death than is disease, starvation, or exposure, which is what would happen to those individuals if the predator were not around.

When a predator attacks, the prey goes into shock, which acts as a natural anesthesia, and therefore does not feel pain. People who have been attacked by sharks or other animals and have even had limbs torn off have stated that they felt no pain at the time of the attack, and in some cases, felt no pain until hours later!

Even among predators there are natural checks for population growth and for insuring that the best genes are passed on to the young. The wolf pack is an excellent example. Wolves live in a family situation that is very similar to its human counterpart, complete with aunts and uncles. Only the dominant male and female propagate, so there is no overpopulation and the young are pro-

176

ducts of the best genes available. However, the pups are loved and cared for by the whole pack. Aunts will happily "puppy-sit" for the mother when she is away hunting or doing whatever. Loving care is taken to properly groom the pups and each other. A strong family bond is formed between all members of the pack insuring the mutual cooperation that is vital to the success of any hunt and, therefore, to the survival of them all.

Mutual Cooperation

Mutual cooperation is evident throughout Nature and not only between members of the same family group. Symbionic relationships (where both parties benefit from the relationship versus parasitic ones where the host is eventually injured or destroyed by its "partner") are very evident on the African grass plains where hundreds of different species coexist harmoniously. Frequently, one sees birds sitting on the backs of water-buffalo or wildebeest. The birds get a free ride and are protected from predators who might attack them on ground level. While on the buffalo's backs, the birds pick off parasitic lice and bugs that would otherwise plague the larger animals. Plus, they serve as an early warning signal against predators for the grazing beasts.

Another example of this symbiosis is seen underwater where certain types of small "dentist" fish clean the teeth, mouth and gill areas of much larger predatory fish. The larger predatory fish swim to so-called "cleaning stations" and will passively wait in line for their turn. They even allow the smaller "dentist" fish to go into their mouths for a thorough cleaning. They would **never** eat the smaller fish as that would destroy the trust between the two species, upon which the mutually beneficial relationship is based.

Cooperation between man and animals has gone on for centuries, too; and this is not just in reference to "draft" animals, such as oxen and horses, or domesticated animals, like cows and sheep, although their help to man should not be underestimated as these animals provide from half to 90% of the energy used for agriculture in the Third World. Not only do they provide this energy within their own lifetime; they also reproduce themselves and are thus a valuable renewable energy resource, consuming no diesel fuel and producing free fertilizer!

The animals' manure is also being used to produce methane gas for cooking, lighting and heating homes in certain Third World countries, and especially in India where bio-gas technology is used widely throughout the country. The manure from just a couple of cows, placed inside a large vat to ferment, produces nitrogen-enriched fertilizer and enough methane gas to fulfill the needs of a modest home. With some tender loving care, proper feeding and comfortable living and working conditions, such as soft horse collars instead of the heavy, choking wooden yokes still used in some countries today, these animals will continue to work for man, without the drawbacks of mechanical breakdowns, pollution or complaints!

The symbol of animals' help to man is often the "Seeing-Eye" dogs who help liberate the blind from the confines of their homes, allowing them to once again walk the streets, eat at restaurants, and generally move about. This same program is being successfully used by deaf people. And little "organ-grinder" monkeys are fast becoming the arms and legs of paralyzed or paraplegic individuals. Responding to voice and/or light requests, these intelligent and talented monkeys not only become loving companions, but also perform many functions for the wheelchair or bedridden person, such as turning on and off lights and appliances, opening doors and windows, and holding straws through which the handicapped can draw liquid nourishment. Thus, through these monkeys, the handicapped are given back some of the mobility and independence that their paralysis had taken away.

But, as stated before, these are not the only animals that cooperate with man. Often "wild" animals have been a great help to man. In Africa, a special relationship has developed between the tribes' honey gatherers and a particular bird called the honey guide. The honey hunters whistle to the birds and bang on the trees to "call" the birds. Then these birds lead the men to trees in which honeybees have built their hives. The men collect the honey and **always** leave a piece of the choicest honeycomb behind for the birds as a "Thank you!"

Just about everyone has heard one story of a dolphin or porpoise saving the life of an exhausted swimmer or shipwrecked sailor. The most recent example of this was reported from Perth, Australia, where an 11-year-old boy was protected by a dolphin for 4 hours in shark-infested waters. The boy had been surfing in Cocos Island Lagoon when a large wave knocked him off his board. The strong current then swept him out to sea. Rescue boats

178

were unable to find him in the rough waters, but the friendly dolphin did. The boy said that the dolphin never left his side throughout his long ordeal, and protected him from the sharks that frequent the area. Without the dolphin's aid, the boy surely would have drowned and/or been a shark's supper!

The dolphin's help to man is even more evident off the coast of Africa. Every year when schools of fish are "running," African tribesmen "call" the dolphins in toward shore by hitting the water with boards. The dolphins then herd the schools of fish closer and closer to shore into the waiting nets of the tribal fishermen. Thus both the dolphins and tribesmen benefit from the abundant catch!

Compare the above to what is happening to the dolphins who are trapped in modern tuna fishing nets and drown by the hundreds of thousands each year, not only off U.S. coasts, but in Latin American and Antarctic waters as well. In the last two decades alone, U.S. tuna boats have killed more than eight million dolphins—and the killing continues, though restricted. Over the next five years, the U.S. government will allow over 100,000 of these gentle, playful creatures to suffocate and drown in these nets as an "incidental kill" to the tuna harvest. But at least the U.S. is restricting its killing; in the Black Sea, the dolphins are on the verge of extinction due to the relentless slaughter of them by Turkish fishermen who hunt and kill them for fertilizer.

Another example of man's tragic insensitivity and inhumanity to the dolphin can be seen in the dolphin's fate on Iki Island in Japan. Here, fishermen are conducting wholesale slaughter operations of the dolphins because they eat the same fish the fishermen hunt. The numbers of fish have declined in recent years, but this is certainly **not** due to the dolphins' appetites: it is due to over-fishing by man and the negative impact his pollutants have had on the fish's breeding grounds. When one man—a member of the environmental group Greenpeace named Dexter Cate—tried to stop the slaughter by freeing 250 dolphins slated to die, the Japanese government arrested him, keeping him in jail for over two-and-a-half months. He who was nonviolent was jailed while those who perpetrated the senseless slaughter were free to continue the killing!

The pictures of the slaughter of the dolphins off Iki Island as well as those of the slaughter of their giant cousins—the whales—reminds us of one of the prophecies of Revelations:

> "The second angel blew his trumpet, and something like a giant mountain, burning with fire, was thrown into the sea; and a third of the sea became blood, a third of the living creatures in the sea died..."[1]

If you have ever seen an explosive harpoon launched, you can see why John said it resembled a burning mountain or great smoking stone. The explosive head of the harpoon detonates upon impact, literally blowing apart the insides of the whale. The sea around the sites of the killings of the whales and dolphins turns to blood. In the past 50 years, over two million whales have been slaughtered. Several species, including the blue (the largest creature on the planet), the right, the sperm, the fin and the humpback are on the brink of extinction. Considering how abundant the whales and dolphins used to be, it is easy to see that **this above prophecy has already been fulfilled: well over one-third of these magnificent sea creatures have already been slaughtered,** with perhaps an equal if not greater number dead or dying as a result of man's pollutions and encroachment on their breeding and feeding grounds. As a matter of fact, according to Jacques Cousteau, **only 6% of these magnificent creatures,** specifically the great whales or leviathans, **are left in the world today.**

Recently, the U.S. led the way toward a total moratorium or ban on commercial whaling as there are synthetic substitutes for every item one may get from the whale (oil, blubber, etc.) that do not require the death of any animal and are actually cheaper in cost. The whale hunting is to be phased out over the next few years and completely stopped by 1986. But several countries, including Japan, Russia, and Norway, have threatened to ignore the ban. Russia has the largest fleet of brutal and inhumane so-called "factory ships" where a whale is slaughtered and hacked to pieces, with half of it being thrown overboard and wasted. What's more, pirate whalers do not recognize **any** restrictions on the size, number or species of whale they kill. In many cases, the members of a herd or "pod" will stay with a wounded whale offering comfort and solace to the injured one. This type of compassionate behavior comes as a boon to the pirate whalers who will slaughter the entire herd, right down to the smallest calf. Often these pirate whalers have official support of countries like Japan and Russia.

It is this kind of senseless, brutal and godless action that will be responsible for bringing man himself to the brink of extinction. It is this type of mentality that we must stop. Certain environmental groups, like Greenpeace, the Cousteau Society, Friends of the Earth, etc., are already using nonviolent tactics to put a stop to the slaughters, often putting themselves between the hunters and the hunted, whether it is whales, dolphins, baby seals or whatever. Other groups have gone even further, taking away the instruments of destruction that these killers use. One group, for example, recently put one of the most notorious pirate whalers out of business for at least six to eight months by ramming their vessel when no one was aboard it while it was in harbor.

This is an example of taking away the aggressor's "stick." This concept can be best understood by the following example: A man who has been taught the ethic of nonviolence is continually assaulted with a stick by another man. Finally, a third man, who is equally nonviolent, steps in between the two. He does not strike the aggressor, but instead, takes away the aggressor's stick, his instrument of aggression and destruction. Thus the aggressor no longer has the means to continue waging his aggression. This is basically the goal of the nuclear freeze movement. It is an attempt to take away the nuclear "sticks" from each side so that no one, especially the innocent bystanders, will be hurt. This concept will be examined in greater detail in later chapters when we discuss what are our responsibilities vis-a-vis the impending tribulation and crises.

The Question of Intelligence

In many cultures, dolphins are known as sacred animals and as omens of good fortune. In ancient Greece one would have been charged with murder for killing a dolphin. Today, however, the idea of a blessed or holy animal does not find much sympathy in our "sophisticated," "civilized(?)," industrialized world. But the idea that animals are intelligent **is** beginning to take hold in the scientific community. And cetacea, which is the class name covering about 87 species of whales and dolphins, are probably the best example.

Cetacea live in an extended family situation where the young are taught by their elders the successful survival techniques that have helped them to thrive on this planet for at least 15 to 35 million years, whereas man has only populated Earth for about 500,000 to a few million years. They are very playful creatures,

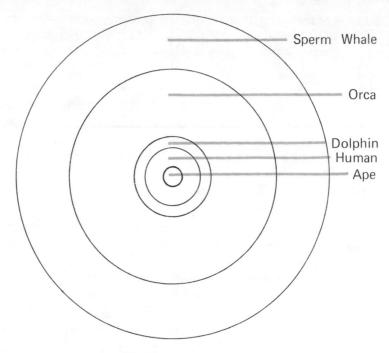

THE BRAIN SCALE

often exhibiting spontaneous reactions to express a wide range of emotions, including ecstasy.

Scientists note that this group of warm-blooded, air-breathing mammals—not fish—have a brain structure that is at least as large and complex, and in some cases much larger and more complex than our own. The size of an animal has nothing to do with the size of its brain. To run a big body does not require a big brain because the part of the brain that actually runs the body is quite small. The whale shark, for example, weights 40 tons, but it has a very small brain.

There are actually two parts to our brain: one part runs our bodily functions—the central motor cortex, a relatively small area—and the other part—the neo-cortex or associational areas—is where memory, learning, communication, spiritual phenomena, etc., are located. It is this second area that varies in size according to the intelligence or "computational capacity" of the species: the larger the area, the more intelligent the species.

In the chart we can see the size of this area in man's brain is enlarged over that of the apes. But the dolphin's area is larger than ours, and those of the orca and sperm whales absolutely dwarf ours!

The question may be raised, "If they are so smart, how come they are on the brink of extinction?" The answer is that cetacea do not use their intelligence for destructive purposes, rather they use their long memories to compose beautiful songs, as with the humpbacks, and to enjoy life to the fullest, quite literally "tripping out" in spiritual ecstasies as their joyous leaps and jumps suggest. As a matter of fact, in the *Shrimad Bhagavatam,* the dolphin's body is recognized as one which is particularly suited for spiritual enjoyments. In one section dealing with the gradual liberation of one's soul from the human body, the scriptures say that, after shaking off all impurity, the spiritual seeker's soul rises upwards, "resembling in shape the figure of a dolphin,"[2] which corresponds to descriptions given by some who have had death experiences of the "new psychic body" in which they found themselves after leaving their physical body behind. Further, in another section of the *Shrimad Bhagavatam,* the sphere of the heavens is said to resemble the shape of a dolphin: "Some people declare the stellar sphere as capable of being meditated upon through deep concentration of the mind as a form of (the) Lord **existing in the shape of a dolphin.**"[3]

Indeed, the intelligence and psychic abilities of cetacea, and in particular, dolphins have fascinated scientists for several years. One woman who attests to the dolphins' abilities is Ms. Estelle Myers who quit a $25,000-a-year job in New York City back in 1976 after having an amazing encounter with a group of dolphins. She relates that on a trip back to her native Australia, she met a number of dolphins off **Cape Tribulation** (interesting it should be called that—"tribulation!"), who communicated several messages to her in a telepathic way that she called "thought transference," which the dolphins encouraged people to use. The dolphins gave her three messages to tell the world:

1) that we must create a planetary pause for peace using the rainbow (the sign that God gave Noah as His Covenant with Man after the Great Flood), and dolphins as a non-verbal unifying visual communication around the world;

2) to initiate an aquarium water-baby program, whereby children are born directly into water from the mother's womb to lessen the shock of the baby going from the water-environment of the womb to the full-gravity environment of the outside world. Using dolphins nearby helps to ease the mother's fear of the water,

too. The process began in Russia under the supervision of Igor Charkovsky, who was responsible for teaching infants to swim before they could even crawl. Through several experiments with different species, including man, Charkovsky has proven that beings born into water and who exercise a lot in water are stronger, and healthier than their land-based kin. Babies born into water learn how to hold their breath immediately with no fear, and turn out to be more gentle, intelligent and stronger than those born straight into the shock of a full-gravity environment. Two years ago, Charkovsky conducted several experiments in the Black Sea with untrained dolphins and several young women with their babies, ranging in age from one month to one year. As long as the dolphins were around, the infants swam and dove underwater even without their mothers, and slept more soundly and peacefully than on land! And, finally,

3) to help free captive cetaceans (dolphins, porpoises, whales) and learn from them in order to create a better and more peaceful world.[4]

Myers believes that we have a chance to either "rebuild our planet" using the lessons of love and cooperation we learn from the dolphins and the rest of Nature as guidance, or it will be destroyed. She has traveled to Egypt, Israel, India, New Zealand, Canada, and the U.S. spreading the dolphin's messages of Peace and Unity. And in eight different places she has gone, dolphins have turned up offshore to help guide her. As an example of just how psychic cetaceans are, Myers points to what happened on her trip to San Francisco last year (1980), where she and 95 other people went whale-watching. The Group was playing Japanese flute music and 15 whales suddenly showed up and surrounded the boat—more whales seen at one time in the area in over ten years! She even has a video-tape to prove the incident occurred.[5]

She says the key to inter-species communication is **Trust:** first a bond of trust must be established between the human and whatever animal he or she is working with, and this can only be done if the animal senses that there is **no fear or aggression** from the human. Myers goes on to state that by learning from the dolphins, especially their telepathy, mankind will have a better chance of rebuilding our planet into a world of Peace and Unity; quite literally a planet of One Universal Mind where techniques for a better life can be passed on telepathically so that all the world can advance simultaneously onto a higher plane of existence. She points to the documented study conducted by naturalist Lyall Watson as an example of how telepathy can change norms and improve life.[6]

Watson taught one three-year-old monkey out of a control group of 100 how to wash a plant root in water before eating it. Soon, the 99 other monkeys followed suit, which was expected. What was unexpected was that shortly thereafter, all the monkeys on the surrounding islands, too, began to wash their food; without any other contact than telepathy, a completely new mode of behavior was transferred or learned. Similar studies have been done teaching monkeys to swim, and, as with the other experiment, monkeys on nearby islands began to swim, too, through sheer telepathy or thought transference.[7]

Myers believes that this same kind of telepathic learning can be used among people to raise the level of consciousness on a planetary basis. And, indeed, she may well be right. Already scientists and parapsychologists have proven that telepathic powers and thought transference between people exist. One experiment proving the above gave amazing results when an individual was told to concentrate on transferring what he saw at an airport to the mind of another person several hundreds of miles away. This second person had no idea of the whereabouts of the first, but was told to draw the images that came to his mind. The picture the second man drew was astounding in that it included all the buildings in the right locations, along with several signs that were at the airport that the first man visited. Thus, the first man's eyes transferred the images accurately to the mind's eye of the second man, proving that we are all intricately linked through consciousness—one to another.

Further, by thinking positive, loving and peaceful thoughts, we can help influence and uplift not only ourselves and our neighbors, but ultimately the world as a whole as the "planetary consciousness network" continues to spread, linking person to person and country to country, until the entire world becomes One Giant Positive Thought of Peace and Love! The positive consequences that this peaceful and loving "consciousness network" effects are illustrated by a recent experiment done in Iowa. Here, a large group of people (about 1600) got together and meditated on and/or chanted the Lord's Name twice a day. Over this same period of time, Iowa experienced a 15% drop in its crime rate while that of the rest of the country continued to rise.[8] Imagine what would happen if there were such groups around the globe!

185

Thus the dolphins and whales surely can teach us a lot, not only about thought transference, telepathy, etc., but also about peace and love. For, in truth, what the cetaceans are doing in their lives is to put into practice what Lord Jesus taught humankind about nonviolence and "turning the other cheek." That is why, out of the hundreds of thousands of whales killed by man in the last century, only **six** have retaliated! Scientists have actually seen other dolphins teach their young the ethic of not hurting man.

So what lessons may we learn from the dolphins and whales? First they are saying that no matter what we do to them, they will not attack us in return; and secondly, that in order to survive on this planet, one cannot be hostile or aggressive. They have recognized the truth of the interdependency of all of us in this world. **We do need one another; not just human beings with human beings, but species with species.** They have transcended their individual egos and know that ego-tripping is self-destructive, not only to the individual, but to the species and, ultimately, to the entire ecosystem of the world.

Man, on the other hand, has yet to recognize this Truth: the same Truth that the Lord has been giving us from time immemorial. Our egos are still way out of control; more often than not, we use our intelligence for destructive rather than constructive and peaceful purposes. Warfare and the means of waging it are still seen as man's topmost priorities and achievements.

As Dr. John Lilly, scientist, brain specialist and dolphin investigator, points out:

> "Man has reached a point where he could eliminate everything on this planet. Apparently, he is willing to take that risk. I would conjecture that a much larger brain (such as that of dolphins and whales) wouldn't...
>
> "...man can no longer act as the experimenter **on** other species: he can only be an experimenter **with** other species. It is by the cooperative effort of two species working together that the really solid scientific data of the future will be generated. People will have to begin to think of cetacea as their peers, or even their superiors...
>
> "We humans tend to set ourselves apart, proud of our knowledge and ashamed of our ignorance, to the point that it gets a little silly. We act as though we were omniscient, omnipotent, omnipresent (in other words, as if **we** were God), and we sit on a mesa, in a very pious way, putting our

selves at the top of the heap of creation. Meanwhile, the universe goes on, ignoring us, and generates all it is going to generate, including us, in a very mysterious way...What makes us so sure man stands alone?"[9]

Clearly our own scientific research has proven that we don't stand alone; we are but **a part** of God's Creation, not the whole of it, and each part is interdependent on the others. It is only man's ego, which stems from ignorance, that refuses to recognize and accept this Truth. It is the ego, then, that clouds our vision and makes us feel this sense of separation from each other and from the rest of Creation, not to mention the Lord. It is in understanding and overcoming the ego that one attains to the Lord. So we must cease to be ignorant and seek to be nonviolent, for as Lord Buddha says:

"It is not by hurting creatures that a man becomes excellent. Only by nonviolence is excellence achieved... Nothing is more impure, O bhikkus (seekers of God) than ignorance. Cast aside ignorance, and all becomes pure."[10]

Chapter 3

THE EGO

Exactly what is the ego? How does one recognize it? And how does one overcome it? The ego can be defined as the sense of I-AM-NESS: "**I AM** great; **I AM** powerful; **I AM** better than others; **I AM, I AM, I, I,...**" The ego is the cause of that sense of separation from others and from God; it is the false identification with our body and individual mind and all of its extensions (**MY** family, **MY** possessions, **MY, MINE,...**), instead of the true identification with the Oneness of the Lord's Spirit that pervades all and is the same in all. It is the source of all sin, suffering and evil in the world.

The ego can be recognized by the emotions and actions that stem from it: greed, selfishness, lust, lies, anger, hatred, aggressiveness and hostility. When we are led away from God and Goodness and Truth, we know the ego is at work, controlling us instead of the other way around. It is characterized by desires and cravings in whatever form these may take. Passion is the ego's mirror image. And it all stems from forgetting God and thinking of worldly things and small, egoistic pleasures.

The mark of egoism is separation; it separates us from God, from one another, from the other manifestations of God's Creation. It pollutes the mind with prejudice, cruelty, slander, hatred and anger. All things that unite us for the good of the whole of humanity and the world are God-oriented; all things that divide us from each other and the rest of God's Creation are ego-oriented. Actions that are done out of selfishness are egoistic and bind us, attach us to the Wheel of Karma. All acts that are done, not for their fruits, but for the sake of the Lord, are liberating and purifying, thus helping to free us from the Wheel of Karma. Lord Buddha describes the ego and its attributes, as well as the virtues and joys of the one who controls his or her ego, as follows:

> "No fire like passion, no sickness like hate, no grief like the ego's, and no joy like peace...No snare like delusion, no torrent like craving...No disease like greed, no sorrow like desire. He who knows this is fit for Nirvana. No gift like health, no wealth like calm of mind, no faith like trust, no peace like Nirvana...

"Take the ego like an autumn lily—and snap it with your fingers! Proceed then on the path to Nirvana (Union with the Lord) with one who has reached as your guide."[1]

The great master Sri Ramana Maharshi has said that the ego is the cause of all evil and suffering in the world:

"Sin and evil of every kind are the result of egoism unrestrained by consideration for the injury caused to others or the deleterious (damaging) effect on the sinner's own character...All egoism has to be renounced...

" 'The Bliss of Self (God) is always yours and you will find it if you seek it earnestly. **The cause of your misery** is not in your outer life; **it is in you, as your ego.** You impose limitations on yourself and then make a vain struggle to transcend them. **All unhappiness is due to the ego. With it comes all your trouble...**

" 'If you would deny the ego and scorch it by ignoring it you would be free. If you accept it, it will impose limitations on you and throw you into a vain struggle to transcend them...To be the Self (God-Realized Soul) that you really are is the only means to realize the Bliss that is ever yours.' "[2]

The whole of spiritual discipline is aimed at controlling and eventually killing the ego within ourselves. For only with its death can we know our true Self and Realize the Divine within and without. All true spiritual teachers have reiterated this Truth, i.e., that the ego must be destroyed before one can truly claim full spiritual transformation. Sri Aurobindo has said that we must search for it in every nook and corner of our being, and then spear it and stab it. He also warns that the ego takes more and more subtle forms as one grows spiritually, and one must therefore be constantly on one's guard against it, especially when one advances spiritually and becomes more "sattvik" or pure. We must persevere until every last taint of the ego has been expunged from our being, and thus that sense of separation will vanish as a matter of course.

For most people, that sense of separation stays with them their entire life, and the only taste they get of true freedom from the ego comes when they leave behind their physical bodies at the moment of death. But one need not wait for physical death to experience ego-free living; on the contrary, the whole Goal of Life

189

is to kill the ego **before** the death of the body, and thus experience the Divine Life on Earth. When one succeeds in doing this, i.e., killing the ego and surrendering one's entire being to God, to become His Instrument to do with as He wills, one is, as Lord Jesus put it, **Reborn.**

The *Shrimad Bhagavatam* explains that man's wisdom is clouded by the five afflictions of ignorance, egotism, attraction, repulsion and fear of death, and that: "the highest state of (God) realization is attained only by those who through their overflowing devotion (to the Lord) succeed in shedding their ego, which obscures the souls."[3]

Guru Nanak explains this concept of devotion and surrender, and again emphasizes the necessity of destroying the ego in all its forms before one can actually become God's instrument:

> "I have heard of the system (of Hatha Yoga, where physical austerities are used as a means to realize God), but I do not believe that merely by outer restraints Yoga (Union with the Lord) can be attained. **What is needed is inner change...**
>
> "Total submission to the Divine Will is more important than all knowledge and virtues, and complete self-surrender is the way to secure Divine Grace...Total submission is entire freedom from subjection to the three Gunas (Modes of Nature or forms of the ego) and becoming an instrument of the divine will with a heart full to the brim with God. Then the sense of I-AM-NESS vanishes and also the sense of separation...
>
> "The world exists in I-AM-NESS, **in forgetting Him is the suffering.** By the Guru's instructions control of mind is obtained, and sense of I-AM-NESS removed...
>
> "The Holy Prophet (Mohammed) has said, 'Learn to die while living'...If the self (ego) dies when we are living, we follow the way of the Prophet (and all other great Teachers of Truth). It is only with the death of the separating self (ego) that we realize all is His."[4]

Sri Ramana Maharshi again speaks of the necessity of killing the ego in order to relieve all suffering and realize our true Self which is always One with God:

> "The way to get rid of grief is not to continue living. Kill

190

the griever, and who will then remain to grieve? The ego must die. That is the only way...All suffering is due to the false notion 'I am the body.' Getting rid of this is knowledge...So long as you consider yourself the body, you see the world as external to you. It is to you that the imperfection appears. God is perfection and His work is also perfection but you see it as imperfect because of your wrong identification with the body or the ego...

"You are not told to shut your eyes to the world, but only to see your Self (the God within you) first and then see the whole world as the Self (God Manifested). If you consider yourself as the body the world appears to be external; if you are the Self (God-Realized) the world appears as Brahman (God the Creator) manifested."[5]

In other words, when one realizes his true Self, then one sees nothing but God within and without. When one has reached this state of God-Realization, one has arrived at the Final Goal, even while the body remains. For, as those who have had death experiences have verified, we are not really the body; it is but a shell or outer garment for the soul which is cast away at the moment of physical death. Our real Self—our Soul—continues on, as It is immortal. If we seek to identify with It, the Soul, instead of the body, then we will realize God within and without and see that we are already at Home in His Heart, even before our bodies drop off. Sri Ramana explained this so simply when he was about to drop his own physical body. Several of his disciples were upset by his approaching physical death as they felt that he was abandoning them, and that they would be lost without his guidance. Sri Ramana said:

"You attach too much importance to the body...The Guru is not the physical form. So contact will remain even after his physical form vanishes...He who has earned the Grace of the Guru will undoubtedly be saved and never forsaken...

"They say that I am dying, but I am not going away. Where could I go? **I am here.**"[6]

Seeing All With An Equal Eye

When we realize that we are all already "Here," then we will literally see God everywhere, or as the *Gita* explains it, we will

191

see all with an equal eye, which is the essence of the teachings of all great masters:

> "The sage views with an equal eye a learned and humble Brahmin (priest) even as a dog, a cow, an outcaste or an elephant. The ones whose minds achieve equality overcome the cosmic world. God who is flawless is the same in all. So are those who live in God...
>
> "One who communes with the Godhead grows serene. He neither grieves nor craves, but **looking with an equal eye on all that lives,** attains deep love for me in the light of which he knows my multitudinous divinity and what I am in essence and thereafter he penetrates into my Being's core. Then, whatever he does, taking refuge in me, through my deep grace he wins the eternal Abode."[7]

When we see the Lord within all things, we realize that all life is part of the Divine and, therefore, sacred and must be treated as such. This includes all plants and animals, for they too are part of the One God. Baha'u'llah emphasized this Unity of the Godhead when he said:

> "He is really a believer in the Unity of God who recognizeth in each and every created thing the sign of the revelation of Him Who is the Eternal Truth, and not he who maintaineth that the creature is distinguishable (separate) from the Creator."[8]

The American Indians have always believed and recognized this Truth as is evidenced by their harmonious lifestyle in Nature. Black Elk, the great holy man of the Oglala Sioux, explains that:

> "We should understand well that all things are the works of the Great Spirit. We should know that He is within all things: the trees, the grasses, the rivers, the mountains, and all the four-legged animals, and the winged peoples; and even more important, we should understand that He is also above all these things and peoples. When we do understand all this deeply in our hearts, then we will fear, and love, and know the Great Spirit, and then we will be and act and live as He intends."[9]

Indeed, the American Indians did do just that! Through Kirlian photography, science has proven the truth the Indians knew, i.e., that all things are from God and have a soul. The aura or energy pattern we see around all living things is the Lord's Life Force, the soul that vivifies all and remains even when the physical parts are cut away. So God is within all and at the same time surrounds all. The idea is to be One with the Kingdom within so that we may also perceive His Kingdom without!

Plants, too, have consciousness as has been proven by science. One example of this proof is a series of experiments conducted by a polygraph expert. He attached his polygraph or lie-detector machine to certain plants in his home, and to his amazement, the plants gave a regular, rhythmic life reading similar to those of humans, i.e., heart beat, respiration, electrical brain waves, etc. What's more, the plants seemed to be able to read his thoughts and reacted to them. For example, whenever he thought of harming the plant itself or any other life form, the life readings of the plants showed a definite change. However, the plants seem to react the most whenever he would think or talk of love!

Other experiments have verified that plants do react to the emotions of people. In one experiment, a scientist set up two boxes of identical bean seeds. To one box, he sent only hate or negative vibrations, telling the seeds that they would never sprout, and that if they did, they would be twisted and stunted. To the other box of seeds, he gave only love and positive vibrations, telling the seeds to spring forth and grow toward the Light, to realize their full potential. And, indeed, the seeds reacted **exactly** as per the vibrations they were given. Those in the first box did not sprout at all, or were stunted or twisted in growth. Whereas those in the second box grew straight and tall, almost twice the height of those in the first!

Communication between plants has also been documented by scientists. Recent experiments have shown that when a plant is threatened by a particular pest, it will change its body chemistry so as to repel and/or discourage the insects from eating it, becoming harder to chew or less tasty. What's more, the same chemical change takes place not only in the individual plant involved, but in all plants near that individual, even before they are attacked by the pest. Trees have exhibited this same type of behavior, i.e., sending out warning signals of approaching danger. In logging areas where trees have been cut down, scientists have found that the trees left standing around the logged area still have a changed body chemistry when compared to those in an area where logging has not taken place. Thus, we can see that thought transference between plants is also a reality.[10]

The Earth is a Living Organism

These experiments confirm what Eastern philosophies and religions have taught for ages, i.e., that all matter and life is a form of consciousness and can be affected positively or negatively by consciousness. Even seemingly inert or "dead" matter houses veiled life. Proof of this was dramatically demonstrated by rocks brought back from the moon by NASA astronauts. These moon rocks have begun to grow—actually increasing in size, and scientists have no explanation for it! On the contrary, the government has been so worried about this inexplicable phenomenon that they finally contacted an American Indian medicine man or holy man—Mad Bear—to look at them![11]

The American Indians believe that this is proof of their traditional view of the Earth as a living, breathing organism. They claim, and rightly so, that the Earth is a living being with a consciousness and will of its own. They believe that what Christians call "The End Times" are in effect the long-awaited fulfillment of Indian prophecy of a period of transition, often called "the Day of Purification." As Rolling Thunder explains it:

> "When you have pollution in one place, it spreads all over. It spreads just as arthritis or cancer spreads in the body. The earth is sick now because the earth is being mistreated, and some of the problems that may occur, some of the natural disasters that might happen in the near future, are only the natural readjustments that have to take place to throw off sickness. A lot of things are on this land that don't belong here. They're foreign objects like viruses or germs. Now, we may not recognize the fact when it happens, but a lot of the things that are going to happen in the future will really be the earth's attempt to throw off some of these sicknesses. This is really going to be like fever or like vomiting, what you might call physiological adjustment.
>
> "It's very important for people to realize this. **The earth is a living organism, the body of a higher individual who has a will and wants to be well,** who is at times less healthy or

194

more healthy, physically and mentally. People should treat their own bodies with respect. It's the same thing with the earth. Too many people don't know that when they harm the earth they harm themselves, nor do they realize that when they harm themselves they harm the earth...

"It's not easy for you (white) people to understand these things because understanding is not knowing the kind of facts that your books and teachers talk about. I can tell you that **understanding begins with love and respect.** It begins with respect for the Great Spirit, and the Great Spirit is the life that is in all things—all the creatures and the plants and even the rocks and the minerals. All things—and I mean **all** things—have their own will and their own purpose; this is what is to be respected.

"Such respect is not a feeling or an attitude only. It's a way of life. Such respect means that we never stop realizing and never neglect to carry out our obligation to ourselves and our environment."[12]

So, then, this period of tribulation/purification is a cleansing, a period of transition during which all that is impure and imperfect will be thrown off, cleansed and purified so that the perfect Perfection, the Divine Life on Earth may be a reality. Sri Aurobindo explains that what is to happen and is, indeed, already happening is but the next logical evolutionary step of the unveiling of Spirit in Material Nature:

"Life evolves out of Matter, Mind out of Life, because they are already involved there: Matter is a form of veiled Life, Life a form of veiled Mind. May not Mind be a form and veil of a higher power, the Spirit, which would be supramental in its nature? Man's highest aspiration would then only indicate the gradual unveiling of the Spirit within, the preparation of a higher life upon earth...(where) Matter will reveal itself as an instrument of the manifestation of Spirit..."[13]

The great question concerning this period of transition is whether the cleansings that are to happen will occur inwardly or outwardly, because the more inward change there is, the less need there will be for outer devastations. In other words, the more people who realize that we must each individually start to cleanse our bodies, minds and hearts, and change our present wasteful, polluting and egotistical way of living to one that is harmonious with God's Laws and with the rest of Nature, the fewer natural disasters will take place. For, as both Sri Aurobindo and Rolling Thunder have pointed out, the kind of love and respect we must inculcate within ourselves must manifest itself outwardly as a way of life—the Divine Life on Earth.

This way of life would be one in which all our activities, on both the micro and macro level, would be in harmony with the Natural Order of things, with respect for one another and all of Nature. This does not mean that we have to go back to living in huts, etc. But it does mean that we have to use our technology **in the right way,** for example, using natural, non-polluting and renewable sources of energy, instead of using those, such as nuclear power, that threaten the very existence of all life on the planet.

If we do not heed the signs of the times, if we do not change our wasteful, polluting and shortsighted ways, we will condemn ourselves to experiencing the greatest tribulations, the greatest natural upheavals and catastrophes that man has ever seen. The more who do change voluntarily, the more these catastrophic blows will be cushioned. God's Protection will surround those who do change and turn to Him, living pure and righteous lives, and encouraging others to do so by their example.

Those who refuse to change voluntarily will be forced to change in due course, or be obliterated. As Edgar Cayce explained it: "Those that have gradually forgotten God entirely have been eliminated...,"[14] and will continue to be so, especially during this period of transition. So the choice is really ours: change voluntarily and be protected from the coming disasters, or stubbornly refuse to change, thus being forced to change through suffering. For change we must as it is the order of the day! As Lao Tzu put it, "Rigidity and hardness (inability to bend and change) are companions of death. Softness and tenderness (the ability to bend and flow with things, the ability to change) are companions of life."[15]

One may raise the question, "Are all of these predicted catastrophes really going to occur? And even if they do, why do I need to worry about them now? The world has gone on as it is for centuries. Why should I believe that these things will occur in my lifetime? And, even if they do, why not wait until I see the start of these tribulations and then change, for surely I'll have ample time to do so."

The answer to all of these questions is that **the changes have already begun, the tribulations are already with us;** they will only intensify with time and come more and more rapidly, like a snowball rolling downhill, gaining size and momentum as it continues to roll. We can wait, if we wish. But the longer we wait, the bigger the snowball gets, the faster it rolls and the harder it will hit!

Plus, there is another reason to change now: **this is the age of Instant Karma.** In the past, the karmic effects of our actions may have taken years, decades, even lifetimes to catch up with us. Not so in this age; in this age, the karmic effects of our actions—both good and bad—are being felt almost immediately. Hence, we haven't much time to dilly-dally around deciding when and how and where to start changing. We must start **NOW** for the cleansings have already begun, as we will see in the remaining chapters of this book. We will first explore the prophecies of the American Indians as most had to do with the changes that are already starting in Nature, and with the peoples who are living in the Indian's native Homeland—America. We will then correlate these prophecies with those of Jesus Christ, Revelations, Edgar Cayce, Nostradamus, Hinduism, and all other relevant materials, proving that almost all, if not all of them have already been fulfilled!

Chapter 4

AMERICAN INDIAN PROPHECIES

The prophecies of the American Indians as well as the secrets of the "Earth Spirit" are kept by the older "medicine" or holy men and women who have, generation to generation, passed them on to younger tribal members who have held fast to their spiritual ways and have rejected the values of the present technological society and world around them. Initially the American Indians were willing to share all of their abundant knowledge of the spiritual and natural worlds with the European immigrants. For example, some of our best medicines were known to the American Indians long before they were "discovered" by Western scientists. Turpentine, quinine, camphor, cocaine, aspirin, and even penicillin were used by the Indians ages before white men started to synthesize them.

But when it became apparent that the Europeans would do whatever it took in order to steal everything away from the Indians, the traditions as well as the secrets of the earth and "spirit world" were hidden away and preserved, some in books, others by word of mouth. Recently, these prophecies and some of the Indians' secrets have been made available to the general public because certain signs have shown the Indians that we are so near to the "Great Day of Purification," which is the time to which these prophecies have pointed.

The American Indian traditions and prophecies have been preserved primarily by the Hopi peoples, "Hopi" meaning "Peace." However, once a year representatives from all Indian tribes come together in the Hopi country to bring out, read, discuss, and interpret the sacred teachings and prophecies.

According to the Hopis, in the beginning, the Great Spirit gave His Life-Plan of Harmony and Balance to two brothers, one of whom was light-skinned and a great inventor, and the younger of whom was red-skinned and understood the secrets of Nature and the Earth. The Great Spirit said that in the future, when the white brother returned to the Broad Land (America), it could mean the beginning of the Great Purification leading to the end of this world or age, **IF** the Life-Plan had not been followed exactly. The Great Spirit stated that when the white brother returned to his red brother's land he was to be welcomed **IF** he brought the sacred symbol with him. The sacred symbol was a cross within a circle. But if he returned with the cross alone, the Indians "should beware and know that the Great Purification was not far off. The missionaries brought only the cross when they came, and the white brothers who followed brought only oppression. They knew nothing of the sacred circle"—which represented the Unity of all life.[1]

The Destroyer's Prophecy

Thus, the Hopi and all other Indians became wary of the white man because his failure to bring with him or at least recognize the sacred symbol of Unity meant the fulfillment of the Destroyer's Prophecy instead. This prophecy had a dual meaning regarding destruction. First, it meant that the white men would destroy everything the Indians held sacred: i.e., their land, the animals, their religion and culture as well as decimating the Indian peoples themselves. Secondly, it meant that these destroyers would ultimately be destroyed themselves when Jesus as the Lost White Brother returned to save the Indians. The prophecy reads as follows:

> "The time would come when they (the Indians) would be overcome by a strange people. They (the Indians) would be forced to develop their land and lives according to the dictates of a new ruler, or else they would be treated as criminals and punished. But they were not to resist. They were to wait for the person who would deliver them.
>
> "This person was the lost white brother, Pahana, who would return...deliver them from their persecutors, and work out with them a new and universal brotherhood of man."[2]

The Christian missionaries, for their part, helped to fulfill this Destroyer's Prophecy as they forced the Indians to convert to **their** form of Christianity. Thus, the horrors of the Spanish Inquisition (during which 300,000 Europeans were burned alive because of "heresy" for threatening the power and authority of the Catholic Church—300,000 people being a lot of people in those days, compared to today's world population) were visited upon the American Indians. An example of this is recorded in Oraibi where, in 1655, Friar Salvadore de Guerra punished a Hopi for "an act of idolatry" by thrashing him publicly until he was covered in blood, and then poured burning turpentine over him.[3]

But the Destroyer's Prophecy was not completely fulfilled with the arrival of the Spanish. It took the birth of the United States as a nation and its government's subsequent actions to do this. For the Spanish and Mexican governments had recognized the Hopis' ancient tradition of common ownership of the land. Only the U.S. forced them to give up this system, which had been the whole basis of their religious and social structure of land tenure, replacing it with an arbitrary allotment system, their purpose being to break up the Hopis' lands and reservations, thereby destroying their way of life and culture, **thus fulfilling the Destroyer's Prophecy.**

The Hopi's Petroglyph

The Hopi prophecies are carved on a rock in Black Mesa in the "Four Corners Area" of Southwestern, U.S.A., and date back at least 2000 years. The petroglyph on the rock shows the Great Spirit pointing to the Spiritual Path. The upper path is that of the White Man as well as those Indians that have adopted the white man's ways. The lower path is the spiritual path of the Hopi. The two paths are joined by a vertical line which represents the first contact between the whites and the Hopis. Close to this vertical line are two large circles which represent World Wars I and II. Remember, these were drawn on the rock 2000 years ago when no one dreamed that there could be such wars!

A third circle follows and represents the Great Purification which we are approaching, after and/or during which the Great Spirit will return, the Earth will be renewed with plenty of food and water, and all will be well. The signs representing this New World all lie on the line representing the Spiritual Path of the Hopi. During and after the Great Purification, the line representing the white man and all who follow his ways becomes very erratic and eventually fades away altogether.[4]

The Hopi were given three signs that were to signal the approach of the Great Purification and trigger the release of certain prophecies and teachings to the general public in a last ditch effort to avert disaster. The three signs were the swastika, the sun and the color red. As with the rest of the universe, the principles of yin and yang, positive and negative, are at play with these three symbols. Originally, the swastika rotated in a clockwise direction

200

and was a spiritual symbol of both the American Indians and the India Indians. It represented the universal life-force emanating from the Great Spirit. The reversal of the swastika's direction by Hitler and his Nazis accurately portrayed the destructive forces that he unleashed, going against the flow of life and disrupting the universal harmony.

The sun represents the East, the seat of spiritual knowledge, and the light and warmth that that knowledge sheds, producing a conducive environment for spiritual growth. Spiritual knowledge from the East was to come in the last days to help the world in its transition to a higher plane of life. The negative aspect of this sign culminated in the power of the nation-state of Japan, "land of the rising sun," whose alliance with Nazi Germany wrought more death and destruction than the world had ever seen, ending with the fiery deaths of hundreds of thousands of Japanese themselves.

The last sign—the color red—had two positive aspects: 1- it represented the teachings and truths of the Red Man himself, teachings which would hopefully help the world avert catastrophe; and 2- the Red Hat Buddhist sects of the East. The Buddhists were to bring great spiritual wisdom and knowledge to the West, the land of the Red Man, and establish centers of spiritual learning and discipline. A Buddhist prophecy concerning this event dates back to the Eighth Century when Padma Sambhava, the great spiritual master of the original Red Hat sect, said: "When the iron bird flies, and horses run on wheels, the Tibetan people will be scattered like ants across the world. And the Dharma (Divine Law) will come to the land of the Red Man."[5]

If the teachings of the Buddhists and Indians were heeded, then the world would be able to make a smooth transition into the New Age. But if they were rejected, the negative aspects of the color red would manifest themselves. The negative aspects of death, destruction and atheism can be seen in world communism, red being the color associated with communism. But the positive aspects of the color red have also been manifesting themselves. In the last few decades, Buddhist monks have been spokesmen and active participants, first as leaders of the Peace Movement against the Vietnam War, and more recently, as vocal advocates for the Nuclear Freeze Movement. Further, is it any coincidence that a television series based on the Dharma (Divine Law) of Buddhist philosophy became popular in the 1970's? Remember *Kung Fu?*

Thus, **both Hopi and Buddhist prophecies** of the Dharma coming to and being taught in the Red Man's Homeland—America—**were fulfilled.** Interestingly enough, the Buddhist monk who was the main character of the television series was named "Kane," which was one of the names given by the American Indians to Jesus, the Pale Prophet!

The Gourd of Ashes

The fourth and final great sign of the imminent approach of the Day of Purification was the discovery and use of atomic power as a weapon. According to the prophecies, man would invent a "gourd of ashes" which, when dropped from the sky, would boil the oceans and burn the land so severely that nothing would be able to grow for many years. The invention and use of this weapon, which is, of course, the atomic bomb, was to be the final signal to the American Indians that certain teachings were to be released to the general public to warn the world that "the third and final event could bring an end to all life unless people correct themselves and their leaders in time."[6]

The time of the Purification is foretold in a song that the Hopi have sung during certain ceremonies for centuries. It was sung in 1914, just before World War I, in 1940 before World War II, and again in 1960, the date to which many point as being the beginning of the last phase of the End Times. The song describes the disunity, corruption and hatred that are spreading all over the world.

Other signs pointing to the Great Day of Purification included:

> "...the recent manipulations of governments in the Far East (Vietnam, Laos, and Cambodia are examples)...the creation of the United Nations headquarters on Manhattan Island (the land of the Iroquois)...moon landings (such as those of the United States in the last two decades), space stations (such as the Russians' Salyut Seven), and the increasing ecological desecration of the continent."[7]

These desecrations include: "...paths in the sky. The paths are airplanes (vapor trails and air lanes)...cobwebs in the air. These are the power lines (giant transmission lines span the desert from Black Mesa to L.A. and Vegas)," etc.[8] These and other desecrations of Nature will cause bizarre weather patterns, earthquakes, volcanic eruptions, droughts, etc. Rolling Thunder explains that:

> "The ultimate hope and help for the oppressed native peoples, say the prophecies, is to come from the light-skinned people themselves, from the sons and daughters of the oppressors. The day would come, it was written, when children of the white man would begin to dress like Indians, when they would begin to wear long hair and headbands as the Hopi do, and these people would be the new friends of the Indians."[9]

This, too, was fulfilled when, in the 1960's and '70's, the children of the oppressors began to wear long hair, headbands, braids, Indian-style clothing, befriended the Indians, and learned from them. Remember, **all of the above prophecies were prophesied over 2000 years ago!**

The Blue Star

The time of the Great Purification is not far off, according to the Hopi, because all prophecies have been fulfilled. It will come, they say, when a blue star, far off and yet invisible, will make its appearance. **This prophecy, too, has already been fulfilled** because in 1981 a super-massive blue star was discovered by astronomers. The star is 3500 times the size of our own sun and is the biggest star known to man. As a matter of fact, the discovery of the blue giant has upset scientists' previous beliefs and theories about stars. It had been believed that a heavenly body of such immense proportions was impossible because it could not form, or could not survive even if it did form. Astronomers will now have to formulate new theories on star formation!

The star itself puts out an incredible amount of energy—in one second, as much energy as our sun does in five years![10] Thus, one of the last Hopi prophecies of the End Times has been fulfilled!

As stated earlier, because of the signs of the End Times manifesting themselves over the last few years, the American Indians have made available certain spiritual teachings and secrets of the Earth Spirit. Most have had to do with the Oneness of all life upon Earth and the interdependency of all creatures of Nature, including man. However, not all of these secrets have been revealed, for in this age of technology, man has yet to harmonize his being and way of living with that of the rest of Nature. He is still caught up with the "shadows" of things, or as the *Shrimad Bhagavatam* puts it, he has failed to or even denies the realities behind things, and, thus, he deals with the shells of things rather than their real substance. Until all humanity starts to live in accordance with the Plan of the Great Spirit (God), in Balance and Harmony with Nature and each other, certain teachings and secrets cannot be revealed. For they might be used for detrimental or egoistic purposes, rather than for the good of the whole of the Earth. As Rolling Thunder explains:

> "As long as so many people accept this modern-day competition, willing to profit at the cost of others and believing it's a good thing; as long as we continue the habit of exploitation, using other people and other life, using Nature in selfish, unnatural ways; as long as we have hunters in these hills drinking whiskey and killing other life for entertainment, spiritual techniques and powers are potentially dangerous. The medicine men and traditional Indians who know many things know also that many things are not to be revealed at this time."[11]

As Jesus Christ said, "Do not give dogs what is holy; and do not throw your pearls before swine, lest they trample them underfoot and turn to attack you!"[12]

The Prophecies of the Pale Prophet

In truth, what the American Indians are doing is following the instructions of the Pale Prophet who foretold the coming of the Europeans to the Americas, even naming the year that they would arrive. He instructed the Indians to write down their history, spiritual teachings and techniques of healing in books, and to take these books and hide them until He returned and helped to usher in the New Age. For He foresaw the burning of the Indians' sacred books, first by the Aztecs, and then by the white invaders. And, indeed, the Spanish did burn all the libraries of the Indians as they moved from the city to city, plundering and pillaging.

The Pale Prophet foretold the fate of the Indians down through the cycles of history. He foresaw the coming of the Aztecs, their conquering of the Toltecs, forcing a return to the abominable practice of human sacrifice, which He had outlawed. He predicted civil wars among different tribes of Indians. As a result of these wars, the Indian nations who turned their back on His warnings to live in Peace or die in war, would fight one another, thereby separating and weakening the Indian race as a whole. Hence, when the white man came, he would find the Indians weak from civil warfare and, therefore, easy to conquer.

Of course, these civil wars were miniscule in size, numbers and brutality when compared to the civil wars of Europe or of the United States. For the American Indians sought only to subdue their rivals, not massacre them. The stronger would merely "touch" or cut the long hair-braids of the weaker as a sign of victory, rather than cutting off their heads! Scalping was unknown among the Indians; it was introduced to this country by the Dutch who paid bounties for every Indian scalp brought in.

As mentioned before, the Pale Prophet or Jesus also prophesied the coming of the white man and the fate of the Indians to this day. Below is a synopsis of His prophecies regarding the Europeans' arrival and the signs of the End Times:

"He repeated the warning given at Tula (sacred city of the Toltecs) against the deeds of the Sacrificers (the Aztecs), and foretold the invasion of White Man...

" 'Further off there is another invasion. In ships many bearded men are coming from across the Sunrise Ocean (the Atlantic)...I see these men taking the Broad Land (America)...They do not respect our trees of cedar. They are but hungry, unenlightened children...

" 'Would that I could speak to those bearded farmers! I have tried. They do not hear me. They go on their way like spoiled children...'

"He repeated again the description: the suits of shining metal, the rods which make much noise and kill at a distance. Then He bowed His head in silence...again He began,

" 'Once I had great hope for these people, for I saw them kneel and kiss the sweet earth, and I saw the shadow of the Great Cross which they carried with them. Yea, I had great faith in these people. Now I must warn you against them.

" 'Carry your great books into the jungles. Place your histories deeply in caverns where none of these men can find them. Nor do you bring them back to the sunlight until the

War-Cycle is over. For children of War are these bearded strangers...They seek naught but the golden metal as if that would buy them passage into the Isles of the Blessed.

" 'They have but one love and that is for weapons. Ever more horrible are these weapons, until they reach for the one which is ultimate. Should they use that, there will be no forgiveness in that vale where there is no turning. Using such a weapon to make man over, is reaching into space for the God-Head. These things are not for man's decision, nor should man presume to think for all things, and thus hurl mockery at the Almighty. Woe to those who do not listen! There are lamps beyond that which you are burning; roads beyond this which you are treading; worlds beyond the one you are seeing. Be humble before the might of the Great Hand which guides the stars within their places. There are many lodges in My Father's Kingdom for it is more vast than Time, and more eternal.

" 'Keep hidden your books, oh my children, all during the Cycle of Warring Strangers. The day will come when they will be precious.

" 'For five full cycles of the Dawn Star (approximately 500 years), the rule of the warring strangers will go on to greater and greater orgies of destruction...Are these bearded ones who are still my children going down war's trail to final destruction, and thus give the last human victory in death to (war)?...Hark well to all I have taught you. Return not to the Sacrificers. Their path will lead to the Last Destruction. Know that the end will come in five full cycles, for five, the difference between the Earth's number and that of the Gleaming Dawn Star, is the number of these children of warfare...(Presently, the U.S.A. has 50 states; its flag contains 50 five-pointed stars; and its center for war planning and strategy is the Pentagon—a five-sided building, where five-starred generals plot strategies for war, five being the highest number of stars a general can receive. The Russians, too, have a five-pointed star on their flag, and the Chinese have five five-pointed stars on theirs...Coincidence?)

" 'Then the heavens growled with reverberations which shook the mountain like a rabbit. A flash of white light crashed beside Him and cracked across the night's darkness. Behold! The old heaven and earth were swept away, as if the cycle He had been seeing was smashed, and He looked into another.

"'The heavens parted and a rising gold sun shone down...The Man (Pale Prophet) was lifted beyond the cold earth. No longer He saw the Age of Destruction. Gone was the horrible Age of Warfare. He was looking beyond the Age of Carnage!...

"'Walk with me through this Age of the Future...Gone is the shadow of fear and suffering, for man no longer sacrifices, and he has outgrown the wars of his childhood. Now he walks full-statured toward his destiny—into the Golden Age of Learning.

"'Carry this vision on through the ages, and remember Kate-Zahl (Quetzal-Coatl), the Prophet.' "[13]

The Cycle of "Warring Strangers"

The American Indians, as well as other ancient peoples, view Venus, the Dawn Star, as a very important heavenly body. As a matter of fact, no North American Indian tribe will make war or go into battle while Venus is shining.[14] Venus or the Dawn Star is also associated with the Pale Prophet, and, interestingly enough, is a name given to Jesus Christ as well—the Morning or Dawn Star. Finally, the recognition of Venus as a star of importance was passed on from the Sumerians to the Babilonians and on to the Jews, who made it the Star of David, whose symbol of two opposing and interlacing pyramids is also the ancient Hindu symbol for the Heart Chakra, the seat of Divine Love, of which Jesus, like Krishna, has been so closely associated. (See Part I, Chapter 5— Chakra Illustration)

The American Indians and the Pale Prophet often measured time according to the Venus Calendar. One full cycle of Venus is approximately 100 years. Thus, the five Full Cycles of which the Pale Prophet spoke are approximately 500 years. Hence, the "Warring Strangers" or the White Man's rule over this land, accompanied with its orgies of destruction, would last 500 years.[15] If one figures from the date that Columbus first landed in the West Indies—1492—the Cycle of Destruction would end in 1992. Of course, Columbus' landing may well have come somewhere **after** the start of the first full cycle. So, **the Age of Destruction is surely due to end at any time from right now to the end of this century!**

This timing also coincides with the prophecies of Edgar Cayce, Nostradamus, the Hopis, the Great Pyramid (Cheops) of Giza in Egypt, and others who all say that this present age of chaos and destruction will come to an end somewhere within the next few years, with the full transformation into the New Age of Enlightenment being completed **before** the turn of this century. Hence, we surely are in the End Times of this system of things, a system whose death throes will, and have already begun to convulse the world in a way never before seen in recorded human history.

Again the Pale Prophet spoke of "the ultimate weapon." Further, He said that there would be no forgiveness for those who use such a weapon. He said that it was a weapon that reached in space toward the Godhead itself and threw mockery at the face of the Lord. Remembering that the root word for "uranium"— "Ourania"—is the same as that for "heavens"—meaning "celestial powers"—it is easy to see that, once again, the discovery of atomic weapons was the turning point in human history in terms of the changing of the ages. The whole purpose of atomic/nuclear weapons is the destruction of the celestial powers, or powers of creation. Further, naming the first atomic explosion "The Trinity," which is the religious term used to describe the Godhead, surely was throwing mockery at the face of God!

The recent experiments with DNA and gene splicing, selective breeding, artificial insemination, test-tube babies, and cloning also bode poorly for the respect or lack of it man gives God. We have presumed to think for all things, redoing life itself, as it were, disrupting the harmonious flow of God's Creation and perverting the purposes He gave to each created thing. As Rolling Thunder mentioned earlier, each and every created thing has a purpose and a mission to fulfill for the Creator of all. When man interferes with that mission through ignorance or arrogance, and/or knowingly perverts that purpose, he disrupts the whole Balance and Harmony of Nature, setting off a chain reaction of catastrophes which will, in the end, blow up in his own face. As Saint Rolling Thunder explains:

> "The establishment people think they have a pretty advanced civilization here. Well, technically maybe they've done a lot, although we know of civilizations that have gone much further in the same direction. In most respects this is a

pretty backward civilization. The establishment people seem completely incapable of learning some of the basic truths.

"The most basic principle of all is that of not harming others, and that includes all people and all life and all things. It means not controlling or manipulating others, not trying to manage their affairs. It means not going off to some other land and killing people over there— not for religion or politics or military exercises or any other excuse. No being has the right to harm or control any other being. No individual or government has the right to force others to join or participate in any group or system or force others to go to school, to church or to war. Every being has the right to live his own life in his own way.

"Every being has an identity and a purpose. To live up to his purpose, every being has the power of self-control, and that's where spiritual power begins. When some of these fundamental things are learned, the time will be right for more to be revealed and spiritual power will come again to this land."[16]

The prophecies and secrets that have recently been revealed were done so as a result of instructions left by the Pale Prophet (Jesus) who told the Indians the signs of His return. When these signs were seen, the Indians were to release certain teachings and prophecies to help pave the way for His return and the dawning of the New Era of Peace and Harmony. As we have seen, the signs He left have been fulfilled. Another sign given to them was that the ancient city of Tula, the sacred city of the Toltecs would be unearthed. The rediscovery and unearthing of this city was to coincide with the start of the Great Purification period. Around 1960, the ancient site of Teotihuacan, which many experts believe is actually the site of ancient Tula, was fully unearthed by archaeologists.[17] Hence, **this prophetic sign given almost 2000 years ago has also been fulfilled.** Indeed, the American Indians started to release their sacred teachings and prophecies around 1960, in accordance with the Pale Prophet's or Jesus' instructions.

The similarities of these teachings and prophecies with those of Revelations, Jesus Christ, Nostradamus, Edgar Cayce, and other Eastern and Western mystics and religions are astounding, as we will see. The parts of the prophecies that interest us today are those that point to the Day of Purification and Punishment of which the Pale Prophet foretold. As Rolling Thunder explained before, it is a time when the Earth will throw off all impurities and unnatural things that are polluting and choking it. It will be a time of great natural upheavals and disasters, a time that is already dawning upon us. The Indians have been preparing for this time in their religious ceremonies for centuries. Their prophecies foretold of the gradual breakdown of the natural cycles of the Earth due to man's interference. The Indians fear that the devastation and polluting of the world has gone so far, especially in the "Spiritual Center" of the Hopi Country, that the entire planet may be destroyed. If people do not start to listen to and follow the teachings of the Great Spirit, they fear that everything will die:

> "Says one Hopi elder, 'If the white man would stop trying to teach us Christianity and begin to listen to what the Great Spirit taught the Hopis, then everything would get back in harmony with Nature. As it is the white man is destroying this country.' "[18]

The Indians hope that the white man will soon heed their warnings, and learn from and use their system of ethics and vision. Otherwise, a complete breakdown in Nature's cycles and the energy systems that hold Mother Earth together is inevitable. This viewpoint, i.e., that the Earth is so polluted and the Natural Balance so upset that it must and will be righted in a violent way, "coincides with the claims of ecologists and scientists who believe that imbalance in Nature has passed the point of no return."[19] But, in truth, the Indians do not fear this day, rather they look upon it with hopeful anticipation as it will bring in the New Era, the New Age, **the New Fifth World.**

Chapter 5

THE FOUR WORLDS OF THE HOPIS

According to Hopi tradition, we have already had three worlds prior to the present one. Their view of the genesis of Earth is strikingly similar to that of the Bible's—the void, the Creator being alone, creating His Nephew or Son—LOGOS—and creating all things from Sound. The first world with which man was blessed was one in Perfect Harmony, in total balance; a world of spiritual purity in which all life was recognized as being a part of the One Whole which is God or the Great Spirit. The four colors of man lived harmoniously, not only with each other, but with all of Nature, where man saw in each created thing a reflection of his own true Self. In other words, it was literally the Garden of Eden of which the Bible speaks.

Problems arose when man's ego started to creep in: first he started to see and emphasize the differences between himself and other animals, instead of seeing the similarities and the One Spirit in all. Next he started noticing the differences between himself and other men, and thus, division and strife, warfare and disharmony began. The corruption of man reached such intensity that the Lord decided to destroy this first world. Hence, He sent fire down upon the earth and destroyed this first world, saving a few "chosen people" who had not abandoned His teachings of Oneness as His "seeds" to plant and repopulate the New World with humanity.

These "chosen ones" had been directed to safety by His Son, who came to them with a sound that was like that of a mighty wind or the roar of many waters—the exact same description given by St. John in Revelations of the sound of Jesus' voice—who led them by **inner vision** to their sanctuary. As in Noah's time, the corrupt people ridiculed these spiritual ones for listening to the Inner Voice and leaving all they had behind them. But, in the end, it was these spiritual ones who had the last laugh!

The second world was exactly the opposite of the first with the great waters and land transposed from the previous one. In this world, man was not allowed to live with the animals, and instead lived in villages and small towns. Everything the people needed was provided for them by Nature/God, but again man's ego got in and greed took over. The people started wanting things that they did not need: greed crept in and overshadowed spirituality. Hence, the Lord again decided to destroy these ungrateful and greedy humans, this time by ice. He shifted the earth's axis and caused an Ice Age which destroyed the ego-ridden people. But, as with the first world, He spared certain spiritual individuals, protecting them and giving them a New World in which to live.

This new third world was not as beautiful as the first two, but it did contain all that humanity needed in order to survive. But again, the ego slipped in, and with it, not only greed this time, but also lust. The people began to overpopulate the Earth in such large numbers that they took away the living spaces from the rest of God's Creation. Hence God's Divine Plan of Balance was disrupted. Because of the number of people, great cities grew, attended with crime and corruption. Eventually the competition for living space got so severe that great wars broke out amongst the people. Sex and materialism, lust and greed, two of the ego's guises had again caused the downfall of man.

This time the Lord chose to destroy humanity with water—the Great Flood of Noah's time, which is recorded throughout the world by different cultures and religions, and has been verified as having been an actual event in history, according to scientists and geologists, as we will see. God saved the righteous this time by putting them in a "hollow reed" that floated above the flood-waters—a boat or ark similar to that of Noah's, which, by the way, was recently discovered on the slopes of Mount Ararat in Turkey.

Scientific Evidence of Former Worlds

Besides the rediscovery of Noah's ark (which in and of itself should be enough physical evidence of the Great Flood and the fact that there have been catastrophic earth changes in the past that have swept away "old" worlds and brought in "new" ones), is there any other scientific evidence to support the Hopis' legend of three previous worlds? Indeed there is!

Scientific journals and publications, such as the *International Geophysical Year*, abound with information that points conclusively to the existence of previous worlds **and** to their destruction. For example, scientific data has shown that the world's oceans rose dramatically in excess of 200 feet 7000 years ago—the time of Noah's flood. Data includes shells, marine fossils and salt deposits from sea water that have been found atop the highest mountains in the world—the Himalayas—as well as other mountain chains.

Further, archaeologists have unearthed massive grave sites where the fossilized remains of literally millions of animals, both tropical and arctic, including bison, mastadon, horses, etc., have all been deposited in one place, along with huge uprooted trees. Examples of this phenomena can be seen in the United Kingdom, Europe, Dinosaur National Park in Northwestern Colorado, and also stream valleys near Fairbanks, Alaska. The fossilized remains of whales have also been found several hundreds of feet above sea level, hundreds of miles inland, in several parts of North America.[1] Plus, archaeologists and geologists state that they have uncovered what seems to be evidence of successive cycles of human civilizations in excavations in the Middle East. Digging deep in the earth, the excavations reveal civilization after civilization, each with a layer of sedimentary rock and mud—sometimes several feet thick—separating it from the previous one, as if each old civilization was buried before the new one could emerge.

The powerful Earth-watching radar carried aboard the space shuttle Columbia a year ago has added further evidence of the above. In a recently published issue of *Science Magazine*, the results of a study conducted by scientists from the U.S. Geological Survey in Flagstaff, Arizona, the University of Arizona, the Egyptian Geological Survey and Mining Authority in Cairo and the Jet Propulsion Lab of Pasadena, California were made available to the public. The report states that the super-powerful radar revealed ancient buried riverbeds in what is now the driest part of Egypt. Evidence points to human occupation of the area dating back 200,000 years or more. The discovery of the buried stream channels, riverbeds with broad flood plains, etc., was a surprise to the scientists as the area is today one of the most barren, featureless expanses of desert-land on Earth. Its discovery may help explain some of the legends about the area, which was supposed to have been the breadbasket of the world at one time.[2]

How could the Earth be changed so dramatically so quickly? Many scientists believe that a shift in the poles may account for the drastic changes. One explanation is that the Earth could have been struck by a giant asteroid or meteorite (perhaps like the one in Nebuchadnezzar's dream that hit the political beast on its feet, causing it to crash to pieces!), shifting the Earth on its axis and causing dramatic floods and other upheavals in Nature in its wake. Evidence for pole-shifting as a result of some giant asteroid colliding with the Earth abounds, and has given scientists new theories on how the Earth's present continents were formed, as well as explanations for the sudden demise of the dinosaurs on Earth.

Klaus J. Schulz of Washington University stated that he has found evidence of a 1700-mile-wide crater beneath the forests and lakes of central Canada. He and other scientists believe that the crater was formed when a giant asteroid the size of the state of Delaware smashed into the Earth aeons ago, setting off volcanic activity, earthquakes and other natural upheavals which helped to form the continents of today.[3]

Other scientific researchers have found an underground layer of an exotic metal—iridium—in eastern Montana. The metal is extremely rare in the Earth's crust, but is found in abundance in matter from outer space. The discovery of the underground layer of iridium supports the theory that a giant meteorite or asteroid, with an estimated diameter of two miles and weight of at least 50 billion tons, hit the Earth some 65 million years ago, thus transporting large amounts of the rare metal to the Earth. The deposits of the metal have been found in layers of the Earth's crust that date back to the time of the dinosaur extinctions. Alongside the iridium are vast deposits of now-extinct, one-celled marine animals and one to ten billion tons of tektites. Tektites are formed by cooled droplets of rock that were melted by the shock of a meteorite impact. The impact of the asteroid and/or meteorite could have sent up a cloud of dust that could affect temperatures dramatically and block out sunlight for months, thereby killing off the vast amounts of vegetation the dinosaurs needed in order to survive.

The impact also could have caused the Earth to shift on its axis. Proof of this theory abounds, too. For example, in the frozen lands of Northeastern Siberia, as well as in other areas encircling the North Pole, quick-frozen or "freeze-dried" bodies of mammoth herds have been found along with vast amounts of vegetation, much of it of a tropical variety, some of the mammoths actually having buttercups still in their mouths! Fossil trees and coral reefs similar to those found in warm tropical areas today have been found only 8°15′ from the cold North Pole! And in one of the ancient tombs of Egypt, the constellations and zodiac of the night sky are shown completely reversed. This correlates to ancient

By permission of Johnny Hart and Field Enterprises, Inc.

writings of various cultures and religions that state that the sun used to rise in the West and set in the East![4]

Even today the Earth is being continually pounded by meteorites, although most are too small to cause much damage. However, scientists are concerned about the possibility of another giant meteorite or asteroid striking the Earth. In the past, the vast majority of these meteorites were burned up in the Earth's atmosphere before hitting the Earth, but because of the depletion of the ozone layer due to man's pollutions, more and more are smashing into the Earth's surface. An example of this was seen near Gallup, New Mexico, where authorities reported the discovery of a massive, smouldering crater believed to have been produced by a giant meteorite. Reports indicate that a "big green ball of fire" followed by at least six sonic booms rocked a 200-mile-wide area. Scientists believe that the booms, etc., were caused by a meteor shower.[5] Concern that a giant asteroid or meteorite may one day strike the Earth again as it did ages ago are so great that in 1968, NASA set up an "Asteroid Watch" called "Project Icarus."

The Lesson of Atlantis

Edgar Cayce has stated that mankind has reached its present technological and spiritual levels many times in the past, only to ignore the teachings of God, thereby failing to enter the Age of Spiritual Purity and committing mass-suicide through warfare, ecological disaster resulting from manmade pollutions, etc.: "Many times has the evolution of the earth reached the stage of development as it has today and then sank again, to rise again the next development..."[6]

Cayce points to the island-continents of Atlantis in the Atlantic and Lemuria in the Pacific as examples of advanced civilizations that were destroyed because they had become corrupt. Atlanteans, in particular, stand out as a people who had evolved great mental and intuitive abilities as well as being very technologically advanced. Cayce said that they understood spiritual laws better than we do today, and worshipped the One God. But the society was destroyed from within by "those who served the dark forces"— the forces of ego, repression, anger, hatred and division.

The destruction of Atlantis was foretold by its prophets well in advance of the actual event, so there was ample time to prepare for it. Thus the important documents and records of Atlantis were gathered together and put in the Hall of Records in Egypt. The Atlanteans knew that the very existence of their culture and civilization would be unknown for centuries, but they also knew that eventually—in this age—their records would be rediscovered and all things would be revealed. And, indeed, recent discoveries in the Atlantic mentioned earlier do support claims of the previous existence of the continent of Atlantis. The reader will remember that part of the submerged Atlantean continent has resurfaced near the Bimini Islands, and underwater divers have brought back pictures of a massive symmetrical sea wall that was obviously made by human hands and probably was one of the walls surrounding the ancient continent.

The survivors from Lemuria and Atlantis were scattered East and West depending on the fortunes of the winds and the seas. Many are said to have gone to Egypt, conquering the native peoples there, and ushering in the Golden Age of Egypt where the arts and sciences, philosophy and religion, and even beautiful architecture such as the Sphinx were greatly emphasized. The commingling of the Atlanteans caused a quantum leap in the evolution of the Egyptians, both materially and spiritually.[7]

Other survivors from the two continents are said to have landed on the shores of the Americas. This theory is supported by the American Indians whose legends say that they are the descendants of the survivors of the now-lost Red Land of Pahn, which was broken up, destroyed and covered over by the waters of the great seas.[8] It is also reported that those Atlanteans who were the most spiritual and, therefore, the most highly evolved, transformed themselves into dolphins to escape the cataclism that engulfed Atlantis. This would help to explain why the ancient Greeks considered it murder to kill a dolphin, and also helps to explain why the Hindu scriptures state that the dolphins are so spiritual and highly evolved.

Mary Ellen Carter, the author of *Edgar Cayce on Prophecy,* states that:

> "The experience of Atlantis, then, is a lesson to this generation in the evolution of the earth, and man's capacity for making a total shambles of his sojourn here. For, says Cayce, not only has this happened to the Atlantean civilization, it has happened to many before it!
>
> " 'You remember a single deluge only,' states the Egyptian priest, in Plato's *Republic.* 'There have been, and will be again, many destructions of mankind arising out of many causes... You remember a single deluge, only, but there were many previous ones.' "[9]

The Fourth World of the Hopi—Today

The fourth world of the Hopis is today's world, with elements of all of the past worlds: extremes of temperature as well as moderate zones. It is a mixed world—mixtures of races and religions as well as temperatures. It represents the midway point of man's spiritual evolution. Mankind can either reverse its downward trend and strive to rise toward God, denouncing greed and the ego in all its forms, or stay at this low point of evolution, possibly even descending further into ego, hatred, greed and lust.

This is the choice we face today. The decision must be made on an individual, grassroots level, which will then affect society and the world as a whole, just as a pebble dropped in water causes ripples to radiate outward, affecting the surface of the entire pond.

Many have already made that decision, changing their ways and striving to live in harmony and balance with Nature and each other. These people have already started to emerge into the fifth world of the Hopis—a world of Peace and Love, Harmony and Cooperation.

It must be understood that the world is but a reflection of the spiritual evolution of humanity. The Indians believe that the world one is born into reflects the spiritual level one has reached in one's evolution. The four worlds of the Hopis mentioned before correspond to the chakras or spiritual energy centers in the individual human being. Thus the first world corresponds to the sixth chakra (the seventh being the doorway to Union with the Lord), located midway between the eyebrows, and represents awareness of the Lord and of the Oneness of All Creation; the second world corresponds to the fifth chakra located at the throat, which represents creativity, but is a step lower than the full awareness of the Oneness of All Life of the first world; the third world corresponds to the fourth chakra—the Heart Chakra—which is the seat of Divine Love, which, in the third world, was perverted into lust.

The present or fourth world corresponds to the three lower chakras of repression, lust and sloth—power, reproduction and elimination—all very physical and ego-oriented qualities. The question is, will we stay at this egoistic level of power, lust, filth and impurity, or will we rise above this level toward the higher realms of reality, toward awareness and Union with God, toward Oneness with All Creation?

218

Chapter 6

FOUR WORLDS—FOUR AGES

The four worlds of the Hopis also correspond precisely to the four ages or worlds of the Sioux Indians. According to the Sioux, at the dawn of each cycle, a buffalo is placed at the west of the American continent to hold back the waters of the Pacific. Each year this buffalo loses one hair, and each age he loses one leg. When all the legs and hair are gone, the waters will rush in again from the west, inundating the U.S., thus bringing the end of the cycle.

This symbolism is paralleled in Hindu legend by the Bull Dharma (Virtue or Divine Law). According to the Hindus, each cycle again contains four ages that correspond to the four legs of the bull. These four legs in turn represent the four cornerstones of true spirituality—Truth, Compassion, Asceticism and Affording Protection to All—which are progressively obscured with the passing of each age. At the end of each age, the bull loses one leg, which means that the four cornerstones of spirituality lose 25% of their strength, while the demonic or dark forces of unrighteousness (Adharma)—violence, discontent, falsehood and hatred—gain strength proportionately.

Today both the American Indians and the Hindus believe that the buffalo or bull is on its last leg and is very nearly bald! This means that we are in the last age—the Kali Yuga or Age of Chaos—before this present world cycle ends in a climactic catastrophe!

The American Indian and Hindu traditions concerning the world's cycles also correspond to the delineation of the ages that Daniel gave while interpreting King Nebuchadnezzar's dream-beast. You will recall that the beast represented the political kingdoms that were to rule the world down through history. The divisions of the beast also represented the four ages of man: the Golden Age, represented by the beast's head and corresponding to the Hopi's first world and the Hindu's Satyayuga or Age of Purity; the Silver Age, represented by the beast's chest and arms; the Copper Age represented by its belly and thighs; and the Iron Age, represented by its legs and feet of iron, which is the present one corresponding to the fourth mixed-metals world of the Hopi and the Kali Age of the Hindus.

The important thing to remember about this dream-beast is that it, too, demonstrates that the present system of things is already beginning to crumble, as the beast's clay toes suggest, and that this Age of Iron or power is soon to come to an end!

The New Century of the Balinese

The people of the island of Bali, Indonesia, also believe that a New Age or Era is upon us. According to the Balinese tradition, which is an outgrowth of Indian Hinduism, at the close of each cycle or century the elements of Nature dissolve themselves and then reorganize, hopefully, on a higher plane of existence. The Balinese perform many ceremonies to help this process along. They believe that the negative forces of decay must be transformed into the positive forces of regeneration, and, thus, a once-in-a-century ceremony is performed by the priests of the island's temples to aid in this transformation. The whole society, however, is involved as offerings to God are sent from all over the island to the site of this purification/transformation ritual. The last transformation ceremony, called *Eka Dashi Rudra,* was performed in March, 1979. Thus, the Balinese, too, believe that we are entering a New Era or Age.

This ceremony and the timing of it should not be taken lightly. During the 1960's, then-dictator Sukarno of Indonesia tried to change the Balinese culture and way of life by introducing various technologies and influences of the West. An example of this was seen when the Western system of agriculture replaced the ancient Temple System that was based on Hindu tradition. The Western system had all of the rice fields planted at the same time, using chemical pesticides and fertilizers in abundance. Instead of increasing the paddies' overall rice yield, the Western system actually decreased it and brought further disasters to the farmers as water shortages, rats and other pests plagued them and their crops. The farmers got together and decided to go back to the Temple System, a system that had yielded two crops year-round for centuries and was in harmony with Nature, being based on the rotational use of the fields as advocated by ancient Hindu scriptures.

The above was paralleled half-a-world away when the Hopi Indians of North America first abandoned, and later returned to their own ancient system of agriculture that was in tune with the

Balance of Nature, and was based on religious ceremonies. When they attempted to follow the white man's system of growing, disaster struck as no rain fell and the entire corn crop was wiped out due to drought, pests and disease.

Sukarno also attempted to change the timing of the *Eka Dashi Rudra* ceremony. He forced the temple priests and the villagers to perform the ritual in 1963—16 years before its scheduled timing—in order to supposedly "unite" the divided Indonesian people, and to impress a Soviet visitor—Nikita Khrushchev. Days after the ceremony was performed, the volcano on Bali erupted for the first time in recorded history in an explosion that devastated several villages, literally wiping them off the face of the earth. Hundreds of people died and hundreds more were left homeless. The people had been warned, according to the temple priests, by two angelic messengers who came to the villagers and told them to leave the area a few days before the eruption. Those who listened, left and were saved; those who did not, were destroyed.

Interestingly enough, the sacred Hindu temple at which the *Eka Dashi Rudra* ceremony is performed was spared in the eruption, even though it stands very close to the peak of the volcano! It was the only thing left on the volcano's slopes as the molten lava literally flowed around the temple's walls!

King Djojobojo's Prophecies

The Indonesians, too, have prophecies concerning the End Times, and as with the prophecies of the American Indians, the trigger that started the unravelling of these prophecies was the coming of the white man. During the 12th Century A.D., the great and righteous Indian King Djojobojo of the Indonesian island of Java had a strange and prophetic vision of the future of the island peoples. The vision is recounted as follows:

> "After a few centuries, he said, the islands would be conquered by white-skinned, fair-haired, blue-eyed men from the northwest who would rule the Indians of the islands with an iron hand for about 350 years. (The colonial rule of the white men or Dutch people, actually lasted from 1610 to 1945 or 332 years.) He foretold that the white men would be driven off the islands by slant-eyed, yellow-skinned dwarfs

from the northeast (these were the Japanese, who conquered the islands in 1942 during the Second World War), but he said the dwarfs would stay on the islands for only a very short time, for little more than one planting of the corn! (The Japanese were quite amazed during the time they ruled the islands to see the East Indians so carefully planting corn! And, sure enough, in four years the Japanese in turn were driven off the islands. This happened in 1946, at the end of World War II.)

"After the dwarfs had left, said the King, the East Indians would be ruled by their own people, but this would be a very bad time for brother would fight against brother, religion against religion, race against race, and social groups against other social groups. Blood would flow."[1] (This is exactly what has been happening to the East Indian Islands since their independence from the white man as those who have been Westernized fight against those who wish to return to the traditions of the past and their ancient culture. Remember, these prophecies were made over 700 years ago, and have been and are being fulfilled today!)

"However, prophesied King Djojobojo, this time also would not last very long. Soon word would come from a great Spiritual King in the west (that is, toward the Holy Land) that would unite all the religions, all the races and social groups, bringing a thousand years of peace."[2]

Thus these prophecies parallel those of other cultures and religions—both East and West—regarding the signs of the End Times and the start of the New Age. The last world rulers of this system of things were to be and have been the white race, as we have seen. Daniel's interpretation of Nebuchadnezzar's dream-beast also verifies this as the last world empires, represented by the beast's feet and toes, were to be outgrowths of the old Roman Empire. It should be remembered that even the rulers of the Soviet Union are of European extraction, and, hence, are also members of the white race.

The Coming of the Mletchhas

The ancient scriptures of Indian Hinduism also foretold the successive rulers of the world, and stated that the last world rulers of the Kali Yuga would be members of the white race, whom they call "Mletchhas." The definition given of Mletchha is as follows: "He is called a Mletchha, who eats the bovine (cow) flesh, speaks much that is self-contradictory and is destitute of all good conduct."[3]

The eating of the cow is against the teachings of orthodox Hinduism as the cow is viewed as a sacred animal representing the Mother. The reason for this reverence, according to some historians, is that ages ago the cow's milk was the only source of food for the people as the land had been devastated by a severe drought. The cow's milk provided the only sustenance left, and hence saved the people from starvation. Thus, she became the symbol of the Earth Mother, and one does not kill one's mother!

The Europeans and their offshoots, specifically the British and Americans, are eaters of the bovine or cow flesh and have indeed ruled the world up to the present day. Regarding India, the British ruled there for over 200 years and brought the custom of beef-eating with them. They often made alliances with the ruling Maharajas of the various Indian provinces, Hindus and Moslem, thus controlling the Indian subcontinent either directly or indirectly through their surrogates who took up the customs, modes of dress and even language of their conquerors. As the *Shrimad Bhagavatam* puts it:

> "Sudras (members of the lowest caste or class), fallen Brahmins (priests) and members of other higher castes who have given up the Vedic courses of conduct and Mletchhas will rule over the banks of the Indus and Chandrabhaga rivers, the city of Kaunti and the territory of Kashmir. (All parts of the Indian subcontinent that were formerly ruled by the British.)
>
> "These kings...who will be contemporaries, will be no better than Mletchhas in their course of conduct and will be given over to unrighteousness and mendacity, illiberal and furious. They will kill women, children, cows and Brahmins (priests), covet others' wives and wealth, experience vicissitudes of fortune in quick succession and will be poor of strength and courage and shortlived too.
>
> "They will cease to perform purificatory rites, will be devoid of righteous actions, and dominated by Rajas (anger) and Tamas (delusion) and, being Mletchhas in the garb of

Ksatriyas (warriors), will suck the blood of their own people. The people ruled over by them will acquire their habits, ways of life and mode of speech and, oppressed by one another as well as their rulers, will go to ruin."[4]

The fulfillment of this prophecy, written approximately 5000 years ago, is easily seen today. Wherever the British have ruled, they have left their mark, changing the customs, dress and even the language of the conquered peoples. English is now one of the two official languages of India and is "THE" international language of the world. Western-style suits and shoes are worn throughout the world, and replicas of the British systems of government and justice are everywhere, the justice system being one of the better legacies of Britain's world dominance.

Having seen that this part of Hindu prophecy has been fulfilled, let's look at what other signs of the End Times are given in the Hindu scriptures and compare them with those of other cultures and religions.

Chapter 7

The Kali Age or Age of Chaos

The description of the Kali Age given in the *Shrimad Bhagavatam* sounds very familiar when read because it so closely parallels the descriptions given by Jesus of the signs of the End Times:

"This earth stands assailed at present by the age of Kali, the helpmate of unrighteousness. There is no truthfulness, askesis, purity of body and mind, and compassion, nor is there liberality to the poor. The people are wretched and engaged only in filling their bellies. They make false statements...

"Those who pose as saints are constantly engaged in preaching false doctrines. Those who have apparently renounced the world are rich in worldly possessions, and have become family men...There are frequent quarrels between husband and wife...All spiritual discipline stands consumed by the wild fire of Kaliyuga...Brahmins (priests) sell the knowledge of the Vedas (or other Holy Scriptures) and women make their living by prostitution...

"Righteous conduct, the path of Yoga (Union with God) and austerities have disappeared under its (the age's) influence...In this age righteous men remain dejected and unrighteous feel overjoyed indeed...

"The learned pandits (scriptural teachers) for their part indulge in sexual commerce with their wives like buffaloes. They are expert in procreating children and are not at all clever in achieving Liberation...the substance of things has disappeared everywhere...

"(In the Kali Age) day after day...righteousness, veracity, purity, forgiveness, compassion, length of life, bodily strength and keenness of memory will decline...wealth alone will be the criterion of pedigree, morality and merit. Again, might (or brute force or power) will be the only factor determining righteousness and fairness...trickery alone will be the motive force in business dealings. Capability of affording sexual delight will be the only criterion of masculine or feminine excellence...Justice will have every chance of being

225

vitiated because of one's inability to gratify those administering it...Want of riches will be the sole test of impiety and hypocrisy will be the only touchstone of goodness...wearing long hair will be regarded as the only sign of beauty...

"Skill will consist in supporting one's family; virtuous deeds will be performed only with the object of gaining fame; and when in this way the terrestrial globe will be overrun by wicked people, the person who would prove to be the most powerful amongst (all)...will become the ruler. Robbed of their wealth and women by greedy and merciless Ksatriyas (politicians and soldiers), behaving like robbers, people will resort to mountains and forests and subsist on leaves, roots, meat, honey, fruits, flowers and seeds. Already oppressed by famine and heavy taxation, people will perish through drought, excessive cold, storms, scorching sunshine, heavy rain, snowfall and mutual conflict. In the age of Kali men will be tormented by hunger and thirst, ailments and worry...

"When through the evil effects of Kali the bodies of men get reduced in size and emaciated, the righteous course chalked out by the Vedas (and other spiritual scriptures)...gets lost, when religion is replaced by heresy to a large extent and rulers mostly turn out to be thieves, when men take to various pursuits like theft, mendacity, wanton destruction of life and so on;...annual plants get stunted in growth and trees are mostly reduced to the size of a Sami (a small tree); ...dwellings will mostly look desolate for want of hospitality to strangers...

"In the Kali Age...a quarter alone of the four feet of Dharma (righteousness, divine law or virtue) remains. Nay, due to the feet of Adharma (unrighteousness) gaining ground that too steadily declines and ultimately disappears altogether. People in that age turn out to be greedy, immoral, and merciless, enter into hostility without cause and are unlucky and extremely covetous...

"When duplicity, mendacity, drowsiness, excessive sleep, violence, dejection, grief, infatuation, fear and wretchedness prevail, that is recognized as the age of Kali, characterized by the predominance of Tamas (sloth, impurity, indolence), as a result of which people become dull-witted, unable to judge things in their proper perspective, and are...voracious, voluptuous and destitute. And women too turn out to be

226

profligate and unchaste. Countries are infested with robbers, the Vedas stand condemned by heretics; rulers exploit the people; and the priests remain devoted to the gratification of sexual desires and intent on filling their belly...

"Householders will take to begging...Low-minded traders will carry on business transactions and practice fraud. Even when they are not in distress people will favour pursuits which are condemned. (Employees) will leave their (employers) when reduced to penury, though superior in every other respect; and (employers) too will discharge their (employee), when incapacitated for service through ailment, etc., even though he may be hereditary (his whole family has worked for the employer as with several coal-mining areas)...

"Those who have no knowledge of (true spiritual) religion will occupy high seats and preach religion. Oppressed by famine and heavy taxation,—land being divested of food grains,—and stricken with fear of droughts, people in the Kali age will ever remain perturbed in mind. Destitute of clothes and ornaments, nay even food and drink, bed and sexual enjoyment, they will go even without a bath and put on the appearance of a fiend. Quarrelling even for a very small sum of money...having cast all goodwill to the winds, people in Kaliyuga will kill even their own people and part with their own dear life. Mean-minded fellows will concern themselves only with the gratification of their lust and satisfaction of their hunger and fail to maintain even their aged parents; while parents will disown their sons, though clever in all matters. With their mind perverted by heretics...mortals in Kaliyuga will not generally worship...the immortal Lord, the highest object of adoration for the whole universe...

"...in this way when the Kali age, whose career is so severe to the people, is well-nigh past, the Lord will appear in His divine form consisting of Sattva (purity) alone, for the protection of virtue."[1]

Jesus' Signs

Jesus Christ also foretold that the last rulers of the world would be members of the white race, whom He called "Gentiles," mean-

227

ing non-Jewish, specifically, descendants of the old Roman Empire, i.e., the Europeans and their offshoots—all members of the white race. He stated that the Jews would be without a homeland until the end of the Gentiles' time or dominance of the Earth. And, indeed, the Jews were without a homeland until 1948, when Israel became a world-recognized nation, this occurring **after** the end of World War II and the explosion of the first atomic weapon—one of the last signs of the End Times that Jesus gave. Compare the rest of the signs of the End Times as given by Jesus Christ with those of other peoples and religions, including those of the Hindus' Kali Age:

"Take heed that no one leads you astray. Many will come in my name, saying, 'I am he!,' and will lead many astray. And you will hear of wars and rumors of wars, do not be alarmed; for these must take place, but the end is not yet. For nation will rise against nation, and kingdom against kingdom, and there will be famine and earthquakes and pestilences in various places; and there will be terrors and great signs from heaven.

"But before all this (and during it) they will lay their hands on you and persecute you, and put you to death for my name's sake. And then many will fall away, and betray one another, and hate one another. You will be delivered up even by parents and brothers and kinsmen and friends. This will be a time for you to bear testimony and the Gospel must first be preached to all nations. And many false prophets will arise and lead many astray. And because wickedness is multiplied, most men's love will grow cold. But he who endures to the end will be saved.

"But when you see the desolating sacrilege set up where it ought not to be, then...flee to the mountains...for these are days of vengeance, to fulfill all that is written. Alas for those who are with child and for those who give suck in those days! For great distress shall be upon the earth...there will be such tribulation as has not been from the beginning of the creation which God created until now, and never will be. And if the Lord had not shortened the days, no living thing would be saved; but for the sake of the elect those days will be shortened...For false Christs and false prophets will arise and show signs and wonders, to lead astray, if possible, even the

228

elect...do not believe them. For as the lightning comes from the east and shines as far as the west, so will be the coming of the Son of Man.

"And there will be signs in sun and moon and stars, the sun will be darkened, and the moon will not give its light, and the stars will be falling from heaven, and upon the earth distress of nations in perplexity at the roaring of the sea and the waves, men fainting with fear and with foreboding of what is coming on the world; for the powers of the heavens shall be shaken. And then they will see the sign of the Son of Man in heaven, and then all the tribes of the earth will mourn, and they will see the Son of Man coming in a cloud with power and great glory. And he will send out the angels, and gather his elect from the four winds, from the ends of the earth to the ends of heaven.

"Now when these things begin to take place, look up and raise your heads, because your redemption is drawing near...when you see these things taking place, you know that the kingdom of God is near. Truly, I say to you, this generation (who sees these signs) will not pass away till all has taken place. Heaven and earth will pass away, but my words will not pass away.

"But take heed to yourselves lest your hearts be weighed down with dissipation and drunkenness and cares of this life, and that day come upon you suddenly like a snare; for it will come upon all who dwell upon the face of the whole earth. But watch at all times, praying that you may have strength to escape all these things that will take place, and to stand before the Son of Man...

"As were the days of Noah, so will be the coming of the Son of Man. For as in those days before the flood they were eating and drinking, marrying and giving in marriage, until the day when Noah entered the ark, and they did not know until the flood came and swept them all away, so will be the coming of the Son of Man...Watch, therefore, for you do not know on what day your Lord is coming; for the Son of Man is coming at an hour you do not expect."[2]

Chapter 8

SIGNS OF THE TIMES COMPARED

There are several common elements in all sets of prophecies. Below is a synopsis of the signs of the End Times, Tribulation/ Purification or Kali Yuga.

False Prophets

All sets of scriptures warn that in the last days of this system of things, there will be an abundance of false prophets and false teachers who claim to have spiritual knowledge but who, in truth, are blasphemers and heretics, with no knowledge of true, spiritual religion. Looking around the globe it is easy to see that this prophecy has been fulfilled. Every organized religion is plagued, at present, with individuals who have twisted God's Words to serve their own selfish purposes: Christianity, Judaism, Islam, Hinduism, and even Buddhism has not escaped.

Without mentioning any names, we will again reiterate the signs of a false prophet and let the reader determine who fits the descriptions. Jesus said that we would know them by their "fruits" or by their actions and the consequences of their actions on others. All those who preach division and hatred are false prophets because, as we have seen, all of God's True Messengers have preached Unity and Love for all, even towards one's "enemy." All those who preach violence versus nonviolence are false for all true teachers have said that one must not return blow for blow, but "turn the other cheek." This does not mean that one should not **defend** one's self, but one must be absolutely sure that one's action is of a defensive, **not** offensive nature.

Whoever preaches intolerance instead of tolerance of other different spiritual paths condemns himself. For all of God's Messengers were the epitome of tolerance and taught that **all** religious practices that are motivated by true faith and love of God **must** be respected. Thus, those who say, "My way and no other," are condemning themselves as false by their own words.

All those who confuse the people with ridiculous ceremonies and silly superstitions are false as they prey on people's fear and give false security of salvation for simply performing some religious act. For one does not attain salvation merely by bowing

230

and bending, nor by giving large sums of money to any organization. The watchman at the gates of heaven cannot be bribed, nor can salvation be "bought" except by a repentant heart, sincere devotion to the Lord, and submission to His Will.

To sum up, all those who speak lies instead of truth; preach hatred instead of love; division of people instead of unity; advocate violence instead of peace; are ego-oriented instead of humble; who only make a practice of receiving material things instead of sharing them; who are more concerned with family life instead of spiritual life—procreation instead of liberation; who are hoarders of wealth instead of distributors of it; who directly or indirectly support Satanic, evil or brutal rulers, individuals or governments instead of denouncing them, as Christ and Lord Krishna did; who complicate rather than simplify God; who use fear of God instead of love of God to control and confuse the people; who, as Jesus said, "cling to the letter of the Law and violate the heart of it," are the false prophets predicted by the various scriptures. As said earlier, the world is already plagued by them; hence, **this prophecy is fulfilled!**

Ruthless Rulers

All scriptures speak of ruthless, cold-hearted, brutal, hateful and egoistic rulers who will control the people of the earth through fear and brute power. These rulers will steal everything from the people: their property, their wealth, even their wives and children, and kill all those who protest their despicable deeds. They will fight without cause and persecute all good people—the persecution of the saints—who would dare to question their authority or their actions.

The world today abounds with such rulers: rulers who have no real concern for anyone but themselves, who have no pity for the plight of the poor and show no liberality toward them. On the contrary, these rulers seek to diminish and/or take away what little the poor have left, even refusing them the basic necessities of life and feeling no pangs of guilt about it.

One organization that keeps track of these ruthless rulers and their barbaric acts is Amnesty International, a London-based, non-profit, Nobel Peace Prize winning group established 21 years ago, whose main concern is the human rights of prisoners around the world, regardless of the political ideology of the countries involved. According to a recently published report, human rights are being violated by governments or extremist groups in **117 of the world's 158 countries.** Of course the degree of the violations depends on the country, but, "Amnesty has established that torture is national policy or is tolerated in 60 countries. The technique varies from one nation to another, but the common characteristic is a disdain for human life and a contempt for the dignity of the individual."[1]

Examples of this can be seen "in Latin America, especially El Salvador and Guatemala, (where) the vast majority of people who are found killed have been mutilated."[2] The victims of both countries include several members of the clergy, such as Archbishop Romero, who was assassinated while serving mass in a hospital chapel, and the three Maryknoll nuns and layworker who were tortured and raped before being murdered, prophetically enough in El Salvador, which, by the way, is the only country in the world named after Jesus Christ, "El Salvador" meaning "The Saviour."

Argentina also has had a horrendous record of human rights violations, detaining nearly 9000 people since 1974. Even more upsetting is the number of people that the military has caused to "disappear"—about 20,000—many of whom were children. The military has set up "death camps" where people who have first been kidnapped undergo interrogation by means of physical and mental torture, followed by periods of time spent in concentration camps and finally "transferred"—actually sedated with a potent drug and dropped alive, but unconscious, into the sea!

Thousands of children have "disappeared" in Argentina, El Salvador, Guatemala and other countries, whose fate usually remains unknown. In one month, fourteen mass grave sites were discovered in Argentina, each containing thousands of bodies. One mother who went to a government office in Argentina to find out what had happened to her daughter was handed a jar containing the child's hands.[3]

Other examples of this type of barbaric, revolting behavior are seen in the Central African Empire, where former Emperor Bokassa massacred over 100 school children; the Soviet Union, where the practice of separating children from religiously-activist parents has gone on for decades; East Germany, who has allowed certain political prisoners to emigrate to West Germany, but has often held back the prisoners' children; South Africa, where children aged 14 and 15 have often been detained in maximum security prisons incommunicado, thus the parents have no information on the whereabouts of their young; Uganda, where hundreds of thousands of orphans still wake up screaming in the middle of the night, having relived the real nightmare they experienced when Idi Amin's troops butchered their parents in front of their eyes; and in U.S.-backed El Salvador,[4] where one out of every four children die before reaching the age of 5, and where the following incident took place, exemplifying the totally inhumane, sick and deranged thinking that characterizes that and other equally repulsive regimes: According to the Washington Post (1/27/82), in December, 1981, the elite, U.S.-trained Atlactl Brigade swept into the small province of Morazan. According to one of the survivors, over 900 defenseless men, women, and children were massacred:

> "I heard the soldiers talking. An order arrived...go ahead and shoot the children too. A soldier said, 'Lieutenant, somebody here says he won't kill children.' 'Who's the son-of-a-bitch who said that?' the lieutenant answered. 'I'm going to kill him.'
> "I could hear the children crying. I could hear my own children. The soldiers had no fury. They just observed the lieutenant's orders. They were cold..."[5]

As Jesus Christ said, "Most men's love will grow cold."[6] And the brutality continues, as a January 21, 1983 article by Sam Dillon of the Knight-Ridder News Service points out:

> "At 2 a.m. on Jan. 5, 18 treasury policemen carrying submachine guns burst into a house in a wealthy San Salvador neighborhood and grabbed 17-year-old Beatriz Alcaine and her 15-year-old sister. The men tied their thumbs behind their backs, blindfolded them and drove away with them. The girls' grandmother remained behind, crying.
> "Hours later...residents discovered the bodies of a young couple lying on a grassy hillside. Their faces had been destroyed by bullets. Their legs had been broken.
> "It was the beginning of another day in El Salvador, a day in which nearly 50 people would fall victim to politi-

cal violence. An unknown number of others would 'disappear.' It was to be a day of higher than average—but not extraordinary—bloodletting.

"Today, the Reagan administration is expected to certify for the third time since early last year to Congress that the government of El Salvador 'is making a concerted and significant effort to comply with internationally recognized human rights,' a requirement imposed by Congress for continued U.S. aid...(even though) U.S. Ambassador Deane Hinton said (in an October speech): 'By no stretch of the imagination can current levels (of political violence) be considered acceptable to any civilized person.' "[7]

Thus, even the United States has dark blemishes on its human rights record, but not only because it has and still does back some of the most ruthless rulers and regimes in the world, such as Zia of Pakistan who has just recently imprisoned and tortured over 15,000 political dissidents without any judicial procedures whatsoever, Park of South Korea, Marcos of the Philippines, D'Aubuisson of El Salvador, Rios Montt of Guatemala,[8] the ex-Shah of Iran, etc., but also because of its disregard for human rights when it comes to many minorities, especially American Indians. As Rolling Thunder explains:

"Even today, in this day and time, we are still losing our land and they are still killing our people, even our young people. Many of them have been found dead in the town of Elko (Nevada) and on the reservations. Sometimes they're found dead in the jail...

"They do not care for a poor person, especially an Indian, who is the poorest of all. Our people are dragged into your courts, and many times there's no pretense of a trial. The recent Indian Bill of Rights doesn't mean anything...

"Only recently a young man was thrown in jail and he was not allowed to have an attorney or witnesses...And this man's actual crime was that he had had the nerve to run for the tribal council.

"The kidnapping of Indian children from their own families goes on all over the country. They kidnap Indian children out on the reservations under the guise of some sort of child care or religious programs. Any excuse is all right provided some white family wants a child or someone likes to convert people. These people will get together with the welfare agents and the sheriffs and the Indian agents and they'll go out on a reservation and take a child. They might say it's because the family is on welfare or has too many children or anything else they can think of as an excuse at the time...

"We have heard that over in some of those European countries they have what they call the 'iron curtain.' We heard about a bamboo curtain in the last big war over in the East. Well, out here we have the buckskin curtain. The public just absolutely does not know and cannot imagine what goes on out on the reservations."[9]

However, in all fairness to the United States, we have had enlightened leaders who have cared for the human rights of **all** people. Examples of this are some of the country's founding fathers, like George Washington, who once said: "To bigotry no sanction, to persecution no assistance;" Thomas Jefferson, who said: "It may be regarded as certain, that not a foot of land will ever be taken from the Indians without their own consent. The sacredness of their rights is felt by all thinking persons in America...;" Abraham Lincoln, who said: "It is for us, the living...to be dedicated to the unfinished work...and the great task remaining before us...that these dead (all those who have died for the Truth and the Unity of all Humankind) shall not have died in vain, that this nation, under God, shall have a new birth of Freedom, and that the government of the people, by the people, and for the people shall not perish from the earth!;" Franklin Delanor Roosevelt, John F. Kennedy, Robert Kennedy, Martin Luther King, and the most prominent example in modern times— former President James Earl Carter who made human rights the cornerstone of his domestic and foreign policy, because of which nearly one billion people in the world were freed from despotic and dictatorial governments. Not since Mahatma Gandhi and former Prime Minister Nehru of India had the world seen such a strong advocate of human rights as President Jimmy Carter. Recently, the International League for Human Rights recognized President Carter's accomplishments in the field of human rights by giving him the organization's human rights award. According to the league's president Jerome Shestack, the league chose Carter because "of his accomplishment in placing human rights prominently on the world agenda and strengthening the human rights community globally. Because of his efforts, human rights issues continue to weigh heavily on the world conscience."[10]

Jimmy Carter helped the United States live up to the ideals enshrined in our Declaration of Independence:

> "We hold these truths to be self-evident, that all (human beings) are created equal, that they are endowed by their Creator with certain unalienable rights, that among these are **life, liberty and the pursuit of happiness.**"[11]

Other examples of ruthless rulers and regimes include Khomeini of Iran who is butchering by the tens of thousands, followers of the Baha'i Faith as well as anyone else he considers as opposition; the military regimes of Honduras, North Korea, East European countries including Poland; war-ravaged Afghanistan; "Baby Doc" of Haiti; China;[12] and the list, unfortunately, goes on and on. Thus, **this prophecy is abundantly fulfilled!**

Since God's Justice is perfect, one shudders to think of the fate that awaits these people and all those who aid them in any manner. The scriptures do give us some glimpses, the details of which we will discuss later when we deal with The Judgement.

Wars and Rumors of Wars

Another prediction common to all sets of prophecies is that there will be wars and rumors of wars, and that people will enter into hostilities without cause. With as many ruthless rulers as there are around the world, it's easy to see why there have been and still are so many wars today.

The year 1914 is pointed to by many historians as a turning point in human history because in that year the first World War began. Almost no part of the world escaped the ravages of that war, and if they did, most failed to escape the consequences of the wars that have followed that first "Great One," or in truth, Horrible One, which had been called "the war to end all wars." In reality, World War I turned out to be the start of global warfare that has not ceased to this day, but rather has intensified and multiplied.

236

The reason World War I was so different from previous wars is that the Industrial Revolution of the 1800's provided the combatants with newer, deadlier and more accurate weapons, including the airplane. Thus total warfare was made possible, with civilian centers becoming easy targets for air bombings, whereas in the past, armies fought primarily outside populated areas. Over 10 million people were killed in World War I, with another 20 million left maimed and wounded.

In between the end of World War I and the start of World War II were numerous "smaller" wars, including the Russian Revolution, in which millions of Russians lost their lives, and the Spanish Revolution, which saw the beginning of Franco's dictatorial reign.

World War II was an even greater orgy of death and destruction. Over 55 million people were killed with even more of the globe embroiled in conflict than in World War I. In this war, whole peoples—ethnos—fought one another, thus fulfilling Jesus' prophecy to His disciples that in the End Times, whole peoples, not just armies, would fight one another. There was nowhere to escape the war as population centers became battlegrounds, and thus, all peoples in the warring countries were involved in the war, either as victims, combatants and/or builders and suppliers of the arms used in the fighting.

During World War II, the first successful atomic chain reaction experiments were conducted on December 2, 1942, and the end of World War II saw the ushering in of the Atomic Age with the first successful atomic tests in 1944—blasphemously code-named "Baby Jesus"—and the first successful atomic explosions—blasphemously code-named "The Trinity"—in 1945. It also saw the first-ever, and so far only use of atomic weapons in war when U.S. airmen dropped atomic bombs over the Japanese cities of Hiroshima and Nagasaki, thereby obliterating them and, again, **fulfilling not only Jesus' prophecy, but also those of the Hopis, Pale Prophet and Nostradamus.**

The effects of these bombs are still being seen today with survivors suffering from cancer and other radiation-related diseases. However, not only are Japanese victims of the bombs suffering, but also military personnel who were involved in atomic testings that took place in the Western part of the U.S., as well as several citizens of the U.S. who were exposed to radioactive fallout that drifted over their towns and farmlands.

It has been estimated that since the end of World War II, 150 wars have been fought with at least 30 million lives lost, 50 of those wars being fought in the last decade alone, according to the Stockholm International Peace Research Institute. The Institute states that in 1981, the world spent over $500 billion—**more than one million dollars a minute**—on arms, with the U.S. and the U.S.S.R. being the two biggest spenders and suppliers (75% of the world arms sales combined.) A partial listing of some of the more well-known wars follows:

1945-54...... Vietnam (French Involvement)	1968 .... Czechoslovakia
	1969-present... Ireland
1955-75...... Vietnam (U.S. involvement)	1969 .... Russian-Chinese border
1948-51...... Malaya	1969-75...... Angola
1950-51...... Korea	1971 .... Bangladesh
1954-62...... Algeria	1973 .... Sinai
1956 .... Hungary	1975 .... Lebanon
1956 .... Suez	1976-79...... Rhodesia (Zimbabwe)
1957 .... Tibet	
1959 .... Laos	1977 .... Ethiopia
1959 .... China-Indian border	1978 .... Zaire
	1979 .... Cambodia and Vietnam
1960 .... Congo	
1962-75...... Iraq	1979 .... Chad
1962 .... Yemen	1979 .... Iran
1965 .... Indian-Pakistan border	1979 .... Yemen
	1979 .... Uganda
1967 .... Arab-Israeli 'Six Days' War'	1979 .... Nicaragua
	1980-present... Afghanistan
1967-69...... Biafra (Nigeria)	1980-present... Iran-Iraq

Other wars being fought in the last two years include the countries of Morroco, El Salvador, Guatemala, Nicaragua, Honduras, Peru, Ecuador, Bolivia, Argentina, Great Britain, Cambodia, Laos, Vietnam, China, Syria, Israel and Lebanon. As in the past with the Christian "Crusades," the Spanish Inquisition and other religious conflicts, many of today's wars are being fought based on religious fanaticism. Examples of this are the conflicts between Israel and the Arab countries, Iran and Iraq where Muslim is fighting Muslim, Pakistan and India, the continuing strife in Northern Ireland where Christians are killing Christians (Catholics versus

Protestants), etc. In most of these conflicts, the warring sides are being encouraged to fight by orthodox priests who do not want to lose their power and control over the people by allowing other forms of religious activity to exist.

The great tragedy of all these conflicts is that brother is fighting brother and cousin is killing cousin. The Arab/Israel/Lebanese-Christian conflict is an excellent example where the world's three most fanatical religions are locked in mortal combat—orthodox Judaism, orthodox Christianity and orthodox Islam. The combatants in this on-going conflict are all descendants from the same human father—Abraham—and their history, religious doctrines and prophecies are all based on those first set down by Moses, not to mention that we all have the same spiritual Father—God! As Dennis Braithwaite of *The Toronto Sun* explains:

> "All that really divides them is religion; the rest is rationalization, propaganda, lies...Take religious fanaticism out of the equation, and what have Arab and Jew (and Christian) left to fight about?...Observe the insanity in Northern Ireland, where two conceptions of the Christian religion have caused people who look alike, talk alike and spring from the same soil, to lock themselves in a death struggle that baffles the outsider...When they're interviewed on television, you can't tell one from the other...religion is but one form of nationalism, the concept of 'them' and 'us'...the greatest threat of all to mankind's future."[13]

Nuclear Holocaust

However, the most terrifying rumor of war today is that of a nuclear holocaust between the two superpowers: the United States and the Soviet Union, who are both presently engaged in the most massive military, specifically, nuclear buildup in history. The U.S. Defense Department has stated that its "modernization program" will cost $1.6 trillion over the next five years. Figures for the Soviet's buildup are somewhere in the same range. One of the weapons systems presently under consideration for deployment in the U.S. today is the MX Missile System, whose call letters literally mean "1000 Christs," "M" being the Roman numeral for 1000 and "X" being an early symbol for "Christ."[14] Ironically, the system has been nicknamed "The Peace-keeper"

By Permission of Johnny Hart and Field Enterprises, Inc.

which, of course, is the exact opposite of its function as it is, in actuality, a weapon of war and destruction, and its effects on the international political scene have been to heighten fears of war—not lessen them.

Recently, Soviet officials stated that the Soviet Union will be forced to build its own version of the MX System if the U.S. does decide to deploy it. Further, the Soviets have said that they "will fire their nuclear rockets at Western Europe on a moment's notice if NATO goes ahead with plans to install 572 new U.S.-made (Pershing 2) missiles," saying that "such a 'launch-on-warning' tactic was 'the only alternative' for the Soviet military if NATO begins deploying the (Pershing and Cruise) rockets in December, 1983."[15] Once these missiles are deployed in Europe, they will be only six minutes from the Soviet Union.

It is estimated that **at least 5 tons of explosive power exists for each person on Earth today!**[16] According to retired Rear Admiral Gene La Rocque, who spent seven years as the strategic nuclear war planner at the Pentagon and who now is the director for the Center for Defense Information, even without adding a

THE ARMS RACE: OVERKILL AND OVERREACTION
Total US and USSR Strategic Nuclear Weapons

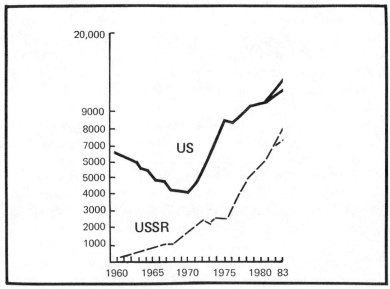

single new missile or weapons system to their arsenals, the U.S. and U.S.S.R. have over 50,000 nuclear weapons of various types which represent 95% of all nuclear weapons in the world, the U.S. accounting for 30,000 and the U.S.S.R. armed with the remaining 20,000.[17] Scientists in both countries estimate that it will take an exchange of only 300 to 500 nuclear ICBM's to obliterate the U.S. and the U.S.S.R., as each nuclear warhead today has several times the destructive power of the bombs that destroyed Hiroshima and Nagasaki.

So why do we have this overkill mentality when both sides already have over 50,000 nuclear weapons combined? Since both countries and probably the rest of the world will be destroyed with the first exchange, as each country will target the other's allies (especially since defense planners for both countries have admitted that they have run out of areas to target because they have so many missiles already, with strategic areas already targeted at least three and four times!), and those areas not directly bombed will cease to have life as we know it due to radioactive fallout, which physicians have called the "final plague" as the lesions left by the fallout resemble those caused by the dreaded bubonic plagues of Europe—why is there any need to stockpile more weapons? The answer is that ego and hate are out of control in those advocating the above in both countries, which needs to be replaced by love and humility in the leaders of both countries— divine attributes without which the world seems headed for Armageddon!

The question is how long are we going to play this egoistic game of one-up-manship? Since God has given mankind only one planet Earth, we must learn to coexist together peacefully, "loving our neighbors as ourselves," replacing evil with good, hate with love, war with peace, the terms "enemy" with "brother," or surely the self-destructive ego will lead to the "final solution," as envisioned by satanic Hitler—a nuclear holocaust and a dead planet!

Retired Admiral Hyman Rickover, the "father" of the U.S. nuclear navy has said that both nuclear weapons and nuclear power should be outlawed, adding, "I think we'll probably destroy ourselves. I'm not proud of the part I played."[18] Admiral Rickover's feelings are shared by George Kistiakowsky, who was an advisor to President Eisenhower and worked on the Manhattan Project (the first A-bomb project). He stated that: "If I knew then what I know now, I never would have helped to develop the bomb."[19]

According to Dr. Marvin Goldberger, president of the California Institute of Technology, "One or two Poseidon submarines could destroy the Soviet Union as a realistic society. We now have a total of 31 such submarines, about 20 of which are on patrol at all times."[20] One Poseidon sub, which is an older and less deadly version of the new Trident subs—one of which is blasphemously named "Corpus Christi," which means "the body of Christ"— has the power to obliterate over 150 large cities as each sub carries 16 Poseidon missiles and each missile has 10 or more nuclear warheads.[21] Thus, one man—the commander of a nuclear submarine—controls the firepower to obliterate an entire country! And the U.S. is planning to build several more.

Given the frequency with which computer errors occur, and understanding that our entire "defense" system is computerized, the chances of a nuclear war being started accidentally are astonishingly high. In 1982 alone, there was a computer error on the average of every other day. And the above does not include the communication blackouts that occur frequently between the submerged nuclear submarines and their land-based defense centers. Nor does it include such accidents as the one that happened recently in West Germany where a U.S. Sidewinder missile fell out of a plane, crashing into the Black Forest below. It is believed that the missile did not explode when it hit the ground, but the reason for the accident remains unknown and unexplained. If that missile had fallen out over an East German forest and exploded, it could have become more than just an accident—it could have become the first bomb blast of the Third World War!

But, unfortunately, there are even more disturbing ways a nuclear holocaust could begin. For example, one shudders to think of the horrifying prospect of a terrorist group taking over or bombing a nuclear facility, which has already been attempted in South Africa, where guerrillas set off four explosions at the country's first nuclear power station. No damage was reported, but the warnings are clear. Recently, the U.S. Nuclear Regulatory Commission expressed concern over the growing prospect of sabotage and vandalism of nuclear power facilities here. Records on file with the commission, "document instances in which vandalism, tampering and sabotage apparently have been done by employees despite strict security measures...Since 1978, the NRC has documented 27 cases of vandalism at the nation's 150 nuclear plants in operation or under construction."[22]

There have been other strange incidents, too, that have not been classified as of yet. Examples of the above include the following:

> 1) In July, 1981, at the Maine Yankee Nuclear Plant, "officials found a message sprayed on the floor of the spent fuel area that said, 'Bomb will go off July 31, 1981,' (along with a note nearby that said), 'So you think your (expletive deleted) security is so good...try to find the bomb.'
> 2) "At the Salem Nuclear Plant in New Jersey...the FBI was called to investigate tampering in August ('82) when workers found valves closed on one of the plant's three diesel generators that provide emergency power for the plant. A week earlier, a control-room operator shut down Salem's Unit 1 after getting a faulty signal from an instrument that

243

had been tampered with. And in April, during union negotiations, the company reported a deliberate effort to trigger a reactor shutdown by disturbing a water-feed pump.

3) "At the Beaver Valley reactor in Shippingport, Pa., workers last year ('81) found that a valve that was supposed to be locked in the open position had been closed and the chain and padlock that normally held it in place were missing. With the valve shut, water was cut off from the emergency core cooling system, which would be needed in an emergency to keep the reactor from overheating...

4) "Three years ago, two operator trainees...were convicted of a felony for pouring a corrosive chemical on nuclear fuel rods (at Virginia Electric Power Co.'s Surry Nuclear Plant.)

5) "Remaining unsolved is a partially cut safety cable last year at the Palisades reactor in South Haven, Michigan, and two mysterious shutdowns in '80 at the Browns Ferry plant in Decatur, Ala., that the FBI blamed on employee sabotage."[23]

6) And the most recent example of sabotage occurring in November, 1982, again, at the Maine Yankee plant, where "an alert worker...noticed metal shavings on a motor that provides cooling water to the radioactive core...some of the small metalic chips had been dropped inside the oil reservoir that lubricates the motor's bearings. If the motor had been operating, metal shards (pieces) would have caused substantial damage to the motor and perhaps triggered the automatic shutdown of the nuclear reactor."[24]

Even these examples do not give the full picture of how frighteningly easy it would be for an accident or sabotage at a nuclear facility to trigger a nuclear war. For they do not take into account the prospect of the leader of a country, with a deranged mind, causing an accident or deliberately starting a nuclear war. For it would only take **one** deranged leader to do so if he had the weapons at his disposal. Further, recent studies have shown that the men in charge of firing a nuclear weapon have a higher rate of alcoholism, drug abuse and mental illness, specifically depression, than the average military person.

But the most immediate threat of a nuclear holocaust comes

NUCLEAR EXPLOSIONS SINCE 1945

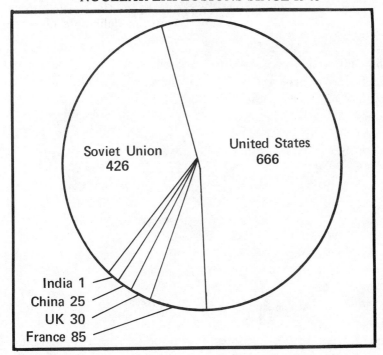

from the perceptions that each superpower has of the other. While the U.S. talks of increasing its nuclear arsenal to close "the window of vulnerability," the Soviet perception can be best understood from an answer Soviet representative Georgi Arbatov gave to a *Time Magazine* interviewer:

> "In the nuclear arms race, we (the Soviets) began as the weaker one. I can't remember a single important weapons system which was not introduced first by you (the U.S., INCLUDING the proposed MX system and new Cruise missiles) and then by us. Right now, because of the Reagan Administration's rhetoric—and maybe it's more than just rhetoric—military people and even some members of the Central Committee believe America is preparing for nuclear war. Even more widespread now is the view that your leaders are determined to change our system and, if that fails, to destroy it."[25]

The Vicious War Cycle

As mentioned earlier, it is the self-destructive ego of man that may ultimately cause the last holocaust. Recently, during the dedication of the Vietnam War Memorial, where the names of the 57,939 men who died in Vietnam were read aloud, America's oldest living war veteran, 108-year-old Harry Chaloner of St. Petersburg, Florida, "sat scowling in his wheelchair and said all wars were just a lot of 'bunk!' 'There should never be any wars at all,' growled Chaloner, who fought in the Spanish-American War and World War I. (He said that) **wars are fought only to serve egos.** 'Ah, it's all bunk. Today, everyone's after the almighty dollar and they don't care how they get it. Just look at them today.' "[26]

Indeed, the vicious cycle of destruction and rebuilding that wars institute reminds us of the words of the Republican President General Dwight D. Eisenhower who, in one of his last public addresses, warned the American people against the "military-industrial complex," he being the first person to coin that phrase having been on the "inside" of that complex as general and president, and thus understanding its methodology and workings.

An example of this "complex" at work was recently revealed when certain U.S. government documents were made public under the Freedom of Information Act. These documents, dating back to the 1950's, show that the Defense Department encouraged the public utility companies to "go nuclear." They did so because they wanted the plutonium that is a by-product of the nuclear process in order to produce more atomic/nuclear weapons, plutonium being the key ingredient of nuclear weapons, tons of which are presently "lost," increasing even more the threat of a terrorist group building and using a nuclear weapon, since it takes only 20 pounds of plutonium to make a nuclear bomb!

Even more incredible is the implication that both the U.S. and Soviet governments covered up evidence of the world's first nuclear accident, known as the Kyshtym Disaster, which occurred in Siberia in 1957 or '58. Apparently a radioactive waste disposal site in the Southern Ural Mountains spontaneously exploded, destroying a 1000-square-kilometer area, literally wiping 30 towns and villages off the map and forcing the evacuation of several thousand people as a mysterious illness began to break out amongst those living near the disaster site. The area, which is still closed to the general public, was left uninhabitable for two centuries, being highly radioactive to this day. Eyewitness accounts of the area say that it is totally desolate, with dead forests surrounding it.

The Soviet accident took place at the same time that debate over nuclear power was beginning in the U.S. Had the public become aware of the devastating accident in Russia, it may not have allowed the wide-spread production of nuclear power plants which, even today, produce only about 12% of the electrical energy generated in the whole United States. The question is, can we in the U.S. afford to lose 1000-square kilometers of America?

Another area where the workings of the military-industrial complex can be seen is in conventional warfare. For many of the corporations that build and supply the world's armaments are the very same corporations that go into a war-ravaged area after the fighting has ceased to bid on reconstruction. As Mahatma Gandhi said:

> "If there were no greed, there would be no occasion for armaments. The principle of nonviolence necessitates complete abstention from exploitation in any form...As soon as the spirit of exploitation is gone, armaments will be felt as a positive unbearable burden. Real disarmament cannot come unless the nations of the world cease to exploit one another."[27]

However, this cycle would not be possible after a nuclear war because there would be no one left to do the rebuilding and no one left for whom to rebuild. Everyone and everything would be destroyed. As Gandhi said, "If the mad race for armaments continues it is bound to result in a slaughter such as has never occurred in history. If there is a victor left the very victory will be a living death for the nation that emerges victorious."[28] Thus we have seen that **the prophecies regarding wars and rumors of wars and the world being on the brink of catastrophe in the End Times have been fulfilled!**

247

Chapter 9

REVELATIONS REVEALED

The prophecies concerning wars and rumors of wars as well as those regarding the dominance of the world by the white race in the End Times are reiterated in even more detail by Saint John in the last book of the Bible—Revelations. While John was meditating in the island prison of Patmos, having been incarcerated there for preaching God's Good News, Jesus came to him in a vision and revealed to him what would happen in the End Times of this man-made system of things.

Jesus first dictated seven letters to John to send to His various churches. The letters contain words of comfort and love as well as warnings against abandoning the True Path. The letters can be understood on at least two levels—from macro (large) to micro (small): 1- the seven stages of the spiritual development of the church and its history, and/or 2- the personal spiritual evolution of seekers of God. Jesus tells God's seekers to have patience, perseverance, and not to be deceived by false prophets; to be faithful in service and love for the Lord, and not to be tempted by the cravings of the senses such as lust, greed and anger; and, finally, to wake up spiritually so as to not die in spiritual darkness.[1]

The last two letters seem to be aimed at two opposite types of people. The first one is directed to those who have kept His Word and been faithful to Him. The Lord promised to keep the door to His Kingdom open for them, saying that no one would be able to shut it. He also promised to keep them from experiencing the coming tribulation and/or to give them the strength to endure it to the end so that they may become pillars of His Church of Love.[2]

The second letter is aimed at those who have become totally apathetic toward God, being neither for or against His Laws and Precepts, and thus they are "to be spewed out" by God for they fail to see that they are, in reality, "blind, wretched, pitiable, poor and naked." He admonishes them to return to doing good works in His Name so that they may be clothed in white linen, representing their good deeds, and to open their eyes to see God, to hear His knocking at their heart's door and to open that door and let Him enter in. In other words, the Lord is saying that in these times one must not be apathetic towards God and His Laws, lest one miss his/her opportunity to enter through the doorway—the crown

248

chakra, which is the doorway to Union with the Lord—and, thus, miss the opportunity for Union with God.[3]

Next, John is shown a vision of God as the Ancient of Days, surrounded by 24 "elders" and four collage-type animal creatures with eyes all over them, which represent all the animal and human life on Earth, and that God is everywhere and sees all. Interestingly enough, one branch of Hinduism believes that there are to be 24 avatars, or Sons of God, prior to the ushering in of the New Age of Light. Presently, 23 have already come, including Jesus, and they are awaiting the twenty-fourth. Could these 24 elders of John's vision represent those same 24 avatars?[4]

Next John sees Jesus as the Lamb of God who was slain for the salvation of man, and brought back to life again. It is He that is deemed worthy to open the scroll of the future in order to show John the events of the End Times.[5]

The Four Horsemen of Apocalypse

The first four seals of the scroll to be opened have been described as the "Four Horsemen of Apocalypse." Basically they represent the international conflicts that are to and have already started to embroil the earth. As with the American Indians, the East Indians and Jesus' prophecies, the trigger that starts the fateful ride of these four horsemen—who, on a macro level represent the bloodshed, death, destruction and economic chaos that wars bring—is the rise to power of the white race and their dominance over the Earth as a whole, subjugating native peoples worldwide, and exploiting the countries under their control. On a micro level, the four horsemen represent the world empires and/or political movements that would dominate the globe in the End Times. One explanation of these four horsemen is as follows:

The first rider on a white horse represents the Western European powers that grew out of the old Roman Empire, who "went out conquering and to conquer" as they colonized most of the world: Great Britain, France, and Spain being the principal colonizers.[6] Thus, **this seal has already been opened.**

The second rider on a red horse represents worldwide communism which has indeed taken peace from the Earth, bringing anarchy, war and killing, red being the color associated with communism.[7] For example, the Russian Communists are not only responsible for the slaughter of their own people (30 million under

Stalin alone), but also for the massacres and suppression of the Hungarian people in 1956, Czechoslovakia in 1968, and Poland and Afghanistan in 1980, not to mention the rest of the Eastern European countries that lie behind their Iron Curtain, as well as other countries round the world. The other communist giant—Red China—not only massacred almost 50 million of their own people under Mao, but waged genocide against the Tibetan people and disrupted peace in the region by attacking India in the late '50's, occupying its territory to this day. Thus, **this seal, too, has been opened.**

The Third Horseman—Economic Chaos

The third rider is on a black horse holding a balance scale, and represents worldwide economic turmoil, with inflation running at ridiculously high levels so that a loaf of bread might end up costing as much as $20. The only items not to be touched by these economic hard times are to be oil and wine.[8] This horseman further represents the worldwide famines that are to occur as a direct result of international strife. For when wars break out, growing cycles are interrupted, distribution patterns are upset and crops are damaged, not to mention the fact that money intended for food is diverted toward building more arms. Plus, it represents the pestilences that are an outgrowth of war as unburied bodies draw insects that spread all kinds of infectious diseases, insects being immune even to nuclear radiation. Hence, once-controlled diseases, like the plague, are another part of the threat to mankind that wars, specifically a nuclear one, present.

Today's world economic condition is the worst it has been in at least 40 years, and in many places, the worst in recorded history. High inflation and bulging budget deficits are causing rising food costs around the globe. This point is illustrated in the following two lists. The first shows which countries are in hock or in debt to foreign banks and/or countries. The second shows the inflation rates of countries round the world.

As we can see, many of the countries hardest hit are from Latin America. But the lists don't tell the whole story. For example, in Bolivia, the peso has plunged to a new low being worth only one-ninth of what it was in February, 1982, having already been devalued in February by a record 76%.[15] Our closest Latin

COUNTRIES IN DEBT[9]		INFLATION RATES	
1-Brazil:	$87.0 billion	1-Argentina:	400%
2-Mexico:	$85.0 billion	2-Israel:	125%
3-Argentina:	$43.0 billion	3-Mexico:	100%[10]
4-S. Korea:	$36.0 billion	4-Brazil:	100%[11]
5-Venezuela:	$28.0 billion	5-Costa Rica:	100%[12]
6-Israel:	$26.7 billion	6-Peru:	72.6%[13]
7-Poland:	$26.0 billion	7-Yugoslavia:	35.7%[14]
8-U.S.S.R.:	$23.0 billion		
9-Egypt:	$19.2 billion		
10-Philippines:	$16.6 billion		

American neighbor—Mexico—is also in deep trouble, its peso having lost three-fourths of its value vis-a-vis the U.S. dollar in the past 10 months alone. Approximately 55% of the country's labor force is either out of work or underemployed. And the problems are sure to get worse as Mexico's population grows at approximately 25% per year. That equates to 800,000 youths joining the work force each year, and projections show that the population will number over 100 million by the end of this century. Severe drought has hit 31 states, thus Mexico will have to import 10.5 million tons of grain by the end of 1983, which will put it into debt even more. This bleak economic picture has caused a run on the banks with people cleaning out accounts and safe deposit boxes, and merchants refusing to open stores.[16]

Millions of abandoned youngsters roam the city streets of Brazil with half of the country's children being undernourished. Columbia's situation is even worse with the annual per capita income running 40% less than in Brazil. And, in Costa Rica, the wages have lost a quarter of their buying power in the last year alone.[17]

This does not even touch the dire situations facing many African and Asian countries. The Sudan, Nigeria, Liberia, Zaire, Zambia, Nepal and Bangladesh are in such horrendous situations economically, with critical food shortages plaguing them, that they are on the brink of economic and political chaos. With international aid declining, high interest rates, the tourist industry down, high inflation and rapidly growing populations, the stage is set in many places for riots, coups, revolutions and general anarchy.

But it is not just poor, underdeveloped or war-ravaged countries that are suffering economic hard times. For example, the communist bloc countries have not escaped this economic plague either. Recently, there were food riots in Poland. In the Soviet Union itself, food shortages are acute, and certain staple food items, like meat and butter, are being rationed. As a matter of fact, certain parts of Russia have been hit so badly that the shelves of food shops contain nothing but dusty jars.

Further, some of the richest countries in the world have been reeling from blow after economic blow. Recently, the stock market in Hong Kong, which is the third largest financial center after New York and London, collapsed. Property values have plummeted and fortunes in the billions of dollars have been wiped out overnight! Japan is suffering from its worst unemployment in 26 years with 1.37 million out of work. The oil-rich Middle Eastern country of Kuwait has also been hit hard. The former strength of the Kuwaiti stock market is illustrated by the rise of stock prices of two companies—the Gulf Cement Co., whose shares climbed over 600% in one year, and the Gulf Co. for Industrial Development, whose stock prices soared 1500% over the same period. However, things are quite different now as the Kuwaiti stock market collapsed in September of 1982! One billionaire affected, who made $4 billion in a few months and threw a party costing $4 million only a few months prior to the collapse, today is in hock to the tune of $14 billion. He and other former billionaires have piled up a debt of over $92 billion in post-dated checks.[18]

West Europe and its colonial offshoots are also facing incredible economic hardships—hardships not seen in recorded history. For example, Australia is suffering from its worst economic situation since the Depression of the '30's, partially brought on by its worst drought in history. An incredible 2 million Aussies live below the poverty line, and soup kitchens and welfare centers are packed daily to overflowing. Canada is experiencing a 36-year jobless high with jobless payments up 79% over a year ago. Great Britain is suffering its worst unemployment since 1886, when employment statistics were first kept. A record of over 14% of the work force are without jobs,[19] and Britain's farmers owe banks a record $6.56 billion with interest payments taking 25% of all farm incomes. Belgium and Ireland have even higher unemployment rates.[20] West Germany, too, is suffering with its worst jobless rate since its official founding as a nation in 1949.

All tolled, 11 million Europeans are currently out of work, according to the Commissioner for Social Affairs of the European Economic Community (EEC or Common Market). What's different about these newly unemployed is that the majority of them are professional skilled workers. Already one out of every six young people in Great Britain is out of work or has never had a paying job,[21] and it is projected that by the mid '80's one-sixth of all Europeans will be out of work with 80% of the entire population having been affected by unemployment.[22]

Presently, one of the hardest hit groups in Europe is women. So scarce are jobs, especially for young women, that some of them are being forced into prostitution in order to earn a decent wage, as the unemployment insurance paycheck in England is only $40 per week—barely enough to buy food much less clothes, shelter, etc. Mind you, we are not talking about poor Third World countries, but Great Britain![23] Hence, **the Hindu prophecy** regarding women making their living by prostitution in the End Times **has been fulfilled.**

Even the Vatican has not escaped the world's economic woes. Currently it is running $28 million in the red, its largest deficit ever reported, and the recent scandal with its connection with the now-defunct Banco Ambrosiano has embarrassed Papal officials. Italian officials have claimed that the Vatican bank, which owned 1.58% of the bankrupt Ambrosiano (which, by the way, was the largest bankruptcy in Italian history), "is liable for $1.2 billion in bad loans left unpaid when the Ambrosiano collapsed," the questionable loans having been made on the strength of "letters of patronage" given by U.S. Archbishop Paul C. Marcinkus to the late Ambrosiano president, Roberto Calvi, who was found hanged June 18, 1982 in London.[24]

And then there is the economic situation in the U.S.A......

The Crumbling Economy of The United States

Today, the United States of America, one of the richest countries in the world, is suffering from one of its worst economic crises in its history. More people are unemployed today than at any time in our history, including the Great Depression. In truth, the problems created by the Great Depression of the '30's are being overshadowed by the Great Global Depression of the 1980's—perhaps the Greatest Depression in world history.

As of December, 1982, in the U.S., one out of every five people, or over 12 million Americans are unemployed. Nationwide, 32% or one out of every three American families has at least one household member who is either out of work or whose workweek or take-home pay has been reduced, according to the latest Harris Survey.[25] But experts agree that these figures are on the low end of the scale because they do not reflect the estimated 2 million or more who have become too discouraged to even look for jobs. Nor do they reflect the incredibly severe unemployment picture plaguing many parts of the country. Some of the hardest hit states include the state of Washington with 12.3% unemployed,[26] Alabama with 14.3% jobless,[27] and Michigan with 17% out of work.[28] (As of January, 1983, Michigan's jobless rate increased to over 24%.)

A special government "hard-times" list contains the names of over 1151 counties and cities suffering from high unemployment. Examples include Yancy County, North Carolina with 17.1% without work,[29] Flint, Michigan, with 19.8% jobless,[30] and Virginia, Minnesota, a mining community with an estimated 85% unemployed!

Jobs are so scarce that incredible numbers of people are lining up hours, sometimes days in advance to fill out applications for a few openings. When 700 postal worker positions opened up in Miami, over 100,000 people applied even though many of the positions may not be available until 1985.[31] When 200 new jobs opened at a department store in Detroit—one of the nation's hardest hit areas—1800 people a day filed in and patiently filled out applications.[32] But Chicago saw the most outpouring of job seekers per day in January of 1983, when more than 20,000 people lined up in freezing weather the first day that applications were being taken for only 2800 full-time and 1000 part-time city jobs, many of the jobs lasting for only 10 weeks.[33]

This past Christmas season (1982) was looking so bleak that Santa was getting some new requests from children. According to Sears Roebuck and Company's latest Santa Claus poll, "small children frequently tell Santa that their fathers are out of work and that they are worried about it," often telling Santa that all they wanted for Christmas is a job for Daddy or Mommy. Others asked for money instead of toys, and one little tot in Lake Grove, N.Y., "asked Santa to bring his father a chain saw so he could cut wood to keep the house warm."[34] Other children, recognizing the connection between money and war asked that "all of the nuclear weapons (would) disappear into thin air." Another said that "the world needs a nuclear weapons trash compactor," adding "Please hurry before the economy goes to the pits!"[35]

Here, however, the beauty of the true American spirit of charity and sharing can be seen, as in several communities, those who still have jobs and the means to do so helped make Christmas a little brighter for the unemployed and their children. For example, in that mining town of Virginia, Minn., some households "adopted" the families of the unemployed, providing food, money, and toys for the little ones during the Christmas season. And in Baton Rouge, La., some of the state's toughest criminals "played Santa" as hundreds of poor children received gifts from the Salvation Army paid for, in part, by donations received from inmates of the Louisianna State Penitentiary at Angola. The prisoners—who earn only 20¢ per day at their prison jobs—collected $3850 and gave it to the charity. Some of the prisoners had heard that donations to the charity were below average in 1982 because of the hard economic times. So they decided to do something about it and started a Christmas fund. "A large percentage of the 4600 convicts at the maximum security prison contributed to the fund."[36] Hence, 1200 poor children benefited from their generosity and kindness.

Often this is the case, i.e., that when people are confronted with suffering and hardship, the very best in them is brought out, and true self-sacrifice for the sake of others, who are in more need than they, is demonstrated. As the national and state unemployment figures continue to rise, more and more such demonstrations of caring and sharing will be needed, especially for the nation's minority groups as the national and state jobless figures do not begin to reflect the suffering that these groups are undergoing.

Most minorities, including women, the elderly and blacks, were the last to be hired, so they are usually the first to be fired. For example, the unemployment rate for blacks is upwards of 20% nationwide—more than twice the rate for white males—and more than 50% of black teenagers are without jobs. The poverty rate for blacks is about 32%—about three times that for whites—even though they account for only 12% of the total population of the country.

The overall poverty population has been increasing rapidly in the last two years. There are currently 31.8 million Americans in the poverty category—about 14% of the population—a large percentage of that number being elderly.[37] About 4 million people over the age of 55 live below the poverty line, existing on only one hot meal per day, and often resorting to dog and cat food for survival. The recent $40 billion cuts in social programs have hit the elderly especially hard, the vast majority of whom are women, **thus fulfilling the Hindu prophecy that the elderly will not be cared for and that there will be no liberality to the poor in the End Times** (the term "bleeding-heart liberal" actually being a reference to the bleeding heart of Jesus Christ!)

As it is, women are paid on an average of 35% to 50% less than men for comparable work, getting only 59¢ for each dollar that men get, and earning less today vis-a-vis men than they did 25 years ago! Almost one female-headed family in three is poor versus one in 18 families headed by a man, with three out of every four poverty-stricken Americans being women.[38]

Of course, if the women are without jobs and have no food, neither do their children. Children make up half of the beneficiaries of food stamps and 70% of welfare. Hence, they have been the hardest hit group overall from the recent cuts in social programs. According to the Census Bureau, 22% or almost a quarter of all American children under the age of six live in poverty. For black children, the poverty rate is one in two.[39] We're not talking about black babies in Africa—these are the children of America—our country's future. When a child is malnourished, his brain becomes damaged—damage that is irreversible for the rest of his life, which brings us to the twin problems facing the unemployed—hunger and homelessness.

Hunger and Homelessness in the U.S.

Across the country, the soup kitchens of the Great Depression of the '30's are again opening up. Many emergency food centers' shelves have already been stripped bare, and with the government cutting aid to charities, the situation is sure to get worse. In Detroit and elsewhere, the unemployed are begging for food and swamping free-meal centers, **thus fulfilling the Hindu prophecy that householders will take to begging in the End Times.** In Tennessee, 10,000 people lined up for food that was once given only

256

to animals, having been deemed unfit for human consumption.[40] Again in Detroit, 80,000 people lined up in freezing temperatures to get free cheese and powdered milk in January of '83. In Lansing, Mich., the jobless are literally selling their life's blood in order to get money to buy food.[41] Finally, in another Michigan town, hunger drove one starving man to kill and eat his neighbor's dog![42] Remember, this didn't happen in the Philippines, Africa or Bangladesh: it happened in the U.S. of A.!

As the cold weather of winter sets in—a winter forecasters predict will be the worst this century—the plight of the growing numbers of homeless Americans is becoming more and more acute. Today there are an estimated two to three million homeless people—more than at any other time in the nation's history, including the Great Depression when one to two million were homeless.[43] People are being evicted from their homes in record numbers, including a 94-year-old woman who has lived in the same house for 75 years, and an elderly woman and her quadriplegic son, whose home of 50-odd years will be torn down in order to make room for a parking lot, having been condemned under the law of "Eminent Domain," which basically says that any government—national, state or local—can seize your private property if it feels that it is in the "interest of the public" to do so: i.e., to make room for a new highway, build a dam, put up a parking lot, etc.

Those who have not been evicted are selling their furniture, cars, etc., in order to pay their heating bills—bills that have shot up over 70% in one year despite the abundant supply of energy. Those who cannot pay their bills are having their heat cut off, even in 26° below zero weather, and hence, **more and more people are literally freezing to death, again, fulfilling prophecy.**[44]

Those who have been evicted from their homes are living wherever they can. Tent villages reminiscent of the Hoovervilles of the '30's are springing up all over the country, this time being dubbed "Reaganvilles" or "Reagan Ranches." Other depression victims are tenting out on neighor's lawns, or are sleeping on street corners, in alleyways, abandoned and condemned buildings, or in transportation center waiting rooms. Here, again, the American heart can be seen as one of the most affluent churches in San Francisco, the Episcopal Grace Cathedral, has opened its doors to house the homeless, the church's officials urging other churches across America to do the same.[45]

Still others that are homeless have turned to the National Parks system for relief, going from park to park in order to comply with residency time restrictions. Some have turned the park sites into permanent homes, staying out the mandatory 24 to 48 hour waiting period, and then returning to the same park. Not all those camping out are poor minorities or unskilled workers; on the contrary, the vast majority of newly-homeless are professional and/or highly skilled workers, including computer programmers and even aerospace engineers. The number turning to the Parks system has increased by 30% in one year, **thus fulfilling Hindu prophecy regarding people resorting to the mountains and forests in order to live,** having been robbed of their wealth, etc., by greedy and merciless politicians and soldiers—**a prophecy made over 5000 years ago and half-a-world away!**

But even this last resort of the unemployed and homeless is threatened as the Interior Department under the direction of James Watt, the plague of the environmentalists, is planning the most massive public lands sale of the century, literally putting thousands and thousands of acres on the auction block. Once the lands are in private hands, the homeless will again be evicted, with nowhere to go.

The American Indians fear that they may be homeless as well, as they believe that Watt's recent critical remarks about the Indians' life-style cloak a sinister design to use that as an excuse to disband the reservation system and deprive them of their lands, in order to open them up for mining exploitation, etc. The above will fulfill the last sign of the Indian prophecies about their lands being taken from them. An American Indian leader responding to Watt's criticism stated that Watt thought that the American Indians were communists since their skin color is red!

Stress, Violence and Crime

With these kinds of pressures facing the unemployed, it is not surprising that some have resorted to theft, suicide, and all forms of violence, particularly within the family and including "mindless violence" such as the Tylenol/Anacin 3-cyanide killings. As Anne Cohn, executive director of the National Committee for the Prevention of Child Abuse, put it, "We do know the unemployment rate has skyrocketed this year as has the number of child deaths."[46] For example, in Colorado, where unemployment

258

increased by 67% over the past four years, there has been a 100% increase in the number of cases of child abuse and a five-fold increase in the number of deaths as a result of abuse.

Others unable to mentally handle the strain have literally gone insane, or sought solace in drugs, specifically alcohol. According to Dr. M. Harvey Benner of the John Hopkins University in Baltimore, when unemployment rises 1%, state prison populations climb 4%, 4.3% more men and 2.3% more women enter mental hospitals, and suicides increase by 4.1%. The longer the unemployment persists, the worse the situation gets with a 1.9% increase in those who die from cirrhosis of the liver, heart disease and other ailments.[47] As Jesus said, "Men's hearts will fail them out of fear for what is coming to the earth."

One funeral home director in Houston said that he saw a higher concentration of suicides in the month of October, '82, than in his 40 years in the business.[48] Some examples of the above include the following:

> "An unemployed petrochemical engineer, unable to find work, shot himself to death at his Houston home. An out-of-work auto mechanic in Mattawan, Mich., strangled his wife and two children, then killed himself. One United Auto Workers local in California said, eight unemployed workers have committed suicide this year. And in Detroit...a suicide prevention center reported calls have tripled."[49]

One unemployed man who shot his wife and himself after losing his home and business left a suicide note saying: "We came to San Antonio (Texas) to work, not to die. But Reagan economics has nothing trickling down to us."[50] Finally, a man dropped from the Social Security disability rolls shot himself outside the Social Security offices in Lansing, Michigan, leaving a note saying: "They cut my Social Security. They are playing God."[51] That same day, the stock market—the mirror that reflects the country's economic image—lost 6.66 points—that number being the mark of the antichrist. Coincidence?

Unfortunately, the tragedies and sufferings endured by individuals affected by joblessness, homelessness, hunger and social program benefit cutbacks, etc., go on and on, with people literally dying for want of bread, a warm shelter, or mental anguish.

As the tragedies multiply, so does the violence. Already, riots,

259

strikes, and protest marches have broken out all over the globe as America's high interest rates affect the world economy so adversely. The unemployed have been rioting in London—the city's worst riots in years—and Manchester, where 1000 youths looted and torched buildings throughout the city; in Berlin, where the eviction of homeless squaters touched off violent street battles between police and youths; in Belgium, where 10,000 steel-workers protesting plant closings ripped out lamp posts and over-turned cars; in Warsaw, Poland, where three people died in riots sparked by food shortages; in Bombay, India, where 22,000 policemen rioted, setting buildings on fire and looting businesses; in Ottawa, Canada, where the largest demonstration ever held in its national capitol was staged to decry the "lunacy" of high interest rates; and finally, in San Franciso, where the largest collective labor demonstration in 32 years was held, with over 35,000 workers marching down the city's streets protesting Reaganomics, and shouting "More Jobs!," and "We can't eat jelly beans!"

Bulging Deficits

The question is why are all these things happening? What is causing this worldwide economic catastrophe? The answer is bulging deficits mainly due to massive spending for the military programs embraced by the present American administration. While social programs for the poor, elderly, handicapped, minorities and children are being cut drastically, spending for military programs has sky-rocketed as the U.S. continues its most massive military buildup in history, surpassing even the defense budgets of the Vietnam War era. This massive spending has raised the U.S. budget deficit to an all-time high—a record $110 billion for 1982 alone, the most red ink ever and far above the previous high of $66 billion under the Ford Administration in 1976, which had been reduced by President Carter to about $27 billion by 1979. Projections are that the deficit will continue to balloon, hitting aproximately $207 billion by 1983, if the present massive military buildup continues. As the conservative *Honolulu Advertiser* in its February 1, 1983 Focus—Economy Section stated:

> "Although he started his term pledging to shrink federal spending and indeed balance the budget by 1984, Reagan in

fact seems likely to roll up a series of deficits during his four-year term that could surpass the total deficits of all other presidents combined—from George Washington to Jimmy Carter."[52]

In order to finance these programs and carry these bulging deficits, the federal government must borrow the money. Currently, the interest (not principal) payment alone on the national debt is costing American taxpayers $119,821.84 per minute![53] The depressed economy caused by the record-high deficits and massive government borrowing has forced a record 50,000 businesses to go bankrupt in 1981 alone,[54] and that dismal trend continued into the first 11 weeks of 1982, with companies folding at a rate 50% more than in the same period of '81. Personal bankruptcies are at epidemic levels as more and more people are being forced to file "Chapters 7, 11 and 13"—the laws concerning bankruptcy. Things have gotten so bad that:

> "A bipartisan group of prominent Americans—including several former Cabinet officers and the chief executives of big U.S. corporations—has bought newspaper advertisements calling on the president to dramatically alter his economic program in an effort to lower the record deficits expected between now and 1985.
> "A draft advertisement being circulated among the businessmen, financiers, lawyers and academicians says that 'The federal budget is now out of control...This fiscal course is senseless.' "[55]

The ad goes on to call for cuts in various areas of the budget, including big cuts in defense spending. As the American economy continues to slump, the economies of the Common Market nations follow suit with business failures at an all-time high. In Great Britain alone, business failures have increased more than 63% in the last two years, according to a recent survey by Dun and Bradstreet.[56] Similarly, the Soviet economy is crumbling along with its allies' due to massive military spending.

The massive military buildup in the U.S. will cost the American taxpayer $38 million an hour over the next five years, and that's only if we remain at peace! The total price tag of this five-year buildup program is upwards of $1.675 trillion! That works out to be more than $20,000 for every taxpayer in the U.S., according to the Center for Defense Information in D.C., and that does not include cost-overruns estimated by experts in the billions.

As stated before, there is absolutely no need for this military buildup or for the building of more nuclear weapons as we can already destroy the entire world several times over with what we have. What's more, it has been estimated that the U.S. can fully maintain its security commitments for at least $135 billion less over the next five years than what the present administration's program calls for as a recent Gallup poll indicated that the American public believes that 25¢ out of every defense dollar spent is wasted. Further, many of the new weapons systems proposed are totally unnecessary and/or will be obsolete even before their completion.[57] Even the Heritage Foundation, a conservative "think tank," has stated that: "High technology weapons that often don't work under battlefield conditions are soaking up dollars from President Reagan's defense budget, leaving the nation with fewer effective weapons and soaring military costs."[58] And Representative Bill Green, Republican of Manhattan, and a member of the House Appropriations Committee, recently stated that: "In short, the current defense program is dangerous both to the U.S.'s economic well-being and future defense. Congress must face up to that reality."[59]

Many proponents of the arms buildup use the lure of jobs to justify the program's ridiculously high cost. In truth, massive military spending does not create jobs; it eliminates them. For every billion dollars spent on military purchases, 18,000 jobs are lost because that money is not spent by consumers, according to a new study by the Employment Research Associates of Lansing, Michigan, the study stating that "Enactment of President Reagan's $238.6 billion defense budget for 1984 would cause a net loss of 2.2 million jobs in the civilian economy."[60] Dollar for dollar, only half as many jobs are created due to military spending versus civilian spending.

Today, more than $550 billion per year is spent on military arms, a sum that is equal to the combined annual income of the poorest half of the world's population, or 4 billion people, as the human race seems bent on rushing headlong toward its own destruction. Most of these arms have been sold by the U.S. and the U.S.S.R. (75% combined). For example, U.S. arms sales to other countries is expected to exceed $30 billion by the end of '82— more than any nation has sold in world history and triple the amount sold in all of 1981.

One of the reasons these sales are so frightening is that many of the world's arms dealers are selling advanced weapons to unstable governments, several of them being military regimes and/or dictatorships, such as Pakistan, Argentina, Brazil, Libya, Iraq, etc. Very often these arms are used not in defense of the country, against some outside threat, but against that nation's own people. Examples of this can be seen all over Latin America where military regimes continue to use arms supplied to them, often by the U.S., to control, suppress and intimidate the general populace. The increase in U.S. arms to dictatorial regimes is a total reversal of former President Carter's policy regarding weapons sales. Under Carter, military aid was tied to the human rights record of the potential buyer. Today, the U.S. is selling arms to just about any country, regardless of its human rights record, provided it declares itself "anti-communist."

The problem with this new policy is that these dictators and regimes who use American-made arms to suppress their own people, won't and don't last forever. Hence, when one dies or is overthrown, as with the former Shah of Iran, America is then faced with an angry nation which is equipped with our own most advanced weapons. Not a very savoury situation!

Guns vs. Butter; Bombs vs. Bread

What's even worse is that each dollar spent on bombs takes bread out of the mouths of countless starving people. In 1953, President Eisenhower said:

> "Every gun that is made, every warship launched, every rocket fired, signifies in a final sense a theft from those who hunger and are not fed—those who are cold and not clothed. This world in arms is not spending money alone—it is spending the sweat of its laborers, the genius of its scientists, the houses of its children."[61]

Nearly 30 years later, India's Prime Minister Indira Gandhi reiterated Eisenhower's words in her keynote address to the Food and Agriculture Organization's 21st Congress, explaining that the cost of one intercontinental missile (ICBM), "could plant 200 million trees, irrigate one million hectares (2.47 million acres), feed 50 million malnourished children...buy a million tons of fertilizers, erect a million small bio-gas plants, build 65,000 health-care centers or 340,000 primary schools."[62]

Mrs. Gandhi re-emphasized this truth, i.e., that money for bombs takes bread from the mouths of the hungry, at the Non-aligned Movement Conference that met in March, 1983 in New Delhi. In her inaugural speech, Mrs. Gandhi said, "Humankind is balancing on the brink of the collapse of the world economic system...We of the developing world have no margin of safety." She added, "We ask not for charity or philanthropy but sound economic sense."

> "It was in the context of the world economic crisis that the Non-aligned Movement (joined other groups and countries around the world giving its) final 'appeal to the great powers' (calling) for an immediate freeze on the production of nuclear weapons by all nations, as well as immediate, concrete steps toward disarmament, (Mrs. Gandhi explaining that): 'The world is a single network. If you think of it as electrical, none can escape its fluctuations, and if there is a blowout, the darkness will shroud all.' "[63]

Today, the world's food situation is reaching a critical stage as over 500 million to one billion people suffer from starvation and/or malnutrition—that's almost one-fifth of the world's total population. Everyday 40,000 children die from lack of food, according to the Executive Director of the United Nations' Children's Fund.[64] Worldwide, 28 people per minute die of starvation, 21 of them being children.[65] In Africa alone, where starvation and malnutrition have reached epidemic levels, more than 150 million are on the brink of starvation with 7 dropping dead every minute for want of food. **The children have arms as thin as sticks, emaciated for lack of proper sustenance, fulfilling the Hindu prophecies regarding men's bodies being emaciated and reduced in size due to lack of food in this age.** Twenty-three out of 26 African nations are suffering from acute food shortages as the worst drought in African history sweeps across that continent.

But it is not only the peoples of Africa that are suffering; famine and food shortages are becoming a worldwide phenomenon. Bangladesh, Cambodia, parts of Latin America and other Third World countries are suffering. In Poland, food rationing of butter, flour and cereals has caused riots, as mentioned earlier. As a matter of fact, all of East Europe is experiencing critical food shortages.

This year's Soviet grain harvest was disastrous as one-fifth of the harvest was lost because it was harvested late or left to rot, and one-third of the potatoes also rotted in the ground, forcing the Russians to import more and more food just to feed their own people, much less anyone else's.

Even in the U.S., food prices continue their steady upward climb. One of the reasons for this is that Americans waste one-fifth of all the food produced in this country. That equates to 137 million tons or $31 billion worth of food thrown away annually, or 23 pounds per week for every man, woman and child in this country. It's no wonder that leaders of countries whose people are starving get upset with the massive food wastage that they see going on every day in the U.S., not to mention the hungry people in the U.S. itself.

Yet, the U.S. is also the world's leading donator of food aid to developing countries—an interesting paradox that again demonstrates the true beauty of the American heart, as well as the political savvy of those in charge. For they know that hungry bellies are often fed on the rhetoric of revolution. As the pangs of hunger grow, so does the anger of the people suffering from them. For a hungry and starving populace is a potential powderkeg waiting for the match of anger to light its short fuse. Thus we see that **the prophecies regarding food shortages and famines during the End Times have been fulfilled.**

Chapter 10

PESTILENCE AND OVERPOPULATION, CRIME AND VIOLENCE IN THE END TIMES

One of the other main reasons there is so much famine today is overpopulation. Man's population was not always out of balance. As a matter of fact, it was not until the onset of the Industrial Revolution of the 1800's that things started to speed up uncontrollably. According to Robert S. MacNamara, former World Bank President, in 1750 there were only 800 million people inhabiting the Earth. But by 1900, that figure had doubled to 1.6 billion; by '64, it had doubled again to 3.2 billion. Today's world population is roughly 4.5 billion, but by the year 2000 it is expected to reach 6.35 billion with 90% of that growth occurring in the poorer countries. That means 80% of the total population of the Earth will be living in the less developed countries, and that 8 out of every 10 people will be suffering from poverty, hunger, stress, crowding and frustration.[1]

For example, India's population increases by one million per month, even though the Indian government has and is making a concerted and sincere effort to control it.[2] China's growth rate is even worse despite the government's massive campaigns supporting family planning and limited growth; in Bangladesh, seven babies are born every minute, which equates to 420 per hour or 10,080 per day or 3,679,200 per year in that one tiny country alone.[3] Worldwide, the population of the Earth grows about 90 million per year.[4] As MacNamara said, "Except for thermonuclear war, population growth is the gravest issue the world faces over the decades immediately ahead."[5]

In Nature, under normal circumstances, no species overpopulates, and if it does, drastic measures are often used to reduce the excess animals. The lemmings of the Arctic are a prime example. Whenever their numbers become too great, they run in masses off cliffs to die on the rocks below.

The consequences of the psychological and physical pressures of overpopulation were graphically illustrated by the experiment of Rat City. Scientists put a few adult rat couples into a plexiglas "city" with ample food, water, and space, but as the rats continued to propagate without any checks on their population growth, pressures for food, water and living space became more and more severe. Soon, mothers, who had been attentive and loving to their pups earlier, began abandoning them and often died while giving birth. Violence, aggression, even murder and cannibalism set in leading to disease and death. In the end, all the rats in the city died! If man does not learn to control his own population growth, he too may end up like the rats in Rat city, or like the lemmings in the Arctic, running off the cliff into the abyss of extinction below.

Pestilence and Epidemics

As we have seen, one of the consequences of overpopulation is disease, caused by filth and crowding. Both Jesus and John in Revelations state that mankind will be plagued by diseases and pestilences in various places during the End Times. And, indeed, we are already experiencing these epidemics. Several of the epidemics hitting the world today have to do with the act of procreation as sexually transmitted diseases are fast becoming the major concern of physicians and scientists alike.

One example of this is what *Time Magazine* called "The New Scarlet Letter: Herpes."[6] In the U.S. alone, 20 to 70 million adults are victims of herpes, which is usually transmitted by sexual contact. Over the last decade or so, there was a 850% increase in the incidence of the disease, with 200,000 to 500,000 new cases reported each year—a disease that stays with you for the rest of your life. It is characterized by open, oozing sores that can affect not only your genital areas and buttocks, but also underarms, mouth and eyes.[7] Thus, **this disease fulfills Revelations' prophecy** regarding people in the End Times being afflicted with open and oozing sores.[8]

Unfortunately, there is no cure as of yet, and even methods of controlling the disease have eluded scientists. What's more, infants can be infected with the disease. Three thousand infants died in 1981 alone from it, with 70% of these dead babies being born to mothers who had no medical history of the disease. Other effects of the disease in babies include mental retardation, cerebral palsy and baldness.

But herpes is not the only sexually transmitted disease affecting infants: syphilis has also been increasing among newborns, up 42% in 1981, according to the Center for Disease Control in D.C.

For women, the increase in syphilis was 21.6%. Other sexually transmitted diseases reaching epidemic proportions include: "Super Gonorrhea," called "super" because it is penicillin-resistant, found in 42 different countries and affecting several U.S. service men in the Philippines and South Korea, as well as people in the U.S.; and the "Gay Plague," so-called because it was first noticed in homosexual males, but has since shown up in heterosexual males and females, being called an epidemic unprecedented in the history of American medicine as it has no known cure and kills four out of every ten who contract it, "threatening to explode in the nation's big cities" as the the number of reported cases increased by 50% during the second quarter of 1982.[9]

Other non-sexual epidemics plaguing the world include:
- A meningitis outbreak in Texas and Connecticut;
- "Pink Eye" infections in Samoa, affecting over one-third of the residents there;
- A viral eye infection in India, affecting 20 million people;
- The worst measles outbreak in decades in the U.S., specifically Florida;
- Flu epidemics in the U.S. (70,000 killed) and Japan ('82 being the worst flu season in four years there);
- A 20% to 30% increase in the incidence of leprosy worldwide, including an increase in the U.S.;
- Typhoid, killed 13,000 people in Guatemala recently;
- Cholera and bubonic plague, all on the rise over the number of cases reported but a few years ago.

Part of the reason for the rise in epidemics is due to the fact that several antibiotic resistant strains of viruses have shown up. This is because of the worldwide overuse of antibiotics. As Nobel Laureate and Harvard University molecular biology professor Dr. Walter Gilbert explained: "We can look forward to a time when 80% to 90% of all infections" are resistant to current treatments.[10] For example, in the 1940's, penicillin cured nearly 100% of all infections caused by staph germs; today it's effective in only 10% of the cases.

In fact, with regard to drug abuse—another modern-day epidemic—abuse of (legal) prescription drugs accounts for 75% of drug-related emergencies versus 25% for illegal drugs.

268

Thus, we can see that **the prophecies regarding plagues and epidemics in the End Times have been abundantly fulfilled.**

The Love of Many to Cool—Crime and Violence

As we have seen, one of the consequences of overpopulation is increased violence and aggression. This is also one of the consequences of unemployment. As mentioned earlier, the Third Seal of Revelations represents the economic chaos that is engulfing the world in these End Times, whose results are unemployment, hunger and violence. This increased violence is one of the common signs of all sets of prophecies regarding the end of this system of things. As Jesus put it, "The love of most people will grow cold due to wickedness multiplying." Hence, crimes of all kinds will increase dramatically.

All one need do is look at any newspaper today to see that **this prophecy has been fulfilled.** Violent crime, in particular, is soaring. For example, **in the U.S., one violent crime is committed every 24 seconds!** There is a murder every 23 minutes, a rape every 9 minutes, a robbery every 58 seconds. And only 19% of all crimes are ever solved and the perpetrators arrested![11]

Across the U.S., as well as in other parts of the world, fear of crime is causing many to literally barricade themselves in their homes. Crimes of all types are on the increase. For example, "The murder rate in Dade County, (Florida) has grown by more than 90% in less than two years, with Miami's homicide rate escalating by 131%;"[12] a bomb wave swept across the East Coast from New York to Boston and Connecticut, with "96 threats in 24 hours...phoned to police (in N.Y.C.)...after the discovery of 5 live bombs in three days;"[13] incest in the U.S. is at epidemic proportions with one out of every 100 women being sexually molested by her father before she reaches adulthood;[14] nationwide, one out of every three young girls will be sexually assaulted by the time she reaches the age of 16, forcing many Girl Scout troops to incorporate self-defense courses in their curriculum; and the prison population in this country has risen 18% since 1981 with the system now operating at 16.7% above its capacity.[15]

Senseless violence is becoming more the rule than the exception. For example, in Los Angeles, "two masked men enter a coffee shop and steal the receipts and valuables from employees and customers, (and then) herd 11 people into a walk-in refrigerator, and open fire, killing three and wounding six; (also in L.A.) a nurse on her way to work is abducted screaming, by three young men who jump into her pickup truck at a red light. She is robbed, raped and beaten to death. Police arrest three suspects because a teenager returned to his neighborhood and 'bragged' about the killing;"[16] (again in L.A.), two young women are accused of 25 random shootings of complete strangers, saying they did it "for fun;" in Ohio, a young man first tries to poison and then shoots at his parents across the breakfast table seriously wounding his mother; and, finally, in Houston, "two friends shot and killed each other in a bar after arguing over how easy it would be to escape arrest for murder in the city."[17]

The recent rash of poisonings involving over-the-counter medications such as the cyanide-Tylenol case, Anacin III poisonings, acid-laced Visine eye drops, poisons found in children's Halloween candies, the recent cyanide poisoning of a Louisiana reservoir that services over 250,000 people, etc., again demonstrate the number of insane, inhuman, sadistic individuals there are out there.

These types of senseless killings are not restricted to city limits. Rural areas, too, are undergoing an epidemic rise in crimes of all kinds, including an incident where two men in a pickup truck fired blasts from their shotgun at drivers and passengers of other vehicles as they passed by. Nor are violent acts restricted to adults. Today, in this country, 4000 babies are murdered every year under one week old, and an additional 14,000 more are killed between the ages of one week to three years.[18]

But the U.S. is not alone. Crime rates are rising all over the world. In China, crimes of every type are rising, according to the *Shanghai Liberation Daily*. In London, the worst crime statistics in its history were recently released by Scotland Yard: violent robbery has increased by 34%, muggings are up 41%, robberies from shops and factories are up a whopping 84%, and the number of armed robberies has doubled, while the English countryside has also been plagued by punks and toughs who have rampaged across Southern England armed with ax handles, machetes and knives. In Ottawa, Canada, violent crime is up 17%, with property crime soaring an average 34%. Police in Victoria, British Columbia are so upset with the amount of residential break-ins (up 30% in one year) that they say they just can't cope anymore.

Of course, the rate of violent crimes committed in the U.S. is still much higher than what is committed in other countries. For example, "a review of 1978 crime statistics reveals 215 times more robberies in this country than in Japan, 10 times more homicides, and 25 times more rapes."[19]

Many believe the reason for this is the easy accessibility to weapons, particularly handguns, in the U.S. Statistics seem to back up this theory. According to Handgun Control, Inc., in all of 1981, there were only 48 handgun deaths in Japan, 8 in Great Britain, 34 in Switzerland, and 52 in Canada compared to **10,728 in the USA!**

According to David Steinberg, the Executive Director of the National Council for a Responsible Firearms Policy, since the assassination of President John F. Kennedy, more than 200,000 Americans have been murdered with guns, with another 190,000 committing suicide and 50,000 more being killed accidentally with guns. In that same period of time, 1.7 million people have been wounded with guns and 2.7 million robbed at gunpoint. One-half of all U.S. households have guns, and as Steinberg put it, "There may be nearly as many guns as there are people (in the U.S.)"[20] Indeed, he may be right as there are an estimated two million handguns added to the U.S. market each year, as the "defense" or "security" business is one of the only "growth industries" left in the U.S. today.

Victims of this crime epidemic include all kinds of famous people, such as John Lennon, Pope John Paul II, and even President Ronald Wilson Reagan, as more and more psychotic killers stalk famous and charismatic people in order to fulfill some bizarre need for recognition or just senseless insanity.

Mass Murder, Racism and Religious Persecution

In the U.S., the most violent crime—murder—has taken an even more bizarre twist, i.e., the rapidly escalating epidemic of mass murders. According to John Godwin, author of *"Murder U.S.A.,"* during the last half of this century, the mass murderer has become the symbol of the crime wave. He says that, "the second half of the 20th Century could be called America's Age of the Mass Murder."[21] So prevalent have these murders become that one English criminologist, Grierson Dirkson, has coined the term "multicide" to describe them.

Godwin conducted a study of mass murders in the U.S. during

the 20th Century, the results of which are frightening. During the first 50 years of this century, the U.S. had only seven recorded multicides with seven or more victims. Over the next 26 years, that number rose sharply to 16, 10 of them occurring between 1970 and 1976, with more than 100 victims killed in those six years. These figures do not include the recent multicides of the last six years. From 1976 to 1982, the American public has been shocked day after day with mass murders becoming almost commonplace. California seems to have been one of the hardest hit sections of this country with several cases of multicides, including the murders of 25 farm workers by one individual, 21 persons by another, and the strangling deaths of 5 teenage girls by a third. In Chicago, 33 young men and boys were killed by one man and buried under his house. In New York City, a single individual has pleaded guilty to murdering six people. And, perhaps the saddest case of all is that of the slaying of over two dozen children in the Atlanta, Georgia area.

As mentioned earlier, the recent dramatic rise in crimes of all types is an indication of the hard economic times we are living in. However, economics is not the only reason lying behind this crime wave. Several of these murders seem to have a perverted sexual motive behind them, while others seem to be racially and/or religiously motivated. The recent riots in Washington, D.C., during a Ku Klux Klan rally and those in Miami illustrate the fever pitch that racial emotions have reached in this country. The recently released video game—Custer's Revenge—where the object of the game is to maneuver "Custer" to an Indian maiden so he can rape her—shows the degree of insensitivity, hatred, and racism toward Indians that still pervades this land. In Europe, especially in Great Britain, random beatings of brown-skinned peoples is becoming an every day occurrence.

Several groups have been attacking various religious organizations. The specter of Nazism has again risen sharply—a 200% increase in violent acts against Jews in one year worldwide—with synagogues and Jewish business establishments often being the targets of snipers, bombers, and vandals. In the U.S. alone, anti-Semitic vandalism and assaults almost tripled in 1980, according to a nationwide survey conducted by the Jewish Anti-Defamation League of B'Nai B'rith. But the Jews are not the only religious group being persecuted. In Iran, members of the Baha'i faith have had their bank accounts and property confiscated, schools and temples closed, children taken away, and are being tortured and killed by the hundreds, if not thousands.

Many of these racially and/or religiously fanatical organizations have set up training camps for children, including Boy Scouts and Civil Air Patrol Cadets. At these camps, the children are taught various techniques of violence including how to fire guns, use knives and bayonnets, and the techniques of strangling a person to death. Other so-called "survival camps" are conducting paramilitary training for adults including practice with M-16 semi-automatic rifles, studies of guerrilla war techniques, how to make bombs, booby traps, chemical explosives, fuses and detonators, grenades, mines, etc.

Mass Media

The minds of many children in this country have been corrupted by the mass media, television in particular. Experts have estimated that the average American child may see over 20,000 shootings, violent deaths, or other acts of violence by the time he/she is 16 years old. There is an average of five to six acts of violence per hour in prime time T.V., and an astounding 26 to 28 violent acts per hour on Saturday morning children's cartoon shows—about one every two minutes! According to a recently released ten-year study by the National Institute of Mental Health, there is now "overwhelming evidence of a causal relationship between violence on television and later aggressive behavior," with other effects of T.V. exposure including "mistrust, fear, alienation, paranoia, and a distorted view of reality."[22]

As historian Arthur Schlessinger, Jr. explains: "The mass media do not create violence. But they (especially T.V. and films) reinforce aggressive and destructive impulses and they may well teach the morality as well as the methods of violence."[23]

Recent studies have shown that many children and young people have become desensitized to violence and, hence, would not help a person in distress, rather, they would just watch. This behavior is carried over to the field of video games, which U.S. Surgeon General C. Evert Koop has said is partly responsible for the increasing violence in this country. In remarks to reporters before a speech he delivered to the University of Pittsburgh's Western Psychiatric Institute, Koop stated that incidents of violence in the U.S. have increased, and he personally believes that video games have contributed to this increase. He is probably right because the whole point of most video games is to "zap the enemy;" in other words, destroy one's opponent. Thus, violent and aggressive actions are encouraged and rewarded.

The video game phenomena has parents, teachers and physicians alike concerned as children addicted to the games are skipping school, stealing and/or begging for money to play them, and stunting their physical, emotional, social and intellectual growth by spending hours in front of those video screens. The stress produced by playing these games is very great. According to the coroner's office in Lake County, Indiana, an 18-year-old suburban Chicago youth died of a heart attack "as a direct result of stress caused by the (video) game" he was playing, which brings us to another common sign of the End Times—**Stress.**[24]

Chapter 11

OUR HUNG-UP, STRESSED-OUT WORLD

According to all sets of prophecies, there is to be great stress upon the Earth in the End Times, both physical and mental. Indeed, the stress of living in the world today does take its toll as physicians warn us of this silent killer which is becoming an epidemic of a variety never before seen in the world. It is estimated that stress is the leading cause of death in tens of millions of people each year. It also makes the body more vulnerable to all kinds of afflictions ranging from skin rashes to the common cold, heart attacks to cancer, ulcers to diabetes.

Russian researchers have stated that they feel there is more stress in the world today than ever before. "They say for every year you are alive today, you live 1000 years of life as it existed 100 years ago. So every lifetime is thousands of lifetimes."[1]

As we have seen, economic chaos, unemployment, hunger, homelessness, and just daily living causes severe pressures on the individual. But the most important psychological reason for stress, especially among the youth today is the specter of a worldwide nuclear holocaust. The Punk Rock movement, attended with its violence, including self-inflicted pain, is the direct result of this stress as the first generation that's had to live with the threat of nuclear obliteration tries to cope. Even the groups' names carry the message of despair and hopelessness as Devo— short for De-evolution—is one of the most popular punk groups. Their message is basically, "Why care about anything? We're all going to die in a nuclear holocaust anyway, so what's the point of going on?" Thus, the sight of dashed dreams and hopelessness turns to rage and violence against others and, finally, against oneself. It certainly doesn't help to alleviate the children's stress when they read banner headlines saying: "Pentagon's Military Agenda: Preparations to Win a Nuclear War,"[2] and "U.S. 'Military Blueprint': Prepare to Battle Soviets."[3]

Stress turns to paranoia and, finally, hopelessness when one reads that there is an actual document entitled "Fiscal 1984-1988 Defense Guidance" which details a military buildup "for winning an extended nuclear war 'effectively' from outer space...(and) for expanding any conventional conflict with the Soviets to a global scale," changing the emphasis from a **defensive** to "an **offensive** military campaign."[4] Examples of this hopelessness can be seen in letters written by young children from different parts of the U.S.A. to the leaders of our nation:

Dear Mr. President,

Please have peace. Why have wars? Nobody needs them. A lot of my relatives have died in them, too many innocent people have died in wars. And with nuclear and atomic bombs coming out, even more innocent people will die. Why not sit down and talk like adults! Please have peace. Now if you press a button, a whole country is leveled out.

—Shaun, age 7, Tacoma, Washington

(Shaun's teacher: "Shaun had tears in his eyes as he wrote this and left saying, 'Mrs._____, I got a lump in my throat while I was writing this. I wish things could be different than they are now but my feeling is that it might never happen!' ")[5]

★★★★★★★★★★★★★★★★★★★★★★

"People do not care enough for each other, that is why all this is happening; pollution, nuclear power plants, nuclear weapons, greed, hate, and a lack of respect for each others' differences. If just half of the money spent on building nuclear weapons was spent on feeding the hungry people of the world, it would be a much better place to live. If people were not hungry and cold, no one would have anything to fight about! When someone asks for peace take the offer and remember that all creatures will go on living. Peace and getting along together is the answer.

"Let's talk about it, let's think about it and let's start doing something about it!!!!!"[6]

—Frank, age 11, Keaau, Hawaii

★★★★★★★★★★★★★★★★★★★★★★

"The Nuclear Nightmare"

"We know that trying to survive through a nuclear war is almost impossible, so what we have to do is to try to prevent this terrible war from happening.

"Can you imagine it? The world could be totally destroyed just by pushing a button or two and some people aren't even aware of this terrible situation...

THIS IS WHAT OUR CHILDREN FEAR

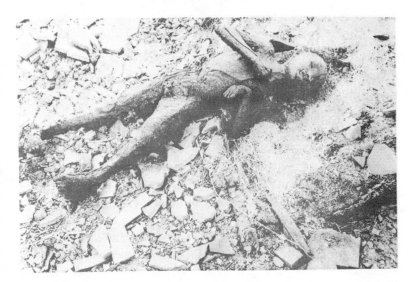

This was a boy   Nagasaki
The charred remains. 700 meters from the hypocenter. August 10, 1945.

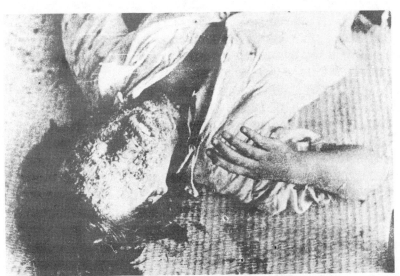

Both photos reprinted with permission from No More Hiroshimas, Japan.

A Schoolgirl   Hiroshima
Nothing could save her. "Water, Water!" Only death ended her suffering.
Red-Cross Hospital. August 10, 1945.

277

"Sometimes the nuclear mechanical warning systems send false alarms that a nuclear bomb is coming and in that case, we would press the button and that would be the beginning of the nuclear war and the end of the world."[7]

—Julietta, age 13, Pahoa, Hawaii

★★★★★★★★★★★★★★★★★★★★★★★

As Jesus Christ said, "Out of the mouths of babes..."

The psychological pressures of living under these stresses were foreseen by Saint Paul who indicated how these pressures would affect the people in the End Times:

> "Understand this, that in the last days there will come times of stress. For men will be lovers of self (ego), lovers of money, proud, arrogant, abusive, disobedient to their parents, ungrateful, unholy, inhuman, implacable, slanderers, profligates, fierce, haters of good, treacherous, reckless, swollen with conceit, lovers of pleasure rather than lovers of God, holding the form of religion but denying the power of it. Avoid such people. For among them are those who make their way into households and capture (the) weak, burdened with sins and swayed by various impulses, who will listen to anybody and can never arrive at a knowledge of the truth...these men also oppose the truth, men of corrupt mind and counterfeit faith; but they will not get very far, for their folly will be plain to all..."[8]

Certainly the above description fits a lot of people in the world today. But why are people like this? The reason is that they have forgotten the One True God, for as the Lord as Guru Nanak stated: "In forgetting Him is the suffering."[9] Most people in the world today are living under a great deal of stress precisely because they have forgotten God and His Teachings, and, hence, are living unspiritual and therefore unnatural lives. Even people that are not overly religious are beginning to recognize "the signs of the times." To quote from an article written by Sammy Amalu of the *Honolulu Advertiser,* on December 19, 1982:

> "It may well be that the frailty of age has overcome me— for heaven knows I am not by inclination or by nature overly religious. But there does come a time in every man's life when it becomes obvious to him that the elements of his life

278

are getting beyond his meager ability to control or to manipulate them to his own advantage.

"When such an hour of realization befalls a man, he then must turn for help to the single source of limitless power who was and is the original architect of all life. He must in such circumstances turn to his God because there is no one else to whom and to which he can turn...

"Recently we have been visited by a hurricane that devastated whole portions of our Islands. Our highly vaunted technologies and safeguards failed before the wrath of nature, and we felt the full power of nature's fury. We were helpless before it—unable to control or to stem it.

"In other parts of our country, storms and floods have taken their full toll in destruction and devastation. Possessions have been swept away; homes have been lost; lives have been lost. In other parts of the world, there have been earthquakes that destroyed lives and property. The whole world seems in convulsion...

"And so for these reasons and only after long and serious consideration, I have come to the conclusion that since we have no other place to turn, we must turn back to the living God and ask for His intervention into our worldly affairs and to help us..."[10]

He goes on to suggest that the nation as a whole choose a day and time to pray together to God for help. As we have seen the easiest way to feel close to God is to get back to God's outer manifestations in Nature. Living in cities with manmade, artificial surroundings dulls the senses and clouds the mind. The constant clangings and bangings and shouting and other irritating noises assault our ears while the drab gray of concrete and steel assaults our eyes, and the noxious fumes of cars and buses and chemical refineries assault our noses. Thus we end up assaulting one another!

For example, according to anthropologist Peggy Reeves Sanday, the incidence of one form of violence—rape—"is more likely to occur when the balance between man and his environment has been disturbed," pointing out that contemporary American culture "may be the most violent the world has ever known." She goes on to state that the Mbuti pygmies of the African forest are a classic example of a rape-free society. These peaceful people live in harmony with Nature, addressing the forest as 'father,' 'mother,' 'lover' and 'friend,' recognizing that "each person and animal is endowed with some spiritual power 'that draws from a single source (God) whose physical manifestation is the forest itself.' "[11] Hence, violence of any kind is virtually unknown to these people because of their reverence for all life, and because they are living in a natural environment.

Doctors have confirmed that living in a noisy, manmade environment causes stress. Recent studies have shown that people who live to be 100 years of age do so because of their environment. These people rarely suffer from heart disease, cancer, stress, or other 20th Century ailments, because they are living in a natural setting. Most of these centenarians are found in the foothills or valleys of mountainous regions, including the Ural Mountains of the Soviet Union and the Kashmir Mountains and valleys of India.

America's Natural Heritage

Our forefathers warned against forgetting our links to Nature. It should be remembered that several of them were farmers, including George Washington, who grew hemp, by the way, and Thomas Jefferson. Indeed, the nation envisioned by our forefathers was not one of brick and concrete, coal and steel, but one of farmlands and orchards, forests and woods. We were meant to be an agrarian society, not an industrial one. In fact, Thomas Jefferson, who lived to see the beginning of the Industrial Age, bewailed its coming, warning that we must not lose touch with the earth and Nature, for to do so would harden our hearts.

The true heart of the American spirit has been seen throughout our history as love for the land has been demonstrated amongst our most prominent leaders. For example, Teddy Roosevelt set up the national parks system—a concept never before seen in modern history. Other American leaders, from Abraham Lincoln to Franklin D. Roosevelt, John F. Kennedy to Richard Nixon (who signed the Clean Air Act) have taken strong actions to protect the environment. The most prominent example of an American leader who understood Nature and, therefore, had a strong environmental record was former President Jimmy Carter. He heavily backed intelligent environmental legislation, including the Alaskan Lands Act, the preservation and expansion of national parks, forests and wildlife refuges.

Of course, in America, the people who understood, loved and lived in harmony with Nature the best were the original, primitive—meaning "first"—peoples of this land—the native American Indians. The Indians recognized the need to be close to Nature, reiterating Jefferson's truth that to lose touch with Nature hardens one's heart. Even more than this, they recognized the need to respect all life, being a "brother" to the rest of the animals in the forest. The Hopis believe that man "lost the privilege of living with the animals," as they put it, when the first world was destroyed due to man's ego seeing differences between himself and the animals.

Indeed, they were right as physicians and psychiatrists are beginning to prescribe pets instead of pills for patients suffering from hypertension, depression, stress and other ailments. Recent studies have found that heart attack and stroke victims who have pets or animal friends have a much lower risk of a second attack than do those without pets. Part of the reason may be due to the fact that one's blood pressure drops when one touches or talks to animals, (in contrast to a rise in pressure when one talks to another human!) as the affection being exchanged between animals and humans helps to relieve stress and anxiety.

Other studies have shown that elderly people, especially those that are in hospitals or nursing homes, benefit greatly from contact with animals. Researchers report significant improvements in the health, moods, morale, self-respect and social skills among those who have pets. The responsibility of caring for the animal stimulates the owner to be more responsible for his own care, as well as helping the individual to become more open to human beings.[12]

Similar studies with autistic or severely withdrawn children and the criminally insane have verified the psychological benefits animal contact gives to man. In one case, a boy who had been withdrawn right up to his teen years suddenly responded to dolphins at a sea-life park to which he had been taken. The boy actually started to squeal and click in a way remarkably similar to the sounds made by dolphins. The dolphins, too, responded, leaping and jumping in joy, tirelessly playing with their new friend.

In one ward for the criminally insane where the attempted-suicide rate was upwards of 85%, not a single suicide attempt was

281

made after the introduction of animals. One man institutionalized in such a hospital explained why he felt so close to the animals. After explaining that dealing with animals had helped him to deal with humans, he added that the animals do not judge you and make no demands upon you, while giving you total unconditional love—the same kind of love the Being of Light or God gave to those who had death experiences. For, after all, what is it that draws people to animals but love—the love that is God, which is within all living things.

Other examples of the animals' help to man also demonstrate their remarkable psychic abilities. For example, in a cold Canadian wilderness, a boy who had become separated from his parents, collapsed from exhaustion. In the morning he awoke to find himself covered by a family of beavers who had kept him warm throughout the bitter cold night. Other examples of animals' psychic abilities given by Bill Schul in his book *The Psychic Power of Animals* include a cow leading a blind farmer around seemingly able to know exactly where the farmer wanted to go without being told; a dog who refused to leave a convict who planned to commit suicide until after the convict's depression had passed; a sick mountain goat who came straight to the door of a doctor who cured her—showing up a year later with her sick kid; and, finally, in Florida, where sick and wounded birds of all kinds seem to "home-in" on a bird hospital, sometimes walking as far as five miles inland to reach it.

Other cases recorded by Schul help to prove that the spirit of departed loved ones—including our pets—is always with us to help guide and protect us from danger. Examples include a father who, after being awakened by the barking of his dog who had died six months earlier, discovered that his house was on fire in time to save himself and his family; and a motorist who, after stopping his car because its headlights revealed his collie, who had died a year earlier, found the mountain road he had been travelling on was washed out—had he gone any further, he would have plunged over a cliff.

Finally, the loyalty of animals to their human friends is demonstrated by the following two examples: after a farmer nursed a sick wild goose back to life, it and its flock migrated to ponds on his property. When the farmer was about to die in a hospital, a large flock of geese was seen circling above the hospital several times. And, in England, a beekeeper who died was so beloved by his bees that they swarmed over his coffin, and then returned to their hives.[13]

The above are verified facts and help to make one thing perfectly clear: it behooves us to make friends with and to protect the animals during the End Times because, as the plagues of Revelations continue to spread and gain strength, the help of the animals will be invaluable. A lesson should be learned from an incident in Utah that took place about 140 years ago. In Salt Lake City, a monument has been erected in memory of sea gulls who came in large flocks and destroyed millions of black crickets that threatened crops in 1848, thus saving the crops and the people from certain starvation!

The American Indians recognized and understood the spirituality of the animals. In fact, their reverence for all life—both plant and animal—and their love for the Earth pervaded their entire culture. As Stewart Udall, former Interior Secretary (1961-'69), explains:

> "The most common trait of all primitive peoples is a reverence for the life-giving Earth, and the native American shared this elemental ethic: the land was alive to his loving touch, and he, its son, was brother to all creatures. His feelings were made visible in medicine bundles and dance rhythms for rain, and all of his religious rites and land attitudes savored the inseparable world of nature and God, the Master of Life. During the long Indian tenure the land remained undefiled save for scars no deeper than scratches of cornfield clearings or the farming canals of the Hohokams on the Arizona desert."[14]

The American Indian prophecies, as well as those of the Hindus and Christians, foretold that this land that the Indians held so sacred and precious would be devastated and defiled, raped and poisoned in the latter days of this system of things. As mentioned earlier, the trigger that was to start this desecration of the Earth was the arrival of the white man to America and his dominance of the world, which brings us the the opening of the fourth seal of Revelations.

Chapter 12

THE FOURTH AND FIFTH SEALS OPENED

The opening of the fourth seal of Revelations actually reveals two riders on pale horses named Death and Hades, representing Great Britain and its offshoot, the U.S.A., it being no coincidence that the American Indians called the British and Americans "pale-face." They are given power over a quarter of the Earth and its population to control and kill with sword and famine, pestilence and animals.[1] If one looks at the history of the British and American Empires it is easy to see that they have controlled well over a quarter of the world's land area and peoples. Indeed, they have been responsible for killing millions over the years with warfare and famine.

In the case of Great Britain, which colonized over half of the world, from China and India in the East, to America, Canada, and even the Hawaiian Islands to the West, the slaughter was direct, while in the case of the U.S., it was more indirect through their support of ruthless dictators, who in turn slaughtered their people with arms obtained from the U.S. Examples of this are General Khan of Pakistan, who slaughtered over three million civilians in East Pakistan prior to their rescue and liberation by the Indian army and their becoming an independent nation—Bangladesh, Marcos in the Philippines, the ex-Shah of Iran, and other dictatorships, primarily in Central and South America, as well as elsewhere. As a matter of fact, Lt. Gen. H. M. Ershad, the general who recently seized power in Bangladesh and declared martial law, says that Washington's "best friends" are authoritarian states. He stated that the U.S. traditionally has supported regimes dominated by the military, pointing to Marcos in the Philippines, Park of South Korea, and Thailand as examples: "They're all martial law governments. Your best friends are the martial law governments in the world."[2] Hence, he now feels that Bangladesh has "earned" the friendship of America since it is now under martial law, too!

As to pestilence, it is a known fact that the British used small pox and other diseases to kill off the American Indians over 200 years ago. In Brazil, greedy European profiteers are still practicing genocide against the Indians of the Amazon interior by giving them "gifts" of small-pox-infested clothes. As many as six million

Indians in Brazil have been killed in this manner since the 16th Century, and the numbers killed in North America must have been equally as great, if not greater.[3]

As to the animals, both countries have used animals as weapons throughout history. Today, even the loving and playful dolphin is being trained by the U.S. Defense Dept. to retrieve and deliver underwater missles and explosives, the dolphins being totally unaware of the dangerous "game" of which they are a part. Thus, we see that **the Fourth Seal of Revelations has been opened.**

The Fifth Seal - The Martyrs

The opening of the Fifth Seal reveals the souls of the saints who had been slain because they believed and bore witness to the Word of God by living it in their lives. Their cry for vengeance is heard by the Lord, who tells them to wait a little longer as there are yet more martyrs to follow them.[4] This corresponds to Jesus' call for endurance by the saints, as throughout the tribulation period more righteous and spiritual people will be slain by the forces of evil before the Day of the Lord dawns. These saints who have already been slain not only represent Christian martyrs like the newly canonized saint—Father Kolbe—but also all followers of God's teachings who have died as a result of believing, living and fighting for the Truth. The American Indians who have been slaughtered over the last few centuries would be the best example of such a group of martyrs. Their population once numbered in the millions, but was reduced to less than 220,000 by 1923, thus **fulfilling the Pale Prophet's prophecy regarding the decimation of the Indian race.**[5]

The Christian missionaries themselves attest to the fact of the Indians' spirituality. As the Rev. C. Van Dusen, a missionary to the Ojibway Indians, put it:

> "The Indian character, in its unadulterated grandeur, is most admirable and attractive. Before it is polluted by the pernicious example of others—the demoralizing and debasing influence of wicked Whitemen—the genuine North American pagan ("pagan" literally meaning "pure" in ancient Greek) presents to the world the most noble specimen of the natural man that can be found on the face of the Earth."[6]

One missionary who had zealously said he was going to convert the "benighted heathens" ended up being converted himself! After having been with a Sioux tribe for some time he admitted that the Medicine Lodge of the Sioux Nation was "a true Church of God, and we have no right to stamp it out."[7] A few years later, he abandoned his role as a missionary and became a lawyer on behalf of the Indians. As explanation for his change, he said:

> "I realized that the Sioux were worshippers of the One True God, and their religion was one of truth and kindness. They do not need a missionary, but they do need a lawyer to defend them in the courts...Of course the missionaries have defrocked me, and the Indian agents (for the U.S. government) hate me...But I glory in the fact that I am devoting the last of my days and my strength to the service of this noble, downtrodden Race."[8]

Even those who fought the American Indians recognized their spiritual character. The legendary Buffalo Bill (so-named because he slaughtered over 100 buffaloes in one day) once said, "I never led an expedition against the Indians but I was ashamed of myself, ashamed of my government, and ashamed of my flag; for they were always in the right and we were always in the wrong. They never broke a treaty, and we never kept one."[9]

An old scout for General Miles of the cavalry, Tom Newcomb, who had the opportunity to live with the Sioux under Crazy Horse (a great Indian holy man) for some years said:

> "I tell you I never saw more kindness or real Christianity anywhere. The poor, the sick, the aged, the widows and the orphans were always looked after first. Whenever we moved camp, someone took care that the widows' lodges were moved first and set up first. After every hunt, a good-sized chunk of meat was dropped at each door where it was most needed. I was treated like a brother; and I tell you I have never seen any community of church people that was as really truly Christian as that band of Indians."[10]

Finally, Captain Bonneville, who visited the Nez Perce and Flathead Indians in 1834, before they had had any contact with whites, summed up the "primitive" (meaning "first") Indians as follows:

"Simply to call these people religious would convey but a faint idea of the deep hue of piety and devotion which pervades their whole conduct. Their honesty is immaculate, and their purity of purpose and their observance of the rites of their religion are most uniform and remarkable. They are certainly more like a nation of saints than a horde of savages."[11]

Modern-day martyrs include Mahatma Gandhi of India, John F. Kennedy, Robert Kennedy and Martin Luther King of the U.S.A., Archbishop Romero and the Maryknoll nuns in El Salvador, as well as other Christian priests and nuns who have been and are still being slaughtered in different Latin American countries, such as Guatemala. Here, the new President, who happens to be a so-called "born-again," Evangelical Christian supported by the current American administration and some evangelical members of the radical right, is continuing to wage genocide against the Indian peasants.

Other individuals who have sought to live God's teachings and help those in need and distress, speaking out against the atrocities and abuses of those in power, include Soviet and Polish dissidents, many of whom are and were members of the clergy—both Christian and Jewish—who are often sent into internal exile or imprisoned in mental institutions; Buddhist monks from Tibet, who were martyred by being slaughtered by the Chinese army when it invaded Tibet, and were given sanctuary by the Indian government who gave them land for farms, homes, equipment and money to build the same; members of the clergy from various faiths in China who suffered greatly and were decimated at the hands of the Chinese communists; and members of the Baha'i faith who are still being massacred by Khomeini and his religious fanatics in Iran.

Finally, the most popular modern-day martyr for the cause of Peace was John Lennon, formerly of the Beatles. It was his songs, like "All we are saying, is give Peace a chance," among others that electrified the youth of the world, especially in the West, making them think of the great moral issues connected with wars in general, and the Vietnam War in particular. Thus, **the prophecies concerning the swelling of the martyrs' ranks have been amply fulfilled!**

The Gospel to be Preached to the Whole World

The only positive side effects of the persecution of the saints have been, 1- that their courage has inspired others to follow the True Path regardless of the consequences, and, 2- the Word of God has been spread to all, just as Jesus had foretold. He stated that the Gospel must first be preached to all peoples before the end of this system of things could come, and the New Age begin.[12] A recent issue of *Time Magazine* (Dec. 27, 1982) illustrates that this prophecy has been fulfilled, and the condition for ushering in the New Age met, as there are more Christian missionaries in the world today than at any other time in history. Of course, one of the reasons for this is that modern technology has given man access to even the most remote areas of the world, **thus fulfilling Daniel's prophecy made over 2500 years ago** that people would travel extensively and, therefore, knowledge would increase in the End Times.[13] Airplanes, automobiles, jeeps, helicopters, etc., have all been employed by missionaries in order to reach the people. The advances in electronic communications have also widened the scope of the audience able to hear the Word of God as T.V. and radio preachers—some true prophets and others false—take to the airwaves to "spread the Word."

Examples of just how far these Christian missionaries have gone are illustrated below:

- In Zaire, Lester Green has trekked deep inside the rain forests to reach the Walese Pygmy tribes.
- In Botswanna, Randy Evert and his wife Roxie cross the forbidding Kalahari Desert to bring the Word and modern farming techniques to impoverished Nomadic Bushmen.
- In Nepal, Father John Dahlheimer counsels Tibetan refugees in search of religious freedom (the Chinese having closed all the Buddhist temples there).
- In the Philippines, Father Brian Gore has been persecuted by the Marcos government for "inciting rebellion" while setting up community-action groups among the poor.
- In Nicaragua, Sister Rachel Pinal endures great hardships in order to help the impoverished *campesinos* there.[14]

Other missionaries have traveled to the Amazon and Indonesian jungles, war-torn Central America, famine-plagued Africa, to Egypt and the Middle East, and to the rain forests of Asia to bring the Word of God to all who would hear. All tolled, there are approximately a quarter of a million Christian missionaries at work in the world today, and their numbers are growing.[15] Many have stopped trying to "convert" their audiences to Christianity; rather, they seek to help alleviate the plight of the poor they come into contact with, thereby setting an example of how a truly Godly person should lead one's life. The best known example of this in the world today would have to be the Nobel Peace Prize winner Mother Theresa, whose tireless dedication to the poor of India and elsewhere has brought her international recognition and renown. Rather than trying to convert people to Christianity, she respects the religious faiths of others, seeking only to touch the hearts of those she meets in a desire to gain new friends and helpers from all faiths and nationalities to aid the poor.

This prophecy is common also to Hinduism and Buddhism as both Lord Krishna and Lord Buddha instructed their disciples to go and spread the Word of God to all people, which they have done all over the world. Thus we can see that the Lord as Jesus, Krishna and Buddha were not saying to convert people to a particular religion, but rather to spread the Eternal Truths contained in all of them. In other words, the Lord wants people to "convert" themselves from leading sinful lives to leading spiritual lives; not from one religion to another, unless they choose to do so. Hence, **this prophecy has also been fulfilled.**

Chapter 13

THE OPENING OF THE SIXTH SEAL—
THE DEVASTATION OF THE EARTH

The opening of the Sixth Seal of Revelations represents the beginning of the plagues upon the inhabitants of the Earth. It also represents the natural disasters that are to and have already begun to happen as we move closer and closer to that final great quake and the return of the Lord. It must be understood that the plagues of Revelations do not necessarily follow one another (although in some instances that is the natural sequence of events), rather the majority of the plagues have been happening simultaneously, growing more and more intense as time goes by, like a snowball rolling downhill, gaining size, momentum and power as it continues its roll.

Basically the plagues fall into two categories—natural upheavals and changes in weather patterns brought on by man's interference with the natural order of things, and unnatural plagues brought on by man's chemicals and pollution, including the unnatural plague of war encompassing the globe.

These plagues correspond to the devastation of the Earth as foretold by the Pale Prophet (Jesus) to the American Indians, as well as the signs of the Kaliyuga or Age of Chaos of the Hindu scriptures. They also correspond to the signs given by Jesus Christ and by several prophets of the Old Testament with regard to the coming of the "Great Day of the Lord," as well as those given by Edgar Cayce regarding Earth changes that are to occur prior to the ushering in of the New Age, and to those of the French physician and prophet—Nostradamus, especially with regard to the rise and fall of the final ruthless, wicked ruler of this system of things—the Antichrist, along with the fall of Babylon—the symbol of false religion throughout the world.

Earthquakes in One Place After Another

Just about all the prophecies say that there will be an increasing number of earthquakes throughout the world prior to the Lord's return and the ushering in of the New Age of Peace. When Jesus said that there would be great stress upon the Earth, He not only meant the emotional stress of the people, but also the physical

290

stress that the Earth is already, and will continue to go through, culminating in one last great quake that will literally shake the entire globe.

The American Indians have already explained that this period of physical upheaval is part of Nature's way of throwing or literally shaking off the unnatural blemishes that are scarring and covering up the Earth's surface. For, since the Earth is a living organism, it must move freely and breathe like any other life form. When she is covered over with asphalt and cement, her natural movements are inhibited. Thus, she will eventually be forced to break these concrete bonds on her "skin" in a more violent way than would have occurred under normal and natural conditions, as man continues to pave over roughly 342 acres per hour of the Earth's surface.

What is even more frightening is that man continues to insist upon building some of his largest cities, as well as nuclear power plants, dams, etc., in earthquake-prone areas, thus setting himself up for even more catastrophes than the quake alone would wrought. The nuclear power plant at Diablo Canyon, California, which is built very close to a fault line, is just one example ("Diablo" meaning "Devil" in Spanish.)

These fault lines act like the seams of the Earth. They are the areas where giant plates of the Earth's crust—twelve in number—meet one another, often forming mountains. According to scientists, these plates sit atop a hot, molten core and are constantly moving or drifting. Usually their movement is so slight—about one inch per year—that no major changes on the Earth's surface are effected. However, when enough stress is generated by these plates moving and rubbing against each other, earthquakes are the inevitable result. Of course, not all quakes are the result of the movement of the Earth's plates, but a lot of them are.

Two other reasons for the recent plague of quakes are the building of huge dams across fault lines, which weakens them, and underground nuclear testing. When nuclear bombs are exploded underground, they create a tremendous amount of pressure within the Earth's crust. That pressure must be released, which it is via an earthquake.

Every year there are nearly 500,000 detectable earthquakes around the globe measuring at least two or more on the Richter scale. Though earthquakes have occurred throughout the Earth's history, according to records, this century has experienced a

291

tremendous increase in their frequency. What's more, in each of the ten-year periods since 1950, the number of earthquakes per decade has roughly doubled.[1] As a matter of fact, the 1970's saw the largest increase of major quakes (registering 7.0 or more on the scale) in recorded history, with many of these quakes hitting populated areas. In 1978 alone, the U.S. experienced a total of 345 quakes in 28 different states.[2]

This phenomena has led many scientists to feel that we are entering a period of great seismic disturbances. Indeed, they are correct as 1980 saw another increase in the number of significant quakes (registering 6.5 or more) round the world. The first six months of 1981 saw a significant increase in the number of quake-related deaths worldwide, too.[3]

Some of the more violent quakes of the last two decades appear on the following page.

Areas rocked by other significant quakes registering 6.0 or more on the Richter scale, or causing a great amount of damage during the first two years of the '80's include: Iran (3 quakes), Sicily (1), Moscow, Russia (1), Mexico (6—the latest series of quakes occurring on January 24, 1983, registering 7. on the scale, shaking half of Mexico and swaying office buildings in Mexico City 318 miles from the epicenter!), China (4), Vancouver Island, Canada (1), Indonesia (2), Greece (6 great and 20 smaller ones), Japan (8 quakes!), the Philippines (2), the South Pacific area (including New Zealand, New Caledonia, Tonga and Vanatu—6 quakes), North India/Pakistan (2), Pakistan (2), Italy (4—one called the "Apocalypse"), Taiwan (2), Aleutians (2), Samoa (1), North Yemen (1), Venezuela-Columbia border (1), Peru (2), Afghanistan (1), Guam (1), Papua, New Guinea (1—registering 7.9, being the greatest quake world-wide in recent years), and Yugoslavia (1—where a dozen people died of heart attacks due to fear and shock, **fulfilling Jesus' prophecy that in the End Times, men's hearts will fail them out of fear**—a quake simultaneously shaking up the Mississippi Valley area in the U.S.—almost opposite points of the world.)

As one can see, the number of quakes is certainly increasing, not only in terms of magnitude or power, but also in terms of frequency. As a matter of fact, during the third week of December, 1982, 6 quakes in 6 separate areas shook the world—the North Yemen quake, registering 6.0, leaving an estimated 1500 to 3000 dead and another 60,000 homeless; Taiwan, registering 6.5,

DATE	LOCATION	RICHTER SCALE	APPROX. # OF DEATHS AND/OR DESTRUCTION
1960	Morocco	5.8	12,000 dead
1962	Iran	7.1	12,230 dead
1964	Alaska (Good Friday)	8.6 (force = to 10,000 atomic bombs	set off 50' high tsunami or tidal wave
1970	Peru	7.7	66,800 dead
1972	Managua, Nicaragua		10,000 dead—70% of city destroyed
1974	Pakistan		5200 dead
1975	Turkey		2312 dead
1975	Haicheng, China	7.3	90 % of city destroyed
1976	Italy		1000 dead
1976	Indonesia	(two quakes)	1000 dead
1976	Philippines	7.8	8000 dead
1976	Turkey		4000 dead
1976	Guatemala	7.7	23,000 dead
1976	China	8.2	700,000 dead
1978	Iran	7.4	12,000 dead
1978	Iran	7.7	25,000 dead
1979	Yugoslavia		80,000 homeless
1979	Mexico	7.9	
1979	Imperial, California	6.4	80% of the business district destroyed
1980	Italy		3000 dead/200,000 homeless
1980	Algeria	7.3	3500 dead
1980	Algeria	6.2	
1980	Italy	7.2	3000 dead
1981	Peru	5.5	
1981	California-Mexican border	6.0	
1981	Iran	6.9	3000 dead
1981	Aleutian Is.	7.0	

causing great panic as high rise buildings swayed to and fro; New Zealand, registering 7.2; a quake near Samoa registering over 6 points; Northern California coast, registering 4.6; and, finally, a very rare quake in Cuba. That's almost one quake per day, and

most of the quakes were of a significant magnitude to cause property damage and loss of life.

The U.S. has been shaking quite a bit, too, lately. Some of the
areas hit by quakes in the last two years include: San Fransisco,
the Imperial Valley (swarm of quakes, one every 20 minutes),
Napa Valley, North L.A., the Mojave Desert (near China Lake
Naval Weapons Center), and Los Angeles proper—all in the state
of California, Tennessee, Utah, Wyoming, Hawaii, Washington
state, Arkansas, the entire New England area including Maine,
New Hampshire, Connecticut, Massachusetts, and New York
state, (being the first significant quakes—4 in 9 days!—in the area
in over 126 years), Nevada, and, finally, the first-ever quake
recorded in Georgia.

Earthquakes can also trigger severe earth changes such as tidal
waves, devastating landslides, and course changes of rivers.
Scientists have been trying out different methods of predicting
earthquakes using various machines, computers, etc. But the most
accurate form of earthquake prediction seems to be the animals.
During a 1969 quake in China, zoo animals exhibited abnormal
behavior such as depression among the tigers, yaks, and pandas,
while other captive animals screamed, moved about nervously,
and refused food. Other examples of pre-quake animal behavior
include birds calling, pigs climbing, and snakes coming up from
the ground. Hence, we can see that it makes sense to protect our
animals if for no other reason than as early warning signs of
natural calamities.

Thus, we see that **the prophecies regarding the literal shaking
up of the earth during the End Times have been abundantly
fulfilled!**

Volcanoes Erupting

Earthquakes are often the warning signals in themselves in that
they very often precede a volcanic eruption. As mentioned earlier,
the Earth's cleansing processes are attempting to throw off or
cover up the poisons that have accumulated within her and on her
surface. Volcanic eruptions are one way in which this is done. An
analogy can be drawn to the vomiting of a sick person or to the skin
eruptions that occur on one's body when it attempts to cleanse
itself of the poisons that have accumulated within it. The
volcanoes are the eruptions of the "skin" or crust of the Earth. As

she tries to cleanse herself, these "blemishes" erupt.

Currently there are a lot of eruptions taking place around the globe. Many are occurring along the fault lines where the Earth's plates meet to form mountains. One area of particular interest to us is the so-called "Ring of Fire," which contains over 75% of the Earth's 850 active volcanoes, stretching all the way from the South Pacific Islands of Fiji, New Zealand, Indonesia, and Japan to the west, up through Asia to Alaska in the north, and down the West Coast of the U.S. to South America and the Antarctic in the east.

This ring has been spewing forth a lot of fire, lately, as once-dormant volcanoes are beginning to stir after centuries of sleep. Others thought to have become extinct ages ago are literally booming back to life. During the first week of April, 1982, three of these volcanoes erupted almost simultaneously: Mt. St. Helens in the state of Washington, Galunggung in Indonesia, and Chichon in Mexico. As geology professor Dr. Leonard Palmer of Portland State University in Oregon said, "What's happening here is that we're beginning to recognize the continual process, that the world is alive..."[4]

The simultaneous eruptions left scientists searching for answers as more and more volcanoes continue to make their presence literally felt after decades or centuries of quiet. For example, Mount St. Helens first erupted on March 20, 1980, with a tremendous explosion 50 times more powerful than the atomic bomb dropped on Hiroshima, after a 123-year slumber, killing 62, hurling 1.3 billion cubic yards of earth skyward, leveling everything for 150 square miles, and shooting ash 63,000 feet into the air.

Chichon Volcano in Mexico first erupted March 29, 1982, after hundreds of years of inactivity, throwing 1.25 billion tons of ash and fumes into the air, closing down highways and airports. It has erupted at least seven times since, spewing forth over 50 billion tons of ash and cinder 120 miles across Southern Mexico. The Pale Prophet foretold that certain volcanoes would come back to life at the time of the Great Purification, several of the survivors of the eruptions being descendants of the Mayan Indians, to whom these prophecies were given almost 2000 years ago.

Galunggung Volcano has erupted over 34 times in 1982 alone after a century of sleep, threatening the lives of 250,000 people as its mud, rocks, lava, gasses and volcanic ash devastated the countryside, covering over hundreds of acres of rice about to be harvested, raising the specter of famine for tens of thousands.

Other volcanoes that have erupted in the last few years include: Japan's Mount Usu, whose August 7, 1977 eruption sounded like a bomb exploding; Mount Sakurajima, also of Japan, whose New Year's Day explosion in 1982 scared worshippers conducting their traditional New Year's prayers at nearby shrines and temples, having erupted an additional 200 times since; Mount Asama, whose two 1982 eruptions after a nine-year slumber blanketed Tokyo with ash; Mount Kusatsu-Shirane, in its first eruption since 1976; Pagan Volcano of the Pacific island bearing the same name, whose eruption in 1981 was the first in recorded history; an Icelandic volcano, whose current eruption was the biggest of seven in the area since 1975; Gamkonora Volcano in Indonesia, whose renewed activity in 1982 has left some 20,000 villagers homeless; Soputan Volcano, also in Indonesia, whose awakening in 1982 from a long period of dormancy came without warning, shooting ash more than a mile into the air, blanketing the Indonesian capitol of Jakarta; Mount Etna of Italy, whose most recent eruption was the worst in ten years, sending streams of lava five miles down its slopes, destroying farmlands and forcing the evacuation of several villages; and finally, the volcanoes in New Guinea and Costa Rica, both of which erupted during the first few months of 1983.

But these are not the only volcanoes that are worrying scientists. In Indonesia, Krakatau Volcano is beginning to stir again. It was this volcano that exploded in 1883 with 26 times the fury of the largest hydrogen bomb, killing more than 36,000 people in the tsunami or tidal waved that ensued. In the Antarctic, a Chilean geologist has found two active volcanoes east of the Antarctic Peninsula. And, in the U.S., geologists and volcanologists are concerned about the possible eruption of Mount Hood in Oregon, and eruptions in Yosemite National Park, especially the Mammoth Lakes area along the Sierra/Nevada border, as the same early warning signs exhibited by Mount St. Helens prior to her first eruption are being seen in both places.

Cayce's Predictions Coming True

What is so significant about the locations of these quakes and eruptions is that they correspond precisely to prophecies given by

Edgar Cayce with regard to the signs of the End Times. Cayce exhibited startling geological accuracy as to fault lines and quakes, and warned that human activities were affecting the crust of the Earth adversely. He stated that the Earth would be broken up in many places, with many lands sinking and/or being inundated, and others rising during the End Times. Cayce predicted that the changes in the Earth would begin to be apparent, "When there is the first breaking up of some conditions in the South Sea (South Pacific)...in the sinking or rising of that which is almost opposite it, or in the Mediterranean, and the Aetna [Etna] area. Then we may know it has begun."[5]

One look at the list of quakes and volcanic eruptions that have hit the South Pacific area proves that **this prophecy has been abundantly fulfilled.** In the last two years alone, the area has been hit by over 30 quakes measuring at least 4 or more on the Richter scale, causing extensive damage and loss of life. Several new islands have thrust up out of the Pacific Ocean recently, too. And the number of volcanoes that have been erupting there is astounding. It's as if the whole region is coming to life.

As to the rising and falling of certain land areas, this too has begun to occur as water levels in several Greek harbors have dropped while that of the Caspian Sea also has decreased, the sea actually sinking, leaving villages and harbors high and dry.[6] In Ancoma, Italy, heavy rains have caused the entire city to start sliding into the Adriatic Sea, buckling roads and destroying houses.

Closer to home, experts are saying that huge areas of the United States, specifically the Sunbelt states, are sinking! According to geophysicist Ronald L. Brooks, satellite data has confirmed that Texas, Arizona and California are slowly sinking, due to the recent population explosion there, increasing the demand on the area's underground aquifers or water supplies. The increased demand has lowered the water table, causing the ground to sink as much as 12.5 feet in Arizona and up to 7.5 feet in Houston, Texas.[7] In Houston, the waters of the Gulf of Mexico are beginning to lap at expensive coastline developments and famous landmarks of yesteryear, such as the battleground where Sam Houston defeated Mexico's Santa Anna a century ago—30% of the battleground is now underwater. Thus we can see that **Cayce's prophecy regarding the sinking of certain lands is already coming true.**

Cayce also said that once the earth changes began, they would grow more and more intense, coming closer and closer to one another. He stated that, "the greater portion of Japan must go into the sea."[8] Indeed, the islands of Japan have been the sites of a lot of activity recently with eight major quakes (registering 6. or more) and 4 volcanoes rocking the islands in the last two years. As mentioned before, one of those volcanoes has erupted over 200 times in 1982 alone! What's more, scientists have discovered a huge fault near Hong Kong. A quake measuring 6.0 or higher would cause catastrophic desolation! Thus, we can see that Cayce was again right on target as to the locations of the coming earth changes: changes that have already begun in earnest.

Further, Cayce predicted the rising of new lands in the Atlantic and Pacific, as well as the re-emergence of parts of Atlantis off the Bimini Islands. As mentioned earlier, this has already happened as parts of old Atlantis have begun to resurface off the Bimini coast, precisely where Cayce predicted. New islands have also surfaced off the coasts of Ecuador, Iceland, Alaska, and Hawaii.

He said that one of the earlier signs would be the shaking up of South America from one end to the other. This prediction could well have two meanings as in recent years South America's countries have been rocked continually by political upheavals. Physically speaking, South America has already been shaken up over the last decade with killer quakes hitting Peru in 1970 and again in '74, Chile in 1975, Argentina in '77, another massive quake measuring 8.2 in 1977 affecting Argentina, Chile, and Southern Brazil, and a quake shaking up Columbia in 1979, and 2 more killer quakes in March, '83.

Cayce stated that, "the upper portion of Europe will be changed as in the twinkling of an eye...Even many of the battlefields of the present [1941] will be ocean...bays,..."[9] This prophecy corresponds to one given by Nostradamus who indicated that the changes occurring in Europe, specifically France, would occur soon after a political upheaval in Iran—the Iranian Revolution led by Khomeini—and the simultaneous rise to power in France of a political party whose symbol was a rose—the Socialist Party, led by Francois Mitterand, whose election to office coincided with Khomeini's defeat of the ex-Shah of Iran and the establishment of an Islamic state there. Perhaps the earth changes have already begun as parts of France are experiencing the worst floods in decades, damaging buildings and destroying crops.

298

Finally, Cayce saw dramatic and drastic changes in the North American continent. He stated that, "All over the country many physical changes of a minor or greater degree" will take place:

"Los Angeles, San Francisco, most all of these will be among those that will be destroyed, before New York even...Portions of the now East Coast of New York, or New York City itself, will in the main disappear...the southern portions of Carolina, Georgia, these will disappear. This will be much sooner. The waters of the Great Lakes will empty into the Gulf of Mexico."[10]

Scientists have been warning for years that the West Coast, specifically the Los Angeles to San Francisco region are well overdue for a massive earthquake, as the San Andreas fault continues to move six times more than what had been previously thought. Officials admit that if one were to happen today, they would be ill-prepared to handle things afterwards. Hundreds of thousands would be killed by falling buildings, downed power lines, etc., not to mention the horrifying thought of what harm a nuclear power plant meltdown might cause if its safety-backup systems were destroyed during the quake.

Cayce warned that, "If there are greater activities in Vesuvius or Pelee, then the Southern Coast of California—and the areas between Salt Lake and the southern portions of Nevada—may expect, within three months following same an inundation caused by the earthquakes."[11] Although Mount Vesuvius and Mount Pelee have not as yet erupted, there has been a very close call as La Soufriere Volcano on the Caribbean Island of Guadeloupe erupted with atomic bomb intensity in 1976. Pelee is only 80 miles south of it. Thus, the region is obviously starting to wake up again after 70 years of dormancy.

Some feel that this prophecy could also refer to Madame Pele (also known as Kilauea), one of the volcanoes on the Big Island of Hawaii. Cayce said, "If there are greater activites;" in other words, if there are sustained eruptions and/or activities such as earthquakes, then the area from the Southern Coast of California up through the southern portions of Nevada to Salt Lake will experience a large number of earthquakes, which will result in some kind of inundation, either by flooding from streams or lakes disturbed, power plant dams broken, lava flow and/or a giant tsunami or tidal wave from the Pacific Ocean generated by the earthquake activity.

During the first week of January, 1983, Madame Pele erupted in a spectacular show of lava fountains leaping hundreds of feet in the air. The eruptions are still going on as of right now (April, 1983). **Days** after the eruptions began, there were swarms of earthquakes in the Mammoth Lakes area in the California-Sierra Nevada Mountains. At one point the quakes were coming at a rate of nearly one per minute. The two largest jolts registered 5.5 on the scale. The quakes were felt 200 miles away and lasted for a 5 hour period. Perhaps these are the early warnings of imminent volcanic eruptions in the area that government officials are concerned may take place similar to those of Mount Saint Helens![12] A few days after these quakes, during the third and fourth weeks of January, 1983, on through the entire month of February and into the first weeks of March, the entire California coast as well as the areas from the Salt Lake through Nevada and Arizona were battered by storm after storm with high winds causing huge waves, inundating vast areas, California being described as an "over-ripe grape," literally splitting at the seams, and falling into the Pacific, **as Cayce had predicted over 50 years ago!**

Cayce did say that the spirituality of the people in an area can help to either cushion the shock or defuse the explosion altogether, with regard to drastic earth changes. Perhaps this is why the San Francisco area has been spared a great quake as it seems to be a mecca for the arts and spiritual endeavors. This is probably why the East Coast will be the area most changed, according to Cayce. It is the area where the seat of our national government is located. It is also the most polluted part of the country, as the recent Environmental Protection Agency toxic dump list reveals, with New Jersey, often referred to as "cancer alley," having 65 of the 400 plus chemical dump sites listed—the highest number of any state in the nation.

Hence, more drastic measures will be needed to "cleanse" the area (East Coast) of the filth that has accumulated there. Cayce stated that, "the greater change will be in the North Atlantic Seaboard. Watch New York, Connecticut, and the like. Many portions of the East Coast will be disturbed, as well as many portions of the West Coast, as well as the central portion of the United States."[13]

300

We have already seen these disturbances begin as there were at least four earthquakes in nine days in 1982, one of them registering 5.9, being the strongest quake in the area in 126 years, literally shaking up the entire New England area from Maine to Connecticut to New York. Few people realize that there is a fault line that runs right down the middle of Manhattan Island (N.Y.C.). Thus we can see why Cayce said New York, on the whole, will disappear.

Further, the floor of the Atlantic Ocean where the American and African continents meet is only one mile thick—the thinnest portion of the Earth's crust known to man. Hence, the area is very earthquake-prone—quakes that may signal the rising of ancient Atlantis and the breaking up and inundation of many areas along the Atlantic Seaboard, as Cayce predicted. Cayce said that one of the places that would be affected the earliest by the earth changes would be Georgia. In 1982, the first-ever earthquake in recorded history struck that state!

As to the heartland of America, Cayce stated that here, too, great changes were to occur. These changes included a shaking up of the area, as well as vast inundations—flooding so great that eventually the Great Lakes would empty into the Gulf of Mexico. Interestingly enough, the most massive quake ever recorded in U.S. history was not in California, but took place in Missouri along the New Madrid Fault Zone on December 16, 1811—a quake so massive that it actually changed the course of the Mississippi River. According to a recent article on the fault zone, scientists are expecting another massive quake to occur there at any time in the near future, as there are minor quakes already in the area every day, usually so minor that they cause no damage. However, in the past, there have been at least three massive quakes: the first around the time of Christ, the second occurring some years later and being the source of Indian legends concerning a great fury in the Earth, and the third occurring in 1811. Apparently, the great Shawnee leader Tecumseh foretold the coming of the quake, for in 1811, he said, "He would stamp his foot and the houses of the white settlers would be shaken down.

"Near the end of that year, a great earthquake centered in that fault zone shook the Mississippi Valley and radiated out with such violence that in Richmond, Va., people 'staggered as they stood.' Clocks stopped in New Orleans. Furniture moved about by itself in rooms in Charleston, S.C. Wells went dry in Columbia, S.C. Plaster ceilings cracked in Chicago. Chimneys fell in Cincinnati. Church bells rang themselves in Washington. Shocks were felt along the Gulf Coast, in Pittsburgh, even in Quebec City 1200 miles from the heart of the quake."[14]

There were three quakes that year that released more energy than 10,000 Hiroshima bombs. The rift zone is actually an area where the American continent tried to split apart at one time aeons ago, similar to the way the continents of South America and Africa split, eventually drifting away from each other. The San Andreas fault is currently blocking the movement of the drift of the American continent, hence pressure builds up and has to be released, as it is with earthquakes in the New Madrid area. When, **NOT**, "if," Cayce's predictions concerning the inundation of the West Coast begin to come true, then there will be nothing stopping the American Continent from splitting itself along the Mississippi Valley area or New Madrid Fault Zone. Thus, the prophecy of the Great Lakes emptying into the Gulf of Mexico becomes much more believable.

When the massive quake happens, there will be a lot more damage than was done during the 1811 quake because there are so many people living there now, and the Mississippi Valley area is the heart of the nation through which most of the food, energy supplies, etc., pass while on their way to the East Coast. The disruption of these supplies could mean catastrophe not only for the Valley area, but also for the people dependent on them living along the East Coast. As Patrick Breheney, the Federal Emergency Management Agency's Regional Director said:

> "We can't sign a peace treaty with God to say it's not going to happen. This is a catastrophe that is going to occur. People have to understand that...One thing for sure is that the more dependent on technology we've become, the more vulnerable we've become...Say a prayer that it doesn't happen in less than 20 years. If it does, we'll be trying to put a Band-Aid on one big, big hurt."[15]

Major quakes in the area happen every 75 years or so. The last one was in 1895, so the area is well overdue for another one.

Another reason that this area is so quake-prone is that there is another supposedly "inactive" rift two times the length of the San Andreas fault intersecting with the New Madrid fault. This fault line stretches from Idaho to the southern Appalachian Mountains—a huge area. Thus, we can see why Cayce said that the central portion of the U.S. would be shaken up a lot in the End Times—a shaking up that has already begun as quakes rocked the states of Tennessee and Arkansas in 1982. It can only get worse!

Further, this same area has been hit with the worst flooding in history the last two winters. From the Great Lakes states of Michigan, Minnesota, Indiana, Illinois, Iowa, Wisconsin, down through Ohio, Missouri, Arkansas, Louisiana and Mississippi, the entire Mississippi River Valley area has been wading in water as high as 42'—as high as the rooftops of two and three story buildings. The '81 floods had been called the worst in our century, but those of '82 were even more severe, as the so-called "once-in-a-century" floodwaters began to look more and more like the rule than the exception. In December of 1982, 44 towns in the Mississippi River Valley area were under water, while floating cylinders containing toxic waste compounded the threat to lives in the flood areas. The toxic chemicals, specifically dioxin, have poisoned the water and land so badly that the federal government has offered to buy the entire town of Times Beach, Mo. (a suburb of St. Louis) as the area has become too contaminated to be safe for human habitation, dioxin being the most deadly substance known to man (170,000 times more deadly than cyanide), scientists saying that 3 ounces of it could kill the entire population of New York City![16] Thus, **the fulfillment of Cayce's prophecies** about the Great Lakes emptying into the Gulf of Mexico via the Mississippi Valley area **is already beginning to occur!**

Chapter 14

BIZARRE WEATHER CHANGES

Edgar Cayce was not the only one who predicted bizarre changes in the weather; just about all of the prophecies state that there will be "crazy weather" as we come closer and closer to the end of this system of things and the beginning of the New Age. In many areas, the weather changes are to be so drastic that the seasons will seem to be completely mixed up.

The *Shrimad Bhagavatam* states that, "people will perish through drought, excessive cold, storms, scorching sunshine, heavy rain, snowfall...(causing) annual plants (to be) stunted in growth..."[1] Jesus Christ states that men will be "in perplexity at the roaring of the sea and the waves."[2] And the American Indians have said that, besides increased volcanic activity and great earthquakes (one which will occur in Los Angeles in mid-April—no year is given), the continent will experience great flooding in several areas, including the New York and Pennsylvania regions, again reiterating Cayce's predictions about many lands being inundated along the Atlantic Seaboard. Further, they state that because the great buffalo placed at the West Coast to hold back the sea is just about ready to fall over, higher and higher waves will plague the West Coast until the great inundation of the West is completed, again echoing Cayce's predictions about the West Coast being flooded. The Indian legend states that when the great buffalo finally falls, this age will come to an end. Finally, many of the plagues of Revelations have to do with bizarre weather changes including incredibly large hail and drought so severe that it "burns up" the grasses and trees as well as tormenting men because of the fierce heat of the sun.[3]

All one needs to do is read the newspapers lately to see that **these prophecies are being fulfilled** and that the great weather changes and plagues are already beginning. All across the U.S., violent storms have been taking their toll in lives lost and property damaged. In the last two years alone, violent rainstorms have caused flooding not only in the Mississippi Valley area, but also Kansas, Nebraska, the entire New England area (again, called "once-in-a-century" rains), Kentucky, Tennessee, Montana (where flood waters caused several small dams to collapse, forcing hundreds of people to flee their homes), Pennsylvania (where a mile-long ice jam sent 6 feet of water pouring into a Pittsburgh suburb), Alabama, the Texas Panhandle (where rains caused one tiny creek to swell into a 350' wide torrent), Utah (again, called a "once-in-a-century" rainstorm), and Washington state (where one river swollen by heavy rainfall caused an entire hill to collapse.)

Some of the hardest hit areas include the entire Atlantic Seaboard where the rainstorms of 1982 have caused severe flooding from the New England states to New York and New Jersey, down to North Carolina, Florida and Alabama. The storms have spawned 10' high waves in North Carolina causing severe coastal flooding, erosion, and wrecking several coastline homes. Huge waves have also battered away at the New England coast, **just as Cayce predicted.**

The West Coast has also been battered by severe rainstorms that have shattered century-old records, washing out bridges, collapsing roofs, and causing mudslides in Marin County, north of San Francisco. During one storm, the slides were so severe that half of a mountain came careening down causing at least $50 million worth of damage to the area's real estate, the storm being called an omen of things to come as giant mudslides due to deforestation become more and more common along the California coastline. Giant waves have often accompanied the storms, the pounding surf during one storm actually breaking off two huge chunks of the outer breakwater surrounding the Diablo Nuclear Power Plant.

Devastating rainstorms have also caused severe flooding in parts of Hawaii as Hurricane Iwa, packing 130 mile-per-hour winds and being the first hurricane to hit the islands in several decades, smashed into Kauai and Oahu, sweeping all kinds of rainfall records before her and wrecking over 20% of all homes on the island of Kauai. The hurricane also stripped certain parts of the islands bare of their protective coral reefs, the reefs having been already weakened due to pollution. Hence, the next severe storm will undoubtedly wash away more and more of the islands' coastlines, including some of the most heavily populated and developed areas of Honolulu.

The U.S. is not the only area to be hit by devastating flooding in the last two years, however. Severe rainstorms causing the worst flooding this century have also struck parts of Canada, with Eastern Canada being continually plagued by high tides and coastal flooding. Other areas hit include Brazil, Peru, Bolivia, El Salvador, Guatemala (where a mudslide triggered by heavy rains crushed an evangelical church, killing 60 people), India (the worst monsoons this century, leaving tens of thousands homeless), Nepal, Japan (where a stone bridge that had withstood severe storms for 350 years could not withstand a storm in 1982 and collapsed—floods in Nagasaki killing 300, being that city's worst disaster since World War II), Thailand, Hong Kong (three days of nonstop rain causing mudslides, flooding and cave ins), Korea, Indonesia, the Philippines (who have been hit again and again this year—'82—by severe storms, causing massive flooding and giant waves 50' high that leveled a coastline village), Taiwan, China (the worst flooding in a century, with rivers rising higher than at any time in history—the floods killing more than 1750 people and leaving almost half-a-million homeless), the Soviet Union, Algeria, South Africa (flooding being called the worst national disaster in history), Poland, and Venice (the city experiencing the highest tides ever.)

High Winds—Tornadoes

Many of these violent rainstorms have been accompanied by high winds. Typhoon after typhoon has plagued the Philippines, Taiwan and Japan with winds over 139 miles-per-hour that have flattened villages, destroyed crops, left hundreds of thousands homeless, thousands of others dead, and spawned massive tidal waves 50' or more in height. The Tonga Islands in the South Pacific were hit with 172-mile-per-hour winds and a tidal wave, the storm destroying 90% of the crops and 95% of the buildings on the northern Ha'apai group. Incredibly high winds have also hit India, Bangladesh, New Caledonia and Mexico.

Several parts of the U.S. have been hit by record high winds including the entire Atlantic Seaboard (Hurricane Harvey packing 148 m.p.h. winds), New Hampshire (175 m.p.h.), Colorado (136 m.p.h. winds that wrecked half of the homes in the city of Boulder), and the Pacific Northwest region (where one woman was killed when winds uprooted a 100' spruce tree and hurled it across her motor home.) Several violent storms have ravaged the California coast in particular as high winds of over 100 m.p.h. caused officials to close San Francisco's Golden Gate Bridge (December of '82) for the second time in its entire history as the

306

winds caused it to sway 5 feet in either direction. High winds also caused a massive blackout by blowing over several giant transmission towers, leaving a million people in the dark in Southern California alone, and affecting cities from San Francisco to Nevada and Arizona as well. The high winds have also caused record high tides and giant waves that have washed away beach houses and ripped off roofs. This storm was followed by several more in the first 3 months of 1983, during which 70 m.p.h. winds helped to raise tides to their highest level ever seen, the giant waves sweeping buildings and trucks into the Pacific, and knocking out power to thousands. The tides and rains were so severe that several levees in the agricultural interior of California actually burst, sending floodwaters over thousands of acres of prime farmland, and routing residents in several communities. The storms moved inland causing severe flooding and blizzards from Salt Lake City, throughout Nevada, Arizona, New Mexico and Colorado, **exactly as Cayce had predicted over 50 years ago.** The flooding was so severe in the desert areas of Nevada that the streets near the famous Las Vegas strip were under 2′ of water. Perhaps the American Indians' buffalo has already started to fall over!

The violent weather over the past few years has spawned innumerable tornadoes across the country, including the first-ever tornadoes recorded in Malibu and Inglewood (a suburb of Los Angeles), California. The tornado that hit Inglewood cut a 3 mile swath of destruction, leveling homes and businesses and ripping off a third of the L.A. Coliseum's roof. On that same day, severe flooding and pounding surf plagued the entire state, topped off by two earthquakes that shook the entire L.A. region.

Other areas not usually visited by tornadoes which have been the unhappy hosts of several over the past two years include Ontario (Canada), New Jersey, Pennsylvania, West Virginia, Georgia, Massachusetts, and even Hawaii, where one tornado ripped apart a military training camp on the Big Island, and another socked the island of Oahu, where one family got together and prayed in their home as the tornado headed straight for their house. The family's son stated that he watched the funnel cloud split into two parts, pass along either side of his house and merge again before going on to destroy most of the other homes in the subdivision, including their next door neighbor's, while leaving their house totally undamaged![4] Thus, we see the power of prayer and the Grace of the Lord vividly illustrated!

Even the areas that are used to tornadoes have seen a tremendous increase in the number and severity of the storms recently, with the first half of 1982 seeing the highest number of insurance casualty claims in history, with losses climbing upwards of $1.15 billion. Waves upon waves of tornadoes have swept across America's heartland (including Texas, Alabama, Oklahoma, Arkansas, Mississippi, Colorado, Kentucky, Illinois, Ohio, Tennessee, Iowa and Missouri.) Examples of the number of tornadoes to hit the area in a short span of time include 20 hitting DeSoto, Mo. on November 5, 1980, 70 on another day and more than 140 on a third, the tornadoes slicing a path across America's mid-section in 1982, literally blowing several towns off the map!

Natural disasters always have a way of humbling people as well as bringing them together in a common effort to help one another. They also point out the naivete and stubbornness of others who, though warned, refuse to believe that the impending catastrophe will ever occur and/or affect them personally. As one man in Hawaii put it after Iwa's devastating winds had passed (the article being entitled, "No one believed til the winds came"):

> "The strange thing...was that people wouldn't believe what was going to happen...I've learned that you can't take it for granted that people will listen. We've had a lot of alerts, but a lot who haven't experienced (catastrophes) felt nothing was going to happen. You'd tell them what to expect and they looked dumbfounded, like they couldn't believe what we were saying...They wouldn't listen to anybody unless they had uniforms...They changed their minds when the big glass doors in the lobby blew in. These were special doors I never dreamt would collapse like paper..."[5]

As Jesus said:

> "Take heed to yourselves lest your hearts be weighed down with dissipation and drunkenness and cares of this life, and that day come upon you suddenly like a snare; for it will come upon all who dwell upon the face of the whole earth. But watch at all times, praying that you may have strength to escape all these things that will be (and already are) taking place...

"As were the days of Noah, so will be the coming of the Son of Man. For as in those days before the flood they were eating and drinking, marrying and giving in marriage, until the day when Noah entered the ark, and (even though they had been warned) they did not know until the flood came and swept them all away, so will be the coming of the Son of Man...Watch, therefore, for the Son of Man is coming at an hour you do not expect."[6]

Extreme Temperatures—Hot and Cold

As we move closer and closer to "The Great Day of the Lord," the world's temperatures have begun to swing back and forth like a pendulum between hot and cold. The deluges of the last one or two years replaced incredible heat waves and droughts in many parts of the globe. Water restrictions were common in several communities, states, and even whole countries. For example:

1) Rajasthan, India received only 50% of its average rainfall in 1981, the ongoing drought—the worst in 50 years—affecting 100 million people or one-seventh of the total population of the country, with 21,365 villages facing famine due to crops drying up for lack of moisture. And, in the state of Bihar, 17 people dropped dead due to the severe heat, **thus fulfilling prophecy.**

2) Italy suffered from its worst heat wave in 36 years, temperatures reaching 111° F. in the shade, causing sunstroke and fits of madness amongst the populace.

3) Parts of China are in their third year of the most intense drought in over 100 years. Water levels in some parts of the country are down 40%, with 80,000 people unable to find water.

4) Spain is into its second year of one of the worst droughts in its history, causing 1.3 million people to take only sponge baths, as reserve supplies of water are down to 9% of capacity. Twenty-five to thirty percent of the livestock have died, and the olive and wine yields have been halved, while the drought spreads to neighboring Portugal.

5) In Indonesia, hundreds have already died of starvation and thousands more are malnourished as the area's worst drought this century continues to burn up crops.

6) Australia is into its fourth year of the most severe drought in its history, raising the specter of food shortages as crops continue to suffer from lack of rain. The ongoing drought has helped cause horrendous fires that raged over 400 miles and wiped out 7 towns.

7) In Winnipeg, Canada, officials are extremely worried as 1981's summer drought turned out to be worse than that of the 1930's.

8) In Mexico, 31 states have been suffering from a continuing drought, adding further troubles to an already troubled country.

9) All over Africa, the ongoing drought of the 1970's continues to spread in the '80's over more and more of the continent, further increasing the number of people dying of starvation or suffering from malnutrition.

10) New Zealand had only 40% of its normal rainfall this year, the ongoing drought being its worst in 100 years.

The U.S., too, has been hit by severe drought conditions in many parts of the country. All over the land, record high temperatures were recorded during 1981 and '82, while water restrictions and water rationing ordinances were enforced as people dropped like flies due to the suffocating heat. The overflowing Mississippi River of the winter of '82 was in sharp contrast to the dried up river bed of the summer of '81. All across the country, triple digit temperatures were the rule: from Florida to Washington, D.C. (June of '81 being the hottest in that city's history), up the Atlantic Coast (where water rationing programs had to be instituted in New York, New Jersey, Pennsylvania, and Delaware because of record low water levels in the reservoirs), inland to the Midwest (where 300 people were felled in St. Louis by heat exhaustion), on to the Western states (where record breaking temperatures caused tinder dry forests and grasslands to literally burst into flames, **fulfilling prophecy once again**), and even out to the Hawaiian Islands, where the city of Hilo on the Big Island (which is normally a pretty wet place) recorded its driest month in history during December of '81, causing several cattle to die from lack of moisture and food as the heat scorched away all the grass. The downpours of '82 were again replaced by severe drought conditions in the first few months of '83 as no significant rainfall was recorded in the area, the pendulum continuing to swing between the two extremes.

Record Cold

Meanwhile, record cold temperatures plagued the entire country during the winter months and continued well into spring in some areas. The month of January, 1982 was the coldest of the 20th Century, with records dating as far back as 1817 being shattered by the bitter cold. Snowfall records were smashed by blizzard after blizzard. The temperatures were so cold in some places that human flesh literally froze instantly when exposed to it! Double digit below zero temperatures engulfed the entire Western two-thirds of the nation, while players in one of the NFL's '81 football season's play-off games tried to keep their hands from being frostbitten as the chill factor dropped to 50° below zero! (Cinncinnati vs. San Diego game) As low temperature records were smashed from coast to coast, scientists named the winter season of '81 to '82 a once-in-a-century blasting of cold air.

But, alas, these terminologies don't seem to mean too much anymore as the winter of '82-'83 got an early jump on things, sending freezing temperatures and the worst blizzard in history across the country's mid-section, knocking out power to thousands of people and dumping so much snow that in the state of Colorado, people were trying to dig themselves out from underneath snowdrifts that were 20' high in some areas. Meanwhile, Northern Texas was being literally hit by hail the size of bricks! And, in the first week of February, '83, the biggest storm of the '82-'83 winter season paralyzed the mid-Atlantic states with two feet of snow, its blizzard force closing government offices, businesses, airports and hundreds of schools along the entire Atlantic Seaboard, as well as knocking out power, leaving thousands in the cold.

Other areas around the world that experienced record cold temperatures and/or record snowfalls during the last two winters include India (where 92 people have died due to the severe cold), Japan, Canada (called the coldest weather in centuries in some regions), the entire European continent, including England (called "back-to-the-Ice Age weather"), Austria, Denmark, Scotland (where the sea actually froze off the Scottish coast), Lebanon (which experienced the worst blizzard in its history in February of '83, snowdrifts reaching 24' in height, burying scores of people in their cars causing dozens to freeze to death), and even Hawaii, where the astronomers in the observatories atop Mauna

Kea Volcano on the Big Island had to break up furniture and burn it in order to keep from freezing to death as the worst blizzard in history hit the mountain in March of '82.

The weather has become so unpredictable that meteorologists are becoming increasingly frustrated as "freak storms" and bizarre temperatures dominate the country, baffling the most modern computers. Along the East Coast, record cold temperatures in October, '82, were replaced by record high temperatures in December. The temperatures were so high that many plants began to put forth leaves, etc., only to be zapped a week later by record cold temperatures that quickly killed the new buds. Thus, the seesawing, pendulum swinging temperatures are mixing up the growing seasons, **again fulfilling prophecy** and being a bad omen for the future. For plants and trees can only take so much of this pendulum swinging before being irreparably damaged or killed altogether.

Thus, we can see that **the prophecies regarding bizarre weather changes,** "freak storms," intense heat and cold, floods and winds **plaguing mankind in the End Times have been fulfilled!**

The question is why are all of these weather changes occurring? Some scientists feel that we are entering another Ice Age as a natural course of the Earth's evolution. Many feel that this has been precipitated by the massive volcanic sulfuric ash cloud spewed into the atmosphere by Mexico's Chichon Volcano. The cloud is said to be blocking 10% of the sunlight, which will naturally lower temperatures on the Earth's surface. It only takes a drop of a few degrees Fahrenheit to usher in another Ice Age. The colder temperatures mean shorter growing seasons in a time when the world's expanding population needs all the food it can get.

Other scientists point to the strange "Mystery Clouds" or "Monster Clouds" that have been encircling the Earth. Experts are not sure as to the origin of these clouds, but do agree that their combined blockage of the sun's life-giving rays and warmth will, and already have started to affect global weather patterns.

Other weather "experts" believe that the bizarre weather is being caused by "El Nino"—a phenomenon that usually begins around Christmas, where equatorial trade winds do not move in their customary patterns, thereby disrupting weather cycles. Scientists do not fully understand the phenomenon or the reason for it, though inadvertantly giving credit where it's due, as "El Nino" literally means "The Christ Child."[7]

Still others say that certain planetary alignments are the root cause of the disruption of weather patterns and increased earth changes currently taking place, which brings us to our next set of prophecies regarding the End Times—the signs in the heavens.

Chapter 15

SIGNS IN THE HEAVENS

As stated before, some scientists believe that the current bizarre weather and earth changes are due to certain planetary alignments, the gravity-pulls of the various planets creating stress on the Earth's crust and disrupting the normal flow of the Earth's atmosphere. Indeed, in 1982, a rare alignment of the nine planets of our solar system took place. At first, nothing seemed to happen at all, but, as if by delayed reaction, suddenly, all "hell" started to break loose: "freak" spring snow and incredibly heavy rain storms, avalanches, blizzards, floods, mudslides, and even volcanic eruptions.

Jesus stated that there would be signs in the heavens indicating His imminent return and the start of the New Age. The Hopis, too, speak of various heavenly signs at the time of the Great Tribulation/Purification. We have previously discussed two of these heavenly signs that have already made themselves known to man: the Triple Conjunction of the planets Saturn and Jupiter, and the recent discovery of the Hopi's Giant Blue Star.

As explained earlier, the triple conjunction of Jupiter and Saturn (the two planets conjuncting or coming close together in the sky three times) took place around the time of the Buddha's birth (563 B.C.) and the year of His Enlightenment (523 B.C.), as well as at the time of Christ's birth (approximately 7 B.C.) and is thought to have been the Star of Bethlehem to which the Bible refers. The Magi, who were expert astronomers/astrologers, interpreted the conjunction at the time to mean the birth of the Messiah or Great King in Judea, Saturn being the Messiah's star, and Jupiter being the King's star, taking place in Pisces—the zodiac sign associated with the House of the Hebrews or Palestine. The conjunction of the planets occurred three times, being joined by the planet Mars—the symbol for war and associated with the enemy of the Jewish nation—during the last conjunction.[1]

In 1981, this same rare conjunction took place on January 14, February 19, and July 30, this time in the zodiac sign of Virgo, which lies directly opposite Pisces and represents the Virgin or Mother, possibly indicating the coming of the feminine aspect of God. During the 1981 conjunction, Jupiter overtook Saturn for the one-hundredth time since they passed in 7 B.C. or since

Christ's birth, since many theologians and astronomers agree that Christ's birth has been miscalculated by 4 to 7 years.

What's more, a month after the last conjunction, Jupiter and Saturn were joined by Venus (August 24th through the 27th, 1981), forming a compact trio—Venus being associated with Christ **and** the Pale Prophet of the American Indians. So perhaps the Lord is coming as both male and female this time!

The Hopi's blue star, as mentioned earlier, was discovered in 1981, the super massive star being the largest ever seen by man, defying his laws of physics as it had been thought that a star could not get so large—3500 times the size of our own sun, emitting a blue light.[2]

Other recent signs in the heavens include a massive solar flare generating a spectacular aurora of red, green and white lights in the sky on the night of June 6, 1982—the Tibetan anniversary of the Buddha's Enlightenment;[3] the reported discovery at UCLA of a mysterious object—possibly a star—that seems to be moving in opposite directions at the same time at extremely high speeds, as much as 31,000 miles a second; the discovery that the largest star in our galaxy—a unique blue supergiant—is about to blow up, which will create a supernova emitting light equal to billions of suns;[4] and the discovery of the fastest pulsar known to man, revolving 642 times per second, putting out ten to 100 million times the energy of our sun, and leading to the possible detection of "gravity waves" theorized by Einstein, which are like ripples in the fabric of space. What effect these waves will have upon the Earth when they reach us is anybody's guess.[5]

Further, Nostradamus makes reference to the coming of a comet during the End Times. Haley's Comet is due to visit the Earth again as it completes its 76-year-cycle. It is already visible through telescopes, but won't be visible to the naked eye until December of 1985, and will make its closest sweep near Earth during the months of February and March of '86. During its far-off first run by the Earth in 1982, it left behind a spectacular red and pink meteor shower that lit up the sky over the Eastern Seaboard.

However, Nostradamus may not have been referring to Haley's Comet at all, rather, he could have meant the appearance of a new comet as Haley's consistent visits to the Earth were well-known and documented even during his lifetime, having been first sighted way back in 240 B.C. Hence, the discovery or appearance of a new comet may well have been what Nostradamus meant, the appearance being a sign of the imminent changes to take place upon the Earth. In June of 1982, a "virgin" comet—one never seen before—was spotted heading toward the Earth. According to scientists, the comet has never visited our skies before and is headed on its first trip around our sun.[6] Perhaps it is this comet to which Nostradamus was referring.

Another sign in the heavens to which Jesus may have been referring is the increasing number of UFO (Unidentified Flying Objects or space ships) sightings that have been taking place recently. Over the last few years, the sightings have started to increase again. For example, in Spain, hundreds of sightings have been reported, many being verified by dozens of people. They include several bright, shining, arrow-shaped objects that take off at incredible speeds giving no sound whatsoever; and one the size of an oil tanker seen in 1981. And, in Tibet, one meteorological official sighted several bright objects surrounded by Saturn-like rings of blue-white lights, moving at 70 to 100 miles per hour for a few minutes before disappearing altogether. His sighting was confirmed by other individuals.

The Hopi prophecies foretold that man would go to the moon, as well as the building of space stations. They further state that man will go no further than this. **This prophecy has already been fulfilled,** as the Russians' Salyut 7 has been orbiting the earth for a few years now. The U.S. is planning to put a multi-million dollar space station in space, too, within the next five years.

One of the very last plagues of Revelations refers to the introduction of various weapons and objects into the heavens encircling our globe.[7] This prophecy was already partially fulfilled when man started to use airplanes as weapons of warfare, dropping bombs—both conventional and atomic—onto populated areas below. The descriptions of the plague of locusts that sting like scorpions from their tails sound remarkably like helicopters used in combat, whose bombs and missiles are launched from the rear of the craft.[8]

But the total fulfillment of this part of Revelations was not complete until man entered outer space, sending up various satellites, space stations, etc., to orbit the Earth. Currently, there are over 4700 various pieces of "litter" orbiting the Earth, 1200 of these being satellites, and the rest being various articles such as spent rockets, wrecked satellites, nuts, bolts, ceramic tiles, etc. The problem is that these objects do eventually come back to Earth. Most burn up in the atmosphere, but some—such as America's Skylab and two Russian satellites of the Cosmos series—don't, crashing into the earth with a tremendous force. Skylab hit Australia in July of '79, and one of the nuclear-powered Russian satellites smashed into the Canadian wilderness in January, 1978. The second nuclear-powered Soviet spy satellite, which developed serious trouble in late '82, has already started to break up above the Earth, a part of it falling into the Indian Ocean in January, 1983. No one knows exactly where or when the remainder of the satellite will fall down, but when it does, "about 100 pounds of dangerous radioactive nuclear fuel is expected to spew out over a wide area," obviously posing a serious health danger to any form of life, including human.[9]

Another blazing fireball plunged from the sky on February 10, 1983, and burrowed into the lawn at the University of New Orleans campus. The 50 pound object was thought to be a satellite and was described as a "red, red, red hot...glowing and smoking" object. It came within 70' of the University's Fine Arts building, again illustrating the danger that these pieces of orbiting "space junk" present to life on Earth.[10]

These space objects are monitored every day by the North American Aerospace Defense Command or NORAD, as a returning piece of "space junk" could easily be mistaken for an enemy missile, thus triggering an unjustified return attack. NORAD's headquarters are located deep within the Rocky Mountains of Colorado, where 15 buildings have been carved out of the mountains' interior, which brings us to two very interesting passages found in the Book of Joel of the Old Testament and in Revelations, regarding one of the last signs in the heavens given by the Bible in reference to the end of this system of things:

> "And I will give portents in the heavens and on the earth, blood and fire and columns of smoke. The sun shall be turned to darkness, and the moon to blood, before the great and terrible day of the Lord comes."[11]

> "When he opened the sixth seal, I looked, and behold, there was a great earthquake; and the sun became black as sackcloth, the full moon became like blood, and the stars of the sky fell to the earth as the fig tree sheds its winter fruit when shaken by a gale; the sky vanished like a scroll that is

rolled up, and every mountain and island was removed from its place.

"Then the kings of the earth and the great men and the generals and the rich and the strong, and everyone, slave and free, hid in the caves and among the rocks of the mountains, calling to the mountains and rocks, 'Fall on us and hide us from the face of Him who is seated on the throne, and from the wrath of the Lamb; for the great day of their wrath has come, and who can stand before it?' "[12]

Part of this prophecy may well have been fulfilled in 1982. That year saw the awakening of both the great Mexican volcano El Chichon, and Indonesia's volcano, Gallunggung, whose spectacular eruptions were preceded by violent earthquakes. When the volcanoes spewed forth their billions of tons of ash and gasses, the sun's light was completely obscured, turning day into night, similar to the way in which Mt. St. Helen's ash cloud threw nearby residents into the dark.

As to the moon turning to blood, the most amazing and spectacular lunar eclipse of the 20th Century happened in July, 1982. On the evening of the 6th of July, the moon turned a dark blood-red surrounded by blue haloes as a result of the volcanic ash cloud sent into the heavens by Galunggung and El Chichon. The eclipse was the longest since 1859, lasting over 100 minutes, being one of seven lunar eclipses during '82. Astronomers called the eclipse a "once-in-a-lifetime event," as the moon actually seemed to disappear altogether at times.[13]

Both volcanoes spewed forth a tremendous number of rocks, some as large as human heads, and cinders that could account for the description of the stars falling from the heavens given in the prophecies. And, as mentioned earlier, the sky seemed to disappear altogether as the volcanic ash cloud threw the areas near the volcanoes into complete darkness.

Of course, the description may also be what one would see in the event of the earth shifting on its axis. So perhaps the first part of the prophecy has been fulfilled; thus we are awaiting the fulfillment of the second.

As to the kings and generals seeking refuge within the mountains, as said before, NORAD's headquarters are indeed deep inside the mountains of the Colorado Rockies. What is perhaps not so well-known is that there is an entire underground city that

318

has been carved out of the interior of the hilly and mountainous areas near Washington, D.C. The city was built as a place of safety for high-ranking officials of the federal government to be used in the event of a nuclear war. The city is complete with living quarters, game rooms and even a huge underground lake, as well as being stocked high with various foodstuffs, including shrimp creole! Thus, if there was a nuclear attack, or any other calamity, not only would the President have the "Doomsday" plane in which to escape (which, during the first two years of his term, while on a practice run, returning from a turkey hunt, President Reagan described the experience as "great, fascinating, reassuring" and giving him a great sense of confidence), but he and his family, along with various senators, congressmen, government officials, cabinet members, etc., would have a supposedly secure shelter to go to until the whole "problem" literally blew over. Meanwhile, the people on the earth's surface would have to make do with shelters and evacuation plans that experts agree are totally unworkable and unrealistic.

It is presumed that the Soviets have constructed similar underground facilities for their top government and military officials, and it is a known fact that China has developed massive underground cities to house their country's leaders. However, these shelters will be useless in a nuclear war because: 1- they may not even withstand a nuclear attack, 2- the amounts of radiation left in the atmosphere after the war would destroy them anyway, so they would be unable to come out, and 3- if they did come out, what would be left? Where would they grow their food, get pure water, air, etc.? Finally, one must realize that no one can hide from the Lord; if He wishes to, these underground mountain cities may well become the final resting places for those within them.

Uranus and Pluto

Other signs in the heavens include the locations of the planets Uranus and Pluto within the sky. The discovery of the planet Uranus in 1781 coincided with the American revolution and America's birth as a nation. It is a planet signifying transformation, transformation having two aspects: on the one hand, it represents atomic power and the destruction it wroughts, transforming matter into ashes; on the other hand, it represents the heavens

319

or spiritual transformation of mankind as it enters into the New Age. "Uranus...rules the sign of Aquarius, which presides over the beginning of the New Age."[14]

The discovery of the planet Pluto in 1930 coincided with the Great Depression, the rise of Hitler, Mussolini and Stalin. It, too, has a dual influence: on the one hand, it represents the underworld, darkness and destruction as the events at the time of its discovery in 1930 attest to the force of that negative influence, the planet actually being named for the "lord" of hell; on the other hand, it represents the positive aspects of regeneration coming from the ashes of the old order, the old world, the old system of things. The phoenix is the symbol used to represent Pluto, indicating the "new birth" or regeneration of the world that this planet helps bring about. For this reason, "Pluto also stands for humanity's ultimate triumph of universal brotherhood."[15]

Pluto's current orbit is bringing it closer to Earth than at any other time, actually coming inside the orbit of Neptune. Its negative aspects have already begun to manifest themselves in economic chaos, political turmoil and unrest, as well as the rise to power of several despotic and demonic leaders round the world—almost a repeat of the '30's era. But, again, Pluto's positive aspects of rebirth and regeneration must prevail. For out of the ashes of catastrophes—both manmade and natural—comes new hope, new birth, transformation to a higher state.

Though initially the world may be ruled by despots, specifically the Beast of Revelations' fame, we must remember that this battle between good and evil, and the period of purification will greatly affect the domain of the Beast. From this will come a release of tremendous energy that will be able to be positively refocalized.

To paraphrase Mahatma Gandhi: Whenever you despair, remember that Truth and Love have always prevailed. There have been despots and murderers who, for a time, have seemed invincible. But they have always fallen in the end. Think of it often, whenever you doubt that Truth and Love is God's Way.

"As the Plutonian cycle culminates, the fledgling Phoenix will preen the ashes of death and destruction from its beautiful feathers, and fly off into the settling dust of a murky sunrise. A new culture will emerge. After all, who can hold back the dawn?"[16]

320

The Age of Aquarius

The concept of the zodiac is one that is common to most ancient civilizations, the word "zodiac" literally meaning "living creatures" in Greek.[17] Basically these 12 signs correspond to a series of 12 star groupings that circle the sky. Each year the Earth moves through the 12 signs of the zodiac.

This same model is seen on a larger level, too. A zodiac age is said to last a little more than 2100 years. The Earth's axis is said to point to a different sign of the zodiac in each age. For the past 2000 or so years we have been in the Age of Pisces. The start of the Piscean Age is said to have coincided with the rise of the Roman Empire, about 200 B.C. or so. The sign for the Piscean Age is the fish, as the word "pisces" means "fish." It is a water sign and the use of water as a religious rite has been clearly demonstrated during this age with baptism in water. Further, the earliest followers of Christ were men dealing with water and fish. Indeed, one of the earliest symbols used by the Christians as a means of identifying themselves to one another was the fish. Several miracles that Jesus performed had to do with fish; i.e., the 4000 and 5000 groups, each fed with loaves and fishes, and Jesus' miracles of filling His disciples nets with so many fish that they nearly burst. On a more worldly level, the Earth was first tied together by water travel as Columbus and others set sail on the oceans, going round the world, navigating by the stars of the heavens.

Today, we are standing on the cusp or transition point of the ages: from Pisces to Aquarius. Aquarius is an air sign, and as we have already seen, scientific advancements during the past century, having to do with the air, abound: radio, T.V., satellite communication, airplanes, space travel, etc. Aquarius literally means "water bearer," and its symbol is a man carrying a pitcher of water in his right hand. To quote the *Aquarian Gospel of Jesus the Christ:*

> "And then the man who bears the pitcher will walk forth across an arc of heaven; the sign and signet of the Son of Man will stand forth in the Eastern sky. The wise will then lift up their heads and know that the redemption of the earth is near."[18]

The Aquarian Age is to be mankind's Age of Enlightenment,

the Age of Spirituality, when all of the spiritual truths that were taught by Jesus Christ and all of God's other Messengers will be available and comprehended **en masse.** In the past, these truths have often been restricted to a tiny minority. But with the advances of technology, air travel, etc., these truths are no longer the sole possession of a handful, but are available to all. What's more, with the mass production and consumption of Nature's Aids in the early '60's, a whole generation is said to have had a religious mystical experience.[19] The timing of this mass mystical experience coincided with the last Kachina dance of the Hopis (1961), the dance signifying the beginning of the Great Purification Period.

Thus, this age **is** the Age of Aquarius, the Age of Spirituality for the multitudes. Hence, our title: **Aquarius or Spirituality Dawns—Liberation Begins!** Hence, also, the author's name: **Kristina Gale-Kumar,** Kristina being the feminine form of "Christopher" (in Greek—"Khristophorus") meaning "Christ-bearer," Gale meaning "strong wind or spirit,"[20] and Kumar meaning "Prince." Therefore, the name means "the Christ-bearing Spirit Prince." Also, Kristina contains two of the Lord's Names: Christ (in Greek-Khrist) and Krishna (or Krisna).

Chapter 16

THE BALANCE OF NATURE PERVERTED

Another reason that the Earth's weather cycles have changed so dramatically, and there has been such an increase in the number of earthquakes and volcanic eruptions recently is that man has interfered with the Balance of Nature. Specifically, he has turned the once-green paradise of the Earth into dust and concrete, literally shaving the Earth of its natural foliage and ground cover as a razor shaves a man's beard. John was told in Revelations that one would have to seek the Lord within as the outer court of the temple of God, or Nature, would be trampled down by the Gentiles, until the end of their time. Indeed, Nature surely has been trampled upon over the last few centuries. This also corresponds to the desecration of the Earth as both the American Indian and Hindu prophecies foretold.

The great sage Sri Aurobindo has perfectly summarized man's present predicament in his beautiful poem *Savitri:*

"An idiot hour destroys what centuries made...
All he has achieved he drags to the precipice.
His grandeur he turns to an epic of doom and fall;
His littleness crawls content through squalor and mud,
He calls heaven's retribution on his head,
And wallows in his self-made misery."[1]

Three areas of particular interest to us today regarding how man has changed the Earth and, therefore, upset the natural order of things, are: 1-species extinction, 2-deforestation, and 3-chemicalization. But first, let's do a quick review of exactly what we mean by the Balance of Nature.

The Balance of Nature can be compared to a spider's web; each strand of the web is like a different species in Nature. It is in the vast diversification of different species that the web of life is held together. When man interferes with or destroys one of these strands, either through arrogance or ignorance, he endangers the entire web of which he himself is a part. Or, as the great American Indian Chief Seattle put it:

"The Earth does not belong to man; man belongs to the Earth. All things are connected like the blood which unites one family. All things are connected. Whatever befalls the Earth befalls the sons of the Earth. Man did not weave the web of life: he is merely a strand in it. Whatever he does to the web, he does to himself."[2]

Again, the Balance of Nature can be compared to a set of building blocks, the security of each block being dependent on the strength of the others. If one continually takes away block after block, the overall structure is weakened and will eventually collapse.

Species Extinctions

In the past, under normal circumstances, species became extinct at about the same rate as new species evolved, thereby preserving the overall structure of Creation and the Balance of Nature. But since the 1600's, the rate of extinction has accelerated upwards of 400 times the norm. Today, over 1,000,000 species are in danger of extinction. By the end of the '80's, the extinction rate will rise to 10,000 species annually—more than one per hour![3]

Although no one can say exactly how many species have already become extinct, estimates range from 30% to 50% of the total number of species that were in the world before 1600. By the year 2000 A.D., over 20% or more of the world's few remaining species of plants and animals could be extinct, with another 20% endangered. Take between 50% to 70% of any building structure away and see how long it stands!

What we have done is to turn the pyramid of life upside down and place it on its point—not a very stable position! In the past, the varieties of other life forms far outnumbered man; the natural diversification gave man a firm, strong and wide foundation upon which to build and grow. But as man's numbers have increased, the number of other life forms has decreased, thereby removing many of the support systems that are vital to the overall ecosystem of the Earth.

Another example of God's Balance is seen on the African grassplains where there are several different species who survive on the surrounding vegetation. Not all species eat the same vegetation. Even the grass itself is eaten by different species at different stages of its growth, some eating only the flowering tops, others the long blades in the middle, and still others the stubble that is left over.

When man introduces a non-indigenous or non-native species into an area, chaos is often the result. The best examples of this would be man's introduction of cattle and sheep into Africa and into America's once-great prairie lands. Cattle eat everything, including tree seedlings and other vegetation that the natural or indigenous animals, such as the antelope and water buffalo, left alone. Sheep have been just as disastrous because they eat grass all the way down to and including its roots, thereby exposing the topsoil and causing severe erosion to take place. The herds of buffalo and antelope migrated from one grazing pasture to another according to the seasons. This allowed the plains to recover from season to season. All too often, man's domesticated herds are not allowed to roam or migrate and, therefore, the land has no chance to grow new grass-covers to protect the soil beneath.

Poor farming techniques have also threatened the earth's topsoil which is vital to the survival of not only man, but all Creation:

> "When American farmers replaced diverse native prairies with vast monocultures of single species of corn and grain, they helped set the stage for the dust bowl of the 1930's. In parts of the Mid-West it was only the remnant areas of natural prairies that kept the soil intact during that terrible drought."[4]

This is what is called a karmic effect. According to Dr. Gerald D. Barney, study director of the 1980 Global Report to the President, which outlines environmental trends until the year 2000, soil deterioration is "the most serious problem facing the world" because of its impact on food production. "For a long time to come, the human species will depend on soil to grow food."[5] It is vital, therefore, that we take the necessary steps to conserve and protect the soil from which we derive our sustenance. Today, one-fifth of the world's cropland is losing topsoil to the tune of about 5.8 billion tons lost annually to soil erosion, and it takes Nature 300 years to build an inch of topsoil naturally! Another 3 million acres a year, that is 342 acres an hour, is lost to urban sprawl and development. That amount of land paved over in one year could form a corridor from New York to California. If we do not heed the warning signals now, we will face the karmic effects later: soil erosion, crop losses, food shortages and, ultimately, starvation.

According to Dr. S. L. Brown, chairman of Pioneer H-Brand International, an agricultural feed company, "About 15 species of cultivated plants literally stand between man and starvation."[6] Farmers need new varieties of wheat every 5 to 15 years because of new diseases and new insect species, insects being the only class of species that is actually on the increase. Because our agriculture is dependent on so little variety of foodstuffs, it is very vulnerable to decimation from a single pest, or climatic change. Without natural or wild strains to replace or rejuvenate our food crops, a worldwide food disaster could easily happen literally overnight.

Reasons for the Extinctions

The principal reasons that there are so many species in danger of extinction are three in number, specifically over-hunting, loss of habitat, and man's pollution. As to hunting, there have been peoples who have played a vital part in the Balance of Nature by keeping in check the population of certain animals. The American Indians would probably be the best example of this. They hunted in harmony with Nature, using every part of the animal killed. As with other predators, they killed only the weak, deformed, diseased, old or excess of young, thereby strengthening the species as a whole by culling out defective individuals so they could not propagate and produce more defective offspring.

There was never a question of so-called "sport hunting." The idea was completely anathema to the Indians because they believed that all living things were made by God and had a soul, and therefore must be respected. One should only kill when necessary for survival. As a matter of fact, the word "animal" is derived from the Latin word "anima," which means "breath, life and soul."[7]

The American Indians were not the only peoples who were taught that all life is sacred and a part of the One God, however. Hindus and Buddhists too believe in the sanctity of life and that God has created all things and indwells in all. The *Shrimad Bhagavatam* states that even plants and animals can achieve liberation through loving God, and the great East Indian saint Sri Ramana Maharshi agreed. He had many animal friends and followers while living on his mountain, and there was one cow in

326

particular called Lakshmi who was his constant companion throughout her life. Sri Ramana said that she obviously was a rare and precious soul in an animal-body, and that when she died, she attained liberation (mukti).[8]

The Buddha once said, "It is not by hurting creatures that a man becomes excellent. Only by nonviolence is excellence a-chieved."[9] Baha'u'llah said, "Know ye that the embodiment of liberty and its symbol is the animal."[10] Mahatma Gandhi once said that you could tell a lot about a particular society and the level of consciousness of its people by observing how they treated their animals and their elderly. And, when offered a camel for sacrifice, Guru Nanak said:

> "If a drop of blood pollutes your garments, how can the spilling of blood be pleasing to God?...The law of love ordains that one should be harmless in thought and action. Treat others as you would have them treat you...We sac-rifice when we deprive the self of what it holds dear, to serve others or to serve a good cause. To kill a sheep and feast on its flesh is no sacrifice. To give what one needs for one's self to another, whose need is greater, is an act of sacri-fice."[11]

Lord Krishna stated that on no account should a seeker of God propitiate Him through the sacrifice of animals.[12] He further stated that "those who kill animals without remorse...are devoured by those animals in their next birth."[13]

The Judeo-Christian tradition teaches this belief, also. Man was to be God's steward, overseeing, protecting and helping the rest of Creation. Why else would the Lord have directed Noah to bring one male and one female of each species onto the Ark if He did not care about them? Noah was to care for and protect these animals so that all of God's created beings would be able to repopulate the New Earth. The Ark was meant to save not only man, but all of God's animals.

In the Old Testament, we find the Lord saying: "I have had enough of burnt offerings of rams and the fat of fed beasts; I do not delight in the blood of bulls, or of lambs, or he-goats."[14] Jesus Christ, too, strongly denounced the concept of animal sacrifice which is why He freed the animals in the temple square in Jerusalem that fateful day. He said that God wanted men to sac-rifice or kill their egos, not innocent animals. He said that one should feed the hungry rather than burn their choicest wheat on sacrificial fires: "Not only must ye refrain from offering human sacrifices, but ye may not lay on the altar any creature to which life has been given."[15]

And, again, He states: "The sacrifices I would bring to thee, O God, are purity in life, a contrite heart, a spirit full of faith and love, and these thou will receive...Let not your altars be accursed again with smoke of innocence. Bring unto God as sacrifice a broken and a contrite heart."[16]

This does not mean that the eating of meat in itself is wrong, although physicians and nutritionists have urged people to eat more vegetables, fruits and grains, and to eat less meat because of various health problems that have been linked to overconsumption of meat. And, Jesus did feed the 5000 with loaves and fishes, not loaves and fruit.

But there is no justification for hunting what few natural animals are left in the wild today even if one is going to eat it. Today, we have more than ample supplies of domesticated animals to fulfill our needs for meat. Even these animals must be treated humanely and not bred in artificial surroundings or killed in cruel ways, as is the case with many "factory farms." They have a right to live in at least somewhat of a natural surrounding and family or herd situation, even if their final destination is to be the dinner table!

Scientists are now warning people against eating meat from factory farms, as the animals are bred in unnatural surroundings, which breed disease. Hence, they are shot-up with excessive amounts of antibiotics, which in turn we consume. These antibiotics become harmful to our system and make our bodies less responsive to these same drugs when we need to take them when we are seriously ill.

As mentioned before, scientists are already warning that new antibiotic resistant strains of various infectious diseases, such as encephalitis, leprosy, malaria, typhoid fever, and even the plague are showing up due to man's excessive use of these antibiotic drugs in medicine and livestock. And we are virtually defenseless against them. **This fulfills prophecies from Revelations that state that in the End Times people will be steeped in "brimstone,"** an old term for sulfur—sulfur being the main ingredient not only of gunpowder and explosives, but also of herbicides, pesticides and many modern medicines.[17] Thus, the answer for those who do eat meat is to eat only organic meat that has been raised naturally and killed humanely.

This part of the Lord's teachings, i.e., that all life is sacred, was apparently forgotten by the early European immigrants though, for when they came to America and elsewhere around the world, they indiscriminantly killed off thousands of species for the sake of "sport" and "fashion," **thus fulfilling prophecy that in the End Times, people will wantonly destroy life.** (NOTE: It takes 5 leopard skins, 10 lynx, and 65 mink pelts to make one fur coat, the animals being killed by a variety of inhumane methods, including cyanide powder squeezed from a syringe into the animal's mouth, poisonous injections, electrocution, physical blows to the head, and the infamous steel leg-hold traps that can cause an animal to suffer for days and even weeks before finally being killed by the returning trapper. In some instances, the animal caught will chew off its own limb in a desperate attempt to free itself. Over 100 species are currently being killed solely for their pelts.)

This mindless destruction threw the entire ecosystem into disarray as well. The most well-known victim of this indiscriminate slaughter that eventually led to its extinction is probably the North American Passenger Pigeon, once the most numerous bird in the world, accounting for nearly 40% of the entire bird population of North America. Even as late as 1870, a single flock still measured one mile (1.6 km.) wide and 320 miles (510 km.) long, and contained not less than 2000 million birds! **Yet, it took man only 50 years to wipe out the entire species!** In a single raid on a nesting area in 1878 hunters destroyed 1000 million birds! The last Passenger Pigeon died in a zoo in 1914.[18]

What's more, animals are often the innocent victims of war. In Uganda, Idi Amin's soldiers used helicopters and machineguns to mow down various animals in the African grasslands and forests, leaving their bodies to rot in the sun.

One may say, "What does it matter?," or may say, "The indiscriminate killing of animals or the killing off of an entire species is wrong, but certainly a few birds or beasts here or there don't count." But this type of attitude belies the ignorance of the speaker. The example of the purple martin swallow illustrates the importance of just one bird in the ecosystem. Just one swallow eats more than 2000 mosquitoes per day! If that one bird is killed, over 2000 mosquitoes will be left to breed, and insects have phenominally high breeding rates. A common housefly is such a prolific breeder that the offspring produced during the average lifespan of just one adult pair would cover the nation of West Germany several feet deep!

Insects like flies, mosquitoes, roaches, and caterpillars—not large predators like wolves and bears—are the greatest threat to mankind for they attack our food supplies and carry all kinds of infectious diseases such as malaria, encephalities, typhoid fever, and even the plague.

It's no coincidence that this is happening. The epidemic outbreaks of gypsy moths, which have chewed up 75% of the hardwood forest preserves along the East Coast of the U.S. and spread a rash among school children in Pennsylvania; the medflies which almost destroyed the prime agricultural areas of California and Florida; the fire ants of the Texas Panhandle that are destroying farm equipment and threaten the impending harvest; termites in Egypt that are devouring $2 million worth of food every month; toads in Florida which are reminding residents of the Biblical plagues as literally billions of them have invaded residential areas; hamsters in North London which are overrunning the community raising the specter of rabies and other diseases (the rodents being immune to all poisons tried); rats which are multiplying so fast in Turkey on the trains officials don't know how to get rid of them; thousands of rats with foot-long tails in Boulder, Colorado, which attacked a police car recently; normally docile honeybees in Missouri which stung a woman to death, refusing to leave the body for 30 minutes; bees in Rio de Janeiro which attacked 200 fans at a soccer match, killing one man—the bees being angered by fireworks; cases of rabies which are at a 26-year high in Illinois; lyme disease—a tick borne ailment causing painful arthritis that stays with the afflicted for the rest of his life, producing basketball size lesions, which has shown up in 14 states along the East Coast; and disease-carrying mosquitoes, which are affecting all parts of the globe, but specifically, Canada and Florida, where the worst mosquito-infestation in 20 years has caused health officials to issue "mosquito alerts": all are examples of the karmic effects of man's actions which destroyed the predators that controlled the populations of these insect and rodent pests, as well as being **the fulfillment of prophecies stating that man will be plagued by various pestilences in the End Times.**

The current Pine Beetle epidemic in the Rocky Mountains of

the U.S. and Canada is another example of the importance of understanding and respecting the laws governing the Balance of Nature. Woodpeckers and other birds are commonly used for "target practice" by hunters. The decimation of their population has severely affected the Rocky Mountain forests. Woodpeckers in particular are vital to the life of the forests because they search out beetles and other parasites that plague the trees. Without woodpeckers to protect them, the trees have become infested with Pine Beetles, which can kill a tree in less than three months. Whole mountainsides of trees have been killed and the tinder-dry trees have literally burst into flames because of intense summer heat. Huge forest fires have ravaged not only the forest, but also housing developments near the mountains. This is what is called a karmic effect.

In California, the horrendous forest fires of 1981 flushed out huge rats infested with bubonic plague-carrying fleas! That's right—bubonic plague—the scourge of the Middle Ages! This would not have happened if the predators, such as hawks, eagles, wolves, etc., had been alive to check the population of the rats. Another karmic effect! Or, as man sowed, so has he reaped!

For those who say we can simply poison our way out of these epidemics and infestations with insecticides, pesticides, etc., a word of caution. A new strain of "super rats" that is immune to the most widely used rodent poisons has developed in areas of California, according to health officials. After being fed supposedly lethal doses of poison, almost 25% of the rats were still alive. And, according to another UPI release (8/6/80), Florida has been invaded by "super termites" which can eat a house in six months, secreting an acid that eats even concrete, and are resistant to most pesticides, even after double doses.

Unfortunately, there's more.....The Sun Belt is being plagued by a new "super roach" which has evolved from years of exposure to the best insecticides science can offer. The strong ones survive and then mate with other hardy roaches, resulting in offspring that inherit resistant traits. Many roaches have been found to be immune to DDT, Dursban, Diazanon, and many other popular bug-killers. To make matters worse, roaches have been known to carry dysentery, typhoid, and even the plague. A single female roach can produce as many as 400,000 offspring during her lifetime, and can go without food for a week at a time.

Doubling the poison dose is not the answer. Children especially have been killed due to exposure to these pesticides. Attempts to check the growing rabbit and coyote populations with poison and "denning" techniques (where men drag out coyote pups from the dens and club them to death) have not worked either. Poison, after all, is indiscriminate and often endangered species, such as hawks, eagles, and wolves—the very predators of these pests—end up being poisoned instead.

The answer is to restore the Balance of Nature by reintroducing predators like different species of birds such as cardinals, peacocks, hawks, eagles, etc., and mammals such as wolves, bears, and mountain lions that feed on various insects, rodents, and similar mammals. An example of a successful reintroduction program was seen in Northern New Jersey where a municipality had a horrendous overpopulation of rats. Poisoning did not work and actually caused more problems as pets and children were being poisoned in the bargain. So they reintroduced the rats' natural predator—the redtailed hawk. The skyscrapers created the same updrafts as the cliffs that are the hawks' natural habitat. Soon after the hawks were introduced, the rat population came under control. This is also a karmic effect—a very good one!

The children of the world are very concerned about the rapid rate of extinction of animals, and the devastation of the Earth. Below are some examples of their feelings on the subject **and** some solutions:

"Since man came to this world, a lot of animals are becoming extinct. Why? Because people don't care. They just kill and kill until there is nothing left. Pretty soon there is not going to be any more animals. Kill and eat—is that all man can do? Yes, because if they cared we would not have to worry. But the children of the Earth Care!

"Why does man have to be so cruel to animals? They have a right to live. That is why God made them—to live."[19]
—Leslie, age 11, Hilo, Hawaii

"It would be really nice to know that all of the creatures God made would have the chance to live a full life."[20]
—Tabetha, age 11, Keaau, Hawaii

"Animals should not be put in the zoo, because they are more beautiful in their own environment. The reason why they put animals in the zoo is because... they are taking their land from them and turning it into concrete jungles.

"Our paradise should stay a paradise!! The land should not be destroyed. The only way to stop, is to stop!!! If there were two trees planted for every tree cut down we would not run out of trees."[21]

—Frank, age 11, Keaau, Hawaii

This brings us to the second reason why there are so many endangered species, namely the loss of natural habitat due to man's overpopulation and deforestation.

Deforestation

As stated before, man's overpopulation has put a severe strain on the entire global ecosystem. As man's numbers have increased, especially in the Third World countries, demands for land on which to live and grow food, wood for homes and fuel, etc., have gone up correspondingly. This has meant the destruction of wildlife habitat and breeding grounds, and therefore the wildlife with it, and corresponding increases in disease-carrying insects and rodents which the displaced birds and animals fed on.

Today, the world's forests are disappearing at a rate of 40,000 square miles each year—an area half the size of the state of California. If the rate continues, half of the remaining tropical forests will disappear by the end of this century. Already vast areas of tropical rain forests have disappeared: 37% of Latin America's, 42% of Asia's and 52% of Africa's once lush forests have now either been paved over or have become deserts, **thus fulfilling prophecy that in the End Times,** virtually no large trees will be left standing, and **the Earth's once beautiful and prolific forests will be drastically reduced.**

The rain forests contain half of the Earth's plant and animal species. Even in the U.S., our forests are rapidly disappearing. There are so few giant redwoods left, that logging businesses have begun to close-up shop. As mentioned earlier, urban sprawl and expansion is paving over 342 acres per hour! It's easy to see why so many species have disappeared already and why so many more will soon be gone. Further, the present administration's Interior Secretary—James Watt—recently withdrew up to two million acres of Western lands from consideration as new wilderness areas, spurring environmentalists to denounce him as a "very dangerous man."

To better comprehend why this action was so disastrous in the long-range scheme of things, and why forests are so essential to the environment, one must understand the life cycle and uses of a single tree. A simple tree performs many functions in the natural world and is an essential part of the overall well-being of the forest. Its roots hold the soil together to prevent mudslides and erosion. They also retain moisture, thereby preventing floods and droughts.

The trunk of the tree provides many homes for various animals and birds, as well as building materials, paper goods, and other products such as rubber and maple syrup for man. The leaves and branches of the tree not only give shade for all, but again provide homes and food for many forest dwellers. They also help to filter the air of various man-made pollutants, absorbing deadly carbon dioxide and giving off life-sustaining oxygen. The fruits and nuts that the trees give off for their own regeneration are delicious treats for animals and humans alike.

When the leaves "die" and fall to the ground, they serve a dual purpose: first, they insulate the ground like a warm blanket, keeping it from freezing too deeply. This protects the seeds that are sleeping deep within the earth waiting for Spring. Secondly, they become a natural mulch or compost, replenishing the soil with necessary nutrients for the trees from which they have come. Thus the cycle is complete, and from death springs new life.

When man does not use moderation when "harvesting" the trees of the forest, or does not replant those he has taken, or replants in unnatural ways, i.e., planting in army-style parade rows as seen in so-called "tree farms," the results are devastating. There are no longer any roots to hold the soil, and massive mudslides, like those of Southern California in 1982, are the result. As mentioned earlier, soil erosion has reached critical stages around the world, and desertification is the inevitable result of deforestation and clear-cutting of woods.

One may ask how lush tropical forests can be turned into deserts so quickly. An example from Brazil will help illustrate the process and its grave consequences. North of Rio de Janeiro is a 300-mile-wide strip of desertland that looks like it belongs more in the Middle East than in the lush forests of the Brazilian Amazon. The area was once lush with abundant life—both plant and animal. Then, three decades ago, some descendants of German Pomeranian immigrants decided to move into the region. They cleared the land for farming, in the process burning several ecologically important trees, and building a road that allowed greedy logging companies access to the surrounding trees. As Brazilian environmentalist Augusto Ruschi put it: "The area went from forest to zero. There were no gradual, intermediate stages. Within 20 years, the Atlantica forest was turned into pasture lands and coffee plantations, and now the area is marching toward desertification."[22]

Without trees, there is less rainfall, and even when it does rain, it doesn't stay because there are no longer any roots to retain the moisture in the soil. Necessary soil nutrients are washed away with the rain. The entire ecosystem is completely out of balance. At least 450 different plants and 204 species of birds have disappeared. With the loss of predatory birds, the pests have proliferated, attacking what few subsistant crops the farmers have planted.

But the karmic effects are not limited to the animals and plants: the people are also suffering as a result of their folly. With no trees to provide shade, the light-skinned Germans are getting skin cancer. Says Dr. Douglas Puppin, Chairman of the Dermatological Department at the Federal University of Espirito Santo: "90% of the people I examine from that area have skin cancer or precancerous lesions."[23] As usual, it's the children who are suffering the most. Thus, **End Times' prophecies are once again fulfilled** as one of the plagues of Revelations is that the people will have open sores and lesions upon their bodies.[24]

Says Ruschi: " 'There are laws prohibiting the killing of rare species, but there are no laws preventing the destruction of the whole forest.' Environmentalists are calling for conservation, but for many Brazilians, economic development remains the top priority—even in the face of ecological devastation."[25]

Another reason that forests are disappearing has to do with one of the gravest plagues mentioned in Revelations: acid rain, which brings us to our next reason for strange weather changes and species extinctions—man's pollution.

Chapter 17

THE POLLUTING OF THE EARTH

Just about all of the prophecies of the End Times state that the Earth will not only be ravaged by deforestation, species extinctions, etc., but that it will also be polluted by man's litter and by dangerous and toxic chemicals. We are living in what Anthropology Professor E. Pierre Morenon called "the Garbage Century," with man depositing about 400,000 pieces of debris on the average acre of land during the past 100 years versus an approximate 158 pieces of debris from the years 2000 B.C. to 1630 A.D.[1]

Every day we read the headlines and see new letters and new unpronounceable names for new chemicals man has "created": PCB's, methane gas, PBB's, propane explosions, ammonia spills, chemical train derailments, asbestos, dioxin, lead and mercury poisonings, acid rain, tons of uranium and plutonium missing, nuclear accidents, radiation sickness, vinyl chloride, or, as the director of Colorado State's Hazardous Materials Division put it when referring to a toxic waste site near Denver, Colorado, "...100 million gallons of God knows what!"[2] And each year that number gets larger and larger.

Currently, there are over 50,000 chemicals on the U.S. market alone, 35,000 of which have already been classified by the EPA as either definitely or potentially hazardous to human health, with 1000 new ones concocted each year, which translates into over 350 billion tons of synthetic chemicals produced per year.[3] This does not even count those produced in the rest of the Industrialized World, or the health hazards generated from nuclear power plants worldwide, which, by the way, only provide about 12% of the electricity produced in the U.S., while costing millions and billions of dollars, being plagued with all kinds of defects and accidents.

For example, there have already been 141 "mishaps" at nuclear facilities that could have led to a meltdown—the most dangerous type of accident—occurring between 1969 and 1979, while 18,000 "events"—a lesser degree of accident, and 2500 to 3500 "minor" incidents per year have continued to plague the plants.[4] The Pentagon recently released data on 32 nuclear accidents that have occurred with regard to nuclear weaponry as well, with the NRC (Nuclear Regulatory Commission) raising new questions about the risk of tons of missing uranium and plutonium being made into nuclear bombs by a terrorist group.

New figures from a government study of potential consequences of a "worst-case" nuclear accident say that the death toll could exceed 100,000 people, and damage could top $300 billion.[5] The possibility of such an accident occurring is continuing to grow as the N.R.C. recently warned that 47 atomic power plants may have defective and corroded bolts that could lead to radioactive water leaks, while the threat of a meltdown due to the cracking of the reactor vessel (which houses the nuclear fuel) looms ever larger. Any sudden temperature change could cause the cracking, as brittling in the power plants, caused by radiation exposure, is occurring much more rapidly than anticipated, with 14 reactors already too brittle to operate safely.[6] Meanwhile, weak tubing in the steam generators is causing an epidemic of radioactive leaks of water and steam into the atmosphere. Most of the nuclear plants operating in the world today have designs similar to those that have been plagued by leaky tubing.

While all of this is going on, scientists and physicians are warning that the levels of safe radiation doses as determined by the nuclear industry and government are overestimated fifty-fold, children being more sensitive than adults to radiation-caused cancer. Finally, Tennessee's Health Dept. is passing out "anti-nuclear pills" in the event of an accident at the Sequoyah Nuclear Power Plant.[7]

In addition, there's the ever-present question of where to put the 2343 tons of nuclear waste spewed out annually just from the 71 U.S. nuclear reactors operating, not to mention the waste produced by those in other countries. Safe waste disposal has been one of the continuing problems presented by the nuclear industry, with Russia's nuclear waste accident in Siberia in the late '50's looming in the background. The waste itself stays radioactive for millions of years, hence the concern. Some have proposed blasting it to the sun at a cost of $3000 per pound, with no explanations of what would happen if the rocket misfired and exploded, releasing radioactivity into the earth's atmosphere.[8]

Currently, the radioactive waste is being trucked all over the country, raising the potential for an accident. Some has been buried in cement containers, but these have been found to be leaking into the ground nearby, threatening groundwater supplies.

DEADLY NUCLEAR RADIATION HAZARDS USA

Women Strike for Peace
201 Massachusetts Ave. NE
Washington, D.C. 20002
202 546-7397

Manmade low level radiation is all about us and IS causing cancer, leukemia, cataracts, premature aging, damage to unborn children, genetic mutations for generations to come, fetal and infant deaths. High level radiation from weapons making, nuclear explosions and nuclear war can bring an end to all life on earth. Plutonium was named for Pluto, the lord of hell. At present over 90% of the volume of manmade radioactivity results from the weapons program. By the year 2000 the worldwide production of long-lived radioactivity will be equal to exploding about 3 million Hiroshima bombs per year. Dr. John Goffman: "It violates minimum morality for any generation of humans to produce a radioactive legacy which IRREVERSIBLY endangers the future of all generations to come."

End the arms race—not the human race.

NUCLEAR WEAPONS
(Design, Testing, Production, Storage, and Army & Air Force Deployment Bases)

NUCLEAR-CAPABLE SHIP AND SUB BASES

NUCLEAR TEST EXPLOSIONS

NUCLEAR INDUSTRIES (Weapons-Related)

NUCLEAR INDUSTRIES (Commercial)

MILITARY AND D.O.E. RESEARCH REACTORS (Operable)*

MILITARY AND D.O.E. RESEARCH REACTORS (Inoperable)* Accounting for 99.2% High-Level Accumulative Radioactive Waste

RADIOACTIVE MATERIALS (Transportation, Packaging, Decontamination, Temporary Storage)

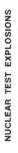

NUCLEAR POWER PLANTS
Accounting for 0.8% High-Level Accumulative Radioactive Waste (not including Spent Fuel)
- ■ **OPERABLE**
- ☢ **INOPERABLE/SHUTDOWN**
- ▲ **UNDER CONSTRUCTION**
- ● **PLANNED**

UNIVERSITY RESEARCH REACTORS (Operable)

UNIVERSITY RESEARCH REACTORS (Inoperable)

URANIUM MINES, MILLS, TAILINGS

PROCESSING FACILITIES (Uranium & plutonium)

PORTS OF ENTRY—Uranium Ore and Spent Fuel

RADIOACTIVE WASTE BURIAL GROUNDS (On Land and Off Shore Long Term Storage)

Original Research from U.S. Government Sources:
Department of Defense (DOD); Department of Energy (DOE); Nuclear Regulatory Commission (NRC); Bureau of Mines. Information also drawn from "State by State Guide to Nuclear Facilities;" Another Mother for Peace; the NARMIC Maps, American Friends Service Committee; "Nuclear America" War Resisters; "The Nuclear News Buyers Guide" American Nuclear Society.
Designed by James True and Carol Gerson, Graphic Artists.
Researched and prepared by Louise Franklin-Ramirez, Virginia Women for Peace and Gray Panthers.

Some has also been dumped into the ocean near San Francisco and 12 miles off the New Jersey coast. But, again, the containers have been found to corrode and leak after a relatively short period of time, raising the specter of dead oceans and dead humans from the cancer-infected fish eaten by humans. Then there is the question of what to do with old nuclear submarines and out-dated nuclear plants—all of which are too highly radioactive to stay around near people.

Beyond the question of nuclear power, there are other toxic chemicals polluting our environment every day, exposure to which can be just as dangerous as radiation exposure. Because these compounds do not occur in the natural environment, they are not biodegradable, or, in other words, sun, wind, water and bacteria do not cause them to decay rapidly. So they linger on in the environment and enter our food chain, and thus enter us. The animals and plants we eat, the water we drink, the air we breathe are all contaminated to some degree by these pollutants. This translates into all kinds of cancers, kidney diseases, neurological disorders, and birth defects, just to mention a few. For example, in 1973, PBB's got mixed in with some animal grains and was fed to various livestock. The people ate the livestock and, hence, the PBB. Today, a decade later, over 90% of the people of Michigan still have PBB in their bodies, and the long range health problems are just beginning to surface.[9] **Thus we see that prophecies regarding pollution causing epidemics in humans in the End Times are fulfilled, again.**

Recently, the Environmental Protection Agency (EPA) released a list of the nation's 418 worst toxic dump sites—sites targeted by the federal government to be cleaned up using money from the federal "Superfund" enacted by Congress under former President Carter. The states with the largest number of sites include Michigan, Pennsylvania and New Jersey, which tops the list with 65 sites.

However, the EPA's administrator Anne Gorsuch Burford admitted that the 418 sites listed are really just the tip of a massive toxic-waste iceberg as there are over 14,000 hazardous chemical dumps in the U.S. today.[10] Not all of these sites or nuclear power plants are located in Love Canal, New York, Three Mile Island, Pa., or Elizabeth, N.J. Toxic landfills and other forms of chemical/nuclear pollution exist in virtually every state of the union and virtually every country in the world. The worst environmental hazard area, according to the E.P.A.,—Tar Creek of Oklahoma—is described as "a foul-smelling **red-colored** stream."[11]

"The third angel poured his bowl into the rivers and the fountains of water, and they became (like) blood."[12]

Yes, the plagues of Revelations are already with us and gaining momentum every day, as we have seen.

Water Pollution

One of the plagues of Revelations has to do with water pollution, specifically, the waters, rivers and oceans of the Earth are to be poisoned by red-colored substances and by "wormwood" or bitterness. We have already seen that several of the polluted streams and rivers around the world have been poisoned by various chemicals turning them red in several instances, as with Tar Creek in Oklahoma. But Oklahoma is not the only area hit by massive water pollution. Other areas, just in the U.S., that have been affected by water pollution include:

- Pennsylvania, where 2-4D herbicide was found in a reservoir, forcing a ban on drinking, bathing and washing clothes;
- Oahu, Hawaii, where DBCP was found in water wells recently, even though it has not been used in the area for 5 years;
- In the early 1980's, wells in 40 states had to be shut down because they were tainted with oozing chemicals; and finally,
- In 1982, a General Accounting Office (GAO) report stated that, "Drinking water contaminated by human waste, chemicals or radioactivity is causing outbreaks of disease (over 100,000 cases to date) and poisoning in thousands of small communities throughout the U.S."[13]

One of the most alarming water problems facing America today is the contamination of aquifers, which are slow-moving underground reservoirs of water, on which well over 50% of the American people depend for drinking water. Because these waters move so slowly, they do not have the same ability to cleanse themselves as do free-flowing streams and rivers. Once tainted, these aquifers remain polluted for centuries. With toxic and nuclear dumping leaching into the soil, it is just a matter of time before these pollutants will reach these underground reservoirs and contaminate them. As a matter of fact, experts believe that many of these aquifers have already been polluted as more and more wells across the country are being shut down because of tainted water. The situation can only get worse![14]

The dumping of raw sewage and toxic/nuclear wastes into the oceans coupled with oil spills, etc., are rebounding on us, too, in the form of red tides, tarred beaches and "mysterious" massive aquatic life kills, such as the recent beachings of whales and dolphins witnessed round the world, which are happening more and more regularly. Red Tides, caused by the sudden explosive increase of a marine organism of a type never before seen by scientists, are so dangerous and powerful that they can kill a fish almost instantaneously and leave humans on shore gasping for breath.[15]

In Australia, "blue bottle" and deadly "box" jelly fish are being seen in larger concentrations than ever before. The shores of Oahu, Hawaii, are being visited by painful man-of-war jellyfish, with over 100 people suffering from welts and rashes. In the Caribbean, over 50% of the islands' protective coral reefs have died due to man's pollution.

In New Jersey, the effects of the ongoing dumping of toxic wastes into the ocean has become so severe that the banning of the consumption of certain species of fish may soon occur. Concentrations of PCB's, a chemical used as a fire retardant that was outlawed in the '70's, are so high in striped bass and bluefish that a ban on fishing for them along the Lower New York Bay, and official warnings to pregnant women and children to avoid eating New Jersey bluefish will soon be forthcoming.[16] Hence, if these fish have been affected, so have all the others. What's more, the New Jersey coast recently saw their shorelines littered with dead sharks, sharks being one of the only animals in Nature that does not get cancer. Hence, if the sharks are dying, what about everything else? **Thus, the prophecies in Revelations regarding the poisoning of the waters and the killing off of the animals in the seas are being fulfilled!**

Acid Rain

One of the other plagues of Revelations mentioned earlier states that man will have to drink water that is tainted with bitterness.[17] John further states that man will be steeped in "brimstone" during the End Times.[18] As explained earlier, brimstone is an old term for sulfer, the main ingredient in herbicides, pesticides, explosives, gunpowder, medicines, **and acid rain!**

John's description fits acid rain so well it's amazing. Acid rain is the result of two pollutants—sulfer dioxide and nitrogen oxide—spewed into the air, mainly by coal-burning power plants and automobile emissions. These pollutants combine with water vapor and fall back to the earth as rainfall, proving the old adage, "What goes up, must come down." It is one of the most corrosive substances known to man, being diluted versions of sulfuric and nitric acids. Very often the rain is as acidic as straight vinegar—not a very tasty substance!

The phenomenon was first documented in Sweden, where 20,000 lakes have become so acidic that clearly one-third of them can no longer support fish. Recently, however, the problem has begun to affect the entire world. For example:

● In Scotland and Pennsylvania, the rain is sometimes more acid than table vinegar;

● In Poland, freight and passenger trains are limited to a speed of 25 m.p.h. because railroad tracks have been so badly corroded and rotted by acid rain, while half of Poland's rivers are said to be contaminated;

● In Greece, the Acropolis and Parthenon have suffered more damage over the last 20 years than they had during all the centuries since they were built, being eaten away by acid rain;

● In Norway, all the fish in an 8000 square mile area have died due to the lakes and streams becoming too acidic;

● In India, the Taj Mahal is being defaced;

● In Rome, the Colosseum is being eroded away;

● In China, the rain is as acidic as lemon juice;

● In New York's Adirondack Mountains, hundreds of lakes are dead or dying;

● In Canada, 40,000 lakes are dead or dying;

- In West Germany, thousands of acres of spruce and fir recently died;
- On Camel's Hump Mountain in Vermont, half of the spruce trees have died;
- In Central Europe, five million acres of forest have been damaged;
- In Brazil, lush tropical forests are being defoliated.

The effects of acid rain are now being seen in the Western States of the U.S.A., as well. **Thus, the plague of Revelations regarding men having to drink water tainted with sulfer or bitterness has been abundantly fulfilled!**

Air Pollution

An even deadlier threat to life has recently been documented in Ankara, Turkey, and in Southern California. In Ankara, a cloud inversion kept that city blanketed under sulfuric acid for several days recently, and in California, acid fog has become the new environmental threat. The fog that is currently plaguing California is said to be hundreds of times worse than acid rain, being so acidic that one scientist said it could burn your eyebrows off! It is more acidic than vinegar or lime, having about the same Ph. or acid rating as toilet bowl cleaner,[19] being similar to the London fog of 1957 which killed more than 12,000 people in three months.[20]

Meanwhile, other airborne threats to mankind's lungs continue to be spewed forth. For example, in New Jersey, airborne carcinogens and chemicals are causing genetic mutations among newborns,[21] and a recent study has concluded that, "11 to 21% of current lung cancer deaths (10,000 to 20,000 per year) could have been prevented by better controls on hazardous pollutants."[22]

As we continue to foul our environment, specifically our water and air, we are also changing the Earth's weather cycles. Scientists are now warning us of two dangers in particular: on the one hand, less sunlight reaching the Earth and, therefore, lower temperatures and the onset of a new Ice Age; and on the other hand, destruction of the ozone layer, which will cause massive outbreaks of skin cancer—a 10% depletion of the ozone translating into a 40% increase in the incidence of skin cancer, **thus fulfilling prophecy again that people will be plagued by open sores in the End Times**[23] —and the buildup of carbon dioxide especially in the Arctic areas, producing the "Greenhouse Effect," where the sun's rays are allowed to penetrate through the Earth's atmosphere, but are not allowed to escape, being reflected back to the earth by the manmade pollutants in the atmosphere, thereby creating warmer temperatures worldwide. These higher temperatures have already started to melt the polar ice caps, which in turn is causing worldwide flooding along coastal regions, including Florida, Japan and New Jersey. Already, nearly one million square miles of the Antarctic's sea ice pack have melted over the last decade alone. **Thus, Cayce's prophecies regarding vast inundations along the Atlantic Seaboard and Japan,** as well as other areas, **again are coming true.** Also, the melting of the ice caps could further help to destabilize the Earth's rotation on its axis, making the threat of an axis shift, and the corresponding natural calamities that go with a shift, that much more possible.

While the present administration lobbies for radical changes in the Clean Water and Clean Air Acts that will greatly weaken both—their argument being that the standards presently set forth in the acts are too costly in both monetary and employment terms—the facts reveal just the opposite. A recent EPA study showed that the Clear Air Act alone has saved between 4 to 20 million work days annually that would have been lost due to illness,[24] while saving the country up to $20 billion per year in health care and other costs.[25] Further, the will of the American people is solidly behind strengthening or at least retaining the standards of air and water quality set in both acts. A recent Lou Harris poll found that an overwhelming 86% of Americans are opposed to weakening air pollution control laws, while an even higher number—a remarkable 94%—believe that the clean water laws should be left as they are or strengthened, even if it means a reduction of jobs.[26]

Jobs and the Environment

In truth, however, stronger environmental laws do not eliminate jobs—they create them. Prior to the Reagan administration's cutbacks in environmental spending, an estimated net increase of 524,000 jobs was expected for the years 1970 to '87. A recent '75 study estimated total employment in pollution control at 1.1 million. And, environmental legislation also helps to save jobs in fishing, forestry, tourism, agriculture and outdoor recreation industries, not to mention keeping business people "economically alive" in the above fields.[27]

As to industry, it is estimated that 600 new industries have sprung up over the years as a direct result of environmental legislation.[28] Some of the largest American businesses are now cashing in on various pollution control devices ranging from smokestack scrubbers to sewage treatment systems to noise mufflers—companies like Boeing, Corning Glass, Union Carbide, etc. Hence, we can see that protecting the environment is not only good for our health; it is good for our pocketbooks as well!

As mentioned earlier, one of the prophets who foresaw the chemical devastation of the planet during the End Times was Michael de Nostradamus. His visions were so accurate that he even predicted the vast polluting of the water systems along the East Coast, specifically New Jersey. He stated that:

"Garden of the world near the New City,
In the road of the hollow mountains,
It will be seized and plunged in the tank,
Forced to drink water poisoned with sulpher."[29]

New Jersey's state logo is "the Garden State," because at one time its principal business was agriculture, the state abounding with orchards, vegetable gardens, etc. It lies near the New City, or New York City, and is reached via the "road of hollow mountains"—skyscrapers—the road being called the Garden State Parkway, which is lined mile after mile by oil refinery storage tanks. As mentioned before, New Jersey has the highest number of toxic waste sites in the Union, and its water supply has indeed been poisoned by sulfur, both through dumping and through acid rainfall. When the authors visited the East Coast in the winter of '81-'82, they found that water from the tap actually smelled like rotten eggs—the smell of sulfur! **Thus we can see that Nostradamus' prophecy has come true.** The amazing thing is that when Nostradamus made the above prophecy over 400 years ago, there was no United States, let alone the "Garden State" of New Jersey.

Nostradamus' prediction regarding chemicalization during the End Times can also be understood on a personal level, too, as the internal consumption of chemicals—both legal and illegal—has mushroomed during the last three decades. He also stated that some time after this intense chemicalization began, the world would see the rise, and ultimate defeat of the most ruthless ruler of them all—the third and last Antichrist!

346

Chapter 18

THE THIRD ANTICHRIST—
A RUTHLESS, WICKED RULER

What exactly is the antichrist? What does the Bible say about this term, and how is it used? In truth, there are very few places in the Bible where the term "antichrist" is actually used. The term appears in only two letters, both written by Saint John. He states that:

> "Children, it is the last hour; and as you have heard that antichrist is coming, so now **many antichrists have come; therefore we know that it is the last hour...**I write to you, not because you do not know the truth, but because you do know it, and know that no lie is of the truth. Who is the liar but he who denies that Jesus is the Christ? **This is the antichrist, he who denies the Father and the Son...**
>
> "Beloved, do not believe every spirit, but test the spirits to see whether they are of God; for many false prophets have gone out into the world. By this you know the Spirit of God; every spirit which confesses that Jesus Christ has come in the flesh is of God, and every spirit which does not confess Jesus is not of God. **This is the spirit of antichrist,** of which you heard that it was coming, and now **it is in the world already.** Little children, you are of God, and have overcome them; for **He who is in you is greater than he who is in the world.** They are of the world, therefore what they say is of the world, and the world listens to them. We are of God, whoever knows God listens to us, and he who is not of God does not listen to us. By this we know the spirit of truth and the spirit of error."[1]

Again John states that:

> "I rejoiced greatly to find some of your children **following the truth,** just as we have been commanded by the Father...**this is the commandment,** as you have heard from the beginning, **that you follow love.** For many deceivers have gone out into the world, **men who will not acknowledge the coming of Jesus Christ in the flesh; such a one is the deceiver and the antichrist...Anyone who goes ahead and**

does not abide in the doctrine of Christ (which is Love) does not have God; he who abides in the doctrine has both the Father and the Son."[2]

In other words, the term antichrist refers not only to certain individuals, but even more to the spirit of hate, lies and disharmony; it means anything or anyone who goes against the doctrines set forth by Jesus Christ, the principal one being that **we love one another.** Hence, anyone who seeks to subvert this feeling of brotherly love, sowing seeds of distrust, hatred, division, lies, violence and deceit, is of the spirit of antichrist or anti-God.

We know through history that God as Jesus, Buddha, Krishna, Guru Nanak, and through other spiritual Great Masters and Divine Messengers of all religions, taught that divine attributes or qualities are Love, Peace, Humility, Compassion, Forgiveness, Truth, Sharing, Caring, Non-violence, Universal Tolerance, Equality, Righteousness, etc. Hence, anything that is opposite to the above is anti-God and, in Christian terminology, antichrist. Further, the person who encourages and follows such satanic behavior is an antichrist. Hence, there have been several antichrists down through history.

It should also be understood that the feeling or movement of antichrist can be viewed on a variety of levels, from macro to micro. On a macro level, the antichrist can be likened to the political dream-beast of Nebuchadnezzar's fame. As a matter of fact, the first reference to the antichrist in the Book of Revelation actually calls it "the Beast." The Beast has seven heads and ten horns with crowns upon each horn. These heads represent the various man-made political empires that have ruled the world down through the ages, the empires being: 1- Egypt, 2- Assyria, 3- Babylon, 4- Medo-Persia (a dual empire, hence the two horns and crowns), 5-Greece, 6- Rome (again, with two horns and crowns, having been split East and West at one time in history), and 7- the joint Anglo-American World Power (again, a dual empire, with the U.S. inheriting the world dominance that its "Mother Country" Great Britain once exercised.) (REVS. 13·1)

These same world empires were prophesied by Daniel of the Old Testament **over 2500 years ago,** as they were shown to him in several visions. In one of his dream-visions he saw four different animals: 1- a lion with eagle's wings, representing the Babylonian Empire of his day; 2- a bear ready to strike, with three ribs in its teeth, representing the Medo-Persian Empire which struck down Babylon during Daniel's lifetime, swallowing up the remnants of it and of the lands of the other two preceding empires of Egypt and Assyria; 3- a leopard with wings and four heads, representing the Greecian Empire, whose conquest of the area was as swift as a bird flying, and was later divided into four smaller empires; and finally, 4- the last beast with ten horns, coming out of the ocean, being far more brutal and vicious than any of the others. This last beast represents the Roman Empire, as well as the ten European powers that grew out of it. Three of the horns of the fourth beast, however, are later uprooted and replaced by a little horn with "a man's eyes" and "a loud, bragging mouth...which was stronger than the others." (DANIEL 7) According to many experts, this little horn represents the U.S.A., which "uprooted" the French, Spanish and British when it became a nation and spread across the American Continent.

This political beast is explained again in Revelations when John is shown the vision of the "Harlot," the symbol of false religion, who is dressed in the colors of royalty—scarlet and purple—bedecked with jewels, and, "drunk with the blood of the saints and the blood of the martyrs of Jesus (God)." This harlot sits on top of a seven-headed, ten-horned beast that represents the kingdoms of man's political system down through the ages, as she, false religion, is the actual "controller" of the beast. Their "fornication" together represents the ungodly union of church and state that has plagued mankind throughout history. John is told that five of the kingdoms have fallen (1- Egypt, 2- Assyria, 3- Babylon, 4- Medo-Persia, 5- Greece), the sixth "is," or was in power at John's time (Rome), and the seventh "has not yet come," being Great Britain, as the country did not exist at John's time, being a part of the Roman Empire. Further, John is told that the beast itself represents an eighth world power that is to come from the original seven preceding powers—again the U.S.A., since it grew out of the European countries, it being no coincidence that Rome's symbol and that of the U.S. is an eagle. (REVS. 17•1-7)

In all three instances, the political beast is given power "to wear down the saints with persecution," making war on them and conquering them. Throughout history, the political empires of man have done exactly that, being allied with false prophets. With regards to the U.S.A., it was allowed to make war on the

American Indians, "the nation of saints," as described by a U.S. Cavalryman.

On another level, the Beast of Revelations and Daniel's visions represents the modern nations that would control the world in the End Times. Many theology experts today agree that the ten-horned beast of Revelations is the European Economic Community (EEC) or Common Market, the EEC being created by a treaty signed in 1957 in Rome, the city of seven hills prophesied in Revelations. However, the controller of these ten horns is really, according to Revelations, the Beast itself, which many theologians agree is the U.S.A., whose economic decisions affect the entire world, as we have seen recently during the Great Depression of the '80's. The fortunes of the American Empire influence not only the "Free World," but also the economies of the Communist-bloc countries, as Stanley Karnov pointed out in a recent editorial, since they depend on trade with the Free World for consumer goods and technology, Karnov stating that: "The U.S. economy is not only the most powerful on Earth, it also is the 'locomotive' that pulls along the rest of the world."[3]

Further, Revelations states that the "kings" of the ten kingdoms of the End Times are to receive authority for a short time, "together with the Beast. These are of one mind and give over their power and authority to the Beast...until the words of God shall be fulfilled." (REVS 17.12-18) In the past there were some doubts as to this interpretation of the ten-horned beast, as the EEC was composed of 9 members. But these doubts were laid to rest when, in January of 1981, Greece joined the EEC, becoming its tenth member. Because of the above, Cayce has said, "The spirituality of the American people would be the criterion for the peace of the world."[4] We can see from recent polls that over 80% of the American public believes in God, with this same vast majority being pro-environment, wanting to defend and protect Nature. Plus, a recent Gallup poll (June, 1982) revealed that over two-thirds now believe in life after death, and over a quarter believe in reincarnation as a fact, illustrating a new openness in the American psyche for spiritual truths found in different religions and sources—a very hopeful sign.[5]

As to the fact that the Beast is to receive a fatal wound and then recover, on a macro scale, this can be understood to mean that world empires were dealt a severe blow to their power over the Earth when Jesus Christ came, spreading His doctrine of Truth

350

and Love throughout the Western World. This doctrine helped to undermine the ancient Roman Empire until King Constantine revived it with a union between the church, led by false prophets, and the state.

However, on a micro level, it is true that there are several references in the Bible that indicate that there will be one particular individual during the End Times who will be the epitomy of the antichrist or anti-God movement. He is referred to variously as "the son of perdition" and "the beast," as well as other uncomplimentary terms. Nostradamus talks about the rise of three notorious and vicious rulers, or antichrists. The first two he actually named—Napolean and Hitler—hundreds of years before they were even born.

In Revelations, one of the plagues refers to the fact that the ruler over a vast military contingent will be called Abaddon in Hebrew, or Apollyon in Greek, which means "the destroyer." The word Napoleon actually means "the new destroyer." Hence, Nostradamus' naming of the first antichrist is verified in the Book of Revelation. (REVS 9.11)

Nostradamus foresaw escalating warfare, and with more and more brutal and inhumane methods. He foresaw the invention of submarines, periscopes and airplanes, as well as the fact that man would use these new inventions to wage war. He also foresaw the coming of atomic weapons, calling them "the contrary of the positive ray," and the destruction of Hiroshima and Nagasaki, as mentioned earlier.

Prior to the discovery of this instrument of war, however, he predicted the rise of the second antichrist—Hitler. He stated that out of the Aryan country would come an inhuman man whose symbol would be topsy-turvy crosses of iron—the swastika. Nostradamus stated that he would be elected to his office by raising false hopes among his people of renewed national greatness, as Hitler was elected to his seat of power in 1933. He gave this second antichrist the name of Hister—Hister being an anagram of Hitler, as well as an old name for the Danube River. Thus, Nostradamus not only named Hitler; he gave the area of the world from which he would come, hundreds of years before his birth.

Nostradamus' prophecies regarding World War II were so accurate and astounding that Goebbels, Hitler's right-hand man, used them as propaganda to deflate the will of the French people. However, the allies, too, used quatrains to support their cause as

351

references to the U.S. and its Statue of Liberty bringing final victory to the Allies helped to spark confidence and hope to the war-weary public.

Experts say that Nostradamus' quatrains indicate that the circumstances surrounding the rise of, and methods used by the three antichrists would be similar. For example, Nostradamus said that the antichrists would come from poor parents—both Hitler and Napoleon came from poor and obscure backgrounds. Further, he said that the antichrists would seduce their countrymen with their tongues, by raising false hopes of greatness among their people. Hitler's inflammatory oratories are well-known, but Napolean's "gift for gab" was also indispensable to him as it was his words that helped inspire his followers to back him, even in doomed pursuits.

As to the last antichrist, there seems to be a good bit of confusion as to his country of origin. Some experts point to certain quatrains that speak of the rise of a great Moslem leader. These verses, however, could refer to Iran's Khomeini whose rise to power brought great distress to the peoples of the Western World, the U.S. in particular, and fears to many Middle Eastern countries, as his fanatical Islamic fundamentalism threatens the thrones of many ruling Arab sheiks. Supporters of this theory point to a quatrain where Nostradamus states that the last antichrist will wear a "blue turban."

However, when Nostradamus was having his visions, the organized church was conducting various forms of persecution on anyone who showed the least bit of so-called "occult powers." After all, the Spanish Inquisition was in full steam, and terror from religious fanatics was rampant across Europe. Clairvoyance, or the ability to see into the future, would have been taken as a "sign of the devil," and Nostradamus surely would have been imprisoned or possibly killed if he had openly written his prophecies. Hence, he cloaked their meanings by using phrases in Latin, old French, anagrams, or references from ages past.

As to the blue turban, around the time of Marco Polo's travels to the Orient (1200-1300 A.D.), the city of Jerusalem was under the control of the Moslems. Before allowing anyone into the city, pilgrims were required to state their religious affiliation, whereupon they were given turbans of different colors to wear according to their faith. The Jews wore yellow, the Moslems wore red, and **the Christians wore blue**—a fact any history buff of Nostradamus' time would have known, having occurred only 200 years beforehand. It is obvious that Nostradamus was well-versed in history, especially with regard to the Holy Land. Hence, his reference to the last antichrist wearing a blue turban could indicate the rise of a Christian to world power, instead of a Moslem.

In any case, Nostradamus states in one of his quatrains that, after a period of intense chemicalization, or chemical pollution, a leader in America will control or greatly influence Great Britain. The quatrain reads as follows:

"Le chef de Londres par regne l'Americh,
L'isle d'ecosse t'empiera par gelee;
Roi Reb aurant, un si faux Antechrist,
Qui les mettra trestous dans la meslee." (10:66)

Rendered by one expert, Stewart Robb, as:

"There will be a head of London from the government of America.
The island of Scotland, he will pave you with ice;
They will have Reb for King, a very false Antichrist,
Who will put them all in an uproar."[6]

This quatrain is so astounding because when Nostradamus wrote it, America as a nation did not even exist, and Britain hadn't even taken a serious interest in the New World or the Americas, as the Spanish were the earliest colonizers. In line 3, "Roi Reb" literally means the "Rebel King," indicating an American leader as the Americans were called "rebels" by the British during their struggle for independence. Robb suggests that line 2, " 'He will pave you with ice,' may refer to a Puritanical regime, with its attendant 'blue laws,' or it may have a more literal meaning,"[7] i.e., that the time of his reign will see severely cold weather visit the land. The line may also indicate a leader who has a very cold heart or lacks compassion. As Franklin D. Roosevelt has said:

"Governments can err, Presidents do make mistakes, but we are told that the Divine Judge weighs the sins of the cold-hearted and the sins of the warm-hearted on different scales. Better the occasional faults of a government operating in the spirit of charity, than the constant omissions of a government frozen in the ice of its own indifference."

Line 3 also states that he will be a very "false" Antichrist. The old French word for "false" comes from the Latin "falsus," meaning "deceptive." Hence he will be a very deceptive Antichrist, saying one thing and doing quite the opposite. Thus, Robb concludes that this quatrain indicates a close association "between the two great English-speaking democracies (the U.S. and Great Britain), headed by a president who appears to be puritanical and in some way associated with 'the isle of Scotland.' This union (or association) should be a reality before Armageddon."[8]

Other descriptions of the final Antichrist can be found in Daniel, who states that:

> "...a king of bold countenance, one who understands riddles, will arise. His power shall be great, and he shall cause fearful destruction, and shall succeed in what he does, and destroy mighty men and the people of the saints. By his cunning he shall make deceit prosper under his hand, and in his own mind he shall magnify himself. He will change the times and the law, changing right to wrong and wrong to right. Without warning he shall destroy many; and he shall even rise up against the Prince of princes; but, **by no human hand, he shall be broken.**"[9]

This line indicates that the Antichrist will be destroyed by God—not by humans. Again, Daniel says:

> "And the king will do exactly as he pleases; he shall exalt himself and magnify himself above every god, and shall speak astonishing things against the God of gods. He shall prosper till his time is up. For God's plans are unshakable. He shall give no heed to the gods of his fathers, or to the one beloved of women; he shall not give heed to any other god, for he shall magnify himself above all. He shall honor the god of fortresses instead of these—a god his fathers never knew—and lavish on him costly gifts! Claiming his help he will have great successes against the strongest fortresses; those who acknowledge him he shall magnify with honor. He shall make them rulers over many and shall divide the land for a price.....
>
> "But, Daniel, keep this prophecy a secret; seal it up so that it will not be understood until the End Times, when travel and education shall be vastly increased...Many shall be purified

354

by great trials and persecutions. But the wicked shall continue in their wickedness, and none of them will understand. Only those who are willing to learn will know what it means."[10]

The angel goes on to tell Daniel that the reign of the Antichrist will be 1290 days. "Blessed is he who waits and comes to the 1335th day."[11] In Revelations, John states that the Beast or "fallen star" is "given the key of the shaft of the bottomless pit, and from the shaft rose smoke like the smoke of a great furnace, and the sun and the air were darkened with smoke from the shaft."[12]

What's so remarkable about this passage is that the description given fits exactly what one sees when an underground nuclear missile is launched. What's more, John says that the Beast is given the key to this shaft. Today we refer to "pushing the button" with regards to launching a nuclear weapon. But, in truth, one does not push a button to launch a missile; one must turn a key to do so. Thus, John's accuracy is astounding! This passage also proves that the Antichrist will have access to nuclear weapons; indeed, he will be given the key that controls them. Thus, this passage confirms Nostradamus' prophecies regarding the last Antichrist. Hence, he will either be the head of one of the six or so present nuclear powers, and/or will gain access to nuclear weapons through an alliance with one of these powers.

The Antichrist lets loose various weapons of war which plague mankind. The descriptions of the weapons sound very similar to helicopters and tanks.[13] John also seems to be describing biological warfare at one point, where he states that the "locusts," or helicopters, are given the power to sting men like scorpions—the power of a scorpion being poison, such as napalm as used in Vietnam, and/or the "yellow rain" of which the Soviets and Vietnamese themselves have been accused of using.[14]

The third Antichrist is to be distinguished by two things, according to Revelations—a severe wound and the number 666:

> "One of its (the Beast's) heads seemed to have a mortal wound, but its mortal wound was healed, and the whole earth followed the beast with wonder...men worshipped...the beast, saying, 'Who is like the beast, and who can fight against it?' "[15]

355

The Beast is given authority to rule for three and one-half years during which he wrecks havoc on the Earth and continually persecutes Godly people. The Beast is joined and helped by the great False Prophet, described as having two small horns like a lamb, but speaking instead like a dragon. Hence, the False Prophet will be one who may look and appear outwardly like Jesus Christ—the Lamb of God—but his words will betray him as he will speak like a dragon, with hatred and fiery words, encouraging warfare. The False Prophet is said to make an image of the Beast that will cause all to see it and hear it, as well as showing great signs and wonders, including making fire come down from heaven. But, as St. Paul emphasizes, these signs and wonders are fakes; they are not real powers as given by God:

> "Let no one deceive you in any way; for that day (the day of the Lord's return) will not come, unless the rebellion comes first, and the man of lawlessness is revealed, the son of perdition...the coming of the lawless one by the activity of Satan will be with all power and with **pretended** signs and wonders, and with all wicked deception for those who are to perish, because they refused to love the truth and so be saved. Therefore God sends upon them a strong delusion, to make them believe what is false, so that all may be condemned who did not believe the truth but had pleasure in unrighteousness."[16]

It must be remembered that John wrote in a very different time than today. Technological inventions that we take for granted today would have appeared to John as being almost miraculous. His descriptions of the "horses of battle"—tanks, "locusts"—helicopters, etc., are quite accurate when viewed from the perspective of one who had never seen or even dreamed of such things before. The image of the Beast that John describes is given the power to speak and appear life-like when in the presence of the Beast. The definition of "image" in the dictionary is: "A reproduction of the appearance of someone or something...An optically formed duplicate, counterpart, or other representative reproduction of an object; **especially, an optical reproduction of an object formed by a lens or mirror.**"[17]

What John was describing was a camera such as those used for movie films or television, as the optical reproduction or image one sees on a movie screen or T.V. screen is accomplished through lenses and mirrors. Hence, the False Prophet will use films, specifically television as a means of furthering the power of himself and the Antichrist, much the same way that Hitler did.

Finally, there is the question of the Beast's number—**666.** Six is the number given man in the Bible, while three is the number used to add emphasis to something. Hence, the imperfections of man—the number 6 being one short of the number 7, representing perfection, heaven or completion—are carried to their fullest measure. Other interpretations of this number are that the computer is actually the Beast. If one takes the alphabet and assigns numerical values to each letter, increasing each by 6 (A=6, B=12, C=18, D=24, etc.), the numbers that correspond to the letters in the word "computer" do add up to 666. Interestingly enough, *Time Magazine* announced on January 3, 1983, that its "Man of the Year" award was going to a machine—the computer, described as, "the greatest influence for good or evil" in the world today.[18] Hence, the computer will likely be an important tool of the Antichrist.

Still others state that the numbers corresponding to the letters in the word "Lateinos" meaning "Latin man" add up to 666 when written in ancient Greek, again indicating a descendant of the old Roman Empire. And, finally, others state that the name of the Antichrist itself will add up to 666:

> "Also it causes all, both small and great, both rich and poor, both free and slave, to be marked on the right hand or the forehead, so that no one can buy or sell unless he has the mark, that is, the name of the beast or the number of its name. This calls for wisdom: let him who has understanding reckon the number of the beast, for it is a human number, its number is six hundred and sixty-six."[19]

> "He required everyone—great and small, rich and poor, slave and free—to be tattooed with a certain mark on the right hand or on the forehead. And no one could get a job or even buy in any store without the permit of that mark, which was either the name of the Creature or the code number of his name. Here is a puzzle that calls for careful thought to solve it. Let those who are able, interpret this code: the numerical values of the letters in his name add to 666!"[20] (Some ancient manuscripts read "616.")[21]

357

It is said that people will have to take the mark of the Beast in order to work, buy food, etc. This could be figuratively speaking, as one would have to help the Antichrist either through money donations, mental or physical aid, etc., or literally speaking as it is conceivable that one would have a surgically-implanted electronic device on one's hand or forehead. This isn't so far fetched as law enforcement officials today state that they are considering the possibility of permanently attaching homing devices on ex-convicts so that they can "home-in" on them in order to keep track of them. Further, scientists are currently experimenting with protein hormones that could be implanted in one's brain and affect one's entire hormonal and thinking processes. Abuse of this by a demonic ruler could result in people being programmed like computers, reminiscent of George Orwell's *1984*.

But do not lose heart and do not give in to the evil and satanic influences that are pervasive in these times. In no way should one give aid in any shape or form to any of the antichrists or false prophets that are so numerous in the world today. For, as Mahatma Gandhi said, "In my humble opinion, non-cooperation with evil is as much a duty as is cooperation with good."[22]

Hence, one must be steadfast in one's resolve to not aid these demonic people in any way, regardless of the consequences. For, as Lord Jesus states, "Here is a call for the endurance and faith of the saints." These times are the times of tribulation and turmoil, but for those who do endure, who do not abandon the Lord's teachings of Love and Peace, Unity and Harmony, Tolerance and Cooperation, Forgiveness and Sharing, awaits the greatest privilege of all: to be in the living presence of the Lord and to serve Him day and night, eternally. These are the ones that John saw as the great multitudes too large to number, coming "from every nation, from all tribes and peoples and tongues," who are dressed in white robes representing their faithfulness to God and their good deeds done in His Name:

> "These are they who have come out of the great tribulation...Therefore are they before the throne of God, and serve Him day and night within His temple; and He who sits upon the throne will shelter them with His presence. They shall hunger no more, neither thirst anymore; the sun shall not strike them, nor any scorching heat. For the Lamb in the midst of the throne will be their shepherd, and He will

358

guide them to springs of living waters; and God will wipe away every tear from their eyes."[23]

In truth, Jesus did teach His followers to obey the laws of the state, providing these laws did not conflict with the laws of God which are, of course, above all manmade laws. But He warned those who rule over others not to abuse their power as, in the end, we all stand before the same Judge—the Eternal Lord and Creator of All. The Legend of St. Issa records the words of Jesus on this subject as follows:

"Just man...tell us if we must continue to do the will of Caesar, or expect our near deliverance?"

And Issa (Jesus)...replied to them: "I have not told you that you would be delivered from Caesar; it is the soul sunk in error which will gain its deliverance.

"There cannot be a family without a head, and there cannot be order in a people without a Caesar, whom ye should implicitly obey, as he will be held to answer for his acts before the Supreme Tribunal."

"Does Caesar possess a divine right?" the spies (of Pilate) asked him again; "and is he the best of mortals?"

"There is no one 'the best' among human beings; but there are many bad, who—even as the sick need physicians— require the care of those chosen for that mission, in which must be used the means given by the sacred law of our Heavenly Father;

"Mercy and justice are the high prerogatives of Caesar, and his name will be illustrious if he exercises them.

"But he who acts otherwise, who transcends the limits of power he has over those under his rule, and even goes so far as to put their lives in danger, offends the great Judge and derogates from his own dignity in the eyes of men."[24]

Again, St. Issa or Jesus states: "Those who deprive their brothers of divine happiness will themselves be deprived of it; and the priests and rulers shall become the peasants of the peasants...In the day of judgement the working classes and poor will be forgiven for they knew not the light, while God will let loose his wrath upon those who arrogated his authority."[25]

Sound familiar? "But many that are first (now) will be last (then), and the last first."[26] Compare the above words of St. Issa's

359

with those of Jesus from the New Testament:

"Are you a wise and faithful servant of the Lord? Have I given you the task of managing my household, to feed my children day by day? Blessings on you if I return and find you faithfully doing your work. I will put such faithful ones in charge of everything I own!

"But if the man begins to think, 'My Lord won't be back for a long time', and begins to whip the men and women he is supposed to protect, oppressing them, and to spend his time partying and getting drunk, well, his master will return without notice and remove him from his position of trust and assign him to the place of the unfaithful, with the hypocrites. He will be severely punished, for though he knew his duty he refused to do it.

"But anyone who is not aware that he is doing wrong will be punished only lightly. Much is required from those to whom much is given, for their responsibility is greater."[27]

Guru Nanak points out that it is only because we do not live up to God's Divine Law of loving one another that we need manmade systems of government and justice at all:

"If we live justly, the need for administering justice does not arise. If we forgive those who harm us, we need invoke no manmade law. If we live as members of one human family, every individual living for the other, then we follow the divine law and if we follow the divine law, we transform this world full of misery into a world of happiness. In such a kingdom there is no need of any law and for any administrators of law. It is because we fail to follow the Divine Law that we submit to manmade law to rectify the self-aggrandisement of men."[28]

Thus we develop our systems of government to help keep our greed and our desires in check. But, as Lord Jesus stated, when those who have been chosen to administer the law refuse to follow it themselves, or put in jeopardy the lives of the very people they are supposed to protect because of some greedy desire or vain ego-trip, woe be to them for the fate that awaits them at the Final Judgement.

This is precisely what the Antichrist and actually all ruthless rulers and false prophets around the world have done and are doing, i.e., putting the lives of millions of innocent people in danger. The Antichrist, in particular, gathers all the kings of the world for war—the final conflict—Armageddon.[29] Many believe that this is to be a real physical war, possibly between the Super-powers directly. Others believe that the Third World War is already being fought through the client nations or the surrogates of the Superpowers. Others feel that this battle is of a more spiritual nature, i.e., the war between good and evil that goes on within each one of us. Whichever interpretation one accepts, it is sure to be a time of struggle and turmoil.

THE FALL OF BABYLON
AND THE RUSSIAN CONNECTION

Before or possibly simultaneously to this great battle, the Earth will experience a final great quake, "such as has never been since men were on the earth." With this quake comes the Fall of Babylon, "and the cities of the nations fell."[1] This would have to be so because if the Earth were struck by an asteroid, or shifted its axis on its own, etc., the corresponding earthquake would have to affect the entire world, as is indicated in Revelations. Further, this is part of the Earth's cleansing process, as explained earlier. The Earth must literally shake off the impurities and scabs that are scarring her surface so that she may breathe and move freely as she was meant. Thus, the great quake will cause the cities round the world to fall, mountains to disappear, islands to sink, great hailstones to fall (perhaps a great meteor shower?), etc.

Then John sees the Harlot—Babylon—on the political beast. Some people feel that Babylon really represents organized religion throughout history. Specifically, they point to the merging of the power of the early Christian Church with that of Constantine's state as an example of the way organized religion has helped to suppress and confuse people throughout the world. Indeed, they are correct, as we have seen, as religions of all varieties have often used the threat of eternal damnation to keep the people under their control. Others state that Babylon is another term for the Catholic Church in particular as Revelations says that the Harlot sits on seven hills; Rome sits on seven hills.

Plus, many wonder why the Pope and the Catholic hierarchy have never released the contents of the third prophecy of Fatima. What does that third prophecy say? One former monk was so determined to have the prophecy revealed that he hijacked a jetliner to try and force the Pope to reveal it. As mentioned earlier, the Holy Mother appeared to three children in a field in Fatima, Portugal, in 1917. Two of the Mother's prophecies have already been revealed, and fulfilled. The first had to do with World War II, as the Lady stated that if people did not change their ways, a second and more deadly war than the one they were experiencing then (World War I) would engulf the globe. The second prophecy had to do with the rise of Russia as a great power and threat to world peace. The Lady stated that if Russia was converted to Her Immaculate Heart, in other words, if Russia followed the teachings of Peace and Love set forth by the Lord, then it would become a great spiritual center and hope for the world. But if the country did not follow this path, then it would become a great power that would bring great misery and suffering to people around the world, especially those who practiced a religious faith.

Of course, both prophecies, unfortunately, did come true, as the world failed to heed the warnings of the Holy Mother. It should be remembered that the prophecies were made long before Russia was anything more than a cold spot on Earth; it had no real international significance at the time, and no one then (1917) guessed it would so rapidly rise to world prominence and dominance.

The third prophecy of Fatima was supposed to be revealed upon the death of Sister Lucia, the only one of the three original children still alive today, or in 1960, whichever came first. Since Sister Lucia was and is still alive, living incommunicado in a convent near Fatima, the letter was opened by Pope John XXIII and a number of cardinals in 1960. According to reports, the faces of the Pope and cardinals turned ashen with horror after reading the prophecy. Many believe that it is a "Doomsday Prophecy" revealing the events that will lead to the end of this sytem of things. Some feel that it also names organized religion, of which the Catholic Church is the largest in the world, as Babylon, the Harlot (prostitute) for prostituting God's teachings. Hence, the horrors that are to befall the Harlot will befall all who prostitute God's Word.

This theory is very interesting as shortly after reading the prophecy Pope John XXIII convened the Second Vatican Council, which instituted sweeping changes in the Catholic Church—changes that are still controversial today. Was the timing of the Council and the scope of the changes merely coincidental? Many think not!

Some of the changes in the Catholic Church begun by the Second Vatican Council include an entire shifting of "the essential perception of the church...from the bishops and clergy to 'all people of God.' Priests began celebrating mass in the language of the people (instead of Latin; thus the people finally understood what was being said)...Meatless Fridays and other time-bound customs were swept away. And other Christian groups suddenly were classified as 'separated brothers and sisters' instead of heretics,"[2] and other such names that had been used to persecute and slaughter hundreds and thousands of people during the Inquisition, Crusades, "Holy Wars," etc.

Pope John XXIII actually allowed 30 official observers from Protestant, Orthodox and Jewish religious traditions to attend as well—a first-ever phenomenon—making him the first Pope ever to address an encyclical beyond Catholic borders, the borders being extended to include "all men of good will." As Msgr. John Egan, an aide to University of Notre Dame's president, put it:

> "Vatican II not only opened itself to the world, but it allowed other groups to search deeply into the traditions of the Catholic faith.
> "We began, all of us, to look to the things which unite us— the primacy of the human conscience, the absolute need for a united moral voice on the issues of war, poverty, hunger and the sacredness of human life and liberty."[3]

It opened the way for Catholics to become interested in non-Catholic cultures and religions; placed a greater emphasis on Jesus Christ and the Holy Spirit, leading to the outgrowth of charismatic movements where faith healing and congregational participation in the service are practiced; allowed Catholics to take a greater interest in social questions of justice, military spending, wars, etc.; and, as one United Methodist observer of the Council put it, the council:

> "...changed the course of modern church history (so that) nothing has been the same since, neither in the Roman Catholic Church nor in the Christian community at large. (It prodded Catholicism from its) preoccupation with immobilism (refusal to change; ultraconservative) to a lively interest in development and renewal. The Council dismayed immobilists, who have never ceased in their efforts to turn the clock back."[4]

And, as another Protestant observer to the Council summed it up, "The four-year council accomplished more concrete ecumenical work than 'had taken place in the preceding four centuries.' "[5]

The timing of the opening of the third prophecy of Fatima and the Second Vatican Council coincided with the Hopis' last

Kachina dance ushering in the period of Purification, with Nostradamus' prophecies concerning the internal and external widespread use of chemicals, and with the date given by several astrologers who believe that we began entering the Aquarian Age astrologically in the early '60's. Thus we can see that the start of the Great Tribulation/Purification, the start of the transformation into the Aquarian Age, really began in the early 1960's. Hence, we must be moving rapidly to the end of this transformation period, as more and more signs of the times seem to be indicating.

The Russian Connection

The Book of Revelations states that the Harlot or Babylon will soon be betrayed by the political beast that she has sat atop for so many generations. It states that the Beast will turn on her and "devour" her, torment her, etc. Many people believe that this has already begun. There is an alternate interpretation of just who the Beast is; some feel that the seven heads of the Beast represent the seven communist countries that are members of the Warsaw Pact. Indeed, they could be correct as the communist countries around the world have turned on religions of all kinds, outlawing them, persecuting the clergy and followers alike, burning shrines and books, defacing religious statues and buildings, and virtually closing the churchs' doors.

It should be remembered that the pre-revolution Czarist regime of Russia was closely allied with a branch of the Catholic Church, led by the manipulative monk—Rasputin. Thus, the church did indeed ride the Russian political beast at that time. The Church was hardly concerned with the ills or troubles of the people as a whole; hence it reaped the wrath of the seeds of discontent, which it had helped to sow, when the Czar was overthrown during the Russian Revolution. The communists, for their part, instead of forcing reforms on the church and allowing the people to worship freely, used the above history as an excuse to close down churches of all faiths, banning religious teachings and practices of any kind, and preaching that the State was the ultimate authority, or God.

As Sri Aurobindo explained, "The exaltation of the collectivity, of the State, only substitutes the collective ego for the individual ego."[6]

Ezekiel states that in the latter days of this system of things, the nation-state of Israel will be rebuilt.[7] And, indeed, Israel as a nation has been rebuilt as it was recognized by the United Nations as a nation in 1948. Further, Ezekiel stated that the House of Israel (or Great Britain and the U.S.A.) would be joined with the House of Judah (the Jews who today make up the nation-state of Israel) in the end days.[8] This, too, has occurred as the Western European countries and the U.S. have been continual backers of the state of Israel. The U.S. in particular has helped to support Israel, and actually signed a treaty with them and Egypt at Camp David, Maryland, in 1979.

Ezekiel goes on to say that after this "joining" takes place, Gog of Magog will lead a huge contingent of soldiers against the land of Israel. He will be joined by other nations in the area who will also come against Israel.[9] Magog is the ancient name for Russia, and the countries mentioned in Ezekiel that are to be allies of Russia's against Israel include Iran, Ethiopia, Libya, Romania, Bulgaria, and Syria. Turkey is also mentioned, and being a Moslem country, it would not be surprising to see them side with the rest of the Arab and Moslem countries against Israel.[10] One of the moderating voices heard in the area is to be Saudi Arabia, and although it too is an Arab nation, it has been one of the most moderate.[11]

Although the ancient boundary lines do not exactly correspond with the borders of these countries today, they are close enough. There is a question as to when this alignment is to take place, as Revelations states that it will occur after the millennial rule of Christ. But, it is clear that it has already happened today; whether it will happen again at some future date, only God knows.

Nostradamus predicted that, in the End Times, the Pope's life would be in danger from certain Moslem factions. This, too, has come true as a Turkish right-wing terrorist, Mehmet Ali Agca, a Moslem, attempted to assassinate the Pope in May of 1981. Agca is said to have been involved with a Bulgarian Secret Service agent. Although there is no evidence, to date, directly linking Russia to the assassination plot, American intelligence sources state that Bulgaria is one of the Soviets' "most obedient" allies, and that it would be unlikely that the Bulgarian intelligence would have done anything like this without Soviet approval.[12]

Though the combination of a right-wing Turkish terrorist working with a left-wing communist government agency sounds an unlikely combination, Italian officials are still investigating the allegations. It is theorized that perhaps the reason the Pope would be targeted is due to his outspoken views on the political situation in his native Poland. **Thus, Nostradamus' prophecy has been fulfilled.**

In any case, the whole situation again proves that the political Beast is turning on organized religion, **as prophesied in Revelations.** Perhaps the Beast actually represents both sides of the political spectrum of the world today, i.e., the ten horns representing the EEC, the seven heads representing the Warsaw Pact, and the Beast itself being the United Nations.

A strange "coincidence" is the fact that Pope John Paul II was shot on May 13, 1981—the 64th anniversary of the first vision of the Holy Mother at Fatima. After being shot, the Pope was heard to call the Mother's Name, and he credited Her direct intervention with saving his life. Because of this, the Pope decided to travel to Fatima, Portugal, in order to thank the Mother the following year. Minutes after praying to the Mother and thanking Her for saving his life, a second assassination attempt was made by a "renegade," right-wing priest who shouted, "Death to Communism! Death to the Second Vatican Council!" as he lunged at the Pope with his bayonnet. The attempt failed, but the priest said he did it "in self-defense of the church," thus illustrating the point made earlier that the changes made by the Second Vatican Council are still not accepted by certain ultraconservative factions of the Catholic Church. The second attempt came, ironically or "coincidentally" enough, almost to the hour of the first attempt on the Pope's life, this time on the 65th anniversary of the first Fatima vision. Perhaps the Lord wants that prophecy released to the public after all!

It's interesting to note that John Paul has continued the changes started by the Second Vatican Council by reducing the large number of different "sins" for which one could be excommunicated down to a mere seven. One important area in which there would be no changes in the Canon Laws was in the question of the ordination of women into the priesthood, even though John Paul credits the Holy Mother with saving his life!

What is clear is that organized religion, and the Catholic Church in particular, have greatly changed their views on many issues over the last few years, including the issue of war. In the past, the Catholic church has gone on record supporting innumerable wars. As a matter of fact, it was the mergence of the church and state back in Constantine's day that changed the early church's totally pacifist stand. Around 400 A.D., or just about the time of Constantine's church/state marriage, the church changed its position of condemning all wars to approving so-called "just wars" or "Holy Wars." The Church has supported virtually every war the various national governments have been involved in ever since, including the war in Vietnam, where Cardinal Francis Spellman was photographed behind a machinegun.

A Change in Stands—The Nuclear Freeze

But maybe all of that **is** changing as Pope John Paul II is speaking out against hatred and violence and for peace, justice and non-violence in his travels around the world. Recently, in Guatemala City and Quetzaltenango he called for an end to "flagrant injustices" there, citing torture, abductions, and the violations against "man's right to life" as crimes and a "very grave offense against God."[13] When President Rios Montt, a so-called "born again" Christian, who ordered the execution of 6 people despite the Pope's plea for clemency, said he had faith in God, the Pope retorted, "Man is justified by his works and not by his faith alone."[14] One American elder of Montt's Church of the Word said that the executions were justified by the Gospel. Obviously it wasn't Jesus' Gospel, since Jesus taught the opposite.

Fortunately, there are other bishops and clergymen of all faiths who have begun to be vocal spokesmen against violence and for the anti-nuclear movement. This positive change has been accompanied with a Catholic pastoral letter that calls nuclear wars "immoral" and raises grave questions about U.S. nuclear strategy. The letter states that:

> " 'Under no circumstances' may nuclear weapons be used against population centers or predominantly civilian targets that are close to populated areas. This applies even if American cities are hit first...because striking back at innocent people serves 'purely as an act of vengeance'...even the threat of using atomic weapons against populated areas is condemned, as well as the first use of atomic weapons."[15]

Other bishops and ministers are encouraging workers in the defense industry to re-evaluate their jobs, and question whether or not what they are doing is morally correct. This reminds us of some of those who have had death experiences who stated that after meeting the Being of Light and evaluating their lives, they came to realize that what they were doing was not in harmony with God's Laws of Peace and Love, that their jobs were actually detrimental to God's Creation and the Goal of Oneness of All Life.

While the Reagan Administration is accusing the Soviets of manipulating and influencing the Nuclear Freeze/Peace Movement in Europe and the U.S., the Russians are accusing the members of the Peace Movement in their country of being manipulated and influenced by the "capitalists." Meanwhile the Peace Movement continues to cut across all cultural, religious, political, economic, social, racial, and national lines, and includes peoples of all ages—young and old. The Catholic Bishops in the U.S. have now been joined by Baptists, Lutherans, Episcopalians, and other Protestants, and even some Evangelicals, including Billy Graham, who recently called for the destruction of all nuclear arms and an end to the "age of fear." Other Protestant leaders have said that, "a moral sea of change in the consciousness of the world on the subject of arms (has emerged). People are getting fed up with spending money on weapons you can never use, and if you use them, history is over." (Rev. Richard McCormick of Georgetown University)[16] And, "We rejoice that there are millions who refuse to accept that we must preserve our selfish security by preparing for collective suicide." (Dr. Philip A. Potter, General Secretary of the World Council of Churches)[17] The Archbishop of Canterbury, the head of the Anglican/Episcopal Church, stated that he could see no circumstances where he could justify the use of nuclear weapons. And, finally, "It is time for a significant effort to break the hold that 30 years of belligerent talk, cold war and military spending have imposed on our minds and spirits." (Rev. Mr. Dudson, United Presbyterian Church)[18]

The theologians and clergy are being joined by scientists, physicians, professors, politicians, laborers, businessmen, students, physicists and ranchers across the country and around the world, as the call for "Peace" spreads. Five U.S. ranchers recently visited Moscow and met with leaders of the Peace Movement there. One of the ranchers, Cecil Garland of Utah, stated that, "he believed that grass-roots Americans must adapt new approaches to end 'the cynicism of 30 years of State Department failures' in weapons negotiations.

369

"We've come here to break the cycle and to say to the Russians, 'For heaven's sake, let's apply a little human intelligence and recognize that we've built enough bombs to destroy the world many times over.' "[19]

Mrs. Kirkbride, a rancher from Wyoming added, "People all over the world seem to think that the U.S. really doesn't care about these issues, but we are here to get the message across that our common enemy is the bomb."[20]

This view was echoed recently by the American Physical Society, a group representing 32,000 physicists from government, industry and academia. The group called for an end to all testing of nuclear weapons worldwide for all time, noting that "Nuclear weapons around the world contain the explosive power of more than one million Hiroshima bombs...," weapons which were developed largely as a result of research by physicists, the group adding that a nuclear war could destroy not only hundreds of millions of people, but civilization itself.[21]

This renewed awareness of the dangers nuclear weapons present to the world was graphically illustrated by a recent (12/82) Harris Poll which found that an overwhelming majority—90%:

"...would like to see 'an end to the production, storage and testing of all nuclear weapons by all countries on Earth...' having become convinced that a nuclear freeze, followed by the reduction and elimination of nuclear weapons must take place...(Further), by a 97% majority, Americans are also unanimous about wanting to see 'a real easing of tensions between the U.S. and the Soviet Union.' "[22]

Meanwhile, Nuclear Freeze and Peace demonstrations have sprung up all over the world:

- West Germany—100,000 at Hamburg, June, '81
- Sicily—30,000 at Comiso, October, '81
- France—40,000 at Paris, October '81
- England—175,000 at London, October '81
- Italy—200,000 at Rome, October '81
- West Germany again—300,000 at Bonn, October, '81
- Netherlands—400,000 at Amsterdam, November, '81
- Spain—400,000 at Madrid, November, '81
- U.S.A.—100,000 at 150 university campuses, November, '81

- Japan—200,000 at three Tokyo rallies, May, '82
- U.S.A.—**700,000** at New York City, June, '82, as well as over 1,000,000 demonstrating that same week in Amsterdam, Antwerp, Berlin, Bonn, Copenhagen, Dublin, London, Madrid and Paris.[23]

Even in the Communist-Bloc countries, the Peace Movement is starting to grow. In Romania, the Orthodox Church recently hosted a Disarmament and Peace convention in Budapest, which was attended by religious representatives from Christian, Jewish and Moslem faiths from 16 countries. In Russia, the Orthodox Church there sponsored the "World Conference of Religious Workers for Saving the Sacred Gift of Life From Nuclear Catastrophe" in May of 1982, and invited 600 clergymen from around the world.[24] In East Germany, 6000 people demonstrated for Peace in Dresden during February, 1982, while Catholic Bishops recently joined Protestant ministers in attacking East German authorities for "thinking in militaristic categories" in schools. They also condemned the use of nuclear weapons and described any war in which they might be used as "immoral."[25] The clergymen are upset by the fact that the East German authorities have set up military training programs throughout the nation's school systems, thus perverting the minds of the young away from Peace and Love, into war, violence and hate.

Even in the U.S., children's minds are being twisted by some who still refuse to recognize the Truths that God's Messengers have repeatedly given us throughout history, i.e., that Peace and Love are the only way to save the world and end fear and war forever. One soon-to-be-ordained minister, Renate Rose, who has lived under Hitler's rule in Germany, survived several allied bombings "by the Grace of God," and also lived under Russian rule before coming to the U.S., reiterated this point recently:

> "A member of the church told me the other day that she would prefer to die in a nuclear holocaust than live under communism—and she added, 'Then I'll have eternal life.' To me that is utter blasphemy of God and His Creation. Our human values, even freedom, are relative. We don't need to die for them. To die in such a way means to die for the freedom and value of self-righteousness.

> "Jesus did not come to bring destruction on Earth and peace in heaven. He died for love of enemies, not in order to

371

prove that He was right. At Christmas we celebrate that Jesus came to bring the qualities of a child—faith (in God, our parent), love (of neighbors and even enemies), and hope in suffering if we renounce violence. And He died on the cross so that we who follow Him would never use violence to achieve our goals...This means to be Peacemakers. 'Blessed are the Peacemakers for they shall be called Sons of God.' "[26]

Thus we must follow His example and be as little children, for Jesus said:

"Truly, I say to you, unless you turn and become like children, you will never enter the kingdom of heaven. Whoever humbles himself like this child, he is the greatest in the kingdom of heaven. Whoever receives one such child in My name receives me...

"See that you do not despise one of these little ones; for I tell you that in heaven their angels always behold the face of my Father who is in heaven...So it is not the will of our Father who is in heaven that one of these little ones should perish."[27]

The children of the world are very concerned about the nuclear arms race as evidenced by the growing number of "Peace Clubs" in various schools. Several students have written letters and even traveled to Washington, D.C., Moscow and Rome to meet with government officials to express their concern for the future of their world, **fulfilling prophecy that "a little child shall lead them."** Mahatma Gandhi once said that, "The law of love could best be understood and learned through little children."[28] Some examples of how children perceive Love and Peace are given below:

—Peace is caring for those around you.
Peace is all nations joining hands.
Peace is not destroying God's Creation.
Peace is knowing the meaning of Love.
Peace will only happen if everyone works together.[29]
                    —Sirena, age 10, Corte Madera, California

—Peace is people talking together with a heart in between them.[30]
                    —Siri Guru Dev Kaur, age 5, Espanola, New Mexico

— Peace is love! Love is the greatest peace I think we have and if it stops, we stop and start fighting.[31]

      — Deanna, age 11, Travis AFB, California

— If I were a teacher to the leaders of the world I would say, "Look at the animals and compare yourself to one of them. An animal only kills to eat. It is kind to its neighbors. Why doesn't the world, as a whole, follow the example of their fellow creatures?"[32]

      —Diane, age 11, Littleton, Colorado

Thus, the children of the world are seeking peace for the Earth and praying that the adults of the world, specifically the leaders of the nations, will allow them to grow up and enjoy their lives in Peace. President Eisenhower once said, "I believe that people, in the long run, are going to do more to promote peace than our governments. Indeed, I think that people want peace so much that one of these days governments had better get out of the way and let them have it."(8/31/59)

Mahatma Gandhi also believed that if people were left to themselves, without governments interfering or false prophets misleading them, there would be Peace and Love throughout the world. After living with and observing Gandhi in his ashram, Swami Rama stated that, "(Gandhi) was a man who constantly prayed for others: who had no hatred for any religion, caste, creed, sex or color. He had three teachers: Christ, Krishna and Buddha."[33]

Swami Rama, speaking about Gandhi's principles, said:

> "Non-violence and cowardice cannot go together because non-violence is a perfect expression of love that casts out fear. To be brave because one is armed implies an element of fear. The power of *ahimsa* (non-violence) is an extremely vital and active force which does not come from physical strength...
>
> "Gandhi did not believe in the barriers created by religions, cultures, superstitions and mistrust. He taught and lived the brotherhood of all religions."[34]

As Gandhi himself said:

> "What I want you to understand is the message of Asia. It is not to be learnt through the Western spectacles or by imitating the atom bomb. If you want to give a message to the

West, it must be the message of love and the message of truth. I do not want merely to appeal to your head. I want to capture your heart.

"In this age of democracy, in this age of awakening of the poorest of the poor, you can redeliver this message with the greatest emphasis. You will complete the conquest of the West not through vengeance because you have been exploited, but with real understanding. I am sanguine if all of you put your hearts together—not merely heads—to understand the secret of the message these wise men of the East have left to us, and if we really become worthy of that great message, the conquest of the West will be completed. This conquest will be loved by the West itself.

"The West is today pining for wisdom. It is despairing of a mutiplication of the atom bombs, because atom bombs mean utter destruction not merely of the West but of the whole world, as if the prophecy of the Bible is going to be fulfilled and there is to be a perfect deluge. It is up to you to tell the world of its wickedness and sin—that is the heritage your teachers and my teachers have taught Asia...

"Nonviolence...is the only thing that the atom bomb cannot destroy...Unless now the world adopts nonviolence, it will spell certain suicide for mankind...

"It has been suggested by American friends that the atom bomb will bring in *ahimsa* (nonviolence) as nothing else can. It will, if it is meant that its destructive power will so disgust the world that it will turn it away from violence for the time being. This is very like a man glutting himself with dainties (sweets) to the point of nausea and turning away from them only to return with redoubled zeal after the effect of nausea is well over. Precisely in the same manner will the world return to violence with renewed zeal after the effect of disgust is worn out...

"So far as I can see, the atomic bomb has deadened the finest feeling that has sustained mankind for ages. There used to be the so-called laws of war which made it tolerable. Now we know the naked truth. War knows no law except that of might...

"The moral to be legitimately drawn from the supreme tragedy of the bomb is that it will not be destroyed by counter-bombs even as violence cannot be by counter-violence. Mankind has to get out of violence only through nonviolence. Hatred can be overcome only by love. Counter-hatred only increases the surface as well as the depth of hatred...

"If we are to reach real peace in this world and if we are to carry on a real war against war, we shall have to begin with children; and if they will grow up in their natural innocence, we won't have to struggle; we won't have to pass fruitless idle resolutions, but we shall go from love to love and peace to peace, until at last all the corners of the world are covered with that peace and love for which consciously or unconsciously the whole world is hungering...

"It may be long before the law of love will be recognized in internal affairs. The machineries of governments stand between and hide the hearts of one people from those of another."[35]

Chapter 20

THE JUDGEMENT

The ruthless rulers and false prophets of the world are still standing between and hiding the hearts of people from each other. For such satanic and demonic acts, these individuals will suffer greatly when the Lord returns and judgement is passed. A glimpse of what awaits these individuals has been given to us in the scriptures of the various religions of the world. Below is a synopsis of what these "children of darkness" may expect:

"Tell the righteous that it shall be well with them, for they shall eat the fruit of their deeds. Woe to the wicked! It shall be ill with him, for what his hands have done shall be done to him. (Karma)

"O my people! Can't you see what fools your rulers are?...True leaders? No, misleaders! Leading you down the...path to destruction.

"The Lord stands up to judge His people...First to feel His wrath will be the elders (priests) and the princes (rulers), for they have defrauded the poor. They have filled their barns with grain extorted from the helpless peasants. 'How dare you grind my people in the dust like that?' the Lord of Hosts will demand of them."[1]

—Isaiah, Old Testament

"Woe unto them (false prophets and ruthless rulers) for the iniquities their hands have formerly wrought! Woe unto them for that which they are now doing!...On their tongue the mention of God hath become an empty name; in their midst His holy Word a dead letter...for they seek no God but their own desire, and tread no path but the path of error...pride and haughtiness as the highest attainments of their hearts' desire. They have placed their sordid machinations above the Divine decree...busied themselves with selfish calculation, and walked in the way of the hypocrite...

"Take warning by what the God of Mercy hath revealed in the *Qur'an (Koran)*: 'Woe unto those who malign and speak evil of their fellows'...God hath forgiven your past ways...Shun reviling, maligning, and whatsoever will offend your fellowmen...

"He forbade conflict and strife—a rigid prohibition in the Book...Meditate on this, O people, and be not of them that wander distraught in the wilderness of error. The day is approaching when its flame will devour the cities, when the Tongue of Grandeur will proclaim: 'The Kingdom is God's, the Almighty, the All-Praised!'"[2]

—Baha'u'llah

"You know that the dark age is like a knife, which kings handle like butchers. Justice has taken wing and flown away. The darkness of untruth obscures even the light of the moon, which cannot be seen...Humanity is groaning under the dread dominion of self...

"Those who profess to be religious indulge in sinful acts...Everyone worships his own self (ego). Such is this dark age...

"Sin occupies the throne, with greed the financier, falsehood the commander, lust and desire as the judges who summon and examine men and pronounce judgements. The people in their ignorance are without power. They too are eager to usurp what others have. Priests have forgotten their craft. They dance, wear masks, beat drums and adorn their bodies. They shout aloud, indulge in battle songs, and uphold war. Ignorant Pandits (scriptural teachers) with subtle reasoning and tricks of their trade strip men and amass wealth...Everyone considers himself perfect but if put to the test, says Nanak, no one could prove true...yet falsehood must fail, and truth prevail.

"Hail, hail...His Light will prevail...Hail, hail to Him, the Lord of all."[3]

—Guru Nanak

"Woe to you! ye adversaries of men, if it is not the favor you await, but rather the wrath of the Most High...their hearts will be the prey of an eternal fire and their flesh shall be given to the beasts of prey...

"And the Spirit of Evil dwells upon the Earth, in the hearts of those who turn the children of God away from the right path. Therefore, I say unto you: Fear the day of judgement, for God will inflict a terrible chastisement upon all those who have led His children astray and beguiled them with

377

superstitions and errors."[4]

—St. Issa (Jesus)

"The man who punishes those who do not deserve punishment, or offends the inoffensive, punishes and offends himself. He suffers one of ten punishments: grief, infirmity, disease, injury, insanity, falling from royal favor, dreadful allegation, loss of precious wealth, death of relatives, or lightning falling on his house; and when he dies, he goes to hell...

"Better for a boorish (false) monk to swallow a red-hot steel ball than in **seeming** goodness to live on people's almsgiving (charity)."[5]

—The Buddha

"These rulers of men...as also others claimed this Earth as their own, but they had to leave it in the end and died...He who perpetrates violence against living beings for the sake of this body, which will be ultimately called by the name of 'worm', 'excrement', or 'ashes', no matter if it enjoys the title of 'king' now, is not alive to his own interests; for such violence surely paves the way to hell."[6]

—Lord Krishna

"Woe to you, scribes (lawyers and/or rulers) and Pharisees (priests), hyprocrites! Because you shut the kingdom of heaven against men; for you neither enter yourselves, nor allow those who would enter to go in. And you pretend to be holy, with all your long, public prayers in the streets, while you are evicting widows from their homes. Hypocrites! Woe to you, for you go to all lengths to make one convert, and then turn him into twice the son of hell you are yourselves. Blind guides!...

"For you tithe down to the last mint leaf in your garden, but ignore the important things—justice, mercy, good faith...Woe to you, scribes and Pharisees, hypocrites! For you cleanse the outside of the cup and the plate, but the inside is foul with extortion and greed...first cleanse the inside of the cup, and then the whole cup will be clean...

"You are like whitewashed tombs, which outwardly appear beautiful, but within they are full of dead men's bones

378

and corruption. So you also outwardly appear righteous to men, but within you are full of hypocrisy and iniquity...You serpents, you brood of vipers, how are you to escape being sentenced to hell!'"[7]

—Lord Jesus Christ

But what exactly does being sentenced to hell mean? What does the Lord mean when He speaks of the lake of fire and brimstone in Revelations? What is Hell? The Lord showed a glimpse of it to the three children of Fatima, Portugal in 1917:

"Our Lady showed us a great sea of fire that seemed to be under the earth. Plunged in this fire were demons and souls in human form, like transparent burning embers, all blackened or burnished bronze, floating about in the conflagration, now raised into air by the flames that issued from within themselves together with great clouds of smoke, now falling back on every side like sparks in a huge fire, without weight or equilibrium, and amid shrieks and groans of pain and despair, which horrified us and made us tremble with fear...

" 'You have seen hell where the souls of poor sinners go,' said the Lady to the children."[8]

Those who have had unpleasant death experiences, i.e., those who tried to commit suicide or were very egoed-out before they "died," have confirmed that there are intermediate states to which certain people go after physical death. The people suffer in these states as long as they refuse to recognize and repent their sins. But after confessing their sins and turning to God for forgiveness and help, He, in His Grace has allowed them to come back into their bodies. Perhaps evil and demonic people will suffer as mentioned above, or in one of these intermediate states of existence, and/or be reborn on Earth as a starving child in Africa or a diseased, starving refugee in Cambodia.

The people who will suffer these torments are not just those who have sinned against other humans, but includes those who have hurt or willfully harmed any part of God's Creation, including the animals and plants of Nature. For those who desecrate God's outer manifestation will surely reap the bitter fruit of their own karmic seeds. For Revelations states that the time has come "for the dead to be judged, for rewarding thy servants, the prophets and saints...and **for destroying the destroyers of the Earth.**"[9]

379

Is there no hope, then, for those who have committed such sins and have caused hardship and suffering for others, or who have been a party to the desecration of the Earth? Remember Lord Krishna's words: "Even if a sinner of sinners turns to me he should be accounted righteous."[10]

This is the Golden Lining of this age: that if one truly turns to the Lord, seeks His forgiveness, and changes his life from one of hatred, violence, deception, and other negative and ungodly things, to one of Love, Truth, Peace, Sharing, Caring and Forgiveness—he will be forgiven by the Lord. **But the change must be sincere and must begin NOW!!**

Karma of Nations

When the Lord returns, He will not only judge individuals; He will also judge the nations according to their collective deeds. The Lord as Jesus Christ, the Buddha, Guru Nanak and Sri Krishna has defined Karma:

"As you sow, so shall you reap."

Mary Ellen Carter, the biographer of the great American prophet Edgar Cayce, summarized Cayce's views of the Karma of Nations as follows:

"The destiny of nations is concerned with man's collective relationships with himself and with God. We can make of the world what we will—and we have! Future wars can be prevented by man's will, just as they are started that way. All evils begin in the hearts of men, and there, they can be resolved."[11]

Thus, the history of nations and their periods of happiness and suffering were no fluke but were caused by the karma of the people of a nation. The saints of the Americas—the American Indians—lived in peace and happiness for thousands of years, due to their leading spiritual lives, following God's laws and living in harmony with all life. Hence, their happiness was due to their good karma. Similarly, the saints of India lived, and many still do, blissful lives as their actions were spiritual and, therefore, karmically excellent with correspondingly excellent, happy and blissful results.

When people in general went astray from God's teachings, espousing unspiritual ways of greed, hate, etc., led by the Moghul kings reigning at that time, their lives changed for the worse with the change in their karma, and they were attacked by foreigners culminating with the British, whose approximately 200-year rule resulted in mass suffering, fragmentation of society, overpopulation, hunger, disease, etc.

Britain found India as perhaps the richest country in the world, and left India as one of the poorest by exploiting it. However, Britain paid dearly for its colonialism, exploitation and destruction of peoples all over the world, too. During the World Wars Britain was bombed to bits by the Germans. The latter committed unspeakable atrocities against the Jews and other nations, but were repaid for their extremely bad karma by being practically destroyed by the Allies during the wars. Other European powers paid for their bad karma, too, by being attacked and devastated during World War I and II.

"It was in misapplying God's laws that the nations have suffered,"[12] Carter said. China, too, paid for its bad karma when it subdued the religious teachings of Taoism, Buddhism, Confucianism and Christianity by suffering through the invasions of the Japanese and other foreigners. China also incurred bad karma when Mao and his "Red Guards" in his "Cultural Revolution" burned temples, books and religious statues. These were followed with the Red Guards themselves being purged, imprisoned or killed, for the Law of Karma is eternal. Japan, for its atrocities during the World Wars, including inhuman biological experiments on prisoners, itself went through acute suffering when it was atom-bombed by the United States.

In 1932, Cayce prophesied that "on Russia's religious development will come the greater hope of the world."[13] It was for lack of the above that Russia suffered under the Czarist regime and the other extreme—Communism. In 1917, in Portugal, where the Lord appeared as "Our Lady of Fatima" to the three children, they were told that to prevent war, famine, persecutions of the Church and of the Holy Father, or in the Lady's own words:

"To prevent this, I shall come to ask for the consecration of Russia to my Immaculate Heart, and the Communion of reparation on the First Saturdays. If my requests are heeded, Russia will be converted, and there will be peace; if not, she will spread her errors throughout the world, causing wars and persecutions of the Church. The good will be martyred; the

381

Holy Father will have much to suffer. Various nations will be annihilated..."[14]

Indeed, the above came true with the Russian Revolution and rise of the Communist Party which outlawed all forms of religious practices. But the communists, too, have suffered for, as Cayce said, "Only when there is freedom of speech, the right to worship according to the dictates of the conscience—until these come about, still turmoils will be within."[15] Since the communists did not allow the above, they in turn paid for their bad karma by suffering and being killed during the Stalin purges. Speaking of Communism, Fascism or Nazism, Cayce said:

"...when there becomes class or mass distinction between this or that group, this or that party, this or that faction, then it becomes...a class rather than 'thy neighbour as Thyself.' For all stand as **one** before Him. For the Lord is **not** a respecter of persons, and these things **cannot** long exist."[16]

The Karma of America

Cayce added, "From the condition in these other lands, then, America—the U.S.—must take warning."[17] And, "Unless we begin within our own selves, and our own household, we are false to ourselves and to the principles that we attempt to declare..."[18]

Saint Rolling Thunder reiterated Cayce's warnings against Fascism. Rolling Thunder was apprehensive about it creeping into the U.S., and considered Fascism "the tool of the dark forces," adding that "people with political power (have begun) to consider themselves priveleged, endowed with special rights, exempt from principles of justice and honesty."[19]

Indeed, during the Watergate Period in the U.S., the American people were shocked at the abuse of power and the use of "Executive Privilege" to keep from Congress and the American people, relevant documents and tapes. More recently, towards the end of 1982, Congress has cited Anne Gorsuch Burford, the head of the E.P.A., with contempt of Congress for failure to give Congress documents relative to hazardous toxic or poisonous wastes in the U.S. She has, at the direction of the White House, again used "Executive Privilege" to withhold from Congress and the American

382

public documents relevant to the same, even though the toxic wastes could adversely affect, injure or even kill people and other life.*

Thus, the responsibility and obligations of people in a democracy, in electing the right leaders believing in justice, human rights, honesty and love, is far more than people living under a dictatorship who have no such rights. Thus when the American people elected leaders with the wrong consciousness, such as Hoover, the karmic result was the awful "Great Depression" of the 1930's, which had been predicted by Cayce who said the causes of the Depression were a "combination of wrath, oppression and sin." When the American people elected leaders like Roosevelt, humane and benevolent, the country came out of the Depression and moved to prosperity. Cayce laid America's problem for these times to her "unbelief":

> "The ideals, the purposes that called the nation into being are well...yet in the present...many conditions that are variance to the First Cause (God) or first principles (Truth, Brotherhood, Peace and Love)..."[20]

It is vital for Americans to go back to the ideals and purposes for which this nation came into being by practicing and living the "first principles" of truth, peace, brotherhood and love in their own lives and by exercising their privilege of voting by electing benevolent leaders who believe and practice the above principles within the U.S. and in our relationships with other countries. Not voting is as bad a karmic thing as voting for unrighteous leaders. Our security does not lie in building more bombs because we, like Russia, already have an "over-kill" capacity to destroy all life on Earth several times over. Our real security lies in living and practicing Divine attributes of Love, Peace and Honesty in order to get Divine protection due to our good karma. If the American people want prosperity and peace, then it is essential to improve our karma for the better by showing kindness, sharing, caring and love to Americans who need it, and by withdrawing our support for ruthless rulers abroad (left, right or any other wing!), who are

---

* Ann Burford resigned on March 9, 1983 as head of E.P.A., and the Administration, bowing to pressure from the public and Congress, is currently working out a deal to hand over the documents in question to a Congressional Committee.

butchering their people, like in El Salvador, Guatemala, Honduras, Chile, Philippines, Pakistan, etc.

We can see the karmic results in our own country with the Depression of the '80's. For if we do not improve our karma in our relationships with other Americans at home and other countries abroad, Nostradamus' and the Hopis' prophecy of great calamity and destruction on this land will come to pass. Both Nostradamus and the Hopis see the U.S.A. devastated by a nuclear war. As the Hopis explain it:

> "The U.S. will be destroyed, land and people, by atomic bombs and radioactivity. Only the Hopi and their homeland will be preserved as an oasis to which refugees will flee. Bomb shelters are a fallacy. 'It is only materialistic people who seek to make shelters. Those who are at peace in their hearts already are in the great shelter of life. There is no shelter for evil. Those who take no part in the making of world division by ideology are ready to resume life in another world, be they of Black, White, Red or Yellow race. They are all one, brothers.'
>
> "The war will be 'a spiritual conflict with material matters. Material matters will be destroyed by spiritual beings who will remain to create one world and one nation under one power, that of the Creator.' "[21]

Since the law of Karma is eternal, unless America improves its actions, it is sure that it will suffer, if for no other reason than for what it did to the original peoples of this land—the American Indians. As Rolling Thunder explains:

> "We were told the day would come when the white man would shake hands with the Indian. But what is needed now between the white man and the Indian is not merely the shaking of hands. What is needed now is for the white man to make some restitution for the wrongs and the crimes that have been committed. What is needed now is the fulfillment of the treaties and agreements that have been made."[22]

> "Turn back, turn back from your evil ways; for why will you die, O house of Israel? (America)...yet if he turns from his sin and does what is lawful and right, **if the wicked restores the pledge, gives back what he has taken away by robbery,** and walks in the statutes of life, committing no

384

NUCLEAR FALLOUT MAP

Fallout areas at 1 hour after a nuclear attack on U.S.

Fallout areas at 24 hours after a nuclear attack on U.S.

NOTE THE ABSENCE OF FALLOUT OVER SACRED HOPI LAND

iniquity; **he shall surely live, he shall not die.** None of the sins that he has committed shall be remembered against him...O house of Israel, I will judge each of you according to his ways."[23]

One place that is sure to be devastated in this war and/or by natural calamities is New York City. Just about all of the prophets—Edgar Cayce, Nostradamus, Hopi Indians, the Bible, and even Mormon scriptures—state that New York City will go. One of the reasons for this belief is that many feel New York City is really the "New Babylon" of which Revelations speaks. In Revelations, it states that Babylon not only represents false religion and the city of Rome, but also "the great city which has dominion over the kings of the Earth."[24]

The United Nations is headquartered in New York City, and the U.N. building has recently been referred to as "the New Tower of Babel" because of the great number of different languages that are spoken within its walls. As the host of the United Nations, New York is, then, the city where representatives of all the nations of the Earth are located. Hence, in this way it is the city that has dominion over the kings of the Earth.

Further, Revelations states that New Babylon will be a great seaport through which the riches of the world have passed:

> "And all shipmasters and seafaring men, sailors and all whose trade is on the sea, stood far off and cried out as they saw the smoke of her burning...'Alas, alas, for the great city where all who had ships at sea grew rich by her wealth! **In one hour she has been laid waste!'** "[25]

Revelations also states that through Babylon will have passed tremendous numbers of weapons, destined for various parts of the Earth, as the corrupt kings of the world use her weapons to destroy the Earth and enslave their own people. It states that Babylon "has become a dwelling place of demons...a haunt of every foul and hateful bird."[26] The word "bird" is a slang term used by the military for "missile." In other words, Babylon will be the area through which many of the Earth's most foul and hateful armaments—specifically, missiles—will be transported. It should be remembered that the United States is the number one arms salesman of the world, even outselling Russia.

Although New Orleans is actually the number one seaport of

the U.S. today, it really does not matter. For it, too, appears doomed according to Edgar Cayce, as it will be part of the area inundated by water when the great earth changes that cause the Great Lakes to flow directly into the Gulf of Mexico are completed.

Since nearly all of Edgar Cayce's, Nostradamus' and the Hopis' prophecies and predictions have come true, our very life depends on ensuring that the above prophecy does not. Since we're running out of time, it is imperative we improve our consciousness and actions for the better, making restitution for the wrongs that have been done, and becoming more spiritual, as well as electing more and more spiritual people to represent us. Leaders who believe and practice truth, honesty, love and non-violence are what we need. For as one of the greatest leaders of our time—Mahatma Gandhi—said, "The force generated by non-violence is infinitely greater than the force of all the arms invented by man's ingenuity."[27] He further states that, "Nonviolence succeeds only when we have a real living faith in God."[28]

Since we can change prophecy, as Nostradamus emphasized, by changing our karma or actions for the better, we can avoid the great calamity predicted for this country. According to Rolling Thunder and Edgar Cayce, one of the main reasons San Francisco has been spared the major earthquake predicted by scientists for that area for years is due to the relatively good consciousness and karma of the people there. As Cayce said:

"...And only those who have set their ideal in Him and practiced it in their dealings with their fellowmen may expect to survive the wrath of the Lord..."[29]

387

Chapter 21

THE TWO WITNESSES
AND THE COMING OF THE LORD

Before the Lord's Return and the Fall of Babylon and the destruction of other cities around the world takes place, the Lord promised He would send two witnesses to the Earth to announce His imminent return, and warn the people to change their ways. This prophecy is found not only in Revelations, but also in the *Shrimad Bhagavatam,* those great ancient Hindu scriptures.

According to Revelations, the two witnesses will have the power to prophecy for three and a half years, during which time the Antichrist will be present on Earth. Their appearance on Earth will also coincide with great natural calamities—droughts, scorching sunshine, pollution of the waterways, pestilences and plagues, great earthquakes, etc.[1]

According to the *Shrimad Bhagavatam,* two great Yogic Masters from ages ago will reappear on Earth at the end of the Kali Age, or at the end of this system of things:

> "Instructed and commanded by Lord Kalki, both will appear once more on Earth at the close of the Kali Age, and propagate virtue as before..."[2]

Interestingly enough, "reports of a mysterious hitchhiker who talks about the Second Coming of Jesus Christ, then disappears into thin air from moving cars"[3] surfaced in Arkansas during late June/early July of 1980. According to one report given to Arkansas' State Police, two couples were driving along the highway from Pine Bluff to Little Rock when,

> "They picked up this neatly dressed man because he looked like he needed transportation, you know. He discussed current events—he knew about the (American) hostages (in Iran)—and all of a sudden he said, 'Jesus Christ is coming again!' and disappeared!
>
> "They stopped the first trooper they saw and told him 'You're going to think we're crazy,' and told him about it. And he said, 'No, you're the fourth party that's told me about it today.' "[4]

According to one state trooper, "There's not much we can do

388

on a report like that. It's not a violation of law and no hazard is involved. It's illegal to hitchhike, but if he disappears, this hitchhiker's going to be hard to arrest."[5]

There's more.....After all, the Lord did say **two** witnesses! A few months after the above incidents, the "highway apostle" began appearing and disappearing again—this time in Sweden. According to a UPI release dated October 31, 1980, the "hitchhiking ghost":

> "...turned up in Southern Sweden...Police said Thursday (October 30, 1980) many drivers have reported picking up a young man who talked about the Second Coming of Christ. Then, without opening the door, the hitchhiker suddenly disappeared without a trace, drivers said."[6]

Could these be the two witnesses of which the Bible and the Hindu scriptures speak? They certainly did display astounding yogic powers in their ability to appear and disappear, and their arrival certainly did coincide with the tremendous increase in natural calamities that have been occurring! Only time will confirm......

The Coming of the Lord

If those were the two witnesses predicted, then the Lord's arrival must be very soon! But exactly how will the Lord come? In what manner should we expect His arrival? According to both Revelations and the *Shrimad Bhagavatam,* the Lord is to come as "The Warrior King"—the Destroyer of Evil:

> "Then I saw heaven opened, and behold, a white horse! He who sat upon it is called Faithful and True, and in righteousness He judges and makes war. His eyes are like a flame of fire, and on His head are many diadems (crowns); and He has a name inscribed which no one knows but Himself. He is clad in a robe dipped in blood, and the name by which He is called is **The Word of God (LOGOS).**
>
> "And the armies of heaven, arrayed in fine linen, white and pure, followed him on white horses. **From His mouth issues a sharp sword with which to smite the nations,** and He will rule them with a rod of iron; He will tread the wine press of the fury of the wrath of God the Almighty. On His

robe and on His thigh He has a name inscribed, **King of kings and Lord of lords.**"[7]

To quote the ancient Indian scriptures:

"...when the Kali age, whose career is so severe to the people, is well-nigh past, **the Lord will appear in His divine form consisting of Sattva (purity) alone for the protection of virtue.**

"Lord Vishnu (the universal Lord) adored of the whole animate and inanimate creation, and the Soul of the universe, appears in this world of matter **for protecting the virtue of the righteous and wiping out the entire stock of their Karma and thereby liberating them.** The Lord will appear under the name of Kalki...Riding a fleet horse...and capable of subduing the wicked, the Lord of the universe, wielding...Divine powers and possessed of endless virtues and matchless splendour, will traverse the globe on that swift horse **and exterminate with His sword in tens of millions robbers wearing the insignia of royalty.**"[6]

Should these passages be taken literally? Is the Lord really going to appear in the heavens and slay the evildoers on the spot? Or are these lines of scripture to be taken in a more symbolic sense? Is the Lord going to use various natural calamities to wipe out evil? Will He just allow the ruthless rulers of the world to destroy each other in warfare? The New Testament does say that every eye shall see Him. And when the apostles were watching Lord Jesus ascend into the heavens after His Resurrection, "Two men stood by them in white robes, and said, 'Men of Galilee, why do you stand looking into heaven? This Jesus, who was taken up from you into heaven, **will come in the same way as you saw Him go into heaven.'** "[9]

And, Edgar Cayce stated:

"For, He shall come as ye have seen Him go, in the **body** He occupied in Galilee. The body that He formed, that was crucified on the Cross..."[10]

Hence, Cayce seems to be saying that Jesus will return in the same form He had 2000 years ago. Maybe this is why He left His image on the Shroud, so that when He returned, people would be able to recognize Him easily. Certainly the Lord materializing on the Earth in physical form would be an easy enough feat for Him, since His two witnesses have already done so with such ease. And Jesus did appear and disappear on several occasions before and after His Resurrection in the past. His physical materialization was so perfect that He ate solid food, drank fluids, etc., according to the scriptures.

Perhaps He will appear in His various froms, simultaneously, so that every Messenger of God will be seen around the world at the same time; thus proving the Oneness of God who comes in His manifold manifestations as per His choice, and that the Eternal Truths contained in all religions are from the same Source. This would be similar to Jesus' transfiguration where Moses and Elijah appeared with Him on the mountain in front of three of His disciples.

In any case, He did give His promise to come again, not only to His fishermen-disciples of Palestine, but also to the American Indians, stating He would "return even as I came, through the Light of the dawning." The Hindu scriptures do seem to indicate a physical incarnation of the Lord. But how He will come, no one knows for sure but the Lord Himself. But come He will, for He has promised it so, and the Lord is as good as His Word! Further, since 99% of the prophecies regarding the events leading up to His return have come true, how can the remaining 1% not come true, especially since it is the most important!

The Question of When

The great question that mankind has asked for centuries is, "When will this New World, the Divine Life on Earth, become a Reality? When will the Lord return to usher in this New Era of Peace?"

The key to the answer can be found in the literal translation of Jesus' words concerning the end of this system of things and the coming of the New Age. He stated that when we saw the start of the various signs of the times—wars, increased crime, natural calamities, etc.—we were to understand that these were the beginnings of the **"birth pangs"** of the New Age.[11]

How does one tell when a child is to be born? The birth pangs come closer and closer together and get more and more intense. Hence, as the number of wars and the amount of violence escalate, economic chaos becomes worldwide and natural calamities increase, we can tell that the birth of the New Age is soon. Another indication of the escalating violence is the increasing number of fanatical religious sects that are cropping up throughout the country, who are ignoring Jesus' teachings of Love and Non-violence and are instead arming themselves to the teeth! As Dr. Lowell Streiker, a leading cult psychologist, recently pointed out:

> "Defectors from ultra-fundamentalist religious sects report many of the groups are heavily armed and training for warfare in the belief a 'great tribulation' is at hand...
>
> " 'I am dealing with phenomena that are unbelievable,' said Streiker. 'They literally believe there are witches and that witches should be burned...'
>
> "He said many of the groups are training in warfare in the belief they will be fighting to defend themselves and their supplies from outsiders whom they consider the Anti-christ...(Streiker describing the sects as) 'ultrafundamen-talist, charismatic deliverance groups.' The psychologist said they grew out of traditional American fundamentalist religions but 'have taken the cardinal doctrines of evangelical fundamentalism to an aberrant extreme.
>
> " 'Such excesses as beating a 6-month-old infant until it dies. I have seen a list recently of eight children who died in an ultra-fundamentalist group because of abuse...'
>
> "A Vietnam War veteran who was in one of the groups told Streiker after leaving that the sect had enough weapons and ammunition to equip 20,000 troops."[12]

Thus we can see that the stress of the Great Tribulation is upon us and is causing people to literally crack up mentally. As a matter of fact, according to the Hopis, the Great Tribulation/Purification period has already begun, and the entry into the New Fifth World is imminent. They state that at the very end of each old world, plants and animals from previous worlds, as well as from the world to come, will make themselves known. Indeed, this is already starting to happen as scientists have been baffled recently by the discoveries of totally new varieties of plants and animals, never before catalogued by man, as well as the re-emergence of various animals into the world thought to have been extinct years and decades ago.

One example of this, appropriately enough, is the recent discovery of several pairs of quetzals—that beautifully colored bird with long tail feathers after whom the Pale Prophet (Jesus) was named—Quetzal-Coatl, the bird itself being the Mayans' sacred symbol of unity between the animals of the earth and the sky. This beautiful bird was thought to have been extinct over half a century ago, but is now being compared to the legendary phoenix, apparently rising out of the ashes of its own funeral pyre to again soar up to the heavens and grace the treetops with its magnificent presence. It is obviously more than just a coincidence that the Lord should choose to resurrect this particular bird—His Namesake!

Off the Kona Coast of Hawaii, a fisherman has caught a strange fish never before seen by marine biologists. The fish is baffling scientists because it exhibits traits that are common to both surface-level and deep-sea fish. It has two stomachs and actually looks like a cross between an eel and a fish. As time goes by, more and more strange and "extinct" plants and animals will appear around the globe.

But the point is not to wait until the Lord returns to change; we must begin our change, our own spiritual transformation **NOW!** For when the Lord returns, it will be too late; we will not have wiped out our karmic debts by doing "good works." Hence His Law of Grace may not apply. Remember, that is the Golden Lining of the Age: irrespective of any sins or wrongs we have done in the past, if one truly asks for forgiveness from the Lord and changes his or her life for the better, putting into practice all the teachings of God's Messengers—not merely giving them lip-service—then one shall be forgiven and will be able to be a part of the New World, experiencing the birth of the Aquarian or Christ Consciousness within and its manifestation without.

Thus we must begin to change **NOW**, become more spiritual **NOW,** prepare to greet our Lord **NOW! For His arrival is imminent.** One of the reasons why Jesus said that no one would know exactly when He would return was so that all would prepare themselves and be ready for His arrival at any time:

> "But of that day and hour no one knows, not even the angels of heaven, but the Father only...Watch, therefore, for you do not know on what day your Lord is coming...Therefore you also must be ready; for the Son of man is coming at an hour you do not expect."[13]

Further, some of us may not be around for the ushering in of the New Age **en masse.** Accidents, sickness, old age, etc., may cause some of us to leave this earthly plane before the transformation of the world as a whole is completed. Hence, it makes all the sense to prepare ourselves NOW. For "the end of the world" or the end of this plane of existence may come sooner for some than for others.

In any case, it is obvious that the end of this system of things is upon us, as almost all, if not all, of the various prophecies have been fulfilled. Even the calendar is heralding in a New Era. It should be remembered that our present calendar is between four to seven years behind, as astronomers and theologians agree that Jesus was actually born between 4 B.C. and 7 B.C. Hence, it is really 1987 or as late as 1990. Cayce and Nostradamus stated that the transformation into the New Age would be complete during the 1990's. And the Great Pyramid of Giza in Egypt, which is a chronicle of mankind's history down to the ushering in of the New Age, states that the New Age will be upon us no later than 2001 A.D.

Jesus said that He would shorten the days before His Coming for the sake of the elect. Perhaps the recent discovery that our dating may be off by four to seven years could have been what He meant. He also said that because of the severity of the tribulation period, He would shorten the time of these days of turmoil prior to His Return, again for the sake of the elect. Therefore, no matter what dates other prophets have given, He may come earlier.

Further, Edgar Cayce said that the Lord would come, "When those that are His have made the way clear, **passable** for Him to come."[14] He also predicted in 1932 that "out of Russia's religious development would come the greater hope of the world."[15] On March 6, 1983, Cable News Network reported that a 12-year-old boy in the Soviet Union had a vision of God in which he was told by the Lord to announce the end of the world and the Lord's imminent return. The boy started a chain letter informing people of the above which has spread like wildfire and is still spreading to thousands of Russians, hungry for spiritual knowledge. **This fulfills both of Cayce's prophecies.**

As unbelievable as the second prophecy sounded 50 years ago, its fulfillment is being seen today as Buddhist, Jewish and Christian youth groups are uniting against religious persecution and demanding more religious freedom in Russia.[16] Further, this boy's vision does indeed fulfill Cayce's prediction as what else could be the greatest hope of the world, especially in countries where religious/spiritual thought and development has been suppressed, than news of the imminent return of the Lord!

From the number of chain letters circulating in Russia, it is obvious that the people are indeed thirsty for such hope, even though the government has tried to suppress and discredit the boy's claim by saying that the letter is a hoax because God has never shown Himself physically. Of course, a major shock and surprise awaits the Russian leaders when the Lord does come and changes their ludicrous and ridiculous unbelief! As Lord Jesus said, "A little child shall lead them!"

Hence it is obvious that the Lord is coming soon, for why else would these "happenings" be taking place all over the world? Two scholars of the Pyramid of Giza in Egypt put it thus:

> "The object of the Pyramid's Message was to proclaim Jesus as Deliverer and Saviour of men, to announce the dated circumstances related to His Coming, and to prepare men by means of its Message...to adapt themselves spiritually to the circumstances of His Coming when the fact of the Message becomes to them a matter of certainty."[17]

As 1983 progresses, being dubbed the "Year of the Bible" by President Reagan,[18] "The Holy Year" by Pope John Paul II, and "The Year of the Computer" by *Time Magazine*, let us prepare ourselves for the coming transition. **For the Lord's Return may be sooner than we think!**

The "Highway Apostle" has been seen again! According to recent UPI reports, several motorists in West Germany have picked up a hitchhiker, "who immediately tells them that he is the Archangel Gabriel. He also informs the drivers that the world will end in 1984 . . . (and then) disappears from the moving car.

"Police in Rosenheim, West Germany, say that the first time such an incident was reported was last fall ('82). A woman driver claimed that a buckled-in 'Gabriel' vanished from her moving car. After he vanished, she said, the seat-belt in his seat was still locked. Police said that since then, 'more than half a dozen' other motorists have told authorities similar stories."[19]

Also, prophecies about the coming transition as well as the timetable for it have recently come from a great yogi living in the Himalayan Mountains of India today. According to his devotees, Hariakhan Babaji, known as the "Eternal Babaji," has been warning that the tribulation has already begun. He states that:

"At present, demonic influences have engulfed man. Man will fight and devour man and they will destroy each other (mankind). Some countries will be totally erased, leaving no sign of their existence. In some 3% to 5% and up to a maximum of 25% of the people will be spared and will survive. The destruction will be brought about by earthquakes, floods, accidents, collisions and wars.

"First destruction will take place, then peace will prevail . . . Prayer will be the only safeguard and savior. Those who pray to their chosen Divinity will not be affected . . . After 1989, when only very few will be left, the Satyayuga (Age of Purity) will commence."[20]

DOONESBURY *by GB Trudeau.*

COMING UP: A CONVERSATION WITH INTERIOR SECRETARY JAMES WATT.

READY?

GO AWAY.

SECRETARY WATT, HAS PUBLIC OPINION FORCED YOU TO MODIFY YOUR PROPOSALS TO OPEN UP FEDERAL LANDS TO OIL AND MINERAL INTERESTS?

NOT AT ALL. WE STILL FEEL THAT THE ENERGY COMPANY OPERATORS HAVE THE SAME RIGHT TO ENJOY THE LAND AS ENVIRONMENTAL EXTREMISTS.

BUT COULDN'T SUCH A POLICY PERMANENTLY RUIN ENVIRONMENTALLY SENSITIVE LANDS FOR FUTURE GENERATIONS?

WELL, AS I SAID IN MY SENATE TESTIMONY, I DON'T KNOW HOW MANY FUTURE GENERATIONS WE CAN COUNT ON BEFORE THE LORD RETURNS.

8-30

COULD YOU BE MORE SPECIFIC, SIR?

WELL, OUR LATEST PROJECTIONS PUT THE SECOND COMING SOMETIME DURING THE 1984 FISCAL YEAR.

THAT SOON?

MAYBE SOONER. NEEDLESS TO SAY, WE'VE GOT A LOT OF STRIP MINING TO DO BEFORE THEN.

PREPARATION FOR THE NEW AGE

The Shrimad Bhagavatam, those magnificent and ancient Hindu scriptures, have given us a Golden Lining for this age: no matter what sins we may have committed in the past, if we will genuinely change our lives and turn to Almighty God, and live according to His teachings, then we will be forgiven all our sins and live happy and blissful lives. That great American prophet—Edgar Cayce—also has told us that even though the Law of Karma is eternal, there is one thing that can supercede it and wipe away our sins due to our wrong karmic actions, and that is **the Lord's Law of Grace.** But for that Grace to descend on us we have to change our lives and become more and more spiritual. The next logical question is how does one change and what must one do to prepare for the New Age?

First of all, one must purify oneself (a) physically, (b) mentally, and (c) spiritually. Since the body is the temple of the soul or God, it is essential to keep it clean and healthy. One must do one's best to eat as much organic food as possible and stop polluting the body or God's Temple by ingesting poisons whether they be foods sprayed with poisonous pesticides, herbicides, etc., or animals injected with excessive amounts of antibiotics, hormones, etc., or whether they be poisonous drugs, legal or illegal. Lord Jesus warned, "Take heed to yourselves lest your hearts be weighed down with dissipation and drunkenness..." As a matter of fact, every religion warns against the consumption of alcohol. Even physicians have been warning the public about the extremely harmful effects and the various cancers alcohol causes, not to mention destroying the brain cells and the pineal gland.

The Federal government through its Health Department has admitted and warned people about alcohol being the most harmful and by far the number one drug problem in this country. Even President Reagan, cognizant of the problem, warned Americans in his 1983 New Year weekly radio broadcast about drunk-driving since over 50% of the deaths occurring in auto accidents are due to drunk drivers.

The Surgeon General of our country has been warning people for years about the harmful effects of cigarettes and tobacco in general. For how could people be ready in the New Age to receive the "breath of life" from the Lord if their lungs are polluted and damaged. For, when one smokes tobacco, one inhales poisons like cyanide, formaldahyde, carbon monoxide and other cancer-causing substances.

Plus, when the body is healthy it is easier for the mind to concentrate on higher things. Also, Jesus and the Hopis warn that times are going to be so severe that unless one is healthy, it will be difficult to withstand the many shocks that will befall the Earth.

Physical fitness through exercises, illustrated in Jane Fonda's best seller *Jane Fonda's Workout Book* and other physical fitness books, gyms, etc., are a very good way to keep fit. But the ancient ways through Yoga are probably the best. Yoga exercises not only strengthen the external parts of the body, but strengthen and massage the internal organs, too.

Another way is through the Japanese art of Aikido whose principles came from the Masters in India. Aikido can be translated as follows: "Ai" means Love, "Ki" is the "Energy" or God, and "Do" is "The Way." Therefore, the way to God is through Love! It not only teaches how to be physically fit, but also teaches how to develop one's "Ki" (Japanese), "Chi" (Chinese), "Prana" (Indian), "Life Force" or "Primal Energy" being Western terminologies. It also teaches one how to coordinate the mind and body since, as the great teacher Kiochi Tohei, President of Ki No Kenkyukai H.Q., founder of Sinshin Toitsu Aikido, says, "Both the mind and body were born of the 'Ki' of the universe...If we realize that the mind and body were originally one and act on this principle, the coordination of mind and body is very easy in the movements of one's daily life."[1]

It is amazing to see how the practice of Aikido helps one not only keep physically fit, but calms the mind and reduces stress as well. It also calms undisciplined children and paves the way for them to lead a healthier and calmer existence. If one learns Ki Hygiene, or how to use Ki or Energy or Life Force, it is possible to cure one's body and others afflicted with diseases/illnesses/wounds, etc., through the use of Ki, or to cure illnesses drug-free, without large bills, the concept being similar to the Western faith-healing technique of the "laying-on-of-hands."

It is also necessary to purify the mind of all ego-oriented thoughts (hate, greed, anger, lust, etc.), for only then can one be ready to receive Divine Bliss and Grace. One of the best ways to achieve liberation and receive the Spirit is through the practice of meditation discussed earlier in this book. For through meditation one achieves Oneness with the Lord. Cleansing of the mind is even more important than cleansing of the body because the natural order of existence is Spirit, Mind and then Body, and not the other way around. For, as Sri Aurobindo has said, "All that denies must be torn out and slain and crushed the many longings for whose sake we lose the One for whom our lives were made."[2]

Return to Nature

The best place to feel and inculcate calmness of mind and love for all is in Nature where God's perfections are manifold. Edgar Cayce advocated as early as 1938 a "return to the soil," or "return to the land" all over the country, "for unless this comes, there must and will come disruption, turmoil and strife."[3] Even those who live in cities should start either rooftop gardens or mini-greenhouses in their apartments, homes, etc., or at least follow the intelligent example set by the Mormons in storing a six month to one year supply of basic food necessities. For times are coming when there may be food shortages, as there is only an estimated three-day supply of food in any given city in the U.S., not to mention the affordability of it!*

Those who are not in the cities should start food and fruit gardens, individually or cooperatively. For as Mahatma Gandhi said, "To forget how to dig the earth and tend the soil is to forget ourselves."[4] Even some of our founding fathers, like Jefferson and Washington, warned us not to go away from the soil or our hearts would harden. And, as has been said again and again throughout this book, Nature is God's outer manifestation. When we return to It, we are in reality, returning to Him. When we protect, preserve and beautify Nature, we are ensuring a close spot in His heart for ourselves.

Creating Something Beautiful

In these times, one should stay away from negative things and

*People who are unemployed and/or need guidance and help in setting up food gardens are urged to contact Gardens For All, a nonprofit group founded in 1972 and located in Burlington, Vermont.

thoughts and get into positive things and thoughts that are beautiful and uplift the human spirit. Creating beautiful things as an artist does, or tending gardens of vegetables, fruits and flowers are some of the positive things to do. Others are helping people who need help in whichever way one can, teaching and learning the right things from children, and most importantly, making "Love thy neighbor as thyself" a reality instead of mere words. As Baha'u'llah said:

"Now is the time to cheer and refresh the down-cast through the invigorating breeze of love and fellowship, and the living waters of friendliness and charity.

"They who are the beloved of God, in whatever place they gather and whomsoever they may meet, must evince, in their attitude towards God...such humility and submissiveness that every atom of the dust beneath their feet may attest the depth of their devotion...

"Every eye, in this Day, should seek what will best promote the cause of God...Nothing whatever can, in this Day, inflict a greater harm upon this Cause than dissension and strife, contention, estrangement and apathy, among the loved ones of God. Flee them, through the power of God and His sovereign aid, and strive to knit together the hearts of men, in His Name, the Unifier, the All-Knowing, the All-Wise."[5]

St. Issa (Jesus) has said that in order to attain Supreme Bliss, "Ye must not only purify yourselves, but must also guide others into the path that will enable them to regain their primitive (first) innocence."[6] In other words, we must not only help others in a physical sense, by relieving pain and suffering whenever and wherever possible, but we must also help guide others back to the Path of Truth and the Lord's Heart. For by guiding others back to the Lord, we help to relieve their sufferings forever. As the great saint—Swami Vivekananda—put it:

"Helping others physically, by removing their physical needs, is indeed great...If a man's wants can be removed for an hour, it is helping him indeed...for a year, it will be rendering him more help, but if his wants can be removed forever, it is surely the greatest help that can be given him.

"Spiritual knowledge is the only thing that can destroy our

THE NEW WORLD

miseries forever; and other knowledge removes wants only for a time."[7]

Further, Meishu Sama, a Japanese contemporary of Edgar Cayce's who also was given visions concerning the end of this system of things and the Dawning of the New Age, said that only those people that have less amounts of negative karma and who do "Good Works," especially with regard to the establishment of the coming "New Order of the Ages," will be protected and saved in the upheavals. He also said that this period of purification is coming about as a direct result of natural and Divine Law so that the world will be cleansed of all disease, strife and impurity. Hence the Earth will become a paradise where peace, plenty and good health will replace all of the negative conditions of the "Old World."[8]

The Outpouring of God's Spirit

The above corresponds to what Joel of the Old Testament stated:

> "In the last days it shall be, God declares, that I (God) will pour out my spirit upon all flesh, and your sons and your daughters shall prophesy, your old men shall dream dreams, and your young men shall see visions. Even upon the menservants and maidservants in those days, I will pour out my spirit. And I will show wonders in the heaven above and signs on the Earth beneath...before the day of the Lord comes, the great and manifest day."[9]

The outpouring of the Spirit of God can be seen everywhere. Miracles and unexplained healings have been taking place around the globe. In the U.S., several examples can be seen:

> • Catholic priest Father D'Orio of Worcester, Massachusetts, has been healing people through faith for over six years now, disclaiming any credit for himself, saying that He is but an instrument, a conduit through whom the Lord's healing energy passes;
> • In Oregon, a 72-year-old man stricken with paralysis five years ago and given up as a hopeless case is now talking and walking on his own, explaining that God had helped him;
> • In Tennessee, a cerebral palsy victim of 18 years who suf-

fered from a paralyzed larynx suddenly recovered his voice on Thanksgiving morning in 1980, the doctors having no medical explanation for his recovery;[10]

• In the Little Havana section of Miami, Florida, a certain tree has been giving off water—not sap—that has cured a number of people, including a 92-year-old blind man who recovered his sight after rubbing his eyes with the tree's water, a woman who claims she was cured of her headaches after seeing a bright glow around a rosary placed on the tree, and a woman who was cured of arthritis after drinking some of the tree's water;

• The well-publicized example of the man who had been deaf and blind for nine years, who received his hearing and sight after being struck by lightning—the first word that he saw upon recovering his sight was "God";

• The waters of the Dead Sea in the Holy Land are being hailed as a miraculous therapy for various skin diseases, clearing up to 90% of the psoriasis plaguing certain people;[11] and there are dozens of other such miraculous healings taking place today all over the globe.

Another example of the Lord's Spirit pouring out onto all is the survival of four victims of a Christmas Eve '81 plane crash, who were lost in the woods during bitter cold weather for five days with no food. The four stated that they survived by eating snow and reading the Book of Job—a part of the Old Testament which describes the ordeals that God put Job through to test his faith.[12] Finally, there is the case of a shadowy image on a garage door that bore a striking resemblance to the head of Christ. The shadow was in the image of a cross topped by the face of a man crowned in thorns. The shadow was first discovered on January 7, 1981, that date being Christmas according to the Julian calendar.

The outpouring of the Lord's Spirit can be seen in much of today's artwork as drawings and paintings depicting the New World as well as the destruction of the old are becoming more and more numerous and popular. Even in cinema films, the Second Coming has become a popular theme as flocks of people turned out to see the *Omen Trilogy*—three films dealing with the rise and fall of the Antichrist and the triumphant return of the Lord, the last section—*The Final Conflict*—being released during the early part of 1981. One astounding incident regarding the above took place during April of 1981 on the shooting set of *Fear No Evil,* a new film about Lucifer (the Devil or Satan) battling three archangels over the Second Coming of the Creator. According to the L.A. Times Service, a mobile home used for makeup and wardrobe exploded in the middle of the night and burned to the ground:

> "The next morning, hair stylist Frank Montesanto searched the rubble for salvage. All he could find was a Bible.
>
> " 'It was slightly charred, but mostly intact,' he said, 'The plastic cover had been melted, and fused to the Bible was a charred copy of the *Fear no Evil* script. I couldn't believe it.'
>
> "Montesanto thinks the episode might have been some secret omen, a bizarre sign of Bible predictions."[13]

Various other films that have been popular over the last two years or so demonstrate the growing desire in the hearts of the American public to feel and express Love. Some of the most outstanding examples of this would be *E.T., the Extraterrestrial,* which touched everyone's hearts and the child within us all, its popularity illustrating the people's desire for spiritual themes and the Lord's Return, the parallelism between the saga of E.T. and Jesus Christ (both Messiah figures, coming from outside our world, with a mission on Earth to perform, being rejected by the authorities, dying, rising from the dead, and ascending to heaven) being no coincidence; *Star Trek II,* which dealt with the love between the commander, crew and especially Mr. Spock, who gave his life so that his friends might live, also dealing with the question of Genesis—generating new life from "dead" matter; and *On Golden Pond,* which demonstrated how important love between family members is, and that Love can bridge any gap. The current smash hit and award-winning film of 1983 is *Gandhi,* which deals with that saint's life, including his politics based on nonviolence and love, demonstrating once again that Love and Nonviolence can achieve more in a shorter period of time than what violence ever can—i.e., the overthrow of the British in a decade or so using a nonviolent campaign which Gandhi accomplished, versus almost two-centuries-worth of unsuccessful violent uprisings.

Even the best selling books today demonstrate this outflowing of the Lord's Spirit. Many of the books that have been on the best sellers list for weeks and months have had to do with (w)holistic healing and cleansing, such as *Jane Fonda's Workout Book,* Marilyn Ferguson's *Aquarian Conspiracy,* several books dealing with the Lord's Coming and the dawning of the Aquarian Age, including various books on prophecies and predictions such as those of Nostradamus, the Hopis and Edgar Cayce, and many more dealing with the subject of **LOVE,** such as Leo Buscaglia's two books *Personhood* and *Living, Loving and Learning.* Thus the above authors, artists, etc., have definitely helped prepare the way for the Coming of the Lord as per Cayce's prediction.

However, none of the above would have been successful if it were not for the active support, participation and interest of the American public, thus proving where the American heart really is. There is a seeking in this country, a seeking after Truth, a seeking after Love, a seeking after Peace which will, in the end, triumph over all the words of hatred and division, violence and lies. **For nothing is stronger than Love and Truth.** The hardships we are experiencing today, and which will no doubt intensify as this age of chaos draws to a close, have often brought out the best in the American soul—caring, sharing, sacrificing for others—and have caused us to reassess our values, our goals in life, making us search deep within ourselves for that part of us that had been covered up and clouded for so long—our Love, specifically, our Love for God and for each other.

This seeking for God, for Love and for Peace and Oneness has often been expressed most vividly in our music. Though spiritual music has been a part of Eastern cultures for ages, it has come to the fore in the West only during the past few decades, where Love of God and visions of the New World or Age are now being sung in songs ranging from Jazz to Country Western, Gospel to Rock, Reggae to Rhythm and Blues. One of the best examples of this is the song "Imagine," sung by John Lennon. Lennon stated in his last interview that most of the lyrics of the song actually came from his wife—Yoko Ono. In the song, John and Yoko give their vision of the New World where nothing exists that can divide mankind: no countries, no organized religion, no greed, no killing—just a Brotherhood/Sisterhood of humanity living in Peace and Harmony as One:

"Imagine there's no countries, it isn't hard to do
Nothing to kill or die for, and no religion too
Imagine all the people living life in Peace...
No need for greed or hunger, a brotherhood of man
Imagine all the people sharing all the world...
You may say I'm a dreamer, but I'm not the only one
I hope someday you'll join us,
And the world will be as One."[14]

Another former member of the Beatles—George Harrison—
sings of his desire to know, love and have Union with the Lord in
his song, "My Sweet Lord." In other words, Harrison is wishing
for a **personal, spiritual experience—gnosis.** Rick Davies and
Roger Hodgson of Supertramp also sing of their need to be with
the Lord, to feel His Love and to seek Him out as the ultimate
Hope of the world and Friend of us all. Examples of this can be
heard in their songs "Even in the Quietest Moments," "Fool's
Overture," and "Lord Is It Mine?"

"The music that you gave me, the language of my soul
Oh Lord, I want to be with you,
Won't you let me come in from the cold?"[15]
—"Even In The Quietest Moments"

"Called the man a fool, stripped Him of His pride
Everyone was laughing up until the day He died
And though the wound went deep
Still He's calling us out of our sleep
My friends, we're not alone
He waits in silence to lead us all home."[16]
—"Fool's Overture"

"I know that there's a reason why I need to be alone,
I need to find a silent place that I can call my own,
Is it mine, Lord, is it mine?
You know I get so weary from the battles in this life,
And many times it seems like
You're the only hope in sight.
Is it mine, Lord, is it mine?
When everthing's dark and nothing seems right,
There's nothing to win and there's no need to fight.

I never cease to wonder at the cruelty of this land
But it seems a time of sadness is a time to understand
Is it mine, Lord, is it mine?...
If only I could find a way
To feel your sweetness through the day
The Love that shines around me could be mine.
So give us an answer, won't you,
We know what we have to do,
There must be a thousand voices
Trying to get through."[17]

—"Lord Is It Mine?"

From this outpouring of spirit, we are again reminded of the Golden Lining of this age, i.e., if we change our lives, recognize and renounce our past wrong actions, and call on the Name of the Lord, we will be saved. For God, in His Mercy, has no wish that any of His children should be lost. He wishes all would turn to Him, for His Mercy and Forgiveness knows no bounds, if we are truly repentant and seek to live our lives according to His Will. *The Shrimad Bhagavatam* says that if people in this age utter the Lord's Name while afflicted or even helplessly dying, they are "freed from all impediment in the shape of Karma and reach the highest goal.

> "Enthroned in the mind of men Lord Sri Hari (the Supreme Person) drives away all evils occasioned by the Kali age...Heard of or glorified, meditated upon and worshipped or even honored, the Lord stays in men's hearts and drives away all their sins committed in thousands of lives..."[18]

In the New Testament, St. Peter assures us that the Lord will save those who turn to Him: "And it shall be that whoever calls on the Name of the Lord shall be saved."[19]

Hence we must cleanse our hearts and minds of all negative, ungodly thoughts and feelings, and fill ourselves with Love and Peace, while performing good works in the Name of the Lord—helping our fellow brothers and sisters, and preserving, protecting and beautifying all parts of the Lord's Creation. For then the Grace of the Lord will descend upon us, protecting us from the tribulations of this time. And we will be worthy to be raptured and become a part of the "New Jerusalem," the New Age or World that is to rise up out of the ashes of the old. As Graeme Edge of the

406

Moody Blues wrote:

"When the white eagle of the North is flying overhead,
The browns, reds and golds of autumn
Lie in the gutter, dead.
Remember then, that summer birds
With wings of fire flaying
Come to witness Spring's new hope,
Born of leaves decaying.
Just as new life will come from death,
Love will come at leisure.
Love of love, love of life and giving without measure
Gives in return a wondrous yearn of promise almost seen
**Live hand-in-hand and together we'll stand
On the threshold of a dream.**"[20]

Chapter 23

THE RAPTURE AND THE NEW WORLD

When the Lord comes, He will usher in the New Age of Light and awaken the Christ or Aquarian Consciousness within us all. It is said that He will rapture those that are His into this New World. But what exactly is the Rapture? What is meant by this term?

According to *The American Heritage Dictionary,* "Rapture" literally means: "The state of being transported by a lofty emotion; ecstasy."[1] It also can mean: "The transporting of a person from one place to another, especially to heaven."[2] Its root word is "raptus," which is Latin for, "one who seizes."[3]

Thus we see that the Rapture spoken of in the Bible can be understood on two levels: 1- as a feeling of ecstasy that transports one to the highest levels of spiritual bliss, and 2- as a physical transporting of the body from the earth to heaven.

But where does "heaven" lie? Is it somewhere above the clouds, or is it, as Jesus said, within us? If we understand Jesus' meaning along this line, then we see that the Rapture is actually God-Realization. When Edgar Cayce was asked to explain the verses from Revelations regarding the New Jerusalem that John saw coming down out of heaven from God, Cayce explained:

> "[To] those then that are come into the new life, the new understanding, the new regeneration, there **is** then the **New Jerusalem...not as a place alone but as a condition, as an experience of the soul.** [i.e., **Gnosis**] Jerusalem has figuratively, symbolically, meant the holy place, the Holy City—for there, the Ark of the Covenant in the minds, the hearts, the understandings, the comprehensions of those who have put away the earthly desires and become as the **new** purposes in their experience, become the New Jerusalem, the new undertakings, the new desires."[4]

Thus, we see that the Rapture, the New Jerusalem, is not only a place or new dimension, but also a condition of the soul, that condition being Union with the Lord:

> "Here we find echoed what Cayce described for the conditions of the New Age, and that it is both of the future, and, for those who are truly One with God's purpose **NOW.**

Jesus told the Samaritan woman that 'the hour is coming, **and NOW is,** when the true worshippers will worship the Father in spirit and truth. Even then, the New Age had begun, and the New Jerusalem was present!'"[5]

Hence, we can now understand why Sri Aurobindo and the other great saints and yogis have said that **the Rapture is Eternal;** there has never been a time when it did not exist, nor will there ever be a time when it will cease to exist. This Rapture, then, is the Union of the individual soul (what the Hindus call "jiva") with the All-Soul, the One, All-Pervading God, and truly does transport one to another dimension, another reality. It exists parallel to our own world, only those who have no spiritual vision are unable to see or perceive it.

This state of Being, this Eternal Rapture, is what Buddhists call "Nirvana," what Hindus call "Samadhi," and what Christians call "Mystical Union." Saints and sages throughout the history of mankind have and still do experience and live in this Rapture. It occurs when we realize in our hearts that we are a part of the One God, when we kill our ego and freely abandon ourselves, our souls, our lives and very bodies to Him to do with as He wills, having full faith that He will resurrect us when He needs us. It is the ultimate surrender of which St. Paul spoke. For when we are willing to surrender to Him, freely, without any attachments or hesitations, then our souls, our beings are freed from the fetters that keep them bound in the prison of the body. We soar ever higher to meet His Light as He descends to touch our hearts and minds with His transmuting Presence. The veil of ignorance is rent and no longer is there any separation between our individual self and the Eternal Self—God.

When this happens, we come to realize that the Lord, our God, our Friend and Sustainer has never left our side. He has always been with us, as a shadow that follows our every step. He is Ever-Present. He is the Friendly Guide, waiting to show us the way back Home, Home in His heart of Eternal Love. He never really went away at all; it was our egos that blinded our eyes from seeing Him, plugged up our ears from hearing Him speaking eternally to our hearts. Thus, through the fire of devotion to Him, the scales that have blinded our eyes and the plugs that have blocked our ears are melted away, and the ropes of the ego that are binding our souls are burnt up and can hold us no longer. Hence, we are released from the prison of our self—our ego—and achieve Union with Him.

When we achieve this Union, we begin to realize that He truly is all and within all. The inner vision becomes the outer reality. We see that all life—human, animal, plant, even the rocks and the skies, the clouds and the sea—are just different faces of the same God. Thus we understand and **actually see** why Jesus said that when we help one another, we are, in reality, helping Him, for He is everyone and everything. It is no longer an intellectual or ethical understanding; it is **a living Reality** which is seen and heard without and felt within. Then the realization of what Sri Aurobindo and the Old Testament of the Bible called "the Ladder of Consciousness" occurs: a network of like-minded individuals interlocked into an all-encompassing Oneness and Awareness of the Love of the Living God. We become part of what Marilyn Ferguson called the Aquarian Conspiracy, "conspiracy" meaning "to breathe together."

This is the New Israel—these seekers of God. Cayce once said that the term "Israel" means the spiritual seekers of the world, no matter if Buddhist, Christian, American, French, German or "Hottentot."[6] The Hopi Indians have said basically the same thing, i.e., that if you do the right things and are seekers of the One True God, then you are "Hopi" too, "hopi" meaning "Peaceful." And this is the difference between ages past and the present one: in the past this Rapturous Union was only experienced by a very few; in this age, it will be experienced **en masse!**

What does this mean, then? Is it "only" going to be a difference in the state of one's mind? Or is there going to be the fulfillment of the second definition of the word "Rapture"? Will we be physically transported to another time, another place, a New World?

The American Indians speak of the Rapture in both senses. In the late 1800's, the great holy man Wovoka had a vision of the Second Coming of Christ. He was shown the New World as well as the fact that it would happen in the not-too-distant future. As a result of this vision, Wovoka created a beautiful dance, called "The Ghost (Holy Ghost) Dance," which was, in essence, a celebration of the promise of the coming of the Lord and the New World. During this dance, Wovoka sang that the Great Spotted Eagle was coming to snatch him away into the sky. What he meant was that Jesus or God, represented by the Great Spotted

Eagle, was coming to Rapture him up to heaven (eagles being "raptors" or birds that snatch away their prey.) For some ridiculous reason this dance was outlawed by the American government back in the 1890's, it being a crime punishable by imprisonment and/or death for taking part in a ceremony that was, ironically enough, dedicated to the Son of God the Americans worshipped![7]

Did Wovoka mean that the Lord would Rapture him only spiritually, or did he mean a literal physical transportation or transformation? Einstein has proven that matter as a form of energy cannot be destroyed; it can only be transformed—its physical nature or form changed. Hence, perhaps an actual physical transformation to a higher level of reality is what is yet to come. Maybe we all will literally be transported to another realm of existence, a New Earth and another level of Reality. In the Bible, St. Paul speaks of this transformation thus:

> "Lo! I tell you a mystery. We shall not all sleep, but we shall all be changed, in a moment, in the twinkling of an eye, at the last trumpet. For the trumpet will sound, and the dead will be raised imperishable, and we shall be changed. For this perishable nature must put on the imperishable, and this mortal nature must put on immortality. When the perishable puts on the imperishable, and the mortal puts on immortality, then shall come to pass the saying that is written: 'Death is swallowed up in victory.' "[8]

Clearly the Lord has already demonstrated His ability to make Himself as well as other physical objects appear and disappear and/or transform them from one substance to another. Perhaps it will be as it is with the highway apostles, where prior to or simultaneously with the last great quake of the Earth, all spiritual and basically good people will be physically transported to another dimension, to be returned to a reborn and renewed Earth. Many yogis of India and the East have had this ability for ages, and some still demonstrate their power of transformation of matter as well, making things appear out of thin air and/or transforming stones and dirt into edible sweets, as witnessed by one of the authors, as Smt. Indira Devi of India demonstrated after entering into an ecstatic spiritual state. Others have seen the remarkable materialization powers of Sathya Sai Baba, also of India, who has caused sacred ash to flow from his hands and other objects.

411

Remember, Sri Aurobindo has stated that these seemingly miraculous powers are normal to one who has reached certain heights of spirituality.

Lord Krishna has assured Arjuna in *The Bhagavad Gita* that:

> "...what seems unreal on the planes of the lower consciousness can become **here and now a rapturous reality**...(uplifting) the soul to the Eternal Union with God which is unending happiness...if only we are vowed to climb to the plateaus of the higher consciousness on the wings of Yoga as outlined by Him...(through) the triune Path of Yoga—knowledge (gnosis), work (actions), and love (devotion)."[9]

Indeed, this is why the great saint Sri Ramana Maharshi stated that although his physical body was going to drop off at his "death," he or his real self, his soul, which is eternal and unaffected by death, was going nowhere as he had already attained Union with the Divine. Hence, he already was dwelling in heaven, even though he still had a physical body.

Science is beginning to recognize this truth, i.e., that there are other realms of reality, other levels of consciousness that are just as real, if not more so than the earthly plane of existence. With the invention of the holograph—a machine that has the ability to project a three-dimensional image that appears to have substance, and can be easily mistaken for a solid object, but is actually mere light waves interacting with one another to produce the illusion of substance—new questions are being raised as to the nature of the universe. Some scientists are beginning to ask the question, "Is the Universe itself a holograph? Is the world of matter actually but one level of reality?" Is it, then, like a cinema show, with all matter and all life (including ourselves) being but light waves speeding through the Universe, being projected on the great screen of the Lord's Spirit?

We know that molecules are in perpetual motion even in seemingly solid substances. We also know that when these molecules increase their speed, the solid substances are changed to liquids and finally gasses. Is it possible that the Rapture will be a speeding up of the molecules that make up our body to the point where the body will be transformed instantaneously into spirit? We know that this is possible, since Jesus' Resurrection, as verified by the image on the Shroud of Turin, has so proven. His body did indeed dissolve into a blaze of light, a tremendous burst of energy which transformed it into pure spirit that had the ability to materialize and change its appearance in accordance with His Will. Is this what the Rapture is to be?

The New World

In any case, it is clear that science is beginning to recognize the Truths revealed in Holy Scriptures for ages, which is only natural as science is, in truth, but an attempt to understand Nature, which is God's outer manifestation. Science discovers these truths by examining external Nature, while spiritual seekers have sought and realized these truths through inner exploration through meditation. *The Vedas* have indeed spoken of other levels of reality, which support the scientific theory that the universe itself is a holograph—a three-dimensional image produced by the reflection of certain light waves on each other:

> "In the heaven of Indra there is said to be a network of pearls so arranged that if you look at one you see all the others reflected in it. In the same way, each object in the world is not merely itself but involves every other object, and in fact **is** every other object."[10]

Hence, the *Vedas* saying that, "Thou art that," is indeed not just a figurative expression but a Truth of the Reality of Being. In Revelations, John too speaks of the New Jerusalem as a different place in time and space. He compares it to many beautiful jewels and crystals, and again draws the same analogy given in the *Vedas* of the gates of heaven being made from pearls that reflect and refract the light of the Lord. He also states that the light or warm glow of the Lord's Presence is seen throughout the "city" and that there is a beautiful stream—"the river of the water of life"—flowing from the throne of God through the middle of the "city."[11]

This description is remarkably similar to the descriptions given by those who have had death experiences regarding the "City of Lights" over which they found themselves. Many stated that there appeared to be jeweled structures, a beautiful flowing river, and a warm, golden glow throughout the "city." They stated that this warm glow filled them and surrounded them with Love—God's Love warming and illuminating all. As we have seen, however, one need not die in order to visit this "city." John had his vision of

413

the "New Jerusalem" while still very much alive. And the saints and seers of India have also seen and held onto this spiritual reality for thousands of years.

Saint Paul, too, speaks of this new level of spirituality, stating that those who have been basically good and spiritual and died, have already gone to this New Land of God's Love. But he also states that those left alive till the Lord's Return will be rapturously transported to this same state, the point being that in this state of Supreme Spiritual Bliss, one does not care whether there is a body or not. For the body, which is the scab of the spirit, is not what is important: **what is important is the spirit or soul within our bodies.**

> "For this we declare to you by the Word of the Lord, that we who are alive, who are left until the coming of the Lord, shall not precede those who have fallen asleep (already died.) For the Lord Himself will descend from heaven with a cry of Command, with the archangel's call, and with the sound of the trumpet of God. And the dead in Christ will rise first; then we who are alive, who are left, shall be caught up together with them in the clouds to meet the Lord in the air; and so we shall always be with the Lord. Therefore comfort one another with these words." (I Thessalonians 4·15-18)

The great Greek philosopher Plato speaks of this new level of consciousness, too, in his play "Republic." In his play, he describes a "world of shadows" in which all human beings live. Then one man decides to seek Truths that lie beyond this "Shadow-land." Through meditation he is brought to a world of light, and realizes that this Light is actually the True Reality and the Source of everything, including the shadows of "Shadow-land."

At this new spiritual level of reality, one sees that all beings are interconnected with one another, that we are all but reflections of the One God. Cayce compares this concept to light passing through a prism:

> "All power is from one Source: God...In this orderly universe, everything has its place and its function. The same God which says 'Love is law...law is love' on the spiritual level, tells us 'Matter doesn't change in chemical transformation' on the scientific level. The various colors thrown out

[of a Prism] are like the various aspects of the universal laws, but all from the same source."[12]

So God is the source of all things in the Universe; He is the original White Light. Our minds are like a prism through which this light is reflected and refracted similar to the way in which water droplets refract the colors of the sun, producing a rainbow. The colors produced when white light goes through a prism depend on the different wavelengths contained in the white light and how those light waves are bent.

God is the source of all light. Our minds are like a prism bending the light and producing various visual images according to the clarity of the mind. When the mind is clouded by the sickness of the ego—what Hindus call "metempsychosis"—then the amount of light allowed to pass through it is limited; hence, our vision is limited. But when the mind is free from the clouds of the ego, then it becomes a perfect mirror of the Light of the Lord: we are able to see with true spiritual vision that we are all but reflections of the Lord and refractions of His Body of Pure Light.

The whole purpose of life is to attain this vast vision, this spiritual vision while still living. Those who have had death experiences have stated that death was actually like an awakening and a remembering, with limitless sight, hearing and comprehension of the secrets of the universe replacing their limited physical senses and mind. And, indeed, they are correct. But one need not die physically to gain this vision, to experience this awakening. As Dr. Raymond Moody explained before, death is but one door through which one gains entry into this New World of Light. Meditation is another. The Goal of life is to enter this New World before death by killing our ego and to bring this vision down to the Earth as a living Reality. And this is what is to happen **en masse** in this age: this New World will not be the sole property of a chosen few, but a Living Reality on Earth for the multitudes. This is what the entire evolution of man has been all about: **to have and experience the Divine Life on Earth.**

The Hopis believe that there is going to be a New World, not only in a consciousness sense, but also in a physical sense, and that this New World will be one of plenty and beauty, where spirituality is the rule, not the exception. The Hindu Scriptures also state that there will be a New World, a physical one, but with everyone totally spiritually aware:

415

"Now when all the robbers are (thus) exterminated, the minds of the people of the cities and the countryside will become pure indeed because of their enjoying the breezes wafting the most sacred fragrance of pigments on the person of Lord Vasudeva (the Universal Lord.) With Lord Vasudeva, the embodiment of strength, in their heart their progeny will grow exceedingly strong.

"When the Lord, the Protector of Dharma (righteousness), appears as Kalki, Satyayuga (the Age of Enlightenment, Spirituality or Aquarius) will prevail once more at that time and the progeny of the people will be of a Sattvic (virtuous) disposition."[13]

Isaiah of the Old Testament, too, foresees a new Divine Life on Earth, stating:

"And they shall beat their swords into plowshares, and their spears into pruning hooks, nation shall not lift up sword against nation, neither shall they learn war any more."[14]

Revelations quotes the Lord as saying: "Behold, I make all things new."[15]

There is no reason to think that this spiritual transformation cannot be accomplished on Earth. On the contrary, as Sri Aurobindo has stated, it would give the truest meaning to terrestrial or earthly existence. Further, according to ancient Indian history, such a spiritual world has existed before. Aeons ago, even before the Lord came as Krishna, He incarnated on Earth as Sri Rama and ruled as King. During His reign there was no sickness, no death or old age, and the people in general were of a spiritual and sattvic (pure or righteous) nature. As a matter of fact, the descriptions of the world under the rule of Lord Rama sound identical to those given by John in Revelations regarding the rule of Lord Jesus in the New World: i.e., the Lord dwelling with the people, no sorrow, no sickness, no death, no pain—only Life and Love and Cooperation between all created beings on Earth.[16]

The tenets of this New World could be summarized from words taken from *The Preamble to the United States Constitution:*

"We the people of the United World, in order to form a more perfect Union, establish justice, insure domestic tranquillity, provide for the common spiritual growth, promote the general welfare, and secure the blessings of liberty

THE RETURN OF THE LORD

to ourselves and our posterity, do ordain and establish this Spiritual Consciousness for the United World of Peace and Love."

Thus the Lord will come in order to make this New World of Peace and Love a reality on Earth. As the great sage Sri D. K. Roy (Dadaji) wrote in the Introduction to his beautiful translation of *The Bhagavad Gita:*

> "One of the reasons why the Lord created the world of matter from stardust was so that He might enjoy His cosmic play (Lila) of transforming...terrestrial darkness into a divine illumination...Krishna, like Christ, came to redeem His pledge to Earth that He would uplead our distracted planet to a harmonious Heaven..."[17]

Hence, He will come again to transform this world of ignorance and death into a world of Purity, Truth and Light. And we must be ready to greet Him by changing NOW, so that we will be eligible to remain in His Loving Presence forever. Sri Aurobindo, perhaps the greatest spiritual master to visit the Earth in ages, was given a vision of this New World and the Life Divine as well as the coming of the Lord. He summarizes his vision in his magnificent epic *Savitri,* a short synopsis of which follows:

Great Man

"To bring God down to the world on earth we came,
 To change the earthly life to life divine...
 A mutual debt binds man to the Supreme:
 His nature we must put on as He put ours;
 We are (children) of God and must be even as He:
 His human portion, we must grow divine.
 Our life is a paradox with God for key.

Since God has made Earth, Earth must make in her God;
 What hides within her breast, she must reveal...

I know my coming was a wave from God.
 For love must soar beyond the very heavens
 And find its secret sense ineffable;
 It must change its human ways to ways divine,
 Yet keep the sovereignty of earthly bliss.

A few shall see what none yet understands;
God shall grow up while the wise men talk and sleep;
For man shall not know the coming till its hour
And belief shall be not till the work is done.
God must be born on Earth and be as man
That man being human may grow even as God...

The Vision

"A mightier race shall inhabit the mortals' world.
On Nature's luminous tops, on the Spirit's ground,
The superman shall reign as king of life,
Make earth almost the mate and peer of heaven
And lead towards God and truth man's ignorant earth
And lift towards godhead his mortality...

The supermind shall claim the world for Light
And thrill with love of God the enamoured heart
And place Light's crown on Nature's lifted head
And found Light's reign on her unshaking base...

When superman is born as Nature's king
His presence shall transfigure Matter's world:
He shall light up Truth's fire in Nature's night,
He shall lay upon the earth Truth's greater law;
Man too shall turn towards the Spirit's call...

The Spirit shall look out through Matter's gaze
And Matter shall reveal the Spirit's face.
Then man and superman shall be at one
And all the earth become a single life.

Even the multitudes shall hear the Voice
And turn to commune with the Spirit within
And strive to obey the high spiritual law:
This earth shall stir with impulses sublime,
Humanity awake to deepest self,
Nature the hidden godhead recognize...

A heavenlier passion shall upheave men's lives,
Their mind shall share in the ineffable gleam,
Their heart shall feel the ecstasy and the fire,
Earth's bodies shall be conscious of a soul;

Mortality's bond-slaves shall unloose their bonds,
Mere men into spiritual beings grow
And see awake the (silent) divinity...

A divine force shall flow through tissue and cell
And take the charge of breath and speech and act
And all the thoughts shall be a glow of suns
And every feeling a celestial thrill...

A sudden bliss shall run through every limb
And Nature with a mightier Presence fill.
Thus shall the earth open to divinity
And common natures feel the wide uplift,
Illumine common acts with the Spirit's ray
And meet the deity in common things.

Nature shall live to manifest secret God,
The Spirit shall take up the human play,
This earthly life become the Life Divine.

Oh, surely one day He shall come to our cry,
One day He shall create our life anew
And utter the magic formula of peace
And bring perfection to the scheme of things.

One day He shall descend to life and earth...
And bring the truth that sets the spirit free,
The job that is the baptism of the soul,
The strength that is the outstretched arm of Love...
Impose delight on the world's beating heart
And bare His secret body of Light and Bliss."[18]

Hopefully, we will all meet in the New World soon.
Until then, we wish everyone:

"OM SHANTI"

Hinduism

"SHALOM ALEICHEM"

Judaism

"PEACE BE WITH YOU"

Christianity

"ASSALAM ALAIKUM"

Islam

Confucianism

Buddhism

American Indian

PEACE

The following is a letter to the authors from the Holy Mother of Hari Krishna Mandir Ashram in Poona, India. Thank you, Ma, for your love and blessings.

What a beautiful book you have written! It fulfills the need of the hour.

You have taken all that is good, holy, and true in all man-made religions—and put them in a spiritual book. You are right: Again and again He comes—to help the devotees, to punish the evil doers and to establish the Kingdom of Heaven on earth. He came as Krishna, as Ram, as Christ, as Nanak, as Buddha, as Moses, and will come again. All religions are off-colour now—what we need is the Spiritual Man—the complete man, above all religions, sects and labels. I want the religion of Love to succeed all others so that when Christ comes or Krishna comes we will see Him not with our outer eyes, but the eyes of love. We will judge Him not with our puny minds, but with our heart's adoration.

We must be ready to receive Him—for, come He will and come He must. Let us prepare ourselves and wait in humility, in joy and hope.

You have done a great service to the West and East. Well done! The Lord be praised.

May the Lord and Dadaji bless you.

15 December 1983   Yours Own,
                          MA

Legend

1) Composite from *The American Heritage Dictionary*, p. 985—"phoenix," p. 950—"paragon," and *The World Book Encyclopedia*, Vol. 15, p. 355 (emphasis added).
2) *Edgar Cayce Reading* #2533-7. Used by permission.
3) *The American Heritage Dictionary*, p. 239.
4) *Ibid.*, p. 703.
5) Revelations 21·5, KJRV.

Introduction

1) Kaur, Sardarni Premka, *The Life and Teachings of Guru Nanak—Guru for the Aquarian Age*, p. 5—Introduction. Hereafter cited as *Guru Nanak*. Used by permission.
2) Ghose, Sri Aurobindo, *Life Divine*, Volume II, Chapters 23 and 28, as quoted by P. B. Saint-Hilaire in *The Future Evolution of Man: The Divine Life Upon Earth* (a compilation of Sri Aurobindo's writings), pp. 27, 31, 52, 54, 130 (emphasis added). Hereafter cited as *Future Evolution*.
3) Attenborough, Sir Richard, *The Words of Gandhi*, pp. 74, 75. Used by permission.
4) Ghose, Sri Aurobindo, *The Human Cycle*, Chapter 17, as quoted by Saint-Hilaire, *op. cit.*, pp. 42, 44 (emphasis added).
5) Luke 17·21, King James Revised Version. Hereafter cited as KJRV.
6) Ghose, Sri Aurobindo, *The Human Cycle*, Chapter 17, and *Life Divine*, Vol. II, Chapter 24, as quoted by Saint-Hilaire, *op. cit.*, pp. 47, 67, 68.
7) John 3·3, KJRV (emphasis added).
8) Matthew 4·17, KJRV.
9) Potter, Rev. Dr. C.F., *The Lost Years of Jesus Revealed*.
10) II Corinthians 6·1-2, all lines except last one from *The Living Bible*. Used by permission. Hereafter cited as *TLB*. Last line from KJRV (emphasis added).

PART I—Chapter 1

1) Prabhavananda, Swami and Manchester, Frederick, *The Upanishads: Breath of the Eternal*, pp. 170, 171. Hereafter cited as *Upanishads*. Used by permission.
2) Composite based on various books and articles relating to near-death experiences, including Dr. Raymond Moody's two books—*Life After Life* and *Reflections on Life After Life*—as well as work done by Dr. Elisabeth Kubler-Ross, and personal experiences relayed to the authors.
3) Brown, Joseph Epes, *The Sacred Pipe: Black Elk's Account of the Seven Rites of the Oglala Sioux*, p. 4, footnote #2. Hereafter cited as *Sacred Pipe*.
4) Composite as per note #2 this chapter.
5) Luke 21·25-26, KJRV (emphasis added).
6) *The American Heritage Dictionary*, p. 609.
7) Matthew 24·30, KJRV.
8) Matthew 24·21-22, KJRV (emphasis added).
9) Luke 21·28, 32, KJRV (emphasis added).
10) Cheetham, Erika, *The Prophecies of Nostradamus*, p. 417.
11) *Ibid.*, p. 417.
12) John 5·28-29, KJRV.

I—Chapter 2

1) Armstrong, Herbert, W., *The United States and Britain in Prophecy.*

I—Chapter 3

1) Lindsey, Hal, *The Late Great Planet Earth,* pp. 39, 40.
2) Matthew 24·2, KJRV.
3) Matthew 24·34, KJRV (emphasis added).
4) Matthew 24·15, 16, KJRV.
5) *Honolulu Advertiser,* 4/19/81, p. A-14.
6) *Ibid.,* 4/19/81, p. A-14.
7) *Ibid.,* 4/19/81, p. A-14.
8) *National Review,* 4/16/82 issue, "The Shroud" by Jerome S. Goldblatt, p. 416.
9) *Ibid.,* 4/16/82 issue, p. 416.
10) *Hawaii Tribune Herald,* 11/20/81, p. 8.
11) *National Geographic Magazine,* June, 1980 issue, "The Mystery of the Shroud" by Kenneth F. Weaver, p. 751.
12) *National Review, op. cit.,* p. 419.
13) Bock, Janet, *The Jesus Mystery: Of Lost Years and Unknown Travels,* p. 158. Hereafter cited as *Jesus Mystery.* Used by permission.
14) *Ibid.,* p. 158.
15) *Ibid.,* p. 159.
16) *Ibid.,* p. 159.

I—Chapter 4

1) *Lost Books of the Bible,* p. 283 (emphasis added).
2) Koester, H., *Introduction to The Gospel of Thomas,* in *The Nag Hammadi Library,* p. 117. Hereafter cited as *NHL.* Used by permission.
3) Moody, Dr. Raymond, *Life After Life,* pp. 95-97. Used by permission.
4) Pagels, Elaine, *The Gnostic Gospels,* p. 90.
5) *Apocalypse of Peter* 81·4-24, in *NHL,* p. 344. Note use of translation by J. Brashler, *The Coptic Apocalypse of Peter* (emphasis added).
6) *Second Treatise of the Great Seth* 56·6-19, in *NHL,* p. 332.
7) *Acts of John* 95·16-96·42, in *New Testament Apocrypha II,* pp. 229-231, hereafter cited as *NTA II,* as quoted by Pagels, Elaine in *The Gnostic Gospels,* p. 89 (emphasis added).
8) *Ibid.,* 97, 101 in *NTA II,* pp. 232, 234, as quoted by Pagels, Elaine, *op. cit.,* pp. 89, 90.

I—Chapter 5

1) John 1·31, KJRV.
2) Levi, *The Aquarian Gospel of Jesus The Christ,* p. 78. Hereafter cited as *Aquarian Gospel.* Used by permission.
3) *Ibid.,* pp. 88-97.
4) Jochmans, J. R., *Rolling Thunder: The Coming Earth Changes,* pg. 15.
5) *Edgar Cayce Readings* #2067-7, #5749-2.
6) Prabhavananda, Swami and Manchester, Frederick, *Upanishads,* pp. 192, 193.
7) Matthew 7·14.
8) *Honolulu Advertiser,* 6/17/82, Global Section.
9) Roy, Sri Dilip Kumar, *The Bhagavad Gita: A Revelation,* pp. 134, 135. Hereafter cited as *Bhagavad Gita.* Used by permission.
10) Roy, Sri Dilip Kumar and Devi, Smt. Indira, *Pilgrims of the Stars,* p. 264. Used by permission.
11) Prabhavananda, Swami and Manchester, Frederick, *op. cit.,* p. 16.

12) *Ibid.,* pp. 90, 189-192 (emphasis added).
13) Paramananda, Swami, *Christ and Oriental Ideals,* pp. 51, 52. Used by permission.
14) Matthew 11·30, KJRV (emphasis added).

I—Chapter 6

1) *Shrimad Bhagavatam,* Vol. I, p. 10.
2) *Ibid.,* Vol. II, p. 1664.
3) Caras, Paul, *The Gospel of Buddha,* p. 245. Used by permission.
4) *Ibid.,* p. 245.
5) Levi, *Aquarian Gospel,* p. 71.
6) Notovitch, Nicolas, *The Legend of St. Issa,* VI·4, hereafter cited as *St. Issa,* as quoted by Bock, Janet in *Jesus Mystery,* p. 213.
7) Bock, Janet, *op. cit.,* pp. 2, 3.
8) Notovitch, Nicolas, *op. cit.,* I·1-4, as quoted by Bock, *op. cit.,* p. 207.
9) *Ibid.,* IV·1-5, 8-9, as quoted by Bock, *op. cit.,* p. 210.
10) *Ibid.,* IV·13, as quoted by Bock, *op. cit.,* p. 210.
11) *Ibid.,* V·1, as quoted by Bock, *op. cit.,* p. 211.

PART II—Chapter 1

1) Roy, Sri D. K., *Bhagavad Gita,* pp. 111, 180.
2) Ghose, Sri Aurobindo, *Essays on the Gita,* pp. 494, 495.
3) Matthew 25·21, KJRV.
4) Matthew 25·26-27, KJRV.
5) Matthew 25·29-30, *TLB.*
6) Roy, Sri D. K., *op. cit.,* p. 108.
7) *Ibid.,* pp. 181, 182.
8) I Corinthians 12·4-27, *TLB* (emphasis added).
9) Malachi 2·10, KJRV.
10) Notovitch, Nicolas, *St. Issa,* V·11-13, 26-27, VI·6, as quoted by Bock, *Jesus Mystery,* pp. 211, 212, 213.
11) Levi, *Aquarian Gospel,* pp. 60-62.

II—Chapter 2

1) Notovitch, Nicolas, *St. Issa,* XII·8-21, as quoted by Bock, Janet in *Jesus Mystery,* pp. 222, 223.
2) As quoted by Ferguson, Marilyn, *The Aquarian Conspiracy,* p. 227.
3) As quoted by Ferguson, Marilyn, *op. cit.,* p. 227.
4) As quoted by Ferguson, Marilyn, *op. cit.,* p. 228.
5) As quoted by Ferguson, Marilyn, *op. cit.,* p. 228.
6) Attenborough, Sir Richard, *The Words of Gandhi,* p. 21.
7) *Honolulu Advertiser,* 10/15/82, p. B-1.
8) Pagels, Elaine, *The Gnostic Gospels,* p. 77.
9) *Dialogue of the Savior,* 139·12-13, in *NHL,* p. 235.
10) Pagels, Elaine, *op. cit.,* p. 78.
11) *Redbook Magazine,* March, 1978 issue, "God and Woman: The Hidden History" by Elizabeth Rodgers Dobell, pp. 37-44.
12) *Ibid.,* March, 1978, p. 44. (New translations of the Book of Genesis 2·18 are now saying that Eve should be considered "a power equal to" Adam—See February issue of *Biblical Archeology Review,* article by R. David Freedman.)
13) Hippolytus, *Refutationis Omnium Haeresium,* 6·18, as quoted by Pagels, Elaine in *The Gnostic Gospels,* p. 60.
14) *Apocryphon of John,* 1·31-2·9-14, in *NHL,* p. 99.

15) Pagels, Elaine, *op. cit.*, p. 62—adapted from *Apocryphon of John* 4·34-5·7, in *NHL*, p. 101.

16) *Gospel to the Hebrews,* cited in Origen, *Commentarium in Johannes,* 2·12, as quoted by Pagels, Elaine in *The Gnostic Gospels,* p. 62.

17) *Gospel of Philip,* 52·24, in *NHL,* p. 136.

18) Ghose, Sri Aurobindo, *Life Divine,* Vol II, Chapter 23, as quoted by Saint-Hilaire in *Future Evolution,* p. 31.

19) Vivekananda, Swami, *Notes of Class Talks and Lectures,* (Vol. VI of the *Complete Works,* p. 90 et. seq.), as quoted by Rolland, Romain in *The Life of Vivekananda and the Universal Gospel,* p. 217.

20) Rolland, Romain, *The Life of Ramakrishna,* pp. 76, 77.

II—Chapter 3

1) Notovitch, Nicolas, *St. Issa,* IV·1-4, as quoted by Bock, Janet in *Jesus Mystery,* p. 210, (emphasis added).

2) Paramananda, Swami, *Christ and Oriental Ideals,* p. 18.

3) Bock, Janet, *op. cit.,* p. 192.

4) *Ibid.,* pp. 33, 34.

5) Roy, Sri Dilip Kumar, *Bhagavad Gita,* p. 110.

6) Kaur, Sardarni Premka, *Guru Nanak,* p. 14.

7) *Ibid.,* p. 14.

8) Caras, Paul, *The Gospel of Buddha,* p. 34.

9) Matthew 4·4, KJRV.

10) Kaur, S. P., *op. cit.,* p. 28.

11) *Ibid.,* pp. 29, 30, 31, (emphasis added).

12) *Ibid.,* pp. 56, 57, (emphasis added).

13) *Ibid.,* p. 57.

14) *The Shrimad Bhagavatam,* Vol. II, p. 1135.

15) Kaur, S. P. *op. cit.,* p. 101.

16) *Ibid.,* p. 57.

17) *Shrimad Bhagavatam,* Vol. II, p. 1191.

18) Kaur, S. P. *op. cit.,* p. 86.

19) *Ibid.,* p. 68.

20) *Ibid.,* p. 68.

21) *Ibid.,* pp. 68, 69.

22) *Acts of John,* 93, in *NTA II,* p. 227, as quoted by Pagels, Elaine in *The Gnostic Gospels,* p. 88.

23) John 3·6, KJRV.

24) *Acts of John,* 88, 89, in *NTA II,* p. 225, as quoted by Pagels, Elaine, *op. cit.,* pp. 87, 88.

25) Roy, Sri D.K. *op. cit.,* p. 131.

26) Caras, Paul, *op. cit.,* p. 225.

27) Matthew 14·31, KJRV.

28) Caras, Paul, *op. cit.,* p. 213.

29) Kaur, S. P. *op. cit.,* p. 93.

30) *Shrimad Bhagavatam,* Vol. II, p. 1164.

31) Matthew 21·21-22, KJRV, (emphasis added).

32) Matthew 17·20, KJRV.

33) *Honolulu Advertiser,* 12/26/82.

34) Hansen, L. Taylor, *He Walked The Americas,* pp. 48, 150. Used by permission.

35) *Ibid.,* pp. 53, 103.

36) John 10·14, 16, KJRV.

37) Hansen, L. Taylor, *op. cit.,* p. 142.

38) *Ibid.,* p. 52.

II—Chapter 4

1) Yogananda, Paramahansa, *Man's Eternal Quest,* p. 306, as quoted by Bock, Janet in *Jesus Mystery,* p. 141.
2) Ghose, Sri Aurobindo, *Life Divine,* Vol. II, Chapter 27, as quoted by Saint-Hilaire in *Future Evolution,* p. 112.
3) Pagels, Elaine, *The Gnostic Gospels,* p. xx of the Introduction.
4) Baha'i World Faith, *Selected Writings of Baha'u'llah and 'Abdu'l-Baha,* pp. 19, 20, 22, 27, 28. Hereafter cited as *Baha'u'llah.* Used by permission.
5) *Ibid.,* p. 63.
6) Matthew 23·13, KJRV.
7) Matthew 23·3-7, 12, KJRV.
8) Matthew 12·11, 12, KJRV.
9) Kaur, S. P. *Guru Nanak,* pp. 19, 20.
10) *Ibid.,* p. 20.
11) *Ibid.,* p. 84.
12) *Ibid.,* pp. 82, 84.
13) Matthew 6·1-6, KJRV.
14) Notovitch, Nicolas, *St. Issa,* IX·12, 13, VI·15, 16, as quoted by Bock, Janet in *Jesus Mystery,* pp. 214, 218.
15) Kaur, *op. cit.,* p. 46.
16) Ghose, Sri Aurobindo, *The Human Cycle,* Chapter 17, as quoted by Saint-Hilaire in *Future Evolution,* pp. 42, 44.
17) Matthew 7·16, KJRV.
18) Seton, Ernest T. and Julia M., *The Gospel of the Redman,* p. 12.
19) *Honolulu Advertiser,* 10/18/82, p. A-3.
20) Kaur, S. P., *op. cit.,* pp. 33, 63.
21) *Ibid.,* p. 67.
22) *Shrimad Bhagavatam,* Vol. II, p. 1528.
23) Lal, P., *The Dhammapada,* p. 18. Used by permission.

II—Chapter 5

1) Roy, Sri D. K., *Bhagavad Gita,* p. 156.
2) Lal, P., *The Dhammapada,* pp. 157, 161, 162, 166.
3) *Ibid.,* pp. 39, 45.
4) Roy, Sri D. K., *op. cit.,* p. 12.
5) *Ibid.,* p. 18.
6) *Ibid.,* p. 18.
7) *Ibid.,* p. 12.
8) *Ibid.,* p. 12.
9) I Corinthians 13·2-10, 13, KJRV, (emphasis added).
10) Kaur, S. P., *Guru Nanak,* p. 14.
11) Ghose, Sri Aurobindo, *Synthesis of Yoga,* Part 3, Chapter 1, p. 523.
12) Ghose, Sri Aurobindo, *Essays on the Gita,* p. 570.
13) Roy, Sri. D. K. *op. cit.,* p. 78.
14) *Ibid.,* pp. 20, 21, 24.
15) *Ibid.,* pp. 60, 61.
16) *Ibid.,* pp. 130, 131, 136, 138, 142, 152.
17) White, Ellen G., *Steps to Christ,* p. 11. Used by permission.
18) Roy, Sri D. K., *op. cit.,* pp. 137, 138, 139, 141, 142, 143, 144, (emphasis added).
19) Baha'i World Faith: *Baha'u'llah,* p. 216.
20) Matthew 19·19, KJRV.
21) Matthew 18·11, KJRV.

22) Hansen, L. Taylor, *He Walked The Americas*, p. 45.

23) Bock, Janet, *Jesus Mystery*, p. 192.

24) Moody, Dr. Raymond, *Reflections on Life After Life*, p. 96. Used by permission.

25) Kaur, S. P., *op. cit.*, pp. 90, 124, (emphasis added).

26) Luke 6·27-31, 35-38, 42, KJRV.

27) Kaur, S. P., *op. cit.*, p. 24.

28) Colossians 3·12-14, *The Good News Bible*, except for last line, KJRV.

29) Das, Bhagavan, *The Essential Unity of All Religions*, pp. 298, 300, as quoted by Bock, Janet, *op. cit.*, pp. 194, 201.

30) *Ibid.*, p. 298, as quoted by Bock, J., *op. cit.*, p. 194.

31) *Ibid.*, p. 298, 311, as quoted by Bock, J., *op. cit.*, p. 194, 200.

32) *Ibid.*, p. 298, as quoted by Bock, J., *op. cit.*, p. 195.

33) Lal, P., *op. cit.*, pp. 75, 83, 102.

34) Satprakashananda, Swami, *Hinduism and Christianity*, p. 23, as quoted by Bock, J., *op. cit.*, p. 197.

35) Lal, P., *op. cit.*, pp. 39, 107.

36) Paramananda, *Christ and Oriental Ideals*, p. 128.

37) *Shrimad Bhagavatam*, Vol. II, p. 1189.

38) Baha'i World Faith, *op. cit.*, pp. 215, 216.

39) Attenborough, Sir Richard, *The Words of Gandhi*, p. 22.

40) Das, Bhagavan, *op. cit.*, p. 309, as quoted by Bock, J., *op. cit.*, p. 201.

41) Kaur, S. P., *op. cit.*, p. 104.

II—Chapter 6

1) Satprakashananda, Swami, *Hinduism and Christianity*, p. 28, as quoted by Bock, Janet in *Jesus Mystery*, p. 194.

2) John 1·1, KJRV.

3) Kaur, Sardarni Premka, *Guru Nanak*, pp. 50, 51, (emphasis added).

4) *Ibid.*, pp. 53, 56.

5) Matthew 6·9, KJRV, (emphasis added).

6) Kaur, S. P., *op. cit.*, p. 96.

7) Das, Bhagavan, *The Essential Unity of All Religions*, p. 60, as quoted by Bock, J., *op. cit.*, p. 203.

8) *Ibid.*, p. 62, as quoted by Bock, J., *op. cit.*, p. 204.

9) *Ibid.*, p. 62, as quoted by Bock, J., *op. cit.*, p. 204.

10) Bock, Janet, *op. cit.*, p. 137.

11) Attenborough, Richard, *The Words of Gandhi*, p. 21.

12) Roy, Sri Dilip Kumar, *Bhagavad Gita*, pp. 108, 109.

13) Attenborough, R., *op. cit.*, p. 17.

14) Romans 13·11-14, composite using *The Good News Bible* and KJRV.

15) Prabhavananda, Swami and Manchester, Frederick, *Upanishads*, p. 142.

16) M., *The Gospel of Sri Ramakrishna*, p. 3.

17) *Ibid.*, p. 5.

18) *Ibid.*, p. 6—Footnote.

19) Kaur, S. P. *op. cit.*, pp. 26, 27, 40.

20) *Ibid.*, p. 40.

21) *Ibid.*, p. 48.

II—Chapter 7

1) Roy, Sri D. K., *Bhagavad Gita*, p. 140.

2) *Ibid.*, pp. 152, 153.

3) Carus, Paul, *The Gospel of Buddha*, pp. 73-75, entire conversation, (emphasis added).

4) *Ibid.,* pp. 75, 76.

5) Luke 11·41, *TLB.*

6) Baha'i World Faith: *Baha'u'llah,* pp. 134, 135, (emphasis added).

7) Matthew 19·24, KJRV.

8) *Sanathana Sarathi,* (Magazine of Prashanthi Nilayamashram), "The Universe as Guru," as seen in the film *The Universal Teacher,* produced by SAI Foundation.

9) Lal, P., *The Dhammapada,* p. 22.

10) Matthew 19·29 and Luke 18·30, KJRV.

11) Matthew 19·21, Luke 12·22-34, KJRV, (emphasis added).

12) Roy, Sri D. K., *op. cit.,* p. 139.

13) II Corinthians 9·9-12, *TLB.*

14) Baha'i World Faith, *op. cit.,* p. 130.

15) Matthew 25·34-36, *TLB.*

16) Matthew 25·40, *TLB.* (emphasis added).

17) Matthew 25·46, *TLB.*

18) Kaur, S. P. *Guru Nanak,* pp. 77, 99.

19) Ghose, Sri Aurobindo, *Life Divine,* Vol. II, Chapter 27, as quoted by Saint-Hilaire in *Future Evolution,* p. 112, (emphasis added).

20) Lal, P., *op. cit.,* p. 22.

II—Chapter 8

1) Lal, P., *The Dhammapada,* pp. 80, 93, 94.

2) Luke 6·38, KJRV.

3) Cayce, Hugh Lynn, *Earth Changes Update,* p. 36.

4) *West Hawaii Today,* July 31, 1979, p. 10.

5) *Ibid.,* 7/31/79, p. 11.

6) *Ibid.,* 7/31/79, pp. 10, 11.

7) *Ibid.,* 7/31/79, p. 10.

8) *Ibid.,* 7/31/79, p. 11.

9) *Rocky Mountain News,* 5/24/78, p. 64.

10) *Ibid.,* 5/24/78, p. 64.

11) Stevenson, Dr. Ian, *Ten Cases in India* and *Twenty Cases Suggestive of Reincarnation,* as recounted in the *National Enquirer,* 2/14/78, p. 37.

12) Roy, Sri D. K. *Bhagavad Gita,* pp. 93-96.

13) *Ibid.,* pp. 133, 134, (emphasis added).

14) *Ibid.,* pp. 139, 140,

15) *Ibid.,* pp. 134, 135, 137, 162-164.

16) *Ibid.,* pp. 126, 127, (emphasis added).

17) *Shrimad Bhagavatam,* Vol. II, p. 1512.

18) Roy, Sri D. K. *op. cit.,* pp. 167-170.

19) *Ibid.,* p. 172.

20) *Ibid.,* pp. 140, 141, (emphasis added).

21) Ezekiel 33·10-11, 14-20, KJRV, (emphasis added).

22) *Shrimad Bhagavatam,* Vol. I, Introduction, p. 27.

23) Luke 15·7, KJRV.

24) Luke 15·24, KJRV.

25) Luke 15·31-32, KJRV.

26) Roy, Sri D. K. *op. cit.,* pp. 97, 99, 120, 121, (emphasis added).

II—Chapter 9

1) Ghose, Sri Aurobindo, *Life Divine,* Vol. II, Chapter 23, as quoted by Saint-Hilaire in *Future Evolution,* p. 27.

2) *Honolulu Advertiser,* 5/20/82, B-3.

3) Ghose, Sri Aurobindo, *Savitri,* Book II, Canto XI, p. 271, and Book VI, Canto II, p. 460.

4) Roy, Sri D. K., *Bhagavad Gita,* p. 135.

5) II Peter 3·8, KJRV.

6) Ghose, Sri Aurobindo, *Life Divine,* Vol. II, Chapters 23, 27, 28, as quoted by Saint-Hilaire, *op. cit.,* pp. 30, 31, 33, 34, 118-120, 137, 139.

7) Bock, Janet, *Jesus Mystery,* p. 143.

8) Matthew 17·5, KJRV.

9) Matthew 17·11-13, KJRV, (emphasis added).

10) Matthew 11·10, 11, 14, 15, KJRV, (emphasis added).

11) John 5·14, KJRV, (emphasis added).

12) John 9·2, 3, KJRV.

13) Bock, J., *op. cit.,* pp. 143, 144.

14) Matthew 18·6, KJRV.

15) Ghose, Sri Aurobindo, *Essays on The Gita,* "Message of the Gita," pp. 569, 570, 571.

PART III—Chapter 1

1) Roy, Sri D. K., *Bhagavad Gita,* p. 138.

2) Ghose, Sri Aurobindo, *Savitri,* Book, VI, Canto I, p. 424, Book X, Canto IV, p. 656, Book II, Canto V, p. 160, Book II, Canto XI, p. 271, and Book VI, Canto II, p. 460.

3) White, Ellen G., *Steps To Christ,* pp. 9, 10, 85, 87.

4) Ghose, Sri Aurobindo, *op. cit.,* Book X, Canto III, p. 624, and Book II, Canto XII, as quoted by Roy, Sri D. K. in *The Message of Savitri: Conveyed Through a few Jewelled Sayings.* Used by permission.

5) Baha'i World Faith, *Baha'u'llah,* pp. 105, 106, (emphasis added).

6) Lal, P., *The Dhammapada,* pp. 59, 152.

7) *Ibid.,* p. 51.

8) White, E. G. *op. cit.,* pp. 85, 86.

9) Bock, J., *Jesus Mystery,* p. 192.

10) Osborne, Arthur, *Ramana Maharshi and the Path of Self-Knowledge,* p. 143. Used by permission.

11) Brown, Joseph Epes, *Sacred Pipe,* pp. 6, 7.

12) *Ibid.,* p. xvii of the Introduction.

13) Schultes, Richard Evans and Hofmann, Albert, *Plants of the Gods,* pp. 9, 61, 82.

14) *Ibid.,* p. 61.

15) *The American Heritage Dictionary,* p. 1055, roots of the word.

16) *Shrimad Bhagavatam,* Vol. II, p. 1111.

17) Schultes and Hofmann, *op. cit.,* p. 99.

18) *Ibid.,* p. 143.

19) *Ibid.,* p. 143, second quote being a quote from J. S. Slotkin, (emphasis added).

20) Ferguson, Marilyn, *The Aquarian Conspiracy,* p. 374. Used by permission.

21) *Ibid.,* p. 375.

22) *Ibid.,* p. 375.

23) *Ibid.,* p. 375, footnote.

24) Boyd, Doug, *Rolling Thunder,* pp. 51, 247, 248. Used by permission.

25) *Ibid.,* p. 248.

26) Moody, Dr. Raymond, *Life After Life,* p. 162.

27) *Ibid.,* p. 162.

28) Prabhavananda, S. and Manchester, F., *Upanishads,* pp. 17, 32-36, 63, 65, 66, (emphasis added).

29) Ghose, Sri Aurobindo, *op. cit.,* Book III, Canto IV, p. 339.

III—Chapter 2
1) Revelations 8·8-9, KJRV.
2) *Shrimad Bhagavatam,* Vol. I, p. 104.
3) *Ibid.,* Vol. I, p. 591, (emphasis added).
4) *Hawaii Tribune Herald,* 9/18/81, p. 24.
5) *Ibid.,* 9/18/81, p.24.
6) *Ibid.,* 9/18/81, p.24.
7) *Ibid.,* 9/18/81, p.24.
8) *Honolulu Advertiser,* 11/9/82, B-2.
9) *New Age Magazine,* July/August, 1976, "Schooling with the Dolphins," pp. 75, 78. Reprinted with permission. All rights reserved.
10) Lal, P., *The Dhammapada,* pp. 122, 129.

III—Chapter 3
1) Lal, P., *The Dhammapada,* pp. 107, 108, 123, 135.
2) Osborne, Arthur, *The Teachings of Ramana Maharshi,* pp. 41, 42, (first paragraph of quote), *Maharshi's Gospel,* Vol. II, p. 49, as quoted by Osborne, A., *op. cit.,* pp. 36, 37 (second and third paragraphs of quote—emphasis added).
3) *Shrimad Bhagavatam,* Vol. II, pp. 1440, 1441.
4) Kaur, S. P., *Guru Nanak,* pp. 67, 77, (emphasis added).
5) *Talks With Sri Ramana Maharshi,* pp. 252, 272, 633, as quoted by Osborne, Arthur, *op. cit.,* pp. 38, 40, 41.
6) Osborne, Arthur, *The Path of Self-Knowledge,* p. 185 (first line of quote), *Day By Day With Bhagavan,* Vol. II, p. 181, (lines 2 and 3 of quote), *Who Am I?,* p. 44 (line 4 of quote), Osborne, A. *The Path of Self-Knowledge,* p. 185 (second paragraph of quote), all as quoted by Osborne, Arthur, in *The Teachings of Ramana Maharshi,* pp. 108-110.
7) Roy, Sri D. K., *Bhagavad Gita,* pp. 118, 183, (emphasis added).
8) Baha'i World Faith, *Baha'u'llah,* p. 100.
9) Brown, J. E., *Sacred Pipe,* p. xx of the Introduction.
10) *Honolulu Advertiser,* 11/25/82, C-6.
11) Boyd, Doug, *Rolling Thunder,* p. 230.
12) *Ibid.,* pp. 51, 52, (emphasis added except for **"all"**).
13) Ghose, Sri Aurobindo, *Life Divine,* Vol. I, Chapter 1 and *Life Divine,* Vol II, Chapter 27, as quoted by Saint-Hilaire, *Future Evolution,* pp. 25, 118.
14) Carter, Mary Ellen, *Edgar Cayce on Prophecy,* p. 37. Used by permission.
15) Prabhavananda, Swami, *The Sermon On The Mount According to Vedanta,* p. 22.

III—Chapter 4
1) Timms, Moira, *Prophecies and Predictions: Everyone's Guide to the Coming Changes,* pp. 136, 137. Hereafter cited as *Prophecies and Predictions.*
2) Waters, Frank, *Book of the Hopi,* pp. 37, 38.
3) *Ibid.,* p. 310.
4) Timms, M., *op. cit.,* p. 138.
5) *Ibid.,* p. 139.
6) *Ibid.,* p. 146.
7) Boyd, Doug, *Rolling Thunder,* p. 139.
8) Timms, M., *op. cit.,* pp. 145, 146.
9) Boyd, D., *op. cit.,* p. 139.
10) *Hawaii Tribune Herald,* 1/19/81, p. 2.

11) Boyd, D., *op. cit.*, p. 199.

12) Matthew 7-6, KJRV.

13) Hansen, L. Taylor, *He Walked The Americas*, pp. 43, 44, 79, 167, 168, 170-172.

14) *Ibid.*, p. 209.

15) *Ibid.*, pp. 223, 224.

16) Boyd, D., *op. cit.*, p. 199.

17) Jochmans, J. R. *Rolling Thunder: The Coming Earth Changes*, p. 39.

18) Timms, M., *op. cit.*, p. 137.

19) Boyd, D., *op. cit.*, p. 51.

III—Chapter 5

1) Timms, Moira, *Prophecies and Predictions*, pp. 81, 82.

2) *Science Magazine*, Vol. 218, 12/3/82, p. 1004.

3) *Honolulu Advertiser*, 1/31/82, A-18.

4) Timms, M., *op. cit.*, pp. 81-83.

5) *Honolulu Advertiser*, 1/14/83.

6) Carter, Mary E., *Edgar Cayce on Prophecy*, p. 180.

7) *Ibid.*, pp. 100-113.

8) Hansen, L. Taylor, *He Walked The Americas*, p. 214.

9) Carter, M. E., *op. cit.*, p. 181.

III—Chapter 6

1) Willoya, William and Brown, Vinson, *Warriors of the Rainbow*, pp. 33, 34. Used by permission.

2) *Ibid.*, p. 34.

3) *Shrimad Bhagavatam*, Vol. II, p. 1592 footnote.

4) *Ibid.*, Vol. II, pp. 1656, 1657.

III—Chapter 7

1) *Shrimad Bhagavatam*, Vol. I, Introduction pp. 4, 5, 7, 9, Vol. II, pp. 1657, 1658, 1664, 1665.

2) Matthew 24-4-44, Mark 13-5-37, Luke 21-8-36, KJRV.

III—Chapter 8

1) *Los Angeles Times*, 8/26/82, Section 2.

2) *Ibid.*, 8/26/82, Section, 2-p. 4.

3) *Hamanitas/International Human Rights Committee*, letter written by Joan Baez, 934 Santa Cruz Ave., Menlo Park, California 94025.

4) Selections of **Ruthless Rulers** made in part from Jack Anderson's article entitled "The World's Worst Leaders," *Parade Magazine*, 1/9/83, pp. 4-7.

5) *Washington Post*, 1/27/82, as quoted by Martin Sheen in a letter from *CISPES*.

6) Matthew 24-12, KJRV.

7) *Honolulu Advertiser*, 1/21/83, A-14.

8) Anderson, Jack, *op. cit.*, as per note #4, this chapter.

9) Boyd, D., *Rolling Thunder*, pp. 146-148.

10) *Honolulu Advertiser*, 12/11/82, C-1.

11) *Our Constitution, Textbook on Citizenship*, p. 335, (emphasis added).

12) Anderson, Jack, *op. cit.*, as per note #4, this chapter.

13) *Toronto Sun*, as quoted by *Watchtower*, Jehovah's Witnesses, 12/15/82 issue, p. 11.

14) *American Heritage Dictionary*, p. 779—m, definition #28, p. 1478—x, definition #1.

15) *Hawaii Tribune Herald*, 11/30/82, p. 1.
16) *Is Planet Earth on the Brink?*, Jehovah's Witnesses.
17) *Honolulu Advertiser*, 1/22/82, A-14.
18) *Ibid.*, 1/30/82.
19) Keyes, Ken, *The Hundredth Monkey*, p. 20.
20) *Honolulu Advertiser*, 11/11/82, A-16.
21) Armstrong, Herbert, *Are We Living in the Last Days?*, Ambassador College, 1971.
22) *Honolulu Advertiser*, 12/12/82, I-7.
23) *Ibid.*, 12/12/82, I-7.
24) *Ibid.*, 12/12/82, I-7.
25) *Time Magazine*, 12/6/82 issue, p. 30.
26) *Honolulu Advertiser*, 11/12/82, (emphasis added).
27) Attenborough, Richard, *The Words of Gandhi*, p. 89.
28) *Ibid.*, p. 91.

III - Chapter 9
1) Revelations 2, 3·1-6.
2) Revelations 3·7-13.
3) Revelations 3·14-22.
4) Revelations 4.
5) Revelations 5.
6) Revelations 6·2.
7) Revelations 6·3-4.
8) Revelations 6·5-6.
9) *Time Magazine*, 1/10/83 issue, p. 43, except for Mexico, *Time* issue 12/20/82, p. 30.
10) *Time Magazine*, 12/20/82, p. 30.
11) *Honolulu Advertiser*, 11/28/82, p. G-3.
12) *Ibid.*, 11/28/82, p. G-3.
13) *Ibid.*, 9/7/82, p. D-6.
14) *Ibid.*, 9/7/82, p. D-6.
15) *Ibid.*, 9/13/82, F-11.
16) *Time Magazine*, 12/20/82, p. 30-32.
17) *Honolulu Advertiser*, 11/28/82, p. G-3.
18) *Wall Street Journal*, Western Edition, 12/2/82, p. 1.
19) *Parade Magazine*, 11/28/82, p. 10.
20) *Awake!*, Jehovah's Witnesses, 12/8/82 issue, p. 29.
21) *Parade Magazine*, 11/28/82, p. 10.
22) *Awake!*, Jehovah's Witnesses, 12/8/82 issue, p. 29.
23) *Parade Magazine*, 11/28/82, p. 10.
24) *Honolulu Advertiser*, 11/27/82, p. G-1.
25) *Ibid.*, 12/12/82.
26) *Ibid.*, 7/15/82, p. D-5.
27) *Ibid.*, 10/17/82, p. A-24.
28) *Ibid.*, 12/17/82, p. A-36.
29) *Ibid.*, 4/3/82, p. C-7.
30) *Ibid.*, 7/17/82, p. D-5.
31) *Ibid.*, 2/27/82, p. C-4.
32) *Ibid.*, 7/15/82, p. D-5.
33) *Ibid.*, 1/7/83.
34) *Ibid.*, 12/16/82, p. A-1.
35) *Ibid.*, 12/25/82, p. A-3.
36) *Ibid.*, 12/19/82.
37) *Ibid.*, 8/19/82, p. A-23.

38) *National Advisory Council on Economic Opportunity,* 12th Report, 8/80; and 1982 Department of Labor statistics.
39) *Honolulu Advertiser,* 12/15/82, p. D-5.
40) *Ibid.,* 10/21/82.
41) *Ibid.,* 12/1/82, p. C-12.
42) *Hawaii Tribune Herald,* 12/2/82.
43) *Honolulu Advertiser,* 12/16/82, p. A-18.
44) *Ibid.,* 3/19/82, p. B-6.
45) *Hawaii Tribune Herald,* 1/24/83, p. 2.
46) *Ibid.,* 1/16/83, p. 14.
47) *Honolulu Advertiser,* 8/11/82, p. E-2.
48) *Ibid.,* 12/12/82, p. D-8.
49) *Ibid.,* 12/12/82, p. D-8.
50) *Ibid.,* 12/12/82, p. D-8.
51) *Ibid.,* 11/7/81, p. B-7.
52) *Ibid.,* 2/1/83, p. C-1.
53) *National Taxpayers Union Newsletter,* 1982.
54) *Los Angeles Times,* 1/10/82, Part IV.
55) *Honolulu Advertiser,* 1/7/83, p. A-1.
56) *Ibid.,* 1/6/83, p. B-5.
57) *Ibid.,* 2/14/82, p. H-1.
58) *Ibid.,* 1/14/82, p. E-12.
59) *Hawaii Tribune Herald,* 1/16/83, p. 6.
60) *Honolulu Advertiser,* 2/7/83, p. A-8.
61) Keyes, Ken, *The Hundredth Monkey,* p. 82.
62) *Honolulu Advertiser,* 11/10/81, p. C-1.
63) *Ibid.,* 3/15/83.
64) *Ibid.,* 12/7/82.
65) *The Hunger Project,* 1982 statistics.

III—Chapter 10

1) *Time Magazine,* 10/24/77 issue.
2) *Ibid.,* 10/24/77 issue.
3) *Honolulu Advertiser,* 12/15/82, p. J-1.
4) *Hawaii Tribune Herald,* 11/23/82.
5) *Time Magazine,* 10/24/77 issue.
6) *Ibid.,* 8/2/82 issue.
7) *Honolulu Advertiser,* 4/2/82, p. E-1.
8) Revelations 16·2.
9) *Honolulu Advertiser,* 7/15/82, p. D-4.
10) *Hawaii Tribune Herald,* 8/9/81, p. 11.
11) *Watchtower,* Jehovah's Witnesses, 12/15/82 issue, p. 3.
12) *Honolulu Advertiser,* 12/29/80, p. C-2.
13) *Ibid.,* 5/20/81, p. A-17.
14) *Newsweek Magazine,* 11/30/82 issue.
15) *Honolulu Advertiser,* 8/11/82, p. E-6.
16) *Ibid.,* 12/29/80, p. C-2.
17) *Ibid.,* 12/6/82, p. C-1.
18) *Ibid.,* 11/23/82.
19) *Parade Magazine,* 1/25/81, Intelligence Report, p. 18.
20) *Honolulu Advertiser,* 11/22/82, p. A-1.
21) *Ibid.,* 5/6/81, p. A-13.
22) *Ibid.,* 5/23/82, T.V. Section, p. 3.

23) *Ibid.*, 4/1/82, p. A-16.
24) *Ibid.*, 4/27/82, p. A-10.

III—Chapter 11
1) *Hawaii Tribune Herald*, 1/26/82, p. 10.
2) *Ibid.*, 1/17/83, p. 1.
3) *Honolulu Advertiser*, 1/17/83, p. A-1.
4) *Ibid.*, 1/17/82, p. A-1, (emphasis added).
5) *Children as Teachers of Peace*, p. 74. Used by permission.
6) Bianchini, Frank, Keaau, Hawaii, written as part of a school assignment on the environment.
7) Ozan, Julietta, Pahoa, Hawaii, written as part of a school assignment on the environment.
8) II Timothy 3-9, KJRV.
9) Kaur, S. P. *Guru Nanak*, p. 77.
10) *Honolulu Advertiser*, 12/18/82, p. F-2.
11) *Ibid.*, 1/10/83, p. B-1.
12) *Hawaii Tribune Herald*, 9/29/82, p. 29.
13) Schul, Bill, *The Psychic Power of Animals.*
14) *Hawaii Tribune Herald*, 12/20/82.

III—Chapter 12
1) Revelations 6·7-8, KJRV.
2) *Honolulu Advertiser*, 11/10/82, p. E-1.
3) *Parade Magazine*, 5/9/82, Significa Section.
4) Revelations 6·9-11, KJRV.
5) Waters, Frank, *Book of the Hopi*, p. 359.
6) Seton, Julia and Ernest T., *The Gospel of the Redman*, p. 35.
7) *Ibid.*, pp. 37, 38.
8) *Ibid.*, p. 38.
9) *Ibid.*, p. 40.
10) *Ibid.*, p. 3.
11) *Ibid.*, p. 2.
12) Matthew 24·14, KJRV.
13) Daniel 12·4, KJRV.
14) *Time Magazine*, 12/27/82 issue.
15) *Ibid.*, 12/27/82 issue.

III—Chapter 13
1) Lindsey, Hal, *The 1980's: Countdown to Armageddon*, p. 29.
2) *Awake!*, Jehovah's Witnesses, 10/8/80 issue, p. 20.
3) *Hawaii Tribune Herald*, 2/1/81, p. 21.
4) *Ibid.*, 4/11/82, p. 1.
5) Carter, Mary Ellen, *Edgar Cayce on Prophecy*, p. 61.
6) Timms, Moira, *Prophecies and Predictions*, p. 153.
7) *Hawaii Tribune Herald*, 2/5/82, p. 16.
8) Carter, M. E., *op. cit.*, p. 61.
9) *Ibid.*, p. 61.
10) *Ibid.*, p. 62.
11) *Ibid.*, p. 62.
12) *Hawaii Tribune Herald*, 1/7/83, p. 2.
13) Carter, M. E., *op. cit.*, p. 62.
14) *Honolulu Advertiser*, 12/25/82, p. E-8, 9.

15) *Ibid.*, 12/25/82, p. E-9.
16) *Ibid.*, 3/20/83, p. F-1.

III—Chapter 14

1) *Shrimad Bhagavatam,* Vol. II, p. 1658.
2) Luke 21·25, KJRV.
3) Revelations 16·8, 9. 21.
4) *Honolulu Advertiser,* 1/9/80, p. 1.
5) *Hawaii Tribune Herald,* 11/25/82.
6) Luke 21·34-36, Matthew 24·36-39, 44, KJRV.
7) *Honolulu Advertiser,* 3/18/83, p. B-7.

III—Chapter 15

1) *Honolulu Advertiser,* 12/12/82, p. G-6.
2) *Hawaii Tribune Herald,* 1/19/81, p. 2.
3) *Ibid.*, 6/6/82, p. 2.
4) *Ibid.*, 4/21/82, p. 32.
5) *Ibid.*, 11/19/82, p. 5.
6) *Honolulu Advertiser,* 7/22/82, p. A-16.
7) Revelations 16·17.
8) Revelations 9·3-10.
9) *Honolulu Advertiser,* 1/6/83, p. B-1.
10) *Hawaii Tribune Herald,* 2/11/83.
11) Joel 2·30, 31, KJRV.
12) Revelations 6·12-17, KJRV.
13) *Hawaii Tribune Herald,* 6/1/82, p. 4.
14) Timms, M., *Prophecies and Predictions,* p. 175.
15) *Ibid.*, p. 181.
16) *Ibid.*, p. 184.
17) *Ibid.*, p. 45.
18) Levi, *Aquarian Gospel,* 157·29, 30.
19) Ferguson, Marilyn, *The Aquarian Conspiracy,* p. 90.

III—Chapter 16

1) Ghose, Sri Aurobindo, *Savitri,* Book VI, Canto II, pp. 440-441.
2) Timms, Moira, *Prophecies and Predictions,* p. 226.
3) *Los Angeles Times,* 12/30/81.
4) *Nature Conservancy,* 1/2/82, p. 6.
5) *Christian Science Monitor,* 9/13/82, pp. 12, 13.
6) *New York Times,* 11/22/81.
7) Berger, Barbara, *Animalia,* inside cover page.
8) Magadevan, T. M. P., *Ramana Maharshi: The Sage of Arunacala,* p. 72.
9) Lal. P., *The Dhammapada,* p. 129.
10) Baha'i World Faith, *Baha'u'llah,* p. 137.
11) Kaur, S. P., *Guru Nanak,* pp. 58, 59.
12) *Shrimad Bhagavatam,* Vol. II, p. 1576.
13) *Ibid.*, Vol. II, p. 1509.
14) Isaiah 1·11, KJRV.
15) Notovitch, Nicolas, *Saint Issa,* VII·14, as quoted by Bock, J., *Jesus Mystery,* p. 215.
16) Levi, *Aquarian Gospel,* p. 174.
17) Revelations 8·11, 9·18, 20·10, 21·8.
18) Day, David, *The Doomsday Book of Animals: A Natural History of Vanished Species,* pp. 32-37.

435

19) Miller, Leslie, Hilo, Hawaii, written as part of a school assignment on the environment.

20) Walther, Tabatha, Keaau, Hawaii, written as part of a school assignment on the environment.

21) Bianchini, Frank, Keaau, Hawaii, written as part of a school assignment on the environment.

22) *Time Magazine*, 5/22/78, p. 95.

23) *Ibid.*, 5/22/78, p. 95

24) Revelations 16·2, KJRV.

25) *Time Magazine*, 5/22/78, p. 95.

III—Chapter 17

1) *Honolulu Advertiser*, 11/22/81.

2) *Ibid.*, 1/25/81.

3) *Time Magazine*, 9/22/80.

4) *Hawaii Tribune Herald*, 7/6/82.

5) *Honolulu Advertiser*, 11/1/82, p. A-1.

6) *Hawaii Tribune Herald*, 3/26/82, p. 16.

7) *Honolulu Advertiser*, 11/27/81, p. A-15.

8) *Ibid.*, 11/10/82, p. A-14.

9) *Ibid.*, 12/5/82, p. A-16.

10) *Ibid.*, 12/21/82, p. A-10.

11) *Ibid.*, 11/14/81, p. B-10.

12) Revelations 16·4, KJRV.

13) *Honolulu Advertiser*, 3/7/82, p. A-16.

14) *Time Magazine*, 9/22/80, p. 58.

15) *Honolulu Advertiser*, 12/14/81, p. C-8.

16) *Asbury Park Press*, 12/13/82, p. B-9.

17) Revelations 8·10-11, KJRV.

18) Revelations 9·17-19, 20·10, 21·8, KJRV.

19) *Honolulu Advertiser*, 12/9/82.

20) *Ibid.*, 11/11/82.

21) *New York Times*, 5/16/82.

22) Natural Resource Defense Council (NRDC), *Annual Report—1981-'82*, p. 7.

23) Revelations 16·2, KJRV.

24) *Honolulu Advertiser*, 3/11/82, p. B-4.

25) *Greenpeace Examiner*, Winter—1982 edition, p. 14.

26) *Honolulu Advertiser*, 12/16/82.

27) *Not Man Apart*, Friends of the Earth (FOE) publication, 11/82, p. 7.

28) *Ibid.*, 11/82 issue, p. 7.

29) Cheetham, Erika, *The Prophecies of Nostradamus*, p. 409.

III—Chapter 18

1) I John 2·18, 21, 22; 4·1-6, KJRV.

2) II John 4, 6, 7, 9, KJRV.

3) *Honolulu Advertiser*, 1/15/83.

4) Carter, Mary E., *Edgar Cayce on Prophecy*, p. 163.

5) *McCall's Magazine*, 6/82 issue, pp. 47, 48.

6) Robb, Stewart, *Prophecies On World Events By Nostradamus*, p. 139.

7) *Ibid.*, p. 139.

8) *Ibid.*, p. 140.

9) Daniel 7·25, 8·24-25, KJRV, and *TLB*—first line and "changing right to wrong" line.

10) Daniel 11·36-39, 12·4, 10, 12, KJRV and *TLB*—first line to "pleases;" "He shall prosper...unshakeable;" "a god his fathers...fortresses;" "But, Daniel,...it means."
11) Daniel 12·12, KJRV.
12) Revelations 9·1-2, KJRV.
13) Revelations 9·3-10, 17-19, KJRV.
14) Revelations 9·5.
15) Revelations 13·3-4.
16) II Thessalonians 2·3, 9-12, KJRV.
17) *The American Heritage Dictionary,* p. 657, definition #1 and #2.
18) *Time Magazine,* 1/3/83, p. 16.
19) Revelations 13·16-18, KJRV.
20) Revelations 13·16-18, *TLB.*
21) Revelations 13·18, footnote, KJRV and *TLB.*
22) Attenborough, Richard, *The Words of Gandhi,* p. 29.
23) Revelations 7·14-17, KJRV.
24) Notovitch, Nicolas, *Saint Issa,* XII·1-7, as quoted by Bock, Janet, *Jesus Mystery,* p. 222.
25) *Ibid.,* V·23-24, as quoted by Bock, J., *op. cit.,* p. 212.
26) Matthew 19·30.
27) Matthew 24·45-51, Luke 12·45-48, *TLB.*
28) Kaur, S. P. *Guru Nanak,* p. 58.
29) Revelations 16·12-16, KJRV.

III—Chapter 19
1) Revelations 16·17-19, KJRV.
2) *Honolulu Advertiser,* 10/10/82, p. A-24.
3) *Ibid.,* 10/10/82, p. A-24.
4) *Ibid.,* 10/10/82, p. A-24.
5) *Ibid.,* 10/10/82, p. A-24.
6) Ghose, Sri Aurobindo, *Life Divine,* Vol. II, Chapter 28, as quoted by Saint-Hilaire, *Future Evolution,* p. 53.
7) Ezekiel 36·33-38.
8) Ezekiel 37·15-28.
9) Ezekiel 38·1-16.
10) Ezekiel 38·5-6.
11) Ezekiel 38·13.
12) *Honolulu Advertiser,* 9/15/82, p. A-21.
13) *Ibid.,* 3/8/83, p. A-1.
14) *Ibid.,* 3/8/83, p. A-1.
15) *Ibid.,* 10/23/82, p. A-6.
16) *Ibid.,* 1/13/82, p. F-1.
17) *Ibid.,* 1/13/82, p. F-1.
18) *Ibid.,* 1/13/82, p. F-1.
19) *New York Times,* 12/19/82, p. 10.
20) *Ibid.,* 12/19/82, p. 10.
21) *Hawaii Tribune Herald,* 1/27/83, p. 18.
22) *Honolulu Advertiser,* 12/25/82.
23) *Awake!,* Jehovah's Witnesses, 1/8/83, p. 4.
24) *Ibid.,* 1/8/83, p. 5.
25) *Honolulu Advertiser,* 1/5/82, p. C-1.
26) *Ibid.,* 12/25/82, p. A-12.
27) Matthew 18·3-5, 10, 11, 14, KJRV.
28) Attenborough, Richard, *The Words of Gandhi,* p. 22.

29) *Children as Teachers of Peace,* p. 15.

30) *Ibid.,* p. 30.

31) *Ibid.,* p. 53.

32) *Ibid.,* p. 88.

33) Rama, Swami, *Living With the Himalayan Masters,* p. 231.

34) *Ibid.,* p. 232.

35) Attenborough, Richard, *op. cit.,* pp. 88, 92, 97, 99, 100, 101, (emphasis added).

III—Chapter 20

1) Isaiah 3·10-11, KJRV, and *TLB,* 3·12, 14, 15.

2) Baha'i World Faith, *Baha'u'llah,* pp. 64, 138, 139, 208, 209.

3) Kaur, S. P. *Guru Nanak,* pp. 45, 72, 101.

4) Notovitch, N., *Saint Issa,* VII·9-10, VIII·19-20, as quoted by Bock, J., *Jesus Mystery,* pp. 215, 217.

5) Lal, P., *The Dhammapada,* pp. 84, 145, (emphasis added).

6) *Shrimad Bhagavatam,* Vol. II, p. 1660.

7) Matthew 23·13, 14, 25, 27, 33, KJRV and Matthew 23·14-16, 23, 25-26, *TLB.*

8) Sister Lucia, *Fatima in Lucia's Own Words,* p. 104.

9) Revelations 11·18, KJRV.

10) Roy, Sri D. K., *Bhagavad Gita,* pp. 140, 141.

11) Carter, M. E., *Edgar Cayce On Prophecy,* p. 85.

12) *Ibid.,* p. 96.

13) *Cayce Reading* #3976-10.

14) Sister Lucia, *op. cit.,* p. 104.

15) *Cayce Reading* #3976-19.

16) *Cayce Reading* #3976-19.

17) *Cayce Reading* #3976-19.

18) *Cayce Reading* #3976-28.

19) Boyd, Doug, *Rolling Thunder,* p. 47.

20) *Cayce Reading* #3976-24.

21) Waters, Frank, *Book of the Hopi,* p. 408.

22) Boyd, D., *op. cit.,* p. 146.

23) Ezekiel 33·11, 14-16, 20, KJRV.

24) Revelations 17·18, KJRV.

25) Revelations 18·17-19, KJRV.

26) Revelations 18·2, KJRV.

27) Attenborough, R., *The Words of Gandhi,* p. 55.

28) *Ibid.,* p. 57.

29) Carter, M. E., *op. cit.,* p. 84.

III—Chapter 21

1) Revelations 11·1-13.

2) *Shrimad Bhagavatam,* Vol. II, p. 1660.

3) *Hawaii Tribune Herald,* 7/25/80, p. 1.

4) *Ibid.,* 7/25/80, p. 1.

5) *Ibid.,* 7/25/80, p. 1.

6) *Ibid.,* 10/31/80.

7) Revelations 19·11-16, KJRV, (emphasis added).

8) *Shrimad Bhagavatam,* Vol. II, p. 1659, (emphasis added).

9) Acts 1·10-11, KJRV.

10) *Cayce Reading* #5749-4.

11) *New American Standard Bible* and *New International Version,* Matthew 24·8.

12) *Hawaii Tribune Herald*, 3/1/83, p. 10.
13) Carter, M. E. *Edgar Cayce On Prophecy*, p. 92.
14) *Ibid.*, p. 96.
15) Matthew 24·36, 42, 44, KJRV.
16) *Cayce Reading* #262-49.
17) Davidson and Aldersmith, *The Great Pyramid: Its Divine Message*, as quoted by
    Carter, M. E., *op. cit.*, pp. 107-108.
18) *Hawaii Tribune Herald*, 2/4/83, p. 14.

III—Chapter 22
1) Tohei, Koichi, *How To Unify Ki: Coordination of Mind and Body*, pp. 2, 3.
2) Ghose, Sri Aurobindo, *Savitri*, Book III, Canto II, p. 316.
3) Carter, Mary Ellen, *Edgar Cayce on Prophecy*, p. 78.
4) Attenborough, Richard, *The Words of Gandhi*, p. 15.
5) Baha'i World Faith, *Baha'u'llah*, pp. 124, 125.
6) Notovitch, Nicolas, *Saint Issa*, VII·18, as quoted by Bock, Janet, *Jesus Mystery*,
   p. 215.
7) Vivekananda, Swami, *The Yogas and Other Works*, as quoted by Bock, J., *op. cit.*,
   pp. 38, 39.
8) Timms, Moira, *Prophecies and Predictions*, p. 131.
9) Joel 2·28-29 and Acts 2·17-20, KJRV.
10) *Honolulu Advertiser*, 11/30/80, p. A-40.
11) *Ibid.*, 2/28/82.
12) *Ibid.*, 12/31/81, p. A-8.
13) *Ibid.*, 4/23/81, p. C-1.
14) Lennon, John, "Imagine," *Shaved Fish*. Used by permission.
15) Hodgson and Davies, "Quietest Moments," *Even In The Quietest Moments*. Used
    by permission.
16) *Ibid.*, "Fool's Overture," *Even In The Quietest Moments*. Used by permission.
17) *Ibid.*, "Lord Is It Mine," *Breakfast in America*. Used by permission.
18) *Shrimad Bhagavatam*, Vol. II, p. 1665.
19) Acts 2·21, KJRV.
20) Edge, Graeme, "The Dream," *On The Threshold of a Dream*, (emphasis added).
    Used by permission.

III—Chapter 23
1) *The American Heritage Dictionary*, p. 1081, definition #1.
2) *Ibid.*, p. 1081, definition #3.
3) *Ibid.*, p. 1081, roots of word.
4) *Cayce Reading* #281-37, (emphasis added on "New Jerusalem..., as an experience
   of the soul...").
5) Carter, M. E., *Edgar Cayce On Prophecy*, p. 166, (emphasis in "and NOW is"
   added).
6) *Ibid.*, p. 99.
7) Seton, Julia and E. T., *Gospel of the Redman*, p. 94.
8) I Corinthians 15·51-54, KJRV.
9) Roy, Sri Dilip Kumar, *Bhagavad Gita*, p. 46, (emphasis added).
10) Ferguson, Marilyn, *The Aquarian Conspiracy*, p. 185.
11) Revelations 21·9-27; 22·1-5, KJRV.
12) Carter, M. E., *op. cit.*, p. 142.
13) *Shrimad Bhagavatam*, Vol. II, p. 1659.
14) Isaiah 2·4, KJRV.

15) Revelations 21·5, KJRV.
16) *Shrimad Bhagavatam,* Vol. I, p. 984; Revelations 21·1-7.
17) Roy, Sri Dilip Kumar, *op. cit.,* p. 59.
18) Ghose, Sri Aurobindo, *Savitri,* **Great Man:** Book XI, Canto I—pp. 692, 693, Book I, Canto IV—pp. 55, 67, Book X, Canto III—p. 633, Book VII, Canto VI—p. 537; **The Vision:** Book XI, Canto I—pp. 706, 707, 709-711, Book II, Canto VI—p. 200, (emphasis added).

Additional footnotes for III—Chapter 21
19) *East West Journal,* May 1983 issue, p. 11.
20) Jand, K.L., *Immortal Babaji and His Lilas,* pp. 113, 114, 115, Haidakhanwale Baba's Ashram, P.O. Haidakhan Vishwa Mahadham, Via Okhaldoonga, Dist. Nainital, V.P., India, 1982.

ACKNOWLEDGEMENTS
AND SUGGESTED READINGS

The authors would like to thank the following for their kind permission to reprint excerpts from previously published materials:

1) *Baha'i World Faith: Selected Writings of Baha'u'llah and 'Abdu'l-Baha,* Baha'i Publishing Trust, Wilmette, Ill. Copyright © 1956 edition.
2) *Children as Teachers of Peace,* copyright © 1982 by Foundation for Spiritual Alternatives, published by Celestial Arts, Millbrae, CA.
3) *Christ and Oriental Ideals* by Swami Paramananda, published by The Vedanta Centre, Cohasset, Mass. Copyright © 1968.
4) *Edgar Cayce on Prophecy* by Mary Ellen Carter. Copyright © 1968 by the Association for Research and Enlightenment, Inc. Reassigned to the Edgar Cayce Foundation, 1978. (Virginia Beach, Virginia)
5) *Edgar Cayce Readings,* copyright © by the Edgar Cayce Foundation. (Virginia Beach, Va.)
6) *He Walked The Americas* by L. Taylor Hansen, published by Amherst Press, Amherst, Wisconsin. Copyright © 1963.
7) *Life After Life* and *Reflections on Life After Life* by Dr. Raymond Moody, Jr., published by Bantam Books, New York. Copyright © Mockingbird Books, Ga. Copyright © 1975 and 1977.
8) *Rolling Thunder* by Douglas Boyd, published by Random House, Inc., New York. Copyright © 1974.
9) *Steps To Christ* by Ellen White, published by Pacific Press Publishing Association, Mountain View, CA. Copyright © 1956. (Reprinted under new title: *The Greatest Love,* by Vision Books.)
10) *The Aquarian Conspiracy: Personal and Social Transformation in the 1980s,* by Marilyn Ferguson, published by J. P. Tarcher, Inc., Los Angeles, CA. Copyright © 1980. (As well as the incident regarding the statue—"The Buddha of the Future.")
11) *The Aquarian Gospel of Jesus The Christ* by Levi,

published by DeVorss and Co., Marina Del Rey, CA. Copyright © 1907.

12) *The Dhammapada,* translated by P. Lal, published by Farrar, Straus and Giroux, Inc., New York. Copyright © 1967.

13) *The Gospel of Buddha* by Paul Caras, published by The Open Court Publishing Co., La Salle, Ill. Copyright © 1973.

14) *The Jesus Mystery: Of Lost Years and Unknown Travels* by Janet Bock, published by Aura Books, Los Angeles, California. Copyright © 1980.

15) *The Life and Teachings of Guru Nanak: Guru For the Aquarian Age* by Sardarni Premka Kaur, published by the Spiritual Community, San Rafael, California. Copyright © 1972.

16) *The Living Bible* (all verses marked in notes *TLB*), copyright © 1971 by Tyndale House Publishers, Wheaton, IL.

17) *The Nag Hammadi Library,* James M. Robinson, General Editor. Copyright © 1978 by E. J. Brill. Harper & Row, Publishers, Inc., New York.

18) *The Teachings of Ramana Maharshi* and *Ramana Maharshi and the Path of Self-Knowledge* by Arthur Osborne, Samuel Weiser, Inc., York Beach, Maine 03910. Copyright © 1978.

19) *The Upanishads: Breath of the Eternal* by Swami Prabhavananda and Frederick Manchester, published by Vedanta Press, Hollywood, CA. Copyright © 1975.

20) *The Words of Gandhi* by Richard Attenborough. Copyright © 1982 by Newmarket Press, New York.

21) *Warriors of the Rainbow* by William Willoya and Vinson Brown, published by Naturegraph Publishers, Happy Camp, CA. 96039. Copyright © 1962.

22) "Even In The Quietest Moments" Words and Music by Rick Davies and Roger Hodgson. Copyright © 1977 ALMO MUSIC CORP. and DELICATE MUSIC (ASCAP). All Rights Reserved—International Copyright Secured. (From the album bearing the same name.)

23) "Fool's Overture" Words and Music by Rick Davies and Roger Hodgson. Copyright © 1977 ALMO MUSIC CORP. and DELICATE MUSIC (ASCAP). All Rights Re-

served—International Copyright Secured. (From the album *Even In The Quietest Moments*.)

24) "Imagine," by John Lennon, copyright © 1971 Northern Songs Limited. All rights for the U.S.A., Mexico and the Philippines controlled by Maclen Music, Inc. Used by permission. All rights reserved. (From the album *Shaved Fish*.)

25) "Lord Is It Mine?" Words and Music by Roger Hodgson and Rick Davies. Copyright © 1979 ALMO MUSIC CORP. and DELICATE MUSIC (ASCAP). All Rights Reserved—International Copyright Secured. (From the album *Breakfast In America*.)

26) "THE DREAM" Words and Music by GRAEME EDGE. Copyright © 1969 by Gymhouse Ltd., London, England. Sole Selling Agent Duchess Music Corporation, New York, N.Y. for USA and Canada. USED BY PERMISSION. ALL RIGHTS RESERVED. (From the album *On The Threshold of a Dream*.)

We would also like to thank the children of Keaau for letting us reprint portions from their school projects on the environment, as well as the children's parents.

We would also like to thank Johnny Hart and Field Enterprises, Inc., for their permission to reprint the two B. C. cartoons that appear in our book, as well as Gary Trudeau and Universal Press Syndicate for their permission to reprint the Doonesbury cartoon that appears in our book.

Further, we would like to thank Dr. Thelma Moss for the Kirlian photographs of the cut-away tomato leaf and the faith-healer's (Olga Worrall's) hands before and during healing. Plus, the illustration appearing on p. 44 is copyrighted by the Philosophical Research Society and is used with their kind permission. (Seven Spinal Chakras)

Finally, this book would not have been possible without the help of certain individuals who spent many hours preparing, researching, typing, proofreading, etc. We would like to thank Barbara and her whole crew for working round-the-clock to typeset this book. Also, we would like to thank Janet and Richard Bock for all of their kindness and great guidance. Many thanks go to Brother Peter and Karmel for the use of several books from their private libraries, as well as to Cheran and Imamu Mohammad for their suggestions and help in cataloguing articles, researching, etc. Our thanks and pranams to Dadaji (Sri Dilip Kumar Roy) and Ma (Smt. Indira Devi) for sending us so many beautiful, helpful and enlightening books from India, as well as answering many of our questions regarding spiritual matters.

Lastly, our greatest thanks go to three young women whose friendship and service to us over the past few years has been invaluable: First, to Sister Danica Terez for her helpful suggestions and tireless efforts in researching, cataloguing articles, typing, proofreading, and general assistance in the preparation of this book; and last, but hardly the least, to our two illustrators—Kae (Wheel of One God, Mother Nature, The Lord's Return, and The New World), and Celeste (Phoenix cover, The Beast, Disembodied Hand, and The New World) who not only illustrated the book and gave us tremendous suggestions and feedback, but also oversaw the actual production of the book, literally putting it all together!

BIBLIOGRAPHY
AND SUGGESTED READINGS

1) Armstrong, Herbert W., *Are We Living In The Last Days?*, Ambassador College, 1971.

2) Armstrong, Herbert W., *The United States and Britain in Prophecy,* Worldwide Church of God, 1967.

3) Berger, Barbara, *Animalia,* Celestial Arts, Millbrae, California, 1982.

4) Brown, Joseph Epes, *The Sacred Pipe: Black Elk's Account of the Seven Rites of the Oglala Sioux,* Penguin Books, New York, 1953.

5) Cayce, Hugh Lynn, *Earth Changes Update,* A.R.E. Press, Virginia Beach, Virginia, 1980.

6) Cheetham, Erika, *The Prophecies of Nostradamus,* Perigee Books, New York, 1973.

7) Day, David, *The Doomsday Book of Animals: A Natural History of Vanished Species,* The Viking Press, New York, 1981.

8) Ghanananda, Swami and Stewart-Wallace, Sir John, (Editorial Advisors), *Women Saints East and West,* Vedanta Press, Hollywood, California, 1955.

9) Ghose, Sri Aurobindo, *Bases of Yoga,* Sri Aurobindo Ashram, Pondicherry, India, 1981.

10) Ghose, Sri Aurobindo, *Essays on the Gita,* Sri Aurobindo Ashram, Pondicherry, India, 1972.

11) Ghose, Sri Aurobindo, *Savitri,* Sri Aurobindo Ashram, Pondicherry, India, 1970.

12) Ghose, Sri Aurobindo, *The Future Evolution of Man: The Divine Life Upon Earth,* compiled by P. B. Saint-Hilaire, The Theosophical Publishing House, Wheaton, Illinois, 1974.

13) Ghose, Sri Aurobindo, *The Synthesis of Yoga,* Sri Aurobindo Ashram, Pondicherry, India, 1972.

14) Gibran, Kahil, *Jesus The Son of Man: His Words and His Deeds as Told and Recorded by Those Who Knew Him,* Alfred A. Knopf, (Borzoi Books), New York, 1956.

15) *Holy Bible,* King James Revised Version, Harper and Row Publishers, New York, 1952.

16) Jochmans, J. R., *Rolling Thunder: The Coming Earth Changes,* Sun Books, Albuquerque, New Mexico, 1980.

17) Keyes, Kenneth, *The Hundredth Monkey,* Vision Books, Coos Bay, Oregon, 1982.

18) Lucia, Sister, *Fatima in Lucia's Own Words,* edited by Fr. Louis Kondor, Svd., Postulation Centre, Fatima, Portugal, 1976.

19) M., *The Gospel of Sri Ramakrishna,* Translated by Swami Mikhilananda, Sri Ramakrishna Math, Madras, India, 1944.

20) Mahadevan, T.M.P., *Ramana Maharshi: The Sage of Arunacala,* Unwin Paperbacks, London, 1977.

21) McLuhan, T. C., *Touch The Earth,* Promontory Press, New York, 1971.

22) Pagels, Elaine, *The Gnostic Gospels,* Vintage Books, New York, 1979.

23) Prabhavananda, Swami, *The Sermon on the Mount According To Vedanta,* Vedanta Press, Hollywood, California, 1963.

24) Ramacharaka, Yogi, *Mystic Christianity,* Yogi Publication Society, Chicago, U.S.A., 1935.

25) Rama, Swami, *Living With the Himalayan Masters,* Himalayan International Institute of Yoga Science and Philosophy, Honesdale, Pa., 1980.

26) Robb, Stewart, *Prophecies on World Events by Nostradamus,* Liveright Publishing Corp., New York, 1961.

27) Rolland, Romain, *The Life of Ramakrishna,* Advaita Ashram, Calcutta, India, (distributed by Vedanta Press, Hollywood, California), 1974.

28) Rolland, Romain, *The Life of Vivekananda and the Universal Gospel,* Advaita Ashram, Calcutta, India, (distributed by Vedanta Press, Hollywood, California), 1970.

29) Roy, Sri Dilip Kumar, *The Bhagavad Gita: A Revelation,* Indian Book Co., New Delhi, India, 1974.

30) Roy, Sri Dilip Kumar and Devi, Smt. Indira, *Pilgrims of the Stars,* Macmillan Publishing Co., New York, 1973.

31) Schell, Jonathan, *The Fate of the Earth,* Avon Publishers, New York, 1982.

32) Schultes, Richard Evans and Hofmann, Albert, *Plants of the Gods,* McGraw-Hill Book Co., New York, 1979.

33) Seton, Ernest T. and Julia M., *The Gospel of the Redman,* Seton Village, New Mexico, 1963, (available through Naturegraph Publishers, Happy Camp, California).

34) *The Lost Books of the Bible,* Bell Publishing Co., New York, 1979.

35) *The Prophecies of Nostradamus,* Avenal Books, New York, 1975.

36) *The Shrimad Bhagavatam,* Volumes I and II, Rendered in English by C.L. Goswami, M.A., Sastri, Motilal Julan Publishers, Gorakhpur, India, 1971.

37) Timms, Moira, *Prophecies and Predictions: Everyone's Guide to the Coming Changes,* Unity Press, Santa Cruz, California, 1980.

38) Tohei, Koichi, *How To Unify Ki (Coordination of Mind and Body),* Kino Kenkyukai, H.Q., Tokyo, Japan, 1978.

39) Waters, Frank, *Book of the Hopi,* Ballantine Books, New York, 1963.

Additional References and Books Used

1) Lindsey, Hal, *The 1980s: Countdown to Armageddon,* Bantam Books, New York, 1980.

2) Lindsey, Hal, *The Late Great Planet Earth,* Zondervan Publishing House, Grand Rapids, Michigan, 1970.

3) *Our Constitution and Government: Textbook on Citizenship,* United States Government Printing Office, Washington, D. C., 1973.

4) Potter, Rev. Dr., C.F., *The Lost Years of Jesus Revealed,* Revised Edition, Fawcett Gold Medal Publishers, Greenwich, Conn., 1962.

5) *The American Heritage Dictionary of the English Language,* New College Edition, Wm. Morris—Editor, Houghton Mifflin Co., Boston, Mass., 1978.

6) *The World Book Encyclopedia,* (Volume 15), World Book—Childcraft International, Chicago, Ill., 1982 revised edition.

shortened and blows cushioned through prayers and penance. For this reason She has stressed the following: 1) **PEACE** - through reconciliation with God, family, neighbors and countries; 2) **PRAYER**; 3) **PENANCE** - for one's sins and the sins of the world through personal sacrifice such as 4) **FASTING**; and 5) **CONVERSION** - or turning back toward God and leading a spiritual life.

According to the Divine Mother, a visible sign will be given to humanity at the location of Her first appearance in Medugorje, **preceded by three admonitions or warnings.** These warnings will be events on earth that will come in rather quick succession. Conversion to God during this brief period of Grace is essential because after the visible sign is given, those still living will have little time to convert.

The Divine Mother has also recently appeared in Detroit (U.S.A.), Vietnam, Nicaragua, Vienna (Austria), Garabandal (Spain), and elsewhere including Poona, India where Smt. Indira Devi (Ma) had a vision of the Holy Mother in March of 1984 during which she was told to set aside Fridays for devotion to Her by reading *The Novena*, which is stories and prayers of Lord Jesus' life. In addition, reports of statues of the Blessed Mother shedding tears have been coming in from around the world, including the May '84 CNN report from St. John of God Church in Chicago, and from Lebanon where a statue of "Our Lady of Fatima" shed tears of blood constantly for two weeks.

The Mother has told the children that these are the last times She will be appearing on Earth, and that we are very close to the events that She has predicted. This timing confirms a vision given to Pope Leo XIII on **October 13, 1884** in which he was shown that the forces of evil would lose their influence on the world within 100 years. Thus, it is imperative for us to turn back to God immediately and start **living** the message the Divine Mother has given in Yugoslavia—the same message She gave in Fatima. For, as She states, **"You have forgotten that with prayer and fasting you can stop a war from happening. You can suspend natural laws."**[3]

A dramatic example of this Truth was given in 1945 when the atomic bomb destroyed Hiroshima. Eight men living near the blinding epicenter of the nuclear explosion not only miraculously survived the searing hurricane blast and gamma rays while everyone within a mile radius perished, but have also shown no effects of the radiation even though others who were further away continue to die from its lethal effects. "For over 30 years, some 200 scientists have examined these 8 men, trying in vain to determine what could have preserved them from incineration. One of the survivors, Father H. Shiffner, S.J., gave the dramatic answer on T.V. in America: **'In that house, we were living the message of Fatima.'** "[4]

Om Shanti — Peace Be With You!

Footnotes to 1984 Update:
1. *The Catholic Standard and Times*, 2/2/84 issue, "Are the Apparitions in Yugoslavia for Real?", by Theresa M. Karminski.
2. *Ibid.*, 2/2/84 issue, same article.
3. *Ibid.*, 2/2/84 issue, same article.
4. Johnston, Francis, *Fatima — The Great Sign*, Ami Press, Washington, N.J., © 1980, back-cover.

MASS-TRANSFER OPERATIONS

Second Edition

ROBERT E. TREYBAL
Professor of Chemical Engineering
New York University

McGRAW-HILL BOOK COMPANY New York
St. Louis San Francisco Toronto London Sydney

PREFACE

In presenting a revised edition of this book, my purpose has
remained unchanged: to provide a vehicle for teaching, either
through a formal course or through self-study, the techniques
of and the principles of equipment design for the mass-transfer
operations of chemical engineering. These operations largely
remain, as they were when the book was first offered, the
responsibility solely of the chemical engineer, who alone is
expected to be thoroughly familiar with their engineering
applications.

There have been profound changes in the training of
chemical engineers since the appearance of the first edition.
Most universities now include more extensive training in
mathematics and also in the fundamentals of the rate or
transport processes upon which the subjects of this book are
based. Students consequently approach the problems of
design with a greater degree of sophistication in these areas
than ever before. At the same time these changes have not
altered, in my experience, their degree of judgment regarding
the suitability and limitations of methods and results nor of
self-confidence in dealing with engineering problems where
detailed information may be lacking. In some cases the time
devoted to practical design matters has been greatly curtailed,
so that self-study is necessary.

In preparing this revision, I have tried to bear all these
developments in mind yet at the same time keep the subject
accessible to those who have not previously studied the
transport processes. As a result, there are many things which
have been changed, and the others which have not. The
basic approach, which treats the major subjects in categories
of gas-liquid, liquid-liquid, and fluid-solid contact, was
somewhat of an innovation when first presented, and is
retained. The development of the design methods progressively,
rather than as completely generalized procedures later to be
particularized, is also largely retained. These I have found
in my own teaching to be most effective. Subject-matter
changes, for purposes of both modernization and improved
presentation, have been made throughout. The greatest of

these is in the introductory material of the first five chapters, which reflects to some extent the matters referred to above, and in the gas-liquid operations, which reflects the greater attention which has been given the development of these most important subjects. Enthalpy-concentration methods for distillation have been added, as well as a quantitative treatment for absorption and distillation of multicomponent systems. There are many new problems for student practice, all thoroughly student tested, and many problem answers are given. The problems require some such collection of physical property data as "The Chemical Engineers' Handbook," to be at hand, since extensive tables of these are not included.

I remain, as before, greatly indebted to many firms and publications for permission to use their material, and these are acknowledged throughout the text. I am also beholden to an anonymous group of chemical engineers who, at my request and with the cooperation of the publishers, generously provided many excellent suggestions as to what would be appropriate for this revision. Keeping the book to a reasonable length was the only reason for not including more of them.

Robert E. Treybal

CONTENTS

CHAPTER ONE
THE MASS-TRANSFER
OPERATIONS

A substantial number of the unit operations of chemical engineering are concerned with the problem of changing the compositions of solutions and mixtures through methods not necessarily involving chemical reactions. Usually these operations are directed toward separating a substance into its component parts. In the case of mixtures, such separations may be entirely mechanical, such as the filtration of a solid from a suspension in a liquid, the classification of a solid into fractions of different particle size by screening, or the separation of particles of a ground solid according to their density. On the other hand, if the operations involve changes in composition of solutions, they are known as the mass-transfer operations and it is these which concern us here.

The importance of these operations is profound. There is scarcely any chemical process which does not require a preliminary purification of raw materials or final separation of products from by-products, and for these the mass-transfer operations are usually used. One can perhaps most readily develop an immediate appreciation of the part these separations play in a processing plant by observing the large number of towers which bristle from a modern petroleum refinery, in each of which a mass-transfer separation operation takes place. Frequently the major part of the cost of a process is that for the separations.   These separation or purification costs depend directly upon the ratio of final to initial concentration of the separated substances, and if this ratio is large, the product costs are large.   Thus, sulfuric acid is a relatively low-priced product in part because sulfur is found naturally in a relatively pure state, whereas pure uranium is expensive because of the low concentration in which it is found in nature.

The mass-transfer operations are characterized by transfer of a substance through another on a molecular scale.   For example, when water evaporates from a pool into an air stream flowing over the water surface, molecules of water vapor diffuse through those of the air at the surface into the main portion of the air stream, whence they are carried away.   It is not bulk movement as a result of a pressure difference, as in the case of pumping a liquid through a pipe, with which we are primarily concerned.   In the problems at hand, the mass transfer is a result of a concentration difference, or gradient, the diffusing substance moving from a place of high to one of low concentration.

CLASSIFICATION OF THE MASS-TRANSFER OPERATIONS

It is useful to classify the operations and to cite examples of each, in order to indicate the scope of the subject matter of this book, and to provide a vehicle for some definitions of terms which are commonly used.

1. Direct contact of two immiscible phases

This category is by far the most important of all and includes the bulk of the mass-transfer operations.   Here we take advantage of the fact that in a two-phase system of several components at equilibrium, with few exceptions the compositions of the phases are different.   The various components, in other words, are differently distributed between the phases.

In some instances, the separation thus afforded leads immediately to a pure substance because one of the phases at equilibrium contains only one constituent. For example, the equilibrium vapor in contact with a liquid aqueous salt solution contains no salt regardless of the concentration of the liquid.   Similarly the equilibrium solid in contact with such a liquid salt solution is either pure water or pure salt, depending upon which side of the eutectic composition the liquid happens to be. Starting with the liquid solution, one may then obtain a complete separation by boiling off the water.   Alternatively, pure salt or pure water may be produced by partly freezing the solution; or, in principle at least, both may be obtained pure by complete solidification followed by mechanical separation of the eutectic mixture of crystals.   In cases like these, when the two phases are first formed, they are immediately at their final equilibrium compositions, and the establishment of equilibrium is not a time-dependent process.   Such separations, with one exception, are not normally considered to be among the mass-transfer operations.

In the mass-transfer operations, neither equilibrium phase consists of only one component.   Consequently when the two phases are initially contacted, they will not (except fortuitously) be of equilibrium compositions. The system then attempts to reach equilibrium by a relatively slow diffusive movement of the constituents, which transfer in part between the phases in the process. Separations are therefore never complete, although, as will be shown, they can be brought to as near completion as desired (but not totally) by appropriate manipulations.

The three states of aggregation, gas, liquid, and solid, permit six possibilities of phase contact.

Gas-gas. Since with very few exceptions all gases are completely soluble in each other, this category is not practically realized.

Gas-liquid. If all components of the system distribute between the phases at equilibrium, the operation is known as *fractional distillation* (or frequently just *distillation*). In this instance the gas phase is created from the liquid by application of heat; or conversely, the liquid is created from the gas by removal of heat. For example, if a liquid solution of acetic acid and water is partially vaporized by heating, it is found that the newly created vapor phase and the residual liquid both contain acetic acid and water but in proportions at equilibrium which are different for the two phases and different from those in the original solution. If the vapor and liquid are separated mechanically from each other and the vapor condensed, two solutions, one richer in acetic acid and the other richer in water, are obtained. In this way a certain degree of separation of the original components has been accomplished.

Both phases may be solutions, each containing, however, only one common component (or group of components) which distributes between the phases. For example, if a mixture of ammonia and air is contacted with liquid water, a large portion of the ammonia, but essentially no air, will dissolve in the liquid, and in this way the air-ammonia mixture may be separated. The operation is known as *gas absorption*. On the other hand, if air is brought into contact with an ammonia-water solution, some of the ammonia leaves the liquid and enters the gas phase, an operation known as *desorption* or *stripping*. The difference is purely in the direction of solute transfer.

If the liquid phase is a pure liquid containing but one component while the gas contains two or more, the operation is *humidification* or *dehumidification*, depending upon the direction of transfer (this is the exception mentioned earlier). For example, contact of dry air with liquid water results in evaporation of some water into the air (humidification of the air). Conversely, contact of very moist air with pure liquid water may result in condensation of part of the moisture in the air (dehumidification). In both cases, diffusion of water vapor through air is involved, and we include these among the mass-transfer operations.

Gas-solid. Classification of the operations in this category according to the number of components which appear in the two phases is again convenient.

If a solid solution were to be partially vaporized without the appearance of a liquid phase, the newly formed vapor phase and the residual solid would each contain all the original components, but in different proportions, and the operation is *fractional sublimation.* As in distillation, the final compositions are established by interdiffusion of the components between the phases. While such an operation is theoretically possible, practically it is not generally done because of the inconvenience of dealing with solid phases in this manner.

All components may not be present in both phases, however. If a solid which is moistened with a volatile liquid is exposed to a relatively dry gas, the liquid leaves the solid and diffuses into the gas, an operation generally known as *drying*, sometimes as *desorption.* A homely example is the drying of laundry by exposure to air, and there are many industrial counterparts such as the drying of lumber or the removal of moisture from a wet filter cake by exposure to dry gas. In this case, the diffusion is, of course, from the solid to the gas phase. If the diffusion takes place in the opposite direction, the operation is known as *adsorption*. For example, if a mixture of water vapor and air is brought into contact with activated silica gel, the water vapor diffuses to the solid, which retains it strongly, and the air is thus dried. In other instances, a gas mixture may contain several components each of which is adsorbed on a solid but to different extents (*fractional adsorption*). For example, if a mixture of propane and propylene gases is brought into contact with activated carbon, the two hydrocarbons are both adsorbed, but to different extents, thus leading to a separation of the gas mixture.

The case where the gas phase is a pure vapor, such as in the sublimation of a volatile solid from a mixture with one which is nonvolatile, is an operation dependent more on the rate of application of heat than on concentration difference and is essentially nondiffusional. The same is true of the condensation of a vapor to the condition of a pure solid, where the rate depends on the rate of heat removal.

Liquid-liquid. Separations involving the contact of two insoluble liquid phases are known as *liquid-extraction* operations. A simple example is the familiar laboratory procedure: if an acetone-water solution is shaken in a separatory funnel with carbon tetrachloride and the liquids allowed to settle, a large portion of the acetone will be found in the carbon tetrachloride-rich phase and will thus have been separated from the water. A small amount of the water will also have been dissolved by the carbon tetrachloride, and a small amount of the latter will have entered the water layer, but these effects are relatively minor. As another possibility, a solution of acetic acid and acetone may be separated by adding it to the insoluble mixture of water and carbon tetrachloride. After shaking and settling, both acetone and acetic acid will be found in both liquid phases, but in different proportions. Such an operation is known as *fractional extraction*. Another form of fractional extraction may be effected by producing two liquid phases from a single-phase solution by cooling the latter below its critical solution temperature. The two phases which form will be of different composition.

Liquid-solid. When all the constituents are present in both phases at equilibrium, we have the operation of *fractional crystallization*. Perhaps the most interesting examples of this are the special techniques of *zone refining*, used to obtain ultrapure metals and semiconductors, and *adductive crystallization*, where a substance, such as urea, has a crystal lattice which will selectively entrap long straight-chain molecules like the paraffin hydrocarbons but which will exclude branched molecules.

Cases where the phases are solutions (or mixtures) containing but one common component occur more frequently. Selective solution of a component from a solid mixture by a liquid solvent is known as *leaching* (sometimes also as solvent extraction), and as examples we cite the leaching of gold from its ores by cyanide solutions and of cottonseed oil from the seeds by hexane. The diffusion is, of course, from the solid to the liquid phase. If the diffusion is in the opposite direction, the operation is known as *adsorption*. Thus, the colored material which contaminates impure cane sugar solutions may be removed by contacting the liquid solutions with activated carbon, whereupon the colored substances are retained on the surface of the solid carbon.

Solid-solid. Because of the extraordinarily slow rates of diffusion within solid phases, there is no industrial separation operation in this category.

2. Phases separated by a membrane

These operations are used relatively infrequently, although they are rapidly increasing in importance. The membranes operate in different ways, depending upon the nature of the separation to be made. In general, however, they serve to prevent intermingling of two miscible phases. They also prevent ordinary hydrodynamic flow, and movement of substances through them is by diffusion. And they permit a component separation by selectively controlling passage of the components from one side to the other.

Gas-gas. In *gaseous diffusion* or *effusion*, the membrane is microporous. If a gas mixture whose components are of different molecular weights is brought into contact with such a diaphragm, the various components of the gas pass through the pores at rates dependent upon the molecular weights. This leads to different compositions on opposite sides of the membrane and consequent separation of the mixture. In this manner large-scale separation of the isotopes of uranium, in the form of gaseous uranium hexafluoride, is carried out. In *permeation*, the membrane is not porous, and the gas which is transmitted through the membrane first dissolves in it and then diffuses through. Separation in this case is brought about principally by difference in solubility of the components. Thus, helium may be separated from natural gas by selective permeation through fluorocarbon-polymer membranes.

Gas-liquid. These are *permeation* separations where, for example, a liquid solution of alcohol and water is brought into contact with a suitable nonporous membrane, in which the alcohol preferentially dissolves. After passage through the membrane the alcohol is vaporized on the far side.

Liquid-liquid. The separation of a crystalline substance from a colloid, by contact of their solution with a liquid solvent with an intervening membrane permeable only to the solvent and the dissolved crystalline substance, is known as *dialysis*. For example, aqueous beet-sugar solutions containing undesired colloidal material are freed of the latter by contact with water with an intervening semipermeable membrane. Sugar and water diffuse through the membrane, but the larger colloidal particles cannot. *Fractional dialysis* for separating two crystalline substances in solution makes use of the difference in membrane permeability for the substances. If an electromotive force is applied across the membrane to assist in the diffusion of charged particles, the operation is *electrodialysis*. If a solution is separated from the pure solvent by a membrane which is permeable only to the solvent, the solvent diffuses into the solution, an operation known as *osmosis*. This is not a separation operation, of course, but by superimposing a pressure to oppose the osmotic pressure the flow of solvent is reversed, and the solvent and solute of a solution may be separated by *reverse osmosis*. This is one of the processes which may be important in the desalination of sea water.

3. Direct contact of miscible phases

The operations in this category, because of the difficulty in maintaining concentration gradients without mixing of the fluid, are not generally considered practical industrially except in unusual circumstances.

Thermal diffusion involves the formation of a concentration difference within a single liquid or gaseous phase by imposition of a temperature gradient upon the fluid, thus making a separation of the components of the solution possible. In this way, He^3 is separated from its mixture with He^4.

If a condensable vapor, such as steam, is allowed to diffuse through a gas mixture, it will preferentially carry one of the components along with it, thus making a separation by the operation known as *sweep diffusion*. If the two zones within the gas phase where the concentrations are different are separated by a screen containing relatively large-size openings, the operation is called *atmolysis*.

If a gas mixture is subjected to a very rapid *centrifugation*, the components will be separated because of the slightly different forces acting on the various molecules owing to their different masses. The heavier molecules thus tend to accumulate at the periphery of the centrifuge.

4. Use of surface phenomena

Substances which when dissolved in a liquid produce a solution of lowered surface tension (in contact with a gas) are known to concentrate in solution at the liquid surface. By forming a foam of large surface, as by bubbling air through the solution, and collecting the foam, the solute may be concentrated. In this manner, detergents have been separated from water, for example. The operation is known as *foam separation*. It is not to be confused with the flotation processes of the ore-dressing industries, where insoluble solid particles are removed from slurries by collection into froths.

Direct and indirect operations. The operations depending upon contact of two immiscible phases particularly may be further subclassified into two types. The *direct* operations produce the two phases from a single-phase solution by addition or removal of heat. Fractional distillation, fractional crystallization, and one form of fractional extraction are of this type. The *indirect* operations involve addition of a foreign substance and include gas absorption and stripping, adsorption, drying, leaching, liquid extraction, and certain types of fractional crystallization.

It is characteristic of the direct operations that the products are obtained directly, free of added substance, and they are therefore sometimes favored over the indirect if they can be used.

If the separated products are required relatively pure, the disadvantages of the indirect operations which are incurred by addition of a foreign substance are several. The removed substance is obtained as a solution, which in this case must in turn be separated, either to obtain the pure substance or the added substance for reuse, and this represents an expense. The separation of added substance and product can rarely be complete, and this may lead to difficulty in meeting product specifications. In any case, addition of a foreign substance may add to the problems of building corrosion-resistant equipment, and the cost of inevitable losses must be borne. Obviously the indirect methods are used only because they are, in the net, less costly than the direct methods if there is a choice. Frequently there is no choice.

When the separated substance need not be obtained pure, many of these disadvantages may disappear. For example, in ordinary drying, the water vapor–air mixture is discarded since neither constituent need be recovered. In the production of hydrochloric acid by washing a hydrogen chloride–containing gas with water, the acid-water solution is sold directly without separation.

CHOICES AMONG SEPARATION METHODS

The chemical engineer faced with the problem of separating the components of a solution must ordinarily choose among several possible methods. While the choice is usually limited owing to peculiar physical characteristics of the materials to be handled, the necessity for making a decision nevertheless almost always exists. Until the fundamentals of the various operations have been clearly understood, of course, no basis for such a decision is available, but it is well at least to establish the nature of the alternatives at the beginning.

One may sometimes choose between using a mass-transfer operation of the sort discussed in this book and a purely mechanical separation method. For example, in the separation of a desired mineral from its ore, it may be possible to use either the mass-transfer operation of leaching with a solvent or the purely mechanical methods of flotation. Vegetable oils may be separated from the seeds in which they occur by expression or by leaching with a solvent. A vapor may be removed from a mixture with a permanent gas by the mechanical operation of compression or by the mass-transfer operations of gas absorption or adsorption. Sometimes both mechanical and mass-transfer operations are used, especially where the former are incomplete, as in processes for recovering vegetable oils wherein expression is followed by leaching. A more commonplace example is the wringing of water from wet laundry followed by air drying.   It is characteristic that at the end of the operation the substance removed by mechanical methods is pure, while if removed by diffusional methods it is associated with another substance.

One may also frequently choose between a purely mass-transfer operation and a chemical reaction, or a combination of both.   Water may be removed from an ethanol-water solution either by causing it to react with unslaked lime or by special methods of distillation, for example.   Hydrogen sulfide may be separated from other gases either by absorption in a liquid solvent with or without simultaneous chemical reaction or by chemical reaction with ferric oxide.   Chemical methods ordinarily destroy the substance removed, while mass-transfer methods usually permit its eventual recovery in unaltered form without great difficulty.

There are also choices to be made within the mass-transfer operations.   For example, a gaseous mixture of oxygen and nitrogen may be separated by preferential adsorption of the oxygen on activated carbon, by adsorption, by distillation, or by gaseous effusion.   A liquid solution of acetic acid may be separated by distillation, by liquid extraction with a suitable solvent, or by adsorption with a suitable adsorbent. The principal basis for choice in any case is cost: that method which costs the least is usually the one to be used.   Occasionally other factors also influence the decision, however.   The simplest operation, while it may not be the least costly, is sometimes desired because it will be trouble-free.   Sometimes a method will be discarded because of imperfect knowledge of design methods or unavailability of data for design, so that results cannot be guaranteed.   Favorable previous experience with one method may be given strong consideration.

METHODS OF CONDUCTING THE MASS-TRANSFER OPERATIONS

Several characteristics of these operations influence our method of dealing with them and are described in terms which require definition at the start.

Solute recovery and fractionation

If the components of a solution fall into two distinct groups of quite different properties, so that one can imagine that one group of components comprises the solvent and the other group the solute, then separation according to these groups is usually relatively easy, and amounts to a *solute-recovery* or *solute-removal* operation.   For example, a gas consisting of methane, pentane, and hexane may be imagined to consist of methane as solvent with pentane plus hexane as solute, the solvent and solute in this case differing considerably in at least one property, vapor pressure. A simple gas-absorption operation, washing the mixture with a nonvolatile hydro-carbon oil, will easily provide a new solution of pentane plus hexane in the oil, essentially methane-free; and the residual methane will be essentially free of pentane and hexane.   On the other hand, a solution consisting of pentane and hexane alone cannot be classified so readily.   While the component properties differ, the differences are small, and to separate them into relatively pure components requires a different technique. Such separations are termed *fractionations*, and in this case we might use fractional distillation as a method.

Whether a solute-recovery or fractionation procedure is used may depend upon the property chosen to be exploited. For example, to separate a mixture of propanol and butanol from water by a gas-liquid contacting method, which depends on vapor pressures, requires fractionation (fractional distillation) because the vapor pressures of the components are not greatly different. But nearly complete separation of the combined alcohols from water can be obtained by liquid extraction of the solution with a hydrocarbon, using solute-recovery methods because the solubility of the alcohols as a group and water in hydrocarbons is greatly different. The separation of propanol from butanol, however, requires a fractionation technique (fractional extraction or fractional distillation, for example), because all their properties are very similar.

Unsteady-state operation

It is characteristic of unsteady-state operation that concentrations at any point in the apparatus change with time. This may result from changes in concentrations of feed materials, flow rates, or conditions of temperature or pressure. In any case, *batch* operations are always of the unsteady-state type. In purely batch operations, all the phases are stationary from a point of view outside the apparatus, i.e., no flow in or out, even though there may be relative motion within. The familiar laboratory extraction procedure of shaking a solution with an immiscible solvent is an example. In *semibatch* operations, one phase is stationary while the other flows continuously in and out of the apparatus. As an example, we may cite the case of a drier where a quantity of wet solid is contacted continuously with fresh air, which carries away the vaporized moisture until the solid is dry.

Steady-state operation

It is characteristic of steady-state operation that concentrations at any position in the apparatus remain constant with passage of time. This requires continuous, invariable flow of all phases into and out of the apparatus, a persistence of the flow regime within the apparatus, constant concentrations of the feed streams, and unchanging conditions of temperature and pressure.

Stagewise operation

If two insoluble phases are first allowed to come into contact so that the various diffusing substances may distribute themselves between the phases, and if the phases are then mechanically separated, the entire operation, and the equipment required to carry it out, are said to constitute one *stage*, e.g., laboratory batch extraction in a separatory funnel. The operation may be carried on in continuous fashion (steady-state) or batchwise fashion, however. For separations requiring greater concentration changes, a series of stages may be arranged so that the phases flow through the assembled stages from one to the other, for example, in countercurrent flow. Such an assemblage is called a *cascade*.   In order to establish a standard for the measurement of performance, the *ideal*, or *theoretical*, stage is defined as one where the effluent phases are in equilibrium, so that a longer time of contact will bring about no additional change of composition.   The approach to equilibrium realized in any stage is then defined as the *stage efficiency*.

Continuous-contact (differential-contact) operation

In this case the phases flow through the equipment in continuous, intimate contact throughout, without repeated physical separation and recontacting.   The nature of the method requires the operation to be either semibatch or steady-state, and the resulting change in compositions may be equivalent to that given by a fraction of an ideal stage or by many stages.   Equilibrium between two phases at any position in the equipment is never established; indeed, should equilibrium occur anywhere in the system, the result would be equivalent to the effect of an infinite number of stages.

The essential difference between stagewise and continuous-contact operation may then be summarized.   In the case of the stagewise operation the diffusional flow of matter between the phases is allowed to reduce the concentration difference which causes the flow.   If allowed to continue long enough, an equilibrium is established, after which no further diffusional flow occurs.   The rate of diffusion and the time then determine the stage efficiency realized in any particular situation.   On the other hand, in the case of the continuous-contact operation the departure from equilibrium is deliberately maintained, and the diffusional flow between the phases may continue without interruption.   Which method will be used depends to some extent on the stage efficiency that can be practically realized.   A high stage efficiency can mean a relatively inexpensive plant and one whose performance can be reliably predicted.   A low stage efficiency, on the other hand, may make the continuous-contact methods more desirable for reasons of cost and certainty.

DESIGN PRINCIPLES

There are four major factors to be established in the design of any plant involving the diffusional operations: the number of ideal stages or their equivalent, the time of phase contact required, the permissible rate of flow, and the energy requirements.

Number of ideal stages

In order to determine the number of ideal stages required in a cascade to bring about a specified degree of separation, or the equivalent quantity for a continuous-contact device, the equilibrium characteristics of the system and material-balance calculations are required.

Time requirement

In stagewise operations the time of contact is intimately connected with stage efficiency, whereas for continuous-contact equipment the time leads ultimately to the volume or length of the required device.   The factors which help establish the time are several.

Material balances permit calculation of the relative quantities required of the various phases. The equilibrium characteristics of the system establish the ultimate concentrations possible, and the rate of transfer of material between phases depends upon the departure from equilibrium which is maintained. The rate of transfer additionally depends upon the physical properties of the phases as well as the flow regime within the equipment.

It is important to recognize that, for a given degree of intimacy of contact of the phases, the time of contact required is independent of the total quantity of the phases to be processed.

Permissible flow rate

This factor enters into consideration of semibatch and steady-state operations, where it leads to the determination of the cross-sectional area of the equipment. Considerations of fluid dynamics establish the permissible flow rate, and material balances determine the absolute quantity of each of the streams required.

Energy requirements

Heat and mechanical energies are ordinarily required to carry out the diffusional operations. Heat is necessary for the production of any temperature changes, for the creation of new phases (such as vaporization of a liquid), and for overcoming heat-of-solution effects. Mechanical energy is required for fluid and solid transport, for dispersing liquids and gases, and for operating moving parts of machinery.

The ultimate design, consequently, requires us to deal with the equilibrium characteristics of the system, material balances, diffusional rates, fluid dynamics, and energy requirements. In what follows, basic considerations of diffusion rates are discussed first (Part 1) and these are later applied to specific operations. The principal operations, in turn, are subdivided into three categories, depending upon the nature of the insoluble phases contacted, gas-liquid (Part 2), liquid-liquid (Part 3), and solid-fluid (Part 4), since the equilibrium and fluid dynamics of the systems are most readily studied in such a grouping. Part 5 considers briefly some of the less frequently used operations.

PART ONE
DIFFUSION AND
MASS TRANSFER

We have seen that most of the mass-transfer operations which
are used for separating the components of a solution achieve
this result by bringing the solution to be separated into contact
with another insoluble phase.   As will be developed, the rate
at which a component is then transferred from one phase to the
other depends upon a so-called mass-transfer, or rate, coefficient and upon the degree of departure of the system from
equilibrium.   The transfer stops when equilibrium is attained.
    Now the rate coefficients for the various components in a
given phase will differ from each other to the greatest extent
under conditions where molecular diffusion prevails, but even
then the difference is not really large.   For example, gases
and vapors diffusing through air will show transfer coefficients
whose ratio at most may be 3 or 4 to 1.   The same is true
when various substances diffuse through a liquid such as water.
Under conditions of turbulence, where molecular diffusion is
relatively unimportant, the transfer coefficients become much
more nearly alike for all components.   Consequently, while
in principle some separation of the components could be
achieved by taking advantage of their different transfer coefficients, the degree of separation attainable in this manner is
small.   This is especially significant when it is considered that
we frequently wish to obtain products which are nearly pure
substances, where the ratio of components may be of the order
of 1,000 or 10,000 to 1, or even larger.
    Therefore we depend almost entirely upon the differences
in concentration which exist at equilibrium, and not upon the
difference in transfer coefficients, for making separations.
Nevertheless, the mass-transfer coefficients are of great
importance, since, as they regulate the rate at which equilibrium
is approached, they control the time required for separation
and therefore the size and cost of the equipment used.   The

transfer coefficients are also important in governing the size of equipment used for entirely different purposes, such as carrying out chemical reactions. For example, the rate at which a reaction between two gases occurs on a solid catalyst is frequently governed by the rate of transfer of the gases to the catalyst surface and the rate of transfer of the product away from the catalyst.

The mass-transfer coefficients, their relationship to the phenomenon of diffusion, fluid motion, and to related rate coefficients, such as those describing heat transfer, are treated in Part 1.

CHAPTER TWO
MOLECULAR DIFFUSION
IN FLUIDS

Molecular diffusion is concerned with the movement of individual molecules through a substance by virtue of their thermal energy. The kinetic theory of gases provides a means of visualizing what occurs, and indeed it was the success of this theory in quantitatively describing the diffusional phenomena which led to its rapid acceptance. In the case of a simplified kinetic theory, a molecule is imagined to travel in a straight line at a uniform velocity until it collides with another molecule, whereupon its velocity changes both in magnitude and direction. The average distance the molecule travels between collisions is its mean free path, and the average velocity is dependent upon the temperature. The molecule thus travels a highly zigzag path, and the net distance in one direction which it moves in a given time, the rate of diffusion, is only a small fraction of the length of its actual path. For this reason the diffusion rate is very slow, although we can expect it to increase with decreasing pressure, which reduces the number of collisions, and with increased temperature, which increases the molecular velocity.

The importance of the barrier which molecular collision presents to diffusive movement is profound. Thus, for example, it can be computed through the kinetic theory that the rate of evaporation of water at 25°C into a complete vacuum is roughly ⅓ g/(sec)(sq cm) of water surface. But placing a layer of stagnant air at 1 atm pressure and only 0.1 mm thick above the water surface reduces the rate by a factor of about 600. The same general mechanism prevails also for the liquid state, but because of the considerably higher molecular concentration, we find even slower diffusion rates than in gases.

The phenomenon of molecular diffusion ultimately leads to a completely uniform concentration of substances throughout a solution which may initially have been nonuniform. Thus, for example, if a drop of blue copper sulfate solution is placed in a beaker of water, the copper sulfate eventually permeates the entire liquid. The blue color in time becomes everywhere uniform, and no subsequent change occurs.

We must distinguish at the start, however, between molecular diffusion, which is a slow process, and the more rapid mixing which can be brought about by mechanical stirring and convective movement of the fluid. Visualize a tank 5 ft in diameter into which has been placed a salt solution to a depth of 2.5 ft. Imagine that a 2.5-ft-deep layer of pure water has been carefully placed over the brine, in such a manner as not to disturb the brine in any way. If the contents of the tank are left completely undisturbed, the salt will, by molecular diffusion, completely permeate the liquid, ultimately coming everywhere to one-half its concentration in the original brine. But the process is very slow, and it can be calculated that the salt concentration at the top surface will still be only 87.5 percent of its final value after 10 years and will reach 99 percent of its final value only after 28 years. On the other hand, it has been demonstrated that a simple paddle agitator rotating in the tank at 60 rpm will bring about complete uniformity in about 30 sec. The mechanical agitation has produced rapid movement of relatively large chunks, or eddies, of fluid characteristic of turbulent motion, and these have carried the salt with them. This method of solute transfer is known as eddy or turbulent diffusion, as opposed to molecular diffusion. Of course, within each eddy, no matter how small, uniformity is achieved only by molecular diffusion, which is the ultimate process. We see then that molecular diffusion is the mechanism of mass transfer in stagnant fluids or in fluids which are moving only in laminar flow, although it is nevertheless always present even in highly developed turbulent flow.

In a two-phase system not at equilibrium, such as a layer of ammonia and air as a gas solution in contact with a layer of liquid water, spontaneous alteration through molecular diffusion also occurs, ultimately bringing the entire system to a state of equilibrium, whereupon alteration stops. At the end, we observe that the concentration of any constituent is the same throughout a phase, but it will not necessarily be the same in both phases. Thus the ammonia concentration will be uniform throughout the liquid and uniform at a different value throughout the gas. On the other hand, the chemical potential of the ammonia (or its activity if the same reference state is used), which is differently dependent upon concentration in the two phases, will be uniform everywhere throughout the system at equilibrium, and it is this uniformity which has brought the diffusive process to a halt. Evidently, then, the true driving force for diffusion is activity or chemical potential, and not concentration. In multiphase systems, however, we customarily deal with diffusional processes in each phase separately, and within one phase it is usually described in terms of that which is most readily observed, namely, concentration changes.

Molecular diffusion

We have noted that if a solution is everywhere uniform in concentration of its constituents, no alteration occurs, but that as long as it is not uniform, the solution is spontaneously brought to uniformity by diffusion, the substances moving from a place of high concentration to one of low. The rate at which a solute moves at any point in any direction must therefore depend on the concentration gradient at that point and in that direction. In describing this quantitatively, we need an appropriate measure of rate.

Rates will be most conveniently described in terms of a molar flux, or moles/ (time)(area), the area being measured in a direction normal to the diffusion. In a nonuniform solution even containing only two constituents, however, both constituents must diffuse if uniformity is the ultimate result, and this leads to the use of two fluxes to describe the motion of one constituent: N, the flux relative to a fixed location in space; and J, the flux of a constituent relative to the average molar velocity of all constituents. The first of these is of importance in the applications to design of equipment, but the second is more characteristic of the nature of the constituent. For example, a fisherman is most interested in the rate at which a fish swims upstream against the flowing current to reach his baited hook (analogous to N), but the velocity of the fish relative to the stream (analogous to J) is more characteristic of the swimming ability of the fish.

The *diffusivity*, or *diffusion coefficient*, D_{AB} of a constituent A in solution in B, which is a measure of its diffusive mobility, is then defined as the ratio of its flux J_A to its concentration gradient

$$J_A = -D_{AB}\frac{\partial c_A}{\partial z} \tag{2.1}$$

which is Fick's first law written for the z direction. The negative sign emphasizes that diffusion occurs in the direction of a drop in concentration. The diffusivity is a characteristic of a constituent and its environment (temperature, pressure, concentration, whether in liquid, gas, or solid solution, and the nature of the other constituents).

Consider the element of fluid of Fig. 2.1, of unit cross-sectional area. To the left of the section at P, the concentration of substance A is higher than on the right, while that of B is higher on the right than on the left. Diffusion of the substances then

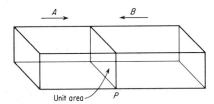

Fig. 2.1 *Diffusion in a binary solution.*

occurs in the directions shown. The volume rate (or velocity for unit cross section) of movement of A is u_A, that of B is $u_B = -u_A$, and the volume on either side of the section at P remains constant. The rate at which moles of A pass an observer at P is $N_A = u_A \rho_A / M_A = u_A c_A$, and for B, $N_B = u_B \rho_B / M_B = u_B c_B$, where c_A and c_B are the molar concentrations of the constituents. The net rate of movement of moles past the observer at P is $N_A + N_B$, and the molar average of the velocities is

$$u_M = \frac{u_A c_A + u_B c_B}{c} = \frac{N_A + N_B}{c} \tag{2.2}$$

where c = total molar concentration or density $= c_A + c_B$. If the observer wished to see no molar flux, he would have to move at a velocity u_M, whereupon the number of moles to his left and right would always be the same. The flux N_A with respect to the fixed position P must be larger than J_A by the amount of A in the volume rate u_M, or

$$N_A = u_M c_A + J_A \tag{2.3}$$

$$N_A = (N_A + N_B)\frac{c_A}{c} - D_{AB}\frac{\partial c_A}{\partial z} \tag{2.4}$$

The counterpart of Eq. (2.4) for B is

$$N_B = (N_A + N_B)\frac{c_B}{c} - D_{BA}\frac{\partial c_B}{\partial z} \tag{2.5}$$

Adding these, there results

$$-D_{AB}\frac{\partial c_A}{\partial z} = D_{BA}\frac{\partial c_B}{\partial z} \tag{2.6}$$

or $J_A = -J_B$. If $c_A + c_B = $ const, it follows that $D_{AB} = D_{BA}$ at the prevailing concentration and temperature.

All the above has considered diffusion in only one direction, but in general concentration gradients, velocities, and diffusional fluxes exist in all directions, so that counterparts of Eqs. (2.1) to (2.6) for all three directions in the cartesian coordinate system exist. In certain solids, the diffusivity D_{AB} may also be direction-sensitive, although in fluids it is not.

The equation of continuity

Consider the volume element of fluid of Fig. 2.2, where a fluid is flowing through the element. We shall need a material balance for a component of the fluid applicable to a differential fluid volume of this type.

The mass rate of flow of component A into the three faces with a common corner at E is

$$M_A[(N_{Ax})_x \, \Delta y \, \Delta z + (N_{Ay})_y \, \Delta x \, \Delta z + (N_{Az})_z \, \Delta x \, \Delta y]$$

where N_{Ax} signifies the x-directed flux and $(N_{Ax})_x$ its value at location x. Similarly the mass rate of flow out of the three faces with a common corner at G is

$$M_A[(N_{Ax})_{x+\Delta x} \, \Delta y \, \Delta z + (N_{Ay})_{y+\Delta y} \, \Delta x \, \Delta z + (N_{Az})_{z+\Delta z} \, \Delta x \, \Delta y]$$

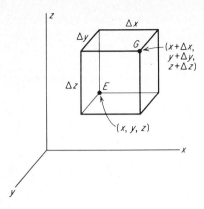

Fig. 2.2 *An elemental fluid volume.*

The total component A in the element is $\Delta x\,\Delta y\,\Delta z\,\rho_A$, and its rate of accumulation is therefore $\Delta x\,\Delta y\,\Delta z\,\partial\rho_A/\partial\theta$. If, in addition, A is generated by chemical reaction at the rate R_A moles/(time)(volume), its production rate is $M_A R_A\,\Delta x\,\Delta y\,\Delta z$, mass/time. Since, in general,

$$\text{Rate out} - \text{rate in} + \text{rate of accumulation} = \text{rate of generation}$$

then

$$M_A\{[(N_{Ax})_{x+\Delta x} - (N_{Ax})_x]\,\Delta y\,\Delta z + [(N_{Ay})_{y+\Delta y} - (N_{Ay})_y]\,\Delta x\,\Delta z$$

$$+ [(N_{Az})_{z+\Delta z} - (N_{Az})_z]\,\Delta x\,\Delta y\} + \Delta x\,\Delta y\,\Delta z\,\frac{\partial\rho_A}{\partial\theta} = M_A R_A\,\Delta x\,\Delta y\,\Delta z \qquad (2.7)$$

Dividing by $\Delta x\,\Delta y\,\Delta z$ and taking the limit as the three distances become zero,

$$M_A\left(\frac{\partial N_{Ax}}{\partial x} + \frac{\partial N_{Ay}}{\partial y} + \frac{\partial N_{Az}}{\partial z}\right) + \frac{\partial\rho_A}{\partial\theta} = M_A R_A \qquad (2.8)$$

Similarly, for component B,

$$M_B\left(\frac{\partial N_{Bx}}{\partial x} + \frac{\partial N_{By}}{\partial y} + \frac{\partial N_{Bz}}{\partial z}\right) + \frac{\partial\rho_B}{\partial\theta} = M_B R_B \qquad (2.9)$$

The total material balance is obtained by adding those for A and B

$$\frac{\partial(M_A N_A + M_B N_B)_x}{\partial x} + \frac{\partial(M_A N_A + M_B N_B)_y}{\partial y} + \frac{\partial(M_A N_A + M_B N_B)_z}{\partial z} + \frac{\partial\rho}{\partial\theta} = 0 \qquad (2.10)$$

where $\rho = \rho_A + \rho_B = $ the solution density, since the mass rate of generation of A and B must equal zero.

Now the counterpart of Eq. (2.3) in terms of masses and in the x direction is

$$M_A N_{Ax} = u_x\rho_A + M_A J_{Ax} \qquad (2.11)$$

where u_x is the mass-average velocity such that

$$\rho u_x = u_{Ax}\rho_A + u_{Bx}\rho_B = M_A N_{Ax} + M_B N_{Bx} \qquad (2.12)$$

Therefore,

$$\frac{\partial(M_A N_A + M_B N_B)_x}{\partial x} = \rho\frac{\partial u_x}{\partial x} + u_x\frac{\partial\rho}{\partial x}$$

Equation (2.10) therefore becomes

$$\rho\left(\frac{\partial u_x}{\partial x} + \frac{\partial u_y}{\partial y} + \frac{\partial u_z}{\partial z}\right) + u_x\frac{\partial \rho}{\partial x} + u_y\frac{\partial \rho}{\partial y} + u_z\frac{\partial \rho}{\partial z} + \frac{\partial \rho}{\partial \theta} = 0 \tag{2.13}$$

which is the "equation of continuity," or a mass balance, for total substance.   If the solution density is constant, it becomes

$$\frac{\partial u_x}{\partial x} + \frac{\partial u_y}{\partial y} + \frac{\partial u_z}{\partial z} = 0 \tag{2.14}$$

Returning to the balance for component A, we see from Eq. (2.11) that

$$M_A\frac{\partial N_{Ax}}{\partial x} = u_x\frac{\partial \rho_A}{\partial x} + \rho_A\frac{\partial u_x}{\partial x} + M_A\frac{\partial J_{Ax}}{\partial x} = u_x\frac{\partial \rho_A}{\partial x} + \rho_A\frac{\partial u_x}{\partial x} - M_A D_{AB}\frac{\partial^2 c_A}{\partial x^2} \tag{2.15}$$

Equation (2.8) then becomes

$$u_x\frac{\partial \rho_A}{\partial x} + u_y\frac{\partial \rho_A}{\partial y} + u_z\frac{\partial \rho_A}{\partial z} + \rho_A\left(\frac{\partial u_x}{\partial x} + \frac{\partial u_y}{\partial y} + \frac{\partial u_z}{\partial z}\right)$$

$$- M_A D_{AB}\left(\frac{\partial^2 c_A}{\partial x^2} + \frac{\partial^2 c_A}{\partial y^2} + \frac{\partial^2 c_A}{\partial z^2}\right) + \frac{\partial \rho_A}{\partial \theta} = M_A R_A \tag{2.16}$$

which is the equation of continuity for substance A.   For a solution of constant density, we can apply Eq. (2.14) to the terms multiplying ρ_A.   Dividing by M_A, we then have

$$u_x\frac{\partial c_A}{\partial x} + u_y\frac{\partial c_A}{\partial y} + u_z\frac{\partial c_A}{\partial z} + \frac{\partial c_A}{\partial \theta} = D_{AB}\left(\frac{\partial^2 c_A}{\partial x^2} + \frac{\partial^2 c_A}{\partial y^2} + \frac{\partial^2 c_A}{\partial z^2}\right) + R_A \tag{2.17}$$

In the special case where the velocity equals zero and there is no chemical reaction, it reduces to Fick's second law

$$\frac{\partial c_A}{\partial \theta} = D_{AB}\left(\frac{\partial^2 c_A}{\partial x^2} + \frac{\partial^2 c_A}{\partial y^2} + \frac{\partial^2 c_A}{\partial z^2}\right) \tag{2.18}$$

This is frequently applicable to diffusion in solids and to limited situations in fluids.
   In similar fashion, it is possible to derive the equations for a differential energy balance.   For a fluid of constant density, the result is

$$u_x\frac{\partial t}{\partial x} + u_y\frac{\partial t}{\partial y} + u_z\frac{\partial t}{\partial z} + \frac{\partial t}{\partial \theta} = \alpha\left(\frac{\partial^2 t}{\partial x^2} + \frac{\partial^2 t}{\partial y^2} + \frac{\partial^2 t}{\partial z^2}\right) + \frac{Q}{\rho C_p} \tag{2.19}$$

where $\alpha = k/\rho C_p$ and Q is the rate of heat generation within the fluid per unit volume from a chemical reaction.   The significance of the similarities between Eqs. (2.17) and (2.19) will be developed in Chap. 3.

STEADY-STATE UNIDIRECTIONAL MOLECULAR DIFFUSION IN FLUIDS AT REST AND IN LAMINAR FLOW

Applying Eq. (2.4) to the case of diffusion only in the z direction, with N_A and N_B both constant (steady state), the variables are readily separated, and if D_{AB} is constant, it may be integrated

$$\int_{c_{A1}}^{c_{A2}}\frac{-dc_A}{N_A c - c_A(N_A + N_B)} = \frac{1}{c D_{AB}}\int_{z_1}^{z_2} dz \tag{2.20}$$

where 1 indicates the beginning of the diffusion path (c_A high), and 2 the end of the diffusion path (c_A low). Letting $z_2 - z_1 = z$,

$$\frac{1}{N_A + N_B} \ln \frac{N_A c - c_{A2}(N_A + N_B)}{N_A c - c_{A1}(N_A + N_B)} = \frac{z}{c D_{AB}} \tag{2.21}$$

or

$$N_A = \frac{N_A}{N_A + N_B} \frac{D_{AB} c}{z} \ln \frac{N_A/(N_A + N_B) - c_{A2}/c}{N_A/(N_A + N_B) - c_{A1}/c} \tag{2.22}$$

Integration under steady-state conditions where the flux N_A is not constant is also possible. Consider radial diffusion from the surface of a solid sphere into a fluid, for example. Equation (2.20) may be applied, but the flux is a function of distance owing to the geometry. Most practical problems which deal with such matters, however, are concerned with diffusion under turbulent conditions, and the transfer coefficients which are then used are based upon a flux expressed in terms of some arbitrarily chosen area, such as the surface of the sphere. These matters are considered in Chap. 3.

Molecular diffusion in gases

When the ideal-gas law can be applied, Eq. (2.21) can be written in a form more convenient for use with gases. Thus,

$$\frac{c_A}{c} = \frac{p_A}{P_t} = y_A \tag{2.23}$$

where p_A = partial pressure of component A
P_t = total pressure
y_A = mole fraction concentration†

Further,

$$c = \frac{n}{V} = \frac{P_t}{RT} \tag{2.24}$$

so that Eq. (2.22) becomes

$$N_A = \frac{N_A}{N_A + N_B} \frac{D_{AB} P_t}{RTz} \ln \frac{[N_A/(N_A + N_B)]P_t - p_{A2}}{[N_A/(N_A + N_B)]P_t - p_{A1}} \tag{2.25}$$

or

$$N_A = \frac{N_A}{N_A + N_B} \frac{D_{AB} P_t}{RTz} \ln \frac{N_A/(N_A + N_B) - y_{A2}}{N_A/(N_A + N_B) - y_{A1}} \tag{2.26}$$

In order to use these, the relation between N_A and N_B must be known. This is usually fixed by other considerations. For example, if methane were being cracked on a catalyst,

$$CH_4 \rightarrow C + 2H_2$$

under circumstances such that CH_4 (A) diffuses to the cracking surface and H_2 (B) diffuses back, then the reaction stoichiometry fixes the relationship $N_B = -2N_A$, and

$$\frac{N_A}{N_A + N_B} = \frac{N_A}{N_A - 2N_A} = -1$$

† The component subscript A on y_A will differentiate mole fraction from the y meaning distance n the y direction.

On other occasions, in the absence of chemical reaction, the ratio may be fixed by enthalpy considerations.   In the case of the purely separational operations, there are two situations which frequently arise.

1. Steady-state diffusion of A through nondiffusing B. This might occur, for example, if ammonia (A) were being absorbed from air (B) into water.   In the gas phase, since air does not dissolve appreciably in water, and if we neglect the evapo-ration of water, only the ammonia diffuses.   Thus, $N_B = 0$, $N_A = \text{const}$,

$$N_A/(N_A + N_B) = 1,$$

and Eq. (2.25) becomes

$$N_A = \frac{D_{AB}P_t}{RTz} \ln \frac{P_t - p_{A2}}{P_t - p_{A1}} \tag{2.27}$$

Since $P_t - p_{A2} = p_{B2}$, $P_t - p_{A1} = p_{B1}$, $p_{B2} - p_{B1} = p_{A1} - p_{A2}$, then

$$N_A = \frac{D_{AB}P_t}{RTz} \frac{p_{A1} - p_{A2}}{p_{B2} - p_{B1}} \ln \frac{p_{B2}}{p_{B1}} \tag{2.28}$$

Letting

$$\frac{p_{B2} - p_{B1}}{\ln (p_{B2}/p_{B1})} = p_{BM} \tag{2.29}$$

then

$$N_A = \frac{D_{AB}P_t}{RTzp_{BM}} (p_{A1} - p_{A2}) \tag{2.30}$$

This equation is shown graphically in Fig. 2.3.   Substance A diffuses by virtue of its concentration gradient, $-dp_A/dz$.   Substance B is also diffusing relative to the average molar velocity at a flux J_B which depends upon $-dp_B/dz$, but like a fish which swims

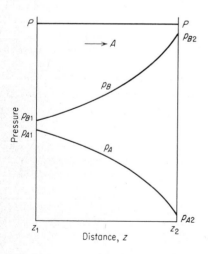

Fig. 2.3   *Diffusion of A through stagnant B.*

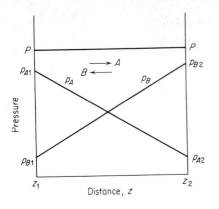

Fig. 2.4 *Equimolal counterdiffusion.*

upstream at the same velocity as the water flows downstream, $N_B = 0$ relative to a fixed place in space.

2. Steady-state equimolal counterdiffusion. This is a situation which frequently pertains in distillation operations. $N_A = -N_B = $ const. Equation (2.25) becomes indeterminate, but we can go back to Eq. (2.4), which, for gases, becomes

$$N_A = (N_A + N_B)\frac{p_A}{P_t} - \frac{D_{AB}}{RT}\frac{dp_A}{dz} \tag{2.31}$$

or, for this case,

$$N_A = -\frac{D_{AB}}{RT}\frac{dp_A}{dz} \tag{2.32}$$

$$\int_{z_1}^{z_2} dz = -\frac{D_{AB}}{RTN_A}\int_{p_{A1}}^{p_{A2}} dp_A \tag{2.33}$$

$$N_A = \frac{D_{AB}}{RTz}(p_{A1} - p_{A2}) \tag{2.34}$$

This is shown graphically in Fig. 2.4.

Steady-state diffusion in multicomponent mixtures. These can frequently be handled by the use of an "effective" diffusivity in Eq. (2.25), where the effective diffusivity of a component can be synthesized from its binary diffusivities with each of the other constituents.[2] Thus, in Eq. (2.25), $N_A + N_B$ is replaced by $\sum\limits_{i=A}^{n} N_i$, where N_i is positive if diffusion is in the same direction as that of A and negative if in the opposite direction, and D_{AB} is replaced by the effective D_{Am}

$$\frac{1}{D_{Am}} = \frac{\sum\limits_{i=A}^{n}\frac{1}{D_{Ai}}(y_i N_A - y_A N_i)}{N_A - y_A\sum\limits_{i=A}^{n} N_i} \tag{2.35}$$

The D_{Ai} are the binary diffusivities. This indicates that D_{Am} may vary considerably from one end of the diffusion path to the other, but a linear variation with distance may usually be assumed for practical calculations.[2]   A commonly arising situation is when all the N's except N_A are zero; i.e., all but one component is stagnant. Equation (2.35) then becomes[14]

$$D_{Am} = \frac{1 - y_A}{\displaystyle\sum_{i=B}^{n} \frac{y_i}{D_{Ai}}} = \frac{1}{\displaystyle\sum_{i=B}^{n} \frac{y_i'}{D_{Ai}}} \tag{2.36}$$

where y_i' is the mole fraction of component i on an A-free basis.

Illustration 2.1. Oxygen (A) is diffusing through carbon monoxide (B) under steady-state conditions, with the carbon monoxide nondiffusing.   The total pressure is 1 atm, and the temperature 0°C.   The partial pressure of oxygen at two planes 0.2 cm apart is, respectively, 100 and 50 mm Hg.   The diffusivity for the mixture is 0.185 sq cm/sec.   Calculate the rate of diffusion of oxygen in g moles/sec through each square centimeter of the two planes.

Solution. Equation (2.30) applies. $D_{AB} = 0.185$ sq cm/sec, $P_t = 1.0$ atm, $z = 0.2$ cm, $R = 82.06$ (cu cm)(atm)/(g mole)(°K), $T = 273°$K, $p_{A1} = 100/760 = 0.1317$ atm, $p_{A2} = 50/760 = 0.0658$ atm, $p_{B1} = 1 - 0.1317 = 0.8683$ atm, $p_{B2} = 1 - 0.0658 = 0.9342$ atm.

$$p_{BM} = \frac{p_{B1} - p_{B2}}{\ln(p_{B1}/p_{B2})} = \frac{0.8683 - 0.9342}{\ln(0.8683/0.9342)} = 0.901 \text{ atm}$$

$$N_A = \frac{D_{AB}P_t}{RTzp_{BM}}(p_{A1} - p_{A2}) = \frac{0.185(1.0)(0.1317 - 0.0658)}{82.06(273)(0.2)(0.901)}$$

$$= 3.01(10^{-6}) \text{ g mole/(sec)(sq cm)} \quad \textbf{Ans.}$$

Illustration 2.2. Recalculate the rate of diffusion of oxygen (A) in Illustration 2.1, assuming that the nondiffusing gas is a mixture of methane (B) and hydrogen (C) in the volume ratio 2:1. The diffusivities are estimated to be $D_{O_2-H_2} = 0.690$, $D_{O_2-CH_4} = 0.184$ sq cm/sec.

Solution. Equation (2.25) will become Eq. (2.30) for this case. $P_t = 1.0$ atm, $T = 273°$K, $p_{A1} = 0.1317$ atm, $p_{A2} = 0.0658$ atm, $p_{iM} = 0.901$ atm, $z = 0.2$ cm, $R = 82.06$ (cu cm)(atm)/(g mole)(°K), as in Illustration 2.1.   In Eq. (2.36), $y_B' = 2/(2 + 1) = 0.667$, $y_C' = 1 - 0.667 = 0.333$, whence

$$D_{AM} = \frac{1}{y_B'/D_{AB} + y_C'/D_{AC}} = \frac{1}{0.667/0.184 + 0.333/0.690} = 0.244 \text{ sq cm/sec}$$

Therefore, Eq. (2.30) becomes

$$N_A = \frac{0.244(1.0)(0.1317 - 0.0658)}{82.06(273)(0.2)(0.901)} = 3.97(10^{-6}) \text{ g mole/(sec)(sq cm)} \quad \textbf{Ans.}$$

Diffusivity of gases

The diffusivity, or diffusion coefficient, D is a property of the system dependent upon the temperature, pressure, and nature of the components.   An advanced kinetic theory[7] predicts that in binary mixtures there would be only a small effect of composition.   Its dimensions may be established from its definition, Eq. (2.1), and are length^2/time.   In the cgs system, sq cm/sec are ordinarily used.   The corresponding English-system units are sq ft/hr.

$$D \text{ sq cm/sec } (3.87) = D \text{ sq ft/hr}$$

A few typical data are listed in Table 2.1; a longer list is available in "The Chemical Engineers' Handbook."[10]

Table 2.1. Diffusivities of gases at atmospheric pressure

System	Temp, °C	Diffusivity, sq cm/sec	Ref.
H_2–CH_4	0	0.625	3
O_2–N_2	0	0.181	3
CO–O_2	0	0.185	3
CO_2–O_2	0	0.139	3
Air–NH_3	0	0.198	17
Air–H_2O	25.9	0.258	4
	59.0	0.305	4
Air–ethanol	0	0.102	8
Air–n-butanol	25.9	0.087	4
	59.0	0.104	4
Air–ethyl acetate	25.9	0.087	4
	59.0	0.106	4
Air–aniline	25.9	0.074	4
	59.0	0.090	4
Air–chlorobenzene	25.9	0.074	4
	59.0	0.090	4
Air–toluene	25.9	0.086	4
	59.0	0.092	4

Expressions for estimating D in the absence of experimental data are based on considerations of the kinetic theory of gases. The Wilke-Lee modification[16] of the Hirschfelder-Bird-Spotz method[6] is recommended for mixtures of nonpolar gases or of a polar with a nonpolar gas†

$$D_{AB} = \frac{(0.00107 - 0.000246\sqrt{1/M_A + 1/M_B})T^{3/2}\sqrt{1/M_A + 1/M_B}}{P_t(r_{AB})^2[f(\mathbf{k}T/\epsilon_{AB})]} \quad (2.37)$$

where D_{AB} = diffusivity, sq cm/sec

T = abs temperature, °K

M_A, M_B = mol wt of A and B, respectively

P_t = abs pressure, atm

r_{AB} = molecular separation at collision, Å

    = $(r_A + r_B)/2$

ϵ_{AB} = energy of molecular interaction, ergs

    = $\sqrt{\epsilon_A \epsilon_B}$

$\mathbf{k}$ = Boltzmann's constant

$f(\mathbf{k}T/\epsilon_{AB})$ = collision function given by Fig. 2.5

† The listed units must be used in Eq. (2.37). For mixtures of polar gases, see Ref. 13.

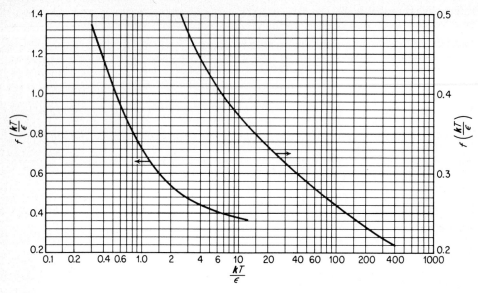

Fig. 2.5 *Collision function for diffusion.*

Table 2.2. Force constants of gases as determined from viscosity data†

Gas	ϵ/k, °K	r, Å
Air	97.0	3.617
H_2	33.3	2.968
N_2	91.46	3.681
CO_2	190	3.996
N_2O	220	3.879
NO	119	3.470
CH_4	136.5	3.882
O_2	113.2	3.433
CO	110.3	3.590
A	124.0	3.418
Ne	35.7	2.80
He	6.03	2.70

† By permission from Hirschfelder, Bird, and Spotz, *Trans. ASME*, **71,** 921 (1949). See also "The Chemical Engineers' Handbook," 4th ed., p. 14-20.

The values of r and ϵ, such as those listed in Table 2.2, can be calculated from other properties of gases, such as viscosity. If necessary, they can be estimated for each component empirically[16]†

$$r = 1.18v^{\frac{1}{3}} \qquad (2.38)$$

$$\frac{\epsilon}{\mathbf{k}} = 1.21T_b \qquad (2.39)$$

where v = molal volume of liquid at normal boiling point, cu cm/g mole (estimate from Table 2.3)

T_b = normal boiling point, °K

In using Table 2.3, the contributions for the constituent atoms are added together. Thus, for toluene, C_7H_8, $v = 7(14.8) + 8(3.7) - 15 = 118.2$. Diffusion through air, when the constituents of the air remain in fixed proportions, is handled as if the air were a single substance.

Table 2.3. Atomic and molecular volumes

Atomic volume		Molecular volume	
Carbon	14.8	H_2	14.3
Hydrogen	3.7	O_2	25.6
Chlorine	24.6	N_2	31.2
Bromine	27.0	Air	29.9
Iodine	37.0	CO	30.7
Sulfur	25.6	CO_2	34.0
Nitrogen	15.6	SO_2	44.8
Nitrogen in primary amines	10.5	NO	23.6
Nitrogen in secondary amines	12.0	N_2O	36.4
Oxygen	7.4	NH_3	25.8
Oxygen in methyl esters	9.1	H_2O	18.9
Oxygen in higher esters	11.0	H_2S	32.9
Oxygen in acids	12.0	COS	51.5
Oxygen in methyl ethers	9.9	Cl_2	48.4
Oxygen in higher ethers	11.0	Br_2	53.2
Benzene ring: subtract	15	I_2	71.5
Naphthalene ring: subtract	30		

Illustration 2.3. Estimate the diffusivity of ethanol vapor (A), C_2H_5OH, through air (B) at 1 atm pressure, 0°C.

Solution. $T = 273°K$, $P_t = 1$ atm, $M_A = 46.07$, $M_B = 29$. From Table 2.2 for air, $\epsilon_B/\mathbf{k} = 97.0$, $r_B = 3.617$. Values for ethanol will be estimated through Eqs. (2.38) and (2.39). From Table

---

† The listed units must be used in Eqs. (2.38) and (2.39).

2.3, $v_A = 2(14.8) + 6(3.7) + 7.4 = 59.2$, whence $r_A = 1.18(59.2)^{1/3} = 4.60$. The normal boiling point is $T_{bA} = 351.4°K$, and $\epsilon_A/k = 1.21(351.4) = 425$.

$$r_{AB} = \frac{r_A + r_B}{2} = \frac{4.60 + 3.617}{2} = 4.11$$

$$\frac{\epsilon_{AB}}{k} = \sqrt{\frac{\epsilon_A}{k}\frac{\epsilon_B}{k}} = \sqrt{425(97.0)} = 203$$

$$\frac{kT}{\epsilon_{AB}} = \frac{273}{203} = 1.345$$

Fig. 2.5: $f(kT/\epsilon_{AB}) = 0.62$. $\sqrt{1/M_A + 1/M_B} = 0.237$. Eq. (2.37):

$$D_{AB} = \frac{[0.00107 - 0.000246(0.237)](273)^{3/2}(0.237)}{1(4.11)^2(0.62)} = 0.103 \text{ sq cm/sec}$$

The observed value (Table 2.1) is 0.102 sq cm/sec.

Equation (2.37) shows D varying almost as $T^{3/2}$ (although a more correct temperature variation is given by considering also the collision function of Fig. 2.5) and inversely as the pressure, which will serve for pressures up to about 15 atm.[11]

The coefficient of self-diffusion, or D for a gas diffusing through itself, can be determined experimentally only by very special techniques involving, for example, the use of radioactive tracers. It can be estimated from Eq. (2.37) by setting $A = B$.

Molecular diffusion in liquids

The integration of Eq. (2.4) to put it in the form of Eq. (2.22) requires the assumption that D_{AB} and c are constant. This is satisfactory for binary gas mixtures but not in the case of liquids, where both may vary considerably with concentration. Nevertheless, in view of our very meager knowledge of the D's, it is customary to use Eq. (2.22), together with an average c and the best average D_{AB} available. Equation (2.22) is also conveniently written†

$$N_A = \frac{N_A}{N_A + N_B} \frac{D_{AB}}{z} \left(\frac{\rho}{M}\right)_{av} \ln \frac{N_A/(N_A + N_B) - x_{A2}}{N_A/(N_A + N_B) - x_{A1}} \tag{2.40}$$

where ρ and M are the solution density and molecular weight, respectively. As in the case of gases, the value of $N_A/(N_A + N_B)$ must be established by the circumstances prevailing. For the most commonly occurring cases, we have, as for gases:

† The component subscript on x_A indicates mole fraction A, to distinguish it from x meaning distance in the x direction.

1. Steady-state diffusion of A through nondiffusing B. $N_A = \text{const}$, $N_B = 0$,

whence
$$N_A = \frac{D_{AB}}{z x_{BM}} \left(\frac{\rho}{M}\right)_{av} (x_{A1} - x_{A2}) \qquad (2.41)$$

where
$$x_{BM} = \frac{x_{B2} - x_{B1}}{\ln (x_{B2}/x_{B1})} \qquad (2.42)$$

2. Steady-state equimolal counterdiffusion. $N_A = -N_B = \text{const}$.

$$N_A = \frac{D_{AB}}{z}(c_{A1} - c_{A2}) = \frac{D_{AB}}{z}\left(\frac{\rho}{M}\right)_{av}(x_{A1} - x_{A2}) \qquad (2.43)$$

Illustration 2.4. Calculate the rate of diffusion of acetic acid (A) across a film of nondiffusing water (B) solution 0.1 cm thick at 17°C when the concentrations on opposite sides of the film are, respectively, 9 and 3 wt % acid. The diffusivity of acetic acid in the solution is $0.95(10^{-5})$ sq cm/sec.

Solution. Equation (2.41) applies. $z = 0.1$ cm, $M_A = 60.03$, $M_B = 18.02$. At 17°C, the density of the 9% solution is 1.0120 g/cu cm. Therefore

$$x_{A1} = \frac{0.09/60.03}{0.09/60.03 + 0.91/18.02} = \frac{0.0015}{0.0520} = 0.0288 \text{ mole fraction acetic acid}$$

$$x_{B1} = 1 - 0.0288 = 0.9712 \text{ mole fraction water}$$

$$M = \frac{1}{0.0520} = 19.21 \text{ g/g mole}$$

$$\frac{\rho}{M} = \frac{1.0121}{19.21} = 0.0527 \text{ g mole/cu cm}$$

Similarly the density of the 3% solution is 1.0032 g/cu cm, $x_{A2} = 0.0092$, $x_{B2} = 0.9908$, $M = 18.40$, and $\rho/M = 0.0545$.

$$\left(\frac{\rho}{M}\right)_{av} = \frac{0.0527 + 0.0545}{2} = 0.0536 \text{ g mole/cu cm}$$

$$x_{BM} = \frac{0.9908 - 0.9712}{\ln (0.9908/0.9712)} = 0.980$$

Eq. (2.41):
$$N_A = \frac{0.95(10^{-5})}{0.1(0.980)} 0.0536(0.0288 - 0.0092)$$

$$= 1.018(10^{-7}) \text{ g mole/(sq cm)(sec)} \quad \textbf{Ans.}$$

Diffusivity of liquids

The dimensions for diffusivity in liquids are the same as those for gases, length²/time. Unlike the case for gases, however, the diffusivity varies appreciably with concentration. A few typical data are listed in Table 2.4, and larger lists are available.[5,9,10]

Estimates of the diffusivity in the absence of data cannot be made with anything like the accuracy with which they can be made for gases, owing to the inadequate development of any sound theory of the structure of liquids. For dilute solutions of

Table 2.4. Liquid diffusivities[8]

Solute	Solvent	Temp, °C	Solute concn, g moles/liter	Diffusivity,† sq cm/sec (10^5)
Cl_2	Water	16	0.12	1.26
HCl	Water	0	9	2.7
			2	1.8
		10	9	3.3
			2.5	2.5
		16	0.5	2.44
NH_3	Water	5	3.5	1.24
		15	1.0	1.77
CO_2	Water	10	0	1.46
		20	0	1.77
NaCl	Water	18	0.05	1.26
			0.2	1.21
			1.0	1.24
			3.0	1.36
			5.4	1.54
Methanol	Water	15	0	1.28
Acetic acid	Water	12.5	1.0	0.82
			0.01	0.91
		18.0	1.0	0.96
Ethanol	Water	10	3.75	0.50
			0.05	0.83
		16	2.0	0.90
n-Butanol	Water	15	0	0.77
CO_2	Ethanol	17	0	3.2
Chloroform	Ethanol	20	2.0	1.25

† For example, D for Cl_2 in water 0.0000126 sq cm/sec.

nonelectrolytes, the empirical correlation of Wilke and Chang[14,15] is recommended†

$$D_{AB} = \frac{7.4(10^{-8})(\phi M_B)^{0.5} T}{\mu' v_A^{0.6}}$$

(2.44)

where D_{AB} = diffusivity of A in dilute soln in solvent B, sq cm/sec
M_B = mol wt of solvent
T = temp, °K
μ' = soln viscosity, centipoises
v_A = solute molal vol at the nbp, cu cm/g mole
= 75.6 for water as solute
ϕ = association factor for solvent
= 2.6 for water as solvent
= 1.9 for methanol as solvent
= 1.5 for ethanol as solvent
= 1.0 for unassociated solvents such as benzene and ethyl ether

† The listed units must be used in Eq. (2.44).

The value of v_A may be estimated from the data of Table 2.3, except when water is the diffusing solute, as noted above.   The association factor for a solvent can be estimated only when diffusivities in that solvent have been experimentally measured.   If a value of ϕ is in doubt, the empirical correlation of Scheibel[12] may be used to estimate D. There is also some doubt about the ability of Eq. (2.44) to handle solvents of very high viscosity, say 100 centipoises or more.

The diffusivity in concentrated solutions differs from that in dilute solutions because of changes in viscosity with concentration and also because of changes in the degree of ideality of the solution.   In the case of strong electrolytes dissolved in water, the diffusion rates are those of the individual ions, which move more rapidly than the large, undissociated molecules, although the positively and negatively charged ions must move at the same rate in order to maintain electrical neutrality of the solution.   Estimations of these effects have been thoroughly reviewed[5,11] but are beyond the scope of this book.

Illustration 2.5. Estimate the diffusivity of mannitol, $CH_2OH(CHOH)_4CH_2OH$, $C_6H_{14}O_6$, in dilute solution in water at 20°C.   Compare with the observed value, $0.56(10^{-5})$ sq cm/sec.
   Solution. From the data of Table 2.3,

$$v_A = 14.8(6) + 3.7(14) + 7.4(6) = 185.0$$

For water as solvent, $\phi = 2.6$. $M_B = 18.02$, $T = 293°K$.   For dilute solutions, the viscosity μ' may be taken as that for water, 1.005 centipoises.

Eq. (2.44):
$$D_{AB} = \frac{7.4(10^{-8})[2.6(18.02)]^{0.5}(293)}{1.005(185)^{0.6}}$$

$$= 0.644(10^{-5}) \text{ sq cm/sec} \quad \textbf{Ans.}$$

Illustration 2.6. Estimate the diffusivity of mannitol in dilute water solution at 70°C, and compare with the observed value, $1.56(10^{-5})$ sq cm/sec.
   Solution. At 20°C, the observed $D_{AB} = 0.56(10^{-5})$ sq cm/sec, and $\mu' = 1.005$ centipoises (Illustration 2.5).   At 70°C, the viscosity of water is 0.4061 centipoise.   Equation (2.44) indicates that $D_{AB}\mu'/T$ should be constant

$$\frac{D_{AB}(0.4061)}{70 + 273} = \frac{0.56(10^{-5})(1.005)}{20 + 273}$$

$$D_{AB} = 1.62(10^{-5}) \text{ sq cm/sec at 70°C} \quad \textbf{Ans.}$$

Applications of molecular diffusion

The expressions developed for the rate of mass transfer under conditions where molecular diffusion defines the mechanism of mass transfer (fluids which are stagnant or in laminar flow) are of course directly applicable to the experimental measurement of the diffusivities, and they are extensively used for this.

In the practical applications of the mass-transfer operations, the fluids are always in motion, even in batch processes, so that we do not have stagnant fluids.   While occasionally the moving fluids are entirely in laminar flow, more frequently the motion is turbulent.   If the fluid is in contact with a solid surface, where the fluid velocity is zero, there will be a region in laminar flow adjacent to the surface.   Mass transfer must then usually take place through the laminar region, and molecular diffusion governs the rate there.   When two immiscible fluids in motion are in contact and mass transfer occurs between them, there may be no laminar region, even at the interface between the fluids.

In practical situations such as these, it has become customary to describe the mass-transfer flux in terms of mass-transfer coefficients.   The relationships of this chapter are then rarely used directly to determine mass-transfer rates, but they are particularly useful in establishing the form of the mass-transfer coefficient-rate equations and in computing the mass-transfer coefficients for laminar flow.

MOMENTUM AND HEAT TRANSFER IN LAMINAR FLOW

In the flow of a fluid past a phase boundary, such as that through which mass transfer occurs, there will be a velocity gradient within the fluid, which results in a transfer of momentum through the fluid.   In some cases there is also a transfer of heat by virtue of a temperature gradient.   The processes of mass, momentum, and heat transfer under these conditions are intimately related, and it is useful briefly to consider this.

Momentum transfer

Consider the velocity profile for the case of a gas flowing past a flat plate, as in Fig. 2.6.   Since the velocity at the solid surface is zero, there must necessarily be a laminar layer (the laminar sublayer) adjacent to the surface.   Within this region, the fluid may be imagined as being made up of thin layers sliding over each other at increasing velocities at increasing distances from the plate.   The force per unit area parallel to the surface, or shearing stress τ, required to maintain their velocities is proportional

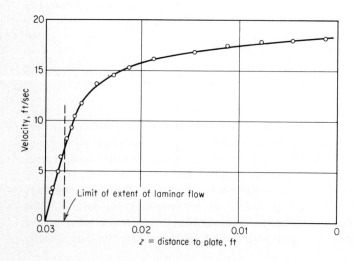

Fig. 2.6   Velocity profile, flow of air along a flat plate.   [Page et al.: Ind. Eng. Chem., 44, 424 (1952).]

to the velocity gradient,

$$\tau g_c = -\mu \frac{du}{dz} \tag{2.45}$$

where μ is the viscosity and z is measured as increasing in the direction toward the surface.   This may be written as

$$\tau g_c = -\frac{\mu}{\rho} \frac{d(u\rho)}{dz} = -\nu \frac{d(u\rho)}{dz} \tag{2.46}$$

where ν is the kinematic viscosity, μ/ρ.

The kinematic viscosity has the same dimensions as diffusivity, length²/time, while the quantity $u\rho$ may be looked upon as a volumetric momentum concentration. The quantity τg_c is the rate of momentum transfer per unit area, or flux of momentum. Equation (2.46) is therefore a rate equation analogous to Eq. (2.1) for mass flux. In the transfer of momentum in this manner there is of course no bulk flow of fluid from one layer to the other in the z direction.   Instead, molecules in one layer, in the course of traveling in random directions, will move from a fast-moving layer to an adjacent, more slowly moving layer, thereby transmitting momentum corresponding to the difference in velocities of the layers.   Diffusion in the z direction occurs by the same mechanism.   At high molecular concentrations, such as in gases at high pressures or even more so in liquids, the molecular diameter becomes appreciable in comparison with the molecular movement between collisions, and momentum may be imagined as being transmitted directly through the molecules themselves.[1]   Visualize, for example, a number of billiard balls arranged in a group in close contact with each other on a table.   A moving cue ball colliding with one of the outermost balls of the packed group will transmit its momentum very rapidly to one of the balls on the opposite side of the group, which will then be propelled from its original position. On the other hand, the cue ball is unlikely to move bodily through the group because of the large number of collisions it would experience.   Thus, at high molecular concentrations the direct parallelism between molecular diffusivity and momentum diffusivity (or kinematic viscosity) breaks down: diffusion is much the slower process. It is interesting to note that a relatively simple kinetic theory predicted that both mass and momentum diffusivities are given by the same expression,

$$D_{AA} = \frac{\mu_A}{\rho_A} = \frac{w\lambda}{3} \tag{2.47}$$

where w is the average molecular velocity and λ is the mean free path of molecule. The Schmidt number, which is the dimensionless ratio of the two diffusivities, Sc $= \mu/\rho D$, should by this theory equal unity for a gas.   A more sophisticated kinetic theory[7] gives values from 0.67 to 0.83, which is just the range found experimentally at moderate pressures.   For binary gas mixtures, Sc may range up to 5. For liquids, as might be expected, Sc is much higher: approximately 297 for self-diffusion in water at 77°F, for example, and ranging into the thousands for more viscous liquids and even for water with slowly diffusing solutes.

Heat transfer

When a temperature gradient exists between the fluid and the plate, the rate of heat transfer in the laminar region of Fig. 2.6 is

$$q = -k \frac{dt}{dz} \tag{2.48}$$

where k is the thermal conductivity of the fluid.   This may also be written as

$$q = -\frac{k}{C_p\rho} \frac{d(tC_p\rho)}{dz} = -\alpha \frac{d(tC_p\rho)}{dz} \tag{2.49}$$

where C_p is the specific heat at constant pressure.   The quantity $tC_p\rho$ may be looked upon as a volumetric thermal concentration, and $\alpha = k/C_p\rho$ is the thermal diffusivity, which, like momentum and mass diffusivities, has dimensions length²/time.   Equation (2.49) is therefore a rate equation analogous to the corresponding equations for momentum and mass transfer.

In a gas at relatively low pressure the heat energy is transferred from one position to another by the molecules traveling from one layer to another at a lower temperature. A simplified kinetic theory leads to the expression

$$\alpha = \frac{k}{C_p\rho} = \frac{1}{3} w\lambda \frac{C_v}{C_p} \tag{2.50}$$

Equations (2.47) and (2.50) would give the dimensionless ratio $v/\alpha = C_p\mu/k$ equal to C_p/C_v.   A more advanced kinetic theory modifies the size of the ratio, known as the Prandtl number Pr, and experimentally it has the range 0.65 to 0.9 for gases at low pressure, depending upon the molecular complexity of the gas.   At high molecular concentrations, the process is modified.   Thus for most liquids, Pr is larger (Pr = 7.02 for water at 68°F, for example).

The third dimensionless group, formed by dividing the thermal by the mass diffusivity, is the Lewis number, Le = α/D = Sc/Pr, and it plays an important part in problems of simultaneous heat and mass transfer, as will be developed later.

We may summarize this brief discussion of the similarity among momentum, heat, and mass transfer as follows.   An elementary consideration of the three processes leads to the conclusion that in certain simplified situations, there is a direct analogy among them.   In general, however, when three- rather than one-dimensional transfer is considered, the momentum-transfer process is of a sufficiently different nature for the analogy to break down.   Modification of the simple analogy is also necessary when, for example, mass and momentum transfer occur simultaneously. Thus, if there were a net mass transfer toward the surface of Fig. 2.6, the momentum transfer of Eq. (2.46) would have to include the effect of the net diffusion.   Similarly, mass transfer must inevitably have an influence on the velocity profile.   Nevertheless, even the limited analogies which exist are put to important practical use.

NOTATION FOR CHAPTER 2

Generally, consistent units in either the cgs or the English system may be used. It has become the custom to express pressure in the diffusion equations as atmospheres, in either system. Certain empirical equations may be used with specific units only, and these are marked in the text and in the following list.

c = concentration, g moles/cu cm or lb moles/cu ft

C_p = heat capacity at constant pressure, cal/(g)(°C) or Btu/(lb)(°F)

C_v = heat capacity at constant volume, cal/(g)(°C) or Btu/(lb)(°F)

d = differential operator

D = diffusivity, sq cm/sec or sq ft/hr; in Eqs. (2.37) and (2.44), only sq cm/sec

f = a function

g_c = conversion factor, 980(g mass)(cm)/(g force)(sec)^2 or 4.17(10^8)(lb mass)(ft)/(lb force)(hr)^2

J = flux of diffusion relative to the molar average velocity, g moles/(sec)(sq cm) or lb moles/(hr)(sq ft)

k = thermal conductivity, (cal)(cm)/(sec)(sq cm)(°C) or (Btu)(ft)/(hr)(sq ft)(°F)

$\mathbf{k}$ = Boltzmann constant = 1.38(10^{-16}) erg/°K [Eqs. (2.37), (2.39), Fig. 2.5, and Table 2.2]

ln = natural logarithm

Le = Lewis number = $k/\rho D C_p$, dimensionless

M = molecular weight, g/g mole or lb/lb mole

n = number of moles

N = flux of diffusion relative to a fixed surface, g moles/(sec)(sq cm) or lb moles/(hr)(sq ft)

p = partial pressure, atm

P_t = total pressure, atm

Pr = Prandtl number = $C_p \mu/k$, dimensionless

q = flux of heat transfer, cal/(sec)(sq cm) or Btu/(hr)(sq ft)

r = molecular separation at collision, Å [Eqs. (2.37), (2.38), and Table 2.2]

R_i = rate of production of component i, g moles/(sec)(cu cm) or lb moles/(hr)(cu ft)

R = (with no subscript) universal gas constant, 82.06 cu cm(atm)/(g mole)(°K) or 0.729 cu ft (atm)/(lb mole)(°R)

Sc = Schmidt number = $\mu/\rho D$, dimensionless

T = absolute temperature, °K or °R; in Eqs. (2.37), (2.39), and (2.44), and Fig. 2.5, only °K

T_b = normal boiling point, °K [Eq. (2.39)]

u = linear velocity, cm/sec or ft/hr

v = liquid molal volume, cu cm/g mole [Eqs. (2.38) and (2.44)]

V = volume, cu cm or cu ft

w = average molecular velocity, cm/sec or ft/hr

x = (with no subscript) distance in the x direction, cm or ft

x_i = mole fraction concentration of component i in a liquid

y = (with no subscript) distance in the y direction, cm or ft

y_i = mole fraction concentration of component i in a gas

y_i' = mole fraction concentration of component i, diffusing-solute-free basis.

z = distance in the z direction, cm or ft

α = thermal diffusivity, sq cm/sec or sq ft/hr

∂ = partial differential operator

Δ = difference

ϵ = energy of molecular interaction, ergs [Eqs. (2.37), (2.39), Table 2.2, and Fig. 2.5]

θ = time, sec or hr

λ = mean free path of a molecule, cm or ft

μ = viscosity, g mass/cm sec or lb mass/ft hr

μ' = viscosity, centipoises [Eq. (2.44)]

v = kinematic viscosity or momentum diffusivity = μ/ρ, sq cm/sec or sq ft/hr

ρ = density, g mass/cu cm or lb mass/cu ft
τ = shearing stress, g force/sq cm or lb force/sq ft
ϕ = dissociation factor for solvent

Subscripts:

A = component A
B = component B
i = component i
n = the last of n components
m = effective
M = mean
x = in the x direction
y = in the y direction
z = in the z direction
1 = beginning of diffusion path
2 = end of diffusion path

REFERENCES

1. Bosworth, R. C. L.: "Physics in the Chemical Industry," Macmillan and Co., Ltd., London, 1950.
2. Bird, R. B., W. E. Stewart, and E. N. Lightfoot: "Transport Phenomena," John Wiley & Sons, Inc., New York, 1960.
3. Chapman, S., and T. G. Cowling: "Mathematical Theory of Non-uniform Gases," Cambridge University Press, London, 1939.
4. Gilliland, E. R.: *Ind. Eng. Chem.*, **26**, 681 (1934).
5. Harned, H. S., and B. B. Owen: "The Physical Chemistry of Electrolytic Solutions," 3d ed., Reinhold Publishing Corporation, New York, 1958.
6. Hirschfelder, J. O., R. B. Bird, and E. L. Spotz: *Trans. ASME*, **71**, 921 (1949); *Chem. Rev.*, **44**, 205 (1949).
7. Hirschfelder, J. O., C. F. Curtis, and R. B. Bird: "Molecular Theory of Gases and Liquids," John Wiley & Sons, Inc., New York, 1954.
8. "International Critical Tables," vol. V, McGraw-Hill Book Co., New York, 1929.
9. Johnson, P. A., and A. L. Babb: *Chem. Rev.*, **56**, 387 (1956).
10. Perry, R. H., C. H. Chilton, and S. D. Kirkpatrick (eds.): "The Chemical Engineers' Handbook," 4th ed., pp. 14-22—14-26, McGraw-Hill Book Co., New York, 1963.
11. Reid, R. C., and T. K. Sherwood: "The Properties of Gases and Liquids," 2d ed., McGraw-Hill Book Co., New York, 1966.
12. Scheibel, E. G.: *Ind. Eng. Chem.*, **46**, 2007 (1954).
13. Stuel, L. I., and G. Thodos: *AIChE J.*, **10**, 266 (1964).
14. Wilke, C. R.: *Chem. Eng. Progr.*, **45**, 218 (1949).
15. Wilke, C. R., and P. Chang: *AIChE J.*, **1**, 264 (1955).
16. Wilke, C. R., and C. Y. Lee: *Ind. Eng. Chem.*, **47**, 1253 (1955).
17. Wintergeist, E.: *Ann. Physik.*, **4**, 323 (1930).

PROBLEMS

2.1. In an oxygen-nitrogen gas mixture at 1 atm, 25°C, the concentrations of oxygen at two planes 0.2 cm apart are 10 and 20 vol%, respectively. Calculate the rate of diffusion of the oxygen, expressed as g moles oxygen/(sq cm)(sec) for the case where:

a. The nitrogen is nondiffusing.

b. There is equimolar counterdiffusion of the two gases.

2.2. Repeat the calculations of Prob. 2.1 for a total pressure of 10 atm.

2.3. Estimate the diffusivities of the following gas mixtures:
a. Acetone–air, 1 atm, 0°C.
b. Nitrogen–carbon dioxide, 1 atm, 25°C.
c. Hydrogen chloride–air, 2 atm, 25°C.
d. Toluene–air, 1 atm, 25°C. **Ans.:** 0.0817 sq cm/sec.
e. Hydrogen–methane, 1 atm, 25°C.

2.4. Ammonia is diffusing through a stagnant gas mixture consisting of one-third nitrogen and two-thirds hydrogen by volume. The total pressure is 30 psia, and the temperature 130°F. Calculate the rate of diffusion of the ammonia, as lb/(hr)(sq ft), through a film of gas 0.5 mm thick when the concentration change across the film is 10 to 5% ammonia by volume.

2.5. Estimate the following liquid diffusivities:
a. Ethyl alcohol in dilute water solution, 10°C.
b. Carbon tetrachloride in dilute solution in methyl alcohol, 15°C [obsvd value $= 1.69(10^{-5})$ sq cm/sec]. **Ans.:** $1.50(10^{-5})$ sq cm/sec.
c. Self-diffusion in water, 25°C.

2.6. Calculate the rate of diffusion of NaCl at 18°C through a stagnant film of water 0.1 cm thick when the concentrations are 20 and 10%, respectively, on either side of the film.

2.7. At 14.7 psia and 212°F, the density of air is 0.0592 lb/cu ft, the viscosity 0.0218 centipoise, the thermal conductivity 0.0183 (Btu)(ft)/(hr)(sq ft)(°F), and the specific heat at constant pressure 0.250 Btu/(lb)(°F). At 77°F, the viscosity is 0.0179 centipoise.
a. Calculate the kinematic viscosity at 212°F, sq ft/hr.
b. Calculate the thermal diffusivity at 212°F, sq ft/hr.
c. Calculate the Prandtl number at 212°F.
d. Assuming that for air at 1 atm Pr = Sc and that Sc is constant with changing temperature, calculate D for air at 77°F, sq ft/hr. Compare with the value of D for the system O_2–N_2, at 1 atm, 77°F, from the data of Table 2.1.

2.8. Ammonia is being cracked on a solid catalyst according to the reaction

$$2NH_3 \rightarrow N_2 + 3H_2$$

At one place in the apparatus, where the pressure is 1 atm abs and the temperature 200°C, the analysis of the bulk gas is 33.33% NH_3 (*A*), 16.67% N_2 (*B*), and 50.00% H_2 (*C*) by volume. The circumstances are such that NH_3 diffuses from the bulk-gas stream to the catalyst surface, and the products of of the reaction diffuse back, as if by molecular diffusion through a gas film in laminar flow 0.1 cm thick. Estimate the maximum local rate of cracking, lb NH_3/(hr) (sq ft catalyst surface), which might be considered to occur if the reaction is diffusion-rate controlled (chemical reaction rate very rapid) with the concentration of NH_3 at the catalyst surface equal to zero. **Ans.:** 9.43 lb/(hr)(sq ft).

2.9. A crystal of copper sulfate $CuSO_4 \cdot 5H_2O$ falls through a large tank of pure water at 20°C. Estimate the rate at which the crystal dissolves, lb/(hr)(sq ft crystal surface).
Data and assumptions. Molecular diffusion occurs through a film of water uniformly $1(10^{-4})$ ft thick, surrounding the crystal. At the inner side of the film, adjacent to the crystal surface, the concentration of copper sulfate is its solubility value, 0.0229 mole fraction $CuSO_4$ (solution density $=$ 74.5 lb/cu ft). The outer surface of the film is pure water. The diffusivity of $CuSO_4$ is $2.82(10^{-5})$ sq ft/hr.

CHAPTER THREE
MASS-TRANSFER
COEFFICIENTS

We have seen that when a fluid flows past a surface under conditions such that turbulence generally prevails, there is a thin film of fluid in laminar flow immediately adjacent to the surface. This is followed by a transition, or buffer, zone where the flow gradually changes to the turbulent condition existing in the outer regions of the fluid. We have noted also that the rate of transfer of dissolved substance through the three regions will necessarily depend upon the nature of the fluid motion prevailing in each region.

In the turbulent region, particles of fluid no longer flow in the orderly manner found in the laminar film. Instead, relatively large portions of the fluid, called eddies, move rapidly from one position to the other with an appreciable component of their velocity in the direction perpendicular to the surface past which the fluid is flowing. These eddies bring with them dissolved material, and the eddy motion thus contributes considerably to the mass-transfer process. Since the eddy motion is rapid, mass transfer in the turbulent region is also rapid, much more so than that resulting from molecular diffusion in the laminar film. Because of the rapid eddy motion, the concentration gradients existing in the turbulent region will be smaller than those in the film, and Fig. 3.1 shows concentration gradients of this sort. In the experiment

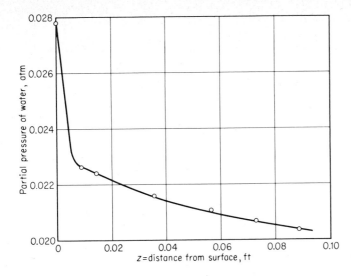

Fig. 3.1 *Evaporation of water into air.*[37]

for which these are the data, air in turbulent motion flowed past a water surface, and water evaporated into the air. Samples of the air were taken at various distances from the surface, and the water-vapor concentration was determined by analysis. At the water surface, the water concentration in the gas was the same as the vapor pressure of pure water at the prevailing temperature. It was not possible to sample the gas very close to the water surface, but the rapid change in concentration in the laminar film, and the slower change in the outer turbulent region, are nevertheless unmistakable. It is important also to note the general similarity of data of this sort to the velocity distribution shown in Fig. 2.6.

It is also useful to compare the data for mass transfer with similar data for heat transfer. Thus, in Fig. 3.2 are plotted the temperatures at various distances from the surface when air flowed past a heated plate. The large temperature gradient in the laminar film and the lesser gradient in the turbulent region are again evident. It will generally be convenient to keep the corresponding heat-transfer process in mind when the mass-transfer process is discussed, since in many instances the methods of reasoning used to describe the latter are borrowed directly from those found to be successful with the former.

Mass-transfer coefficients

The mechanism of the flow process involving the movements of the eddies in the turbulent region is not thoroughly understood. On the other hand, the mechanism of molecular diffusion, at least for gases, is fairly well known, since it can be described in terms of a kinetic theory to give results which agree well with experience. It is natural therefore to attempt to describe the rate of mass transfer through a combination of laminar film and turbulent zone, including the intervening buffer zone, in the same manner found useful for laminar flow. Thus, the $D_{AB}c/z$ of Eq. (2.22), which is

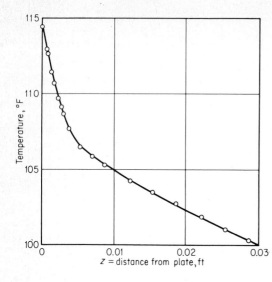

Fig. 3.2 *Heat transfer, flow of air past a heated plate.*[25]

characteristic of molecular diffusion, is replaced by F, a mass-transfer coefficient.[1,6] For binary solutions,

$$N_A = \frac{N_A}{N_A + N_B} F \ln \frac{N_A/(N_A + N_B) - c_{A2}/c}{N_A/(N_A + N_B) - c_{A1}/c} \tag{3.1}$$

where c_A/c is the mole-fraction concentration, x_A for liquids, y_A for gases. As in the case of molecular diffusion, the ratio $N_A/(N_A + N_B)$ is ordinarily established by nondiffusional considerations.

Since the surface through which the transfer takes place may not be plane, so that the diffusion path in the fluid may be of variable cross section, N is defined as the *flux at the phase interface*, or *boundary*, where substance leaves or enters the phase for which F is the mass-transfer coefficient. N_A is positive when c_{A1} is at the beginning of the transfer path and c_{A2} at the end. In any case, one of these concentrations will be at the phase boundary. The manner of defining the concentration of A in the fluid will influence the value of F, and this is usually established arbitrarily. If mass transfer takes place between a phase boundary and a large quantity of unconfined fluid, as, for example, when a drop of water evaporates while falling through a great volume of air, the concentration of diffusing substance in the fluid is usually taken as the constant value found at large distances from the phase boundary. If the fluid is in a confining duct, so that the concentration is not constant along any position of the transfer path, the bulk-average concentration $\bar{c}_A$, as found by mixing all the fluid passing a given point, is usually used. In Fig. 3.3, where a liquid evaporates into the flowing gas, the concentration c_A of the vapor in the gas varies continuously from c_{A1} at the liquid surface to the value at $z = Z$. In this case c_{A2} in Eq. (3.1) would usually be taken as $\bar{c}_A$, defined by

$$\bar{c}_A = \frac{1}{\bar{u}_y S} \int_0^S u_y c_A \, dS \tag{3.2}$$

where $u_y(z)$ is the velocity distribution in the gas across the duct (the time average of u_y in the case of turbulence), $\bar{u}_y$ is the bulk-average velocity (volumetric rate/duct cross section), and S is the duct cross-sectional area.   In any case, one must know how the mass-transfer coefficient is defined in order to use it properly.

The F of Eq. (3.1) is a *local* mass-transfer coefficient, defined for a particular location on the phase-boundary surface.   Since the value of F depends on the local nature of the fluid motion, which may vary along the surface, an average value F_{av} is sometimes used in Eq. (3.1) with constant c_{A1} and c_{A2}, which takes into account these variations in F.   The effect of variation in c_{A1} and c_{A2} on the flux must be accounted for separately.

Equation (3.1) is adapted to multicomponent systems by replacing $N_A + N_B$ by $\sum_{i=1}^{n} N_i$, where n is the number of components.

The two situations noted in Chap. 2, equimolar counterdiffusion and transfer of one substance through another which is not transferred, occur so frequently that special mass-transfer coefficients are usually used for them.   These are defined by equations of the form

$$\text{Flux} = \text{coefficient (concentration difference)}$$

Since concentration may be defined in a number of ways and standards have not been established, we have a variety of coefficients for each situation:

Transfer of A through Nontransferring B $[N_B = 0, N_A/(N_A + N_B) = 1]$

Gases: $N_A = k_G(p_{A1} - p_{A2}) = k_y(y_{A1} - y_{A2}) = k_c(c_{A1} - c_{A2})$ (3.3)

Liquids: $N_A = k_x(x_{A1} - x_{A2}) = k_L(c_{A1} - c_{A2})$ (3.4)

Equimolar Countertransfer $[N_A = -N_B, N_A/(N_A + N_B) = \infty]$

Gases: $N_A = k_G'(p_{A1} - p_{A2}) = k_y'(y_{A1} - y_{A2}) = k_c'(c_{A1} - c_{A2})$ (3.5)

Liquids: $N_A = k_x'(x_{A1} - x_{A2}) = k_L'(c_{A1} - c_{A2})$ (3.6)

These are, of course, analogous to the definition of a heat-transfer coefficient $h: q = h(t_1 - t_2)$.   Whereas the concept of the heat-transfer coefficient is generally applicable, at least in the absence of mass transfer, the coefficients of Eqs. (3.3) and

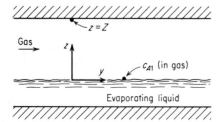

Fig. 3.3   *Mass transfer to a confined fluid.*

(3.4) are more restricted. Thus, k_c of Eq. (3.3) can be considered as a replacement of D_{AB}/z in an integration of Eq. (2.1), and the bulk-flow term of Eq. (2.4) has been ignored in equating this to N_A. The coefficients of Eqs. (3.3) and (3.4) are therefore generally useful only for low mass-transfer rates. Values measured under one level of transfer rate should be converted to F for use with Eq. (3.1) before being applied to another. To obtain the relation between F and the k's, note that for gases, for example, F replaces $D_{AB}P_t/RTz$ in Eq. (2.25) and that k_G replaces $D_{AB}P_t/RTzp_{BM}$ in Eq. (2.30). From this it follows that $F = k_G p_{BM}$. In this manner the conversions of Table 3.1 have been obtained. Since the bulk-flow term $N_A + N_B$ of Eq. (2.4) is zero for equimolal countertransfer, $F = k'_y$ (gases) and $F = k'_x$ (liquids), and Eqs. (3.5) and (3.6) are identical with Eq. (3.1) for this case.

Table 3.1 Relations among mass-transfer coefficients

Rate equation		Units of coefficient
Equimolal counterdiffusion	Diffusion of A through nondiffusing B	
Gases		
$N_A = k'_G \, \Delta p_A$	$N_A = k_G \, \Delta p_A$	$\dfrac{\text{Moles transferred}}{\text{Time(area)(pressure)}}$
$N_A = k'_y \, \Delta y_A$	$N_A = k_y \, \Delta y_A$	$\dfrac{\text{Moles transferred}}{\text{Time(area)(mole fraction)}}$
$N_A = k'_c \, \Delta c_A$	$N_A = k_c \, \Delta c_A$	$\dfrac{\text{Moles transferred}}{\text{Time(area)(moles/vol)}}$
	$W_A = k_Y \, \Delta Y_A$	$\dfrac{\text{Mass transferred}}{\text{Time(area)(mass } A/\text{mass } B)}$

Conversions

$$F = k_G p_{BM} = k_y \frac{p_{BM}}{P_t} = k_c \frac{p_{BM}}{RT} = \frac{k_Y}{M_B} = k'_G P_t = k'_y = k'_c \frac{P_t}{RT} = k'_c c$$

Liquids		
$N_A = k'_L \, \Delta c_A$	$N_A = k_L \, \Delta c_A$	$\dfrac{\text{Moles transferred}}{\text{Time(area)(moles/vol)}}$
$N_A = k'_x \, \Delta x_A$	$N_A = k_x \, \Delta x_A$	$\dfrac{\text{Moles transferred}}{\text{Time(area)(mole fraction)}}$

Conversions

$$F = k_x x_{BM} = k_L x_{BM} c = k'_L c = k'_L \frac{\rho}{M} = k'_x$$

Many data on mass transfer where $N_A/(N_A + N_B)$ is neither unity nor infinity have nevertheless been described in terms of the k-type coefficients.   Before these can be used for other situations, they must be converted to F's.

Mass-transfer coefficients can, in a few limited situations, be deduced from theoretical principles.   In the great majority of cases, however, we depend upon direct measurement under known conditions, for use later in design.

MASS-TRANSFER COEFFICIENTS IN LAMINAR FLOW

In principle, at least, we do not need mass-transfer coefficients for laminar flow, since molecular diffusion prevails, and the relationships of Chap. 2 can be used to compute mass-transfer rates.   A uniform method of dealing with both laminar and turbulent flow is nevertheless desirable.

Mass-transfer coefficients for laminar flow should be capable of computation. To the extent that the flow conditions are capable of description and the mathematics remains tractable, this is so.   These are, however, severe requirements, and frequently the simplification required to permit mathematical manipulation is such that the results fall somewhat short of reality.   It is not our purpose to develop these methods in detail, since they are dealt with extensively elsewhere.[2,3]   We shall choose one relatively simple situation to illustrate the general technique and to provide some basis for considering turbulent flow.

Mass transfer from a gas into a falling liquid film

Figure 3.4 shows a liquid falling in a thin film in laminar flow down a vertical flat surface while being exposed to a gas A, which dissolves in the liquid.   The liquid contains a uniform concentration of A, c_{A0}, at the top.   At the liquid surface, the concentration of the dissolved gas is c_{Ai}, in equilibrium with the pressure of A in the gas phase.   Since $c_{Ai} > c_{A0}$, gas dissolves in the liquid.   The problem is

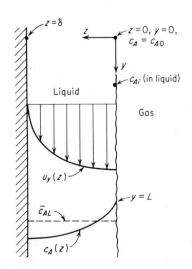

Fig. 3.4   *Falling liquid film.*

to obtain the mass-transfer coefficient k_L, with which the amount of gas dissolved after the liquid falls the distance L can be computed.

The problem is solved by simultaneous solution of the equation of continuity for component A, Eq. (2.17), with the equations describing the liquid motion, the Navier-Stokes equations. The simultaneous solution of this formidable set of partial differential equations becomes possible only when several simplifying assumptions are made. For present purposes, assume the following:

1. There is no chemical reaction. R_A of Eq. (2.17) $= 0$.
2. Conditions do not change in the x direction (perpendicular to the plane of the paper, Fig. 3.4). All derivatives with respect to x of Eq. (2.17) $= 0$.
3. Steady-state conditions prevail. $\partial c_A / \partial \theta = 0$.
4. The rate of absorption of gas is very small. This means that u_z in Eq. (2.17) due to diffusion of A is essentially zero.
5. Diffusion of A in the y direction is negligible in comparison with the movement of A downward due to bulk flow. Therefore, $D_{AB} \, \partial^2 c_A / \partial y^2 = 0$.
6. Physical properties (D_{AB}, ρ, μ) are constant.

Equation (2.17) then reduces to

$$u_y \frac{\partial c_A}{\partial y} = D_{AB} \frac{\partial^2 c_A}{\partial z^2} \tag{3.7}$$

which states that any A added to the liquid running down at any location z, over an increment in y, got there by diffusion in the z direction. The equations of motion under these conditions reduce to

$$\mu \frac{d^2 u_y}{dz^2} + \rho g = 0 \tag{3.8}$$

The solution to Eq. (3.8), with the conditions that $u_y = 0$ at $z = \delta$ and that $du_y/dz = 0$ at $z = 0$, is well known

$$u_y = \frac{\rho g \delta^2}{2\mu} \left[1 - \left(\frac{z}{\delta}\right)^2 \right] = \frac{3}{2} \bar{u}_y \left[1 - \left(\frac{z}{\delta}\right)^2 \right] \tag{3.9}$$

where $\bar{u}_y$ is the bulk-average velocity. The film thickness is then

$$\delta = \left(\frac{3\bar{u}_y \mu}{\rho g}\right)^{1/2} = \left(\frac{3\mu\Gamma}{\rho^2 g}\right)^{1/3} \tag{3.10}$$

where Γ is the mass rate of liquid flow per unit of film width in the x direction. Substituting Eq. (3.9) into (3.7),

$$\frac{3}{2} \bar{u}_y \left[1 - \left(\frac{z}{\delta}\right)^2 \right] \frac{\partial c_A}{\partial y} = D_{AB} \frac{\partial^2 c_A}{\partial z^2} \tag{3.11}$$

which is to be solved under the following conditions:

1. At $z = 0$, $c_A = c_{Ai}$ at all values of y.
2. At $z = \delta$, $\partial c_A / \partial z = 0$ at all values of y, since no diffusion takes place into the solid wall.
3. At $y = 0$, $c_A = c_{A0}$ at all values of z.

The solution results in a general expression (an infinite series) giving c_A for any z and y, thus providing a concentration distribution $c_A(z)$ at $y = L$, as shown in Fig. 3.4. The bulk-average $\bar{c}_{AL}$ at $y = L$ can then be found in the manner of Eq. (3.2). The result is[17]

$$\frac{c_{Ai} - \bar{c}_{AL}}{c_{Ai} - c_{A0}} = 0.7857 e^{-5.1213\eta} + 0.1001 e^{-39.318\eta} + 0.03599 e^{-105.64\eta} + \cdots \tag{3.12}$$

where $\eta = 2D_{AB}L/3\delta^2\bar{u}_y$. The total rate of absorption is then $\bar{u}_y\delta(\bar{c}_{AL} - c_{A0})$ per unit width of liquid film.

Alternatively, to obtain a local mass-transfer coefficient, we can combine Eq. (2.4) for the case of negligible bulk flow in the z direction ($N_A + N_B = 0$) with Eq. (3.4), keeping in mind that mass-transfer coefficients use fluxes at the phase interface ($z = 0$)

$$N_A = -D_{AB}\left(\frac{\partial c_A}{\partial z}\right)_{z=0} = k_L(c_{Ai} - \bar{c}_{AL}) \tag{3.13}$$

In this case, however, because of the nature of the series which describes c_A, the derivative is un-defined at $z = 0$. It is better therefore to proceed with an average coefficient for the entire liquid-gas surface. The rate at which A is carried by the liquid at any y, per unit width in the x direction, is $\bar{u}_y\delta\bar{c}_A$ moles/time. Over a distance dy, per unit width, therefore, the rate of solute absorption is, in moles/time,

$$\bar{u}_y\delta\,d\bar{c}_A = k_L(c_{Ai} - \bar{c}_A)\,dy \tag{3.14}$$

$$\bar{u}_y\delta\int_{\bar{c}_A=\bar{c}_{A0}}^{\bar{c}_A=\bar{c}_{AL}}\frac{d\bar{c}_A}{c_{Ai} - \bar{c}_A} = \int_0^L k_L\,dy = k_{L,\mathrm{av}}\int_0^L dy \tag{3.15}$$

$$k_{L,\mathrm{av}} = \frac{\bar{u}_y\delta}{L}\ln\frac{c_{Ai} - c_{A0}}{c_{Ai} - \bar{c}_{AL}} \tag{3.16}$$

which defines the average coefficient. Now for small rates of flow or long times of contact of the liquid with the gas (usually for film Reynolds numbers Re $= 4\Gamma/\mu$ less than 100), only the first term of the series of Eq. (3.12) need be used. Substituting in Eq. (3.16),

$$k_{L,\mathrm{av}} = \frac{\bar{u}_y\delta}{L}\ln\frac{e^{5.1213\eta}}{0.7857} = \frac{\bar{u}_y\delta}{L}(0.241 + 5.1213\eta) \doteq 3.41\frac{D_{AB}}{\delta} \tag{3.17}$$

$$\frac{k_{L,\mathrm{av}}\delta}{D_{AB}} = \mathrm{Sh}_{\mathrm{av}} \doteq 3.41 \tag{3.18}$$

where Sh represents the Sherwood number, the mass-transfer analog to the Nusselt number of heat transfer. A similar development for large Reynolds numbers or short contact time[31] leads to

$$k_{L,\mathrm{av}} = \left(\frac{6D_{AB}\Gamma}{\pi\rho\delta L}\right)^{1/2} \tag{3.19}$$

$$\mathrm{Sh}_{\mathrm{av}} = \left(\frac{3}{2\pi}\frac{\delta}{L}\,\mathrm{Re}\,\mathrm{Sc}\right)^{1/2} \tag{3.20}$$

The product Re Sc is the Péclet number Pe.

These average k_L's may be used to compute the total absorption rate. Thus the average flux $N_{A,\mathrm{av}}$ for the entire gas-liquid surface, per unit width, is the difference in rate of flow of A in the liquid at $y = L$ and at $y = 0$, divided by the liquid surface. This may be used with some mean concentra-tion difference

$$N_{A,\mathrm{av}} = \frac{\bar{u}_y\delta}{L}(\bar{c}_{AL} - c_{A0}) = k_{L,\mathrm{av}}(c_{Ai} - \bar{c}_A)_M \tag{3.21}$$

Substitution for $k_{L,\mathrm{av}}$ from Eq. (3.16) shows that the logarithmic average of the difference at the top and bottom of the film is required

$$(c_{Ai} - \bar{c}_A)_M = \frac{(c_{Ai} - c_{A0}) - (c_{Ai} - \bar{c}_{AL})}{\ln[c_{Ai} - c_{A0})/(c_{Ai} - \bar{c}_{AL})]} \tag{3.22}$$

The experimental data[31] show that the $k_{L,\mathrm{av}}$ realized may be as much as twice as large as the above theoretical values at high film Reynolds numbers, even for low mass-transfer rates, owing to ripples and waves formed in the liquid surface which were not considered in the mathematical analysis. Rapid absorption, as for very soluble gases, produces important values of u_z, and this will cause further discrepancies, owing to alteration of the velocity profile in the film. The velocity profile may also be altered by flow of the gas, so that even in the simplest case, when both fluids move, k_L should depend on both flow rates.

Illustration 3.1. Estimate the rate of absorption of carbon dioxide into a water film flowing down a vertical wall 2 ft long at the rate of 150 lb/hr per ft of width, at 25°C. The gas is pure CO_2 at 1 atm. The water is initially CO_2-free.

Solution. The solubility of CO_2 in water at 25°C, 1 atm, is $c_{Ai} = 0.0021$ lb mole/cu ft soln; $D_{AB} = 7.59(10^{-5})$ sq ft/hr; soln density $\rho = 62.3$ lb/cu ft; and viscosity $\mu = 0.894$ centipoise $= 2.16$ lb/(ft)(hr). $\Gamma = 150$ lb/(hr)(ft), $L = 2$ ft.

$$\delta = \left(\frac{3\mu\Gamma}{\rho^2 g}\right)^{1/3} = \left[\frac{3(2.16)150}{(62.3)^2(4.17)(10^8)}\right]^{1/3} = 0.000843 \text{ ft}$$

$$\mathrm{Re} = \frac{4\Gamma}{\mu} = \frac{4(150)}{2.16} = 278$$

Consequently Eq. (3.19) should apply.

$$k_{L,\mathrm{av}} = \left(\frac{6 D_{AB}\Gamma}{\pi\rho\delta L}\right)^{1/2} = \left[\frac{6(7.59)(10^{-5})(150)}{\pi(62.3)(0.000843)(2)}\right]^{1/2}$$

$$= 0.455 \frac{\text{lb mole}}{\text{hr(sq ft)(lb mole/cu ft)}}$$

$$\bar{u}_y = \frac{\Gamma}{\rho\delta} = \frac{150}{62.3(0.000843)} = 2,850 \text{ ft/hr}$$

At the top, $c_{Ai} - \bar{c}_A = c_{Ai} - c_{A0} = c_{Ai} = 0.0021$ lb mole/cu ft.
At the bottom, $c_{Ai} - \bar{c}_{AL} = 0.0021 - \bar{c}_{AL}$ lb mole/cu ft.
The flux of absorption is given by Eqs. (3.21) and (3.22)

$$\frac{2,850(0.000843)\bar{c}_{AL}}{2} = \frac{0.455[0.0021 - (0.0021 - \bar{c}_{AL})]}{\ln[0.0021/(0.0021 - \bar{c}_{AL})]}$$

$$\therefore \quad \bar{c}_{AL} = 0.00066 \text{ lb mole/cu ft}$$

The rate of absorption is therefore estimated to be

$$\bar{u}_y\delta(\bar{c}_{AL} - c_{A0}) = 2,850(0.000843)(0.00066 - 0) = 0.001585 \text{ lb mole/(hr)(ft width)}$$

The actual value may be substantially larger.

MASS-TRANSFER COEFFICIENTS IN TURBULENT FLOW

Most practically useful situations involve turbulent flow, and for these it is generally not possible to compute mass-transfer coefficients owing to inability to describe the flow conditions mathematically. Instead, we rely principally on experimental data. The data are, however, limited in scope, with respect to circumstances and situations as well as to range of fluid properties. Therefore it is important to be able to extend their applicability to situations not covered experimentally and to draw upon knowledge of other transfer processes (of heat, particularly) for help.

To this end, there are many theories which attempt to interpret or explain the behavior of mass-transfer coefficients, such as the film, penetration, surface-renewal, and other theories.   They are all speculations, and are continually being revised.   It is helpful to keep in mind that transfer coefficients, for both heat and mass transfer, are expedients used to deal with situations which are not fully understood.   They include in one quantity effects which are the result of both molecular and turbulent diffusion.   The relative contribution of these effects, and indeed the detailed character of the turbulent diffusion itself, differs from one situation to another.   The ultimate interpretation or explanation of the transfer coefficients will come only when the problems of the fluid mechanics are solved, at which time it will be possible to abandon the concept of the transfer coefficient.

Eddy diffusion

It will be useful first to describe briefly an elementary view of fluid turbulence, as a means of introducing the definitions of terms used in describing transfer under turbulent conditions.   Turbulence is characterized by motion of the fluid particles which is irregular with respect both to direction and time.   Thus, for a fluid flowing turbulently in a duct (Fig. 3.5), the flow is, in the net, in the axial (or x) direction.   At any location 2 within the central region of the cross section, the time average of the velocity may be u_x, but at any instant the velocity will actually be $u_x + u'_{ix}$, where u'_{ix} is the *deviating* or *fluctuating* velocity.   Values of u'_{ix} will vary with time through a range of positive and negative values, the time average being zero, although u'_x, the square root of the time average of $(u'_{ix})^2$, will be finite.   Although the time-average value of $u_z = 0$, since the net flow is axially directed, the deviating velocity in the z direction will be u'_{iz} at any instant.

In Fig. 3.5, consider a second location 1, where the x velocity is larger than at 2 by an amount $\Delta u_x = -l \, du_x/dz$.   The distance l, the *Prandtl mixing length*, is defined such that $u'_x = \Delta u_x = -l \, du_x/dz$.   Owing to the z-directed fluctuating velocity, a particle of fluid, an eddy, may move from 2 to 1 at a velocity u'_{iz}, but it will be replaced by an eddy of equal volume moving from 1 to 2.   It is imagined, in the Prandtl theory, that the eddies retain their identity during the interchange but

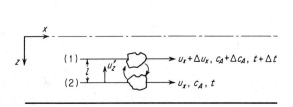

Fig. 3.5 *Eddy diffusion.*

blend into the fluid at their new locations.   This is recognized as a great oversimplification, since an eddy must likely lose at least part of its identity as soon as it moves from its original location even an infinitesimal distance (G. I. Taylor theory[16]).

The mass velocity of eddy interchange is then $\rho u'_{iz}$, and owing to the different velocities at 1 and 2, there will be a momentum transfer flux $\rho u'_{iz} u'_{ix}$.   If u'_{iz} and u'_{ix} are essentially equal, there results an average shear stress due to the turbulent eddy interchange,

$$\tau_{\text{turb}} g_c = \rho \,|u'_{iz} u'_{ix}| = \rho u'_z u'_x = \rho(u'_x)^2 = \rho l^2 \left(\frac{du_x}{dz}\right)^2 \tag{3.23}$$

Molecular motion, of course, still also contributes to the shear stress, as given by Eq. (2.45), so that the *total* shear stress becomes

$$\tau g_c = -\mu \frac{du_x}{dz} + \rho l^2 \left(\frac{du_x}{dz}\right)^2 = -\left[\mu + \rho l^2 \left(-\frac{du_x}{dz}\right)\right] \frac{du_x}{dz} = -\left(\frac{\mu}{\rho} + E_v\right) \frac{d(u_x \rho)}{dz} \tag{3.24}$$

E_v is the eddy momentum diffusivity, length^2/time.   While μ or $v = \mu/\rho$ is a constant for a given fluid at fixed temperature and pressure, E_v will depend on the local degree of turbulence.   In the various regions of the duct, v predominates near the wall, while in the turbulent core E_v predominates, to an extent depending upon the degree of turbulence.

The eddies bring about a transfer of dissolved solute, as we have mentioned before.   The average concentration gradient between 1 and 2 in Fig. 3.5 is $\Delta c_A/l$, proportional to a local gradient, $-dc_A/dz$.   The flux of A due to the interchange, $u'_z \Delta c_A$, and the concentration gradient may be used to define an eddy diffusivity of mass E_D, length^2/time

$$E_D = \frac{b_1 u'_z \Delta c_A}{\Delta c_A/l} = \frac{J_{A,\text{turb}}}{-dc_A/dz} \tag{3.25}$$

where b_1 is a proportionality constant.   The *total* flux of A, due both to molecular and eddy diffusion, then will be

$$J_A = -(D_{AB} + E_D) \frac{dc_A}{dz} \tag{3.26}$$

As in the case of momentum transfer, D is a constant for a particular solution at fixed conditions of temperature and pressure, while E_D depends on the local turbulence intensity. D predominates in the region near the wall, E_D in the turbulent core.

In similar fashion, an eddy thermal diffusivity E_H, length^2/time, can be used to describe the flux of heat as a result of a temperature gradient,

$$E_H = \frac{b_2 u'_z \Delta(\rho C_p t)}{\Delta(\rho C_p t)/l} = \frac{q_{\text{turb}}}{-d(\rho C_p t)/dz} \tag{3.27}$$

where b_2 is a proportionality constant.   The *total* heat flux due to conduction and eddy motion is

$$q = -(k + E_H \rho C_p) \frac{dt}{dz} = -(\alpha + E_H) \frac{d(t \rho C_p)}{dz} \tag{3.28}$$

As before, α for a given fluid is fixed for fixed conditions of temperature and pressure, but E_H varies with the degree of turbulence and hence with location.

The three eddy diffusivities of momentum, heat, and mass are then each proportional to $u'_z l$. They may be computed from measured velocity, temperature, and concentration gradients, respectively, in that order of increasing difficulty of measurement. The data, very meager, indicate that the proportionality constants are not all the same. For ordinary fluids flowing in a pipe, E_D/E_v and E_H/E_v may be in the range 1.2 to 1.8, varying with position, while for liquid metals (high k, low Pr), E_H/E_v is much less than unity because of heat leak from the metal eddies as they move from place to place.[24,32] Within the limitations of the data, except for liquid metals, it appears that E_D is, for a given situation, essentially the same as E_H.

Just as for laminar flow or for stagnant fluids, the ratios of the diffusivities are significant. Thus, we may speak of a molecular Schmidt number $Sc = v/D_{AB}$, a turbulent Schmidt number E_v/E_D, and a total Schmidt number $(v + E_v)/(D_{AB} + E_D)$. Similarly, the ratios of total to molecular diffusivity,

$$\frac{v + E_v}{v} = 1 + \frac{E_v}{v} \tag{3.29}$$

$$\frac{\alpha + E_H}{\alpha} = 1 + \text{Pr}\,\frac{E_H}{v} \tag{3.30}$$

$$\frac{D + E_D}{D} = 1 + \text{Sc}\,\frac{E_D}{v} \tag{3.31}$$

are significant in that they indicate the relative importance of turbulence and laminar flow. Assuming that the eddy diffusivities are about the same, then a small amount of turbulence, as near a solid surface ($E_v/v \ll 1$), will not influence the ratio of Eq. (3.29) and therefore the velocity distribution very greatly. If Pr and Sc both equal unity, the influence on the heat and mass transfer will also be small. But for large Pr and Sc, the influence will be profound, and the relative influence on heat and mass transfer will clearly depend upon the relative size of Pr and Sc. Only for fluids whose Pr = Sc will the percentage change in heat- and mass-transfer flux be the same for a given change in the degree of turbulence, and only for Pr = Sc = 1 will all three total diffusivities be the same.

Mass-transfer coefficients covering the transfer of material from an interface to the turbulent zone will clearly depend upon the total diffusivity $D + E_D$. Success in estimating this theoretically in the manner used for laminar flow will depend on knowledge of how the ratio E_D/D varies throughout the diffusion path. Knowledge of how the ratio E_v/v varies will be of direct help only provided $E_D = E_v$, which is evidently not generally true. But knowledge of the heat-transfer coefficients, which depend upon E_H/v, should be useful in predicting the mass-transfer coefficient, since E_H and E_D are evidently essentially equal except for the liquid metals.

Film theory

This is the oldest[18] and most obvious picture of the meaning of the mass-transfer coefficients. When a fluid flows in turbulent flow past a solid surface, the fluid

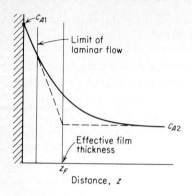

Fig. 3.6   *Film theory.*

velocity being zero at the surface itself, there must be a viscous layer, or film, in the fluid adjacent to the surface. Since the eddy diffusivity is not infinite in the turbulent region of the fluid, there is a concentration gradient for any diffusing solute between the surface and the fluid which extends into the turbulent core. That part lying within the viscous layer is characteristic of molecular diffusion. This is shown by the full curve of Fig. 3.6 for the case of a solute diffusing into the fluid. The film theory imagines the concentration to follow the broken curve of the figure, such that the entire concentration difference, $c_{A1} - c_{A2}$, is described by molecular diffusion, and defines an "effective" film thickness z_F whose resistance to molecular diffusion is the same as the actual resistance to mass transfer in the true viscous layer, buffer region, and turbulent core combined. It was early recognized[19] that if this picture were to be valid, the effective film would have to be very thin, so that the quantity of solute within the film would be small relative to the amount passing through it or that the concentration gradient would have to be set up quickly. The concentration gradient in the film is that characteristic of steady state.

In Eq. (3.1), it is clear that F has merely replaced the group $D_{AB}c/z$ of Eq. (2.22). The film theory states that z of Eq. (2.21) is z_F, the effective film thickness, whose thickness depends upon the nature of the flow conditions. Similarly, the z's of Eqs. (2.26), (2.30), (2.34), (2.40), (2.41), and (2.43) are interpreted to be z_F, incorporated into the k's of Eqs. (3.3) to (3.6).

The film theory predicts therefore that F and the k-type mass-transfer coefficients for different solutes being transferred under the same fluid-flow conditions are directly proportional to the D's for the solutes. On the other hand, we observe for turbulent flow a much smaller dependency, proportional to D^n, where n may be anything from nearly zero to 0.8 or 0.9, depending upon the circumstances. The simple film theory has therefore been largely discredited, except as a limiting case. Nevertheless, mass-transfer coefficients are still frequently called "film" coefficients.

Penetration theory

Higbie[15] emphasized that in many situations the time of exposure of a fluid to mass transfer is short, so that the concentration gradient of the film theory, characteristic of steady state, would not have time to develop.   His theory was actually conceived to describe the contact of two fluids, as in Fig. 3.7.   Here, as Higbie depicted it in Fig. 3.7a, a bubble of gas rises through a liquid which absorbs the gas.   A particle of the liquid b, initially at the top of the bubble, is in contact with the gas for the time θ required for the bubble to rise a distance equal to its diameter while the liquid particle slips along the surface of the bubble.   An extension to cases where the liquid may be in turbulent motion, as in Fig. 3.7b,[7] shows an eddy b rising from the turbulent depths of the liquid and remaining exposed for a time θ to the action of the gas.   In this theory the time of exposure is taken as constant for all such eddies or particles of liquid.

Initially, the concentration of dissolved gas in the eddy is uniformly c_{A0}, and internally the eddy is considered to be stagnant.   When the eddy is exposed to the gas at the surface, the concentration in the liquid at the gas-liquid surface is c_{Ai}, which may be taken as the equilibrium solubility of the gas in the liquid.   During the time θ, the liquid particle is subject to unsteady-state diffusion or penetration of solute in the z direction, and, as an approximation, Eq. (2.18) may be applied

$$\frac{\partial c_A}{\partial \theta} = D_{AB} \frac{\partial^2 c_A}{\partial z^2} \tag{3.32}$$

For short exposure times, and with slow diffusion in the liquid, the molecules of dissolving solute are never able to reach the depth z_b corresponding to the thickness of the eddy, so that from the solute point of view, z_b is essentially infinite.   The conditions on Eq. (3.32) then are

$$c_A = \begin{cases} c_{A0} & \text{at } \theta = 0 \text{ for all } z \\ c_{Ai} & \text{at } z = 0 \text{ for } \theta > 0 \\ c_{A0} & \text{at } z = \infty \text{ for all } \theta \end{cases}$$

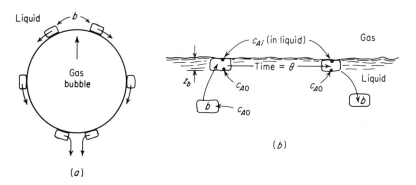

Fig. 3.7 *Penetration theory.*

and its solution is

$$c_A = c_{A0} + (c_{Ai} - c_{A0})\left(1 - \frac{2}{\pi}\int_0^{z/2(\theta D_{AB})^{0.5}} e^{-\eta^2}\,d\eta\right) \tag{3.33}$$

which gives the concentration profile $c_A(z)$ for any time.   The flux at the surface at time θ, if absorption rates are small ($N_A + N_B \to 0$), is

$$N_{A,z=0} = -D_{AB}\left(\frac{\partial c_A}{\partial z}\right)_{z=0} = (c_{Ai} - c_{A0})\sqrt{\frac{D_{AB}}{\pi\theta}} \tag{3.34}$$

where the concentration gradient has been obtained by differentiating Eq. (3.33). The average flux over the time of exposure is then

$$N_{A,av} = \frac{\displaystyle\int_0^\theta (c_{Ai} - c_{A0})\sqrt{\frac{D_{AB}}{\pi\theta}}\,d\theta}{\theta - 0} = 2(c_{Ai} - c_{A0})\sqrt{\frac{D_{AB}}{\pi\theta}} \tag{3.35}$$

and comparison with Eq. (3.4) shows

$$k_{L,av} = 2\sqrt{\frac{D_{AB}}{\pi\theta}} \tag{3.36}$$

with $k_{L,av}$ proportional to $D_{AB}^{0.5}$ for different solutes under the same circumstances. This indicated dependence on D is typical of short exposure times, where the depth of solute penetration is small relative to the depth of the absorbing pool [compare Eq. (3.19)].   As pointed out above, experience shows a range of exponents on D from nearly zero to 0.8 or 0.9.

Surface-renewal theory

Danckwerts[7] pointed out that the Higbie theory with its constant time of exposure of the eddies of fluid at the surface is a special case of what may be a more realistic picture, where the eddies are exposed for varying lengths of time.   The liquid-gas interface is then a mosaic of surface elements of different exposure-time histories, and since the rate of solute penetration depends on the exposure time, the average rate for unit surface area must be determined by summing up the individual values.   If $\phi\,d\theta$ is the area of surface elements having residence times between θ and $\theta + d\theta$, then unit surface area becomes $1 = \displaystyle\int_0^\infty \phi\,d\theta$.   On the assumption that the chance of a surface element's being replaced by another is quite independent of how long it has been in the surface, and if s is the fractional rate of replacement of elements belonging to any age group, Danckwerts finds $\phi = se^{-s\theta}$.   Consequently, the mean rate of absorption per unit of surface is, using Eq. (3.35),

$$N_{A,av} = (c_{Ai} - c_{A0})\int_0^\infty \sqrt{\frac{D_{AB}}{\pi\theta}}\,se^{-s\theta}\,d\theta = (c_{Ai} - c_{A0})\sqrt{D_{AB}s} \tag{3.37}$$

and therefore

$$k_{L,\text{av}} = \sqrt{D_{AB}s} \tag{3.38}$$

Danckwerts pointed out that all theories of this sort, derived with the original boundary conditions on Eq. (3.33), will lead to $k_{L,\text{av}}$ proportional to $D_{AB}^{0.5}$, regardless of the nature of the surface-renewal rate s which may apply.

Combination film–surface-renewal theory

Dobbins,[9] concerned with the rate of absorption of oxygen into flowing streams and rivers, pointed out that the film theory ($k_L \propto D_{AB}$) assumes a time of exposure of the surface elements sufficiently long for the concentration profile within the film to be characteristic of steady state, whereas the penetration and surface-renewal theories ($k_L \propto D_{AB}^{0.5}$) assume the surface elements to be of essentially infinite depth, the diffusing solute never reaching the region of constant concentration below. The observed dependency, $k_L \propto D_{AB}^n$ with n dependent upon circumstances, might be explained by allowing for a finite depth of the surface elements or eddies for a limited time.

Accordingly he replaced the third boundary condition on Eq. (3.32) by $c_A = c_{A0}$ for $z = z_b$, where z_b is finite. Higbie's requirement of constant exposure time then produced

$$k_{L,\text{av}} = \frac{D_{AB}}{z_b}\left(1 - \frac{z_b^2}{3 D_{AB}\theta} - \frac{2 z_b^2}{\pi^2 D_{AB}\theta}\sum_{n=1}^{\infty}\frac{1}{n^2}e^{-\pi^2 n^2 D_{AB}\theta/z_b^2}\right) \tag{3.39}$$

which, as Fig. 3.8a shows, reduces to $k_{L,\text{av}} = D_{AB}/z_b$ for values of $D_{AB}\theta/z_b^2$ greater than about 0.6. In other words, for rapid penetration (D_{AB} large), long exposure time (θ large), or thin surface elements, a steady-state concentration gradient within the surface element is produced, and the penetration theory reverts to the film theory. Similarly, with Danckwerts' rate of renewal of the surface elements, he obtained

$$k_{L,\text{av}} = \sqrt{D_{AB}s}\,\coth\sqrt{\frac{s z_b^2}{D_{AB}}} \tag{3.40}$$

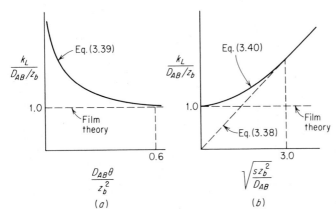

Fig. 3.8 *Film-surface renewal theory.* (a) *Constant exposure time.* (b) *Random replacement of surface elements.* (*After Dobbins.*[9])

which is shown in Fig. 3.8*b*.   Here, as the rate of surface renewal becomes small (*s* approaches zero) or with large diffusivities, the mass-transfer coefficient takes on the character of the film theory, whereas for slow penetration (D_{AB} small) or rapid surface renewal (*s* large), it follows Eq. (3.38).   Consequently $k_L \propto D_{AB}^n$, where *n* may have any value between the limits of 0.5 and 1.0, which will account for many observations.   Toor and Marchello[36] have made similar suggestions.

By simulating the turbulences developed in a river, Dobbins[10] has absorbed gases into water and observed values of *n* in the range 0.985 to 0.65, smaller with increasing turbulence (larger *s*), and has measured both *s* and z_b by writing Eq. (3.40) with measured k_L's for gases of different diffusivities and solving simultaneously.   The observations could not be accounted for by Eq. (3.39).

Flow past solids; boundary layers

In the case of the theories discussed above, where the interfacial surface is formed between two fluids, the velocity at that surface will not normally be zero.   But when one of the phases is a solid, the fluid velocity parallel to the surface at the interface must of necessity be zero, and consequently the two circumstances are inherently different.

In Fig. 3.9 a fluid with uniform velocity u_0 and uniform solute concentration c_{A0} meets up with a flat solid surface AK.   Since the velocity u_x is zero at the surface and rises to u_0 at some distance above the plate, the curve $ABCD$ separates the region of velocity u_0 from the region of lower velocity, called the boundary layer.   The boundary layer may be characterized by laminar flow, as below the curve AB, but if the velocity u_0 is sufficiently large, for values of $\mathrm{Re}_x = xu_0\rho/\mu$ in excess of about $5(10^5)$ the flow in the bulk of the boundary layer will be turbulent, as below the curve CD.   Below the turbulent boundary layer there will be a thinner region, the viscous sublayer, extending from the plate to the curve FG.   The equations of motion (Navier-Stokes equations) have been solved to provide the velocity distribution, u_x and u_z as functions

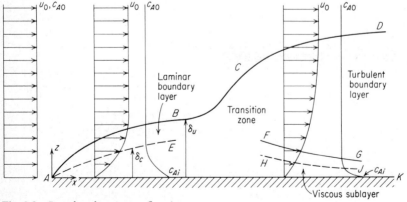

Fig. 3.9   *Boundary layers on a flat plate.*

of x and z, within the laminar boundary layer. For the turbulent region, exact solutions are not known for lack of complete knowledge of the turbulence, although approximations can be made. Boundary layers also occur for flow at the entrance to circular pipes, for flow along the outside of cylinders, and the like.

If mass transfer from the surface into the fluid occurs, as with a solid subliming into a gas or a solid dissolving into a liquid, the solute concentration in the fluid at the solid surface is everywhere c_{Ai}, greater than c_{A0}. There will be a curve AE, and also one HJ, which separates regions of uniform concentration c_{A0} from regions of higher values of c_A, corresponding to a concentration boundary layer. In the region where only a laminar velocity boundary layer exists, the equations of motion and of mass transfer can be solved simultaneously to yield the concentration profile and, from its slope at the surface, the laminar mass-transfer coefficient.[3] This is a fairly complex problem particularly if account is taken of the influence of the flux of mass of A in the z direction on the velocity profile. If this influence is negligible, and if mass transfer begins at the leading edge A, it develops that the thickness of the velocity boundary layer δ_u and that of the concentration boundary layer δ_c are in the ratio $\delta_u/\delta_c = \mathrm{Sc}^{1/3}$. The average mass-transfer coefficient from the leading edge to a distance x is given by

$$\mathrm{Sh}_{av} = \frac{k_{L,av} x}{D_{AB}} = 0.664\,\mathrm{Re}_x^{1/2}\,\mathrm{Sc}^{1/3} \qquad (3.41)$$

This shows the mass-transfer coefficient to vary as $D_{AB}^{2/3}$, which is typical of the results of boundary-layer calculations.

In the regions where a turbulent boundary layer and a viscous sublayer exist, similar calculations cannot be made because the fluid motion cannot be described, except after rather drastic simplifying assumptions. While it has usually been assumed that the viscous sublayer is a *laminar* sublayer, attempts have been made to describe the mass-transfer characteristics by picturing eddies entering the sublayer from the turbulent region, even to the solid surface, somewhat in the manner of the surface-renewal theory. This idea was first proposed by Murphree[23] in 1932 and has more recently been revived by others.[8,14,20,29,38] As explained earlier (see page 49), such eddies may have important influence on the mass-transfer rate without strongly affecting the velocity profile.

When the surface over which the fluid passes is curved convexly in the direction of flow, as in flow at right angles to the outside of a cylinder and past a sphere, well-developed boundary layers form at very low rates of flow, which are amenable to theoretical treatment. At higher rates of flow, however, the boundary layer separates from the surface, and eddies form in the wake behind the object. Theoretical computation of the mass-transfer coefficient cannot then be made.

MASS-, HEAT-, AND MOMENTUM-TRANSFER ANALOGIES

In laminar flow past a solid surface, as for the two-dimensional laminar boundary layer of Fig. 3.9, for example, the momentum balance or equation of motion

(Navier-Stokes equation) for the x direction becomes[3]

$$u_x \frac{\partial u_x}{\partial x} + u_z \frac{\partial u_x}{\partial z} = \nu \left(\frac{\partial^2 u_x}{\partial x^2} + \frac{\partial^2 u_x}{\partial z^2} \right) \tag{3.42}$$

If there is mass transfer without chemical reaction, Eq. (2.17) gives the equation of continuity for substance A

$$u_x \frac{\partial c_A}{\partial x} + u_z \frac{\partial c_A}{\partial z} = D_{AB} \left(\frac{\partial^2 c_A}{\partial x^2} + \frac{\partial^2 c_A}{\partial z^2} \right) \tag{3.43}$$

and if there is heat transfer between the fluid and the plate, Eq. (2.19) provides

$$u_x \frac{\partial t}{\partial x} + u_z \frac{\partial t}{\partial z} = \alpha \left(\frac{\partial^2 t}{\partial x^2} + \frac{\partial^2 t}{\partial z^2} \right) \tag{3.44}$$

which are to be solved simultaneously, together with the equation of continuity (2.14). It is clear that these equations are all of the same form, with u_x, c_A, and t and the three diffusivities of momentum ν, mass D_{AB}, and heat α replacing each other in appropriate places in the equations.

In solving these, dimensionless forms of the variables are usually substituted

$$\frac{u_x - (u_{x,z=0} = 0)}{u_0 - (u_{x,z=0} = 0)}$$

$$\frac{c_A - c_{Ai}}{c_{A0} - c_{Ai}} \quad \text{and} \quad \frac{t - t_i}{t_0 - t_i}$$

Then the boundary conditions become identical. Thus, for Fig. 3.9, at $z = 0$ all three dimensionless variables are zero, and at $z = \infty$, all three equal unity. Consequently the form of the solutions, which provide dimensionless velocity, concentration, and temperature profiles, are the same. Indeed, if all three diffusivities are equal, so that $Sc = Pr = 1$, the profiles in dimensionless form are identical. The initial slopes of the concentration, temperature, and velocity profiles provide the means of computing the corresponding local transfer coefficients

$$N_A = -D_{AB} \left(\frac{\partial c_A}{\partial z} \right)_{z=0} = k_L(c_{Ai} - c_{A0}) \tag{3.45}$$

$$q = -\alpha \left[\frac{\partial (t C_p \rho)}{\partial z} \right]_{z=0} = h(t_i - t_0) \tag{3.46}$$

$$\tau_i g_c = \nu \left[\frac{\partial (u_x \rho)}{\partial z} \right]_{z=0} = \frac{f}{2} u_0(\rho u_0 - 0) \tag{3.47}$$

where f is the dimensionless friction factor and $f u_0/2$ might be considered a momentum-transfer coefficient. When the coefficients are computed and arranged as dimensionless groups, the results are all of the same form, as might be expected. In particular, for the flat plate of Fig. 3.9 at low mass-transfer rates,

$$\frac{Nu}{Re_x\, Pr^{1/3}} = \frac{Sh}{Re_x\, Sc^{1/3}} = \frac{f}{2} = 0.332\ Re_x^{-1/2} \qquad (3.48)$$

and the average coefficients provide Nu_{av} and Sh_{av} given by the same expressions with 0.332 replaced by 0.664 [compare Eq. (3.41)]. The same procedure may be followed with any laminar-flow case, with similarly analogous expressions resulting. In these cases, the friction factor corresponds to a skin-friction drag along the surface. For flow where separation occurs, such as for flow past a sphere or at right angles to a cylinder or any bluff object, one might expect the friction factor based on total drag, which includes not only skin friction but form drag due to flow separation as well, to follow a function different from that of the mass- and heat-transfer groups.

In the case of turbulent flow, the differential equations will contain time-averaged velocities and in addition the eddy diffusivities of momentum, mass, and heat transfer. The resulting equations cannot be solved for lack of information about the eddy diffusivities, but one might expect results of the form

$$\frac{Sh}{Re\ Sc} = \psi_1\!\left(\frac{f}{2},\, Sc,\, \frac{E_v}{E_D}\right) = \psi_2\!\left(\frac{f}{2},\, Sc,\, \frac{E_D}{v}\right) \qquad (3.49)$$

$$\frac{Nu}{Re\ Pr} = \psi_1\!\left(\frac{f}{2},\, Pr,\, \frac{E_v}{E_H}\right) = \psi_2\!\left(\frac{f}{2},\, Pr,\, \frac{E_H}{v}\right) \qquad (3.50)$$

Successful completion of an analogy requires, therefore, knowledge of how the ratios E_v/v, E_D/E_v, and E_H/E_v vary with distance from the fluid interface. It is customary arbitrarily to set $E_D/E_v = E_H/E_v = 1$, despite experimental evidence to the contrary (see page 49) and to make some arbitrary decision about E_v/v. With these assumptions, however, experimental velocity profiles permit prediction of the profiles and coefficients for mass and heat transfer. Further, assuming only $E_D = E_H$ (which is much more reasonable) permits information on heat transfer to be converted directly for use in mass-transfer calculations and vice versa.

Let us sum up and further generalize what can be done with the analogies:

1. For analogous circumstances, temperature and concentration profiles in dimensionless form and heat- and mass-transfer coefficients in the form of dimensionless groups, respectively, are given by the same functions. To convert equations or correlations of data on heat transfer and temperatures to corresponding mass transfer and concentrations, the dimensionless groups of the former are replaced by the corresponding groups of the latter. Table 3.2 lists the commonly appearing dimensionless groups. The limitations are:

a. The flow conditions and geometry must be the same.

b. Most heat-transfer data are based on situations involving no mass transfer. Use of the analogy would then produce mass-transfer coefficients corresponding to no net mass transfer, in turn corresponding most closely to k'_G, k'_c, or k'_y $(= F)$. Sherwood numbers are commonly written in terms of any of the coefficients, but when

Table 3.2. Corresponding dimensionless groups of mass and heat transfer

No.	Mass transfer	Heat transfer
1	$\dfrac{c_A - c_{A1}}{c_{A2} - c_{A1}}$	$\dfrac{t - t_1}{t_2 - t_1}$
2	Reynolds number $$\mathrm{Re} = \frac{lu\rho}{\mu}$$	Reynolds number $$\mathrm{Re} = \frac{lu\rho}{\mu}$$
3	Schmidt number $$\mathrm{Sc} = \frac{\mu}{\rho D_{AB}} = \frac{\nu}{D_{AB}}$$	Prandtl number $$\mathrm{Pr} = \frac{C_p\mu}{k} = \frac{\nu}{\alpha}$$
4	Sherwood number $$\mathrm{Sh} = \frac{Fl}{cD_{AB}}, \frac{k_G p_{BM} RTl}{P_t D_{AB}},$$ $$\frac{k_c p_{BM} l}{P_t D_{AB}}, \frac{k_c' l}{D_{AB}}, \frac{k_y' RTl}{P_t D_{AB}}, \text{etc.}$$	Nusselt number $$\mathrm{Nu} = \frac{hl}{k}$$
5	Grashof number† $$\mathrm{Gr} = \frac{gl^3 \,\Delta\rho}{\rho}\left(\frac{\rho}{\mu}\right)^2$$	Grashof number† $$\mathrm{Gr} = gl^3\beta \,\Delta t \left(\frac{\rho}{\mu}\right)^2$$
6	Péclet number $$\mathrm{Pe} = \mathrm{Re}\,\mathrm{Sc} = \frac{lu}{D_{AB}}$$	Péclet number $$\mathrm{Pe} = \mathrm{Re}\,\mathrm{Pr} = \frac{C_p lu\rho}{k} = \frac{lu}{\alpha}$$
7	Stanton number $$\mathrm{St} = \frac{\mathrm{Sh}}{\mathrm{Re}\,\mathrm{Sc}} = \frac{\mathrm{Sh}}{\mathrm{Pe}} = \frac{F}{cu},$$ $$\frac{F}{G}, \frac{k_G p_{BM} M_{\mathrm{av}}}{\rho u}, \text{etc.}$$	Stanton number $$\mathrm{St} = \frac{\mathrm{Nu}}{\mathrm{Re}\,\mathrm{Pr}} = \frac{\mathrm{Nu}}{\mathrm{Pe}} = \frac{h}{C_p u\rho}$$
8	$j_D = \mathrm{St}\,\mathrm{Sc}^{2/3}$	$j_H = \mathrm{St}\,\mathrm{Pr}^{2/3}$

† The Grashof number appears in cases involving natural convection; $\Delta\rho = |\rho_1 - \rho_2|$, $\Delta t = |t_1 - t_2|$, in the same phase.

derived by replacement of Nusselt numbers for use where the net mass transfer is not zero, they should be taken as $\mathrm{Sh} = Fl/cD_{AB}$, and the F used with Eq. (3.1). Further, the result will be useful only in the absence of chemical reaction.

 c. The boundary conditions which would be used to solve the corresponding differential equations must be analogous. For example, in the case of the mass-transfer problem of the falling film of Fig. 3.4, the analogous circumstances for heat transfer would require heat transfer from the gas (not from the solid wall) to the liquid, the wall to be impervious to the transfer of heat, heat transfer beginning at the same value of y as mass transfer (in this case at $y = 0$), a constant temperature for the liquid-gas interface, and constant fluid properties.

d. For turbulent flow, $E_H = E_D$ at any location.

2. Friction factors and velocity profiles can be expected to correlate with the corresponding heat- and mass-transfer quantities only if $E_v = E_H = E_D$ in turbulent flow, and in extension to viscous sublayers only if $E_v/v = E_H/\alpha = E_D/D_{AB}$. For either laminar or turbulent flow, the friction factors must indicate skin friction and not form drag as well. In general, it is safest to avoid the friction analogy to mass and heat transfer.

These analogies are particularly useful in extending the very considerable amount of information on heat transfer to yield corresponding information on mass transfer, which is more likely to be lacking. Alternatively, local mass-transfer coefficients can be measured with relative ease through sublimation or dissolution of solids, and these can be converted to the analogous local heat-transfer coefficients, which are difficult to obtain.[34]

Illustration 3.2. What is the heat-transfer analog to Eq. (3.12)?

Solution. The equation remains the same with the dimensionless concentration ratio replaced by $(t_i - t_L)/(t_i - t_0)$; the dimensionless group

$$\eta = \frac{2D_{AB}L}{3\delta^2 \bar{u}_y} = \frac{2}{3} \frac{D_{AB}}{\delta \bar{u}_y} \frac{L}{\delta} = \frac{2}{3} \frac{L}{Pe} \frac{L}{\delta}$$

for mass transfer is replaced by

$$\eta = \frac{2}{3} \frac{L}{Pe} \frac{L}{\delta} = \frac{2}{3} \frac{\alpha}{\delta \bar{u}_y} \frac{L}{\delta} = \frac{2\alpha L}{3\delta^2 \bar{u}_y} \quad \textbf{Ans.}$$

Illustration 3.3. For flow of a fluid at right angles to a circular cylinder, the average heat-transfer coefficient (averaged around the periphery) for fluid Reynolds numbers in the range 1 to 4,000 is given by[11]

$$Nu_{av} = 0.43 + 0.532\ Re^{0.5}\ Pr^{0.31}$$

where Nu and Re are computed with the cylinder diameter and fluid properties are taken at the mean of the cylinder and bulk-fluid temperatures.

Estimate the rate of sublimation of a cylinder of uranium hexafluoride, UF_6, $\frac{1}{4}$ in. diam, exposed to an air stream flowing at a velocity of 10 ft/sec. The surface temperature of the solid is 43°C, at which temperature the vapor pressure of UF_6 is 400 mm Hg. The bulk air is at 1 atm pressure, 60°C.

Solution. The analogous expression for the mass-transfer coefficient is

$$Sh_{av} = 0.43 + 0.532\ Re^{0.5}\ Sc^{0.31}$$

Along the mass-transfer path (cylinder surface to bulk air) the average temperature is 51.5°C, and the average partial pressure of UF_6 is 200 mm Hg, corresponding to $200/760 = 0.263$ mole fraction UF_6, 0.737 mole fraction air. The corresponding physical properties of the gas, at the mean temperature and composition, are estimated to be: density $= 0.256$ lb/cu ft, viscosity $= 0.027$ centipoise $= 0.0653$ lb/(ft)(hr), diffusivity $= 0.35$ sq ft/hr.

$$\text{Re} = \frac{du\rho}{\mu} = \frac{(0.25/12)(10)(3600)(0.256)}{0.0653} = 2{,}940$$

$$\text{Sc} = \frac{\mu}{\rho D} = \frac{0.0653}{0.256(0.35)} = 0.728$$

$$\therefore \quad \text{Sh}_{\text{av}} = 0.43 + 0.532(2{,}940)^{0.5}(0.728)^{0.31} = 26.5 = \frac{F_{\text{av}}d}{cD_{AB}}$$

$$c = \frac{1}{359}\frac{492}{460 + 124.7} = 0.00234 \text{ lb mole/cu ft}$$

$$F_{\text{av}} = \frac{\text{Sh}_{\text{av}}\, cD_{AB}}{d} = \frac{26.5(0.00234)(0.35)}{0.25/12} = 10.4 \text{ lb moles/(hr)(sq ft)}$$

In this case, N_B (air) $= 0$, so that $N_A/(N_A + N_B) = 1.0$. Since $c_A/c = p_A$ atm, Eq. (3.1) provides

$$N_A = 10.4 \ln \frac{1 - 0}{1 - {}^{400}/_{760}} = 7.78 \text{ lb moles UF}_6/(\text{hr})(\text{sq ft})$$

which is the mass-transfer flux based on the entire cylinder area.

Note 1: The calculated N_A is an instantaneous flux. Mass transfer will rapidly reduce the cylinder diameter, so that the Reynolds number and hence F will change with time. Furthermore, the surface will not remain in the form of a circular cylinder owing to the variation of the local F about the perimeter, so that the empirical correlation for Nu_{av} and Sh_{av} will then no longer apply.

Note 2: Use of k_c or k_G computed from a simple definition of Sh produces incorrect results because of the relatively high mass-transfer rate, which is not allowed for in the heat-transfer correlation. Thus, $k_c = k_G RT = \text{Sh}_{\text{av}} D_{AB}/d = 26.5(0.35)/(0.25/12) = 4{,}440$ lb moles/(hr)(sq ft)(lb mole/cu ft), or $k_G = 4{,}440/0.729(460 + 124.7) = 10.4$ lb moles/(hr)(sq ft)(atm). This leads to [Eq. (3.3)] $N_A = 10.4({}^{400}/_{760} - 0) = 5.48$ lb moles/(hr)(sq ft), which is too low. However, if k_G is taken to be $10.4P_t/p_{BM}$, the correct answer will be given by Eq. (3.3).

Turbulent flow in circular pipes

A prodigious amount of effort has been spent in developing the analogies among the three transport phenomena for this case, beginning with Reynolds' original concept of the analogy between momentum and heat transfer in 1874.[28]   The number of well-known relationships proposed is in the dozens, and new ones of increasing complexity are continually being proposed.   Space limitations will not permit discussion of this interesting development, and we shall confine ourselves to a few of the results.

Although fairly elaborate measurements have been made of velocity distributions for this case, which should permit determination of the eddy viscosity and its variation with distance from the pipe wall and Reynolds number, nevertheless the quality of the data does not permit very accurate determination of this quantity, especially near the pipe wall.   Even the assumption that all three eddy diffusivities are everywhere the same is then not enough to establish a good basis from which to compute mass or heat transfer from friction data.   This is because for large values of Sc and Pr the computed mass- and heat-transfer coefficients are very sensitive to the variations of eddy diffusivity of mass and heat with distance from the wall (see page 49). Consequently either the variation of eddy viscosity with distance must be assumed, empirically or with the help of some other theory or other, for extension of the friction data, or the variations of those for heat and mass must be assumed.

Assuming that in the viscous sublayer E_v and E_H are both zero and that elsewhere the molecular diffusivities are of negligible importance, with $E_v = E_H$, Prandtl[27] and Taylor[35] deduced

$$\text{St}_{\text{av}} = \frac{\text{Nu}_{\text{av}}}{\text{Re Pr}} = \frac{h_{\text{av}}}{C_p \bar{u}_x \rho} = \frac{\frac{1}{2}f}{1 - u_{xF}/\bar{u}_x + (u_{xF}/\bar{u}_x)\,\text{Pr}} \tag{3.51}$$

where u_{xF} is the axially directed velocity at the edge of the viscous sublayer. The mass-transfer analog can be immediately written. As a result of the assumptions, including neglect of the gradual, rather than abrupt, transition from the viscous sublayer to the turbulent core, the equation does not represent the observed data very well except for Pr (and Sc) near unity. The remarkably simple empirical modification by Colburn[5] represents the data extremely well (Colburn analogy)

$$\text{St}_{\text{av}} = \frac{h_{\text{av}}}{C_p \bar{u}_x \rho} = \frac{\frac{1}{2}f}{\text{Pr}^{\frac{2}{3}}} \tag{3.52}$$

The group $\text{St}_{\text{av}}\,\text{Pr}^{\frac{2}{3}}$ is called j_H

$$\text{St}_{\text{av}}\,\text{Pr}^{\frac{2}{3}} = \frac{h_{\text{av}}}{C_p \bar{u}_x \rho}\,\text{Pr}^{\frac{2}{3}} = j_H = \frac{1}{2}f = \psi(\text{Re}) \tag{3.53}$$

The mass-transfer analog (Chilton-Colburn analogy)[4] is

$$\text{St}_{\text{av}}\,\text{Sc}^{\frac{2}{3}} = \frac{\text{Sh}_{\text{av}}}{\text{Re Sc}}\,\text{Sc}^{\frac{2}{3}} = \frac{F_{\text{av}}}{c\bar{u}_x}\,\text{Sc}^{\frac{2}{3}} = j_D = \frac{1}{2}f = \psi(\text{Re}) \tag{3.54}$$

which, as will be shown, agrees well with experimental data. Many much more elaborate analogies have been proposed,[8,20] based on a variety of assumed relations between E_D/ν and distance from the wall, even in the viscous sublayer [Eq. (3.54) has been shown[38] to be consistent with Murphree's early suggestion[23] that E_D/ν varies as the cube of the distance from the wall in the sublayer]. For most purposes, Eq. (3.54) serves amply well.

Experimental data have come from so-called wetted-wall towers (Fig. 3.10) and flow of liquids through soluble pipes. In Fig. 3.10, a volatile pure liquid is permitted to flow down the inside surface of a circular pipe while a gas is blown upward or downward through the central core. Measurement of the rate of evaporation of the liquid into the gas stream over the known surface permits calculation of the mass-transfer coefficients for the gas phase. Use of different gases and liquids provides variation of Sc. In this way, Sherwood and Gilliland[30] covered values of Re from 2,000 to 35,000, Sc from 0.6 to 2.5, and gas pressures from 0.1 to 3 atm. Linton and Sherwood[21] caused water to flow through a series of pipes made by casting molten benzoic acid and other sparingly soluble solids. In this way the range of Sc was extended to

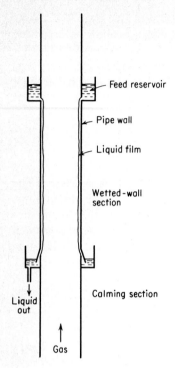

Feed reservoir

Pipe wall

Liquid film

Wetted-wall
section

Calming section

Liquid
out

Gas

Fig. 3.10 *Wetted-wall tower.*

3,000. All the data are empirically correlated by†

$$\text{Sh}_{\text{av}} = \frac{k_{c,\text{av}} p_{BM} d}{P_t D_{AB}} = \frac{k_{L,\text{av}} d}{D_{AB}} = 0.023 \text{ Re}^{0.83} \text{ Sc}^{\frac{1}{3}} \tag{3.55}$$

Over the range of Re = 5,000 to 200,000, the friction factor for flow in smooth pipes can be expressed as

$$\tfrac{1}{2} f = 0.023 \text{ Re}^{-0.20} \tag{3.56}$$

Substitution in Eq. (3.55) then gives

$$\frac{\text{Sh}_{\text{av}}}{\text{Re}^{1.03} \text{ Sc}} \text{Sc}^{\frac{2}{3}} = \tfrac{1}{2} f \tag{3.57}$$

which may be compared with Eq. (3.54).

MASS-TRANSFER DATA FOR SIMPLE SITUATIONS

Table 3.3 provides a few of the correlations taken from the literature for relatively simple situations. Others more appropriate to particular types of mass-transfer equipment will be introduced as needed.

† $k_c p_{BM}/P_t = k'_c$, which then corrects for the mass-transfer flux. Consequently, Sh_{av} may be written also as $F_{\text{av}} d / c D_{AB}$ for cases where Eq. (3.1) must be applied. The data for gases only are better correlated with 0.44 replacing $\frac{1}{3}$ as the exponent on Sc.

Table 3.3. Mass transfer[a] for simple situations

Fluid motion	Range of conditions	Equation	Ref.
1. Inside circular pipes	Re = 4,000–60,000 Sc = 0.6–3,000	$j_D = 0.023\ \text{Re}^{-0.17}$ $\text{Sh}_{av} = 0.023\ \text{Re}^{0.83}\ \text{Sc}^{1/3}$	21, 30
2. Perpendicular to circular cylinders (gases only)	Re′ = 400–25,000 Sc = 0.6–2.6	$\dfrac{k_{G,av} P_t}{G}\ \text{Sc}^{0.56} = 0.281\ \text{Re}'^{-0.4}$	1, 26
3. Parallel to flat plates[b]	Transfer begins at leading edge $\text{Re}_x < 80,000$ $\text{Re}_x > 500,000$	$j_H = 0.664\ \text{Re}_x^{-0.5}$ $j_H = 0.036\ \text{Re}_x^{-0.2}$	22, 31
4. Past single spheres	Sc = 0.6–3,200 $\text{Re}''\ \text{Sc}^{0.5} = 1.8$–600,000	$\text{Sh}_{av} = \text{Sh}_o + 0.347(\text{Re}''\ \text{Sc}^{0.5})^{0.62}$ Gr Sc < 10^8: $\text{Sh}_o = 2.0 + 0.569(\text{Gr Sc})^{0.250}$ Gr Sc > 10^8: $\text{Sh}_o = 2.0 + 0.0254(\text{Gr Sc})^{0.333}\ \text{Sc}^{0.244}$	33
5. Through fixed beds of pellets (gases only)[c,d]	Sc = 0.6 $\dfrac{\text{Re}''}{\epsilon} = 90$–4,000 $\dfrac{\text{Re}''}{\epsilon} = 5,000$–10,300	$j_D = \dfrac{2.06}{\epsilon}\left(\dfrac{\text{Re}''}{\epsilon}\right)^{-0.575}$ $j_D = \dfrac{20.4}{\epsilon}\left(\dfrac{\text{Re}''}{\epsilon}\right)^{-0.815}$	13
6. Through fixed beds of pellets (liquids only)[d,e]	Sc = 159–13,260 $\dfrac{\text{Re}''}{\epsilon} = 0.08$–125 $\dfrac{\text{Re}''}{\epsilon} = 125$–5,000	$\dfrac{F}{G}\text{Sc}^{0.58} = 2.40\left(\dfrac{\text{Re}''}{\epsilon}\right)^{-0.66}$ $\dfrac{F}{G}\text{Sc}^{0.58} = 0.442\left(\dfrac{\text{Re}''}{\epsilon}\right)^{-0.31}$	12, 39

[a] Average mass-transfer coefficients throughout, for constant solute concentrations at the phase surface. Generally, fluid properties are evaluated at the average conditions between the phase surface and the bulk fluid. The heat-mass-transfer analogy is valid throughout except for flow of fluids through fixed beds of pellets.

[b] Mass-transfer data for this case scatter badly but are reasonably well represented by setting $j_D = j_H$.

[c] A transition in the range Re = 4,000–5,000 is indicated. Not all investigators confirm this. For a complete review, see J. J. Barker, *Ind. Eng. Chem.*, **57**(4), 43; (5), 33 (1965).

[d] For fixed beds, the relation between ϵ and d_p is

$$a = \frac{6(1-\epsilon)}{d_p}$$

where a is the specific solid surface, sq ft/cu ft of bed.

[e] The heat-mass-transfer analogy is not confirmed in this case.

Experimental data are usually obtained by blowing gases over various shapes wet with evaporating liquids or causing liquids to flow past solids which dissolve. Average, rather than local, mass-transfer coefficients are usually obtained. In most cases, the data are reported in terms of k_G, k_c, k_L, and the like, coefficients applicable to the binary systems used with $N_B = 0$, without details concerning the actual concentrations of solute during the experiments. Fortunately, the solute concentrations during the experiments are usually fairly low, so that if necessary, conversion of the data to the corresponding F is usually at least approximately possible by simply taking p_{BM}/P_t, x_{BM}, etc., equal to unity (see Table 3.1).

In many cases, particularly when only gases have been studied, the range of Schmidt numbers covered is relatively small; sometimes only one Sc (0.6 for air-water vapor) is studied. The j_D of Eq. (3.54) has been so successful in dealing with turbulent flow in pipes that many data of small Sc range have been put in this form without actually establishing the validity of the $\frac{2}{3}$ exponent on Sc for the situation at hand. Extension to values of Sc far outside the original range of the experiments, particularly for liquids, must therefore be made with the understanding that a considerable approximation may be involved. Some data, as for flow past spheres, for example, cannot be put in the j_D form, and it is likely that many of the correlations using j_D may not be very general.

For situations not covered by the available data, it seems reasonable to assume that the mass-transfer coefficients can be estimated as functions of Re from the corresponding heat-transfer data, if available. If necessary, in the absence of a known effect of Pr, the heat-transfer data may be put in the j_H form and the analog completed by equating j_D to j_H at the same Re. This should serve reasonably well if the range of extrapolation of Sc (or Pr) is not too large.

Illustration 3.4. It is desired to estimate the rate at which water will evaporate from a wetted surface of unusual shape when hydrogen at 1 atm, 100°F, is blown over the surface at a superficial velocity of 50 ft/sec. No mass-transfer measurements have been made, but heat-transfer measurements indicate that for air at 100°F, 1 atm, the heat-transfer coefficient h between air and the surface is given empirically by

$$h = 0.072 G'^{0.6}$$

where G' is the superficial air mass velocity, lb/(hr)(sq ft). Estimate the required mass-transfer coefficient. Physical-property data are:

	100°F, 1 atm	
	Air	H₂
Density ρ, lb/cu ft	0.071	0.00495
Viscosity μ, centipoise	0.0185	0.009
Thermal conductivity k, (Btu)(ft)/(hr)(sq ft)(°F)	0.01576	0.1069
Heat capacity C_p, Btu/(lb)(°F)	0.24	3.45
Diffusivity with water vapor, sq ft/hr		3.0

Solution. The experimental heat-transfer data do not include effects of changing Prandtl number. It will therefore be necessary to assume that the j_H group will satisfactorily describe the effect.

$$j_H = \frac{h}{C_p \rho u} \text{Pr}^{2/3} = \frac{h}{C_p G'} \text{Pr}^{2/3} = \psi(\text{Re})$$

$$h = \frac{C_p G'}{\text{Pr}^{2/3}} \psi(\text{Re}) = 0.072 G'^{0.6} \quad \text{for air}$$

The $\psi(\text{Re})$ must be compatible with $0.072 G'^{0.6}$. Therefore, let $\psi(\text{Re}) = b \, \text{Re}^n$ and define Re as lG'/μ, where l is a characteristic linear dimension of the solid body.

$$\therefore \quad h = \frac{C_p G'}{\text{Pr}^{2/3}} b \, \text{Re}^n = \frac{C_p G'}{\text{Pr}^{2/3}} b \left(\frac{lG'}{\mu}\right)^n = \frac{bC_p}{\text{Pr}^{2/3}} \left(\frac{l}{\mu}\right)^n G'^{1+n} = 0.072 G'^{0.6}$$

$$\therefore \quad 1 + n = 0.6 \qquad n = -0.4$$

$$\frac{bC_p}{\text{Pr}^{2/3}} \left(\frac{l}{\mu}\right)^{-0.4} = 0.072$$

$$b = \frac{0.072 \, \text{Pr}^{2/3}}{C_p} \left(\frac{l}{\mu}\right)^{0.4}$$

Using the data for air at 100°F, 1 atm,

$$\text{Pr} = \frac{C_p \mu}{k} = \frac{0.24(0.0185)(2.42)}{0.01576} = 0.681$$

$$b = \frac{0.072(0.681)^{2/3}}{0.24} \left[\frac{l}{0.0185(2.42)}\right]^{0.4} = 0.810 l^{0.4}$$

$$j_H = \frac{h}{C_p G} \text{Pr}^{2/3} = \frac{0.810 l^{0.4}}{\text{Re}^{0.4}} = \psi(\text{Re})$$

The heat- mass-transfer analogy will be used to estimate the mass-transfer coefficient ($j_D = j_H$).

$$j_D = \frac{k_G p_{BM} M_{av}}{\rho u} \text{Sc}^{2/3} = \psi(\text{Re}) = \frac{0.810 l^{0.4}}{\text{Re}^{0.4}}$$

$$k_G p_{BM} = F = \frac{0.810 l^{0.4} \rho u}{\text{Re}^{0.4} M_{av} \text{Sc}^{2/3}} = \frac{0.810 (\rho u)^{0.6} \mu^{0.4}}{M_{av} \text{Sc}^{2/3}}$$

For H_2–H_2O, 100°F, 1 atm, Sc $= \mu/\rho D = 0.009(2.42)/0.00495(3) = 1.468$. At $u = 50(3,600) = 180,000$ ft/hr, and assuming the density, mol wt, and viscosity of the gas are essentially those of H_2,

$$k_G p_{BM} = F = \frac{0.810[0.00495(180,000)]^{0.6}[0.009(2.42)]^{0.4}}{2.02(1.468)^{2/3}}$$

$$= 3.98 \text{ lb moles/(hr)(sq ft)} \quad \textbf{Ans.}$$

Flux variation with concentration

In many situations the concentrations of solute in the bulk fluid, and even at the fluid interface, may vary in the direction of flow. Further, the mass-transfer coefficients depend upon fluid properties and rate of flow, and if these vary in the direction of flow, the coefficients will also. The flux N_A of Eqs. (3.1) and (3.3) to (3.6) is therefore a local flux and will generally vary with distance in the direction of flow. This problem was dealt with, in part, in the development leading to Illustration 3.1.   In solving problems where something other than the local flux is required, allowance must be made for these variations.   This normally requires some considerations of material balances, but there is no standard procedure.   An example is offered below, but it must be emphasized that generally some sort of improvisation for the circumstances at hand will be required.

Illustration 3.5. Nickel carbonyl is to be produced by passing carbon monoxide gas downward through a bed of nickel spheres, 0.5 in. diam.   The bed is 1 sq ft in cross section and is packed so that there are 30% voids.   Pure CO enters at 50°C, 1 atm, at the rate of 15 lb moles/hr.   The reaction is

$$Ni + 4CO \rightarrow Ni(CO)_4$$

For present purposes, the following simplifying assumptions will be made:

1. The reaction is very rapid, so that the partial pressure of CO at the metal surface is essentially zero.   The carbonyl forms as a gas, which diffuses as fast as it forms from the metal surface to the bulk-gas stream.   The rate of reaction is controlled entirely by the rate of mass transfer of CO from the bulk gas to the metal surface and that of the $Ni(CO)_4$ to the bulk gas.
2. The temperature remains at 50°C and the pressure at 1 atm throughout.
3. The viscosity of the gas = 0.024 centipoise, and the Schmidt number = 2.0 throughout.
4. The size of the nickel spheres remains constant.

Estimate the bed depth required to reduce the CO content of the gas to 0.5%.
Solution. Let $A = CO$, $B = Ni(CO)_4$. $N_B = -N_A/4$, and $N_A/(N_A + N_B) = \frac{1}{3}$.   In   Eq. (3.1), $c_{A2}/c = y_{Ai}$ at the metal interface = 0, and $c_{A1}/c = y_A$ = mole fraction CO in the bulk gas. Equation (3.1) therefore becomes

$$N_A = \tfrac{1}{3} F \ln \frac{\tfrac{1}{3}}{\tfrac{1}{3} - y_A} = \tfrac{1}{3} F \ln \frac{4}{4 - 3y_A} \tag{3.58}$$

where N_A is the mass-transfer flux based on the metal surface.   Since y_A varies with position in the bed, Eq. (3.58) gives a local flux N_A, and to determine the total mass transfer, allowance must be made for the variation of y_A and F with bed depth.
Let G = moles of gas/(hr)(sq ft bed cross section) flowing at any depth z from the top.   The CO content of this gas is $y_A G$ moles CO/(hr)(sq ft bed).   The change in CO content in passing through a depth dz of bed is $-d(y_A G)$ moles/(hr)(sq ft).   If a is the specific metal surface, sq ft/cu ft of bed, a depth dz and a cross section of 1 sq ft (volume = dz cu ft) has a metal surface $a\,dz$ sq ft.   Therefore $N_A = -d(y_A G)/a\,dz$ moles CO/(hr)(sq ft metal surface).   For each mole of CO consumed, $\frac{1}{4}$ mole $Ni(CO)_4$ forms, representing a net loss of $\frac{3}{4}$ mole per mole CO consumed.   The CO consumed through bed depth z is therefore $(G_0 - G)4/3$ moles, where G_0 is the molar superficial mass velocity at the top, and the CO content at depth z is $G_0 - (G_0 - G)4/3$.   Therefore,

$$y_A = \frac{G_0 - (G_0 - G)4/3}{G} \qquad G = \frac{G_0}{4 - 3y_A}$$

$$d(y_A G) = \frac{4G_0\,dy_A}{(4 - 3y_A)^2}$$

Substituting in Eq. (3.58),

$$-\frac{4G_0\,dy_A}{(4 - 3y_A)^2 a\,dz} = \frac{4}{3} F \ln \frac{4}{4 - 3y_A} \tag{3.59}$$

F is given by item 5 of Table 3.3 and is dependent upon y_A. At depth z, the CO mass velocity $= [G_0 - (G_0 - G)4/3]28.0$, and the Ni(CO)$_4$ mass velocity $= [(G_0 - G)1/3]170.7$, making a total mass velocity $G' = 47.6G_0 - 19.6G$ lb/(hr)(sq ft). Substituting for G,

$$G' = 47.6G_0 - \frac{19.6G_0}{4 - 3y_A} = G_0\left(47.6 - \frac{19.6}{4 - 3y_A}\right) \text{lb/(hr)(sq ft)}$$

With 0.5-in. spheres, $d_p = 0.5/12 = 0.0416$ ft; $\mu = 0.024(2.42) = 0.0580$ lb/(ft)(hr).

$$\text{Re}'' = \frac{d_p G'}{\mu} = 0.0416G_0 \frac{47.6 - 19.6/(4 - 3y_A)}{0.0580}$$

$$= G_0\left(34.2 - \frac{14.06}{4 - 3y_A}\right)$$

With $G_0 = 15$ lb moles/(hr)(sq ft) and y_A in the range 1 to 0.005, the range of Re$''$ is 302 to 461. Therefore (Table 3.3),

$$j_D = \frac{F}{G} \text{Sc}^{2/3} = \frac{2.06}{\epsilon} \text{Re}''^{-0.575}$$

For Sc $= 2$ and $\epsilon = 0.3$ void fraction, this becomes

$$F = \frac{2.06}{0.3(2)^{2/3}}\left(\frac{G_0}{4 - 3y_A}\right)\left[G_0\left(34.2 - \frac{14.06}{4 - 3y_A}\right)\right]^{-0.575} \tag{3.60}$$

Equation (3.60) may be substituted in Eq. (3.59). Since $a = 6(1 - \epsilon)/d_p = 6(1 - 0.3)/0.0416 = 101$ sq ft/cu ft and $G_0 = 15$ lb moles/(hr)(sq ft), the result, after consolidation and rearrangement for integration, is

$$Z = \int_0^Z dz = -0.0325 \int_{1.0}^{0.005} \frac{[34.2 - 14.06/(4 - 3y_A)]^{0.575}}{(4 - 3y_A)\ln[4/(4 - 3y_A)]} dy_A$$

The integration is most readily done graphically, by plotting the integrand as ordinate vs. y_A as abscissa and determining the area under the resulting curve between the indicated limits. As a result, $Z = 0.475$ ft, or say 6-in. bed depth. **Ans.**

SIMULTANEOUS MASS AND HEAT TRANSFER

Mass transfer may occur simultaneously with the transfer of heat, either as a result of an externally imposed temperature difference or because of the absorption or evolution of heat which generally occurs when a substance is transferred from one phase to another. In such cases, within one phase, the heat transferred is a result not only of the conduction (convection) by virtue of the temperature difference which would happen in the absence of mass transfer but also includes the sensible heat carried by the diffusing matter.

Consider the situation shown in Fig. 3.11. Here a fluid consisting of substances A and B flows past a second phase under conditions causing mass transfer. The total mass transferred is given by the following variation of Eq. (3.1):

$$N_A + N_B = F \ln \frac{N_A/(N_A + N_B) - c_{Ai}/c}{N_A/(N_A + N_B) - c_{A1}/c} \tag{3.61}$$

As usual, the relationship between N_A and N_B is fixed by other considerations. As a result of the temperature difference, there is a heat flux described by the ordinary

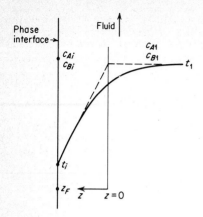

Fig. 3.11   *Effect of mass transfer on heat transfer.*[6]

heat-transfer coefficient h in the absence of mass transfer.   If we think in terms of the film theory, this heat flux is $h(-dt/dz)z_F$.   The total sensible heat flux q_s to the interface must include in addition the sensible heat brought there by the movement of matter through the temperature difference.   Thus,

$$q_s = h\left(-\frac{dt}{dz}\right)z_F + (N_A M_A C_{pA} + N_B M_B C_{pB})(t - t_i) \tag{3.62}$$

Rearranging and integrating,

$$\int_{t_i}^{t_1} \frac{dt}{q_s - (N_A M_A C_{pA} + N_B M_B C_{pB})(t - t_i)} = \frac{1}{h z_F} \int_{z_F}^{0} dz \tag{3.63}$$

$$q_s = \frac{N_A M_A C_{pA} + N_B M_B C_{pB}}{1 - e^{-(N_A M_A C_{pA} + N_B M_B C_{pB})/h}} (t_1 - t_i) \tag{3.64}$$

The first term after the equals sign in Eq. (3.64) may be considered as a heat-transfer coefficient corrected for mass transfer.

The *total* heat release at the interface q_t will then include additionally the effect produced when the transferred mass passes through the interface.   This may be a latent heat of vaporization, a heat of solution, or both, depending upon the circumstances.   Thus,

$$q_t = q_s + \lambda_A N_A + \lambda_B N_B \tag{3.65}$$

where λ is the molar heat evolution.   In some cases the heat released at the interface continues to flow to the left in Fig. 3.11, owing to a temperature drop in the adjacent phase.   In others, where the mass transfer in the fluid is in the opposite direction to the sensible heat transfer, it is possible that the diffusing mass may carry heat from the interface into the fluid as fast as it is released, in which case no heat enters the adjacent phase.

Illustration 3.6. An air–water vapor mixture flows upward through a vertical copper tube, 1 in. OD, 0.065 in. wall thickness, which is surrounded by flowing cold water.   As a result, the water vapor condenses and flows as a liquid down the inside surface of the tube.   At one level in the appara-tus, the average velocity of the gas is 15 ft/sec, its bulk-average temperature 150°F, the pressure 1 atm, and the bulk-average partial pressure of water vapor $= 0.24$ atm.   The film of condensed liquid is such that its heat-transfer coefficient $= 2,000$ Btu/(hr)(sq ft)(°F).   The cooling water has a bulk-average temperature of 75°F and a heat-transfer coefficient $= 100$ Btu/(hr)(sq ft)(°F) (see Fig. 3.12). Compute the local rate of condensation of water from the air stream.

Solution. For the metal tube, ID $= 1 - 0.065(2) = 0.870$ in. $= 0.0725$ ft.   Av diam $=$ $(1 + 0.870)/2 = 0.935$ in.

For the gas mixture, $A =$ water, $B =$ air. $N_B = 0$, $N_A/(N_A + N_B) = 1$; $y_{A1} = 0.24$, $y_{Ai} = p_{Ai} =$ vapor pressure of water at the interface temperature t_i. $M_{av} = 0.24(18.02) + 0.76(29) = 26.4$; $\rho = (26.4/359)[492/(460 + 150)] = 0.0594$ lb/cu ft; $\mu = (0.0175$ centipoise)$(2.42) = 0.0424$ lb/(ft)(hr). $C_{pA} = 0.45$, C_p of the mixture $= 0.274$ Btu/(lb)(°F). Sc $= 0.60$, Pr $= 0.75$.

$$G' = \text{mass velocity} = u\rho = 15(3,600)(0.0594) = 3,205 \text{ lb/(hr)(sq ft)}$$

$$G = \text{molar mass velocity} = \frac{G'}{M_{av}} = \frac{3,205}{26.4} = 121.5$$

$$\text{Re} = \frac{dG'}{\mu} = \frac{0.0725(3,205)}{0.0424} = 5,490$$

The mass-transfer coefficient is given by item 1, Table 3.3

$$j_D = \text{St Sc}^{\frac{2}{3}} = \frac{F}{G}\text{Sc}^{\frac{2}{3}} = 0.023\ \text{Re}^{-0.17} = 0.023(5,490)^{-0.17} = 0.00532$$

$$F = \frac{0.00532G}{\text{Sc}^{\frac{2}{3}}} = \frac{0.00532(121.5)}{(0.60)^{\frac{2}{3}}} = 0.910 \text{ lb mole/(hr)(sq ft)}$$

The heat-transfer coefficient in the absence of mass transfer will be estimated through $j_D = j_H$.

$$j_H = \text{St Pr}^{\frac{2}{3}} = \frac{h}{C_pG'}\text{Pr}^{\frac{2}{3}} = 0.00532$$

$$h = \frac{0.00532C_pG'}{\text{Pr}^{\frac{2}{3}}} = \frac{0.00532(0.274)(3,205)}{(0.75)^{\frac{2}{3}}} = 5.66 \text{ Btu/(hr)(sq ft)(°F)}$$

The sensible heat-transfer flux to the interface is given by Eq. (3.64), with $N_B = 0$.   This is com-bined with Eq. (3.65) to produce

$$q_t = \frac{N_A(18.02)(0.45)}{1 - e^{-N_A(18.02)(0.45)/5.66}}(150 - t_i) + \lambda_{Ai}N_A \qquad (3.66)$$

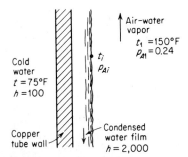

Cold
water
$t = 75°F$
$h = 100$

Copper
tube wall

t_i
p_{Ai}

Condensed
water film
$h = 2,000$

Air–water
vapor
$t_1 = 150°F$
$p_{A1} = 0.24$

Fig. 3.12 *Illustration* 3.6.

where λ_{Ai} is the molal latent heat of vaporization of water at t_i. All the heat arriving at the interface is carried to the cold water. U is the overall heat-transfer coefficient, interface to cold water, based on the inside tube surface

$$\frac{1}{U} = \frac{1}{2{,}000} + \frac{0.065/12}{220}\frac{0.870}{0.935} + \frac{1}{100}\frac{0.870}{1.00}$$

where 220 is the thermal conductivity of the copper.

$$U = 108.5 \text{ Btu/(hr)(sq ft)(°F)}$$

$$q_t = 108.5(t_i - 75) \tag{3.67}$$

The rate of mass transfer is given by Eq. (3.61) with $N_B = 0$, $c_{Ai}/c = p_{Ai}$, $c_{A1}/c = y_{A1} = 0.24$.

$$N_A = 0.910 \ln \frac{1 - p_{Ai}}{1 - 0.24} \tag{3.68}$$

Equations (3.66) to (3.68) are solved simultaneously by trial with the vapor-pressure curve for water, which relates p_{Ai} and t_i, and the latent-heat data. It is easiest to assume t_i, which is checked when q_t from Eqs. (3.66) and (3.67) agree.

As a final trial, assume $t_i = 107.5°F$, whence $p_{Ai} = 0.0806$ atm, $\lambda_{Ai} = 18{,}630$ Btu/lb mole, and [Eq. (3.68)] $N_A = 0.1740$ lb mole/(hr)(sq ft). By Eq. (3.67) $q_t = 3{,}520$; by Eq. (3.66) $q_t = 3{,}512$ Btu/(hr)(sq ft), a sufficiently close check. The local rate of condensation of water is therefore 0.1740 lb mole/(hr)(sq ft). **Ans.**

Note: In this case, the true q_s [Eq. (3.62)] $= 272$ Btu/(hr)(sq ft), whereas the uncorrected h gives $5.66(150 - 107.5) = 240$ Btu/(hr)(sq ft).

Illustration 3.7. Recalculate the example of Illustration 3.6 under the following circumstances. The bulk air stream is free of water vapor, at 150°F, 1 atm, and flowing at $G' = 3{,}205$ lb/(hr)(sq ft). The tube is thoroughly insulated on the outside against transfer of heat. The liquid film at the tube wall is supplied from the top.

Solution. In this case, sensible heat transfers by convection from the warm gas to the cooler liquid surface. Heat does not penetrate the liquid. Water evaporates into the gas at a rate sufficient to take away the heat arriving at the surface. q_t of Eq. (3.65) $= 0$.

For the gas, $G' = 3{,}205$, $G = 3{,}205/29 = 110.5$ lb moles/(hr)(sq ft); $\mu = (0.0195$ centipoise) $(2.42) = 0.0472$ lb/(ft)(hr); Re $= 0.0725(3{,}205)/(0.0472) = 4{,}930$; $N_B = 0$; $N_A/(N_A + N_B) = 1.0$.

$$j_D = \frac{F}{G} Sc^{2/3} = 0.023 \text{ Re}^{-0.17} = 0.023(4{,}930)^{-0.17} = 0.0054$$

$$F = \frac{0.0054G}{Sc^{2/3}} = \frac{0.0054(110.5)}{(0.60)^{2/3}} = 0.84 \text{ lb mole/(hr)(sq ft)}$$

$$j_H = j_D = \frac{h}{C_p G'} Pr^{2/3} = 0.0054$$

$$h = \frac{0.0054 C_p G'}{Pr^{2/3}} = \frac{0.0054(0.24)(3{,}205)}{(0.75)^{2/3}} = 5.04 \text{ Btu/(hr)(sq ft)}$$

Eqs. (3.64) and (3.65):

$$q_t = \frac{N_A(18.02)(0.45)}{1 - e^{-N_A(18.02)(0.45)/5.04}}(150 - t_i) + \lambda_{Ai} N_A = 0$$

Eq. (3.61):

$$N_A = 0.84 \ln \frac{1 - p_{Ai}}{1 - 0}$$

These are solved by trial. As a final trial, assume $t_i = 70°F$, whence $\lambda_{Ai} = 19{,}000$ Btu/lb mole, $p_{Ai} = 0.0247$ atm, $N_A = -0.0210$ lb mole/(hr)(sq ft), and $q_t = 0$ (check). The local rate of evaporation is 0.0210 lb mole/(hr)(sq ft). **Ans.**

NOTATION FOR CHAPTER 3

Consistent units in either cgs or the English system may be used.   Pressures in mass-transfer equations are ordinarily expressed in atmospheres in either system.

a = specific surface of a fixed bed of pellets, pellet surface/volume of bed, sq cm/cu cm or sq ft/ cu ft

b_1, b_2 = constants

c = solute concentration (if subscripted), molar density of a solution (if not subscripted), g moles/cu cm or lb moles/cu ft

$\bar{c}$ = bulk-average concentration, g moles/cu cm or lb moles/cu ft

C_p = heat capacity at constant pressure, cal/(g)($°$C) or Btu/(lb)($°$F)

d = differential operator

   = diameter, cm or ft

d_c = diameter of a cylinder, cm or ft

d_p = diameter of a sphere; for nonspherical particles, diameter of a sphere of the same surface as the particle; cm or ft

D = molecular diffusivity, sq cm/sec or sq ft/hr

E_D = eddy mass diffusivity, sq cm/sec or sq ft/hr

E_H = eddy thermal diffusivity, sq cm/sec or sq ft/hr

E_v = eddy momentum diffusivity, sq cm/sec or sq ft/hr

f = friction factor; Fanning friction factor for flow through circular pipes; dimensionless

F = mass-transfer coefficient, g moles/(sec)(sq cm) or lb moles/(hr)(sq ft)

g = acceleration due to gravity, cm/sq sec or ft/sq hr

g_c = conversion factor, 980 (g mass)(cm)/(g force)(sq sec), or $4.17(10^8)$(lb mass)(ft)/(lb force) (sq hr)

G = molar mass velocity, g moles/(sec)(sq cm) or lb moles/(hr)(sq ft)

G' = mass velocity, g mass/(sec)(sq cm) or lb mass/(hr)(sq ft)

Gr = Grashof number, dimensionless

h = heat-transfer coefficient, cal/(sec)(sq cm)($°$C) or Btu/(hr)(sq ft)($°$F)

j_D = mass-transfer dimensionless group, St Sc$^{2/3}$

j_H = heat-transfer dimensionless group, St Pr$^{2/3}$

J = mass-transfer flux, g moles/(sec)(sq cm) or lb moles/(hr)(sq ft)

k = thermal conductivity, (cal)(cm)/(sec)(sq cm)($°$C) or (Btu)(ft)/(hr)(sq ft)($°$F)

k_c, k_G, k_x, k_y, etc. = mass-transfer coefficients, g moles/(sec)(sq cm)(concentration difference) or lb moles/(hr)(sq ft)(concentration difference); see Table 3.1

l = a length; Prandtl mixing length, cm or ft

L = length of wetted-wall tower, cm or ft

M = molecular weight, g mass/g mole or lb mass/lb mole

n = a number, dimensionless

N = mass-transfer flux at a phase boundary, g moles/(sec)(sq cm) or lb moles/(hr)(sq ft)

Nu = Nusselt number, dimensionless

p = partial pressure, atm

P_t = total pressure, atm

Pe = Péclet number, dimensionless

Pr = Prandtl number, dimensionless

q = heat-transfer flux, cal/(sec)(sq cm) or Btu/(hr)(sq ft)

R = universal gas constant, 82.06 (cu cm)(atm)/(g mole)($°$K) or 0.729 (cu ft)(atm)/(lb mole)($°$R)

Re = Reynolds number, dimensionless

Re′ = Reynolds number for flow outside a cylinder, $d_c G'/\mu$, dimensionless

Re″ = Reynolds number for flow past a sphere, $d_p G'/\mu$, dimensionless

Re$_x$ = Reynolds number computed with x as the length dimension, dimensionless

s = fractional rate of surface-element replacement, 1/sec or 1/hr

S = cross-sectional area of a duct, sq cm or sq ft
Sh = Sherwood number, dimensionless
St = Stanton number, dimensionless
t = temperature, °C or °F
T = absolute temperature, °K or °R
u = local velocity, cm/sec or ft/hr
$\bar{u}$ = bulk-average velocity, cm/sec or ft/hr
u' = root-mean-square deviating velocity, cm/sec or ft/hr
u'_i = instantaneous deviating velocity, cm/sec or ft/hr
x, y, z (no subscript) = distances in the x, y, z direction, respectively, cm or ft
x_A = concentration of component A in a liquid, mole fraction
y_A = concentration of component A in a gas, mole fraction
z_b = depth of penetration (film and surface-renewal theories), cm or ft
z_F = effective film thickness (film theory), cm or ft
α = thermal diffusivity = $k/C_p\rho$, sq cm/sec or sq ft/hr
β = volumetric coefficient of expansion, 1/°C or 1/°F
Γ = mass rate of flow per unit width, g mass/(cm)(sec) or lb mass/(ft)(hr)
δ = thickness of a layer, cm or ft
Δ = difference
ϵ = fractional void volume in a fixed bed of pellets = $1 - d_p a/6$, dimensionless
θ = time, sec or hr
λ = molar heat evolution on passing through an interface, cal/g mole or Btu/lb mole
μ = viscosity, g mass/(cm)(sec) or lb mass/(ft)(hr)
ν = kinematic viscosity = μ/ρ, sq cm/sec or sq ft/hr
π = 3.1416
ρ = density, g mass/cu cm or lb mass/cu ft
τ = shear stress, g force/sq cm or lb force/sq ft
ϕ = area of surface elements (surface-renewal theory), sq cm/(sq cm)(sec) or sq ft/(sq ft)(hr)
ψ_1, ψ_2 = functions

Subscripts:

av = average
A = component A
B = component B
c = concentration
i = interface; instantaneous when used for velocity
M = logarithmic mean
s = sensible heat
t = total
turb = turbulent
x, y, z = in the $x, y,$ and z direction, respectively
0 = approach, or initial, value
1 = at beginning of mass-transfer path
2 = at end of mass-transfer path

REFERENCES

1. Bedingfield, C. H., and T. B. Drew: *Ind. Eng. Chem.*, **42**, 1164 (1950).

2. Bennett, C. O., and J. E. Myers: "Momentum, Heat, and Mass Transfer," McGraw-Hill Book Company, New York, 1962.

3. Bird, R. B., W. E. Stewart, and E. N. Lightfoot: "Transport Phenomena," John Wiley & Sons, Inc., New York, 1960.

4. Chilton, T. H., and A. P. Colburn: *Ind. Eng. Chem.*, **26,** 1183 (1934).
5. Colburn, A. P.: *Trans. AIChE,* **29,** 174 (1933).
6. Colburn, A. P., and T. B. Drew: *Trans. AIChE,* **33,** 197 (1937).
7. Danckwerts, P. V.: *AIChE J.,* **1,** 456 (1955); *Ind. Eng. Chem.,* **43,** 1460 (1951).
8. Deissler, R. G.: *NACA Rept.* **1210,** 1955.
9. Dobbins, W. E.: pt. 2-1, in McCabe and Eckenfelder (eds.), "Biological Treatment of Sewage and Industrial Wastes," Reinhold Publishing Corporation, New York, 1956.
10. Dobbins, W. E.: "International Conference on Water Pollution Research, London, September, 1962," p. 61, Pergamon Press, New York, 1964.
11. Eckert, E. R. G., and R. M. Drake: "Heat and Mass Transfer," 2d ed., McGraw-Hill Book Company, New York, 1959.
12. Gaffney, B. J., and T. B. Drew: *Ind. Eng. Chem.,* **42,** 1120 (1950).
13. Gupta, A. S., and G. Thodos: *AIChE J.,* **9,** 751 (1963); *Ind. Eng. Chem. Fundamentals,* **3,** 218 (1964).
14. Hanratty, T. J.: *AIChE J.,* **2,** 359 (1956).
15. Higbie, R.: *Trans. AIChE,* **31,** 365 (1935).
16. Hinze, J. O.: "Turbulence," McGraw-Hill Book Company, New York, 1959.
17. Johnstone, H. F., and R. L. Pigford: *Trans. AIChE,* **38,** 25 (1952).
18. Lewis, W. K.: *Ind. Eng. Chem.,* **8,** 825 (1916).
19. Lewis, W. K., and W. Whitman: *Ind. Eng. Chem.,* **16,**1215 (1924).
20. Lin, C. S., R. W. Moulton, and G. L. Putnam: *Ind. Eng. Chem.,* **45,** 636 (1953).
21. Linton, W. H., and T. K. Sherwood: *Chem. Eng. Progr.,* **46,** 258 (1950).
22. McAdams, W. H.: "Heat Transmission," 3d ed., McGraw-Hill Book Company, New York, 1954.
23. Murphree, E. V.: *Ind. Eng. Chem.,* **24,** 726 (1932).
24. Opfell, J. B., and B. H. Sage: in T. B. Drew and J. W. Hoopes (eds.), "Advances in Chemical Engineering," vol. 1, p. 241, Academic Press, Inc., New York, 1956.
25. Page, F., W. G. Schlinger, D. K. Breaux, and B. H. Sage: *Ind. Eng. Chem.,* **44,** 424 (1952).
26. Powell, R. W.: *Trans. Inst. Chem. Engrs.* (*London*), **13,** 175 (1935); **18,** 36 (1940).
27. Prandtl, T. L.: *Z. Physik,* **11,** 1072 (1910); **29,** 487 (1928).
28. Reynolds, O.: "Scientific Papers of Osborne Reynolds," vol. II, Cambridge University Press, New York, 1901.
29. Ruckenstein, E.: *Chem. Eng. Sci.,* **7,** 265 (1958); **18,** 233 (1963).
30. Sherwood, T. K., and E. R. Gilliland: *Ind. Eng. Chem.,* **26,** 516 (1934).
31. Sherwood, T. K., and R. L. Pigford: "Absorption and Extraction," 2d ed., McGraw-Hill Book Company, New York, 1952.
32. Sleicher, C. A.: in A. Acrivos (ed.), "Modern Chemical Engineering," vol. I, p. 45, Reinhold Publishing Corporation, New York, 1963.
33. Steinberger, R. L., and R. E. Treybal: *AIChE J.,* **6,** 227 (1960).
34. Stynes, S. K., and J. E. Myers: *AIChE J.,* **10,** 437 (1964).
35. Taylor, G. I.: *Rept. Mem., Brit. Advisory Comm. Aeronaut.,* **272,** 423 (1916).
36. Toor, H. L., and J. M. Marchello: *AIChE J.,* **4,** 97 (1958).
37. Towle, W. L., and T. K. Sherwood: *Ind. Eng. Chem.,* **31,** 457 (1939).
38. Vieth, W. R., J. H. Porter, and T. K. Sherwood: *Ind. Eng. Chem. Fundamentals,* **2,** 1 (1963).
39. Williams, J. E., K. E. Bazaire, and C. J. Geankoplis: *Ind. Eng. Chem. Fundamentals,* **2,** 126 (1963).

PROBLEMS

3.1. Estimate the mass-transfer coefficient and effective film thickness to be expected in the absorption of ammonia from air by a 2 N sulfuric acid solution in a wetted-wall tower under the following circumstances:

Air flow = 41.4 g/min (air only)
Av partial pressure ammonia in air = 30.8 mm Hg
Total pressure = 760 mm Hg
Av gas temp = 25°C
Av liquid temp = 25°C
Diam tower = 1.46 cm

For absorption of ammonia in sulfuric acid of this concentration, the entire mass-transfer resistance lies within the gas, and the partial pressure of ammonia at the interface is negligible. *Note:* The circumstances correspond to run 47 of Chambers and Sherwood [*Trans. AIChE*, **33**, 579 (1937)], who observed $d/z_F = 16.6$.

3.2.   Powell[26] evaporated water from the outside of cylinders into an air stream flowing parallel to the axes of the cylinders.   The air temperature was 25°C, and the total pressure atmospheric. The results are given by

$$\frac{wl}{p_w - p_a} = 3.17(10^{-8})(ul)^{0.8}$$

where w = water evaporated, g/(sec)(sq cm)
 p_a = partial pressure of water in air stream, mm Hg
 p_w = water vapor pressure at surface temp, mm Hg
 u = velocity of air stream, cm/sec
 l = length cylinder, cm

 a.   Transform the equation into the form $j_D = \psi(Re_l)$, where Re_l is a Reynolds number based on the cylinder length.

 b.   Calculate the rate of sublimation from a cylinder of naphthalene 3 in. in diam, 24 in. long, into a stream of pure carbon dioxide at a velocity of 20 ft/sec, 1 atm, 100°C.   The vapor pressure of naphthalene at the surface temperature may be taken as 10 mm Hg, and its diffusivity in carbon dioxide as 0.0515 sq cm/sec at 0°C, 1 atm.   Express the results as grams naphthalene evaporated/hr. **Ans.:** 345.

3.3.   Water flows down the inside wall of a wetted-wall tower of the design of Fig. 3.10, while air flows upward through the core.   In a particular case, the inside diameter is 1 in., and dry air enters at the rate 5,000 lb/(hr)(sq ft of inside cross section).   Assume the air is everywhere at its average temperature, 97°F, the water at 70°F, and the mass-transfer coefficient constant.   Pressure = 1 atm. Compute the average partial pressure of water in the air leaving, if the tower is 3 ft long.   **Ans.:** 0.015 atm.

3.4.   Winding and Cheney [*Ind. Eng. Chem.*, **40**, 1087 (1948)] passed air through a bank of rods of naphthalene.   The rods were of "streamline" cross section, arranged in staggered array, with the air flowing at right angles to the axes of the rods.   The mass-transfer coefficient was determined by measuring the rate of sublimation of the naphthalene.   For a particular shape, size, and spacing of the rods, with air at 100°F, 1 atm, the data could be correlated empirically by

$$k_G = 0.00663 G'^{0.56}$$

where G' = superficial mass velocity of air, lb/(hr)(sq ft)
 k_G = lb moles/(hr)(sq ft)(atm)

Estimate the mass-transfer coefficient to be expected for evaporation of water into hydrogen gas for the same geometrical arrangement, when the hydrogen flows at a superficial velocity of 50 ft/sec, 100°F, 2 atm pressure. D for naphthalene–air, 1 atm, 100°F = 0.272 sq ft/hr; for water–hydrogen, 32°F, 1 atm = 2.9 sq ft/hr.

3.5.   For the dissolution of crystals of soluble anhydrous solids into water in an agitated tank, Barker and Treybal [*AIChE J.*, **6**, 289 (1960)] obtained the following expression for the mass-transfer coefficient:

$$\frac{k_{L,av}T}{D_{AB}} = 0.052 \, Re_s^{0.833} \, Sc^{0.5}$$

where T = tank diameter

$\quad\quad\quad$ Re_s = Reynolds number of stirrer

c_{A1}[Eq. (3.4)] = solubility of solute in water

$\quad\quad\quad$ c_{A2} = solute concentration in the bulk liquid, lb moles/cu ft

A tank 3 ft in diameter, 4 ft deep, contains 1,250 lb water and is agitated with the 8-in.-diam stirrer at a stirrer Reynolds number Re_s = 100,000. Two hundred fifty pounds $CuSO_4 \cdot 5H_2O$ in the form of uniform crystals, $\frac{1}{4}$ in. diam, are suddenly dropped into the tank.

$\quad$ *a.* Estimate the initial rate of dissolving, lb hydrate/hr.

$\quad$ *b.* Estimate the time required to (1) dissolve all but 10 lb of the crystals and (2) completely dissolve the crystals. **Ans.:** (1) 0.328 hr, (2) 0.548 hr.

$\quad$ *Data and assumptions.* Assume the temperature remains at 20°C. For $CuSO_4$ in water D = 0.73(10⁻⁵) sq cm/sec. The density of the hydrate crystals = 143 lb/cu ft. For present purposes, assume that the kinematic viscosity of the solution remains at 1 centistoke and the solution density at 62.4 lb/cu ft. The crystals are assumed to be uniform spheres which remain spherical as they dissolve, without break-up of the crystals. Assume F remains constant for all crystal sizes. The solubility of $CuSO_4$ in water = 0.0229 mole fraction $CuSO_4$ at 20°C.

3.6. The free-fall terminal velocity of water drops in air at atmospheric pressure is given by the following table of data:[31]

Diam, mm	0.05	0.2	0.5	1.0	2.0	3.0
Velocity, ft/sec	0.18	2.3	7.0	12.7	19.2	23.8

A water drop of initial diam 1.0 mm falls in quiet dry air at 1 atm, 100°F. The liquid temperature may be taken as 58°F. Assume the drop remains spherical and that the atmospheric pressure remains constant at 1 atm.

$\quad$ *a.* Calculate the initial rate of evaporation.

$\quad$ *b.* Calculate the time and distance of free fall for the drop to evaporate to a diameter of 0.2 mm. **Ans.:** 0.0276 hr, 830 ft.

$\quad$ *c.* Calculate the time for the above evaporation, assuming that the drop is suspended without motion (as from a fine thread) in still air.

3.7. The temperature variation of rate of a chemical reaction which involves mass transfer is sometimes used to determine whether the rate of mass transfer or that of the chemical reaction "controls" or is the dominating mechanism.

$\quad$ Consider a fluid flowing through a 1.0-in.-ID circular tube, where the transferred solute is ammonia in dilute solution. Compute the mass-transfer coefficient for each of the following cases:

$\quad$ *a.* The fluid is a dilute solution of ammonia in air, 25°C, 1 atm, flowing at a Reynolds number = 10,000. D_{AB} = 0.226 sq cm/sec.

$\quad$ *b.* Same as (*a*) (same mass velocity), but temperature = 35°C.

$\quad$ *c.* The fluid is a dilute solution of ammonia in liquid water, 25°C, flowing at a Reynolds number = 10,000. D_{AB} = 2.65(10⁻⁵) sq cm/sec.

$\quad$ *d.* Same as (*c*) (same mass velocity), but temperature = 35°C.

$\quad$ In the case of both gas and liquid, assuming that the mass-transfer coefficient follows an Arrhenius-type equation, compute the "energy of activation" of mass transfer. Are these high or low, in comparison with the energy of activation of typical chemical reactions? Note that, for dilute solutions, the identity of the diffusing solute need not have been specified in order to obtain the "energy of activation" of mass transfer. What other method might be used to determine whether reaction rate or mass-transfer rate controls?

3.8. A gas consisting of 50% air, 50% steam, by volume, flows at 200°F, 1 atm pressure at 25 ft/sec av velocity through a horizontal, square duct 1 ft wide. A horizontal copper tube, 1 in. OD, 0.065 in. wall thickness, passes through the center of the duct from one side to the other, at right angles to the duct axis, piercing the duct walls. Cold water flows inside the tube at an average temperature of 60°F, velocity 10 ft/sec. Estimate the rate of condensation on the outside of the copper tube. **Ans.: 5.54 lb/hr.**

Data. McAdams,[22] p. 338, gives the heat-transfer coefficient for the condensate film on the tube as

$$h_{av} = 1.51 \left(\frac{k^3 \rho^2 g}{\mu^2} \right)^{1/3} \left(\frac{\mu L}{4W} \right)^{1/3}$$

where W = lb/hr condensate
$\quad\quad\ L$ = tube length, ft

The fluid properties are to be evaluated at the mean temperature of the condensate film. Data for the group $(k^3 \rho^2 g/\mu^2)^{1/3}$ for water are listed in McAdams, Table A-27, p. 484, for convenience.

CHAPTER FOUR
DIFFUSION IN SOLIDS

It was indicated in Chap. 1 that certain of the diffusional operations such as leaching, drying, adsorption, and the "membrane" operations of dialysis and gaseous effusion involve contact of fluids with solids. In such operations the diffusion must involve the solid phase and may proceed according to several mechanisms. Diffusion through a solid when the solute is dissolved to form a homogeneous solid solution may be termed "structure-insensitive" diffusion, and this form is most nearly similar to diffusion through fluids. A porous or granular solid, however, may permit flow of a liquid or gas through the interstices and capillaries, and diffusion by this mechanism may be termed "structure-sensitive." Diffusion may occur even along the surface of a solid with nothing but superficial penetration of the solute into the solid itself, which may be important in certain adsorption operations.

STRUCTURE-INSENSITIVE DIFFUSION

This type of diffusion may occur when the diffusing substance dissolves in the solid to form a homogeneous solution. The actual mechanisms of the diffusion may be quite complex and very different for diverse substances. For example, in the diffusion of hydrogen through palladium metal the hydrogen molecules evidently dissociate and enter the metal crystal lattice as atoms. On the other hand, nitrogen or oxygen when diffusing through metals forms compounds, and it is the progressive decomposition of these nitrides or oxides which results in the passage of the gas.   Helium and hydrogen may diffuse through the anionic network of a glass, while gases such as argon and air diffuse along faults in the structure.   The diffusion of metals into each other, such as the diffusion of gold through silver, follows a different mechanism from that of the diffusion of gases through membranes or rubber and other polymers or of ammonia and water through certain zeolitic crystals.

Steady-state diffusion

When the concentration gradient remains unchanged with passage of time, so that the rate of diffusion is constant, Fick's law may be applied in the form used in Chap. 2 for cases where the diffusivity is independent of concentration and where there is no bulk flow.   Thus N_A, the rate of diffusion of substance A per unit cross section of solid, is proportional to the concentration gradient in the direction of diffusion, $-dc_A/dz$,

$$N_A = -D_{AB}\frac{dc_A}{dz} \tag{4.1}$$

where D_{AB} is the diffusivity of A through B.   If D_{AB} is constant, integration of Eq. (4.1) for *diffusion through a flat slab* of thickness z results in

$$N_A = \frac{D_{AB}(c_{A1} - c_{A2})}{z} \tag{4.2}$$

which parallels the expressions obtained for fluids in a similar situation.   Here c_{A1} and c_{A2} are the concentrations at opposite sides of the slab.   For other solid shapes, the rate is given by

$$w = N_A S_{av} = \frac{D_{AB}S_{av}(c_{A1} - c_{A2})}{z} \tag{4.3}$$

with appropriate values of the average cross section for diffusion, S_{av}, to be applied. Thus, for *radial diffusion through a solid cylinder* of inner and outer radii a_1 and a_2, respectively, and of length l,

$$S_{av} = \frac{2\pi l(a_2 - a_1)}{\ln (a_2/a_1)} \tag{4.4}$$

and

$$z = a_2 - a_1 \tag{4.5}$$

For *radial diffusion through a spherical shell* of inner and outer radii a_1 and a_2,

$$S_{av} = 4\pi a_1 a_2 \tag{4.6}$$

$$z = a_2 - a_1 \tag{4.7}$$

Illustration 4.1. Hydrogen gas at 2 atm pressure, 25°C, is flowing through a pipe made of a vulcanized neoprene rubber, whose ID and OD are 1 and 2 in., respectively.   The solubility of the hydrogen is 0.053 cu cm H_2 at standard conditions per cubic centimeter rubber per atmosphere, and the diffusivity of the hydrogen through the rubber is $0.18(10^{-5})$ sq cm/sec.   Estimate the rate of loss of hydrogen by diffusion per foot of pipe length.

Solution. At 2 atm hydrogen pressure, the solubility is $0.053(2) = 0.106$ cu ft H_2 at standard conditions per cubic foot rubber. Therefore concentration c_{A1} at the inner surface of the pipe $= 0.106/359 = 0.000295$ lb mole H_2/cu ft.

At the outer surface, $c_{A2} = 0$ (assuming that the resistance to diffusion of the H_2 away from the surface is negligible).

$$D_{AB} = 0.18(10^{-5})(3.87) = 0.696(10^{-5}) \text{ sq ft/hr}$$

$$z = a_2 - a_1 = \frac{2-1}{2(12)} = 0.0417 \text{ ft} \qquad l = 1 \text{ ft}$$

Eq. (4.4): $\quad S_{av} = \dfrac{2\pi(1)(1-0.5)}{12 \ln (1/0.5)} = 0.377 \text{ sq ft}$

Eq. (4.3): $\quad w = \dfrac{D_{AB}S_{av}(c_{A1} - c_{A2})}{z} = \dfrac{0.696(10^{-5})(0.377)(0.000295 - 0)}{0.0417}$

$$= 1.86(10^{-8}) \text{ lb mole } H_2/\text{hr} \quad \textbf{Ans.}$$

Unsteady-state diffusion

Since solids are not so readily transported through equipment as fluids are, the application of batch and semibatch processes and consequently unsteady-state diffusional conditions arise much more frequently than in the case of fluids. Even in continuous operation, as in the case of a continuous drier, the history of each solid piece as it passes through equipment is representative of the unsteady state. These cases are therefore of considerable importance.

For the case where there is no bulk flow, and in the absence of chemical reaction, Fick's second law, Eq. (2.18), can be used to solve problems of unsteady-state diffusion by integration with appropriate boundary conditions. For some simple cases, Newman[6] has summarized the results most conveniently.

1. *Diffusion from a slab with sealed edges.* Consider a slab of thickness $2a$, with sealed edges on four sides, so that diffusion can take place only toward and from the flat parallel faces, a cross section of which is shown in Fig. 4.1. Suppose initially the concentration of solute throughout the slab is uniform, c_{A0}, and that the slab is immersed in a medium so that the solute will diffuse out of the slab. Let the concentration at the surfaces be $c_{A\infty}$, invariant with passage of time. If the diffusion were allowed to continue indefinitely, the concentration would fall to the uniform value $c_{A\infty}$, and $c_{A0} - c_{A\infty}$ is a measure of the amount of solute removed. On the other hand, if diffusion from the slab were stopped at time θ, the distribution of solute would be given by the curve marked c, which by internal diffusion would level off to the uniform concentration $c_{A\theta}$, where $c_{A\theta}$ is the average concentration at time θ. The quantity $c_{A\theta} - c_{A\infty}$ is a measure of the amount of solute still unremoved. The fraction unremoved, E, is given by integration of Eq. (2.18),

$$E = \frac{c_{A\theta} - c_{A\infty}}{c_{A\theta} - c_{A\infty}} = f\left(\frac{D\theta}{a^2}\right)$$

$$= \frac{8}{\pi^2}\left(e^{-D\theta\pi^2/4a^2} + \tfrac{1}{9} e^{-9D\theta\pi^2/4a^2} + \tfrac{1}{25} e^{-25D\theta\pi^2/4a^2} + \cdots\right) = E_a \qquad (4.8)$$

The function is shown graphically in Fig. 4.2.

2. *Diffusion from a rectangular bar with sealed ends.* For a rectangular bar of thickness $2a$ and width $2b$, with sealed ends,

$$E = f\left(\frac{D\theta}{a^2}\right) f\left(\frac{D\theta}{b^2}\right) = E_a E_b \tag{4.9}$$

3. *Diffusion for a rectangular parallelepiped.* For a brick-shaped bar, of dimensions $2a$, $2b$, and $2c$, with diffusion from all six faces,

$$E = f\left(\frac{D\theta}{a^2}\right) f\left(\frac{D\theta}{b^2}\right) f\left(\frac{D\theta}{c^2}\right) = E_a E_b E_c \tag{4.10}$$

4. *Diffusion from a sphere.* For a sphere of radius a,

$$E = f'\left(\frac{D\theta}{a^2}\right) = E_s \tag{4.11}$$

5. *Diffusion from a cylinder with sealed ends.* For a cylinder of radius a, with plane ends sealed,

$$E = f''\left(\frac{D\theta}{a^2}\right) = E_r \tag{4.12}$$

6. *Diffusion from a cylinder.* For a cylinder of radius a and length $2c$, with diffusion from both ends as well as from the cylindrical surface,

$$E = f\left(\frac{D\theta}{c^2}\right) f''\left(\frac{D\theta}{a^2}\right) = E_c E_r \tag{4.13}$$

The functions $f'(D\theta/a^2)$ and $f''(D\theta/a^2)$ are also shown in Fig. 4.2.

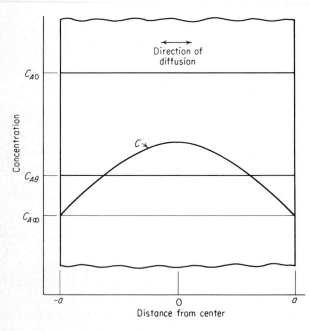

Fig. 4.1 *Unsteady-state diffusion in a slab.*

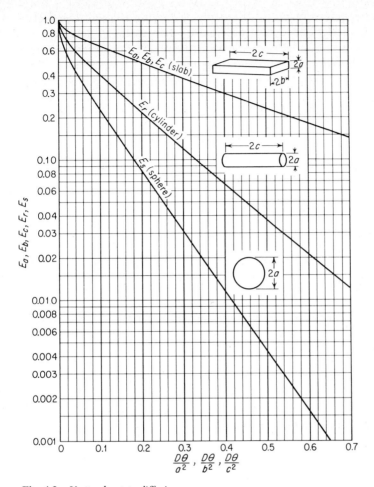

Fig. 4.2 *Unsteady-state diffusion.*

For solid shapes where the diffusion takes place from one rather than two oppo-site faces, the functions are calculated as if the thickness were twice the true value. For example, if diffusion occurs through only one face of the flat slab of thickness $2a$, edges sealed, the calculation is made with $D\theta/4a^2$. The equations may also be used for diffusion into, as well as out of, the various shapes.

It is important to note that Eqs. (4.8) to (4.13) and Fig. 4.2 all assume constant diffusivity, initially uniform concentration within the solid, and constancy of the edge concentration $c_{A\infty}$. The last is the same as assuming (1) that there is no resistance to diffusion in the fluid surrounding the solid and (2) that the quantity of such fluid is so large that its concentration does not change with time or (3) that the fluid is contin-uously replenished. In many instances, the diffusional resistance within the solid is so large that the assumption of absence of any in the fluid is quite reasonable. In any case, however, integrations of Eq. (2.18) involving varying D^{11} and the effect of added diffusional resistance[1,4-6] have been developed. It is useful to note that Eq. (2.18) is of the same form as Fourier's equation for heat conduction, with molecular rather than thermal diffusivity and concentration rather than temperature. Consequently the lengthy catalog of solutions to the problems of heat transfer of Carslaw and Jaeger[3] may be made applicable to diffusion by appropriate substitutions. Crank's book[4] deals particularly with problems of this sort for diffusion.

Illustration 4.2. A 5% agar gel containing a uniform concentration of 5 g urea/100 cu cm is molded in the form of a 3-cm cube. One face of the cube is exposed to a running supply of fresh water into which the urea diffuses. The other faces are protected by the mold. The temperature is 5°C. At the end of 68 hr, the average urea concentration in the gel has fallen to 3 g/100 cu cm. The resistance to diffusion may be considered as residing wholly within the gel.

a. Calculate the diffusivity of the urea in the gel.

b. How long would it have taken for the average concentration to fall to 1 g/100 cu cm?

c. Repeat (*b*) for the case where two opposite faces of the cube are exposed.

Solution. a. c_A can be calculated in terms of g/100 cu cm. $c_{A0} = 5$ g/100 cu cm; $c_{A\theta} = 3$, $c_{A\infty} = 0$ since pure water was the leaching agent. $a = \frac{3}{2} = 1.5$ cm; $\theta = 68(3,600) = 245,000$ sec.

$$\frac{c_{A\theta} - c_{A\infty}}{c_{A0} - c_{A\infty}} = \frac{3}{5} = 0.6 = E$$

The abscissa read from Fig. 4.2, which is $D\theta/4a^2$ for diffusion from only one exposed face, is 0.128

$$D = \frac{0.128(4)a^2}{\theta} = \frac{0.128(4)(1.5)^2}{245,000} = 4.70(10^{-6}) \text{ sq cm/sec}$$

b. For $c_{A\theta} = 1$ g/100 cu cm

$$\frac{c_{A\theta} - c_{A\infty}}{c_{A0} - c_{A\infty}} = \frac{1}{5} = 0.20 \qquad \frac{D\theta}{4a^2} = 0.568 \qquad \text{from Fig. 4.2}$$

$$\theta = \frac{0.568(4)a^2}{D} = \frac{0.568(4)(1.5)^2}{4.70(10^{-6})} = 1,087,000 \text{ sec, or 302 hr}$$

c. For two opposite faces exposed, $a = 1.5$ cm, $c_{A\theta}/c_{A0} = 0.2$, and $D\theta/a^2 = 0.568$.

$$\theta = \frac{0.568a^2}{D} = \frac{0.568(1.5)^2}{4.70(10^{-6})} = 222,000 \text{ sec, or 61.5 hr}$$

Diffusivity and permeability

While a great many measurements of diffusivity have been made, these are largely in connection with systems not of immediate interest here. The diffusivity in metals, for example, is of great interest to the metallurgist in problems of carburizing, nitriding or powder metallurgy, but of little value in the diffusional operations of the chemical engineer. A great many data on the diffusivity of gases through membranes have been gathered, a few typical values of which are listed in Table 4.1 in order to indicate order of magnitude. In connection with diffusion through membranes particularly, it is common to cite the so-called permeability P, rather than the diffusivity.[10] Permeability is defined as

$$P = \frac{V}{-dp/dz} \tag{4.14}$$

Table 4.1. Diffusivity of gases in vulcanized rubber,[1] 25°C

Diffusing substance (A)	D_{AB}, sq cm/sec	Solubility, cu cm gas, 0°C, 1 atm
		(cu cm rubber)(atm)
H_2	$0.85(10^{-5})$	0.040
O_2	$0.21(10^{-5})$	0.070
N_2	$0.15(10^{-5})$	0.035
CO_2	$0.11(10^{-5})$	0.90

where V is the volume of gas (at some specified temperature and pressure, frequently 1 atm, 0°C) diffusing per unit time (area) under the pressure gradient $-dp/dz$. The maximum concentration of solute gas in the solid is its solubility, which varies with the pressure of the gas in contact with the membrane.

Illustration 4.3. From the data of Table 4.1, calculate the rate of diffusion of carbon dioxide, CO_2, through a membrane of the rubber 1 mm thick at 25°C if the partial pressure of the CO_2 is 1 cm Hg on one side and zero on the other. Calculate also the permeability of the membrane.

Solution. At a pressure of 1 cm Hg ($\frac{1}{76}$ atm) the solubility of CO_2 in the rubber is 0.90/76 = 0.01184 cu cm gas (measured at 0°C, 1 atm) per cu cm rubber, or 0.01184/22,400 g mole CO_2/cu cm. On the downstream face of the membrane the CO_2 concentration is zero. The thickness $z = 0.1$ cm. Therefore

$$V = 22{,}400 N_A = \frac{22{,}400 D_{AB} \, \Delta c}{z} = \frac{0.11(10^{-5})(0.01184)}{0.1}$$

$$= 0.13(10^{-6}) \text{ cu cm (0°C, 1 atm) per sec/sq cm}$$

Eq. (4.14): $$P = \frac{V}{-dp/dz} = \frac{0.13(10^{-6})}{(1/76)/0.1}$$

$$= 0.99(10^{-6}) \text{ cu cm (0°C, 1 atm) per sec/(sq cm)(atm/cm)}$$

Note that $P = D_{AB}$ (solubility) $= 0.11(10^{-5})(0.90) = 0.99(10^{-6})$.

Diffusivities in solids may vary very rapidly with temperature, much more so than with liquids or gases. For example, D for nitrogen through a vulcanized chloroprene-polymer membrane is cited as $0.019(10^{-5})$ sq cm/sec at 27.1°C and $0.450(10^{-5})$ sq cm/sec at 84.3°C.[1] Usually, log D is linear with reciprocal absolute temperature for solid diffusion. The diffusivity may vary considerably with concentration; it may be anisotropic; for example, the diffusivity through crystals may vary depending upon the direction with respect to the various crystallographic axes. Observations such as these make it understandable that it is now impossible to predict the diffusivity in solids, as we did for liquids or gases, and it is necessary in practice to measure the diffusivity experimentally under the desired conditions.

STRUCTURE-SENSITIVE DIFFUSION

This is a most complex subject, owing to the great variety of solid structures and diffusing solutes which may have to be studied. Only a few of the situations can be considered in any detail.

Diffusion through a uniformly porous solid

Consider a rigid solid which is uniformly porous throughout, i.e., where the nature and percentage of voids are constant in all directions and in every part of the solid, as might be the case with an idealized clay brick. Suppose the pores and interstices of such a solid are filled with a solution, such as a solution of salt in water. If the solid is now immersed in water, one may imagine a continuous liquid path leading from the depths within the solid to the surrounding liquid through the myriad interstices formed by the rigid solid structure. Since a concentration gradient of dissolved salt exists within the liquid path, diffusion occurs, and in time the salt will completely diffuse from the solid into the surrounding fresh water.

To such a system the previous equations applicable to solid solutions may be applied. Since the liquid path along which the diffusion takes place is relatively very long and in general not known, one may characterize the operation by use of an effective diffusivity to be used in the equations of the preceding section, which could be expected to be smaller than the ordinary diffusivities for the solute in the solvent in the absence of a constraining solid structure. As an alternative,[7] one may define a "pore-shape factor" K, characteristic of the number, size, and nature of the pores in the solid, which when multiplied by the ordinary solid thickness provides a measure of the true length of the diffusion path. The factor is independent of solute and solvent, concentration, time, or any other variable affecting the rate of diffusion. Use of the preceding equations then requires, as before, constancy of the diffusivity, or the use of a correct average or integral diffusivity, over the concentration range experienced.

Under certain limited conditions, the previous relations may also be used to describe the change in average moisture content of a solid during drying: under conditions such that internal diffusion of moisture controls the rate of drying, and in cases where the solid structure contains very fine interstices. Coarse sands do not fall into the latter category, and the drying of wood on occasions may be complicated by the variation of diffusivity with direction, i.e., with or across the grain. These matters are considered in greater detail in Chap. 12. Applications to leaching are discussed in Chap. 13. For applications in catalysis, see the book by Satterfield and Sherwood.[8]

Illustration 4.4. Porous alumina spheres, 1 cm diameter, 25% voids, were thoroughly impregnated with an aqueous potassium chloride, KCl, solution concentration 0.25 g/cu cm. When immersed in pure running water, they lost 90% of their salt content in 4.75 hr. The temperature was 25°C. At this temperature the average diffusivity of KCl in water over the indicated concentration range is $1.84(10^{-5})$ sq cm/sec.

Estimate the time for removal of 90% of the dissolved solute if the spheres had been impregnated with potassium chromate, K_2CrO_4, solution at a concentration 0.28 g/cu cm, when immersed in a running stream of water containing 0.02 g K_2CrO_4/cu cm. The average diffusivity of K_2CrO_4 in water at 25°C is $1.14(10^{-5})$ sq cm/sec.

Solution. For these spheres, $a = 0.5$ cm, and, for the KCl diffusion, $\theta = 4.75(3,600) = 17,000$ sec. When the spheres are surrounded by pure water, the ultimate concentration in the spheres, $c_{A\infty} = 0$.

$$\therefore \quad \frac{c_{A\theta} - c_{A\infty}}{c_{A0} - c_{A\infty}} = 0.1 \qquad \text{for 90\% removal of KCl}$$

From Fig. 4.2, $D\theta/(Ka)^2 = 0.18$, where K is the pore-shape factor.

$$K^2 = \frac{D\theta}{a^2(0.18)} = \frac{1.84(10^{-5})(17,000)}{0.5^2(0.18)} = 6.95$$

For the K_2CrO_4 diffusion, $c_{A0} = 0.28$ g/cu cm; $c_{A\infty} = 0.02$, and $c_{A\theta} = 0.1(0.28) = 0.028$.

$$\therefore \quad E = \frac{c_{A\theta} - c_{A\infty}}{c_{A0} - c_{A\infty}} = \frac{0.028 - 0.02}{0.28 - 0.02} = 0.0308 = E_s$$

From Fig. 4.2, $D\theta/(Ka)^2 = 0.30$.

$$\theta = \frac{0.30(Ka)^2}{D} = \frac{0.30(6.95)(0.5)^2}{1.14(10^{-5})} = 45,800 \text{ sec, or } 12.2 \text{ hr} \quad \textbf{Ans.}$$

Illustration 4.5. A slab of wood, 15.2 by 15.2 by 1.90 cm, of initial uniform moisture content 39.7% water, was exposed to relatively dry air.[9] The thin edges were sealed, and drying took place from the two large flat faces by internal diffusion of liquid water to the surface and evaporation at the surface. The moisture content at the surface remained constant at 8.0%. At the end of 7 hr 40 min, the average moisture content had fallen to 24.0%.

a. Calculate the effective diffusivity, sq cm/sec.

b. Assuming D remains constant and is the same for diffusion in all directions, what average water content would have resulted had the slab been dried from one face only, and from all six faces, for the same length of time?

c. What average water content would be had for a cylinder 1 ft long, 6 in. diameter, drying from all surfaces for a period of 7 days?

Solution. a. Let ρ = dry density of wood, lb dry wood/cu ft, assumed constant. If X is mass fraction of water, concentration in lb moles/cu ft $= \rho \dfrac{X}{1 - X} \dfrac{1}{18.02}$. Since the factor $\rho/18.02$ then appears in all such concentrations, E may be computed in terms of lb water/lb dry wood, $X/(1 - X)$.

$$c_{A0} = \frac{0.397}{1 - 0.397} = 0.658 \text{ lb water/lb dry wood}$$

$$c_{A\infty} = \frac{0.08}{1 - 0.08} = 0.087 \text{ lb water/lb dry wood}$$

$$c_{A\theta} = \frac{0.240}{1 - 0.240} = 0.316 \text{ lb water/lb dry wood}$$

At $\theta = 7.67(3,600) = 27,600$ sec,

$$E = \frac{c_{A\theta} - c_{A\infty}}{c_{A0} - c_{A\infty}} = \frac{0.316 - 0.087}{0.658 - 0.087} = 0.40 = E_a$$

From Fig. 4.2, $D\theta/a^2 = 0.287$. Since $a = 1.90/2 = 0.95$ cm,

$$\text{Effective diffusivity} = D = \frac{0.287a^2}{\theta} = \frac{0.287(0.95)^2}{27,600} = 9.38(10^{-6}) \text{ sq cm/sec}$$

b. For diffusion through one face only,

$$\frac{D\theta}{4a^2} = \frac{9.38(10^{-6})(27,600)}{4(0.95)^2} = 0.0718$$

From Fig. 4.2, $E = E_a = 0.7$.

$$\therefore \quad 0.7 = \frac{c_{A\theta} - 0.087}{0.658 - 0.087} \qquad c_{A\theta} = 0.487 \text{ lb water/lb dry wood}$$

corresponding to

$$\frac{0.487}{1.487} \, 100 = 32.8\% \text{ water}$$

For diffusion through six faces, $a = 0.95$ cm, $b = c = 15.2/2 = 7.6$ cm.

$$\frac{D\theta}{a^2} = \frac{9.38(10^{-6})(27,600)}{(0.95)^2} = 0.287$$

$$\frac{D\theta}{b^2} = \frac{D\theta}{c^2} = \frac{9.38(10^{-6})(27,600)}{(7.6)^2} = 0.00448$$

From Fig. 4.2, $E_a = 0.4$, $E_b = E_c = 0.94$.

Eq. (4.10): $\qquad\qquad E = E_a E_b E_c = 0.4(0.94)(0.94) = 0.353$

$$0.353 = \frac{c_{A\theta} - 0.087}{0.658 - 0.087}$$

$$c_{A\theta} = 0.291 \text{ lb water/lb dry wood } (22.5\% \text{ water})$$

c. For 7 days, $\theta = 7(24) = 168$ hr.

$$D = 9.38(10^{-6})(3.87) = 36.3(10^{-6}) \text{ sq ft/hr}$$

$$a = \frac{0.5}{2} = 0.25 \text{ ft} \qquad c = \frac{1}{2} = 0.5 \text{ ft}$$

$$\frac{D\theta}{a^2} = \frac{36.3(10^{-6})(168)}{(0.25)^2} = 0.0975 \qquad E_r = 0.405$$

$$\frac{D\theta}{c^2} = \frac{36.3(10^{-6})(168)}{(0.5)^2} = 0.0244 \qquad E_c = 0.82$$

Eq. (4.13): $\quad E = E_c E_r = 0.82(0.405) = 0.332$

$$0.332 = \frac{c_{A\theta} - 0.087}{0.658 - 0.087} \qquad c_{A\theta} = 0.277 \text{ lb water/lb dry wood } (21.7\% \text{ water})$$

Flow of gases through porous solids[2]

If there exists a concentration difference, i.e., a pressure difference, for a gas across a porous solid, a flow of the gas through the solid will take place. Under ordinary conditions, this is not a diffusional flow in the usual sense; yet since it may be described according to the methods of diffusion, it is sometimes so considered. Let us for the moment simplify the structure of the porous solid and consider it to be a series of straight capillary tubes of constant diameter d, and of length l, reaching from the high-pressure to the low-pressure side of the solid. At ordinary pressures, the flow of the gas in the capillaries may be either streamline or turbulent, depending upon whether the dimensionless Reynolds number, $du\rho/\mu$, is below or above 2,100. For the present purposes, where the diameter of the capillaries is small, and the pressure difference and hence the velocity are small, flow will be streamline and is described by

Poiseuille's law for a compressible fluid obeying the perfect-gas law,

$$N_A = \frac{d^2 g_c}{32 \mu l R T} p_{av}(p_1 - p_2) \tag{4.15}$$

where

$$p_{av} = \frac{p_1 + p_2}{2} \tag{4.16}$$

This assumes that the entire pressure difference is due to friction in the capillaries and ignores entrance and exit losses and kinetic-energy effects, which is satisfactory for present purposes. The capillaries leading through the porous solid are not of constant diameter, and their length is on the average some multiple of the solid thickness z. Only a fraction of the surface of the solid is open to the gas. The equation may then be written

$$RTN_A = \frac{k p_{av}(p_1 - p_2)}{z} \tag{4.17}$$

If the rate of flow is measured in terms of a gas volume V at the average pressure flowing per unit time per unit cross section of the solid, then Eq. (4.17) becomes

$$p_{av}V = \frac{P p_{av}(p_1 - p_2)}{z} \tag{4.18}$$

where P is the permeability of the solid to gas flow by Poiseuille's law. It is possible to compute average capillary sizes in membranes and porous barriers by measurements made according to this equation.

Under certain conditions, a different type of flow will occur, however. If the capillary diameters are small in comparison with the mean free path of the gas molecules λ (say $d \le 0.1\lambda$), flow takes place by molecular effusion, following Knudsen's law. For a single straight capillary, this becomes

$$N_A = k' \sqrt{\frac{g_c}{2\pi M R T}} \frac{d}{l} (p_1 - p_2) \tag{4.19}$$

where k' is a correction to take care of reflection of the molecule from the capillary wall. This may be written

$$RTN_A = k' \sqrt{\frac{g_c R T}{2\pi M}} \frac{d}{l} (p_1 - p_2) \tag{4.20}$$

or since, as before, the capillaries are of variable diameter nor is their length the same as the thickness of the solid,

$$p_{av}V = \frac{P'(p_1 - p_2)}{z} \tag{4.21}$$

where P' is now the permeability of the solid to molecular streaming. The mean free path of the molecules can be estimated from the relation

$$\lambda = \frac{3.2\mu}{p} \sqrt{\frac{R T}{2\pi g_c M}} \tag{4.22}$$

Flow according to Knudsen's law is a function of the molecular weight of the gas, and consequently the components of a gas mixture will pass through a porous solid barrier at different rates. This has been used as a method for analyzing gas mixtures and is the basis of the separation process of gaseous effusion.

In a given capillary, flow will occur according to both laws: at very low pressures or in extremely fine capillaries Knudsen flow predominates, while at higher pressures Poiseuille flow predominates. In a porous solid with capillaries of various diameters, the different types may predominate in different capillaries within the same solid. In any case, the equations show that the rate of flow as measured by the quantity $p_{av}V$ is proportional to the pressure difference and inversely proportional to the thickness, as in true diffusion in solution. The effect of temperature on the permeability may be used to indicate which type of flow predominates.[1] For flow according to Poiseuille's law, the permeability varies inversely as the gas viscosity, which in turn increases with temperature; P then decreases with increased temperature. For Knudsen flow, P' varies as $\sqrt{T}$ and therefore increases with increased temperature. Further, it will be remembered that, should diffusion in solid solution occur, the temperature dependence of P depends upon those of D and the solubility. All these effects may occur at once and the resulting temperature dependence may therefore be very complex.

Finally it should be remembered that, should the pressure difference become very large, the possibility of turbulent flow exists, which follows still a different law.

Illustration 4.6. A porous carbon diaphragm 1 in. thick, of average pore diameter 100 μ, permitted the flow of nitrogen at the rate of 9.0 cu ft (measured at 1 atm, 80°F) per square foot per minute with a pressure difference across the diaphragm of 2 in. of water. The temperature was 80°F, and the downstream pressure was 1 atm. Calculate the flow to be expected at 250°F, with the same pressure difference.

Solution. At 80°F, 1 atm, the viscosity of nitrogen is 0.018 centipoise.

$$\mu = 0.018(\tfrac{1}{100}) = 0.00018 \text{ g/(cm)(sec)} \qquad R = 84,780 \text{ (g force)(cm)/(°K)(g mole)}$$

$$p = 1(1,033.2) = 1,033.2 \text{ g/sq cm} \qquad g_c = 980 \text{ (g mass)(cm)/(g force)(sq sec)}$$

$$T = (80 + 460)\frac{1}{1.8} = 300°\text{K} \qquad M = 28.02$$

Eq. (4.22):
$$\lambda = \frac{3.2\mu}{p}\sqrt{\frac{RT}{2\pi g_c M}} = \frac{3.2(0.00018)}{1,033.2}\sqrt{\frac{84,780(300)}{2\pi(980)(28.02)}}$$

$$= 0.00000557 \text{ cm, or } 0.0557\mu$$

With capillary diameters of 100 μ, flow is therefore according to Poiseuille's law. For the first condition,

$$V_2 = 9.0 \text{ cu ft/(sq ft)(min)} \qquad \text{at 80°F, 1 atm}$$

$$p_2 = 1 \text{ atm} = 14.7(144) = 2,120 \text{ lb/sq ft}$$

$$p_1 - p_2 = \tfrac{2}{12}(62.2) = 10.4 \text{ lb/sq ft}$$

$$p_{av} = 2,120 + \frac{10.4}{2} = 2,125 \text{ lb/sq ft}$$

Eq. (4.18):
$$\frac{P}{z} = \frac{p_2 V_2}{p_{av}(p_1 - p_2)} = \frac{2,120(9.0)}{2,125(10.4)} \cdot$$

$$= 0.864 \text{ cu ft/(min)(sq ft)(lb/sq ft) for 1-in. thickness at 80°F}$$

At 250°F, the viscosity of nitrogen is 0.022 centipoise, and the new permeability becomes

$$\frac{P}{z} = 0.864 \frac{0.018}{0.022} = 0.706$$

$$\therefore \quad V_2 = P\frac{p_{av}(p_1 - p_2)}{zp_2} = \frac{0.706(2,125)(10.4)}{2,120}$$

$$= 7.36 \text{ cu ft/(min)(sq ft)}$$

measured at 250°F, 1 atm

NOTATION FOR CHAPTER 4

Consistent units in either the cgs or the English system may be used throughout.

a = one-half thickness or radius, cm or ft
b = one-half width, cm or ft
c = concentration, g moles/cu cm or lb moles/cu ft
= one-half length, cm or ft
d = diameter of a capillary, cm or ft
= differential operator
D = diffusivity, sq cm/sec or sq ft/hr
e = 2.7183
E = fraction of solute unremoved, dimensionless
f, f', f'' = functions
g_c = conversion factor, 980 (g mass)(cm)/(g force)(sq sec) or 4.17(10^8)(lb mass)(ft)/(lb force)(sq hr)
k, k' = constants
K = pore-shape factor, dimensionless
l = length, cm or ft
ln = natural logarithm
M = molecular weight, g/g mole or lb/lb mole
N = rate of diffusion, g moles/(sec)(sq cm) or lb moles/(hr)(sq ft)
p = pressure, g force/sq cm or lb force/sq ft (unless otherwise indicated)
P = permeability = rate of diffusion per unit pressure gradient, cu cm/(sec)(sq cm)(g force/sq cm/cm) or cu ft/(hr)(sq ft)(lb force/sq ft/ft) (frequently also in other pressure units)
R = universal gas constant, 84,780 (g force)(cm)/(g mole)(°K) or 1,543 ft-lb force/(lb mole)(°R)
S = cross-sectional area, sq cm or sq ft
T = absolute temperature, °K or °R
u = linear velocity, cm/sec or ft/hr
V = volumetric rate of flow, cu cm/(sec)(sq cm) or cu ft/(hr)(sq ft)
w = rate of diffusion, g moles/sec or lb moles/hr
z = distance in the direction of diffusion, cm or ft
Δ = difference
θ = time, sec or hr
λ = molecular mean free path, cm or ft
μ = viscosity, g mass/(cm)(sec)(= poises) or lb mass/(ft)(hr)
π = 3.1416
ρ = density, g mass/cu cm or lb mass/cu ft

Subscripts:

av = average
A, B = components A, B

θ = at time θ
0 = initial (at time zero)
1, 2 = positions 1, 2
∞ = at time ∞; at equilibrium

REFERENCES

1.   Barrer, R. M.: "Diffusion in and through Solids," Cambridge University Press, London, 1941.

2.   Carman, P. C.: "Flow of Gases through Porous Media," Academic Press Inc., New York, 1956.

3.   Carslaw, H. S., and J. C. Jaeger: "Conduction of Heat in Solids," 2d ed., Oxford University Press, Fair Lawn, N.J., 1959.

4.   Crank, J.: "The Mathematics of Diffusion," Oxford University Press, Fair Lawn, N.J., 1956.

5.   Jost, W.: "Diffusion in Solids, Liquids, and Gases," Academic Press Inc., New York, 1952.

6.   Newman, A. B.: *Trans. AIChE*, **27**, 203, 310 (1931).

7.   Piret, E. L., R. A. Ebel, C. T. Kiang, and W. P. Armstrong: *Chem. Eng. Progr.*, **47**, 405, 628 (1951).

8.   Satterfield, C. N., and T. K. Sherwood: "The Role of Diffusion in Catalysts," Addison-Wesley Publishing Company, Inc., Reading, Mass., 1963.

9.   Sherwood, T. K.: *Ind. Eng. Chem.*, **21**, 12, 976 (1929).

10.   Tuwiner, S. B.: "Diffusion and Membrane Technology," Reinhold Publishing Corporation, New York, 1962.

11.   Van Arsdel, W. B.: *Chem. Eng. Progr.*, **43**, 13 (1947).

PROBLEMS

4.1.   Removal of soybean oil impregnating a porous clay plate by contact with a solvent for the oil has been shown to be a matter of internal diffusion of the oil through the solid [Boucher, Brier, and Osburn, *Trans. AIChE*, **38**, 967 (1942)].   Such a clay plate, $\frac{1}{16}$ in. thick by 1.80 in. long by 1.08 in. wide, thin edges sealed, was impregnated with soybean oil to a uniform concentration of 0.229 lb oil/lb dry clay.   It was immersed in a flowing stream of pure tetrachloroethylene at 120°F, whereupon the oil content of the plate was reduced to 0.048 lb oil/lb dry clay in 1 hr.   The resistance to diffusion may be taken as residing wholly within the plate and the final ultimate oil content of the clay as zero when contacted with pure solvent.

a.   Calculate the effective diffusivity.

b.   A cylinder of the same clay, 0.5-in. diameter, 1 in. long, both ends sealed, contains an initial uniform concentration of 0.17 lb oil/lb clay.   When immersed in a flowing stream of pure tetrachloroethylene at 120°F, to what concentration will the oil content fall in 10 hr?   **Ans.: 0.0748.**

c.   Recalculate (*b*) for the cases where only one end of the cylinder is sealed and where neither end is sealed.

d.   How long will it take for the concentration to fall to 0.01 lb oil/lb clay for the cylinder of (*b*) with neither end sealed?

4.2.   A slab of clay, such as that used to make brick, 2 in. thick, was dried from both flat surfaces with the four thin edges sealed, by exposure to dry air.   The initial uniform moisture content was 15%.   The drying took place by internal diffusion of the liquid water to the surface, followed by evaporation at the surface.   The diffusivity may be assumed to be constant with varying water concentration, and uniform in all directions.   The surface moisture content was 3%.   In 5 hr the average moisture content had fallen to 10.2%.

a.   Calculate the diffusivity, sq ft/hr.

b. Under the same drying conditions, how much longer would it have taken to reduce the average water content to 6%?

c. How long would it require to dry a sphere of 6-in. radius from 15 to 6% under the same drying conditions?

d. How long would it require to dry a cylinder 1 ft long, 6-in. diameter, drying from all surfaces, to a moisture content of 6%? **Ans.:** 47.5 hr.

4.3. An unglazed porcelain plate 0.5 cm thick has an average pore diameter of 0.2 μ. Pure oxygen gas at an absolute pressure of 2 cm Hg, 100°C, on one side of the plate passed through at a rate of 0.093 cu cm (at 2 cm Hg, 100°C) per second per square centimeter when the pressure on the downstream side was so low as to be considered negligible. Estimate the rate of passage of hydrogen gas at 25°C and a pressure of 1 cm Hg abs, with negligible downstream pressure.

CHAPTER FIVE
INTERPHASE
MASS TRANSFER

Thus far we have considered only the diffusion of substances within a single phase. In most of the mass-transfer operations, however, two insoluble phases are brought into contact in order to permit transfer of constituent substances between them. Therefore we are now concerned with the simultaneous application of the diffusional mechanism for each phase to the combined system. We have seen that the rate of diffusion within each phase is dependent upon the concentration gradient existing within it. At the same time the concentration gradients of the two-phase system are indicative of the departure from equilibrium which exists between the phases. Should equilibrium be established, the concentration gradients and hence the rate of diffusion will fall to zero. It is necessary, therefore, to consider both the diffusional phenomena and the equilibria in order to describe the various situations fully.

EQUILIBRIUM

It is convenient first to consider the equilibrium characteristics of a particular operation and then to generalize the result for others. As an example, consider the gas-absorption operation which occurs when ammonia is dissolved from an ammonia-air mixture by liquid water. Suppose a fixed amount of liquid water is placed in a closed container together with a gaseous mixture of ammonia and air, the whole arranged so that the system can be maintained at constant temperature and pressure. Since ammonia is very soluble in water, some ammonia molecules will instantly transfer from the gas into the liquid, crossing the interfacial surface separating the two phases. A portion of the ammonia molecules escapes back into the gas, at a rate proportional to their concentration in the liquid. As more ammonia enters the liquid, with consequent increase in concentration within the liquid, the rate at which ammonia returns to the gas increases, until eventually the rate at which it enters the liquid exactly equals that at which it leaves. At the same time, through the mechanism of diffusion, the concentrations throughout each phase become uniform. A dynamic equilibrium now exists, and while ammonia molecules continue to transfer back and forth from one phase to the other, the net transfer falls to zero. The concentrations within each phase no longer change. To the observer who cannot see the individual molecules the diffusion has apparently stopped.

If we now inject additional ammonia into the container, a new set of equilibrium concentrations will eventually be established, with higher concentrations in each phase than were at first obtained. In this manner we can eventually obtain the complete relationship between the equilibrium concentrations in both phases. If the ammonia is designated as substance A, the equilibrium concentrations in the gas and liquid, y_A and x_A mole fractions, respectively, give rise to an *equilibrium-distribution curve* of the type shown in Fig. 5.1. This curve results irrespective of the amounts of water and air that we start with and is influenced only by the conditions, such as temperature and pressure, imposed upon the three-component system. It is important to note that at equilibrium the concentrations in the two phases are not equal; rather the chemical potential of the ammonia is the same in both phases, and it will be recalled (Chap. 2) that it is equality of chemical potentials, not concentrations, which cause the net transfer of solute to stop.

The curve of Fig. 5.1 does not of course show all the equilibrium concentrations existing within the system. For example, the water will partially vaporize into the

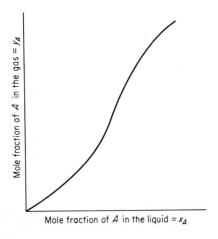

Fig. 5.1   *Equilibrium distribution of a solute between a gas and a liquid phase at constant temperature.*

gas phase, the components of the air will also dissolve to a small extent in the liquid, and equilibrium concentrations for these substances will also be established. For the moment we need not consider these equilibria, since they are of minor importance to the discussion at hand. Obviously also, concentration units other than mole fractions may be used to describe the equilibria.

Generally speaking, whenever a substance is distributed between two insoluble phases, a dynamic equilibrium of this type can be established. The various equilibria are peculiar to the particular system considered. For example, replacement of the water in the example considered above with another liquid such as benzene, or with a solid adsorbent such as activated carbon, or replacement of the ammonia with another solute such as sulfur dioxide will each result in new curves not at all related to the first. The equilibrium resulting for a two-liquid-phase system bears no relation to that for a liquid-solid system. A discussion of the characteristic shapes of the equilibrium curves for the various situations and the influence of conditions such as temperature and pressure must be left for the studies of the individual unit operations. Nevertheless the following principles are common to all systems involving the distribution of a substance between two insoluble phases:

1. At a fixed set of conditions, referring to temperature and pressure, there exists a set of equilibrium relationships which may be shown graphically in the form of an equilibrium-distribution curve by plotting the equilibrium concentrations in the two phases one against the other.

2. For a system in equilibrium, there is no net diffusion of the components between the phases.

3. For a system not in equilibrium, diffusion of the components between the phases will occur in such a manner as to bring the system to a condition of equilibrium. If sufficient time is available, equilibrium concentrations will eventually prevail.

DIFFUSION BETWEEN PHASES

Having established that departure from equilibrium provides the driving force for diffusion, the rates of diffusion in terms of the driving forces may now be studied. Many of the mass-transfer operations are carried out in steady-flow fashion, with continuous and invariant flow of the contacted phases, and under circumstances such that concentrations at any position in the equipment used do not change with time. It will be convenient to use one of these as an example with which to establish the principles and to generalize respecting other operations later. For this purpose, let us consider the absorption of a soluble gas such as ammonia (substance A) from a mixture such as air and ammonia, by liquid water as the absorbent, in one of the simplest of apparatus, the wetted-wall tower previously described in Chap. 3 (Fig. 3.10). The ammonia-air mixture may enter at the bottom and flow upward while the water flows downward around the inside of the pipe. The gas mixture changes its composition from a high- to a low-solute concentration as it flows upward, while the water dissolves the ammonia and leaves at the bottom as an aqueous ammonia

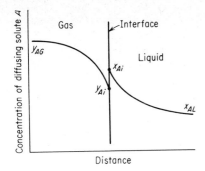

Fig. 5.2 *The two-resistance concept.*

solution. Under steady-state conditions, the concentrations at any point in the apparatus do not change with passage of time.

Local two-phase mass transfer

Let us investigate the situation at a particular level along the tower, e.g., at a point midway between top and bottom. Since the solute is diffusing from the gas phase into the liquid, there must be a concentration gradient in the direction of mass transfer within each phase. This can be shown graphically in terms of the distance through the phases as in Fig. 5.2, where a section through the two phases in contact is shown. It will be assumed that no chemical reaction occurs. The concentration of A in the main body of the gas is y_{AG} mole fraction, and it falls to y_{Ai} at the interface. In the liquid, the concentration falls from x_{Ai} at the interface to x_{AL} in the bulk liquid. The bulk concentrations y_{AG} and x_{AL} are clearly not equilibrium values, since otherwise diffusion of the solute would not occur. At the same time, these bulk concentrations cannot be used directly with a mass-transfer coefficient to describe the rate of interphase mass transfer, since the two concentrations are differently related to the chemical potential, which is the real "driving force" of mass transfer.

To get around this problem, Lewis and Whitman[5,10] assumed that the only diffusional resistances are those residing in the fluids themselves. There is then no resistance to solute transfer across the interface separating the phases, and as a result the concentrations y_{Ai} and x_{Ai} are equilibrium values, given by the system's equilibrium-distribution curve.† The reliability of this theory has been subjected to many tests. As a result, it is now known that there are special situations where it is invalid. For example, if a solute diffuses to a solid interface, where it crystallizes, the molecules must orient themselves to fit into the crystal lattice, and since this is a time-consuming process, an interfacial "resistance" may result. Certain substances tend to concentrate at the interface, and these may hinder the interphase transfer of solute. For example, cetyl alcohol, when spread upon water in remarkably small concentrations, reduces the rate of evaporation of the water into air by as much as 95 percent. It is

---

† This has been called the "two-film" theory, improperly so, because it is not related to, or dependent upon, the film theory of mass-transfer coefficients described in Chap. 3. A more appropriate name would be the "two-resistance" theory.

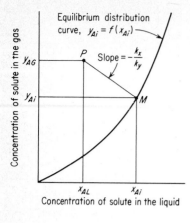

Fig. **5.3** *Departure of bulk-phase concentrations from equilibrium.*

thought that this may occur by virtue of its adsorption at the surface, which then reduces the net area available for the mass transfer of the water.   Certain high-molecular-weight substances tend to adsorb at the interface between two insoluble liquids, and these tend to reduce the rate of transfer of an extractable solute.   These effects may be profound, but they are very specific; the theories of the actions are highly speculative.   In ordinary situations, the evidence is that equilibrium does indeed exist at the interface, and the interfacial concentrations of Fig. 5.2 are those given by a point on the equilibrium-distribution curve.

Referring again to Fig. 5.2, it is clear that the concentration rise at the interface, from y_{Ai} to x_{Ai}, is not a barrier to diffusion in the direction gas to liquid.   They are equilibrium concentrations, and hence correspond to equal chemical potentials of substance A in both phases at the interface.

The various concentrations may also be shown graphically, as in Fig. 5.3, whose coordinates are those of the equilibrium-distribution curve.   Point P represents the two bulk-phase concentrations and point M those at the interface.   For steady-state mass transfer, the rate at which A reaches the interface from the gas must equal that at which it diffuses to the bulk liquid, so that no accumulation or depletion of A at the interface occurs.   We may therefore write the flux of A in terms of the mass-transfer coefficients for each phase and the concentration changes appropriate to each (the development will be done in terms of the k-type coefficients, since this is simpler, and the results for F-type coefficients will be indicated later).   Thus, when k_y and k_x are the locally applicable coefficients,

$$N_A = k_y(y_{AG} - y_{Ai}) = k_x(x_{Ai} - x_{AL}) \tag{5.1}$$

and the differences in y's or x's are considered the "driving forces" for the mass transfer.   Rearrangement as

$$\frac{y_{AG} - y_{Ai}}{x_{AL} - x_{Ai}} = -\frac{k_x}{k_y} \tag{5.2}$$

provides the slope of the line PM.   If the mass-transfer coefficients are known, the interfacial concentrations and hence the flux N_A may be determined, either graphically by plotting the line *PM* or analytically by solving Eq. (5.2) with an algebraic expression for the equilibrium-distribution curve,

$$y_{Ai} = f(x_{Ai}) \tag{5.3}$$

Local overall mass-transfer coefficients

In experimental determinations of the rate of mass transfer, it is usually possible to determine the solute concentrations in the bulk of the fluids by sampling and analyzing. Successful sampling of the fluids at the interface, however, is ordinarily impossible, since the greatest part of the concentration differences, such as $y_{AG} - y_{Ai}$, takes place over extremely small distances. Any ordinary sampling device will be so large in comparison with this distance that it is impossible to approach the interface sufficiently closely. Sampling and analyzing, then, will provide y_{AG} and x_{AL} but not y_{Ai} and x_{Ai}. Under these circumstances, only an overall effect, in terms of the bulk concentrations, can be determined. The bulk concentrations are, however, not by themselves on the same basis in terms of chemical potential.

Consider the situation as shown in Fig. 5.4. Since the equilibrium-distribution curve for the system is unique at fixed temperature and pressure, then y_A^*, in equilibrium with x_{AL}, is as good a measure of x_{AL} as x_{AL} itself, and moreover it is on the same basis as y_{AG}. The entire two-phase mass-transfer effect may then be measured in terms of an overall mass-transfer coefficient K_y

$$N_A = K_y(y_{AG} - y_A^*) \tag{5.4}$$

From the geometry of the figure,

$$y_{AG} - y_A^* = (y_{AG} - y_{Ai}) + (y_{Ai} - y_A^*) = (y_{AG} - y_{Ai}) + m'(x_{Ai} - x_{AL}) \tag{5.5}$$

where m' is the slope of the chord *CM*. Substituting for the concentration differences

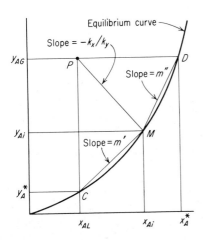

Fig. 5.4   *Overall concentration differences.*

their equivalents (flux/coefficient) as given by Eqs. (5.1) and (5.4),

$$\frac{N_A}{K_y} = \frac{N_A}{k_y} + \frac{m'N_A}{k_x} \tag{5.6}$$

or

$$\frac{1}{K_y} = \frac{1}{k_y} + \frac{m'}{k_x} \tag{5.7}$$

This shows the relationship among the individual-phase transfer coefficients and the overall coefficient to take the form of addition of resistances (hence the term "two-resistance" theory). In similar fashion, x_A^* is a measure of y_{AG} and may be used to define another overall coefficient K_x

$$N_A = K_x(x_A^* - x_{AL}) \tag{5.8}$$

and it is readily shown that

$$\frac{1}{K_x} = \frac{1}{m''k_y} + \frac{1}{k_x} \tag{5.9}$$

where m'' is the slope of the chord MD on Fig. 5.4.   Equations (5.7) and (5.9) lead to the following relationships among the mass-transfer resistances:

$$\frac{\text{Resistance in gas phase}}{\text{Total resistance, both phases}} = \frac{1/k_y}{1/K_y} \tag{5.10}$$

$$\frac{\text{Resistance in liquid phase}}{\text{Total resistance, both phases}} = \frac{1/k_x}{1/K_x} \tag{5.11}$$

Assuming that the numerical values of k_x and k_y are roughly the same, the importance of the slope of the equilibrium-curve chords can readily be demonstrated. If m' is small (equilibrium-distribution curve very flat), so that at equilibrium only a small concentration of A in the gas will provide a very large concentration in the liquid (solute A is very soluble in the liquid), the term m'/k_x of Eq. (5.7) becomes minor, the major resistance is represented by $1/k_y$, and it is said that the rate of mass transfer is gas-phase-controlled.   In the extreme, this becomes

$$\frac{1}{K_y} \doteq \frac{1}{k_y} \tag{5.12}$$

or

$$y_{AG} - y_A^* \doteq y_{AG} - y_{Ai} \tag{5.13}$$

Under such circumstances, even fairly large percentage changes in k_x will not significantly affect K_y, and efforts to increase the rate of mass transfer would best be directed toward decreasing the gas-phase resistance. Conversely, when m'' is very large (solute A relatively insoluble in the liquid), with k_x and k_y nearly equal, the first term on the right of Eq. (5.9) becomes minor, and the major resistance to mass transfer resides within the liquid, which is then said to control the rate. Ultimately, this becomes

$$\frac{1}{K_x} \doteq \frac{1}{k_x} \tag{5.14}$$

$$x_A^* - x_{AL} \doteq x_{Ai} - x_{AL} \tag{5.15}$$

In such cases efforts to effect large changes in the rate of mass transfer are best directed to conditions influencing the liquid coefficient k_x. For cases where k_x and k_y are not nearly equal, Fig. 5.4 shows that it will be the relative size of the ratio k_x/k_y and of m' (or m'') which will determine the location of the controlling mass-transfer resistance.

It is sometimes useful to note that the effect of temperature is much larger for liquid mass-transfer coefficients than for those for gases (see Prob. 3.7, for example). Consequently a large effect of temperature on the overall coefficient, when it is determined experimentally, is usually a fairly clear indication that the controlling mass-transfer resistance is in the liquid phase.

For purposes of establishing the nature of the two-resistance theory and the overall coefficient concept, gas absorption was chosen as an example. The principles are applicable to any of the mass-transfer operations, however, and may be applied in terms of k-type coefficients using any concentration units, as listed in Table 3.1 (the F-type coefficients are considered separately below). For each case, the values of m' and m'' must be appropriately defined and used consistently with the coefficients. Thus, if the generalized phases are termed E (with concentrations expressed as i) and R (with concentrations expressed as j),

$$\frac{1}{K_E} = \frac{1}{k_E} + \frac{m'}{k_R} \tag{5.16}$$

$$\frac{1}{K_R} = \frac{1}{m''k_E} + \frac{1}{k_R} \tag{5.17}$$

$$m' = \frac{i_{Ai} - i_A^*}{j_{Ai} - j_{AR}} \qquad m'' = \frac{i_{AE} - i_{Ai}}{j_A^* - j_{Ai}} \tag{5.18}$$

$$i_A^* = f(j_{AR}) \qquad i_{AE} = f(j_A^*) \tag{5.19}$$

where f is the equilibrium-distribution function.

Local coefficients—General case

When we deal with situations which do not involve either diffusion of only one substance or equimolar counterdiffusion, or if mass-transfer rates are large, the F-type coefficients should be used. The general approach is the same, although the resulting expressions are more cumbersome than those developed above. Thus, in the case of a situation such as that shown in Figs. 5.2 to 5.4, the mass-transfer flux is

$$N_A = \frac{N_A}{\Sigma N} F_G \ln \frac{N_A/\Sigma N - y_{Ai}}{N_A/\Sigma N - y_{AG}} = \frac{N_A}{\Sigma N} F_L \ln \frac{N_A/\Sigma N - x_{AL}}{N_A/\Sigma N - x_{Ai}} \tag{5.20}$$

where F_G and F_L are the gas- and liquid-phase coefficients for substance A and $\Sigma N = N_A + N_B + N_C + \cdots$. Equation (5.20) then becomes[2]

$$\frac{N_A/\Sigma N - y_{Ai}}{N_A/\Sigma N - y_{AG}} = \left(\frac{N_A/\Sigma N - x_{AL}}{N_A/\Sigma N - x_{Ai}}\right)^{F_L/F_G} \tag{5.21}$$

The interfacial compositions y_{Ai} and x_{Ai} may be found by plotting Eq. (5.21) (with y_{Ai} replaced by y_A and x_{Ai} by x_A) on the distribution diagram (Fig. 5.3) and determining the intersection of the resulting curve with the distribution curve. This is, in general, a trial-and-error procedure, since $N_A/\Sigma N$ may not be known, and must be done in conjunction with Eq. (5.20). In the special cases for diffusion only of A and of equimolar counterdiffusion in two-components phases, no trial and error is required.

We may also define the overall coefficients F_{OG} and F_{OL} as

$$N_A = \frac{N_A}{\Sigma N} F_{OG} \ln \frac{N_A/\Sigma N - y_A^*}{N_A/\Sigma N - y_{AG}} = \frac{N_A}{\Sigma N} F_{OL} \ln \frac{N_A/\Sigma N - x_{AL}}{N_A/\Sigma N - x_A^*} \qquad (5.22)$$

By a procedure similar to that used for the K's, it may be shown that the overall and individual phase F's are related:

$$\exp\left[\frac{N_A}{(N_A/\Sigma N)F_{OG}}\right] = \exp\left[\frac{N_A}{(N_A/\Sigma N)F_G}\right]$$

$$+ m' \frac{N_A/\Sigma N - x_{AL}}{N_A/\Sigma N - y_{AG}} \left\{ 1 - \exp\left[-\frac{N_A}{(N_A/\Sigma N)F_L}\right]\right\} \qquad (5.23)$$

$$\exp\left[-\frac{N_A}{(N_A/\Sigma N)F_{OL}}\right] = \frac{1}{m''}\left(\frac{N_A/\Sigma N - y_{AG}}{N_A/\Sigma N - x_{AL}}\right)\left\{ 1 - \exp\left[\frac{N_A}{(N_A/\Sigma N)F_G}\right]\right\}$$

$$+ \exp\left[-\frac{N_A}{(N_A/\Sigma N)F_L}\right] \qquad (5.24)$$

where $\exp Z$ means e^Z. These fortunately simplify for the two important special cases:

(a) *Diffusion of one component* ($\Sigma N = N_A, N_A/\Sigma N = 1.0$)†

$$e^{N_A/F_{OG}} = e^{N_A/F_G} + m'\left(\frac{1 - x_{AL}}{1 - y_{AG}}\right)(1 - e^{-N_A/F_L}) \qquad (5.25)$$

$$e^{-N_A/F_{OL}} = \frac{1}{m''}\left(\frac{1 - y_{AG}}{1 - x_{AL}}\right)(1 - e^{N_A/F_G}) + e^{-N_A/F_L} \qquad (5.26)$$

† Equations (5.25) and (5.26) may also be written in the following forms:

$$\frac{1}{F_{OG}} = \frac{1}{F_G}\frac{(1 - y_A)_{iM}}{(1 - y_A)_{*M}} + \frac{m'(1 - x_A)_{iM}}{F_L(1 - y_A)_{*M}} \qquad (5.25a)$$

$$\frac{1}{F_{OL}} = \frac{1}{m''F_G}\frac{(1 - y_A)_{iM}}{(1 - x_A)_{*M}} + \frac{1}{F_L}\frac{(1 - x_A)_{iM}}{(1 - x_A)_{*M}} \qquad (5.26a)$$

where

$(1 - y_A)_{iM}$ = logarithmic mean of $1 - y_{AG}$ and $1 - y_{Ai}$
$(1 - y_A)_{*M}$ = logarithmic mean of $1 - y_{AG}$ and $1 - y_A^*$
$(1 - x_A)_{iM}$ = logarithmic mean of $1 - x_{AL}$ and $1 - x_{Ai}$
$(1 - x_A)_{*M}$ = logarithmic mean of $1 - x_{AL}$ and $1 - x_A^*$

(b) *Equimolar counterdiffusion* $[\Sigma N = 0 \ (F_G = k'_y, F_L = k'_x)]$

$$\frac{1}{F_{OG}} = \frac{1}{F_G} + \frac{m'}{F_L} \tag{5.27}$$

$$\frac{1}{F_{OL}} = \frac{1}{m''F_G} + \frac{1}{F_L} \tag{5.28}$$

Use of local overall coefficients

The concept of overall mass-transfer coefficients is in many ways similar to that of overall heat-transfer coefficients in the case of heat-exchanger design. And, as is the practice in heat transfer, the overall coefficients of mass transfer are frequently synthesized through the relationships developed above from the individual coefficients for the separate phases. These may be taken, for example, from the correlations of Chap. 3 or from those developed in later chapters for specific types of mass-transfer equipment. It is important to recognize the limitations inherent in this procedure.[3]

The hydrodynamic circumstances must be the same as those for which the correlations were developed. Especially in the case of two fluids, where motion in one may influence motion in the other, the individual correlations may make inadequate allowances for the effect on the transfer coefficients. On occasion, particularly in the transfer of solute between two liquids, an "interfacial turbulence," or extraordinary motion of the interface, occurs as a result of interfacial tension gradients peculiar to the two-phase system at hand, and this leads to unexpectedly high interphase mass transfer.[1,8] On other occasions adsorption of surface-active substances at the interface has caused a rigidity, or reduction of mobility, at the interface with consequent reduction in the expected mass-transfer rate.[1]

The mere presence of a mass-transfer resistance in one phase must have no influence on that in the other: the resistances must not interact, in other words. This may be important, since the individual-phase coefficient correlations are frequently developed under conditions where mass-transfer resistance in the second phase is nil, as when the second phase is a pure substance. The analysis of such situations is dependent upon the mechanism assumed for mass transfer (film, surface-renewal, etc., theories), and has been incompletely developed.

Average overall coefficients

As will be shown, in practical mass-transfer apparatus the bulk concentrations in the contacted phases normally vary considerably from place to place, so that a point such as P in Figs. 5.3 and 5.4 is just one of an infinite number which forms a curve on these figures. Thus, in the countercurrent wetted-wall gas absorber considered earlier, the solute concentrations in both fluids are small at the top and large at the bottom. In such situations, we may speak of an average overall coefficient applicable to the entire device. Such an average coefficient can be synthesized from constituent individual-phase coefficients by the same equations as developed above for local overall coefficients only, provided the quantity $m'k_E/k_R$ (or $m''k_R/k_E$) remains everywhere constant.[3]   Of course, variations in values of the coefficients and slope m' may occur in such a way that they are self-compensating.   But in practice, since average phase coefficients, assumed constant for the entire apparatus, are the only ones usually available, average overall coefficients generally will have meaning only when $m' = m'' = $ const, in other words, for cases of straight-line equilibrium-distribution curves. Obviously, also, the same hydrodynamic regime must exist throughout the apparatus for an average overall coefficient to have meaning.

Illustration 5.1. A wetted-wall absorption tower, 1 in. ID, is fed with water as the wall liquid and an ammonia-air mixture as the central-core gas.   At a particular level in the tower, the ammonia concentration in the bulk gas is 0.80 mole fraction, that in the bulk liquid 0.05 mole fraction.   The temperature $= 80°F$, the pressure 1 atm.   The rates of flow are such that the local mass-transfer coefficient in the liquid, from a correlation obtained with dilute solutions, is $k_L = 0.34$ lb mole/ (hr)(sq ft)(lb mole/cu ft), and the local Sherwood number for the gas is 40.   The diffusivity of ammonia in air $= 0.890$ sq ft/hr.   Compute the local mass-transfer flux for the absorption of ammonia, ignoring the vaporization of water.

Solution. $y_{AG} = 0.80$, $x_{AL} = 0.05$ mole fraction ammonia.   Because of the large concentration of ammonia in the gas, F's rather than k's will be used.   Notation is that of Chap. 3.

Liquid. From Table 3.1, $F_L = k_L x_{BM} c$.   Since the molecular weight of ammonia and water are so nearly the same, and the density of a dilute solution is practically that of water, the molar density $c = 62.3/18 = 3.44$ lb moles/cu ft.   Since the k_L was determined for dilute solutions, where x_{BM} is practically 1.0,

$$F_L = 0.34(1.0)(3.44) = 1.170 \text{ lb moles/(hr)(sq ft)}$$

Gas.

$$\text{Sh} = \frac{F_G d}{c D_A} = 40 \qquad d = \tfrac{1}{12} = 0.0833 \text{ ft}$$

$$c = \frac{1}{359} \frac{492}{460 + 80} = 0.00254 \text{ lb mole/cu ft}$$

$$D_A = 0.890 \text{ sq ft/hr}$$

$$F_G = \frac{40 c D_A}{d} = \frac{40(0.00254)(0.890)}{0.0833} = 1.085 \text{ lb moles/(hr)(sq ft)}$$

Mass-transfer flux. The equilibrium distribution of ammonia is taken from the data at 80°F in "The Chemical Engineers' Handbook," 4th ed., p. 3-66:

NH$_3$ mole fraction x_A	NH$_3$ partial pressure p_A, lb/sq in.	$y_A = \dfrac{p_A}{14.7}$
0	0	0
0.05	1.04	0.0707
0.10	1.98	0.1347
0.25	8.69	0.590
0.30	13.52	0.920

These are plotted as the equilibrium curve in Fig. 5.5.

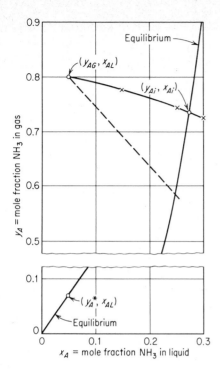

Fig. 5.5 *Construction for Illustration 5.1.*

For transfer of only one component, $N_A/\Sigma N = 1.0$. Equation (5.21), with y_{Ai} and x_{Ai} replaced by y_A and x_A, becomes

$$y_A = 1 - (1 - y_{AG})\left(\frac{1 - x_{AL}}{1 - x_A}\right)^{F_L/F_G} = 1 - (1 - 0.8)\left(\frac{1 - 0.05}{1 - x_A}\right)^{1.078}$$

from which the following are computed:

x_A	0.05	0.15	0.25	0.30
y_A	0.80	0.780	0.742	0.722

These are plotted (as crosses) on Fig. 5.5, and the resulting curve intersects the equilibrium curve to give the interface compositions, $x_{Ai} = 0.274$, $y_{Ai} = 0.732$. Therefore, Eq. (5.20) provides

$$N_A = 1(1.170)\ln\frac{1 - 0.05}{1 - 0.274} = 1(1.085)\ln\frac{1 - 0.732}{1 - 0.80} = 0.316 \text{ lb mole NH}_3$$

$$\text{absorbed/(hr)(sq ft), local flux} \quad \textbf{Ans.}$$

Overall coefficient. Although it is not particularly useful in this case, the overall coefficient will be computed to demonstrate the method. The gas concentration in equilibrium with the bulk liquid ($x_{AL} = 0.05$) is, from Fig. 5.5, $y_A^* = 0.0707$. The chord slope m' is therefore

$$m' = \frac{y_{Ai} - y_A^*}{x_{Ai} - x_{AL}} = \frac{0.732 - 0.0707}{0.274 - 0.05} = 2.95$$

Note that, unless the equilibrium curve is straight, this cannot be obtained without first obtaining (y_{Ai}, x_{Ai}), in which case there is no need for an overall coefficient. In Eq. (5.25), normally we would obtain F_{OG} by trial, by assuming N_A. Thus (with one eye on the answer obtained above), assume $N_A = 0.316$.   Then Eq. (5.25) becomes

$$e^{0.316/F_{OG}} = e^{0.316/1.085} + 2.95\,\frac{1 - 0.05}{1 - 0.80}\,(1 - e^{-0.316/1.170}) = 4.658$$

$$\therefore\quad F_{OG} = 0.205 \text{ lb mole/(hr)(sq ft)}$$

As a check of the trial value of N_A, Eq. (5.22) is

$$N_A = 1(0.205)\ln\frac{1 - 0.0707}{1 - 0.80} = 0.316\quad\text{(check)}$$

Use of k-type coefficients. There are, of course, k's which are consistent with the F's and which will produce the correct result. Thus, $k_y = F_G P_t/p_{BM} = 4.64$ and $k_x = F_L/x_{BM} = 1.39$ will produce the same result as above. But these k's are specific for the concentration levels at hand, and the p_{BM} and x_{BM} terms, which correct for the bulk-flow flux [the $(N_A + N_B)$ term of Eq. (2.4)], cannot be obtained until x_{Ai} and y_{Ai} are first obtained as above.

However, if it had been assumed that the concentrations were dilute and that the bulk-flow terms were negligible, the Sherwood number *might* have been (incorrectly) interpreted as

$$\text{Sh} = \frac{k_y RTd}{P_t D_A} = 40 = \frac{k_y(0.729)(460 + 80)(0.0833)}{1(0.890)}$$

$$k_y = 1.085 \text{ lb moles/(hr)(sq ft)(mole fraction)}$$

and, in the case of the liquid,

$$k_x = k_L c = 0.34(3.44) = 1.170 \text{ lb moles/(hr)(sq ft)(mole fraction)}$$

These k's are suitable for small driving forces but are unsuitable here.   Thus

$$-\frac{k_x}{k_y} = -\frac{1.170}{1.085} = -1.078$$

and a line of this slope (the dashed line of Fig. 5.5) drawn from (x_{AL}, y_{AG}) intersects the equilibrium curve at $x_A = 0.250$, $y_A = 0.585$.   If this is interpreted to be (x_{Ai}, y_{Ai}), the calculated flux would be

$$N_A = k_x(x_{Ai} - x_{AL}) = 1.170(0.250 - 0.05) = 0.234$$

or

$$N_A = k_y(y_{AG} - y_{Ai}) = 1.085(0.8 - 0.585) = 0.234$$

The corresponding overall coefficient, with $m' = (0.585 - 0.0707)/(0.250 - 0.05) = 2.57$, would be

$$\frac{1}{K_y} = \frac{1}{k_y} + \frac{m'}{k_x} = \frac{1}{1.085} + \frac{2.57}{1.170}$$

$$K_y = 0.321 \text{ lb mole/(hr)(sq ft)(mole fraction)}$$

and

$$N_A = K_y(y_{AG} - y_A^*) = 0.321(0.8 - 0.0707) = 0.234$$

This value of N_A is of course incorrect.   However, had the gas concentration been low, say 0.10 mole fraction NH_3, these k's would have been satisfactory and would have given the same flux as the F's.

MATERIAL BALANCES

The concentration-difference driving forces discussed above, as has been pointed out, are those existing at one position in the equipment used to contact the immiscible phases.   In the case of a steady-state process, because of the transfer of solute from one phase to the other, the concentration within each phase changes as it moves through the equipment.   Similarly, in the case of a batch process, the concentration in each phase changes with time.   These changes produce corresponding variations in the driving forces, and these can be followed with the help of material balances. In what follows, all concentrations are the bulk-average values for the indicated streams.

Steady-state cocurrent processes

Consider any mass-transfer operation whatsoever conducted in a steady-state co-current fashion, as in Fig. 5.6, in which the apparatus used is represented simply as a rectangular box.   Let the two insoluble phases be identified as phase E and phase R, and for the present consider only the case where a single substance A diffuses from phase R to phase E during their contact.   The other constituents of the phases, solvents for the diffusing solutes, are then considered not to diffuse.

At the entrance to the device in which the phases are contacted, phase R contains R_1 moles per unit time of total substances, consisting of nondiffusing solvent R_S moles per unit time and diffusing solute A, whose concentration is x_1 mole fraction.   As phase R moves through the equipment, A diffuses to phase E and consequently the total quantity of R falls to R_2 moles per unit time at the exit, although the rate of flow of nondiffusing solvent R_S is the same as at the entrance.   The concentration of A has fallen to x_2 mole fraction.   Similarly, phase E at the entrance contains E_1 moles per unit time total substances, of which E_S moles is nondiffusing solvent, and an A concentration of y_1 mole fraction.   Owing to the accumulation of A to a concentration

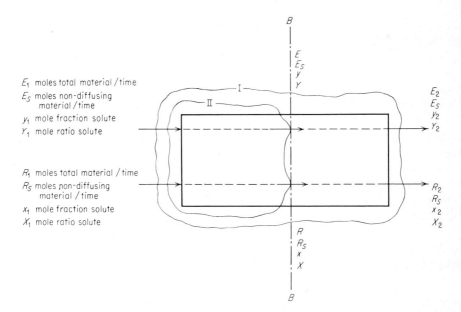

Fig. 5.6   *Steady-state cocurrent processes.*

y_2 mole fraction, phase E increases in amount to E_2 moles per unit time at the exit, although the solvent content E_S has remained constant.

Envelope I, the closed, irregular line drawn about the equipment, will help to establish a material balance for substance A, since an accounting for substance A must be made wherever the envelope is crossed by an arrow representing a flowing stream. The A content of the entering R phase is R_1x_1, that of the E phase is E_1y_1. Similarly the A content of the leaving streams is R_2x_2 and E_2y_2, respectively.

Thus,
$$R_1x_1 + E_1y_1 = R_2x_2 + E_2y_2 \tag{5.29}$$

or
$$R_1x_1 - R_2x_2 = E_2y_2 - E_1y_1 \tag{5.30}$$

But
$$R_1x_1 = R_S \frac{x_1}{1 - x_1} = R_S X_1 \tag{5.31}$$

where X_1 is the mole-ratio concentration of A at the entrance, moles A/mole non-A. The other terms may be similarly described, and Eq. (5.30) becomes

$$R_S(X_1 - X_2) = E_S(Y_2 - Y_1) \tag{5.32}$$

The last is the equation of a straight line on X, Y coordinates, of slope $-R_S/E_S$, passing through two points whose coordinates are (X_1,Y_1) and (X_2,Y_2), respectively.

At any section B-B through the apparatus, the mole fractions of A are x and y and the mole ratios X and Y, in phases R and E, respectively, and if an envelope II is drawn so as to include all the device from the entrance to section B-B, the A balance becomes

$$R_S(X_1 - X) = E_S(Y - Y_1) \tag{5.33}$$

This is also the equation of a straight line on X, Y coordinates, of slope $-R_S/E_S$, through the points (X_1,Y_1) and (X,Y). Since the two straight lines have the same slope and a point in common, they are the same straight line, and Eq. (5.33) is therefore a general expression relating the compositions of the phases in the equipment at any distance from the entrance.†

Since X and Y represent concentrations in the two phases, the equilibrium relationship may also be expressed in terms of these coordinates. Figure 5.7 shows a representation of the equilibrium relationship as well as the straight line QP of Eqs. (5.32) and (5.33). The line QP, called an *operating line*, should not be confused with the driving-force lines of the earlier discussion. At the entrance to the apparatus, for example, the mass-transfer coefficients in the two phases may give rise to the driving-force line KP, where K represents the interface compositions at the entrance and the distances KM and MP represent, respectively, the driving forces in phase E and phase R. Similarly, at the exit, point L may represent the interface composition and LQ the line representative of the driving forces. If the apparatus were longer than that indicated in Fig. 5.6, so that eventually an equilibrium between the two phases

---

† Masses, mass fractions, and mass ratios may be substituted consistently for moles, mole fractions, and mole ratios in Eqs. (5.29) to (5.33).

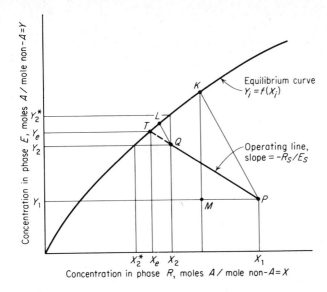

Fig. 5.7 *Steady-state cocurrent process, transfer of solute from phase R to phase E.*

were established, the corresponding equilibrium compositions X_e and Y_e are given by an extension of the operating line to intersection with the equilibrium curve at T.   The driving forces, and therefore the diffusion rate, at this point will have fallen to zero. Should the diffusion be in the opposite direction, i.e., from phase E to phase R, the operating line will fall on the opposite side of the equilibrium curve, as in Fig. 5.8.

It must be emphasized that the graphical representation of the operating line as as a *straight* line is greatly dependent upon the units in which the concentrations of

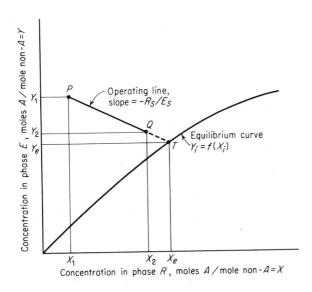

Fig. 5.8 *Steady-state cocurrent process, transfer of solute from phase E to phase R.*

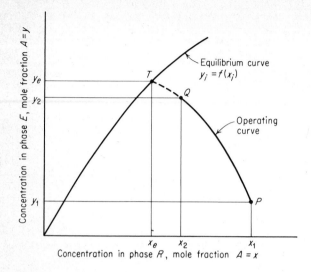

Fig. 5.9 *Steady-state cocurrent process, transfer of solute from phase R to phase E.*

the material balance are expressed. The representations of Figs. 5.7 and 5.8 are straight lines because the mole-ratio concentrations are based on the unchanging quantities E_S and R_S. If Eq. (5.30) is plotted on mole-fraction coordinates, or if any concentration unit proportional to mole fractions such as partial pressure is used, for example, Fig. 5.9 indicates the nature of the operating *curve* obtained. Extrapolation to locate the ultimate equilibrium conditions at T is of course much more difficult than for mole-ratio coordinates. On the other hand, in any operation where the total quantities of each of the phases E and R remain constant while the compositions change owing to diffusion of several components, a diagram in terms of mole fraction will provide a straight-line operating line, as Eq. (5.30) indicates (let $E_2 = E_1 = E$; $R_2 = R_1 = R$). If all the components diffuse so that the total quantities of each phase do not remain constant, the operating line will generally be curved.

To sum up, the cocurrent operating line is a graphical representation of the material balance. A point on the line represents the bulk-average concentrations of the streams in contact with each other at any section in the apparatus. Consequently the line passes from the point representing the streams entering the apparatus to that representing the effluent streams.

Steady-state countercurrent processes

If the same process as previously considered is carried out in countercurrent fashion, as in Fig. 5.10, where the subscripts 1 indicate that end of the apparatus where phase R enters and 2 that end where phase R leaves, the material balances become, by envelope I,†

$$E_2 y_2 + R_1 x_1 = E_1 y_1 + R_2 x_2 \qquad (5.34)$$

† Masses, mass ratios, and mass fractions may be substituted consistently for moles, mole ratios, and mole fractions in Eqs. (5.34) to (5.37).

and
$$R_S(X_1 - X_2) = E_S(Y_1 - Y_2) \tag{5.35}$$

and, for envelope II,
$$Ey + R_1 x_1 = E_1 y_1 + Rx \tag{5.36}$$

and
$$R_S(X_1 - X) = E_S(Y_1 - Y) \tag{5.37}$$

Equations (5.36) and (5.37) give the general relationship between concentrations in the phases at any section, while Eqs. (5.34) and (5.35) establish the entire material balance.   Equation (5.35) is that of a straight line on X, Y coordinates, of slope R_S/E_S, through points of coordinates (X_1,Y_1), (X_2,Y_2), as shown in Fig. 5.11.   The line will lie above the equilibrium-distribution curve if diffusion proceeds from phase E to phase R, below for diffusion in the opposite direction.   For the former case, at a point where the concentrations in the phases are given by the point P, the driving-force line may be indicated by line PM, whose slope depends upon the relative diffusional resistances of the phases.   The driving forces obviously change in magnitude from one end of the equipment to the other.   If the operating line should touch the equilibrium curve anywhere, so that the contacted phases are in equilibrium, the driving force and hence the rate of mass transfer would become zero, and the time required for a finite material transfer would be infinite.   This may be interpreted in terms of a limiting ratio of flow rates of the phases for the concentration changes specified.

As in the cocurrent case, linearity of the operating line depends upon the method of expressing the concentrations.   The operating lines of Fig. 5.11 are straight because the mole-ratio concentrations X and Y are based on the quantities R_S and

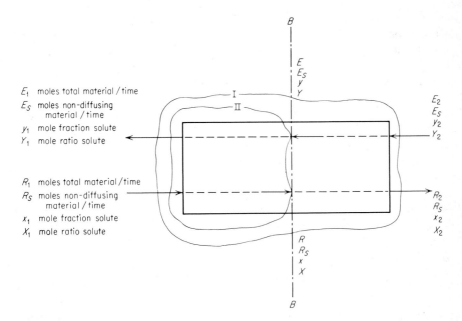

E_1 moles total material / time
E_S moles non-diffusing material / time
y_1 mole fraction solute
Y_1 mole ratio solute

R_1 moles total material / time
R_S moles non-diffusing material / time
x_1 mole fraction solute
X_1 mole ratio solute

Fig. 5.10   *Steady-state countercurrent process.*

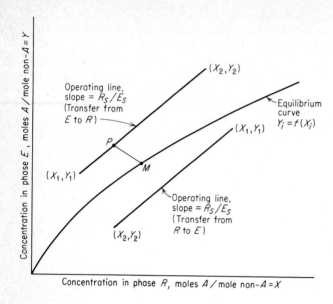

Fig. 5.11 *Steady-state counter-current process.*

E_S, which are stipulated to be constant. If for this situation mole fractions (or quantities such as partial pressures, which are proportional to mole fractions) are used, the operating lines are curved, as indicated in Fig. 5.12. However, for some operations should the total quantity of each of the phases E and R be constant while the compositions change, the mole-fraction diagram will provide the straight-line operating lines, as Eq. (5.34) would indicate (let $E = E_1 = E_2$; $R = R_1 = R_2$). As

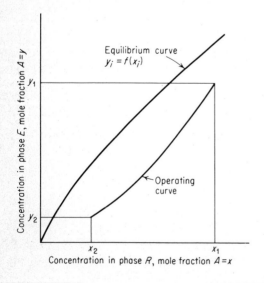

Fig. 5.12 *Steady-state countercurrent process, transfer of solute from phase R to phase E.*

in the cocurrent case, however, the operating line will generally be curved if all the components diffuse so that the total quantities of each phase do not remain constant.

The countercurrent operating line is a graphical representation of the material balance, passing from the point representing the streams at one end of the apparatus to the point representing the streams at the other. A point on the line represents the bulk-average concentrations of the streams passing each other at any section in the apparatus. It is useful to rearrange Eq. (5.36) to read

$$Ey - Rx = E_1 y_1 - R_1 x_1 \qquad (5.38)$$

The left-hand side represents the *net* flow rate of solute A to the left at section $B\text{-}B$ in Fig. 5.10. The right-hand side is the net flow rate of solute out at the left end of the apparatus, or the difference in solute flow, out — in, and for steady state this is constant. Since the section $B\text{-}B$ was taken to represent any section of the apparatus, at every point on the operating line the *net* flow rate of solute is constant, equal to the net flow out at the end.

STAGES

A *stage* is defined as any device or combination of devices in which two insoluble phases are brought into intimate contact, where mass transfer occurs between the phases tending to bring them to equilibrium, and where the phases are then mechanically separated. A process carried out in this manner is a *single-stage* process. An *ideal*, or *theoretical*, stage is one where the time of contact between phases is sufficient so that the effluents are indeed in equilibrium, and although in principle this cannot be attained, in practice we can frequently approach so close to equilibrium that the difference is unimportant.

Continuous cocurrent processes

Quite obviously the cocurrent process and apparatus of Fig. 5.6 is that of a single stage, and if the stage were ideal, the effluent compositions would be at point T on Fig. 5.7 or 5.8.

A *stage efficiency* is defined as the fractional approach to equilibrium which a real stage produces. Referring to Fig. 5.7, this might be taken as the fraction which the line QP represents of the line TP, or the rate of actual solute transfer to that if equilibrium were attained. The most frequently used expression, however, is the Murphree stage efficiency, the fractional approach of one leaving stream to equilibrium with the actual concentration in the other leaving stream.[6] Referring to Fig. 5.7, this may be expressed in terms of the concentrations in phase E or in phase R,

$$\mathbf{E}_{ME} = \frac{Y_2 - Y_1}{Y_2^* - Y_1} \qquad \mathbf{E}_{MR} = \frac{X_1 - X_2}{X_1 - X_2^*} \qquad (5.39)$$

These definitions are somewhat arbitrary since, in the case of a truly cocurrent operation such as that of Fig. 5.7, it would be impossible to obtain a leaving concentration in phase E higher than Y_e or one in phase R lower than X_e. They are nevertheless useful, as will be developed in later chapters. The two Murphree efficiencies are not normally equal for a given stage, and they can be simply related only when the equilibrium relation is a straight line. Thus, for a straight equilibrium line of slope $m = (Y_2^* - Y_2)/(X_2 - X_2^*)$, it can be shown that

$$E_{ME} = \frac{E_{MR}}{E_{MR}(1 - S) + S} = \frac{E_{MR}}{E_{MR}(1 - 1/A) + 1/A} \qquad (5.40)$$

The derivation is left to the student (Prob. 5.6). Here $A = R_S/mE_S$ is called the *absorption factor*, and its reciprocal, $S = mE_S/R_S$, is the *stripping factor*. As will be shown, these have great economic importance.

Batch processes

It is characteristic of batch processes that while there is no flow of the phases into and out of the equipment used, the concentrations within each phase change with time. When initially brought into contact, the phases will not be of equilibrium compositions, but they will approach equilibrium with passage of time. The material-balance equation (5.33) for the cocurrent steady-state operation then shows the relation between the concentrations X and Y in the phases which coexist at any time after the start of the operation, and Figs. 5.7 and 5.8 give the graphical representation of these compositions. Point T on these figures represents the ultimate compositions which are obtained at equilibrium. The batch operation is a single stage.

Cascades

A group of stages interconnected so that the various streams flow from one to the other is called a cascade. Its purpose is to increase the extent of mass transfer over and above that which is possible with a single stage. The fractional overall stage efficiency of a cascade is then defined as the number of ideal stages to which the cascade is equivalent divided by the number of real stages.

Two or more stages connected so that the flow is cocurrent between stages will, of course, never be equivalent to more than one ideal stage, although the overall stage efficiency can thereby be increased. For effects greater than one ideal stage, they may be connected for cross flow or countercurrent flow.

Cross-flow cascades

In Fig. 5.13, each stage is represented simply by a circle, and within each the flow is cocurrent. The R phase flows from one stage to the next, being contacted in each stage by fresh E phase. There may be different flow rates of the E to each stage, and each stage may have a different Murphree stage efficiency. The material balances are obviously merely a repetition of that for a single stage and the construction on the distribution diagram is obvious. Cross flow is used sometimes in adsorption, leaching, drying, and extraction operations but rarely in the others.

Countercurrent cascades

These are the most efficient arrangements, requiring fewest stages for a given change of composition and ratio of flow rates, and they are therefore most frequently used.

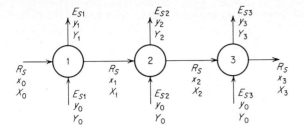

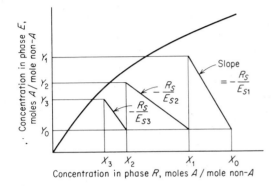

Fig. 5.13 *A cross-flow cascade of three real stages.*

Refer to Fig. 5.14, where a cascade of N_p ideal stages is shown. The flow rates and compositions are numbered corresponding to the effluent from a stage, so that Y_2 is the concentration in the E phase leaving stage 2, etc. Each stage is identical in its action to the cocurrent process of Fig. 5.6; yet the cascade as a whole has the characteristics of the countercurrent process of Fig. 5.10. The cocurrent operating lines for the first two stages are written beneath them on the figure, and since the stages are ideal, the effluents are in equilibrium (Y_2 in equilibrium with X_2, etc.). The graphical relations are shown in Fig. 5.15. Line PQ is the operating line for stage 1, MN for

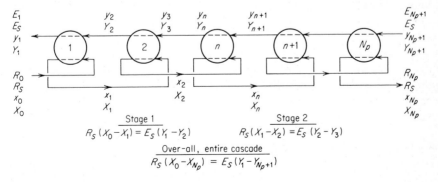

Fig. 5.14 *Countercurrent multistage cascade.*

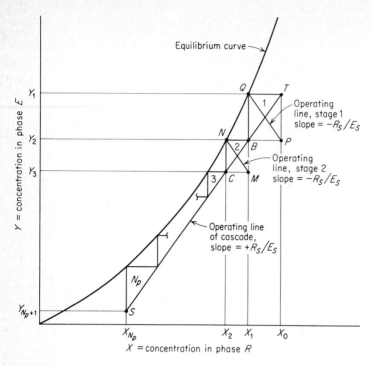

Fig. 5.15 *Countercurrent multistage cascade, solute transfer from phase R to phase E.*

stage 2, etc., and the coordinates (X_1, Y_1) fall on the equilibrium curve because the stage is ideal. Line ST is the operating line for the entire cascade, and points such as B, C, etc., represent compositions of streams passing each other between stages. We may therefore determine the number of ideal stages required for a countercurrent process by drawing the stairlike construction $TQBNC \cdots S$ (Fig. 5.15). If anywhere the equilibrium curve and cascade operating line should touch, the stages become *pinched*, and an infinite number are required to bring about the desired composition change. If the solute transfer is from E to R, the entire construction falls above the equilibrium curve of Fig. 5.15.

For most cases, because of either a curved operating line or equilibrium curve, the relation among number of stages, compositions, and flow ratio must be determined graphically, as shown. For the *special* case where both are straight, however, with the equilibrium curve continuing straight to the origin of the distribution graph, an analytical solution can be developed which will be most useful.

In Fig. 5.14, a solute balance for stages $n + 1$ through N_p is

$$E_S(Y_{n+1} - Y_{Np+1}) = R_S(X_n - X_{Np}) \tag{5.41}$$

If the equilibrium curve slope is $m = Y_{n+1}/X_{n+1}$, and if the absorption factor $A = R_S/mE_S$, then by substitution and rearrangement, Eq. (5.41) becomes

$$X_{n+1} - AX_n = \frac{Y_{Np+1}}{m} - AX_{Np} \tag{5.42}$$

This is a linear first-order finite-difference equation, whose solution is handled much like that of ordinary differential equations.[11]   Thus, putting it in operator form,

$$(D - A)X_n = \frac{Y_{Np+1}}{m} - AX_{Np} \tag{5.43}$$

where the operator D indicates the finite difference.   The characteristic equation is then

$$M - A = 0 \tag{5.44}$$

from which $M = A$.   Hence the general solution (here a little different from ordinary differential equations) is

$$X_n = C_1 A^n \tag{5.45}$$

with C_1 a constant.   Since the right-hand side of Eq. (5.43) is a constant, the particular solution is $X = C_2$, where C_2 is a constant.   Substituting this into the original finite-difference equation (5.42) provides

$$C_2 - AC_2 = \frac{Y_{Np+1}}{m} - AX_{Np} \tag{5.46}$$

from which

$$C_2 = \frac{Y_{Np+1}/m - AX_{Np}}{1 - A} \tag{5.47}$$

The complete solution is therefore

$$X_n = C_1 A^n + \frac{Y_{Np+1}/m - AX_{Np}}{1 - A} \tag{5.48}$$

To determine C_1, we set $n = 0$:

$$C_1 = X_0 - \frac{Y_{Np+1}/m - AX_{Np}}{1 - A}$$

and therefore we have

$$X_n = \left(X_0 - \frac{Y_{Np+1}/m - AX_{Np}}{1 - A} \right) A^n + \frac{Y_{Np+1}/m - AX_{Np}}{1 - A} \tag{5.49}$$

This result is useful to get the concentration X_n at any stage in the cascade, knowing the terminal concentrations.   Putting $n = N_p$ and rearranging provide the very useful forms which follow.

For transfer from R to E (stripping of R)

$A \neq 1:$
$$\frac{X_0 - X_{Np}}{X_0 - Y_{Np+1}/m} = \frac{(1/A)^{Np+1} - 1/A}{(1/A)^{Np+1} - 1} \tag{5.50}$$

$$N_p = \frac{\log \left[\dfrac{X_0 - Y_{Np+1}/m}{X_{Np} - Y_{Np+1}/m} (1 - A) + A \right]}{\log 1/A} \tag{5.51}$$

$A = 1:$
$$\frac{X_0 - X_{Np}}{X_0 - Y_{Np+1}/m} = \frac{N_p}{N_p + 1} \tag{5.52}$$

$$N_p = \frac{X_0 - X_{Np}}{X_{Np} - Y_{Np+1}/m} \tag{5.53}$$

For transfer from E to R (absorption into R). A similar treatment yields

$A \neq 1$:

$$\frac{Y_{Np+1} - Y_1}{Y_{Np+1} - mX_0} = \frac{A^{Np+1} - A}{A^{Np+1} - 1} \tag{5.54}$$

$$N_p = \frac{\log\left[\dfrac{Y_{Np+1} - mX_0}{Y_1 - mX_0}\left(1 - \dfrac{1}{A}\right) + \dfrac{1}{A}\right]}{\log A} \tag{5.55}$$

$A = 1$:

$$\frac{Y_{Np+1} - Y_1}{Y_{Np+1} - mX_0} = \frac{N_p}{N_p + 1} \tag{5.56}$$

$$N_p = \frac{Y_{Np+1} - Y_1}{Y_1 - mX_0} \tag{5.57}$$

These are called the Kremser-Brown-Souders (or simply Kremser) equations. after those who derived them for gas absorption,[4,7] although apparently Turner[9] had used them earlier for leaching and solids washing. They are plotted in Fig. 5.16, which then becomes very convenient for quick solutions. We shall have many opportunities to use them for different operations. In order to make them so generally useful, it is important to note that in the derivation, $A = R_S/mE_S =$ const, where R_S and E_S are the nonsolute molar flow rates with concentrations (X in R and Y in E) defined as mole ratios and $m = Y/X$ at equilibrium. However, as necessary to keep A constant, A may be defined as R/mE, with R and E either as total molar flow rates, concentrations (x in R and y in E) as mole fractions, $m = y/x$, or as total mass flow rates and weight fractions, respectively.

We shall delay using the equations until specific opportunity arises.

Stages and mass-transfer rates

It is clear from the previous discussion that each process may be considered either in terms of the number of stages it represents or in terms of the appropriate mass-transfer rates. A batch or continuous cocurrent operation, for example, is a single-stage operation, but the stage efficiency realized in the available contact time will depend upon the average mass-transfer rates prevailing. A change of composition greater than that possible with one stage may be brought about by repetition of the cocurrent process, where one of the effluents from the first stage is brought again into contact with fresh treating phase. Alternatively, a countercurrent multistage cascade can be arranged. If, however, the countercurrent operation is carried out in continuous-contact fashion without repeated separation and recontacting of the phases in a stepwise manner, it is still possible to describe the operation in terms of the number of ideal stages to which it is equivalent. But in view of the differential changes in composition which occur in such cases, it is more correct to characterize them in terms of average mass-transfer coefficients or equivalent. Integration of the point mass-transfer rate equations must be delayed until the characteristics of each operation can be considered, but the computation of the number of ideal stages requires only the equilibrium and material-balance relationships.

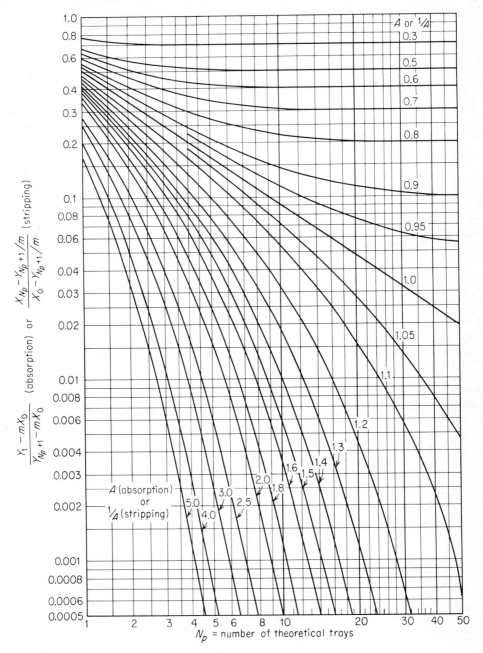

Fig. 5.16 *Number of theoretical stages for countercurrent cascades, with Henry's law equilibrium and constant absorption or stripping factors.* [*After Hachmuth and Vance, Chem. Eng. Progr.*, **48**, 523, 570, 617 (1952).]

Illustration 5.2. When a certain sample of moist soap is exposed to air at 120°F, 1 atm pressure, the equilibrium distribution of moisture between the air and soap is as follows:

Wt % moisture in soap	0	2.40	3.76	4.76	6.10	7.83	9.90	12.63	15.40	19.02
Partial pressure water in air, mm Hg	0	9.66	19.20	28.4	37.2	46.4	55.0	63.2	71.9	79.5

a. Ten pounds of wet soap containing 16.7% moisture by weight is placed in a vessel containing 150 cu ft moist air whose initial moisture content corresponds to a water-vapor partial pressure of 12 mm Hg. After the soap has reached a moisture content of 13.0%, the air in the vessel is entirely replaced by fresh air of the original moisture content and the system is then allowed to reach equilibrium. The total pressure and temperature are maintained at 1 atm and 120°F, respectively. What will be the ultimate moisture content of the soap?

b. It is desired to dry the soap from 16.7 to 4% moisture continuously in a countercurrent stream of air whose initial water-vapor partial pressure is 12 mm Hg. The pressure and temperature will be maintained throughout at 1 atm and 120°F. Per 1 lb initial wet soap per hour, what is the minimum amount of air required per hour?

c. If 30% more air than that determined in (*b*) is used, what will be the moisture content of the air leaving the drier? To how many ideal stages will the process be equivalent?

Solution. a. The process is a batch operation. Since air and soap are mutually insoluble, with water distributing between them, Eq. (5.32) applies. Let the E phase be air–water and the R phase be soap–water. Define Y as lb water/lb dry air and X as lb water/lb dry soap. It will be necessary to convert the equilibrium data to these units.

For a partial pressure of moisture $= p$ mm Hg and a total pressure of 760 mm Hg, $p/(760 - p)$ is the mole ratio of water to dry air. Multiplying this by the ratio of molecular weights of water to air then gives Y: $Y = [p/(760 - p)](18.02/29)$. Thus, at $p = 71.9$ mm Hg,

$$Y = \frac{71.9}{760 - 71.9} \frac{18.02}{29} = 0.0650 \text{ lb water/lb dry air}$$

In similar fashion the percent moisture content of the soap is converted to units of X. Thus, at 15.40% moisture,

$$X = \frac{15.40}{100 - 15.40} = 0.182 \text{ lb water/lb dry soap}$$

In this manner all the equilibrium data are converted to these units and the data plotted as the equilibrium curve of Fig. 5.17.

First operation. Initial air, $p = 12$ mm Hg:

$$Y_1 = \frac{12}{760 - 12} \frac{18.02}{29} = 0.00996 \text{ lb water/lb dry air}$$

Initial soap, 16.7% water:

$$X_1 = \frac{16.7}{100 - 16.7} = 0.2 \text{ lb water/lb dry soap}$$

Final soap, 13% water:

$$X_2 = \frac{13.0}{100 - 13.0} = 0.1493 \text{ lb water/lb dry soap}$$

$$R_s = 10(1 - 0.167) = 8.33 \text{ lb dry soap}$$

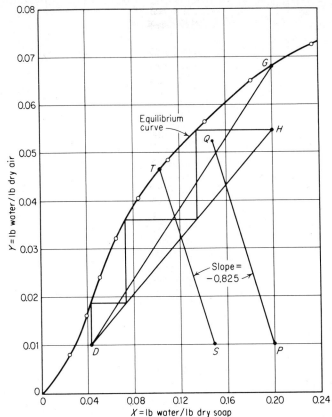

Fig. 5.17 *Solution to Illustration 5.2.*

E_s, the mass of dry air, is found by use of the perfect-gas law,

$$E_s = 150 \frac{760 - 12}{760} \frac{492}{460 + 120} \frac{29}{359} = 10.1 \text{ lb dry air}$$

$$\text{Slope of operating line} = \frac{-R_s}{E_s} = \frac{-8.33}{10.1} = -0.825$$

From point P, coordinates (X_1, Y_1), on Fig. 5.17, the operating line of slope -0.825 is drawn, to reach the abscissa $X_2 = 0.1493$ at point Q. The conditions at Q correspond to the end of the first operation.

   Second operation. $X_1 = 0.1493$, $Y_1 = 0.00996$, which locate point S on the figure. The operating line is drawn parallel to the line PQ since the ratio $-R_s/E_s$ is the same as in the first operation. Extension of the line to the equilibrium curve at T provides the final value of $X_2 = 0.103$ lb water/lb dry soap.

$$\text{Final moisture content of soap} = \frac{0.103}{1.103} 100 = 9.33 \%$$

  b. Equation (5.35) and Fig. 5.10 apply

$$R_S = 1(1 - 0.167) = 0.833 \text{ lb dry soap/hr}$$

Entering soap: $X_1 = 0.20$ lb water/lb dry soap

Leaving soap: $X_2 = \dfrac{0.04}{1 - 0.04} = 0.0417$ lb water/lb dry soap

Entering air: $Y_2 = 0.00996$ lb water/lb dry air

$$\text{Slope of operating line} = \frac{R_S}{E_S} = \frac{\text{lb dry soap/hr}}{\text{lb dry air/hr}}$$

Point D, coordinates (X_2, Y_2), is plotted on Fig 5.17. The operating line of least slope giving rise to equilibrium conditions will indicate the least amount of air usable. Such a line is DG, which provides equilibrium conditions at $X_1 = 0.20$. The corresponding value of $Y_1 = 0.068$ lb water/lb dry air is read from the figure at G.

Eq. (5.35): $\qquad\qquad 0.833(0.20 - 0.0417) = E_S(0.068 - 0.00996)$

$$E_S = 2.27 \text{ lb dry air/hr}$$

This corresponds to

$$\frac{2.27}{29} \, 359 \, \frac{760}{760 - 12} \, \frac{460 + 120}{492} = 33.6 \text{ cu ft air/lb soap}$$

  c. $E_S = 1.30(2.27) = 2.95$ lb dry air/hr

Eq. (5.35) $\qquad\qquad 0.833(0.20 - 0.0417) = 2.95(Y_1 - 0.00996)$

$$Y_1 = 0.0547 \text{ lb water/lb dry air}$$

This corresponds to operating line DH, where H has the coordinates $X_1 = 0.20$, $Y_1 = 0.0547$. The ideal stages are marked on the figure and total three.

NOTATION FOR CHAPTER 5

Consistent units in either the cgs or the English system may be used. In either system, pressures are customarily expressed as atmospheres in the mass-transfer equations.

A = substance A, the diffusing solute
  = absorption factor, dimensionless
e = 2.7183
E = phase E; total rate of flow of phase E, g moles/sec or lb moles/hr
E_S = rate of flow of nondiffusing solvent in phase E, g moles/sec or lb moles/hr
E_{ME} = fractional Murphree stage efficiency for phase E
E_{MR} = fractional Murphree stage efficiency for phase R
f = equilibrium-distribution function
F_G = gas-phase mass-transfer coefficient, g moles/(sec)(sq cm) or lb moles/(hr)(sq ft)
F_L = liquid-phase mass-transfer coefficient, g moles/(sec)(sq cm) or lb moles/(hr)(sq ft)
F_{OG} = overall gas mass-transfer coefficient, g moles/(sec)(sq cm) or lb moles/(hr)(sq ft)
F_{OL} = overall liquid mass-transfer coefficient, g moles/(sec)(sq cm) or lb moles/(hr)(sq ft)
i = generalized concentration in phase R
j = generalized concentration in phase E
k_x = liquid mass-transfer coefficient, g moles/(sec)(sq ft)(mole fraction) or lb moles/(hr)(sq ft) (mole fraction)
k_y = gas mass-transfer coefficient, g moles/(sec)(sq ft)(mole fraction) or lb moles/(hr)(sq ft) (mole fraction)

K_x = overall liquid mass-transfer coefficient, g moles/(sec)(sq cm)(mole fraction) or lb moles/(hr)(sq ft)(mole fraction)

K_y = overall gas mass-transfer coefficient, g moles/(sec)(sq cm)(mole fraction) or lb moles/(hr)(sq ft)(mole fraction)

m = equilibrium curve slope, dimensionless

m', m'' = slopes of chords of the equilibrium curve, dimensionless

n = stage n

N = mass-transfer flux, g moles/(sec)(sq cm) or lb moles/(hr)(sq ft)

N_p = total number of ideal stages in a cascade

R = phase R; total rate of flow of phase R, g moles/sec or lb moles/hr

R_s = rate of flow of nondiffusing solvent in phase R, g moles/sec or lb moles/hr

S = stripping factor, dimensionless

x = concentration of A in a liquid or in phase R, mole fraction

X = concentration of A in phase R, moles A/mole non-A

y = concentration of A in a gas or in phase E, mole fraction

Y = concentration of A in phase E, moles A/mole non-A

Subscripts:

A = substance A

e = equilibrium

E = phase E

G = gas

i = interface

L = liquid

n = stage n

O = overall

R = phase R

0 = entering stage 1

$1, 2$ = positions 1 and 2; stages 1 and 2

Superscript:

$*$ = in equilibrium with bulk concentration in other phase

REFERENCES

1. Davies, T. J.: in T. B. Drew, J. W. Hoopes, and T. Vermeulen (eds.), "Advances in Chemical Engineering," vol. 4, p. 1, Academic Press Inc., New York, 1963.

2. Kent, E. R., and R. L. Pigford: *AIChE J.*, **2**, 363 (1956).

3. King, C. J.: *AIChE J.*, **10**, 671 (1964).

4. Kremser, A.: *Natl. Petrol. News*, **22**(21), 42 (1930).

5. Lewis, W. K., and W. G. Whitman: *Ind. Eng. Chem.*, **16**, 1215 (1924).

6. Murphree, E. V.: *Ind. Eng. Chem.*, **17**, 747 (1925).

7. Souders, M., and G. G. Brown: *Ind. Eng. Chem.*, **24**, 519 (1932).

8. Sternling, C. V., and L. E. Scriven: *AIChE J.*, **5**, 514 (1958).

9. Turner, S. D.: *Ind. Eng. Chem.*, **21**, 190 (1929).

10. Whitman, W. G.: *Chem. Met. Eng.*, **29**, 147 (1923).

11. Wylie, C. R., Jr.: "Advanced Engineering Mathematics," 3d ed., McGraw-Hill Book Company, New York, 1966.

PROBLEMS

5.1. Repeat the calculations for the local mass-transfer flux of ammonia in Illustration 5.1, on the assumption that the gas pressure is 2 atm. The gas mass velocity, bulk-average gas and liquid concentrations, liquid flow rate, and temperature are unchanged.

5.2. In a certain apparatus used for the absorption of sulfur dioxide, SO_2, from air by means of water, at one point in the equipment the gas contained 10% SO_2 by volume and was in contact with liquid containing 0.4% SO_2 by weight (density = 61.8 lb/cu ft). The temperature was 50°C and the total pressure 1 atm. The overall mass-transfer coefficient based on gas concentrations was K_G = 0.055 lb mole SO_2 absorbed/(hr)(sq ft)(atm). Of the diffusional resistance 47% lay in the gas phase, 53% in the liquid. Equilibrium data at 50°C are as follows:

G SO_2/100 g water	0.2	0.3	0.5	0.7
Partial pressure SO_2, mm Hg	29	46	83	119

a. Calculate the overall coefficient based on liquid concentrations in terms of lb moles/cu ft.

b. Calculate the individual film coefficients for the gas film [expressed as k_G lb moles/(hr)(sq ft)(atm), k_y lb moles/(hr)(sq ft)(mole fraction), and k_c lb moles/(hr)(sq ft)(lb mole/cu ft)] and for the liquid film [expressed as k_L lb moles/(hr)(sq ft)(lb mole/cu ft) and k_x lb moles/(hr)(sq ft)(mole fraction)].

c. Determine the interfacial compositions in both phases.

5.3. The equilibrium partial pressure of water vapor in contact with a certain silica gel on which water is adsorbed is, at 25°C, as follows:

Partial pressure of water, mm Hg	0	2.14	4.74	7.13	9.05	10.9	12.6	14.3	16.7
Lb water/100 lb dry gel	0	5	10	15	20	25	30	35	40

a. Plot the equilibrium data as p = partial pressure of water vapor, mm Hg, against x = wt fraction water in the gel.

b. Plot the equilibrium data as X = lb moles water/lb dry gel, Y = lb moles water vapor/lb mole dry air, for a total pressure of 1 atm.

c. Ten pounds of silica gel containing 5 wt% adsorbed water is placed in a flowing air stream containing a partial pressure of water vapor of 12 mm Hg. The total pressure is 1 atm and the temperature 25°C. When equilibrium is reached, how many pounds of additional water will the gel have adsorbed? Air is not adsorbed.

d. One pound of silica gel containing 5 wt % adsorbed water is placed in a vessel in which there are 400 cu ft moist air whose partial pressure of water is 15 mm Hg. The total pressure and temperature are kept at 1 atm and 25°C, respectively. At equilibrium, what will be the moisture content of the air and gel and the weight of water adsorbed by the gel? **Ans.: 0.1335 lb water.**

e. Write the equation of the operating line for (*d*) in terms of X and Y. Convert this into an equation in terms of p and x, and plot the operating curve on the p, x coordinates.

f. One pound of silica gel containing 18% adsorbed moisture is placed in a vessel containing 500 cu ft dry air. The temperature and pressure are maintained at 1 atm and 25°C, respectively. Compute the final equilibrium moisture content of the air and gel.

g. Repeat (*f*) for a total pressure of 2 atm. (Note that the equilibrium curve in terms of X and Y previously used is not applicable.)

5.4. The equilibrium adsorption of benzene vapor on a certain activated charcoal at 33.3°C is as follows:

Cu cm benzene vapor adsorbed (measured at standard conditions)/g C	15	25	40	50	65	80	90	100
Partial pressure benzene, mm Hg	0.0010	0.0045	0.0251	0.115	0.251	1.00	2.81	7.82

a.   A nitrogen–benzene vapor mixture containing 1.0% benzene by volume is to be passed countercurrently at the rate of 100 cu ft/min in contact with a moving stream of the activated charcoal so as to remove 95% of the benzene from the gas in a continuous process.   The entering charcoal contains 15 cu cm benzene vapor (at standard conditions) adsorbed per gram charcoal.   The temperature and total pressure are to be maintained at 33.3°C and 1 atm, respectively, throughout. The nitrogen is not adsorbed.   What is the least amount of charcoal which may be used per hour? If twice as much is used, what will be the concentration of adsorbed benzene upon the charcoal leaving?

b.   Repeat (*a*) for a cocurrent flow of gas and charcoal.

c.   Charcoal which has adsorbed upon it 100 cu cm (at standard conditions) benzene vapor per gram charcoal is to be stripped at the rate of 100 lb/hr of its benzene to a concentration of 55 cu cm adsorbed benzene/g charcoal by continuous countercurrent contact with a stream of pure nitrogen gas at 1 atm.   The temperature will be maintained at 33.3°C.   What is the minimum rate of nitrogen flow, cu ft/hr?   What will be the benzene content of the exit gas if twice as much nitrogen is fed? What will be the number of ideal stages?   **Ans.: Three ideal stages.**

5.5.   A mixture of hydrogen and air, 4 atm pressure, bulk-average concentration 50% H_2 by volume, flows through a circular reinforced tube of vulcanized rubber whose ID and OD are 1 and 1.125 in., respectively, at an average velocity of 10 ft/sec.   Outside the pipe, hydrogen-free air at 1atm flows at right angles to the pipe at a velocity of 10 ft/sec.   The temperature is everywhere 25°C.   The solubility of hydrogen in the rubber is 0.053 cu cm H_2 (at standard conditions) per cu cm rubber per atm partial pressure, and its diffusivity in the rubber $= 0.18(10^{-5})$ sq cm/sec.   The diffusivity of H_2–air $= 0.161$ sq cm/sec at 0°C, 1 atm.   Estimate the rate of loss of hydrogen from the pipe per foot of pipe length.

5.6.   Assuming the equilibrium curve of Fig. 5.7 is straight, of slope *m*, derive the relation between the Murphree stage efficiencies E_{ME} and E_{MR}.

5.7.   If the equilibrium distribution curve of the cross-flow plant of Fig. 5.13 is everywhere straight, of slope *m*, make a solute material balance about stage $n + 1$, and by following the procedures used to derive Eq. (5.51) show that

$$N_p = \frac{\log\,[(X_0 - Y_0/m)/(X_{Np} - Y_0/m)]}{\log\,(S + 1)}$$

where S is the stripping factor, mE_S/R_S, constant for all stages, and N_p is the total number of ideal stages.

PART TWO
GAS-LIQUID
OPERATIONS

The operations which include humidification and dehumidification, gas absorption and desorption, and distillation in its various forms all have in common the requirement that a gas and a liquid phase be brought into contact for the purpose of a diffusional interchange between them.

The order listed above is in many respects that of increasing complexity of the operations, and this is therefore the order in which they will be considered. Since in humidification the liquid is a pure substance, concentration gradients exist and diffusion of matter occurs only within the gas phase. In absorption, concentration gradients exist within both the liquid and the gas, and diffusion of at least one component occurs within both. In distillation, all the substances comprising the phases diffuse. These operations are also characterized by an especially intimate relationship between heat and mass transfer. The evaporation or condensation of a substance introduces consideration of latent heats of vaporization, sometimes heats of solution as well. In distillation, the new phase necessary for mass-transfer separation is created from the original by addition or withdrawal of heat. Our discussion must necessarily include consideration of these important heat quantities and their effects.

In the case of all these operations, the equipment used has as its principal function the contact of the gas and liquid in as efficient a fashion as possible, commensurate with the cost. In principle, at least, any type of equipment satisfactory for one of these operations is also suitable for the others, and the major types are indeed used for all. For this reason, our discussion begins with equipment.

CHAPTER SIX
EQUIPMENT FOR
GAS-LIQUID OPERATIONS

The purpose of the equipment used for the gas-liquid operations is to provide intimate contact of the two fluids in order to permit interphase diffusion of the constituents. The rate of mass transfer is directly dependent upon the interfacial surface exposed between the phases, and the nature and degree of dispersion of one fluid in the other are therefore of prime importance. The equipment may be broadly classified according to whether its principal action is to disperse the gas or the liquid, although in many devices both phases become dispersed.

I. GAS DISPERSED

In this group are included those devices, such as agitated vessels and the various types of tray towers, in which the gas phase is dispersed into bubbles or drops. The most important of the group are the tray towers.

Agitated vessels

The simplest method of dispersing the gas into a batch of liquid is to discharge it beneath the liquid surface through a perforated pipe, or sparger. The gas bubbles from such a sparger are relatively large, and the interfacial surface is correspondingly small therefore. The degree of dispersion may be increased by forcing the gas through smaller openings such as those in porous ceramic or metallic plates, but the small openings require high gas pressures and are subject to clogging. It is preferable to increase the degree of dispersion by use of a mechanical agitator, as in Fig. 6.1. Here the agitation is brought about by a turbine-type impeller. The gas is introduced through submerged pipes against a "target," an open sleeve, which leads the gas into the bottom of the impeller at a position about halfway from the center to the periphery. This prevents formation of large gas bubbles at the center of the impeller and assists in the shearing of the gas into bubbles of small sizes by the impeller. The hooded ring surrounding the impeller aids in projecting the stream downward and therefore provides a longer time of contact between gas and liquid. In other arrangements the hooded ring is omitted, and instead four vertical baffles, projecting radially inward from the wall to a distance of one-tenth the tank diameter, extending for the full depth of the liquid, are used. When a large part of the gas does not dissolve in one pass through the liquid, an impeller is sometimes used near the liquid surface to draw the gas down into the liquid from the gas space above.

Turbine impellers will finely subdivide gas introduced at superficial linear velocities less than 0.1 ft/sec based on vessel cross sections. Agitated vessels are therefore primarily useful for dispersing small quantities into liquids, on a batch, semibatch, or continuous basis. They are also especially useful for cases where the liquid contains a suspended solid, as, for example, in the precipitation of calcium carbonate by the absorption of carbon dioxide from flue gas into a lime slurry or in the hydrogenation of a liquid in the presence of a suspended solid catalyst. They are frequently used in fermentation processes of the pharmaceutical industry, where oxygen from air is absorbed into liquids containing suspended microorganisms such as yeasts and molds, which require the oxygen for their life processes.

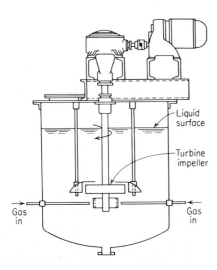

Liquid
surface

Turbine
impeller

Gas
in

Gas
in

Fig. 6.1 *Turbo gas absorber. (General American Transportation Corporation.)*

Since a well-designed turbine impeller provides very thorough mixing of the liquid, it may reasonably be assumed that the concentration throughout the liquid phase in such devices is quite uniform. The benefits of countercurrent flow for continuous operation cannot therefore be had with a single tank and agitator. Multistage arrangements, with countercurrent flow of gas and liquid, require multiple vessels and agitators, piped to lead the gas from the top of one tank to the bottom of the next and the liquid from vessel to vessel in the opposite direction.

TRAY TOWERS

Tray towers are vertical cylinders in which the liquid and gas are contacted in stepwise fashion on trays or plates, in a manner shown schematically for one type (bubble-cap trays) in Fig. 6.2. The liquid enters at the top and flows downward by gravity. On the way, it flows across each tray and through a downspout to the tray below. The gas passes upward through openings of one sort or another in the tray, then bubbles through the liquid to form a froth, disengages from the froth, and passes on to the next tray above. The overall effect is a multiple countercurrent contact of gas and liquid, although each tray is characterized by a cross flow of the two. Each tray of the tower is a stage, since on the tray the fluids are brought into intimate contact, interphase diffusion occurs, and the fluids are separated.

The number of theoretical trays (or stages) in a column or tower is dependent only upon the difficulty of the separation to be carried out and is determined solely from material balances and equilibrium considerations. The stage or tray efficiency, and therefore the number of real trays, is determined by the mechanical design used and the conditions of operation. The diameter of the tower, on the other hand, depends upon the quantities of liquid and gas flowing through the tower per unit time. Once the number of theoretical trays required has been determined, the principal problem in the design of the tower is to choose dimensions and arrangements which will represent the best compromise among several opposing tendencies, for it is generally found that conditions leading to high tray efficiencies will ultimately lead to operational difficulties.

In order that stage or tray efficiencies be high, the time of contact should be long, so as to permit the diffusion to occur, the interfacial surface between phases must be made large, and a relatively high intensity of turbulence is required to obtain high mass-transfer coefficients. In order to provide long contact time, the liquid pool on each tray should be deep, so that bubbles of gas will require a relatively long time to rise through the liquid. When the gas bubbles only slowly through the openings on the tray, the bubbles are large and the interfacial surface per unit of gas volume is small, the liquid is relatively quiescent, and much of it may even pass over the tray without having contacted the gas. On the other hand, when the gas velocity is relatively high, it is dispersed very thoroughly into the liquid, which in turn is agitated into a froth. This provides large interfacial surface areas. For high tray efficiencies, therefore, we require deep pools of liquid and relatively high gas velocities.

These conditions, however, lead to a number of difficulties. One of these is the

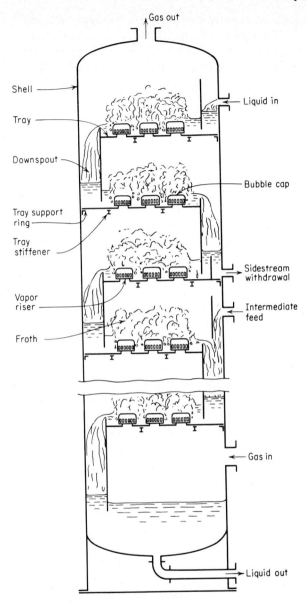

Gas out

Shell

Tray

Downspout

Tray support
ring

Tray
stiffener

Vapor
riser

Froth

Liquid in

Bubble cap

Sidestream
withdrawal

Intermediate
feed

Gas in

Liquid out

Fig. 6.2 *Schematic section through
a bubble-cap tray tower.*

mechanical entrainment of droplets of liquid in the rising gas stream. At high gas
velocities, when the gas is disengaged from the froth, small droplets of liquid will be
carried by the gas to the tray above. Liquid carried up the tower in this manner
reduces the concentration change which is brought about by the mass transfer, and
consequently adversely affects the tray efficiency. And so the gas velocity may be
limited by the reduction in tray efficiency due to liquid entrainment.

Furthermore, great liquid depths on the tray and high gas velocities both result in high pressure drop for the gas in flowing through the tray, and this in turn leads to a number of difficulties.   In the case of absorbers and humidifiers, high pressure drop results in high fan power to blow or draw the gas through the tower, and consequently high operating cost.   In the case of distillation, high pressure at the bottom of the tower results in high boiling temperatures, which in turn may lead to heating difficulties and possibly damage to heat-sensitive compounds.

Ultimately, purely mechanical difficulties arise.   High pressure drop may lead directly to a condition of *flooding*.   With a large pressure difference in the space between trays, the level of liquid leaving a tray at relatively low pressure and entering one of high pressure must necessarily assume an elevated position in the downspouts, as shown in Fig. 6.2.   As the pressure difference is increased owing to increased rate of flow of either gas or liquid, the level in the downspout will rise further to permit the liquid to enter the lower tray.   Ultimately the liquid level may reach that on the tray above.   Further increase in either flow rate then aggravates the condition rapidly, and the liquid will fill the entire space between the trays.   The tower is then flooded, the tray efficiency falls to a low value, the flow of gas is erratic, and liquid may be forced out of the exit pipe at the top of the tower.

For liquid-gas combinations which tend to foam excessively, high gas velocities may lead to a condition of *priming*, which is also an inoperative situation.   Here the foam persists throughout the space between trays, and a great deal of liquid is carried by the gas from one tray to the tray above.   This is an exaggerated condition of entrainment.   The liquid so carried recirculates between trays, and the added liquid-handling load increases the gas pressure drop sufficiently to lead to flooding.

We may summarize these opposing tendencies as follows.   Great depths of liquid on the trays lead to high tray efficiencies through long time of contact but also to high pressure drop per tray.   High gas velocities, within limits, provide good vapor-liquid contact through excellence of dispersion but lead to excessive entrainment and high pressure drop.   The various arrangements and dimensions chosen for design are those which experience has proved to be reasonably good compromises.   The general design procedure involves a somewhat empirical application of these followed by computational check to ensure that pressure drop and flexibility, i.e., ability of the tower to handle more than the immediately expected fluid quantities, are satisfactory.

General characteristics

Certain design features are common to the most frequently used types of trays (bubble-cap and sieve trays), and these will be dealt with first.

Shell and trays. The tower may be made of any of a number of materials, depending upon the corrosion conditions encountered.   Glass, glass-lined metal, impervious carbon, plastics, even wood, but most frequently metals are used.   For metal towers, the shells are usually cylindrical for reasons of cost.   If made in one piece, they are fitted with handholes or manholes to permit installation of trays and cleaning. Alternatively, they may be made of a number of flanged sections bolted together.

The trays of modern installations are ordinarily made of sheet metal, of special alloys if necessary, the thickness governed by the anticipated corrosion rate. The trays must be stiffened or supported, as in Fig. 6.2, and must be fastened to the shell to prevent movement due to surges of gas, with allowance for thermal expansion. This can be arranged by use of tray-support rings with slotted bolt holes, to which the trays are bolted. Large trays are made in sections for ease in installation and so that a man can climb from one tray to another during repair and cleaning. They should be installed level to within ¼ in.

Tray spacing. Tray spacing is usually chosen first on the basis of expediency in construction, maintenance, and cost, and later checked to be certain that adequate insurance against flooding is present. For special cases where headroom is a most important consideration, spacings of 6 in. have been used. For all except the smallest tower diameters, 18 in. would seem to be a more workable minimum from the point of view of cleaning the trays. Most petroleum-refinery installations use 18 to 20 in. for tower diameters up to 4 ft and increased spacing for greater diameters in order to facilitate cleaning and removal of trays through manholes in the shell. See Table 6.1 for a summary of recommended values.

Tower diameter. The tower diameter and consequently its cross section must be sufficiently large to handle the gas and liquid at velocities which will not cause flooding or excessive entrainment. For a given type of tray at flooding, the superficial velocity of the gas V_F (cu ft gas/sec divided by the "net" cross section for gas flow, A_n sq ft) is related to fluid densities by

$$V_F = C_F \left(\frac{\rho_L - \rho_G}{\rho_G} \right)^{1/2} \tag{6.1}$$

The net cross section A_n is the tower cross section A_t minus the area taken up by downspouts (one A_d in the case of a cross-flow tray as in Fig. 6.2). C_F is an empirical constant which will be considered later for individual tray types. Some appropriately smaller value of V is used for actual design, for nonfoaming liquids 80 to 85 percent of V_F (75 percent or less for foaming liquids), subject to check of entrainment and pressure-drop characteristics. For most circumstances, the diameter so chosen will be adequate, although occasionally the liquid flow may be limiting. A well-designed single-pass cross-flow tray can ordinarily be expected to handle up to 75 gal/min of liquid per foot of diameter [$q/d = 0.165$ cu ft/(sec)(ft)] without excessive liquid gradient. For most installations, considerations of cost make it impractical to vary the tower diameter to accommodate variations in liquid or gas flow from one end of the tower to the other, and the maximum flow quantities are used to set the design. When the variation in flow is considerable, and especially when expensive alloys are used in construction, two diameters are sometimes used.

The tower diameters may clearly be decreased by use of increased tray spacing so that tower cost, which depends on height as well as diameter, passes through a minimum at some optimum tray spacing.

Downspouts. The liquid is led from one tray to the next by means of downspouts, or downcomers. These may be circular pipes or, preferably, simply portions of the tower cross section set aside for liquid flow by vertical plates, as in Fig. 6.2. Since

Table 6.1. Recommended conditions and dimensions for tray towers

General

1. Tray spacing:

Tower diameter d, ft	Tray spacing t, in.
	6 in. minimum
4 or less	18–20
4–10	24
10–12	30
12–24	36

2. Liquid flow:
    a. Not over 0.165 cu ft/(sec)(ft diam) for single-pass cross-flow trays
    b. Not over 0.35 cu ft/(sec)(ft weir length) for others

3. Downspout holdup: 8 sec minimum (superficial)

4. Downspout seal: 0.5 in. minimum at no liquid flow

5. Weir length: Straight, rectangular weirs of cross-flow trays, $0.6d$–$0.8d$

6. Liquid gradient: 0.5 in. (1.25 in. maximum)

7. Pressure drop per tray:

Pressure	Pressure drop
35 mm Hg abs	3 mm Hg or less
Atm	0.07–0.12 psi
300 psi	0.15 psi

Bubble-cap trays

1. Liquid seal:

Pressure	Seal, in.
Vacuum	0.5–1.5
Atm	1.0–2.0
50–100 psi	1.5–3.0
200–500 psi	2.0–4.0

2. Skirt clearance: 0.5 in. minimum, 1.5 in. for dirty liquids

Table 6.1. Recommended conditions and dimensions for tray towers (*Continued*)

3. Flooding constant C_F [Eqs. (6.1), (6.2)]:

Range of $\dfrac{L'}{G'}\left(\dfrac{\rho_G}{\rho_L}\right)^{0.5}$	a	b
0.01–0.03 use values at 0.03		
0.03–0.2	$0.0041t + 0.0135$	$0.0047t + 0.068$
0.2–1.0	$0.0068t + 0.049$	$0.0028t + 0.044$

Perforated trays

Flooding constant C_F [Eqs. (6.1), (6.3)]

Range of $\dfrac{L'}{G'}\left(\dfrac{\rho_G}{\rho_L}\right)^{0.5}$	a	b
0.01–0.1 use values at 0.1		
0.1–1.0	$0.0062t + 0.0385$	$0.00253t + 0.05$

the liquid is agitated into a froth on the tray, adequate residence time must be allowed in the downspout to permit disengaging of the gas from the liquid so that only clear liquid enters the tray below. A minimum residence, or holdup, time for the liquid of 8 sec [= total volume of downspout in cu ft/(cu ft liquid/sec)] will ordinarily ensure this. Foamy liquids require more time. The downspout must be brought sufficiently close to the tray below so as to seal into the liquid on that tray (½ to 1 in. below the outlet weir level), thus preventing gas bubbles from rising up the downspout to short-circuit the tray above. Seal pots and seal-pot dams (inlet weirs) may be used, as in Fig. 6.3, but not if there is any tendency to accumulate sediment.

Weirs. The depth of liquid on the tray required for gas contacting is maintained by an overflow weir (outlet weir), which may or may not be a continuation of the downspout plate. The weir may be straight, rectangular, or notched; circular weirs which are extensions of circular pipes used as downspouts are not recommended.

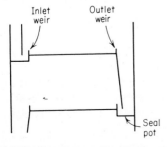

Fig. 6.3 *Seal-pot arrangement.*

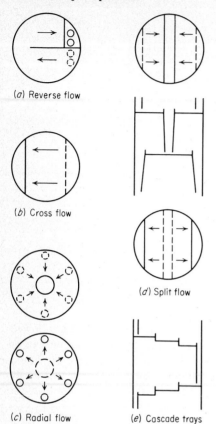

(a) Reverse flow

(b) Cross flow

(c) Radial flow

(d) Split flow

(e) Cascade trays

Fig. 6.4 *Tray arrangements. Arrows show direction of liquid flow.*

In order to ensure reasonably uniform distribution of liquid flow on single-pass trays, a weir length of 60 to 75 percent of the tower diameter is used.   To assist the weir action, the openings on the tray for gas flow (particularly for bubble caps) are set from 3 to 5 in. from the weir, so that some vapor-disengaging space is provided before the liquid flows over the weir.

Liquid flow. An increase in liquid depth from the outlet to the inlet of the tray, the liquid *gradient* (by which is meant merely the difference in liquid depth), results from the resistance offered to flow of liquid by devices on the tray and the flow of gas. Excessive liquid gradient, as will be shown, leads to maldistribution of gas and other difficulties.

The liquid gradient may be minimized by reducing the distance along the tray through which the liquid must flow.   For large-diameter towers, radial or split flow may be substituted for the simple cross flow thus far considered (see Fig. 6.4), although every attempt is usually made to use the cross-flow tray by reason of its lower cost. For very large diameters, cascade trays of several levels, each with its own weir, can be used, although their cost is considerable. For towers up to 4 ft in diameter, simple cross flow is probably best. In any case, the liquid gradient should be kept to about 0.5 in. with perhaps 1.25 in. as a maximum.

Bubble-cap trays

These have been known for well over a century. Because they can operate at high efficiency over a wide range of flow rates, they have been the most commonly used type of tray in the past, and their technology is probably the most advanced of all vapor-liquid contacting devices. A schematic arrangement is shown in Fig. 6.2. The vapor or gas rises through the openings in the tray (vapor risers) into bubble caps which surmount each riser. The periphery of each cap is slotted or serrated with a number of openings (slots) through which the gas bubbles into the liquid.

Tower diameter. The diameter is determined through the use of a gas velocity, appropriately smaller than that which causes flooding, as indicated earlier. The constant C_F of Eq. (6.1) has been correlated for the available data on flooding for nonfoaming systems, for cases where the weir height is less than 15 percent of the tray spacing, and for tray spacings $t = 12$ to 36 in.[17,19] The curves of the original papers can be adequately expressed by

$$C_F = \left[a \log \frac{1}{(L'/G')(\rho_G/\rho_L)^{0.5}} + b \right] \left(\frac{\sigma'}{20} \right)^{0.2} \tag{6.2}$$

and values of a and b are given in Table 6.1.

The caps are ordinarily circular, 3 to 6 in. diameter, or sometimes rectangular (tunnel caps), 3 to 6 in. wide by 12 in. or more long. They are most frequently made of thin metal by punching or spinning, less frequently by casting, but also from other materials such as plastics, glass, or carbon. Figure 6.5 shows some typical designs. The slots are arranged around the periphery (skirt) and are either of sawtooth design or cut so that they do not extend to the edge of the cap, leaving a *shroud ring*. Slots may be rectangular or triangular; the shape does not seem particularly important in influencing tray efficiency. The slots should be covered by a depth of liquid, the *liquid seal*, so as to ensure contact of liquid and gas. Typical values of liquid seal[4] are given in Table 6.1. The skirt of the cap may be placed directly on the tray, but it is preferable to allow at least 0.5 in. skirt clearance to prevent accumulation of sediment from the liquid and to allow for means of passing more than the expected amount of gas under the skirt if necessary. The vapor risers under the cap should extend above the top of the slots to reduce the tendency to *back trap* or *dump* (flow of liquid through the riser).

A typical cross-flow tray layout is shown in Fig. 6.6. The caps are set at the corners of equilateral triangles, arranged so that the liquid is adequately contacted by gas. The gas issuing from the slots is usually not projected more than about 1 in. from the cap, so that the distance between caps should be from 1 to 3 in., and for the same reason the clearance between caps and tower shell should be kept small. The

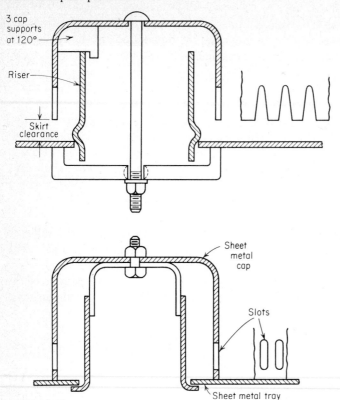

Fig. 6.5 *Typical bubble-cap designs. (With permission of The Pressed Steel Company.)*

arrangement is usually chosen by trial and error.   After the first arrangement is made, with perhaps 60 to 70 percent of the tray area allocated to bubble caps, a computation is made of the gas pressure drop, liquid gradient, the increase in level of liquid in the downspout, and gas distribution among the caps.   If not satisfactory, a new layout is chosen.   Detailed computation of the hydraulic characteristics of bubble-cap trays has been thoroughly developed by Bolles[4] and others,[48] and will not be covered here.

The difficulties that excessive liquid gradient can cause are shown schematically in Fig. 6.7.   The bulk of the gas flows through the row of caps nearest the outlet weir, while those caps nearest the liquid inlet do not function properly because the pressure due to liquid depth prevents the gas from opening the slots.   Back trapping is most injurious to tray efficiency, since on cross-flow trays the back-trapped liquid bypasses two trays.   In an existing tower, the difficulties are sometimes alleviated by raising the level of the caps and risers near the liquid inlet of the trays.

Properly designed bubble trays are able to handle a four- to fivefold range of gas flow, as well as liquid flows ranging from the maximum causing flooding to very low values (the ratio of maximum to minimum flow is termed *turndown*) since at all times the liquid level on the trays is maintained by the weir and the cap slots are covered.

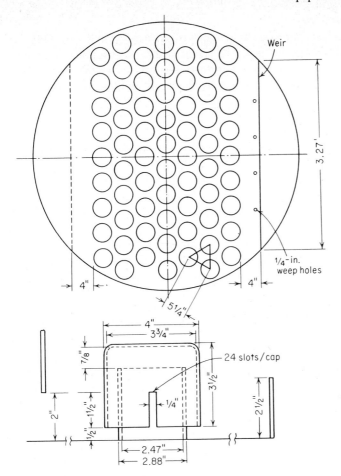

Weir

3.27'

¼-in.
weep holes

4"   4"

5¼"

4"
3¾"
⅞"
24 slots/cap
3½"
2"
1½"
½"
¼"
2½"
2.47"
2.88"

Fig. 6.6 *Typical bubble-cap tray arrangement.*

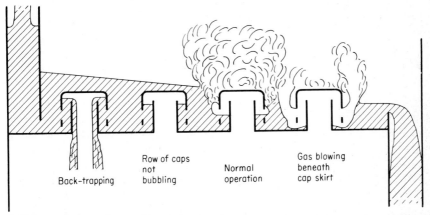

Back-trapping

Row of caps
not
bubbling

Normal
operation

Gas blowing
beneath
cap skirt

Fig. 6.7 *Effect of excessive liquid gradient.*

Perforated (sieve) trays

These have been known almost as long as bubble-cap trays, but they fell out of favor, particularly in the first half of this century.   In recent years, because they are much less expensive than bubble-cap trays, interest in them has revived to the extent that they (or proprietary modifications) have nearly replaced bubble caps for new installations.

Perforated trays are built in the same general fashion as bubble-cap trays except that the area normally devoted to caps and risers is replaced by a sheet of metal perforated with small circular holes.   If it were not for the rapid flow of gas up through the holes, liquid would rain down (weep) through them.   The gas, dispersed into bubbles by the perforations, expands the liquid into a turbulent froth, characterized by very large interfacial surface for mass transfer.   The trays are subject to flooding due to backup of liquid in the downspouts or excessive entrainment (priming) much as bubble-cap trays are.

Hole diameters from $\frac{1}{8}$ to $\frac{1}{2}$ in. are used, $\frac{3}{16}$ in. perhaps most frequently, and the holes are placed on the corners of equilateral triangles at distances between centers (pitch) of from 2.5 to 5 hole diameters.[48]   For most installations, stainless steel or other alloy perforated sheet, which is commercially available, is used rather than carbon steel, even though not particularly required for corrosion resistance.   Sheet thickness is usually four-tenths to eight-tenths the hole diameter for stainless steel, somewhat larger for carbon steel or copper alloys.

Tower diameter. The flooding constant C_F of Eq. (6.1) has been correlated for the data available on flooding.[17,18]   The original curves can be represented by

$$C_F = \left[a \log \frac{1}{(L'/G')(\rho_G/\rho_L)^{0.5}} + b \right] \left(\frac{\sigma'}{20} \right)^{0.2} \left(5 \frac{A_h}{A_a} + 0.5 \right) \tag{6.3}$$

and the constants a and b are given in Table 6.1.   The expression is limited to hole diameters not larger than $\frac{1}{4}$ in., to cases where the weir height does not exceed 15 percent of the tray spacing, and to nonfoaming systems. A_a is the active area of the tray, taken to be that between inlet downspout and the outlet weir on a cross-flow tray, and A_h is the hole area per tray.   A velocity appropriately smaller than the flooding velocity of Eq. (6.1) is then chosen to fix the diameter of the tower (see Illustration 6.1).

Perforated-tray hydraulics

The design of a perforated tray must include not only the tray layout but also estimates of the gas pressure drop and approach to flooding as well as insurance against weeping and excessive entrainment.

Liquid depth. Liquid depths should not ordinarily be less than 2 in., to ensure good froth formation, or probably much greater than 4 in.,[28] although the recent tendency is to make the maximum figure larger.   These limits refer to the sum of the weir height h_W plus the crest over the weir h_1, although the evidence is that in the perforated area the actual equivalent clear-liquid depth will be smaller than this.

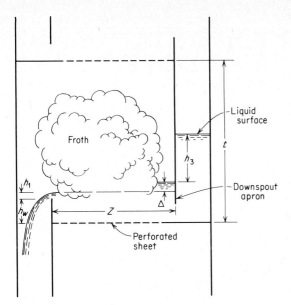

Fig. 6.8 *Schematic diagram of a cross-flow perforated tray.*

Weirs. Refer to Fig. 6.8, where a schematic representation of a cross-flow tray is shown. The crest of liquid over a straight rectangular weir may be estimated by the familiar Francis formula,

$$\frac{q}{W_{\text{eff}}} = 3.33 \left(\frac{h_1}{12}\right)^{3/2} \qquad (6.4)$$

where q = rate of liquid flow, cu ft/sec
$\quad W_{\text{eff}}$ = effective length of weir, ft
$\quad h_1$ = liquid crest over weir, in.

Owing to the fact that the weir action is hampered by the curved sides of the circular tower, it is recommended[13] that W_{eff} be represented as a chord of the circle of diameter d, a distance h_1 farther from the center than the actual weir, as in Fig. 6.9. Equation (6.4) may then be rearranged to

$$h_1 = 5.38 \left(\frac{W}{W_{\text{eff}}}\right)^{2/3} \left(\frac{q}{W}\right)^{2/3} \qquad (6.5)$$

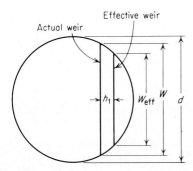

Fig. 6.9 *Effective weir length.*

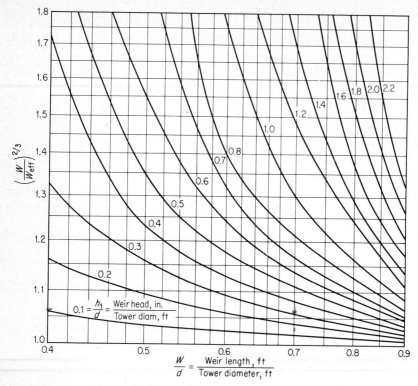

$$\frac{W}{d} = \frac{\text{Weir length, ft}}{\text{Tower diameter, ft}}$$

Fig. 6.10   *Correction for effective weir length.*

The effective lengths of weirs have been calculated from the geometry of Fig. 6.9, and the correction is given by Fig. 6.10.

Pressure drop for the gas.   For convenience, all gas-pressure drops will be expressed as equivalent heads, in inches, of clear liquid of density ρ_L lb/cu ft on the tray.   The pressure drop for the gas h_G is the sum of the effects for flow of gas through the dry plate and those caused by the presence of liquid:

$$h_G = h_D + h_L + h_R \tag{6.6}$$

where h_D = dry-plate pressure drop

h_L = pressure drop due to the depth of liquid on the tray

h_R = "residual" pressure drop

Although Fig. 6.8 shows a hydraulic gradient Δ, half of which should be used in Eq. (6.6), in practice this is so small, except for the very largest of trays, that it may reasonably be neglected.[24,33]   Estimates of the gas-pressure drop summarized here are based on a critical study by Madigan[32] of all available data and the generally accepted methods.   Most of the available data are for the air–water system, and extension to others is somewhat uncertain.

Dry pressure drop h_D.   This is calculated on the basis that it is the result of a loss in pressure on entrance to the perforations, friction within the short tube formed by the perforation due to plate thickness, and an exit loss:[25]

$$h_D = 12C_0 \frac{V_h^2 \rho_G}{2g\rho_L}\left[0.40\left(1.25 - \frac{A_h}{A_n}\right) + \frac{4lf}{d_h} + \left(1 - \frac{A_h}{A_n}\right)^2\right] \tag{6.7}$$

The Fanning friction factor f is taken from a standard chart.[2] C_0 is an orifice coefficient which depends upon the plate thickness/hole diameter ratio.[34]   Over the range $l/d_h = 0.2$ to 2.0,

$$C_O = 1.09 \left(\frac{d_h}{l}\right)^{0.25} \tag{6.8}$$

Hydraulic head h_L. In the perforated area of the tray, the liquid is actually in the form of a froth. The equivalent depth of clear liquid h_L is that which would be obtained if the froth collapsed.   This is usually actually less than the height of the outlet weir, decreasing with increased gas rate.   The methods available for estimating h_L are not well developed, and this is the poorest known of the several gas pressure drops.   The recommended relationship is[21]

$$h_L = 0.24 + 0.725 h_W - 0.29 h_W V_a \rho_G^{0.5} + 4.48 \frac{q}{z} \tag{6.9}$$

where z is the average liquid flow width, which may be taken as $(d + W)/2$.

Residual gas pressure drop h_R. This is believed to be due largely to the necessity of overcoming surface tension as the gas issues from a perforation.   A balance of the internal force in a static bubble required to overcome surface tension is

$$\frac{\pi d_p^2}{4} \Delta P_B = \pi d_p \sigma \tag{6.10}$$

or

$$\Delta P_B = \frac{4\sigma}{d_p} \tag{6.11}$$

where ΔP_B is the excess pressure in the bubble owing to surface tension.   But the bubble of gas grows over a finite time when the gas flows, and by averaging over time[16] it develops that the appropriate value is ΔP_R:

$$\Delta P_R = \frac{6\sigma}{d_p} \tag{6.12}$$

Since d_p is not readily computed, we substitute as an approximation the diameter of the perforation, $d_h/12$, which leads to

$$h_R = 12 \frac{\Delta P_R}{\rho_L} \frac{g_c}{g} = 144(6) \frac{\sigma}{\rho_L d_h} \frac{g_c}{g} = 0.06 \frac{\sigma'}{\rho_L d_h} \tag{6.13}$$

where g_c/g is taken as 1.0.

Comparison of observed data with values of h_G calculated by these methods shows a standard deviation of 14.7 percent.[32]

Pressure loss at liquid entrance h_2. The flow of liquid under the downspout apron as it enters the tray incurs a pressure loss which may be estimated as three velocity heads:[10]

$$h_2 = \frac{12(3)}{2g} \left(\frac{q}{A_{da}}\right)^2 = 0.558 \left(\frac{q}{A_{da}}\right)^2 \tag{6.14}$$

where A_{da} is the smaller of the two areas, the downspout cross section or the free area between the downspout apron and the tray, and g is taken as 32.2 ft/sq sec.   Friction in the downspout is negligible.

Backup in the downspout. Refer to Fig. 6.8.   The distance h_3, the difference in liquid level inside and immediately outside the downspout, will be the sum of the pressure losses due to liquid and gas flow

$$h_3 = h_G + h_2 \tag{6.15}$$

Since the mass in the downspout will be partly froth carried over the weir from the tray above, not yet disengaged, whose average density may be estimated roughly as half of the clear liquid, safe design requires that the level of equivalent clear liquid in the downspout be no more than half the tray spacing. Neglecting Δ, the requirement is

$$h_W + h_1 + h_3 \leqslant \frac{t}{2} \tag{6.16}$$

Weeping. If the gas velocity through the holes is too small, liquid will drain through them and short-circuit part of the tray. The data on incipient weeping are meager, particularly for large liquid depths on the tray. A study of the available data[32] led to the following as the best representation of V_{hW}, the minimum gas velocity below which liquid weeping will occur,

$$\frac{V_{hW}\mu_G}{\sigma g_c} = 2.92(10^{-4})\left(\frac{\mu_G^2}{\sigma g_c \rho_G d_h'}\frac{\rho_L}{\rho_G}10^5\right)^{0.379}\left(\frac{l}{d_h}\right)^{0.293}\left(\frac{2A_a d_h'}{\sqrt{3}p'^3}\right)^{2.8/(Z/d_h')^{0.724}} \tag{6.17}$$

where each of the ratios in parentheses is dimensionless. Available data for h_L, in the range 0.9 to 1.9 in., do not indicate h_L to be of influence. It may be for higher values.

Liquid entrainment. When liquid is carried by the gas up to the tray above, the entrained liquid is caught in the liquid on the upper tray, and the liquid flowing downward is then larger in amount by the entrainment. A convenient definition of the degree or extent of entrainment is the fraction of the liquid entering a tray which is carried by the gas to the tray above,[17]

$$\text{Fractional entrainment} = E = \frac{\text{moles liquid entrained/(hr)(sq ft)}}{L + \text{moles liquid entrained/(hr)(sq ft)}}$$

The important influence of entrainment on tray efficiency will be discussed later. Figure 6.11 represents a summary of sieve-tray entrainment data[17,18] with an accuracy of ± 20 percent.

Illustration 6.1. A dilute aqueous solution of methanol and water is to be stripped with steam in a perforated tray tower. The conditions chosen for design are (1) vapor, 700 moles/hr, 18 mole % methanol; (2) liquid, 2,100 moles/hr, 5 wt. % (2.9 mole %) methanol; (3) temperature 95°C, pressure 1 atm. Design a suitable perforated tray.

Solution. Mol wt methanol = 32, mol wt water = 18. Av mol wt gas = 0.18(32) + 0.82(18) = 20.5 lb/lb mole.

$$\rho_G = \frac{20.5}{359}\frac{273}{273 + 95} = 0.0424 \text{ lb/cu ft}$$

$$Q = \frac{700}{3,600}359\frac{273 + 95}{273} = 94 \text{ cu ft/sec, vapor rate}$$

$$\rho_L = 60 \text{ lb/cu ft}$$

Av mol wt liquid = $100/(\frac{5}{32} + \frac{95}{18})$ = 18.43 lb/lb mole

$$q = \frac{2,100(18.43)}{60(3,600)} = 0.1794 \text{ cu ft liquid/sec}$$

Perforations. Take $d_h = \frac{3}{16}$-in.-diameter (0.1875-in.) holes, on equilateral triangular pitch, 0.5 in. between hole centers, punched in sheet metal 0.078 in. thick (14 U.S. standard gauge). Each triangle has an area $(3)^{0.5}(0.5)^2/4 = 0.1085$ sq in., and contains one-half a hole of area $\pi(0.1875)^2/4 = 0.0276$ sq in. The perforated sheet has a ratio of hole to total area = 0.0276/2(0.1085) = 0.1275.

Tower diameter. Tentatively take $t = 20$ in tray spacing.

$$\frac{L'}{G'}\left(\frac{\rho_G}{\rho_L}\right)^{0.5} = \frac{q\rho_L}{Q\rho_G}\left(\frac{\rho_G}{\rho_L}\right)^{0.5} = \frac{q}{Q}\left(\frac{\rho_L}{\rho_G}\right)^{0.5} = \frac{0.1794}{94}\left(\frac{60}{0.0424}\right)^{0.5} = 0.0719$$

Table 6.1:

$$a = 0.0062(20) + 0.0385 = 0.1625$$
$$b = 0.00253(20) + 0.05 = 0.1006$$

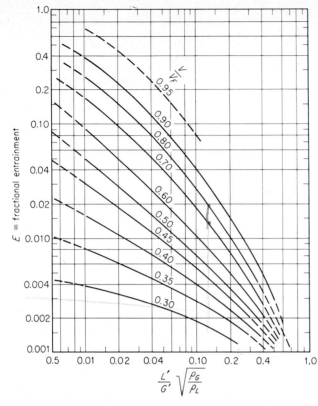

Fig. **6.11** *Entrainment, sieve trays.*[17] *(With permission of Petro/Chemical Engineering.)*

In Eq. (6.3), since $\dfrac{L'}{G'}\left(\dfrac{\rho_G}{\rho_L}\right)^{0.5}$ is less than 0.1, use 0.1 (see Table 6.1). Tentatively take $A_h/A_a = 0.1275$. The surface tension is estimated as 40 dynes/cm.

$$C_F = \left(0.1625 \log \frac{1}{0.1} + 0.1006\right)\left(\frac{40}{20}\right)^{0.2}[5(0.1275) + 0.5] = 0.354$$

Eq. (6.1): $\qquad V_F = 0.354\left(\dfrac{60 - 0.0424}{0.0424}\right)^{0.5} = 13.31$ ft/sec at flooding

Using 80% of flooding, $V = 0.80(13.31) = 10.65$ ft/sec based on area A_n.

$$A_n = \frac{Q}{V} = \frac{94}{10.65} = 8.82 \text{ sq ft}$$

Tentatively choose a weir length $W = 0.7d$. This makes the segmental area of one downspout 8.8% of the cross section of the circular tower.

$$A_t = \frac{8.82}{1 - 0.088} = 9.65 \text{ sq ft}$$

$$d = [4(9.65)/\pi]^{0.5} = 3.5 \text{ ft, tower diam}$$

$$W = 0.7(3.5) = 2.45 \text{ ft weir length}$$

$$A_d = 0.088(9.65) = 0.850 \text{ sq ft downspout cross section}$$

$$A_a = A_t - 2A_d = 9.65 - 2(0.850) = 7.95 \text{ sq ft active area}$$

Hole area A_h. Taking $A_h/A_t = 0.09$ to allow for a tray support ring, $A_h = 0.09(9.65) = 0.866$ sq ft hole area.

$$\text{Total area of perforated sheet} = \frac{0.866}{0.1275} = 6.80 \text{ sq ft}$$

True $A_h/A_a = 0.866/7.95 = 0.1095$, which will not alter the flooding coefficient C_F significantly.

Weir crest h_1. Try $h_1 = 1.0$ in. ∴ $h_1/d = 1/3.5 = 0.286$, and $W/d = 0.7$. From Fig. 6.10, $(W/W_{\text{eff}})^{2/3} = 1.05$.

Eq. (6.5):
$$h_1 = 5.38(1.05)\left(\frac{0.1794}{2.45}\right)^{2/3} = 0.98 \text{ in.} \quad \text{OK}$$

Set weir height $h_W = 2.0$ in.

Dry pressure drop h_D

Eq. (6.8):
$$C_O = 1.09\left(\frac{0.1875}{0.078}\right)^{0.25} = 1.360$$

$$V_h = \frac{VA_n}{A_h} = 10.65\,\frac{8.82}{0.866} = 108.4 \text{ ft/sec}$$

$$\mu_G' = 0.0125 \text{ centipoise}$$

$$\text{Hole Reynolds number} = \frac{d_h' V_h \rho_G}{\mu_G} = \frac{0.1875(108.4)(0.0424)}{12(0.0125)(0.000672)} = 8{,}550$$

∴ $f = 0.008$ ("The Chemical Engineers' Handbook," 4th ed., Fig. 5.25).

$$g = 32.2 \text{ ft/sec}^2 \qquad l = 0.078 \text{ in. plate thickness}$$

Substituting in Eq. (6.7) yields $h_D = 2.10$ in. liquid.

Hydraulic head h_L

$$V_a = \frac{VA_n}{A_a} = 10.65\,\frac{8.82}{7.95} = 11.81 \text{ ft/sec}$$

$$\rho_G = 0.0424 \text{ lb/cu ft} \qquad h_W = 2.0 \text{ in.}$$

$$q = 0.1794 \text{ cu ft/sec} \qquad z = \frac{d+W}{2} = 2.975 \text{ ft}$$

Substituting in Eq. (6.9) yields $h_L = 0.55$ in. liquid.

Residual pressure drop h_R. Eq. (6.13):

$$h_R = \frac{0.06(40)}{60(0.1875)} = 0.213 \text{ in. liquid}$$

Total gas-pressure drop h_G. Eq. (6.6):

$$h_G = 2.10 + 0.55 + 0.213 = 2.86 \text{ in. liquid}$$

Pressure loss at liquid entrance h_2. The downspout apron will be set at $h_W - 0.5 = 1.5$ in. above the tray. The area for liquid flow under the apron $= 1.5W/12 = 1.5(2.45)/12 = 0.306$ sq ft. Since this is smaller than A_d, $A_{da} = 0.306$ sq ft.

Eq. (6.14):
$$h_2 = 0.558\left(\frac{0.1749}{0.306}\right)^2 = 0.192 \text{ in. liquid}$$

Backup in downspout. Eq. (6.15): $h_3 = 2.86 + 0.192 = 3.05$ in.

Check on flooding. $h_W + h_1 + h_3 = 2.0 + 0.98 + 3.05 = 6.03$ in., which is well below $t/2 = 10$ in. OK.

Weeping velocity

$$\mu_G = 0.0125(0.000672) = 8.40(10^{-6}) \text{ lb/(ft)(sec)}$$

$$\sigma = 40(6.85)(10^{-5}) = 274(10^{-5}) \text{ lb/ft}$$

$$d'_h = \frac{0.1875}{12} = 0.0156 \text{ ft} \qquad p' = \frac{0.5}{12} = 0.0417 \text{ ft}$$

For $W/d = 0.7$, the weir is set 1.25 ft from the center of the tower.   Therefore $Z = 2(1.25) = 2.50$ ft. All the other items of Eq. (6.17) have been previously evaluated, and the equation then yields $V_{hW} = 20$ ft/sec.   The tray will not weep until the gas velocity through the holes is reduced to something close to this value.

Downspout residence time. The volume of the downspout $= A_d(t + h_W)/12 = 0.850(20 + 2)/12 = 1.56$ cu ft.   Since the liquid flow rate is $q = 0.1794$ cu ft/sec, the superficial residence time $= 1.56/0.1794 = 8.7$ sec, which should be satisfactory.

Entrainment

$$\frac{V}{V_F} = 0.80 \qquad \frac{L'}{G'}\left(\frac{\rho_G}{\rho_L}\right)^{0.5} = 0.0719 \text{ (see Tower diameter)}$$

Fig. 6.11: $\qquad\qquad\qquad\qquad\qquad E = 0.042$

The recycling of liquid resulting from such entrainment is too small to influence the tray hydraulics appreciably.

The mass-transfer efficiency of this tray is estimated in Illustration 6.2.

Proprietary trays

Although for many decades the basic design of tray-tower internals remained relatively static, recent years have seen a great many innovations, only a few of which can be mentioned here.   Figure 6.12 is a variation of the bubble-cap arrangement,[3,36] wherein the vapor issues from the slots in the direction of liquid flow.   The structure shown extends across the entire area of the tray.   As a result the backward splashing of liquid in the direction of the liquid inlet to the tray is much reduced in comparison with that for bubble caps.   There is also a great variety of *valve trays*, which are, in effect, perforated trays with variable area of openings for gas flow.   The perforations are relatively large, roughly 1.5 in. in diameter if circular, and they are covered with movable caps which rise as the flow rate of gas increases.   At low gas rates and correspondingly small openings, the tendency to weep is reduced; at high gas rates the

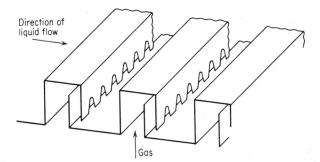

Direction of liquid flow

Gas

Fig. 6.12 *Socony-Mobil Uniflux tray (schematic).*

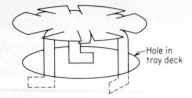

Fig. 6.13 *Glitsch Ballast Tray (schematic), a form of valve tray. (Fritz W. Glitsch and Sons, Inc.)*

pressure drop remains low. Figure 6.13 shows one variety, and there are many others.[38,42,50] In most cases, the design of proprietary trays must be left to the supplier.

Tray efficiency

Tray efficiency is the fractional approach to an ideal or theoretical tray (see Chap. 5) which is attained by a real tray. Ultimately, we require a measure of approach to equilibrium of all the vapor and liquid from the tray, but since the conditions at various locations on the tray may differ, we begin by considering the local, or *point*, efficiency of mass transfer at a particular place on the tray surface.

Point efficiency. Figure 6.14 is a schematic representation of one tray of a multitray tower. The tray n is fed from tray $n - 1$ above by liquid of average composition x_{n-1} mole fraction of transferred component, and it delivers liquid of average composition x_n to the tray below. At the place under consideration, a pencil of gas of composition $y_{n+1,\text{local}}$ rises from below, and as a result of mass transfer, leaves with a concentration $y_{n,\text{local}}$. At the place in question, it is assumed that the local liquid concentration x_{local} is constant in the vertical direction. The point

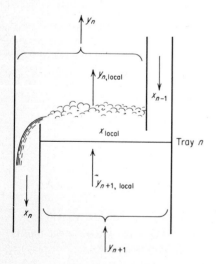

Fig. 6.14 *Tray efficiency.*

efficiency is then defined by

$$\mathbf{E}_{OG} = \frac{y_{n,\text{local}} - y_{n+1,\text{local}}}{y^*_{\text{local}} - y_{n+1,\text{local}}} \tag{6.18}$$

Here y^*_{local} is the concentration in equilibrium with x_{local}, and Eq. (6.18) then represents the change in gas concentration which actually occurs as a fraction of that which would occur if equilibrium were established.   The subscript G signifies that gas concentrations are used, and the O emphasizes that $\mathbf{E}_{OG}$ is a measure of the overall resistance to mass transfer for both phases.   As the gas passes through the openings of the tray and through the liquid and foam, it encounters several hydrodynamic regimes, each with different rates of mass transfer.   The danger in attempting to describe the entire effect in terms of a single quantity, in cases of this sort, was pointed out in Chap. 5, but present information permits nothing better.

Consider that the gas rises at a rate G lb moles/(hr)(sq ft).   Let the interfacial surface between gas and liquid be a sq ft/cu ft of liquid-gas foam.   As the gas rises a differential height dh_L, the area of contact is $a\,dh_L$ per square feet of tray.   If, while of concentration y, it undergoes a concentration change dy in this height, and if the total quantity of gas remains essentially constant, the rate of solute transfer is $G\,dy$:

$$G\,dy = K_y(a\,dh_L)(y^*_{\text{local}} - y) \tag{6.19}$$

Then

$$\int_{y_{n+1,\text{local}}}^{y_{n,\text{local}}} \frac{dy}{y^*_{\text{local}} - y} = \int_0^{h_L} \frac{K_y a\,dh_L}{G} \tag{6.20}$$

Since y^*_{local} is constant for constant x_{local},

$$-\ln \frac{y^*_{\text{local}} - y_{n,\text{local}}}{y^*_{\text{local}} - y_{n+1,\text{local}}} = -\ln\left(1 - \frac{y_{n,\text{local}} - y_{n+1,\text{local}}}{y^*_{\text{local}} - y_{n+1,\text{local}}}\right)$$

$$= -\ln(1 - \mathbf{E}_{OG}) = \frac{K_y a h_L}{G} \tag{6.21}$$

Therefore

$$\mathbf{E}_{OG} = 1 - e^{-K_y a h_L/G} = 1 - e^{-N_{tOG}} \tag{6.22}$$

The exponent on e is simplified to N_{tOG}, the number of overall gas-transfer units. Just as K_y contains both gas and liquid resistance to mass transfer, so also N_{tOG} is made up of the transfer units for the gas N_{tG} and those for the liquid N_{tL}.   As will be shown in Chap. 8, these may be combined in the manner of Eq. (5.7):

$$\frac{1}{N_{tOG}} = \frac{1}{N_{tG}} + \frac{mG}{L}\frac{1}{N_{tL}} \tag{6.23}$$

The terms on the right represent, respectively, the gas and liquid mass-transfer resistances, which must be obtained experimentally.   For example, by contacting a gas with a pure liquid on a tray, so that vaporization of the liquid occurs without mass-transfer resistance in the liquid, the vaporization efficiency provides N_{tG}, which may then be correlated in terms of fluid properties, tray design, and operating conditions.   Values of N_{tL} obtained through absorption of relatively insoluble gases into liquids (see Chap. 5) may be similarly correlated.

Murphree tray efficiency. The bulk-average concentrations of all the local pencils of gas of Fig. 6.14 are y_{n+1} and y_n.   The Murphree efficiency of the entire tray is then [see Eq. (5.39)]

$$\mathbf{E}_{MG} = \frac{y_n - y_{n+1}}{y_n^* - y_{n+1}} \tag{6.24}$$

where y_n^* is the value in equilibrium with the leaving liquid of concentration x_n.

The relationship between $\mathbf{E}_{MG}$ and $\mathbf{E}_{OG}$ can then be derived by integrating the local $\mathbf{E}_{OG}$'s over the surface of the tray.   Clearly, if all the gas entering were uniformly mixed and fed uniformly to the entire tray cross section, and if the mechanical contacting of gas and liquid were everywhere uniform, the uniformity of concentration of exit gas $y_{n+1,\text{local}}$ would then depend on the uniformity of liquid concentration on the tray.   Liquid on the tray is splashed about by the action of the gas, some of it even being thrown backward in the direction from which it enters the tray (back mixing).   The two extreme cases which might be visualized are:

1. Liquid completely back mixed, everywhere of uniform concentration x_n. In this case, Eq. (6.24) reverts to Eq. (6.18), and

$$\mathbf{E}_{MG} = \mathbf{E}_{OG} \tag{6.25}$$

2. Liquid in "plug flow," with no mixing, each particle remaining on the tray for the same length of time.   In this case, it has been shown that[30]

$$\mathbf{E}_{MG} = \frac{L}{mG} (e^{\mathbf{E}_{OG} mG/L} - 1) \tag{6.26}$$

and $\mathbf{E}_{MG} > \mathbf{E}_{OG}$.

In the more likely intermediate case, the transport of solute by the mixing process can be described in terms of an eddy diffusivity D_E, whereupon[7]

$$\frac{\mathbf{E}_{MG}}{\mathbf{E}_{OG}} = \frac{1 - e^{-(\eta + \mathrm{Pe})}}{(\eta + \mathrm{Pe})[1 + (\eta + \mathrm{Pe})/\eta]} + \frac{e^\eta - 1}{\eta[1 + \eta/(\eta + \mathrm{Pe})]} \tag{6.27}$$

where

$$\eta = \frac{\mathrm{Pe}}{2}\left[\left(1 + \frac{4mG\mathbf{E}_{OG}}{L\,\mathrm{Pe}}\right)^{0.5} - 1\right] \tag{6.28}$$

$$\mathrm{Pe} = \frac{Z^2}{D_E \theta_L} \tag{6.29}$$

Here θ_L is the liquid residence time on tray and Z the length of liquid travel.   Pe is a Péclet number (see Chap. 3), as can be seen better by writing it as $\dfrac{Z}{D_E}\dfrac{Z}{\theta_L}$, whence

Z/θ_L becomes the average liquid velocity. Pe $= 0$ corresponds to complete back mixing ($D_E = \infty$), while Pe $= \infty$ corresponds to plug flow ($D_E = 0$). Large values of Pe result when mixing is not extensive and for large values of Z (large tower diameters).

Entrainment. A further correction is required for the damage done by entrainment. Entrainment represents a form of back mixing, which acts to destroy the concentration changes produced by the trays. It can be shown[11,18] that the Murphree efficiency corrected for entrainment is

$$\mathbf{E}_{MGE} = \frac{\mathbf{E}_{MG}}{1 + \mathbf{E}_{MG}[E/(1-E)]} \tag{6.30}$$

Data. Experimental information on N_{tG}, N_{tL}, and D_E is needed to use the relations developed above. Many data have been published, particularly for bubble-cap trays, and an excellent review is available.[48] Perhaps the best-organized information results from a research program sponsored by the American Institute of Chemical Engineers.[7] Most of the work was done with bubble-cap trays, but the relatively fewer data together with subsequent information from sieve trays[22] indicate that the empirical expressions below represent the performance of sieve trays reasonably well. No attempt will be made here to outline in detail the range of conditions covered by these expressions, which should be used with caution, especially if the original report is not consulted.

Sieve Trays

$$N_{tG} = \frac{0.776 + 0.116h_W - 0.290V_a\rho_G^{0.5} + 9.72q/Z}{Sc_G^{0.5}} \tag{6.31}$$

$$N_{tL} = 7.31(10^5)D_L^{0.5}(0.26V_a\rho_G^{0.5} + 0.15)\theta_L \tag{6.32}$$

$$D_E = \left(0.774 + 1.026V_a + 67.2\frac{q}{Z} + 0.900h_W\right)^2 \tag{6.33}$$

$$\theta_L = \frac{\text{cu ft liquid on tray}}{\text{liquid rate, cu ft/hr}} = \frac{(h_L/12)zZ}{3{,}600q} = \frac{2.31(10^{-5})h_L zZ}{q} \tag{6.34}$$

Illustration 6.2. Estimate the tray efficiency of the stripping tray of Illustration 6.1. *Solution.* From the results of Illustration 6.1, we have

Vapor rate = 700 lb moles/hr	Liquid rate = 2,100 lb moles/hr
$\rho_G = 0.0424$ lb/cu ft	$h_L = 0.55$ in.
$q = 0.1794$ cu ft/sec	$h_W = 2.0$ in.
$V_a = 11.81$ ft/sec	$Z = 2.50$ ft
$z = 2.975$ ft	$E = 0.042$

In addition, by the methods of Chap. 2, the following may be estimated: $Sc_G = 0.865$, $D_L = 2.3(10^{-4})$ sq ft/hr. The vapor-liquid equilibria yield $m = 6.2$ ("The Chemical Engineers' Handbook," 4th ed.,

p. 13-5).   Substitution of these directly in Eqs. (6.31) to (6.34) then yields

$$\theta_L = 52.7(10)^{-5} \text{ hr} \qquad N_{tG} = 0.955$$
$$N_{tL} = 3.79 \qquad\qquad D_E = 351 \text{ sq ft/hr}$$

Eq. (6.23):
$$\frac{1}{N_{tOG}} = \frac{1}{0.955} + \frac{6.2(700)}{2,100} \frac{1}{3.79}$$

$$N_{tOG} = 0.628$$

Eq. (6.22):
$$\mathbf{E}_{OG} = 1 - e^{-0.628} = 0.466$$

Eq. (6.29):
$$\text{Pe} = \frac{(2.50)^2}{351(52.7)(10^{-5})} = 33.7$$

Eq. (6.28):
$$\eta = 0.944$$

Eq. (6.27):
$$\frac{\mathbf{E}_{MG}}{\mathbf{E}_{OG}} = 1.55 \qquad \mathbf{E}_{MG} = 1.55(0.466) = 0.727$$

Eq. (6.30):
$$\mathbf{E}_{MGE} = 0.70 \quad \textbf{Ans.}$$

Overall tray efficiency. Another method of describing the performance of a tray tower is through the overall tray efficiency,

$$\mathbf{E}_O = \frac{\text{number of ideal trays required}}{\text{number of real trays required}} \tag{6.35}$$

While reliable information on such an efficiency is most desirable and convenient to use, it must be obvious that so many variables enter into such a measure that really reliable values of $\mathbf{E}_O$ for design purposes would be most difficult to come by.   As will be shown in Chap. 8, $\mathbf{E}_O$ may be derived from the individual tray efficiencies in certain simple situations.

Provided that only standard tray designs are used and operation is within the standard ranges of liquid and gas rates, some success in correlating $\mathbf{E}_O$ with conditions might be expected.   O'Connell[39] was successful in doing this for absorption and distillation in bubble-cap-tray towers, and his correlations are shown in Figs. 6.15 and 6.16.   These must be used with great caution, but for rough estimates they are most useful.

II. LIQUID DISPERSED

In this group are included those devices in which the liquid is dispersed into thin films or drops, such as wetted-wall towers, sprays and spray towers, the various packed towers, and the like.   The packed towers are the most important of the group.

Venturi scrubbers

In these devices, which are similar to ejectors, the gas is drawn into the throat of a venturi by a stream of absorbing liquid sprayed into the convergent duct section.

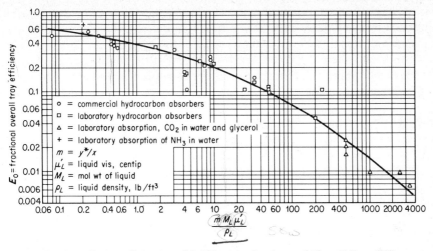

Fig. 6.15 *Overall tray efficiencies of bubble-tray absorbers. (After O'Connell.[39])*

The cocurrent flow produces a single stage,[23] although multistage countercurrent effects may be obtained by using several venturis.

Wetted-wall towers

A thin film of liquid running down the inside of a vertical pipe, with gas flowing either cocurrently or countercurrently, constitutes a wetted-wall tower.   Such devices have been used for theoretical studies of mass transfer, as described in Chap. 3, because the interfacial surface between the phases is readily kept under control and is measurable.

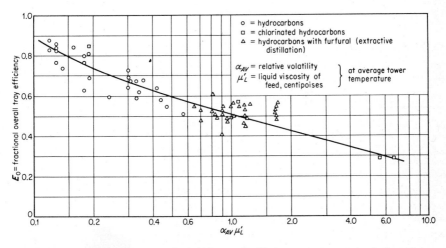

Fig. 6.16 *Overall tray efficiencies for bubble-tray distillation towers separating hydrocarbons and similar mixtures. (After O'Connell.[39])*

Industrially, they have been used as absorbers for hydrochloric acid, where absorption is accompanied by a very large evolution of heat. In this case the wetted-wall tower is surrounded with rapidly flowing cooling water. Multitube devices have also been used for distillation, where the liquid film is generated at the top by partial condensation of the rising vapor. Gas pressure drop in these towers is probably lower than in any other gas-liquid contacting device, for a given set of operating conditions.

Spray towers and spray chambers

The liquid may be sprayed into a gas stream by means of a nozzle which disperses the liquid into a fine spray of drops. The flow may be countercurrent, as in vertical towers with the liquid sprayed downward, or parallel, as in horizontal spray chambers (see Chap. 7). These devices have the advantage of low pressure drop for the gas but also have a number of disadvantages. There is a relatively high pumping cost for the liquid, owing to the pressure drop through the spray nozzle. The tendency for entrainment of liquid by the gas leaving is considerable, and mist eliminators will almost always be necessary. Unless the diameter/length ratio is very small, the gas will be fairly thoroughly mixed by the spray, and full advantage of countercurrent flow cannot be taken. The diameter/length ratio, however, cannot ordinarily be made very small since then the spray would quickly reach the walls of the tower and become ineffective as a spray.

Baffle towers and shower trays

In a tower of the design shown in Fig. 6.17, the gas flows upward through curtains of liquid falling from the edges of the baffles. The liquid dispersion is not so good as with sprays, but countercurrent contact is more readily maintained. The shower tray of Fig. 6.18, for which pressure drops as low as 0.015 psi (0.75 mm Hg) are possible,[27] is sometimes used in vacuum distillations.

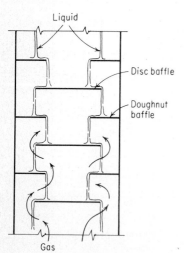

Fig. 6.17 *Section through disk-and-doughnut baffle column.*

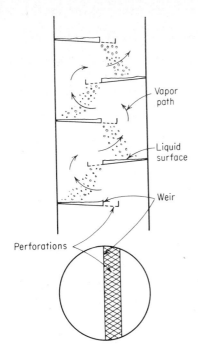

Fig. 6.18 *Shower tray.*

Packed towers

Packed towers, used for continuous countercurrent contact of liquid and gas, are vertical columns which have been filled with packing or devices of large surface, as in Fig. 6.19.   The liquid is distributed over, and trickles down through, the packed bed, thus exposing a large surface to contact the gas.

Packing. The tower packing, or *fill*, should offer the following characteristics:

1. Provide for large interfacial surface between liquid and gas.   The surface of the packing per unit volume of packed space a_p should be large but not in a microscopic sense.   Lumps of coke, for example, have a large surface owing to their porous structure, but most of this would be covered by the trickling film of liquid.   The specific packing surface a_p in any event is almost always larger than the interfacial liquid-gas surface.

2. Possess desirable fluid-flow characteristics.   This ordinarily means that the fractional void volume ϵ, or fraction of empty space, in the packed bed should be large.   The packing must permit passage of large volumes of fluid through small tower cross sections without loading or flooding (see below) and with low pressure drop for the gas.   Furthermore, gas pressure drop should be largely the result of skin friction if possible, since this is more effective than form drag in promoting high values of the mass-transfer coefficients (see Wetted-wall towers, page 151).

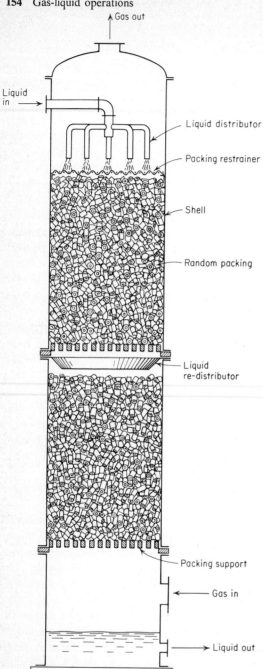

Gas out

Liquid in →

Liquid distributor

Packing restrainer

Shell

Random packing

Liquid re-distributor

Packing support

← Gas in

→ Liquid out

Fig. 6.19   *Packed tower.*

3. Be chemically inert to fluids being processed.
4. Have structural strength to permit easy handling and installation.
5. Represent low cost.

Packings are of two major types, random and regular.

Random packings. Random packings are those which are simply dumped into the tower during installation and allowed to fall at random. In the past such readily available materials as broken stone, gravel, or lumps of coke were used, but although inexpensive, these are not desirable for reasons of small surface and poor fluid-flow characteristics. Random packings most frequently used at present are manufactured, and the common types are shown in Fig. 6.20. Raschig rings are hollow cylinders, as shown, of diameters ranging from ¼ to 4 in. or more. They may be made of chemical stoneware or porcelain, which are useful in contact with most liquids except alkalies and hydrofluoric acid; of carbon, which is useful except in strongly oxidizing atmospheres; of metals; or of plastics. Thin-walled metal rings offer the advantage of lightness in weight. Lessing rings and others with internal partitions are less frequently used. The saddle-shaped packings, Berl and Intalox saddles, are available in sizes from ½ to 3 in., ordinarily made of chemical stoneware although they may be made of any material which can be stamped into shape. Generally the random packings offer larger specific surface (and larger gas pressure drop) in the smaller sizes, but they cost less per cubic foot in the larger sizes. For industrial work the 1- to 2-in. sizes are most popular. During installation the packings are poured into

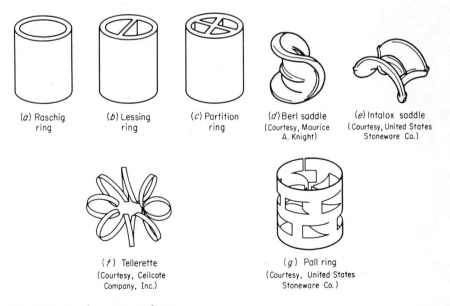

(*a*) Raschig
ring

(*b*) Lessing
ring

(*c*) Partition
ring

(*d*) Berl saddle
(Courtesy, Maurice
A. Knight)

(*e*) Intalox saddle
(Courtesy, United States
Stoneware Co.)

(*f*) Tellerette
(Courtesy, Ceilcote
Company, Inc.)

(*g*) Pall ring
(Courtesy, United States
Stoneware Co.)

Fig. 6.20   *Random tower packings.*

the tower to fall at random, and in order to prevent breakage of the more fragile packings, the tower may be first filled with water to reduce the velocity of fall.

Regular packings. These may be of the type shown in Fig. 6.21, or they may be those devices known generally as *counterflow trays*, which will be mentioned later. The regular packings offer the advantages of lower pressure drop and greater possible throughput of fluids, usually at the expense at least of more costly installation than random packings. The larger sizes of Raschig rings (3 in. or larger) may be carefully stacked, as in Fig. 6.21*a*. Rings are also available with internal spirals, as in Fig. 6.21*b*, and these may be stacked one upon the other to provide continuous passages for the gas. The packing of Fig. 6.21*c*, Spraypak and Panapak, is made of sheets of several layers of expanded metal lath which have been formed into wave-shaped surfaces.[43] Wood grids (Fig. 6.21*d*) or hurdles are inexpensive, and both the arrangement shown and many variants are used in filling water-cooling towers. Drip-point ceramic grid tiles are large and easily stacked; they provide very effective contact at low gas pressure drop.

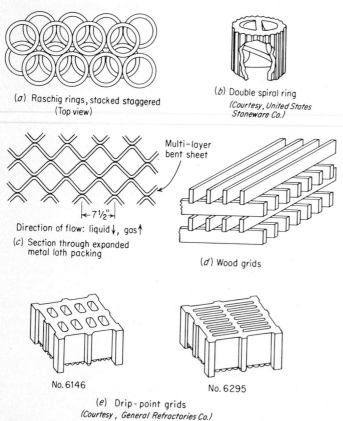

(*a*) Raschig rings, stacked staggered
(Top view)

(*b*) Double spiral ring
(Courtesy, United States
Stoneware Co.)

Multi-layer
bent sheet

|←— 7½" —→|

Direction of flow: liquid↓, gas↑
(*c*) Section through expanded
metal lath packing

(*d*) Wood grids

No. 6146

No. 6295

(*e*) Drip-point grids
(Courtesy, General Refractories Co.)

Fig. 6.21 *Regular, or stacked, packings.*

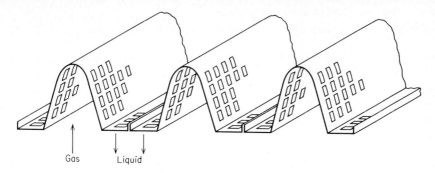

Gas   Liquid

Fig. 6.22 *Multibeam support plate. (The United States Stoneware Company.)*

The packings shown in Figs. 6.20 and 6.21 are by no means the only ones used, but they are probably the most popular.   Many others offer particular advantages, e.g., low pressure drop or very effective gas-liquid contact.   Among these are packings made of Fiberglas[52] and Dowpac[1] for large towers.   For laboratory or pilot-plant installations, there are McMahon packing,[35] a sort of Berl saddle made of wire gauze; Cannon packing,[8] a semiring of punched metal; and Heli-Pak and Heli-Grid of wound-wire construction.[40]

Tower shells. These may be of wood, metal, chemical stoneware, acidproof brick, glass, plastic, plastic- or glass-lined metal, or other material depending upon the corrosion conditions.   For ease of construction, they are usually circular in cross section.

Packing supports. An open space at the bottom of the tower is necessary for ensuring good distribution of the gas into the packing.   Consequently the packing must be supported above the open space.   The support must, of course, be sufficiently strong to carry the weight of a reasonable height of packing, and it must have ample free area to allow for flow of liquid and gas with a minimum of restriction.   A bar grid, of the sort shown in Fig. 6.19, may be used, but specially designed supports which provide separate passageways for gas and liquid are preferred.   Figure 6.22 shows one variety whose free area for flow is of the order of 85 percent, which may be made in various modifications and of many different materials including metals, ceramics, and plastics.

Liquid distribution. The importance of adequate initial distribution of the liquid at the top of the packing is indicated in Fig. 6.23.   Dry packing is of course completely ineffective for mass transfer, and various devices are used for liquid distribution.   Spray nozzles generally result in too much entrainment of liquid in the gas to be useful.   The arrangement shown in Fig. 6.19 or a ring of perforated pipe may be used

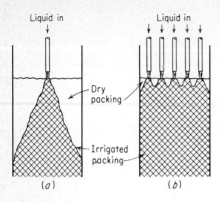

Fig. 6.23 *Liquid distribution and packing irrigation.*
(a) Inadequate; (b) adequate.

in small towers. For large diameters, a distributor of the type shown in Fig. 6.24 may be used. It is generally considered necessary to provide at least five points of introduction of liquid for each square foot of tower cross section for large towers ($d \geqslant 4$ ft) and a greater number for smaller diameters.

Random packing size and liquid redistribution. In the case of random packings, the packing density, i.e., the number of packing pieces per cubic foot, is ordinarily less in the immediate vicinity of the tower walls, and this leads to a tendency of the liquid to segregate toward the walls and the gas to flow in the center of the tower (channeling). This tendency is much less pronounced provided the diameter of the individual packing pieces is smaller than at least one-eighth the tower diameter, but it is recommended that, if possible, the ratio d_p/d not exceed 1:15.[12] Even so it is customary to provide for redistribution of the liquid at intervals varying from three

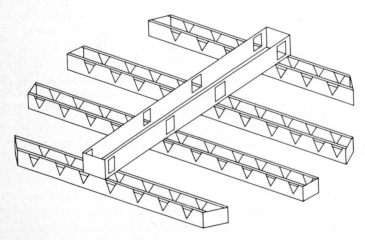

Fig. 6.24 *Weir-trough liquid distributor.* (*The United States Stoneware Company.*)

to ten times the tower diameter, but at least every 20 ft. With proper attention to liquid distribution, packed towers are successfully built to diameters of 20 ft or more.

Packing restrainers. These are necessary when gas velocities are high, and they are generally desirable to guard against lifting of packing during a sudden gas surge. Heavy screens or bars may be used.

Entrainment eliminators. Especially at high gas velocities, the gas leaving the top of the packing may carry off droplets of liquid as a mist. This may be removed by mist eliminators, through which the gas must pass, installed above the liquid inlet. A layer of wire mesh several inches thick[9,53] or 2 or 3 ft of dry random packing are very effective.

Flow of fluids through packing. For most random packings, the pressure drop suffered by the gas is influenced by the gas and liquid flow rates in a manner similar to that shown in Fig. 6.25. The slope of the line for dry packing is usually in the range 1.8 to 2.0, indicating turbulent flow for most practical gas velocities.

At a fixed gas velocity, the gas pressure drop increases with increased liquid rate, owing principally to the reduced free cross section available for flow of gas resulting from the presence of the liquid. In the region of Fig. 6.25 below A, the liquid holdup, i.e., the quantity of liquid contained in the packed bed, is reasonably constant with changing gas velocity, although it increases with liquid rate. In the region between A and B, the liquid holdup increases rapidly with gas rate, the free area for gas flow becomes smaller, and the pressure drop rises more rapidly. This is known as *loading*. As the gas rate is increased to B at fixed liquid rate, one of a number of changes occurs: (1) a layer of liquid, through which the gas bubbles, may appear at the top of the packing; (2) liquid may fill the tower, starting at the bottom or at any intermediate restriction such as a packing support, so that there is a change from gas–continuous liquid–dispersed to liquid–continuous gas–dispersed (inversion);

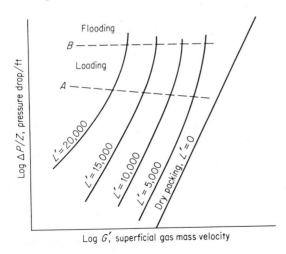

Fig. 6.25 *Typical gas pressure drop for counterflow of liquid and gas in random packings.*

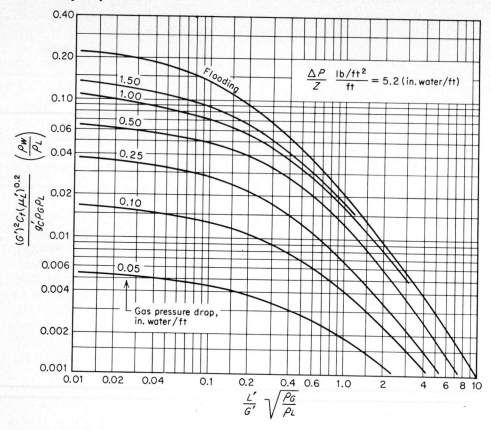

Fig. 6.26 *Flooding and pressure drop in packed towers.* (*The United States Stoneware Company.*)

or (3) slugs of foam may rise rapidly upward through the packing.   At the same time, entrainment of liquid by the effluent gas increases rapidly, and the tower is *flooded*. The gas pressure drop then increases very rapidly.   The change in conditions in the region *A* to *B* of Fig. 6.25 is gradual, and initial loading and flooding are frequently determined by the change in slope of the pressure-drop curves rather than through any visible effect.   It is not practical to operate a tower in a flooded condition; most towers operate just below, or in the lower part of, the loading region.

Flooding and loading. Flooding velocities in random packings are well correlated by the upper curve of Fig. 6.26.[12,51]†   The lower limit of loading will occur at a gas

† The generalized correlation of flooding in this basic form was first made by Sherwood et al.,[45] who used a_p/ε^3 calculated from the packing geometry as the method of characterizing the packings. Later it was found that this quantity varied greatly, depending upon the method of packing (wet or dry) and with settling of the packing,[31] and finally it was found best to use an empirical characterization C_f chosen to fit the data.[12]   The original correlation did not include ρ_W/ρ_L.   This was added as $(\rho_W/\rho_L)^2$ to handle the pressure-drop data,[29] but subsequently it was found better[12] to reduce the exponent on this group to 1.

pressure drop of about 0.5 in. water/ft of packed depth, and flooding at about 2 to 3 in. water/ft. Values of C_f, which characterize the packing, are given in Table 6.2. They depend strongly on the method of installing the packing. Flooding velocities for regular or stacked packings will generally be considerably greater than for random packing.

Pressure drop for single-phase flow. The pressure drop suffered by a single fluid in flowing through a bed of packed solids, when it alone fills the voids in the bed, is reasonably well correlated by the Ergun equation[15]

$$\frac{\Delta P}{Z} \frac{g_c \epsilon^3}{(1-\epsilon)G'^2} \frac{d_p \rho_G}{} = \frac{\Delta P}{Z} \frac{6g_c \rho_G}{C_f'G'^2} = \frac{150(1-\epsilon)}{\text{Re}} + 1.75 \qquad (6.36)$$

Here the terms on the right are friction factors, the first for purely laminar flow, the second for completely turbulent flow. There is a gradual transition from one type of flow to the other, the two terms changing their relative importance as the flow rate increases. $\text{Re} = d_p G'/\mu_G$, and d_p is the effective diameter of the particle, the diameter of a sphere of the same surface/volume ratio as the packing in place. If the packing surface is a_p sq ft/cu ft of packed bed, the surface per unit volume of the particles is $a_p/(1-\epsilon)$, and from the properties of a sphere,

$$d_p = \frac{6(1-\epsilon)}{a_p} \qquad (6.37)$$

This will not normally be the same as the nominal size of the particles. For the hollow manufactured packings of Table 6.2, operating at gas rates above 500 lb/(hr)(sq ft), the right-hand side of Eq. (6.36) may be taken simply as 1.75. Reasonably good results are then obtained by using values of C_f' about twice those for C_f in Table 6.2.

Pressure drop for two-phase flow. For simultaneous countercurrent flow of liquid and gas, the pressure-drop data of various investigators show wide discrepancies, sometimes as much as 60 percent for the same type of packing and rates of flow, presumably owing to differences in packing density. Estimates cannot therefore be expected to be very accurate. For most purposes, the generalized correlation of Leva[29] shown as modified in Fig. 6.26 will serve. Here the value of C_f in Table 6.2 should be used directly. More elaborate data for particular packings are available from the manufacturers.

Illustration 6.3. Sulfur dioxide is to be removed from gas of the characteristics of air by scrubbing with an aqueous ammonium salt solution in a tower packed with 1-in. ceramic Raschig rings. The gas, entering at the rate of 100,000 cu ft/hr (80°F, 1 atm), contains 7.0% SO_2, which is to be nearly completely removed. The washing solution will enter at the rate of 30,000 lb/hr and has a density 77 lb/cu ft, viscosity 2.5 centipoises.

　　a. Choose a suitable tower diameter.

　　b. If the irrigated packed height is 25 ft, and if 3 ft of 1-in. Raschig rings is used above the liquid inlet as an entrainment separator, estimate the power requirement to overcome the gas pressure drop. The overall efficiency of fan and motor is 60%.

Table 6.2. Characteristics of random packings†

Packing	Nominal size, in.										
	¼	⅜	½	⅝	¾	1	1¼	1½	2	3	3½
Raschig rings:											
Ceramic:‡											
C_f	1,000	750	640	380	255	160	125	95	65	37	
ϵ	0.73	0.68	0.63	0.68	0.73	0.73	0.74	0.71	0.74	0.78	
a_p	240	155	111	100	80	58	45	38	28	19	
Metal:											
¹⁄₃₂-in. wall:											
C_f	700		300	258	185	115					
ϵ	0.69		0.84		0.88	0.92					
a_p	236		128		83.5	62.7					
¹⁄₁₆-in. wall:											
C_f			340	290	230	145	110	82	57	37	
ϵ			0.73		0.78	0.85	0.87	0.90	0.92	0.95	
a_p			118		71.8	56.7	49.3	41.2	31.4	20.6	
Pall rings:											
Plastic:											
C_f			97			52		32	25		16
ϵ			0.88			0.90		0.905	0.91		
a_p			110			63.0		39	31		23.4
Metal:											
C_f			71			48		28	20		
ϵ			0.902			0.938		0.953	0.964		
a_p			131.2			66.3		48.1	36.6		
Intalox saddles, ceramic											
C_f	600		265		130	98		52	40		
ϵ	0.75		0.78		0.77	0.775		0.81	0.79		
a_p	300		190		102	78		59.5	36		
Berl saddles, ceramic:											
C_f	900		380		170	110		65	45		
ϵ	0.60		0.63		0.66	0.69		0.75	0.72		
a_p	274		142		82	76		44	32		

Tellerettes,§ ¾ × 2 in., plastic:
High density:
$C_f = 57$
$\epsilon = 0.87$
Low density:
$C_f = 65$
$\epsilon = 0.83$

† Table from the United States Stoneware Company.   Data are for wet dumped packing in 16- and 30-in. ID towers.

‡ Nominal size and wall thickness, in inches, for ceramic Raschig rings are, respectively, ¼, ¹⁄₃₂; ⅜, ¹⁄₁₆; ½ to ¾, ³⁄₃₂; 1, ⅛; 1¼ and 1½, ³⁄₁₆; 2, ¼; 3, ⅜.

§ Teller and Ford: *Ind. Eng. Chem.*, **50**, 1201 (1958).

Solution. a. Since the larger flow quantities are at the bottom for an absorber, the diameter will be chosen for the bottom conditions.

$$\text{Av mol wt gas in} = 0.07(64) + 0.93(29) = 31.4 \text{ lb/lb mole}$$

$$\text{Gas in} = 100,000(^{492}\!/_{520})(^1\!/_{359}) = 254 \text{ lb moles/hr or } 254(31.4) = 7,980 \text{ lb/hr}$$

$$\rho_G = \frac{7,980}{100,000} = 0.0798 \text{ lb/cu ft}$$

Assuming essentially complete absorption, SO_2 removed $= 254(0.07)(64) = 1,139$ lb/hr.

$$\text{Liquid leaving} = 30,000 + 1,139 = 31,140 \text{ lb/hr}$$

$$\frac{L'}{G'}\left(\frac{\rho_G}{\rho_L}\right)^{0.5} = \frac{31,140}{7,980}\left(\frac{0.0798}{77}\right)^{0.5} = 0.126$$

At flooding the ordinate of Fig. 6.26 is 0.13. For 1-in. ceramic Raschig rings, $C_f = 160$ (Table 6.2). Therefore,

$$G' \text{ at flooding} = \left(\frac{0.13 g'_c \rho_G \rho_L}{C_f \mu_L'^{0.2}}\frac{\rho_L}{\rho_W}\right)^{0.5}$$

$$= \left[\frac{0.13(4.18)(10^8)(0.0798)(77)^2}{160(2.5)^{0.2}(62.3)}\right]^{0.5}$$

$$= 1,470 \text{ lb/(hr)(sq ft)}$$

For 60% of the flooding rate, $G' = 0.60(1,470) = 882$ lb/(hr)(sq ft). The tower cross section is therefore $7,980/882 = 9.05$ sq ft.

$d = [4(9.05)/\pi]^{0.5} = 3.37$ ft, or say $d = 3.5$ ft diam. **Ans.**

b. For 3.5-ft diameter, the cross section $= 9.60$ sq ft.

$$G' = \frac{7,980}{9.6} = 830 \text{ lb/(hr)(sq ft)}$$

$$\frac{G'^2 C_f \mu_L'^{0.2}}{g'_c \rho_G \rho_L}\frac{\rho_W}{\rho_L} = \frac{(830)^2(160)(2.5)^{0.2}(62.3)}{4.18(10^8)(0.0798)(77)^2} = 0.0418$$

With this ordinate and 0.126 as abscissa, the pressure drop for the irrigated packing is estimated from Fig. 6.26 as 0.4 in. water/ft or $0.4(5.2)(25) = 52$ lb/sq ft for the 25 ft of packing.

For the dry packing, the gas flow rate is $(7,980 - 1,139)/9.60 = 713$ lb/(hr)(sq ft), at a pressure $14.7 - ^{52}\!/_{144} = 14.3$ psi. The gas density is

$$\rho_G = \frac{29}{359}\frac{492}{540}\frac{14.3}{14.7} = 0.0682 \text{ lb/cu ft}$$

Using Eq. (6.36) with the right-hand side simplified to 1.75 since $G' > 500$ and with $C_f' = 2C_f = 320$, we have

$$\frac{\Delta P}{Z}\frac{6(4.18)(10^8)(0.0682)}{320(713)^2} = 1.75$$

$$\frac{\Delta P}{Z} = 1.66 \text{ lb/(sq ft)(ft)}$$

For a 3-ft packed depth, $\Delta P = 1.66(3) = 5.0$ lb/sq ft.

The total pressure drop for the packing is therefore $52 + 5 = 57$ lb/sq ft. To estimate fan power, to this must be added the pressure drop for the packing supports and liquid distributor and inlet expansion and outlet contraction losses for the gas. For a well-designed packing support (85% free area) and liquid distributor, the pressure drop should be negligible. For a gas velocity in the inlet and outlet pipes of 25 ft/sec, the expansion and contraction losses would amount to, at most, 1.5 velocity heads, or $1.5(25)^2/2(32.2) = 14.6$ ft-lb/lb or $14.6(0.0682) = 1.0$ lb/sq ft.

The fan power output for the tower is therefore estimated to be

$$\frac{(57 + 1)(7,980)}{0.0682(3,600)} = 1,885 \text{ ft-lb/sec}$$

The power for the fan motor is then $1,885/(550)(0.6) = 5.7$ hp.   **Ans.**

Mass-transfer coefficients for packed towers

When a packed tower is operated in the usual manner as a countercurrent absorber or stripper for transfer of solute between the gas and liquid, the rate of solute transfer may be computed from measured values of the rate of gas and liquid flow and the bulk concentrations of solute in the entering and leaving streams. As explained in Chap. 5, because of the impossibility of measuring solute concentrations at the gas-liquid interface, the resulting rates of mass transfer can be expressed only as overall coefficients, rather than as coefficients for the individual fluids. Further, since the interfacial area between gas and liquid is not directly measured in such experiments, the *flux* of mass transfer cannot be determined, but instead only the rate as the product of the flux and the total interfacial area. By dividing these rates by the volume of the packing, the results appear as "volumetric overall coefficients," $K_x a$, $K_y a$, $K_G a$, $F_{OG} a$, $F_{OL} a$, etc., where a is the interfacial surface per cubic foot of packed volume.

The individual fluid mass-transfer coefficients (k_x, k_y, F_L, F_G) and the interfacial area a which make up these overall volumetric coefficients are differently dependent upon fluid properties, flow rates, and type of packing. The overall volumetric coefficients are therefore useful only in the design of towers filled with the same packing and handling the same chemical system at the same flow rates and concentrations as existed during the measurements. For general design purposes, the individual coefficients and the interfacial area are necessary.

To obtain individual coefficients, the general approach has been to choose experimental conditions such that the resistance to mass transfer in the gas phase is negligible in comparison with that in the liquid. This is the case for the absorption or desorption of very insoluble gases, e.g., oxygen or hydrogen in water [see Eq. (5.14)].[44] Measurements in such systems then lead to values of $k_x a$, $k_L a$, and $F_L a$, which can be correlated in terms of system variables. There are evidently no systems involving absorption or desorption where the solute is so soluble in the liquid that the liquid-phase resistance is entirely negligible. But by subtracting the known liquid resistance from the overall resistances (see Chap. 5), it is possible to arrive at the gas-phase coefficients $k_y a$, $k_G a$, and $F_G a$, and to correlate these in terms of system variables.

Another approach to obtaining pure gas-phase coefficients is to make measurements when a pure liquid evaporates into a gas. Here there is no liquid resistance since there is no concentration gradient within the liquid. The resulting volumetric coefficients $k_y a$ and $F_G a$, however, do not agree with those obtained in the manner first described above.   The reason is the different effective interfacial areas, as explained below.

Liquid holdup. Holdup refers to the liquid retained in the tower as films wetting the packing and as pools caught in the crevices between packing particles.   It is found that the total holdup ϕ_t is made up of two parts,

$$\phi_t = \phi_o + \phi_s \tag{6.38}$$

where ϕ_s is the "static" and ϕ_o the operating, or moving, holdup, each expressed as cu ft liquid/cu ft packed volume.   The moving holdup consists of liquid which continually moves through the packing, continually replaced regularly and rapidly by new liquid flowing from above.   On stopping the gas and liquid flow, the moving holdup drains from the packing.   The static holdup is liquid retained as pools in protected interstices in the packing, largely stagnant, and only slowly replaced by fresh liquid.   On stopping the flows, the static holdup does not drain.

When absorption or desorption of a solute occurs, involving transfer of a solute between the bulk liquid and gas, the liquid of the static holdup rapidly comes to equilibrium with the adjacent gas, and thereafter its interfacial surface contributes nothing to mass transfer except as it is slowly replaced.   For absorption and desorption, therefore, the smaller area offered by the moving holdup is effective.   When evaporation or condensation occurs with the liquid phase a single, pure component, however, the area offered by the total holdup is effective since the liquid then offers no resistance to mass transfer.

Mass transfer. Shulman[46] and his coworkers, in an extensive work, have established the nature of the gas-phase mass-transfer coefficients characteristic of Raschig rings and Berl saddles by passing gases through beds packed with packings made with naphthalene, which sublimes into the gas.   By comparing these with $k_G a$'s from aqueous absorption[20] and other systems, the interfacial areas for absorption and vaporization were obtained.   The data on $k_L a$'s[44] then provided the correlation for k_L, the liquid-phase coefficient.   Their work is summarized as follows.

For Raschig rings and Berl saddles, the gas-phase coefficient is given by[†]

$$\frac{F_G \, \mathrm{Sc}_G^{\,2/3}}{G} = \frac{k_G p_{BM} \, \mathrm{Sc}_G^{\,2/3}}{G} = 1.195 \left[\frac{d_s G'}{\mu_G''(1 - \epsilon_o)} \right]^{-0.36} \tag{6.39}$$

where ϵ_o, the operating void space in the packing, is given by

$$\epsilon_o = \epsilon - \phi_t \tag{6.40}$$

and d_s is the diameter of a sphere of the same surface as a single packing particle (not the same as d_p).   The fluid properties should be evaluated at the average conditions

---

† The j form of Eq. (6.39), with the $2/3$ exponent on Sc_G, correlates the data well, although it has been pointed out that, in principle at least, the nature of the function should probably change with degree of turbulence.[49]

between interface and bulk gas. The liquid coefficient is given by

$$\frac{k_L d_s}{D_L} = 25.1 \left(\frac{d_s L'}{\mu_L''}\right)^{0.45} Sc_L^{0.5} \tag{6.41}$$

Since the liquid data were obtained at very low solute concentrations, k_L may be converted to F_L through $F_L = k_L c$, where c is the molar density of the solvent liquid.

Table 6.3. Interfacial areas for absorption, desorption, aqueous liquids†

For gases of density approximating 0.075 lb/cu ft, and below loading, $a_{AW} = mG'^n L'^p$. For other gases, substitute $G'(0.075/\rho_G)^{0.5}$ for G'. (Note: The original data cover L' up to 4,500 lb/(hr)(sq ft). Extrapolation to $L' = 7,500$ has been suggested.[46])

Packing	Size, in.	Range of L', lb/(hr)(sq ft)	m	n	p
Raschig rings	0.5	500–1,500	8,200	$3.15(10^{-4})L' - 0.30$	-1.04
		1,500–4,500	9.32	$0.151(10^{-4})L' + 0.148$	-0.111
	1	500–1,500	0.274	0	0.552
		1,500–4,500	463	$0.528(10^{-4})L' - 0.0793$	-0.47
	1.5	500–1,500	1.82	$0.675(10^{-4})L' - 0.1013$	0.274
		1,500–4,500	4.85	$0.148(10^{-4})L' - 0.022$	0.140
	2	500–1,500	0.401	0	0.481
		1,500–4,500	0.95	0	0.362
Berl saddles	0.5	500–1,500	0.0336	0.0529	0.761
		1,500–4,500	2.54	0.0529	0.170
	1‡	500–1,500	15.89	$0.686(10^{-4})L' - 0.1029$	0
		1,500–4,500	238	$0.420(10^{-4})L' - 0.0630$	-0.359
	1.5‡	500–1,500	0.613	-0.0508	0.455
		1,500–4,500	46.5	$0.325(10^{-4})L' - 0.0996$	-0.1355

† Data of Shulman et al.[46]

‡ For $G' < 800$ lb/(hr)(sq ft) only. For higher values, see Shulman, *AIChE J.*, **1**, 253 (1955), Figs. 16 and 17.

The interfacial areas for absorption and desorption with water (or very dilute aqueous solutions) a_{AW} are given for conditions below loading by Shulman in an extensive series of graphs. These are well represented by the empirical expressions of Table 6.3. For absorption or desorption with nonaqueous liquids, the area is a_A, given by

$$a_A = a_{AW} \frac{\phi_o}{\phi_{oW}} \tag{6.42}$$

and for contact of a gas with a pure liquid, as in vaporization, the areas are

$$a_V = 0.85 a_A \frac{\phi_t}{\phi_o} \tag{6.43a}$$

$$a_{VW} = 0.85 a_{AW} \frac{\phi_{tW}}{\phi_{oW}} \tag{6.43b}$$

The subscript W indicates water as the liquid. The holdup data are summarized in Table 6.4. Although these data are based on work with absorption, desorption, and vaporization, the evidence is that the same coefficients apply to distillation in packed towers.[37] In distillation, a_A's should be used.

Many other volumetric mass-transfer-coefficient data are available, often covering wider ranges of flow rates and for packings other than those given here. Excellent summaries of these are available.[14,48]

Illustration 6.4. A tower packed with 1.5-in. Berl saddles is to used for absorbing benzene vapor from a dilute mixture with an inert gas. The circumstances are:

Gas: Av mol wt = 11, viscosity = 0.01 centipoise, 80°F, 800 mm Hg, $D_G = 0.504$ sq ft/hr, flow rate = $G' = 528$ lb/(hr)(sq ft).

Liquid: Av mol wt = 260, viscosity = 2.0 centipoises, sp gr = 0.84 g/cu cm, surface tension = 30 dynes/cm, $D_L = 1.85(10^{-5})$ sq ft/hr, flow rate = 2,000 lb/(hr)(sq ft).

Compute the volumetric mass-transfer coefficients.

Solution. For the gas,

$$\mu_G'' = 0.01(2.42) = 0.0242 \text{ lb/(ft)(hr)}$$

$$\rho_G = \frac{11}{359} \frac{800}{760} \frac{492}{460 + 80} = 0.0294 \text{ lb/cu ft}$$

$$Sc_G = \frac{\mu_G''}{\rho_G D_G} = \frac{0.0262}{0.0294(0.504)} = 1.63$$

$$G' = 528 \text{ lb/(hr)(sq ft)} \qquad G = {}^{528}\!/_{11} = 48.0 \text{ lb moles/(hr)(sq ft)}$$

For the liquid,

$$L' = 2,000 \text{ lb/(hr)(sq ft)}$$

$$\rho_L = 62.3(0.84) = 52.4 \text{ lb/cu ft} \qquad \mu_L' = 2.0 \text{ centipoises}$$

$$Sc_L = \frac{\mu_L''}{\rho_L D_L} = \frac{2(2.42)}{52.4(1.85)(10^{-5})} = 5,000$$

$$\sigma' = 30 \text{ dynes/cm}$$

Holdup. Table 6.4:

$$d_s = 0.155 \text{ ft}$$

$$\beta = 0.965 d_s^{0.376} = 0.477$$

$$\phi_{tW} = \frac{2.55(10^{-5}) L'^{0.477}}{d_s^2} = 0.0394 \text{ cu ft/cu ft}$$

$$\phi_{sW} = \frac{0.00032}{d_s^{1.56}} = 0.000428 \text{ cu ft/cu ft}$$

$$\phi_{oW} = \phi_{tW} - \phi_{sW} = 0.0394 - 0.00043 = 0.0390$$

$$H = \frac{1.291 L'^{0.57} \mu_L'^{0.13}}{\rho_L^{0.84}(0.212 L'^{0.413} - 1)} \left(\frac{\sigma'}{73}\right)^{1.033 - 0.262 \log L'} = 1.375$$

$$\phi_o = \phi_{oW} H = 0.0390(1.375) = 0.0536 \text{ cu ft/cu ft}$$

$$\phi_s = \frac{1.641(10^{-4}) \mu_L'^{0.04} \sigma'^{0.55}}{d_s^{1.56} \rho_L^{0.37}} = 0.00034 \text{ cu ft/cu ft}$$

$$\phi_t = \phi_o + \phi_s = 0.0536 + 0.00034 = 0.0539 \text{ cu ft/cu ft}$$

Table 6.4. Liquid holdup in packed towers†

$\phi_t = \phi_o + \phi_s \qquad \phi_{tW} = \phi_{oW} + \phi_{sW} \qquad \phi_o = \phi_{oW}H$

Packing	Nominal size, in.	d_s, ft	ϕ_s	Water (ordinary temperatures)	μ'_L, centipoise	H
Ceramic Raschig rings	0.5 1 1.5 2	0.0582 0.1167 0.1740 0.238	$\dfrac{6.85(10^{-5})\mu_L'^{0.02}\sigma'^{0.99}}{d_s^{1.21}\rho_L^{0.37}}$	$\phi_{tW}=\dfrac{2.25(10^{-5})L'^{\beta}}{d_s^2}$ $\phi_{sW}=\dfrac{0.00104}{d_s^{1.21}}$ $\beta=0.965d_s^{0.376}$	<12 >12	$\dfrac{0.897L'^{0.57}\mu_L'^{0.13}}{\rho_L^{0.84}(0.1183L'^{0.430}-1)}\left(\dfrac{\sigma'}{73}\right)^{0.925-0.262\log L'}$ $\dfrac{0.575L'^{0.57}\mu_L'^{0.31}}{\rho_L^{0.84}(0.1183L'^{0.430}-1)}\left(\dfrac{\sigma'}{73}\right)^{0.925-0.262\log L'}$
Carbon Raschig rings	1 1.5 2	0.0427 0.178 0.235	$\dfrac{6.36(10^{-8})\mu_L'^{0.02}\sigma'^{0.23}}{d_s^{1.21}\rho_L^{0.37}}$	$\phi_{tW}=\dfrac{7.90(10^{-5})L'^{\beta}}{d_s^2}$ $\phi_{sW}=\dfrac{0.00250}{d_s^{1.21}}$ $\beta=0.706d_s^{0.376}$	<12 >12	$\dfrac{0.375L'^{0.57}\mu_L'^{0.13}}{\rho_L^{0.84}(0.174L'^{0.315}-1)}\left(\dfrac{\sigma'}{73}\right)^{0.925-0.262\log L'}$ $\dfrac{0.239L'^{0.57}\mu_L'^{0.31}}{\rho_L^{0.84}(0.174L'^{0.315}-1)}\left(\dfrac{\sigma'}{73}\right)^{0.925-0.262\log L'}$
Ceramic Berl saddles	0.5 1 1.5	0.0532 0.1050 0.155	$\dfrac{1.641(10^{-4})\mu_L'^{0.04}\sigma'^{0.55}}{d_s^{1.56}\rho_L^{0.37}}$	$\phi_{tW}=\dfrac{2.50(10^{-5})L'^{\beta}}{d_s^2}$ $\phi_{sW}=\dfrac{0.00032}{d_s^{1.56}}$ $\beta=0.965d_s^{0.376}$	<20 >20	$\dfrac{1.291L'^{0.57}\mu_L'^{0.13}}{\rho_L^{0.84}(0.212L'^{0.413}-1)}\left(\dfrac{\sigma'}{73}\right)^{1.033-0.262\log L'}$ $\dfrac{0.752L'^{0.57}\mu_L'^{0.31}}{\rho_L^{0.84}(0.212L'^{0.413}-1)}\left(\dfrac{\sigma'}{73}\right)^{1.033-0.262\log L'}$

† Data of Shulman et al.[46]

Interfacial area. Use

$$G' = 528\left(\frac{0.075}{0.0294}\right)^{0.5} = 843$$

$$m = 46.5 \qquad n = 0.325(10^{-4})L' - 0.0996 = -0.0346$$

$$p = -0.1355 \qquad a_{AW} = mG'^n L'^p = 13.13 \text{ sq ft/cu ft}$$

Eq. (6.42):

$$a_A = a_{AW}\frac{\phi_o}{\phi_{oW}} = 13.13\frac{0.0536}{0.0390} = 18.1 \text{ sq ft/cu ft}$$

Table 6.2:

$$\epsilon = 0.75$$

Eq. (6.40):

$$\epsilon_o = \epsilon - \phi_t = 0.75 - 0.0539 = 0.696$$

Eq. (6.39):

$$\frac{F_G(1.63)^{2/3}}{48} = 1.195\left[\frac{0.155(528)}{0.0242(1 - 0.696)}\right]^{-0.36}$$

$$F_G = 1.443 \text{ lb moles/(hr)(sq ft)} = k_G p_{BM}$$

Eq. (6.41):

$$\frac{k_L(0.155)}{1.85(10^{-5})} = 25.1\left[\frac{0.155(2,000)}{2(2.42)}\right]^{0.45}(5,000)^{0.5}$$

$$k_L = 1.375 \text{ lb moles/(hr)(sq ft)(lb mole/cu ft)}$$

Since the data for k_L were taken at very low concentrations, this may be converted to $F_L = k_L c$ where here $c = 0.84(62.3)/260 = 0.201$ lb mole/cu ft molar density. Therefore $F_L = 1.375(0.201) = 0.276$ lb mole/(hr)(sq ft) $= k_L x_{BM} c$.

The volumetric coefficients are

$$F_G a_A = 1.443(18.1) = 26.1 \text{ lb moles/(hr)(cu ft)} = k_G a_A p_{BM}$$

$$F_L a_A = 0.276(18.1) = 5.00 \text{ lb moles/(hr)(cu ft)} = k_L a_A x_{BM} c$$

Illustration 6.5. A tower packed with 2-in. ceramic Raschig rings is to be used for dehumidification of air by countercurrent contact with water. At the top of the tower, the conditions are to be: water flow rate = 4,000 lb/(hr)(sq ft), temp = 60°F; air flow rate = 800 lb/(hr)(sq ft), at 70°F, 1 atm, essentially dry. Compute the transfer coefficients for the top of the tower.

Solution. For the gas, $G' = 800$ lb/(hr)(sq ft), $G = 800/_{29} = 27.6$ lb moles/(hr)(sq ft). $\mu'_G = 0.018$ centipoise, $Sc_G = 0.6$ for air–water vapor, and

$$\rho_G = \frac{29}{359}\left(\frac{492}{530}\right) = 0.0750 \text{ lb/cu ft}$$

For the liquid, $L' = 4,000$ lb/(hr)(sq ft).

Table 6.4:

$$d_s = 0.238 \text{ ft}$$

$$\beta = 0.965 d_s^{0.376} = 0.541$$

$$\phi_{tW} = \frac{2.25(10^{-5})L'^\beta}{d_s^2} = 0.0353 \text{ cu ft/cu ft}$$

$$\phi_{sW} = \frac{0.00104}{d_s^{1.21}} = 0.0059 \text{ cu ft/cu ft}$$

$$\phi_{oW} = \phi_{tW} - \phi_{sW} = 0.0353 - 0.0059 = 0.0294 \text{ cu ft/cu ft}$$

Table 6.3: $m = 0.95$ $n = 0$ $p = 0.362$

$$a_{AW} = mG'^n L'^p = 19.1 \text{ sq ft/cu ft}$$

Eq. (6.43b): $a_{VW} = 0.85a_{AW} \dfrac{\phi_{tW}}{\phi_{oW}} = 0.85(19.1)\dfrac{0.0353}{0.0294}$

$$= 19.5 \text{ sq ft/cu ft}$$

Table 6.2: $\epsilon = 0.74$ $\epsilon_o = \epsilon - \phi_t = 0.74 - 0.0353 = 0.705$

Eq. (6.39): $\dfrac{F_G(0.6)^{2/3}}{27.6} = 1.195 \left[\dfrac{0.238(800)}{0.018(2.42)(1 - 0.705)} \right]^{-0.36} = 0.0393$

$$F_G = 1.527 \text{ lb moles/(hr)(sq ft)}$$

$$F_G a_{VW} = 1.527(19.5) = 29.8 \text{ lb moles/(hr)(cu ft)}$$

$$= k_G a_{VW} p_{BM}$$

There is no mass-transfer coefficient for the liquid, since it is pure water. However, for such processes (see Chap. 7), we need convection heat-transfer coefficients for both gas and liquid. These may be estimated, in the absence of directly applicable data, through the heat- mass-transfer analogy. Thus, from Eq. (6.39), $j_D = 0.0393$, and assuming $j_H = j_D$,

$$j_H = \frac{h_G}{C_p G'} \Pr_G^{2/3} = 0.0393$$

For air, $C_p = 0.24$ Btu/(lb)($°$F), $\Pr_G = 0.74$.

$$h_G = \frac{0.0393 C_p G'}{\Pr_G^{2/3}} = \frac{0.0393(0.24)(800)}{(0.74)^{2/3}} = 9.24 \text{ Btu/(hr)(sq ft)(°F)}$$

Similarly, the heat-transfer analog of Eq. (6.41) is

$$\text{Nu} = \frac{h_L d_s}{k} = 25.1 \left(\frac{d_s L'}{\mu_L''} \right)^{0.45} \Pr_L^{0.5}$$

where $k =$ thermal conductivity of water $= 0.339$ (Btu)(ft)/(hr)(sq ft)($°$F), and $\Pr_L = C_p \mu_L''/k = 1.0(1.12)(2.42)/0.339 = 8.0$. Therefore,

$$h_L = 25.1 \frac{k}{d_s} \left(\frac{d_s L'}{\mu_L''} \right)^{0.45} \Pr_L^{0.5}$$

$$= \frac{25.1(0.339)}{0.238} \left[\frac{0.238(4,000)}{1.12(2.42)} \right]^{0.45} (8.0)^{0.5}$$

$$= 1415 \text{ Btu/(hr)(sq ft)(°F)}$$

The corresponding volumetric coefficients are

$$h_G a_V = 9.24(19.5) = 180 \text{ Btu/(hr)(cu ft)(°F)}$$

$$h_L a_V = 1415(19.5) = 27,600 \text{ Btu/(hr)(cu ft)(°F)}$$

End Effects and Axial Mixing. In addition to that which occurs within the packed volume, there will be mass transfer where the liquid is introduced by sprays or other distributors and where it drips off the lower packing support. These constitute the "end effects." For proper evaluation of the packing itself, correction of experimental data must be made for these, usually by operating at several packing heights followed by extrapolation of the results to zero height. New equipment designed with uncorrected data will be conservatively designed if shorter than the experimental equipment but underdesigned if taller. Alternatively, equipment designed with corrected data will include a small factor of safety represented by the end effects. The data represented by Eqs. (6.38) to (6.43) and Tables 6.3 and 6.4 are believed to be reasonably free of end effects.

As will be clear in later chapters, the equations usually used for design, which are the same as those used for computing mass-transfer coefficients from laboratory measurements, are based on the assumption that the gas and liquid flow in "piston," or "plug," flow, with a flat velocity profile across the tower and with each portion of the gas or liquid having the same residence time in the tower. Such is not actually the case. Nonuniformity of packing and maldistribution of liquid may lead to "channeling," or regions where the liquid flow is abnormally great; the liquid in the static holdup moves forward much more slowly than that in the moving holdup; drops of liquid falling from a packing piece may be blown upward by the gas. Similarly the resistance to gas flow at the tower walls, and in relatively dry regions of the packing, is different from that elsewhere; the downward movement of liquid induces downward movement of the gas. As a result, the purely piston-type flow does not occur, and there is a relative movement within each fluid parallel to the axis of the tower, described as "axial mixing." The transport of solute by axial mixing tends to reduce the concentration differences for interphase mass transfer. The axial solute transport has been described in terms of an eddy diffusivity, although the precise method of incorporating this idea into the mass-transfer equations is not yet certain. In any event, the true mass-transfer coefficients for interphase solute transfer are undoubtedly larger than those which we customarily use, since the latter have not been corrected for axial mixing. A good introduction to the literature and some experimental data are given by Brittan and Woodburn.[6]

Counterflow trays

These are proprietary traylike devices which resemble packings in the sense that the gas and liquid flow countercurrently through the same openings. Separate liquid downspouts are not used. Turbo-Grids[47] are of several varieties: parallel rods or bars arranged horizontally across the tower or sheet metal stamped with slotted openings form the trays, and these are installed so that alternate trays have the openings at right angles. Kittel trays[41,54] are slotted double trays arranged so that liquid movement on the tray is influenced by passage of the gas. Ripple trays[26] are perforated sheets bent into a sinusoidal wave, and alternate trays are installed with the waves at right angles. These devices all have low gas pressure drop and high liquid-flow capacity.

NOTATION FOR CHAPTER 6

a = specific interfacial surface for mass transfer, sq ft/cu ft

a_A = specific interfacial surface for absorption, desorption, and distillation, sq ft/cu ft packed volume

a_p = specific packing surface, sq ft/cu ft packed volume

a_V = specific interfacial surface for contact of a gas with a pure liquid, sq ft/cu ft packed volume

A_a = active area of a tray = $A_t - 2A_d$ for cross-flow trays, sq ft/tray

A_d = downspout cross-sectional area, sq ft

A_{da} = smaller of the two areas, A_d or free area between downspout apron and tray, sq ft

A_h = perforation area, sq ft/tray

A_n = net tower cross-sectional area for gas flow = $A_t - A_d$ for cross-flow trays, sq ft/tray

A_t = tower cross-sectional area, sq ft

c = concentration, lb moles/cu ft

C_f = characterization factor of packing, two-phase flow

C_f' = characterization factor of packing, single-phase flow

C_F = flooding constant for trays

C_o = orifice constant, dimensionless

d = tower diameter, ft

d_h = hole diameter, in.

d_h' = hole diameter, ft

d_p = bubble or particle diameter, ft; for particles, d_p is given by Eq. (6.37)

d_s = diameter of a sphere of same surface as a single packing particle, ft

D = molecular diffusivity, sq ft/hr

D_E = eddy diffusivity of back mixing, sq ft/hr

E = fractional entrainment, moles entrained liquid/moles (entrained liquid + net liquid flow)

$\mathbf{E}_{MG}$ = Murphree gas-phase tray efficiency, fractional

$\mathbf{E}_{MGE}$ = Murphree gas-phase tray efficiency, corrected for entrainment, fractional

$\mathbf{E}_O$ = overall tray efficiency, fractional

$\mathbf{E}_{OG}$ = point gas-phase tray efficiency, fractional

f = Fanning friction factor, dimensionless

F = mass-transfer coefficient, lb moles/(hr)(sq ft)

F_O = overall mass-transfer coefficient, lb moles/(hr)(sq ft)

g = acceleration due to gravity, ft/sq sec

g_c = conversion constant, 32.2 (lb mass)(ft)/(lb force)(sq sec)

g_c' = conversion constant, 4.18(10⁸)(lb mass)(ft)/(lb force)(sq hr)

G = superficial molar gas velocity, lb moles/(hr)(sq ft)

G' = superficial gas mass velocity, lb/(hr)(sq ft)

h_D = dry-plate gas pressure drop, as head of clear liquid, in.

h_G = gas pressure drop for a perforated tray, as head of clear liquid, in.

h_L = gas pressure drop due to liquid holdup on a tray, as head of clear liquid, in.

h_R = residual gas pressure drop, as head of clear liquid, in.

h_W = weir height, in.

h_1 = weir crest, in.

h_2 = head loss due to liquid flow under downspout apron, in.

h_3 = backup of liquid in downspout, in.

H = correction factor, dimensionless

k_G = gas-phase mass-transfer coefficient, lb moles/(hr)(sq ft)(atm)

k_L = liquid-phase mass-transfer coefficient, lb moles/(hr)(sq ft)(lb mole/cu ft)

k_x = liquid-phase mass-transfer coefficient, lb moles/(hr)(sq ft)(mole fraction)

k_y = gas-phase mass-transfer coefficient, lb moles/(hr)(sq ft)(mole fraction)

K_x = overall liquid mass-transfer coefficient, lb moles/(hr)(sq ft)(mole fraction)

K_y = overall gas mass-transfer coefficient, lb moles/(hr)(sq ft)(mole fraction)

l = plate thickness, in.

ln = natural logarithm

log = common logarithm

L = superficial molar liquid velocity, lb moles/(hr)(sq ft)

L' = superficial liquid mass velocity, lb/(hr)(sq ft)

m = slope of chord of equilibrium curve (see Chap. 5), mole fraction in gas/mole fraction in liquid, for Eqs. (6.23) to (6.28)

= empirical constant, for Table 6.3

n = empirical constant

N_{tG} = number of gas-phase transfer units

N_{tL} = number of liquid-phase transfer units

N_{tOG} = number of overall gas transfer units

p = empirical constant

p' = pitch; center-to-center hole spacing, ft

p_{BM} = logarithmic mean partial pressure of nondiffusing gas, atm

ΔP = gas pressure drop, lb force/sq ft

ΔP_R = residual gas pressure drop, lb force/sq ft

Pe = Péclet number for liquid mixing, dimensionless

q = liquid flow rate, cu ft/sec

Q = gas flow rate, cu ft/sec

Sc = Schmidt number, $\mu''/\rho D$, dimensionless

t = tray spacing, in.

V = velocity of gas through net tower area A_n, ft/sec

V_a = velocity of gas through active tray area A_a, ft/sec

V_F = velocity of gas through net tower area A_n at flooding, ft/sec

V_h = velocity of gas through perforations, ft/sec

V_{hW} = velocity of gas through perforations at incipient weeping, ft/sec

W = weir length, ft

W_{eff} = effective weir length, ft

x = concentration in liquid, mole fraction

y = concentration in gas, mole fraction

z = average flow width for liquid on a tray, ft

Z = length of travel on a tray, ft

= depth of packing, ft

Δ = hydraulic gradient, in.

ϵ = fractional void volume in a dry packed bed, cu ft voids/cu ft packed volume

ϵ_o = fractional void volume in irrigated packing, cu ft voids/cu ft packed volume

θ_L = time of residence of liquid on a tray, hr

μ = viscosity, lb mass/(ft)(sec) = $0.000672\mu'$

μ' = viscosity, centipoises

μ'' = viscosity, lb mass/(ft)(hr) = $2.42\mu'$

ρ = density, lb mass/cu ft

σ = surface tension, lb force/ft = $6.85(10^{-5})\sigma'$

σ' = surface tension, dynes/cm

ϕ = volume fraction liquid, cu ft liquid/cu ft packed volume

Other subscripts;

G = gas

L = liquid

n = tray number

o = operating, or moving

s = static

W = water

Superscript:

* = in equilibrium with bulk liquid

REFERENCES

1. Anon.: *Chem. Eng. News*, Oct. 23, 1961, p. 58.
2. Bolles, W. L.: *Petrol. Process.*, **11**(2), 64; (3), 82; (4), 72; (5), 109 (1956).
3. Bolles, W. L.: in B. D. Smith, "Design of Equilibrium Stage Processes," chap. 14, McGraw-Hill Book Company, New York, 1963.
4. Boucher, D. F., and G. E. Alves: in "The Chemical Engineers' Handbook," 4th ed., p. 5-20, McGraw-Hill Book Company, New York, 1963.
5. Bowles, V. O.: *Petrol. Refiner*, **34**(7), 118 (1955).
6. Brittan, M. I., and E. T. Woodburn: *AIChE J.*, **12**, 541 (1966).
7. "Bubble-tray Design Manual," American Institute of Chemical Engineers, New York, 1958.
8. Cannon, M. R.: *Ind. Eng. Chem.*, **41**, 1953 (1949).
9. Carpenter, C. L., and D. F. Othmer: *AIChE J.*, **1**, 549 (1955).
10. Cicalese, J. J., J. A. Davies, P. J. Harrington, G. S. Houghland, A. J. L. Huchinson, and T. J. Walsh: *Proc. Am. Petrol. Inst.*, **26**, sec. III, 180 (1946).
11. Colburn, A. P.: *Ind. Eng. Chem.*, **28**, 526 (1936).
12. Eckert, J. S.: *Chem. Eng. Progr.*, **57**(9), 54 (1961); **59**(5), 76 (1963).
13. Edmister, W. C.: *Petrol. Engr.*, **1948**(12), 193.
14. Emmett, R. E., and R. L. Pigford: sec. 14 in "The Chemical Engineers' Handbook," 4th ed., McGraw-Hill Book Company, New York, 1963.
15. Ergun, S.: *Chem. Eng. Progr.*, **48**, 89 (1952).
16. Eversole, W. G., G. H. Wagner, and E. Stackhouse: *Ind. Eng. Chem.*, **33**, 1459 (1941).
17. Fair, J. R.: *Petro/Chem. Eng.*, **33** (Sept.), 210 (1961).
18. Fair, J. R.: chap. 15 in B. D. Smith, "Design of Equilibrium Stage Processes," McGraw-Hill Book Company, New York, 1963.
19. Fair, J. R., and R. L. Matthews: *Petrol. Refiner*, **37**(4), 153 (1958).
20. Fellinger, L.: reported by T. K. Sherwood and R. L. Pigford, "Absorption and Extraction," 2d ed., McGraw-Hill Book Company, New York, 1952.
21. Foss, A. S., and J. A. Gerster: *Chem. Eng. Progr.*, **52**, 28 (1956).
22. Gerster, J. A.: *Chem. Eng. Progr.*, **59**, 35 (1963).
23. Harris, L. S., and G. S. Haun: *Chem. Eng. Progr.*, **60**(5), 100 (1964).
24. Hughmark, G. A., and H. E. O'Connell: *Chem. Eng. Progr.*, **53**, 127 (1957).
25. Hunt, C. d'A., D. N. Hanson, and C. R. Wilke: *AIChE J.*, **1**, 441 (1955).
26. Hutchinson, M. H., and R. F. Baddour: *Chem. Eng. Progr.*, **52**, 503 (1956).
27. Kraft, W. W.: *Ind. Eng. Chem.*, **40**, 807 (1948).
28. Liebson, I., R. E. Kelley, and L. A. Bullington: *Petrol. Refiner*, **36**(2), 127 (1957).
29. Leva, M.: *Chem. Eng. Progr. Symp. Ser.*, **50**(10), 51 (1954).
30. Lewis, W. K., Jr.: *Ind. Eng. Chem.*, **28**, 399 (1936).
31. Lobo, W. E., L. Friend, F. Hashmall, and F. Zenz: *Trans. AIChE*, **41**, 693 (1945).
32. Madigan, C. M.: Master of Chemical Engineering thesis, New York University, 1964.
33. Mayfield, F. D., W. L. Church, A. C. Green, D. C. Lee, and R. S. Rasmussen; *Ind. Eng. Chem.*, **44**, 2238 (1952).
34. McAllister, R. A., P. H. McGinnis, and C. A. Planck: *Chem. Eng. Sci.*, **9**, 25 (1958).
35. McMahon, H. O.: *Ind. Eng. Chem.*, **39**, 712 (1947).
36. Muller, H. M., and D. F. Othmer: *Ind. Eng. Chem.*, **51**, 625 (1959).
37. Norman, W. S., T. Cakaloz, A. Z. Fresco, and D. H. Sutcliffe: *Trans. Inst. Chem. Engrs.* (*London*), **41**, 61 (1963).
38. Nutter, I. E.: *Chem. Eng.*, **61**(5), 176 (1954).
39. O'Connell, H. E.: *Trans. AIChE*, **42**, 741 (1946).
40. Podbielniak, W.: *Ind. Eng. Chem., Anal. Ed.*, **13**, 639 (1941).
41. Pollard, B.: *Chem. Ind.* (*London*), **1958**, 1414.
42. Robin, B. J.: *Brit. Chem. Eng.*, **4**, 351 (1959).

43. Scofield, R. C.: *Chem. Eng. Progr.*, **46**, 405 (1950).

44. Sherwood, T. K., and F. A. L. Holloway: *Trans. AIChE*, **36**, 39 (1940).

45. Sherwood, T. K., G. H. Shipley, and F. A. L. Holloway: *Ind. Eng. Chem.*, **30**, 765 (1938).

46. Shulman, H. L. et al.: *AIChE J.*, **1**, 247, 253, 259 (1955); **3**, 157 (1957); **5**, 280, (1959); **6**, 175, 469 (1960); **9**, 479 (1963).

47. Staff, Shell Development Co.: *Chem. Eng. Progr.*, **50**, 57 (1954).

48. Teller, A. J., S. A. Miller, and E. G. Scheibel: sec. 18 in "The Chemical Engineers' Handbook," 4th ed., McGraw-Hill Book Company, New York, 1963.

49. Thoenes, D., and H. Kramers: *Chem. Eng. Sci.*, **8**, 271 (1958).

50. Thrift, G. C.: *Oil Gas J.*, **52**(51), 165 (1954); *Chem. Eng.*, **61**(5), 177 (1954).

51. United States Stoneware Company: "Packed Tower Design Manual," p. GR-109R4, Akron, Ohio, 1963.

52. Williams, G. C., R. B. Akell, and C. P. Talbott: *Chem. Eng. Progr.*, **43**, 585 (1947).

53. York, O. H.: *Chem. Eng. Progr.*, **50**, 421 (1954).

54. Zuiderweg, F. J., H. Verburg, and F. A. H. Gilissen: *Proc. Intern. Symp. Distillation, London, 1960*, p. 201.

PROBLEMS

Problems associated with tray efficiencies and mass-transfer coefficients for packed towers are to be found with Chaps. 7 to 9.

6.1. For the stripping operation of Illustration 6.1, determine suitable diameters of towers of the following designs, and compare with that of the perforated tray tower of Illustration 6.1:

a. Bubble-cap tray tower.

b. Tower packed with (1) 1-in. ceramic Raschig rings, (2) 1-in. Berl saddles, and (3) 1-in. Pall rings. For these use a gas pressure drop of 0.4 in. water/ft of packing.

6.2. A gas containing methane, propane, and butane is to be scrubbed countercurrently in a perforated-tray tower with a hydrocarbon oil to absorb principally the butane. It is agreed to design a tray for the circumstances existing at the bottom of the tower, where the conditions are:

Pressure = 50 psia

Temperature = 100°F

Gas—1,750 lb moles/hr, containing 85% methane, 10% propane, and 5% butane by volume.

Liquid—1,000 lb moles/hr, av mol wt = 150, density = 53.0 lb/cu ft, surface tension = 25 dynes/cm, viscosity = 1.60 centipoises.

Design a suitable perforated tray, and check for flooding by downspout backup, weeping, and downspout residence time.

6.3. A packed tower is to be designed for the countercurrent contact of a benzene–nitrogen gas mixture with kerosene to wash out the benzene from the gas. The circumstances are:

Gas in = 20 cu ft/sec, containing 5 mole % benzene, at 800 mm Hg abs, 75°F

Gas out = substantially pure nitrogen

Liquid in = 3.0 lb/sec, benzene-free, sp gr = 0.80, viscosity = 2.3 centipoises

The packing will be 1-in. Intalox saddles, and the tower diameter will be set to produce 0.4 in. water pressure drop per foot of irrigated packing.

a. Calculate the tower diameter to be used.

b. Assume that, for the diameter chosen, the irrigated packed depth will be 20 ft and that 3 ft of unirrigated packing will be placed above the liquid inlet to act as an entrainment separator. The blower-motor combination to be used at the gas inlet will have an overall efficiency of 60%. Calculate the power required to blow the gas through the packing.

6.4. A small water-cooling tower, 3 ft in diameter, packed with 2-in. ceramic Raschig rings, is fed with water at the rate of 20,000 lb/(hr)(sq ft), in at 105°F, out at 80°F. The water is contacted with air (85°F, 1 atm, essentially dry) drawn upward countercurrently to the water flow. Neglecting evaporation of the water, estimate the rate of air flow, cu ft/min, which would flood the tower.

CHAPTER SEVEN
HUMIDIFICATION
OPERATIONS

The operations considered in this chapter are concerned with the interphase transfer of mass and of energy which result when a gas is brought into contact with a pure liquid in which it is essentially insoluble. While the term "humidification operations" is used to characterize these in a general fashion, the purpose of such operations may include not only humidification of the gas but dehumidification and cooling of the gas, measurement of its vapor content, and cooling of the liquid as well. The matter transferred between phases in such cases is the substance comprising the liquid phase, which either vaporizes or condenses. As in all mass-transfer problems, it is necessary for a complete understanding of the operation to be familiar with the equilibrium characteristics of the systems. But since the mass transfer in these cases will invariably be accompanied by a simultaneous transfer of heat energy as well, some consideration must also be given to the enthalpy characteristics of the systems.

VAPOR-LIQUID EQUILIBRIUM AND ENTHALPY FOR A PURE SUBSTANCE

As indicated above, the substance undergoing interphase transfer in these operations is the material comprising the liquid phase, which diffuses in the form of a vapor.

The equilibrium vapor-pressure characteristics of the liquid are therefore of importance.

Vapor-pressure curve

Every liquid exerts an equilibrium pressure, the vapor pressure, to an extent depending upon the temperature. When the vapor pressures of a liquid are plotted against the corresponding temperatures, a curve such as *TBDC* (Fig. 7.1) results. The vapor-pressure curve for each substance is unique, but each exhibits characteristics generally similar to that in the figure. The curve separates two areas of the plot, representing, respectively, conditions where the substance exists wholly in the liquid state and wholly in the vapor state. If the conditions imposed upon the substance are in the liquid-state area, such as at point *A*, the substance will be entirely liquid. Under all conditions in the lower area, such as those at point *E*, the substance is entirely a vapor. At all conditions corresponding to points on the curve *TBDC*, however, liquid and vapor may coexist in any proportions indefinitely. Liquid and vapor represented by points on the vapor-pressure curve are called *saturated liquid* and *saturated vapor*, respectively. Vapor or gas at a temperature above that corresponding to saturation is termed *superheated*. The vapor-pressure curve has two abrupt end points, at *T* and *C*. Point *T*, from which originate curves *LT* and *ST* separating the conditions for the solid state from those for the liquid and vapor, is the *triple point*, at which all three states of aggregation may coexist. Point *C* is the *critical point*, or *state*, whose coordinates are the *critical pressure* and *critical temperature*. At the critical point, distinction between the liquid and vapor phases disappears, and all the properties of the liquid, such as density, viscosity, refractive index, etc., are identical with those of the vapor. The substance at a temperature above the

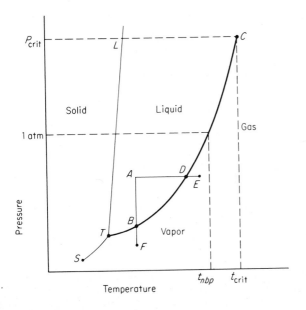

Fig. 7.1 *Vapor pressure of a pure liquid.*

critical is called a *gas*, and it will then not be liquefied regardless of how high a pressure may be imposed.   This distinction between a gas and a vapor, however, is not always strictly adhered to, and the term gas is frequently used to designate merely a condition relatively far removed from the vapor-pressure curve.   The temperature corresponding to each pressure on the curve is termed the boiling point of the liquid at the pressure in question, and that corresponding to 1 atm in particular is known as the *normal boiling point*, as at t_{nbp} on Fig. 7.1.

Whenever a process involves bringing a sample of fluid across the vapor-pressure curve, such as the isobaric process *ADE* or the isothermal process *ABF*, there will be a change of phase.   This will be accompanied by the evolution (for condensation) or absorption (for vaporization) of the *latent heat of vaporization* at constant tempera-ture, for example, at points *B* or *D* in the processes mentioned above.   Heat added or given up with changing temperatures is called *sensible heat*.

Interpolation between data.   For such common liquids as water, many refrigerants, and others, the vapor pressure–temperature curve has been established at many points.   For most liquids, however, only relatively few data are available, so that it is necessary frequently to interpolate between, or extrapolate beyond, the measure-ments.   The curve on arithmetic coordinates (Fig. 7.1) is very inconvenient for this because of the curvature, and some method of linearizing the curve is needed.   Most of the common methods stem from the Clausius-Clapeyron equation, which relates the slope of the vapor-pressure curve to the latent heat of vaporization

$$\frac{dP}{dT} = \frac{\lambda'}{T(v_G - v_L)} \tag{7.1}$$

where v_G and v_L are molal specific volumes of the saturated vapor and liquid, respec-tively, and λ' is the molal latent heat in units consistent with the rest of the equation. As a simplification, we may neglect v_L in comparison with v_G and express the latter by the ideal-gas law, to obtain

$$d \ln P = \frac{dP}{P} = \frac{\lambda' \, dT}{RT^2} \tag{7.2}$$

and if λ' may be considered reasonably constant over a short range of temperature,

$$\ln P = -\frac{\lambda'}{RT} + \text{const} \tag{7.3}$$

Equation (7.3) suggests that a plot of log P against $1/T$ will be straight for short temperature ranges.   It also suggests a method of interpolating between points listed in a table of data.

Illustration 7.1.   A table lists the vapor pressure of benzene to be 100 mm Hg at 26.1°C and 400 mm Hg at 60.6°C.   At what temperature is the vapor pressure 200 mm Hg?

Solution. At 26.1°C, $1/T = 1/299.1$ reciprocal °K; at 60.6°C, $1/T = 1/333.6$.

$$\frac{1/299.1 - 1/T}{1/299.1 - 1/333.6} = \frac{\log 100 - \log 200}{\log 100 - \log 400}$$

$$T = 315.4°K = 42.4°C$$

The correct value is 42.2°C. Linear interpolation would have given 37.6°C.

Reference-substance plots[15]

Equation (7.2) may be rewritten for a second substance, a *reference substance*, at the same temperature,

$$d \ln P_r = \frac{\lambda'_r \, dT}{RT^2} \tag{7.4}$$

where the subscript r denotes the reference substance. Dividing Eq. (7.2) by (7.4) provides

$$\frac{d \ln P}{d \ln P_r} = \frac{\lambda'}{\lambda'_r} = \frac{M\lambda}{M_r \lambda_r} \tag{7.5}$$

which, upon integration, becomes

$$\log P = \frac{M\lambda}{M_r \lambda_r} \log P_r + \text{const} \tag{7.6}$$

Equation (7.6) suggests that a linear graph will result if $\log P$ as ordinate is plotted against $\log P_r$ for the reference substance as abscissa, where for each plotted point the vapor pressures are taken at the same temperature. Such a plot is straight over larger temperature ranges (but not near the critical temperature) than that based on Eq. (7.3) and, moreover, the slope of the curve gives the ratio of the latent heats at the same temperature. The reference substance chosen is one whose vapor-pressure data are well known.

Illustration 7.2. (*a*) Plot the vapor pressure of benzene over the range 15 to 180°C using water as reference substance according to Eq. (7.6). (*b*) Determine the vapor pressure of benzene at 100°C. (*c*) Determine the latent heat of vaporization of benzene at 25°C.

Solution. a. Logarithmic graph paper is marked with scales for the vapor pressure of benzene and for water, as in Fig. 7.2. The vapor pressure of benzene at 15.4°C is 60 mm Hg, and that for water at this temperature is 13.1 mm Hg. These pressures provide the coordinates of the lowest point on the plot. In similar fashion, additional data for benzene are plotted with the help of a steam table, thus providing the curve shown. The line is very nearly straight over the temperature range used.

b. At 100°C, the vapor pressure of water is 760 mm Hg. Entering the plot at this value for the abscissa, the vapor pressure of benzene is read as 1,400 mm Hg. Alternatively the abscissa can be marked with the temperatures corresponding to the vapor pressures of water, as shown, thus eliminating the necessity of referring to the steam table.

c. The slope of the curve at 25°C is 0.775. (*Note:* This is most conveniently determined with a millimeter rule. If the coordinates are used, the slope will be $\Delta \log P / \Delta \log P_r$.) At 25°C, the latent

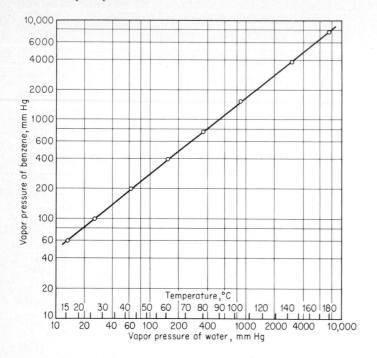

Fig. 7.2   *Reference-substance plot for the vapor pressure of benzene.*

heat of vaporization of water is 1049.8 Btu/lb.   From Eq. (7.6),

$$\frac{\lambda M}{\lambda_r M_r} = \frac{\lambda(78.05)}{1,049.8(18.02)} = 0.775$$

$$\lambda = 187.5 \text{ Btu/lb} \quad \text{for benzene at } 25°C$$

(The accepted value is 186.5 Btu/lb.)

Enthalpy

The internal energy U of a substance is the total energy residing in the substance owing to the motion and relative position of the constituent atoms and molecules. Absolute values of internal energy are not known, but numerical values relative to some arbitrarily defined standard state for the substance can be computed.   The sum of the internal energy and the product of pressure and volume of the substance, when both quantities are expressed in the same units, is defined as the *enthalpy* of the substance,

$$H = U + Pv$$

In a batch process at constant pressure, where work is done only in expansion against the pressure, the heat absorbed by the system is the gain in enthalpy,

$$Q = \Delta H = \Delta(U + Pv) \tag{7.7}$$

In a steady-state continuous-flow process, the net transfer of energy to the system as heat and work will be the sum of its gains in enthalpy and potential and kinetic energies.   It frequently happens that the changes in potential and kinetic energies are insignificant in comparison with the enthalpy change and that there is no mechanical work done.   In such cases, Eq. (7.7) can be used to compute the heat added to the system, and such a calculation is termed a *heat balance*.   In *adiabatic* operations, where no exchange of heat between the system and its surroundings occurs, the heat balance becomes simply an equality of enthalpies in the initial and final condition.

Absolute values of the enthalpy of a substance, like the internal energy, are not known.   However, by arbitrarily setting the enthalpy of a substance at zero when it is in a convenient reference state, relative values of enthalpy at other conditions may be calculated.   To define the reference state, the temperature, pressure, and state of aggregation must be established.   For the substance water, the ordinary steam tables list the relative enthalpy at various conditions referred to the enthalpy of the substance at 32°F, the equilibrium vapor pressure at this temperature, and in the liquid state. For other substances, other reference conditions may be more convenient.

Figure 7.3 is a graphical representation of the relative enthalpy of a typical substance where the liquid, vapor, and gaseous states are shown.   The data are most conveniently shown on lines of constant pressure.   The curves marked "saturated liquid" and "saturated vapor," however, cut across the constant-pressure lines and show the enthalpies for these conditions at temperatures and pressures corresponding

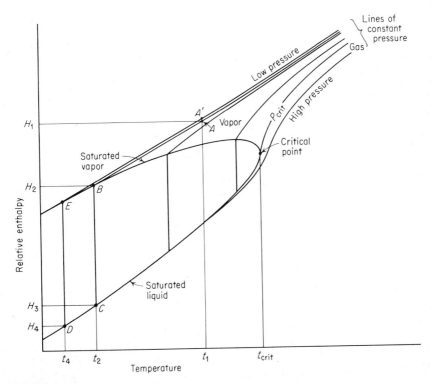

Fig. 7.3   *Typical enthalpy-temperature diagram for a pure substance.*

to the equilibrium vapor-pressure relationship for the substance. The vertical distance between the saturated-vapor and -liquid curves, such as the distance BC, represents the latent heat of vaporization at the corresponding temperature. The latent heat thus decreases with increased temperature, becoming zero at the critical point. In the vapor state at low pressures, the enthalpy is essentially a function of temperature; at all pressures where the ideal-gas law may be used to describe the Pvt relation, the lines of constant pressure are superimposed and the enthalpy is independent of pressure. Except near the critical temperature, the enthalpy of the liquid is also substantially independent of pressure until exceedingly high pressures are reached.

The change in enthalpy between two conditions, such as those at A and D, may be taken simply as the difference in ordinates corresponding to the points. Thus, to calculate the enthalpy of the substance in the superheated condition at point A relative to the saturated liquid at D, or $H_1 - H_4$, we may add the enthalpy change $H_1 - H_2$, the sensible heat of the vapor from the saturation temperature t_2 at the same pressure to the superheated condition at A; $H_2 - H_3$, the latent heat of vaporization at t_2; and $H_3 - H_4$, the sensible heat of the liquid from the final condition at D to the boiling point at the prevailing pressure t_2. For a liquid or vapor, the slope of the constant-pressure lines at any temperature is termed the *heat capacity*. The lines are not strictly straight, so that the heat capacity changes with temperature. By use of an average heat capacity or average slope, however, sensible heats are readily calculated. Thus, referring again to Fig. 7.3,

$$H_1 - H_2 = C(t_1 - t_2)$$

where C is the average heat capacity of the vapor at constant pressure over the indicated temperature range.

Illustration 7.3. Compute the heat evolved when 10 lb of benzene as a superheated vapor at 94 mm Hg, 100°C, is cooled and condensed to a liquid at 10°C. The average heat capacity for the vapor may be taken as 0.30 and for the liquid 0.36 Btu/(lb)(°F).

Solution. Refer to Fig. 7.2. When the pressure is 94 mm Hg, the saturation temperature for benzene is 25°C. The latent heat of vaporization at this temperature is 186.5 Btu/lb (Illustration 7.2). The initial condition corresponds to a point such as A on Fig. 7.3, the final condition to point D, the path of the process to $ABCD$. Using the notation of Fig. 7.3,

$$H_1 - H_2 = C(t_1 - t_2) = 0.30(100 - 25)(1.8) = 40.5 \text{ Btu/lb}$$
$$H_2 - H_3 = 186.5 \text{ Btu/lb}$$
$$H_3 - H_4 = C(t_2 - t_4) = 0.36(25 - 10)(1.8) = 9.7 \text{ Btu/lb}$$
$$\therefore \quad H_1 - H_4 = 40.5 + 186.5 + 9.7 = 236.7 \text{ Btu/lb}$$
$$\therefore \quad \text{Heat evolved for 10 lb benzene} = 10(236.7) = 2367 \text{ Btu}$$

VAPOR-GAS MIXTURES

In what follows, the term *vapor* will be applied to that substance, designated as substance A, in the vaporous state which is relatively near its condensation temperature at the prevailing pressure. The term *gas* will be applied to substance B, which is a relatively highly superheated gas.

Absolute humidity

While the common concentration units (partial pressure, mole fraction, etc.) which are based on total quantity are useful, when operations involve changes in vapor content of a vapor-gas mixture without changes in the gas content, it is more convenient to use a unit based on the unchanging amount of gas. The ratio mass of vapor/mass of gas is the *absolute humidity* Y'. If the quantities are expressed in moles, the ratio is the *molal* absolute humidity Y.

$$Y = \frac{y_A}{y_B} = \frac{p_A}{p_B} = \frac{p_A}{P_t - p_A} \frac{\text{moles } A}{\text{moles } B}$$

$$Y' = Y\frac{M_A}{M_B} = \frac{p_A}{P_t - p_A} \frac{M_A}{M_B} \frac{\text{mass } A}{\text{mass } B}$$

(7.8)

In many respects the molal ratio is the more convenient, owing to the ease with which moles and volumes may be interrelated through the gas law, but the mass ratio has nevertheless become firmly established in the humidification literature. The mass absolute humidity was first introduced by Grosvenor[5] and is sometimes called the Grosvenor humidity.

Illustration 7.4. In a mixture of benzene vapor (A) and nitrogen gas (B) at a total pressure of 800 mm Hg and a temperature of 60°C, the partial pressure of benzene is 100 mm Hg. Express the benzene concentration in other terms.

Solution. $p_A = 100$, $p_B = 800 - 100 = 700$ mm Hg.

a. Mole fraction. Since the pressure fraction and mole fraction are identical for gas mixtures, $y_A = p_A/P_t = {}^{100}\!/_{800} = 0.125$ mole fraction benzene. The mole fraction nitrogen $= y_B = 1 - 0.125 = {}^{700}\!/_{800} = 0.875$.

b. Volume fraction of benzene equals the mole fraction, 0.125.

c. Absolute humidity.

$$Y = \frac{y_A}{y_B} = \frac{p_A}{p_B} = \frac{0.125}{0.875} = \frac{100}{700} = 0.143 \text{ mole benzene/mole nitrogen}$$

$$Y' = Y\frac{M_A}{M_B} = 0.143\frac{78.05}{28.08} = 0.398 \text{ lb benzene/lb nitrogen}$$

Saturated vapor-gas mixtures

If an insoluble dry gas B is brought into contact with sufficient liquid A, the liquid will evaporate into the gas until ultimately, at equilibrium, the partial pressure of A in the vapor-gas mixture reaches its saturation value, the vapor pressure P_A at the prevailing temperature. So long as the gas can be considered insoluble in the liquid, the partial pressure of vapor in the saturated mixture is independent of the nature of the gas and total pressure (except at very high pressures) and is dependent only upon the temperature and identity of the liquid. However, the saturated molal absolute humidity $Y_s = P_A/(P_t - P_A)$ will depend upon the total pressure, and the saturated absolute humidity $Y'_s = Y_s M_A/M_B$ upon the identity of the gas as well. Both saturated humidities become infinite at the boiling point of the liquid at the prevailing total pressure.

Illustration 7.5. A gas (B)–benzene (A) mixture is saturated at 1 atm, 50°C. Calculate the absolute humidity if (a) B is nitrogen and (b) if B is oxygen.

Solution. Since the mixture is saturated, the partial pressure of benzene p_A equals the equilibrium vapor pressure P_A of benzene at 50°C. From Fig. 7.2, $P_A = 275$ mm Hg, or 0.362 atm.

$a.$ $\quad Y_s = \dfrac{P_A}{P_t - P_A} = \dfrac{0.362}{1 - 0.362} = 0.568$ mole benzene/mole nitrogen

$\quad Y_s' = \dfrac{Y_s M_A}{M_B} = \dfrac{0.568(78.05)}{28.02} = 1.583$ lb benzene/lb nitrogen

$b.$ $\quad Y_s = \dfrac{P_A}{P_t - P_A} = \dfrac{0.362}{1 - 0.362} = 0.568$ mole benzene/mole oxygen

$\quad Y_s' = \dfrac{Y_s M_A}{M_B} = \dfrac{0.568(78.05)}{32.00} = 1.387$ lb benzene/lb oxygen

Unsaturated vapor-gas mixtures

If the partial pressure of the vapor in a vapor-gas mixture is for any reason less than the equilibrium vapor pressure of the liquid at the same temperature, the mixture is unsaturated.

1. *Dry-bulb temperature.* This is the temperature of a vapor-gas mixture as ordinarily determined by immersion of a thermometer in the mixture.

2. *Relative saturation.* *Relative saturation*, also called *relative humidity*, expressed as a percentage is defined as $100 p_A/P_A$, where P_A is the vapor pressure at the dry-bulb temperature of the mixture. For any vapor, the graphical representation of conditions of constant relative saturation may be easily constructed on a vapor pressure–temperature chart, as in Fig. 7.4a, by dividing the ordinates of the vapor-pressure

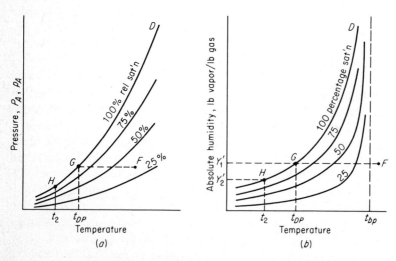

Fig. 7.4 *Forms of psychrometric charts.*

curve into appropriate intervals. Thus the curve for 50 percent relative saturation shows a vapor partial pressure equal to one-half the equilibrium vapor pressure at any temperature. A reference-substance plot, such as Fig. 7.2, could also be used for this.

3. *Percentage saturation. Percentage saturation,* or *percentage absolute humidity,* is defined as $100\,Y/Y_s$ and $100\,Y'/Y'_s$, where the saturated values are computed at the dry-bulb temperature of the mixture. Graphical representation of the quantity for any vapor may be made on a chart of Y vs. t (in which case the chart must be limited to a single total pressure) or one of Y' vs. t (for a single total pressure and a specific gas), as in Fig. 7.4*b*. On this chart, the saturation humidities are plotted from vapor-pressure data with the help of Eq. (7.8), to give curve GD. The curve for humidities at 50 percentage saturation is plotted at half the ordinate of curve GD, etc. All the curves of constant percentage saturation reach infinity at the boiling point of the liquid at the prevailing pressure.†

4. *Dew point.* This is the temperature at which a vapor-gas mixture becomes saturated when cooled at constant total pressure out of contact with a liquid. For example, if an unsaturated mixture such as that at F (Fig. 7.4) is cooled at constant pressure out of contact with liquid, the path of the cooling process follows the line FG, the mixture becoming more nearly saturated as the temperature is lowered, and fully saturated at t_{DP}, the dew-point temperature. All mixtures of absolute humidity Y'_1 on this figure have the same dew point. If the temperature is reduced only an infinitesimal amount below t_{DP}, vapor will condense as a liquid dew. This is used as a method of humidity determination: a shiny metal surface is cooled in the presence of the gas mixture, and the appearance of a fog which clouds the mirrorlike surface indicates that the dew point has been reached.

If the mixture is cooled to a lower temperature, the vapor-gas mixture will continue to precipitate liquid, itself always remaining saturated, until at the final temperature t_2 (Fig. 7.4) the residual vapor-gas mixture will be at point H. The mass of vapor condensed per unit mass of dry gas will be $Y'_1 - Y'_2$. Except under specially controlled circumstances supersaturation will not occur, and no vapor-gas mixture whose coordinates lie to the left of curve GD will result.

5. *Humid volume.* The humid volume v_H of a vapor-gas mixture is the volume in cubic feet of 1 lb of dry gas and its accompanying vapor at the prevailing temperature and pressure. For a mixture of absolute humidity Y' at $t_G°$F and P_t atm, the ideal-gas law gives the humid volume as

$$v_H = \left(\frac{1}{M_B} + \frac{Y'}{M_A}\right)359\frac{t_G + 460}{492}\frac{1}{P_t} = 0.730\left(\frac{1}{M_B} + \frac{Y'}{M_A}\right)\frac{t_G + 460}{P_t} \qquad (7.9)$$

The humid volume of a saturated mixture is computed with $Y' = Y'_s$ and that for a

---

† For this reason curves of constant relative saturation are sometimes drawn on absolute humidity–temperature charts. Since relative saturation and percentage saturation are not numerically equal for an unsaturated mixture, the position of such curves must be computed by the methods of Illustration 7.6.

dry gas with $Y' = 0$. These values may then be plotted against temperature on a psychrometric chart. For partially saturated mixtures, v_H may be interpolated between values for 0 and 100 percentage saturation at the same temperature according to percentage saturation. When the mass of *dry* gas in a mixture is multiplied by the humid volume, the volume of *mixture* results.

6. *Humid heat.* The humid heat C_S is the heat required to raise the temperature of 1 lb of gas and its accompanying vapor 1°F at constant pressure. For a mixture of absolute humidity Y',

$$C_S = C_B + Y'C_A \tag{7.10}$$

Provided neither vaporation nor condensation occurs, the heat in Btu required to raise the temperature of W_B lb dry gas *and* its accompanying vapor Δt°F will be

$$Q = W_B C_S \Delta t \tag{7.11}$$

7. *Enthalpy.* The (relative) enthalpy of a vapor-gas mixture is the sum of the (relative) enthalpies of the gas and of the vapor content. Imagine 1 lb of a gas containing Y' lb vapor at dry-bulb temperature t_G°F. If the mixture is unsaturated, the vapor is in a superheated state, and we may calculate the enthalpy relative to the reference states gas and saturated liquid at t_0°F. The enthalpy of the gas alone is $C_B(t_G - t_0)$. The vapor at t_G is at a condition corresponding to point A on Fig. 7.3, and its reference state corresponds to point D. If t_{DP} is the dew point of the mixture (t_2 on Fig. 7.3) and λ_{DP} the latent heat of vaporization of the vapor at that temperature, the enthalpy per pound of vapor will be $C_A(t_G - t_{DP}) + \lambda_{DP} + C_{AL}(t_{DP} - t_0)$. Then the total enthalpy for the mixture, per pound of dry gas, is

$$H' = C_B(t_G - t_0) + Y'[C_A(t_G - t_{DP}) + \lambda_{DP} + C_{AL}(t_{DP} - t_0)] \tag{7.12}$$

Refer again to Fig. 7.3. For the low pressures ordinarily encountered in humidification work, the point A which actually lies on a line of constant pressure corresponding to the partial pressure of the vapor in the mixture may, for all practical purposes, be considered as lying on the line whose pressure is the saturation pressure of the vapor at the reference temperature, or at A'. The vapor enthalpy may then be computed by following the path $A'ED$ and becomes, per pound of vapor, $C_A(t_G - t_0) + \lambda_0$, where λ_0 is the latent heat of vaporization at the reference temperature. The enthalpy of the mixture, per pound of dry gas, is then

$$H' = C_B(t_G - t_0) + Y'[C_A(t_G - t_0) + \lambda_0] = C_S(t - t_0) + Y'\lambda_0 \tag{7.13}$$

Occasionally different reference temperatures are chosen for the dry gas and for the vapor. Note that the enthalpy H' for a mixture may be increased by increasing the temperature at constant humidity, by increasing the humidity at constant temperature, or by increasing both. Alternatively, under certain conditions H' may remain constant as t and Y' vary in opposite directions.

By substitution of Y'_s and the appropriate humid heat in Eq. (7.13), the enthalpy of saturated mixtures H'_s may be computed and plotted against temperature on the

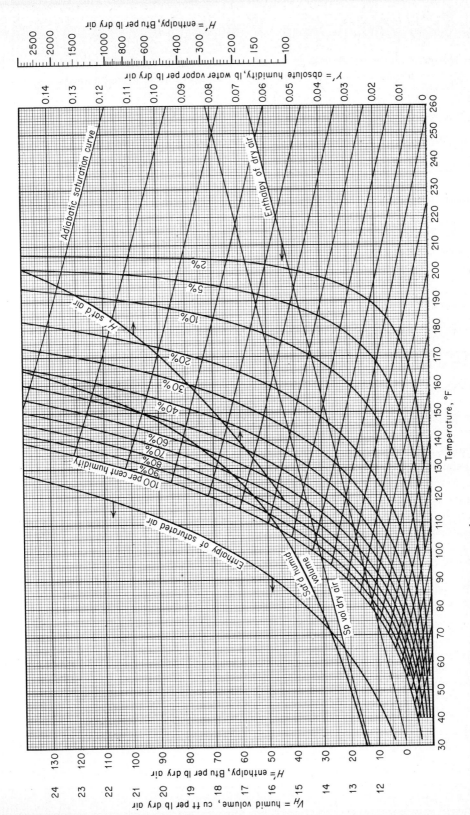

Fig. 7.5 *Psychrometric chart for air–water vapor, 1 atm abs.*

psychrometric chart. Similarly H for the dry gas may be plotted. Enthalpies for unsaturated mixtures may then be interpolated between the saturated and dry values at the same temperature according to the percentage saturation.

The system air–water

While psychrometric charts for any vapor-gas mixture may be prepared when circumstances warrant, the system air–water vapor occurs so frequently that unusually complete charts for this mixture are available. Figure 7.5 is one such chart prepared for a total pressure of 1 atm. For convenient reference, the various equations representing the curves are listed in Table 7.1. It should be noted that all the

Table 7.1. Psychrometric relations for the system air (B)–water (A) at 1 atm pressure

$M_A = 18.02$, mol wt water

$M_B = 28.97$, mol wt air

$$Y' = 0.622 \frac{p_{H_2O}}{1 - p_{H_2O}} \qquad \text{lb water vapor/lb air}$$

$$Y'_s = 0.622 \frac{p_{H_2O}}{1 - p_{H_2O}} \qquad \text{lb water vapor/lb air at saturation}$$

$v_H = (0.0252 + 0.0405Y')(t_G + 460) \qquad \text{cu ft mixture/lb air}$

$C_S = 0.24 + 0.45Y' \qquad \text{Btu for mixture/(lb air)(°F)}$

$t_0 = 32°F.$

$\lambda_0 = 1075.8$ Btu/lb, latent heat of vaporization of water, 32°F

$H' = (0.24 + 0.45Y')(t_G - 32) + 1,075.8Y'$, relative enthalpy, Btu for mixture/lb air, referred to gaseous air and saturated liquid water at 32°F

quantities (absolute humidity, enthalpies, humid volumes) are plotted against temperature. In the case of the enthalpies, gaseous air and saturated liquid water at 32°F were the reference conditions used so that the chart may be used in conjunction with the steam tables. The data for enthalpy of saturated air were then plotted with two enthalpy scales to provide for the large range of values necessary. The series of curves marked "adiabatic-saturation curves" on the chart were plotted according to Eq. (7.21), to be considered later. For most purposes these may be considered as curves of constant enthalpy for the vapor-gas mixture per pound of gas.

Illustration 7.6. An air (B)–water vapor (A) sample has a dry-bulb temperature of 135°F and an absolute humidity 0.030 lb water/lb dry air at 1 atm pressure. Tabulate its characteristics.

Solution. The point of coordinates $t = 135°F$, $Y' = 0.030$ is located on the psychrometric chart (Fig. 7.5), a schematic version of which is shown in Fig. 7.6. This is point D on Fig. 7.6.

a. By vertical interpolation between the adjacent curves of constant percent humidity, the sample has a percent humidity of 22.9%. Alternatively, the saturation humidity at 135°F is $Y'_s = 0.131$, and the percent humidity at D is therefore $(0.030/0.131)100 = 22.9\%$.

b. The molal absolute humidity $= Y = Y'(M_B/M_A) = 0.030(28.97/18.02) = 0.0482$ mole water/mole dry air.

c. The partial pressure of water vapor in the sample, by Eq. (7.8), is

$$p_A = \frac{YP_t}{1 + Y} = \frac{0.0482(1)}{1.0482} = 0.0460 \text{ atm}$$

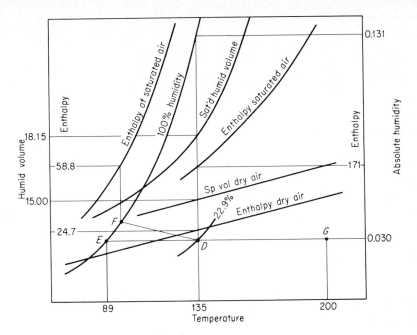

Fig. 7.6   *Solution to Illustrations 7.6 and 7.7.*

d. The vapor pressure of water at 135°F is 0.1727 atm $= P_A$ (steam tables). The relative humidity $= p_A(100)/P_A = 0.0460(100)/0.1727 = 26.6\%$.

e. Dew point. From point D proceed at constant humidity to the saturation curve at point E, at which the dew-point temperature is 89°F.

f. Humid volume. At 135°F, the specific volume of dry air is 15.00 cu ft/lb dry air. The humid volume of saturated air is 18.15 cu ft/lb dry air. Interpolating for 22.9% humidity,

$$v_H = 15.00 + (18.15 - 15.00)(0.229) = 15.72 \text{ cu ft wet air/lb dry air}$$

g. Humid heat, Eq. (7.10)

$$C_S = C_B + Y'C_A = 0.24 + 0.45(0.030) = 0.254 \text{ Btu for wet air/(lb dry air)(°F)}$$

h. Enthalpy. At 135°F, the enthalpy of dry air is 24.7 Btu/lb dry air: that for saturated air is 171 Btu/lb dry air. Interpolating for 22.9% humidity,

$$H' = 24.7 + (171 - 24.7)0.229 = 58.2 \text{ Btu for wet air/lb dry air}$$

Alternatively, Eq. (7.13),

$$H' = C_S(t_G - t_0) + Y'\lambda_0 = 0.254(135 - 32) + 0.030(1,075.8) = 58.4 \text{ Btu/lb dry air}$$

Alternatively, line DF is drawn parallel to the adjacent adiabatic saturation curves. At F, the enthalpy is nearly the same as at D, or 58.8 Btu/lb dry air.

Illustration 7.7. One hundred cubic feet of the moist air of Illustration 7.6 is heated to 200°F. How many Btu are required?

Solution. After heating, the mixture will be at point G (Fig. 7.6).   The mass of dry air $= w_B = 100/v_H = 100/15.72 = 6.35$ lb.

Eq. (7.11): $Q = w_B C_S \Delta t = 6.35(0.254)(200 - 135) = 105$ Btu

Alternatively, the enthalpy of the mixture at G, computed by the methods of Illustration 7.6, is 74.9 Btu/lb dry air.

$$Q = w_B(H'_G - H'_D) = 6.35(74.9 - 58.4) = 105 \text{ Btu}$$

Adiabatic-saturation curves

Consider the operation indicated schematically in Fig. 7.7.   Here the entering gas is contacted with liquid, for example, in a spray, and as a result of diffusion and heat transfer between gas and liquid the gas leaves at conditions of humidity and temperature different from those at the entrance.   The operation is adiabatic inasmuch as no heat is gained or lost to the surroundings.   A mass balance for substance A,

$$L' = G'_S(Y'_2 - Y'_1) \tag{7.14}$$

An enthalpy balance,

$$G'_S H'_1 + L' H_L = G'_S H'_2 \tag{7.15}$$

$$\therefore \quad H'_1 + (Y'_2 - Y'_1)H_L = H'_2 \tag{7.16}$$

This may be expanded by the definition of H' given in Eq. (7.13),

$$C_{S1}(t_{G1} - t_0) + Y'_1 \lambda_0 + (Y'_2 - Y'_1)C_{AL}(t_L - t_0) = C_{S2}(t_{G2} - t_0) + Y'_2 \lambda_0 \tag{7.17}$$

In the special case where the leaving gas-vapor mixture is saturated, and therefore at conditions t_{as}, Y'_{as}, H'_{as}, and the liquid enters at t_{as}, the gas is humidified by evaporation of liquid and cooled.   Equation (7.17) becomes, on expansion of the humid-heat terms,

$$C_B(t_{G1} - t_0) + Y'_1 C_A(t_{G1} - t_0) + Y'_1 \lambda_0 + (Y'_{as} - Y'_1)C_{AL}(t_{as} - t_0)$$
$$= C_B(t_{as} - t_0) + Y'_{as} C_A(t_{as} - t_0) + Y'_{as} \lambda_0 \tag{7.18}$$

By subtracting $Y'_1 C_A t_{as}$ from both sides and simplifying, this becomes

$$(C_B + Y'_1 C_A)(t_{G1} - t_{as}) = C_{S1}(t_{G1} - t_{as})$$
$$= (Y'_{as} - Y'_1)[C_A(t_{as} - t_0) + \lambda_0 - C_{AL}(t_{as} - t_0)] \tag{7.19}$$

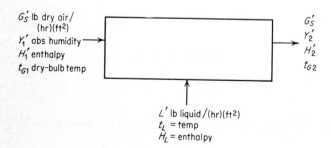

G'_S lb dry air/ (hr)(ft2)
Y'_1 abs humidity
H'_1 enthalpy
t_{G1} dry-bulb temp

G'_S
Y'_2
H'_2
t_{G2}

L' lb liquid /(hr)(ft2)
t_L = temp
H_L = enthalpy

Fig. 7.7   *Adiabatic gas-liquid contact.*

Reference to Fig. 7.3 shows the quantity in brackets to be equal to λ_{as}. Consequently,

$$C_{S1}(t_{G1} - t_{as}) = (Y'_{as} - Y'_1)\lambda_{as} \qquad (7.20)$$

or
$$t_{G1} - t_{as} = (Y'_{as} - Y'_1)\frac{\lambda_{as}}{C_{S1}} \qquad (7.21)$$

This is the equation of a curve on the psychrometric chart, the "adiabatic-saturation curve"† which passes through the points (Y'_{as}, t_{as}) on the 100 percent saturation curve and (Y'_1, t_{G1}). Since the humid heat C_{S1} contains the term Y'_1, the curve is not straight but instead slightly concave upward. For any vapor-gas mixture there is an *adiabatic-saturation temperature* t_{as} such that if contacted with liquid at t_{as}, the gas will become humidified and cooled. If sufficient contact time is available, the gas will become saturated at (Y'_{as}, t_{as}) but otherwise will leave unsaturated at (Y'_2, t_{G2}), a point on the adiabatic-saturation curve for the initial mixture. Eventually, as Eq. (7.20) indicates, the sensible heat given up by the gas in cooling equals the latent heat required to evaporate the added vapor.

The psychrometric chart (Fig. 7.5) for air–water contains a family of adiabatic-saturation curves, as previously noted. Each point on the curve represents a mixture whose adiabatic-saturation temperature is at the intersection of the curve with the 100 percent humidity curve.

Illustration 7.8. Air at 190°F, $Y' = 0.030$ lb water/lb dry air, 1 atm is contacted with water at the adiabatic-saturation temperature and is thereby humidified and cooled to 90% saturation. What are the final temperature and humidity of the air?

Solution. The point representing the original air is located on the psychrometric chart (Fig. 7.5). The adiabatic-saturation curve through the point reaches the 100% saturation curve at 105°F, the adiabatic-saturation temperature. This is the water temperature. On this curve, 90% saturation occurs at 108°F, $Y' = 0.0504$ lb water/lb air, the exit-air conditions.

Wet-bulb temperature

The wet-bulb temperature is the steady-state temperature reached by a small amount of liquid evaporating into a large amount of unsaturated vapor-gas mixture. Under properly controlled conditions it can be used to measure the humidity of the mixture. For this purpose a thermometer whose bulb has been covered with a wick kept wet with the liquid is immersed in a rapidly moving stream of the gas mixture. The temperature indicated by this thermometer will ultimately reach a value lower than the dry-bulb temperature of the gas if the latter is unsaturated, and from a knowledge of this the humidity is computed.

Consider a drop of liquid immersed in a rapidly moving stream of unsaturated vapor-gas mixture. If the liquid is initially at a temperature higher than the gas dew point, the vapor pressure of the liquid will be higher at the drop surface than the

---

† The adiabatic-saturation curve is nearly one of constant enthalpy per pound of dry gas. As Eq. (7.16) indicates, H'_{as} differs from H'_1 by the enthalpy of the evaporated liquid at its entering temperature t_{as} but this difference is usually unimportant.

partial pressure of vapor in the gas, and the liquid will evaporate and diffuse into the gas. The latent heat required for the evaporation will at first be supplied at the expense of the sensible heat of the liquid drop, which will then cool down. As soon as the liquid temperature is reduced below the dry-bulb temperature of the gas, heat will flow from the gas to the liquid, at an increasing rate as the temperature difference becomes larger. Eventually the rate of heat transfer from the gas to the liquid will equal the rate of heat requirement for the evaporation, and the temperature of the liquid will remain constant at some low value, the wet-bulb temperature t_w. The mechanism of the wet-bulb process is essentially the same as that governing the adiabatic saturation, except that in the case of the former the humidity of the gas is assumed not to change during the process.

Refer to Fig. 7.8, sketched in the manner of the film theory, where a drop of liquid is shown already at the steady-state conditions, and the mass of gas is so large as it passes the drop that its humidity is not measurably affected by the evaporation. The problem is very similar to that of Illustration 3.7, and Eq. (3.65) applies with $q_T = 0$ since no heat passes through the gas-liquid interface, and $N_B = 0$. Therefore†

$$q_s = \frac{N_A M_A C_A}{1 - e^{-N_A M_A C_A / h_G}} (t_G - t_w) \doteq h_G(t_G - t_w) \tag{7.22}$$

and the approximation of the right-hand side is usually satisfactory since ordinarily the rate of mass transfer is small. Further,

$$N_A = F \ln \frac{1 - P_{Aw}/P_t}{1 - p_{AG}/P_t} \doteq k_G(p_{AG} - P_{Aw}) \tag{7.23}$$

where the approximation on the right is usually satisfactory since N_A is small [the form of Eq. (7.23) reflects the fact that N_A is negative if q_s is taken to be positive]. P_{Aw} is the vapor pressure of A at t_w. Substituting Eqs. (7.22) and (7.23) into Eq. (3.65) with N_B and q_T equal to zero,

$$h_G(t_G - t_w) + \lambda_w M_A k_G(p_{AG} - P_{Aw}) = 0 \tag{7.24}$$

where λ_w is the latent heat at the wet-bulb temperature per unit of mass. From this,

$$t_G - t_w = \frac{\lambda_w M_A k_G(P_{Aw} - p_{AG})}{h_G} = \frac{\lambda_w M_B p_{BM} k_G(Y'_w - Y')}{h_G} \tag{7.25}$$

† For very careful measurements, the possibility of the liquid surface's receiving heat by radiation from either the gas itself or from the surroundings must also be considered. Assuming that the source of radiation is at temperature t_G, we then have

$$q_s = (h_G + h_R)(t_G - t_w)$$

where the radiative heat transfer is described by an equivalent convection-type coefficient h_R. In wet-bulb thermometry, the effect of radiation may be minimized by using radiation shields and maintaining a high velocity of gas to keep h_G relatively high (at least 15 to 20 ft/sec in the case of air–water vapor mixtures at ordinary temperatures). The relative size of h_G and h_R in any case may be estimated by standard methods.[9] It is necessary to observe the additional precaution of feeding the wick surrounding the thermometer bulb with an adequate supply of liquid preadjusted as nearly as practicable to the wet-bulb temperature.

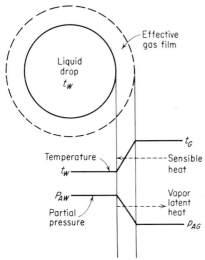

Vapor-gas mixture $\begin{cases} t_G = \text{dry-bulb temp.} \\ p_{AG} = \text{part. pres. of vapor} \\ Y' = \text{abs. humidity} \end{cases}$

Effective gas film

Liquid drop t_w

Temperature t_w

t_G

Sensible heat

Partial pressure p_{Aw}

Vapor latent heat

p_{AG}

Fig. 7.8 *The wet-bulb temperature.*

where p_{BM} is the average partial pressure of the gas.   Since (Table 3.1) $M_B p_{BM} k_G = k_Y$, Eq. (7.25) becomes

$$t_G - t_w = \frac{\lambda_w(Y'_w - Y')}{h_G/k_Y} \tag{7.26}$$

which is the form of the relationship commonly used.   The quantity $t_G - t_w$ is the *wet-bulb depression*.

In order to use Eq. (7.26) for determination of Y', it is necessary to have at hand appropriate values of h_G/k_Y, the *psychrometric ratio*.   Values of h_G and k_Y may be independently estimated for the particular shape of the wetted surface by correlations such as those of Table 3.3.   Alternatively, experimental values of the ratio for special circumstances may be employed.   For the case of *flow of gases past a wetted cylinder such as a wet-bulb thermometer*, a limited number of investigations have been made for a variety of vapors in several gases.   The best of the data show that so long as turbulent flow prevails there is no apparent effect of Reynolds number on the ratio. This is because for most gas-vapor mixtures the ratio Sc/Pr is not very far removed from unity (see page 49).   Bedingfield and Drew[2] made measurements over an extended range of Schmidt numbers, using cast cylinders of a volatile solid which sublimed into the gas stream.   They found, for air as the gas,

$$\frac{h_G}{k_Y} = 0.294 \, \text{Sc}^{0.56} \tag{7.27}$$

and, for other gases (see Table 3.3, item 2),

$$\frac{h_G}{k_Y} = C_S \left(\frac{k}{C_S \rho D_{AB}}\right)^{0.56} = C_S \left(\frac{\text{Sc}}{\text{Pr}}\right)^{0.56} \tag{7.28}$$

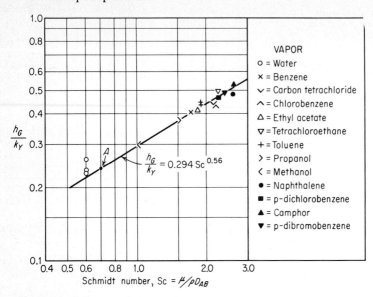

VAPOR

o = Water
x = Benzene
v = Carbon tetrachloride
∧ = Chlorobenzene
△ = Ethyl acetate
∇ = Tetrachloroethane
+ = Toluene
> = Propanol
< = Methanol
● = Naphthalene
■ = p-dichlorobenzene
▲ = Camphor
▼ = p-dibromobenzene

$$\frac{h_G}{k_Y} = 0.294 \, Sc^{0.56}$$

Schmidt number, $Sc = \mu/\rho D_{AB}$

Fig. 7.9 *The ratio h_G/k_Y for wet-bulb thermometry in air–vapor systems.*

The ratio Sc/Pr is the Lewis number Le. Figure 7.9 compares Eq. (7.27) with some of the better data culled from the literature, each different plotted symbol representing a different vapor. For pure air, for which $Sc = Pr = 0.702$, h_G/k_Y should equal $C_S = 0.24$, and the line has been drawn through this point at A on the figure.[2]

A thorough study[16,17] of Dropkin's[3] carefully measured data on wet-bulb thermometers with air–water vapor led to the value $h_G/k_Y = 0.227$, which is recommended for this system. This agrees very closely with Eq. (7.27) and also with the correlation of Lynch and Wilke.[8]

It will be noted that Eq. (7.26) is identical with Eq. (7.21) for the adiabatic-saturation temperature with, however, the replacement of C_{S1} by h_G/k_Y. In the case of the air–water system at moderate humidities, C_{S1} is not greatly different from 0.227, and for many practical purposes the adiabatic-saturation curves of Fig. 7.5 may be used instead of Eq. (7.26). For most other systems, however, the wet-bulb temperature of an unsaturated mixture will be higher than the corresponding adiabatic-saturation temperature.

Illustration 7.9. For an air–water vapor mixture of dry-bulb temperature 150°F, a wet-bulb temperature of 90°F was determined under such conditions that the radiation coefficient may be considered negligible. The total pressure was 1 atm. Compute the humidity of the air.
Solution. At $t_w = 90°F$, $\lambda_w = 1042.9$ Btu/lb, and $Y'_w = 0.031$ lb H_2O/lb dry air (Fig. 7.5); $h_G/k_Y = 0.227$, $t_G = 150°F$.

Eq. (7.26):
$$150 - 90 = \frac{1,042.9}{0.227}(0.031 - Y')$$

$$Y' = 0.0179 \text{ lb water/lb air}$$

Alternatively as an approximation, the adiabatic-saturation curve for $t_{as} = 90°F$ on Fig. 7.5 is followed down to a dry-bulb temperature 150°F, where Y' is read as 0.0170.

Illustration 7.10. Estimate the wet-bulb and adiabatic-saturation temperatures for a toluene–air mixture of 140°F dry-bulb temperature, $Y' = 0.050$ lb vapor/lb air, 1 atm.

Solution. a. Wet bulb temperature. $t_G = 140°F$ (60°C), $Y' = 0.050$ lb vapor/lb air. From Table 2.1 $D_{AB} = 0.092$ sq cm/sec at 59.0°C, 1 atm, or 0.092(3.87) = 0.356 sq ft/hr. At 140°F, ρ for air = 0.0663 lb/cu ft, and $\mu = 0.0195$ centipoise, or 0.0472 lb/(ft)(hr).

Sc *should* be calculated for mean conditions between those of the gas-vapor mixture and the wet-bulb saturation conditions, but for dilute gas mixtures the values of ρ and μ for air are satisfactory.

$$\text{Sc} = \frac{\mu}{\rho D_{AB}} = \frac{0.0472}{0.0663(0.356)} = 2.00$$

Eq. (7.27): $\dfrac{h_G}{k_Y} = 0.294(2.00)^{0.56} = 0.431$ Btu/(lb)(°F)   (obsvd value = 0.44)

Eq. (7.26): $$140 - t_w = \frac{\lambda_w}{0.431}(Y'_w - 0.050)$$

Solution for t_w is by trial and error. Try $t_w = 90°F$. $\lambda_w = 183$ Btu/lb. The vapor pressure of toluene at 90°F = 41.3 mm Hg.

$$\therefore \quad Y'_w = \frac{41.3}{760 - 41.3}\frac{92.1}{29} = 0.1827 \text{ lb vapor/lb air}$$

and the equation gives $t_w = 83.8°F$ instead of the 90°F assumed. On repeated trials, t_w is computed to be 88°F.

b. Adiabatic-saturation temperature. $t_1 = 140°F$, $Y'_1 = 0.050$. C for toluene vapor = 0.30 Btu/(lb)(°F). $C_{S1} = 0.24 + 0.05(0.30) = 0.255$ Btu/(lb air)(°F).

Eq. (7.21): $$140 - t_{as} = (Y'_{as} - 0.05)\frac{\lambda_{as}}{0.255}$$

In the same fashion as the wet-bulb temperature, t_{as} is calculated by trial and found to be 79°F.

The Lewis relation

We have seen that *for the system air–water vapor, h_G/k_Y is approximately equal to C_S*, or, approximately, $h_G/k_Y C_S = 1$. This is the so-called Lewis relation (after W. K. Lewis). Not only does this lead to near equality of the wet-bulb and adiabatic-saturation temperatures (as in the case of air–water vapor), but also to other simplifications to be developed later. It is important to recognize the circumstances which bring this about.

The heat-transfer coefficient h_G may be defined through Eq. (3.28):

$$h_G = \frac{q}{\Delta t} = -\frac{\alpha + E_H}{\Delta t}\frac{d(t\rho C)}{dz} = \frac{(\alpha + E_H)\rho C}{\Delta z} \tag{7.29}$$

Similarly, Eq. (3.26), if bulk flow is neglected ($J_A = N_A$), leads to the mass-transfer coefficient

$$k_c = \frac{N_A}{\Delta c} = -\frac{D + E_D}{\Delta c_A}\frac{dc_A}{dz} = \frac{D + E_D}{\Delta z} = \frac{k_Y RT}{p_{BM}M_B} \tag{7.30}$$

Consequently,

$$\frac{h_G}{k_Y} = \frac{(\alpha + E_H)\rho CRT}{(D + E_D)p_{BM}M_B} \tag{7.31}$$

and since $p_{BM}M_B/RT = \rho$, and $C \doteq C_s$,

$$\frac{h_G}{k_Y C_s} = \frac{\alpha + E_H}{D + E_D} \qquad (7.32)$$

Now we have seen (page 49) that $E_D = E_H$. Consequently $h_G/k_Y C_s = 1$ only if $\alpha = D$, or $\text{Pr} = \text{Sc}$, or $\text{Le} = 1.0$. For low concentrations of water vapor in air, $\text{Sc} = 0.60$ and $\text{Pr} = 0.702$, so that the Lewis relation is nearly followed. For other systems, Lewis numbers are roughly in the range 0.3 to 5, and the simplifications resulting from the Lewis relation will only rarely accrue.

GAS-LIQUID CONTACT OPERATIONS

Direct contact of a gas with a pure liquid may have any of several purposes:

1. *Cooling a hot gas.* Direct contact provides a nonfouling heat exchanger which is very effective, providing vaporization of some of the liquid into the gas is not objectionable.

2. *Humidifying a gas.* This may be used for controlling the moisture content of air for drying, for example.

3. *Dehumidifying a gas.* Contact of a warm vapor-gas mixture with cold liquid results in condensation of the vapor. This has applications in air conditioning, recovery of solvent vapors from gases used in drying, and the like.

4. *Cooling a liquid.* The cooling occurs by transfer of sensible heat and also by evaporation. The principal application is cooling of water by contact with atmospheric air (water cooling).

Although operations of this sort are simple in the sense that mass transfer is confined to the gas phase (there can be no mass transfer within the pure liquid), they are nevertheless complex owing to the very large heat effects which accompany evaporation or condensation. The discussion here will be confined to adiabatic operations, i.e., where no heat is added to, or removed from, the system except by the liquid and gas being contacted. There are important nonadiabatic operations also: "evaporative cooling,"[17] for example, where a liquid inside a pipe is cooled by water flowing in a film about the outside, the latter in turn being cooled by direct contact with air; dehumidification of a gas by contact with refrigerated tubes; and many others.

Fundamental relationships

The adiabatic operations are usually carried out countercurrently in a packed tower of some sort. Refer to Fig. 7.10, which shows a tower of unit cross-sectional area. A mass balance for substance A over the lower part of the tower (envelope I) is

$$L' - L'_1 = G'_S(Y' - Y'_1) \qquad (7.33)$$

or

$$dL' = G'_S \, dY' \qquad (7.34)$$

Similarly, an enthalpy balance is

$$L'H_L + G'_S H'_1 = L'_1 H_{L1} + G'_S H' \qquad (7.35)$$

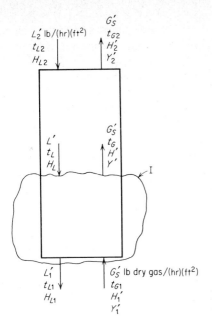

Fig. 7.10 *Continuous countercurrent adiabatic gas-liquid contact.*

These may be applied to the entire tower by putting subscript 2 on the unnumbered terms.

The rate relationships are fairly complex and will be developed in the manner of Olander.[14]   Refer to Fig. 7.11, which represents a section of the tower of differential height dZ and shows the liquid and gas flowing side by side, separated by the gas-liquid interface.   The changes in temperature, humidity, etc., are all differential over this section.

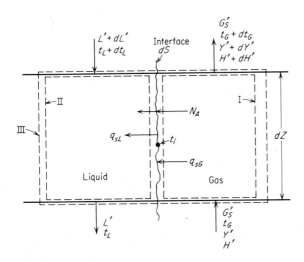

Fig. 7.11 *Differential section of a packed tower.*

The interfacial surface of the section is dS. If the interfacial surface per unit volume of packing is a sq ft/cu ft (not the same as the packing surface a_p), since the volume of packing per unit tower cross section is dZ cu ft, then $dS = a\,dZ$. If the packing is incompletely wetted by the liquid, the surface for mass transfer a_M, which is the liquid-gas interface, will be smaller than that for heat transfer a_H, since heat transfer may also occur between the packing and the fluids. Note that a_M corresponds to a_V of Chap. 6. The transfer rates are then:

Mass, as lb vapor/(hr)(sq ft tower cross section)

$$N_A M_A a_M\,dZ = -G_S'\,dY' = M_A F_G\left(\ln\frac{1 - P_{Ai}/P_t}{1 - p_{AG}/P_t}\right)a_M\,dZ \qquad (7.36)$$

Sensible heat, as Btu/(hr)(sq ft tower cross section)

Gas: $\quad q_{sG}a_H\,dZ = \dfrac{N_A M_A C_A}{1 - e^{-N_A M_A C_A/h_G}}\,(t_G - t_i)a_H\,dZ = h_G'a_H(t_G - t_i)\,dZ \qquad (7.37)$

Liquid: $\qquad\qquad q_{sL}a_H\,dZ = h_L a_H(t_i - t_L)\,dZ \qquad\qquad\qquad (7.38)$

In Eq. (7.36), P_{Ai} is the vapor pressure of A at the interface temperature t_i, and p_{AG} is the partial pressure in the bulk gas. In Eq. (7.37), radiation has been neglected, and the coefficient h_G', which accounts for the effect of mass transfer on heat transfer, replaces the ordinary convection coefficient h_G (see Chap. 3). The rate equations are written as if transfer were in the direction gas to interface to liquid, but they are directly applicable as written to all situations; correct signs for the fluxes will develop automatically.

We now require a series of enthalpy balances based on the envelopes sketched in Fig. 7.11.

Envelope I

Rate enthalpy in $= G_S'H'$

Rate enthalpy out $= G_S'(H' + dH') - (G_S'\,dY')[C_A(t_G - t_0) + \lambda_0]$

The second term is the enthalpy of the transferred vapor [recall N_A and $G_S\,dY$ have opposite signs in Eq. (7.36)].

Rate in — rate out = heat-transfer rate

$$G_S'H' - G_S'(H' + dH') + (G_S'\,dY')[C_A(t_G - t_0) + \lambda_0] = h_G'a_H(t_G - t_i)\,dZ \quad (7.39)$$

If dH', obtained by differentiation of Eq. (7.13), is substituted, this reduces to

$$-G_S'C_S\,dt_G = h_G'a_H(t_G - t_i)\,dZ \qquad (7.40)$$

Envelope II

Rate enthalpy in $= (L' + dL')C_{AL}(t_L + dt_L - t_0) + (-G'_S dY')C_{AL}(t_i - t_0)$

Here the second term is the enthalpy of the material transferred, now a liquid.

$$\text{Rate enthalpy out} = L'C_{AL}(t_L - t_0)$$

Rate out = rate in + heat-transfer rate

$$L'C_{AL}(t_L - t_0) = (L' + dL')C_{AL}(t_L + dt_L - t_0) - (G'_S dY')C_{AL}(t_i - t_0)$$

$$+ h_L a_H (t_i - t_L) dZ \tag{7.41}$$

If Eq. (7.34) is substituted and the second-order differential $dY' dt_L$ ignored, this becomes

$$L'C_{AL} dt_L = (G'_S C_{AL} dY' - h_L a_H dZ)(t_i - t_L) \tag{7.42}$$

Envelope III

$$\text{Rate enthalpy in} = G'_S H' + (L' + dL')C_{AL}(t_L + dt_L - t_0)$$

$$\text{Rate enthalpy out} = L'C_{AL}(t_L - t_0) + G'_S(H' + dH')$$

Rate in = rate out (adiabatic operation)

$$G'_S H' + (L' + dL')C_{AL}(t_L + dt_L - t_0) = L'C_{AL}(t_L - t_0) + G'_S(H' + dH') \tag{7.43}$$

Substitutions of Eq. (7.34) and the differential of Eq. (7.13) for dH' are made, and the term $dH' dt_L$ is ignored, whereupon this becomes

$$L'C_{AL} dt_L = G'_S\{C_S dt_G + [C_A(t_G - t_0) - C_{AL}(t_L - t_0) + \lambda_0] dY'\} \tag{7.44}$$

These will now be applied to the adiabatic operations.

Water cooling with air

This is without question the most important of the operations. Water, warmed by passage through heat exchangers, condensers, and the like, is cooled by contact with atmospheric air for reuse. The latent heat of water is so large that only a small amount of evaporation produces large cooling effects. Since the rate of mass transfer is usually small, the temperature level is generally fairly low, and the Lewis relation applies reasonably well for the air–water system, the relationships of the previous section may be greatly simplified by making reasonable approximations.

Thus, if the sensible heat terms of Eq. (7.44) are ignored in comparison with the latent heat, we have

$$L'C_{AL} dt_L = G'_S C_S dt_G + G'_S \lambda_0 dY' \doteq G'_S dH \tag{7.45}$$

Here the last term on the right ignores the Y' which appears in the definition of C_S. Integrating, on the further assumption that L' is essentially constant (little evaporation),

$$L'C_{AL}(t_{L2} - t_{L1}) = G'_S(H'_2 - H'_1) \tag{7.46}$$

This enthalpy balance may be represented graphically by plotting the gas enthalpy H' against t_L, as in Fig. 7.12.   The line ON on the chart represents Eq. (7.46), and it passes through the points representing the terminal conditions for the two fluids. Insofar as $L'_2 - L'_1$ is small in comparison with L', the line is straight and of slope $L'C_{AL}/G'_S$.   The equilibrium curve in the figure is plotted for conditions of the gas at the gas-liquid interface, i.e., the enthalpy of saturated gas at each temperature.

If the mass-transfer rate is small, as it usually is, Eq. (7.36) may be written as

$$G'_S \, dY' = k_Y a_M (Y'_i - Y') \, dZ \tag{7.47}$$

and Eq. (7.40) as

$$G'_S C_S \, dt_G = h_G a_H (t_i - t_G) \, dZ \tag{7.48}$$

Ignoring the sensible heat of the transferred vapor, Eq. (7.42) becomes

$$L'C_{AL} \, dt_L = h_L a_H (t_L - t_i) \, dZ \tag{7.49}$$

Substituting Eqs. (7.47) and (7.48) into (7.45):

$$G'_S \, dH' = h_G a_H (t_i - t_G) \, dZ + \lambda_0 k_Y a_M (Y'_i - Y') \, dZ \tag{7.50}$$

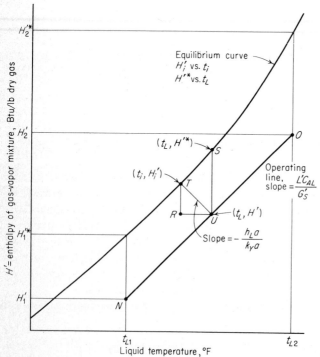

Fig. 7.12 *Operating diagram for a water cooler.*

If $h_G a_H / C_S k_Y a_M = r$, this becomes

$$G_S' \, dH' = k_Y a_M [(C_S r t_i + \lambda_0 Y_i') - (C_S r t_G + \lambda_0 Y')] \, dZ \tag{7.51}$$

For the special case where r = 1,[11,12] the terms in parentheses are gas enthalpies. The restriction that $r = 1$ requires Le = 1 (air–water), and $a_M = a_H = a$ (the latter will be true only for thoroughly irrigated tower filling; even for air–water contacting, values of r as high as 2 have been observed with low liquid rates[6]). With these understood, Eq. (7.51) is

$$G_S' \, dH' = k_Y a (H_i' - H') \, dZ \tag{7.52}$$

which is remarkable in that the mass-transfer coefficient is used with an enthalpy driving force. Combining Eqs. (7.45), (7.49), and (7.52) then provides

$$G_S' \, dH' = k_Y a (H_i' - H') \, dZ = h_L a (t_L - t_i) \, dZ \tag{7.53}$$

At a position in the apparatus corresponding to point U on the operating line (Fig. 7.12), point T represents the interface conditions and the distance TR the enthalpy driving force $H_i' - H'$ within the gas phase. By making constructions like the triangle RTU at several places along the operating line, corresponding H_i' and H' values may be obtained. Equation (7.53) then provides, assuming $k_Y a$ is constant,

$$\int_{H_1'}^{H_2'} \frac{dH'}{H_i' - H'} = \frac{k_Y a}{G_S'} \int_0^Z dZ = \frac{k_Y a Z}{G_S'} \tag{7.54}$$

The integral may be evaluated graphically and the packed height Z computed. The enthalpy integral of Eq. (7.54) is sometimes given another interpretation. Thus,

$$\int_{H_1'}^{H_2'} \frac{dH'}{H_i' - H'} = \frac{H_2' - H_1'}{(H_i' - H')_{\text{av}}} = N_{tG} \tag{7.55}$$

where the middle part of the equation is the number of times the average driving force divides into the enthalpy change. This is a measure of the difficulty of enthalpy transfer, called the *number of gas-enthalpy transfer units* N_{tG}. Consequently,

$$Z = H_{tG} N_{tG} \tag{7.56}$$

where the height of a gas-enthalpy transfer unit $= H_{tG} = G_S' / k_Y a$. H_{tG} is frequently preferred over $k_Y a$ as a measure of packing performance since it is less dependent upon rates of flow and has the simple dimension of length.

As discussed in Chap. 5, an overall driving force representing the enthalpy difference for the bulk phases but expressed in terms of H' may be used, such as the vertical distance SU (Fig. 7.12). This requires a corresponding overall coefficient and leads to overall numbers and heights of transfer units:†

$$N_{tOG} = \int_{H_1'}^{H_2'} \frac{dH'}{H'^* - H'} = \frac{K_Y a Z}{G_S'} = \frac{Z}{H_{tOG}} \tag{7.57}$$

† The water-cooling-tower industry frequently uses Eq. (7.57) in another form:

$$\frac{K_Y a Z}{L'} = \int_{t_{L1}}^{t_{L2}} \frac{dt_L}{H'^* - H'}$$

which results from combining Eqs. (7.45) and (7.57) and setting C_{AL} for water $= 1$.

The use of Eq. (7.56) is satisfactory (see Chap. 5) only if the equilibrium enthalpy curve of Fig. 7.12 is straight, which is not strictly so, or if $h_L a$ is infinite, so that the interface temperature equals the bulk-liquid temperature. Although the few data available indicate that $h_L a$ is usually quite large (see, for example, Illustration 6.5), there are uncertainties owing to the fact that many have been taken under conditions such that $h_G a_H / C_S k_Y a_M = r$ was *not* unity even though assumed to be so. In any case, it frequently happens that, for cooling-tower packings, only $K_Y a$ or H_{tOG}, and not the individual phase coefficients, are available.

Just as with concentrations (Chap. 5), an operating line on the enthalpy co-ordinates of Fig. 7.12 which anywhere touches the equilibrium curve results in a zero driving force and consequently an infinite interfacial surface, or infinite height Z, to accomplish a given temperature change in the liquid. This condition would then represent the limiting ratio of L'/G_S' permissible. It is also clear that point N, for example, will be below the equilibrium curve so long as the entering-air enthalpy H_1' is less than the saturation enthalpy $H_1'^*$ for air at t_{L1}. Since the enthalpy H' is for most practical purposes only a function of the adiabatic-saturation temperature (or, for air–water, the wet-bulb temperature), the entering-air wet-bulb temperature must be below t_{L1} *but its dry-bulb temperature need not be*. For this reason, it is perfectly possible to cool water to a value of t_{L1} less than the entering-air dry-bulb temperature t_{G1}. It is also possible to operate a cooler with entering air saturated, so long as its temperature is less than t_{L1}. The difference between the exit-liquid temperature and the entering-air wet-bulb temperature, $t_{L1} - t_{w1}$, called the "wet-bulb temperature approach," is then a measure of the driving force available for diffusion at the lower end of the equipment. In the design of cooling towers, this is ordinarily specified to be from 5 to 10°F, with t_{w1} set at the "5 percent wet-bulb temperature" (the wet-bulb temperature which is exceeded only 5 percent of the time on the average during the summer months). "Makeup" fresh water in recirculating water systems must be added to replace losses from entrainment, evaporation losses, and "blowdown." If makeup water introduces dissolved salts ("hardness") which will otherwise accumulate, a small amount of the water is deliberately discarded (blow-down) to keep the salt concentration at some predetermined level. Many other practical details are available.[10,13] Some cooling towers use a cross flow of water and air, for which the methods of computation are also available.[1]

The use of overall mass-transfer coefficients does not distinguish between convec-tive and evaporative cooling of the liquid and will not permit computation of the humidity or dry-bulb temperature of the exit air. The air will ordinarily be very nearly saturated, and for purposes of estimating makeup requirements it may be so assumed. The temperature-humidity history of the air as it passes through the tower may be estimated by a graphical method on the $H't_L$ diagram (Fig. 7.12) if $h_L a$ and $k_Y a$ are known,[12] but approach of the gas to saturation is very critical to the compu-tations, and it is recommended instead that these be done by the methods outlined later (see page 208) which make no assumptions. Cooling towers for systems other than air–water (Le $\neq$ 1), or when $a_M \neq a_H$, must also be treated by the general methods discussed later.

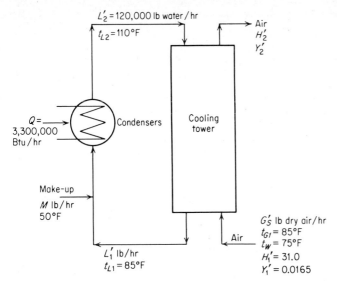

$L'_2 = 120,000$ lb water / hr
$t_{L2} = 110°F$

→ Air
H'_2
Y'_2

$Q = $ 3,300,000 Btu / hr

Condensers

Cooling tower

Make-up
M lb / hr
50°F

L'_1 lb/hr
$t_{L1} = 85°F$

Air

G'_S lb dry air/hr
$t_{G1} = 85°F$
$t_w = 75°F$
$H'_1 = 31.0$
$Y'_1 = 0.0165$

Fig. 7.13 *Flow sheet for Illustration 7.11.*

Illustration 7.11. A plant requires 2,000 lb/min of cooling water to flow through its distillation-equipment condensers, thereby removing 55,000 Btu/min from the condensers. The water will leave the condensers at 110°F. It is planned to cool it for reuse by contact with air in an induced-draft cooling tower. Makeup water will come from a well at 50°F. The design conditions chosen are entering air at 85°F dry-bulb, 75°F wet-bulb temperature; water cooled to within 10°F of the inlet-air wet-bulb temperature, i.e., to 85°F; an air/water ratio of 1.5 times the minimum. For the packing to be used, $K_Y a$ is expected to be 200 lb/(hr)(cu ft)($\Delta Y'$), provided the liquid rate is at least 2,000 lb/(hr)(sq ft) and the gas rate 1,500 lb/(hr)(sq ft). Compute the required cross section and packed height of the cooling tower, and estimate the makeup water required.

Solution. Refer to Fig. 7.13, which represents the flow sheet of the operation. The entering-air humidity and enthalpy are taken from Fig. 7.5. The operating diagram (Fig. 7.14) contains the saturated air-enthalpy curve, and on this plot is point N representing the conditions at the bottom of the tower ($t_{L1} = 85°F$, $H'_1 = 31.0$). The operating line will pass through N and end at $t_{L2} = 110°F$. For the minimum value of G'_s, the operating line will have the least slope which causes it to touch the equilibrium curve and will consequently pass through point O', where $H'_2 = 84.7$ Btu/lb dry air. The slope of line $O'N$ is therefore

$$\frac{L'C_{AL}}{G'_{s,min}} = \frac{120,000(1)}{G'_{s,min}} = \frac{84.7 - 31.0}{110 - 85}$$

and $G'_{s,min} = 55,900$ lb dry air/hr. For a gas rate of 1.5 times the minimum, $G'_s = 1.5(55,900) = 83,800$ lb dry air/hr. Therefore

$$\frac{H'_2 - 31.0}{110 - 85} = \frac{120,000(1)}{83,800}$$

and $H'_2 = 66.8$ Btu/lb dry air, plotted at point O. The operating line is therefore line ON. For a liquid rate of at least 2,000 lb/(hr)(sq ft), the tower cross section would be $120,000/2,000 = 60$ sq ft. For a gas rate of at least 1,500 lb/(hr)(sq ft), the cross section will be $83,800/1,500 = 56$ sq ft. The latter will therefore be used, since the liquid rate will then exceed the minimum to ensure $K_Y a = 200$.

Basis: 1 sq ft cross section. $G'_s = 1{,}500$ lb dry gas/hr.   The driving force $H'^* - H'$ is computed at frequent intervals of t_L from Fig. 7.14 as listed below:

t_L, °F	H'^* (equilibrium curve)	H' (operating line)	$1/(H'^* - H')$
85	41.9	31.0	0.0917
90	48.2	38.3	0.1011
95	55.7	45.3	0.0980
100	64.0	52.5	0.0885
105	74.2	59.5	0.0680
110	84.7	66.8	0.0558

The data of the last two columns are plotted against each other, H' as abscissa, and the area under the curve is 3.18.   From Eq. (7.57),

$$3.18 = \frac{K_y a Z}{G'_s} = \frac{200 Z}{1{,}500} \qquad Z = 23.8 \text{ ft of packed height}$$

(*Note:* For this case, $N_{tOG} = 3.18$, and $H_{tOG} = G'_s / K_y a = 1{,}500/200 = 7.5$ ft.)
The makeup water requirement, M lb/hr, can only be estimated.   Refer to Fig. 7.13.   If the exit air is assumed to be saturated, its humidity Y'_2 must be that for saturated air at $H'_s = H'_2 = 66.8$, or $Y'_2 = 0.0453$.   Since G'_s was calculated on the assumption that $L'_2 = L'_1$ (a straight operating line), thus not allowing for evaporation, it is best to eliminate G'_s in estimating M.   An enthalpy balance for the entire plant,

$$3{,}300{,}000 + M(1)(50 - 32) + G'_s(31.0) = G'_s H'_2$$

A water balance,

$$M = G'_s(Y'_2 - 0.0165)$$

Eliminating G'_s, and substituting for H'_2 and Y'_2, $M = 2{,}690$ lb/hr.   **Ans.**

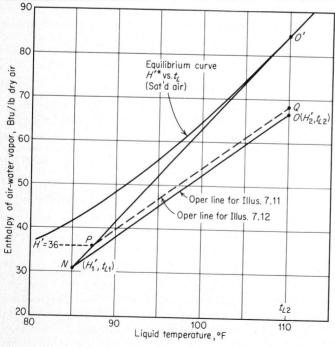

Fig. 7.14   *Solutions to Illustrations 7.11 and 7.12.*

Illustration 7.12. In the cooler of Illustration 7.11, to what temperature would the water be cooled if, after the tower was built and operated at the design L'/G'_S ratio, the entering air should enter at dry-bulb temperature $t_{G1} = 85°F$ and wet-bulb temperature $t_{w1} = 80°F$?

Solution. For the new conditions, $t_{L2} = 110°F$ and $H_1 = 36.0$ Btu/lb dry air, and the slope of the operating line is the same as that for Illustration 7.11. Refer to Fig. 7.14. The new operating line will be parallel to line ON and end at $H'_1 = 36.0$ and at $t_{L2} = 110°F$. Since the coefficient K_Ya is unchanged, the line is located by trial and error so that the area under the curve of $1/(H'^* - H')$ vs. H' remains at 3.18, the value found previously. The line PQ (Fig. 7.14) is found to satisfy these conditions, and t_{L1} is read at point P as 87.4°F, the new outlet-water temperature.

Alternatively, it might have been assumed that the heat load of the tower, the same as the heat load of the plant which uses the circulating water, remains constant, so that

$$83,800(66.8 - 31.0) = 83,800(H'_2 - 36)$$

whence $H'_2 = 71.8$. This, by a procedure similar to that above, results in $t_{L1} = 86.0°F$ and $t_{L2} = 111°F$.

Dehumidification of air–water vapor

If a warm vapor-gas mixture is contacted with cold liquid so that the humidity of the gas is greater than that at the gas-liquid interface, vapor will diffuse toward the liquid, and the gas will be dehumidified. In addition, sensible heat may be transferred as a result of temperature differences within the system. For air–water vapor mixtures (Le = 1) contacted with cold water, the methods of water cooling apply with only obvious modification. The operating line on the gas enthalpy–liquid temperature graph will be above the equilibrium curve, the driving force is $H' - H'^*$, and Eq. (7.57) may be used with this driving force. For all other systems, for which Le $\neq$ 1, the general methods below must be used.

Tray towers. Water cooling may be carried out in stagewise fashion in any of the tray towers discussed in Chap. 6, although it is not generally the custom to do so. The determination of the number of ideal trays, following the principles of Chap. 5, is done on the $H't_L$ diagram.

Recirculating liquid.   Gas humidification-cooling

This is a special case where the liquid enters the equipment at the adiabatic-saturation temperature of the entering gas. This may be achieved by continuously reintroducing the exit liquid to the contactor immediately, without addition or removal of heat on the way, as in Fig. 7.15. The development which follows applies to any liquid-gas system, regardless of the Lewis number. In such a system, the temperature of the entire liquid will fall to, and remain at, the adiabatic-saturation temperature. The gas will be cooled and humidified, following along the path of the adiabatic-saturation curve on the psychrometric chart which passes through the entering-gas conditions. Depending upon the degree of contact, the gas will approach more or less closely equilibrium with the liquid, or its adiabatic-saturation conditions. This supposes that the makeup liquid enters at the adiabatic-saturation temperature also, but for most purposes the quantity of evaporation is so small relative to the total liquid circulation that minor deviations from this temperature for the makeup liquid may be ignored.

As has been shown previously, the enthalpy of the gas is practically a function only of its adiabatic-saturation temperature, which remains constant throughout the operation. The enthalpy of the liquid at constant temperature is also constant, so that an operating "line" on a plot such as Fig. 7.12 would be merely a single point on the equilibrium curve. This diagram cannot therefore be used for design purposes. The temperature and humidity changes, which lie entirely within the gas phase, can be used, however, and these are shown schematically in Fig. 7.15. If mass transfer is used as a basis for design, Eq. (7.47) becomes

$$G'_S \, dY = k_Y a(Y'_{as} - Y') \, dZ \tag{7.58}$$

$$\int_{Y'_1}^{Y'_2} \frac{dY'}{Y_{as} - Y'} = \frac{k_Y a}{G_S} \int_0^Z dZ \tag{7.59}$$

and since Y'_{as} is constant,

$$\ln \frac{Y'_{as} - Y'_1}{Y'_{as} - Y'_2} = \frac{k_Y a Z}{G_S} \tag{7.60}$$

Equation (7.60) may be used directly, or it may be rearranged by solving for G'_S and multiplying each side by $Y'_2 - Y'_1$ or its equivalent,

$$G'_S(Y'_2 - Y'_1) = \frac{k_Y a Z[(Y'_{as} - Y'_1) - (Y'_{as} - Y'_2)]}{\ln[(Y'_{as} - Y'_1)/(Y'_{as} - Y'_2)]} = k_Y a Z(\Delta Y')_{av} \tag{7.61}$$

where $(\Delta Y')_{av}$ is the logarithmic average of the humidity-difference driving forces a the ends of the equipment. Alternatively,

$$N_{tG} = \frac{Y'_2 - Y'_1}{(\Delta Y')_{av}} = \ln \frac{Y'_{as} - Y'_1}{Y'_{as} - Y'_2} \tag{7.62}$$

and

$$H_{tG} = \frac{G'_S}{k_Y a} = \frac{Z}{N_{tG}} \tag{7.63}$$

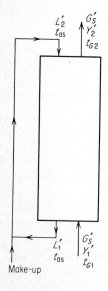

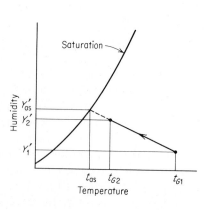

Fig. 7.15 Recirculating liquid, gas humidification-cooling.

where N_{tG} is the number of gas-phase transfer units and H_{tG} the corresponding height of a transfer unit.†

In contacting operations of this sort, where one phase approaches equilibrium with the other under conditions such that the characteristics of the latter do not change, the maximum change in the first phase corresponds to the operation of one theoretical stage (see Chap. 5). Since the humidity in adiabatic equilibrium with the liquid is Y'_{as}, the Murphree gas-phase stage efficiency is then

$$E_{MG} = \frac{Y'_2 - Y'_1}{Y'_{as} - Y'_1} = 1 - \frac{Y'_{as} - Y'_2}{Y'_{as} - Y'_1} = 1 - e^{-k_Y a Z/G'_S} = 1 - e^{-N_{tG}} \quad (7.64)$$

If heat transfer is used as the basis for design, similar treatment of Eq. (7.48) leads to

$$G'_S C_{S1}(t_{G1} - t_{G2}) = \frac{h_G a Z[(t_{G1} - t_{as}) - (t_{G2} - t_{as})]}{\ln [(t_{G1} - t_{as})/(t_{G2} - t_{as})]} = h_G a Z (\Delta t)_{av} \quad (7.65)$$

where $h_G a$ is the volumetric-heat-transfer coefficient of sensible-heat transfer between the bulk of the gas and the liquid surface.

Illustration 7.13. A horizontal spray chamber (Fig. 7.19) with recirculated water is to be used for the adiabatic humidification and cooling of air. The active part of the chamber is 5 ft long and has a cross section of 20 sq ft. With the nozzle arrangement provided, and when operated with the water-circulation rate recommended by the nozzle manufacturer, the coefficient of heat transfer is expected to be $h_G a = 85$ Btu/(hr)(cu ft)(°F). An amount 7,500 cu ft/min of air at 150°F, $Y' = 0.0170$ lb water/lb dry air, is to be blown through the spray.

    a.   What exit temperature and humidity can be expected for the air?

    b.   What makeup water will be needed?

    c.   Express the performance in terms of $k_Y a$, N_{tG}, H_{tG}, and stage efficiency.

    d.   If a duplicate spray chamber, operated in the same manner, were to be added in series with the first, what exit conditions would be expected for the air?

    Solution. a.   From the psychrometric chart (Fig. 7.5), the initial air has a percentage humidity of 8.0%. The dry specific volume of air at 150°F = 15.38, and the saturated volume = 20.60 cu ft/lb dry air. The humid volume of the entering air is therefore

$$v_H = 15.38 + 0.08(20.60 - 15.38) = 15.80 \text{ cu ft humid air/lb dry air}$$

$$G'_S = \frac{7,500(60)}{15.80(20)} = 1,422 \text{ lb dry air/(hr)(sq ft)}$$

The initial humid heat = $C_{S1} = 0.24 + 0.45Y' = 0.24 + 0.45(0.017) = 0.248$ Btu/(lb dry air)(°F). $t_{G1} = 150$°F, and the air lies on the adiabatic-saturation line for $t_{as} = 90$°F. $Z = 5$ ft.

Eq. (7.65):
$$1,422(0.248)(150 - t_{G2}) = \frac{85(5)[(150 - 90) - (t_{G2} - 90)]}{\ln [(150 - 90)/(t_{G2} - 90)]}$$

$$= \frac{85(5)(150 - t_{G2})}{\ln [60/(t_{G2} - 90)]}$$

$$t_{G2} = 108°F$$

---

† To be entirely consistent with the definition of Chap. 8, Eq. (7.63) should read $H_{tG} = G'_S/k_Y a(1 - y_A)$. The value of $1 - y_A$ in the present application is, however, ordinarily very close to unity.

On the 90°F adiabatic-saturation curve, the humidity at this temperature is $Y_2' = 0.0268$ lb water/lb dry air.

b. The makeup water,

$$G_S'(20)(Y_2' - Y_1') = 1{,}422(20)(0.0268 - 0.0170) = 278 \text{ lb/hr}$$

c. Y_{as}' (at 90°F) = 0.0312 lb water/lb dry air.

Eq. (7.62): $$N_{tG} = \ln \frac{Y_{as}' - Y_1'}{Y_{as}' - Y_2'} = \ln \frac{0.0312 - 0.0170}{0.0312 - 0.0268} = 1.15 \text{ transfer units}$$

Eq. (7.60): $$k_Y a = \frac{G_S'}{Z} \ln \frac{Y_{as}' - Y_1'}{Y_{as}' - Y_2'} = \frac{1{,}422}{5}\, 1.15 = 327 \text{ lb water evapd/(hr)(cu ft)}(\Delta Y')$$

Eq. (7.63): $$H_{tG} = \frac{Z}{N_{tG}} = \frac{5}{1.15} = 4.35 \text{ ft}$$

Eq. (7.64): $$E_{MG} = 1 - e^{-N_{tG}} = 1 - \frac{1}{e^{1.15}} = 0.684, \text{ or } 68.4\%$$

d. $Z = 10$ ft.   At the same air rate and spray density, the coefficients are unchanged.

Eq. (7.65): $$1{,}422(0.248)(150 - t_{G2}) = \frac{85(10)(150 - t_{G2})}{\ln [60/(t_{G2} - 90)]}$$

$$t_{G2} = 95.4°F$$

Y_2', read from the adiabatic-saturation curve as before, is 0.0298 lb water/lb dry air.

General methods

For all other countercurrent operations, and even for those discussed above when the approximations are not appropriate or when Le $\ne$ 1, we must return to the equations on page 198.   Equating the right-hand sides of Eqs. (7.42) and (7.44) provides

$$t_i = t_L + \frac{G_S'\{C_S(dt_G/dZ) + [C_A t_G - C_{AL}t_L + (C_{AL} - C_A)t_0 + \lambda_0](dY'/dZ)\}}{G_S' C_{AL}(dY'/dZ) - h_L a_H} \tag{7.66}$$

The humidity gradient in this expression is obtained from Eq. (7.36):

$$\frac{dY'}{dZ} = -\frac{M_A F_G a_M}{G_S'} \ln \frac{1 - p_{Ai}/P_t}{1 - p_{AG}/P_t} = -\frac{M_A F_G a_M}{G_S'} \ln \frac{Y' + M_A/M_B}{Y_i' + M_A/M_B} \tag{7.67}$$

$$\doteq -\frac{M_A k_G a_M}{G_S'}(p_{AG} - p_{Ai}) \doteq -\frac{k_Y a_M}{G_S'}(Y' - Y_i') \tag{7.67a}$$

where the approximations of Eq. (7.67a) are suitable for low vapor concentrations. The temperature gradient is taken from Eq. (7.40):

$$\frac{dt_G}{dZ} = -\frac{h_G' a_H(t_G - t_i)}{G_S' C_S} \doteq -\frac{h_G a_H(t_G - t_i)}{G_S' C_S} \tag{7.68}$$

where $h_G a_H$ rather than $h'_G a_H$ may be used at low transfer rates. Unless a_H and a_M are separately known (which is not usual), there will be difficulty in evaluating h'_G exactly. Here we must assume $a_H = a_M$:

$$h'_G a_H = \frac{N_A M_A C_A a_H}{1 - e^{-N_A M_A C_A a_H / h_G a_H}} \doteq \frac{N_A M_A C_A a_M}{1 - e^{-N_A M_A C_A a_M / h_G a_H}} \tag{7.69}$$

$$\doteq -\frac{G'_S C_A (dY'/dZ)}{1 - e^{G'_S C_A (dY'/dZ)/h_G a_H}}$$

The effect of the approximation is not normally important.

Equations (7.67) and (7.68) are integrated numerically, using a procedure outlined in Illustration 7.14. Extensive trial and error is required, since t_i from Eq. (7.66) is necessary before P_{Ai} (or Y'_i) can be computed. The t_i-P_{Ai} relationship is that of the vapor-pressure curve. If at any point in the course of the calculations p_{AG} (or Y') at a given t_G calculates to be larger than the corresponding saturation vapor concentration, a fog will form in the gas phase, the entire analysis is invalid, and new conditions at the terminals of the tower must be chosen.

Illustration 7.14. A producer gas, 65% nitrogen, 35% carbon monoxide, 1 atm, 600°F, initially dry, is to be cooled to 80°F by countercurrent contact with water entering at 65°F. A hurdle-packed tower will be used, with $G'_S = 500$ lb/(hr)(sq ft), $L'_2 = 1,000$ lb/(hr)(sq ft), for which the transfer coefficients (assumed constant) are

$$h_G a_H = 150 \text{ Btu/(hr)(cu ft)(°F)}$$

$$h_L a_H = 1000 \text{ Btu/(hr)(cu ft)(°F)}$$

$$F_G a_M = 21.8 \text{ lb moles/(hr)(cu ft)}$$

Compute the required height of the packed section.

Solution. For convenience, the base temperature will be taken as $t_0 = 65°F$. The heat capacities will be assumed constant throughout: $C_{AL} = 1.0$, $C_A = 0.45$, $C_B(N_2 + CO) = 0.26$. (*Note:* It is not necessary to assume these, or the transfer coefficients, to be constant.) The given data provide $Y'_1 = 0$, $L'_2 = 1,000$, $G'_S = 500$, $t_{L2} = 65°F$, $t_{G1} = 600°F$, $t_{G2} = 80°F$, $C_{S1} = 0.26$, $\lambda_0 = 1,057.1$, $M_A = 18.02$, $M_B = 28.0$, $P_t = 1$ atm.

Calculations will be started at the bottom, for which L'_1 and t_{L1} must be known. These will be determined by assuming an outlet gas humidity, to be checked at the end of the calculation. Since the exit gas is likely to be nearly saturated ($Y'_s = 0.023$), estimate its humidity to be $Y'_2 = 0.02$, for which $C_{S2} = 0.26 + 0.02(0.45) = 0.269$. An overall water balance [Eq. (7.33)]:

$$1,000 - L'_1 = 500(0.02 - 0)$$

$$L'_1 = 990 \text{ lb/(hr)(sq ft)}$$

An overall enthalpy balance [Eq. (7.35)]:

$$1,000(1)(65 - 65) + 500(0.26)(600 - 65) = 990(1)(t_{L1} - 65)$$

$$+ 500[0.269(80 - 65) + 0.02(1,057.1)]$$

$$t_{L1} = 122.5°F$$

At the bottom $(Z = 0)$, t_i will be estimated by trial and error. After several trials, assume $t_i = 124.5°F$. $P_{Ai} = 0.1303$ atm.

Eq. (7.67):
$$\frac{dY'}{dZ} = -\frac{18.02(21.8)}{500} \ln \frac{1 - 0.1303}{1 - 0} = 0.1705 \text{ lb H}_2\text{O/(lb dry gas)(ft)}$$

Eq. (7.69):
$$h'_G a_H = -\frac{500(0.45)(0.1075)}{1 - e^{500(0.45)(0.1075)/150}} = 139 \text{ Btu/(hr)(cu ft)(°F)}$$

Eq. (7.68):
$$\frac{dt_G}{dZ} = -\frac{139(600 - 124.5)}{500(0.26)} = -510°\text{F/ft}$$

For use in Eq. (7.66):

$$C_A t_G - C_{AL} t_L + (C_{AL} - C_A)t_0 + \lambda_0 = 0.45(600) - 1.0(122.5) + (1 - 0.45)65 + 1{,}057.1 = 1{,}240$$

Eq. (7.66): $$t_i = 122.5 + \frac{500[0.26(-510) + 1{,}240(0.1075)]}{500(1.0)(0.1075) - 1{,}000} = 124.5°\text{F}   \text{(check)}$$

$$\frac{dY'}{dt_G} = \frac{dY'/dZ}{dt_G/dZ} = \frac{0.1075}{-510} = -0.000211$$

A suitably small increment in gas temperature is now chosen, and with the computed gradient assumed constant over a small range, the conditions at the end of the increment are computed. In this case, take $\Delta t_G = -60°F$.

$$\Delta Z = \frac{\Delta t_G}{dt_G/dZ} = \frac{-60}{-510} = 0.1178 \text{ ft}$$

$$t_G = t_G \text{ (at } Z = 0) + \Delta t_G = 600 - 60 = 540°\text{F}$$

$$Y' = Y' \text{ (at } Z = 0) + \frac{dY'}{dt_G} \Delta t_G = 0 + (-0.000211)(-60) = 0.01266$$

$$p_{AG} = \frac{Y'}{Y' + M_A/M_B} = \frac{0.01266}{0.01266 + 18/28} = 0.0193 \text{ atm}$$

$$C_S = 0.26 + 0.45(0.01266) = 0.266$$

L' is calculated by a water balance [Eq. (7.33)] over the increment:

$$L' - 990 = 500(0.01266 - 0)$$
$$L' = 996.3$$

t_L is calculated by an enthalpy balance [Eq. (7.35)]:

$$996.3(1.0)(t_L - 65) + 500(0.26)(600 - 65) = 990(1)(122.5 - 65)$$
$$+ 500[0.266(540 - 65) + 1{,}057.1(0.01266)]$$
$$t_L = 122.3°\text{F}$$

New gradients dY'/dZ and dt_G/dZ at this level in the tower and another interval are then computed in exactly the same manner. The process is repeated until the gas temperature falls to 80°F. The intervals of Δt_G chosen must be small as the gas approaches saturation, and in this case they were ultimately reduced to $-10°F$. The computed t_G-Y' results are shown in Fig. 7.16 (the plotted points are those calculated at each interval) along with the saturation humidity curve. At $t_G = 80°F$, the sum of the ΔZ's $= Z = 6.7$ ft. However, Y'_2 calculated to be 0.0222 and $t_{L2} = 66.2°F$, whereas

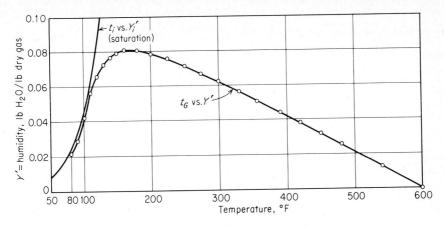

Fig. 7.16 *Gas temperatures and humidities for Illustration 7.14.*

the initially assumed Y_2' was 0.02 (and $t_{L2} = 65°$F).   The result is therefore not exact, and the entire computation should be repeated with a new assumed Y_2' until assumed and calculated values agree.

In this problem, the gas is initially humidified as it cools, but below 160°F it becomes dehumidified as it meets cold water.   The maximum bulk-liquid temperature is at the bottom, and the interface never rises above 125.4°F, despite the fact that the gas is initially very hot.

EQUIPMENT

Any of the gas-liquid contact devices described in Chap. '6 are applicable to the operations described here, and conventional packed and tray towers are very effective in these services.   Air and water are low-cost materials, however, and when large volumes must be handled, as in many water-cooling operations, equipment of low initial cost and low operating cost is essential.   For this reason large-scale installations are more frequently of the type described below.

Water-cooling towers

The framework and internal packing is frequently redwood, a material which is very durable in continuous contact with water.   Impregnation of the wood with fungicides is common practice, and coating with neoprene for protection against fungus attack has also been done.   Siding for the towers is commonly redwood, asbestos cement, glass-reinforced polyester plastic, and the like.   Towers have been built entirely of plastic.   The internal packing ("fill") is usually a modified form of hurdle (see Chap. 6), horizontal slats arranged staggered or with alternate tiers at right angles.   A great many arrangements are used.[7,10]   Plastic packing may be molded in grid form.[4] The void space is very large, usually greater than 90 percent, in order that the gas pressure drop be as low as possible.   The air–water interfacial surface consequently includes not only that of the liquid films which wet the slats but also the surface of the droplets which fall as rain from each tier of slats to the next.

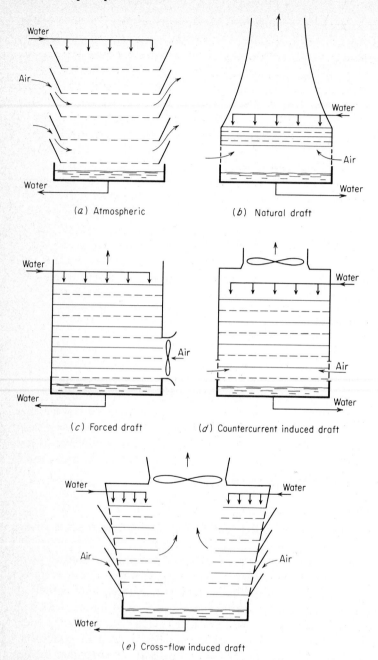

Fig. 7.17   *Cooling-tower arrangements.*

The common arrangements are shown schematically in Fig. 7.17. Of the *natural-circulation* towers (Fig. 7.17a and b), the atmospheric towers depend on prevailing winds for air movement. The natural-draft design ensures more positive air movement even in calm weather by depending upon the displacement of the warm air inside the tower by the cooler outside air. Fairly tall chimneys are then required. Both these tower types must be relatively tall in order to operate at a small wet-bulb-temperature approach. Natural-draft equipment is used commonly in the southwestern United States and in the Middle East, where the air humidity is usually low, and in parts of Europe where air temperatures are generally low. In most of the United States, mechanical-draft equipment is commonly used.

Mechanical-draft towers may be of the forced-draft type (Fig. 7.17c), where the air is blown into the tower by a fan at the bottom. These are particularly subject to recirculation of the hot, humid discharged air into the fan intake owing to the low discharge velocity, which materially reduces the tower effectiveness. Induced draft, with the fan at the top, avoids this and also permits more uniform internal distribution of air. The arrangements of Fig. 7.17d and e are most commonly used, and a more detailed drawing is shown in Fig. 7.18. Liquid rates are ordinarily in the range 1 to 5

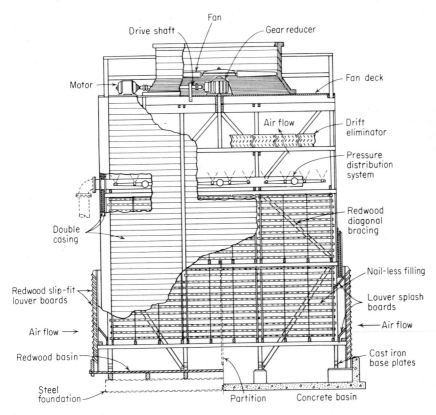

Fig. 7.18 *Induced-draft cooling tower.* (*The Marley Co., Inc.*)

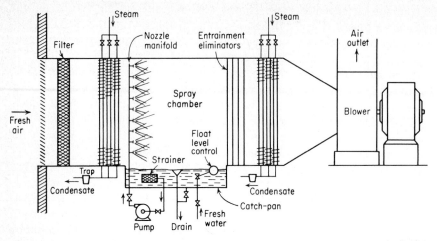

Fig. 7.19 *Schematic arrangement of a spray chamber.*

gal/(min)(sq ft)($L' = 500$ to $2,500$), and superficial air velocities are of the order of 4 to 7 ft/sec ($G'_S = 1,200$ to $2,100$), whereupon the air pressure drop is ordinarily less than 1 in. of water. Entrainment, or "drift," eliminators at the top can maintain loss of water from this cause to less than 0.3 percent of the circulated water.

Spray chambers

These are essentially horizontal spray towers and may be arranged as in Fig. 7.19. They are frequently used for adiabatic humidification-cooling operations with recirculating liquid. With large liquid drops, gas rates up to roughly 600 to 900 lb/(hr)(sq ft) are possible, but in any case entrainment eliminators are necessary.

Heat-transfer surfaces at the inlet and outlet provide for preheating and after-heating of the air, so that processes of the type shown in Fig. 7.20 may be carried out.

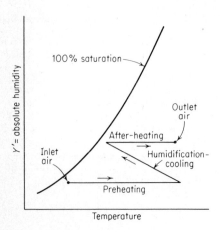

Fig. 7.20 *A simple conditioning process.*

If large humidity changes by this method are required, preheating of the air to unusually high temperatures is necessary, however. As an alternative, the spray water may be heated above the adiabatic-saturation temperature to which it will tend to come by direct injection of steam or by heating coils. Dehumidification may be practiced by cooling the water prior to spraying or by using refrigerating coils directly in the spray chamber. Operations of this sort cannot be followed with assurance on the enthalpy-temperature diagrams described earlier owing to the departure from strictly countercurrent-flow conditions which prevail. When an adequate spray density is maintained, it may be assumed that three banks of sprays in series will bring the gas to substantial equilibrium with the incoming spray liquid.

For comfort air conditioning, many compact devices are provided with a variety of these facilities, and automatic controls are available.

Spray ponds

These are sometimes used for water cooling where close approach to the air wet-bulb temperature is not required. Spray ponds are essentially fountains, where the water is sprayed upward into the air and allowed to fall back into a collection basin. They are subject to high windage losses of water.

Mass-transfer rates

The correlations of mass-transfer coefficients for the standard packings discussed in Chap. 6 are suitable for the operations discussed here (see particularly Illustration 6.5). Data for some of the special tower fillings usually used for water-cooling towers are available in texts specializing in this type of equipment,[10,13] and in some manufacturers' bulletins. Sieve and bubble-tray towers are very effective but are not commonly used in humidification, dehumidification, or gas-cooling operations for reasons of cost and relatively high gas pressure drop.

Dehumidification by other methods

Adsorption, such as those methods using activated silica gel or alumina as adsorbents (see Chap. 11), and washing gases with water solutions containing dissolved substances which appreciably lower the partial pressure of the water (see Chap. 8) are other commonly used dehumidifying processes, particularly when very dry gases are required.

NOTATION FOR CHAPTER 7

a = interfacial surface per unit volume of packing, sq ft/cu ft
a_H = interfacial surface for heat transfer, sq ft/cu ft
a_M = interfacial surface for mass transfer, sq ft/cu ft
c = concentration, lb moles/cu ft
C = heat capacity (of a gas or vapor unless otherwise indicated) at constant pressure, Btu/(lb)(°F)
C_L = heat capacity of a liquid at constant pressure, Btu/(lb)(°F)
C_S = humid heat, Btu (of a vapor-gas mixture)/(lb dry gas)(°F)
d = differential operator

D = diffusivity, sq ft/hr

e = 2.7183

E_D = eddy diffusivity of mass, sq ft/hr

E_H = eddy diffusivity of heat, sq ft/hr

E_{MG} = Murphree gas-phase stage efficiency, fractional

F = mass-transfer coefficient, lb moles/(hr)(sq ft)

G'_s = superficial mass velocity of gas, lb dry gas/(hr)(sq ft cross section)

h = convection heat-transfer coefficient, Btu/(hr)(sq ft)(°F)

h' = convection heat-transfer coefficient corrected for simultaneous mass transfer, Btu/(hr)(sq ft)(°F)

h_R = radiation heat-transfer coefficient in convection form, Btu/(hr)(sq ft)(°F)

H = enthalpy, Btu/lb

H' = enthalpy of a vapor-gas mixture, Btu/lb dry gas

H'^* = enthalpy of a saturated vapor-gas mixture in equilibrium with the bulk liquid, Btu/lb dry gas

H'_{as} = enthalpy of a saturated vapor-gas mixture at t_{as}, Btu/lb dry gas

H_{tG} = height of a gas-enthalpy transfer unit, ft

H_{tOG} = overall height of a gas-enthalpy transfer unit, ft

k = thermal conductivity, (Btu)(ft)/(hr)(sq ft)(°F)

k_c = mass-transfer coefficient, lb moles A transferred/(hr)(sq ft)(Δc)

k_G = mass-transfer coefficient, lb moles A transferred/(hr)(sq ft)(atm)

k_Y = mass-transfer coefficient, lb A transferred/(hr)(sq ft)($\Delta Y'$)

K_Y = overall mass-transfer coefficient, lb A transferred/(hr)(sq ft)($\Delta Y'$)

ln = natural logarithm

log = common logarithm

L' = superficial mass velocity of liquid, lb/(hr)(sq ft cross section)

Le = Lewis number = Sc/Pr

M = molecular weight, lb/lb mole

N = mass-transfer flux, lb moles/(hr)(sq ft)

N_{tG} = number of gas-enthalpy transfer units

N_{tOG} = number of overall gas-enthalpy transfer units

p = partial pressure, atm

p_{BM} = average partial pressure of component B, atm

P = vapor pressure of a pure substance, atm

P_t = total pressure, atm

Pr = Prandtl number = $C\mu/k$

Pv = product of pressure and specific volume, Btu/lb

q_s = heat-transfer flux for sensible heat, Btu/(hr)(sq ft)

Q = gain in enthalpy, Btu/lb

r = $h_G a_H / C_s k_Y a_M$

R = uhiversal gas constant, 0.729 (cu ft)(atm)/(lb mole)(°R)

S = interfacial surface, sq ft

Sc = Schmidt number = $\mu/\rho D$

t = temperature, °F

t_{as} = adiabatic-saturation temperature, °F

t_{DP} = dew-point temperature, °F

t_0 = reference temperature, °F

T = absolute temperature, °R

U = internal energy, Btu/lb

v = molal volume, cu ft/lb mole

v_H = humid volume, cu ft of vapor-gas mixture/lb dry gas

y = concentration in gas, mole fraction

Y = molal absolute humidity, lb moles vapor/lb mole dry gas

Y' = absolute humidity, lb vapor/lb dry gas
Y'_{as} = saturated absolute humidity at adiabatic-saturation temperature, lb vapor/lb dry gas
z = distance, ft
Z = length or height of active part of equipment, ft
α = thermal diffusivity, sq ft/hr
Δ = difference
λ = latent heat of vaporization, Btu/lb
λ' = molal latent heat of vaporization, (cu ft)(atm)/lb mole
λ_{as} = latent heat of vaporization at t_{as}, Btu/lb
λ_0 = latent heat of vaporization at t_0, Btu/lb
μ = viscosity, lb mass/(ft)(hr)
ρ = density, lb mass/cu ft

Subscripts:

1, 2 = positions 1, 2
as = adiabatic saturation
av = average
A = substance A, the vapor
B = substance B, the gas
G = pertaining to the gas
i = interface
L = pertaining to the liquid
min = minimum
r = reference substance
s = saturated
w = at the wet-bulb temperature
0 = at the reference temperature

REFERENCES

1. Baker, D. R., and H. A. Skyrock: *J. Heat Transfer,* **83,** 339 (1961).
2. Bedingfield, C. H., and T. B. Drew: *Ind. Eng. Chem.,* **42,** 1164 (1950).
3. Dropkin, D.: *Cornell Univ. Eng. Expt. Sta. Bull.,* **23** (1936); **26** (1939).
4. Fuller, A. L., A. L. Kohl, and E. Butcher: *Chem. Eng. Progr.,* **53,** 501 (1957).
5. Grosvenor, W. M.: *Trans. AIChE,* **1,** 184 (1908).
6. Hensel, S. L., and R. E. Treybal: *Chem. Eng. Progr.,* **48,** 362 (1952).
7. Kelly, N. W., and L. K. Swenson: *Chem. Eng. Progr.,* **52,** 263 (1956).
8. Lynch, E. J., and C. R. Wilke: *AIChE J.,* **1,** 9 (1955).
9. McAdams, W. H.: "Heat Transmission," 3d ed., McGraw-Hill Book Company, New York, 1954.
10. McKelvey, K. K., and M. Brooke: "The Industrial Cooling Tower," D. Van Nostrand Company, Inc., Princeton, N.J., 1959.
11. Merkel, F.: *Ver. Deut. Forschungsarb.,* 275 (1925).
12. Mickley, H. S.: *Chem. Eng. Progr.,* **45,** 739 (1949).
13. Norman, W. S.: "Absorption, Distillation, and Cooling Towers," Longmans, Green & Co., Ltd., London, 1961.
14. Olander, D. R.: *AIChE J.,* **6,** 346 (1960); *Ind. Eng. Chem.,* **53,** 121 (1961).
15. Othmer, D. F., et al.: *Ind. Eng. Chem.,* **32,** 841 (1940); **34,** 952 (1942).
16. Parker, R. O.: Doctor of Engineering Science thesis, New York University, 1959; "The Psychrometric Ratio for the System Air–Water Vapor," *First Inter-Am. Congr. Chem. Eng.,* San Juan, Puerto Rico, October, 1961.
17. Parker, R. O., and R. E. Treybal: *Chem. Eng. Prog. Symp. Ser.,* **57**(32), 138 (1960).

PROBLEMS

7.1. Prepare a logarithmic reference-substance plot of the vapor pressure of acetone over a temperature range of 10°C to its critical temperature, 235°C, with water as reference substance. With the help of the plot, determine (*a*) the vapor pressure of acetone at 65°C, (*b*) the temperature at which acetone has a vapor pressure of 500 mm Hg, and (*c*) the latent heat of vaporization of acetone at 40°C (accepted value = 230.5 Btu/lb).

7.2. *a.* Compute the heat required to convert 5 lb acetone from a condition of saturated liquid at 10°C to superheated vapor at 500 mm Hg abs, and 100°C. The heat capacity of acetone as a liquid is 0.52, as a vapor 0.35 Btu/(lb)(°F).

b. Calculate the enthalpy of the acetone in the superheated condition of part *a* relative to liquid acetone at the same temperature, Btu/lb.

7.3. A mixture of nitrogen and acetone vapor at 800 mm Hg total pressure, 80°F, has a percentage saturation of 80%. Calculate (*a*) the absolute molal humidity, (*b*) the absolute humidity, lb acetone/lb nitrogen, (*c*) the partial pressure of acetone, (*d*) the relative humidity, (*e*) the volume percent acetone, and (*f*) the dew point.

7.4. In a plant for the recovery of acetone which has been used as a solvent, the acetone is evaporated into a stream of nitrogen gas. A mixture of acetone vapor and nitrogen is flowing through a duct, 12- by 12-in. cross section. The pressure and temperature at one point in the duct are 800 mm Hg, 100°F, and at this point the average velocity is 10 ft/sec. A wet-bulb thermometer (wick wet with acetone) indicates a wet-bulb temperature at this point of 80°F. Calculate lb acetone/hr carried by the duct. **Ans.:** 1,615.

7.5. An air–water vapor mixture, 1 atm, 350°F, flows in a duct (wall temperature = 350°F) at 10 ft/sec average velocity. A wet-bulb temperature, measured with an ordinary, unshielded thermometer covered with a wetted wick (⅜-in. outside diameter) and inserted in the duct at right angles to the duct axis, is 125°F. Under these conditions, the adiabatic-saturation curves of the psychrometric chart do not approximate wet-bulb lines, radiation to the wet bulb and the effect of mass transfer on heat transfer are not negligible, nor should *k*-type (rather than *F*) mass-transfer coefficients be used.

a. Make the best estimate you can of the humidity of the air, taking these matters into consideration.

b. Compute the humidity using the ordinary wet-bulb equation (7.26) with the usual h_G/k_Y, and compare.

7.6. Derive Eq. (7.28), the psychrometric ratio, from item 2, Table 3.2, using the heat- mass-transfer analogy.

7.7. Prepare a psychrometric chart of the mixture acetone-nitrogen at a pressure of 800 mm Hg over the ranges 0 to 140°F, $Y' = 0$ to 3 lb vapor/lb dry gas. Include the following curves, all plotted against temperature: (*a*) 100, 75, 50, and 25% humidity; (*b*) dry and saturated humid volumes; (*c*) enthalpy of dry and saturated mixtures expressed as Btu/lb dry gas, referred to liquid acetone and nitrogen gas at 0°F; (*d*) wet-bulb curve for $t_w = 80°F$; (*e*) adiabatic-saturation curves for $t_{as} = 80$ and 100°F.

7.8. A drier requires 3,000 cu ft/min of air at 150°F, 20% humidity. This is to be prepared from air at 80°F dry-bulb, 65° wet-bulb temperature by direct injection of steam into the air stream followed by passage of the air over steam-heated finned tubes. The available steam is saturated at 5 psig. Compute the lb of steam/hr required (*a*) for direct injection and (*b*) for the heat exchange.

7.9. Air in an amount 1,000 cu ft/min at 150°F, 20% humidity (condition 1), is passed over a refrigerated coil and thereby brought to 60°F, 90% humidity (condition 2), with the condensed moisture withdrawn at an average temperature of 55°F. The air is then reheated by means of a steam coil to 150°F (condition 3).

a. Tabulate the absolute humidity, wet-bulb temperature, dew point, enthalpy, and volume in cu ft/min for the moist air at each of the three conditions.

b. Compute the moisture removed, lb/min.

c. Compute the heat removed by the refrigerated coil, expressed as tons of refrigeration (1 ton of refrigeration = 200 Btu/min removed). **Ans.:** 18.

7.10. A recently installed induced-draft cooling tower was guaranteed by the manufacturer to cool 2,000 gal/min of water at 110°F to 85°F when the available air has a wet-bulb temperature of 75°F. A test on the tower, when operated at full fan capacity, provided the following data:

Inlet water, 2,000 gal/min, 115.0°F

Outlet water, 78.0°F

Inlet air 75°F dry-bulb, 60°F wet-bulb temperature

Outlet air, 99.8°F

a. What is the fan capacity, cu ft/min?

b. Can the tower be expected to meet the guarantee conditions?

7.11. *a.* Calculate the height of a 1-in.-ID wetted-wall tower required to bring dry air at 140°F to 90% saturation with water by adiabatic gas humidification-cooling with recirculated liquid. The air rate is to be 3,000 lb/(hr)(sq ft), and the thickness of the liquid film may be neglected. Use gas properties at the average conditions between bulk gas and interface.

b. Calculate the depth of 1-in. ceramic Raschig rings in a packed tower for the same humidification. L' will be set at 1,600 and G'_S at 500 lb/(hr)(sq ft). **Ans.:** 1.7 ft.

c. Compare the pressure drop, lb/sq ft, for the gas in both cases.

d. Compare the two devices by calculating $N_{tG}/\Delta P$ for each. What other factors should be considered in comparing the two?

7.12. It is desired to dehumidify 2,500 cu ft air/min, available at 100°F dry-bulb, 85°F wet-bulb temperature, to a wet-bulb temperature of 60°F in a countercurrent tower using water chilled to 50°F. The packing will be 2-in. ceramic Raschig rings. To keep entrainment at a minimum, G'_s will be 900 lb air/(hr)(sq ft), and a liquid rate of 1.5 times the minimum will be used. (*a*) Specify the cross section and height of the packed portion of the tower. (*b*) What will be the temperature of the outlet water? **Ans.:** (*a*) 3.9 ft.

7.13. Acetone is to be removed from a product in a continuous process by evaporation into a stream of inert (nonflammable) gas, essentially nitrogen. The resulting vapor-gas mixture, at 80°F, 1 atm total pressure, will have a partial pressure of acetone equal to 150 mm Hg. A scheme for recovering the acetone from the nitrogen involves washing the gas countercurrently with cold liquid acetone (entering at 10°F) in a packed tower. The vapor-gas mixture will enter the tower at a rate $G'_1 = 500$ lb total/(hr)(sq ft) and will leave with an acetone partial pressure of 40 mm Hg. This mixture will be returned to the evaporator. The cold acetone will enter at a rate $L'_2 = 1,500$ lb/(hr)(sq ft). Compute the depth of packing required. **Ans.:** 3 ft.

Data. For the packing, $k_G a_V p_{BM} = 0.038 G'^{0.6} L'^{0.4}$, where G' and L' are the mass velocities of *total* gas and liquid, respectively, and the coefficient will not be constant. The heat-transfer coefficient $h_G a$ will be estimated from this through the heat- mass-transfer analogy,

$$St_{\text{mass transfer}} \; Sc^{0.5} = St_{\text{heat transfer}} \; Pr^{0.5}$$

where St is the Stanton number. The Lewis number $Sc/Pr = Le$ for nitrogen-acetone is 0.63. It will be assumed for lack of better information that $a_M = a_H = a$. The circumstances are such that the liquid-phase heat-transfer coefficient $h_L a$ is so large that it may be assumed infinite for calculation purposes ($t_i = t_L$). Use $t_0 = 10°F$, and $\lambda_0 = 244.5$ Btu/lb. The heat capacities may be taken as $C_{AL} = 0.514$, $C_A = 0.35$, $C_B = 0.26$ Btu/(lb)(°F).

CHAPTER EIGHT
GAS ABSORPTION

Gas absorption is an operation in which a gas mixture is contacted with a liquid for the purposes of preferentially dissolving one or more components of the gas and to provide a solution of these in the liquid. For example, the gas from by-product coke ovens is washed with water to remove ammonia and again with an oil to remove benzene and toluene vapors. Objectionable hydrogen sulfide is removed from such a gas or from naturally occurring hydrocarbon gases by washing with various alkaline solutions in which it is absorbed. Valuable solvent vapors carried by a gas stream may be recovered for reuse by washing the gas with an appropriate solvent for the vapors. Such operations require mass transfer of a substance from the gas stream to the liquid. When mass transfer occurs in the opposite direction, i.e., from the liquid to the gas, the operation is called desorption, or stripping. For example, the benzene and toluene are removed from the absorption oil mentioned above by contacting the liquid solution with steam, whereupon the vapors enter the gas stream and are carried away, and the absorption oil may be used again. The principles of both absorption and desorption are basically the same, and we may study both operations at the same time.

Ordinarily, these operations are used only for solute recovery or solute removal. Separation of solutes from each other to any important extent requires the fractionation techniques of distillation.

EQUILIBRIUM SOLUBILITY OF GASES IN LIQUIDS

The rate at which a gaseous constituent of a mixture will dissolve in an absorbent liquid depends upon the departure from equilibrium which is maintained, and therefore it is necessary to consider the equilibrium characteristics of gas-liquid systems. A very brief discussion of such matters was presented in Chap. 5, but some elaboration will be required here.

Two-component systems

If a quantity of a single gas and a relatively nonvolatile liquid are brought to equilibrium in the manner described in Chap. 5, the resulting concentration of dissolved gas in the liquid is said to be the gas solubility at the prevailing temperature and pressure. At fixed temperature, the solubility concentration will increase with pressure in the manner, for example, of curve A, Fig. 8.1, which shows the solubility of ammonia in water at 30°C.

Different gases and liquids yield separate solubility curves, which must ordinarily be determined experimentally for each system. If the equilibrium pressure of a gas at a given liquid concentration is high, as in the case of curve B (Fig. 8.1), the gas is

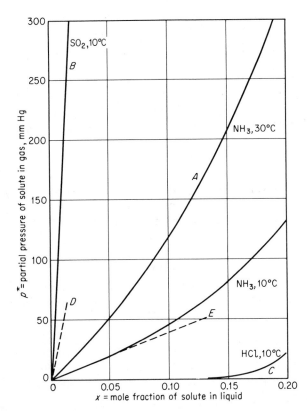

Fig. 8.1 *Solubilities of gases in water.*

said to be relatively insoluble in the liquid, while if it is low, as for curve C, the solubility is said to be high.   But these are relative matters only, for it is possible to produce any ultimate gas concentration in the liquid if sufficient pressure is applied, so long as the liquefied form of the gas is completely soluble in the liquid.

The solubility of any gas is influenced by the temperature, in a manner which is described by van't Hoff's law of mobile equilibrium: If the temperature of a system at equilibrium is raised, that change will occur which will absorb heat.   Usually, but not always, the solution of a gas results in an evolution of heat, and it follows that in most cases the solubility of a gas decreases with increasing temperature.   As an example, curve A (Fig. 8.1) for ammonia in water at 30°C lies above the corresponding curve for 10°C.   At the boiling point of the solvent, provided its vapor pressure is less than that of the gas or vapor solute, the gas solubility will be zero.

Multicomponent systems

If a mixture of gases is brought into contact with a liquid, under certain conditions the equilibrium solubilities of each gas will be independent of the others, provided, however, that the equilibrium is described in terms of the *partial pressures* in the gas mixture.   If all but one of the components of the gas are substantially insoluble, their concentrations in the liquid will be so small that they cannot influence the solubility of the relatively soluble component, and the generalization applies.   For example, curve A (Fig. 8.1) will also describe the solubility of ammonia in water when the ammonia is diluted with air, since air is so insoluble in water, provided that the ordinate of the plot be considered as the partial pressure of ammonia in the gas mixture.   This is most fortunate, since the amount of experimental work in gathering useful solubility data is thereby considerably reduced.   If several components of the mixture are appreciably soluble, the generalization will be applicable only provided that the solute gases are indifferent to the nature of the liquid, which will be the case only for ideal solutions.   For example, a mixture of propane and butane gases will dissolve in a nonvolatile paraffin oil independently since the solutions that result are substantially ideal.   On the other hand, the solubility of ammonia in water can be expected to be influenced by the presence of methylamine, since the resulting solutions of these gases are not ideal.   The solubility of a gas will also be influenced by the presence of a nonvolatile solute in the liquid, such as a salt in water solution, when such solutions are nonideal.

Ideal liquid solutions

When the liquid phase may be considered ideal, we may compute the equilibrium partial pressure of a gas from the solution without resort to experimental determination.

There are four significant characteristics of ideal solutions, all interrelated:

1. The average intermolecular forces of attraction and repulsion in the solution are unchanged on mixing the constituents.

2. The volume of the solution varies linearly with composition.

3. There is neither absorption nor evolution of heat in mixing of the constituents. In the case of gases dissolving in liquids, however, this criterion should not include the heat of condensation of the gas to the liquid state.

4. The total vapor pressure of the solution varies linearly with composition expressed as mole fractions.

In reality there are no ideal solutions, and actual mixtures only approach ideality as a limit. Ideality would require that the molecules of the constituents be similar in size, structure, and chemical nature, and the nearest approach to such a condition is perhaps exemplified by solutions of optical isomers of organic compounds. Practically, however, many solutions are so nearly ideal that for engineering purposes they may be so considered. Adjacent or nearly adjacent members of a homologous series of organic compounds particularly fall in this category. So, for example, solutions of benzene in toluene, of ethyl and propyl alcohols, or the paraffin hydrocarbon gases in paraffin oils may ordinarily be considered as ideal solutions.

When the gas mixture in equilibrium with an ideal liquid solution also follows the ideal-gas law, the partial pressure p^* of a solute gas A equals the product of its vapor pressure P at the same temperature and its mole fraction in the solution x. This is *Raoult's law*.

$$p^* = Px \qquad (8.1)$$

The nature of the solvent liquid does not enter into consideration except insofar as it establishes the ideality of the solution, and it follows that the solubility of a particular gas in ideal solution in any solvent is always the same.

Illustration 8.1. A gas mixture, after long contact with a hydrocarbon oil and establishment of equilibrium, has the following composition at 2 atm total pressure, 75°F: methane 60%, ethane 20%, propane 8%, n-butane 6%, n-pentane 6%. Calculate the composition of the equilibrium solution.

Solution. The equilibrium partial pressure p^* of each constituent in the gas is its volume fraction multiplied by the total pressure. These and the vapor pressures P of the constituents at 75°F are tabulated below. The prevailing temperature is above the critical value for methane, and at this low total pressure its solubility may be considered negligible. For each constituent its mole fraction in the liquid is calculated by Eq. (8.1), $x = p^*/P$, and the last column of the table lists these as the answers to the problem. The remaining liquid, $1 - 0.264 = 0.736$ mole fraction, is the solvent oil.

Component	p^*, equilibrium partial pressure, atm	P, vapor pressure at 75°F, atm	Mole fraction in the liquid, $x = \dfrac{p^*}{P}$
Methane	$1.20 = 0.6(2.0)$		
Ethane	0.40	41.5	0.0097
Propane	0.16	8.84	0.018
n-Butane	0.12	2.33	0.052
n-Pentane	0.12	0.65	0.184
Total			0.264

For total pressures in excess of those for which the ideal-gas law applies, Raoult's law may frequently be used with fugacities substituted for the pressure terms.[13]

Nonideal liquid solutions

For liquid solutions which are not ideal, Eq. (8.1) will give highly incorrect results. Line D (Fig. 8.1), for example, is the calculated partial pressure of ammonia in equilibrium with water solutions at 10°C, assuming Raoult's law to be applicable, and it clearly does not represent the data. On the other hand, the straight line E is seen to represent the 10°C ammonia–water data very well up to mole fractions of 0.06 in the liquid. The equation of such a line is

$$y^* = \frac{p^*}{P_t} = mx \tag{8.2}$$

where m is a constant. This is *Henry's law*,† and it is seen to be applicable with different values of m for each of the gases in the figure over at least a modest liquid-concentration range. Failure to follow Henry's law over wide concentration ranges may be the result of chemical interaction with the liquid or electrolytic dissociation, as is the case with ammonia–water, or nonideality in the gas phase. The less soluble gases, such as nitrogen or oxygen in water, can be expected to follow the law up to equilibrium partial pressures of 1 atm, and gases of the vapor type (which are below their critical temperature) will generally follow the law up to pressures of approximately 50 percent of the saturation value at the prevailing temperature provided no chemical action occurs in the liquid. In any case m must be established experimentally.

The advantages of straight-line plotting for interpolation and extrapolating experimental data are, of course, very great, and an empirical method of wide utility is an extension of the "reference-substance" vapor-pressure plot described in Chap. 7.[11] As an example of this, Fig. 8.2 shows the data for ammonia–water solutions, covering a wide range of concentrations and temperatures. The coordinates are logarithmic. The abscissa is marked with the vapor pressure of a convenient reference substance, in this case water, and the ordinate is the equilibrium partial pressure of the solute gas. Points are plotted where the corresponding temperatures for the vapor pressure of the reference substance and the partial pressure of solute are identical. For example, at 90°F the vapor pressure of water is 36 mm Hg, and the partial pressure of ammonia for a 10 mole percent solution is 130 mm Hg, and these pressures locate point A on the figure. The lines for constant liquid composition are straight with few exceptions. A temperature scale may later be substituted for the reference vapor-pressure scale, using the steam tables in the case of water as reference substance.

---

† For conditions under which Henry's law is inapplicable, Eq. (8.2) may be used in empirical fashion to describe experimental data, but the value of m (or $K = y^*/x$, which is sometimes used) will then be expected to vary with temperature, pressure, and concentration and must be listed as a function of these variables.

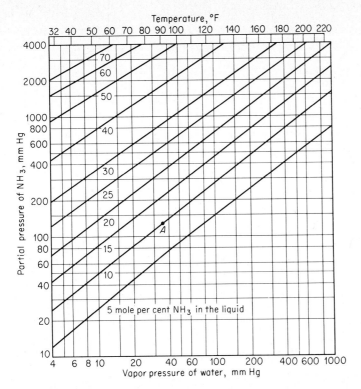

Fig. 8.2 *Reference-substance plot for gas solubility. The system ammonia–water, water as reference.*

Choice of solvent for absorption

If the principal purpose of the absorption operation is to produce a specific solution, as in the manufacture of hydrochloric acid, for example, the solvent is specified by the nature of the product. If the principal purpose is to remove some constituent from the gas, some choice is frequently possible. Water is, of course, the cheapest and most plentiful solvent, but the following properties are important considerations:

1. *Gas solubility*. The gas solubility should be high, thus increasing the rate of absorption and decreasing the quantity of solvent required. Generally solvents of a chemical nature similar to that of the solute to be absorbed will provide good solubility. Thus hydrocarbon oils, and not water, are used to remove benzene from coke-oven gas. For cases where the solutions formed are ideal, the solubility of the gas is the same in terms of mole fractions for all solvents. But it is greater in terms of weight fractions for solvents of low molecular weight, and smaller weights of such solvents, as measured in pounds, need to be used. Chemical reaction of solvent with the solute will frequently result in very high gas solubility, but if the solvent is to be recovered for reuse, the reaction must be reversible. For example, hydrogen sulfide may be removed from gas mixtures using ethanolamine solutions since the sulfide is readily absorbed at low temperatures and easily stripped at high temperatures.

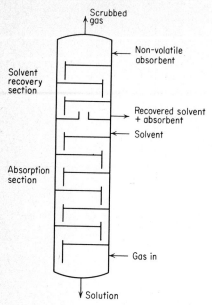

Fig. 8.3 *Tray absorber with volatile-solvent recovery section.*

Caustic soda absorbs hydrogen sulfide excellently but will not release it in a stripping operation.

2. *Volatility.* The solvent should have a low vapor pressure since the gas leaving an absorption operation is ordinarily saturated with the solvent and much may thereby be lost. If necessary, a second, less volatile liquid may be used to recover the evaporated portion of the first, as in Fig. 8.3. This is sometimes done, for example, in the case of hydrocarbon absorbers, where a relatively volatile solvent oil is used in the principal portion of the absorber because of the superior solubility characteristics and the volatilized solvent is recovered from the gas by a nonvolatile oil. Similarly, hydrogen sulfide may be absorbed by a water solution of sodium phenolate, but the desulfurized gas is further washed with water to recover the evaporated phenol.

3. *Corrosiveness.* The materials of construction required for the equipment should not be unusual or expensive.

4. *Cost.* The solvent should be inexpensive, so that losses are not costly, and should be readily available.

5. *Viscosity.* Low viscosity is preferred for reasons of rapid absorption rates, improved flooding characteristics in absorption towers, low pressure drops on pumping, and good heat-transfer characteristics.

6. *Miscellaneous.* The solvent if possible should be nontoxic, nonflammable, and chemically stable and should have a low freezing point.

MATERIAL BALANCES

The basic expressions for material balances and their graphical interpretation were presented for any mass-transfer operation in Chap. 5. Here they are adapted to the problems of gas absorption and stripping.

Countercurrent flow

Figure 8.4 shows a countercurrent tower which may be either a packed or spray tower, filled with bubble-cap trays, or of any internal construction to bring about liquid-gas contact. The gas stream at any point in the tower consists of G total moles/(hr)(sq ft tower cross section), made up of diffusing solute A of mole fraction y, partial pressure p, or mole ratio Y, and nondiffusing, essentially insoluble gas G_S moles/(hr)(sq ft). The relationship among these are

$$Y = \frac{y}{1 - y} = \frac{p}{P_t - p} \tag{8.3}$$

$$G_S = G(1 - y) = \frac{G}{1 + Y} \tag{8.4}$$

Similarly the liquid stream consists of L total moles/(hr)(sq ft), containing x mole fraction soluble gas, or mole ratio X, and essentially nonvolatile solvent L_S moles/(hr)(sq ft).

$$X = \frac{x}{1 - x} \tag{8.5}$$

$$L_S = L(1 - x) = \frac{L}{1 + X} \tag{8.6}$$

Since the solvent gas and solvent liquid are essentially unchanged in quantity as they

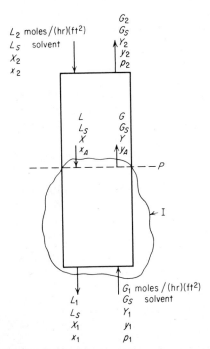

L_2 moles/(hr)(ft²)
L_S solvent
X_2
x_2

G_2
G_S
Y_2
y_2
p_2

L
L_S
X
x_A

G
G_S
Y
y_A

—— P

← I

L_1
L_S
X_1
x_1

G_1 moles/(hr)(ft²)
G_S solvent
Y_1
y_1
p_1

Fig. 8.4 *Flow quantities for an absorber or stripper.*

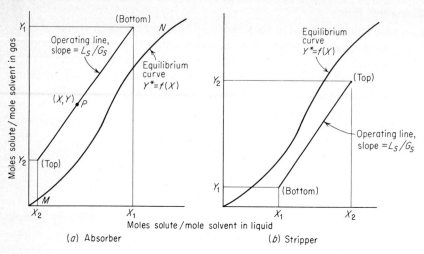

Fig. 8.5 *Operating lines for absorber and stripper.*

pass through the tower, it is convenient to express the material balance in terms of these.   A solute balance about the lower part of the tower (envelope I) is†

$$G_S(Y_1 - Y) = L_S(X_1 - X) \tag{8.7}$$

This is the equation of a straight line (the operating line) on X, Y coordinates, of slope L_S/G_S, which passes through (X_1, Y_1).   Substitution of X_2 and Y_2 for X and Y shows the line to pass through (X_2, Y_2), as on Fig. 8.5a for an absorber.   This line indicates the relation between the liquid and gas concentration at any level in the tower, as at point P.

The equilibrium-solubility data for the solute gas in the solvent liquid may also be plotted in terms of these concentration units on the same diagram, as curve MN, for example.   Each point on this curve represents the gas concentration in equilibrium with the corresponding liquid at its local concentration and temperature.   For an absorber (mass transfer from gas to liquid) the operating line always lies above the equilibrium-solubility curve, while for a stripper (mass transfer from liquid to gas) the line is always below, as in Fig. 8.5b.

The operating line is straight only when plotted in terms of the mole-ratio units. In terms of mole fractions or partial pressures the line is curved, as in Fig. 8.6 for an

---

† Equations (8.7) and (8.8) and the corresponding Figs. 8.4 to 8.8 are written as for packed towers, with 1 indicating the streams at the bottom and 2 those at the top.   For tray towers, where tray numbers are used as subscripts, as in Fig. 8.12, the same equations apply, but changes in subscripts must be made.   Thus Eq. (8.7) becomes, when applied to an entire tray tower,

$$G_S(Y_{N_p+1} - Y_1) = L_S(X_{N_p} - X_0)$$

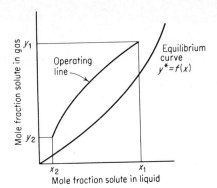

Fig. 8.6 *Operating line in mole fractions.*

absorber. The equation of the line is then

$$G_S\left(\frac{y_1}{1-y_1}-\frac{y}{1-y}\right)=G_S\left(\frac{p_1}{P_t-p_1}-\frac{p}{P_t-p}\right)$$

$$=L_S\left(\frac{x_1}{1-x_1}-\frac{x}{1-x}\right) \tag{8.8}$$

The total pressure P_t at any point may ordinarily be considered constant throughout the tower for this purpose.

Minimum liquid-gas ratio for absorbers

In the design of absorbers, the quantity of gas to be treated G or G_S, the terminal concentrations Y_1 and Y_2, and the composition of the entering liquid X_2 are ordinarily fixed by process requirements, but the quantity of liquid to be used is subject to choice. Refer to Fig. 8.7a. The operating line must pass through point D and must end at the

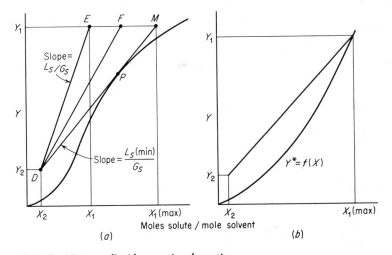

Fig. 8.7 *Minimum liquid-gas ratio, absorption.*

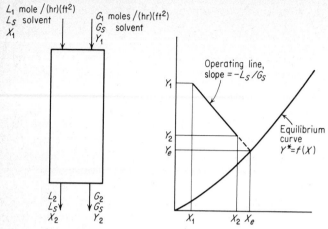

Fig. 8.8 *Cocurrent absorber.*

ordinate Y_1.   If such a quantity of liquid is used to give operating line DE, the exit liquid will have the composition X_1.   If less liquid is used, the exit-liquid composition will clearly be greater, as at point F, but since the driving forces for diffusion are less, the absorption is more difficult.   The time of contact between gas and liquid must then be greater, and the absorber must be correspondingly taller.   The minimum liquid which may be used corresponds to the operating line DM, which has the greatest slope for any line touching the equilibrium curve and is tangent to the curve at P. At P the diffusional driving force is zero, the required time of contact for the concentration change desired is infinite, and an infinitely tall tower results.   This then represents the limiting liquid-gas ratio.

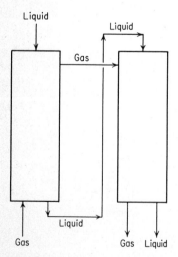

Fig. 8.9 *Countercurrent-cocurrent arrangement for very tall towers.*

The equilibrium curve is frequently concave upward, as in Fig. 8.7b, and the minimum liquid-gas ratio then corresponds to an exit-liquid concentration in equilibrium with the entering gas.

These principles also apply to strippers, where an operating line which anywhere touches the equilibrium curve represents a maximum ratio of liquid to gas and a maximum exit-gas concentration.

Cocurrent flow

When gas and liquid flow cocurrently, as in Fig. 8.8, the operating line has a negative slope $-L_S/G_S$. There is no limit on this ratio, but an infinitely tall tower would produce an exit liquid and gas in equilibrium, as at (X_e, Y_e). Cocurrent flow is used in the case where an exceptionally tall tower is built in two sections, as in Fig. 8.9, with the second section operated in cocurrent flow to save on the large-diameter gas pipe connecting the two. It may also be used if the gas to be dissolved in the liquid is a pure substance, where there is no advantage to countercurrent operation.

Illustration 8.2. A coal gas is to be freed of its light oil by scrubbing with wash oil as an absorbent and the light oil recovered by stripping the resulting solution with steam. The circumstances are:

a. Absorber. Gas in, 30,000 cu ft/hr at 800 mm Hg, 80°F, containing 2.0% by volume of light oil. The light oil will be assumed to be entirely benzene, and a 95% removal is required. The wash oil enters the absorber at 80°F, containing 0.005 mole fraction benzene, and has an average molecular weight of 260. An oil circulation rate of 1.5 times the minimum is to be used. Wash oil–benzene solutions are ideal. The temperature will be constant at 80°F.

b. Stripper. The solution from the absorber is heated to 250°F and enters the stripper at 1 atm pressure. Stripping steam is at atmospheric pressure, superheated to 250°F. The debenzolized oil, 0.005 mole fraction benzene, is cooled to 80°F and returned to the absorber. A steam rate of 1.5 times the minimum is to be used. The temperature will be constant at 250°F.

Compute the oil-circulation rate and the steam rate required.

Solution. a. Absorber. Basis: 1 hr. Define L, L_S, G, G_S in terms of moles/hr.

$$G_1 = 30,000 \frac{492}{460 + 80} \frac{800}{760} \frac{1}{359} = 80.8 \text{ moles gas in/hr}$$

$$y_1 = 0.02, \; Y_1 = \frac{0.02}{1 - 0.02} = 0.0204 \text{ mole benzene/mole dry gas}$$

$$G_S = 80.8(1 - 0.02) = 79.1 \text{ moles dry gas/hr}$$

For 95% removal of benzene,

$$Y_2 = 0.05(0.0204) = 0.00102 \text{ mole benzene/mole dry gas}$$

$$x_2 = 0.005, \; X_2 = \frac{0.005}{1 - 0.005} = 0.00502 \text{ mole benzene/mole oil}$$

At 80°F, the vapor pressure of benzene,

$$P = 100 \text{ mm Hg} = {}^{100}\!/_{760} = 0.1315 \text{ atm}$$

Eq. (8.1) for ideal solutions: $p^* = 0.1315x$

$$y^* = \frac{p^*}{P_t} \qquad P_t = \tfrac{800}{760} = 1.053 \text{ atm} \qquad Y^* = \frac{y^*}{1 - y^*} \qquad X = \frac{x}{1 - x}$$

Substitution in Eq. (8.1) yields

$$\frac{Y^*}{1 + Y^*} = \frac{0.1250X}{1 + X}$$

which is the equilibrium curve for the absorber, and it is plotted in Fig. 8.10. Operating lines originate at point D in this figure.   For the minimum oil rate, line DE is drawn as the line of maximum slope which touches the equilibrium curve (tangent to the curve).   At $Y_1 = 0.0204$, $X_1 = 0.176$ mole benzene/mole wash oil (point E).

$$\text{Min } L_S = \frac{G_S(Y_1 - Y_2)}{X_1 - X_2} = \frac{79.1(0.0204 - 0.00102)}{0.176 - 0.00502} = 8.95 \text{ moles oil/hr}$$

For 1.5 times the minimum, $L_S = 1.5(8.95) = 13.43$ moles oil/hr

$$X_1 = \frac{G_S(Y_1 - Y_2)}{L_S} + X_2 = \frac{79.1(0.0204 - 0.00102)}{13.43} + 0.00502 = 0.1192 \text{ mole benzene/mole oil}$$

The operating line is DF.

b.   Stripper.   At 250°F the vapor pressure of benzene is 2,400 mm Hg, or 3.16 atm.   The equilibrium curve for the stripper is therefore

$$\frac{Y^*}{1 + Y^*} = \frac{3.16X}{1 + X}$$

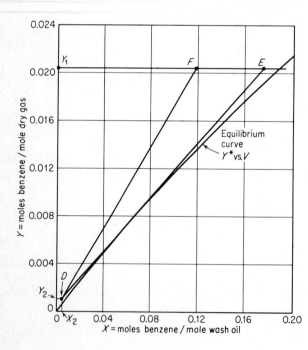

Fig. 8.10   *Solution to Illustration 8.2, absorption.*

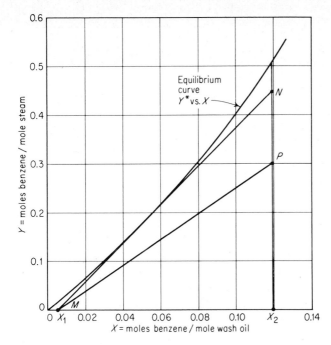

Fig. 8.11   *Solution to Illustration 8.2, stripping*.

which is drawn in Fig. 8.11.   For the stripper, $X_2 = 0.1192$, $X_1 = 0.00502$ mole benzene/mole oil. $Y_1 = 0$ mole benzene/mole steam.   For the minimum steam rate, line MN is drawn tangent to the equilibrium curve, and at N the value of $Y_2 = 0.45$ mole benzene/mole steam.

$$\text{Min } G_s = \frac{L_s(X_2 - X_1)}{Y_2 - Y_1} = \frac{13.43(0.1192 - 0.00502)}{0.45 - 0} = 3.41 \text{ mole steam/hr}$$

For 1.5 times the minimum, the steam rate is $1.5(3.41) = 5.11$ moles steam/hr, corresponding to line MP.

COUNTERCURRENT MULTISTAGE OPERATION

Tray towers and similar devices bring about stepwise contact of the liquid and gas and are therefore countercurrent multistage cascades.   On each tray of a bubble-cap tower, for example, the gas and liquid are brought into intimate contact and separated, somewhat in the manner of Fig. 5.14, and the tray thus constitutes a stage.   Few of the tray devices described in Chap. 6 actually provide the parallel flow on each tray as shown in Fig. 5.14.   Nevertheless it is convenient to use the latter as an arbitrary standard for design and for measurement of performance of actual trays regardless of their method of operation.   For this purpose a *theoretical*, or *ideal*, tray is defined as one where the average composition of all the gas leaving the tray is in equilibrium with the average composition of all the liquid leaving the tray.

The number of ideal trays required to bring about a given change in composition

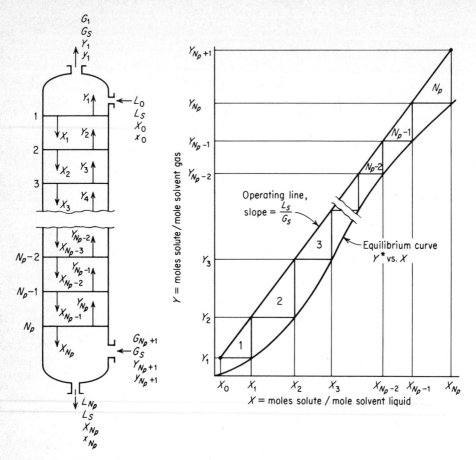

Fig. 8.12 *Tray absorber.*

of the liquid or the gas, for either absorbers or strippers, may then be determined graphically in the manner of Fig. 5.15. This is illustrated for an absorber in Fig. 8.12, where the liquid and gas compositions corresponding to each tray are marked on the operating diagram. Ideal tray 1, for example, brings about a change in liquid composition from X_0 to X_1 and of gas composition from Y_2 to Y_1. The step marked 1 on the operating diagram therefore represents this ideal tray. The nearer the operating line to the equilibrium curve, the more steps will be required, and should the two curves touch at any point corresponding to a minimum L_S/G_S ratio, the number of steps will be infinite. The steps may equally be constructed on diagrams plotted in terms of any concentration units, such as mole fractions or partial pressures. The construction for strippers is the same, with the exception, of course, that the operating line lies below the equilibrium curve.

It is usually convenient, for tray towers, to define the flow rates L and G simply as moles/hr, rather than to base them on unit tower cross section.

Dilute gas mixtures

For cases where both operating line and equilibrium curve may be considered straight, the number of ideal trays may be determined without recourse to graphical methods. This will frequently be the case for relatively dilute gas and liquid mixtures.   Henry's law [Eq. (8.2)] often applies to dilute solutions, for example.   If the quantity of gas absorbed is small, the total flow of liquid entering and leaving the absorber remains substantially constant, $L_0 \doteq L_{Np} \doteq L$ total moles/(hr)(sq ft), and similarly the total flow of gas is substantially constant at G total moles/(hr)(sq ft).   An operating line plotted in terms of mole fractions will then be substantially straight.   For such cases, the Kremser equations (5.50) to (5.57) and Fig. 5.16 apply.†   Small variations in A from one end of the tower to the other due to changing L/G as a result of absorption or stripping or to change in gas solubility with concentration or temperature may be roughly allowed for by use of the geometric average of the values of A at top and bottom.[7]   For large variations, either more elaborate corrections[5,9] for A, graphical computations, or tray-to-tray numerical calculations as developed below must be used.

The absorption factor A

The absorption factor $A = L/mG$ is the ratio of the slope of the operating line to that of the equilibrium curve.   For values of A less than unity, corresponding to convergence of the operating line and equilibrium curve for the lower end of the absorber, Fig. 5.16 indicates clearly that the fractional absorption of solute is definitely limited, even for infinite theoretical trays.   On the other hand, for values of A greater than unity, any degree of absorption is possible if sufficient trays are provided.   For a fixed degree of absorption from a fixed amount of gas, as A increases beyond unity, the absorbed solute is dissolved in more and more liquid and becomes therefore less valuable.   At the same time, the number of trays decreases, so that the equipment cost

---

† These become, in terms of mole fractions,

Absorption:
$$\frac{y_{Np+1} - y_1}{y_{Np+1} - mx_0} = \frac{A^{Np+1} - A}{A^{Np+1} - 1}$$

$$N_p = \frac{\log\left[\dfrac{y_{Np+1} - mx_0}{y_1 - mx_0}\left(1 - \dfrac{1}{A}\right) + \dfrac{1}{A}\right]}{\log A}$$

Stripping:
$$\frac{x_0 - x_{Np}}{x_0 - y_{Np+1}/m} = \frac{S^{Np+1} - S}{S^{Np+1} - 1}$$

$$N_p = \frac{\log\left[\dfrac{x_0 - y_{Np+1}/m}{x_{Np} - y_{Np+1}/m}\left(1 - \dfrac{1}{S}\right) + \dfrac{1}{S}\right]}{\log S}$$

where $A = L/mG$, and $S = mG/L$.

decreases.   From these opposing cost tendencies it follows that in all such cases, there will be a value of A, or of L/G, for which the most economical absorption results. This should be obtained generally by computing the total costs for several values of A and observing the minimum.   As a rule of thumb for purposes of rapid estimates, it has been frequently found[3] that the most economical A will be in the range from 1.25 to 2.0.

The reciprocal of the absorption factor is called the stripping factor S.

Illustration 8.3. Determine the number of theoretical trays required for the absorber and the stripper of Illustration 8.2.

Solution. a. Absorber. Since the tower will be a tray device, the following notation changes will be made (compare Figs. 8.4 and 8.12):

L_1 is changed to L_{Np}		G_1 is changed to G_{Np+1}	
L_2	L_0	G_2	G_1
X_1	X_{Np}	Y_1	Y_{Np+1}
X_2	X_0	Y_2	Y_1
x_1	x_{Np}	y_1	y_{Np+1}
x_2	x_0	y_2	y_1

The operating diagram is established in Illustration 8.2, and is replotted in Fig. 8.13, where the theoretical trays are stepped off.   Between 7 and 8 (approximately 7.6) theoretical trays are required.

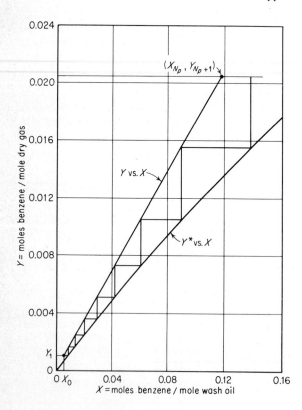

Fig. 8.13 *Illustration 8.3, the absorber.*

Alternatively, the number of theoretical trays may be computed analytically.

$$y_{Np+1} = 0.02 \qquad y_1 = \frac{0.00102}{1 + 0.00102} = 0.00102$$

$$x_0 = 0.005 \qquad m = \frac{y^*}{x} = 0.125$$

$$L_{Np} = L_S(1 + X_{Np}) = 13.43(1 + 0.1192) = 15.0 \text{ moles/hr}$$

$$A_{Np} = \frac{L_{Np}}{mG_{Np}} \doteq \frac{L_{Np}}{mG_{Np+1}} = \frac{15.0}{0.125(80.8)} = 1.485$$

$$L_0 = L_S(1 + X_0) = 13.43(1 + 0.005) = 13.5 \text{ moles/hr}$$

$$G_1 = G_S(1 + Y_1) = 79.1(1 + 0.00102) = 79.1 \text{ moles/hr}$$

$$A_1 = \frac{L_1}{mG_1} \doteq \frac{L_0}{mG_1} = \frac{13.5}{0.125(79.1)} = 1.368$$

$$\text{Av } A = [1.485(1.368)]^{0.5} = 1.425$$

$$\frac{y_1 - mx_0}{y_{Np+1} - mx_0} = \frac{0.00102 - 0.125(0.005)}{0.02 - 0.125(0.005)} = 0.0204$$

From Fig. 5.16 or Eq. (5.55), $N_p = 7.7$ theoretical trays.

b. Stripper. The trays were determined graphically in the same manner as for the absorber and found to be 6.7. Figure 5.16 for this case gave 6.0 trays owing to the relative nonconstancy of the stripping factor, $1/A_{Np} = S_{Np} = 1.197$, $1/A_1 = S_1 = 1.561$. The graphical method should be used.

Nonisothermal operation

Many absorbers and strippers deal with dilute gas mixtures and liquids, and it is frequently satisfactory in these cases to assume that the operation is isothermal. But actually absorption operations are usually exothermic, and when large quantities of solute gas are absorbed to form concentrated solutions, the temperature effects cannot be ignored. If by absorption the temperature of the liquid is raised to a considerable extent, the equilibrium solubility of the solute will be appreciably reduced and the capacity of the absorber decreased (or else much larger flow rates of liquid will be required). If the heat evolved is excessive, cooling coils may be installed in the absorber, or the liquid may be removed at intervals, cooled, and returned to the absorber. In the case of stripping, an endothermic action, the temperature tends to fall.

Consider the tray tower of Fig. 8.14. If Q_T Btu/hr is the heat removed from the entire tower by any means whatsoever, an enthalpy balance for the entire tower is

$$L_0 H_{L0} + G_{Np+1} H_{G,Np+1} = L_{Np} H_{L,Np} + G_1 H_{G1} + Q_T \qquad (8.9)$$

where H represents in each case the molal enthalpy of the stream at its particular concentration and condition. It is convenient to refer all enthalpies to the condition of pure liquid solvent, pure diluent (or solvent) gas, and pure solute at some base temperature t_o, with each substance assigned zero enthalpy for its normal state of aggregation at t_o and 1 atm pressure. Thus, the molal enthalpy of a liquid solution,

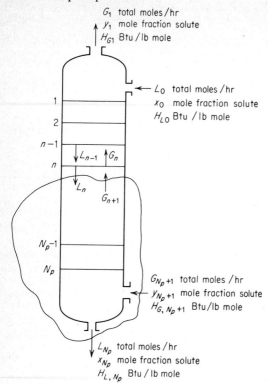

G_1 total moles/hr
y_1 mole fraction solute
H_{G1} Btu/lb mole

L_0 total moles/hr
x_0 mole fraction solute
H_{L0} Btu/lb mole

1

2

$n-1$

L_{n-1} G_n

n

L_n

G_{n+1}

N_p-1

N_p

G_{N_p+1} total moles/hr
y_{N_p+1} mole fraction solute
H_{G, N_p+1} Btu/lb mole

L_{N_p} total moles/hr
x_{N_p} mole fraction solute
H_{L, N_p} Btu/lb mole

Fig. 8.14 *Nonisothermal operation.*

temperature t_L, composition x mole fraction solute, is

$$H_L = C_L(t_L - t_o)M_{av} + \Delta H_S \qquad (8.10)$$

where the first term on the right represents the sensible heat and the second the molal enthalpy of mixing, or integral heat of solution, at the prevailing concentration and at the base temperature t_o, *per mole of solution*.   If heat is evolved on mixing, ΔH_S will be a negative quantity.   If the absorbed solute is a gas at t_o, 1 atm, the gas enthalpy will include only sensible heat.   If the absorbed solute is a liquid at the reference conditions, as in the case of many vapors, the enthalpy of the gas stream must include also the latent heat of vaporization of the solute vapor (see Chap. 7).   For ideal solutions, ΔH_S for mixing liquids is zero, and the enthalpy of the solution is the sum of the enthalpies of the separate, unmixed constituents.   If the ideal liquid solution is formed from a gaseous solute, the heat evolved is the latent heat of condensation of the absorbed solute.

For *adiabatic* operation, Q_T of Eq. (8.9) is zero, and the temperature of the streams leaving an absorber will generally be higher than the entering temperatures owing to the heat of solution.   The rise in temperature causes a decrease in solute solubility, which in turn results in a larger minimum L/G, and a larger number of trays

than for isothermal absorption. The design of such absorbers must be done numerically, calculating tray by tray from the bottom to the top. The principle of an ideal
tray, that the effluent streams from the tray are in equilibrium both with respect to
composition and temperature, is utilized for each tray. Thus, total and solute
balances up to tray n, envelope I, Fig. 8.14, are

$$L_n + G_{Np+1} = L_{Np} + G_{n+1} \tag{8.11}$$

$$L_n x_n + G_{Np+1} y_{Np+1} = L_{Np} x_{Np} + G_{n+1} y_{n+1} \tag{8.12}$$

from which L_n and x_n are computed. An enthalpy balance is

$$L_n H_{L,n} + G_{Np+1} H_{G,Np+1} = L_{Np} H_{L,Np} + G_{n+1} H_{G,n+1} \tag{8.13}$$

from which the temperature of stream L_n may be obtained. Stream G_n is then at the
same temperature as L_n and in composition equilibrium with it. Equations (8.11) to
(8.13) are then applied to tray $n - 1$, and so forth. To get started, since usually only
the temperatures of the entering streams L_0 and G_{Np+1} are known, it is usually necessary to estimate the temperature t_1 of the gas G_1 (which is the same as the top tray
temperature), and use Eq. (8.9) to compute the temperature of the liquid leaving at
the bottom of the tower. The estimate is checked when the calculations reach the top
tray, and if necessary the entire computation is repeated. The method is best illustrated by an example.

Illustration 8.4. One lb mole per unit time of a gas consisting of 75% methane CH_4 and 25%
n-pentane vapor, n-C_5H_{12}, 80°F, 1 atm, is to be scrubbed with 2 lb moles/unit time of a nonvolatile
paraffin oil, mol wt 200, specific heat 0.45 Btu/(lb)(°F), entering the absorber free of pentane at 95°F.
Compute the number of theoretical trays for adiabatic absorption of 98% of the pentane. Neglect
the solubility of CH_4 in the oil, and assume operation to be at 1 atm (neglect pressure drop for flow
through the trays). The pentane forms ideal solutions with the paraffin oil.

Solution. Heat capacities over the temperature range 0 to 150°F are

$$CH_4: 8.5 \text{ Btu/(lb mole)(°F)}$$

$$n\text{-}C_5H_{12}: 28.6 \text{ Btu/(lb mole)(°F) as vapor}$$

$$42.4 \text{ Btu/(lb mole)(°F) as liquid}$$

The latent heat of vaporization of n-C_5H_{12} at 0°F = 12,550 Btu/lb mole. Use a base temperature
$t_o = 0$°F. Enthalpies referred to 0°F, liquid pentane, liquid paraffin oil, and gaseous methane, are
then

$$H_L = (1 - x)(0.45)(200)(t_L - 0) + x(42.4)(t_L - 0)$$
$$= t_L(90 - 47.6x) \text{ Btu/lb mole liquid solution}$$

$$H_G = (1 - y)(8.5)(t_G - 0) + y(28.6)(t_G - 0) + 12,550y$$
$$= t_G(8.5 + 20.1y) + 12,550y \text{ Btu/lb mole gas-vapor mixture}$$

For solutions which follow Raoult's law, combine Eqs. (8.1) and (8.2)

$$y^* = \frac{Px}{P_t} = mx$$

where P = vapor pressure of n-pentane. Thus, the vapor pressure of n-C_5H_{12} is 400 mm Hg at 65.8°F, whence $m = P/P_t = {}^{400}\!/_{760} = 0.53$. Similarly,

t, °F	70	80	90	100	110
m	0.60	0.73	0.87	1.05	1.25

It is convenient to prepare a graph of these.

Basis: unit time. From the given data,

$$G_{Np+1} = 1 \text{ lb mole} \qquad y_{Np+1} = 0.25$$

$$H_{G,Np+1} = 80[8.5 + 20.1(0.25)] + 12,550(0.25) = 4,220 \text{ Btu/lb mole}$$

$$L_0 = 2 \text{ lb moles} \qquad x_0 = 0$$

$$H_{L0} = 95(90) = 8,550 \text{ Btu/lb mole}$$

$$n\text{-}C_5H_{12} \text{ absorbed} = 0.98(0.25) = 0.245 \text{ lb mole}$$

$$n\text{-}C_5H_{12} \text{ in } G_1 = 0.25 - 0.245 = 0.005 \text{ lb mole}$$

$$G_1 = 0.75 + 0.005 = 0.755 \text{ lb mole}$$

$$\text{Required } y_1 = \frac{0.005}{0.755} = 0.00662$$

$$L_{Np} = 2 + 0.245 = 2.245 \text{ lb moles} \qquad x_{Np} = \frac{0.245}{2.245} = 0.1091$$

Assume $t_1 = 96°F$ (to be checked later).

$$H_{G1} = 96[8.5 + 20.1(0.00662)] + 12,550(0.00662) = 911.9 \text{ Btu/lb mole}$$

Eq. (8.9), with $Q_T = 0$:

$$2(8,550) + 4,220 = L_{Np}H_{L,Np} + 0.755(911.9)$$

$$L_{Np}H_{L,Np} = 20,632 \text{ Btu}$$

$$H_{L,Np} = \frac{20,632}{2.245} = t_{Np}[90 - 47.6(0.1091)]$$

$$t_{Np} = 108.5°F$$

$$\therefore \quad m_{Np} = 1.22 \quad \text{and} \quad y_{Np} = m_{Np}x_{Np} = 1.22(0.1091) = 0.1332$$

$$G_{Np} = \frac{0.75}{1 - 0.1332} = 0.865 \text{ lb mole}$$

$$H_{G,Np} = 108.5[8.5 + 20.1(0.1332)] + 12,550(0.1332) = 2,886 \text{ Btu/lb mole}$$

Eq. (8.11) with $n = N_p - 1$:

$$L_{Np-1} + G_{Np+1} = L_{Np} + G_{Np}$$

$$L_{Np-1} + 1 = 2.245 + 0.865$$

$$L_{Np-1} = 2.110 \text{ lb moles}$$

Eq. (8.12) with $n = N_p - 1$:

$$2.110x_{Np-1} + 0.25 = 0.245 + 0.865(0.1332)$$

$$x_{Np-1} = 0.0521$$

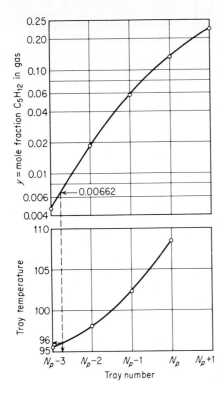

Fig. 8.15 *Solution to Illustration 8.4.*

Eq. (8.13) with $n = N_p - 1$:

$$2.110 H_{L, N_p - 1} + 4,220 = 20,632 + 0.865(2,886)$$
$$H_{L, N_p - 1} = 8,960 \text{ Btu/lb mole}$$
$$8,960 = t_{N_p - 1}[90 - 47.6(0.0521)]$$
$$t_{N_p - 1} = 102.3°\text{F}$$

The computation is continued upward through the tower in this manner until the gas composition falls at least to $y = 0.00662$.   The results are:

n = tray no.	t_n, °F	x_n	y_n
$N_p = 4$	108.5	0.1091	0.1332
$N_p - 1 = 3$	102.3	0.0521	0.0568
$N_p - 2 = 2$	98.2	0.0184	0.01875
$N_p - 3 = 1$	95.6	0.00463	0.00450

Figure 8.15 shows the calculated gas compositions and tray temperatures plotted against tray number. The required $y_1 = 0.00662$ occurs at 3.75 theoretical trays, and the temperature on the top tray is 96°F, as assumed initially.   Had this temperature been other than 96°F, a new assumed value of t_1 and a new calculation would have been required.   An integral number of trays will require a slightly greater (for $N_p = 3$) or less (for $N_p = 4$) liquid flow L_0, but since a tray efficiency must still be applied to obtain the number of real trays, the nonintegral number is ordinarily accepted.

When the temperature rise for the liquid is large, as with concentrated gases entering and small values of L/G, calculations of this sort become very tedious since the rate of convergence of the calculated and assumed t_1 is very slow.   There may be a temperature maximum at some tray other than the bottom tray.   If the number of trays is fixed, the outlet-gas composition and top-tray temperature must both be determined by trial and error.

Real trays and tray efficiency

Methods for estimating the Murphree tray efficiency corrected for entrainment $\mathbf{E}_{MGE}$ for sieve trays are discussed in detail in Chap. 6.   For a given absorber or stripper, these permit estimation of the tray efficiency as a function of fluid compositions and temperature as they vary from one end of the tower to the other.   Usually it is sufficient to make such computations at only three or four locations, and then proceed as in Fig. 8.16.   The broken line is drawn between equilibrium curve and operating line at a fractional vertical distance from the operating line equal to the prevailing Murphree gas efficiency.   Thus the value of $\mathbf{E}_{MGE}$ for the bottom tray is the ratio of the lengths of lines, AB/AC.   Since the broken line then represents the real effluent compositions from the trays, it is used instead of the equilibrium curve to complete the tray construction, which now provides the number of real trays.

When the Murphree efficiency is constant for all trays, and under conditions such that the operating line and equilibrium curves are straight (Henry's law, isothermal operation, dilute solutions), then the overall tray efficiency can be computed, and the number of real trays may be determined analytically:

$$\mathbf{E}_O = \frac{\text{ideal trays}}{\text{real trays}} = \frac{\log\,[1 + \mathbf{E}_{MGE}(1/A - 1)]}{\log\,(1/A)} \tag{8.14}$$

For rough estimates, Fig. 6.15 is useful for bubble-cap trays.

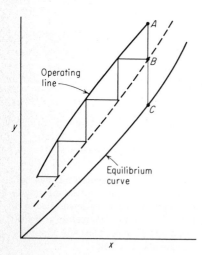

y

Operating line

A

B

C

Equilibrium curve

x

Fig. 8.16   *Use of Murphree efficiencies for an absorber.*

Illustration 8.5. A process for making small amounts of hydrogen by cracking ammonia is being considered, and it is desired to remove residual uncracked ammonia from the resulting gas. The gas will consist of H_2 and N_2 in the molar ratio of $3:1$, containing 3% NH_3 by volume, at 2 atm, 80°F.

There is available a sieve-tray tower, 30-in. diameter, containing 14 cross-flow trays at 18-in. tray spacing. On each tray, the downflow weir is 21 in. long and extends 2.0 in. above the tray floor. The perforations are $\frac{3}{16}$-in. diameter, arranged in triangular pitch on 0.5-in. centers, punched in sheet metal 0.078 in. thick. The total perforation area is 0.4 sq ft/tray. Estimate the capacity of the tower to remove ammonia from the gas by scrubbing with water. Assume isothermal operation at 80°F.

Solution. From the geometry of the tray arrangement, in the notation of Chap. 6, the following are calculated:

$$d = \text{tower diameter} = 30/12 = 2.50 \text{ ft}$$
$$A_t = \text{tower cross section} = 4.90 \text{ sq ft}$$
$$A_d = \text{downspout cross section} = 0.431 \text{ sq ft}$$
$$A_n = A_t - A_d = 4.47 \text{ sq ft} \qquad A_a = A_t - 2A_d = 4.04 \text{ sq ft}$$
$$A_h = 0.40 \text{ sq ft}$$
$$Z = \text{distance between downspouts} = 1.78 \text{ ft}$$
$$W = \text{weir length} = \frac{21}{12} = 1.75 \text{ ft}$$
$$h_W = \text{weir height} = 2.0 \text{ in.}$$
$$t = \text{tray spacing} = 18.0 \text{ in.}$$
$$z = \text{av flow width} = \frac{d + W}{2} = 2.12 \text{ ft}$$

Use a weir head $h_1 = 0.75$ in. $W/d = 21/30 = 0.7$, $h_1/d = 0.75/2.5 = 0.30$ in./ft. From Fig. 6.10, $(W/W_{\text{eff}})^{2/3} = 1.06$.

Eq. (6.5): $\qquad 0.75 = 5.38(1.06)\left(\dfrac{q}{W}\right)^{2/3} \qquad \dfrac{q}{W} = 0.0516 \text{ cu ft/(sec)(ft)}$

$q = 0.0516(1.75) = 0.0905$ cu ft/sec liquid, or 5.15 lb/sec, or 0.286 lb mole/sec. This is a reasonable, but not the maximum possible, liquid flow rate.

$$\text{Liquid density} = \rho_L = 62.3 \text{ lb/cu ft}$$
$$\text{Av mol wt gas} = 0.03(17.03) + 0.97(0.25)(28.02) + 0.97(0.75)(2.02)$$
$$= 8.78 \text{ lb/lb mole}$$
$$\rho_G = \frac{8.78}{359}\frac{2}{1}\frac{492}{460 + 80} = 0.0466 \text{ lb/cu ft}$$

The flooding gas rate is found by simultaneous solution of Eqs. (6.1) and (6.3) by trial and error. Table 6.1: $a = 0.1535$, $b = 0.0935$. For these solutions, $\sigma' = 68$ dynes/cm surface tension. A gas rate of 1.82 lb/sec provides, through Eq. (6.3), $C_F = 0.366$; Eq. (6.1): $V_F = 13.40$ ft/sec at flooding. Using 65% of the flood rate, $V = 0.65(13.40) = 8.75$ ft/sec, whence the gas rate $= VA_n\rho_G = 8.75(4.47)(0.0466) = 1.82$ lb/sec, or 0.207 lb moles/sec.

The methods of Chap. 6 then provide $h_D = 2.37$ in., $V_a = VA_n/A_a = 9.68$ ft/sec, $h_L = 0.77$ in., $h_R = 0.35$ in., $h_G = 3.47$ in., $h_2 = 0.2$ in., $h_3 = 3.67$ in.

$$h_W + h_1 + h_3 = 6.42 \text{ in.}$$

This is below $t/2 = 9.0$ in., flooding will not occur, and the flow rates are reasonable.

$$\frac{V}{V_F} = 0.65 \qquad \frac{L'}{G'}\left(\frac{\rho_G}{\rho_L}\right)^{0.5} = 0.078$$

and from Fig. 6.11, the fractional entrainment $E = 0.019$.

The methods of Chap. 2 provide D_G, the diffusivity of ammonia through the N_2–H_2 mixture, equal to 1.0 sq ft/hr. The gas viscosity $= 0.01125$ centipoise, whence $Sc_G = \mu_G/\rho_G D_G = 0.01125(2.42)/0.0466(1.0) = 0.585$.

The diffusivity of ammonia in the water solution $D_L = 9.38(10^{-5})$ sq ft/hr. For dilute solutions, NH_3–H_2O follows Henry's law, and at 80°F, the Henry-law constant $= m = y^*/x = 0.707$. The absorption factor $= A = L/mG = 0.286/0.707(0.207) = 1.955$.

Eq. (6.31): $N_{tG} = 0.817$ Eq. (6.34): $\theta_L = 0.00074$ hr

Eq. (6.32): $N_{tL} = 2.86$ Eq. (6.33): $D_E = 236$ sq ft/hr

Eq. (6.23): $N_{tOG} = 0.705$ Eq. (6.22): $E_{OG} = 0.506$

Eq. (6.29): $Pe = 18.1$ Eq. (6.28): $\eta = 0.253$

Eq. (6.27): $E_{MG} = 0.568$ Eq. (6.30): $E_{MGE} = 0.566$

Since the quantity of gas absorbed is small relative to the total gas flow and the liquid solutions all dilute, the Murphree tray efficiency will be taken as constant for all trays. For the dilute solutions encountered here, the operating line is essentially straight. Consequently, Eq. (8.14):

$$E_O = \frac{\log\,[1 + 0.566(1/1.955 - 1)]}{\log\,(1/1.955)} = 0.482$$

(*Note:* for bubble-cap trays, Fig. 6.15 provides, as a rough estimate, $E_O = 0.55$.)

Eq. (8.14): $N_p = 14(0.482) = 6.75$ ideal trays

From Fig. 5.16,

$$\frac{y_1 - mx_0}{y_{Np+1} - mx_0} = \frac{y_1}{y_{Np+1}} = \frac{y_1}{0.03} = 0.0048$$

$y_1 = 0.000144$ mole fraction NH_3 in the effluent gas   **Ans.**

CONTINUOUS-CONTACT EQUIPMENT

Countercurrent packed and spray towers operate in a different manner from plate towers in that the fluids are in contact continuously in their path through the tower, rather than intermittently. Thus, in a packed tower the liquid and gas compositions change continuously with height of packing. Every point on an operating line therefore represents conditions found somewhere in the tower, whereas for tray towers, only the isolated points on the operating line corresponding to trays have real significance.

Height equivalent to a theoretical plate

A simple method for designing packed towers, which was introduced many years ago, ignores the differences between stagewise and continuous contact. In this method the number of theoretical trays or plates required for a given change in concentration is computed by the methods of the previous section. This is then multiplied by a quantity, the height equivalent to a theoretical tray or plate (HETP) to give the required height of packing to do the same job. The HETP must be an experimentally determined quantity characteristic for each packing. Unfortunately it is found that the HETP varies, not only with the type and size of the packing but also very strongly with flow rates of each fluid and for every system with concentration as well, so that an enormous amount of experimental data would have to be accumulated to permit utilization of the method. The difficulty lies in the failure to account for the fundamentally different action of tray and packed towers, and the method has now largely been abandoned.

Absorption of one component

Consider a packed tower of unit cross section, as in Fig. 8.17. The total effective interfacial surface for mass transfer, as a result of spreading of the liquid in a film over the packing, is S sq ft/sq ft tower cross section. This is conveniently described as the product of a sq ft interfacial surface/cu ft packed volume by the packed volume, Z cu ft/sq ft tower cross section (the quantity a is the a_A of Chap. 6). In the differential volume dZ cu ft, the interface surface is

$$dS = a\,dZ \tag{8.15}$$

The quantity of solute A in the gas passing the differential section of the tower under consideration is Gy moles/(hr)(sq ft), and the rate of mass transfer is therefore $d(Gy)$ moles A/(hr)(differential volume). Since $N_B = 0$ and $N_A/(N_A + N_B) = 1.0$, application of Eq. (5.20) provides

$$N_A = \frac{\text{moles } A \text{ absorbed}}{\text{(hr)(interfacial surface)}} = \frac{d(Gy)}{a\,dZ} = F_G \ln \frac{1 - y_i}{1 - y} \tag{8.16}$$

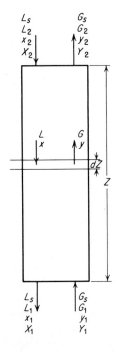

Fig. 8.17 *Packed tower.*

Both G and y vary from one end of the tower to the other, but G_S, the solvent gas which is essentially insoluble, does not.   Therefore,

$$d(Gy) = d\left(\frac{G_S y}{1-y}\right) = \frac{G_S \, dy}{(1-y)^2} = \frac{G \, dy}{1-y} \tag{8.17}$$

Substituting in Eq. (8.16), rearranging, and integrating,

$$Z = \int_0^Z dZ = \int_{y_2}^{y_1} \frac{G \, dy}{F_G a (1-y) \ln \left[(1-y_i)/(1-y)\right]} \tag{8.18}$$

The value of y_i may be found by the methods of Chap. 5, using Eq. (5.21) with $N_A/\Sigma N = 1$:

$$\frac{1-y_i}{1-y} = \left(\frac{1-x}{1-x_i}\right)^{F_L/F_G} = \left(\frac{1-x}{1-x_i}\right)^{F_{La}/F_{Ga}} \tag{8.19}$$

For any value of (x,y) on the operating curve plotted in terms of mole fractions, a curve of x_i vs. y_i from Eq. (8.19) is plotted to determine the intersection with the equilibrium curve.   This provides the local y and y_i for use in Eq. (8.18).† Equation (8.18) may then be integrated graphically after plotting the integrand as ordinate vs. y as abscissa.

However, it is more customary to proceed as follows.[2]   Since

$$y - y_i = (1-y_i) - (1-y) \tag{8.20}$$

the numerator and denominator of the integral of Eq. (8.18) may be multiplied respectively by the right- and left-hand sides of Eq. (8.20) to provide

$$Z = \int_{y_2}^{y_1} \frac{G(1-y)_{iM} \, dy}{F_G a (1-y)(y-y_i)} \tag{8.21}$$

where $(1-y)_{iM}$ is the logarithmic mean of $1-y_i$ and $1-y$.   Defining a *height of a gas transfer unit* H_{tG} as

$$H_{tG} = \frac{G}{F_G a} = \frac{G}{k_y a (1-y)_{iM}} = \frac{G}{k_G a P_t (1-y)_{iM}} \tag{8.22}$$

Eq. (8.21) becomes

$$Z = \int_{y_2}^{y_1} H_{tG} \frac{(1-y)_{iM} \, dy}{(1-y)(y-y_i)} \doteq H_{tG} \int_{y_2}^{y_1} \frac{(1-y)_{iM} \, dy}{(1-y)(y-y_i)} \tag{8.23}$$

$$= H_{tG} N_{tG}$$

Here advantage is taken of the fact that the ratio $G/F_G a = H_{tG}$ is very much more constant than either G or $F_G a$, and in many cases may be considered constant within the accuracy of the available data.   In the integral of Eq. (8.23) containing only the y terms, if we disregard the ratio $(1-y)_{iM}/(1-y)$, the remainder is seen to be the

---

† As demonstrated in Illustration 8.6, for moderately dilute solutions it is satisfactory to determine y_i by a line of slope $-k_x a/k_y a$ drawn from (x,y) on the operating line to intersection with the equilibrium curve, in accordance with Eq. (5.2).

number of times the average $y - y_i$ divides into the change of gas concentration $y_1 - y_2$. As in Chap. 7, this is a measure of the difficulty of the absorption, and the integral is called the *number of gas transfer units* N_{tG}. Equation (8.23) can be further simplified by substituting the arithmetic average for the logarithmic average $(1 - y)_{iM}$:[4]

$$(1 - y)_{iM} = \frac{(1 - y_i) - (1 - y)}{\ln [(1 - y_i)/(1 - y)]} \doteq \frac{(1 - y_i) + (1 - y)}{2} \tag{8.24}$$

which involves very little error. N_{tG} then becomes

$$N_{tG} = \int_{y_2}^{y_1} \frac{dy}{y - y_i} + \frac{1}{2} \ln \frac{1 - y_2}{1 - y_1} \tag{8.25}$$

which makes for simpler graphical integration.† For dilute solutions, the second term on the right of Eq. (8.25) is negligible, $F_G a \doteq k_y a$, and y_i may be obtained by plotting a line of slope $-k_x a/k_y a$ from points (x,y) on the operating line to intersection with the equilibrium curve.

The above relationships all have their counterparts in terms of liquid concentrations, derived in exactly the same way

$$Z = \int_{x_2}^{x_1} \frac{L \, dx}{F_L a(1 - x) \ln [(1 - x)/(1 - x_i)]} = \int_{x_2}^{x_1} \frac{L(1 - x)_{iM} \, dx}{F_L a(1 - x)(x_i - x)} \tag{8.26}$$

$$Z = \int_{x_2}^{x_1} H_{tL} \frac{(1 - x)_{iM} \, dx}{(1 - x)(x_i - x)} \doteq H_{tL} \int_{x_2}^{x_1} \frac{(1 - x)_{iM} \, dx}{(1 - x)(x_i - x)} = H_{tL} N_{tL} \tag{8.27}$$

$$H_{tL} = \frac{L}{F_L a} = \frac{L}{k_x a(1 - x)_{iM}} = \frac{L}{k_L ac(1 - x)_{iM}} \tag{8.28}$$

$$N_{tL} = \int_{x_2}^{x_1} \frac{dx}{x_i - x} + \frac{1}{2} \ln \frac{1 - x_1}{1 - x_2} \tag{8.29}$$

where H_{tL} = height of a liquid transfer unit
N_{tL} = number of liquid transfer units
$(1 - x)_{iM}$ = logarithmic mean of $1 - x$ and $1 - x_i$

Either set of equations leads to the same value of Z.

Strippers. The same relationships apply as for absorption. The "driving forces" $y - y_i$ and $x_i - x$ which appear in the above equations are then negative, but since for strippers $x_2 > x_1$, and $y_2 > y_1$, the result is a positive Z as before.

† In the graphical integration of Eq. (8.25), the plot of $1/(y - y_i)$ vs. y often covers awkwardly large ranges of the ordinate. This may be avoided[12] by replacing dy by its equal $y \, d \ln y$, so that

$$N_{tG} = 2.303 \int_{\log y_2}^{\log y_1} \frac{y}{y - y_i} \, d \log y + 1.152 \log \frac{1 - y_2}{1 - y_1} \tag{8.25a}$$

Illustration 8.6. The absorber of Illustrations 8.2 and 8.3 is to be a packed tower, 1.5 ft in diameter, filled with 1.5-in. Berl saddles. The circumstances are:

Gas

Benzene content: in, $y_1 = 0.02$ mole fraction, $Y_1 = 0.0204$ mole/mole dry gas.

Out, $y_2 = 0.00102$ mole fraction, $Y_2 = 0.00102$ mole/mole dry gas.

Nonabsorbed gas: av mol wt $= 11.0$.

Rate in $= 80.8$ lb moles total/hr; 79.1 moles/hr nonbenzene.

Temperature $= 80°F$; pressure $= 800$ mm Hg.

Viscosity $= 0.01$ centipoise; $D_{AG} = 0.504$ sq ft/hr.

Liquid

Benzene content: in, $x_2 = 0.005$ mole fraction, $X_2 = 0.00502$ moles vapor/mole dry gas.

Out, $x_1 = 0.1065$ mole fraction, $X_1 = 0.1192$ mole vapor/mole gas.

Benzene-free oil: mol wt $= 260$, viscosity $= 2.0$ centipoises; sp gr 0.84; rate $= 13.43$ lb moles/hr.

Temp $= 80°F$; $D_{AL} = 1.85(10^{-5})$ sq ft/hr.

Surface tension $= 30$ dynes/cm; $m = y^*/x = 0.1250$.

Compute the depth of packing required.

Solution. To plot the operating line, use Eq. (8.7) to calculate X and Y values (or read from Fig. 8.10), and convert to $x = X/(1 + X)$ and $y = Y/(1 + Y)$. Thus,

$$79.1(0.0204 - Y) = 13.43(0.1192 - X)$$

X	x	Y	y
0.00502	0.00500	0.00102	0.00102
0.02	0.01961	0.00356	0.00355
0.04	0.0385	0.00695	0.00690
0.06	0.0566	0.01035	0.01024
0.08	0.0741	0.01374	0.01355
0.10	0.0909	0.01714	0.01685
0.1192	0.1065	0.0204	0.0200

Values of y and x (the operating line) are plotted along with the equilibrium line, $y = 0.1250x$, in Fig. 8.18. Although the curvature in this case is not great, the operating line is not straight on mole-fraction coordinates.

The cross-sectional area of the absorber is $(1.5)^2\pi/4 = 1.77$ sq ft. At the bottom,

$$L' = \frac{13.43(260) + 0.1192(13.43)(78)}{1.77} = 2,040 \text{ lb/(hr)(sq ft)}$$

Similarly at the top, $L' = 1,970$. Av $L' = 2,005$ lb/(hr)(sq ft). Also at the bottom

$$G' = \frac{80.8(0.98)(11) + 80.8(0.02)(78)}{1.77} = 563 \text{ lb/(hr)(sq ft)}$$

Similarly at the top, $G' = 493$. Av $G' = 528$ lb/(hr)(sq ft).

The flow quantities change so little from one end of the tower to the other that the average values may be used to compute the mass-transfer coefficients, which may then be taken as constant. The circumstances are precisely those of Illustration 6.4, where it was found that

$$F_G a = 26.1 \text{ lb moles/(hr)(cu ft)} \qquad F_L a = 5.0 \text{ lb moles/(hr)(cu ft)}$$

For each plotted point on the operating line, Eq. (8.19) is then used to determine the interface compositions. Thus, at $(x = 0.1065, y = 0.0200)$ on the operating line (point A, Fig. 8.18), Eq. (8.19) becomes

$$\frac{1 - y_i}{1 - 0.0200} = \left(\frac{1 - 0.1065}{1 - x_i}\right)^{5.0/26.1}$$

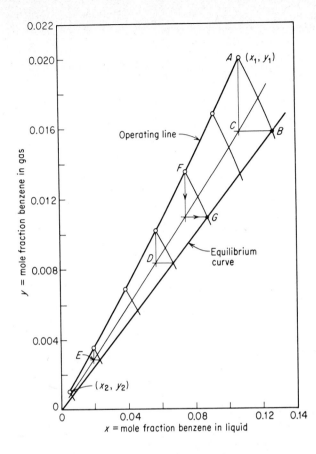

Fig. 8.18 *Solution to Illustration 8.6.*

This is plotted (y_i vs. x_i) as curve AB on Fig. 8.18, to intersect the equilibrium curve at B, where $y_i = 0.01580$.

Note: In this case, since the concentrations are low, an essentially correct value of y_i may be obtained by the following less tedious calculation.   Table 3.1 shows

$$k_y a = \frac{F_G a}{p_{BM}/P_t} = \frac{F_G a}{(1 - y)_{iM}} \qquad k_x a = \frac{F_L a}{(1 - x)_{iM}}$$

At point A on the operating line, $1 - y = 1 - 0.02 = 0.98$, $1 - x = 1 - 0.1065 = 0.8935$.   As an approximation, these may be taken as $(1 - y)_{iM}$ and $(1 - x)_{iM}$, respectively, whence

$$k_y a = \frac{26.1}{0.98} = 26.4 \text{ moles/(hr)(cu ft)(mole fraction)}$$

$$k_x a = \frac{5.0}{0.8935} = 5.60 \text{ moles/(hr)(cu ft)(mole fraction)}$$

In accordance with Eq. (5.2), $-k_x a/k_y a = -5.60/26.4 = -0.210$, and if a straight line of this slope is drawn from point A, it intersects the equilibrium curve at $y_i = 0.01585$.   Curve AB, in other words, is nearly a straight line of slope -0.210.   The error by this method becomes even less at lower solute concentrations.   Where the F's must be used, it is sufficient to proceed as follows.   On Fig. 8.18,

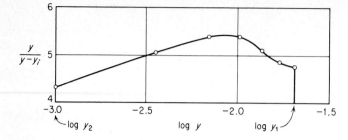

Fig. 8.19 *Graphical integration for Illustration 8.6.*

draw the vertical line *AC* to intersection with the horizontal line *CB*, thus locating the intersection *C*. Repeat the calculation at two other locations, such as at *D* and *E*, and draw the curve *EDC*. Interfacial concentrations *G* corresponding to any point *F* on the operating line may then be obtained by the construction shown on the figure leading to point *G*.

In a similar manner, the values of y_i tabulated below were determined, as shown on Fig. 8.18.

y	y_i	$\dfrac{y}{y - y_i}$	$\log y$
0.00102	0.000784	4.32	$-2.9999 = \log y_2$
0.00355	0.00285	5.03	-2.4498
0.00690	0.00562	5.39	-2.1612
0.01024	0.00830	5.39	-1.9897
0.01355	0.01090	5.11	-1.8681
0.01685	0.01337	4.84	-1.7734
0.0200	0.01580	4.76	$-1.6990 = \log y_1$

Since the mass-transfer coefficients are essentially constant, Eq. (8.25a) will be used to determine N_{tG}. From the data of the above tabulation, the curve for graphical integration of Eq. (8.25a) is plotted in Fig. 8.19.   The area under the curve (to the zero ordinate) is 6.556.   Then by Eq. (8.25a),

$$N_{tG} = 2.303(6.556) + 1.152 \log \frac{1 - 0.00102}{1 - 0.0200} = 15.11$$

The average gas rate is

$$G = \frac{80.8 + 79.1/(1 - 0.00102)}{2(1.77)} = 45.2 \text{ lb moles/(hr)(sq ft)}$$

Eq. (8.22): $H_{tG} = \dfrac{G}{F_G a} = \dfrac{45.2}{26.1} = 1.735 \text{ ft}$

$Z = H_{tG} N_{tG} = 1.735(15.11) = 26.0$ ft packed depth   **Ans.**

Note: The circumstances are such that, for this problem, the simpler computations of Illustration 8.7 are entirely adequate.   The method used above, however, is suitable for solutions of any concentration and where the equilibrium curve is not straight.   If flow rates vary appreciably from top to bottom of the tower, so that mass-transfer coefficients vary, this is easily allowed for in determining values of y_i.   In such cases, Eq. (8.18) would be used to compute Z.

Overall coefficients and transfer units $(m = dy_i/dx_i = \text{const})$

In cases where the equilibrium-distribution curve is straight and the ratio of mass-transfer coefficients is constant, it was shown in Chap. 5 that overall mass-transfer coefficients are convenient. The expressions for the height of packing may then be written

$$Z = N_{tOG} H_{tOG} \tag{8.30}$$

$$N_{tOG} = \int_{y_2}^{y_1} \frac{(1-y)_{*M} \, dy}{(1-y)(y-y^*)} \tag{8.31}$$

$$N_{tOG} = \int_{y_2}^{y_1} \frac{dy}{y-y^*} + \frac{1}{2} \ln \frac{1-y_2}{1-y_1} \tag{8.32}$$

$$N_{tOG} = \int_{Y_2}^{Y_1} \frac{dY}{Y-Y^*} + \frac{1}{2} \ln \frac{1+Y_2}{1+Y_1} \tag{8.33}$$

$$H_{tOG} = \frac{G}{F_{OG}a} = \frac{G}{K_y a(1-y)_{*M}} = \frac{G}{K_G a P_t (1-y)_{*M}} \tag{8.34}$$

Here y^* (or Y^*) is the solute concentration in the gas corresponding to equilibrium with the bulk liquid concentration x (or X), so that $y - y^*$ (or $Y - Y^*$) is simply the vertical distance between operating line and equilibrium curve. $(1-y)_{*M}$ is the logarithmic average of $1-y$ and $1-y^*$. These methods are convenient since interfacial concentrations need not be obtained, and Eq. (8.33) is especially convenient since the operating line on X, Y coordinates is straight. N_{tOG} is the *number of overall gas transfer units*, H_{tOG} the *height of an overall gas transfer unit*.

Equations (8.30) to (8.34) are usually used when the principal mass-transfer resistance resides within the gas. For cases where the principal mass-transfer resistance lies within the liquid, it is more convenient to use

$$Z = N_{tOL} H_{tOL} \tag{8.35}$$

$$N_{tOL} = \int_{x_2}^{x_1} \frac{(1-x)_{*M} \, dx}{(1-x)(x^*-x)} \tag{8.36}$$

$$N_{tOL} = \int_{x_2}^{x_1} \frac{dx}{x^*-x} + \frac{1}{2} \ln \frac{1-x_1}{1-x_2} \tag{8.37}$$

$$N_{tOL} = \int_{X_2}^{X_1} \frac{dX}{X^*-X} + \frac{1}{2} \ln \frac{1+X_1}{1+X_2} \tag{8.38}$$

$$H_{tOL} = \frac{L}{F_{OL}a} = \frac{L}{K_x a(1-x)_{*M}} = \frac{L}{K_L ac(1-x)_{*M}} \tag{8.39}$$

Dilute solutions

The computation of the number of transfer units for dilute mixtures can be greatly simplified. When the gas mixture is dilute, for example, the second term of the definition of N_{tOG} [Eq. (8.32)] becomes entirely negligible and may be discarded

$$N_{tOG} = \int_{y_2}^{y_1} \frac{dy}{y-y^*} \tag{8.40}$$

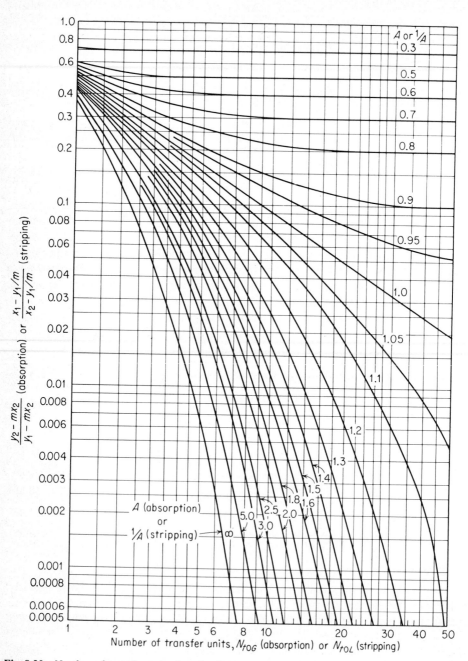

Fig. 8.20 *Number of transfer units for absorbers or strippers with constant absorption or stripping factor.*

If the equilibrium curve in terms of mole fractions is linear over the range of compositions x_1 to x_2, then

$$y^* = mx + r \qquad (8.41)$$

If the solutions are dilute, the operating line may be considered as a straight line as well

$$y = \frac{L}{G}(x - x_2) + y_2 \qquad (8.42)$$

so that the driving force $y - y^*$ is then linear in x

$$y - y^* = qx + s \qquad (8.43)$$

where q, r, and s are constants. Therefore Eq. (8.40) becomes

$$N_{tOG} = \frac{L}{G} \int_{x_2}^{x_1} \frac{dx}{qx + s} = \frac{L}{Gq} \ln \frac{(y - y^*)_1}{(y - y^*)_2} = \frac{y_1 - y_2}{\dfrac{(y - y^*)_1 - (y - y^*)_2}{\ln\left[(y - y^*)_1/(y - y^*)_2\right]}} \qquad (8.44)$$

$$N_{tOG} = \frac{y_1 - y_2}{(y - y^*)_M} \qquad (8.45)$$

where $(y - y^*)_M$ is the logarithmic average of the concentration differences at the ends of the tower. This equation is sometimes used in the familiar rate form obtained by substituting the definition of N_{tOG}

$$G(y_1 - y_2) = K_G a Z P_t (y - y^*)_M \qquad (8.46)$$

Dilute solutions, Henry's law

If Henry's law applies [r of Eq. (8.41) $= 0$], by elimination of x between Eqs. (8.41) and (8.42) and substitution of y^* in Eq. (8.40) there results for absorbers[4]

$$N_{tOG} = \frac{\ln\left[\left(\dfrac{y_1 - mx_2}{y_2 - mx_2}\right)\left(1 - \dfrac{1}{A}\right) + \dfrac{1}{A}\right]}{1 - 1/A} \qquad (8.47)$$

where $A = L/mG$, as before. For strippers, the corresponding expression in terms of N_{tOL} is similar

$$N_{tOL} = \frac{\ln\left[\left(\dfrac{x_2 - y_1/m}{x_1 - y_1/m}\right)(1 - A) + A\right]}{1 - A} \qquad (8.48)$$

These are shown in convenient graphical form in Fig. 8.20.

Graphical construction for transfer units[1]

Equation (8.45) demonstrates that one overall gas transfer unit results when the change in gas composition equals the average overall driving force causing the change. Consider now the operating diagram of Fig. 8.21, where line KB has been drawn so as to be everywhere vertically halfway between the operating line and equilibrium

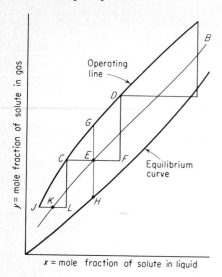

x = mole fraction of solute in liquid

Fig. 8.21 *Graphical determination of transfer units.*

curve. The step *CFD*, which corresponds to one transfer unit, has been constructed by drawing the horizontal line *CEF* so that line *CE* = *EF* and continuing vertically to *D*. $y_G - y_H$ may be considered as the average driving force for the change in gas composition $y_D - y_F$ corresponding to this step. Since *GE* = *EH*, and if the operating line may be considered straight, *DF* = 2(*GE*) = *GH*, the step *CFD* corresponds to one transfer unit. In similar fashion the other transfer units were stepped off (*JK* = *KL*, etc.). For computing N_{tOL}, the line *KB* would be drawn horizontally halfway between equilibrium curve and operating line and would bisect the vertical portions of the steps.

Overall heights of transfer units

When overall numbers of transfer units are appropriate, the overall heights of transfer units may be synthesized from those for the individual phases through the relationships developed in Chap. 5. Thus, Eq. (5.25a), with $m' = m'' = m = $ const, may be written

$$\frac{G}{F_{OG}a} = \frac{G(1-y)_{iM}}{F_{G}a(1-y)_{*M}} + \frac{mG}{L}\frac{L}{F_{L}a}\frac{(1-x)_{iM}}{(1-y)_{*M}} \tag{8.49}$$

whence, by definition of the heights of transfer units,

$$H_{tOG} = H_{tG}\frac{(1-y)_{iM}}{(1-y)_{*M}} + \frac{mG}{L}H_{tL}\frac{(1-x)_{iM}}{(1-y)_{*M}} \tag{8.50}$$

If the mass-transfer resistance is essentially all in the gas, $y_i \doteq y^*$, and

$$H_{tOG} = H_{tG} + \frac{mG}{L}H_{tL}\frac{(1-x)_{iM}}{(1-y)_{*M}} \tag{8.51}$$

and, for dilute solutions, the concentration ratio of the last equation may be dropped. In similar fashion, Eq. (5.26a) yields

$$H_{tOL} = H_{tL} \frac{(1 - x)_{iM}}{(1 - x)_{*M}} + \frac{L}{mG} \grave{H}_{tG} \frac{(1 - y)_{iM}}{(1 - x)_{*M}} \qquad (8.52)$$

and if the mass-transfer resistance is essentially all in the liquid,

$$H_{tOL} = H_{tL} + \frac{L}{mG} H_{tG} \frac{(1 - y)_{iM}}{(1 - x)_{*M}} \qquad (8.53)$$

The concentration ratio of the last equation may be dropped for dilute solutions. Data for the individual phase coefficients are summarized for standard packings in Chap. 6.

Illustration 8.7. Repeat the computation of Illustration 8.6, using the simplified procedures for dilute mixtures.

Solution. Number of transfer units. a. Use Eq. (8.45). $y_1 = 0.02$, $x_1 = 0.1065$, $y_1^* = mx_1 = 0.125(0.1065) = 0.01331$, $(y - y^*)_1 = 0.02 - 0.01331 = 0.00669$. $y_2 = 0.00102$, $x_2 = 0.0050$, $y_2^* = mx_2 = 0.125(0.0050) = 0.000625$, $(y - y^*)_2 = 0.00102 - 0.000625 = 0.000395$.

$$(y - y^*)_M = \frac{0.00669 - 0.000395}{\ln (0.00669/0.000395)} = 0.00223$$

$$N_{tOG} = \frac{0.02 - 0.00102}{0.00223} = 8.55 \quad \textbf{Ans.}$$

b. Eq. (8.47) or Fig. 8.20. Av $A = 1.425$ (Illustration 8.3).

$$\frac{y_2 - mx_2}{y_1 - mx_2} = \frac{0.00102 - 0.125(0.005)}{0.02 - 0.125(0.005)} = 0.0204.$$

From either Eq. (8.47) or Fig. 8.20, $N_{tOG} = 8.8$. **Ans.**

c. The graphical construction for transfer units is shown in Fig. 8.22. The mole-ratio coordinates are satisfactory for dilute mixtures, and the operating line and equilibrium curve were redrawn from Fig. 8.10. The line *BD* was drawn everywhere vertically midway between operating line and equilibrium curve, and the transfer-unit steps constructed by making the horizontal-line segments such as *AB* and *BC* equal. The number of transfer units required is 8⅔. **Ans.**

d. Eq. (8.33). From Fig. 8.10, for each value of *X*, values of *Y* are read from the operating line *DF* and *Y** from the equilibrium curve (or these may be computed from the equations of these lines).

X	Y	Y^*	$\dfrac{1}{Y - Y^*}$
$X_2 = 0.00502$	0.00102	0.00062	2,500
0.02	0.00356	0.00245	901
0.04	0.00695	0.00483	462
0.06	0.01035	0.00712	310
0.08	0.01374	0.00935	228
0.10	0.01714	0.01150	177.5
$X_1 = 0.1192$	0.0204	0.01350	145.0

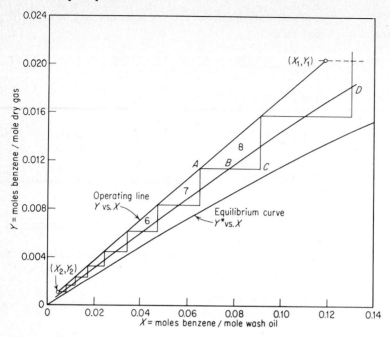

Fig. 8.22 *Solution to Illustration 8.7.*

The integral of Eq. (8.23) may be evaluated graphically from a plot of $1/(Y - Y^*)$ as ordinate vs. Y as abscissa, or, following the suggestion of Eq. (8.25a), from a plot of $Y/(Y - Y^*)$ as ordinate vs. log Y as abscissa. The integral term is then 8.63. Then

$$N_{toG} = 8.63 + \frac{1}{2} \ln \frac{1 + 0.00102}{1 + 0.0204} = 8.62 \quad \textbf{Ans.}$$

Height of a transfer unit. Since the solutions are dilute, Eq. (8.51) becomes

$$H_{toG} = H_{tG} + \frac{mG}{L} H_{tL} = H_{tG} + \frac{H_{tL}}{A}$$

From Illustration 6.4, $F_G a = 26.1$, $F_L a = 5.0$ lb moles/(hr)(cu ft). Av $G = 45.2$ lb moles/(hr)(sq ft) (Illustration 8.6). Av $L = (15.0 + 13.5)/2(1.77) = 8.05$ lb moles/(hr)(sq ft).

Eq. (8.22): $\qquad\qquad H_{tG} = \dfrac{G}{F_G a} = \dfrac{45.2}{26.1} = 1.735$ ft

Eq. (8.28): $\qquad\qquad H_{tL} = \dfrac{L}{F_L a} = \dfrac{8.05}{5.00} = 1.61$ ft

$$H_{toG} = 1.735 + \frac{1.61}{1.425} = 2.87 \text{ ft}$$

$$Z = H_{toG} N_{toG} = 2.87(8.8) = 25.3 \text{ ft} \quad \textbf{Ans.}$$

Nonisothermal operation

All the relationships above for packed towers are correct for either isothermal or non-isothermal operation.   For the nonisothermal case, as in adiabatic tray absorbers, the only difficulty will be in the location of the equilibrium curve owing to the temperature rise.   For packed towers, the differential equations for heat and mass transfer, together with mass and enthalpy balances, must be integrated numerically in a manner similar to that described for adiabatic contact of a pure liquid with a gas (Chap. 7).   This is beyond the scope of this book but is described elsewhere.[13]   For relatively dilute solutions, a conservative approximation can be made by assuming that all the heat evolved on absorption is taken up by the liquid, thus neglecting any temperature rise of the gas.   This results in a higher liquid temperature than is likely, which will lead to a tower slightly taller than need be used.   This method is used in the following example.

Illustration 8.8. In a plant for manufacturing ethyl alcohol by molasses fermentation, the carbon dioxide, CO_2, evolved during fermentation, which contains ethanol vapor, is presently discarded without attempt to recover the ethanol.   The CO_2 issues from the fermenters at 1 atm, av temp 80°F, and may be assumed to be in equilibrium at this temperature with an alcohol-water solution containing 6.5 wt % ethanol.   The gas volume is 15,000 cu ft/hr.   The fermentation liquor (beer) is presently distilled to recover the ethanol, which has a value of $0.10 per pound in the dilute solution (before distillation).

It is proposed to recover the ethanol in the CO_2 by washing the gas with water at 80°F and to use the resultant dilute ethanol solution in making up the fresh fermentation liquor.   The plant operates 350 days per year.   Duct work presently used to lead the gas away from the fermenters will be adapted to the new absorber.   Design the absorber.

Solution. Partial pressures of ethanol and water of aqueous ethanol solutions are shown, in the manner of Othmer and White,[11] in Fig. 8.23.   The ethanol pressure from pure water is, of course,

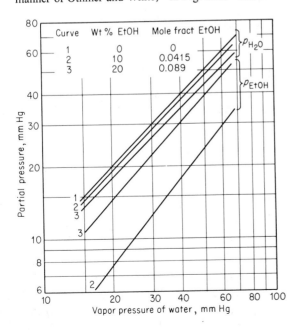

Curve	Wt % EtOH	Mole fract EtOH
1	0	0
2	10	0.0415
3	20	0.089

Fig. 8.23 *Equilibrium partial pressure of ethanol-water solutions.*

zero.   The data are from "International Critical Tables," vol. III, p. 290.   Interpolating for 6.5 wt %
ethanol at 80°F (vapor pressure pure $H_2O = 26.3$ mm Hg), $p_{EtOH} = 7.5$ mm Hg, $p_{H_2O} = 25.5$ mm Hg.
For the gas entering the absorber, therefore, $y_1 = 7.5/760 = 0.00986$ mole fraction ethanol.

Gas in

$$15,000(\tfrac{492}{640})(\tfrac{1}{359}) = 38.1 \text{ moles/hr}$$
$$\text{Ethanol in} = 38.1(0.00986) = 0.376 \text{ mole/hr} = 17.3 \text{ lb/hr}$$
$$\text{Water vapor in} = 38.1(25.5/760) = 1.28 \text{ moles/hr} = 23.1 \text{ lb/hr}$$
$$CO_2 \text{ in} = 38.1 - 0.376 - 1.28 = 36.4 \text{ moles/hr} = 1,600 \text{ lb/hr}$$
$$\text{Total wt} = 1,640 \text{ lb/hr}$$
$$\text{Value of ethanol presently lost} = 17.3(350)(24)(0.10) = \$14,550 \text{ per year}$$

Gas out. Assume temporarily that all ethanol is removed, that the pressure is 1 atm, and that
the gas leaving is saturated with water.   The CO_2 absorption will be negligible.

$$CO_2 \text{ out} = 36.4 \text{ moles/hr} = 1,600 \text{ lb/hr}$$

$$\text{Water vapor out} = \frac{36.4(26.3)}{760 - 26.3} = 1.305 \text{ moles/hr}$$

$$\text{Total gas out} = 36.4 + 1.305 = 37.7 \text{ moles/hr}$$

$$\text{Av gas rate} = \frac{38.1 + 37.7}{2} = 37.9 \text{ moles/hr}$$

Enthalpy, or heat, balance. "International Critical Tables," vol. V, pp. 159–160, lists heats of
solution of ethanol in water.   For 80°F, expressed in engineering units, some of these are as follows:

x of ethanol	0.05	0.10	0.15	0.20	0.25
Ht of soln at 80°F, Btu/mole ethanol	−3350	−2750	−2020	−1463	−1075

The heats of solution are referred to liquid water and liquid ethanol at 80°F.   Use a base
temperature $t_o = 80°F$.   Rewrite Eq. (8.13) with packed-tower notation

$$H_L L - H_{L2}L_2 = H_G H - H_{G2}G_2 = G_S(H'_G - H'_{G2})$$

where H'_G is molal enthalpy gas/mole dry gas, CO_2.   The water content of the gas will be essentially
constant throughout the absorber, and, neglecting any sensible-heat change of the gas (gas temperature constant at 80°F), the enthalpy of the gas is only the latent heat of vaporization of the
ethanol content, 17,920 Btu/mole ethanol at 80°F. $Y =$ moles ethanol/mole CO_2.

$$G_S(H'_G - H'_{G2}) = G_S(17,920)(Y - Y_2)$$

Ethanol balance:
$$G_S(Y - Y_2) = L_S(X - X_2) = L_S X$$

Since the entering liquid is pure water at 80°F, $H_{L2} = 0$.   The heat balance then becomes

$$H_L \frac{L}{L_S} = 17,920X$$

Let $X = 0.01$ mole ethanol/mole water.

$$\therefore \quad L/L_S = 1.01 \qquad x_{EtOH} = \frac{0.01}{1.01} = 0.00989$$

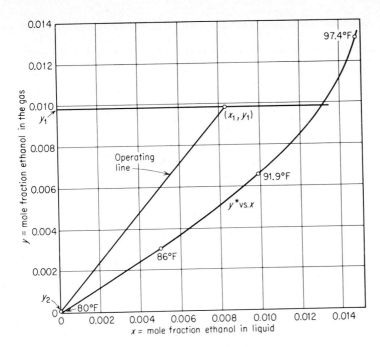

Fig. 8.24 *Adiabatic equilibrium curve, Illustration 8.8.*

From the preceding table, by extrapolation, the heat of solution is −3830 Btu/mole ethanol.   This is converted to Btu/mole solution by multiplying by moles ethanol/mole solution or $X/(1 + X)$.

$$\Delta H_S = -\frac{3{,}850(0.01)}{1 + 0.01} = -38.2 \text{ Btu/mole solution}$$

$$M_{av} = \frac{0.01(46.05) + 1(18.02)}{1.01} = 18.31 \text{ lb/mole}$$

Eq. (8.10):
$$C_L = 1.0 \text{ Btu/(lb)}(°F)$$
$$H_L = 1.0(t_L - 80)18.31 - 38.2$$
$$\therefore \quad [1.0(t_L - 80)18.31 - 38.2]1.01 = 17{,}920(0.01)$$
$$t_L = 91.9°F$$

From Fig. 8.23 at this temperature and concentration, the partial pressure of ethanol = 5.0 mm Hg. $y^*_{\text{EtOH}} = 5.0/760 = 0.00658$.   In similar fashion,

x_{EtOH}	0	0.00497	0.00989	0.01475
t_L, °F	80	86	91.9	97.4
y^*_{EtOH}	0	0.00302	0.00658	0.01316

This provides the equilibrium curve of Fig. 8.24.

Diameter of absorber. Use 1-in. stoneware Berl saddles.   The average slope of the equilibrium curve is approximately 0.73.   For an economical liquid rate, take $A = L/mG = 1.6$.   Therefore

$L/G = 1.6(0.73) = 1.17$ moles water/mole gas.   Therefore use $1.17(37.9) = 44.5$ moles water/hr $= 804$ lb/hr.

At the bottom of the tower, assuming all ethanol is absorbed, the liquid rate is $804 + 17.3 = 821$ lb/hr.

$$\rho_G = \frac{1,640}{15,000} = 0.1093 \text{ lb/cu ft} \qquad \rho_L = 62.0 \text{ lb/cu ft}$$

$$\frac{L'}{G'}\left(\frac{\rho_G}{\rho_L}\right)^{0.5} = \frac{821}{1,640}\left(\frac{0.1093}{62.0}\right)^{0.5} = 0.021$$

At flooding, the ordinate of Fig. 6.26 $= 0.2$.   For 1-in. Berl saddles, $C_f = 110$ (Table 6.2). $\mu'_L = 0.95$ centipoise, $\rho_W/\rho_L \doteq 1$.   With the notation of Fig. 6.26, at flooding,

$$G' = \left(\frac{0.2 g'_c \rho_G \rho_L}{C_f \mu_L'^{0.2}}\frac{\rho_L}{\rho_W}\right)^{0.5} = \left[\frac{0.2(4.17)(10^8)(0.1093)(62.0)}{110(0.95)^{0.2}}\right]^{0.5}$$

$$= 2,300 \text{ lb/(hr)(sq ft)}$$

To allow for future expansion of the process, use $G' = 800$ lb/(hr)(sq ft).   Therefore $L' = 800(821)/1,640 = 400$ lb/(hr)(sq ft).   Cross section of tower $= 1,640/800 = 2.05$ sq ft.

$$\text{Tower diam} = \left[\frac{4(2.05)}{\pi}\right]^{0.5} = 1.62 \text{ ft} = 19.5 \text{ in.}$$

Use 20-in. standard pipe.

Tower height. No value of the exit-gas concentration of ethanol y_2 is specified.   This is typical, and y_2 must be established by the design engineer.

The greater the extent of absorption of ethanol (the lower the y_2), the taller (and more costly) will be the tower, yet the greater will be the savings from recovery of presently lost ethanol.   Clearly there is a most economical value of y_2 which, if the value of lost ethanol is counted as a cost, will correspond to the minimum cost.   Ordinarily to determine this, several values of y_2 must be assumed, the corresponding costs determined, and the y_2 for least cost determined from the resulting data. Here, since the solutions are dilute, an analytical expression can be developed for the cost in terms of y_2 which can then be treated formally for determining the economic optimum.

On Fig. 8.24, with y_2 anticipated to be very small, a typical operating line is drawn.   The outlet concentration in the liquid is then in the neighborhood of 0.008 mole fraction.   The great majority of the transfer units are clearly located at the dilute end of the tower, and the slope of the equilibrium curve at the dilute end (up to $x = 0.007$) is 0.607.   Therefore, use the dilute-end absorption factor, $A = L_2/mG_2 = 44.5/0.607(37.7) = 1.94$ to determine the N_{tOG}.

Eq. (8.47):
$$N_{tOG} = \frac{\ln\left[(0.00986/y_2)(1 - 1/1.94) + 1/1.94\right]}{1 - 1/1.94}$$

$$= 2.06 \ln\left(\frac{0.00479}{y_2} + 0.515\right)$$

To determine the mass-transfer coefficients and H_{tOG}, the correlations of Chap. 6 will be used, for which diffusivities are needed.   The average liquid temperature $= 85°F = 29.4°C$.   "International Critical Tables," vol. V, p. 70, gives the diffusivity of ethanol in water at $x = 0.004$ and $10°C$ as $0.8(10^{-5})$ sq cm/sec.   The viscosity of water at $10°C = 1.308$, at $29.4°C = 0.80$ centipoise. Refer to Chap. 2. $T/D_L\mu_L = \text{const}$.

$$\therefore \quad D_L \text{ at } 29.4°C = \frac{29.4 + 273}{10 + 273}\frac{1.308}{0.80}\, 0.8(10^{-5})$$

$$= 1.4(10^{-5}) \text{ sq cm/sec, or } 5.34(10^{-5}) \text{ sq ft/hr}$$

$$Sc_L = \frac{\mu_L}{\rho_L D_L} = \frac{0.80(2.42)}{62.0(5.34)(10^{-5})} = 575$$

Similarly, by the methods of Chap. 2, $D_G = D_{\text{EtOH-CO}_2} = 0.304$ sq ft/hr.

$$\mu_G \text{ for } CO_2 = 0.015 \text{ centipoise at } 85°F$$

$$\text{Sc}_G = \frac{\mu_G}{\rho_G D_G} = \frac{0.015(2.42)}{0.1093(0.304)} = 1.092$$

Table 6.2: $\epsilon = 0.69$.   Table 6.4: $d_s = 0.1050$ ft.   Since the solutions are so dilute, their properties are essentially those of water.   Therefore

$$\beta = 0.965 d_s^{0.376} = 0.412$$

$$\phi_{tw} = \frac{2.50(10^{-5})(400)^{0.412}}{(0.1050)^2} = 0.0267$$

Eq. (6.40):
$$\epsilon_o = \epsilon - \phi_t = 0.69 - 0.0267 = 0.663$$

$$G = \frac{37.9 \text{ moles/hr}}{2.05 \text{ sq ft}} = 18.5 \text{ moles/(hr)(sq ft)}$$

Eq. (6.39):
$$\frac{F_G(1.092)^{\frac{2}{3}}}{18.5} = 1.195 \left[\frac{0.1050(800)}{0.015(2.42)(1-0.663)} \right]^{-0.36}$$

$$F_G = 0.93 \text{ lb moles/(hr)(sq ft)}$$

Table 6.3:
$$a_{AW} = a = 15.89(800)^{0.686(10^{-4})(400)-0.1029}$$
$$= 9.48 \text{ sq ft/cu ft}$$

Eq. (8.22):
$$H_{tG} = \frac{G}{F_G a} = \frac{18.5}{0.93(9.48)} = 2.10 \text{ ft}$$

For the liquid, Eq. (6.41):

$$\frac{k_L(0.1050)}{5.34(10^{-5})} = 25.1 \left[\frac{0.1050(400)}{0.80(2.42)} \right]^{0.45} (575)^{0.5}$$

$$k_L = 1.15 \text{ lb moles/(hr)(cu ft)(lb mole/cu ft)}$$

$$\text{Av } L = \frac{44.5 \text{ moles } H_2O/hr + 0.376/2 \text{ moles EtOH/hr}}{2.05} = 21.8 \text{ moles/(hr)(sq ft)}$$

$$c = \frac{62.0}{18.2} = 3.44 \text{ lb moles/cu ft}$$

For the dilute solutions used to determine k_L, $(1-x)_{iM} \doteq 1$

Eq. (8.28):
$$H_{tL} = \frac{L}{k_L a c (1-x)_{iM}} = \frac{21.8}{1.15(9.48)(3.44)} = 0.58 \text{ ft}$$

Eq. (8.51), neglecting the concentration ratio,

$$H_{tOG} = 2.10 + \frac{0.58}{1.94} = 2.40 \text{ ft}$$

$$Z = H_{tOG} N_{tOG} = 2.40(2.06) \ln \left(\frac{0.00479}{y_2} + 0.515 \right) = 4.90 \ln \left(\frac{0.00479}{y_2} + 0.515 \right)$$

Cost for power. For $G' = 800$, $L' = 400$ lb/(sq ft), the abscissa of Fig. 6.26 = 0.021, the ordinate = 0.0242.   Therefore $\Delta P/Z = (0.175 \text{ in } H_2O/ft)(5.2) = 0.91$ lb/(sq ft)(ft).

$$\Delta P = 0.91Z$$

With an overall efficiency of blower and motor = 50%, the power required for gas flow is

$$\frac{0.91Z(15,000)}{3,600(550)(0.50)} = 0.0138Z \text{ hp}$$

The height of the shell = $Z + 4$ ft, allowing for gas and liquid inlets at the ends. Power for pumping liquid is essentially that to elevate it to the top of the tower, since pipe friction is negligible. For a motor-pump efficiency of 80%, the power for liquid flow is

$$\frac{(Z + 4)(804)}{3,600(550)(0.80)} = 0.000506(Z + 4) \text{ hp}$$

At $0.015 per kilowatt-hour the annual power cost is

$$[0.0138Z + 0.000506(Z + 4)](0.7457)(350)(24)(0.015) = 13.48Z + 1.90 \quad \text{\$/yr}$$

Cost of equipment. This must be expressed as an annual cost to make it additive with the power cost.

$$\text{Cost of packing} = \$10/\text{cu ft or } 2.05Z(10) = \$20.5Z$$

Twenty-inch pipe weighs 123 lb/ft, and at $0.20 per pound, the tower shell cost is $123(0.20)(Z + 4) = \$24.6(Z + 4)$.

Allowing a factor of 100% for end closures, foundation, piping, and installation, the cost of the tower is

$$[20.5Z + 24.6(Z + 4)]2 = \$(90.2Z + 196.8)$$

If the cost of the installation is amortized over 3 years, and the maintenance cost is 5% annually, the annual cost of the tower is

$$\frac{90.2Z + 196.8}{3} + 0.05[20.5Z + 24.6(Z + 4)] = 32.3Z + 70.5 \quad \text{\$/yr}$$

To this must be added the annual cost P of installed pump, blower, and motors. Since such equipment is available in incremental sizes, the choice will not depend on Z for substantial ranges of Z, and need not be evaluated now.

Cost of alcohol. The value of the lost alcohol (mol wt 46.05) in the scrubbed gas is

$$y_2(37.7)(46.05)(0.10)(350)(24) = 1,460,000y_2 \quad \text{\$/yr}$$

Total annual cost C

$$C = (32.3Z + 70.5 + P) + (13.48Z + 1.90) + 1,460,000y_2 \quad \text{\$/yr}$$

Substituting the value of Z, this becomes

$$C = 225 \ln \left(\frac{0.00479}{y_2} + 0.515 \right) + 72.4 + P + 1,460,000y_2$$

To make this a minimum, dC/dy_2 is set equal to zero:

$$\frac{dC}{dy_2} = \frac{-225(0.00479)/y_2{}^2}{0.00479/y_2 + 0.515} + 1,460,000 = 0$$

Optimum $y_2 = 0.0001515$ mole fraction ethanol in the exit gas.

$$Z = 4.90 \ln (0.00479/0.0001515 + 0.515) = 17 \text{ ft packed height.}$$

The annual cost is then $C = 1,074 + P$ dollars per year. If the pump, blower, and motors cost $300, with 100% allowed for installation and 5% for maintenance, $P = 300(\frac{2}{3} + 0.05) = \$215$ per year, and the annual cost is $1,289, representing a savings over present practice of $14,550 - 1,289 = \$13,261$.

There are other economic balances which may be made for this design. Thus, the absorption factor was chosen arbitrarily here, but it influences the cost. Larger packing sizes cost less per cubic foot and offer less gas pressure drop per foot, but their H_{toG} is greater, and therefore an optimum packing size exists. Other packing types may be investigated. If there is no concern about future expansion of the process, a closer approach to flooding will lead to lower H_{toG} but higher gas pressure drop, and the gas mass velocity then is subject to economic balance.

MULTICOMPONENT SYSTEMS

The previous discussion has assumed that only one component of the gas stream has an appreciable solubility in the absorbent liquid. When the gas contains more than one soluble component, or where the solvent gas itself has an appreciable solubility, some modifications are necessary. The almost complete lack of solubility data for multicomponent systems, except where ideal solutions are formed in the liquid phase and the solubilities of the various components are therefore mutually independent, unfortunately makes estimates of even the ordinary cases very difficult. However, some of the more important industrial applications fall in the ideal-solution category, e.g., the absorption of hydrocarbons from gas mixtures in nonvolatile hydrocarbon oils as in the recovery of natural gasoline.

In principle, the problem for tray towers should be capable of solution by the same tray-to-tray methods used in Illustration 8.4 for one component absorbed, through Eqs. (8.9) to (8.13). These expressions are indeed valid. If, as with one component absorbed, computations are to be started at the bottom of the tower, the outlet-liquid temperature and composition must be known. This, as before, requires that the outlet-gas temperature be estimated, but in addition, in order to complete the enthalpy balance of Eq. (8.9), also requires that the complete outlet-gas composition with respect to each component be estimated at the start. Herein lies the difficulty.

The quantities which are ordinarily fixed before an absorber design is started are the following:

1. Rate of flow, composition, and temperature of entering gas.
2. Composition and temperature of entering liquid (but not flow rate).
3. Pressure of operation.
4. Heat gain or loss (even if set at zero, as for adiabatic operation).

Under these circumstances it can be shown[10] that the principal variables still remaining are:

1. The liquid flow rate (or liquid/gas ratio).
2. The number of ideal trays.
3. The fractional absorption of any one component.

Any *two of these last, but not all three*, may be arbitrarily fixed for a given design. Having specified two, the third is automatically fixed, as is the extent of absorption of all substances not already specified and the outlet-stream temperatures. For example, if the liquid rate and number of ideal trays are specified, the extent of absorption of each substance of the gas is automatically fixed and may not be arbitrarily chosen. Or, if the liquid rate and extent of absorption of one substance are specified, the number of ideal trays and the extent of absorption of all components are automatically fixed and may not be chosen arbitrarily.

As a result, for the tray-to-tray calculations suggested above, not only must the outlet-gas temperature be guessed, but also the complete outlet-gas composition, all to be checked at the end of the calculation. This becomes so hopeless a trial-and-error procedure that it cannot be done practically without some guidance. This is provided through an approximate procedure, either that offered by the Kremser equations, which apply only for constant absorption factor, or through some procedure allowing for variation of the absorption factor with tray number. To establish the latter, we first need an exact expression for the absorber with varying absorption factor. This was first derived by Horton and Franklin,[9] as outlined below.

Refer to Fig. 8.25, which shows a multitray absorber or stripper. Since all components may transfer between gas and liquid, there may be no substance which passes through at constant rate in the gas, for example. It is convenient, therefore, to define all gas compositions in terms of the entering gas, and similarly all liquid compositions in terms of the entering liquid. Thus, for any component in the liquid leaving any tray n,

$$X_n' = \frac{\text{moles component in } L_n/\text{time}}{L_0} = \frac{x_n L_n}{L_0}$$

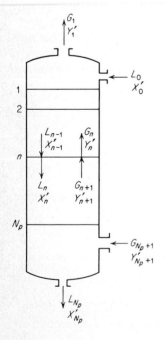

Fig. 8.25 *Multicomponent absorber or stripper.*

and for any component in the gas G_n,

$$Y_n' = \frac{\text{moles component in } G_n/\text{time}}{G_{Np+1}} = \frac{y_n G_n}{G_{Np+1}}$$

where x and y are the usual mole fractions.

The equations which follow may all be written separately for each component. Consider the tower of Fig. 8.25 to be an absorber. A material balance for any component about ideal tray n is

$$L_0(X_n' - X_{n-1}') = G_{Np+1}(Y_{n+1}' - Y_n') \tag{8.54}$$

The equilibrium relation for the ideal tray is†

$$y_n = m_n x_n \tag{8.55}$$

or, in terms of the new concentrations,

$$Y_n' \frac{G_{Np+1}}{G_n} = m_n X_n' \frac{L_0}{L_n} \tag{8.56}$$

Similarly, for tray $n - 1$,

$$Y_{n-1}' \frac{G_{Np+1}}{G_{n-1}} = m_{n-1} X_{n-1}' \frac{L_0}{L_{n-1}} \tag{8.57}$$

Solving Eqs. (8.56) and (8.57) for the X's, substituting in Eq. (8.54), and rearranging, we have

$$Y_n' = \frac{Y_{n+1}' + A_{n-1} Y_{n-1}'}{1 + A_n} \tag{8.58}$$

where $A_n = L_n/m_n G_n$ and $A_{n-1} = L_{n-1}/m_{n-1} G_{n-1}$ are the component absorption factors on the two trays.

If the absorber contained only one tray ($n = 1$), Eq. (8.58) would read

$$Y_1' = \frac{Y_2' + A_0 Y_0'}{1 + A_1} \tag{8.59}$$

From Eq. (8.57),

$$Y_0' = m_0 X_0' \frac{L_0}{L_0} \frac{G_0}{G_{Np+1}} = \frac{m_0 X_0' G_0}{G_{Np+1}} \tag{8.60}$$

and

$$A_0 Y_0' = \frac{L_0}{m_0 G_0} \frac{m_0 X_0' G_0}{G_{Np+1}} = \frac{L_0 X_0'}{G_{Np+1}} \tag{8.61}$$

Substituting this into Eq. (8.59) provides

$$Y_1' = \frac{Y_2' + L_0 X_0'/G_{Np+1}}{1 + A_1} \tag{8.62}$$

If the absorber contained two trays, Eq. (8.58) with $n = 2$ would become

$$Y_2' = \frac{Y_3' + A_1 Y_1'}{1 + A_2} \tag{8.63}$$

Substituting Y_1' from Eq. (8.62) and rearranging,

$$Y_2' = \frac{(A_1 + 1) Y_3' + A_1 L_0 X_0'/G_{Np+1}}{A_1 A_2 + A_2 + 1} \tag{8.64}$$

Similarly, for a three-tray absorber,

$$Y_3' = \frac{(A_1 A_2 + A_2 + 1) Y_4' + A_1 A_2 L_0 X_0'/G_{Np+1}}{A_1 A_2 A_3 + A_2 A_3 + A_3 + 1} \tag{8.65}$$

---

† The ratio y/x at equilibrium is usually written as K, but here we use m to distinguish this from the mass-transfer coefficients.

and for N_p trays,

$$Y'_{Np}$$
$$= \frac{(A_1 A_2 A_3 \cdots A_{Np-1} + A_2 A_3 \cdots A_{Np-1} + \cdots + A_{Np-1} + 1)Y'_{Np+1} + A_1 A_2 \cdots A_{Np-1} L_0 X_0 / G_{Np+1}}{A_1 A_2 A_3 \cdots A_{Np} + A_2 A_3 \cdots A_{Np} + \cdots + A_{Np} + 1} \tag{8.66}$$

In order to eliminate Y'_{Np}, which is inside the absorber, a component material balance about the entire absorber,

$$L_0(X'_{Np} - X'_0) = G_{Np+1}(Y'_{Np+1} - Y'_1) \tag{8.67}$$

and Eq. (8.56) for $n = N_p$,

$$Y'_{Np} = m_{Np} X'_{Np} \frac{L_0}{L_{Np}} \frac{G_{Np}}{G_{Np+1}} = \frac{L_0 X'_{Np}}{A_{Np} G_{Np+1}} \tag{8.68}$$

are solved simultaneously to eliminate X'_{Np}, the result substituted for Y'_{Np} in Eq. (8.68), whence rearrangement yields

$$\frac{Y'_{Np+1} - Y'_1}{Y'_{Np+1}} = \frac{A_1 A_2 A_3 \cdots A_{Np} + A_2 A_3 \cdots A_{Np} + \cdots + A_{Np}}{A_1 A_2 A_3 \cdots A_{Np} + A_2 A_3 \cdots A_{Np} + \cdots + A_{Np} + 1}$$
$$- \frac{L_0 X'_0}{G_{Np+1} Y'_{Np+1}} \frac{A_2 A_3 A_4 \cdots A_{Np} + A_3 A_4 \cdots A_{Np} + \cdots + A_{Np} + 1}{A_1 A_2 A_3 \cdots A_{Np} + A_2 A_3 \cdots A_{Np} + \cdots + A_{Np} + 1} \tag{8.69}$$

Equation (8.69) is an expression for the fractional absorption of any component, exact because it is based only upon material balances and the condition of equilibrium which defines an ideal tray.

A similar expression for strippers is

$$\frac{X'_0 - X'_{Np}}{X'_0} = \frac{S_1 S_2 \cdots S_{Np} + S_1 S_2 \cdots S_{Np-1} + \cdots + S_1}{S_1 S_2 \cdots S_{Np} + S_1 S_2 \cdots S_{Np-1} + \cdots + S_1 + 1}$$
$$- \frac{G_{Np+1} Y'_{Np+1}}{L_0 X'_0} \frac{S_1 S_2 \cdots S_{Np-1} + S_1 S_2 \cdots S_{Np-2} + \cdots + S_1 + 1}{S_1 S_2 \cdots S_{Np} + S_1 S_2 \cdots S_{Np-1} + \cdots + S_1 + 1} \tag{8.70}$$

In order to use Eqs. (8.69) or (8.70), the L/G ratio for each tray and the tray temperatures (which determine the m's) are required to compute the A's or the S's. If the liquids are not ideal, m for any component on any tray additionally depends upon the complete liquid composition on the tray.   The same is true for the gas compositions under conditions for which the gas solutions are not ideal.   The equations are practically useful, therefore, only for ideal solutions.

As an approximation,[9] the gas rate G_n for tray n of an absorber may be estimated on the assumption that the fractional absorption is the same for each tray:

$$\frac{G_n}{G_{n+1}} \doteq \left(\frac{G_1}{G_{Np+1}}\right)^{1/N_p} \tag{8.71}$$

or

$$G_n \doteq G_{Np+1}\left(\frac{G_1}{G_{Np+1}}\right)^{(N_p+1-n)/N_p} \tag{8.72}$$

The liquid rate L_n may then be obtained by material balance to the end of the tower. Similarly in strippers,

$$L_n \doteq L_0\left(\frac{L_{Np}}{L_0}\right)^{n/N_p} \tag{8.73}$$

where G_n is determined by material balance. If the molar latent heats and heat capacities are all alike for all components, and if no heat of solution is evolved, the temperature rise on absorption is roughly proportional to the amount of absorption, so that, approximately,

$$\frac{G_{Np+1} - G_{n+1}}{G_{Np+1} - G_1} \doteq \frac{t_{Np} - t_n}{t_{Np} - t_0} \tag{8.74}$$

and similarly for stripping,

$$\frac{L_0 - L_n}{L_0 - L_{Np}} \doteq \frac{t_0 - t_n}{t_0 - t_{Np}} \tag{8.75}$$

In order further to simplify the computations, Edmister[5] has writtten the Horton-Franklin equations in terms of average or "effective" absorption and stripping factors instead of the A's and S's for each tray. Thus, for absorption, Eq. (8.69) becomes

$$\frac{Y'_{Np+1} - Y'_1}{Y'_{Np+1}} = \left(1 - \frac{L_0 X'_0}{A' G_{Np+1} Y'_{Np+1}}\right) \frac{A_E^{Np+1} - A_E}{A_E^{Np+1} - 1} \tag{8.76}$$

For a two-tray absorber, it develops that

$$A' = \frac{A_{Np}(A_1 + 1)}{A_{Np} + 1} \tag{8.77}$$

and
$$A_E = [A_{Np}(A_1 + 1) + 0.25]^{0.5} - 0.5 \tag{8.78}$$

These are exact, but it is found that Eqs. (8.76) to (8.78) apply reasonably well for any number of trays, provided that unusual temperature profiles (such as a maximum temperature on an intermediate tray) do not develop. If $X'_0 = 0$, Eq. (8.76) is the Kremser equation. It is also convenient to note that $(A_E^{Np+1} - A_E)/(A_E^{Np+1} - 1)$ is the Kremser function [Eq. (5.54)], and the ordinate of Fig. 5.16 is 1 minus this function.

Similarly for stripping,

$$\frac{X'_0 - X'_{Np}}{X'_0} = \left(1 - \frac{G_{Np+1} Y'_{Np+1}}{S' L_0 X'_0}\right) \frac{S_E^{Np+1} - S_E}{S_E^{Np+1} - 1} \tag{8.79}$$

with
$$S' = \frac{S_1(S_{Np} + 1)}{S_1 + 1} \tag{8.80}$$

and
$$S_E = [S_1(S_{Np} + 1) + 0.25]^{0.5} - 0.5 \tag{8.81}$$

Equation (8.79) becomes the Kremser equation if $Y'_{Np+1} = 0$.

Components present only in the entering gas will be absorbed, and those present only in the entering liquid will be stripped. If a component is present in both streams, the terms in the parentheses of the right-hand sides of Eqs. (8.76) and (8.79) are computed, and the equation is used which provides the positive quantity.

Equations (8.76) and (8.79) may be used to determine the number of ideal trays required to absorb or strip a component to a specified extent and to estimate the extent of absorption or stripping of all other components. This then provides a basis for using the exact equations of Horton and Franklin, Eqs. (8.69) and (8.70). These latter may be used only for an integral number of ideal trays. A change of L_0/G_{Np+1} may be necessary to meet the specifications exactly with such an integral number; alternatively the nearest larger integral number of trays may be accepted.

Illustration 8.9. A gas analyzing 70 mole % CH_4, 15% C_2H_6, 10% $n\text{-}C_3H_8$, and 5% $n\text{-}C_4H_{10}$, at 75°F, 2 atm, is to be scrubbed in an adiabatic tray absorber with a liquid containing 1 mole % $n\text{-}C_4H_{10}$, 99% nonvolatile hydrocarbon oil, at 75°F, using 3.5 moles liquid/mole entering gas. The pressure is to be 2 atm, and at least 70% of the C_3H_8 of the entering gas is to be absorbed. The solubility of CH_4 in the liquid will be considered negligible, and the other components form ideal solutions. Estimate the number of ideal trays required and the composition of the effluent streams.

Solution. In what follows, CH_4, C_2H_6, C_3H_8, and C_4H_{10} will be identified as C_1, C_2, C_3, and C_4, respectively. Physical properties are:

Component	Av sp ht, 0 to 100°F, Btu/(lb mole)(°F)		Latent heat of vaporization, 0°F, Btu/lb mole	$m = \dfrac{y^{*\dagger}}{x}$		
	Gas	Liquid		75°F	80°F	85°F
C_1	8.50					
C_2	12.71	25.10	5,100	13.1	13.5	14.0
C_3	18.16	27.8	7,600	4.00	4.25	4.50
C_4	24.45	33.1	10,100	1.15	1.25	1.35
Oil		90.0				

† Values of m from C. L. Depriester, *Chem. Eng. Progr. Symp. Ser.*, **49** (7), 1 (1953).

Basis: 1 lb mole entering gas; $t_o = 0°F$; enthalpies are referred to gaseous C_1 and other components liquid at 0°F. Gas in: $G_{Np+1} = 1.0$ lb mole, $t_{Np+1} = 75°F$.

Component	$Y'_{Np+1} = y_{Np+1}$	Enthalpy, Btu/lb mole	$H_{G,Np+1}y_{Np+1}$
C_1	0.70	$8.50(75 - 0) = 638$	$446 = 638(0.70)$
C_2	0.15	$12.71(75 - 0) + 5,100 = 6,055$	910
C_3	0.10	$18.16(75 - 0) + 7,600 = 8,960$	896
C_4	0.05	$24.45(75 - 0) + 10,000 = 11,930$	596
	1.00		$2,848 = H_{G,Np+1}$

Liquid in: $L_0 = 3.5$ lb moles, $t_0 = 75°F$.

Component	$X'_0 = x_0$	$L_0 X'_0$	Enthalpy, Btu/lb mole	$H_{L0}L_0X'_0$
C_4	0.01	0.035	$33.1(75 - 0) = 2,480$	$86.9 = 2,480(0.035)$
Oil	0.99	3.465	$90.0(75 - 0) = 6,750$	23,400
	1.00	3.50		$23,487 = H_{L0}L_0$

Preliminary calculations. The total absorption is estimated to be 0.15 lb mole, and an average temperature 80°F is assumed. A rough value of L/G at the top is then $3.5/(1 - 0.15) = 4.20$, and at the bottom $(3.5 + 0.15)/1.0 = 3.65$, with an average of 3.93. The number of ideal trays is fixed by the C_3 absorption specified. For C_3, m at 80°F $= 4.25$, rough $A = 3.93/4.25 = 0.925$. Equation (8.76), with fractional absorption $= 0.7$ and $X_0' = 0$,

$$0.7 = \frac{0.925^{N_p+1} - 0.925}{0.925^{N_p+1} - 1}$$

This can be solved for N_p directly. Alternatively, since Fig. 5.16 has as its ordinate $(1 -$ Kremser function$) = 0.3$, then with $A = 0.925$, $N_p = 2.8$. Since the Horton-Franklin equations will be used later, an integral number of trays $N_p = 3$ is chosen. Figure 5.16 with $N_p = 3$, $A = 0.925$, shows an ordinate of 0.28, or 0.72 fraction of C_3 absorbed.

$$\frac{Y_{N_p+1}' - Y_1'}{Y_{N_p+1}'} = \frac{0.10 - Y_1'}{0.10} = 0.72$$

$$Y_1' = 0.028 \text{ lb mole } C_3 \text{ in } G_1$$

For C_2, $m = 13.5$ at 80°F, rough $A = 3.93/13.5 = 0.291$. At low A's, Fig. 5.16 shows the ordinate to be $1 - A$, and the fractional absorption $= 0.291$.

$$\frac{Y_{N_p+1}' - Y_1'}{Y_{N_p+1}'} = \frac{0.15 - Y_1'}{0.15} = 0.291$$

$$Y_1' = 0.1064 \text{ lb mole } C_2 \text{ in } G_1$$

C_4 is present in both entering liquid and gas. At 80°F, $m = 1.25$, rough $A = 3.93/1.25 = 3.15$, rough $S = 1/3.15 = 0.317$. Then

$$1 - \frac{L_0 X_0'}{A' G_{N_p+1} Y_{N_p+1}'} = 1 - \frac{3.5(0.01)}{3.15(1.0)(0.05)} = +0.778$$

$$1 - \frac{G_{N_p+1} Y_{N_p+1}'}{S' L_0 X_0'} = 1 - \frac{1(0.05)}{0.317(3.5)(0.01)} = -3.48$$

The C_4 will therefore be absorbed. Equation (8.76):

$$\frac{0.05 - Y_1'}{0.05} = 0.778 \frac{3.15^4 - 3.15}{3.15^4 - 1}$$

At $N_p = 3$, $A = 3.15$, Fig. 5.16 provides an ordinate of 0.023. Therefore

$$\frac{0.05 - Y_1'}{0.05} = 0.778(1 - 0.023)$$

$$Y_1' = 0.0120 \text{ lb mole } C_4 \text{ in } G_1$$

Edmister method. Estimate the top-tray temperature $t_1 = 77$°F. This is to be verified later. The results of the preliminary calculations then give the following approximate results:

G_1

Component	Y_1'	Enthalpy, Btu/lb mole	$H_{G1} Y_1'$
C_1	0.70	$8.5(77 - 0) = 655$	$459 = 655(0.70)$
C_2	0.1064	$12.71(77 - 0) + 5,100 = 6,080$	648
C_3	0.0280	$18.16(77 - 0) + 7,600 = 9,000$	252
C_4	0.0120	$24.4(77 - 0) + 10,000 = 11,982$	144
	$0.8464 = G_1$		$1,503 = H_{G1} G_1$

L_3

Component	Lb moles $= L_3x_3$	Enthalpy	$H_{L3}L_3x_3$
C_2	$0.15 - 0.1064 = 0.0436$	$25.0t_3$	$1.093t_3 = 0.0436(25.0)t_3$
C_3	$0.10 - 0.028 = 0.0720$	$27.8t_3$	$2.00t_3$
C_4	$0.035 + 0.05 - 0.012 = 0.0730$	$33.1t_3$	$2.42t_3$
Oil	3.465	$90.0t_3$	$312t_3$
	$L_3 = 3.654$		$317.5t_3 = H_{L3}L_3$

Overall enthalpy balance, Eq. (8.9) with $Q_T = 0$, $G_{Np+1} = 1.0$, $N_p = 3$:

$$23,487 + 2,848 = 317.5t_3 + 1,503$$
$$t_3 = 78.5°F$$

Equation (8.76) may now be used to obtain a second approximation of the effluent compositions.

Eq. (8.72) with $n = 2$: $G_2 = 1.0\left(\dfrac{0.8464}{1.0}\right)^{(3+1-2)/3} = 0.894$

Eq. (8.11) with $n = 1$: $L_1 + 1.0 = 3.654 + 0.894$

$$L_1 = 3.548$$

$$\frac{L_1}{G_1} = \frac{3.548}{0.8464} = 4.195$$

Eq. (8.72) with $n = 3$: $G_3 = 1.0\left(\dfrac{0.8464}{1.0}\right)^{(3+1-3)/3} = 0.947$

$$\frac{L_3}{G_3} = \frac{4.654}{0.947} = 3.86$$

For C_4: m at $77°F = 1.19$ $A_1 = \dfrac{4.195}{1.19} = 3.51$

m at $78.5°F = 1.22$ $A_3 = \dfrac{3.86}{1.22} = 3.16 = A_{Np}$

Eq. (8.77): $A' = 3.43$
Eq. (8.78): $A_E = 3.31$
Eq. (8.76): $Y_1' = 0.0110$ lb mole C_4 in G_1

C_4 in $L_3 = 0.035 + 0.05 - 0.0110 = 0.0740$ lb mole $= L_3x_3$

In similar fashion, the Y_1''s for the other components, together with outlet gas and outlet liquid enthalpies, may be computed:

Component	Y_1'	$H_{G1}Y_1'$, $77°F$	L_3x_3	$H_{L3}L_3x_3$
C_1	0.700	459	0	0
C_2	0.1064	645	0.044	$1.10t_3$
C_3	0.0278	250	0.0722	$2.01t_3$
C_4	0.0110	132	0.0740	$2.45t_3$
Oil			3.465	$312t_3$
	$0.8448 = G_1$	$1,486 = H_{G1}G_1$	$3.655 = L_3$	$317.6t_3 = H_{L3}L_3$

Equation (8.9) again shows $t_3 = 78.5°F$. The results are sufficiently close to those of the first estimate that we may proceed with Eq. (8.69).

Horton-Franklin method. Equations (8.72) and (8.11), used as above with $G_1 = 0.8448$, now show

Tray n	G_n	L_n	$\dfrac{L_n}{G_n}$	t_n, °F
1	0.8448	3.548	4.20	77
2	0.893	3.583	4.01	77
3	0.928	3.655	3.94	78.5

t_2 is estimated through Eq. (8.74) with $n = 2$:

$$\frac{1 - 0.928}{1 - 0.8448} = \frac{78.5 - t_2}{78.5 - 75}$$

The temperatures permit tabulation of m's, and the L_n/G_n's permit calculation of A for each component on each tray. Equation (8.69) then gives Y_1' and a material balance the moles of each component in L_3:

Component	A_1	A_2	A_3	Y_1' [Eq. (8.69)]	L_3x_3
C_1				0.700	0
C_2	0.318	0.304	0.294	0.1062	0.0448
C_3	1.025	0.979	0.938	0.0263	0.0737
C_4	3.53	3.37	3.23	0.0108	0.0742
Oil					3.465
				$0.8433 = G_1$	$3.658 = L_3$

An enthalpy balance again shows $t_3 = 78.5°F$.

For most purposes, the preceding results will be reasonably satisfactory. But they are correct only if the A values for each component on each tray are correct. These may be checked by first verifying the L/G ratios. For the components found in both liquid and gas,

$$A_n = \frac{L_n}{m_n G_n} = \frac{L_n}{(y_n/x_n)G_n} \tag{8.82}$$

or

$$G_n y_n = \frac{L_n x_n}{A_n} \tag{8.83}$$

If there are G_S moles/time of nonabsorbed gas, then

$$G_n = G_S + \Sigma \frac{L_n x_n}{A_n} \tag{8.84}$$

and Eq. (8.11) will provide $L_n x_n$, whose sum is L_n. The L_n/G_n ratios may then be compared with those used previously.

Illustration 8.9, continued. For tray 3, $G_s = 0.7$ lb mole C_1. For C_2, $G_3 y_3 = 0.0448/0.294 = 0.1522$, and Eq. (8.11) with $n = 2$ provides $L_2 x_2 = 0.0448 + 0.1522 - 0.15 = 0.0470$. Similarly,

Component	$G_3 y_3$	$L_2 x_2$
C_1	0.700	
C_2	0.1522	0.0470
C_3	0.0785	0.0522
C_4	0.0230	0.0472
Oil		3.465
	$0.9537 = G_3$	$3.6114 = L_2$

The value of $L_2 x_2$ is similarly used with the previous A_2's to obtain G_2, etc. In this way it is found that

$$\frac{L_3}{G_3} = \frac{3.658}{0.9537} = 3.84 \qquad \frac{L_2}{G_2} = 3.82 \qquad \frac{L_1}{G_1} = 3.98$$

which are different from those used before.

The procedure then to be followed is to repeat the use of Eq. (8.69) with the new L/G ratios to provide A's, repeating the check of L/G and use of Eq. (8.69) until agreement is reached. This still leaves the temperatures to be checked. For an assumed top-tray temperature, an overall tower enthalpy balance provides t_{Np}. With the compositions and flow rates for each stream as last determined, individual tray enthalpy balances provide the temperature of each tray. These are repeated until the assumed t_1 agrees with that calculated. New m's and A's are then used with Eq. (8.69), and the entire procedure repeated until a completely consistent set of L/G's and temperatures are obtained, at which time the problem is solved. The procedure is very tedious, and methods for reducing the work, including the use of high-speed computers, have been given much study.[6,8,14]

Use of reflux—reboiled absorbers

Refer again to the preceding illustration. Considering only the three substances absorbed, the wet gas contained these roughly in the proportions $C_2H_6 : C_3H_8 : C_4H_{10} = 50 : 33 : 17$. The rich oil leaving the absorber contained the same substances in the approximate ratio $23 : 38 : 39$. Despite its low solubility, the proportion of absorbed gas which is ethane is high, owing to the relatively high proportion of this substance in the original wet gas. If it is desired to reduce the relative proportions of ethane in the rich oil, the oil just as it leaves the tower must be in contact with a gas relatively leaner in ethane and richer in propane and butane. Such a gas can be

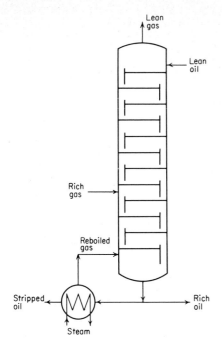

Lean
gas

Lean
oil

Rich
gas

Reboiled
gas

Stripped
oil

Rich
oil

Steam

Fig. 8.26   *Reboiled absorber.*

obtained by heating a part of the rich oil, which will then evolve a gas of the required low ethane content.   This evolved gas may then be returned to an extension of the absorber below the inlet of the wet gas, where in rising past the oil it will strip out the ethane (and also any methane which may have been absorbed as well).   The ethane not absorbed will now, of course, leave with the lean gas.   The heat exchanger where a portion of the rich oil is heated is called a *reboiler*, and the arrangement of Fig. 8.26 may be used.

A stream returned to a cascade of stages, as represented by the trays in the absorber, for the purposes of obtaining an enrichment beyond that obtained by counter-current contact with the feed to the cascade, is called *reflux*.   This principle is used extensively in distillation, liquid extraction, and adsorption, but it is applicable to any countercurrent enrichment operation.

NOTATION FOR CHAPTER 8

a = interfacial surface, sq ft/cu ft active volume
A = absorption factor = L/mG, dimensionless
c = concentration, lb moles/cu ft
C_L = specific heat of the liquid, Btu/(lb)(°F)
d = differential operator

D = diffusivity, sq ft/hr

E_{MGE} = Murphree gas tray efficiency, corrected for entrainment, fractional

E_O = overall tray efficiency, fractional

F = mass-transfer coefficient, lb moles/(hr)(sq ft)

F_O = overall mass-transfer coefficient, lb moles/(hr)(sq ft)

G = total gas rate, lb moles/hr for tray towers, lb moles/(hr)(sq ft) for packed towers

G' = total gas rate, lb/(hr)(sq ft)

G_S = rate of solvent gas, lb mole/hr for tray towers, lb moles/(hr)(sq ft) for packed towers

H_G = gas enthalpy, Btu/lb mole

H_G' = gas enthalpy, Btu for the gas/lb mole solvent gas

H_L = liquid enthalpy, Btu/lb mole liquid

H_t = height of a transfer unit, ft

H_{to} = overall height of a transfer unit, ft

ΔH_s = integral heat of solution, Btu/lb mole solution

k_G = gas mass-transfer coefficient, lb moles/(hr)(sq ft)(atm)

k_L = liquid mass-transfer coefficient, lb moles/(hr)(sq ft)(lb moles/cu ft)

k_x = liquid mass-transfer coefficient, lb moles/(hr)(sq ft)(mole fraction)

k_y = gas mass-transfer coefficient, lb moles/(hr)(sq ft)(mole fraction)

K = overall mass-transfer coefficient (units indicated by subscript as for k's)

ln = natural logarithm

log = common logarithm

L = total liquid rate, lb moles/hr for tray towers, lb moles/(hr)(sq ft) for packed towers

L' = total liquid rate, lb moles/(hr)(sq ft)

L_S = rate of solvent liquid, lb moles/hr for tray towers, lb moles/(hr)(sq ft) for packed towers

m = slope of the equilibrium curve = dy^*/dx

M = molecular weight, lb/lb mole

N_A = mass-transfer flux of A, lb moles/(hr)(sq ft)

N_p = number of ideal trays, plates, or stages

N_t = number of transfer units

N_{to} = overall number of transfer units

p = partial pressure, atm

p^* = partial pressure in equilibrium with a liquid solution, atm

P = vapor pressure, atm

P_t = total pressure, atm

q, r, s = constants

S = interfacial surface, sq ft/sq ft tower cross section

= stripping factor, mG/L

t_L = liquid temperature, °F

t_o = base temperature for enthalpy, °F

x = concentration in the bulk liquid, mole fraction

x^* = concentration in equilibrium with the bulk gas, mole fraction

x_i = concentration in the liquid at the interface, mole fraction

X = concentration in the bulk liquid, lb moles solute/lb mole solvent

X^* = concentration in equilibrium with bulk gas concentration, lb moles solute/lb mole solvent

X' = concentration in the bulk liquid, lb moles/lb mole entering liquid

y = concentration in the bulk gas, mole fraction

y^* = concentration in the gas in equilibrium with the bulk liquid, mole fraction

y_i = concentration in the gas at the interface, mole fraction

Y = concentration in the bulk gas, lb moles solute/lb mole solvent gas

Y^* = concentration in equilibrium with the bulk liquid, lb moles solute/lb mole solvent gas

Y' = concentration in the bulk gas, lb moles/lb mole entering gas

Z = height of packing

Subscripts

av	= average
G	= gas
i	= interface
L	= liquid
M	= logarithmic mean
n	= effluent from tray n
$n + 1$	= effluent from tray $n + 1$
Np	= effluent from tray N_p
$Np + 1$	= effluent from tray $N_p + 1$
O	= overall (transfer units and mass-transfer coefficients)
0	= entering liquid (tray tower)
1	= bottom (of a packed tower); effluent from tray 1 (tray tower)
2	= top (of a packed tower); effluent from tray 2 (tray tower)

REFERENCES

1. Baker, T. C.: *Ind. Eng. Chem.*, **27,** 977 (1935).
2. Chilton, T. H., and A. P. Colburn: *Ind. Eng. Chem.*, **27,** 255 (1935).
3. Colburn, A. P.: *Trans. AIChE*, **35,** 211 (1939).
4. Colburn, A. P.: *Ind. Eng. Chem.*, **33,** 111 (1941).
5. Edmister, W. C.: *Ind. Eng. Chem.*, **35,** 837 (1943).
6. Friday, J. R., and B. D. Smith: *AIChE J.*, **10,** 698 (1964).
7. Hachmuth, K. H.: *Chem. Eng. Progr.*, **45,** 716 (1949); **47,** 523, 621 (1951).
8. Holland, C. D.: "Multicomponent Distillation," Prentice-Hall, Inc., Englewood Cliffs, N.J., 1963.
9. Horton, G., and W. B. Franklin: *Ind. Eng. Chem.*, **32,** 1384 (1940).
10. Kwauk, M.: *AIChE J.*, **2,** 240 (1956).
11. Othmer, D. F., and R. E. White: *Ind. Eng. Chem.*, **34,** 952 (1942).
12. Rackett, H. G.: *Chem. Eng.*, Dec. 21, 1964, p. 108.
13. Sherwood, T. K., and R. L. Pigford: "Absorption and Extraction," 2d ed., McGraw-Hill Book Company, New York, 1952.
14. Smith, B. D.: "Design of Equilibrium Stage Processes," McGraw-Hill Book Company, New York, 1963.

PROBLEMS

8.1. A scheme for removal of hydrogen sulfide from a gas by scrubbing with water at 75°F is being considered. The gas contains 2% H_2S and is to be scrubbed to a concentration of 0.1% H_2S. The water is H_2S-free. Henry's law describes the solubility, and $p^*/x = 545$ atm/mole fraction.

a. For a countercurrent absorber, calculate the liquid/gas ratio, moles water/mole gas for 1.2 times the minimum, and the composition of the exit liquid, (1) if the pressure is 1 atm, and (2) if the pressure is 10 atm.

b. The absorber for (*a*) would have to be excessively tall, and the various schemes in Fig. 8.27 are being considered as means of using two shorter absorbers. Make freehand sketches of operating diagrams, one for each scheme, showing the relation between operating lines for the two absorbers and the equilibrium curve. Mark the concentrations of Fig. 8.27 on each diagram, but do not compute the concentrations.

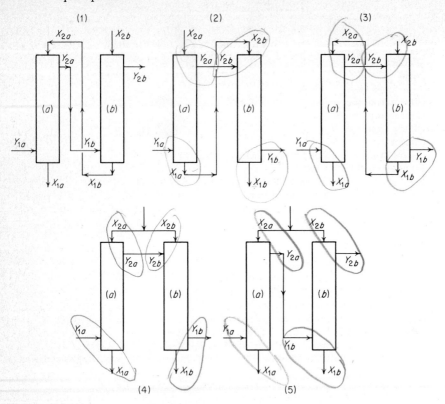

Fig. 8.27   *Absorber arrangement for Prob.* 8.1.

8.2.   The equilibrium partial pressures of carbon dioxide over aqueous solutions of monoethanolamine (30 wt %) [Mason and Dodge, *Trans. AIChE*, **32**, 27 (1936)] are as follows:

Moles CO_2	Partial pressure CO_2, mm Hg		
Mole solution	77°F	122°F	167°F
0.050			65
0.052		7.5	93.5
0.054		13.6	142.6
0.056		25.0	245
0.058	5.6	47.1	600
0.060	12.8	96.0	
0.062	29.0	259	
0.064	56.0		
0.066	98.7		
0.068	155		
0.070	232		

A plant for manufacturing dry ice will burn coke in air to produce a flue gas, which when cleaned and cooled will contain 15% CO_2, 6% O_2, 79% N_2. The gas will be blown into a bubble-tray scrubber at 1.2 atm, 77°F, to be scrubbed with 30% ethanolamine solution entering at 77°F. The scrubbing liquid, which is recycled from a stripper, will contain 0.058 mole CO_2/mole solution. The gas leaving the scrubber is to contain 2% CO_2. Assume isothermal operation.

a. Determine the minimum liquid/gas ratio, moles/mole.

b. Determine the number of pounds of solution to enter the absorber per cubic foot of entering gas, for an L/G ratio of 1.2 times the minimum. **Ans.**: 1.165.

c. Determine the number of theoretical trays for the conditions of (*b*). **Ans.**: 2.5.

d. The viscosity of the solution is 6.0 centipoises; sp gr = 1.012. Estimate the average *m*, and the overall tray efficiency to be expected. How many real trays are required?

8.3. *a.* Determine the number of ideal trays for the absorption of Prob. 8.2, assuming adiabatic operation. Use 1.6 lb absorbent solution/cu ft gas in, which will be about 1.2 times the minimum. The heat of solution of CO_2 in the solution is 720 Btu evolved/lb CO_2 absorbed, referred to gaseous CO_2 and liquid solution. The specific heat of the solution is 0.82 Btu/(lb solution)(°F) at all CO_2 concentrations. **Ans.**: 2.6.

b. Suppose the absorber planned for isothermal operation (L/G and theoretical trays of Prob. 8.2) were operated adiabatically. What concentration of CO_2 in the exit gas could be expected? [Note that this normally requires trial-and-error determination of both the top-tray temperature and exit-gas concentration. However, study of the calculations of part (*a*) should indicate that, in this case, the top-tray temperature need not be determined by trial.]

8.4. Carbon disulfide, CS_2, used as a solvent in a chemical plant is evaporated from the product in a drier into an inert gas (essentially nitrogen, N_2) in order to avoid an explosion hazard. The vapor-nitrogen mixture is to be scrubbed with an absorbent hydrocarbon oil, which will be subsequently steam-stripped to recover the CS_2. The CS_2–N_2 mixture has a partial pressure of CS_2 equal to 50 mm Hg at 75°F and is to be blown into the absorber at essentially atmospheric pressure at the rate of 50,000 cu ft/hr. The vapor content of the gas is to be reduced to 0.5%. The absorption oil has an average molecular weight 180, viscosity 2 centipoises, and specific gravity 0.81 at 75°F. The oil enters the absorber essentially stripped of all CS_2, and solutions of oil and CS_2 are ideal. The vapor pressure of CS_2 at 75°F = 346 mm Hg. Assume isothermal operation.

a. Determine the minimum liquid/gas ratio.

b. For a liquid/gas ratio of 1.5 times the minimum, determine the pounds of oil per hour to enter the absorber.

c. Determine the number of theoretical trays required, both graphically and analytically.

d. For a conventional bubble-cap-tray tower, estimate the overall tray efficiency to be expected and the number of real trays required.

8.5. Design a suitable perforated tray for the absorber of Prob. 8.4, and compute its hydraulics. Determine the tray efficiency (which may be considered constant for all the trays) and the number of real trays required graphically, and also through Eq. (8.14). Take the surface tension as 30 dynes/cm.

8.6. Determine the number of ideal trays for the absorber of Prob. 8.4, assuming adiabatic operation. Use a liquid rate of 18,000 lb/hr, which is about 1.5 times the minimum. The specific heat of the oil = 86.5, of liquid CS_2 = 18.2, and of CS_2 vapor = 11.2, all Btu/(lb mole)(°F). The latent heat of CS_2 = 12,000 Btu/lb mole at 75°F. **Ans.**: 3.8.

8.7. Starting with Eq. (8.31), replace the *y*'s by equivalent *Y*'s and derive Eq. (8.33).

8.8. With the help of the Kremser equations and Eq. (8.47), derive the relation between N_p and N_{tOG} for constant absorption factor. Establish the conditions when $N_p = N_{tOG}$.

8.9. Design a tower packed with 2-in. ceramic Raschig rings for the carbon disulfide scrubber of Prob. 8.4. Assume isothermal operation, use a liquid/gas ratio of 1.5 times the minimum, and a gas pressure drop not exceeding 0.40 in. water per foot of packing. Tower shells are available in diameter increments of 2 in. The liquid surface tension = 30 dynes/cm. A procedure follows:

   a. Determine the diameter of the tower.

   b. Using average (top and bottom) flow rates and fluid properties, compute the mass-transfer coefficients F_Ga and F_La and heights of transfer units H_{tG}, H_{tL}, and H_{toG}.

   c. Compute N_{tG}, and with H_{tG}, the packing height. **Ans.:** 15.5 ft.

   d. Compute N_{toG} through the following methods, and the corresponding packing height for each: Eq. (8.33), Eq. (8.45), and Fig. 8.20.

   e. Compare the gas pressure drop for the full depth of packing with that for all the trays of Prob. 8.5. At a power cost of $0.015 per kilowatt-hour, and a blower-motor efficiency of 50%, calculate the annual (350 days) difference in power cost for the two towers.

   8.10. It is desired to reduce the ammonia content of 6,000 cu ft/hr (80°F, 1 atm) of an ammonia-air mixture from 5.0 to 0.04% by volume by water scrubbing. There is available a 1-ft-diameter tower packed to a depth of 12 ft with 1-in. Berl saddles. Is the tower satisfactory, and if so, what water rate should be used? At 80°F, ammonia-water solutions follow Henry's law up to 5 mole % ammonia in the liquid, and $m = 1.414$.

   8.11. A tower, 1-ft diameter, is packed with 1-in. Berl saddles to a depth of 12 ft. It is to be fed with 6,000 cu ft/hr (80°F, 1 atm) of an ammonia-air mixture containing 5% ammonia by volume, and with pure water at 80°F. In what follows, operation may be considered isothermal, and Henry's law applies up to 5 mole % ammonia in the liquid, with $m = 1.414$.

   a. If the water rate is set at 400 lb/hr, calculate the concentration of ammonia in the effluents.

   Since at the low water rate in part (*a*) the liquid mass-transfer coefficient and the interfacial area are both low, consideration is also being given to the following two schemes, each of which provides the same substantial increase in liquid irrigation rate. In each case, calculate the effluent compositions to be expected, and compare the rate of absorption with that of (*a*).

   b. Fresh water is to be used at the rate of 3,500 lb/hr.

   c. Fresh water is to be used at the rate of 400 lb/hr, but 3,100 lb/hr of the liquid will be continuously recycled from the bottom to the top of the tower.

   8.12. As a result of an absorption process, there are two solutions which must be stripped of absorbed solute. The first, 25 moles/hr, is a solution of benzene in a nonvolatile oil, containing 0.10 mole, fraction benzene. The second, 10 moles/hr, is a solution of benzene in oil of the same type, 0.05 mole fraction benzene. Each will be preheated to 250°F and will be stripped in the same tower at 1 atm abs, with superheated steam at 250°F. The liquid effluent from the stripper is to contain no more than 0.005 mole fraction benzene. Assume isothermal operation. Raoult's law applies, and at 250°F, the vapor pressure of benzene = 2,400 mm Hg.

   a. The more concentrated solution will enter the top tray of the stripper, and the less concentrated will be fed to that tray where the benzene concentration most nearly matches its concentration. Determine the minimum steam rate, the number of ideal trays required for 1.25 times the minimum steam rate, and the ideal tray number for feeding the less-concentrated solution.

                                                                 Ans.: Nine ideal trays.

   b. How many ideal trays would be required if both liquids were fed to the top tray of the stripper, using the same steam rate as in part (*a*)?

   c. Suppose, with the same steam rate as in part (*a*), the more dilute feed had to be introduced onto the fifth ideal tray from the top. What then would be the total number of ideal trays required?

   8.13. A process is being considered which involves crystallizing a product from methanol and drying the wet crystals by evaporation of the methanol into air. The resulting air-methanol mixture, estimated as 25,000 cu ft/hr at 80°F, 1 atm, will contain 5% methanol by volume. This is to be recovered by countercurrent scrubbing in a packed tower with water, available at 80°F. The scrubbed gas will be returned to the driers, and its methanol content must be no greater than 0.1%. The methanol-water solution will be distilled to recover the methanol.

   It is agreed that the absorber will be a tower packed with 1.5-in. ceramic Raschig rings, and will operate essentially adiabatically. Its cost, including the shell and packing, will be $25 per cubic foot.

It will be designed to operate at 70% of the flooding gas rate.   Allow 150% of the tower cost for installation and piping, amortized over a 2-yr period.   Allow 5% of the tower cost for annual maintenance.   Fan and motor for moving the gas will operate at 50% overall efficiency, pump and motor for moving liquid at 80%.   Power costs $0.015 per kilowatt-hour.   Operation is expected for 350 twenty-four-hour days per year.   The heat cost for distillation of the methanol solution is estimated to be $(7,500/x - 33,000)10^{-6}$ dollars per pound mole contained methanol, where x is the mole fraction methanol in the feed to the still (absorber effluent).   The cost of fan, pump, motors, and distillation equipment is not expected to be dependent upon variations in absorber design covered in this problem.

Determine the most economical water rate for the absorber.

The following were interpolated from the listings in "International Critical Tables," vol. III, p. 290; vol. V, p. 159:

Mole % methanol in water solution	Equilibrium partial pressure of methanol, mm Hg		Heat of soln in water, 80°F, Btu/lb mole methanol
	39.9°C	59.4°C	
0	0	0	
5	25.0	50	−2715
10	46.0	102	−2370
15	66.5	151	−2030

The heat of solution is referred to liquid water and liquid methanol at 80°F.   Extend the partial-pressure data by the methods of Fig. 8.2.

8.14.   A gas containing 88% CH_4, 4% C_2H_6, 5% n-C_3H_8, and 3% n-C_4H_{10} is to be scrubbed isothermally at 100°F, 5 atm pressure, in a tower containing the equivalent of eight ideal trays.   It is desired to remove 80% of the C_3H_8.   The lean oil will contain 0.5 mole % of C_4H_{10} but none of the other gaseous constituents.   What quantity of lean oil, moles/mole wet gas, should be used, and what will be the composition of the rich oil and scrubbed gas?   The Henry's law constants m are: CH_4, 32; C_2H_6, 6.7; n-C_3H_8, 2.4; n-C_4H_{10}, 0.74.

8.15.   An absorber of four ideal trays, to operate adiabatically at 150 psia, is fed with 1 mole/time each of liquid and gas, each entering at 90°F, as follows:

Component	Liquid mole fraction	Gas mole fraction
CH_4		0.70
C_2H_6		0.12
n-C_3H_8		0.08
n-C_4H_{10}	0.02	0.06
n-C_5H_{12}	0.01	0.04
Nonvolatile oil	0.97	

Estimate the composition and rate (mole/time) of the exit gas.   Necessary data follow.

Henry's law constants [Depriester: *Chem. Eng. Progr. Symp. Ser.*, **49** (7), 1 (1953)], enthalpies in Btu/lb mole at 90°F relative to saturated liquid at −200°F (Maxwell, "Data Book on Hydrocarbons," D. Van Nostrand Company, Inc., Princeton, N.J., 1950) and molar heat capacities are:

Component	90°F			100°F	110°F	C_p, Btu/(lb mole)(°F)	
	m	H_G	H_L	m	m	Gas	Liquid
CH_4	16.5	5,550	4,200	17.0	17.8	9.0	12.0
C_2H_6	3.40	9,700	6,700	3.80	4.03	15.0	20.0
$n\text{-}C_3H_8$	1.16	13,350	7,250	1.30	1.44	19.0	31.0
$n\text{-}C_4H_{10}$	0.35	17,650	8,900	0.41	0.47	23.0	38.0
$n\text{-}C_5H_{12}$	0.123	21,900	10,600	0.140	0.165	28.0	44.0
Oil							90.0

CHAPTER NINE
DISTILLATION

Distillation is a method of separating the components of a solution which depends upon the distribution of the substances between a gas and a liquid phase, applied to cases where all components are present in both phases. Instead of introducing a new substance into the mixture in order to provide the second phase, as is done in gas absorption or desorption, the new phase is created from the original solution by vaporization or condensation.

In order to make clear the distinction among distillation and the other operations, let us cite a few specific examples. In the separation of a solution of common salt and water, the water may be completely vaporized from the solution without removal of salt since the latter is for all practical purposes quite nonvolatile at the prevailing conditions. This is the operation of evaporation. Distillation, on the other hand, is concerned with the separation of solutions where all the components are appreciably volatile. In this category, consider the separation of the components of a liquid solution of ammonia and water. By contacting the ammonia-water solution with air, which is essentially insoluble in the liquid, the ammonia may be stripped or desorbed by processes which were discussed in Chap. 8, but the ammonia is then mixed with water vapor and air and is not obtained in pure form. On the other hand, by application of heat, we may partially vaporize the solution and thereby create a gas phase consisting of nothing but water and ammonia. And since the gas will be richer in ammonia than the residual liquid, a certain amount of separation will have resulted. By appropriate manipulation of the phases, or by repeated vaporizations and condensations, it is then ordinarily possible to make as complete a separation as may be desired, recovering both components of the mixture in as pure a state as we wish.

The advantages of such a separation method are clear. In distillation the new phase differs from the original by its heat content, but heat is readily added or removed without difficulty, although of course the cost of doing this must inevitably be considered. Absorption or desorption operations, on the other hand, which depend upon the introduction of a foreign substance, provide us with a new solution which in turn may have to be separated by one of the diffusional operations unless it happens that the new solution is useful directly.

There are in turn certain limitations to distillation as a separation process. In absorption or similar operations, where it has been agreed to introduce a foreign substance to provide a new phase for distribution purposes, we may ordinarily choose from a great variety of solvents in order to provide the greatest possible separation effect. For example, since water is ineffectual in absorbing hydrocarbon gases from a gas mixture, we choose instead a hydrocarbon oil which provides a high solubility. But in distillation there is no such choice. The gas which may be created from a liquid by application of heat inevitably consists only of the components comprising the liquid. Since the gas is therefore chemically very similar to the liquid, the change in composition resulting from the distribution of the components between the two phases is ordinarily not very great. Indeed, in some cases the change in composition is so small that the process becomes impractical; it may even happen that there is no change in composition whatsoever.

Nevertheless the direct separation which is ordinarily possible by distillation, into pure products requiring no further processing, has made this perhaps the most important of all the mass-transfer operations.

VAPOR-LIQUID EQUILIBRIA

The successful application of distillation methods depends greatly upon an understanding of the equilibria which exist between the vapor and liquid phases of the mixtures encountered. A brief review of these is therefore essential. The emphasis here will be on binary mixtures.

Pressure-temperature-concentration phase diagram

Let us first consider binary mixtures which we shall term "ordinary," by which is meant that the liquid components dissolve in all proportions to form homogeneous solutions which are not necessarily ideal and that no complications of maximum or minimum boiling points occur. We shall consider component A of the binary mixture A-B as the more volatile, i.e., the vapor pressure of pure A at any temperature is higher than the vapor pressure of pure B. The vapor-liquid equilibrium for each pure substance of the mixture is of course its vapor pressure–temperature relationship, as indicated in Fig. 7.1. For binary mixtures an additional variable, concentration, must

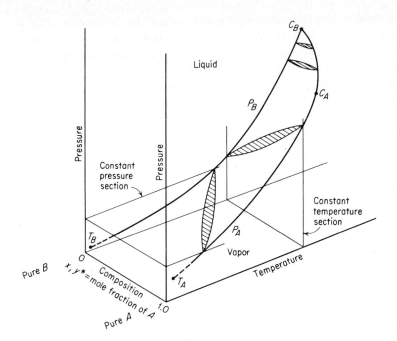

Fig. 9.1 *Binary vapor-liquid equilibria.*

likewise be considered. Mole fractions are the most convenient concentration terms to use, and throughout this discussion x will be the mole fraction of the more volatile substance A in the liquid and $y*$ the corresponding equilibrium mole fraction of A in the vapor.

Complete graphical representation of the equilibria requires a three-dimensional diagram, as in Fig. 9.1. The curve marked P_A is the vapor-pressure curve of A, lying entirely in the nearest composition plane at $x = 1.0$. The curve extends from its critical point C_A to its triple point T_A, but the complications of the solid phase which do not enter into distillation operations will not be considered. Similarly curve P_B is the vapor pressure of pure B, in the far plane at $x = 0$. The liquid and vapor regions at compositions between $x = 0$ and 1.0 are separated by a double surface which extends smoothly from P_A to P_B. The shape of this double surface is most readily studied by considering sections at constant pressure and constant temperature, examples of which are shown in the figure.

Constant-pressure equilibria

Consider first a typical section at constant pressure (Fig. 9.2a). The intersection of the double surface of Fig. 9.1 with the constant-pressure plane produces a looped curve without maxima or minima extending from the boiling point of pure B to that of pure A at the pressure in question. The upper curve provides the temperature-vapor composition (t-y^*) relationship, the lower that of the temperature-liquid composition (t-x). Liquid and vapor mixtures at equilibrium are at the same temperature and pressure throughout, so that horizontal *tie lines* such as line DF join equilibrium mixtures at D and F. There are an infinite number of such tie lines for this diagram. A mixture on the lower curve, as at point D, is a saturated liquid; a mixture on the upper curve, as at F, is a saturated vapor. A mixture at E is a two-phase mixture, consisting of a liquid phase of composition at D and a vapor phase of composition at F, in such proportions that the average composition of the entire mixture is represented by E. The relative amounts of the equilibrium phases are related to the segments of the tie line,

$$\frac{\text{Moles of } D}{\text{Moles of } F} = \frac{\text{line } EF}{\text{line } DE} \tag{9.1}$$

Consider a solution at G in a closed container which may be kept at constant pressure by moving a piston. The solution is entirely liquid. If it is heated, the first bubble of vapor forms at H and has the composition at J, richer in the more volatile substance, and hence the lower curve is called the bubble-point temperature curve. As more of the mixture is vaporized, more of the vapor forms at the expense of the liquid, giving rise, for example, to liquid L and its equilibrium vapor K, although the composition of the entire mass is still the original as at G. The last drop of liquid vaporizes at M and has the composition at N. Superheating the mixture follows the path MO. The mixture has vaporized over a temperature range from H to M, unlike the single vaporization temperature of a pure substance. Thus, the term *boiling point* for a solution ordinarily has no meaning since vaporization occurs over a temperature

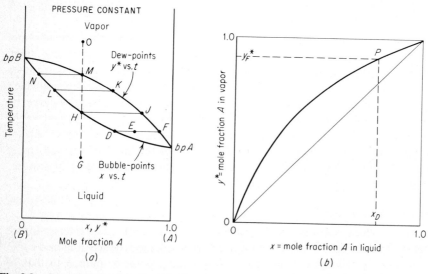

Fig. 9.2 *Constant-pressure vapor-liquid equilibria.*

range, i.e., from the bubble point to the dew point. If the mixture at O is cooled, all the phenomena reappear in reverse order. Condensation, for example, starts at M, whence the upper curve is termed the dew-point curve, and continues to H.

If a solution such as that at H is boiled in an open vessel, on the other hand, with the vapors escaping into the atmosphere, since the vapor is richer in the more volatile substance, the liquid residue must therefore become leaner. The temperature and composition of the saturated residual liquid therefore move along the lower curve toward N as the distillation proceeds.

The vapor-liquid equilibrium compositions may be shown also on a distribution diagram (x vs. y^*) as in Fig. 9.2b. Point P on the diagram represents the tie line DF, for example. Since the vapor is richer in the more volatile substance, the curve lies above the 45° diagonal line, which has been drawn in for comparison.

Relative volatility

The greater the distance between the equilibrium curve and the diagonal of Fig. 9.2b, the greater the difference in liquid and vapor compositions and the more readily is the separation by distillation made. One numerical measure of this is called the *separation factor*, or, particularly in the case of distillation, the *relative volatility* α. This is the ratio of the concentration ratio of A and B in one phase to that in the other and is a measure of the separability,

$$\alpha = \frac{y^*/(1 - y^*)}{x/(1 - x)} = \frac{y^*(1 - x)}{x(1 - y^*)} \tag{9.2}$$

The value of α will ordinarily change as x varies from 0 to 1.0. If $y^* = x$ (except at $x = 0$ or 1), $\alpha = 1.0$, and no separation is possible. The larger the value of α above unity, the greater the degree of separability.

Increased pressures

At higher pressures the sections at constant pressure will of course intersect the double surface of Fig. 9.1 at increased temperatures. The intersections may be projected onto a single plane, as in Fig. 9.3a. It should be noted that not only do the looped curves occur at higher temperatures, but also they usually become narrower. This is readily seen from the corresponding distribution curves of Fig. 9.3b. The relative volatilities, and hence the separability, therefore usually become less at higher pressures. As the critical pressure of one component is exceeded, there is no longer a distinction between vapor and liquid for that component, and for mixtures the looped curves are therefore shorter, as at pressures above P_{t3}, the critical for A in the figure. Distillation separations can be made only in the region where a looped curve exists.

For particular systems, the critical pressure of the less volatile substance may be reached before that of the more volatile, and it is also possible that the double surface of Fig. 9.1 will extend at intermediate compositions to a small extent beyond the critical pressures of either substance.

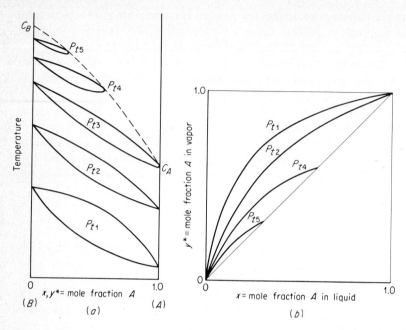

Fig. 9.3 *Vapor-liquid equilibria at increased pressure.*

Constant-temperature equilibria

A typical constant-temperature section of the three-dimensional phase diagram is shown in Fig. 9.4.   The intersection of the constant-temperature plane with the double surface of Fig. 9.1 provides the two curves which extend without maxima or minima from the vapor pressure of pure B to that of pure A.   As before, there are an infinite number of horizontal tie lines, such as TV, which join an equilibrium vapor as at V to its corresponding liquid at T.   A solution in a closed container at W is entirely a liquid, and if the pressure is reduced at constant temperature, the first bubble of vapor forms at U, complete vaporization occurs at S, and further reduction in pressure results in a superheated vapor as at R.

Ideal solutions—Raoult's law

Before studying the characteristics of mixtures which deviate markedly from those just described, let us consider the equilibria for the limiting case of mixtures whose vapors and liquids are ideal.   The nature of ideal solutions and the types of mixtures which approach ideality were discussed in Chap. 8.

For an ideal solution, the equilibrium partial pressure p^* of a constituent at a fixed temperature equals the product of its vapor pressure P when pure at this temperature and its mole fraction in the liquid.   This is Raoult's law.

$$p_A^* = P_A x \qquad p_B^* = P_B(1 - x) \qquad (9.3)$$

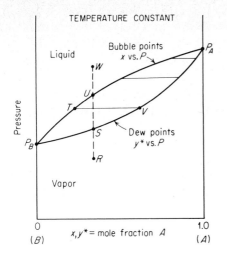

Fig. **9.4** *Constant-temperature vapor-liquid equilibria.*

If the vapor phase is also ideal,

$$P_t = p_A^* + p_B^* = P_A x + P_B(1 - x) \tag{9.4}$$

and the total as well as the partial pressures are linear in x at a fixed temperature. These relationships are shown graphically in Fig. 9.5. The equilibrium vapor composition may then be computed at this temperature. For example, the value of y^* at point D on the figure equals the ratio of the distances FG to EG,

$$y^* = \frac{p_A^*}{P_t} = \frac{P_A x}{P_t} \tag{9.5}$$

$$1 - y^* = \frac{p_B^*}{P_t} = \frac{P_B(1 - x)}{P_t} \tag{9.6}$$

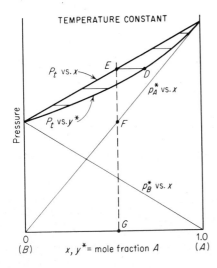

Fig. **9.5** *Ideal solutions.*

The relative volatility α is, by substitution in Eq. (9.2),

$$\alpha = \frac{P_A}{P_B} \tag{9.7}$$

For ideal solutions, it is possible then to compute the entire vapor-liquid equilibria from the vapor pressures of the pure substances. For all other mixtures, however, it is necessary to obtain the data experimentally.

Illustration 9.1. Compute the vapor-liquid equilibria at constant pressure of 1 atm for mixtures of n-heptane with n-octane, which may be expected to form ideal solutions.

Solution. The boiling points at 1 atm of the substances are n-heptane (A), 98.4°C; n-octane (B), 125.6°C. Computations are therefore made between these temperatures. For example, at 110°C, $P_A = 1{,}050$ mm Hg, $P_B = 484$ mm Hg, $P_t = 760$ mm Hg.

Eq. (9.4): $x = \dfrac{P_t - P_B}{P_A - P_B} = \dfrac{760 - 484}{1{,}050 - 484} = 0.487$ mole fraction heptane in liquid

Eq. (9.5): $y^* = \dfrac{P_A x}{P_t} = \dfrac{1{,}050(0.487)}{760} = 0.674$ mole fraction heptane in vapor

Eq. (9.7): $\alpha = \dfrac{P_A}{P_B} = \dfrac{1{,}050}{484} = 2.17$

In similar fashion, the data of the following table may be computed:

t, °C	P_A, mm Hg	P_B, mm Hg	x	y^*	α
98.4	760	333	1.0	1.0	2.28
105	940	417	0.655	0.810	2.25
110	1,050	484	0.487	0.674	2.17
115	1,200	561	0.312	0.492	2.14
120	1,350	650	0.1571	0.279	2.08
125.6	1,540	760	0	0	2.02

Curves of the type of Fig. 9.2 may now be plotted. Note that although the vapor pressures of the pure substances vary considerably with temperature, α for ideal solutions does not. In this case, an average of the computed α's is 2.16, and substituting this in Eq. (9.2), rearranged,

$$y^* = \frac{\alpha x}{1 + x(\alpha - 1)} = \frac{2.16x}{1 + 1.16x}$$

provides an expression which for many purposes is a satisfactory empirical relation between y^* and x for this system at 1 atm.

Positive deviations from ideality

A mixture whose total pressure is greater than that computed for ideality [Eq. (9.4)] is said to show positive deviations from Raoult's law. Most mixtures fall into this category. In these cases the partial pressures of each component are larger than the

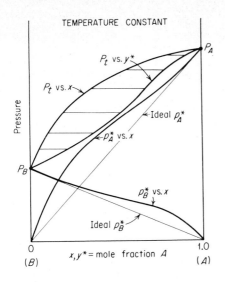

P_t vs. y^*

P_t vs. x

Pressure

$\leftarrow$ Ideal p_A^*

$\leftarrow p_A^*$ vs. x

P_B

p_B^* vs. x

Ideal p_B^*

0
(B) $x, y^* = $ mole fraction A 1.0
(A)

Fig. 9.6 *Positive deviation from ideality.*

ideal, as shown in Fig. 9.6.† It should be noted that as the concentration for each component approaches unity mole fraction, the partial pressures for that substance approach ideality tangentially. Raoult's law, in other words, is nearly applicable to the substance present in very large concentrations. This is the case for all substances except where association within the vapor or electrolytic dissociation within the liquid occurs.

The distribution diagram (x vs. y^*) for systems of this type appears much the same as that of Fig. 9.2b.

Minimum-boiling mixtures—azeotropes. When the positive deviations from ideality are sufficiently large and the vapor pressures of the two components are not too far apart, the total-pressure curves at constant temperature may rise through a maximum at some concentration, as in Fig. 9.7a. Such a mixture is said to form an azeotrope, or constant-boiling mixture. The significance of this is more readily seen by study of the constant-pressure section (Fig. 9.7b or c). The liquid- and vapor-composition curves are tangent at point L, the point of azeotropism at this pressure, which represents the minimum-boiling temperature for this system. For all mixtures of composition less than L, such as those at C, the equilibrium vapor (E) is richer in the more volatile component than the liquid (D). For all mixtures richer than L, however, such as at F, the equilibrium vapor (G) is less rich in the more volatile substance than the liquid (H). A mixture of composition L gives rise to a vapor of composition identical with the liquid, and it consequently boils at constant temperature

† The ratio of the actual equilibrium partial pressure of a component p^* to the ideal value Px is the activity coefficient referred to the pure substance: $\gamma = p^*/Px$. Since γ is greater than unity in these cases and log γ is positive, the deviations are termed *positive* deviations from ideality. A very extensive science of the treatment of nonideal solutions through activity coefficients has been developed by which, from a very small number of data, all the vapor-liquid equilibria of a system may be predicted.[4,12]

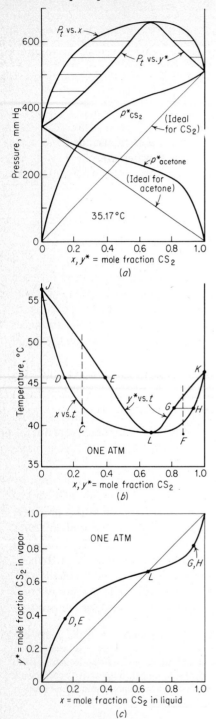

Fig. 9.7 *Minimum-boiling azeotropism in the system carbon disulfide–acetone.* (*a*) *At constant temperature;* (*b*) *and* (*c*) *at constant pressure.*

and without change in composition. If solutions either at D or H are boiled in an open vessel with continual escape of the vapors, the temperature and composition of the residual liquids in each case move along the lower curve away from point L (toward K for a liquid at H, and toward J for one at D).

Solutions such as these cannot be completely separated by ordinary distillation methods at this pressure, since at the azeotropic composition $y^* = x$ and $\alpha = 1.0$.† The azeotropic composition as well as its boiling point changes with pressure. In some cases, changing the pressure may eliminate azeotropism from the system.

Azeotropic mixtures of this sort are very common, and thousands have been recorded.[19,20] One of the most important is the ethanol-water azeotrope which at 1 atm occurs at 89.4 mole percent ethanol and 78.2°C. Azeotropism disappears in this system at pressures below 70 mm Hg.

Partial liquid miscibility. Some substances exhibit such large positive deviations from ideality that they do not dissolve completely in the liquid state, as in the case of isobutanol-water (Fig. 9.8). The curves through points C and E represent the solubility limits of the constituents at relatively low temperatures. Mixtures of composition and temperature represented by points within the central area, such as point D, form two liquid phases at equilibrium at C and E, and line CE is a liquid tie line. Mixtures in the regions on either side of the solubility limits such as at F are homogeneous liquids. The solubility ordinarily increases with increased temperature, and the central area consequently decreases in width. If the pressure were sufficiently high so that vaporization did not occur, the liquid-solubility curves would continue along the broken extensions as shown. At the prevailing pressure, however, vaporization occurs before this can happen, giving rise to the branched vapor-liquid equilibrium curves. For homogeneous liquids such as that at F, the vapor-liquid equilibrium phenomena are normal, and such a mixture boils initially at H to give the first bubble of vapor of composition J. The same is true of any solution richer than M, except that here the vapor is leaner in the more volatile component. Any two-phase liquid mixture within the composition range from K to M will boil at the temperature of the line KM, and all these give rise to the same vapor of composition L. A liquid mixture of average composition L, which produces a vapor of the same composition, is sometimes called a *heteroazeotrope*. The corresponding distribution diagram with the tie line HJ, solubility limits at the boiling point K and M, and the azeotropic point L, is shown in Fig. 9.8b.

In relatively few instances the azeotropic composition lies outside the limits of insolubility. One such case is the system methyl ethyl ketone–water.

Insoluble liquids; steam distillation. The mutual solubility of some liquids is so small that they may be considered substantially insoluble: points K and M (Fig. 9.8) are then for all practical purposes on the vertical axes of these diagrams. This is the case for a mixture such as a hydrocarbon and water, for example. If the liquids are

---

† For compositions to the right of L (Fig. 9.7) α as usually computed is less than unity, and the reciprocal of α is then ordinarily used.

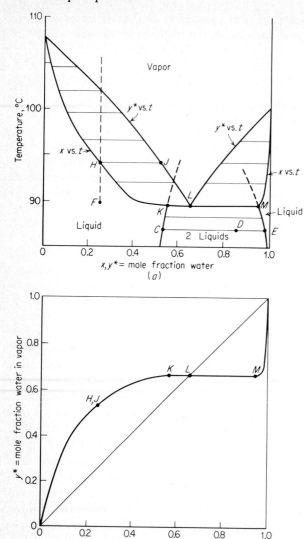

Fig. 9.8 *Isobutanol–water at 1 atm.*

completely insoluble, the vapor pressure of either component cannot be influenced by the presence of the other, and each exerts its true vapor pressure at the prevailing temperature.   When the sum of the separate vapor pressures equals the total pressure, the mixture boils, and the vapor composition is readily computed, assuming the applicability of the simple gas law,

$$P_A + P_B = P_t \tag{9.8}$$

$$y^* = \frac{P_A}{P_t} \tag{9.9}$$

So long as two liquid phases are present, the mixture will boil at the same temperature and produce a vapor of constant composition.

Illustration 9.2. A mixture containing 50 g water and 50 g ethylaniline, which may be assumed to be essentially insoluble, is boiled at atmospheric pressure. Describe the phenomena that occur.

Solution. Since the liquids are insoluble, each exerts its own vapor pressure, and when the sum of these equals 760 mm Hg, the mixture boils.

t, °C	P_A (water), mm Hg	P_B (ethylaniline), mm Hg	$P_t = P_A + P_B$, mm Hg
38.5	51.1	1	52.1
64.4	199.7	5	205
80.6	363.9	10	374
96.0	657.6	20	678
99.15	737.2	22.8	760
113.2	1,225	40	1,265
204		760	

The mixture boils at 99.15°C.

$$y^* = \frac{P_A}{P_t} = \frac{737.2}{760} = 0.97 \text{ mole fraction water}$$

$$1 - y^* = \frac{P_B}{P_t} = \frac{22.8}{760} = 0.03 \text{ mole fraction ethylaniline}$$

The original mixture contained $50/18.02 = 2.78$ g moles water and $50/121.1 = 0.412$ g mole ethylaniline. The mixture will continue to boil at 99.15°C, with an equilibrium vapor of the indicated composition, until all the water has evaporated together with $2.78(0.03/0.97) = 0.086$ g mole of the ethylaniline. The temperature will then rise to 204°C, and the equilibrium vapor will be pure ethylaniline.

Note that by this method of distillation with steam, so long as liquid water is present, the high-boiling organic liquid can be made to vaporize at a temperature much lower than its normal boiling point without the necessity of a vacuum-pump equipment operating at 22.8 mm Hg.   If boiled at 204°C, this compound will undergo considerable decomposition.   However, the heat requirements of the steam-distillation process are great since such a large amount of water must be evaporated simultaneously.   Alternatives would be (1) to operate at a different total pressure in the presence of liquid water where the ratio of the vapor pressures of the substances may be more favorable and (2) to bubble superheated steam (or other insoluble gas) through the mixture in the absence of liquid water and to vaporize the ethylaniline by allowing it to saturate the steam.

Negative deviations from ideality
When the total pressure of a system at equilibrium is less than the ideal value, the system is said to deviate negatively from Raoult's law.   Such a situation is shown in

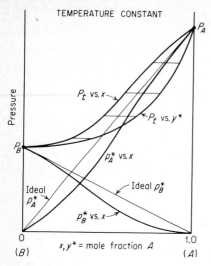

Fig. 9.9   *Negative deviations from ideality.*

Fig. 9.9 at constant temperature.   Note that in this case, as with positive deviations, where neither vapor association nor liquid dissociation occurs, the partial pressures of the constituents of the solution approach ideality as their concentrations approach 100 percent.   The constant-pressure diagram for such a case has the same general appearance as the diagrams shown in Fig. 9.2.

Maximum-boiling mixtures—azeotropes

When the difference in vapor pressures of the components is not too great and in addition the negative deviations are large, the curve for total pressure against composition may pass through a minimum, as in Fig. 9.10*a*.   This condition gives rise to a maximum in the boiling temperatures, as at point *L* (Fig. 9.10*b*), and a condition of azeotropism.   The equilibrium vapor is leaner in the more volatile substance for liquids whose *x* is less than the azeotropic composition and greater if *x* is larger. Solutions on either side of the azeotrope, if boiled in an open vessel with escape of the vapor, will ultimately leave a residual liquid of the azeotropic composition in the vessel.

Maximum-boiling azeotropes are less common than the minimum type.   One which is very well known is that of hydrochloric acid–water (11.1 mole % HCl, 110°C, at 1 atm), which may be prepared simply by boiling a solution of any strength of the acid in an open vessel.   This is one method of standardizing hydrochloric acid.

Enthalpy-concentration diagrams

Binary vapor-liquid equilibria may also be plotted on coordinates of enthalpy vs. concentration at constant pressure.   Liquid-solution enthalpies include both sensible heat and the heat of mixing the components

$$H_L = C_L(t_L - t_o)M_{av} + \Delta H_S \tag{9.10}$$

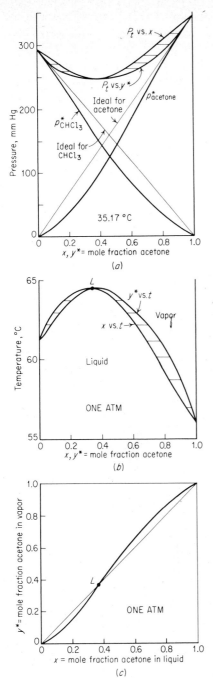

Fig. 9.10 *Maximum-boiling azeotropism in the system acetone–chloroform.* (a) *At constant temperature;* (b) *and* (c) *at constant pressure.*

where C_L is the heat capacity of the solution, Btu/(lb)(°F), and ΔH_S is the heat of solution at t_o and the prevailing concentration referred to the pure liquid components, Btu/lb mole *solution*. For saturated liquids, t_L is the bubble point corresponding to the liquid concentration at the prevailing pressure. Heat-of-solution data vary in form, and some adjustment of the units of tabulated data may be necessary. If heat is evolved on mixing, ΔH_S will be negative, and for ideal solutions it is zero. For ideal solutions, the heat capacity is the weighted average of those for the pure components.

For present purposes, saturated-vapor enthalpies may be calculated adequately by assuming that the unmixed liquids are heated separately as liquids to the gas temperature t_G (the dew point), each vaporized at this temperature, and the vapors mixed

$$H_G = y[C_{LA}M_A(t_G - t_o) + \lambda_A M_A] + (1 - y)[C_{LB}M_B(t_G - t_o) + \lambda_B M_B] \quad (9.11)$$

where λ_A, λ_B = latent heats of vaporization of pure substances at t_G, Btu/lb

C_{LA}, C_{LB} = heat capacities of pure liquids, Btu/(lb)(°F)

In the upper part of Fig. 9.11, which represents a typical binary mixture, the enthalpies of saturated vapors at their dew points have been plotted vs. y and those of the saturated liquids at their bubble points vs. x. The vertical distances between the

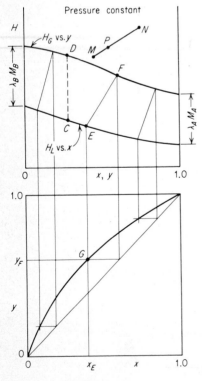

Fig. 9.11 *Enthalpy-concentration coordinates.*

two curves at $x = 0$ and 1 represent, respectively, the molar latent heats of B and A. The heat required for complete vaporization of solution C is $H_D - H_C$ Btu/lb mole solution. Equilibrium liquids and vapors may be joined by tie lines, of which line EF is typical. The relation between this equilibrium phase diagram and the xy plot is shown in the lower part of Fig. 9.11. Here the point G represents the tie line EF, located on the lower plot in the manner shown. Other tie lines, when projected to the xy plot, produce the complete equilibrium-distribution curve.

Characteristics of the Hxy and xy diagrams.[31] Let point M on Fig. 9.11 represent M moles of a mixture of enthalpy H_M and concentration z_M, and similarly N is N moles of a mixture of properties H_N, z_N. Adiabatic mixing of M and N will produce P moles of a mixture of enthalpy H_P and concentration z_P. A total material balance is

$$M + N = P \tag{9.12}$$

and a balance for component A is

$$Mz_M + Nz_N = Pz_P \tag{9.13}$$

An enthalpy balance is

$$MH_M + NH_N = PH_P \tag{9.14}$$

Elimination of P between Eqs. (9.12) and (9.13) and between (9.12) and (9.14) yields

$$\frac{M}{N} = \frac{z_N - z_P}{z_P - z_M} = \frac{H_N - H_P}{H_P - H_M} \tag{9.15}$$

This is the equation of a straight line on the enthalpy-concentration plot, passing through points (H_M, z_M), (H_N, z_N), and (H_P, z_P). Point P is therefore on the straight line MN, located so that $M/N =$ line NP/line PM. Similarly if mixture N were *removed* adiabatically from mixture P, the mixture M would result.

Consider now mixture C (H_C, z_C) on Fig. 9.12. It will be useful to describe such a mixture in terms of saturated vapors and liquids, since distillation is mostly concerned with such mixtures. C may be considered the result of adiabatically removing saturated liquid D from saturated vapor E (DE is *not* a tie line), and x_D and y_E may be located on the lower diagram as shown. But C may equally well be considered as having been produced by adiabatically subtracting F from G, or J from K, or indeed by such a combination of saturated liquids and vapors given by any line from C which intersects the saturated-enthalpy curves. These, when projected to the lower diagram, form the curve shown there. Thus any point C on the Hxy diagram may be represented by the difference between saturated vapors and liquids, and in turn also by a curve on the xy plot. For the combination $E - D = C$, a material balance shows

$$\frac{D}{E} = \frac{z_C - y_E}{z_C - x_D} = \frac{\text{line } CE}{\text{line } CD} \tag{9.16}$$

This is the equation on the xy diagram of the chord of slope D/E drawn between point (y_E, x_D) and $y = x = z_C$ on the 45° line. Similarly, the ratios F/G and J/K would be shown by the slopes of chords drawn from these points to $y = x = z_C$.

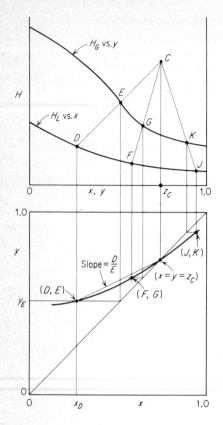

Fig. 9.12   *Relation between the diagrams.*

Consideration of the geometry of the diagram will readily show the following:

1. If the $H_G y$ and $H_L x$ curves are straight parallel lines (which will occur if the molar latent heats of A and B are equal, if the heat capacities are constant over the prevailing temperature range, and if there is no heat of solution), then $D/E = F/G = J/K$ for adiabatic subtraction, since the line-segment ratios are then equal, and the curve on xy representing C becomes a straight line.

2. If point C is moved upward, the curve on xy becomes more steep, ultimately coinciding with the 45° line when C is at infinite enthalpy.

3. If point C is on the $H_G y$ curve, the curve on xy becomes a horizontal straight line; if C is on the $H_L x$ curve, the curve on xy becomes a vertical straight line.

These concepts will be useful in understanding the applications of these diagrams.

Multicomponent systems

Nonideal systems of three components may be treated graphically, using triangular coordinates to express the compositions in the manner of Chap. 10, but for more than three components graphical treatment becomes very complicated.   Actually our knowledge of nonideal systems of this type is extremely limited, and very few data have been accumulated. It is generally unsafe to predict detailed behavior of a multicomponent system from considerations of the pure components alone, or even from a knowledge of the simple binary systems that may be formed from the components. For example, three-component systems sometimes form ternary azeotropes, whose equilibrium vapor and liquid phases have identical composition. But the fact that one, two, or three binary azeotropes are known among the components does not make the formation of a ternary azeotrope certain, and a ternary azeotrope need not necessarily coincide with the composition of minimum or maximum boiling temperature for the system at constant pressure.

Ideal systems. Many of the multicomponent systems of industrial importance may be considered nearly ideal in the liquid phase for all practical purposes. This is particularly true for hydrocarbon mixtures of the same homologous series, such as those of the paraffin series or the lower-boiling aromatic hydrocarbons.† In such cases Raoult's law may be applied. If the components are A, B, C, etc., then, at a fixed temperature,

$$p_A^* = P_A x_A \qquad p_B^* = P_B x_B \qquad p_C^* = P_C x_C \qquad p_J^* = P_J x_J \qquad (9.17)$$

and, for an ideal vapor,

$$P_t = p_A^* + p_B^* + p_C^* + \cdots = \Sigma p^* \qquad (9.18)$$

Since $y_A^* = p_A^*/P_t$, etc., then, for any component J,

$$y_J^* = \frac{p_J^*}{\Sigma p^*} = \frac{P_J x_J}{\Sigma P x} \qquad (9.19)$$

The relative volatility of two substances forming an ideal solution is the ratio of their vapor pressures [Eq. (9.7)], so that the relative volatility of substance J with respect to substance C, for example, is

$$\alpha_{JC} = \frac{P_J}{P_C} \qquad (9.20)$$

Dividing numerator and denominator of Eq. (9.19) by P_C, we obtain, since $\alpha_{CC} = 1$,

$$y_J^* = \frac{\alpha_{JC} x_J}{\alpha_{AC} x_A + \alpha_{BC} x_B + x_C + \alpha_{DC} x_D + \cdots} = \frac{\alpha_{JC} x_J}{\Sigma \alpha x} \qquad (9.21)$$

This form of the equation is sometimes more convenient for computing compositions than Eq. (9.19) since, as has been demonstrated, the relative volatilities change much more slowly with temperature than do vapor pressures.

† Hydrocarbons of different molecular structure, however, frequently form such nonideal solutions that azeotropism occurs, as, for example, in the binary systems hexane–methyl cyclopentane, hexane–benzene, and benzene–cyclohexane.

Illustration 9.3. A liquid contains 50 mole % benzene, 25 mole % toluene, and 25 mole % o-xylene. At 1 atm pressure, compute its bubble point and the composition of the equilibrium vapor. The solution may be considered ideal.

Solution. For a first estimate the temperature of initial boiling (bubble point) will be assumed to be 90°C. This will be the bubble point provided the sum of the partial pressures equals the prevailing total pressure, 760 mm Hg. The following table shows the sum to be only 652.5 mm Hg, and subsequent trials show 95°C to be the correct temperature. The vapor composition is then calculated with the final partial pressures.

| Substance | x | Temp = 90°C | | Temp = 95°C | | y^* |
		Vapor pressure P, mm Hg	$p^* = Px$, mm Hg	Vapor pressure P, mm Hg	$p^* = Px$, mm Hg	
Benzene	0.50	1,030	515 = 0.5(1,030)	1,200	600	0.789 = $^{600}/_{760}$
Toluene	0.25	410	102.5	475	118.5	0.156
o-Xylene	0.25	140	35.0	166	41.5	0.0545
			652.5 = Σp^*		760 = Σp^*	1.0 = Σy^*

Had it been desired to obtain the vapor composition only, the first estimate of the temperature would for many purposes have been satisfactory. As an alternative calculation, relative volatilities may be based on toluene (taken arbitrarily; any of the three substances would have served equally well) and y^* calculated by means of Eq. (9.21) as follows:

Substance	x	P, 90°C, mm Hg	α	αx	y^*
Benzene	0.50	1,030	2.51 = 1,030/410	1.255 = 2.51(0.5)	0.789 = 1.255/1.5905
Toluene	0.25	410	1.0	0.250	0.157
o-Xylene	0.25	140	0.342	0.0855	0.0537
				$\Sigma \alpha x = 1.5905$	$\Sigma y^* = 1.0$

Note that the y^*'s are practically the same as those computed at the correct temperature, 95°C.

For purposes of computing liquid compositions in equilibrium with a given vapor and the dew point, the Raoult's law equations may be written for any component J as

$$x_J = \frac{p_J^*}{P_J} = \frac{P_t y_J^*}{P_J} = \frac{y_J^*/\alpha_{JC}}{\Sigma(y^*/\alpha)} \qquad (9.22)$$

and

$$\Sigma x = 1.0 \qquad (9.23)$$

For cases where the ideal-gas law is inapplicable, fugacities may be used instead of vapor pressures and total pressures, and the ideal-solution law becomes at constant temperature†

$$y_J^* = m_J x_J \tag{9.24}$$

where m for a particular component changes with temperature and pressure, but not with composition.[4]   In this case,

$$\alpha_{JC} = \frac{m_J}{m_C} \tag{9.25}$$

and the expressions for computing bubble points and dew points containing α may still be used.   If in addition the liquid is nonideal, Eq. (9.24) may be used as an empirical relationship with m varying with temperature, pressure, and composition.

It must be emphasized that for all ordinary purposes the vapor-liquid equilibria should be experimentally determined.   Very few systems can be considered sufficiently close to ideality to permit computation of the data from vapor pressures.   The techniques for experimental determination have been reasonably well established, and methods of extending data, which depend on thermodynamic treatment, are also available.[4,12]

SINGLE-STAGE OPERATION—FLASH VAPORIZATION

Flash vaporization, or equilibrium distillation as it is sometimes called, is a single-stage operation wherein a liquid mixture is partially vaporized, the vapor allowed to come to equilibrium with the residual liquid, and the resulting vapor and liquid phases are separated and removed from the apparatus.   It may be carried out batchwise or in continuous fashion.

A typical flow sheet is shown schematically in Fig. 9.13 for continuous operation. Here the liquid feed is heated in a conventional tubular heat exchanger or by passing it through the heated tubes of a fuel-fired furnace.   The pressure is then reduced, vapor forms at the expense of the liquid adiabatically, and the mixture is introduced into a vapor-liquid separating vessel.   The separator shown is of the cyclone type, where the feed is introduced tangentially into a covered annular space.   The liquid portion of the mixture is thrown by centrifugal force to the outer wall and leaves at the bottom, while the vapor rises through the central chimney and leaves at the top. The vapor may then pass to a condenser, not shown in the figure.   Particularly for flash vaporization of a volatile substance from a relatively nonvolatile one, operation in the separator may be carried out under reduced pressure, but not so low that ordinary cooling water will not condense the vapor product.

The product, D moles/hr, richer in the more volatile substance, is in this case entirely a vapor.   The material and enthalpy balances are

$$F = D + W \tag{9.26}$$

$$Fz_F = Dy_D + Wx_W \tag{9.27}$$

$$FH_F + Q = DH_D + WH_W \tag{9.28}$$

---

† K rather than m is frequently used to denote the proportionality between y^* and x.

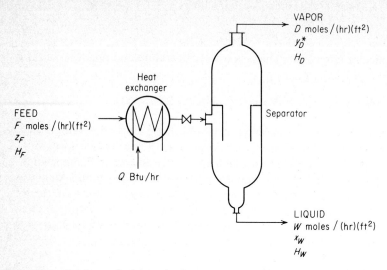

Fig. 9.13 *Continuous flash vaporization.*

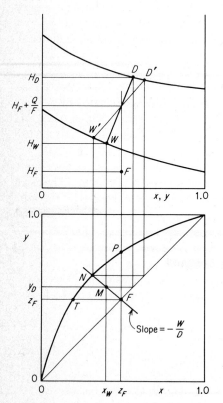

Fig. 9.14 *Flash vaporization.*

These, when solved simultaneously, yield

$$-\frac{W}{D} = \frac{y_D - z_F}{x_W - z_F} = \frac{H_D - (H_F + Q/F)}{H_W - (H_F + Q/F)} \tag{9.29}$$

On the *Hxy* diagram, this represents a straight line through points of coordinates (H_D, y_D) representing D, (H_W, x_W) representing W, and $(H_F + Q/F, z_F)$ representing the feed mixture after it leaves the heat exchanger of Fig. 9.13. It is shown on the upper part of Fig. 9.14 as the line DW. The two left-hand members of Eq. (9.29) represent the usual single-stage operating line on distribution coordinates, of negative slope as for all single-stage (cocurrent) operations (see Chap. 5), passing through compositions representing the influent and effluent streams, points F and M on the lower figure. If the effluent streams were in equilibrium, the device would be an ideal stage, and the products D' and W' would be on a tie line in the upper figure and on the equilibrium curve at N on the lower figure. The richest vapor, but infinitesimal in amount, is that corresponding to P at the bubble point of the feed; and the leanest liquid, but also infinitesimal in amount, is that corresponding to T at the dew point of the feed. The compositions of the actual products will be between these limits, depending upon the extent of vaporization of the feed and the stage efficiency.

Partial condensation

All the equations apply equally well to the case where the feed is a vapor, and Q, the heat removed in the heat exchanger to produce incomplete condensation, is taken as negative. On the upper part of Fig. 9.14, point F is then either a saturated or superheated vapor.

Illustration 9.4. A liquid mixture containing 50 mole % *n*-heptane (*A*), 50 mole % *n*-octane (*B*), at 80°F, is to be continuously flash-vaporized at 1 atm pressure to vaporize 60 mole % of the feed. What will be the composition of the vapor and liquid and the temperature in the separator for an ideal stage?

Solution. *Basis:* $F = 100$ moles feed, $z_F = 0.50$. $D = 60$ moles, $W = 40$ moles, $-W/D = -^{40}\!/_{60} = -0.667$.

The equilibrium data were determined in Illustration 9.1 and are plotted in Fig. 9.15. The point representing the feed composition is plotted at P, and the operating line is drawn with a slope -0.667 to intersect the equilibrium curve at T, where $y_D^* = 0.575$ mole fraction heptane and $x_W = 0.387$ mole fraction heptane. The temperature at T is 113°C (235.4°F $= t_L = t_G$).

Multicomponent systems—ideal solutions

For mixtures which form ideal liquid solutions containing components A, B, C, etc., the equilibrium relation for any component J may be written as

$$y^*_{JD} = m_J x_{JW} \tag{9.30}$$

Equation (9.29) also applies for each of the components, and when combined with Eq. (9.30) for any component J, for an ideal stage

$$\frac{W}{D} = \frac{m_J x_{JW} - z_{JF}}{z_{JF} - x_{JW}} = \frac{y^*_{JD} - z_{JF}}{z_{JF} - y^*_{JD}/m_J} \tag{9.31}$$

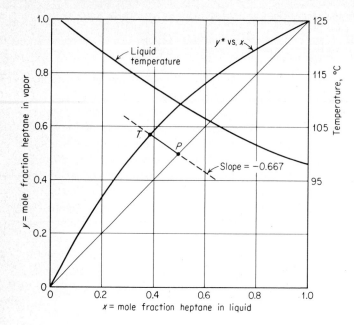

Fig. 9.15   *Solution to Illustration 9.4.*

This provides the following, useful for equilibrium vaporization,

$$y_{JD}^* = \frac{z_{JF}(W/D + 1)}{1 + W/Dm_J} \tag{9.32}$$

$$\Sigma y_D^* = 1.0 \tag{9.33}$$

and for condensation,

$$x_{JW} = \frac{z_{JF}(W/D + 1)}{m_J + W/D} \tag{9.34}$$

$$\Sigma x_W = 1.0 \tag{9.35}$$

Thus Eq. (9.32) may be used for each of the components with appropriate values of m and z_F, and the sum of the y_D^*'s so calculated must equal unity if the correct conditions of W/D, temperature, and pressure have been chosen. A similar interpretation is used for Eqs. (9.34) and (9.35). These expressions reduce in the limit to the dew-point and bubble-point equations (9.22) and (9.21), respectively.

Illustration 9.5. A liquid containing 50 mole % benzene (A), 25 mole % toluene (B), and 25 mole % o-xylene (C) is flash-vaporized at 1 atm pressure and 100°C. Compute the amounts of liquid and vapor products and their compositions. The solutions follow Raoult's law.

Solution. For Raoult's law, $y^* = Px/P_t = mx$, so that for each component $m = P/P_t$. $P_t = 760$ mm Hg. In the following table, column 2 lists the vapor pressures P at 100°C for each substance and column 3 the corresponding value of m. The feed composition is listed in column 4. A value of W/D is arbitrarily chosen as 3.0 and Eq. (9.32) used to compute y_D^*'s in column 5. Since the sum of the y_D^*'s is not unity, a new value of W/D is chosen until finally (column 6) $W/D = 2.08$ is seen to be correct.

Basis: $F = 100$ moles.

$$100 = W + D \qquad \frac{W}{D} = 2.08$$

$$\therefore \quad D = 32.5 \text{ moles} \qquad W = 67.5 \text{ moles}$$

The composition of the residual liquid may be found by material balance or by equilibrium relation, as in column 7.

Substance	$P =$ vapor pressure, mm Hg	$m = \dfrac{P}{760}$	z_F	$\dfrac{W}{D} = 3.0$ $\dfrac{z_F(W/D + 1)}{1 + W/Dm} = y_D^*$	$\dfrac{W}{D} = 2.08$ y_D^*	$x_W = \dfrac{Fz_F - Dy_D^*}{W}$ $= \dfrac{y_D^*}{m}$
(1)	(2)	(3)	(4)	(5)	(6)	(7)
A	1,370	1.803	0.50	$\dfrac{0.5(3 + 1)}{1 + 3/1.803} = 0.750$	0.715	0.397
B	550	0.724	0.25	0.1940	0.1983	0.274
C	200	0.263	0.25	0.0805	0.0865	0.329
				$\Sigma = 1.0245$	0.9998	1.000

Successive flash vaporizations may be made on the residual liquids in a series of single-stage operations, whereupon the separation will be better than that obtained if the same amount of vapor were formed in a single operation. As the amount of vapor formed in each stage becomes smaller and the total number of vaporizations larger, the operation approaches differential distillation in the limit.

DIFFERENTIAL OR SIMPLE DISTILLATION

If during an infinite number of successive flash vaporizations of a liquid only an infinitesimal portion of the liquid were flashed each time, the net result would be equivalent to a differential or simple distillation.

In practice this can only be approximated. A batch of liquid is charged to a kettle or still fitted with some sort of heating device such as a steam jacket, as in Fig. 9.16. The charge is boiled slowly, and the vapors are withdrawn as rapidly as they form to a condenser, where they are liquefied, and the condensate (distillate) is collected in the receiver. The apparatus is essentially a large-scale replica of the ordinary laboratory distillation flask and condenser. The first portion of the distillate will be the richest in the more volatile substance, and as distillation proceeds, the vaporized product becomes leaner. The distillate may therefore be collected in several separate batches, called "cuts," to give a series of distilled products of various purities. Thus, for example, if a ternary mixture contained a small amount of a very

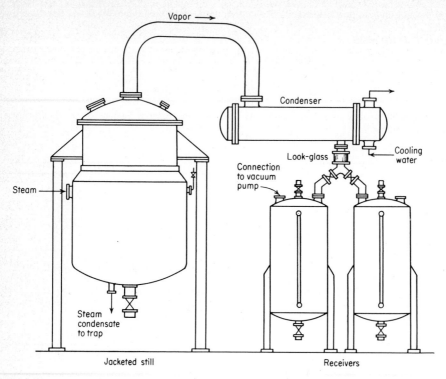

Fig. 9.16 *Batch still.*

volatile substance A, a majority of substance B of intermediate volatility, and a small amount of C of low volatility, the first cut, which would be small, would contain the majority of A. A large second cut would contain the majority of B reasonably pure but nevertheless contaminated with A and C, and the residue left in the kettle would be largely C. While all three cuts would contain all three substances, nevertheless some separation would have been obtained.

For such an operation to approach even approximately the theoretical characteristics of a differential distillation, it would have to proceed infinitely slowly so that the vapor issuing from the liquid would at all times be in equilibrium with the liquid. All entrainment would have to be eliminated, and there could be no cooling and condensation of the vapor prior to its entering the condenser. Despite the fact that these conditions are substantially impossible to attain, it is nevertheless useful to study the limiting results which a differential distillation could produce as a standard for comparison.

Binary mixtures

The vapor issuing from a true differential distillation is at any time in equilibrium with the liquid from which it rises, but changes continuously in composition. The mathematical approach must therefore be differential. Assume that at any time during the course of the distillation there are L moles of liquid in the still of composition x mole fraction A and that an amount dD moles of distillate is vaporized, of mole fraction y^* in equilibrium with the liquid. Then we have the following material balances:

	Total material	Component A
Moles in	0	0
Moles out	dD	$y^* \, dD$
Moles accumulated	dL	$d(Lx) = L \, dx + x \, dL$
In − out = accumulation	$0 - dD = dL$	$0 - y^* \, dD = L \, dx + x \, dL$

The last two equations become

$$y^* \, dL = L \, dx + x \, dL \tag{9.36}$$

$$\int_W^F \frac{dL}{L} = \ln \frac{F}{W} = \int_{x_W}^{x_F} \frac{dx}{y^* - x} \tag{9.37}$$

where F is the moles of charge of composition x_F and W the moles of residual liquid of composition x_W. This is known as the Rayleigh equation, after Lord Rayleigh, who first derived it. It may be used to determine F, W, x_F, or x_W when three of these are known. Integration of the right-hand side of Eq. (9.37), unless an algebraic equilibrium relationship between y^* and x is available, is done graphically by plotting $1/(y^* - x)$ as ordinate against x as abscissa and determining the area under the curve between the indicated limits. The data for this are taken from the vapor-liquid equilibrium relationship. The *composited* distillate composition $y_{D,\mathrm{av}}$ can be determined by a simple material balance,

$$Fx_F = Dy_{D,\mathrm{av}} + Wx_W \tag{9.38}$$

Differential condensation

This is a similar operation where a vapor feed is slowly condensed under equilibrium conditions and the condensate withdrawn as rapidly as it forms. As in the case of distillation, the results can only be approximated in practice. A derivation similar to that above leads to

$$\ln \frac{F}{D} = \int_{y_F}^{y_D} \frac{dy}{y - x^*} \tag{9.39}$$

where F is the moles of feed vapor of composition y_F and D the vaporous residue of composition y_D.

The heat requirements of such processes may be worked out on enthalpy-concentration diagrams.[4]

Constant relative volatility

If Eq. (9.2) can describe the equilibrium relation at constant pressure by use of some average relative volatility α over the concentration range involved, this may be substituted in Eq. (9.37) to yield

$$\ln \frac{F}{W} = \frac{1}{\alpha - 1} \ln \frac{x_F(1 - x_W)}{x_W(1 - x_F)} + \ln \frac{1 - x_W}{1 - x_F} \qquad (9.40)$$

and graphical integration can be avoided. This may be rearranged to another useful form,

$$\log \frac{Fx_F}{Wx_W} = \alpha \log \frac{F(1 - x_F)}{W(1 - x_W)} \qquad (9.41)$$

which relates the number of moles of A remaining in the residue, Wx_W, to that of B remaining, $W(1 - x_W)$. These expressions are most likely to be valid for ideal mixtures, for which α is most nearly constant.

Illustration 9.6. Suppose the liquid of Illustration 9.4 [50 mole % n-heptane (A), 50 mole % n-octane (B)] were subjected to a differential distillation at atmospheric pressure, with 60 mole % of the liquid distilled. Compute the composition of the composited distillate and the residue.

Solution. Basis: $F = 100$ moles. $x_F = 0.50$, $D = 60$ moles, $W = 40$ moles.

Eq. (9.37):
$$\ln \frac{100}{40} = 0.916 = \int_{x_W}^{0.50} \frac{dx}{y^* - x}$$

The equilibrium data are given in Illustrations 9.1 and 9.4. From these, the following are calculated:

x	0.50	0.46	0.42	0.38	0.34	0.32
y^*	0.689	0.648	0.608	0.567	0.523	0.497
$1/(y^* - x)$	5.29	5.32	5.32	5.35	5.50	5.65

x as abscissa is plotted against $1/(y^* - x)$ as ordinate, and the area under the curve obtained beginning at $x_F = 0.50$. When the area equals 0.916, integration is stopped, and this occurs at $x_W = 0.33$ mole fraction heptane in the residue. The composited distillate composition is obtained through Eq. (9.38),

$$100(0.50) = 60y_{D,\text{av}} + 40(0.33)$$

$$y_{D,\text{av}} = 0.614 \text{ mole fraction heptane}$$

Note that, for the same percentage vaporization, the separation in this case is better than that obtained by flash vaporization, i.e., each product is purer in its majority component.

Alternatively, since for this system the average $\alpha = 2.16$ at 1 atm (Illustration 9.1),

Eq. (9.41):
$$\log \frac{100(0.5)}{40x_W} = 2.16 \log \frac{100(1 - 0.5)}{40(1 - x_W)}$$

from which by trial and error $x_W = 0.33$.

Multicomponent systems—ideal solutions

For multicomponent systems forming ideal liquid solutions, Eq. (9.41) can be written for any two components. Ordinarily one component is chosen on which to base the relative volatilities, whereupon Eq. (9.41) is written once for each of the others. For example, for substance J, with relative volatility based on substance B,

$$\log \frac{Fx_{JF}}{Wx_{JW}} = \alpha_{JB} \log \frac{Fx_{BF}}{Wx_{BW}} \tag{9.42}$$

and
$$\Sigma x_W = 1.0 \tag{9.43}$$

where x_{JF} is the mole fraction of J in the feed, x_{JW} that in the residue.

Illustration 9.7. A liquid containing 50 mole % benzene (A), 25 mole % toluene (B), and 25 mole % o-xylene (C) is differentially distilled at 1 atm, with vaporization of 32.5 mole % of the charge. Raoult's law applies. Compute the distillate and residue compositions. Note that this is the same degree of vaporization as in Illustration 9.5.

Solution. The average temperature will be somewhat higher than the bubble point of the feed (see Illustration 9.3) but is unknown. It will be taken as 100°C. Corrections can later be made by computing the bubble point of the residue and repeating the work, but α's vary little with moderate changes in temperature. The vapor pressures at 100°C are tabulated and α's calculated relative to toluene, as follows:

Substance	$P =$ vapor pressure, 100°C, mm Hg	α	x_F
A	1,370	1,370/550 = 2.49	0.50
B	550	1.0	0.25
C	200	0.364	0.25

Basis: $F = 100$ moles, $D = 32.5$ moles, $W = 67.5$ moles.

Eq. (9.42): For A, $\log \dfrac{100(0.50)}{67.5x_{AW}} = 2.49 \log \dfrac{100(0.25)}{67.5x_{BW}}$

For C, $\log \dfrac{100(0.25)}{67.5x_{CW}} = 0.364 \log \dfrac{100(0.25)}{67.5x_{BW}}$

Eq. (9.43): $x_{AW} + x_{BW} + x_{CW} = 1.0$

Solving simultaneously by assuming values of x_{BW}, computing x_{AW} and x_{CW}, and checking their sum until it equals unity, there is obtained $x_{AW} = 0.385$, $x_{BW} = 0.285$, $x_{CW} = 0.335$. The sum is 1.005, which is taken as satisfactory.

The composited distillate composition is computed by material balances.

For A, $100(0.50) = 32.5y_{AD,av} + 67.5(0.385)$ $y_{AD,av} = 0.742$

Similarly,
$$y_{BD,av} = 0.178 \quad \text{and} \quad y_{CD,av} = 0.075$$

Note the improved separation over that obtained by flash vaporization (Illustration 9.5).

CONTINUOUS RECTIFICATION—BINARY SYSTEMS

Continuous rectification, or fractionation, is a multistage countercurrent distillation operation. For a binary solution, with certain exceptions it is ordinarily possible by this method to separate the solution into its components, recovering each in any state of purity that is desired.

The fractionation operation

In order to understand how such an operation is carried out, recall the discussion of reboiled absorbers in Chap. 8 and Fig. 8.26. There, because the liquid leaving the bottom of an absorber is at best in equilibrium with the feed and may therefore contain substantial concentrations of volatile component, trays installed below the feed point were provided with vapor generated by a reboiler to strip out the volatile component from the liquid. This component then entered the vapor and left the tower at the top. The upper section of the tower served to wash the gas free of less volatile component, which entered the liquid to leave at the bottom.

So, too, with distillation. Refer to Fig. 9.17. Here the feed is introduced more or less centrally into a vertical cascade of stages. Vapor rising in the section above the feed (called the *absorption*, *enriching*, or *rectifying* section) is washed with liquid to remove or absorb the less volatile component. Since no extraneous material is added, as in the case of absorption, the washing liquid in this case is provided by condensing the vapor issuing from the top, which is rich in more volatile component. The liquid returned to the top of the tower is called *reflux*, and the material permanently removed is the *distillate*, which may be a vapor or a liquid, rich in more volatile component. In the section below the feed (*stripping* or *exhausting* section), the liquid is stripped of volatile component by vapor produced at the bottom by partial vaporization of the bottom liquid in the reboiler. The liquid removed, rich in less volatile component, is the *residue*, or *bottoms*. Inside the tower, the liquids and vapors are always at their bubble points and dew points, respectively, so that the highest temperatures are at the bottom, the lowest at the top. The entire device is called a *fractionator*.

The purities obtained for the two withdrawn products will depend upon the liquid/gas ratios used and the number of ideal stages provided in the two sections of the tower, and the interrelation of these must now be established. The cross-sectional area of the tower, however, is governed entirely by the quantities of materials handled, in accordance with the principles of Chap. 6.

Overall enthalpy balances

In Fig. 9.17, the ideal trays are numbered from the top down, and subscripts generally indicate the tray from which a stream originates: for example, L_n is moles liquid/hr falling from the nth tray. A bar over the quantity indicates that it applies to the section of the column below the point of introduction of the feed. The distillate product may be liquid, vapor, or a mixture. The reflux, however, must be liquid. The molar ratio of reflux to withdrawn distillate is the *reflux ratio*, sometimes called

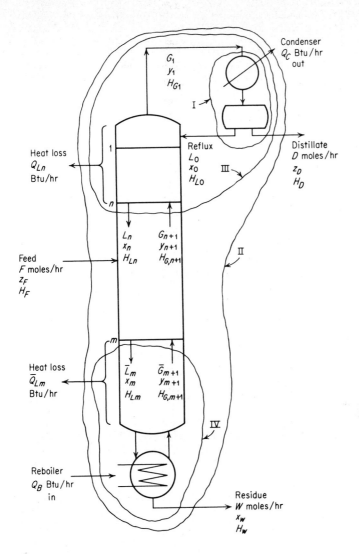

Fig. 9.17 *Material and enthalpy balance of a fractionator.*

the *external* reflux ratio,

$$R = \frac{L_0}{D} \tag{9.44}$$

which is specified in accordance with principles to be established later.

Consider the condenser, envelope I (Fig. 9.17). A total material balance is

$$G_1 = D + L_0 \tag{9.45}$$

or

$$G_1 = D + RD = D(R + 1) \tag{9.46}$$

For substance A

$$G_1 y_1 = D z_D + L_0 x_0 \tag{9.47}$$

Equations (9.45) to (9.47) establish the concentrations and quantities at the top of the tower.   An enthalpy balance, envelope I,

$$G_1 H_{G1} = Q_C + L_0 H_{L0} + D H_D \tag{9.48}$$

$$Q_C = D[(R + 1)H_{G1} - R H_{L0} - H_D] \tag{9.49}$$

provides the heat load of the condenser.   The reboiler heat is then obtained by a complete enthalpy balance about the entire apparatus, envelope II,

$$Q_B = D H_D + W H_W + Q_C + Q_L - F H_F \tag{9.50}$$

where Q_L is the sum of all the heat losses.   Heat economy is frequently obtained by heat exchange between the residue product, which issues from the column at its bubble point, and the feed for purposes of preheating the feed.   Equation (9.50) still applies provided that any such exchanger is included inside envelope II.

Two methods will be used to develop the relationship among numbers of trays, liquid/vapor ratios, and product compositions.   The first of these, the method of Ponchon and Savarit,[4,29,31,33] is rigorous and can handle all situations, but it requires detailed enthalpy data for its application.   The second, the method of McCabe and Thiele,[26] a simplification requiring only concentration equilibria, is less rigorous yet nevertheless adequate for many purposes.†

MULTISTAGE (TRAY) TOWERS—THE METHOD OF PONCHON AND SAVARIT

The method will first be developed for the case of negligible heat losses.

The enriching section

Consider the enriching section through tray n, envelope III, Fig. 9.17.   Tray n is any tray in this section.   Material balances for the section are, for total material,

$$G_{n+1} = L_n + D \tag{9.51}$$

and for component A,

$$G_{n+1} y_{n+1} = L_n x_n + D z_D \tag{9.52}$$

$$G_{n+1} y_{n+1} - L_n x_n = D z_D \tag{9.53}$$

The left-hand side of Eq. (9.53) represents the difference in rate of flow of component A, up − down, or the net flow upward.   Since for a given distillation the right-hand side is constant, it follows that the difference, or net rate of flow of A upward, is constant, independent of tray number in this section of the tower, and equal to that permanently withdrawn at the top.

An enthalpy balance, envelope III, with *heat loss negligible*, is

$$G_{n+1} H_{G,n+1} = L_n H_{Ln} + Q_C + D H_D \tag{9.54}$$

† The treatment of the McCabe-Thiele method is complete in itself, and may be referred to directly, if desired.

Let Q' be the heat removed in the condenser and the permanently removed distillate, per mole of distillate.   Then

$$Q' = \frac{Q_C + DH_D}{D} = \frac{Q_C}{D} + H_D \tag{9.55}$$

and

$$G_{n+1}H_{G,n+1} - L_n H_{Ln} = DQ' \tag{9.56}$$

The left-hand side of Eq. (9.56) represents the difference in rate of flow of heat, up — down, or the net flow upward.   Since for a given set of circumstances the right-hand side is constant, then the difference, or net rate of flow upward, is constant, independent of tray number in this section of the tower, and equal to that permanently taken out at the top with the distillate and at the condenser.

Elimination of D between Eqs. (9.51) and (9.52) and between Eqs. (9.51) and (9.56) yields

$$\frac{L_n}{G_{n+1}} = \frac{z_D - y_{n+1}}{z_D - x_n} = \frac{Q' - H_{G,n+1}}{Q' - H_{Ln}} \tag{9.57}$$

L_n/G_{n+1} is called the *internal reflux ratio*.

On the *Hxy* diagram, Eq. (9.57) is the equation of a straight line through $(H_{G,n+1}, y_{n+1})$ at G_{n+1}, (H_{Ln}, x_n) at L_n, and (Q', z_D) at Δ_D.   The last is called a *difference point*, since its coordinates represent differences in rates of flow:

$$\Delta_D \begin{cases} Q' = \dfrac{\text{difference in heat flow, up} - \text{down}}{\text{net moles total substance out}} = \dfrac{\text{net heat out}}{\text{net moles out}} \\[3mm] z_D = \dfrac{\text{difference in flow of component } A, \text{ up} - \text{down}}{\text{net moles total substance out}} = \dfrac{\text{net moles } A \text{ out}}{\text{net moles out}} \end{cases}$$

Δ_D then represents a fictitious stream, in amount equal to the net flow outward (in this case D) and of properties (Q', z_D) such that

$$G_{n+1} - L_n = \Delta_D \tag{9.58}$$

On the *xy* diagram, Eq. (9.57) is the equation of a straight line of slope L_n/G_{n+1}, through (y_{n+1}, x_n) and $y = x = z_D$.   These are plotted on Fig. 9.18, where both diagrams are shown.

Figure 9.18 is drawn for the case of a total condenser.   The distillate D and reflux L_0 then have identical coordinates and are plotted at point D.   The location shown indicates that they are below the bubble point.   If they were at the bubble point, D would be on the saturated-liquid curve.   The saturated vapor G_1 from the top tray, when totally condensed, has the same composition as D and L_0.   Liquid L_1 leaving ideal tray 1 is in equilibrium with G_1 and is located at the end of tie line 1. Since Eq. (9.57) applies to all trays in this section, G_2 can be located on the saturated-vapor curve by a line drawn from L_1 to Δ_D; tie line 2 through G_2 locates L_2, etc. Thus, alternate tie lines (each representing the effluents from an ideal tray) and construction lines through Δ_D provide the stepwise changes in concentration occurring

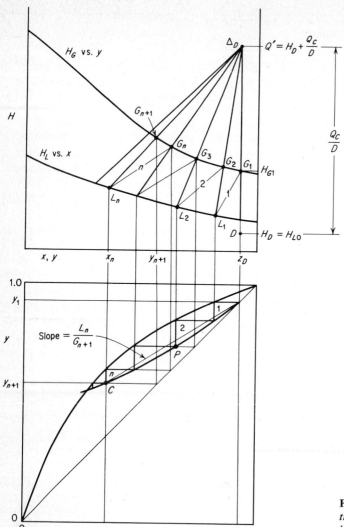

Fig. 9.18 *Enriching section, total condenser, reflux below the bubble point.*

in the enriching section. Intersections of the lines radiating from Δ_D with the saturated-enthalpy curves, such as points G_3 and L_2, when projected to the lower diagram, produce points such as P. These in turn produce the operating curve CP, which passes through $y = x = z_D$. The tie lines, when projected downward, produce the equilibrium-distribution curve, and the stepwise nature of the concentration changes with tray number then becomes obvious. The difference point Δ_D is used in this manner for all trays in the enriching section, working downward until the feed tray is reached.

Enriching trays may thus be located on the Hxy diagram alone by alternating construction lines to Δ_D and tie lines, each tie line representing an ideal tray. As an alternative, random lines radiating from Δ_D may be drawn, their intersections with the $H_G y$ and $H_L x$ curves plotted on the xy diagram to produce the operating curve, and the trays determined by the step construction typical of such diagrams.

At any tray n (compare Fig. 9.12) the L_n/G_{n+1} ratio is given by the ratio of line lengths $\Delta_D G_{n+1}/\Delta_D L_n$ on the upper diagram of Fig. 9.18 or by the slope of the chord as shown on the lower diagram. Substituting Eq. (9.51) into Eq. (9.57) provides

$$\frac{L_n}{L_n + D} = \frac{H_{G,n+1} - Q'}{H_{Ln} - Q'} = \frac{y_{n+1} - z_D}{x_n - z_D} \tag{9.59}$$

which can be arranged to

$$\frac{L_n}{D} = \frac{Q' - H_{G,n+1}}{H_{G,n+1} - H_{Ln}} = \frac{z_D - y_{n+1}}{y_{n+1} - x_n} \tag{9.60}$$

Applying this to the top tray provides the external reflux ratio, which is usually the one specified:

$$R = \frac{L_0}{D} = \frac{Q' - H_{G1}}{H_{G1} - H_{L0}} = \frac{\text{line } \Delta_D G_1}{\text{line } G_1 L_0} = \frac{\text{line } \Delta_D G_1}{\text{line } G_1 D} \tag{9.61}$$

For a given reflux ratio, the line-length ratio of Eq. (9.61) may be used to locate Δ_D vertically on Fig. 9.18, and the ordinate Q' may then be used to compute the condenser heat load.

In some cases a *partial condenser* is used, as in Fig. 9.19. Here a saturated vapor distillate D is withdrawn, and the condensate provides the reflux. This is frequently done when the pressure required for complete condensation of the vapor G_1, at reasonable condenser temperatures, would be too large. The Δ_D is plotted at an abscissa y_D corresponding to the composition of the withdrawn distillate. Assuming that an equilibrium condensation is realized, reflux L_0 is at the end of the tie line C. G_1 is located by the construction line $L_0\Delta_D$, etc. In the lower diagram, the line MN solves the equilibrium-condensation problem (compare Fig. 9.14). The reflux ratio $R = L_0/D = \text{line } \Delta_D G_1/\text{line } G_1 L_0$, by application of Eq. (9.61). It is seen that the equilibrium partial condenser provides one ideal tray's worth of rectification. However, it is safest not to rely on such complete enrichment by the condenser and instead to provide trays in the tower equivalent to all the stages required.

The stripping section

Consider the envelope IV, Fig. 9.17, where tray m is any tray in the stripping section. A balance for total material is

$$\bar{L}_m = \bar{G}_{m+1} + W \tag{9.62}$$

and, for component A,

$$\bar{L}_m x_m = \bar{G}_{m+1} y_{m+1} + W x_W \tag{9.63}$$

$$\bar{L}_m x_m - \bar{G}_{m+1} y_{m+1} = W x_W \tag{9.64}$$

The left-hand side of Eq. (9.64) represents the difference in rate of flow of component A, down $-$ up, or the net flow downward. Since the right-hand side is a constant

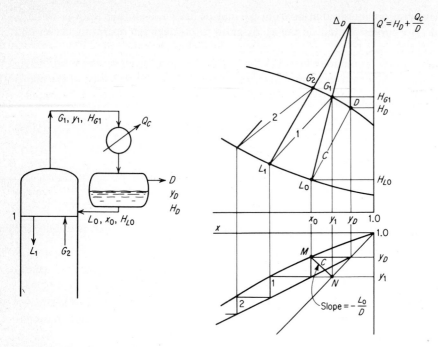

Fig. 9.19   *Partial condenser.*

for a given distillation, the difference is independent of tray number in this section of the tower and equal to the rate of permanent removal of A out the bottom.   An enthalpy balance is

$$L_m H_{Lm} + Q_B = \bar{G}_{m+1} H_{G,m+1} + W H_W \tag{9.65}$$

Define Q'' as the net flow of heat outward at the bottom, per mole of residue

$$Q'' = \frac{W H_W - Q_B}{W} = H_W - \frac{Q_B}{W} \tag{9.66}$$

whence

$$L_m H_{Lm} - \bar{G}_{m+1} H_{G,m+1} = W Q'' \tag{9.67}$$

The left-hand side of Eq. (9.67) is the difference in rate of flow of heat, down — up, which then equals the constant net rate of heat flow out the bottom for all trays in this section.

Elimination of W between Eqs. (9.62) and (9.63) and between Eqs. (9.62) and (9.67) provides

$$\frac{L_m}{\bar{G}_{m+1}} = \frac{y_{m+1} - x_W}{x_m - x_W} = \frac{H_{G,m+1} - Q''}{H_{Lm} - Q''} \tag{9.68}$$

On the Hxy diagram, Eq. (9.68) is a straight line through $(H_{G,m+1}, y_{m+1})$ at $\bar{G}_{m+1}$, (H_{Lm}, x_m) at L_m, and (Q'', x_W) at Δ_W. Δ_W is a *difference* point, whose coordinates mean

$$\Delta_W \begin{cases} Q'' = \dfrac{\text{difference in heat flow, down } - \text{ up}}{\text{net moles of total substance out}} = \dfrac{\text{net heat out}}{\text{net moles out}} \\[2em] x_W = \dfrac{\text{difference in flow of component } A, \text{ down } - \text{ up}}{\text{net moles of total substance out}} = \dfrac{\text{moles } A \text{ out}}{\text{net moles out}} \end{cases}$$

Thus, Δ_W is a fictitious stream, in amount equal to the net flow outward (in this case W), of properties (Q'',x_W),

$$\bar{L}_m - \bar{G}_{m+1} = \Delta_W \qquad (9.69)$$

On the xy diagram, Eq. (9.68) is a straight line of slope $\bar{L}_m/\bar{G}_{m+1}$, through (y_{m+1},x_m) and $y = x = x_W$. These straight lines are plotted on Fig. 9.20 for both diagrams.

Since Eq. (9.68) applies to all trays of the stripping section, the line on the Hxy plot of Fig. 9.20 from $\bar{G}_{Np+1}$ (vapor leaving the reboiler and entering the bottom tray N_p of the tower) to Δ_W intersects the saturated-liquid–enthalpy curve at $\bar{L}_{Np}$, the liquid leaving the bottom tray. Vapor $\bar{G}_{Np}$ leaving the bottom tray is in equilibrium with liquid $\bar{L}_{Np}$ and is located on the tie line N_p. Tie lines projected to the xy diagram produce points on the equilibrium curve, and lines through Δ_W provide points such as T on the operating curve. Substitution of Eq. (9.62) into Eq. (9.68) provides

$$\frac{\bar{L}_m}{W} = \frac{H_{G,m+1} - Q''}{H_{G,m+1} - H_{Lm}} = \frac{y_{m+1} - x_W}{y_{m+1} - x_m} \qquad (9.70)$$

The diagrams have been drawn for the type of reboiler shown in Fig. 9.17, where the vapor leaving the reboiler is in equilibrium with the residue, the reboiler thus providing an ideal stage of enrichment (tie line B, Fig. 9.20). Other methods of applying heat at the bottom of the still are considered later.

Stripping-section trays may thus be determined entirely on the Hxy diagram by alternating construction lines to Δ_W and tie lines, each tie line accounting for an ideal stage. Alternatively, random lines radiating from Δ_W may be drawn, their intersections with curves $H_G y$ and $H_L x$ plotted on the xy diagram to produce the operating curve, and the stages determined by the usual step construction.

The complete fractionator

Envelope II of Fig. 9.17 may be used for material balances over the entire device

$$F = D + W \qquad (9.71)$$

$$Fz_F = Dz_D + Wx_W \qquad (9.72)$$

Equation (9.50) is a complete enthalpy balance. If, in the absence of heat losses ($Q_L = 0$), the definitions of Q' and Q'' are substituted into Eq. (9.50), it becomes

$$FH_F = DQ' + WQ'' \qquad (9.73)$$

If F is eliminated from Eqs. (9.71) to (9.73), there results

$$\frac{D}{W} = \frac{z_F - x_W}{z_D - z_F} = \frac{H_F - Q''}{Q' - H_F} \qquad (9.74)$$

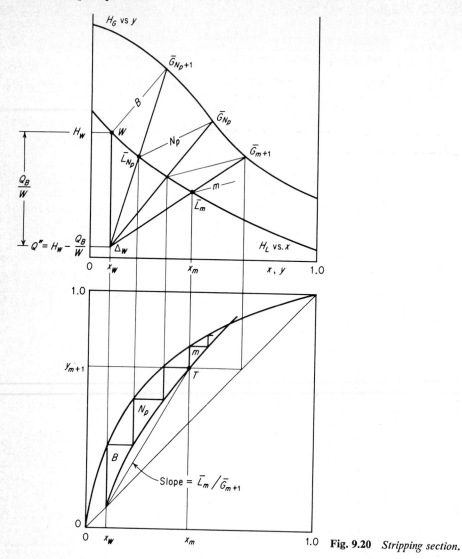

Fig. 9.20 *Stripping section.*

This is the equation of a straight line on the Hxy diagram, through (Q', z_D) at Δ_D, (H_F, z_F) at F, and (Q'', x_W) at Δ_W, as plotted in Fig. 9.21. In other words,

$$F = \Delta_D + \Delta_W \tag{9.75}$$

The location of F, representing the feed, on Fig. 9.21 shows the feed in this case to be a liquid below the bubble point. In other situations, F may be on the saturated-liquid or vapor curve, between them, or above the saturated-vapor curve. In any event, the two Δ points and F must lie on a single straight line.

The construction for trays is now clear. After locating F and the concentration

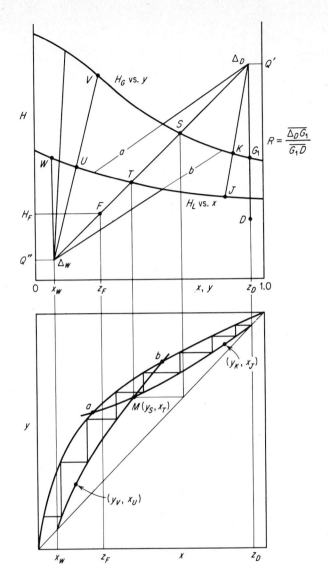

$$R = \frac{\overline{\Delta_D G_1}}{\overline{G_1 D}}$$

Fig. 9.21 *The entire fractionator. Feed below the bubble point and a total condenser.*

abscissas z_D and x_W corresponding to the products on the *Hxy* diagram, Δ_D is located vertically on line $x = z_D$ by computation of Q' or by the line-length ratio of Eq. (9.61) using the specified reflux ratio R. The line $\Delta_D F$ extended to $x = x_W$ locates Δ_W, whose ordinate may be used to compute Q_B. Random lines such as $\Delta_D J$ are drawn from Δ_D to locate the enriching-section operating curve on the *xy* diagram, and random lines such as $\Delta_W V$ are used to locate the stripping-section operating curve on the lower diagram. The operating curves intersect at M, related to the line $\Delta_D F \Delta_W$ in the manner shown. They intersect the equilibrium curve at a and b, corresponding to the tie lines on the *Hxy* diagram which, when extended, pass through

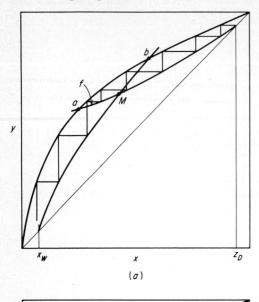

(a)

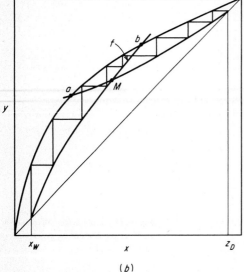

(b)

Fig. 9.22 *Delayed and early feed entries.*

Δ_D and Δ_W, respectively, as shown.   Steps are drawn on the xy diagram between operating curves and equilibrium curve, beginning usually at $x = y = z_D$ (or at $x = y = x_W$ if desired), each step representing an ideal stage or tray.   A change is made from the enriching to the stripping operating curve *at the tray on which the feed is introduced;* in the case shown the feed is to be introduced on the tray whose step straddles point M.   The step construction is then continued to $x = y = x_W$.

Liquid and vapor flow rates may be computed throughout the fractionator from the line-length ratios [Eqs. (9.57), (9.60), (9.68), and (9.70)] on the Hxy diagram.

Feed-tray location

The material and enthalpy balances from which the operating curves are derived dictate that the stepwise construction of Fig. 9.21 must change operating lines at the tray where the feed is to be introduced. Refer to Fig. 9.22, where the equilibrium and operating curves of Fig. 9.21 are reproduced. In stepping down from the top of the fractionator, it is clear that, as shown in Fig. 9.22a, the enriching curve could have been used to a position as close to point a as desired. As point a is approached, however, the change in composition produced by each tray diminishes, and at a a *pinch* develops. As shown, tray f is the feed tray. Alternatively, the stripping operating curve could have been used at the first opportunity after passing point b, to provide the feed tray f of Fig. 9.22b (had the construction begun at x_W, introduction of feed might have been delayed to as near point b as desired, whereupon a pinch would develop at b).

In the design of a new fractionator, the smallest number of trays for the circumstances at hand is desired. This requires that the distance between operating and equilibrium curves be kept always as large as possible, which will occur if the feed tray is taken as that which straddles the operating-curve intersection at M, as in Fig. 9.21. The total number of trays for either Fig. 9.22a or b is of necessity larger. Delayed or early feed entry, as shown in these figures, is used only in cases where a separation is being adapted to an existing tower equipped with a feed-tray entry nozzle on a particular tray, which must then be used.

Consider again the feed tray of Fig. 9.21. It is understood that if the feed is all liquid, it is introduced above the tray in such a manner that it enters the tray along with the liquid from the tray above. Conversely, if the feed is all vapor, it is introduced underneath the feed tray. Should the feed be a mixed liquid and vapor, in principle it should be separated outside the column and the liquid portion introduced above, the vapor portion below, the feed tray. This is rarely done, and the mixed feed is usually introduced into the column without prior separation for reasons of economy. This will have only a small influence on the number of trays required.[3]

Increased reflux ratio

As the reflux ratio $R = L_0/D$ is increased, the Δ_D difference point on Fig. 9.21 must be located at higher values of Q'. Since Δ_D, F, and Δ_W are always on the same line, increasing the reflux ratio lowers the location of Δ_W. These changes result in larger values of L_n/G_{n+1} and smaller values of $\bar{L}_m/\bar{G}_{m+1}$, and the operating curves on the *xy* diagram move closer to the 45° diagonal. Fewer trays are then required, but Q_C, Q_W, L, $\bar{L}$, G, and $\bar{G}$ all increase; condenser and reboiler surfaces and tower cross section must be increased to accommodate the larger loads.

Total reflux

Ultimately, when $R = \infty$, $L_n/G_{n+1} = \bar{L}_m/\bar{G}_{m+1} = 1$, the operating curves both coincide with the 45° line on the *xy* plot, the Δ points are at infinity on the *Hxy* plot, and the number of trays required is the minimum value, N_m. This is shown on Fig. 9.23. The condition may be realized practically by returning all the distillate to the

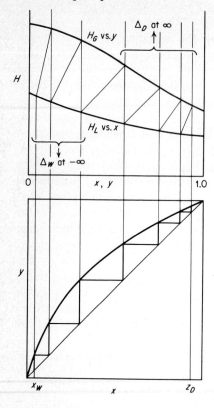

Fig. 9.23 *Total reflux and minimum stages.*

top tray as reflux and reboiling all the residue, whereupon the feed to the tower must be stopped.

Constant relative volatility

A useful analytical expression for the minimum number of theoretical stages can be obtained for cases where the relative volatility is reasonably constant.[9,39] Applying Eq. (9.2) to the residue product,

$$\frac{y_W}{1 - y_W} = \alpha_W \frac{x_W}{1 - x_W} \tag{9.76}$$

where α_W is the relative volatility at the reboiler. At total reflux the operating line coincides with the 45° diagonal so that $y_W = x_{Nm}$. Therefore

$$\frac{x_{Nm}}{1 - x_{Nm}} = \alpha_W \frac{x_W}{1 - x_W} \tag{9.77}$$

Similarly for the last tray of the column, where α_{Nm} pertains,

$$\frac{y_{Nm}}{1 - y_{Nm}} = \alpha_{Nm} \frac{x_{Nm}}{1 - x_{Nm}} = \alpha_{Nm}\alpha_W \frac{x_W}{1 - x_W} \tag{9.78}$$

This procedure may be continued up the column until ultimately

$$\frac{y_1}{1 - y_1} = \frac{x_D}{1 - x_D} = \alpha_1 \alpha_2 \cdots \alpha_{Nm} \alpha_W \frac{x_W}{1 - x_W} \tag{9.79}$$

If some average relative volatility α_{av} can be used,

$$\frac{x_D}{1 - x_D} = \alpha_{av}^{N_m+1} \frac{x_W}{1 - x_W} \tag{9.80}$$

or

$$N_m + 1 = \frac{\log \dfrac{x_D}{1 - x_D} \dfrac{1 - x_W}{x_W}}{\log \alpha_{av}} \tag{9.81}$$

which is known as Fenske's equation.   The total minimum number of theoretical stages to produce products x_D and x_W is $N_m + 1$, which then includes the reboiler.   For small variations in α, α_{av} may be taken as the geometric average of the values for the overhead and bottom products $\sqrt{\alpha_1 \alpha_W}$. The expression may be used only with nearly ideal mixtures, for which α is nearly constant.

Minimum reflux ratio

The minimum reflux ratio R_m is the maximum ratio which will require an infinite number of trays for the separation desired, and it corresponds to the minimum reboiler heat load and condenser cooling load for the separation.

Refer to Fig. 9.24a, where the lightly drawn lines are tie lines which have been extended to intersect lines $x = z_D$ and $x = x_W$.   It is clear that if Δ_D were located at point K, alternate tie lines and construction lines to Δ_D at the tie line k would coincide, and an infinite number of stages would be required to reach tie line k from the top of the tower.   The same is true if Δ_W is located at point J.   Since as Δ_D is moved upward and Δ_W downward the reflux ratio increases, the definition of minimum reflux ratio requires Δ_{Dm} and Δ_{Wm} for the minimum reflux ratio to be located as shown, with Δ_{Dm} at the highest tie-line intersection and Δ_{Wm} at the lowest tie-line intersection.   In this case, it is the tie line which, when extended, passes through F, the feed, that determines both, and this is always the case when the xy equilibrium distribution curve is everywhere concave downward.

For some positively deviating mixtures with a tendency to form an azeotrope, an enriching-section tie line m in Fig. 9.24b gives the highest intersection with $x = z_D$, not that which passes through F.   Similarly, as in Fig. 9.24c for some negatively deviating mixtures, a stripping-section tie line p gives the lowest intersection with $x = x_W$.   These then govern the location of Δ_{Dm} as shown.   For the minimum reflux ratio, either Δ_{Dm} is located at the highest intersection of an enriching-section tie line with $x = z_D$, or Δ_{Wm} is at the lowest intersection of a stripping-section tie line with $x = x_W$, consistent with the requirements that Δ_{Dm}, Δ_{Wm}, and F all be on the same straight line and Δ_{Dm} be at the highest position resulting in a pinch.

Once Q'_m is determined, the minimum reflux ratio may be computed through Eq. (9.61).   Some larger reflux ratio must obviously be used for practical separations, whereupon Δ_D is located above Δ_{Dm}.

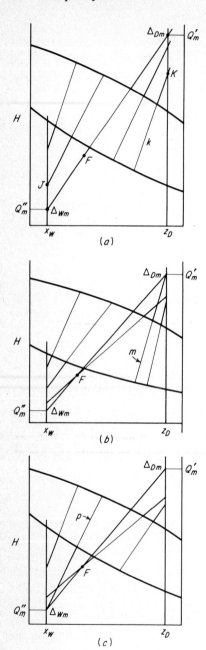

Fig. 9.24 *Minimum reflux ratio.*

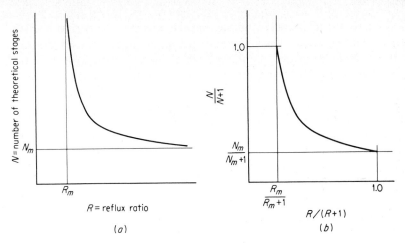

Fig. 9.25 *Reflux ratio–stage relation.*

Optimum reflux ratio

Any reflux ratio between the minimum and infinity will provide the desired separation, with the corresponding number of theoretical trays required varying from infinity to the minimum number, as in Fig. 9.25a. Determination of the number of trays at several values of R, together with the limiting values of N_m and R_m, will usually permit plotting the entire curve with sufficient accuracy for most purposes. The coordinate system of Fig. 9.25b[11] will permit locating the ends of the curve readily by avoiding the awkward asymptotes. There have been several attempts at generalizing the curves of Fig. 9.25,[2,7,11,13] but the resulting charts yield only approximate results.

The reflux ratio which should be used for a new design should be the optimum, or the most economical, reflux ratio, for which the costs will be the least. Refer to Fig. 9.26. At the minimum reflux ratio the column requires an infinite number of

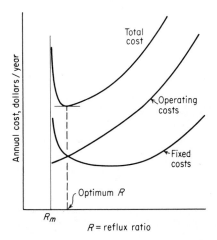

Fig. 9.26 *Most economical (optimum) reflux ratio.*

trays, and consequently the fixed cost is infinite, but the operating costs (heat for the reboiler, condenser cooling water, power for reflux pump) are least. As R increases, the number of trays rapidly decreases, but the column diameter increases owing to the larger quantities of recycled liquid and vapor per unit quantity of feed. The condenser, reflux pump, and reboiler must also be larger. The fixed costs therefore fall through a minimum and rise to infinity again at total reflux. The heat and cooling requirements increase almost directly with reflux ratio, as shown. The total cost, which is the sum of operating and fixed costs, must therefore pass through a minimum at the optimum reflux ratio. This will frequently but not always occur at a reflux ratio near the minimum value ($1.2R_m$ to $1.5R_m$).

Illustration 9.8. Five thousand pounds per hour of a methanol (A)–water (B) solution containing 50 wt % methanol at 80°F is to be continuously rectified at 1 atm pressure to provide a distillate containing 95% methanol and a residue containing 1.0% methanol (by weight). The feed is to be preheated by heat exchange with the residue, which will leave the system at 100°F. The distillate is to be totally condensed to a liquid and the reflux returned at the bubble point. The withdrawn distillate will be separately cooled before storage. A reflux ratio of 1.5 times the minimum will be used. Determine (*a*) quantity of the products; (*b*) enthalpy of feed and of products; (*c*) minimum reflux ratio; (*d*) minimum number of theoretical trays; (*e*) condenser and reboiler heat loads for specified reflux ratio; (*f*) number of theoretical trays for specified reflux ratio, and liquid and vapor quantities inside the tower.

Solution. a. Mol wt methanol = 32.04, mol wt water = 18.02. *Basis:* 1 hr. Define quantities in terms of moles/hr.

$$F = \frac{5{,}000(0.50)}{32.04} + \frac{5{,}000(0.50)}{18.02} = 78.0 + 138.8 = 216.8 \text{ moles/hr}$$

$$z_F = \frac{78}{216.8} = 0.360 \text{ mole fraction methanol}$$

$$M_{av} \text{ for feed} = \frac{5{,}000}{216.8} = 23.1 \text{ lb/mole}$$

$$x_D = \frac{95/32.04}{95/32.04 + 5/18.02} = \frac{2.94}{3.217} = 0.915 \text{ mole fraction methanol}$$

$$M_{av} \text{ for distillate} = \frac{100}{3.217} = 31.1 \text{ lb/mole}$$

$$x_W = \frac{1/32.04}{1/32.04 + 99/18.02} = \frac{0.0312}{5.53} = 0.00565 \text{ mole fraction methanol}$$

$$M_{av} \text{ for residue} = \frac{100}{5.53} = 18.08 \text{ lb/mole}$$

Eq. (9.71): $$216.8 = D + W$$

Eq. (9.72): $$216.8(0.360) = D(0.915) + W(0.00565)$$

Solving simultaneously,

$$D = 84.4 \text{ moles/hr, or } 84.4(31.1) = 2{,}620 \text{ lb/hr}$$

$$W = 132.4 \text{ moles/hr, or } 132.4(18.08) = 2{,}380 \text{ lb/hr}$$

b. The vapor-liquid equilibria at 1 atm pressure are given in "The Chemical Engineers' Handbook," 4th ed., p. 13-5, specific heats of liquid solutions on p. 3-133, and latent heats of vaporization of methanol on p. 3-114. Heats of solution are available in "International Critical Tables," vol. V, p. 159, at 19.69°C = 67.5°F, which will be used as t_o, the base temperature for computing enthalpies.

To compute enthalpies of saturated liquids, consider the case of $x = 0.3$ mole fraction methanol, $M_{av} = 22.2$. The bubble point = 172.4°F, specific heat = 0.92 Btu/lb°F, and the heat of solution is listed as 3.055 kilojoules evolved per gram mole methanol.

$$\Delta H_s = -3.055(238.9)(0.3)(1.8) = -394 \text{ Btu/lb mole solution}$$

where 238.9 converts from kilojoules to calories, 0.3 converts g moles methanol to g moles solution, and 1.8 to Btu/lb mole. Therefore, Eq. (9.10):

$$H_L = 0.92(172.4 - 67.5)22.2 - 394 = 1,746 \text{ Btu/lb mole}$$

To compute the enthalpy of saturated vapors, consider the case of $y = 0.665$ mole fraction methanol. The dew point is 172.4°F. At this temperature, the latent heat of methanol is 450 Btu/lb, that of water is 994.9 Btu/lb. The specific heat of methanol is 0.617, of water 0.999 Btu/lb°F. Equation (9.11):

$$H_G = 0.665[0.617(32.04)(172.4 - 67.5) + 450(32.04)]$$
$$+ (1 - 0.665)[0.999(18.02)(172.4 - 67.5) + 994.9(18.02)]$$
$$= 17,600 \text{ Btu/lb mole}$$

The enthalpy data of Fig. 9.27 were computed in this manner.

From the vapor-liquid equilibria, the bubble point of the residue is 210°F. Specific heat of residue is 0.998; of feed, 0.920. Enthalpy balance for feed preheat exchanger:

$$5,000(0.92)(t_F - 80) = 2,380(0.998)(210 - 100)$$
$$t_F = 136°F, \text{ temp at which feed enters tower}$$

(*Note:* The bubble point of the feed is 169°F. Had t_F as computed above been higher than the bubble point, the above enthalpy balance would have been discarded and made in accordance with flash-vaporization methods.) For the feed, $\Delta H_s = -388$ Btu/lb mole. Enthalpy of feed at 136°F is

$$H_F = 0.92(136 - 67.5)(23.1) - 388 = 1,070 \text{ Btu/lb mole}$$

From Fig. 9.27, $H_D = H_{L0} = 1,565$, $H_W = 2,580$ Btu/lb mole.

c. Since the *xy* diagram (Fig. 9.28) is everywhere concave downward, the minimum reflux ratio is established by the tie line on Fig. 9.27 ($x = 0.37$, $y = 0.71$) which, when extended, passes through F, the feed. At Δ_{Dm}, $Q_m = 26,900$ Btu/lb mole. $H_{G1} = 16,600$ Btu/lb mole. Eq. (9.61):

$$R_m = \frac{26,900 - 16,600}{16,600 - 1,565} = 0.685$$

d. The minimum number of trays was determined on the *xy* diagram in the manner of the lower part of Fig. 9.23; and 4.9 ideal stages, including the reboiler, were obtained. $N_m = 4.9 - 1 = 3.9$.

e. For $R = 1.5(0.685) = 1.029$, Eq. (9.61) becomes

$$1.029 = \frac{Q' - 16,600}{16,600 - 1,565}$$

$$Q' = 32,070 = H_D + \frac{Q_c}{D} = 1,565 + \frac{Q_c}{84.4}$$

$$Q_c = 2,575,000 \text{ Btu/hr condenser heat load}$$

Eq. (9.73):
$$216.8(1,070) = 84.4(32,070) + 132.4Q''$$

$$Q'' = -18,690 = H_W - \frac{Q_B}{W} = 2,580 - \frac{Q_B}{132.4}$$

$$Q_B = 2,816,000 \text{ Btu/hr reboiler heat load}$$

f. On Fig. 9.27, Δ_D at ($x_D = 0.915$, $Q' = 32,070$) and Δ_W at ($x_W = 0.00565$, $Q'' = -18,690$) are plotted. Random lines from the Δ points, as shown, intersect the saturated-vapor and saturated-liquid curves at values of y and x, respectively, corresponding to points on the operating curve (note that for accurate results a large-scale graph and a sharp pencil are needed). These are plotted on Fig. 9.28 to provide the operating curves, which are nearly, but not exactly, straight. A total of nine ideal stages including the reboiler, or eight ideal trays in the tower, are required when the feed tray is the optimum (No. 5) as shown.

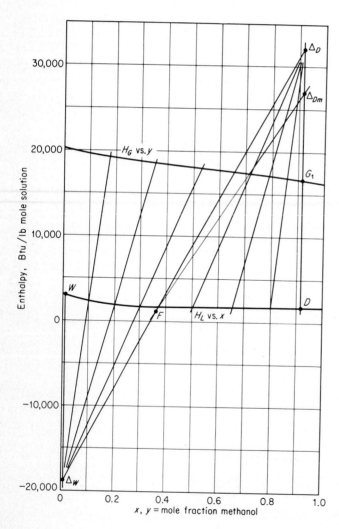

Fig. 9.27 *Enthalpy-concentration diagram for Illustration 9.8.*

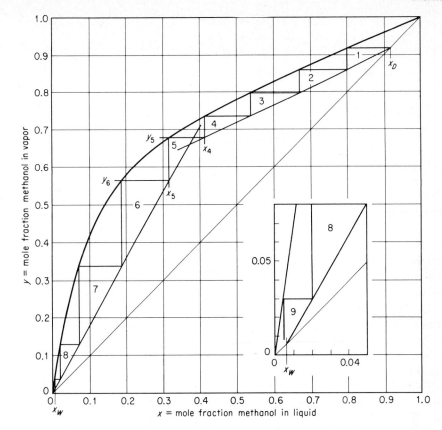

Fig. 9.28 *xy diagram for Illustration 9.8.*

At the top of the tower, $G_1 = D(R + 1) = 84.4(1.029 + 1) = 171.3$ lb moles/hr.

$$L_0 = DR = 84.4(1.029) = 86.7 \text{ lb moles/hr}$$

At the feed tray, $x_4 = 0.415$, $y_5 = 0.676$, $x_5 = 0.318$, $y_6 = 0.554$ (Fig. 9.28).

Eq. (9.60):
$$\frac{L_4}{D} = \frac{L_4}{84.4} = \frac{0.915 - 0.676}{0.676 - 0.415}$$

$$L_4 = 77.2 \text{ lb moles/hr}$$

Eq. (9.57):
$$\frac{L_4}{G_5} = \frac{77.2}{G_5} = \frac{0.915 - 0.676}{0.915 - 0.415}$$

$$G_5 = 161.5 \text{ lb moles/hr}$$

Eq. (9.70):
$$\frac{L_5}{W} = \frac{L_5}{132.4} = \frac{0.554 - 0.00565}{0.554 - 0.318}$$

$$L_5 = 308 \text{ lb moles/hr}$$

Eq. (9.68):
$$\frac{L_5}{\bar{G}_6} = \frac{308}{\bar{G}_6} = \frac{0.554 - 0.00565}{0.318 - 0.00565}$$

$$\bar{G}_6 = 175.7 \text{ lb moles/hr}$$

At the bottom of the tower, Eq. (9.62): $L_{Np} = \bar{G}_W + W$

$$L_8 = \bar{G}_W + 132.4$$

Further, $y_W = 0.035$, $x_8 = 0.02$ (Fig. 9.28).

Eq. (9.68):
$$\frac{L_8}{\bar{G}_W} = \frac{0.035 - 0.00565}{0.02 - 0.00565}$$

Solving simultaneously, $\bar{G}_W = 127.6$, $L_8 = 260$ lb moles/hr.

Reboilers

The heat-exchanger arrangements to provide the necessary heat and vapor return at the bottom of the fractionator may take several forms.   Small fractionators used for pilot-plant work may merely require a jacketed kettle, as shown schematically in Fig. 9.29a, but the heat-transfer surface and the corresponding vapor capacity will necessarily be small.   The tubular heat exchanger built into the bottom of the tower (Fig. 9.29b) is a variation which provides larger surface, but cleaning requires shutdown of the distillation operation.   This type may also be built with an internal floating head.   Both of these provide a vapor entering the bottom tray essentially in equilibrium with the residue product, so that the last stage of the previous computations represents the enrichment owing to the reboiler.

External reboilers of several varieties are commonly used for large installations, and these may be arranged with spares for cleaning.   The kettle reboiler (Fig. 9.29c), with heating medium inside the tubes, provides a vapor to the tower essentially in equilibrium with the residue product and then behaves like an ideal stage.   The vertical thermosiphon reboiler of Fig. 9.29d, with the heating medium outside the tubes, may be operated so as to vaporize all the liquid entering it to produce a vapor of the same composition as the residue product, in which case there is no enrichment provided.   However, owing to fouling of the tubes, which may occur with this type of operation, it is more customary to provide for only partial vaporization, the mixture issuing from the reboiler comprising both liquid and vapor.   The reboiler of Fig. 9.29e receives liquid from the trapout of the bottom tray, which it partially vaporizes. Other arrangements are discussed by Hengstebeck,[14] and Fair[8] reviews their design. It is safest not to assume that an ideal stage's worth of fractionation will occur with thermosiphon reboilers but instead to provide the necessary stages in the tower itself. In Fig. 9.29, the reservoir at the foot of the tower customarily holds a 5- to 10-min flow of liquid to provide for reasonably steady operation of the reboiler.

Reboilers may be heated by steam, heat-transfer oil, or other hot fluids.   For some high-boiling liquids, the reboiler may be a fuel-fired furnace.

Use of open steam

When a water solution in which the nonaqueous component is the more volatile is fractionated, so that the water is removed as the residue product, the heat required may

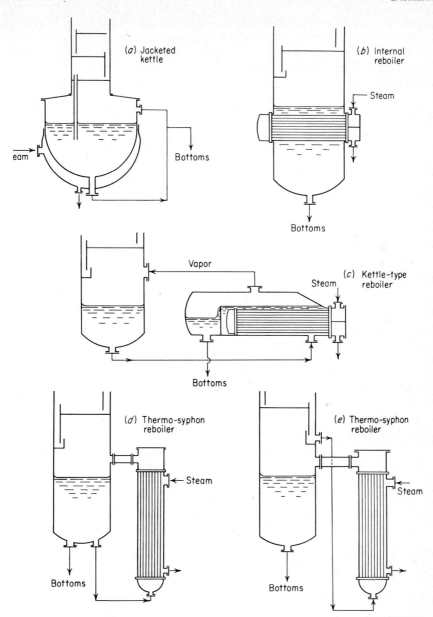

Fig. 9.29 *Reboiler arrangements.*

be provided by admission of steam directly to the bottom of the tower. The reboiler is then dispensed with. For a given reflux ratio and distillate composition, more trays will usually be required in the tower, but these are usually cheaper than the replaced reboiler and its cleaning costs.

Refer to Fig. 9.30. While the enriching section of the tower is unaffected by the use of open steam and is not shown, nevertheless the overall material and enthalpy balances are influenced. Thus, in the absence of important heat loss,

$$F + \bar{G}_{Np+1} = D + W \tag{9.82}$$

$$Fz_F = Dz_D + Wx_W \tag{9.83}$$

$$FH_F + \bar{G}_{Np+1}H_{G,Np+1} = WH_W + DH_D + Q_C \tag{9.84}$$

where $\bar{G}_{Np+1}$ is the molar rate of introducing steam. On the Hxy diagram, the Δ_D difference point is located in the usual manner. For the stripping section, Δ_W has its usual meaning, a fictitious stream of size equal to the net flow outward

$$\underline{\Delta_W = \bar{L}_m - \bar{G}_{m+1} = W - \bar{G}_{Np+1}} \tag{9.85}$$

of coordinates

$$\Delta_W \begin{cases} x_{\Delta W} = \dfrac{\text{net moles } A \text{ out}}{\text{net moles out}} = \dfrac{Wx_W}{W - \bar{G}_{Np+1}} \\[3mm] Q'' = \dfrac{\text{net heat out}}{\text{net moles out}} = \dfrac{WH_W - \bar{G}_{Np+1}H_{G,Np+1}}{W - \bar{G}_{Np+1}} \end{cases}$$

where $H_{G,Np+1}$ is the enthalpy of the steam. The point is shown on Fig. 9.31. Thus,

$$\bar{L}_m x_m - \bar{G}_{m+1}y_{m+1} = \Delta_W x_W \tag{9.86}$$

$$\bar{L}_m H_{Lm} - \bar{G}_{m+1}H_{G,m+1} = \Delta_W Q'' \tag{9.87}$$

and

$$\frac{\bar{L}_m}{\bar{G}_{m+1}} = \frac{y_{m+1} - x_{\Delta W}}{x_m - x_{\Delta W}} = \frac{H_{G,m+1} - Q''}{H_{Lm} - Q''} \tag{9.88}$$

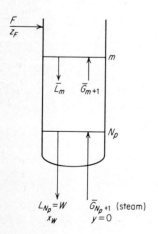

Fig. 9.30 *Use of open steam.*

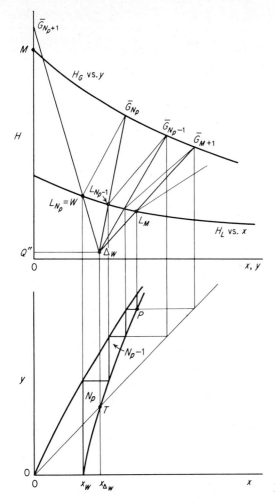

Fig. 9.31   *Use of open steam.*

The construction is shown on Fig. 9.31.   Equation (9.88) is the slope of a chord (not shown) between points P and T.   Here, the steam introduced is shown slightly superheated ($H_{G,Np+1} >$ saturated enthalpy); had saturated steam been used, $\bar{G}_{Np+1}$ would be located at point M.   Note that the operating curve on the x, y diagram passes through the 45° diagonal at T ($x = x_{\Delta W}$) and through the point ($x_W, y = 0$) corresponding to the fluids passing each other at the bottom of the tower.

Illustration 9.9.   Open steam, initially saturated at 10 psig pressure, will be used for the methanol fractionator of Illustration 9.8, with the same distillate rate and composition and the same reflux ratio.   Assuming that the feed enters the tower at the same enthalpy as in Illustration 9.8, determine the steam rate, bottoms composition, and the number of ideal trays.

Solution. From Illustration 9.8, $F = 216.8$, $z_F = 0.360$, $H_F = 1,070$, $D = 84.4$, $z_D = 0.915$, $H_D = 1,565$, and $Q_C = 2,575,000$, each in the usual units.   From the steam tables, the enthalpy of saturated steam at 10 psig = 1,160.4 Btu/lb referred to liquid water at 32°F.   On expanding adia-batically through a control valve to the tower pressure, it will be superheated with the same enthalpy. The enthalpy of liquid water at 67.5°F (t_o for Illustration 9.8) = 35.55 Btu/lb referred to 32°F. Therefore $H_{G,Np+1}$ = (1,160.4 − 35.55)(18.02) = 20,280 Btu/lb mole.

Eq. (9.82): $$216.8 + \bar{G}_{Np+1} = 84.4 + W$$

Eq. (9.83): $$216.8(0.360) = 84.4(0.915) + Wx_W$$

Eq. (9.84): $$216.8(1,070) + 20,280\bar{G}_{Np+1} = WH_W + 84.4(1,565) + 2,575,000$$

Since the bottoms will be essentially pure water, H_W is tentatively estimated as the enthalpy of satu-rated water (Fig. 9.28), 2,620 Btu/lb mole.   Solving the equations simultaneously with this value for H_W, the steam rate is $\bar{G}_{Np+1}$ = 159.4 and W = 291.8 lb moles/hr, with x_W = 0.00281.   The enthalpy of this solution at the bubble point is 2,600 Btu/lb mole, sufficiently close to the assumed 2,620 to be acceptable.   (Note that had the same interchange of heat between bottoms and feed been used as in Illustration 9.8, with bottoms discharged at 100°F, the feed enthalpy would no longer be 1,070 Btu/lb mole.)   For Δ_W,

$$x_{\Delta W} = \frac{Wx_W}{W - \bar{G}_{Np+1}} = \frac{291.8(0.00281)}{291.8 - 159.4} = 0.0062$$

$$Q'' = \frac{WH_W - \bar{G}_{Np+1}H_{G,Np+1}}{W - \bar{G}_{Np+1}}$$

$$= \frac{291.8(2,600) - 159.4(20,280)}{291.8 - 159.4} = -18,650$$

The Hxy and xy diagrams for the enriching section are the same as in Illustration 9.8.   For the stripping section, they resemble Fig. 9.31.   The number of ideal stages is N_p = 9.5, and these must now all be included in the tower.

Multiple feeds

There are occasions when two or more feeds composed of the same substances but of different concentrations require distillation to give the same distillate and residue products.   A single fractionator will then suffice for all.

Consider the two-feed fractionator of Fig. 9.32.   The construction on the Hxy diagram for the sections of the column above F_1 and below F_2 are the same as for a single-feed column, with the Δ_D and Δ_W points located in the usual manner.   For the middle section between the feeds, the difference point Δ_M may be located by con-sideration of material and enthalpy balances either toward the top, as indicated by the envelope shown on Fig. 9.32, or toward the bottom; the net result will be the same. Consider the envelope shown in the figure, with Δ_M representing a fictitious stream of quantity equal to the net flow upward and out

$$G'_{r+1} - L'_r = D - F_1 = \Delta_M \qquad (9.89)$$

whose coordinates are

$$\Delta_M \begin{cases} x_{\Delta M} = \dfrac{\text{net moles } A \text{ out}}{\text{net moles out}} = \dfrac{Dz_D - F_1z_{F_1}}{D - F_1} \\[2ex] Q_M = \dfrac{\text{net heat out}}{\text{net moles out}} = \dfrac{Q_C + DH_D - F_1H_{F_1}}{D - F_1} \end{cases}$$

Δ_M may be either a positive or negative quantity.

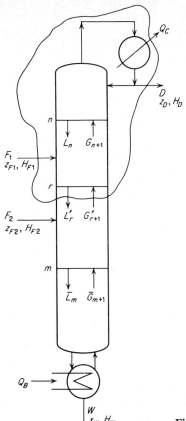

Fig. 9.32 *Fractionator with two feeds.*

Equation (9.89) may be used as a basis for component-A and enthalpy balances

$$G'_{r+1}y_{r+1} - L'_r x_r = \Delta_M x_{\Delta M} \qquad (9.90)$$

$$G'_{r+1}H_{G,r+1} - L_r H_{Lr} = \Delta_M Q_M \qquad (9.91)$$

whence

$$\frac{L'_r}{G'_{r+1}} = \frac{y_{r+1} - x_{\Delta M}}{x_r - x_{\Delta M}} = \frac{H_{G,r+1} - Q_M}{H_{Lr} - Q_M} \qquad (9.92)$$

Since

$$F_1 + F_2 = D + W = \Delta_D + \Delta_W \qquad (9.93)$$

then

$$\Delta_M = F_2 - W \qquad (9.94)$$

The construction (both feeds liquid) is shown on Fig. 9.33, where Δ_M lies on the line $\overline{\Delta_D F_1}$ [Eq. (9.89)] and on the line $\overline{\Delta_W F_2}$ [Eq. (9.94)]. A solution representing

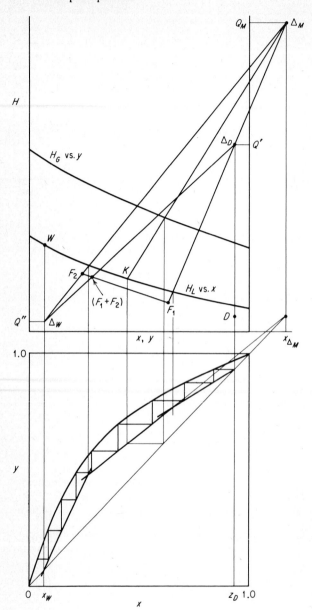

Fig. 9.33 *Construction for two feeds.*

the composited feed, with

$$z_{F,av} = \frac{F_1 z_{F1} + F_2 z_{F2}}{F_1 + F_2}, \qquad H_{F,av} = \frac{F_1 H_{F1} + F_2 H_{F2}}{F_1 + F_2}$$

must lie on the line $\Delta_D \Delta_W$ [Eq. (9.93)]. It is also possible for Δ_M to lie below and to the left of Δ_W. The operating curve for the middle section on the xy diagram is located by lines such as $\Delta_M K$, as shown. Trays are best drawn in the usual step fashion on the xy diagram, and for optimum location, the feed trays straddle the intersections of the operating curves, as shown.

Side streams

Side streams are products of intermediate composition withdrawn from the inter-mediate trays of the column. They are used frequently in the distillation of petroleum products, where intermediate properties not obtainable merely by mixing distillate or bottoms with feed are desired. They are used only infrequently in the case of binary mixtures, and are not treated here (see Prob. 9.17).

Heat losses

Most fractionators operate above ambient temperature, and heat losses along the column are inevitable since insulating materials have a finite thermal conductivity. The importance of the heat losses and their influence on fractionators need now to be considered.

Consider the fractionator of Fig. 9.17. A heat balance for the top n trays of the enriching section (envelope III) which includes the heat loss is[4]

$$G_{n+1} H_{G,n+1} = Q_C + D H_D + L_n H_{Ln} + Q_{Ln} \qquad (9.95)$$

where Q_{Ln} is the heat loss for trays 1 through n. Defining

$$Q_L' = \frac{Q_C + D H_D + Q_{Ln}}{D} = Q' + \frac{Q_{Ln}}{D} \qquad (9.96)$$

we have

$$G_{n+1} H_{G,n+1} - L_n H_{Ln} = D Q_L' \qquad (9.97)$$

Q_L' is a variable since it depends upon how many trays are included in the heat balance. If only the top tray ($n = 1$) is included, the heat loss is small, and Q_L' is nearly equal to Q'. As more trays are included, Q_{Ln} and Q_L' increase, ultimately reaching their largest values when all enriching-section trays are included. Separate difference points are therefore needed for each tray.

For the stripping section up to tray m (envelope IV, Fig. 9.17),

$$\bar{L}_m H_{Lm} + Q_B = W H_W + \bar{G}_{m+1} H_{G,m+1} + \bar{Q}_{Lm} \qquad (9.98)$$

Letting

$$Q_L'' = \frac{W H_W - Q_B + \bar{Q}_{Lm}}{W} = Q'' + \frac{\bar{Q}_{Lm}}{W} \qquad (9.99)$$

there results

$$\bar{L}_m H_{Lm} - \bar{G}_{m+1} H_{G,m+1} = W Q_L'' \qquad (9.100)$$

If the heat balance includes only the bottom tray, the heat loss is small, and Q_L'' nearly equals Q''. As more trays are included, $\bar{Q}_{Lm}$ and therefore Q_L'' increase, reaching their largest values when the balance is made over the entire stripping section.   Separate difference points are needed for each tray.

The construction on the Hxy diagram is shown on Fig. 9.34 for a six-tray column and reboiler, liquid feed on to the fourth tray, and distillate at the bubble point.   The procedure for design is one of trial and error.   For example, as a first trial, heat losses might be neglected and trays calculated with fixed difference points, and after the size of the resulting column is determined, the first estimate of the heat losses for the two column sections may be made by the usual methods of heat-transfer

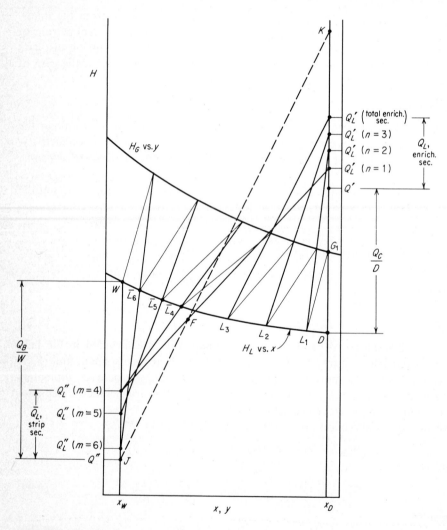

Fig. 9.34   *Heat losses.*

calculations.   The heat losses may then be apportioned among the trays and the number of trays redetermined with the appropriate difference points.   This leads to a second approximation of the heat loss, and so forth.

As Fig. 9.34 shows, heat losses increase the internal-reflux ratio, and *for a given condenser heat load*, fewer trays for a given separation are required (recall that the higher the enriching-section difference point and the lower the stripping-section difference point, the fewer the trays).   However, the reboiler must provide not only the heat removed in the condenser but also the heat losses.   Consequently, for the same reboiler heat load as shown on Fig. 9.34 but with complete insulation against heat loss, all the heat would be removed in the condenser, all the stripping trays would use point J, and all the enriching trays would use point K as their respective difference points.   It therefore follows that, *for a given reboiler heat load or heat expenditure*, fewer trays are required for a given separation if heat losses are eliminated.   For this reason, fractionators are usually well insulated.

High-purity products and tray efficiencies

Methods of dealing with these problems are considered following the McCabe-Thiele method and are equally applicable to Ponchon-Savarit calculations.

MULTISTAGE (TRAY) TOWERS—METHOD OF McCABE AND THIELE

This method, although less rigorous than that of Ponchon and Savarit, is nevertheless most useful since it does not require detailed enthalpy data.   If such data must be approximated from fragmentary information, much of the exactness of the Ponchon-Savarit method is lost in any case.   Except where heat losses or heats of solution are unusually large, the McCabe-Thiele method will be found adequate for most purposes.   It hinges upon the fact that, as an approximation, the operating lines on the xy diagram may be considered straight for each section of a fractionator between points of addition or withdrawal of streams.

Equimolal overflow and vaporization

Consider the enriching section of the fractionator of Fig. 9.17.   In the absence of heat losses, which can be (and usually are) made very small by thermal insulation for reasons of economy if for no other, Eq. (9.56) may be written

$$\frac{L_n}{G_{n+1}} = 1 - \frac{H_{G,n+1} - H_{Ln}}{Q' - H_{Ln}} \tag{9.101}$$

where Q' includes the condenser heat load and the enthalpy of the distillate, per mole of distillate. The liquid enthalpy H_{Ln} is ordinarily small in comparison with Q' since the condenser heat load must include the latent heat of condensation of at least the reflux liquid.   If then $H_{G,n+1} - H_{Ln}$ is substantially constant, L_n/G_{n+1} will be constant also for a given fractionation.[32]   From Eq. (9.11),

$$H_{G,n+1} = [y_{n+1}C_{LA}M_A + (1 - y_{n+1})C_{LB}M_B](t_{n+1} - t_o)$$
$$+ y_{n+1}\lambda_A M_A + (1 - y_{n+1})\lambda_B M_B \tag{9.102}$$

where t_{n+1} is the temperature of the vapor from tray $n + 1$ and the λ's are the latent heats of vaporization at this temperature.   If the deviation from ideality of liquid solutions is not great, the first term in brackets of Eq. (9.102) is

$$y_{n+1}C_{LA}M_A + (1 - y_{n+1})C_{LB}M_B \doteq C_LM_{av} \tag{9.103}$$

From Eq. (9.10),

$$H_{Ln} = C_L(t_n - t_o)M_{av} + \Delta H_S \tag{9.104}$$

and

$$H_{G,n+1} - H_{Ln} = C_LM_{av}(t_{n+1} - t_n) + y_{n+1}\lambda_AM_A + (1 - y_{n+1})\lambda_BM_B - \Delta H_S \tag{9.105}$$

For all but unusual cases, the only important terms of Eq. (9.105) are those containing the latent heats. The temperature change between adjacent trays is usually small, so that the sensible-heat term is insignificant. The heat of solution can in most cases be measured in terms of hundreds of Btu/lb mole of solution, whereas the latent heats at ordinary pressures are usually of the order of 10,000 to 20,000 Btu/mole. Therefore, for all practical purposes,

$$H_{G,n+1} - H_{Ln} = (\lambda M)_{av} \tag{9.106}$$

where the last term is the weighted average of the molal latent heats. For many pairs of substances, the molal latent heats are nearly identical, so that averaging is unnecessary. If their inequality is the only barrier to application of these simplifying assumptions, it is possible to assign a fictitious molecular weight to one of the components so that the molal latent heats are then forced to be the same (if this is done, the entire computation must be made with the fictitious molecular weight, including operating lines and equilibrium data). This is, however, rarely necessary.

If it is sufficiently important, therefore, one can be persuaded that, for all but exceptional cases, the ratio L/G in the enriching section of the fractionator is essentially constant. The same reasoning can be applied to any section of a fractionator between points of addition or withdrawal of streams, although each section will have its own ratio.

Consider next two adjacent trays n and r, between which neither addition nor withdrawal of material from the tower occurs. A material balance provides

$$L_{r-1} + G_{n+1} = L_n + G_r \tag{9.107}$$

Since $L_{r-1}/G_r = L_n/G_{n+1}$, it follows that $L_n = L_{r-1}$ and $G_{n+1} = G_r$, which is the "principle of equimolal overflow and vaporization." The rate of liquid flow from each tray in a section of the tower is constant on a molar basis, but since the average molecular weight changes with tray number, the weight rates of flow are different.

It should be noted that, as shown in the discussion of Fig. 9.12, if the H_Gy and H_Lx lines on the Hxy diagram are straight and parallel, then in the absence of heat loss the L/G ratio for a given tower section will be constant regardless of the relative size of H_{Ln} and Q' in Eq. (9.101).

The general assumptions involved in the foregoing are customarily called the "usual simplifying assumptions."

Enriching section; total condenser—reflux at the bubble point

Consider a section of the fractionator entirely above the point of introduction of feed, shown schematically in Fig. 9.35a. The condenser removes all the latent heat from the overhead vapor but does not cool the resulting liquid further. The reflux and distillate product are therefore liquids at the bubble point, and $y_1 = x_D = x_0$. Since the liquid, L moles/hr, falling from each tray and the vapor, G moles/hr, rising from each tray are each constant if the usual simplifying assumptions pertain, subscripts are not needed to identify the source of these streams. The compositions, however, change. The trays shown are theoretical trays, so that the composition y_n of the vapor from the nth tray is in equilibrium with the liquid of composition x_n leaving

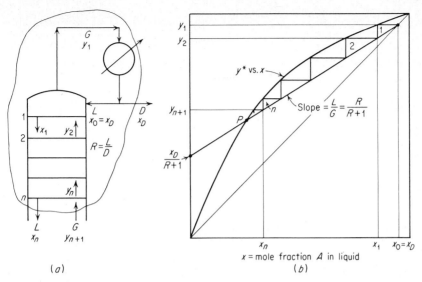

Fig. 9.35 *Enriching section.*

the same tray. The point (x_n, y_n), on x, y coordinates, therefore falls on the equilibrium curve.

A total material balance for the envelope in the figure is

$$G = L + D = D(R + 1) \tag{9.108}$$

For component A,

$$Gy_{n+1} = Lx_n + Dx_D \tag{9.109}$$

from which the enriching-section operating line is

$$y_{n+1} = \frac{L}{G} x_n + \frac{D}{G} x_D \tag{9.110}$$

$$y_{n+1} = \frac{R}{R+1} x_n + \frac{x_D}{R+1} \tag{9.111}$$

This is the equation of a straight line on x, y coordinates (Fig. 9.35b) of slope $L/G = R/(R + 1)$, and with a y intercept of $x_D/(R + 1)$. Setting $x_n = x_D$ shows $y_{n+1} = x_D$, so that the line passes through the point $y = x = x_D$ on the 45° diagonal. This point and the y intercept permit easy construction of the line. The concentration of liquids and vapors for each tray is shown in accordance with the principles of Chap. 5, and the usual "staircase" construction between operating line and equilibrium curve is seen to provide the theoretical tray-concentration variation. The construction obviously cannot be carried farther than point P.

In plotting the equilibrium curve of the figure, it is generally assumed that the pressure is constant throughout the tower. If necessary, the variation in pressure from tray to tray may be allowed for after determining the number of real trays, but this will require a trial-and-error procedure. It is ordinarily unnecessary except for operation under very low pressures.

Exhausting section; reboiled vapor in equilibrium with residue

Consider next a section of the fractionator below the point of introducing the feed, shown schematically in Fig. 9.36a. The trays are again theoretical trays. The rates of flow $\bar{L}$ and $\bar{G}$ are each constant from tray to tray, but not necessarily equal to the values for the enriching section. A total material balance,

$$\bar{L} = \bar{G} + W \tag{9.112}$$

and, for component A,

$$\bar{L}x_m = \bar{G}y_{m+1} + Wx_W \tag{9.113}$$

These provide the equation of the exhausting-section operating line,

$$y_{m+1} = \frac{\bar{L}}{\bar{G}} x_m - \frac{W}{\bar{G}} x_W \tag{9.114}$$

operating line

$$y_{m+1} = \frac{\bar{L}}{\bar{L} - \bar{W}} x_m - \frac{W}{\bar{L} - W} x_W \tag{9.115}$$

This is a straight line of slope $\bar{L}/\bar{G} = \bar{L}(\bar{L} - W)$, and since when $x_m = x_W$, $y_{m+1} = x_W$, it passes through $x = y = x_W$ on the 45° diagonal (Fig. 9.36b). If the reboiled vapor y_W is in equilibrium with the residue x_W, the first step of the staircase construction represents the reboiler. The steps can be carried no farther than point T.

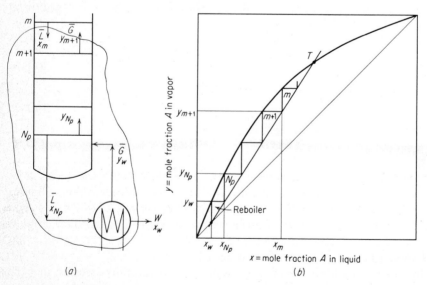

(a)

(b)

Fig. 9.36 *Exhausting section.*

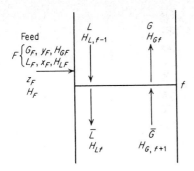

Fig. 9.37   *Introduction of feed.*

Introduction of feed

It is convenient before proceeding further to establish how the introduction of the feed influences the change in slope of the operating lines as we pass from the enriching to the exhausting sections of the fractionator.

Consider the section of the column at the tray where the feed is introduced (Fig. 9.37). The quantities of the liquid and vapor streams change abruptly at this tray, since the feed may consist of liquid, vapor, or a mixture of both. If, for example, the feed is a saturated liquid, $\bar{L}$ will exceed L by the amount of the added feed liquid. To establish the general relationship, an overall material balance about this section is

$$F + L + \bar{G} = G + \bar{L} \tag{9.116}$$

and an enthalpy balance,

$$FH_F + LH_{L,f-1} + \bar{G}H_{G,f+1} = GH_{Gf} + \bar{L}H_{Lf} \tag{9.117}$$

The vapors and liquids inside the tower are all saturated, and the molal enthalpies of all saturated vapors at this section are essentially identical since the temperature and composition changes over one tray are small. The same is true of the molal enthalpies of the saturated liquids, so that $H_{Gf} = H_{G,f+1}$ and $H_{L,f-1} = H_{Lf}$. Equation (9.117) then becomes

$$(\bar{L} - L)H_L = (\bar{G} - G)H_G + FH_F \tag{9.118}$$

Combining this with Eq. (9.116),

$$\frac{\bar{L} - L}{F} = \frac{H_G - H_F}{H_G - H_L} = q \tag{9.119}$$

The quantity q is thus seen to be the heat required to convert 1 mole of feed from its condition H_F to a saturated vapor, divided by the molal latent heat $H_G - H_L$. The feed may be introduced under any of a variety of thermal conditions ranging from a liquid well below its bubble point to a superheated vapor, for each of which the value of q will be different. Typical circumstances are listed in Table 9.1, with the corresponding range of values of q. Combining Eqs. (9.116) and (9.119),

$$\bar{G} - G = F(q - 1) \tag{9.120}$$

which provides a convenient method for determining $\bar{G}$.

Table 9.1. Thermal conditions for the feed

Feed condition	G_F, moles/(hr)(sq ft)	L_F, moles/(hr)(sq ft)	H_{GF}, Btu/mole	H_{LF}, Btu/mole	H_F, Btu/mole	$q = \dfrac{H_G - H_F}{H_G - H_L}$	$\dfrac{q}{q-1}$
Liquid below bubble point	0	F		H_F	$H_F < H_L$	> 1.0	> 1.0
Saturated liquid	0	F		H_F	H_L	1.0	∞
Mixture of liquid and vapor†	G_F $F = G_F + L_F$	L_F	H_G	H_L	$H_G > H_F > H_L$	$\Big\}\dfrac{L_F}{F}$ $1.0 > q > 0$	$\dfrac{L_F}{L_F - F}$
Saturated vapor	F	0	H_F		H_G	0	0
Superheated vapor	F	0	H_F		$H_F > H_G$	< 0	$1.0 > \dfrac{q}{q-1} > 0$

† In this case the intersection of the q line with the equilibrium curve gives the compositions of the equilibrium liquid and vapor which comprise the feed. The q line is the flash-vaporization operating line for the feed.

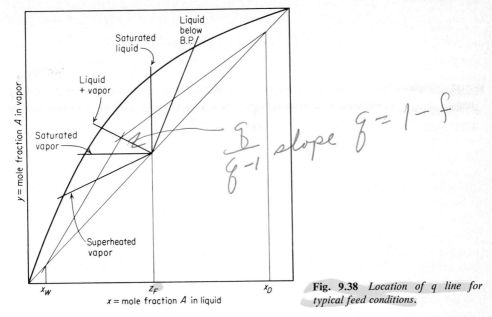

Fig. 9.38 *Location of q line for typical feed conditions.*

The point of intersection of the two operating lines will help locate the exhausting-section operating line.   This may be established as follows.   Rewriting Eqs. (9.110) and (9.114) without the tray subscripts,

$$yG = Lx + Dx_D \tag{9.121}$$

$$y\bar{G} = \bar{L}x - Wx_W \tag{9.122}$$

Subtracting,

$$(\bar{G} - G)y = (\bar{L} - L)x - (Wx_W + Dx_D) \tag{9.123}$$

Further, by an overall material balance,

$$Fz_F = Dx_D + Wx_W \tag{9.72}$$

Substituting this and Eqs. (9.119) and (9.120) in (9.123)

$$y = \frac{q}{q-1}x - \frac{z_F}{q-1} \tag{9.124}$$

This, the locus of intersection of operating lines (the q line), is a straight line of slope $q/(q-1)$, and since $y = z_F$ when $x = z_F$, it passes through the point $x = y = z_F$ on the 45° diagonal.   The range of the values of the slope $q/(q-1)$ is listed in Table 9.1, and the graphical interpretation for typical cases is shown in Fig. 9.38.   Here the operating-line intersection is shown for a particular case of feed as a mixture of liquid and vapor.   It is clear that, for a given feed condition, fixing the reflux ratio at the top of the column automatically establishes the liquid/vapor ratio in the exhausting section and the reboiler heat load as well.

Location of the feed tray

The q line is useful in simplifying the graphical location of the exhausting line, but the point of intersection of the two operating lines does not necessarily establish the demarcation between the enriching and exhausting sections of the tower. Rather it is the introduction of feed which governs the change from one operating line to the other and establishes the demarcation, and at least in the design of a new column some latitude in the introduction of the feed is available.

Consider the separation shown partially in Fig. 9.39, for example. For a given feed, z_F and the q line are fixed. For particular overhead and residue products, x_D and x_W are fixed. If the reflux ratio is specified, the location of the enriching line DG is fixed, and the exhausting line KC must pass through the q line at E. If the feed is introduced upon the seventh tray from the top (Fig. 9.39a), line DG is used for trays 1 through 6, and, beginning with the seventh tray, the line KC must be used. If, on the other hand, the feed is introduced upon the fourth from the top (Fig. 9.39b), line KC is used for all trays below the fourth. Clearly a transition from one operating line to the other must be made somewhere between points C and D, but anywhere within these limits will serve. The least total number of trays will result if the steps on the diagram are kept as large as possible, or if the transition is made at the first opportunity after passing the operating-line intersection, as shown in Fig. 9.39c. In the design of a new column, this is the practice to be followed.

In the adaptation of an existing column to a new separation, the point of introducing the feed is limited to the location of existing nozzles in the column wall. The

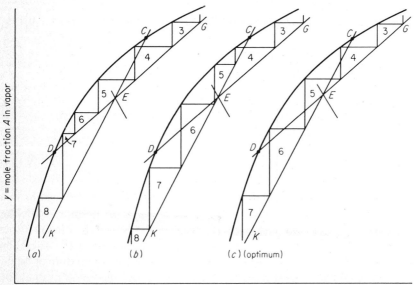

Fig. 9.39 *Location of feed tray.*

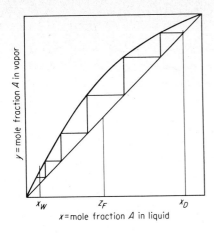

y = mole fraction A in vapor

x = mole fraction A in liquid

x_W z_F x_D

Fig. 9.40   *Total reflux and minimum trays.*

slope of the operating lines (or reflux ratio) and the product compositions to be realized must then be determined by trial and error, in order to obtain numbers of theoretical trays in the two sections of the column consistent with the number of real trays in each section and the expected tray efficiency.

Total reflux, or infinite reflux ratio

As the reflux ratio $R = L/D$ is increased, the ratio L/G increases, until ultimately, when $R = \infty$, $L/G = 1$ and the operating lines of both sections of the column coincide with the 45° diagonal as in Fig. 9.40. In practice this can be realized by returning all the overhead product back to the column as reflux (total reflux) and reboiling all the residue product, whereupon the forward flow of fresh feed must be reduced to zero. Alternatively such a condition may be interpreted as requiring infinite reboiler heat and condenser cooling capacity for a given rate of feed.

As the operating lines move farther away from the equilibrium curve with increased reflux ratio, the number of theoretical trays required to produce a given separation becomes less, until at total reflux the number of trays is the minimum N_m.

If the relative volatility is constant or nearly so, the analytical expression of Fenske, Eq. (9.81), may be used.

Minimum reflux ratio

The minimum reflux ratio R_m is the maximum ratio which will require an infinite number of trays for the separation desired, and it corresponds to the minimum reboiler heat and condenser cooling capacity for the separation. Refer to Fig. 9.41a. As the reflux ratio is decreased, the slope of the enriching operating line becomes less, and the number of trays required increases. Operating line MN, which passes through the point of intersection of the q line and the equilibrium curve, corresponds to the minimum reflux ratio, and an infinite number of trays would be required to reach point N from either end of the tower. In some cases, as in Fig. 9.41b, the minimum-reflux operating line will be tangent to the equilibrium curve in

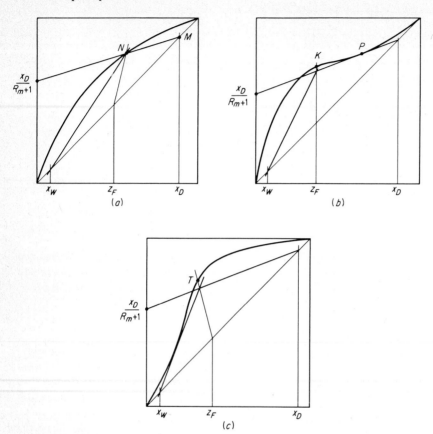

Fig. 9.41   *Minimum reflux ratio and infinite stages.*

the enriching section as at point P, while a line through K would clearly represent too small a reflux ratio.   Owing to the interdependence of the liquid/vapor ratios in the two sections of the column, a tangent operating line in the exhausting section may also set the minimum reflux ratio, as in Fig. 9.41c.

For cases when the equilibrium curve is always concave downward, the minimum reflux ratio may be conveniently calculated analytically.[39]   The required relationship may be developed by solving Eqs. (9.111) and (9.124) simultaneously to obtain the coordinates (x_a, y_a) of the point of intersection of the enriching operating line and the q line.   Dropping the tray-number designation in Eq. (9.111), these are

$$x_a = \frac{x_D(q-1) + z_F(R+1)}{R+q} \qquad y_a = \frac{Rz_F + qx_D}{R+q}$$

At the minimum reflux ratio R_m, these coordinates are equilibrium values since they occur on the equilibrium curve.   Substituting them into the definition of α, Eq. (9.2),

$$\frac{R_m z_F + q x_D}{R_m(1 - z_F) + q(1 - x_D)} = \frac{\alpha[x_D(q-1) + z_F(R_m+1)]}{(R_m+1)(1 - z_F) + (q-1)(1 - x_D)} \tag{9.125}$$

This may be conveniently solved for R_m for any value of q. Thus, for example,
$q = 1$ (*feed liquid at the bubble point*)

$$R_m = \frac{1}{\alpha - 1}\left[\frac{x_D}{x_F} - \frac{\alpha(1 - x_D)}{1 - x_F}\right] \tag{9.126}$$

$q = 0$ (*feed vapor at the dew point*)

$$R_m = \frac{1}{\alpha - 1}\left(\frac{\alpha x_D}{y_F} - \frac{1 - x_D}{1 - y_F}\right) - 1 \tag{9.127}$$

In each case, the α is that prevailing at the intersection of the q line and the equilibrium curve.

Optimum reflux ratio

The discussion given under the Ponchon-Savarit method applies.

Illustration 9.10. Redesign the methanol-water fractionator of Illustration 9.8, using the simplifying assumptions of the McCabe-Thiele method. The circumstances are:

Feed: 5,000 lb/hr, 216.8 lb moles/hr, $x_F = 0.360$ mole fraction methanol, av mol wt = 23.1, temperature entering the fractionator = 136°F.

Distillate: 2,620 lb/hr, 84.4 lb moles/hr, $x_D = 0.915$ mole fraction methanol, liquid at the bubble point.

Residue: 2,380 lb/hr, 132.4 lb moles/hr, $x_W = 0.00565$ mole fraction methanol.

Reflux ratio: 1.5 times the minimum.

Solution. Refer to Fig. 9.42. From the *txy* diagram, the bubble point of the feed at 0.360 mole fraction methanol is 169°F, and its dew point is 193°F. The latent heats of vaporization at 193°F are $\lambda_A = 450$ Btu/lb for methanol, $\lambda_B = 982$ Btu/lb for water. Specific heat of liquid methanol = 0.65, of liquid water = 1.0, of feed solution = 0.92. Ignoring heats of solution, as is customary with the McCabe-Thiele method, the enthalpy of the feed at 169°F (the bubble point) referred to 136°F (the feed temperature) is

$$0.92(23.1)(169 - 136) = 702 \text{ Btu/lb mole}$$

The enthalpy of the saturated vapor at 193°F referred to liquids at 136°F is

$$0.36[0.65(32.04)(193 - 136) + 450(32.04)]$$
$$+ (1 - 0.36)[1(18.02)(193 - 136) + 982(18.02)] = 17,110 \text{ Btu/lb mole}$$

$$q = \frac{\text{heat to convert to a saturated vapor}}{\text{heat of vaporization}} = \frac{17,110 - 0}{17,110 - 702} = 1.04$$

(The same value, within slide-rule precision, is obtained if the heat of solution is considered.)

$$\frac{q}{q - 1} = \frac{1.04}{1.04 - 1} = 26$$

On Fig. 9.42, x_D, x_W, and z_F are located on the 45° diagonal, and the q line is drawn with slope = 26. The operating line for minimum reflux ratio in this case passes through the intersection of the q line and equilibrium curve, as shown.

$$\frac{x_D}{R_m + 1} = \frac{0.915}{R_m + 1} = 0.57$$

$$R_m = 0.605 \text{ mole reflux/mole } D$$

The minimum number of ideal trays is determined using the 45° diagonal as operating lines (Fig. 9.42). Theoretical stages to the number of 4.9, including the reboiler, are determined.

For $R = 1.5R_m = 1.5(0.605) = 0.908$ mole reflux/mole D, and for equimolal overflow and vaporization,

Eq. (9.44):
$$L = L_0 = RD = 0.908(84.4) = 76.5 \text{ lb moles/hr}$$

Eq. (9.108):
$$G = D(R + 1) = 85.4(0.908 + 1) = 160.9 \text{ lb moles/hr}$$

Eq. (9.119):
$$L = qF + L = 1.04(216.8) + 76.5 = 302.5 \text{ lb moles/hr}$$

Eq. (9.120):
$$\bar{G} = F(q - 1) + G = 216.8(1.04 - 1) + 160.9 = 169.7 \text{ lb moles/hr}$$

$$\frac{x_D}{R + 1} = \frac{0.915}{0.908 + 1} = 0.480$$

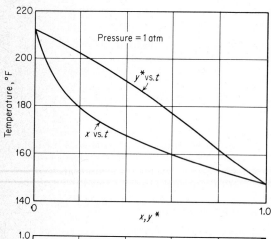

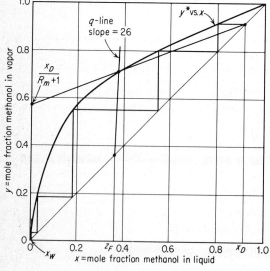

Fig. 9.42 *Solution to Illustration 9.10. Minimum reflux ratio and minimum trays.*

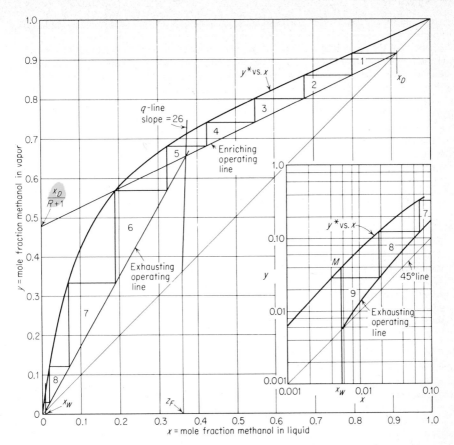

Fig. 9.43 *Solution to Illustration 9.10.* $R = 0.908$ *mole reflux/mole distillate product.*

Refer to Fig. 9.43.   The y intercept 0.480 and enriching and exhausting operating lines are plotted. Steps are drawn to determine the number of ideal trays, as shown.   The exhausting operating line is used immediately after crossing the operating-line intersection, and the feed is therefore to be introduced on the fifth ideal tray from the top.   A total of 8.8 ideal trays, including the reboiler, is required, and the tower must therefore contain 7.8 ideal trays.   An integral number can be obtained by very slight adjustment of the reflux ratio, but since a tray efficiency must still be applied to obtain the number of real trays, this need not be done.

   For cases where the residue composition is very small, it will be necessary to enlarge the scale of the lower left-hand part of the diagram in order to obtain the number of trays.   In some cases the graphical determination may still be difficult because of the closeness of the exhausting line and the equilibrium curve.   Logarithmic coordinates may then be used to maintain a satisfactory separation of the lines, as in the insert of Fig. 9.43.   On such a graph, for very low values of x, the equilibrium curve will be substantially given by $y^* = \alpha x$, which is a straight line of unit slope.   The exhausting operating line will, however, be curved and must be plotted from its equation.   In this example, the equation is [Eq. (9.114)]

$$y = \frac{302.5}{169.7} x - \frac{132.4}{169.7} 0.00565 = 1.785x - 0.0044$$

The steps representing the ideal stages are made in the usual manner on these coordinates, continued down from the last made on the arithmetic coordinates (see also page 358).

The diameter of the tower and the tray design are established through the methods of Chap. 6. Note the substantially different liquid loads in the enriching and exhausting sections. A column of constant diameter for all sections is usually desired for reasons of simplicity in construction and lower cost. If, however, the discrepancy between liquid or vapor quantities in the two sections is considerable, and particularly if expensive alloy or nonferrous metal is used, different diameters for the two sections may be warranted.

Computations for other reflux ratios are easily and quickly made once the diagram and equations have been set up for one value of R. These provide data for determining the most economical R. The following table lists the important quantities for this separation at various values of R:

R	L	G	$\bar{L}$	$\bar{G}$	No. ideal stages
$R_m = 0.605$	51.0	135.4	277	144.1	∞
0.70	59.0	143.4	285	152.1	11.5
0.80	67.5	151.9	294	160.6	10
0.908	76.5	160.9	303	169.7	8.8
1.029	86.7	171.3	313	180	8.3
2.0	168.8	253	395	262	6.5
4.0	338	422	564	431	5.5
∞	∞	∞	∞	∞	$4.9 = N_m + 1$

Included in the table are the data for the McCabe-Thiele method at $R = 1.029$, the reflux ratio used in Illustration 9.8 for the exact Ponchon-Savarit calculation. Illustration 9.8 showed nine ideal stages. It is noteworthy that for either method each at 1.5 times its respective value of R_m, the number of stages is essentially the same, and the maximum flow rates which would be used to set the mechanical design of the tower are sufficiently similar for the same final design to result.

Use of open steam

Ordinarily, heat is applied at the base of the tower by means of a heat exchanger (see page 330). When, however, a water solution is fractionated to give the nonaqueous solute as the distillate and the water is removed as the residue product, the heat required may be provided by the use of open steam at the bottom of the tower. The reboiler is then dispensed with. For a given reflux ratio and overhead composition, however, more trays will be required in the tower.

Refer to Fig. 9.44. Overall material balances for both components and for the more volatile substance are

$$F + \bar{G} = D + W \tag{9.128}$$

$$Fz_F = Dx_D + Wx_W \tag{9.129}$$

where $\bar{G}$ is moles/hr of steam used, assumed saturated at the tower pressure. The enriching operating line is located as usual, and the slope of the exhausting line $\bar{L}/\bar{G}$ is related to L/G and the feed conditions in the same manner as before. A material balance for the more volatile substance below tray m in the exhausting

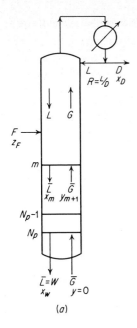

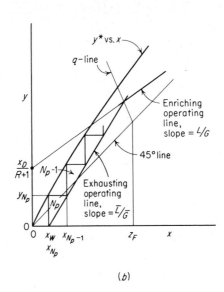

Fig. 9.44 *Use of open steam.*

section is

$$\bar{L}x_m + \bar{G}(0) = \bar{G}y_{m+1} + Wx_W \tag{9.130}$$

and since $\bar{L} = W$ in this case,

$$\frac{\bar{L}}{\bar{G}} = \frac{y_{m+1}}{x_m - x_W} \tag{9.131}$$

The exhausting line therefore passes through the point ($y = 0$, $x = x_W$) as shown in Fig. 9.44b. The graphical tray construction must therefore be continued to the x axis of the diagram.

If the steam entering the tower, $\bar{G}_{Np+1}$, is superheated, it will vaporize liquid on tray N_p to the extent necessary to bring it to saturation, $\bar{G}_{Np+1}(H_{G,Np+1} - H_{G,\text{sat}})/\lambda M$, where $H_{G,\text{sat}}$ is the enthalpy of saturated steam and λM the molar latent heat at the tower pressure.

$$\bar{G} = \bar{G}_{Np+1}\left(1 + \frac{H_{G,Np+1} - H_{G,\text{sat}}}{\lambda M}\right) \tag{9.132}$$

and

$$\bar{L} = \bar{G} - \bar{G}_{Np+1} + L_{Np} \tag{9.133}$$

from which the internal $\bar{L}/\bar{G}$ ratio may be computed.

Condensers

Condensers are usually conventional tubular heat exchangers, arranged horizontally with the coolant inside the tubes. The condenser may be placed above the tower for gravity flow of the condensed reflux to the top tray.   But it is usually more convenient for purposes of construction and cleaning to place the condenser nearer the ground and to return the reflux from an accumulator drum to the top tray by pumping. This procedure also provides more pressure drop for operation of control valves on the reflux line.

The condenser coolant is most frequently water.   The pressure of the distillation must then be sufficiently high so that the available cooling water can condense the overhead vapor with an adequate temperature difference to provide reasonably rapid heat-transfer rates.   The cost of the fractionator will, however, increase with increased pressure of operation, and in the case of very volatile distillates some low-temperature refrigerant may be used as a coolant.

If the condensate is cooled only to the bubble point, the withdrawn distillate is then usually further cooled in a separate heat exchanger to avoid vaporization loss on storage.

Partial condensers

It is occasionally desired to withdraw a distillate product in the vapor state, especially when the low boiling point of the distillate makes complete condensation difficult. In this case the overhead vapor is cooled sufficiently to condense the necessary liquid reflux and the residual vapor provides the product, as in Fig. 9.45.

A partial condenser may produce any of several results.   (1) If time of contact between vapor product and liquid reflux is sufficient, the two will be in equilibrium with each other and the condenser provides an equilibrium condensation.   (2) If the condensate is removed as rapidly as it forms, a differential condensation may

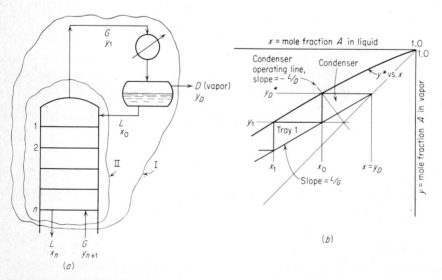

Fig. 9.45 *Partial equilibrium condenser.*

occur. (3) If cooling is very rapid, little mass transfer between vapor and condensate results, and the two will have essentially the same composition.

In case the first pertains, the condenser acts as one theoretical stage for the separation. The compositions y_D and x_0 may be computed by the methods of equilibrium condensation, as shown in Fig. 9.45b. The enriching operating line is then given as usual by material balances.

Envelope I

$$G = L + D \tag{9.134}$$

$$Gy_{n+1} = Lx_n + Dy_D \tag{9.135}$$

Envelope II

$$Gy_{n+1} + Lx_0 = Gy_1 + Lx_n \tag{9.136}$$

In the design of new equipment it is safer to ignore the enrichment which may be obtained by a partial condenser and to include the additional theoretical tray in the column, since it is difficult to ensure that equilibrium condensation will occur.

Cold reflux

If the overhead vapor is condensed and cooled below its bubble point so that the reflux liquid is cold, vapor G_1 rising from the top tray will be less in quantity than that for the rest of the enriching section since some will be required to condense and heat the reflux to its bubble point. External reflux L_0 will require $L_0 C_{L0} M_{av}(t_{bpR} - t_R)$ Btu/hr, where t_{bpR} and t_R are the reflux bubble point and actual temperatures, respectively. An amount of vapor, $L_0 C_{L0} M_{av}(t_{bpR} - t_R)/(\lambda M)_{av}$ will condense to provide the heat, and the condensed vapor adds to L_0 to provide L, the liquid flow rate below the top tray. Therefore

$$L = L_0 + \frac{L_0 C_{L0} M_{av}(t_{bpR} - t_R)}{(\lambda M)_{av}} = RD\left[1 + \frac{C_{L0} M_{av}(t_{bpR} - t_R)}{(\lambda M)_{av}}\right] \tag{9.137}$$

where R is the usual external reflux ratio, L_0/D. Defining an *apparent* reflux ratio R' by

$$R' = \frac{L}{D} = \frac{L}{G - L} \tag{9.138}$$

gives

$$R' = R\left[1 + \frac{C_{L0} M_{av}(t_{bpR} - t_R)}{(\lambda M)_{av}}\right] \tag{9.139}$$

The enriching operating line becomes

$$y_{n+1} = \frac{R'}{R' + 1} x_n + \frac{x_D}{R' + 1} \tag{9.140}$$

and it is plotted through $y = x = x_D$, with a y intercept at $x_D/(R' + 1)$ and a slope $R'/(R' + 1)$.

Rectification of azeotropic mixtures

Minimum- and maximum-boiling azeotropic mixtures of the type shown in Figs. 9.7 and 9.10 may be treated by the methods already described, except that it will be impossible to obtain two products of compositions which fall on opposite sides of the azeotropic composition. In the rectification of a minimum-boiling azeotrope (Fig. 9.7), for example, the distillate product may be as close to the azeotropic composition as desired. But the residue product will be either rich in A or rich in B depending upon whether the feed is richer or leaner in A than the azeotropic mixture. In the case of maximum-boiling mixtures (Fig. 9.10) the residue product will always approach the azeotropic composition. These mixtures may sometimes be separated completely by addition of a third substance, as described later.

Insoluble mixtures which form two-liquid-phase azeotropes may, however, be readily separated completely, provided two fractionators are used. This depends upon the fact that the condensed distillate forms two liquid solutions on opposite sides of the azeotropic composition. Consider the separation of the mixture whose vapor-liquid equilibrium diagram is shown in Fig. 9.46, where the feed has the composition z_F and the solubility limits are x_{RI} and x_{RII} at the boiling point. If the feed is introduced into fractionator I of Fig. 9.47, it is evident that the residue product of composition x_{WI} may be as nearly pure B as desired. The enriching section may contain sufficient trays to produce an overhead vapor approaching the azeotropic composition M, such as vapor y_{DI}. This vapor, when totally condensed to mixture K at its boiling point, will form two insoluble liquids of composition x_{RI} and x_{RII}, which may be decanted as shown. The layer which is richer in B is returned to the

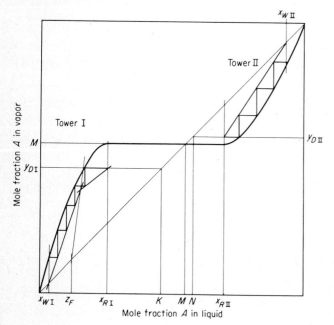

Fig. 9.46 *Fractionation of partially miscible mixtures.*

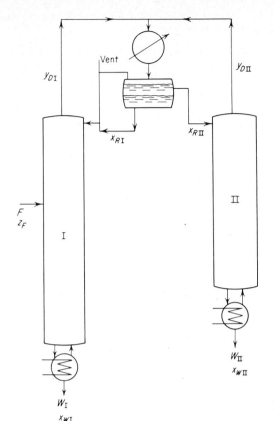

Fig. 9.47 *Two-tower system for partially miscible mixtures.*

top tray of column I as reflux. The enriching operating line for column I then passes through the point $(y = y_{DI}, x = x_{RI})$, as shown in Fig. 9.46, and its slope will be the liquid/vapor ratio in the enriching section.

The A-rich layer from the decanter (Fig. 9.47) is sent to the top tray of fractionator II, which contains only a stripping or exhausting section. It is clear from Fig. 9.46 that the residue product composition x_{WII} may be as nearly pure A as desired (turn the figure upside down to give it its usual appearance). The overhead vapor from tower II will be of composition y_{DII}, which, when totally condensed as mixture N, produces the same two insoluble liquids as the first distillate. Consequently a common condenser may be used for both towers.

In practice it will be desirable to cool the distillate below its bubble point to prevent excessive loss of vapor from the vent of the decanter. This changes the compositions x_{RI} and x_{RII} slightly and provides somewhat larger internal reflux ratios. If the feed itself consists of two insoluble liquids, it may be fed to the decanter, whereupon both fractionators then consist of exhausting sections only. When it is desired to remove the last traces of water from a substance such as a hydrocarbon, it is common practice to use only one tower from which the dry hydrocarbon is removed as the residue product. The hydrocarbon-rich layer from the decanter is returned as reflux, but the water layer, which contains very little hydrocarbon, is normally discarded.

The Ponchon-Savarit method may also be used,[31] but the necessary enthalpy data are rarely available for these systems.

Multiple feeds

If two solutions of different concentrations are to be fractionated to give the same products, both may be handled in the same fractionator. The McCabe-Thiele diagram for a two-feed column will resemble the lower part of Fig. 9.33, with operating lines straight. Each feed is considered separately (as if neither "knew" of the other's presence). The upper operating line is located as usual. The intermediate operating line, for the section of the column between feeds, intersects the enriching line at the q line for the richer feed and has a slope given by the L and G quantities computed through Eqs. (9.119) and (9.120). The lowermost operating line intersects the intermediate one at the q line for the less rich feed. For the least number of stages at a given reflux ratio, the feeds are each introduced at the stage whose construction on the diagram straddles their respective q line.

High-purity products

In Illustration 9.10 it was shown that for very low concentrations of more volatile substance in the residue, the graphical construction for stripping-section trays can be completed on logarithmic coordinates. This is readily done, since at very low concentrations the equilibrium curve is essentially linear, given by $y^* = \alpha x$. This plots as a straight $45°$ line on logarithmic coordinates, and α is taken for very low concentrations. The operating line is curved on such a graph, however, and must be plotted from its equation, (9.114). For very pure distillates a similar logarithmic graph can be constructed by turning the graph paper upside down and re-marking the coordinates as $(1 -$ printed marking).[21] Thus, the printed 0.0001 is marked as 0.9999, etc. On such a graph the equilibrium curve is also straight at $45°$ for high concentrations, but the operating line is curved and must be plotted from its equation, (9.111). Specially drawn graph paper can be used for the complete diagram.[24]

As an alternative to these methods, calculations may be made analytically using the Kremser equations (5.50) to (5.57) or Fig. 5.16, since even for systems where the McCabe-Thiele assumptions are not generally applicable, the operating lines are straight at the extreme concentrations now under consideration. The *exhausting section* is considered as a stripper for the more volatile component, whence, for a kettle-type reboiler,

$$N_p - m + 1 = \frac{\log\left[\frac{(x_m - x_W/\alpha)}{(x_W - x_W/\alpha)}(1 - \bar{A}) + \bar{A}\right]}{\log(1/\bar{A})} \tag{9.141}$$

where x_m is the composition of the liquid leaving tray m, the last ideal tray obtained by graphical work, and $\bar{A} = L/\alpha G$. For a thermosiphon reboiler which totally vaporizes the liquid, the left-hand side of Eq. (9.141) is $N_p - m$. For open steam, the left-hand side is $N_p - m$, and x_W/α is omitted ($y_{Np+1} = 0$). The *enriching section* is considered as an absorber for the less volatile component

$$n - 1 = \frac{\log \left[\frac{(1 - y_n) - (1 - x_0)/\alpha}{(1 - y_1) - (1 - x_0)/\alpha} \left(1 - \frac{1}{A} \right) + \frac{1}{A} \right]}{\log A} \tag{9.142}$$

where y_n is the vapor leaving tray n, the last ideal tray obtained by graphical construction upward from the feed, x_0 is the reflux composition, and $A = \alpha L/G$.

For many ideal liquids, where α is nearly constant for all concentrations, the analytical calculation of Smoker[36] applies to the entire fractionator.

Tray efficiencies

Methods for estimating tray efficiencies are discussed in Chap. 6. Murphree vapor efficiencies are most simply used graphically on the xy diagram, whether this is derived from the exact Ponchon-Savarit calculation or with the simplifying assumptions, as shown in Illustration 9.11. Overall efficiencies E_O strictly have meaning only when the Murphree efficiency of all trays is the same and when the equilibrium and operating lines are both straight over the concentrations considered. The latter requirement can be met only over limited concentration ranges in distillation, but nevertheless the empirical correlation of Fig. 6.16 is useful for rough estimates, if not for final designs, with the exception that values of E_O for aqueous solutions are usually higher than the correlation shows.

Illustration 9.11. In the development of a new process, it will be necessary to fractionate 2,000 lb/hr of an ethanol-water solution containing 0.3 mole fraction ethanol, available at the bubble point. It is desired to produce a distillate containing 0.80 mole fraction ethanol, with a substantially negligible loss of ethanol in the residue.

There is available a tower containing 20 identical cross-flow sieve trays, 30-in. diameter, with provision for introducing the feed only on the twelfth tray from the top. The tower is suitable for use at 1-atm pressure. The tray spacing is 18 in., the weir on each tray is 21 in. long, extending 2.25 in. above the tray floor, and the area of perforations is 0.5 sq ft/tray.

Determine a suitable reflux ratio for use with this tower, and estimate the corresponding alcohol loss, assuming that open steam at 10 psig will be used for heating and that adequate condenser capacity will be supplied.

Solution. The McCabe-Thiele method will be used. Mol wt ethanol = 46.05, of water = 18.02. $z_F = 0.30$.

Basis: 100 lb moles feed. Ethanol = 30 lb moles = 1,383 lb; water = 70 lb moles = 1,263 lb. Total feed = 2,646 lb.

Basis: 1 hr. Feed contains 2,000(30/2,646) = 22.7 lb moles ethanol and 2,000(70/2,646) = 52.9 lb moles water, total = 75.6 lb moles. If essentially all the ethanol is removed from the residue, the distillate $D = 22.7/0.80 = 28.4$ lb moles/hr, or 1,172 lb/hr. Vapor-liquid equilibrium data are available in "The Chemical Engineers' Handbook," 4th ed., p. 13-5.

Preliminary calculations indicate that the capacity of the tower is governed by the top vapor rate. At tray 1, av mol wt vapor = 0.8(46.05) + 0.2(18.02) = 40.5 lb/lb mole, temp = 78.2°C. Using Chap. 6 notation,

$$\rho_G = \frac{40.5}{359} \frac{273}{273 + 78.2} = 0.0876 \text{ lb/cu ft}$$

$$\rho_L = 46.5 \text{ lb/cu ft} \qquad \sigma' \text{ (estd)} = 21 \text{ dynes/cm}$$

Table 6.1: for $t = 18$ in., $a = 0.1503$, $b = 0.0955$. The tower cross-sectional area $= A_t = \pi(30)^2/4(144) = 4.90$ sq ft, and for a 21-in. weir, $A_d = 0.088A_t = 0.43$ sq ft. The active area $A_a = 4.90 - 2(0.43) = 4.04$ sq ft. With $A_h = 0.5$ sq ft, and tentatively taking $(L'/G')(\rho_G/\rho_L)^{0.5} = 0.1$, Eq. (6.3) provides $C_F = 0.278$, and Eq. (6.1) shows $V_F = 6.40$ ft/sec as the flooding gas velocity based on $A_t - A_d = 4.90 - 0.43 = 4.47$ sq ft.

Calculations will be made for a reflux ratio $R = 3.0$, corresponding to $G = D(R + 1) = 28.4(3 + 1) = 113.6$ lb moles/hr vapor at the top, or

$$\frac{113.6(359)}{3,600} \frac{273 + 78.2}{273} = 14.6 \text{ cu ft/sec}$$

The vapor velocity is then $14.6/4.47 = 3.26$ ft/sec, or 51% of the flooding value (amply safe). $L = 3(28.4) = 85.2$ lb moles/hr, or 3,518 lb/hr. Therefore

$$\frac{L'}{G'}\left(\frac{\rho_G}{\rho_L}\right)^{0.5} = \frac{3,518}{14.6(3,600)(0.0876)}\left(\frac{0.0876}{46.5}\right)^{0.5} = 0.0332$$

Since for values of this quantity less than 0.1, Eq. (6.3) nevertheless uses 0.1, the calculated C_F is correct.

Since the feed is at the bubble point, $q = 1$, and Eq. (9.119):

$$\bar{L} = L + qF = 85.2 + 1(79.6) = 160.8 \text{ lb moles/hr}$$

Eq. (9.120):

$$\bar{G} = G + F(q - 1) = G = 113.6 \text{ lb moles/hr}$$

The enthalpy of saturated steam (referred to 32°F) at 10 psig gage $= 1160.4$ Btu/lb, and this will be its enthalpy as it enters the tower if expanded to the tower pressure adiabatically. The enthalpy of saturated steam at 1 atm (neglecting tower pressure drop) $= 1150.4$ Btu/lb, and the latent heat $= 970.3$ Btu/lb.

Eq. (9.132):

$$113.6 = \bar{G}_{Np+1}\left[1 + \frac{(1160.4 - 1150.4)18.02}{970.3(18.02)}\right]$$

$$\bar{G}_{Np+1} = 112.0 \text{ lb moles steam/hr}$$

Eq. (9.133):

$$160.8 = 113.6 - 112.0 + L_{Np}$$

$$L_{Np} = W = 158.2 \text{ lb moles residue/hr}$$

Tray Efficiencies. Consider the situation at $x = 0.5$, $y^* = 0.654$, $t = 79.8°C$, which is in the enriching section. Here (Chap. 6 notation) $\rho_L = 49.4$, $\rho_G = 0.0780$ lb/cu ft, m (from equilibrium data) $= 0.42$, and by the methods of Chap. 2, $Sc_G = 0.930$, $D_L = 8(10^{-5})$ sq ft/hr. For $L = 85.2$ lb moles/hr, $q = 0.0154$ cu ft/sec, and for $G = 113.6$ lb moles/hr, $V_a = 3.63$ ft/sec. From the tray dimensions, $z = 2.12$ ft, $Z = 2.14$ ft, and $h_W = 2.25$ in.

Eq. (6.31): $N_{tG} = 1.275$ Eq. (6.9): $h_L = 1.838$

Eq. (6.34): $\theta_L = 0.01252$ Eq. (6.32): $N_{tL} = 34$

Eq. (6.23): $N_{tOG} = 1.250$ Eq. (6.22): $E_{OG} = 0.714$

Eq. (6.33): $D_E = 49$ Eq. (6.29): Pe $= 748$

Eq. (6.27): $E_{MG} = 0.82$

Entrainment is negligible. Similarly,

x	0	0.1	0.3	0.5	0.7
E_{MG}	0.65	0.70	0.82	0.82	0.82

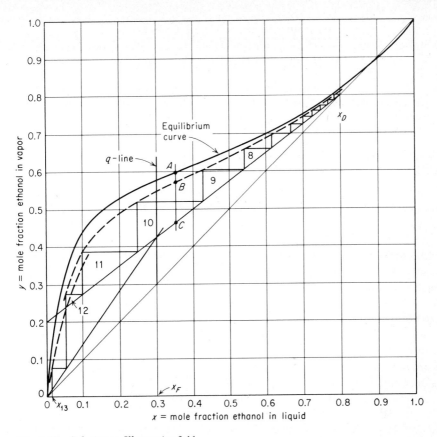

Fig. 9.48 *Solution to Illustration 9.11.*

Tray calculations. The operating-line intercept $= x_D/(R + 1) = 0.8/(3 + 1) = 0.2$, $q/(q - 1) = \infty$. The operating line for the enriching section and the q line are located as usual (Fig. 9.48). The exhausting-section operating line, on this scale of plot, passes through the origin for all practical purposes. The broken curve is located so that at each concentration, vertical distances corresponding to line BC and line AC are in the ratio E_{MG}. The curve is used instead of the equilibrium curve to locate real trays, as shown. The feed tray is the twelfth.

Below tray 13, calculations can be made on logarithmic coordinates as in Illustration 9.10, but this will necessitate trial-and-error location of the operating line since x_W is unknown. It is easier to proceed as follows.

From Fig. 9.48, $x_{13} = 0.0150$, and from this concentration down, the equilibrium curve is essentially straight ($\alpha = m = 8.95$), $E_{MG} = 0.65 = $ const, $\bar{A} = L/\alpha\bar{G} = 160.8/8.95(113.6) = 0.1582$. Equation (8.14) then provides the overall tray efficiency

$$E_O = \frac{\log\,[1 + 0.65(1/0.1582 - 1)]}{\log\,(1/0.1582)} = 0.897$$

There are 7 real or $7(0.897) = 6.28$ ideal trays to the bottom of the tower, whence Eq. (9.141) provides, for open steam,

$$6.28 = \frac{\log \left[(0.0150/x_W)(1 - 0.1582) + 0.1582 \right]}{\log (1/0.1582)}$$

$x_W = 12(10^{-8})$ mole fraction ethanol in the residue.

This corresponds to an ethanol loss of approximately 0.02 lb/day. Larger reflux ratios would reduce this further, but the cost of additional steam will likely make them not worthwhile. Smaller values of R, with corresponding reduced steam cost but larger ethanol loss, should be considered, but care should be taken to ensure gas velocities above the weeping velocity [Eq. (6.17)].

CONTINUOUS-CONTACT EQUIPMENT (PACKED TOWERS)

Towers filled with the various types of packings described in Chap. 6 are frequently competitive in cost with trays, and they are particularly useful in cases where pressure drop must be low, as in low-pressure distillations, and where liquid holdup must be small, as in distillation of heat-sensitive materials whose exposure to high temperatures must be minimized. There are also available extremely effective packings for use in bench-scale work, capable of producing the equivalent of many stages in packed heights of only a few feet.[28]

The transfer unit

As in the case of packed absorbers, the changes in concentration with height produced by these towers are continuous rather than stepwise as for tray towers, and the computation procedure must take this into consideration. Figure 9.49a shows a schematic drawing of a packed-tower fractionator. As in the case of tray towers, it must be provided with a reboiler at the bottom (or open steam may be used if an aqueous residue is produced), a condenser, means of returning reflux and reboiled vapor, as well as means for introducing feed. The last may be accomplished by providing a short unpacked section at the feed entry, with adequate distribution of liquid over the top of the exhausting section (see Chap. 6).

The operating diagram, Fig. 9.49b, is determined in exactly the same fashion as for tray towers, using either the Ponchon-Savarit method, or, where applicable, the McCabe-Thiele simplifying assumptions. Equations for operating lines and enthalpy balances previously derived for trays are all directly applicable, with the exception that tray-number subscripts may be omitted. The operating lines are then simply the relation between x and y, the bulk liquid and gas compositions, prevailing at each horizontal section of the tower. As before, the change from enriching- to exhausting-section operating lines is made at the point where the feed is actually introduced, and for new designs a shorter column results, for a given reflux ratio, if this is done at the intersection of the operating lines. In what follows, this practice is assumed.

For packed towers, rates of flow are based on unit tower cross-sectional area, lb moles/(hr)(sq ft). As for absorbers, in the differential volume dZ cu ft, Fig. 9.49a, the interface surface is $a\,dZ$ sq ft, where a is the a_A of Chap. 6. The quantity of substance A in the vapor passing through the differential section is Gy moles/(hr)(sq ft), and the rate of mass transfer is $d(Gy)$ moles A/(hr)(differential volume).

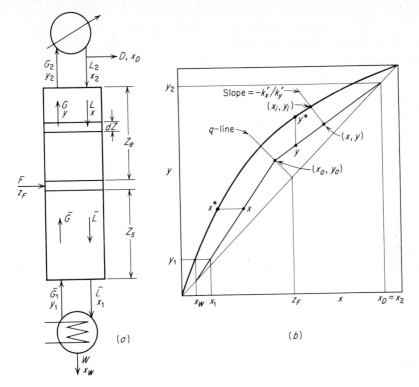

Fig. 9.49 *Fractionation in a packed tower.*

Similarly, the rate of mass transfer is $d(Lx)$. Even in those cases where the usual simplifying assumptions are not strictly applicable, G and L are, within a section of the column, each sufficiently constant so that equimolar counterdiffusion between phases is practically true: $N_A = -N_B$. Consequently (see Table 3.1), $F_G = k_y'$, $F_L = k_x'$, and the mass-transfer flux is

$$N_A = \frac{d(Gy)}{a\,dZ} = k_y'(y_i - y) = \frac{d(Lx)}{a\,dZ} = k_x'(x - x_i) \qquad (9.143)$$

Therefore

$$Z_e = \int_0^{Z_e} dZ = \int_{(Gy)_a}^{(Gy)_2} \frac{d(Gy)}{k_y'a(y_i - y)} = \int_{(Lx)_a}^{(Lx)_2} \frac{d(Lx)}{k_x'a(x - x_i)} \qquad (9.144)$$

A similar expression, with appropriate integration limits, applies to the stripping section.

For any point (x,y) on the operating line, the corresponding point (x_i,y_i) on the equilibrium curve is obtained at the intersection with a line of slope $-k_x'/k_y' = -k_x'a/k_y'a$ drawn from (x,y), as shown in Fig. 9.49b. For $k_x' > k_y'$, so that the principal mass-transfer resistance lies within the vapor, $y_i - y$ is more accurately read than $x - x_i$. The middle integral of Eq. (9.144) is then best used, evaluated graphically as the area under a curve of $1/k_y'a(y_i - y)$ as ordinate, Gy as abscissa, within the appropriate limits. For $k_x' < k_y'$, it is better to use the last integral. In this manner, variations in G, L, the coefficients, and the interfacial area with location on the operating lines are readily dealt with.

For cases where the usual simplifying assumptions apply, G and L within any section of the tower are each constant, and the heights of transfer units

$$H_{tG} = \frac{G}{k_y'a} \qquad H_{tL} = \frac{L}{k_x'a} \tag{9.145}$$

are sometimes sufficiently constant (or else average values for the section may be used) so that Eq. (9.144) may be written

$$Z_e = H_{tG} \int_{y_a}^{y_2} \frac{dy}{y_i - y} = H_{tG}N_{tG} \tag{9.146}$$

$$Z_e = H_{tL} \int_{x_a}^{x_2} \frac{dx}{x - x_i} = H_{tL}N_{tL} \tag{9.147}$$

with similar expressions for Z_s. The number of transfer units N_{tG} and N_{tL} are given by the integrals of Eqs. (9.146) and (9.147). It should be kept in mind, however, that the interfacial area a and the mass-transfer coefficients depend upon the mass rates of flow, which, because of changing average molecular weights with concentration, may vary considerably even if the molar rates of flow are constant. The constancy of H_{tG} and H_{tL} should therefore not be assumed without check.

Ordinarily the equilibrium curve for any section of the tower varies in slope sufficiently that overall mass-transfer coefficients and heights of transfer units cannot be used. If, however, the curve is essentially straight, we may write

$$Z_e = H_{tOG} \int_{y_a}^{y_2} \frac{dy}{y^* - y} = H_{tOG}N_{tOG} \tag{9.148}$$

$$Z_e = H_{tOL} \int_{x_a}^{x_2} \frac{dx}{x - x^*} = H_{tOL}N_{tOL} \tag{9.149}$$

where

$$H_{tOG} = \frac{G}{K_y'a} \qquad H_{tOL} = \frac{L}{K_x'a} \tag{9.150}$$

Here, $y^* - y$ is an overall "driving force" in terms of vapor compositions, and $x - x^*$ is a similar one for the liquid (see Fig. 9.49b). For such cases, Eqs. (8.45), (8.47), and (8.48) may be used to determine the number of overall transfer units without graphical integration. As shown in Chap. 5, with F's equal to the corresponding k''s,

$$\frac{1}{K'_y} = \frac{1}{k'_y} + \frac{m}{k'_x} \tag{9.151}$$

$$\frac{1}{K'_x} = \frac{1}{mk'_y} + \frac{1}{k'_x} \tag{9.152}$$

$$H_{tOG} = H_{tG} + \frac{mG}{L} H_{tL} \tag{9.153}$$

$$H_{tOL} = H_{tL} + \frac{L}{mG} H_{tG} \tag{9.154}$$

where, in Eqs. (5.27) and (5.28), $m = m' = m'' =$ slope of a straight equilibrium curve.

Although practically all the meaningful data on mass-transfer coefficients in packings were obtained at relatively low temperatures, the limited evidence is that they may be used for distillation as well, where the temperatures are normally relatively high. Reviews of data specifically for distillation are available;[5,37] research in this area is badly needed.

Illustration 9.12. Determine suitable dimensions of packed sections of a tower for the methanol-water separation of Illustration 9.8, using 1.5-in. Raschig rings.

Solution. Vapor and liquid quantities throughout the tower, calculated in the manner of Illustration 9.8, with Eqs. (9.57), (9.60), (9.68), and (9.70) are:

Enriching section

x	t_L, °F	y	t_G, °F	Vapor		Liquid	
				moles/hr	lb/hr	moles/hr	lb/hr
0.915	150	0.915	154	171.3	5,303	86.7	2,723
0.600	160	0.762	165.5	164.0	4,684	79.6	2,104
0.370	169	0.656	173	160.9	4,378	76.5	1,779

Stripping section

0.370	169	0.656	173	168.6	4,585	301	7,000
0.200	179	0.360	193	161.6	3,721	294	6,138
0.100	189	0.178	203	160.6	3,296	293	5,690
0.02	206	0.032	210.5	127.6	2,360	260	4,767

The x and y values are those on the operating line (Fig. 9.28). The temperatures are bubble and dew points for the liquids and vapors, respectively. The operating lines intersect at $x = 0.370$, the dividing point between enriching and stripping sections.

The tower diameter will be set by the conditions at the top of the stripping section because of the large liquid flow at this point.   Here (Chap. 6 notation),

$$\rho_G = \frac{4{,}585}{168.6(359)} \frac{492}{460 + 173} = 0.059 \text{ lb/cu ft}$$

$$\rho_L = 56.5 \text{ lb/cu ft}$$

and

$$\frac{L'}{G'}\left(\frac{\rho_G}{\rho_L}\right)^{0.5} = \frac{7{,}000}{4{,}185}\left(\frac{0.059}{56.5}\right)^{0.5} = 0.0495$$

Figure 6.26: loading (0.5 in H_2O/ft) provides an ordinate of 0.055.   Since C_f (Table 6.2) = 95, $\mu'_L = 0.45$ centipoise, and $\rho_W = 60.7$ lb/cu ft,

$$G' \text{ at loading} = \left[\frac{0.055 g'_c \rho_G \rho_L}{C_f \mu_L'^{0.2}(\rho_W/\rho_L)}\right]^{0.5} = 940 \text{ lb/(hr)(sq ft)}$$

Choose a tower diameter of 2.5 ft (cross section = 4.90 sq ft), for which $G' = 4{,}585/4.90 = 932$ lb/(hr)(sq ft), $L' = 7{,}000/4.90 = 1{,}430$ lb/(hr)(sq ft), which are satisfactory.

Mass-transfer coefficients will be computed for this same location.

Table 6.3: $m = 1.82$, $n = -0.0048$, $p = 0.274$.   Use $G' = 932(0.075/0.059)^{0.5} = 1{,}043$, whence $a_{AW} = 12.85$ sq ft/cu ft.

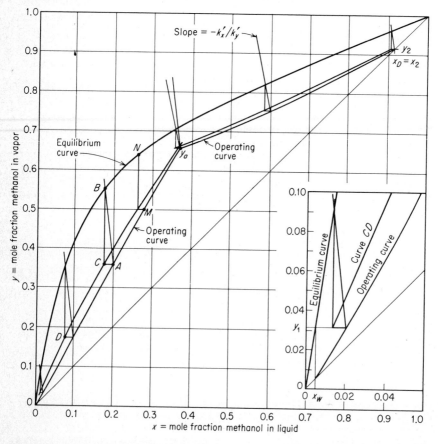

Fig. 9.50   *Solution to Illustration 9.12.*

Table 6.4: $d_s = 0.1740$ ft, $\beta = 0.499$, $\phi_{sW} = 0.0086$, $\phi_{tW} = 0.0279$, $\phi_{oW} = 0.0193$, $\phi_s = 0.00362$ (with $\mu'_L = 0.45$ centipoise, $\sigma' \doteq 29$ dynes/cm), $H = 0.90$, $\phi_o = 0.0174$, $\phi_t = 0.0210$.

Equation (6.42): $a_A = a = 12.85(0.0174/0.0193) = 11.55$ sq ft/cu ft.   Table 6.2: $\epsilon = 0.71$; Eq. (6.40) $\epsilon_o = 0.71 - 0.0210 = 0.689$.   By the methods of Chap. 2, $Sc_G = 1.0$. $G = 168.6/4.90 = 34.4$ lb moles/(hr)(sq ft), $\mu''_G = 0.0296$ lb/(ft)(hr), and by Eq. (6.39), $F_G = k'_y = 1.210$ lb moles/(hr)(sq ft)(mole fraction).

$$D_L = 18.6(10^{-5}) \text{ sq ft/hr}$$

$$Sc_L = 103.5$$

and by Eq. (6.41), $k_L = 3.12$ lb moles/(hr)(sq ft)(lb mole/cu ft)

Since the molar density of water at 169°F is 3.36 lb moles/cu ft, $F_L = k'_x = 3.12(3.36) = 10.5$ lb moles/(hr)(sq ft)(mole fraction).   Similarly, values were calculated at each of the entries of the above table.

x	G	a	k'_y	k'_x
0.915	35.0	6.15	1.125	7.75
0.600	33.5	6.57	1.138	6.35
0.370	32.8	6.68	1.140	5.70
0.370	34.4	11.58	1.210	10.50
0.200	33.0	10.00	1.248	10.95
0.100	32.7	9.75	1.303	10.75
0.02	26.0	6.78	1.170	11.05

Figure 9.50 shows the equilibrium curve and operating curves as determined in Illustration 9.8. At $x = 0.2$, $y = 0.36$, on the operating curve, line AB was drawn with slope $= -k'_x/k'_y = -10.95/1.248 = -8.77$.   Point B then provides the value of y_i for $y = 0.36$.   Similarly the lines are erected at each of the x values of the table.   Points such as C and D are joined by the curve CD.   Then, at any point M, the corresponding y_i at N is easily located.   The enlarged inset of the figure shows y_1 for the vapor entering the packed section to be in equilibrium with the reboiler liquid x_W.   Since $k'_x > k'_y$, the middle integral of Eq. (9.144) will be used.   The following values of y_i were determined in the manner described, with values of G, k'_y, and a obtained from a plot of these against y.

y	y_i	$\dfrac{1}{k'_y a(y_i - y)}$	Gy
$y_2 = 0.915$	0.960	2.82	$32.0 = (Gy)_2$
0.85	0.906	2.37	29.1
0.80	0.862	2.14	27.0
0.70	0.760	2.22	23.2
$y_a = 0.656$	0.702	3.50	$21.6 = (Gy)_a$
$y_a = 0.656$	0.707	1.40	$22.6 = (Gy)_a$
0.50	0.639	0.554	16.65
0.40	0.580	0.443	13.20
0.30	0.500	0.396	9.90
0.20	0.390	0.412	6.56
0.10	0.230	0.687	3.07
$y_1 = 0.032$	0.091	2.14	$0.83 = (Gy)_1$

Graphical integration (not shown) according to Eq. (9.144) provides $Z_e = 24.7$ ft for the enriching section, $Z_s = 14.9$ ft for the stripping section.

Berl saddles of the 1.5-in. size, because they provide substantially larger interfacial areas, lead to packed depths equal to roughly six-tenths of the above values, with approximately a 30% reduction of the gas pressure drop per foot, at the same mass velocities (although in this instance pressure drop is not important). A choice between such packings then revolves about their relative costs.

In the above example, H_{tG} for the stripping section varies from $34.4/1.210(11.58) = 2.46$ ft at the top to 3.27 ft at the bottom. Using Eq. (9.146) with an average $H_{tG} = 2.9$ yields $Z_s = 15.3$ rather than 14.9 ft as first computed. The equilibrium-curve slope varies so greatly that the use of H_{tOG} here is not recommended.

MULTICOMPONENT SYSTEMS

Many of the distillations of industry involve more than two components. While the principles established for binary solutions generally apply to such distillations, new problems of design are introduced which require special consideration.

Consider the continuous separation of a ternary solution consisting of components A, B, and C whose relative volatilities are in that order (A most volatile). In order to obtain the three substances in substantially pure form, either of the schemes of Fig. 9.51 may be used. According to scheme (a), the first column is used to separate C as a residue from the rest of the solution. The residue is necessarily contaminated with a small amount of B and with an even smaller amount of A, although if relative volatilities are reasonably large, the amount of the latter may be

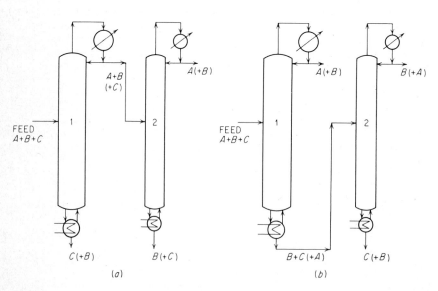

Fig. 9.51 *Separation of a ternary system.*

exceedingly small. The distillate, which is necessarily contaminated with at least a small amount of C, is then fractionated in a second column to provide nearly pure A and B. According to scheme (b), the first tower provides nearly pure A directly, and the residue is separated in the second. Which of the two schemes would be used depends upon the relative difficulty of the separation according to the two methods, but generally scheme (b) will be the more economical since it requires only one vaporization of substance A.

An important principle to be emphasized is that a single fractionator cannot separate more than one component in reasonably pure form from a multicomponent solution and that a total of $n - 1$ fractionators will be required for complete separation of a system of n components. It might at first be thought, for example, that the component of intermediate volatility B would tend to concentrate in reasonably pure form in the central parts of the first tower, from which it might be withdrawn as a *side stream*, thus allowing pure A and pure C to be withdrawn as distillate and residue, respectively. But this cannot occur. The feed tray of column 1, scheme (a), for example, will necessarily contain all three components in proportions not far from those prevailing in the feed itself. Trays immediately above the feed will therefore also contain appreciable quantities of all three substances, with the proportion of C gradually diminishing as we go higher in the enriching section. Similarly, trays immediately below the feed necessarily contain large proportions of all substances, with decreasing amounts of A and B as we penetrate more deeply into the exhausting section. While side streams are indeed sometimes withdrawn from fractionating towers, these streams must be further processed if they are to provide pure products.

The general principles of design of multicomponent fractionators are the same in many respects as those for binary systems, but the dearth of adequate vapor-liquid equilibrium data imposes severe restrictions on their application. These are especially needed for liquids which are not ideal, and the danger of attempting new designs without adequate equilibrium data or pilot-plant study for such solutions cannot be overemphasized. Inadequate methods of dealing with tray efficiencies for multicomponents represent another serious problem still to be solved.

Since the design calculations involve extensive trial and error, high-speed computers are frequently used. Except in extraordinary cases, it is not impossible to carry them out by hand, however, and this may be necessary when only a few designs are to be made. In what follows, hand calculations are assumed, and these will in any case provide an introduction to the computer methods. The most reliable design procedure is that of Thiele and Geddes.[38] This, or modifications of it, is the basis for many of the computer procedures. The method assumes that, for a given feed, the number of trays, position of the feed tray, and the liquid/vapor ratio and temperature for each tray are all known at the start, and it proceeds to compute the resulting distillate and residue products. In most cases, of course, at the beginning of a computation the necessary quantities are ordinarily unknown. The scheme outlined here begins by developing, with a minimum of trials, information necessary to use the Thiele-Geddes method, which then provides the final design.

Specification limitations

It will be assumed at the beginning that at least the following are established:

1. Temperature, pressure, composition, and rate of flow of the feed.

2. Pressure of the distillation (frequently fixed by the temperature of the available cooling water, which must be able to condense the distillate vapor to provide reflux).

3. Feed to be introduced on that tray which will result in the least total number of trays (optimum feed-tray location).

4. Heat losses (even if assumed to be zero).

Under these circumstances it has been shown[22] that there are left to the designer only three additional items which he may specify. Having chosen the three, all other characteristics of the fractionator are fixed. The designer may only calculate what they will be, and may arbitrarily assign values to them only temporarily for purposes of trial calculations and later verification. The three may be chosen from the following list, each item counting one:

1. Total number of trays.

2. Reflux ratio.

3. Reboil ratio, i.e., ratio of vapor produced by the reboiler to residue withdrawn.

4. Concentration of one component in one product (a maximum of two may be chosen).

5. Ratio of flow of one component in the distillate to the flow of the same component in the residue, or "split" of the component (a maximum of two may be chosen).

6. Ratio of total distillate to total residue.

In what follows, it will be assumed that the reflux ratio and splits of two components are specified. Modifications of the procedures are readily made for other cases. It is clear that, with more than two components in the feed, neither the complete compositions nor the rates of flow of either product are then known.

Key components

It is convenient first to list the feed components in order of their relative volatility. The more volatile components are called "light," the less volatile are "heavy." There will frequently be one component, the *light key component*, which is present in the residue in important amounts while components lighter than the light key are present in only very small amounts. If all components are present in the residue at important concentrations, then the most volatile is the light key. Similarly there will usually be one component, the *heavy key component*, present in the distillate in important amounts while components heavier than the heavy key are present only in small amounts. If all components are found in the distillate at important concentrations, then the least volatile is the heavy key.

The difficulty of the separation, as measured by the number of trays required for a given reflux ratio, is fixed by the key-component concentrations in the products. It is therefore important to establish which are the keys, and these may or may not be those whose splits have been specified.

Relative volatilities will be computed always with respect to the heavy key

$$\alpha_J = \frac{m_J}{m_{hk}} \qquad (9.155)$$

where J represents any component and hk the heavy key. Thus, $\alpha_{hk} = 1$, α's for components lighter than the heavy key are greater than 1, and those for heavier components are less than 1.

Minimum reflux ratio

This is the largest reflux ratio requiring an infinite number of trays to separate the key components.

With an infinite number of trays, it is possible to exclude from the distillate all components heavier than the heavy key. Since all components are present at the feed tray, and since it requires several enriching trays to reduce these heavy components to negligible concentrations, the "pinch" for these components, above which their concentration is zero, lies somewhere above the feed tray. Similarly an infinite number of trays permits exclusion from the residue of all components lighter than the light key, and there is a "pinch" for these several trays below the feed tray. The situation is therefore different from that for binary distillation, where at minimum reflux ratio there is only one pinch, usually at the feed tray.

Because of the possibility of excluding components from the products, computations at minimum reflux ratio help decide which are the key components. Components between the keys in volatility are found importantly in both products, and they are said to "distribute." Shiras et al.[34] show that at minimum reflux ratio, approximately

$$\frac{x_{JD}D}{z_{JF}F} = \frac{\alpha_J - 1}{\alpha_{lk} - 1} \frac{x_{lkD}D}{z_{lkF}F} + \frac{\alpha_{lk} - \alpha_J}{\alpha_{lk} - 1} \frac{x_{hkD}D}{z_{hkF}F} \qquad (9.156)$$

For $x_{JD}D/z_{JF}F$ less than -0.01 or greater than 1.01, component J will probably not distribute. For $x_{JD}D/z_{JF}F$ between 0.01 and 0.99, component J will undoubtedly distribute. The computations are made with first estimates of what the keys are, to be corrected as necessary.

Many methods of estimating the minimum reflux ratio R_m have been proposed, most of which are tedious to use and not necessarily very accurate. Since the only purpose of obtaining R_m is to estimate the product compositions at R_m and to ensure that the specified R is reasonable, an exact value is not required. Underwood's method,[40] which uses constant average α's and assumes constant L/G, is not exact but provides reasonable values without great effort; it is recommended (refer to the original papers for a derivation, which is lengthy). Two equations must be solved:

$$\sum \frac{\alpha_J z_{JF} F}{\alpha_J - \phi} = F(1 - q) \tag{9.157}$$

and

$$\sum \frac{\alpha_J x_{JD} D}{\alpha_J - \phi} = D(R_m + 1) \tag{9.158}$$

The first of these is written for all J components of the feed and solved for the necessary values of ϕ. There are $J - 1$ real, positive values of ϕ which satisfy the expression, and each lies between the α's of the components. However, the equation need be solved for only enough values of ϕ to determine, through Eq. (9.158), R_m and $x_{JD}D$ for components whose distribution is unknown. We thus require one more value of ϕ than there are components between the keys, and these will lie between α_{lk} and $\alpha_{hk} = 1$. Equation (9.158) is then written once for each value of ϕ so obtained, including the heavy key and all lighter components in the summations. These are solved simultaneously for R_m and the unknown $x_{JD}D$'s. If $x_{JD}D$ computes to be negative or greater than $z_{JF}F$, component J will not distribute, and the keys have been incorrectly chosen.

The α's are all computed at the average of the distillate dew point and the residue bubble point, which may require a few trial estimates. It is useful to note that in making dew-point calculations through Eq. (9.22), $\Sigma y_J / \alpha_J = m_{hk}$, and for bubble-point calculations through Eq. (9.21), $\Sigma \alpha_J x_J = 1/m_{hk}$, which helps determine the temperature.

Illustration 9.13. The following feed, at 180°F, 150 psi, is to be fractionated at that pressure so that the vapor distillate contains 98% of the C_3H_8 but only 1% of the C_5H_{12}:

Component	CH_4	C_2H_6	$n\text{-}C_3H_8$	$n\text{-}C_4H_{10}$	$n\text{-}C_5H_{12}$	$n\text{-}C_6H_{14}$
z_F, mole fraction	0.03	0.07	0.15	0.33	0.30	0.12

Estimate the minimum reflux ratio and the corresponding products.

Solution. The components will be identified as C_1, C_2, etc. Subscript numerals on m's, α's, etc., are temperatures, °F, if larger than 100; otherwise they represent tray numbers. Liquid solutions are assumed to be ideal. Values of m are taken from Depriester, *Chem. Eng. Progr. Symp. Ser.*, **49** (7), 1 (1953). Values of H, all as Btu/lb mole referred to the saturated liquid at $-200°F$, are taken from Maxwell, "Data Book on Hydrocarbons," D. Van Nostrand Company, Inc., Princeton, N.J., 1950. In the case of H_G for temperatures below the dew point, the enthalpy is that of the saturated vapor. In the case of H_L for temperatures above the critical, the enthalpy is that of the gas in solution. Values of m are conveniently plotted as $\log m$ vs. $t°F$ for interpolation. Enthalpy may be plotted vs. t on arithmetic coordinates.

	100°F	150°F	200°F	250°F
C_1:				
m	17.0	19.7	22.0	24.0
H_G	5,610	6,050	6,550	7,000
H_L	4,390	4,950	5,550	6,200
C_2:				
m	3.80	5.12	6.45	8.10
H_G	9,820	10,580	11,330	12,120
H_L	7,200	7,800	8,600	9,400
C_3:				
m	1.30	2.03	2.96	4.00
H_G	13,550	14,530	15,600	16,800
H_L	7,550	9,180	11,300	13,380
C_4:				
m	0.41	0.75	1.20	1.80
H_G	17,900	18,950	20,050	21,630
H_L	9,250	11,100	13,100	15,250
C_5:				
m	0.140	0.297	0.520	0.85
H_G	22,180	23,550	24,930	26,300
H_L	11,000	13,200	15,500	17,950
C_6:				
m	0.056	0.150	0.250	0.450
H_G	25,900	27,700	29,500	31,300
H_L	12,550	15,150	17,850	20,750

Basis: 1 lb mole feed throughout.

Flash vaporization of the feed. Use Eq. (9.32). After several trials, assume $G_F/F = 0.333$, $L_F/G_F = 0.667/0.333 = 2.0$.

Component	z_F	m_{180}	$y = \dfrac{z_F(2+1)}{1+2/m}$
C_1	0.03	21.0	0.0829
C_2	0.07	5.90	0.1578
C_3	0.15	2.56	0.2530
C_4	0.33	1.00	0.3300
C_5	0.30	0.42	0.1559
C_6	0.12	0.19	0.0312
	1.00		1.0108

Σy is sufficiently close to 1.0. Therefore $q = L_F/F = 0.67$. Tentatively assume C_3 = light key, C_5 = heavy key. Therefore specifications require $x_{lkD}D = 0.98(0.15) = 0.1470$ lb mole, $x_{hkD}D = 0.01(0.30) = 0.0030$ lb mole. Estimate the average temperature to be 175°F (to be checked).

Component	$z_F F$	m_{175}	α_{175}
C_1	0.03	21.0	$53.2 = 21.0/0.395$
C_2	0.07	5.90	14.94
lk C_3	0.15	2.49	6.30
C_4	0.33	0.95	2.405
hk C_5	0.30	0.395	1.0
C_6	0.12	0.180	0.456

Equation (9.156) is to be used for C_1, C_2, and C_6; the others distribute at R_m. Use y_{JD} instead of x_{JD} since distillate is a vapor.

C_1:
$$\frac{y_D D}{z_F F} = \left(\frac{53.2 - 1}{6.30 - 1}\right)\frac{0.1470}{0.15} + \left(\frac{6.30 - 53.2}{6.30 - 1}\right)\frac{0.0030}{0.30} = 9.761$$

Similarly, for C_2 and C_6 the values are 2.744 and -0.0892, respectively. None of these components will distribute at R_m, and the chosen keys are correct. The distillate contains 0.03 lb mole C_1, 0.07 lb mole C_2, and no C_6. The distribution of only C_4 to the products is unknown. Equation (9.157):

$$\frac{53.2(0.03)}{53.2 - \phi} + \frac{14.94(0.07)}{14.94 - \phi} + \frac{6.30(0.15)}{6.30 - \phi} + \frac{2.405(0.33)}{2.405 - \phi}$$

$$+ \frac{1.0(0.30)}{1.0 - \phi} + \frac{0.456(0.12)}{0.456 - \phi} = 1(1 - 0.67)$$

This is to be solved for the two values of ϕ lying between α_{C_3} and α_{C_4}, and α_{C_4} and α_{C_5}. Therefore, $\phi = 4.7760$ and 1.4177. Equation (9.158) is then written for each value of ϕ and for components C_1 through C_5. For $\phi = 4.776$,

$$\frac{53.2(0.03)}{53.2 - 4.776} + \frac{14.94(0.07)}{14.94 - 4.776} + \frac{6.30(0.1470)}{6.30 - 4.776} + \frac{2.405(y_{C_4 D} D)}{2.405 - 4.776} + \frac{1.0(0.0030)}{1.0 - 4.776} = D(R_m + 1)$$

This is repeated with $\phi = 1.4177$, and the two solved simultaneously. $y_{C_4 D} D = 0.1306$ lb mole C_4 in the distillate, $D(R_m + 1) = 0.6099$. For the distillate, try a dew point $= 115°F$:

Component	$y_D D$	y_D	m_{115}	α_{115}	$\dfrac{y_D}{\alpha_{115}}$
C_1	0.03	0.0789	18.0	100	0.000789
C_2	0.07	0.1840	4.2	23.3	0.00789
lk C_3	0.1470	0.3861	1.50	8.34	0.0463
C_4	0.1306	0.3431	0.500	2.78	0.1234
hk C_5	0.0030	0.0079	0.180	1.0	0.0079
	$D = 0.3806$	1.0000			0.1863

$m_{hk} = m_{C_5} = 0.1863$ at 116°F, and the assumed 115° was close enough. For the residue, try a bubble point = 235°F. The amount of residue is obtained from $x_{JW}W = z_{JF}F - y_{JD}D$:

Component	$x_W W$	x_W	m_{235}	α_{235}	$\alpha_{235}x_W$
lk C_3	0.0030	0.00484	3.65	5.00	0.0242
C_4	0.1994	0.3219	1.60	2.19	0.7050
hk C_5	0.2970	0.4795	0.730	1.00	0.4800
C_6	0.1200	0.1937	0.380	0.521	0.1010
	$W = 0.6194$	1.0000			1.3102

$m_{hk} = m_{C_5} = 1/1.3102 = 0.763$ at 237°F, and the assumed 235°F was close enough.

Average temperature $= (237 + 116)/2 = 176.5°$F (assumed 175° is close enough). Therefore,

$$D(R_m + 1) = 0.3806(R_m + 1) = 0.6099$$

$$R_m = 0.58 \text{ mole reflux/mole distillate}$$

Total reflux

The product compositions change with reflux ratio, and computations at total reflux will help decide the ultimate compositions.

Fenske's equation (9.81) is not limited to binary mixtures, and it may be applied to the key components to determine the minimum number of trays,

$$N_m + 1 = \frac{\log \left[(x_{lkD}D/x_{hkD}D)(x_{hkW}W/x_{lkW}W)\right]}{\log \alpha_{lk,av}} \tag{9.159}$$

where $N_m + 1$ is the total number of ideal stages including the reboiler (and a partial condenser if credit is taken for its fractionating ability). The equation may then be applied to determine the distribution of other components at total reflux,

$$\frac{x_{JD}D}{x_{JW}W} = \alpha_{J,av}^{N_m+1} \frac{x_{hkD}D}{x_{hkW}W} \tag{9.160}$$

The average α is the geometric mean of the values at the distillate dew point and residue bubble point, which may require a few trials to estimate. Winn[42] suggests a method to reduce the number of trials required.

Having obtained N_m and R_m, reference may be made to any of the several empirical correlations mentioned earlier[2,7,11,13] for an estimate of the number of trays at reflux ratio R. These can be unreliable, however, particularly if the majority of the trays are in the exhausting section of the tower.

Illustration 9.13, continued. Compute the number of ideal trays at total reflux and the corresponding products.

Solution. Tentatively assume the same distillate and residue temperatures as obtained for the minimum reflux ratio.

Component	α_{115}	α_{235}	$\alpha_{av} = (\alpha_{115}\alpha_{235})^{0.5}$
C_1	100	31.9	56.4
C_2	23.3	10.43	15.6
lk C_3	8.34	5.00	6.45
C_4	2.78	2.19	2.465
hk C_5	1.0	1.0	1.0
C_6	0.415	0.521	0.465

Eq. (9.159):
$$N_m + 1 = \frac{\log\,[(0.147/0.003)(0.297/0.003)]}{\log 6.45} = 4.55$$

Eq. (9.160) for C_4:
$$\frac{y_{C_4D}D}{x_{C_4W}W} = (2.465)^{4.55}\frac{0.003}{0.297} = 0.611$$

A C_4 balance:
$$y_{C_4D}D + x_{C_4W}W = z_{C_4F}F = 0.33$$

Solving simultaneously,
$$y_{C_4D}D = 0.1255 \text{ lb mole} \qquad x_{C_4W}W = 0.2045 \text{ lb mole}$$

Similarly,

C_1: $\qquad\qquad x_{C_1W}W \doteq 0 \qquad y_{C_1D}D = 0.03$

C_2: $\qquad\qquad x_{C_2W}W \doteq 0 \qquad y_{C_2D}D = 0.07$

C_6: $\qquad y_{C_6D}D = 0.00003$ (negligible; assume 0) $\qquad x_{C_6W}W = 0.12$

Therefore, at total reflux,

Component	$y_D D$	$x_W W$
C_1	0.03	Nil
C_2	0.07	Nil
C_3	0.1470	0.0030
C_4	0.1255	0.2045
C_5	0.0030	0.2970
C_6	Nil	0.12
	0.3755 = D	0.6245 = W

The distillate dew point computes to be 115.5°F and the residue bubble point 234°F. The assumed 115 and 235 are close enough.

Product compositions

For components between the keys, a reasonable estimate of their distribution at reflux ratio R may be obtained by linear interpolation of $x_{JD}D$ between R_m and total reflux according to $R/(R + 1)$. For components lighter than the light key and heavier than the heavy key, unless there is clear indication of important distribution at total reflux and unless R is to be very large, it is best at this time to assume they do not distribute. Even very small amounts of light components in the residue or of heavy components in the distillate enormously disturb the computations to follow.

Illustration 9.13, continued. A reflux ratio $R = 0.8$ will be used. Estimate the product compositions at this reflux ratio.

Solution. Since C_1 and C_2 do not enter the residue (nor C_6 the distillate) appreciably at either total reflux or minimum reflux ratio, it is assumed that they will not at $R = 0.8$. C_3 and C_5 distributions are fixed by the specifications. Only that of C_4 remains to be estimated.

R	$\dfrac{R}{R+1}$	$y_{C_4D}D$
∞	1.0	0.1255
0.8	0.445	?
0.58	0.367	0.1306

Using a linear interpolation,

$$y_{C_4D}D = \frac{1 - 0.445}{1 - 0.367}(0.1306 - 0.1255) + 0.1255 = 0.1300$$

Therefore, for the distillate,

Component	$y_D D$	y_D	$\dfrac{y_D}{\alpha_{115}}$	$x_0 = \dfrac{y_D/\alpha}{\Sigma y_D/\alpha}$
C_1	0.03	0.0789	0.00079	0.00425
C_2	0.07	0.1842	0.0079	0.0425
lk C_3	0.1470	0.3870	0.0464	0.2495
C_4	0.1300	0.3420	0.1230	0.6612
hk C_5	0.0030	0.0079	0.0079	0.0425
	$D = 0.3800$	1.0000	0.1860	1.0000

$m_{C_5} = 0.1860$; $t = 115°F$ distillate dew point. The last column of the table shows the liquid reflux in equilibrium with the distillate vapor [Eq. (9.22)].

For the residue,

Component	$x_W W$	x_W	$\alpha_{235}x_W$	$y_{Np+1} = \dfrac{\alpha x_W}{\Sigma \alpha x_W}$
lk C_3	0.003	0.00484	0.0242	0.01855
C_4	0.200	0.3226	0.7060	0.5411
hk C_5	0.2970	0.4790	0.4790	0.3671
C_6	0.1200	0.1935	0.0955	0.0732
	$W = 0.6200$	1.0000	1.3047	1.0000

$m_{C_5} = 1/1.3047 = 0.767$; $t = 236°F$, residue bubble point. The last column shows the reboiler vapor in equilibrium with the residue [Eq. (9.21)].

Feed-tray location

Just as with binary mixtures, the change from enriching to exhausting section should be made as soon as greater enrichment is thereby produced. This ultimately can be determined only by trial in the Thiele-Geddes calculation,[10] but in the meantime some guidance is required. The following assumes constant L/G, neglects interference of components other than the keys, and assumes that the optimum feed tray occurs at the intersection of operating lines of the key components.[32]

Equation (9.109), the operating line for the enriching section, omitting the tray-number designations, may be written for each key component

$$x_{lk} = y_{lk} \frac{G}{L} - \frac{D}{L} x_{lkD} \tag{9.161}$$

$$x_{hk} = y_{hk} \frac{G}{L} - \frac{D}{L} x_{hkD} \tag{9.162}$$

Elimination of L provides

$$y_{lk} = \frac{x_{lk}}{x_{hk}} \left(y_{hk} - \frac{D}{G} x_{hkD} \right) + \frac{D}{G} x_{lkD} \tag{9.163}$$

Similarly, Eq. (9.113) for the exhausting section yields

$$y_{lk} = \frac{x_{lk}}{x_{hk}} \left(y_{hk} + \frac{W}{\bar{G}} x_{hkW} \right) - \frac{W}{\bar{G}} x_{lkW} \tag{9.164}$$

At the operating-line intersection, y_{lk} from Eqs. (9.163) and (9.164) are the same, as are y_{hk} and x_{lk}/x_{hk}. Equating the right-hand sides of the two expressions then produces

$$\left(\frac{x_{lk}}{x_{hk}} \right)_{\text{intersection}} = \frac{Wx_{lkW}/\bar{G} + Dx_{lkD}/G}{Wx_{hkW}/\bar{G} + Dx_{hkD}/G} \tag{9.165}$$

Combining Eqs. (9.72) and (9.120) for the light key produces

$$\frac{W}{\bar{G}} x_{lkW} + \frac{D}{G} x_{lkD} = \frac{GFz_{lkF} - DF(1-q)x_{lkD}}{[G - F(1-q)]G} \tag{9.166}$$

and a similar result is obtained for the heavy key. Putting these into Eq. (9.165) then yields, with $G/D = R + 1$,

$$\left(\frac{x_{lk}}{x_{hk}} \right)_{\text{intersection}} = \frac{z_{lkF} - x_{lkD}(1-q)/(R+1)}{z_{hkF} - x_{hkD}(1-q)/(R+1)} \tag{9.167}$$

Recall from the treatment of binaries that the feed tray f is the uppermost step on the exhausting-section operating line and that it rarely happens that the feed step exactly coincides with the operating-line intersection. The feed-tray location is then given by

$$\left(\frac{x_{lk}}{x_{hk}}\right)_{f-1} \geqslant \left(\frac{x_{lk}}{x_{hk}}\right)_{\text{intersection}} \geqslant \left(\frac{x_{lk}}{x_{hk}}\right)_{f} \tag{9.168}$$

Ultimately, the best feed-tray location is obtained through the Thiele-Geddes calculation.

Lewis and Matheson calculation[23]

This establishes the first (and usually the final) estimate of the number of trays required. Although it is possible to allow for variations in the L/G ratio with tray number by tray-to-tray enthalpy balances at the same time, since the products are not yet firmly established, it is best to omit this refinement.

With constant L/G, the McCabe-Thiele operating lines, which are merely material balances, are applicable to each component. Thus, for the enriching section, Eq. (9.109) is

$$y_{J,n+1} = \frac{L}{G} x_{Jn} + \frac{D}{G} z_{JD} \tag{9.169}$$

This is used alternately with dew-point (equilibrium) calculations to compute tray by tray for each component from the top down to the feed tray. For components heavier than the heavy key, there will be no z_{JD} available, and these components cannot be included.

For the exhausting section, it is convenient to solve Eq. (9.113) for x:

$$x_{Jm} = y_{J,m+1} \frac{\bar{G}}{\bar{L}} + \frac{W}{\bar{L}} x_{JW} \tag{9.170}$$

This is used alternately with bubble-point (equilibrium) calculations to compute tray by tray for each component from the bottom up to the feed tray. There are no values of x_{JW} for components lighter than the light key, and these cannot be included.

If, in the first estimate of product compositions, it is found that one product contains all components (lk = most volatile or hk = least volatile component of the feed), the computation can be started with this product and continued past the feed tray to the other end of the column. The operating-line equations appropriate to each section must of course be used. This will avoid the composition corrections discussed later.

Illustration 9.13, continued. Determine the number of ideal trays and the location of the feed tray for $R = 0.8$.

Solution. For locating the feed tray, Eq. (9.167):

$$\left(\frac{x_{lk}}{x_{hk}}\right)_{\text{intersection}} = \frac{0.15 - 0.3870(1 - 0.67)/1.8}{0.30 - 0.0079(1 - 0.67)/1.8} = 0.264$$

Enriching section:

$$D = 0.3800, \; L = RD = 0.8(0.3800) = 0.3040$$

$$G = L + D = 0.3040 + 0.3800 = 0.6840$$

$$\frac{L}{G} = \frac{0.3040}{0.6840} = 0.445 \qquad \frac{D}{G} = \frac{0.3800}{0.6840} = 0.555$$

Eq. (9.169):

C_1:
$$y_{n+1} = 0.445x_n + 0.555(0.0789) = 0.455x_n + 0.0438$$

Similarly,

C_2
$$y_{n+1} = 0.455x_n + 0.1022$$

C_3:
$$y_{n+1} = 0.445x_n + 0.2148$$

C_4:
$$y_{n+1} = 0.445x_n + 0.1898$$

C_5:
$$y_{n+1} = 0.445x_n + 0.0044$$

Estimate $t_1 = 135°F$.

Component	x_0	y_1 [Eq. (9.169), $n = 0$]	α_{135}	$\dfrac{y_1}{\alpha}$	$x_1 = \dfrac{y_1/\alpha}{\Sigma y_1/\alpha}$
C_1	0.00425	0.0457	79.1	0.00058	0.00226
C_2	0.0425	0.1211	19.6	0.00618	0.0241
lk C_3	0.2495	0.3259	7.50	0.0435	0.1698
C_4	0.6612	0.4840	2.66	0.1820	0.7104
hk C_5	0.0425	0.0233	1.00	0.0239	0.0933
	1.0000	1.0000		0.2562	1.0000

$m_{C_5} = 0.2562$, $t_1 = 138°F$. Liquid x_1's in equilibrium with y_1. $(x_{lk}/x_{hk})_1 = 0.1698/0.0933 = 1.82$. Tray 1 is not the feed tray. Estimate $t_2 = 145°F$.

Component	y_2 [Eq. (9.169), $n = 1$]	α_{145}	$\dfrac{y_2}{\alpha}$	$x_2 = \dfrac{y_2/\alpha}{\Sigma y_2/\alpha}$
C_1	0.0448	68.9	0.00065	0.00221
C_2	0.1129	17.85	0.00632	0.0214
lk C_3	0.2904	6.95	0.0418	0.1419
C_4	0.5060	2.53	0.2000	0.6787
hk C_5	0.0459	1.00	0.0459	0.1557
	1.0000		0.2947	1.0000

$m_{C_5} = 0.2947$, $t_2 = 149°F$. $(x_{lk}/x_{hk})_2 = 0.1419/0.1557 = 0.910$. The tray calculations are continued downward in this manner. The results for trays 5 and 6 are:

Component	x_5	x_6
C_1	0.00210	0.00204
C_2	0.0195	0.0187
lk C_3	0.1125	0.1045
C_4	0.4800	0.4247
hk C_5	0.3859	0.4500
t, °F	168	174
x_{lk}/x_{hk}	0.292	0.232

Applying Eq. (9.168), it is seen that tray 6 is the feed tray. Exhausting section:

$$L = L + qF = 0.3040 + 0.67(1) = 0.9740$$
$$\bar{G} = L - W = 0.9740 - 0.6200 = 0.3540$$
$$\frac{\bar{G}}{L} = \frac{0.3540}{0.9740} = 0.364 \qquad \frac{W}{L} = \frac{0.6200}{0.9740} = 0.636$$

Eq. (9.170): C_3: $\qquad x_m = 0.364 y_{m+1} + 0.636(0.00484) = 0.364 y_{m+1} + 0.00308$
Similarly,
C_4: $\qquad\qquad\qquad x_m = 0.364 y_{m+1} + 0.2052$
C_5: $\qquad\qquad\qquad x_m = 0.364 y_{m+1} + 0.3046$
C_6: $\qquad\qquad\qquad x_m = 0.364 y_{m+1} + 0.1231$

Estimate $t_{Np} = 230$°F.

Component	y_{Np+1}	x_{Np} [Eq. (9.170), $m = N_p$]	α_{230}	αx_{Np}	$y_{Np} = \dfrac{\alpha x_{Np}}{\Sigma \alpha x_{Np}}$
lk C_3	0.01855	0.00983	5.00	0.0492	0.0340
C_4	0.5411	0.4023	2.20	0.885	0.6118
hk C_5	0.3671	0.4382	1.0	0.4382	0.3028
C_6	0.0732	0.1497	0.501	0.0750	0.0514
	1.0000	1.0000		1.4474	1.0000

$m_{C_5} = 1/1.447 = 0.691$, $t_{Np} = 227$°F. y_{Np} in equilibrium with x_{Np}. $(x_{lk}/x_{hk})_{Np} = 0.00983/0.4382 = 0.0224$. N_p is not the feed tray. In like fashion, x_{Np-1} is obtained from y_{Np} with Eq. (9.170), and the computations continued up the tower. The results for trays $N_p - 7$ to $N_p - 9$ are:

Component	x_{Np-7}	x_{Np-8}	x_{Np-9}
lk C_3	0.0790	0.0915	0.1032
C_4	0.3994	0.3897	0.3812
hk C_5	0.3850	0.3826	0.3801
C_6	0.1366	0.1362	0.1355
t, °F	204	202	201
x_{lk}/x_{hk}	0.205	0.239	0.272

Application of Eq. (9.168) shows tray $N_p - 8$ as the feed tray. The data for $N_p - 9$ are discarded. Then $N_p - 8 = 6$, and $N_p = 14$ trays.

Composition corrections

The previous computations provide two feed-tray liquids, computed from opposite directions, which do not agree. In most cases, the number of trays will be satisfactory nevertheless, but in order to get suitable tray temperatures and L/G ratios for subsequent calculations, it is best to try to patch up the discrepancies for trays near the feed tray, at least. The following, due to Underwood,[39] is reasonably satisfactory.

Starting with the feed-tray liquid as computed from the enriching section, which shows no heavy components, the mole fractions are all reduced proportionately so that their sum, plus the mole fractions of the missing components (as shown in the feed-tray composition as computed from the exhausting section) is unity. The bubble point is then recalculated. The justification for this somewhat arbitrary procedure is that the *relative* concentrations of the light components in the vapor will remain about the same so long as their relative concentrations in the liquid are unchanged.

The concentrations of the missing heavy components on trays above the feed tray are next estimated. For these, z_{JD} should be very small, and Eq. (9.169) shows

Since

$$\frac{y_{J,n+1}}{y_{hk,n+1}} = \frac{Lx_{Jn}/G + Dz_{JD}/G}{Lx_{hk,n}/G + Dz_{hkD}/G} \doteq \frac{x_{Jn}}{x_{hkn}} \tag{9.171}$$

$$\frac{y_{J,n+1}}{y_{hk,n+1}} = \frac{m_{J,n+1}x_{J,n+1}}{m_{hk,n+1}x_{hk,n+1}} = \frac{\alpha_{J,n+1}x_{J,n+1}}{x_{hk,n+1}} \tag{9.172}$$

then

$$x_{Jn} = \frac{\alpha_{J,n+1}x_{J,n+1}x_{hkn}}{x_{hk,n+1}} \tag{9.173}$$

The liquid mole fractions on tray n as previously determined are then reduced proportionately to accommodate those of the heavy components, and a new bubble point is calculated. This is continued upward until the concentrations on upper trays as previously computed are no longer changed importantly.

Missing light components are added to trays below the feed in much the same manner. Thus, Eq. (9.170) for these provides

$$\frac{y_{J,m+1}}{y_{lk,m+1}} = \frac{x_{Jm} - Wx_{JW}/\bar{L}}{x_{lkm} - Wx_{lkW}/\bar{L}} \doteq \frac{x_{Jm}}{x_{lkm}} \tag{9.174}$$

where advantage is taken of the fact that x_{JW} must be small for these components. As before,

$$\frac{y_{J,m+1}}{y_{lk,m+1}} = \frac{m_{J,m+1}x_{J,m+1}}{m_{lk,m+1}x_{lk,m+1}} = \frac{\alpha_{J,m+1}x_{J,m+1}}{\alpha_{lk,m+1}x_{lk,m+1}} \doteq \frac{\alpha_{Jm}x_{J,m+1}}{\alpha_{lkm}x_{lk,m+1}} \tag{9.175}$$

The last approximation results from assuming that the ratio of α's stays reasonably constant with small temperature changes.   Then

$$x_{J,m+1} = \frac{x_{Jm}\alpha_{lkm}x_{lk,m+1}}{\alpha_{Jm}x_{lkm}} \tag{9.176}$$

The mole fractions of the components on the lower tray are then proportionately reduced to accommodate the light components, and the bubble point is recalculated.

Illustration 9.13, continued. Compositions at the feed tray as previously determined are listed in the first two columns.   The old x_6's are reduced to accommodate the C_6 from $N_p - 8$, and the new x_6's are determined.   The new bubble point is 188°F.

Component	x_{Np-8}	Old x_6	$x_6(1 - 0.1362)$	New x_6	α_{188}
C_1		0.00204	0.00176	0.00176	46.5
C_2		0.0187	0.0162	0.0162	13.5
lk C_3	0.0915	0.1045	0.0903	0.0903	5.87
C_4	0.3897	0.4247	0.3668	0.3668	2.39
hk C_5	0.3826	0.4500	0.3887	0.3887	1.00
C_6	0.1362			0.1362	0.467
	1.0000	1.0000	0.8638	1.0000	

For tray 5, x_{C_6} is estimated, through Eq. (9.173),

$$x_{C_6,5} = \frac{0.467(0.1362)(0.3859)}{0.3887} = 0.0631$$

where 0.3859 is the concentration of the heavy key on tray 5 as previously calculated.   The old x_5's are all reduced by multiplying them by $1 - 0.0631$, whence their new sum plus 0.0631 for $C_6 = 1$. The new tray 5 has a bubble point of 176°F, and its equilibrium vapor may be obtained from the bubble-point calculation, as usual.   In similar fashion, the calculations are continued upward. Results for the top trays and the distillate are:

Component	x_2	y_2	x_1	y_1	x_0	y_D
C_1	0.00221	0.0444	0.00226	0.0451	0.00425	0.0789
C_2	0.0214	0.1111	0.0241	0.1209	0.0425	0.1842
C_3	0.1418	0.2885	0.1697	0.3259	0.2495	0.3870
C_4	0.6786	0.5099	0.7100	0.4840	0.6611	0.3420
C_5	0.1553	0.0458	0.0932	0.0239	0.0425	0.0079
C_6	0.00262	0.00034	0.00079	0.00009	0.00015	0.00001
t, °F	150		138		115	

To correct tray $N_p - 7 =$ tray 7, use Eq. (9.176) to determine the concentrations of C_1 and C_2 on tray 7. $x_{1k, m+1}$ is taken from the old $N_p - 7$.

$$x_{C_1, 7} = \frac{0.00176(5.87)(0.0790)}{46.5(0.0903)} = 0.000194$$

$$x_{C_2, 7} = \frac{0.0162(5.87)(0.0790)}{13.5(0.0903)} = 0.00615$$

The old x_{N_p-7} must be reduced by multiplying by $1 - 0.000194 - 0.00615$. The adjusted values together with those above constitute the new x_7's. The new bubble point is 202°F.

The calculations are continued downward in the same fashion. The new tray 6 has $x_{C_1} = 0.000023$, $x_{C_2} = 0.00236$. It is clear that concentrations for these components are reducing so rapidly that there is no need to go further.

Liquid/vapor ratios

With the corrected temperatures and compositions, it is now possible to estimate the L/G ratios on the trays reasonably well.

For the enriching section, Eq. (9.54) may be solved simultaneously with Eq. (9.51) to provide

$$G_{n+1} = \frac{Q_C + D(H_D - H_{Ln})}{H_{G, n+1} - H_{Ln}} \qquad (9.177)$$

Equation (9.51) then provides L_n; G_n is computed through another application of Eq. (9.177), and hence L_n/G_n is obtained. Similarly for the exhausting section, Eqs. (9.62) and (9.65) provide

$$\bar{G}_{m+1} = \frac{Q_B + W(H_{Lm} - H_W)}{H_{G, m+1} - H_{Lm}} \qquad (9.178)$$

and Eq. (9.62) gives the liquid rate. Usually it is necessary to compute only a few such ratios in each section and interpolate the rest from a plot of L/G vs. tray number.

It must be remembered that if the enthalpies are computed from temperatures and concentrations taken from the Lewis-Matheson data, even though corrected in the manner previously shown, the L/G ratios will still be estimates only, since the data upon which they are based assume constant L/G in each section.

Illustration 9.13, continued. Compute the condenser and reboiler heat loads and the L/G ratios.
Solution. The condenser heat load is given by Eq. (9.49). Values of x_0, y_D, and y_1 are taken from the corrected concentrations previously obtained.

Component	H_D, vapor, 115°F	$y_D H_D$	H_{L0}, 115°F	$x_0 H_{L0}$	H_{G1}, 138°F	$y_1 H_{G1}$
C_1	5,800	458	4,500	19.1	6,000	270.5
C_2	10,050	1,851	7,400	314.5	10,400	1,258
C_3	13,800	5,340	8,000	1,996	14,300	4,660
C_4	18,200	6,220	9,800	6,490	18,700	9,050
C_5	22,600	178.5	11,650	495	23,200	555
C_6	26,430	0.3	13,350	2	27,300	4.1
		$14,048 = H_D$		$9,307 = H_{L0}$		$15,798 = H_{G1}$

Eq. (9.49):
$$Q_C = 0.3800[(0.8 + 1)(15,798) - 0.8(9,307) - 14,048]$$
$$= 2640 \text{ Btu/lb mole feed}$$

In similar fashion, $H_W = 16,863$, $H_F = 14,730$, and Q_B [Eq. (9.50)] $= 3700$ Btu/lb mole feed.
For tray $n = 1$, $G_1 = L_0 + D = D(R + 1) = 0.3800(0.8 + 1) = 0.684$ lb mole. With x_1 and y_2 from the corrected compositions,

Component	H_{G2}, 150°F	$H_{G2}y_2$	H_{L1}, 138°F	$H_{L1}x_1$
C_1	6,050	268.5	4,800	10.9
C_2	10,580	1,178	7,700	185.8
C_3	14,530	4,200	8,800	1,493
C_4	18,950	9,660	10,700	7,600
C_5	23,550	1,081	12,700	1,183
C_6	27,700	9.4	14,550	11.5
		$16,397 = H_{G2}$		$10,484 = H_{L1}$

Eq. (9.177):
$$G_2 = \frac{2,640 + 0.38(14,048 - 10,484)}{16,397 - 10,484} = 0.675 \text{ lb mole}$$

$$L_2 = G_2 - D = 0.675 - 0.380 = 0.295 \text{ lb mole}$$

$$\frac{L_2}{G_2} = \frac{0.295}{0.675} = 0.437$$

Similarly, the calculations may be made for other trays in the enriching section.
For tray $N_p = 14$,

Component	$H_{G,15}$, 236°F	$y_{15}H_{G,15}$	$H_{L,14}$, 227°F	$x_{14}H_{L,14}$
C_1		Nil		Nil
C_2		Nil		Nil
C_3	16,450	305	12,600	123.7
C_4	21,200	11,480	13,700	5,500
C_5	25,900	9,500	16,200	7,100
C_6	30,800	2,255	18,700	2,780
		$23,540 = H_{G,15}$		$15,504 = H_{L,14}$

Similarly, $H_{L,13} = 15,818$, and $H_{G,14} = 22,619$.

Eq. (9.178):
$$\bar{G}_{15} = \frac{3,700 + 0.62(15,504 - 16,863)}{23,540 - 15,504} = 0.358$$

$$L_{14} = W + \bar{G}_{15} = 0.620 + 0.358 = 0.978$$

$$\bar{G}_{14} = \frac{3,700 + 0.62(15,818 - 16,863)}{22,619 - 15,818} = 0.448$$

$$\frac{L_{14}}{\bar{G}_{14}} = \frac{0.978}{0.448} = 2.18$$

and similarly for other exhausting-section trays.   Thus,

Tray no.	$\dfrac{L}{G}$ or $\dfrac{L}{\bar{G}}$	t, °F	Tray no.	$\dfrac{L}{\bar{G}}$	t, °F
Condenser	0.80	115	8	3.25	206
1	0.432	138	9	2.88	208
2	0.437	150	10	2.58	210
3	0.369	158	11	2.48	212
4	0.305	165	12	2.47	217
5	0.310	176	13	2.42	221
6	1.53	188	14	2.18	227
7	4.05	202	Reboiler	1.73	236

These values are not final.   They scatter erratically because they are based on the temperatures and concentrations computed with the assumption of constant L/G.

Method of Thiele and Geddes

With number of trays, position of the feed tray, temperatures, and L/G ratios, the Thiele-Geddes method proceeds to compute the products which will result, thus ultimately permitting a check of all previous calculations.   The following is Edmister's[6] variation of the original.[38]

All the equations which follow apply separately for each component, and component designations are omitted.   For the enriching section, consider first the condenser.

$$G_1 y_1 = L_0 x_0 + D z_D \tag{9.179}$$

$$\frac{G_1 y_1}{D z_D} = \frac{L_0 x_0}{D z_D} + 1 \tag{9.180}$$

For a total condenser, $x_0 = z_D = x_D$, and $L_0/D = R$.   Therefore

$$\frac{G_1 y_1}{D z_D} = R + 1 = A_0 + 1 \tag{9.181}$$

For a partial condenser behaving like an ideal stage, $z_D = y_D$, $z_D/x_0 = y_D/x_0 = m_0$, and

$$\frac{G_1 y_1}{D z_D} = \frac{R}{m_0} + 1 = A_0 + 1 \tag{9.182}$$

A_0 is therefore either R or R/m_0, depending upon the type of condenser.   For tray 1,

$$\frac{L_1 x_1}{G_1 y_1} = \frac{L_1}{G_1 m_1} = A_1 \tag{9.183}$$

where A_1 is the absorption factor for tray 1.   Then

$$L_1 x_1 = A_1 G_1 y_1 \tag{9.184}$$

For tray 2,

$$G_2 y_2 = L_1 x_1 + D z_D \tag{9.185}$$

$$\frac{G_2 y_2}{D z_D} = \frac{L_1 x_1}{D z_D} + 1 = \frac{A_1 G_1 y_1}{D z_D} + 1 = A_1(A_0 + 1) + 1 = A_0 A_1 + A_1 + 1 \tag{9.186}$$

Generally, for any tray,

$$\frac{G_n y_n}{Dz_D} = \frac{A_{n-1}G_{n-1}y_{n-1}}{Dz_D} + 1 = A_0 A_1 A_2 \cdots A_{n-1} + A_1 A_2 \cdots A_{n-1} + \cdots + A_{n-1} + 1 \quad (9.187)$$

and for the feed tray,

$$\frac{G_f y_f}{Dz_D} = A_0 A_1 A_2 \cdots A_{f-1} + A_1 A_2 \cdots A_{f-1} + \cdots + A_{f-1} + 1 \quad (9.188)$$

Consider next the exhausting section. For a kettle-type reboiler,

$$\frac{\bar{G}_{Np+1}y_{Np+1}}{Wx_W} = \frac{\bar{G}_{Np+1}m_W}{W} = S_W \quad (9.189)$$

where S_W is the reboiler stripping factor. Since

$$L_{Np}x_{Np} = \bar{G}_{Np+1}y_{Np+1} + Wx_W \quad (9.190)$$

then

$$\frac{L_{Np}x_{Np}}{Wx_W} = \frac{\bar{G}_{Np+1}y_{Np+1}}{Wx_W} + 1 = S_W + 1 \quad (9.191)$$

For a thermosiphon reboiler, $y_{Np+1} = x_W$, and

$$S_W = \frac{\bar{G}_{Np+1}}{W} \quad (9.192)$$

S_W is therefore defined by either Eq. (9.189) or (9.192), depending upon the type of reboiler. For the bottom tray,

$$\frac{\bar{G}_{Np}y_{Np}}{\bar{L}_{Np}x_{Np}} = \frac{\bar{G}_{Np}m_{Np}}{\bar{L}_{Np}} = S_{Np} \quad (9.193)$$

$$\bar{G}_{Np}y_{Np} = S_{Np}\bar{L}_{Np}x_{Np} \quad (9.194)$$

$$\bar{L}_{Np-1}x_{Np-1} = \bar{G}_{Np}y_{Np} + Wx_W \quad (9.195)$$

Then

and

$$\frac{L_{Np-1}x_{Np-1}}{Wx_W} = \frac{\bar{G}_{Np}y_{Np}}{Wx_W} + 1 = \frac{S_{Np}\bar{L}_{Np}x_{Np}}{Wx_W} + 1 = S_{Np}(S_W + 1) = S_{Np}S_W + S_{Np} + 1 \quad (9.196)$$

In general, for any tray,

$$\frac{L_m x_m}{Wx_W} = \frac{S_{m+1}L_{m+1}x_{m+1}}{Wx_W} + 1 = S_{m+1} \cdots S_{Np-1}S_{Np}S_W + S_{m+1} \cdots S_{Np-1}S_{Np}$$
$$+ S_{m+1} \cdots S_{Np-1} + \cdots + S_{m+1} + 1 \quad (9.197)$$

and at the feed tray,

$$\frac{L_f x_f}{Wx_W} = S_{f+1} \cdots S_{Np}S_W + S_{f+1} \cdots S_{Np} + \cdots + S_{f+1} + 1 \quad (9.198)$$

Edmister[6] provides shortcut methods involving "effective" A's and S's for use in Eqs. (9.188) and (9.198), much as for gas absorption.

At the feed tray,

$$A_f = \frac{L_f}{G_f m_f} = \frac{L_f x_f}{G_f y_f} \quad (9.199)$$

and

$$\frac{Wx_W}{Dz_D} = \frac{L_f x_f}{G_f y_f}\frac{G_f y_f / Dz_D}{L_f x_f / Wx_D} = A_f \left(\frac{G_f y_f / Dz_D}{L_f x_f / Wx_W} \right) \quad (9.200)$$

Since
$$Fz_D = Wx_W + Dz_D \qquad (9.201)$$

$$Dz_D = \frac{Fz_F}{Wx_W/Dz_D + 1} \qquad (9.202)$$

For each component, Eqs. (9.188) and (9.198) are then used to compute the numerator and denominator, respectively, of the term in parentheses of Eq. (9.200), whence Wx_W/Dz_D, or the split of the component, is found. Equation (9.202) then provides Dz_D and Eq. (9.201), Wx_W.

The products thus computed are completely consistent with the number of trays, feed-tray position, and reflux ratio used, provided the A's and S's (or L/G's and temperatures) are correct. For checking these, it is necessary to use the general equations (9.187) and (9.197) for each tray in the appropriate section of the tower. To check tray n in the enriching section,

$$\frac{G_n y_n}{Dz_D} \frac{Dz_D}{G_n} = y_n \qquad (9.203)$$

and this may be obtained from the data already accumulated. If $\Sigma y_{Jn} = 1$, the temperature is satisfactory. If not, a new temperature is obtained by adjusting the y's proportionately until they add to unity and computing the corresponding dew point. To check a tray in the exhausting section,

$$\frac{L_m x_m}{Wx_W} \frac{Wx_W}{L_m} = x_m \qquad (9.204)$$

which is obtainable from the data. If $\Sigma x_{Jm} = 1$, the temperature is correct. If not, the x's are adjusted to add to unity and the bubble point computed. The new temperatures and compositions permit new enthalpy balances to obtain corrected L/G's for each tray, and the Thiele-Geddes calculation may be redone. Problems of convergence of this trial-and-error procedure are considered by Holland,[18] Lyster et al.,[25] and Smith.[35]

The true optimum feed-tray location is obtained by trial, altering the location and observing which location produces the smallest number of trays for the desired products.

Illustration 9.13, concluded. Reestimate the products through the Thiele-Geddes method.
   Solution. The temperature and L/G profiles as previously estimated will be used. Computations will be shown for only one component, C_4; all other components are treated in the same manner.
   Using the tray temperatures to obtain m, $A = L/mG$ for the enriching trays and $S = m\bar{G}/L$ for the exhausting trays are computed. Since a partial condenser is used, $A_0 = R/m_0$. For the kettle-type reboiler, $S_W = \bar{G}_{15}m_W/W$. Then, for C_4,

Tray	Condenser	1	2	3	4	5	6 = f
m	0.50	0.66	0.75	0.81	0.86	0.95	1.07
A	1.600	0.655	0.584	0.455	0.355	0.326	1.431

Tray	7 = f + 1	8	9	10	11	12	13	14	Reboiler
m	1.22	1.27	1.29	1.30	1.32	1.40	1.45	1.51	1.65
S	0.301	0.390	0.447	0.503	0.532	0.566	0.599	0.693	0.954

With these data

Eq. (9.188): $$\frac{G_f y_f}{D z_D} = 1.5778$$

Eq. (9.198): $$\frac{L_f x_f}{W x_W} = 1.5306$$

Eq. (9.200): $$\frac{W x_W}{D z_D} = 1.431 \frac{1.5778}{1.5306} = 1.475$$

Eq. (9.202): $$D y_D = \frac{0.33}{1.475 + 1} = 0.1335$$

Eq. (9.201): $$W x_W = 0.33 - 0.1335 = 0.1965$$

Similarly,

Component	$\dfrac{G_f y_f}{D z_D}$	$\dfrac{L_f x_f}{W x_W}$	$\dfrac{W x_W}{D y_D}$	$D y_D$	$W x_W$
C_1	1.0150	254(10⁶)	288(10⁻¹⁰)	0.03	Nil
C_2	1.0567	8,750	2.98(10⁻⁵)	0.07	Nil
C_3	1.1440	17.241	0.0376	0.1447	0.0053
C_4	1.5778	1.5306	1.475	0.1335	0.1965
C_5	15.580	1.1595	45.7	0.00643	0.29357
C_6	1,080	1.0687	7,230	0.0000166	0.11998
				$0.3846 = D$	$0.6154 = W$

These show that $0.1447(100)/0.15 = 96.3\%$ of the C_3 and 2.14% of the C_5 are in the distillate. These do not quite meet the original specifications. The temperatures and L/G's must still be corrected, however. Thus for tray 2 and component C_4, Eq. (9.187) yields $G_2 y_2 / D z_D = 2.705$. From the enthalpy balances, $G_2 = 0.675$. Therefore, by Eq. (9.203),

$$y_2 = \frac{2.705(0.1335)}{0.675} = 0.5349$$

Similarly,

Component	$\dfrac{G_2 y_2}{D z_D}$	y_2	Adjusted y_2
C_1	1.0235	0.0454	0.0419
C_2	1.1062	0.1147	0.1059
C_3	1.351	0.2896	0.2675
C_4	2.705	0.5349	0.4939
C_5	10.18	0.0970	0.0896
C_6	46.9	0.00115	0.00106
		1.0828	1.0000

Since Σy_2 does not equal 1, the original temperature is incorrect. After adjusting the y's to add to unity as shown, the dew point = $160°F$ instead of the $150°F$ used. Similarly all tray compositions and temperatures must be corrected, new L/G's obtained by enthalpy balances with the new compositions, temperatures, and L/G's, and the Thiele-Geddes calculations repeated.

Multicomponent fractionation finds its most complex applications in the field of petroleum refining. Petroleum products such as gasoline, naphthas, kerosenes, gas oils, fuel oils, and lubricating oils are each mixtures of hundreds of hydrocarbons, so many that their identity and actual number cannot readily be established.   For-tunately, it is not usually specific substances that are desired in these products, but rather *properties*, so that specifications may be made as to boiling range, specific gravity, viscosity, and the like.   Fractionators for these products cannot be designed by the detailed methods just described but must instead be based upon laboratory studies in small-scale equipment.   As an example which illustrates the complex nature of some of these separations, consider the schematic diagram of a topping plant for the initial distillation of a crude oil (Fig. 9.52).   The crude oil, after preliminary heat exchange with several of the products from the plant, is passed through the tubes of a gas-fired furnace, the tube-still heater.   Here a portion of the oil is vaporized, somewhat larger in amount than that ultimately to be taken as vaporized products. The mixture of liquid and vapor then enters the large tray tower.   Open steam is introduced at the bottom to strip the last traces of volatile substances from the residue product, and this steam passes up the column, where it lowers the effective pressure

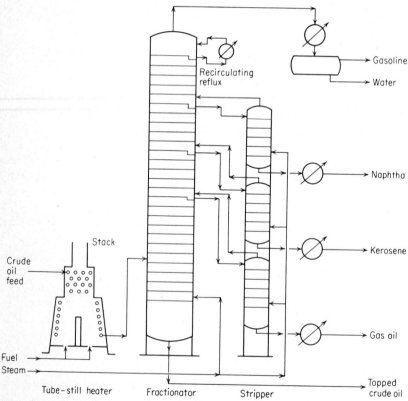

Fig. 9.52   *Schematic arrangement, petroleum topping plant.*

and hence the temperature of the distillation. The steam and most volatile substances (crude gasoline) leaving the top tray are condensed, the water separated, and the gasoline sent to storage. Reflux in the scheme shown here is provided by withdrawing a portion of the liquid from the top tray and returning it after it has been cooled. The cold liquid condenses some of the rising vapors to provide internal reflux. Several trays down from the top of the tower, a side stream may be withdrawn which will contain the hydrocarbons characteristic of a desired naphtha product. Since the components of the more volatile gasoline are also present at this point, the liquid is steam-stripped in a short auxiliary tray tower, the steam and vaporized gasoline being sent back to the main fractionator. The stripped naphtha is then withdrawn to storage. In similar fashion kerosene and gas oil cuts may be withdrawn, but each must be separately steam-stripped. The individual steam strippers are frequently built into a single shell, as shown, for reasons of economy, so that from the outside the multipurpose nature of the smaller tower is not readily evident. The withdrawn products must ordinarily be further processed before they are considered finished.

The design, method of operation, and number of products from topping units of this sort may vary considerably from refinery to refinery. Indeed, any individual unit will be built for maximum flexibility of operation, with, for example, multiple nozzles for introducing the feed at various trays and multiple side-stream withdrawal nozzles, to allow for variations in the nature of the feed and in the products to be made.

Azeotropic distillation

This is a special case of multicomponent distillation used for separation of binary mixtures which are either difficult or impossible to separate by ordinary fractionation. If the relative volatility of a binary mixture is very low, the continuous rectification of the mixture to give nearly pure products will require high reflux ratios and correspondingly high heat requirements, as well as towers of large cross section and numbers of trays. In other cases the formation of a binary azeotrope may make it impossible to produce nearly pure products by ordinary fractionation. Under these circumstances a third component, sometimes called an "entrainer," may be added to the binary mixture to form a new low-boiling azeotrope with one of the original constituents, whose volatility is such that it may be easily separated from the other original constituent.

As an example of such an operation, consider the flow sheet of Fig. 9.53 for the azeotropic separation of acetic acid–water solutions, using butyl acetate as entrainer.[27] Acetic acid may be separated from water by ordinary methods, but only at great expense owing to the low relative volatility of the constituents despite their fairly large difference in boiling points at atmospheric pressure (nbp acetic acid = 118.1°C, nbp water = 100°C). Butyl acetate is only slightly soluble in water and consequently forms a heteroazeotrope with it (bp = 90.2°C). Therefore if at least sufficient butyl acetate is added to the top of the distillation column (1) to form the azeotrope with all the water in the binary feed, the azeotrope may be readily distilled from the high-boiling acetic acid which leaves as a residue product. The heteroazeotrope on

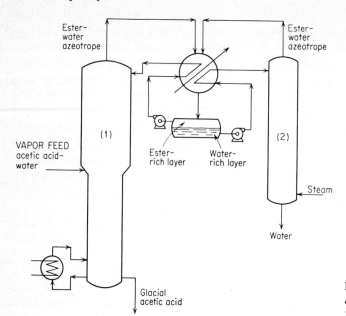

Fig. 9.53 *Azeotropic distillation of acetic acid–water with butyl acetate.*

condensation forms two insoluble liquid layers, one nearly pure water but saturated with ester, the other nearly pure ester saturated with water. The latter is returned to the top of the column as reflux and is the source of the entrainer in the column. The former may be stripped of its small entrainer content in a second small column (2). The separation of the heteroazeotrope from acetic acid is readily done, so that relatively few trays are required in the principal tower. On the other hand, heat must be supplied, not only to vaporize the water in the overhead distillate, but to vaporize the entrainer as well. The operation may also be done batchwise, in which case sufficient entrainer is charged to the still kettle, together with the feed, to azeotrope the water. The azeotrope is then distilled overhead.

Sometimes the new azeotrope which is formed contains all three constituents. The dehydration of ethanol-water mixture with benzene as added substance is an example. Dilute ethanol-water solutions may be continuously rectified to give at best mixtures containing 89.4 mole percent ethanol at atmospheric pressure, since this is the composition of the minimum-boiling azeotrope in the binary system. By introducing benzene into the top of a column fed with an ethanol-water mixture, the ternary azeotrope containing benzene (53.9 mole %), water (23.3 mole %), ethanol (22.8 mole %), boiling at 64.9°C, is readily separated from the ethanol (bp = 78.4°C) which leaves as a residue product. In this case also the azeotropic overhead product separates into two liquid layers, one rich in benzene which is returned to the top of the column as reflux, the other rich in water which is withdrawn. Since the latter contains appreciable quantities of both benzene and ethanol, it must be separately rectified. The ternary azeotrope contains nearly equal molar proportions of ethanol and water, and consequently dilute ethanol-water solutions must be given a preliminary rectification to produce substantially the alcohol-rich binary azeotrope which is used as a feed.

In still other cases the new azeotrope which is formed does not separate into two insoluble liquids, and special means for separating it, such as liquid extraction, must be provided, but this is less desirable.

It is clear that the choice of entrainer is a most important consideration. The added substance should preferably form a low-boiling azeotrope with only one of the constituents of the binary mixture it is desired to separate, preferably the constituent present in the minority so as to reduce the heat requirements of the process. The new azeotrope must be of sufficient volatility to make it readily separable from the remaining constituent and so that inappreciable amounts of entrainer will appear in the residue product. It should preferably be lean in entrainer content, to reduce the amount of vaporization necessary in the distillation. It should preferably be of the heterogeneous-liquid type, which then simplifies greatly the recovery of the entrainer. In addition, a satisfactory entrainer must be (1) cheap and readily available, (2) chemically stable and inactive toward the solution to be separated, (3) noncorrosive toward common construction materials, (4) nontoxic, (5) of low latent heat of vaporization, (6) of low freezing point to facilitate storage and outdoor handling, and (7) of low viscosity to provide high tray efficiencies.

Extractive distillation

This is a multicomponent-rectification method similar in purpose to azeotropic distillation. To a binary mixture which is difficult or impossible to separate by ordinary means a third component, termed a "solvent," is added which alters the relative volatility of the original constituents, thus permitting the separation. The added solvent is, however, of low volatility and is itself not appreciably vaporized in the fractionator.

As an example of such an operation, consider the process of Fig. 9.54. The separation of toluene (bp = 110.8°C) from paraffin hydrocarbons of approximately the same molecular weight is either very difficult or impossible, owing to low relative volatility or azeotropism, yet such a separation is necessary in the recovery of toluene from certain petroleum hydrocarbon mixtures. Using isooctane (bp = 99.3°C) as an example of a paraffin hydrocarbon, Fig. 9.54a shows that isooctane in this mixture is the more volatile, but the separation is obviously difficult. In the presence of phenol (bp = 181.4°C), however, the isooctane relative volatility increases, so that, with as much as 83 mole percent phenol in the liquid, the separation from toluene is relatively easy. A flow sheet for accomplishing this is shown in Fig. 9.54b, where the binary mixture is introduced more or less centrally into the extractive distillation tower (1), and phenol as the solvent is introduced near the top so as to be present in high concentration upon most of the trays in the tower. Under these conditions isooctane is readily distilled as an overhead product, while toluene and phenol are removed as a residue. Although phenol is relatively high-boiling, its vapor pressure is nevertheless sufficient so that its appearance in the overhead product must be

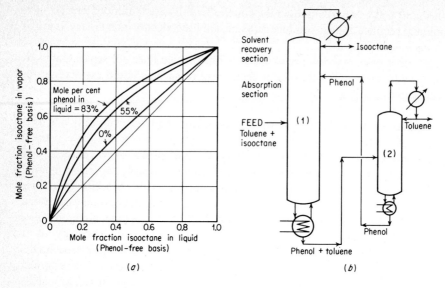

Fig. 9.54 *Extractive distillation of toluene–isooctane with phenol.* [*Vapor-liquid equilibria from Drickamer, Brown, and White, Trans. AIChE,* **41**, 555 (1945).]

prevented. The solvent-recovery section of the tower, which may be relatively short, serves to separate the phenol from the isooctane. The residue from the tower must be rectified in the auxiliary tower (2) to separate toluene from the phenol which is recycled, but this is a relatively easy separation. In practice, the paraffin hydrocarbon is a mixture rather than the pure substance isooctane, but the principle of the operation remains the same.

Such a process depends upon the difference in departure from ideality between the solvent and the components of the binary mixture to be separated. In the example given, both toluene and isooctane separately form nonideal liquid solutions with phenol, but the extent of the nonideality with isooctane is greater than that with toluene. When all three substances are present, therefore, the toluene and isooctane themselves behave as a nonideal mixture, and their relative volatility becomes high. Considerations of this sort form the basis for the choice of an extractive-distillation solvent. If, for example, a mixture of acetone (bp $= 56.4°$C) and methanol (bp $=$ 64.7°C), which form a binary azeotrope, were to be separated by extractive distillation, a suitable solvent could probably be chosen from the group of aliphatic alcohols. Butanol (bp $= 117.8°$C), since it is a member of the same homologous series but not far removed, forms substantially ideal solutions with methanol, which are themselves readily separated. It will form solutions of positive deviation from ideality with acetone, however, and the acetone-methanol vapor-liquid equilibria will therefore be substantially altered in ternary mixtures. If butanol forms no azeotrope with acetone, and if it alters the vapor-liquid equilibrium of acetone-methanol sufficiently to destroy the azeotrope in this system, it will serve as an extractive-distillation solvent.

When both substances of the binary mixture to be separated are themselves chemically very similar, a solvent of an entirely different chemical nature will be necessary. Acetone and furfural, for example, are useful as extractive-distillation solvents for separating the hydrocarbons butene-2 and *n*-butane.

Generally the requirements of a satisfactory extractive-distillation solvent are:

1. High selectivity, or ability to alter the vapor-liquid equilibria of the original mixture sufficiently to permit its easy separation, with, however, use of only small quantities of solvent.

2. High capacity, or ability to dissolve the components in the mixture to be separated. It frequently happens that substances which are incompletely miscible with the mixture are very selective; yet if sufficiently high concentrations of solvent cannot be obtained in the liquid phase, the separation ability cannot be fully developed.

3. Low volatility in order to prevent vaporization of the solvent with the overhead product and to maintain high concentration in the liquid phase.

4. Separability. The solvent must be readily separated from the mixture to which it is added, and particularly it must form no azeotropes with the original substances.

5. The same considerations of cost, toxicity, corrosive character, chemical stability, freezing point, and viscosity apply as for entrainers for azeotropic distillation.

Extractive distillation is usually more desirable a process than azeotropic distillation since no large quantities of solvent must be vaporized. Furthermore, a greater choice of added component is possible since the process is not dependent upon the accident of azeotropic formation. It cannot be conveniently carried out in batch operations, however.

Azeotropic and extractive-distillation equipment can be designed using the general methods for multicomponent distillation, and detailed discussion is available.[1,17,32,35]

LOW-PRESSURE DISTILLATION

Many organic substances cannot be heated to temperatures which even approach their normal boiling points without chemical decomposition. If such substances are to be separated by distillation, then the pressure and the corresponding temperature must be kept low. The time of exposure of the substances to the distillation temperature must also be kept to a minimum, since the extent of thermal decomposition will thereby be reduced. For distillation under absolute pressures of the order of several lb/sq in., packed towers may be used, bubble-cap and sieve trays can be designed with pressure drops approaching 0.05 psi (2.6 mm Hg), and other simpler designs, such as the shower tray of Fig. 6.18, for which the pressure drops are of the order of 0.015 psi (0.75 mm Hg) are possible. Mechanically stirred spray and wetted-wall columns provide even smaller pressure drops.[30]

In the distillation of many natural products, such as the separation of vitamins from animal and fish oils as well as the separation of many synthetic industrial products such as plasticizers, the temperature may not exceed perhaps 200 to 300°C, where the vapor pressures of the substances may be a fraction of a millimeter of mercury. The conventional equipment is, of course, wholly unsuitable for such separations, not only because the pressure drop would result in high temperatures at the bottom of columns, but also because of the long exposure time to the prevailing temperatures resulting from high holdup.

Molecular distillation

This is a form of very-low-pressure distillation, conducted at absolute pressures of the order of 0.003 mm Hg, suitable for the heat-sensitive substances described above.

The rate at which evaporation takes place from a liquid surface is given by the Langmuir equation,

$$N'_A = 1006 p_A \left(\frac{1}{2\pi M_A R'' T} \right)^{0.5} \tag{9.205}$$

where N'_A = g moles substance A evaporated/(sec)(sq cm)

p_A = partial pressure of A, atm

M_A = mol wt of A

R'' = universal gas const, 82.07 (cu cm) (atm)/(g mole)(°K)

T = abs temp, °K

At ordinary pressures the net rate of evaporation is, however, very much less than this, owing to the fact that the evaporated molecules are reflected back to the liquid after collisions occurring in the vapor. By reducing the absolute pressure to values used in molecular distillation, the mean free path of the molecules becomes very large, of the order of 1 cm. If the condensing surface is then placed at a distance from the vaporizing liquid surface not exceeding a few centimeters, very few molecules will return to the liquid, and the net rate of evaporation of each substance of a binary mixture will approach that given by Eq. (9.205). The vapor composition, or the composition of the distillate, will now be different from that given by ordinary equilibrium vaporization, and the ratio of the constituents in the distillate will approach

$$\frac{N'_A}{N'_B} = \frac{\text{moles of } A}{\text{moles of } B} = \frac{p_A/M_A^{0.5}}{p_B/M_B^{0.5}} \tag{9.206}$$

If this ratio is to be maintained, however, the surface of the liquid must be rapidly renewed, since otherwise the ratio of constituents in the surface will change as evaporation proceeds. The vigorous agitation or boiling present during ordinary distillations is absent under conditions of molecular distillation, and in most devices the liquid is caused to flow in a thin film over a solid surface, thus continually renewing the surface but at the same time maintaining low holdup of liquid.

Figure 9.55 shows a device which is used industrially for accomplishing a molecular distillation.[15] The degassed liquid to be distilled is introduced continuously at the bottom of the inner surface of the rotor, a rotating conical-shaped surface. The rotor may be as large as 5 ft in diameter at the top and may revolve at speeds of 400 to 500 rpm. A thin layer of liquid to be distilled, 0.05 to 0.1 mm thick, then

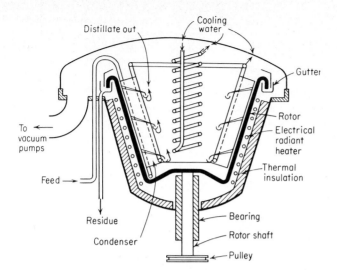

Distillate out

Cooling water

Gutter

To vacuum pumps

Rotor

Electrical radiant heater

Thermal insulation

Feed →

Residue

Bearing

Rotor shaft

Condenser

Pulley

Fig. 9.55 *Schematic section, centrifugal molecular still of Hickman.*[15]

spreads over the inner surface and travels rapidly to the upper periphery under the action of centrifugal force.   Heat is supplied to the liquid through the rotor by radiant electrical heaters, and the vaporized material is condensed upon the water-cooled louver-shaped condenser.   This is maintained at temperatures sufficiently low to prevent reevaporation or reflection of the vaporized molecules.   The residue liquid is caught in the collection gutter at the top of the rotor, and the distillate is drained from the collection troughs on the condenser.   Each product is pumped from the still body, which is evacuated to the low pressures necessary for molecular distillation, and the time of residence of the substances in the still may be as low as several seconds or less.   Such a device is capable of handling 50 to 250 gal/hr of liquid to be distilled and gives a separation of 80 to 95% of that indicated by Eq. (9.206).   Multiple distillations are necessary for multistage separation effects.

NOTATION FOR CHAPTER 9

a = interfacial surface, sq ft/cu ft of packed section

A = more volatile component of a binary mixture

= absorption factor = L/mG, dimensionless

B = less volatile component of a binary mixture

C = heat capacity at constant pressure, Btu/(lb)(°F)

d = differential operator

D = distillate rate, lb moles/hr for tray towers, lb moles/(hr)(sq ft) for packed towers

E_O = overall tray efficiency, as a fraction

E_{MG} = Murphree vapor tray efficiency, as a fraction

F = feed rate, lb moles/hr for tray towers, lb moles/(hr)(sq ft) for packed towers

= quantity of feed, lb moles (batch distillation)

= (with subscript) mass-transfer coefficient, lb moles/(hr)(sq ft)

G = vapor rate, lb moles/hr for tray towers, lb moles/(hr)(sq ft) for packed towers

H = enthalpy, Btu/lb mole of solution

H_{tG} = height of a gas transfer unit, ft
H_{tL} = height of a liquid transfer unit, ft
H_{tOG} = height of an overall gas transfer unit, ft
H_{tOL} = height of an overall liquid transfer unit, ft
ΔH_S = integral heat of solution, Btu/lb mole solution
k_x' = liquid mass-transfer coefficient, lb moles/(hr)(sq ft)(mole fraction)
k_y' = gas mass-transfer coefficient, lb moles/(hr)(sq ft)(mole fraction)
K_x' = liquid overall mass-transfer coefficient, lb moles/(hr)(sq ft)(mole fraction)
K_y' = gas overall mass-transfer coefficient, lb moles/(hr)(sq ft)(mole fraction)
ln = natural logarithm
log = common logarithm
L = liquid rate, lb moles/hr for tray towers, lb moles/(hr)(sq ft) for packed towers
L_0 = external reflux rate, lb moles/hr for tray towers, lb moles/(hr)(sq ft) for packed towers
m = slope of the equilibrium curve, dy^*/dx
M = molecular weight, lb/lb mole
N = mass-transfer flux, lb moles/(hr)(sq ft interface)
N' = mass-transfer flux, g moles/(sec)(sq cm interface)
N_m = minimum number of ideal trays
N_p = number of ideal trays
N_{tG} = number of gas transfer units
N_{tL} = number of liquid transfer units
N_{tOG} = number of overall gas transfer units
N_{tOL} = number of overall liquid transfer units
p = partial pressure, atm
P = vapor pressure, atm
P_t = total pressure, atm
q = quantity defined by Eq. (9.119)
Q = net heat added, Btu/hr
Q_B = heat added at reboiler, Btu/hr for tray towers, Btu/(hr)(sq ft) for packed towers
Q_C = heat removed at condenser, Btu/hr for tray towers, Btu/(hr)(sq ft) for packed towers
Q_L = heat loss, Btu/hr for tray towers, Btu/(hr)(sq ft) for packed towers
Q' = quantity defined by Eq. (9.55)
Q'' = quantity defined by Eq. (9.66)
R = external reflux ratio, lb moles reflux/lb mole distillate
R' = apparent reflux ratio, defined by Eq. (9.138)
R'' = universal gas constant, 82.07 (cu cm)(atm)/(g mole)(°K)
R_m = minimum reflux ratio, lb moles reflux/lb mole distillate
S = stripping factor = mG/L, dimensionless
t = temperature, °F
t_o = base temperature for enthalpy computations, °F
T = absolute temperature, °K
W = residue rate, lb moles/hr for tray towers, lb moles/(hr)(sq ft) for packed towers; quantity of residue for batch distillation
x = concentration in the liquid (of A in binaries), mole fraction
x^* = liquid concentration in equilibrium with y, mole fraction
y = concentration in the vapor (of A in binaries), mole fraction
y^* = vapor concentration in equilibrium with x, mole fraction
z = average concentration in a solution or mixture, mole fraction
Z = height of packing, ft
α = relative volatility, defined by Eq. (9.2), dimensionless
α_{JC} = relative volatility of component J with respect to component C
Δ = difference point, representing a fictitious stream
λ = latent heat of vaporization, Btu/lb

Σ = summation
ϕ = root of Eq. (9.157)

Subscripts:

a = operating-line intersection
av   = average
A, B = components A, B
D = distillate
e = enriching section
f = feed tray
F = feed
G = gas
hk = heavy key component
i = interface
lk = light key component
L = liquid
m = tray m; minimum
n = tray n
r = tray r
s = stripping section
W = residue
1   = bottom of packed tower; tray 1
2   = top of packed tower; tray 2

REFERENCES

1. Benedict, M., and L. C. Rubin: *Trans. AIChE,* **41,** 353 (1945).
2. Brown, G. G., and H. Z. Martin: *Trans. AIChE,* **35,** 679 (1939).
3. Cavers, S. D.: *Ind. Eng. Chem. Fundamentals,* **4,** 229 (1965).
4. Dodge, B. F.: "Chemical Engineering Thermodynamics," McGraw-Hill Book Company, New York, 1944.
5. Eckert, J. S.: *Chem. Eng. Progr.,* **59**(5), 76 (1963).
6. Edmister, W. C.: *AIChE J.,* **3,** 165 (1957).
7. Erbar, J. H., and R. N. Maddox: *Petr. Refiner,* **40**(5), 183 (1961).
8. Fair, J. R.: *Chem. Eng.,* **69,** July 8, 119; Aug. 5, 101 (1963).
9. Fenske, M. R.: *Ind. Eng. Chem.,* **24,** 482 (1931).
10. Floyd, R. B., and H. G. Higgins: *Ind. Eng. Chem.,* **55**(6), 34 (1963).
11. Gilliland, E. R.: *Ind. Eng. Chem.,* **32,** 1220 (1940).
12. Gilmont, R.: "Thermodynamic Principles for Chemical Engineers," Prentice-Hall, Inc., Englewood Cliffs, N.J., 1959.
13. Hachmuth, K. H.: *Chem. Eng. Progr.,* **48,** 523, 570, 617 (1952).
14. Hengstebeck, R. J.: "Distillation, Principles and Design Procedures," Reinhold Publishing Corporation, New York, 1961.
15. Hickman, K. C. D.: *Ind. Eng. Chem.,* **39,** 686 (1947).
16. Hickman, K. C. D.: sec. 17 in "The Chemical Engineers' Handbook," 4th ed., McGraw-Hill Book Company, New York, 1963.
17. Hoffman, E. J.: "Azeotropic and Extractive Distillation," Interscience Publishers, Inc., New York, 1964.
18. Holland, C. D.: "Multicomponent Distillation," Prentice-Hall, Inc., Englewood Cliffs, N.J., 1963.
19. Horsley, L. H.: "Azeotropic Data," *Advan. Chem. Ser.,* **6** (1952).
20. Horsley, L. H., and W. S. Tamplin: "Azeotropic Data II," *Advan. Chem. Ser.,* **35** (1963).

21. Horvath, P. J., and R. F. Schubert: *Chem. Eng.*, **64**, Feb. 10, 129 (1958).

22. Kwauk, M.: *AIChE J.*, **2**, 240 (1956).

23. Lewis, W. K., and G. L. Matheson: *Ind. Eng. Chem.*, **24**, 494 (1932).

24. Lowenstein, J. G.: *Ind. Eng. Chem.*, **54**(1), 61 (1962).

25. Lyster, W. N., S. L. Sullivan, D. S. Billingsley, and C. D. Holland: *Petr. Refiner*, **38**(6), 221; (7), 151; (10), 139 (1959).

26. McCabe, W. L., and E. W. Thiele: *Ind. Eng. Chem.*, **17**, 605 (1925).

27. Othmer, D. F.: *Chem. Eng. Progr.*, **59**(6), 67 (1963).

28. Perry, E. S., and A. Weissberger (eds.): "Distillation," Techniques of Organic Chemistry, vol. IV, Interscience Publishers, Inc., New York, 1965.

29. Ponchon, M.: *Tech. Mod.*, **13**, 20, 55 (1921).

30. Raichle, L., and R. Billet: *Ind. Eng. Chem.*, **57**(4), 52 (1965).

31. Randall, M., and B. Longtin: *Ind. Eng. Chem.*, **30**, 1063, 1188, 1311 (1938); **31**, 908, 1295 (1939); **32**, 125 (1940).

32. Robinson, C. S., and E. R. Gilliland: "Elements of Fractional Distillation," 4th ed., McGraw-Hill Book Company, New York, 1950.

33. Savarit, R.: *Arts Métiers*, **1922**, 65, 142, 178, 241, 266, 307.

34. Shiras, R. N., D. N. Hanson, and C. H. Gibson: *Ind. Eng. Chem.*, **42**, 871 (1950).

35. Smith, B. D.: "Design of Equilibrium Stage Processes," McGraw-Hill Book Company, New York, 1963.

36. Smoker, E. H.: *Trans. AIChE*, **34**, 165 (1938).

37. Teller, A. J., S. A. Miller, and E. G. Scheibel: sec. 18 in "The Chemical Engineers' Handbook," 4th ed., McGraw-Hill Book Company, New York, 1963.

38. Thiele, E. W., and R. L. Geddes: *Ind. Eng. Chem.*, **25**, 289 (1933).

39. Underwood, A. J. V.: *Trans. Inst. Chem. Engrs.* (*London*), **10**, 112 (1932).

40. Underwood, A. J. V.: *Chem. Eng. Progr.*, **44**, 603 (1948); **45**, 609 (1949).

41. Watt, P. Ridgeway: "Molecular Stills," Reinhold Publishing Corporation, New York, 1963.

42. Winn, F. W.: *Petr. Refiner*, **37**, 216 (1950).

PROBLEMS

9.1. Solutions of methanol and ethanol are substantially ideal.

a. Compute the vapor-liquid equilibria for this system at 1 and at 5 atm abs pressure, and plot *xy* and *txy* diagrams at each pressure.

b. For each pressure compute relative volatilities, and determine an average value.

c. Using Eq. (9.2) with the average volatilities, compare the values of y^* at each value of x so obtained with those computed directly from the vapor pressures.

9.2. A 1,000-lb batch of nitrobenzene is to be steam-distilled from a very small amount of a nonvolatile impurity, insufficient to influence the vapor pressure of the nitrobenzene. The operation is to be carried out in a jacketed kettle fitted with a condenser and distillate receiver. Saturated steam at 5 psig is introduced into the kettle jacket for heating. The nitrobenzene is charged to the kettle at 80°F, and it is substantially insoluble in water.

Liquid water at 80°F is continuously introduced into the nitrobenzene in the kettle, so as always to maintain a liquid water level. The mixture is distilled at atmospheric pressure. (*a*) At what temperature does the distillation proceed? (*b*) How much water is vaporized? (*c*) How much steam must be condensed in the kettle jacket? Neglect the heat required to bring the still up to operating temperature. The heat capacity of nitrobenzene is 0.33 Btu/(lb)(°F), and its latent heat of vaporization may be determined by the methods of Chap. 7.

9.3. A mixture contains 40 mole % methanol, 35 mole % ethanol, and 25 mole % *n*-propanol. Liquid solutions of these substances are substantially ideal. Assuming the applicability of the perfect-gas law, for a total pressure of 1 atm abs compute:

  a. The bubble point and the equilibrium vapor composition.

  b. The dew point and the equilibrium liquid composition.

9.4. Vapor-liquid equilibrium data at 1 atm abs and heats of solution for the system acetone (*A*)–water (*B*), in addition to heat-capacity and latent-heat data for acetone, are as follows:

x mole fraction acetone in liquid	Integral ht soln at 59°F, Btu/lb mole soln	y^* equil mole fraction acetone in vapor	Vapor-liquid temp, °F	Ht capacity at 63°F, Btu/(lb soln)(°F)
0.00	0	0.00	212	1.00
0.01		0.253	197.1	0.998
0.02	−81.0	0.425	187.8	0.994
0.05	−192.3	0.624	168.3	0.985
0.10	−287.5	0.755	151.9	0.96
0.15	−331	0.798	146.2	0.93
0.20	−338	0.815	143.9	0.91
0.30	−309	0.830	141.8	0.85
0.40	−219	0.839	140.8	0.80
0.50	−150.5	0.849	140.0	0.75
0.60	−108.6	0.859	139.1	0.70
0.70		0.874	138.1	0.66
0.80		0.898	136.8	0.61
0.90		0.935	135.5	0.57
0.95		0.963	134.6	0.55
1.00		1.000	133.7	

t, °F	68	100	150	200	212
Ht capacity acetone, Btu/(lb)(°F)	0.53	0.54	0.56	0.58	
Latent ht vaporization, Btu/lb	242	233	219	206	203

Compute the enthalpies of saturated liquids and vapors relative to pure acetone and water at 59°F, and plot the enthalpy-concentration diagram, for 1 atm abs. Retain for use in Probs. 9.5, 9.6, and 9.12.

9.5. A liquid mixture containing 60 mole % acetone, 40 mole % water, at 80°F, is to be continuously flash-vaporized at 1 atm pressure, to vaporize 30 mole % of the feed.

  a. What will be the composition of the products and the temperature in the separator, if equilibrium is established?

  b. How much heat, Btu/lb mole of feed, is required? **Ans.:** 5849.

  c. If the products are each cooled to 80°F, how much heat, Btu/lb mole of feed, must be removed from each?

9.6. A saturated vapor at 1 atm pressure, containing 50 mole % acetone and 50 mole % water, is subject to equilibrium condensation to yield 50 mole % of the feed as liquid. Compute the equilibrium vapor and liquid compositions, the equilibrium temperature, and the heat to be removed, Btu/lb mole of feed.

9.7. The liquid solution of Prob. 9.5 is differentially distilled at 1 atm pressure to vaporize 30 mole % of the feed. Compute the composition of the composited distillate and the residue. Compare with the results of Prob. 9.5. **Ans.:** $y_D = 0.857$.

9.8. The ideal mixture containing 40 mole % methanol, 35 mole % ethanol, 25 mole % n-propanol is flash-vaporized to vaporize 60 mole % of the feed.   Determine the compositions of the liquid and vapor products and their equilibrium temperature for 1 atm pressure.

9.9. The ideal solution containing 10 mole % methanol, 80 mole % ethanol, and 10 mole % n-propanol is to be differentially distilled at 1 atm pressure.   The first 20 mole % of vapor will be discarded, following which a "heart cut" of 60 mole % will be distilled and separately retained.   The 20 mole % of residue will be discarded.   Compute the yield of ethanol in the heart cut and the composition of this product.   **Ans.**: 60.5% yield ethanol at 0.822 mole fraction.

9.10.   A jacketed kettle is originally charged with 30 moles of a mixture containing 40 mole % benzene, 60 mole % toluene.   The vapors from the kettle pass directly to a total condenser, and the condensate is withdrawn.   Liquid of the same composition as the charge is continuously added to the kettle at the rate of 15 moles/hr.   Heat to the kettle is regulated to generate 15 moles vapor/hr, so that the total molar content of the kettle remains constant.   The mixture is ideal, and the average relative volatility is 2.51.   The distillation is essentially differential.

a. How long will the still have to be operated before vapor containing 50 mole % benzene is produced, and what is the composition of the composited distillate?   **Ans.**: 1.466 hr, 0.555 mole fraction benzene.

b. If the rate at which heat is supplied to the kettle is incorrectly regulated so that 18 moles/hr of vapor are generated, how long will it take until vapor containing 50 mole % benzene is produced?   **Ans.**: 1.08 hr.

9.11.   An open kettle contains 50 lb moles of a dilute aqueous solution of methanol, mole fraction methanol = 0.02, at the bubble point, into which steam is continuously sparged.   The entering steam agitates the kettle contents so that they are always of uniform composition, and the vapor produced, always in equilibrium with the liquid, is led away.   Operation is adiabatic.   For the concentrations encountered it may be assumed that the enthalpy of the steam and evolved vapor are the same, the enthalpy of the liquid in the kettle is essentially constant, and the relative volatility is constant at 7.6.   Compute the quantity of steam to be introduced in order to reduce the concentration of methanol in the kettle contents to 0.001 mole fraction.   **Ans.**: 20.5 lb moles.

Continuous fractionation: Savarit-Ponchon method

9.12.   Ten thousand pounds per hour of an acetone-water solution, containing 25 wt % acetone, is to be fractionated at 1 atm pressure.   It is desired to recover 99.5% of the acetone in the distillate at a concentration of 99 wt %.   The feed will be available at 80°F and will be preheated by heat exchange with the residue product from the fractionator, which in turn will be cooled to 125°F.   The distilled vapors will be condensed and cooled to 100°F by cooling water entering at 80°F and leaving at 105°F.   Reflux will be returned at 100°F, at a reflux ratio $L_0/D = 1.8$.   Open steam, available at 10 psig, will be used at the base of the tower.   The tower will be insulated to reduce heat losses to negligible values.   Physical property data are given in Prob. 9.4.   Determine:

a. The hourly rate and composition of distillate and reflux.

b. The hourly condenser heat load and cooling water rate.

c. The hourly rate of steam and residue and the composition of the residue.

d. The enthalpy of the feed as it enters the tower and its condition (express quantitatively).

e. The number of ideal trays required if the feed is introduced at the optimum location.   Use large-size graph paper and a sharp pencil.   **Ans.**: 13.1.

f. The rates of flow, lb/hr, of liquid and vapor at the top, at $x = 0.6$, 0.1, 0.025, and at the bottom tray.   For a tower of uniform diameter, the conditions on which tray control the diameter, if the criterion is a 75% approach to flooding?

9.13.   Design a suitable sieve-tray tower for the fractionator of Prob. 9.12, determine the tray efficiencies, and the number of real trays required.   **Ans.**: There is no single answer.   For a diameter of 2.5 ft, tray spacing 20 in., $A_h/A_a = 0.1$, the Murphree efficiencies vary from 0.60 at the top to 0.78 at the bottom, 25 trays are required, with the feed on to the twentieth.

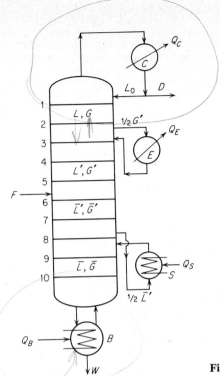

Fig. 9.56 *Arrangement for Prob.* 9.14.

9.14. In a certain binary distillation, the overhead vapor condenser must be run at a temperature requiring mild refrigeration, and the available refrigeration capacity is very limited. The reboiler temperature is very high, and the available high-temperature heat supply is also limited. Consequently the scheme shown in Fig. 9.56 is adopted, where the intermediate condenser E and reboiler S operate at moderate temperatures. Condensers C and E are total condensers, delivering liquids at their bubble points. Reboiler S is a total vaporizer, delivering saturated vapor. Heat losses are negligible, $D = W$, the external reflux ratio $R = L_0/D = 1.0$, and other conditions are shown on the figure. The system is one which follows the McCabe-Thiele assumptions ($H_L x$ and $H_G y$ curves are straight and parallel). Feed is liquid at the bubble point.

   a. Per mole of feed, compute the rates of flow of all streams, the relative size of the two condenser heat loads, and the relative size of the two vaporizer heat loads.

   b. Establish the coordinates of all difference points. Sketch the Hxy diagram and locate the difference points, showing how they are related to the feed. Show the construction for trays.

   c. Sketch the xy diagram, show all operating lines, and locate their intersections with the 45° diagonal. Show the construction for trays.

9.15. A distillation column is operated at a temperature below that of the surroundings (as in the distillation of air). Owing to imperfect insulation, the entire enriching section is subject to a heat leak inward of Q_E Btu/hr, while the entire stripping section is subject to a heat leak inward of Q_S Btu/hr. Aside from the heat leaks, the system has all the characteristics which satisfy the McCabe-Thiele requirements.

   a. Sketch the Hxy and the xy diagrams, labeling the coordinates of all significant points. Are the operating curves on the xy diagram concave upward or downward?

   b. For a given condenser heat load, explain which is better: to design a new column with the inward heat leak minimized, or to take any possible advantage of a heat leak. Consider the reboiler heat load free, available from the surroundings.

c. Suppose the column with the inward heat leak is operated at full reboiler heat load, limited by the available heat-transfer surface. The column is then insulated thoroughly, essentially eliminating the heat leak, but without provision to alter the heat load of the reboiler or otherwise to alter the operation. Explain whether the separation obtained will be better than, worse than, or the same as, before the insulation was installed.

Continuous fractionation: McCabe-Thiele method

9.16. A solution of carbon tetrachloride and carbon disulfide containing 50 wt % each is to be continuously fractionated at atmospheric pressure at the rate of 4,000 lb/hr. The distillate product is to contain 95 wt % carbon disulfide, the residue 0.5%. The feed will be 30 mole % vaporized before it enters the tower. A total condenser will be used, and reflux will be returned at the bubble point. Equilibrium data are available in "The Chemical Engineers' Handbook," 4th ed., p. 13-5.

a. Determine the quantities of products, lb/hr and lb moles/hr.

b. Determine the minimum reflux ratio.

c. Determine the minimum number of ideal trays, graphically and by means of Eq. (9.81).

d. Determine the number of theoretical trays required at a reflux ratio equal to twice the minimum and the position of the feed tray. **Ans.:** 12.5 ideal stages.

e. Estimate the overall tray efficiency of a bubble-cap-tray tower of conventional design and the number of real trays.

f. Using the distillate temperature as the base temperature, determine the enthalpy of the feed, the products, and the vapor entering the condenser. Determine the heat loads of the condenser and reboiler. Latent and specific heats are available in "The Chemical Engineers' Handbook," 4th ed., pp. 3-113 and 3-126.

9.17. An acetone-water solution, 0.2 mole fraction acetone and at the bubble point, is to be fractionated at 1 atm pressure. No more than 0.1% of the acetone content of the feed is to be lost to the residue. Two products other than the residue are required, each containing half of the recovered acetone: the first at 0.98, the second at 0.80 mole fraction acetone. Two schemes are being considered as outlined below. In both, open steam at 10 psig at the base of the tower and a total condenser delivering liquid at the bubble point will be used, with an external reflux ratio 1.5 times the minimum value. Equilibrium vapor-liquid data are given in Prob. 9.4. Use 100 lb moles of feed as a basis for computation.

a. The first scheme is to fractionate the entire feed, to remove the rich product as overhead distillate and the less rich product as a liquid side stream from an appropriate tray between the feed and the top tray.

1. Determine the quantities of distillate D and side stream S.

2. Determine the reflux ratio (use a large graph), and plot the enriching operating line.

3. For the section between side stream and feed, write the operating-line equation (make an acetone balance to the top, noting that for this section $G = G_1$ and $L = L_0 - S$), determine the point where $x = y$, the y intercept, and the point of intersection with the enriching line. $S = $ molar side-stream rate.

4. Determine the quantity of steam, x_W, and the total number of ideal trays required. **Ans.:** 18.2 ideal trays.

b. The second scheme will fractionate only part of the feed to produce the residue and a single distillate, $x_D = 0.98$. The product of $x = 0.8$ will be obtained by mixing the undistilled portion of the feed with part of the distillate. Total acetone loss to the residue is to be the same as in *a*. Determine the quantity of feed to be fractionated, the quantities of distillate, steam, residue, x_W, and the number of ideal trays. **Ans.:** 17.8 ideal trays.

c. Which scheme is to be preferred?

9.18. An aqueous solution of furfural contains 4 mole % furfural. It is to be continuously fractionated at 1 atm pressure to provide solutions containing 0.1 and 99.5 mole % furfural, respectively. Feed is liquid at the bubble point. Equilibrium data are available in "The Chemical Engineers' Handbook," 4th ed., p. 13-5.

a. Arrange a scheme for the separation using kettle-type reboilers, and determine the number of ideal trays required for a vapor boilup rate of 1.25 times the minimum for an infinite number of trays.

b. Repeat *a*, but use open steam at essentially atmospheric pressure for the tower delivering the water-rich product, with 1.25 times the minimum steam and vapor boilup rates.

c. Which scheme incurs the greater furfural loss to the water-rich product?

9.19. One thousand pounds per hour of an aniline-water solution containing 7 wt % aniline, at the bubble point, is to be steam-stripped in a tower packed with 1-in. Berl saddles with open steam to remove 99% of the aniline. The condensed overhead vapor will be decanted at 98.5°C, and the water-rich layer returned to the column. The aniline-rich layer will be withdrawn as distillate product. The steam rate will be 1.3 times the minimum. Design the tower so as not to exceed loading, and use standard pipe ("The Chemical Engineers" Handbook," 4th ed., p. 6-45) for the shell. *Note:* For concentrations where the equilibrium curve is nearly straight, it should be possible to use overall numbers and heights of transfer units. **Ans.:** 18.5 ft of packing.

Data. At 98.5°C, the solubility of aniline in water is 7.02 and 89.90 wt % aniline. The vapor-liquid equilibria at 745 mm Hg, at which pressure the tower will be operated, are [Griswold et al., *Ind. Eng. Chem.*, **32**, 878 (1940)]:

x = mole fraction aniline	0.002	0.004	0.006	0.008	0.010	0.012	Two liquid phases, 98.5°C
y^* = mole fraction aniline	0.01025	0.0185	0.0263	0.0338	0.03575	0.03585	0.0360

9.20. The following feed, liquid at the bubble point at 120 psia, is to be fractionated at 120 psia to provide no more than 7.45% of the n-C_5H_{12} in the distillate and no more than 7.6% of the n-C_4H_{10} in the bottoms, with a total condenser and reflux returned at the bubble point:

Component	x_F	150°F	200°F	250°F
n-C_3H_8	0.05			
m		2.50	3.7	5.2
H_G		14,700	15,700	16,850
H_L		9,200	11,300	13,400
i-C_4H_{10}	0.15			
m		1.31	1.91	2.96
H_G		17,600	19,100	20,600
H_L		10,700	12,600	14,950
n-C_4H_{10}	0.25			
m		0.90	1.50	2.50
H_G		19,000	20,200	21,700
H_L		11,100	13,100	15,200
i-C_5H_{12}	0.20			
m		0.44	0.76	1.31
H_G		22,500	23,900	25,600
H_L		12,900	15,100	17,500
n-C_5H_{12}	0.35			
m		0.35	0.65	1.16
H_G		23,550	25,000	26,300
H_L		13,200	15,500	18,000

The above table provides Henry's law constants and enthalpies as Btu/lb mole, from the same sources and with the same base as the data of Illustration 9.13.

Compute the minimum reflux ratio, the minimum number of ideal trays, and, for a reflux ratio $R = 2.58$, estimate the product analyses, condenser and reboiler heat loads, vapor and liquid rates per mole of feed throughout, and the number of ideal trays.   **Ans.:** 8 ideal trays + reboiler.

PART THREE
LIQUID-LIQUID
OPERATIONS

Liquid extraction, the only operation in this category, is basically very similar to the operations of gas-liquid contact described in the previous part. The creation of a new insoluble liquid phase by addition of a solvent to a mixture accomplishes in many respects the same result as the creation of a new phase by the addition of heat in distillation operations, for example, or by addition of gas in desorption operations. The separations produced by single stages, the use of countercurrent cascades and reflux to enhance the extent of separation—all have their liquid-extraction counterparts. The similarity among these will be exploited in explaining what liquid extraction can accomplish.

Certain differences in the operations nevertheless make it expedient to provide a separate treatment for liquid extraction. The considerably greater change in mutual solubility of the contacted liquid phases which may occur during passage through a cascade of stages requires somewhat different techniques of computation than are necessary for gas absorption or stripping. The considerably smaller differences in density of the contacted phases and their relatively low interfacial tension, as compared with the corresponding gas-liquid systems, require consideration in the design of apparatus. The larger number of variables which apparently influence the rate of mass transfer in countercurrent equipment makes the correlation of design data much more difficult. For these reasons separate treatment is desirable, at least for the present.

CHAPTER TEN
LIQUID EXTRACTION

Liquid extraction, sometimes called solvent extraction, is the separation of the constituents of a liquid solution by contact with another insoluble liquid. If the substances comprising the original solution distribute themselves differently between the two liquid phases, a certain degree of separation will result, and this may be enhanced by use of multiple contacts or their equivalent in the manner of gas absorption and distillation.

A simple example will indicate the scope of the operation and some of its characteristics. If a solution of acetic acid in water is agitated with a liquid such as ethyl acetate, some of the acid but relatively little water will enter the ester phase. Since at equilibrium the densities of the aqueous and ester layers are different, they will settle on cessation of agitation and may be decanted from each other. Since now the ratio of acid to water in the ester layer is different from that in the original solution and also different from that in the residual water solution, a certain degree of separation will have occurred. This is an example of stagewise contact, and it may be carried out either in batch or in continuous fashion. The residual water may be repeatedly extracted with more ester to reduce still further the acid content, or we may arrange a countercurrent cascade of stages. Another possibility is to use some sort of countercurrent continuous-contact device, where discrete stages are not involved. The use of reflux, as in distillation, may enhance still further the ultimate separation.

In all such operations, the solution which is to be extracted is called the *feed*, and the liquid with which the feed is contacted is the *solvent*. The solvent-rich product of the operation is called the *extract*, and the residual liquid from which solute has been removed is the *raffinate*.

More complicated processes may use two solvents to separate the components of a feed. For example, a mixture of *p*- and *o*-nitrobenzoic acids may be separated by distributing them between the insoluble liquids chloroform and water. The chloroform preferentially dissolves the para isomer and the water the ortho isomer. This is called *double-solvent*, or *fractional*, extraction.

Fields of usefulness

In distillation, where the vapor phase with which a liquid is contacted is created from the liquid by addition of heat, the vapor and liquid are necessarily of the same substances and are therefore chemically very similar. The separations produced depend on the vapor pressures of the substances. In the case of liquid extraction, on the other hand, the two phases are chemically quite different, and this leads to a separation of substances according to chemical type. There are therefore the following major fields of application for liquid extraction:

1. As a substitute for distillation or evaporation, particularly when the substances to be separated are chemically different. Here the relative costs are important, since extraction produces new solutions which must be separated, frequently by distillation or evaporation. Thus, for example, acetic acid may be separated from dilute solutions with water with difficulty by distillation, or with relative ease by extraction followed by distillation of the extract. For the more dilute solutions particularly, when much water must be vaporized in distillation, extraction is more economical, particularly since the heat of vaporization of most organic solvents is substantially less than that of water. Extraction may also be attractive as an alternative to distillation or evaporation when very low temperatures would be required to avoid thermal decomposition. For example, long-chain fatty acids may be separated from vegetable oils by high-vacuum distillation but more economically by extraction with liquid propane.

2. For separations not readily done by other methods. For example, aromatic and paraffinic hydrocarbons of nearly the same molecular weight can be separated readily by extraction with any of a number of solvents, e.g., sulfur dioxide, diethylene glycol, and sulfolane, but are impossible to separate by distillation since their vapor pressures are nearly the same. Many pharmaceutical products, e.g., penicillin, occur naturally in mixtures which are so complex that only liquid extraction is a feasible separation device. Many metal separations, particularly those which are expensive by chemical methods, such as uranium-vanadium, tantalum-columbium, and hafnium-zirconium, are economically done by extraction. Even low-cost inorganic chemicals such as phosphoric acid, boric acid, sodium hydroxide, and the like, can be economically purified by liquid-extraction means, despite the fact that the cost of solvent recovery must be included in the final reckoning.

EQUIPMENT

There are two major categories of equipment for liquid extraction:

1. Single-stage equipment, which provides one stage of contact in a single device or combination of devices. In such an apparatus, the liquids are mixed, extraction occurs, and the insoluble liquids are settled and separated. A countercurrent cascade of stages may be arranged for enhancement of the separation.

2. Multistage equipment, where the equivalent of many stages may be incorporated into a single device or apparatus.

SINGLE-STAGE EQUIPMENT

A single stage must provide facilities for mixing the insoluble liquids and for settling and decanting the emulsion or dispersion which results. In batch operation, mixing together with settling and decanting may take place in the same or in separate vessels. In continuous operation, different vessels are required, and the combination is called a *mixer-settler*.

Mixers

For efficient extraction, the mixing device must bring about intimate contact of the liquids. This usually requires that one liquid be dispersed in the form of small droplets into the other and that sufficient time of contact ("holding time") be provided to allow extraction to take place. The smaller the droplets and the larger their number, the greater will be the interfacial area produced, the more rapid will be the interphase mass transfer, and the less holding time will be required. It is, however, essential that the dispersion not be made so fine that subsequent settling is too slow.

To effect the dispersion requires the expenditure of mechanical work or power upon the system. The mere application of large amounts of power through some mixing device will not necessarily ensure adequate mixing, however. The mixing effectiveness, which may be loosely defined as the degree of dispersion produced per unit of power applied, depends greatly upon the design of the mixing device. As yet no really adequate measurements of this have been made, and we must rely instead on the stage efficiency as indication of the success of the mixing. This will include the influence of degree of dispersion, holding time, and rate of mass transfer upon the operation as a whole. It is known, however, that the degree of dispersion which results from the application of a fixed amount of power through a given mixer depends upon the properties of the liquids involved, including their densities, viscosities, and interfacial tension.

There are two major varieties of mixers, agitated vessels and flow mixers. The former are by far the more important.

Agitated vessels

These consist of a vessel to contain the liquids and a mechanical agitator to provide the mixing, as in Fig. 10.1. In such vessels strong vertical currents within the liquid

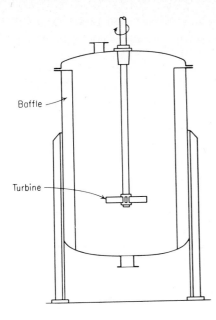

Baffle

Turbine

Fig. 10.1   *Agitated vessel for batch or continuous extraction.*

are necessary to ensure that the heavy liquid will not stratify at the bottom.   Radial rather than circular motion is desired, since the latter tends to stratify the liquids by centrifugal force, causing the heavy liquid to be flung to the side wall of the vessel. The circulation currents developed will depend upon the vessel shape, the presence of baffles, and the design, location, and speed of the agitation impeller.

The vessels are ordinarily vertical cylinders, circular rather than rectangular in cross section.   They may be fitted with internal baffles, which are necessary in cases where the liquid is in contact with air to prevent vortexing.   Four equally spaced vertical baffles, arranged radially as shown in the figure, of length equal to the liquid depth and width equal to one-tenth the tank diameter, are sufficient.   Baffles are customarily used also with full vessels, where there is no air-liquid interface, although the meager evidence is that in these cases the same extraction rates are given with less impeller power if baffles are omitted.[17]

Impellers of many designs are effective, and Fig. 10.2 shows several types.   The impeller diameter is usually one-third to one-half that of the vessel, and the shaft is best placed along the vessel axis.   Agitation power in the range 0.05 to 0.3 hp/cu ft vessel volume may be used, rarely more, depending upon how difficult it is to disperse the liquids: high interfacial tension and density difference make dispersion more difficult.   Impeller speeds for a given power may be estimated from standard correlations.[13,22,27]

For continuous operation, which is most common, the two liquids to be contacted usually flow upward through the vessel, and the dispersion produced is led from the top to a settling device.   Now the rate of extraction is proportional to an overall mass-transfer coefficient and the interfacial area, which should be as large as practical.   The area is governed by the size of the droplets produced (usually in the range 0.1 to 1 mm diameter, depending upon the liquid properties and the agitation power) and the volume fraction ϕ_D of dispersed phase in the vessel (dispersed-phase holdup). Droplet diameters cannot be made too small, since difficulty in subsequent settling results, and consequently it is desirable to maintain a high value of ϕ_D. Ordinarily the liquid flowing at the smaller volume rate (the minority liquid) will be dispersed in the other, and at the agitator-power levels mentioned above, the value of ϕ_D will usually be the same as the volume fraction that the dispersed liquid represents of the total liquid entering the vessel. When the volume ratio of liquids to the vessel is small, say 0.1, for example, as may be the case when a particularly excellent solvent is used, only small values of ϕ_D will result. In this case, the interfacial area and hence the rate of mass transfer may be substantially increased by recycling part of the minority liquid flowing from the settler back to the mixer.[28] It is difficult, however, to maintain ϕ_D at values much above 0.6 to 0.7,[19] and attempts to increase it beyond these values usually result in inversion of the dispersion.

Methods for estimating the droplet size, the interfacial area, and the mass-transfer coefficients, from which the stage efficiency may be computed, have been the subject of much study,[27] but many questions remain unanswered. Fortunately, stage efficiencies are usually very high. Particularly when extraction consists of diffusive mass transfer alone, a residence time within the mixing vessel (vessel volume/total volumetric rate of flow) of the order of 1 min or less is usually sufficient to produce fractional stage efficiencies greater than 0.9. Slow chemical reaction accompanying the extraction may increase the required time substantially.

Flow mixers

The power required for dispersion by flow mixers, or "line mixers," comes from pumping the liquids through the device. They have small volumes and consequently

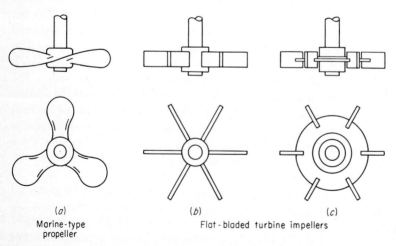

(a)
Marine-type
propeller

(b)

(c)

Flat-bladed turbine impellers

Fig. 10.2 *Mixing impellers.*

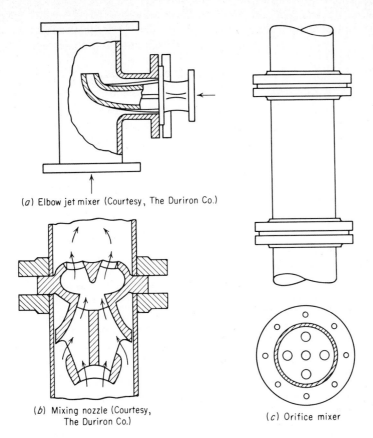

(*a*) Elbow jet mixer (Courtesy, The Duriron Co.)

(*b*) Mixing nozzle (Courtesy,
The Duriron Co.)

(*c*) Orifice mixer

Fig. 10.3 *Flow mixers.*

provide little holding time.   They are especially useful for liquids of low viscosity and low interfacial tension, for which dispersion is not difficult.

Several types are shown in Fig. 10.3.   Jet mixers depend for their action upon impingement of one liquid, which is caused to flow through a small opening, upon the other when both are pumped into the mixer.   Mixing nozzles and orifices bring about mixing and dispersion by causing great turbulence when both liquids are pumped through the device.   Even ordinary globe valves may be used.   Each of these devices is effective and inexpensive to install but may incur high pressure drop and consequently may be expensive to operate.

Emulsions

The mixture of liquids issuing from any mixing device, an emulsion, consists of small droplets of one liquid dispersed throughout a continuum of the other.   The stability, or permanence, of the emulsion is of the utmost importance in liquid extraction, since it is necessary to separate the phases at each extraction stage.   Stable emulsions, those which do not settle and coalesce rapidly, must be avoided For an emulsion to "break," or separate into its phases in bulk, both sedimentation and coalescence of the dispersed phase must occur.

The rate of sedimentation of a quiescent emulsion is the more rapid if the size of the droplets and the density difference of the liquids are large and if the viscosity of the continuous phase is small. Stable emulsions, those which settle only over long periods of time, are usually formed when the diameter of the dispersed droplets is of the order of 1 to 1.5 μ, whereas dispersions of particle diameter 1 mm or larger usually sedimentate rapidly.

Coalescence of the settled droplets is the more rapid the higher the interfacial tension. Interfacial tension is ordinarily low for liquids of high mutual solubility and is lowered by the presence of emulsifying or wetting agents. In addition, high viscosity of the continuous phase hinders coalescence by reducing the rate at which the residual film between drops is removed. Dust particles, which usually accumulate at the interface between liquids, also hinder coalescence.

In the case of an unstable emulsion, after agitation has stopped, the mixture settles and coalesces rapidly into two liquid phases unless the viscosity is high. The appearance of a sharply defined interface between the phases (primary break) is usually very rapid, but one of the phases, ordinarily that in the majority, may remain clouded by a very fine fog or haze, a dispersion of the other phase. The cloud will eventually settle and leave the clouded phase clear (secondary break), but this may take a considerable time. The primary break of an unstable emulsion is usually so rapid that merely stopping agitation for a very short time, a matter of minutes, is sufficient to bring it about. In continuous multistage operation, it is usually impractical to hold the mixture between stages long enough to attain the secondary break.

Settlers

In continuous extraction, the dispersion from the mixer is allowed to flow through a vessel of sufficient size so that the time of residence is great enough to permit primary break. The cross section of such a device should be large so that turbulence is reduced to a minimum. An empty vessel may be employed, but baffles are often included, as in Fig. 10.4. Horizontal baffles reduce turbulence and also the distance through which the dispersed droplets must settle before coalescence. Other more elaborate devices are also in use.[27]

Neglecting the pressure drop for flow through the exit pipes, which should be kept to a minimum, the level of the interface within the settler (Fig. 10.4) will adjust itself so that

$$s\rho_H = t\rho_H + u\rho_L \tag{10.1}$$

For operation under pressure and with elimination of the siphon vents, a liquid-level controller activated by the interface position and operating a regulating valve in the exit pipe for the heavy liquid may be used.

Continuous centrifuges are sometimes used for decreasing the settling time, but they will not influence in any way the rate of coalescence of the settled dispersed phase.

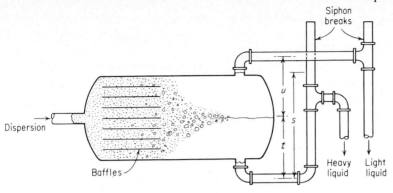

Fig. 10.4 *Gravity settler.*

The latter may be assisted by causing the emulsion to flow through a bed of porous substance which is preferentially wetted by the dispersed phase. Glass fibers, steel wool, and coarse wire mesh have been successfully used as coalescers, and these should be placed upstream from the settling vessel.[23]

Multistage extraction

A continuous multistage extraction plant will consist of the required number of stages arranged according to the desired flow sheet. Each stage will consist of at least a mixer and a settler, as in the countercurrent plant of Fig. 10.5. The liquids will generally be pumped from one stage to the next, but occasionally gravity flow can be arranged if sufficient headroom is available. Many arrangements have been designed to reduce the amount of interstage piping and the corresponding cost.[27] Figure 10.6 is one such: the mixing vessels are immersed in the large circular settling tanks, heavy liquid flows by gravity, light liquid by air lift, and recycling of settled light liquid to the mixer is accomplished by overflow.

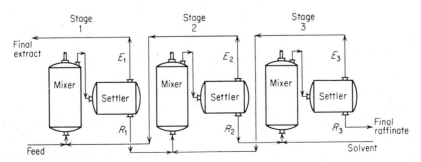

Fig. 10.5 *Flow sheet of three-stage countercurrent mixer-settler extraction cascade.*

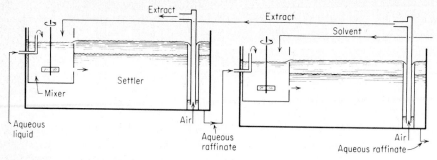

Fig. 10.6 *Kerr-McGee uranium extractor.*

MULTISTAGE EQUIPMENT

When the liquids flow countercurrently through a single piece of equipment, the equivalent of as many ideal stages may be had as desired. In such devices, the countercurrent flow is produced by virtue of the difference in densities of the liquids, and if the motivating force is the force of gravity, the extractor takes the form of a vertical tower, the light liquid entering at the bottom, the heavy liquid at the top. As an alternative, a larger centrifugal force may be generated by rapidly rotating the extractor, in which case the counterflow is radial with respect to the axis of revolution.

There are several characteristics common to countercurrent extractors which have an important bearing upon their design and performance. It is typical that only one of the liquids may be pumped through the device at any desired rate. The maximum rate for the other will depend upon, among other things, the density difference of the liquids. If an attempt is made to exceed this rate for the second liquid, the extractor will reject one of the liquids, and it is said to be *flooded*. The same is true, of course, for gas-liquid contactors, but since the density difference is much smaller than for a gas and liquid, the flooding velocities of extractors are much lower. For a given volumetric rate of liquids to be handled, the extractor cross section must be sufficiently large so that the flooding velocities are not reached. The more open the cross section, the greater the flow rates before flooding occurs. Internal structures, packing, mechanical agitators, and the like normally reduce the velocities at which flooding occurs.

Most of these devices are also subject to *axial mixing*, commonly called back mixing, which severely reduces the extraction rates. Several phenomena are recognized to be involved.[31] Because the velocity profile for a liquid across the tower cross section is not flat ("plug flow"), the dissolved solute is carried by the liquid at different rates in different locations in the cross section. Where pockets of liquid within the extractor become mixed, the solute concentrations do not change regularly with axial distance. Some liquid is caused to circulate in the wrong direction, movement which is induced by the flow of the other liquid. The net result is a reduction in the concentration difference between the liquids, upon which the mass transfer depends. The mathematical description of axial mixing has been fairly completely developed, but only recently has its importance been fully realized, and our quantitative knowledge of its effects is meager.

Spray towers

These, the simplest of the continuous-contact devices, consist merely of an empty vertical shell with provisions for introducing and removing the liquids. Refer to Fig. 10.7a, where operation is shown with the light liquid dispersed. Heavy liquid enters at the top, fills the tower completely (continuous phase), and flows out at the bottom. Light liquid enters at the bottom through a distributor which disperses it into small droplets. These rise through the downward-flowing heavy liquid and coalesce into a layer at the top. The heavy liquid is shown leaving through a looped pipe A, and the head of heavy liquid at the bottom of the pipe (static pressure + friction resulting from flow) must balance the head of combined light and heavy liquids in the tower. In this manner the interface B is maintained in the position shown. The position of the interface may be regulated by the elevation of A, but it is more satisfactorily controlled in large-scale equipment by the valve C, which may be operated by a liquid-level controller actuated by the position of the interface itself. The tap D is used periodically to withdraw scum and dust particles which accumulate at the interface and interfere with coalescence of the droplets of dispersed liquid. The exit streams from this and other types of countercurrent towers are frequently passed through settlers of the sort shown in Fig. 10.4, to remove entrained droplets from the product liquids.

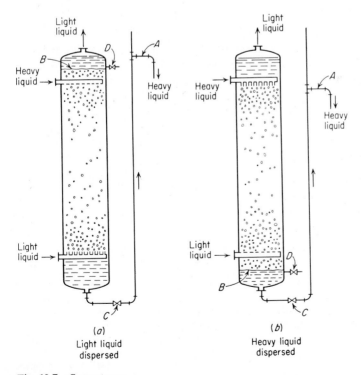

(a) Light liquid dispersed

(b) Heavy liquid dispersed

Fig. 10.7 *Spray tower.*

By reducing the height of pipe *A* or by opening the valve *C* the interface may be lowered to the position shown in Fig. 10.7*b*. The heavy liquid is now dispersed and the light liquid continuous. As an additional alternative the interface may be located more or less centrally in the tower.

The spray tower is inexpensive to build, easy to keep clean, and has a high flow capacity. The freedom with which the continuous phase can circulate leads to such severe axial-mixing effects and reduced extraction efficiency, however, that it is not normally used for industrial purposes. We have used it here principally to describe the methods of operating extraction towers generally.

Packed towers

Towers filled with the same random packings used for gas-liquid contact are also used for liquid extraction. The packing serves to reduce axial mixing and also to jostle and distort the droplets of dispersed phase, in this way improving somewhat the mass-transfer rates. A typical packed tower, arranged for light liquid dispersed, is shown schematically in Fig. 10.8. By lowering the interface (see page 417) it may be arranged for heavy liquid dispersed. The tower is usually straight-sided, as shown; some have been made with an expanded end section where the dispersed phase enters.[4]

The nature of the liquid flow in such towers requires that the choice of packing and arrangement of dispersed-phase distributor be given careful attention. If the dispersed liquid preferentially wets the packing, it will pass through in rivulets on the packing, not as droplets, and the interfacial area produced will be small. For this reason, the packing material should be preferentially wetted by the continuous phase. Usually, ceramics are preferentially wet by aqueous liquids, carbon and plastics by organic liquids. The packing should be sufficiently small, no greater than one-eighth the tower diameter, so that the packing density is fully developed yet larger than a certain critical size (see below). In cases where the material of the packing support is not wet by the dispersed droplets and where the distributor is placed outside the packing, the drops will have difficulty in entering the packing, and premature flooding results. For this reason it is always desirable to embed the dispersed-phase distributor in the packing, as in Fig. 10.8.

Dispersed-phase holdup[18]

For packing sizes d_F larger than a critical size d_{FC},

$$d_{FC} = 2.42 \left(\frac{\sigma g_c}{\Delta \rho g} \right)^{0.5} \tag{10.2}$$

there is a characteristic mean diameter of dispersed-phase droplet d_p which is nearly independent of packing size and shape. For smaller packings, the drop size is larger, and interfacial areas are smaller. Packings smaller than d_{FC} should not be used, and what follows is strictly for $d_F > d_{FC}$.

Flow rates are conveniently described as superficial velocities (volumetric rate/tower cross-sectional area), V_C and V_D ft/hr for the continuous and dispersed phases, respectively. Dispersed-phase holdup ϕ_D is an "operating" holdup, that which drains from the packing if liquid flow is stopped, and is expressed as a fraction of the void volume ϵ within the packed bed (see Table 6.2). At low

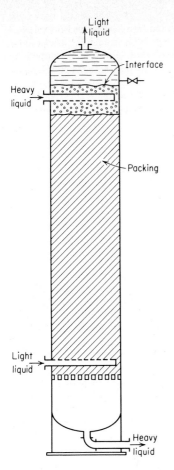

Light
liquid

Interface

Heavy
liquid

Packing

Light
liquid

Heavy
liquid

Fig. 10.8   *Packed extraction tower, light liquid dispersed.*

values of V_D, ϕ_D varies linearly with V_D up to a lower "transition point" reminiscent of loading in gas-liquid contact. With further increase in V_D, ϕ_D increases rapidly, the dispersed droplets tend to coalesce, and a second transition occurs. V_D can increase a small amount beyond this without marked increase in ϕ_D, but flooding ultimately results. Below the upper transition, the holdup is described by

$$\frac{V_D}{\epsilon\phi_D} + \frac{V_C}{\epsilon(1 - \phi_D)} = V_K(1 - \phi_D) \tag{10.3}$$

Here, were it not for the additional permanent holdup, which is not included in ϕ_D, the left-hand side of Eq. (10.3) would represent a *slip* velocity, or superficial relative velocity. V_K is a "characteristic" velocity, a limiting mean drop velocity at $V_C = 0$ for low values of V_D, and is correlated from the experimental data by Fig. 10.9. For design purposes, it is recommended that ϕ_D be set in the range 0.10 to 0.20, the low value for V_D/V_C below 0.5, the flow rates being further checked for flooding.

The mean characteristic drop diameter d_p for liquids at equilibrium is given by

$$d_p = 0.92\left(\frac{\sigma g_c}{\Delta\rho\,g}\right)^{0.5}\frac{V_K\epsilon\phi_D}{V_D} \tag{10.4}$$

For liquids which are not mutually saturated, or if extraction occurs from a dispersed organic to a continuous aqueous liquid, d_p will be larger to an extent which cannot be estimated. If extraction occurs in the reverse direction, d_p is evidently not altered. If the drops formed at the distributor nozzles are smaller than d_p, they grow very slowly by coalescence to the characteristic size, but premature flooding may result. It is best therefore to produce drops initially somewhat larger than those of Eq. (10.4), whereupon they are broken up within the packing to the characteristic size. In any case, the holes in the distributor should be at least sufficiently large (say ³⁄₁₆ to ¼ in. diameter) to avoid plugging.

Flooding

There have been a great many studies of flooding, and the results are not in good agreement. The studies were all made in the absence of mass transfer, and in view of the influence of mass transfer on d_p, it can be expected that there is an influence on flooding as well. The recommended work is that of Crawford and Wilke,[6] whose results are shown in Fig. 10.10. It is recommended that actual velocities be no larger than 50 to 60 percent of the flooding values in view of the uncertainties involved. Packing characteristics a_p and ϵ are given in Table 6.2.

Drop terminal velocities

Figure 10.9 contains the term V_t, the terminal velocity of a liquid drop in a liquid medium. This is the free-fall (or rise, depending on the relative density) velocity of a single isolated drop in the gravitational field. The terminal velocities of small drops, which are essentially spherical, are larger than those of solid spheres of the same diameter and density, owing to the mobility and internal circulation within the drop: the surface velocity is not zero, as it is for a solid. With increasing diameter, there occurs a transition drop size, beyond which the drop shape is no longer spherical (although it is nevertheless described with d_p as the diameter of a sphere of the same volume), and the drop oscillates and distorts. The terminal velocity of the transition size is a maximum, and for larger sizes the velocity falls slowly with increased diameter. Dimensional analysis shows $\text{Re} = f(C_D, \text{We})$, where Re is the drop Reynolds number at terminal velocity, We is the drop Weber number, and C_D is the usual drag coefficient. For very pure liquids (no surface-active agents, no mass transfer),

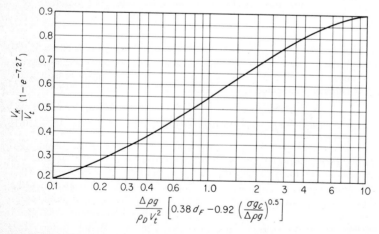

Fig. 10.9 *Characteristic drop velocities for packings.* [*Gaylor, Roberts, and Pratt: Trans. Inst. Chem. Engrs.* (*London*), **31**, 57 (1953).] *Not to be used for $T < 0.25$ ft or $d_F < d_{FC}$.*

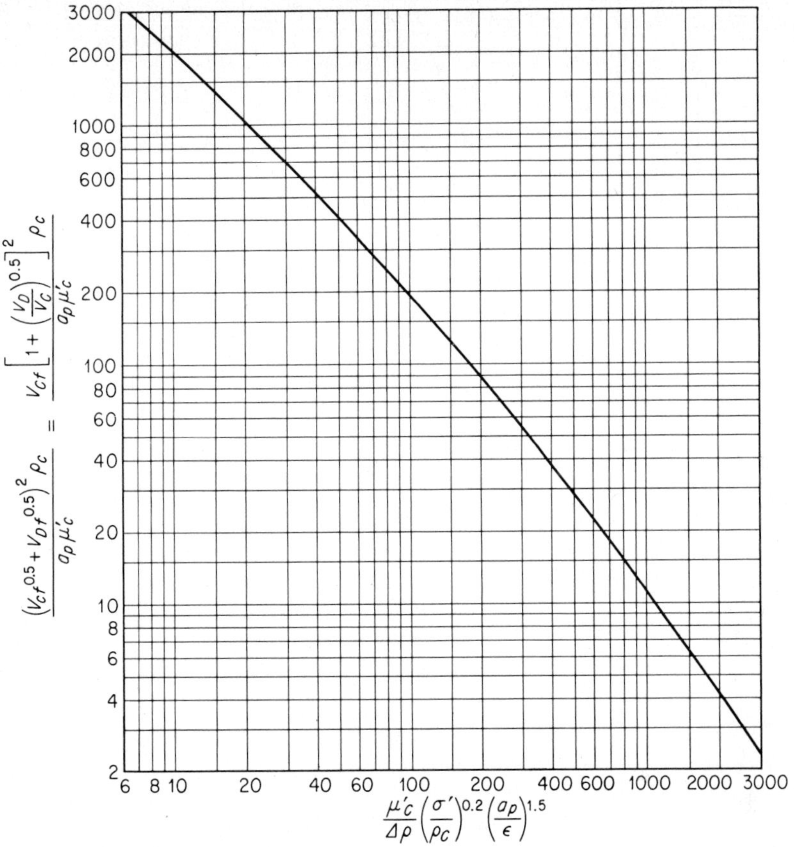

Fig. 10.10 *Flooding in packed towers.*[6]

and continuous phase viscosities less than 5 centipoises, the Hu-Kintner correlation[9] (Fig. 10.11) provides the functional relation. P is defined as

$$P = \frac{4\text{Re}^4}{3C_D \text{We}^3} = \frac{\rho_C^2(\sigma g_c)^3}{g\mu_C^4 \, \Delta\rho} \tag{10.5}$$

and the transition maximum velocity occurs at an ordinate of Fig. 10.11 equal to approximately 70. For larger continuous phase viscosities, but not exceeding 30 centipoises, the ordinate of Fig. 10.11 should be multiplied by $(\mu_W/\mu_C)^{0.14}$, where μ_W is the viscosity of water.[11] Minute amounts of impurities which are frequently present in practice can alter the terminal velocities profoundly (usually to lower values), and the effect of mass transfer is unknown.†

† The curve of Fig. 10.11 should not be extrapolated to lower values. For values of the ordinate below 1.0, the equation of Klee and Treybal, *AIChE J.*, **2,** 444 (1956), will give more correct results:

$$V_t = \frac{53{,}000\Delta\rho^{0.58} d_p^{0.70}}{\rho_c^{0.45}\mu_c^{0.11}}$$

This equation will serve also for all drop sizes less than the transition size and continuous phase viscosity not exceeding 2 centipoises.

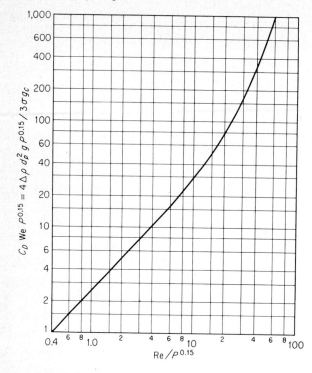

Fig. 10.11 *Terminal settling velocities of single liquid drops in infinite liquid media.*[9]

Drop formation

A liquid may be dispersed into drops by passage through perforations in plates or pipes or by causing it to issue from a short open tube or nozzle. If the drop preferentially wets the material of the plate, the drop size is uncontrollably large, and it is best to use small nozzles which project from the surface. These may be punched in a flat plate in the manner of Fig. 10.12, with the burr left in place facing in the direction of drop formation.

In the absence of mass transfer, whose effect is not known, when the dispersed phase issues from a nozzle or perforated plate which is not preferentially wetted by the dispersed liquid, drop size will be uniform at a given velocity up to nozzle or perforation velocities of 0.3 ft/sec. At higher velocities jets or "streamers" of dispersed liquid issue from the openings, and these break up at some distance from the opening into relatively large drops of nonuniform size. For openings up to 0.31 in. diameter, Fig. 10.13 provides the uniform drop size d_p for nozzle velocities V'_o up to 0.3 ft/sec, and the diameter of the largest drop for $V'_o = 0.3$ to 1.0 ft/sec.[8] For velocities larger than this there is a tendency for the liquid to "atomize," and small but very nonuniform drops are produced.[12]

Despite the fact that packings reduce the axial mixing to much lower values than are found in spray towers, packed towers are still subject to it.[31] Packed towers are not very satisfactory when the ratio of flow rates to the tower is outside the range 0.5

Fig. 10.12 *Punched perforations for dispersed phase.*[15]

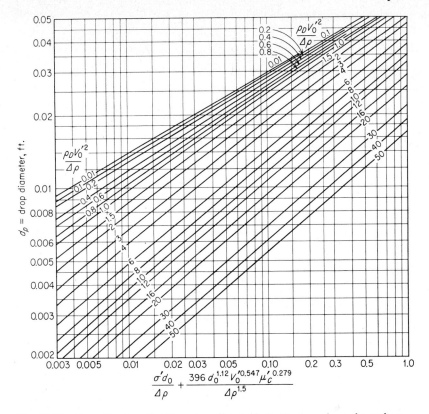

Fig. 10.13 *Drop diameters for dispersion of insoluble liquids through nozzles and per-forations.*[8]

to 2.0, since then suitable dispersed phase holdup and interfacial area are difficult to establish and still avoid flooding.   Mass-transfer rates will generally be low except for systems of low interfacial tension.

Illustration 10.1. Isopropyl ether, 180 cu ft/hr, is to be used to extract acetic acid from a dilute solution in water, 120 cu ft/hr, in a tower packed with 1-in. Berl saddles.   The ether is to be dispersed. Physical properties are, for the aqueous phase, density = 63.0 lb/cu ft, viscosity = 3.1 centipoises; for the ether phase, density = 45.6 lb/cu ft; interfacial tension = 13 dynes/cm.   Determine the tower diameter to be used and the distributor characteristics.

Solution. $\sigma = (13 \text{ dynes/cm})(6.85)(10^{-5}) = 8.90(10^{-4})$ lb/ft, $\Delta\rho = 63.0 - 45.6 = 17.4$ lb/cu ft, $g_c/g = 1$.   Equation (10.2):

$$d_{FO} = 2.42 \left[\frac{8.90(10^{-4})}{17.4} \right]^{0.5} = 0.0173 \text{ ft}$$

This corresponds to 0.21 in., so that the 1-in. Berl saddles are therefore satisfactory.   The saddles should be ceramic, preferentially wet by the continuous aqueous phase.   Table 6.2: $\epsilon = 0.69$, $a_p = 76$.

Flooding. The abscissa of Fig. 10.10 is

$$\frac{\mu_C'}{\Delta\rho}\left(\frac{\sigma'}{\rho_C}\right)^{0.2}\left(\frac{a_p}{\epsilon}\right)^{1.5} = \frac{3.1}{17.4}\left(\frac{13}{63.0}\right)^{0.2}\left(\frac{76}{0.69}\right)^{1.5} = 149.3$$

and the corresponding ordinate is 125. Therefore

$$V_{Of} = \frac{125 a_p \mu_C'}{[1 + (V_D/V_C)^{0.5}]^2 \rho_C} = \frac{125(76)(3.1)}{[1 + (180/120)^{0.5}]^2 63.0} = 94.4 \text{ ft/hr}$$

$$V_{Df} = 94.4(180/120) = 141.5 \text{ ft/hr}$$

Tower diameter. Set $\phi_D = 0.20$. Equation (10.3), with $V_C = 120V_D/180$:

$$\frac{V_D}{0.69(0.20)} + \frac{120V_D/180}{0.69(1-0.20)} = V_K(1-0.20) \qquad \frac{V_K}{V_D} = 10.56$$

Eq. (10.4): $$d_p = 0.92\left[\frac{8.90(10^{-4})}{17.4}\right]^{0.5} 10.56(0.69)(0.20) = 0.00958 \text{ ft}$$

Eq. (10.5): $$P = \frac{(63.0)^2[8.90(10^{-4})(4.18)(10^8)]^3}{4.18(10^8)[3.1(2.42)]^4(17.4)} = 885(10^4)$$

and $P^{0.15} = 11.03$. The ordinate of Fig. 10.11 is, with $g/g_c = 1$,

$$\frac{4\Delta\rho \, d_p{}^2 g P^{0.15}}{3\sigma g_c} = \frac{4(17.4)(0.00958)^2(11.03)}{3(8.90)(10^{-4})} = 26.4$$

and therefore the abscissa = 9.

$$\frac{\text{Re}}{P^{0.15}} = \frac{d_p V_t \rho_C}{\mu_C P^{0.15}} = \frac{0.00958 V_t(63.0)}{3.1(2.42)(11.03)} = 9$$

$$V_t = 1,240 \text{ ft/hr, terminal drop velocity}$$

The abscissa of Fig. 10.9, with $d_F = 1/12 = 0.0833$ ft, is 2.6, and the corresponding ordinate is $0.725 = V_K/V_t$, since the exponential term will be negligible. Therefore $V_K = 0.725(1,240) = 900$ ft/hr.

$$V_D = \frac{V_K}{10.56} = \frac{900}{10.56} = 85.1 \text{ ft/hr}$$

This is 60% of the flooding velocity, and will be accepted. The tower cross section is therefore $180/85.1 = 2.11$ sq ft, corresponding to a diameter of 1.6 ft, say 1 ft, 8 in.

Dispersed-phase distributors. Since $d_p = 0.00958$ ft, the distributor nozzles should produce somewhat larger drops. For nozzle diameters of $1/4$ in., $d_o = 0.25/12 = 0.0208$ ft, and with a hole velocity $V_O' = 0.3$ ft/sec, the abscissa of Fig. 10.13 is 0.0651. The parameter is 0.236, whence d_p at the nozzle is 0.022 ft, which should be satisfactory. The volumetric rate through one hole is

$$(\pi/4)(0.0205)^2(0.3)(3,600) = 0.368 \text{ cu ft/hr}$$

so that $180/0.368 = 490$ holes are required.

Perforated-plate (sieve-plate) towers

These have proven very effective, both with respect to liquid-handling capacity and efficiency of extraction, particularly for systems of low interfacial tension. This is

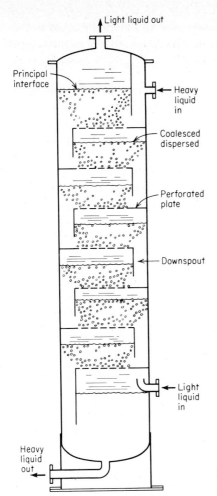

Light liquid out

Principal interface

Heavy liquid in

Coalesced dispersed

Perforated plate

Downspout

Light liquid in

Heavy liquid out

Fig. 10.14 *Perforated-plate extractor, arranged for light liquid dispersed.*

because (1) axial mixing of the continuous phase is confined to the region between trays and does not spread throughout the tower, and (2) the dispersed-phase droplets coalesce and are re-formed at each tray, destroying the tendency to establish concentration gradients within the drops which persist for the entire tower height. A tower of simple design is shown in Fig. 10.14, where the general arrangement of plates and downspouts is much the same as for gas-liquid contact except that no weir is required. The figure shows the arrangement for light liquid dispersed. Light liquid passes through the perforations, and the bubbles rise through the heavy continuous phase and coalesce into a layer, which accumulates beneath each plate. The heavy liquid flows across each plate through the rising droplets and passes through the downspouts to the plate below. By turning the tower as shown upside down, the downspouts become "upspouts" and carry the light liquid from plate to plate, while the heavy liquid flows through the perforations and is dispersed into drops. As an alternative, the heavy liquid may be dispersed in one part of the tower and the light liquid in the other, while the principal interface is maintained in the central portion of the tower. Interface taps to remove scum accumulating at the interface may be included between each tray, or special bypasses may be arranged.[15]

Perforation diameters of ⅛ to ¼ in., ½ to ¾ in. apart, may be used, and these may either be drilled or better punched (Fig. 10.12) to eliminate wetting of the plate by the dispersed liquid which interferes with drop formation. The best velocity of liquid through the perforations ought to be established by pilot-plant tests, but in the absence of experimental information it is recommended that it be kept within the range 0.4 to 1.0 ft/sec. At lower velocities the diameter of the tower will be unnecessarily large, and all perforations may not operate, while at higher velocities the many fine droplets which form will be likely to be carried from tray to tray through the downspout by the continuous phase. At the recommended velocities the liquid flowing through the perforations will probably "stream," and droplets will not form at the perforations, but rather at the ends of jets which extend from the plate.

The tower will flood if excessive quantities of dispersed-phase droplets are carried through the downspout, entrained in the continuous phase. The velocity of the liquid in the downspouts, V_d, should therefore be lower than the settling velocity of all except the smallest droplets, those smaller than 1/32 in. diameter, for example.[15] The settling velocity of the drops may be estimated through Fig. 10.11. The plate spacing should be sufficient so that (1) the "streamers" of dispersed liquid from the perforations break up into drops before coalescing into the layer of liquid on the next plate; (2) the linear velocity of the continuous liquid is not greater than that in the downspout, to avoid excessive entrainment; and (3) the tower may be entered through hand- or manholes in the sides for cleaning.

The tower will also flood if the dispersed liquid accumulates to a depth greater than the length of the downspout. The depth of dispersed liquid accumulating on each tray is determined by the pressure drop required for counterflow of the liquids,[5]

$$h = h_C + h_D \tag{10.6}$$

where h is the total thickness of the layer, while h_C and h_D are the contributions from the flow of each liquid. The head required for the dispersed phase h_D is that necessary to overcome interfacial tension effects at the perforations h_σ plus that necessary to cause flow through the orifices h_o,

$$h_D = h_\sigma + h_o \tag{10.7}$$

The value of h_o may be computed from the usual orifice equation with a coefficient of 0.67,

$$h_o = \frac{(V_o{}^2 - V_n{}^2)\rho_D}{2g_C(0.67)^2 \, \Delta\rho} \tag{10.8}$$

where V_n is based on A_n, the net tower cross section, $A_t - A_d$. h_σ, which is important only when the dispersed phase flows slowly, may be computed from

$$h_\sigma = \frac{6\sigma}{d_{p,0.1} \, \Delta\rho} \tag{10.9}$$

where $d_{p,0.1}$ is the drop diameter produced at perforation velocities $V_o' = 0.1$ ft/sec. At perforation velocities where jets of dispersed liquid issue from the perforations, h_σ may be omitted, and $h_D = h_o$.

The head required for flow of the continuous phase h_C includes losses owing to (1) friction in the downspout, which is ordinarily negligible, (2) contraction and expansion upon entering and leaving the downspout, equal to 0.5 and 1.0 "velocity heads," respectively, and (3) the two abrupt changes in direction each equivalent to 1.47 velocity heads. The value of h_C is therefore substantially 4.5 velocity heads, or

$$h_C = \frac{4.5 V_d^2 \rho_C}{2 g_c \Delta \rho} \tag{10.10}$$

Illustration 10.2. Design a perforated tray tower for the extraction of illustration 10.1 with ether as the dispersed phase.

Solution. The perforations will be made $\frac{3}{16}$ in. diameter. $d_o = 3/16(12) = 0.01561$ ft, and the area of each perforation $= \pi(0.01561)^2/4 = 0.000191$ sq ft. A perforation velocity $V_o' = 1.0$ ft/sec will be used, and $V_o = 3,600$ ft/hr.

For 180 cu ft ether/hr, $180/3,600(0.000191) = 262$ perforations per plate. If placed on the corners of $\frac{3}{4}$-in. equilateral triangles, 0.89 sq ft of the tower cross section must be devoted to perforations.

The velocity of the aqueous phase in the downspout will be set at the settling velocity of ether droplets $\frac{1}{32}$ in. diameter, $d_p = 1/32(12) = 0.0026$ ft. $P^{0.15} = 11.03$, as in Illustration 10.1. The ordinate of Fig. 10.11 becomes $4(17.4)(0.0026^2)(11.03)/3(8.90)(10^{-4}) = 1.95$, and the abscissa is therefore 0.8. Therefore,

$$\frac{Re}{P^{0.15}} = \frac{0.0026 V_t(63.0)}{3.1(2.42)(11.03)} = 0.8$$

$$V_t = 405 \text{ ft/hr}$$

and V_d will be set at this value.

For 120 cu ft/hr of aqueous liquid, the downspout cross section is therefore $A_d = \frac{120}{405} = 0.296$ sq ft. The tower cross section devoted to downspouts and perforations $= 2(0.296) + 0.89 = 1.482$ sq ft. Keeping the perforations at least 1 in. from the walls of the tower to allow for a ring support for the plate, and 1 in. from the downspouts brings the total tower cross section to $A_t = 1.71$ sq ft, corresponding to a diameter 1.475 or 1.5 ft. For a tower arranged as in Fig. 10.14, the segmental downspouts are formed of chords 15 in. long, set at 5 in. from the tower center. The distance between trays will be set at 12 in., and the downspouts will extend 6 in. below each plate.

The net area $A_n = A_t - A_d = 1.5 - 0.296 = 1.204$ sq ft, and the dispersed-phase velocity based on this is $V_n = 180/1.204 = 149.5$ ft/hr.

Eq. (10.8):

$$h_O = \frac{[(3,600)^2 - (149.5)^2]45.6}{2(4.18)(10^8)(0.67)^2(17.4)} = 0.0905 \text{ ft}$$

At this perforation velocity, h_σ may be omitted, and $h_D = 0.0905$ ft.

Eq. (10.10):

$$h_C = \frac{4.5(405)^2(63.0)}{2(4.18)(10^8)(17.4)} = 0.00321 \text{ ft}$$

Eq. (10.6): $\qquad\qquad h = 0.00312 + 0.0905 = 0.0936$ ft

This corresponds to 1.12 in., and the tower will therefore not flood.

Agitated countercurrent extractors

The extraction towers previously described are very similar to towers used for gas-liquid contact, where density differences between liquid and gas are of the order of 50 lb/cu ft or more, available to provide the energy for adequate dispersion of one fluid in the other. In liquid extraction, where density differences are likely to be one-tenth as large or less, good dispersion of systems with high interfacial tension is impossible in such towers, and mass-transfer rates are poor. For such systems, dispersion is best brought about by mechanical agitation of the liquids, whereupon good mass-transfer rates are developed. Some examples of such extractors follow. Except for pulse columns, they are proprietary devices for which complete design procedures have not been made publicly available, and the manufacturers are best consulted. Some of their characteristics have been reviewed.[27]

The *Mixco Lightnin CMContactor (Oldshue-Rushton extractor)*[3,16] of Fig. 10.15 uses flat-blade turbine impellers to disperse and mix the liquids and depends upon the horizontal compartmenting plates to reduce vertical axial mixing.

The *Rotating-disk Contactor (RDC)*[20,26] (Fig. 10.16) is somewhat similar, except that the vertical baffles are omitted and the agitation is brought about by rotating flat disks, which usually turn at higher speeds than turbine-type impellers.

The *Scheibel-York* extractor[24] is shown only in a short section in Fig. 10.17. The paddle-type impellers are surrounded by a shroud baffle. For systems of low interfacial tension, the agitation sections may be alternated with sections filled with woven

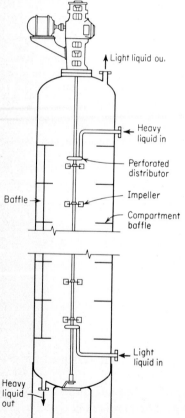

Fig. 10.15 *Mixco Lightnin CMContactor (Mixing Equipment Co.).*

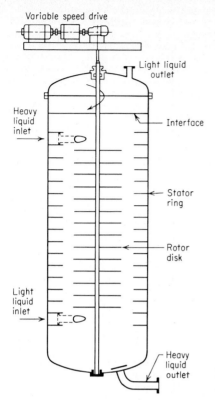

Variable speed drive

Light liquid
outlet

Heavy
liquid
inlet

Interface

Stator
ring

Rotor
disk

Light
liquid
inlet

Heavy
liquid
outlet

Fig. 10.16 *Rotating-disk Contactor (RDC) (General American Transportation Corp.).*

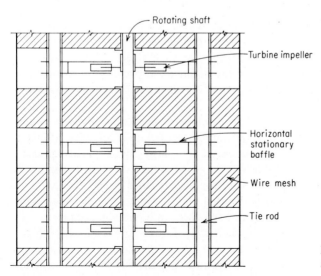

Rotating shaft

Turbine impeller

Horizontal
stationary
baffle

Wire mesh

Tie rod

Fig. 10.17 *Scheibel-York extractor (York Process Equipment Co.).*

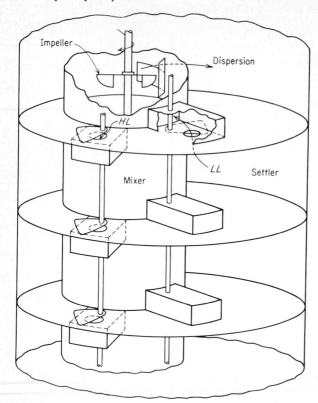

Fig. 10.18 *Treybal extractor (schematic). Recycle provisions not shown. LL = light liquid, HL = heavy liquid. (U.S. Stoneware, Inc.)*

wire mesh, as shown.   For systems of high interfacial tension the wire-mesh sections are omitted.

The *Treybal* extractor[29] (Fig. 10.18) is in reality a vertically arranged mixer-settler cascade, thus essentially eliminating axial mixing.   The mixing compartments, vertically in line, are surrounded by the settlers for each stage.   Baffles within the mixers assist the turbine impellers to pump the liquids, and provision is available for interface-level control and intrastage recycling of liquids between settler and mixer of the same stage (see page 412).

In *pulsed extractors*,[14,32] a rapid (30 to 250/min) reciprocating motion of short amplitude (¼ to 1 in.) is hydraulically transmitted to the liquid contents.   Since no moving parts are present within the extractors, they have found particular use in handling radioactive solutions in atomic-energy work, where they can be put behind heavy radiation shields without the necessity for maintenance.   The most common arrangement is that of Fig. 10.19; the perforated plates, which have no downspouts, are drilled with very small holes so that ordinarily flow of liquid will not occur.   The pulsing superimposed upon the liquids alternately forces light and heavy liquids through the perforations.   Packed columns may also be pulsed,[7] as indeed may any type of extractor.   Although the mass-transfer rates are thereby improved, the flow capacities become lower.

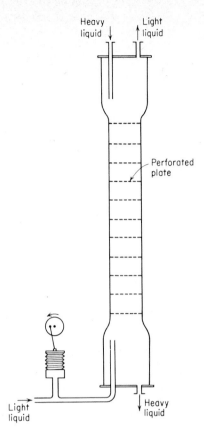

Fig. **10.19** *Pulse column.*

Centrifugal extractors

The most important of these is the Podbielniak extractor[2,10] (Fig. 10.20).   The cylindrical drum contains perforated, concentric shells, and is rapidly rotated on the horizontal shaft (2,000 to 5,000 rpm).   Liquids enter through the shaft: heavy liquid is led to the center of the drum, light liquid to the periphery.   The heavy liquid flows radially outward, displacing the light liquid inwardly, and both are led out through the shaft.   These extractors are especially useful for liquids of very small density difference and where very short residence times are essential, as in some pharmaceutical applications.

LIQUID EQUILIBRIA

Extraction involves the use of systems composed of at least three substances, and in most cases all three components appear in both insoluble phases.   The following notation scheme will be used to describe the concentrations and amounts of these ternary mixtures, for purposes of discussing both equilibria and material balances.

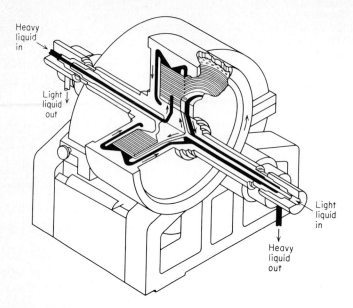

Heavy liquid in

Light liquid out

Light liquid in

Heavy liquid out

Fig. 10.20 *Podbielniak centrifugal extractor (schematic).* (*Podbielniak, Inc.*)

Notation scheme

1. *A* and *B* are pure, substantially insoluble liquids, and *C* is the distributed solute. Mixtures to be separated by extraction are composed of *A* and *C*, and *B* is the extracting solvent.

2. The same letter will be used to indicate the quantity of a solution or mixture and the location of the mixture on a phase diagram. Quantities are measured in pounds for batch operations, lb/hr for continuous operation. Thus,

E = lb/hr of solution E, an extract, shown on a phase diagram by point E
R = lb/hr of solution R, a raffinate, shown on a phase diagram by point R
B = lb/hr of solvent B

Solvent-free (*B*-free) quantities are indicated by primed letters. Thus,

E' = lb *B*-free solution/hr, shown on a phase diagram by point E
$E = E'(1 + N_E)$

3. x = weight fraction C in the solvent-lean (*A*-rich), or raffinate, liquids
y = weight fraction C in the solvent-rich (*B*-rich), or extract, liquids
$x' = x/(1 - x)$ = lb C/lb non-C in the raffinate liquids
$y' = y/(1 - y)$ = lb C/lb non-C in the extract liquids
X = weight fraction C in the raffinate liquids on a *B*-free basis, lb C/(lb A + lb C)
Y = weight fraction C in the extract liquids on a *B*-free basis, lb C/(lb A + lb C)
N = weight fraction B on a *B*-free basis, lb B/(lb A + lb C)

Subscripts identify the solution or mixture to which the concentration terms refer. Stages are identified by number. Thus, x_3 = wt fraction C in the raffinate from stage 3, Y_3 = wt fraction C (B-free basis) in the extract from stage 3, etc. For other solutions identified by a letter on a phase diagram, the same letter is used as an identifying subscript. Thus, x_M = wt fraction C in the mixture M.

An asterisk specifically identifies equilibrium concentrations where the condition of equilibrium is emphasized. Thus, y_E^* = wt fraction C in the equilibrium solution E.

4. Throughout the discussion of equilibria, material balances, and stagewise calculations, mole fractions, mole ratios, and pound moles may be consistently substituted for weight fractions, weight ratios, and pounds, respectively.

Equilateral-triangular coordinates

These are used extensively in the chemical literature to describe graphically the concentrations in ternary systems. It is the property of an equilateral triangle that the sum of the perpendicular distances from any point within the triangle to the three sides equals the altitude of the triangle. We may therefore let the altitude represent 100 percent composition and the distances to the three sides the percents or fractions of the three components. Refer to Fig. 10.21. Each apex of the triangle represents one of the pure components, as marked. The perpendicular distance from any point such as K to the base AB represents the percentage of C in the mixture at K, the distance to the base AC the percentage of B, and that to the base CB the percentage of A. Thus $x_K = 0.4$. Any point on a side of the triangle represents a binary mixture. Point D, for example, is a binary containing 80% A, 20% B. All points on the line DC represent mixtures containing the same ratio of A to B and may be considered as mixtures originally at D to which C has been added. If R lb of a mixture at point R is added to E lb of a mixture at E, the new mixture is shown on the straight line RE at point M, such that

$$\frac{R}{E} = \frac{\text{line } ME}{\text{line } RM} = \frac{x_E - x_M}{x_M - x_R} \tag{10.11}$$

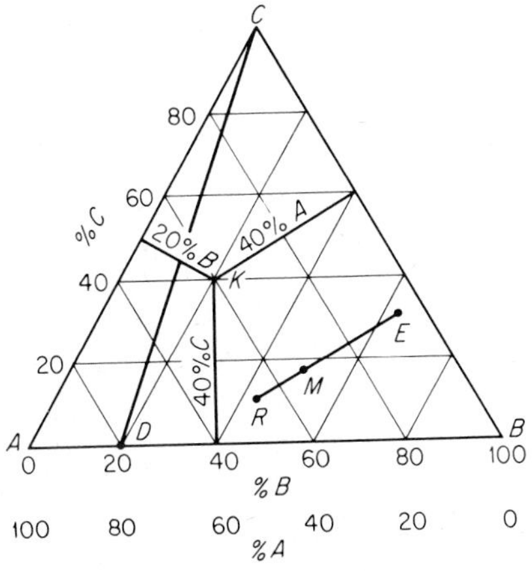

Fig. 10.21 Equilateral-triangular coordinates.

Alternatively the composition corresponding to point M can be computed by material balances, as will be shown later. Similarly, if a mixture at M has removed from it a mixture of composition E, the new mixture is on the straight line EM extended in the direction away from E, and located at R so that Eq. (10.11) applies.

Equation (10.11) is readily established. Refer to Fig. 10.22, which again shows R lb of mixture at R added to E lb of mixture at E. Let M represent the pounds of new mixture as well as the composition on the figure. Line RL = wt fraction C in $R = x_R$, line MO = wt fraction C in $M = x_M$, and line ET = wt fraction C in $E = x_E$. A total material balance,

$$R + E = M$$

A balance for component C,

$$R(\text{line } RL) + E(\text{line } ET) = M(\text{line } MO)$$

$$Rx_R + Ex_E = Mx_M$$

Eliminating M,

$$\frac{R}{E} = \frac{\text{line } ET - \text{line } MO}{\text{line } MO - \text{line } RL} = \frac{x_E - x_M}{x_M - x_R}$$

But line ET − line MO = line EP, and line MO − line RL = line MK = line PS. Therefore

$$\frac{R}{E} = \frac{\text{line } EP}{\text{line } PS} = \frac{\text{line } ME}{\text{line } RM}$$

The following discussion is limited to those types of systems which most frequently occur in liquid-extraction operations. For a complete consideration of the very many types of systems which may be encountered, the student is referred to one of the more comprehensive texts on the phase rule.[21]

Systems of three liquids—one pair partially soluble

This is the most commonly encountered type of system in extraction, and typical examples are water (A)–chloroform (B)–acetone (C), and benzene (A)–water (B)–acetic acid (C). The triangular coordinates are used as *isotherms*, or diagrams at constant temperature. Refer to Fig. 10.23a. Liquid C dissolves completely in A and B, but A and B dissolve only to a limited extent in each other to give rise to the saturated liquid solutions at L (A-rich) and at K (B-rich). The more insoluble the liquids A

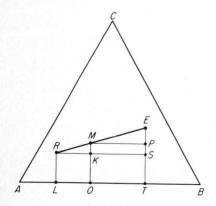

Fig. 10.22 *The mixture rule.*

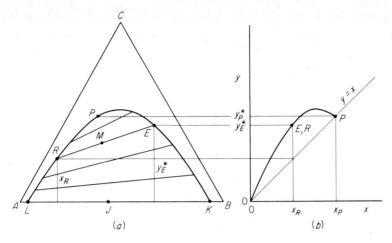

Fig. 10.23 *System of three liquids, A and B partially miscible.*

and B, the nearer the apexes of the triangle will points L and K be located.   A binary mixture J, anywhere between L and K, will separate into two insoluble liquid phases of compositions at L and K, the relative amounts of the phases depending upon the position of J, according to the principle of Eq. (10.11).

Curve $LRPEK$ is the binodal solubility curve, indicating the change in solubility of the A- and B-rich phases upon addition of C.   Any mixture outside this curve will be a homogeneous solution of one liquid phase.   Any ternary mixture underneath the curve, such as M, will form two insoluble, saturated liquid phases of equilibrium compositions indicated by R (A-rich) and E (B-rich).   The line RE joining these equilibrium compositions is a tie line, which must necessarily pass through point M representing the mixture as a whole.   There are an infinite number of tie lines in the two-phase region, and only a few are shown.   They are rarely parallel and usually change their slope slowly in one direction as shown.   In a relatively few systems the direction of the tie-line slope changes, and one tie line will be horizontal.   Such systems are said to be "solutropic."   Point P, the *plait point, the last of the tie lines and the point where the A-rich and B-rich solubility curves merge, is ordinarily not at the maximum value of C on the solubility curve.*

The percentage of C in solution E is clearly greater than that in R, and it is said that in this case the distribution of C favors the B-rich phase.   This is conveniently shown on the distribution diagram (Fig. 10.23b), where the point (E,R) lies above the diagonal $y = x$.   The ratio y^*/x, the *distribution coefficient*, is in this case greater than unity.   The concentrations of C at the ends of the tie lines, when plotted against each other, give rise to the distribution curve shown.   Should the tie lines on Fig. 10.23a slope in the opposite direction, with C favoring A at equilibrium, the distribution curve will lie below the diagonal.   The distribution curve may be used for interpolating between tie lines when only a few have been experimentally determined.   Other methods of interpolation are also available.[27]

Effect of temperature. To show the effect of temperature in detail requires a three-dimensional figure, as in Fig. 10.24a. In this diagram, temperature is plotted vertically, and the isothermal triangles are seen to be sections through the prism. For most systems of this type, the mutual solubility of A and B increases with increasing temperature, and above some temperature t_4, the critical solution temperature, they dissolve completely. The increased solubility at higher temperatures influences the ternary equilibria considerably, and this is best shown by projection of the isotherms onto the base triangle as in Fig. 10.24b. Not only does the area of heterogeneity decrease at higher temperatures, but the slopes of the tie lines may also change. Liquid-extraction operations, which depend upon the formation of insoluble liquid phases, must be carried on at temperatures below t_4. Other temperature effects, which are less common, are also known.[21,27]

Effect of pressure. Except at very high pressures, the influence of pressure on the liquid equilibrium is so small that it may generally be ignored. All the diagrams shown are therefore to be considered as having been plotted at sufficiently high pressure to maintain a completely condensed system, i.e., above the vapor pressures of the solutions. However, should the pressure be sufficiently reduced so that it becomes less than the vapor pressure of the solutions, a vapor phase will appear, and the liquid equilibrium will be interrupted. Such an effect on a binary solubility curve of the type APB of Fig. 10.24a is shown in Fig. 9.8.

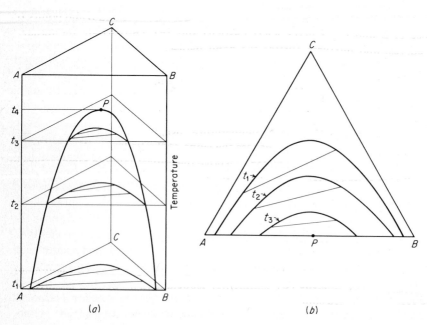

Fig. 10.24 *Effect of temperature on ternary equilibria.*

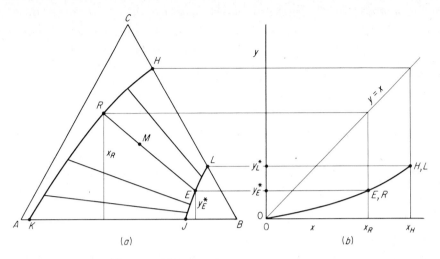

Fig. 10.25   *System of three liquids, A-B and B-C partially miscible.*

Systems of three liquids—two pairs partially soluble

This type is exemplified by the system chlorobenzene (*A*)–water (*B*)–methyl ethyl ketone (*C*), where *A* and *C* are completely soluble, while the pairs *A-B* and *B-C* show only limited solubility.   Refer to Fig. 10.25*a*, a typical isotherm.   At the prevailing temperature, points *K* and *J* represent the mutual solubilities of *A* and *B* and points *H* and *L* those of *B* and *C*.   Curves *KRH* (*A*-rich) and *JEL* (*B*-rich) are the ternary solubility curves, and mixtures outside the band between these curves form homogeneous single-phase liquid solutions.   Mixtures such as *M*, inside the heterogeneous area, form two liquid phases at equilibrium at *E* and *R*, joined on the diagram by a tie line.   The corresponding distribution curve is shown in Fig. 10.25*b*.

Effect of temperature. Increased temperature usually increases the mutual solubilities and at the same time influences the slope of the tie lines.   Figure 10.26 is typical of the effect that may be expected.   Above the critical solution temperature of the binary *B-C* at t_3, the system is similar to the first type discussed.   Other temperature effects are also possible.[21,27]

Systems of two partially soluble liquids and one solid

When the solid does not form compounds such as hydrates with the liquids, the system will frequently have the characteristics of the isotherm of Fig. 10.27, an example of which is the system naphthalene (*C*)–aniline (*A*)–isooctane (*B*).   Solid *C* dissolves in liquid *A* to form a saturated solution at *K* and in liquid *B* to give the saturated solution at *L*.   *A* and *B* are soluble only to the extent shown at *H* and *J*.   Mixtures in the regions *AKDH* and *BLGJ* are homogeneous liquid solutions.   The curves *KD* and

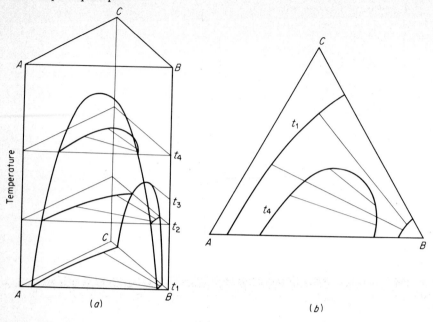

Fig. 10.26   *Effect of temperature on ternary liquid equilibria.*

GL show the effect of adding A and B upon the solubilities of the solid.   In the region $HDGJ$ two liquid phases form: if C is added to the insoluble liquids H and J to give a mixture M, the equilibrium liquid phases will be R and E, joined by a tie line.   All mixtures in the region CDG consist of three phases, solid C, and saturated liquid solutions at D and G.   Liquid-extraction operations are usually confined to the region of the two liquid phases, which is that corresponding to the distribution curve shown.

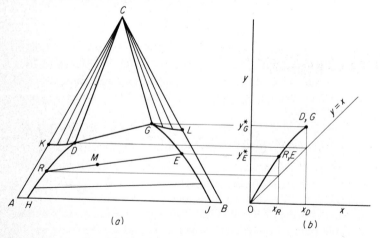

Fig. 10.27   *System of two partially soluble liquids A, B and one solid C.*

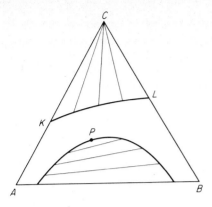

Fig. 10.28 *System of two partially soluble liquids A, B and one solid C.*

Increased temperature frequently changes these systems to the configuration shown in Fig. 10.28.

Other coordinates

Because the equilibrium relationship can rarely be expressed algebraically with any convenience, extraction computations must usually be made graphically on a phase diagram.   The coordinate scales of equilateral triangles are necessarily always the same, and in order to be able to expand one concentration scale relative to the other, rectangular coordinates may be used.   One of these is formed by plotting concentrations of B as abscissa against concentrations of C (x and y) as ordinate, as in Fig. 10.29a.   Unequal scales may be used in order to expand the plot as desired.   Equation (10.11) applies for mixtures on Fig. 10.29a, regardless of any inequality of the scales.

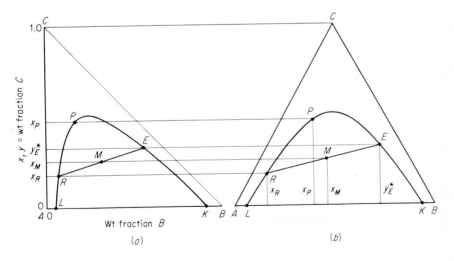

Fig. 10.29 *Rectangular coordinates.*

Another rectangular coordinate system involves plotting as abscissa the weight fraction C on a B-free basis, X and Y in the A- and B-rich phases, respectively, against N, the B-concentration on a B-free basis, as ordinate, as shown in the upper part of Fig. 10.30. This has been plotted for a system of two partly miscible pairs, such as that of Fig. 10.25.

The similarity of such diagrams to the enthalpy-concentration diagrams of Chap. 9 is clear. In extraction, the two phases are produced by addition of solvent, in distillation by addition of heat, and solvent becomes the analog of heat. This is emphasized by the ordinate of the upper part of Fig. 10.30. Tie lines such as QS can be projected to X, Y coordinates, as shown in the lower figure, to produce a solvent-free distribution graph similar to those of distillation. The mixture rule on these coordinates (see the upper part of Fig. 10.30) is

$$\frac{M'}{N'} = \frac{Y_N - Y_P}{Y_P - Y_M} = \frac{X_N - X_P}{X_P - X_M} = \frac{\text{line } NP}{\text{line } PM} \qquad (10.12)$$

where M' and N' are the B-free weights of these mixtures.

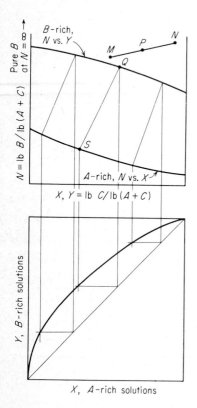

Fig. 10.30 *Rectangular coordinates, solvent-free basis, for a system of two partly miscible liquid pairs.*

Multicomponent systems

The simplest system of four components occurs when two solutes distribute between two solvents, e.g., the distribution of formic and acetic acids between the partly soluble solvents water and carbon tetrachloride.   Complete display of such equilibria requires a three-dimensional graph[27] which is difficult to work with, but frequently we can simplify this to the distribution (*xy*) curves, one for each solute, such as that for a single solute in Fig. 10.23*b*.   More than four components cannot be conveniently dealt with graphically.

Choice of solvent

There is usually a wide choice among liquids to be used as solvents for extraction operations.   It is unlikely that any particular liquid will exhibit all the properties considered desirable for extraction, and some compromise is usually necessary.   The following are the quantities to be given consideration in making a choice:

1. *Selectivity.*   The effectiveness of solvent *B* for separating a solution of *A* and *C* into its components is measured by comparing the ratio of *C* to *A* in the *B*-rich phase to that in the *A*-rich phase at equilibrium.   The ratio of the ratios, the separation factor, or selectivity, *β*, is analogous to the relative volatility of distillation.   If *E* and *R* are the equilibrium phases,

$$\beta = \frac{(\text{wt fraction } C \text{ in } E)/(\text{wt fraction } A \text{ in } E)}{(\text{wt fraction } C \text{ in } R)/(\text{wt fraction } A \text{ in } R)}$$

$$= \frac{y_E^*(\text{wt fraction } A \text{ in } R)}{x_R(\text{wt fraction } A \text{ in } E)} \tag{10.13}$$

For all useful extraction operations the selectivity must exceed unity, the more so the better.   If the selectivity is unity, no separation is possible.

Selectivity usually varies considerably with solute concentration, and in systems of the type shown in Fig. 10.23 it will be unity at the plait point.   In some systems it passes from large values through unity to fractional values, and these are analogous to azeotropic systems of distillation.

2. *Distribution coefficient.*   This is the ratio y^*/x at equilibrium.   While it is not necessary that the distribution coefficient be larger than 1, large values are very desirable since less solvent will then be required for the extraction.

3. *Insolubility of solvent.*   Refer to Fig. 10.31.   For both systems shown, only those *A-C* mixtures between *D* and *A* can be separated by use of the solvents *B* or *B'*, since mixtures richer in *C* will not form two liquid phases with the solvents.   Clearly the solvent in Fig. 10.31*a*, which is the more insoluble of the two, will be the more useful.   In systems of the type shown in Figs. 10.25*a* and 10.27*a*, if the solubility of *C* in *B* is small (point *L* near the *B* apex), the *capacity* of solvent *B* to extract *C* is small, and large amounts of solvent are then required.

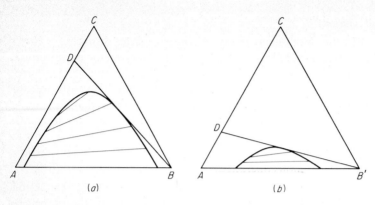

Fig. 10.31   *Influence of solvent solubility on extraction.*

4. *Recoverability.*   It is always necessary to recover the solvent for reuse, and this must ordinarily be done by another of the mass-transfer operations, most frequently distillation.   If distillation is to be used, the solvent should form no azeotrope with the extracted solute, and mixtures should show high relative volatility for low-cost recovery.   That substance in the extract, either solvent or solute, which is present as the lesser quantity should be the more volatile in order to reduce heat costs.   If the solvent must be volatilized, its latent heat of vaporization should be small.

5. *Density.*   A difference in densities of the saturated liquid phases is necessary, both for stagewise and continuous-contact equipment operation.   The larger this difference the better.   In systems of the type shown in Fig. 10.23, the density difference for equilibrium phases will become less as C concentrations increase and will be zero at the plait point.   It may reverse in sign before reaching the plait point, in which case continuous-contact equipment cannot be specified to operate at the concentrations at which the density difference passes through zero.

6. *Interfacial tension.*   The larger the interfacial tension, the more readily will coalescence of emulsions occur, but the more difficult will the dispersion of one liquid in the other be.   Coalescence is usually of greater importance, and interfacial tension should therefore be high.   Interfacial tension between equilibrium phases in systems of the type shown in Fig. 10.23 falls to zero at the plait point.

7. *Chemical reactivity.*   The solvent should be stable chemically and inert toward the other components of the system and toward the common materials of construction.

8. *Viscosity, vapor pressure, and freezing point.*   These should be low for ease in handling and storage.

9. The solvent should be *nontoxic, nonflammable,* and of *low cost.*

STAGEWISE CONTACT

Extraction in equipment of the stage type may be carried on according to a variety of flow sheets, depending upon the nature of the system and the extent of separation desired. In the discussion which follows it is to be understood that each stage is a *theoretical* or *ideal* stage, such that the effluent extract and raffinate solutions are in equilibrium with each other. Each stage must include facilities for contacting the insoluble liquids and separating the product streams. A combination of a mixer and a settler may therefore constitute a stage, and in multistage operation these may be arranged in cascades as desired. In the case of countercurrent multistage operation, it is also possible to use towers of the multistage type, as described earlier.

Single-stage extraction

This may be a batch or a continuous operation. Refer to Fig. 10.32. The flow sheet shows the extraction stage. Feed F lb (if batch) or F lb/hr (if continuous) contains substances A and C at x_F weight fraction C. This is contacted with S_1 lb (or lb/hr) of a solvent, principally B, containing y_S weight fraction C, to give the equilibrium extract E_1 and raffinate R_1, each measured in pounds or pounds per hour. Solvent recovery then involves separate removal of solvent B from each product·stream (not shown).

The operation may be followed in either of the phase diagrams as shown. If the solvent is pure B ($y_S = 0$), it will be plotted at the B apex, but sometimes it has been recovered from a previous extraction and therefore contains a little A and C as well, as shown by the location of S. Adding S to F produces in the extraction stage a mixture M_1 which, on settling, forms the equilibrium phases E_1 and R_1 joined by the tie

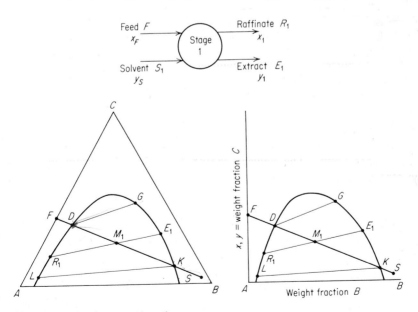

Fig. 10.32 *Single-stage extraction.*

line through M_1. A total material balance is

$$F + S_1 = M_1 = E_1 + R_1 \tag{10.14}$$

and point M_1 may be located on line FS by the mixture rule, Eq. (10.11), but it is usually more satisfactory to locate M_1 by computing its C concentration. Thus, a C balance provides

$$Fx_F + S_1 y_S = M_1 x_{M1} \tag{10.15}$$

from which x_{M1} may be computed. Alternatively, the amount of solvent to provide a given location for M_1 on the line FS may be computed:

$$\frac{S_1}{F} = \frac{x_F - x_{M1}}{x_{M1} - y_S} \tag{10.16}$$

The quantities of extract and raffinate may be computed by the mixture rule, Eq. (10.11), or by the material balance for C:

$$E_1 y_1 + R_1 x_1 = M_1 x_{M1} \tag{10.17}$$

$$E_1 = \frac{M_1(x_{M1} - x_1)}{y_1 - x_1} \tag{10.18}$$

and R_1 can be determined through Eq. (10.14).

Since two insoluble phases must form for an extraction operation, point M_1 must lie within the heterogeneous liquid area, as shown. The minimum amount of solvent is thus found by locating M_1 at D, which would then provide an infinitesimal amount of extract at G, and the maximum amount of solvent is found by locating M_1 at K, which provides an infinitesimal amount of raffinate at L. Point L represents also the raffinate with the lowest possible C concentration, and if a lower value were required, the recovered solvent S would have to have a lower C concentration.

Computations for systems of two insoluble liquid pairs, or with a distributed solute which is a solid, are made in exactly the same manner, and Eqs. (10.14) to (10.18) all apply.

All the computations may also be made on a solvent-free basis, as in the upper part of Fig. 10.33, if the nature of this diagram makes it convenient. If solvent S is pure B, its N value is infinite, and the line FS is then vertical. Products E_1 and R_1 lie on a tie line through M_1 representing the entire mixture in the extractor. Material balances for use with this diagram must be made on a B-free basis. Thus,

$$F' + S' = M_1' = E_1' + R_1' \tag{10.19}$$

where the primes indicate B-free weight (the feed is normally B-free, and $F = F'$). A balance for C is

$$F'X_F + S'Y_S = M_1' X_{M1} = E_1' Y_1 + R_1' X_1 \tag{10.20}$$

and for B,

$$F'N_F + S'N_S = M_1' N_{M1} = E_1' N_{E1} + R_1' N_{R1} \tag{10.21}$$

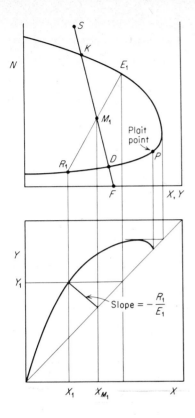

Fig. 10.33 *Single-stage extraction, solvent-free coordinates.*

(ordinarily, $N_F = 0$ since the feed contains no B). The coordinates of M_1' may be computed, point M_1 located on line FS, the tie line located, and the B-free weights, E_1' and R_1', computed:

$$E_1' = \frac{M_1'(X_{M1} - X_1)}{Y_1 - X_1}$$

(10.22)

and R_1' is obtained through Eq. (10.19). The total weights of the saturated extract and raffinate are then

$$E_1 = E_1'(1 + N_{E1}) \qquad R_1 = R_1'(1 + N_{R1})$$

(10.23)

If the solvent is pure B, whence $N_S = \infty$, these equations still apply, with the simplification that $S' = 0$, $Y_S = 0$, $S'N_S = B$, and $F' = M_1'$. Minimum and maximum amounts of solvent correspond to putting M_1 at D and K on the figure, as before.

Equations (10.19) and (10.20) lead to

$$\frac{R_1'}{E_1'} = \frac{Y_1 - X_{M1}}{X_{M1} - X_1}$$

(10.24)

When the equilibrium extract and raffinate are located on the lower diagram of Fig. 10.33, Eq. (10.24) is seen to be that of the operating line shown, of slope $-R_1'/E_1'$.

The single stage is seen to be analogous to the flash vaporization of distillation, with solvent replacing heat. If pure B is used as solvent, the operating line on the lower figure passes through the 45° line at X_F, which completes the analogy (see Fig. 9.14).

Multistage crosscurrent extraction

This is an extension of single-stage extraction, wherein the raffinate is successively contacted with fresh solvent, and may be done continuously or in batch. Refer to Fig. 10.34, which shows the flow sheet for a three-stage extraction. A single final raffinate results, and the extracts may be combined to provide the composited extract, as shown. As many stages as may be used as desired.

Computations are shown on triangular and on solvent-free coordinates. All the material balances for a single stage of course now apply to the first stage. Subsequent stages are dealt with in the same manner, except of course that the "feed" to any stage is the raffinate from the preceding stage. Thus, for any stage n,

Total balance:
$$R_{n-1} + S_n = M_n = E_n + R_n \tag{10.25}$$

C balance:
$$R_{n-1}x_{n-1} + S_n y_S = M_n x_{Mn} = E_n y_n + R_n x_n \tag{10.26}$$

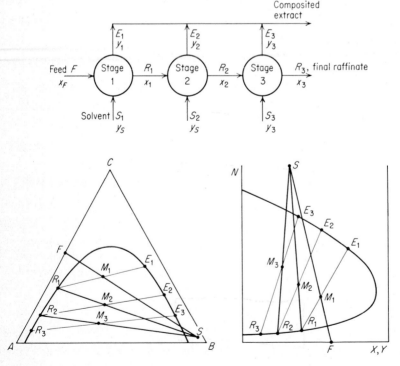

Fig. 10.34 *Crosscurrent extraction.*

For the solvent-free coordinates,

$A + C$ balance:
$$R'_{n-1} + S'_n = M'_n = E'_n + R'_n \qquad (10.27)$$

C balance:
$$R'_{n-1}X_{n-1} + S'_n Y_S = M'_n X_{Mn} = E'_n Y_n + R'_n X_n \qquad (10.28)$$

B balance:
$$R'_{n-1}N_{R,n-1} + S'_n N_S = M'_n N_{Mn} = E'_n N_{En} + R'_n N_{Rn} \qquad (10.29)$$

from which the quantities can be calculated for either type of graph.

Unequal amounts of solvent may be used in the various stages, and even different temperatures, in which case each stage must be computed with the help of a phase diagram at the appropriate temperature. For a given final raffinate concentration, less total solvent will be used the greater the number of stages.

Look over

Illustration 10.3. One hundred pounds of a solution of acetic acid (C) and water (A) containing 30% acid is to be extracted three times with isopropyl ether (B) at 20°C, using 40 lb of solvent in each stage. Determine the quantities and compositions of the various streams. How much solvent would be required if the same final raffinate concentration were to be obtained with one stage?

Solution. The equilibrium data at 20°C are listed below [*Trans. AIChE*, **36**, 628 (1940), with permission]. The horizontal rows give the concentrations in equilibrium solutions. The system is of the type shown in Fig. 10.29, except that the tie lines slope downward toward the B apex. The rectangular coordinates of Fig. 10.29a will be used, but only for acid concentrations up to $x = 0.30$. These are plotted in Fig. 10.35.

Water layer			Isopropyl ether layer		
Wt % acetic acid $100x$	Water	Isopropyl ether	Acetic acid $100y*$	Water	Isopropyl ether
0.69	98.1	1.2	0.18	0.5	99.3
1.41	97.1	1.5	0.37	0.7	98.9
2.89	95.5	1.6	0.79	0.8	98.4
6.42	91.7	1.9	1.93	1.0	97.1
13.30	84.4	2.3	4.82	1.9	93.3
25.50	71.1	3.4	11.40	3.9	84.7
36.70	58.9	4.4	21.60	6.9	71.5
44.30	45.1	10.6	31.10	10.8	58.1
46.40	37.1	16.5	36.20	15.1	48.7

Stage 1. $F = 100$ lb, $x_F = 0.30$, $y_S = 0$, $S_1 = B_1 = 40$ lb.

Eq. (10.14):
$$M_1 = 100 + 40 = 140 \text{ lb}$$

Eq. (10.15):
$$100(0.30) + 40(0) = 140x_{M1} \qquad x_{M1} = 0.214$$

Point M_1 is located on line FB. With the help of a distribution curve, the tie line passing through M_1 is located as shown, and $x_1 = 0.258$, $y_1 = 0.117$ wt fraction acetic acid.

Eq. (10.18):
$$E_1 = \frac{140(0.214 - 0.258)}{0.117 - 0.258} = 43.6 \text{ lb}$$

Eq. (10.14):
$$R_1 = 140 - 43.6 = 96.4 \text{ lb}$$

Stage 2. $S_2 = B_2 = 40$ lb.

Eq. (10.25): $\qquad M_2 = R_1 + B_2 = 96.4 + 40 = 136.4$ lb

Eq. (10.26): $\qquad 96.4(0.258) + 40(0) = 136.4x_{M2} \qquad x_{M2} = 0.1822$

Point M_2 is located on line R_1B and the tie line R_2E_2 through M_2. $x_2 = 0.227$, $y_2 = 0.095$. Eq. (10.18) becomes

$$E_2 = \frac{M_2(x_{M2} - x_2)}{y_2 - x_2} = \frac{136.4(0.1822 - 0.227)}{0.095 - 0.227} = 46.3 \text{ lb}$$

Eq. (10.25): $\qquad R_2 = M_2 - E_2 = 136.4 - 46.3 = 90.1$ lb

Stage 3. In a similar manner, $B_3 = 40$, $M_3 = 130.1$, $x_{M3} = 0.1572$, $x_3 = 0.20$, $y_3 = 0.078$, $E_3 = 45.7$, and $R_3 = 84.4$. The acid content of the final raffinate is $0.20(84.4) = 16.88$ lb.

The composited extract is $E_1 + E_2 + E_3 = 43.6 + 46.3 + 45.7 = 135.6$ lb, and its acid content $= E_1y_1 + E_2y_2 + E_3y_3 = 13.12$ lb.

If an extraction to give the same final raffinate concentration, $x = 0.20$, were to be done in one stage, the point M would be at the intersection of tie line R_3E_3 and line BF of Fig. 10.35, or at $x_M = 0.12$. The solvent required would then be, by Eq. (10.16), $S_1 = 100(0.30 - 0.12)/(0.12 - 0) = 150$ lb, instead of the total of 120 required in the three-stage extraction.

Insoluble liquids. When the extraction solvent and feed solution are insoluble and remain so at all concentrations of the distributed solute which are encountered in the operation, the computations may be simplified. For this purpose, the equilibrium

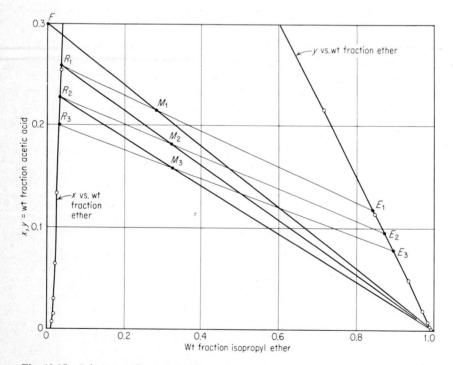

Fig. 10.35 *Solution to Illustration 10.3.*

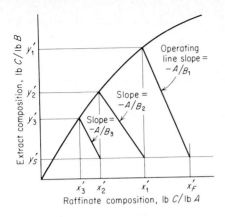

Extract composition, lb $C/$lb B

Raffinate composition, lb $C/$lb A

Fig. 10.36 *Crosscurrent extraction with an insoluble solvent.*

concentrations are plotted as in Fig. 10.36, $x' = x/(1 - x)$ against $y' = y/(1 - y)$. Since the liquids A and B are insoluble, there are A lb of this substance in all raffinates. Similarly, the extract from each stage contains all the solvent B fed to that stage. A solute-C balance about any stage n is then

$$Ax'_{n-1} + B_n y'_S = B_n y'_n + Ax'_n \tag{10.30}$$

$$-\frac{A}{B_n} = \frac{y'_S - y'_n}{x'_{n-1} - x'_n} \tag{10.31}$$

This is the operating-line equation for stage n, of slope $-A/B_n$, passing through points (x'_{n-1}, y'_S) and (x'_n, y'_n).   The construction for a three-stage extraction is shown in Fig. 10.36, where for each stage a line is drawn of slope appropriate to that stage. Each operating line intersects the equilibrium curve at the raffinate and extract compositions.   No raffinate of concentration smaller than that in equilibrium with the entering solvent is possible.

Solute concentrations for these cases are sometimes also conveniently expressed as mass/volume.   Equations (10.30) and (10.31) then apply with x' and y' expressed as mass solute/volume, and A and B as volume/time (or volumes for batch operations).

Illustration 10.4. Nicotine (C) in a water (A) solution containing 1 % nicotine is to be extracted with kerosene (B) at 20°C.   Water and kerosene are essentially insoluble.   (*a*) Determine the percentage extraction of nicotine if 100 lb of feed solution is extracted once with 150-lb solvent.   (*b*) Repeat for three ideal extractions using 50-lb solvent each.

Solution. Equilibrium data are provided by Claffey et al., *Ind. Eng. Chem.*, **42**, 166 (1950), and expressed as lb nicotine/lb liquid, they are as follows:

$x' = \dfrac{\text{lb nicotine}}{\text{lb water}}$	0	0.001011	0.00246	0.00502	0.00751	0.00998	0.0204
$y'^* = \dfrac{\text{lb nicotine}}{\text{lb kerosene}}$	0	0.000807	0.001961	0.00456	0.00686	0.00913	0.01870

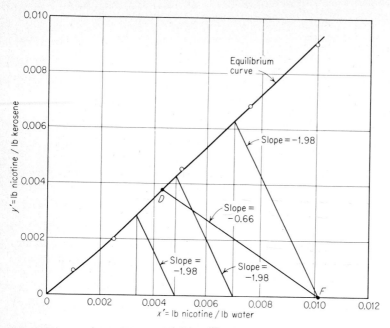

Fig. 10.37   *Solution to Illustration* 10.4.

a. $x_F = 0.01$ wt fraction nicotine, $x_F' = 0.01/(1 - 0.01) = 0.0101$ lb nicotine/lb water. $F = 100$ lb. $A = 100(1 - 0.01) = 99$ lb water. $A/B = {}^{99}\!/_{150} = 0.66$.

Refer to Fig. 10.37, which shows the equilibrium data and the point F representing the composition of the feed.   From F, line FD is drawn of slope -0.66, intersecting the equilibrium curve at D, where $x_1' = 0.00425$ and $y_1' = 0.00380$ lb nicotine/lb liquid.   The nicotine removed from the water is therefore $99(0.0101 - 0.00425) = 0.580$ lb, or 58% of that in the feed.

b. For each stage, $A/B = {}^{99}\!/_{50} = 1.98$.   The construction is started at F, with operating lines of slope -1.98.   The final raffinate composition is $x_3' = 0.0034$, and the nicotine extracted is $99(0.0101 - 0.0034) = 0.663$ lb, or 66.3% of that in the feed.

Continuous countercurrent multistage extraction

The flow sheet for this type of operation is shown in Fig. 10.38.   Extract and raffinate streams flow from stage to stage in countercurrent and provide two final products, raffinate R_{N_p} and extract E_1.   For a given degree of separation, this type of operation requires fewer stages for a given amount of solvent, or less solvent for a fixed number of stages, than the crosscurrent methods described above.

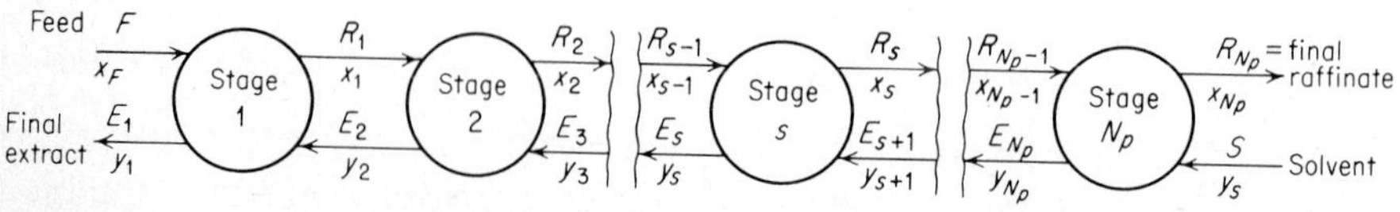

Fig. 10.38   *Countercurrent multistage extraction.*

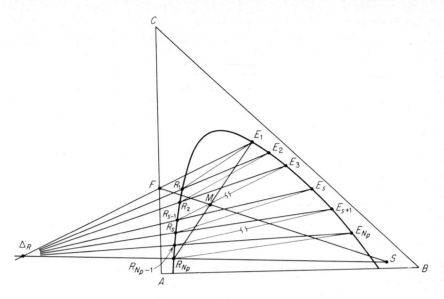

Fig. 10.39   *Countercurrent multistage extraction.*

The graphical treatment is developed in Fig. 10.39 on rectangular coordinates. Construction on the equilateral triangle is identical with this. A total material balance about the entire plant is

$$F + S = E_1 + R_1 = M \qquad (10.32)$$

Point M may be located on line FS through a balance for substance C,

$$Fx_F + Sy_S = E_1y_1 + R_{N_p}x_{N_p} = Mx_M \qquad (10.33)$$

$$x_M = \frac{Fx_F + Sy_S}{F + S} \qquad (10.34)$$

Equation (10.32) indicates that M must lie on line $R_{N_p}E_1$, as shown. Rearrangement of Eq. (10.32) provides

$$R_{N_p} - S = F - E_1 = \Delta_R \qquad (10.35)$$

where Δ_R, a difference point, is the net flow outward at the last stage N_p. According to Eq. (10.35), the extended lines E_1F and SR_{N_p} must intersect at Δ_R, as shown in Fig. 10.39. This intersection may in some cases be located at the right of the triangle. A material balance for stages s through N_p is

$$R_{s-1} + S = R_{N_p} + E_s \qquad (10.36)$$

or

$$R_{N_p} - S = R_{s-1} - E_s = \Delta_R \qquad (10.37)$$

so that the difference in flow rates at a location between any two adjacent stages is constant, Δ_R. Line E_sR_{s-1} extended must therefore pass through Δ_R, as on the figure.

The graphical construction is then as follows. After location of points F, S, M, E_1, R_{Np}, and Δ_R, a tie line from E_1 provides R_1 since extract and raffinate from the first ideal stage are in equilibrium. A line from Δ_R through R_1 when extended provides E_2, a tie line from E_2 provides R_2, etc. The lowest possible value of x_{Np} is that given by the A-rich end of a tie line which, when extended, passes through S.

As the amount of solvent is increased, point M representing the overall plant balance moves toward S on Fig. 10.39 and point Δ_R moves farther to the left. At an amount of solvent such that lines E_1F and SR_{Np} are parallel, point Δ_R will be at an infinite distance. Greater amounts of solvent will cause these lines to intersect on the right-hand side of the diagram rather than as shown, with point Δ_R nearer B for increasing solvent quantities. The interpretation of the difference point is, however, still the same: a line from Δ_R intersects the two branches of the solubility curve at points representing extract and raffinate from adjacent stages.

If a line from point Δ_R should coincide with a tie line, an infinite number of stages will be required to reach this condition. The maximum amount of solvent for which this occurs corresponds to the minimum solvent/feed ratio which may be used for the specified products. The procedure for determining the minimum amount of solvent is indicated in Fig. 10.40. All tie lines below that marked JK are extended to line SR_{Np}, to give intersections with line SR_{Np} as shown. The intersection farthest from S (if on the left-hand side of the diagram) or nearest S (if on the right) represents the difference point for minimum solvent, as at point Δ_{Rm} (Fig. 10.40). The actual position of Δ_R must be farther from S (if on the left) or nearer to S (if on the right) for a finite number of stages. The larger the amount of solvent, the fewer the number of stages. Usually, but not in the instance shown, the tie lines which when extended pass through F, i.e., tie line JK, will locate Δ_{Rm} for minimum solvent.

When the number of stages is very large, the construction indicated in Fig. 10.41 may be more convenient. A few lines are drawn at random from point Δ_R to intersect the two branches of the solubility curve as shown, where the intersections do not now necessarily indicate streams between two actual adjacent stages. The C

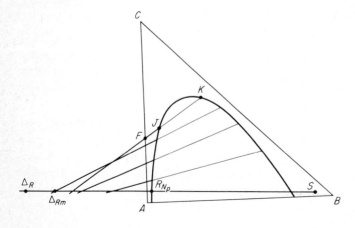

Fig. 10.40 *Minimum solvent for countercurrent extraction.*

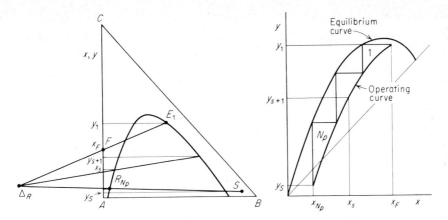

Fig. 10.41 *Transfer of coordinates to distribution diagram.*

concentrations x_s and y_{s+1} corresponding to these are plotted on x, y coordinates as shown to provide an operating curve. Tie-line data provide the equilibrium curve y^* vs. x, and the theoretical stages are stepped off in the manner used for gas absorption and distillation.

Figure 10.42 shows the construction for solvent-free coordinates. The B-free material balance for the entire plant is

$$F' + S' = E_1' + R_{Np}' = M' \tag{10.38}$$

where ordinarily $F = F'$ since the feed is usually B-free. M' is therefore on the line FS at X_M calculated by a C balance

$$F'X_F + S'Y_S = M'X_M \tag{10.39}$$

If pure B is used as solvent, $S' = 0$, $S'Y_S = 0$, $F' = M'$, $X_M = X_F$, and point M is vertically above F.

Line E_1R_{Np} must pass through M. Then

$$R_{Np}' - S' = F' - E_1' = \Delta_R' \tag{10.40}$$

The balance for stages s through N_p is

$$R_{Np}' - S' = R_{s-1}' - E_s' = \Delta_R' \tag{10.41}$$

where Δ_R' is the difference in solvent-free flow, out $-$ in, at stage N_p, and the constant difference in solvent-free flows of the streams between any two adjacent stages. Line E_sR_{s-1} extended, where s is any stage, must therefore pass through Δ_R on the graph.

The graphical construction is then as follows. After locating points $F, S, M, E_1, R_{Np},$ and Δ_R, a tie line from E_1 provides R_1, line $\Delta_R R_1$ extended locates E_2, etc. If the solvent is pure B ($N_S = \infty$), line $R_{Np}\Delta_R$ is vertical.

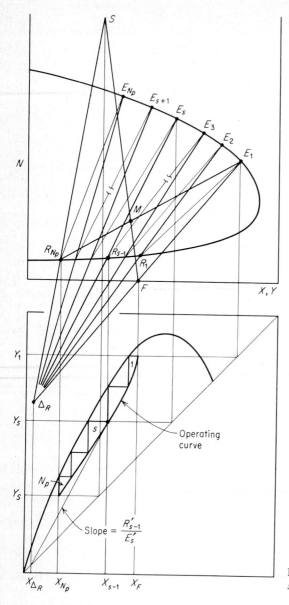

Fig. 10.42 *Countercurrent extraction solvent-free coordinates.*

A C balance, stages s through N_p, following Eq. (10.40) is

$$R'_{s-1}X_{s-1} - E'_sY_s = \Delta'_RX_{\Delta R} \tag{10.42}$$

A B balance is

$$R'_{s-1}N_{R,s-1} - E'_sN_{Es} = \Delta'_RN_{\Delta R} \tag{10.43}$$

Elimination of Δ'_R between Eqs. (10.40) to (10.42) provides

$$\frac{R'_{s-1}}{E'_s} = \frac{Y_s - X_{\Delta R}}{X_{s-1} - X_{\Delta R}} = \frac{N_{Es} - N_{\Delta R}}{N_{R,n-1} - N_{\Delta R}} \tag{10.44}$$

Thus, the ratio of flows R'_{s-1}/E'_s may be obtained from the ratio of line lengths $E_s\Delta_R/R_{s-1}\Delta_R$ on the upper part of Fig. 10.42, or as the slope of the chord from (X_{s-1}, Y_s) to $X_{\Delta R}$ on the 45° diagonal of the lower diagram, as shown. The difference-point coordinates are

$$\Delta'_R \begin{cases} N_{\Delta R} = \dfrac{\text{difference in } B \text{ flow, out } - \text{ in, at stage } N_p}{\text{net flow out, } B\text{-free}} \\[2em] X_{\Delta R} = \dfrac{\text{difference in } C \text{ flow, out } - \text{ in, at stage } N_p}{\text{net flow out, } B\text{-free}} \end{cases}$$

and Δ'_R is analogous to the Δ_W of distillation (see Chap. 9).

As the solvent/feed ratio is increased, Δ_R on Fig. 10.42 moves lower, and the minimum solvent is determined by the lowest point of intersection of all extended tie lines with the line SR_{Np}. A practical Δ_R must be located below this, corresponding to larger amounts of solvent.

Solvent recovery by extraction. While most processes use distillation or evaporation to recover the solvent from the product solutions of liquid extraction, it is not uncommon to recover solvent by liquid extraction. A typical example is the recovery of penicillin from the acidified fermentation broth in which it occurs by extraction with amyl acetate as solvent, followed by stripping of the penicillin from the solvent by extracting it into an aqueous buffer solution. The amyl acetate is then returned to the first extraction. The calculations of such solvent-recovery operations are made in the same manner as those for the first extraction.

Illustration 10.5. Two thousand pounds per hour of an acetic acid (C)–water (A) solution, containing 30% acid, is to be countercurrently extracted with isopropyl ether (B) to reduce the acid concentration to 2% in the solvent-free raffinate product. (a) Determine the minimum amount of solvent which may be used. (b) Determine the number of theoretical stages if 5,000 lb/hr of solvent is used.

Solution. The equilibrium data of Illustration 10.3 are plotted on triangular coordinates in Fig. 10.43. The tie lines have been omitted for reasons of clarity.

a. $F = 2,000$ lb/hr; $x_F = 0.30$ wt fraction acetic acid, corresponding to point F on the figure. R'_{Np} is located on the AC base at 2% acid, and line BR'_{Np} intersects the water-rich solubility curve at R_{Np}, as shown. In this case the tie line J which when extended passes through F provides the conditions for minimum solvent, and this intersects line $R_{Np}B$ on the right of the figure nearer B than

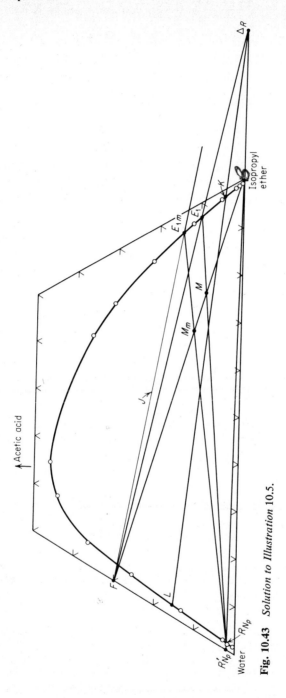

Fig. 10.43 *Solution to Illustration 10.5.*

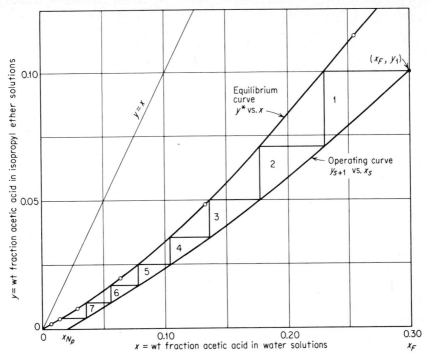

Fig. 10.44 *Solution to Illustration 10.5.*

any other lower tie line. Tie line *J* provides the minimum E_1 as shown at $y_1 = 0.143$. Line $E_{1m}R_{N_p}$ intersects line *FB* at M_m, for which $x_M = 0.114$.

Eq. (10.34), with $y_s = 0$ and $S = B$:

$$B_m = \frac{Fx_F}{x_M} - F = \frac{2{,}000(0.30)}{0.114} - 2{,}000 = 3{,}260 \text{ lb/hr, min solvent rate}$$

b. For $B = 5{,}000$ lb solvent/hr [Eq. (10.34) with $y_s = 0$ and $S = B$],

$$x_M = \frac{Fx_F}{F + B} = \frac{2{,}000(0.30)}{2{,}000 + 5{,}000} = 0.0857$$

and point *M* is located as shown on line *FB*. Line $R_{N_p}M$ extended provides E_1 at $y_1 = 0.10$. Line FE_1 is extended to intersect line $R_{N_p}B$ at Δ_R. Random lines such as *OKL* are drawn to provide y_{s+1} at *K* and x_s at *L*, as follows:

y_{s+1}	0	0.01	0.02	0.04	0.06	0.08	0.10 = y_1
x_s	0.02	0.055	0.090	0.150	0.205	0.250	0.30 = x_F

These are plotted on Fig. 10.44 as the operating curve, along with the tie-line data as the equilibrium curve. There are required 7.6 theoretical stages. The weight of extract may be obtained by an

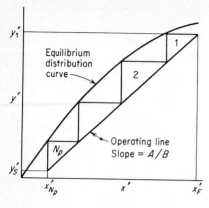

Fig. 10.45   *Countercurrent extraction, insoluble solvent.*

acid balance,

$$E_1 = \frac{M(x_M - x_{Np})}{y_1 - x_{Np}} = \frac{7,000(0.0857 - 0.02)}{0.10 - 0.02} = 5,750 \text{ lb/hr}$$

and

$$R_{Np} = M - E_1 = 7,000 - 5,750 = 1,250 \text{ lb/hr}$$

Insoluble liquids. When the liquids A and B are insoluble over the range of solute concentrations encountered, the stage computation is made more simply on x', y' coordinates. For this case, the solvent content of all extracts and the A content of all raffinates are constant. An overall plant balance for substance C is

$$By'_S + Ax'_F = Ax'_{Np} + By'_1 \tag{10.45}$$

or

$$\frac{A}{B} = \frac{y'_1 - y'_S}{x'_F - x'_{Np}} \tag{10.46}$$

which is the equation of a straight line, the operating line, of slope A/B, through points (y'_1, x'_F), (y'_S, x'_{Np}). For stages 1 through s, similarly,

$$\frac{A}{B} = \frac{y'_1 - y'_{s+1}}{x'_F - x'_s} \tag{10.47}$$

and Fig. 10.45 shows the construction for stages. x' and y' may also be expressed as mass/volume, with A and B as volume/time.

For the special case where the equilibrium curve is of constant slope $m' = y'^*/x'$, Eq. (5.50) applies,

$$\frac{x'_F - x'_{Np}}{x'_F - y'_S/m'} = \frac{(m'B/A)^{Np+1} - m'B/A}{(m'B/A)^{Np+1} - 1} \tag{10.48}$$

where $m'B/A$ is the extraction factor. This may be used in conjunction with Fig. 5.16, with $(x'_{Np} - y'_S/m')/(x'_F - y'_S/m')$ as ordinate and $m'B/A$ as parameter.

Illustration 10.6. One thousand pounds per hour of a nicotine (C)–water (A) solution containing 1% nicotine is to be countercurrently extracted with kerosene at 20°C to reduce the nicotine content to 0.1%. (*a*) Determine the minimum kerosene rate. (*b*) Determine the number of theoretical stages required if 1,150 lb of kerosene is used per hour.

Solution. The equilibrium data of Illustration 10.4 are plotted in Fig. 10.46.
a. $F = 1,000$ lb/hr, $x_F = 0.01$, $A = 1,000(1 - 0.01) = 990$ lb water/hr, $y_S = 0$.

$$x_F' = \frac{0.01}{1 - 0.01} = 0.0101 \text{ lb nicotine/lb water}$$

$$x_{Np} = 0.001 \qquad x_{Np}' = \frac{0.001}{1 - 0.001} = 0.001001 \text{ lb nicotine/lb water}$$

The operating line starts at point L ($y' = 0$, $x' = 0.001001$) and for infinite stages passes through K on the equilibrium curve at x_F'. $y_K' = 0.0093$. Therefore

$$A/B_m = (0.0093 - 0)/(0.0101 - 0.001001) = 1.021,$$

and $B_m = A/1.021 = 990/1.021 = 969$ lb kerosene/hr.
b. $B = 1,150$ lb/hr, $A/B = 990/1,150 = 0.860$.

Eq. (10.46): $$\frac{y_1'}{x_F' - x_{Np}'} = \frac{y_1'}{0.0101 - 0.001001} = 0.860$$

$$y_1' = 0.00782 \text{ lb nicotine/lb kerosene}$$

The operating line is drawn through (y_1', x_F'), and 8.3 theoretical stages are determined graphically. Alternatively, at the dilute end of the system, $m' = dy'^*/dx' = 0.798$, and

$$m'B/A = 0.798(1,150)/990 = 0.928.$$

At the concentrated end, $m' = 0.953$, and $m'B/A = 0.953(1,150)/990 = 1.110$. The average is $[0.928(1.110)]^{0.5} = 1.01$. $x_{Np}'/x_F' = 0.001001/0.0101 = 0.099$, and Fig. 5.16 indicates 8.4 theoretical stages.

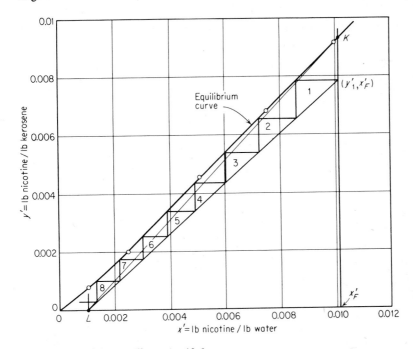

Fig. 10.46 *Solution to Illustration* 10.6.

Continuous countercurrent extraction with reflux

Whereas in ordinary countercurrent operation the richest possible extract product leaving the plant is at best only in equilibrium with the feed solution, the use of reflux at the extract end of the plant can provide a product even richer, as in the case of the rectifying section of a distillation column. Reflux is not needed at the raffinate end of the cascade since, unlike the case of distillation, where heat must be carried in from the reboiler by a vapor reflux, in extraction the solvent (the analog of heat) may enter without need for a carrier stream.

An arrangement for this is shown in Fig. 10.47. The feed to be separated into its components is introduced more or less centrally into the cascade, through which extract and raffinate liquids are passing countercurrently. The concentration of solute C is increased in the extract-enriching section by countercurrent contact with a raffinate liquid rich in C. This is provided by removing the solvent from extract E_1 to produce the solvent-free stream E', part of which is removed as extract product P'_E and part returned as reflux R_0. The raffinate-stripping section of the cascade is the same as the countercurrent extractor of Fig. 10.38, and C is stripped from the raffinate by countercurrent contact with solvent.

Graphical determination of stages required for such operations is usually inconvenient to carry out on triangular coordinates[27] because of crowding, and only the use of N, X, Y coordinates will be described. For the stages in the raffinate stripping section, Fig. 10.47, the developments for simple countercurrent extraction, Eqs. (10.41) to (10.44) apply, and this section of the plant needs no further consideration.

In the extract-enriching section, an $A + C$ balance about the solvent separator is

$$E'_1 = E' = P'_E + R'_0 \tag{10.49}$$

Let Δ_E represent the net rate of flow outward from this section. Then, for its $A + C$ content,

$$\Delta'_E = P'_E \tag{10.50}$$

and for its C content,

$$X_{\Delta E} = X_{PE} \tag{10.51}$$

while for its B content,

$$B_E = \Delta'_E N_{\Delta E} \tag{10.52}$$

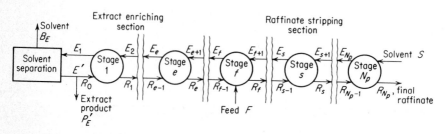

Fig. 10.47 *Countercurrent extraction with reflux.*

The point Δ_E is plotted on Fig. 10.48, which is drawn for a system of two partly miscible component pairs. For all stages through e, an $A + C$ balance is

$$E'_{e+1} = P'_E + R'_e = \Delta'_E + R'_e \tag{10.53}$$

or

$$\Delta'_E = E'_{e+1} - R'_e \tag{10.54}$$

A C balance,

$$\Delta'_E X_{\Delta E} = E'_{e+1} Y_{e+1} - R'_e X_{Re} \tag{10.55}$$

and a B balance,

$$\Delta'_E N_{\Delta E} = E'_{e+1} N'_{E,e+1} - R'_e N_{Re} \tag{10.56}$$

Since e is any stage in this section, lines radiating from point Δ_E cut the solubility curves of Fig. 10.48 at points representing extract and raffinate flowing between any two adjacent stages. Δ_E is therefore a difference point, constant for all stages in this section, whose coordinates mean

$$\Delta'_E \begin{cases} N_{\Delta E} = \dfrac{\text{difference in } B \text{ flow, out } - \text{ in}}{\text{net flow out, } B\text{-free}} = \dfrac{B \text{ out}}{(A + C) \text{ out}} \\[2ex] X_{\Delta E} = \dfrac{\text{difference in } C \text{ flow, out } - \text{ in}}{\text{net flow out, } B\text{-free}} = \dfrac{C \text{ out}}{(A + C) \text{ out}} \end{cases}$$

Alternating tie lines and lines from Δ_E then establish the stages, starting with stage 1 and continuing to the feed stage. Figure 10.48 also shows the raffinate-stripping stages as well, developed as before for countercurrent extraction.

Solving Eq. (10.53) with (10.55) and (10.56) produces the internal reflux ratio at any stage,

$$\frac{R'_e}{E'_{e+1}} = \frac{N_{\Delta E} - N_{E,e+1}}{N_{\Delta E} - N_{Re}} = \frac{X_{\Delta E} - Y_{e+1}}{X_{\Delta E} - X_{Re}} = \frac{\text{line } \Delta_E E_{e+1}}{\text{line } \Delta_E R_e} \tag{10.57}$$

This may be computed from line lengths on the upper diagram of Fig. 10.48 or from the slope of a chord on the lower diagram, as shown. The external reflux ratio is

$$\frac{R'_0}{P'_E} = \frac{R_0}{P'_E} = \frac{N_{\Delta E} - N_{E1}}{N_{E1}} \tag{10.58}$$

which may be used to locate Δ_E for any specified reflux ratio.

Material balances may also be made over the entire plant. For $A + C$,

$$F' + S' = P'_E + R'_{Np} \tag{10.59}$$

Using Eqs. (10.40) and (10.50), this becomes

$$F' = \Delta'_R + \Delta'_E \tag{10.60}$$

where normally $F = F'$. Point F must therefore lie on a line joining the two difference points, and the optimum location of the feed stage is represented by the tie line which

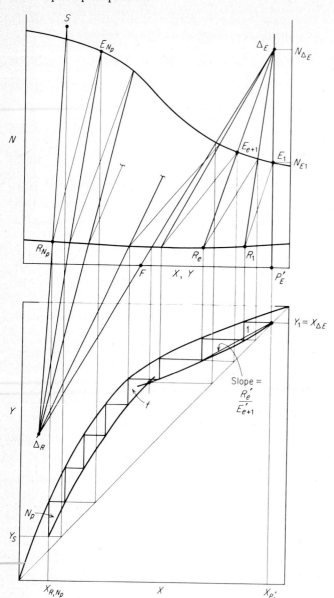

Fig. 10.48 *Countercurrent extraction with reflux.*

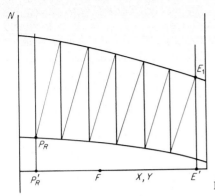

Fig. 10.49   *Total reflux.*

crosses line $\Delta_R F \Delta_E$, as shown.   The similarity of Fig. 10.48 to the enthalpy-concentration diagram of distillation is clear, and the two become completely analogous when solvent S is pure B.

The higher the location of Δ_E (and the lower Δ_R), the larger the reflux ratio and the smaller the number of stages.   When R_0/P'_E is infinite (infinite reflux ratio or total reflux), $N_{\Delta E} = \infty$, and the minimum number of stages results.   The capacity of the plant falls to zero, feed must be stopped, and solvent B_E is recirculated to become S. The configuration is shown in Fig. 10.49 on N, X, Y coordinates.   The corresponding XY diagram uses the 45° diagonal as operating lines for both sections of the cascade.

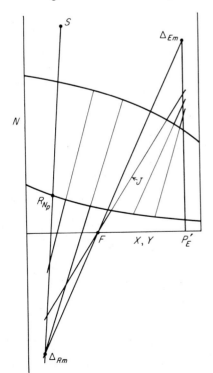

Fig. 10.50   *Determination of minimum reflux ratio.*

An infinity of stages is required if a line radiating from either Δ_E or Δ_R coincides with a tie line, and the greatest reflux ratio for which this occurs is the *minimum reflux ratio*. This may be determined as in Fig. 10.50. Tie lines to the left of J are extended to intersect line SR_{Np+1}, and those to the right of J are extended to line $P'_E E_1$. Points Δ_{Em} and Δ_{Rm} for the minimum reflux ratio are established by selecting the intersections farthest from $N = 0$, consistent with the requirement that Δ_R, Δ_E, and F must always lie on the same straight line. Frequently tie line J, which when extended passes through F, will establish the minimum reflux ratio, and always if the XY equilibrium distribution curve is everywhere concave downward.

Illustration 10.7. One thousand pounds per hour of a solution containing 50% ethylbenzene (A) and 50% styrene (C) is to be separated at 25°C into products containing 10% and 90% styrene, respectively, with diethylene glycol (B) as solvent. (a) Determine the minimum number of theoretical stages. (b) Determine the minimum extract reflux ratio. (c) Determine the number of theoretical stages and the important flow quantities at an extract reflux ratio of 1.5 times the minimum value.

Solution. Equilibrium data of Boobar et al., *Ind. Eng. Chem.*, **43**, 2922 (1951), have been converted to a solvent-free basis and are tabulated below.

Hydrocarbon-rich solutions		Solvent-rich solutions	
X, lb styrene lb hydrocarbon	N, lb glycol lb hydrocarbon	Y^*, lb styrene lb hydrocarbon	N, lb glycol lb hydrocarbon
0	0.00675	0	8.62
0.0870	0.00817	0.1429	7.71
0.1883	0.00938	0.273	6.81
0.288	0.01010	0.386	6.04
0.384	0.01101	0.480	5.44
0.458	0.01215	0.557	5.02
0.464	0.01215	0.565	4.95
0.561	0.01410	0.655	4.46
0.573	0.01405	0.674	4.37
0.781	0.01833	0.833	3.47
1.00	0.0256	1.00	2.69

These are plotted on the solvent-free coordinate system of Fig. 10.51. The tie lines corresponding to these points are not drawn in, for purposes of clarity. $F = 1,000$ lb/hr, $X_F = 0.5$ wt fraction styrene, $X_{P'E} = 0.9$, $X_{R,Np} = 0.1$, all on a solvent-free basis. Point E_1 is located as shown. $N_{E1} = 3.10$.

a. Minimum theoretical stages are determined by drawing a tie line from E_1, a vertical line from R_1, a tie line from E_2, etc., until the raffinate product is reached, as shown. The minimum number of stages, corresponding to the constructed tie lines, is 9.5.

b. The tie line which when extended passes through F provides the minimum reflux ratios, since it provides intersections Δ_{Em} and Δ_{Rm} farthest from the line $N = 0$. From the plot, $N_{\Delta Em} = 20.76$.

Eq. (10.58):
$$\left(\frac{R_0}{P'_E}\right)_m = \frac{20.76 - 3.1}{3.1} = 5.70 \text{ lb reflux/lb extract product}$$

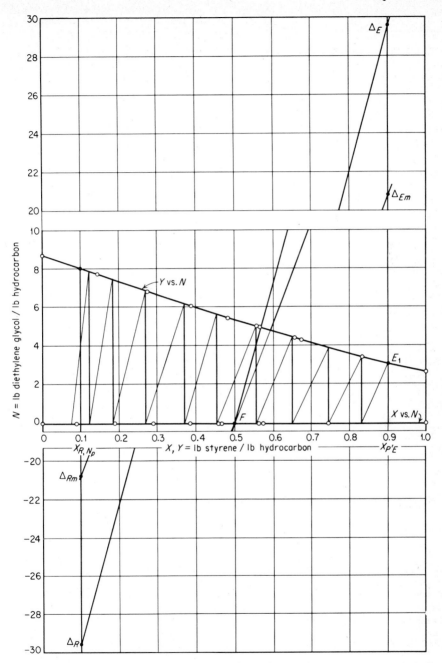

Fig. 10.51 *Solution to Illustration* 10.7. *Minimum ideal stages at total reflux and location of difference points.*

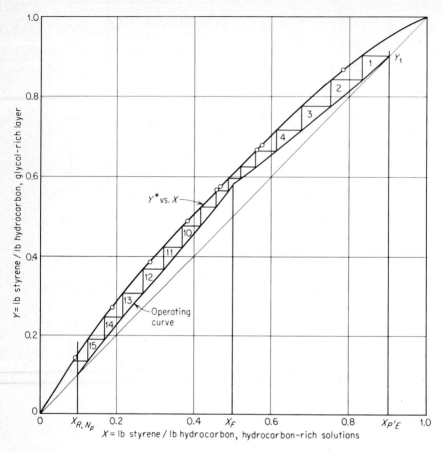

Fig. 10.52 *Solution to Illustration 10.7.*

c. For $R_0/P'_E = 1.5(5.70) = 8.55$ lb reflux/lb extract product [Eq. (10.58)],

$$8.55 = \frac{N_{\Delta E} - 3.1}{3.1}$$

and $N_{\Delta E} = 29.6$. Point Δ_E is plotted as shown. A straight line from Δ_E through F intersects line $X = 0.10$ at Δ_R. $N_{\Delta R} = -29.6$. Random lines are drawn from Δ_E for concentrations to the right of F, and from Δ_R for those to the left, and intersections of these with the solubility curves provide the coordinates of the operating curve (Fig. 10.52). The tie-line data plotted directly provide the equilibrium curve. The number of theoretical stages is seen to be 15.5, and the feed is to be introduced into the seventh from the extract-product end of the cascade.

From Fig. 10.51, $X_{R,N_p} = 0.10$, $N_{R,N_p} = 0.0082$. On the basis of 1 hr, an overall plant balance is

$$F = 1,000 = P'_E + R'_{N_p}$$

A *C* balance,

$$FX_F = 500 = P'_E(0.9) + R'_{N_p}(0.1)$$

Solving simultaneously, $P'_E = R'_{Np} = 500$ lb/hr.

$$R_0 = R'_0 = 8.55 P'_E = 8.55(500) = 4,275 \text{ lb/hr}$$

Eq. (10.49): $\quad E'_1 = R'_0 + P'_E = 4,275 + 500 = 4,775 \text{ lb/hr}$

$$B_E = E'_1 N_{E1} = 4,775(3.10) = 14,800 \text{ lb/hr}$$

$$E_1 = B_E + E'_1 = 14,800 + 4,775 = 19,575 \text{ lb/hr}$$

$$R_{Np} = R'_{Np}(1 + N_{R,Np}) = 500(1.0082) = 504 \text{ lb/hr}$$

$$S = B_E + R'_{Np} N_{R,Np} = 14,800 + 500(0.0082) = 14,804 \text{ lb/hr}$$

Economic balances

Several types of economic balances may be made for the various flow sheets just described. For example, the amount of solute extracted for a fixed solvent/feed ratio increases with increased number of stages, and therefore the value of the unextracted solute may be balanced against the cost of the extraction equipment required to recover it. The amount of solvent per unit of feed, or reflux ratio in the case of the last flow sheet described, is also subject to economic balance. For a fixed extent of extraction, the number of stages required decreases as solvent rate or reflux ratio increases. Since the capacity of the equipment for handling the larger liquid flow must at the same time increase, the cost of equipment must then pass through a minimum. The extract solutions become more dilute as solvent rate is increased, and consequently the cost of solvent removal increases. The total cost, which is the sum of investment and operating costs, must pass through a minimum at the optimum solvent rate or reflux ratio. In all such economic balances, the cost of solvent recovery will always be a major item and usually must include consideration of recovery from the saturated raffinate product as well as the extract.

Fractional extraction—separation of two solutes

If a solution contains two extractable solutes, both may be removed from the solution by countercurrent extraction with a suitable solvent, but it is impossible to produce any great degree of separation of the solutes by this method unless the ratio of their distribution coefficients is very large.

Separation to any extent may, however, be achieved, so long as their distribution coefficients are different, by the techniques of fractional extraction. The simplest flow sheet for this is shown in Fig. 10.53. Here solutes B and C, which constitute the

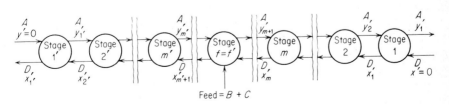

Fig. 10.53 *Fractional extraction.*

feed, are introduced into a countercurrent cascade where partly miscible solvents A and D flow countercurrently. At the feed stage, both solutes distribute between the solvents, with solute B favoring solvent A, solute C favoring solvent D. In the section to the left of the feed stage, solvent A preferentially extracts the B from D, and D leaves this section with a solute content rich in C. In the section to the right of the feed stage, solvent D preferentially extracts the C from A, and A leaves with a solute content rich in B.

This operation will be considered only in its simplest form, where the solvents A and D are essentially immiscible and enter free of solutes and where solutes B and C distribute independently, i.e., the distribution of each is uninfluenced by the presence of the other. A and D will represent the weight rates of flow of these solvents, lb/hr, and concentrations will be expressed as

$$y' = \text{lb solute/lb } A \ (y'_B \text{ for solute } B, \ y'_C \text{ for solute } C)$$

$$x' = \text{lb solute/lb } D \ (x'_B \text{ for solute } B, \ x'_C \text{ for solute } C)$$

Consider the stages $1'$ through m'. For *either* solute, a solute material balance is

$$Dx'_{m'+1} = Ay'_{m'} + Dx'_{1'} \tag{10.61}$$

or

$$\frac{D}{A} = \frac{y'_{m'} - 0}{x'_{m'+1} - x'_{1'}} \tag{10.62}$$

and we need only add the subscripts B or C to the concentrations to apply these to particular solutes. Similarly, for stages 1 through m, for *either* solute, the balance is

$$Ay'_{m+1} = Dx'_m + Ay'_1 \tag{10.63}$$

$$\frac{D}{A} = \frac{y'_{m+1} - y'_1}{x'_m - 0} \tag{10.64}$$

Equations (10.62) and (10.64) represent the operating lines for each solute, one for each section of the cascade, of slope D/A. Figure 10.54 shows the distribution diagrams

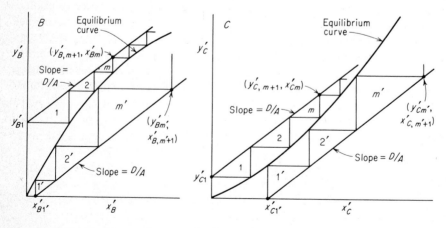

Fig. 10.54 *Fractional extraction, operating lines and stages.*

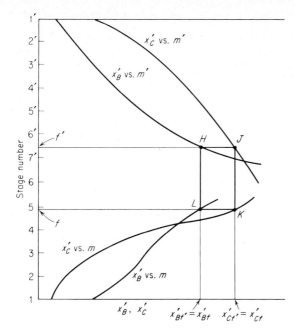

Fig. 10.55 *Feed-stage matching.*

for the solutes, each of which distrbiutes independently of the other.   The operating lines are also drawn on the figure, and the stages stepped off in the usual manner, beginning at stages 1 and 1'.

To determine the number of stages required in each section of the cascade, a match of concentrations and stage numbers at the point of feed introduction must be made.   At the feed stage (which is numbered f and f') for either solute f must be the same, f' must be the same, and the concentration must be the same when computed from each end of the cascade.   The match may be established by plotting the concentrations of both B and C in one of the solvents against stage number, as in Fig. 10.55.   The requirements listed above are then met where the rectangle $HJKL$ can be drawn in the manner shown.

It can be seen from Fig. 10.55 that the concentrations of both solutes is greatest at the feed stage, least at stages 1 and 1'.   Sufficient rates of solvent flow must be used to ensure that solute solubilities are not exceeded at the feed stage.   Changing the solvent ratio changes the total number of stages and the relative position of the feed stage, and there is always a solvent ratio for which the total number of stages is the least.

The number of stages may be reduced by use of solute reflux at either or both ends of the cascade.   Computation of this effect, treatment of cases where solute distributions are interdependent or solvent miscibility varies, and other special flow sheets are beyond the scope of this book, but these have been thoroughly worked out.[25,27]

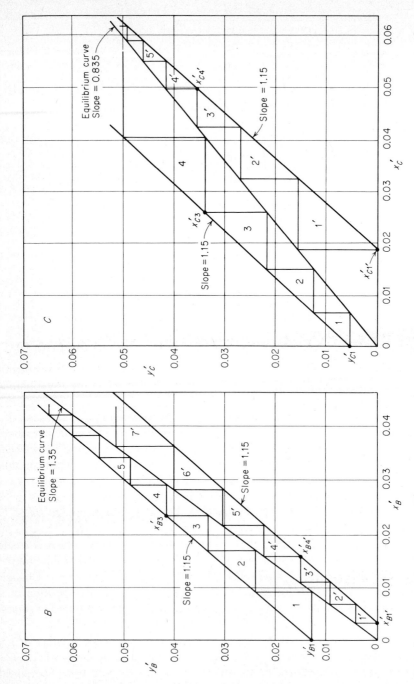

Fig. 10.56   *Solution to Illustration 10.8.*

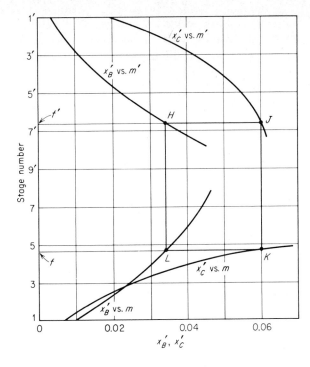

Fig. 10.57 *Solution to Illustration 10.8, feed-stage matching.*

Illustration 10.8. A mixture containing 40% p-chloronitrobenzene (B) and 60% o-chloronitrobenzene (C) is to be separated at the rate of 100 lb/hr into products containing 80 and 15%, respectively, of the para isomer after removal of solvents. The insoluble solvents to be used are 2,400 lb/hr heptane (A) and 2,760 lb/hr aqueous methanol (D). The distribution coefficients are constant and independent, $y_B'^*/x_B' = 1.35$ and $y_C'^*/x_C' = 0.835$. Determine the number of ideal stages required and the position of the feed stage.

Solution. The para isomer (B) favors the heptane (A), and the ortho (C) favors the methanol (D). *Basis:* 1 hr. Feed $= 100$ lb $= 40$ lb B, 60 lb C. Let $W =$ lb A-rich product, $Z =$ lb D-rich product, after solvent removal. Then B and C balances are, respectively,

$$0.80W + 0.15Z = 40 \qquad 0.20W + 0.85Z = 60$$

from which $W = 38.5$ lb (30.8 lb B, 7.7 lb C), and $Z = 61.5$ lb (9.23 lb B, 52.27 lb C).

$$x_{B1}' = \frac{9.23}{2,760} = 0.00334 \qquad x_{C1}' = \frac{52.27}{2,760} = 0.01895$$

$$y_{B1}' = \frac{30.8}{2,400} = 0.01283 \qquad y_{C1}' = \frac{7.7}{2,400} = 0.00321$$

$D/A = 2,760/2,400 = 1.15$. The stages are constructed on Fig. 10.56, and the feed-stage match is shown on Fig. 10.57. From the latter, the feed stage is $f' = 6.6$ and $f = 4.6$. Therefore the total number of ideal stages is $6.6 + 4.6 - 1 = 10.2$ and the feed stage is the 4.6th from the solvent-D inlet.

Multicomponent systems

For most systems containing more than four components, the display of equilibrium data and the computation of stages is very difficult. Some of our most important separations involve hundreds of components whose identity is not even firmly established, as in the extraction of petroleum lubricating oils. In such cases, the stage requirements are best obtained in the laboratory, without detailed study of the equilibria. There are available small-scale mixer-settler extractors of stage efficiency essentially 100 percent, which may be used to study extraction processes,[27] but these must be run continuously to steady state. Countercurrent flow sheets, which are necessarily for continuous operation, can be simulated with small batches of feed and solvent in separatory funnels, however, and this is frequently most convenient and least costly.

Suppose, for example, it is desired to determine what products will be obtained from a five-stage countercurrent extraction of a complex feed flowing at F lb/hr with a solvent flowing at S lb/hr. Refer to Fig. 10.58. Here each circle represents a separatory funnel which, when adequately shaken and the liquids allowed to settle, will represent one ideal stage. Into funnel a are placed suitable amounts of feed and solvent in the ratio F/S, the mixture is shaken, settled, and the two phases separated. Extract layer E' is removed and raffinate R_a is contacted in funnel b with precisely the same amount of solvent S as used in funnel a. Raffinates and extracts, feeds and solvents, are moved and contacted in the manner indicated in the figure, care being taken each time to use precisely the same amount of feed and solvent at streams marked F and S as in funnel a.

Clearly extract E' and raffinate R' will not be the same as those produced by a continuous countercurrent extraction. Subsequent raffinates R'', R''', and extracts E'', E''', etc., will approach the desired result, however. One can follow the approach to steady state by observing any conveniently measured property of the raffinates and extracts (density, refractive index, etc.). The properties of R', R'', etc., will approach a constant value, as will those of E', E'', etc. If this has occurred by the time extract E_1 and raffinate R_5 in the upper part of Fig. 10.58 is reached, then funnels 1 through 5 represent in every detail the stages of the continuous cascade just below. Thus, for example, raffinate R_3 from funnel 3 will have all the properties and relative volume of raffinate R_3 of the continuous plant.

In a similar manner, flow sheets involving reflux and fractional extraction may also be studied.[1,27]

Stage efficiency

As in the case of gas-liquid contact, the performance of individual extraction stages can be described in terms of the approach to equilibrium actually realized by the effluent extract and raffinate streams. The Murphree stage efficiency may be expressed in terms of extract compositions as $\mathbf{E}_{ME}$ or in terms of raffinate compositions as $\mathbf{E}_{MR}$. Applying Eq. (5.39) to stage m of the countercurrent cascade of Fig. 10.59, for example,

$$\mathbf{E}_{ME} = \frac{y_m - y_{m+1}}{y_m^* - y_{m+1}} \qquad \mathbf{E}_{MR} = \frac{x_{m-1} - x_m}{x_{m-1} - x_m^*} \tag{10.65}$$

where x_m and y_m represent the actual average effluent compositions and y_{m+1} and

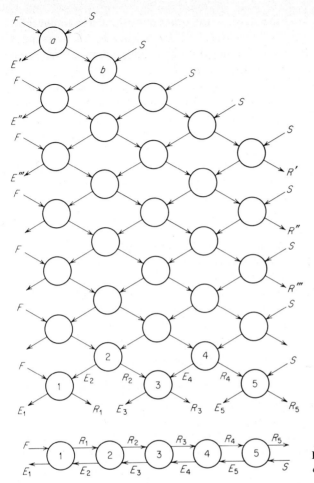

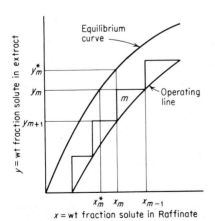

Fig. 10.58 *Batch simulation of a countercurrent cascade.*

Fig. 10.59 *Murphree stage efficiency.*

x_{m-1} those of the streams entering the stage. Any other consistent set of concentration units may equally well be used. The overall stage efficiency E_O of a cascade is defined simply as the ratio of the number of ideal stages to the number of real stages required to bring about a given concentration change.

The available experimental data are so meager that few generalizations can be made. Pilot-plant experimentation for new designs is therefore essential.[30] Overall stage efficiencies for cascades of the mixer-settler type have been reported ranging from 0.75 to 1.0. On the other hand, individual Murphree stage efficiencies of 1.0 are easily obtained with agitated vessels, especially if they are baffled, even with systems of high interfacial tension for which dispersion is difficult. It seems quite probable, therefore, that overall efficiencies as low as the 0.75 occasionally reported for cascades may well be the result of incomplete settling of the liquids between stages.

The few data reported for perforated-tray towers have all been taken from small laboratory devices of only a few inches diameter, and the direct application of these data to the design of large-scale equipment is most risky. Overall efficiencies range from as low as 0.02 for systems of high interfacial tension which are difficultly dispersed to 1.0 for easily dispersed systems of low interfacial tension, with the bulk of the data falling in the range 0.25 to 0.50. There appears to be little effect of perforation size, up to 0.25 in., for any given system. Tray efficiencies increase with tray spacing, owing to the corresponding increased time of contact of the phases, but there is little improvement for spacing larger than 16 or 18 in. As will be shown later, it appears that the most rapid mass transfer occurs during the formation of droplets, owing probably to the continual formation of new interfacial surface, while that occurring during the passage of the drop through a layer of continuous liquid is slow owing to the relatively stagnant conditions inside the drop. For these reasons very large tray spacings offer no advantage.

Overall stage efficiencies for agitated equipment of the type shown in Figs. 10.15 to 10.17 and 10.19 depend to some extent on arbitrary definitions as to what constitutes real stages in these devices, and they are perhaps better treated as continuous-contact devices. The centrifugal extractor of Fig. 10.20 has been reported to offer the equivalent of 1 to 13 theoretical stages, depending upon the circumstances of operation.[2]

CONTINUOUS CONTACT

Countercurrent extraction as shown in Figs. 10.38, 10.47, and 10.53 may be carried out in any of the continuous-contact devices such as the spray, packed, and agitated towers previously described, as well as in the centrifugal-type extractors, although for the last, two extractors are needed for cases where feed is introduced into other than the ends of the cascade.

Consider the continuous-contact tower of Fig. 10.60, where extract and raffinate phases flow countercurrently. Although in the diagram the raffinate is shown flowing downward as if it were the more dense phase, it is to be understood that in some instances the solvent-rich, or extract, phase will be the heavier and will enter at the top. In either case, in what follows subscript 1 will always represent that end of the tower where the raffinate enters and extract leaves, while subscript 2 will indicate where

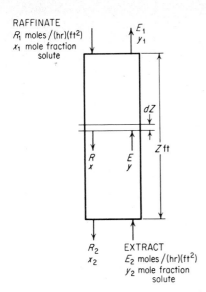

RAFFINATE
R_1 moles /(hr)(ft²)
x_1 mole fraction
solute

E_1
y_1

dZ

Z ft

R
x

E
y

R_2
x_2

EXTRACT
E_2 moles /(hr)(ft²)
y_2 mole fraction
solute

Fig. 10.60   *Continuous-contact tower.*

extract enters and raffinate leaves. We are presently unconcerned with the matter of which phase is dispersed and which is continuous. If the extractor is fed along the side, Fig. 10.60 and the relationships which follow apply separately to each section above and below the feed inlet.

Throughout this discussion, *unless otherwise specified*, x and y will refer to solute concentrations expressed as mole fractions in the raffinate and extract, respectively, and rates of flow of raffinate R and of extract E will be expressed as lb moles/(hr) (sq ft tower cross section). Except in special cases, the transfer of solute usually results in changes of mutual solubility of the contacted liquids, so that in general all components of the systems transfer from one phase to the other. The F-type mass-transfer coefficients are capable of handling this problem, but in reality our knowledge of mass-transfer rates in extractors is so poorly developed that we can ordinarily consider only the transfer of a single solute. This discussion is therefore limited to cases where the liquids are insoluble, only solute is transferred, and mutual solubility unchanged. In practice, however, the expressions developed are used for all cases.

It then follows that the equations derived for gas absorption apply. Thus, for the raffinate (which corresponds to the gas in gas absorption), we have the counterparts of Eqs. (8.21) to (8.25)

$$Z = \int_{x_2}^{x_1} \frac{R(1-x)_{iM}\, dx}{F_R a(1-x)(x-x_i)} = H_{tR} \int_{x_2}^{x_1} \frac{(1-x)_{iM}\, dx}{(1-x)(x-x_i)} = H_{tR} N_{tR} \quad (10.66)$$

$$H_{tR} = \frac{R}{F_R a} = \frac{R}{k_R a(1-x)_{iM}} \quad (10.67)$$

$$N_{tR} = \int_{x_2}^{x_1} \frac{(1-x)_{iM}\, dx}{(1-x)(x-x_i)} = \int_{x_2}^{x_1} \frac{dx}{x-x_i} + \frac{1}{2}\ln\frac{1-x_2}{1-x_1} \quad (10.68)$$

where x_i = interface concentration of solute
   F_R, k_R = transfer coefficients for the raffinate phase
   H_{tR} = raffinate height of transfer unit
   N_{tR} = number of raffinate transfer units
$(1 - x)_{iM}$ = logarithmic mean of $1 - x$ and $1 - x_i$

The interface concentration corresponding to any bulk raffinate concentration x is found through Eq. (5.21) adapted to the present situation

$$\frac{1 - x_i}{1 - x} = \left(\frac{1 - y}{1 - y_i}\right)^{F_E/F_R} \tag{10.69}$$

This equation is plotted, for any value of (x,y) on the operating curve, to determine its intersection with the equilibrium curve at (x_i,y_i), just as for gas absorption.   As an approximation, a straight line of slope $-k_R/k_E$ is plotted from (x,y) on the operating line to obtain the intersection at (x_i,y_i).

Similarly, we have the corresponding expressions for the extract (corresponding to the liquid in gas absorption).

In reality, we know so little about the mass-transfer coefficients that the above expressions are of little use.   For practical reasons, even though not strictly applicable unless the equilibrium curve is of constant slope, it is usually necessary to deal with overall coefficients and transfer units.   These we may take from their gas-absorption counterparts:

$$Z = H_{tOR}N_{tOR} = H_{tOE}N_{tOE} \tag{10.70}$$

$$H_{tOR} = \frac{R}{F_{OR}a} = \frac{R}{K_R a(1 - x)_{*M}} \tag{10.71}$$

$$H_{tOE} = \frac{E}{F_{OE}a} = \frac{E}{K_E a(1 - y)_{*M}} \tag{10.72}$$

$$N_{tOR} = \int_{x_2}^{x_1} \frac{(1 - x)_{*M}\,dx}{(1 - x)(x - x^*)} = \int_{x_2}^{x_1} \frac{dx}{x - x^*} + \frac{1}{2}\ln\frac{1 - x_2}{1 - x_1} \tag{10.73}$$

$$N_{tOE} = \int_{y_2}^{y_1} \frac{(1 - y)_{*M}\,dy}{(1 - y)(y^* - y)} = \int_{y_2}^{y_1} \frac{dy}{y^* - y} + \frac{1}{2}\ln\frac{1 - y_1}{1 - y_2} \tag{10.74}$$

$$(1 - x)_{*M} = \frac{(1 - x^*) - (1 - x)}{\ln\left[(1 - x^*)/(1 - x)\right]} \tag{10.75}$$

$$(1 - y)_{*M} = \frac{(1 - y) - (1 - y^*)}{\ln\left[(1 - y)/(1 - y^*)\right]} \tag{10.76}$$

where x^* is the concentration in equilibrium with y, and y^* that in equilibrium with x.

Concentrations in Eqs. (10.70) to (10.76) are in mole fractions.   *If x and y are expressed as weight fractions*, for convenience in use with the stage-calculation operating diagrams in terms of weight fractions,

$$N_{tOR} = \int_{x_2}^{x_1} \frac{dx}{x - x^*} + \frac{1}{2} \ln \frac{1 - x_2}{1 - x_1} + \frac{1}{2} \ln \frac{x_2(r - 1) + 1}{x_1(r - 1) + 1} \tag{10.77}$$

$$N_{tOE} = \int_{y_2}^{y_1} \frac{dy}{y^* - y} + \frac{1}{2} \ln \frac{1 - y_1}{1 - y_2} + \frac{1}{2} \ln \frac{y_1(r - 1) + 1}{y_2(r - 1) + 1} \tag{10.78}$$

where r is the ratio of molecular weights of nonsolute to solute.   For weight-ratio concentrations,

$$N_{tOR} = \int_{x_2'}^{x_1'} \frac{dx'}{x' - x'^*} + \frac{1}{2} \ln \frac{1 + rx_2'}{1 + rx_1'} \tag{10.79}$$

$$N_{tOE} = \int_{y_2'}^{y_1'} \frac{dy'}{y'^* - y'} + \frac{1}{2} \ln \frac{1 + ry_1'}{1 + ry_2'} \tag{10.80}$$

Dilute solutions

For dilute solutions, only the integral terms of the above equations for N_{tOE} and N_{tOR} are important.   If in addition the equilibrium curve and operating line are straight over the concentration range encountered, it is readily shown in the manner of Chap. 8 that logarithmic averages of the terminal concentration differences are applicable

$$N_{tOR} = \frac{x_1 - x_2}{(x - x^*)_M} \qquad N_{tOE} = \frac{y_1 - y_2}{(y^* - y)_M} \tag{10.81}$$

The equivalent expressions in terms of mass-transfer coefficients are

$$R(x_1 - x_2) = E(y_1 - y_2) = K_R aZ(x - x^*)_M = K_E aZ(y - y^*)_M \tag{10.82}$$

If in addition the equivalent of Henry's law applies, so that the equilibrium-distribution curve is a straight line passing through the origin ($m = y^*/x = y/x^* = $ const), there is obtained, by a procedure exactly similar to that used previously in the case of gas absorption,

$$N_{tOR} = \frac{\ln \left[\frac{x_1 - y_2/m}{x_2 - y_2/m} \left(1 - \frac{R}{mE} \right) + \frac{R}{mE} \right]}{1 - R/mE} \tag{10.83}$$

Figure 8.20 represents a graphical solution, provided $(x_2 - y_2/m)/(x_1 - y_2/m)$ is considered the ordinate and mE/R the parameter.   Similarly for the extract-enriching section of a tower used with reflux, the same circumstances provide

$$N_{tOE} = \frac{\ln \left[\frac{y_2 - mx_1}{y_1 - mx_1} \left(1 - \frac{mE}{R} \right) + \frac{mE}{R} \right]}{1 - mE/R} \tag{10.84}$$

which is also solved graphically in Fig. 8.20 provided $(y_1 - mx_1)/(y_2 - mx_1)$ is the ordinate and R/mE the parameter.

For these dilute solutions, Eqs. (10.81), (10.83), and (10.84) may be used with concentrations in terms of weight fractions, in which case m must be defined in these terms as well while E and R are measured in lb/(hr)(sq ft).   Weight ratios may also be used.   Equations (10.81) and (10.82) are frequently used with concentrations expressed as c lb moles/cu ft, in which case the extract and raffinate flow rates are measured in terms of V cu ft/(hr)(sq ft) and the units of the appropriate mass-transfer coefficients are K_{LE} and K_{LR} lb moles/(hr)(sq ft)(Δc).   The requirements of constant m (in whatever units it is measured) and straight line operating lines still of course apply.

Illustration 10.9. Determine the number of transfer units N_{tOR} for the extraction of Illustration 10.5, for the case where 5,000 lb/hr of solvent are used.

Solution. Define x and y in terms of weight fractions acetic acid. $x_1 = x_F = 0.30$; $y_2 = 0$; $x_2 = 0.02$; $y_1 = 0.10$.   The operating diagram is already plotted in Fig. 10.43.   From this plot, values of x and x^* are taken from the operating line and equilibrium curve at various values of y, as follows:

x	x^*	$\dfrac{1}{x - x^*}$
0.30	0.230	14.30
0.25	0.192	17.25
0.20	0.154	20.75
0.15	0.114	27.8
0.10	0.075	40.0
0.05	0.030	50.0
0.02	0	50.0

The area under a curve of x as abscissa against $1/(x - x^*)$ as ordinate (not shown) between $x = 0.30$ and $x = 0.02$ is determined to be 8.40.   In these solutions, the mutual solubility of water and isopropyl ether is very small, so that r may be taken as $^{18}\!/_{60} = 0.30$.   Eq. (10.77):

$$N_{tOR} = 8.40 + \frac{1}{2} \ln \frac{1 - 0.02}{1 - 0.30} + \frac{1}{2} \ln \frac{0.02(0.3 - 1) + 1}{0.30(0.3 - 1) + 1} = 8.46$$

The operating and equilibrium curves are nearly parallel in this case, so that N_{tOR} and N_p are nearly the same.   The curvature of the lines makes the simplified methods for N_{tOR} inapplicable, however.

Illustration 10.10. Determine the number of transfer units N_{tOR} for the extraction of Illustration 10.6, when 1,150 lb/hr of kerosene are used.

Solution. Use weight-ratio concentrations, as in Illustration 10.6. $x_1' = x_F' = 0.0101$; $y_2' = 0$; $x_2' = 0.001001$; $y_1' = 0.0782$.   The calculation may be done through Eq. (10.83) or the equivalent, Fig. 8.20.

$$\frac{x_2' - y_2'/m'}{x_1' - y_2'/m'} = \frac{0.001001}{0.0101} = 0.0909$$

The average $mE/R = m'B/A = 1.01$ (Illustration 10.6).   From Fig. 8.20, $N_{tOR} = 8.8$.

Illustration 10.11. Leibson and Beckmann [*Chem. Eng. Progr.*, **49**, 405 (1953)] extracted di-ethylamine from water [20.4 cu ft/(hr) (sq ft)] with toluene [3.05 cu ft/(hr)(sq ft)] at 30.8°C, toluene dispersed, in a 6-in.-ID tower packed to a depth of 4 ft with ½-in. Rasching rings.   The observed concentrations of diethylamine, in lb moles/cu ft, were water in $= 0.01574$, out $= 0.01450$; toluene in $= 0$, out 0.00860.   At this temperature the distribution coefficient $=$ concn in water/concn in toluene $= 1.156$, and water and toluene are substantially insoluble at these diethylamine concentra-tions.   (*a*) Determine the extraction characteristics of the packing for these conditions.   (*b*) Com-pute the effluent concentrations if 8 ft of packing had been used.

Solution. a. The water solution is the raffinate and toluene the extract.   Define $m'' = c_E^*/c_R = 1/1.156 = 0.865$.

$c_{E1} = 0.00860$, $c_{E2} = 0$, $c_{R1} = 0.01574$, $c_{R2} = 0.01450$ lb moles diethylamine/cu ft. Owing to the insolubility of the water and toluene, Eq. (10.82) may be written for this case as

$$V_E(c_{E1} - c_{E2}) = K_{LE}aZ(c_E^* - c_E)_M$$

where $V_E = 3.05$ cu ft extract/(hr)(sq ft), constant at these concentrations

$Z = 4$ ft

$C_{E1}^* = m''c_{R1} = 0.865(0.01574) = 0.01363$

$c_{E2}^* = m''c_{R2} = 0.865(0.01450) = 0.01254$

$$(c_E^* - c_E)_M = \frac{(c_{E2}^* - c_{E2}) - (c_{E1}^* - c_{E1})}{\ln\left[(c_{E2}^* - c_{E2})/(c_{E1}^* - c_{E1})\right]} = \frac{(0.01254 - 0) - (0.01363 - 0.00860)}{\ln\left[(0.01254 - 0)/(0.01363 - 0.00860)\right]}$$

$$= 0.00825 \text{ lb mole/cu ft.}$$

$$\therefore 3.05(0.00860 - 0) = K_{LE}a(4)(0.00825)$$

$$K_{LE}a = 0.795 \text{ lb mole/(hr)(cu ft)}(\Delta c_E)$$

Applying Eqs. (5.16) and (5.17) to this case, $K_{LR}a = m''K_{LE}a = 0.865(0.795) = 0.687$ lb mole/ (hr)(cu ft)(Δc_R).

From Table 3.1, $K_E a = cK_{LE}a$, where c is the molar density, lb moles/cu ft, of the extract phase.   For these dilute solutions, the density (0.856 g/cu cm) and average molecular weight (92.1) of the extract are the same as those for pure toluene, so that $c = 0.856(62.3)/92.1 = 0.58$ lb mole/cu ft.   Therefore $K_E a = 0.58(0.795) = 0.461$ lb mole/(hr)(cu ft)(mole fraction).

$$E = V_E c = 3.05(0.58) = 1.77 \text{ lb moles extract/(hr)(sq ft)}$$

$$H_{tOE} = \frac{E}{K_E a} = \frac{1.77}{0.461} = 3.84 \text{ ft}$$

Alternatively,

$$H_{tOE} = \frac{V_E}{K_{LE}a} \qquad H_{tOR} = \frac{V_R}{K_{LR}a} = \frac{20.4}{0.687} = 29.7 \text{ ft}$$

b. For 8 ft of packing let c_{R2} be the exit concentration in the water and c_{E1} the exit concentration in the toluene.   Equation (10.83) can be adapted to these units.

$$\frac{V_R}{m''V_E} = \frac{20.4}{0.865(3.05)} = 7.73$$

$$N_{tOR} = \frac{Z}{H_{tOR}} = \frac{8}{29.7} = 0.269 \qquad c_{R1} = 0.01574 \qquad c_{E2} = 0$$

$$\therefore 0.269 = \frac{\ln\left[(0.01574/c_{R2})(1 - 7.73) + 7.73\right]}{1 - 7.73}$$

$$c_{R2} = 0.01400 \text{ lb mole diethylamine/cu ft}$$

A material balance for diethylamine,

$$V_E(c_{E1} - c_{E2}) = V_R(c_{R1} - c_{R2})$$
$$3.05(c_{E1} - 0) = 20.4(0.01574 - 0.01400)$$
$$c_{E1} = 0.01163 \text{ lb mole/cu ft}$$

Performance of continuous-contact equipment

While over the past 30 years a considerable number of data has been accumulated, taken almost entirely from laboratory-size equipment of a few inches diameter, no satisfactory correlation of them has as yet been possible owing to the very large number of variables which influence extraction rates. For the design of new extractors it is essential that pilot-plant experiments be performed under conditions as nearly like those expected in the large-scale equipment as possible.[30] This discussion will therefore be limited to a brief consideration of the important variables, but no data for design will be presented. Detailed study of many of the data is available elsewhere.[27]

The principal difficulty in obtaining an understanding of extractor performance lies with the very large number of variables which influence the performance. The following at least have influence.

1. The liquid system.
    a. Chemical identity and corresponding physical properties. In this category may be included the presence or absence of surface-active agents, finely divided solids, and the like.
    b. Concentration of solute, since this influences physical properties.
    c. Direction of extraction, whether from aqueous to organic, from continuous to dispersed phase.
    d. Total flow rate of the liquids.
    e. Ratio of liquid flows.
    f. What liquid is dispersed.
2. The equipment.
    a. Design, which includes not only the gross and obvious design such as whether the extractor is a packed- or sieve-tray tower, but also the details such as size and shape of packing and number of perforations in a plate.
    b. Nature and extent of mechanical agitation, whether rotary or pulsating, whether fast or slow.
    c. Materials of construction, which influence the relative wetting by the liquids.
    d. Height of the extractor and the end effects.
    e. Diameter of extractor and extent of axial mixing.

Except for possible interface effects due to surface-active substances, the overall resistance to mass transfer is made up of those residing in each of the fluids. Thus Eqs. (5.16) and (5.17) provide the relation between mass-transfer coefficients, and in terms of heights of transfer units we have

$$H_{tOR} = H_{tR} + \frac{R}{mE} H_{tE} \tag{10.85}$$

$$H_{tOE} = H_{tE} + \frac{mE}{R} H_{tR} \tag{10.86}$$

It must be understood that in any equipment of this sort the dispersed phase may be either the extract or the raffinate and either the light or the heavy phase.   The resistances to mass transfer in the contacted fluids are likely to depend strongly upon whether the phases in question are dispersed or continuous.   It is best therefore to describe the equipment characteristics in terms of mass-transfer coefficients or heights of tranfer units written in terms of the continuous or dispersed phase, $K_C a$ and $K_D a$, or H_{tOC} and H_{tOD}, so that the resistance equations become

$$H_{tOD} = H_{tD} + \frac{L_D}{mL_C} H_{tC} \tag{10.87}$$

$$H_{tOC} = H_{tC} + \frac{mL_C}{L_D} H_{tD} \tag{10.88}$$

Some work has been done to establish the individual mass-transfer resistances by use of a technique similar to that found useful in humidification work.   Thus, by allowing pure water and pure butanol in the absence of a third distributed substance to flow countercurrently through a tower and mutually to saturate each other, values of H_{tC} and H_{tD} can be obtained.   A limited number of such studies with spray and packed towers has been made, but insufficient to permit regularization of the data.

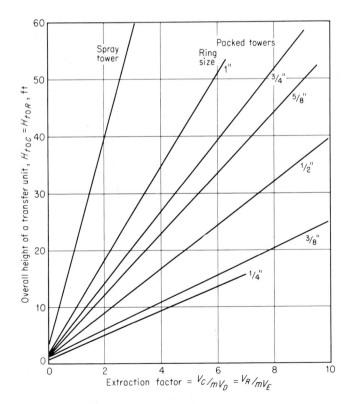

Fig. 10.61 *Extraction of diethylamine from water into toluene, toluene dispersed, in a 6-in.-diameter tower.* [*Data of Leibson and Beckmann:* Chem. Eng. Progr., **49**, 405 (1953).]

In packed towers, H_{tD} for a given packing and system appears to be fairly constant, while H_{tC} varies with the ratio of liquid flow rates. Despite this, Eq. (10.88) has frequently been successful in the empirical correlation of data for a given packing and system, as shown in Fig. 10.61. Despite the linearity of the data, the slope and intercept of such lines should *not* be interpreted as H_{tD} and H_{tC}.[30] The figure shows clearly the improved, i.e., lower, values of H_{tOC} for small packings as compared to large and the poor performance of a spray tower. Economic considerations would generally put the extraction factor V_R/mV_E of the figure in the region of 1 or 2, so that for the smaller packings, values of H_{tOR} are not too unreasonably large. Mechanically agitated extractors will show substantially lower values, however.

NOTATION FOR CHAPTER 10

a = interfacial surface, sq ft/cu ft active volume

a_p = surface of packing, sq ft/cu ft

A = component A, lb liquid A/hr or lb (batch operations)

A_d = downspout cross section, sq ft

A_n = net tower cross section = $A_t - A_d$, sq ft

A_t = tower cross section, sq ft

B = component B, lb liquid B/hr or lb (batch operations)

c = concentration of solute, lb moles/cu ft solution

C = component C, lb substance C/hr or lb (batch operations)

C_D = drag coefficient = $4\Delta\rho\, d_p g/3\rho_d V_t^2$, dimensionless

d = differential operator

d_F = packing size, ft

d_{FC} = critical packing size, ft

d_O = nozzle or perforation diameter, ft

d_p = drop diameter, ft

D = component D, lb liquid D/hr

E = extract solution, lb/hr (staged extractors), lb (batch operations), lb moles/(hr)(sq ft) (continuous-contact extractors)

E' = solvent-free extract, lb/hr or lb (batch operation)

$\mathbf{E}_{ME}$ = Murphree extract-stage efficiency, fractional

$\mathbf{E}_{MR}$ = Murphee raffinate-stage efficiency, fractional

$\mathbf{E}_O$ = overall stage efficiency, fractional

F = feed or solution to be extracted, lb/hr or lb (batch operations)

= mass-transfer coefficient, lb moles/(hr)(sq ft)

F' = feed, solvent-free basis, lb/hr or lb (batch operations)

g = acceleration due to gravity, ft/hr²

g_c = conversion factor, $4.17(10^8)$(lb mass)(ft)/(lb force)(hr²)

h = depth of dispersed liquid accumulating on a tray, ft

h_C = depth of dispersed liquid on a tray owing to flow of continuous liquid, ft

h_D = depth of dispersed liquid on a tray owing to flow of dispersed liquid, ft

h_O = head required to cause flow through an orifice, ft

h_σ = head required to overcome effect of interfacial tension, ft

H_t = height of a transfer unit, ft

k = mass-transfer coefficient, lb moles/(hr)(sq ft)(mole fraction)

K = overall mass-transfer coefficient, lb moles/(hr)(sq ft)(mole fraction)

K_L = overall mass-transfer coefficient, lb moles/(hr)(sq ft)(lb mole/cu ft)

ln = natural logarithm

L = superficial mass velocity, lb/(hr)(sq ft)

m = slope of the equilibrium-distribution curve = $dy^*/dx = dy/dx^*$, dimensionless

m' = slope of the equilibrium-distribution curve = $dy'^*/dx' = dy'/dx'^*$, dimensionless

M = mixture M, lb/hr or lb (batch operations)

M' = solvent-free mixture M, lb/hr or lb (batch operations)

N = solvent concentration, solvent-free basis, lb B/lb $(A + C)$

N_p = number of ideal stages, dimensionless

N_t = number of transfer units, dimensionless

P = dimensionless group defined by Eq. (10.5)

P'_E = solvent-free extract product, lb/hr

r = molecular weight nonsolute/molecular weight solute, dimensionless

R = raffinate solution, lb/hr (staged extractors), lb (batch operations), lb moles/(hr)(sq ft) (continuous-contact extractors)

R' = solvent-free raffinate, lb/hr or lb (batch operations)

Re = drop Reynolds number = $d_p V_t \rho_C / \mu_C$, dimensionless

s = a distance, Fig. 10.4 and Eq. (10.1), ft

= stage s

S = solvent, lb/hr or lb (batch operations)

t = a distance, ft

T = tower diameter, ft

u = a distance, ft

V = superficial velocity based on tower cross section, ft/hr

V' = superficial velocity based on tower cross section, ft/sec

V_d = velocity through downspout, ft/hr

V_K = characteristic velocity, ft/hr

V_n = velocity based on A_n, ft/hr

V_O = velocity through orifice, ft/hr

V'_O = velocity through orifice, ft/sec

V_t = terminal settling velocity, ft/hr

We = drop Weber number = $d_p V_t^2 \rho_C / \sigma g_c$, dimensionless

x = concentration of C in A-rich (raffinate) phase, weight fraction (staged extractors), mole fraction (continuous-contact extractors)

x' = concentration of C in A-rich (raffinate) phase, lb C/lb non-C

= concentration of solute in D-rich phase (fractional extraction), lb solute/lb nonsolute

X = concentration of C in A-rich (raffinate) phase, solvent-free basis, lb C/lb $(A + C)$

y = concentration of C in B-rich (extract) phase, weight fraction (staged extractors), mole fraction (continuous-contact extractors)

y' = concentration of C in B-rich (extract) phase, lb C/lb non-C

= concentration of solute in A-rich phase (fractional extraction), lb solute/lb nonsolute

Y = concentration of C in B-rich (extract) phase, solvent-free basis, lb C/lb $(A + C)$

Z = active height, ft

β = selectivity, dimensionless

Δ = difference

Δ'_E = difference in flow rate, solvent-free basis, defined by Eq. (10.50)

Δ_R = difference in flow rate, defined by Eq. (10.35)

Δ'_R = difference in flow rate, solvent-free basis, defined by Eq. (10.41)

ϵ = volume void fraction in a packed bed, dimensionless

μ = viscosity, lb mass/(ft)(hr) = $2.42\mu'$

μ_W = viscosity of water, lb mass/(ft)(hr)

μ' = viscosity, centipoises

π = 3.1416

ρ = density, lb mass/cu ft

σ = interfacial tension, lb force/ft = $6.85(10^{-5})\sigma'$

σ' = interfacial tension, dynes/cm

ϕ_D = volume fraction dispersed phase, dimensionless

Subscripts:

C = continuous phase

D = dispersed phase

e = stage e

E = extract

f = flooding condition

F = feed

H = heavy, or more dense, phase

i = interface

L = light, or less dense, phase

m = stage m; minimum (reflux ratio or solvent/feed ratio)

M = mixture M; logarithmic mean

N_p = last stage of a cascade

O = orifice or nozzle

= overall (with $\mathbf{E}$, H_t, and N_t)

R = raffinate

s = stage s

S = solvent

1 = stage 1; that end of a continuous-contact tower where feed or raffinate enters

2 = stage 2; that end of a continuous-contact tower where extract or solvent enters

Superscript:

* = in equilibrium with bulk concentration of other phase

REFERENCES

1. Alders, L.: "Liquid-Liquid Extraction," 2d ed., Elsevier Publishing Company, Amsterdam, 1959.

2. Barson, N., and G. H. Beyer: *Chem. Eng. Progr.*, **49**, 243 (1953).

3. Bibaud, R. E., and R. E. Treybal: *AIChE J.*, **12**, 472 (1966).

4. Blanding, F. H., and J. C. Elgin: *Trans. AIChE*, **38**, 305 (1942).

5. Bussolari, R., S. Schiff, and R. E. Treybal: *Ind. Eng. Chem.*, **45**, 2413 (1953).

6. Crawford, J. W., and C. R. Wilke: *Chem. Eng. Progr.*, **47**, 423 (1951).

7. Feick, G., and H. M. Anderson: *Ind. Eng. Chem.*, **44**, 404 (1952).

8. Hayworth, C. B., and R. E. Treybal: *Ind. Eng. Chem.*, **42**, 1174 (1950).

9. Hu, S., and R. C. Kintner: *AIChE J.*, **1**, 42 (1955).

10. Jacobson, F. M., and G. H. Beyer: *AIChE J.*, **2**, 283 (1956).

11. Johnson, A. I., and L. Braida: *Can. J. Chem. Eng.*, **35**, 165 (1957).

12. Keith, F. W., and A. N. Hixson: *Ind. Eng. Chem.*, **47**, 258 (1955).

13. Laity, D. S., and R. E. Treybal: *AIChE J.*, **3**, 176 (1957).

14. Mar, B. W., and A. L. Babb: *Ind. Eng. Chem.*, **51**, 1011 (1959).

15. Mayfield, F. D., and W. L. Church: *Ind. Eng. Chem.*, **44**, 2253 (1952).

16. Oldshue, J. Y., and J. H. Rushton: *Chem. Eng. Progr.*, **48**, 297 (1952).

17. Overcashier, R., H. A. Kingsley, and R. B. Olney: *AIChE J.*, **2**, 529 (1956).

18. Pratt, H. R. C., and coworkers: *Trans. Inst. Chem. Engrs. (London)*, **29**, 89, 110, 126 (1951); **31**, 57, 70, 78 (1953); **35**, 267 (1957).

19. Quinn, J. A., and D. B. Sigloh: *Can. J. Chem. Eng.*, **41**, 15 (1963).

20. Reman, G. H., and R. B. Olney: *Chem. Eng. Progr.*, **51**, 141 (1955).

21. Ricci, J. E.: "The Phase Rule and Heterogeneous Equilibrium," D. Van Nostrand Company, Inc., Princeton, N.J., 1951.

22. Rushton, J. H., E. W. Costich, and H. J. Everett: *Chem. Eng. Progr.*, **46**, 395, 467 (1950).
23. Sareen, S. S., P. M. Rose, R. C. Gudeson, and R. C. Kintner: *AIChE J.*, **12**, 1045 (1966).
24. Scheibel, E. G.: *AIChE J.*, **2**, 74 (1956).
25. Scheibel, E. G.: *Chem. Eng. Progr.*, **62**(9), 76 (1966).
26. Strand, C. P., R. B. Olney, and G. H. Ackerman: *AIChE J.*, **8**, 252 (1962).
27. Treybal, R. E.: "Liquid Extraction," 2d ed., McGraw-Hill Book Co., New York, 1963.
28. Treybal, R. E.: *Ind. Eng. Chem. Fundamentals*, **3**, 185 (1964).
29. Treybal, R. E.: *Chem. Eng. Progr.*, **60**(5), 77 (1964).
30. Treybal, R. E.: *Chem. Eng. Progr.*, **62**(9), 67 (1966).
31. Vermeulen, T., J. S. Moon, A. Hennico, and T. Miyauchi: *Chem. Eng. Progr.*, **62**(9), 95 (1966).
32. Woodfield, F. N., and G. Sege: *Chem. Eng. Progr. Symp. Ser.*, **50**(13), 14 (1954).

PROBLEMS

Problems 10.1 to 10.7 refer to the system water (A)–chlorobenzene (B)–pyridine (C) at 25°C. Equilibrium tie-line data, interpolated from those of Peake and Thompson, *Ind. Eng. Chem.*, **44**, 2439 (1952), are in weight percents.

C	B	A	C	B	A
Pyridine	Chlorobenzene	Water	Pyridine	Chlorobenzene	Water
0	99.95	0.05	0	0.08	99.92
11.05	88.28	0.67	5.02	0.16	94.82
18.95	79.90	1.15	11.05	0.24	88.71
24.10	74.28	1.62	18.90	0.38	80.72
28.60	69.15	2.25	25.50	0.58	73.92
31.55	65.58	2.87	36.10	1.85	62.05
35.05	61.00	3.95	44.95	4.18	50.87
40.60	53.00	6.40	53.20	8.90	37.90
49.0	37.8	13.2	49.0	37.8	13.2

10.1. Plot the equilibrium data on the following coordinate systems: (*a*) triangular; (*b*) x and y against weight fraction B; (*c*) x against y.

10.2. Compute the selectivity of chlorobenzene for pyridine at each tie line, and plot selectivity against concentration of pyridine in water.

10.3. It is desired to reduce the pyridine concentration of 2,000 lb of an aqueous solution from 50 to 2% in a single batch extraction with chlorobenzene. What amount of solvent is required? Solve on triangular coordinates.

10.4. A 2,000-lb batch of pyridine-water solution, 50% pyridine, is to be extracted with an equal weight of chlorobenzene. The raffinate from the first extraction is to be reextracted with a weight of solvent equal to the raffinate weight, and so on $(B_2 = R_1, B_3 = R_2,$ etc.). How many theoretical stages and what total solvent will be required to reduce the concentration of pyridine to 2% in the final raffinate? Solve on triangular coordinates.

10.5. Two thousand pounds per hour of a 50% pyridine–50% water solution is to be continuously and countercurrently extracted with chlorobenzene to reduce the pyridine concentration to 2%. Using the coordinate systems plotted in (*b*) and (*c*) of Prob. 10.1:
   a. Determine the minimum solvent rate required, lb/hr.

  b.   If 2,040 lb solvent/hr is used, what are the number of theoretical stages and the saturated weights of extract and raffinate?   **Ans.:** 3 ideal stages.
  c.   Determine the number of transfer units N_{tOR} for the extraction of (b).   **Ans.:** 4.89.

10.6.   The properties of the solutions have not been completely studied, but from those of the pure constituents the following properties are estimated:

	Density, lb/cu ft	Viscosity, centipoises	Interfacial tension, dynes/cm
Feed	62.1	1.0	8
Extract	65	1.3	
Raffinate	62.2	0.89	35
Solvent	68.5	1.25	

For the extraction of Prob. 10.5b and c, chlorobenzene as dispersed phase,
  a.   Recommend a diameter of a tower packed with 1-in. ceramic rings, operating with a dispersed-phase holdup of 10%.   What approach to flooding does this represent?   **Ans.:** 1 ft 9 in.
  b.   Design a perforated tray suitable for the lower part of a tower.   Use $\frac{3}{16}$-in.-diameter perforations and a perforation velocity of 0.5 ft/sec.   Estimate the depth of dispersed liquid accumulating on the tray.

10.7.   Can the separation of Prob. 10.5 be made by distillation at atmospheric pressure?

10.8.   Water-dioxane solutions form a minimum-boiling azeotrope at atmospheric pressure and cannot be separated by ordinary distillation methods.   Benzene forms no azeotrope with dioxane and may be used as an extraction solvent.   At 25°C, the equilibrium distribution of dioxane between water and benzene [*J. Am. Chem. Soc.*, **66**, 282 (1944)] is as follows:

Wt % dioxane in water	5.1	18.9	25.2
Wt % dioxane in benzene	5.2	22.5	32.0

At these concentrations water and benzene are substantially insoluble.   One thousand pounds of a 25% dioxane–75% water solution is to be extracted with benzene to remove 95% of the dioxane.   The benzene is dioxane-free.
  a.   Calculate the solvent requirement for a single batch operation.
  b.   If the extraction were done with equal amounts of solvent in five crosscurrent stages, how much solvent would be required?

10.9.   One thousand pounds per hour of a 25% solution of dioxane in water is to be continuously extracted in countercurrent fashion with benzene to remove 95% of the dioxane.   Equilibrium data are given in Prob. 10.8.
  a.   What is the minimum solvent requirement, lb/hr?
  b.   If 900 lb/hr of solvent is used, how many theoretical stages are required?   **Ans.:** 6.1 ideal stages.
  c.   How many transfer units N_{tOR} correspond to the extraction of (b)?

10.10.   An aqueous solution contains 25% acetone by weight together with a small amount of an undesired contaminant.   For the purpose of a later process, it is necessary to have the acetone dissolved in water without the impurity.   To accomplish this, the solution will be extracted countercurrently with trichloroethane, which extracts the acetone but not the impurity.   The extract will then be countercurrently extracted with pure water in a second extractor to give the desired product water solution, and the recovered solvent will be returned to the first extractor. It is required to obtain 98% of the acetone in the final product. Water and trichloroethane are insoluble over the acetone-concentration range involved, and the distribution coefficient (lb acetone/lb trichloro-ethane)/(lb acetone/lb water) = 1.65 = const.

    a. What is the largest concentration of acetone possible in the recovered solvent?

    b. How many stages would be required in each extractor to obtain the acetone in the final water solution at the same concentration as in the original solution?

    c. If recovered solvent contains 0.005 lb acetone/lb trichloroethane, if 1 lb trichloroethane/lb water is used in the first extractor, and if the same number of stages is used in each extractor, what concentration of acetone in the final product will result?

    10.11. Twenty-four cubic feet per hour of water, containing 0.02 lb mole diethylamine/cu ft, is to be extracted countercurrently with 27.7 cu ft toluene/hr at 30.8°C, in order to remove 90% of the diethylamine. Determine the required height and diameter of a tower packed with 1-in. unglazed porcelain rings, operated at 50% of the flooding velocity.

    Equilibrium distribution data are given in Illustration 10.11 and values of H_{tOR} in Fig. 10.61. The densities and viscosities of the liquids may be taken as those of pure water and toluene, and the interfacial tension is estimated to be 30 dynes/cm.

Problems 10.12 to 10.14 refer to the system cottonseed oil (*A*)–liquid propane (*B*)–oleic acid (*C*) at 98.5°C, 625 psia. Smoothed equilibrium tie-line data of Hixson and Bockelmann, *Trans. AIChE,* **38,** 891 (1942), in weight percents, are as follows:

Cottonseed oil	Oleic acid	Propane	Cottonseed oil	Oleic acid	Propane
63.5	0	36.5	2.30	0	97.7
57.2	5.5	37.3	1.95	0.76	97.3
52.0	9.0	39.0	1.78	1.21	97.0
46.7	13.8	39.5	1.50	1.90	96.6
39.8	18.7	41.5	1.36	2.73	95.9
31.0	26.3	42.7	1.20	3.8	95.0
26.9	29.4	43.7	1.10	4.4	94.5
21.0	32.4	46.6	1.0	5.1	93.9
14.2	37.4	48.4	0.8	6.1	93.1
8.3	39.5	52.2	0.7	7.2	92.1
4.5	41.1	54.4	0.4	6.1	93.5
0.8	43.7	55.5	0.2	5.5	94.3

    10.12. Plot the equilibrium data on the following coordinate systems: (*a*) *N* against *X* and *Y*; (*b*) *X* against *Y*.

    10.13. One hundred pounds of a cottonseed oil–oleic acid solution containing 25% acid is to be extracted twice in crosscurrent fashion, each time with 1,000 lb of propane. Determine the compositions, percent by weight, and the weights of the mixed extracts and the final raffinate. Determine the compositions and weights of the solvent-free products. Make the computations on the coordinates plotted in Prob. 10.12*a*.

    10.14. One thousand pounds per hour of a cottonseed oil–oleic acid solution containing 25% acid is to be continuously separated into products containing 2 and 90% acid (solvent-free compositions) by countercurrent extraction with propane. Make the following computations on the coordinate systems of Prob. 10.12a and b:

a. What is the minimum number of theoretical stages required? **Ans.:** 5.

b. What is the minimum external extract-reflux ratio required? **Ans.:** 3.08.

c. For an external extract-reflux ratio of 4.5, determine the number of theoretical stages, the position of the feed stage, and the quantities, in lb/hr, of the following streams: E_1, B_E, E', R_0, R_{Np}, P'_E, and S. **Ans.:** 10.5 ideal stages.

d. What do the equilibrium data indicate as to the maximum purity of oleic acid that could be obtained?

Problems 10.15 and 10.16 refer to the system oxalic and succinic acids distributed between water and *n*-amyl alcohol. The acids distribute practically independently of each other, and for present purposes they will be considered to do so. Equilibrium concentrations, expressed as g acid/liter, are:

Either acid in water	0	20	40	60
Oxalic in alcohol	0	6.0	13.0	21.5
Succinic in alcohol	0	12.0	23.5	35.0

The water and amyl alcohol are essentially immiscible. In the calculations, express acid concentrations as g/liter and solvent rates as liters/time.

10.15. A water solution containing 50 g each of oxalic and succinic acids per liter of water is to be extracted countercurrently with *n*-amyl alcohol (free of acid) to recover 95% of the oxalic acid.

a. Compute the minimum solvent required, liters alcohol/liter water.

b. If an alcohol/water ratio of 3.8 liters/liter is used, compute the number of ideal stages required and the solvent-free analysis of the extract product. **Ans.:** 9 ideal stages.

10.16. A mixture of succinic (*B*) and oxalic (*C*) acids containing 50% of each is to be separated into products each 90% pure on a solvent-free basis, using *n*-amyl alcohol (*A*) and water (*D*) by a fractional extraction.

a. Calculate the number of ideal stages and the location of the feed stage if 9 liters of alcohol and 4 liters of water are used per 100 g of acid feed. **Ans.:** 12.75 stages.

b. Investigate the effect of solvent ratio on the number of stages, keeping the total liquid flow constant. What is the least number of stages required and the corresponding solvent ratio?

PART FOUR
SOLID-FLUID
OPERATIONS

The mass-transfer operations in this category to be considered in detail are adsorption, drying, and leaching. Others which are less frequently used are included in Part 5. Adsorption involves contact of solids with either liquids or gases, with mass transfer in the direction fluid to solid. Drying involves gas-solid, and leaching liquid-solid, contact, with mass transfer in each case in the direction solid to fluid. In many but not all applications, the last two may be considered as special cases of desorption, the reverse of adsorption. Adsorption is thus more general, in principle at least, and is considered first.

Theoretically, at least, the same apparatus and equipment useful for gas-solid or liquid-solid contact in adsorption should also be useful in the corresponding operations of drying and leaching. In practice, however, we find special types of apparatus in all three categories. This is probably the result of many years of development of the practical applications of these operations without the realization that basically they are very similar. For example, we find considerable inventive genius applied to the development of equipment for the continuous gas-solid operations of adsorption, but little application of the results to the problem of drying. Many clever devices have been developed for continuous leaching of solids with liquids, but there is little application of these to the practical problems of adsorption from liquids. Ideal devices have not yet been invented. But we may reasonably expect a reduction in the number of equipment types and greater interapplication among the three operations as the many problems of solids handling are eventually solved.

In developing the quantitative treatment of these operations, particularly the diverse applications of adsorption, considerable simplification results if advantage is taken of the resemblances to the gas and liquid operations previously considered. This introduces many problems of mathematical notation, however, and the student is advised to pay more than ordinary attention to the tables of notation at the end of each chapter. Complete consistency with the notation of the previous chapters seemed impossible to realize.

CHAPTER ELEVEN
ADSORPTION AND
ION EXCHANGE

The adsorption operations exploit the ability of certain solids preferentially to concentrate specific substances from solution onto their surfaces. In this manner, the components of either gaseous or liquid solutions may be separated from each other. A few examples will indicate the general nature of the separations possible and at the same time demonstrate the great variety of practical applications. In the field of gaseous separations, adsorption is used to dehumidify air and other gases, to remove objectionable odors and impurities from industrial gases such as carbon dioxide, to recover valuable solvent vapors from dilute mixtures with air and other gases, and to fractionate mixtures of hydrocarbon gases containing such substances as methane, ethylene, ethane, propylene, and propane. Typical liquid separations include the removal of moisture dissolved in gasoline, decolorization of petroleum products and aqueous sugar solutions, removal of objectionable taste and odor from water, and the fractionation of mixtures of aromatic and paraffinic hydrocarbons.

These operations are all similar in that the mixture to be separated is brought into contact with another insoluble phase, the adsorbent solid, and the unequal distribution of the original constituents between the adsorbed phase on the solid surface and the bulk of the fluid then permits a separation to be made. All the techniques previously found valuable in the contact of insoluble fluids are useful in adsorption. Thus we have batchwise single-stage and continuous multistage separations and separations analogous to countercurrent absorption and stripping in the field of gas-liquid contact and to rectification and extraction with the use of reflux. In addition, the rigidity and immobility of a bed of solid adsorbent particles makes possible useful application of semicontinuous methods which are not at all practicable when two fluids are contacted.

Another solid-liquid operation of great importance is ion exchange, the reversible exchange of ions between certain solids and an electrolyte solution, which permits the separation and fractionation of electrolytic solutes. It is, of course, chemical in nature but involves not only the interaction of the ions with the solid but also diffusion of ions within the solid phase. Although the phenomenon may be more complex than adsorption, the general techniques and the results obtained are very similar. The special features of ion exchange are considered separately at the end of this chapter.

Types of adsorption

We must distinguish at the start between two types of adsorption phenomena, physical and chemical.

Physical adsorption, or "van der Waals" adsorption, a readily reversible phenomenon, is the result of intermolecular forces of attraction between molecules of the solid and the substance adsorbed. When, for example, the intermolecular attractive forces between a solid and a gas are greater than those existing between molecules of the gas itself, the gas will condense upon the surface of the solid even though its pressure may be lower than the vapor pressure corresponding to the prevailing temperature. Such a condensation will be accompanied by an evolution of heat, in amount usually somewhat larger than the latent heat of vaporization and of the order of the heat of sublimation of the gas. The adsorbed substance does not penetrate within the crystal lattice of the solid and does not dissolve in it but remains entirely upon the surface. If, however, the solid is highly porous, containing many fine capillaries, the adsorbed substance will penetrate these interstices if it wets the solid. The equilibrium vapor pressure of a concave liquid surface of very small radius of curvature is lower than that of a large flat surface, and the extent of adsorption is correspondingly increased. In any case, at equilibrium the partial pressure of the adsorbed substance equals that of the contacting gas phase, and by lowering the pressure of the gas phase or by raising the temperature the adsorbed gas is readily removed or desorbed in unchanged form. Industrial adsorption operations of the type we shall consider depend upon this reversibility for recovery of the adsorbent for reuse, for recovery of the adsorbed substance, or for the fractionation of mixtures. Reversible adsorption is not confined to gases but is observed in the case of liquids as well.

Chemisorption, or activated adsorption, is the result of chemical interaction between the solid and the adsorbed substance. The strength of the chemical bond may vary considerably, and identifiable chemical compounds in the usual sense may not actually form, but the adhesive force is generally much greater than that found in physical adsorption. The heat liberated during chemisorption is usually large, of the order of the heat of chemical reaction. The process is frequently irreversible, and on desorption the original substance will often be found to have undergone a chemical change. The same substance which, under conditions of low temperature, will undergo substantially only physical adsorption upon a solid will sometimes exhibit chemisorption at higher temperatures, and both phenomena may occur at the same time. Chemisorption is of particular importance in catalysis but will not be considered here.

Nature of adsorbents

Adsorbent solids are usually used in granular form, varying in size from roughly $\frac{1}{2}$ in. in diameter to as small as 50 μ. The solids must possess certain engineering properties depending upon the application to which they are put If they are used in a fixed bed through which a liquid or gas is to flow, for example, they must not offer too great a pressure drop for flow nor must they easily be carried away by the flowing stream. They must have adequate strength and hardness so as not to be reduced in size during handling or crushed in supporting their own weight in beds of the required thickness. If they are to be transported frequently in and out of bins, they should be free-flowing. These are properties which are readily recognized.

The adsorptive ability of solids is quite another matter. Adsorption is a very general phenomenon, and even common solids will adsorb gases and vapors at least to a certain extent. For example, every student of analytical chemistry has observed with annoyance the increase in weight of a dried porcelain crucible on a humid day during an analytical weighing, owing to the adsorption of moisture from the air upon the crucible surface. But only certain solids exhibit sufficient specificity and adsorptive capacity to make them useful as industrial adsorbents. Since solids are frequently very specific in their ability to adsorb certain substances in large amounts, the chemical nature of the solid evidently has much to do with its adsorption characteristics. But mere chemical identity is insufficient to characterize its usefulness. In liquid extraction, all samples of pure butyl acetate will extract acetic acid from a water solution with identical ability. The same is not true for the adsorption characteristics of silica gel with respect to water vapor, for example. Much depends on its method of manufacture and on its prior history of adsorption and desorption.

Large surface per unit weight seems essential to all useful adsorbents. Particularly in the case of gas adsorption, the significant surface is not the gross surface of the granular particles which are ordinarily used but rather the very much larger surface of the internal pores of the particles. The pores are usually very small, sometimes of the order of a few molecular diameters in width, but their large number provides an enormous surface for adsorption. It is estimated, for example, that a typical gasmask charcoal has an effective surface of 1,000,000 sq m/kg.[33] There are many other properties evidently of great importance which are not at all understood, and we must depend largely on empirical observation for recognition of adsorptive ability. The following is a list of the principal adsorbents in general use. For a complete description the student is referred to a more extensive treatment of the subject.[21,33]

1. *Fuller's earths.* These are natural clays, the American varieties coming largely from Florida and Georgia. They are chiefly magnesium aluminum silicates in the form of the minerals attapulgite and montmorillonite. The clay is heated and dried, during which operation it develops a porous structure, ground, and screened. Commercially available sizes range from coarse granules to fine powders. The clays are particularly useful in decolorizing, neutralizing, and drying such petroleum products as lubricating oils, transformer oils, kerosenes, and gasolines, as well as vegetable and animal oils. By washing and burning the adsorbed organic matter accumulating upon the clay during use, the adsorbent may be reused many times.

2. *Activated clays.* These are bentonite or other clays which show essentially no adsorptive ability unless activated by treatment with sulfuric or hydrochloric acid. Following such treatment, the clay is washed, dried, and ground to a fine powder. It is particularly useful for decolorizing petroleum products and is ordinarily discarded after a single application.

3. *Bauxite.* This is a certain form of naturally occurring hydrated alumina which must be activated by heating to temperatures varying from 450 to 1500°F in order to develop its adsorptive ability. It is used for decolorizing petroleum products and for drying of gases and may be reactivated by heating.

4. *Alumina.* This is a hard, hydrated aluminum oxide which is activated by heating to drive off the moisture. The porous product is available as granules or powders, and it is used chiefly as a desiccant for gases and liquids. It may be reactivated for reuse.

5. *Bone char.* This is obtained by the destructive distillation of crushed, dried bones at temperatures in the range 1100 to 1600°F. It is used chiefly in the refining of sugar and may be reused after washing and burning.

6. *Decolorizing carbons.* These are variously made by (*a*) mixing vegetable matter with inorganic substances such as calcium chloride, carbonizing, and leaching away the inorganic matter, (*b*) mixing organic matter such as sawdust, etc., with porous substances such as pumice stone, followed by heating and carbonizing to deposit the carbonaceous matter throughout the porous particles, and (*c*) carbonizing wood, sawdust, and the like, followed by activation with hot air or steam. They are used for a great variety of purposes, including the decolorizing of solutions of sugar, industrial chemicals, drugs, and dry-cleaning liquids, water purification, and refining of vegetable and animal oils.·

7. *Gas-adsorbent carbon.* This is made by carbonization of coconut shells, fruit pits, coal, and wood. It must be activated, essentially a partial oxidation process, by treatment with hot air or steam. It is available in granular or pelleted form and is used for recovery of solvent vapors from gas mixtures, in gas masks, and for the fractionation of hydrocarbon gases. It is revivified for reuse by evaporation of the adsorbed gas.

8. *Silica gel.* This is a hard, granular, very porous product made from the gel precipitated by acid treatment of sodium silicate solution. Its moisture content prior to use varies from roughly 4 to 7 percent, and it is used principally for dehydration of air and other gases, in gas masks, and for fractionation of hydrocarbons. It is revivified for reuse by evaporation of the adsorbed matter.

9. *Molecular sieves.* These are porous, synthetic zeolite crystals, metal aluminosilicates. The "cages" of the crystal cells can entrap adsorbed matter, and the diameter of the passageways, controlled by the crystal composition, regulates the size of the molecules which may enter or be excluded. The sieves can thus separate according to molecular size, but they also separate by adsorption according to molecular polarity and degree of unsaturation. They are used for dehydration of gases and liquids, separation of gas and liquid hydrocarbon mixtures, and in a great variety of processes. They are regenerated by heating or elution.

ADSORPTION EQUILIBRIA

The great bulk of the experimental data pertaining to adsorption represents equilibrium measurements. Many of them were gathered in an attempt to provide corroboration for one or another of the many theories which have been advanced in an

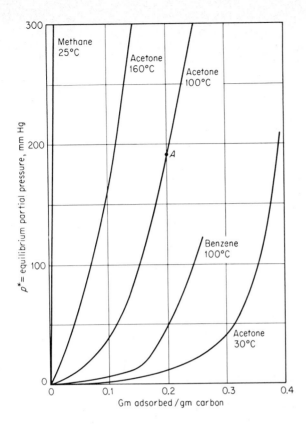

Fig. 11.1 *Equilibrium adsorption on an activated carbon.*

attempt to explain the adsorption phenomena. No one theory has yet been devised which satisfactorily explains even a majority of the observations, and this discussion is therefore limited simply to a description of the more commonly observed adsorption characteristics. The theories are reviewed elsewhere.[5,6,43]

SINGLE GASES AND VAPORS

In many respects the equilibrium adsorption characteristics of a gas or vapor upon a solid resemble the equilibrium solubility of a gas in a liquid. Figure 11.1 shows several equilibrium adsorption isotherms for a particular activated carbon as adsorbent, where the concentration of adsorbed gas (the adsorbate) on the solid is plotted against the equilibrium partial pressure p^* of the vapor or gas at constant temperature. Curves of this sort are analogous to those of Fig. 8.1. At 100°C, for example, pure acetone vapor at a pressure of 190 mm Hg is in equilibrium with an adsorbate concentration of 0.2 g adsorbed acetone/g carbon, point A. Increasing the pressure of the acetone will cause more to be adsorbed, as the rising curve indicates, and decreasing the pressure of the system at A will cause acetone to be desorbed from the carbon.

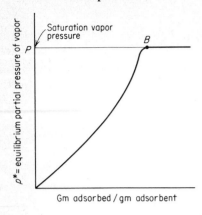

Gm adsorbed / gm adsorbent   **Fig. 11.2** *Typical complete-adsorption isotherm.*

While not determined experimentally in this case, it is known that the 100°C isotherm for acetone will continue to rise only to a pressure of 2,790 mm Hg, the saturation vapor pressure of acetone at this temperature. At higher pressures, no acetone can exist in the vapor state at this temperature but instead will condense entirely to a liquid. It will thus be possible to obtain indefinitely large concentrations of the substance on the solid at pressures higher than the vapor pressure, as at point *B* (Fig. 11.2). However, concentrations in excess of that corresponding to point *B* indicate liquefaction, but not necessarily adsorption of the vapor. Gases above their critical temperature, of course, do not show this characteristic.

Different gases and vapors are adsorbed to different extents under comparable conditions. Thus benzene (Fig. 11.1) is more readily adsorbed than acetone at the same temperature and gives a higher adsorbate concentration for a given equilibrium pressure. As a general rule, vapors and gases are more readily adsorbed the higher their molecular weight and the lower their critical temperature, although chemical differences such as the extent of unsaturation in the molecule also influence the extent of adsorption. The so-called permanent gases are usually adsorbed only to a relatively small extent, as the methane isotherm of Fig. 11.1 indicates.

Adsorption isotherms are not always concave to the pressure axis. The shapes shown in Fig. 11.3 have all been observed for various systems. Here the ordinate is plotted as equilibrium partial pressure p^* divided by the saturation vapor pressure P of the adsorbed substance (actually, the relative saturation) in order to place all the curves on a comparable basis.

It will be recalled that a change of liquid solvent alters profoundly the equilibrium solubility of a gas except in the case of ideal liquid solutions. In a similar fashion the equilibrium curves for acetone, benzene, and methane on silica gel as adsorbent would be entirely different from those of Fig. 11.1. Indeed, differences in the origin and method of preparation of an adsorbent will result in significant differences in the equilibrium adsorption as well. For this reason, many of the data gathered years ago are no longer of practical value, since methods of preparing adsorbents, and consequently the corresponding adsorbent capacities, have improved greatly over the

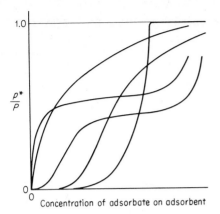

Fig. 11.3 *Types of adsorption isotherms for vapors.*

years. Repeated adsorption and desorption will also frequently alter the characteristics of a particular adsorbent, owing perhaps to progressive changes in the pore structure within the solid.

Adsorption hysteresis

The curves of Fig. 11.1 are true equilibrium curves and therefore represent completely reversible phenomena. The conditions corresponding to point A on the figure, for example, can be obtained either by adsorption onto fresh carbon or by desorption of a sample with an initially higher adsorbate concentration. Occasionally, however, different equilibria result, at least over a part of an isotherm, depending upon whether the vapor is adsorbed or desorbed, and this gives rise to the hysteresis phenomenon indicated in Fig. 11.4. This may be the result of the shape of the openings to the capillaries and pores of the solid or of complex phenomena of wetting of the solid by the adsorbate. In any case, when hysteresis is observed, the desorption equilibrium pressure is always lower than that obtained by adsorption.

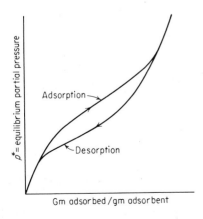

Fig. 11.4 *Adsorption isotherms showing hysteresis.*

Effect of temperature

Since adsorption is an exothermic process, the concentration of adsorbed gas decreases with increased temperature at a given equilibrium pressure, as the several acetone isotherms of Fig. 11.1 indicate.

The reference-substance method of plotting, described in Chap. 8 for gas-liquid solubilities, is conveniently applicable also to adsorption data.[36]   As reference substance it is best to use the pure substance being adsorbed, unless the temperatures are above the critical temperature.   Figure 11.5, for example, was prepared for the adsorption of acetone vapor on activated carbon with acetone as reference substance. The abscissa of the logarithmic coordinates was marked with the vapor pressure of pure acetone, and the corresponding saturation temperatures were also marked.   The equilibrium partial pressure of adsorbate was plotted on the ordinate.   Points of equal temperature for the vapor pressure of pure acetone and the partial pressure of adsorbate were then plotted.   Thus, point A of Fig. 11.1 ($p^* = 190$ mm Hg, 100°C) was plotted on Fig. 11.5 at A, where $P = 2,790$ mm Hg, the vapor pressure of acetone at 100°C. Points of constant adsorbate concentration (isosteres) form straight lines with few exceptions, and thus only two points are required to establish each.

Figure 11.6 shows all the same data plotted in such a manner as to reduce all the measurements to a single curve, thereby permitting considerable extension of meager

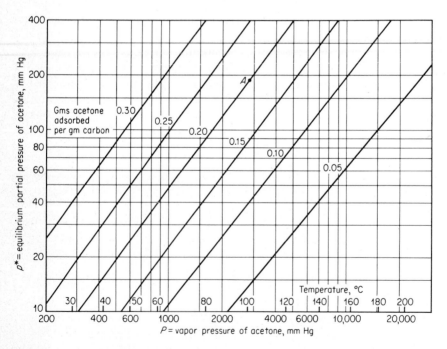

Fig. 11.5 *Reference-substance plot of equilibrium adsorption of acetone on an activated carbon.* [*Data of Josefewitz and Othmer: Ind. Eng. Chem.,* **40,** 739 (1948).]

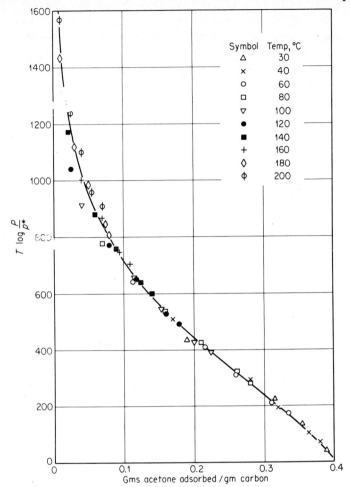

Fig. 11.6 *Adsorption of acetone on an activated carbon, 30 to 200°C.*

data.   The free energy of compression of 1 mole of a gas from the equilibrium adsorption pressure p^* to the vapor pressure P, the "adsorption potential," is $RT \ln (P/p^*)$. In the case of single substances, when this quantity is plotted against adsorbate concentration, a single curve results for all temperatures, at least over a moderate temperature range.[14]   The ordinate of Fig. 11.6 is proportional to this quantity.   More complex methods of expressing the adsorbate concentration may be used to provide improved and extended correlations of the data.

Heat of adsorption

The *differential heat of adsorption* $(-\bar{H})$ is defined as the heat liberated at constant temperature when unit quantity of vapor is adsorbed upon a large quantity of solid already containing adsorbate.   Such a large quantity of solid is used that the adsorbate concentration is unchanged.   The *integral heat of adsorption* at any concentration X

of adsorbate upon the solid is defined as the enthalpy of the adsorbate-adsorbent combination minus the sum of the enthalpies of unit weight of pure solid adsorbent and sufficient pure adsorbed substance (before adsorption) to provide the required concentration X, all at the same temperature. These are both functions of temperature and adsorbate concentration for any system.

Othmer and Sawyer[36] have shown that plots of the type shown in Fig. 11.5 are useful in estimating the heat of adsorption, which may be calculated in a manner similar to that for the latent heat of vaporization of a pure liquid (see Chap. 7). Thus, the slope of an isostere of Fig. 11.5 is

$$\frac{d \ln p^*}{d \ln P} = \frac{(-\bar{H})M}{\lambda_r M_r} \tag{11.1}$$

where $\bar{H}$, Btu/lb of vapor adsorbed, is referred to the pure vapor and λ_r is the latent heat of vaporization of the reference substance at the same temperature, Btu/lb. M and M_r are the molecular weights of the vapor and reference substance, respectively. If $\bar{H}$ is computed at constant temperature for each isostere, then the integral heat of adsorption at this temperature may be computed from the relation

$$\Delta H'_A = \int_0^X \bar{H} \, dX \tag{11.2}$$

$\Delta H'_A$, Btu/lb of adsorbate-free solid, is referred to the pure vapor, and X is the adsorbate concentration, lb adsorbate/lb solid. The integral may be evaluated graphically by determining the area under a curve of $\bar{H}$ against X. The integral heat of adsorption referred to solid and the adsorbed substance in the liquid state is $\Delta H_A = \Delta H'_A + \lambda X$, Btu/lb solid. The quantities $\bar{H}$, ΔH_A, and $\Delta H'_A$ are negative quantities if heat is evolved during adsorption.

Illustration 11.1. Estimate the integral heat of adsorption of acetone upon activated carbon at 30°C as a function of adsorbate concentration.

Solution. Refer to Fig. 11.5. The isosteres for various concentrations are straight on this diagram, and their slopes are measured with the help of a millimeter rule. In the accompanying table, column 1 lists the adsorbate concentrate of each isostere and column 2 the corresponding slope.

X, $\dfrac{\text{lb acetone}}{\text{lb carbon}}$	Slope of isostere	Differential heat of adsorption, $\bar{H}$, Btu/lb acetone	Integral heat of adsorption, Btu/lb carbon	
			$\Delta H'_A$, referred to acetone vapor	ΔH_A, referred to acetone liquid
(1)	(2)	(3)	(4)	(5)
0.05	1.170	−275	−12.8	−0.9
0.10	1.245	−295	−27.1	−3.4
0.15	1.300	−308	−42.1	−6.5
0.20	1.310	−310	−57.6	−10.2
0.25	1.340	−318	−73.3	−14.0
0.30	1.327	−314	−89.1	−18.0

Since in this case the adsorbate and reference substance are the same, $M = M_r$ and consequently $\bar{H} = -\lambda_r$ (slope of isostere). At 30°C, $\lambda_r = \lambda$, the latent heat of vaporization of acetone $= 237$ Btu/lb. Column 3 of the table lists values of $\bar{H}$ calculated in this manner.

Column 3 was plotted as ordinate against column 1 as abscissa (not shown). The area under the curve between $X = 0$ and any value of X is listed in column 4 as the corresponding integral heat of adsorption, referred to acetone vapor. Thus the area under the curve between $X = 0$ and $X = 0.20 = -57.6$. If 0.20 lb acetone vapor at 30°C is adsorbed on 1 lb fresh carbon at 30°C and the product brought to 30°C, 57.6 Btu will be evolved.

Column 5, the integral heat of adsorption referred to liquid acetone, is computed from the relation $\Delta H_A = \Delta H_A' + \lambda X$. Thus, at $X = 0.20$, $\Delta H_A = -57.6 + 237(0.20) = -10.2$ Btu/lb carbon.

VAPOR AND GAS MIXTURES

It is necessary to distinguish between mixtures depending upon whether one or several of the components are adsorbed.

One component adsorbed

In the case of many mixtures, particularly vapor-gas mixtures, only one component is appreciably adsorbed. This would be the circumstance for a mixture of acetone vapor and methane in contact with activated carbon (Fig. 11.1), for example. In such instances, the adsorption of the vapor will be substantially unaffected by the presence of the poorly adsorbed gas, and the adsorption isotherm for the pure vapor will be applicable provided the equilibrium pressure is taken as the *partial* pressure of the vapor in the vapor-gas mixture. The isotherms for acetone (Fig. 11.1) thus apply for mixtures of acetone with any poorly adsorbed gas such as nitrogen, hydrogen, and the like. This is similar to the corresponding case of gas-liquid solubility.

Binary gas or vapor mixtures, both components appreciably adsorbed

When both components of a binary gas or vapor mixture are separately adsorbed to roughly the same extent, the amount of either one adsorbed from the mixture will be affected by the presence of the other. Since such systems are composed of three components when the adsorbent is included, the equilibrium data are conveniently shown in the manner used for ternary liquid equilibria in Chap. 10. For this purpose it is convenient to consider the solid adsorbent as being analogous to liquid solvent in extraction operations. However, adsorption is greatly influenced by both temperature and pressure, unlike liquid solubility, which is scarcely affected by pressure under ordinary circumstances. Equilibrium diagrams are consequently best plotted at constant temperature and constant total pressure, and they are therefore simultaneously *isotherms* and *isobars*.

A typical system is shown in Fig. 11.7 on triangular and rectangular coordinates. The properties of these coordinate systems and the relations between them were considered in detail in Chap. 10. Even though mole fraction is generally a more convenient concentration unit in dealing with gases, the figure is plotted in terms of weight-fraction compositions since the molecular weight of the adsorbent is uncertain.†

---

† Alternatively, some arbitrary molecular weight could be assigned to the adsorbent.

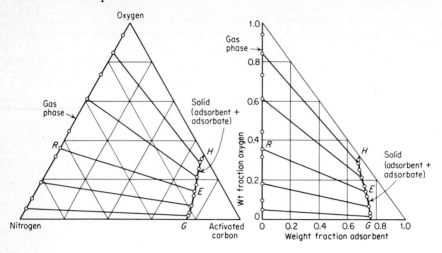

Fig. 11.7 *System oxygen–nitrogen–activated carbon, −150°C, 1 atm, concentrations expressed as weight fractions. [Data of Maslan, Altman, and Aberth: J. Phys. Chem., 57, 106 (1953).]*

Since the adsorbent is not volatile and does not appear in the gas phase, the equilibrium gas compositions fall upon one axis of either graph, as shown.   Points *G* and *H* represent the adsorbate concentration for the individual pure gases and the curve *GEH* that of gas mixtures.   Tie lines such as line *RE* join equilibrium compositions of the gas and adsorbate.   The fact that the tie lines do not, when extended, pass through the adsorbent apex indicates that under the prevailing conditions the adsorbent can be used to separate the binary gas mixture into its components.   The separation factor, or *relative adsorptivity,* similar to relative volatility in distillation or selectivity in liquid extraction, is obtained by dividing the equilibrium ratio of gas compositions in the adsorbate (as at point *E*) by the ratio in the gas (as at *R*).   The relative adsorptivity must be larger than unity if the adsorbent is to be useful for separating the components of the gas mixture.   In the system of Fig. 11.7 the more strongly adsorbed of the two pure gases (oxygen) is also selectively adsorbed from any mixture. This appears to be true for most mixtures, although an inversion of the relative adsorptivity in some systems (analogous to azeotropism in distillation) is certainly a possibility.

Especially when the extent of adsorption is small, it will be more convenient to express compositions on an adsorbent-free basis and to plot them in the manner of Fig. 11.8.   Such diagrams are also analogous to those used in liquid extraction (Fig. 10.30, for example), where adsorbent solid and extraction solvent play an analogous role, and to the enthalpy-concentration diagrams of distillation, where heat is analogous to adsorbent.   The adsorption characteristics of the binary gas mixture acetylene-ethylene on silica gel for one temperature and pressure are shown in Fig. 11.8a.   In the upper portion of this figure, the gas phase appears entirely along the abscissa of the plot owing to the absence of adsorbent in the gas.   The adsorbent-free equilibrium compositions corresponding to the tie lines may be plotted in the lower half of the diagram, as at point (R,E), to produce a figure analogous to the xy diagram of distillation. Silica gel selectively adsorbs acetylene from these gas mixtures.

The powerful influence of the adsorbent on the equilibrium is demonstrated with the same gas mixture by Fig. 11.8*b*, where activated carbon is the adsorbent. Not only is the extent of adsorption greater than for silica gel so that the curve GH is lower than the corresponding curve for silica gel, but in addition the relative adsorptivity is reversed: ethylene is selectively adsorbed on activated carbon. In both cases, however, that gas which is separately more strongly adsorbed on each adsorbent is selectively adsorbed from mixtures. If a condition corresponding to azeotropism should arise, the curve of the lower half of these figures would cross the 45° diagonal line. In cases such as Fig. 11.8*b*, it will generally be preferable to plot compositions

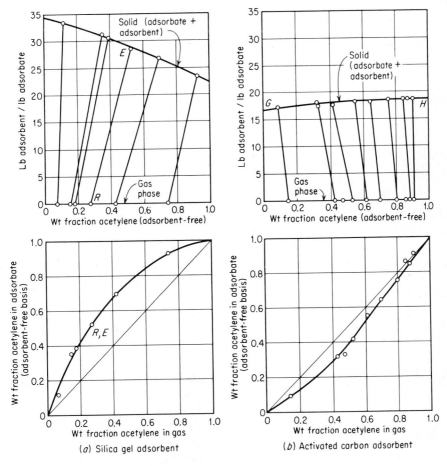

Fig. 11.8 *Adsorption of acetylene-ethylene on (a) silica gel and (b) activated carbon, at 25°C, 1 atm. [Data of Lewis et al.: J. Am. Chem. Soc., **72**, 1157 (1950).]*

in terms of the more strongly adsorbed gas (ethylene), to keep the appearance of the diagram similar to those used previously in liquid extraction.

Effect of change of pressure or temperature

The available data are meager, and generalizations are very difficult to make. Lowering the pressure will of course reduce the amount of adsorbate upon the adsorbent, as shown in the upper half of Fig. 11.9.   In those cases investigated over

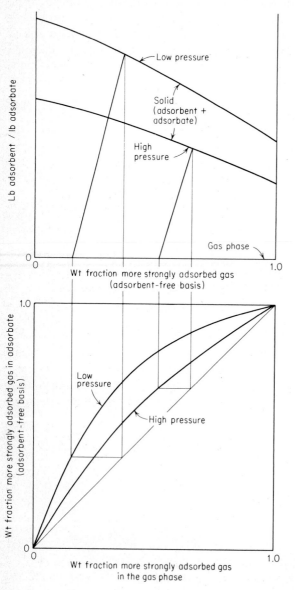

Fig. 11.9 *Effect of pressure on adsorption isotherms for binary gas mixtures.*

any appreciable pressure range[12,30] the relative adsorptivity of paraffin hydrocarbons on carbon decreased at increased pressure, as shown in the lower part of this figure, just as it does in the case of distillation.   Owing to the increased tendency toward liquid condensation in the absorbent capillaries at higher pressures, the equilibrium may simply be shifting toward the ordinary vapor-liquid equilibrium with increased pressure, and in each of the investigated cases this corresponded to lower separation factor.   Increasing the temperature at constant pressure will decrease the amount adsorbed from a mixture and will influence the relative adsorptivity as well, but in a manner for which no generalizations can now be made.   A beginning has been made on the estimation of the adsorption of mixed vapors whose liquid solutions are not ideal.[20]

LIQUIDS

When an adsorbent solid is immersed in a pure liquid, the evolution of heat, known as the heat of wetting, is evidence that adsorption of the liquid does occur.   But immersion does not provide an effective method of measuring the extent of adsorption. No appreciable volume change of the liquid which might be used as a measure of adsorption is ordinarily observed, while withdrawal of the solid and weighing it will not distinguish between the adsorbed liquid and that which is mechanically occluded. This problem does not exist in the case of adsorption of gases, where the change in weight of the solid owing to adsorption is readily measured.

Adsorption of solute from dilute solution

When an adsorbent is mixed with a binary solution, adsorption of both solute and solvent occurs.   Since the total adsorption cannot be measured, the relative or apparent adsorption of solute is determined instead.   The customary procedure is to treat a known volume of solution with a known weight of adsorbent, V cu ft solution/lb adsorbent.   As a result of preferential adsorption of solute, the solute concentration of the liquid is observed to fall from the initial value c_0 to the final equilibrium value $c*$ lb solute/cu ft liquid.   The apparent adsorption of solute, neglecting any volume change in the solution, is then $V(c_0 - c*)$ lb solute adsorbed/lb adsorbent.   This is satisfactory for dilute solutions when the fraction of the original solvent which may be adsorbed is small.

Correction is sometimes made for the volume of the solute apparently adsorbed.   Thus, the initial solvent content of this solution is $V(1 - c_0/\rho)$, and on the assumption that no solvent is adsorbed, the volume of residual solution is $V(1 - c_0/\rho)/(1 - c*/\rho)$.   The apparent solute adsorption is then the difference between initial and final solute content of the liquid, $Vc_0 - [V(1 - c_0/\rho)/(1 - c*/\rho)]c*$ or $V(c_0 - c*)/(1 - c*/\rho)$.   This, of course, still neglects solvent adsorption.

The apparent adsorption of a given solute depends upon the concentration of solute, the temperature, the solvent, and the type of adsorbent.   Typical isotherms are shown in Fig. 11.10.   Isotherms of all the indicated forms have been observed, for example, when a given solute is adsorbed on the same adsorbent, but from different

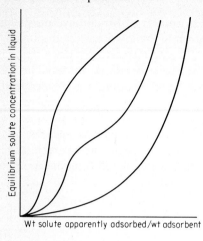

Fig. 11.10 *Typical adsorption isotherms for dilute solutions.*

solvents.   The extent of adsorption of a given solute practically always decreases at increased temperature and usually is greater the smaller the solubility in the solvent. It is usually reversible, so that the same isotherm results whether solute is desorbed or adsorbed.

The Freundlich equation

Over a small concentration range, and particularly for dilute solutions, the adsorption isotherms may frequently be described by an empirical expression usually attributed to Freundlich,

$$c^* = k[V(c_0 - c^*)]^n \tag{11.3}$$

where $V(c_0 - c^*)$ is the apparent adsorption per unit weight of adsorbent and k and n are constants.   Other concentration units are frequently used also, and while these

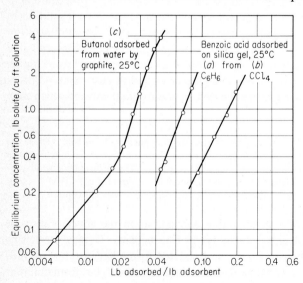

Fig. 11.11 *Adsorption from a dilute solution.*   [*Data of Bartell, et al.: J. Phys. Chem.*, **33**, 676 (1929); *J. Phys. Colloid. Chem.*, **55**, 1456 (1951).*]

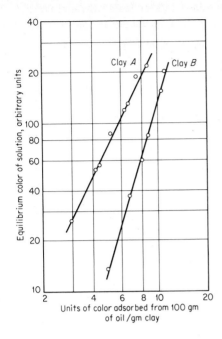

Fig. 11.12 *Decolorization of cylinder oil with clay.* [*Data of Rogers, et al.: Ind. Eng. Chem.,* **18**, 164 (1926).]

will result in different values of k, for the dilute solutions for which the equation is applicable the value of n will be unaffected. The form of the equation indicates that plotting the equilibrium solute concentration as ordinate against adsorbate content of the solid as abscissa on logarithmic coordinates will provide a straight line of slope n and intercept k. Several typical isotherms are plotted in this manner in Fig. 11.11. The effect of the nature of the solvent on adsorption of benzoic acid on silica gel is shown by curves a and b, which follow Eq. (11.3) excellently over the concentration range shown. The adsorption is less strong from benzene solutions, which is to be expected in view of the higher solubility of the acid in this solvent. Curve c of this figure shows the deviation from linearity to be expected over large concentration ranges, although Eq. (11.3) is applicable for the lower concentration ranges. Failure of the data to follow the equation at high solute concentrations may be the result of appreciable adsorption of the solvent which is not taken into account or simply general inapplicability of the expression.

The Freundlich equation is also frequently useful in cases where the actual identity of the solute is not known, as in the adsorption of colored substances from such materials as sugar solutions and mineral or vegetable oils. In such cases, the concentration of solute may be measured by means of a colorimeter or spectrophotometer and expressed in terms of arbitrary units of color intensity, provided that the color scale used varies linearly with the concentration of the responsible solute. Figure 11.12 illustrates the application of this method of plotting the adsorption of colored substances from a petroleum fraction on two adsorbent clays. Here the color concentrations of the solutions are measured on an arbitrary scale, and the concentration of adsorbate on the clay determined by measuring the change in color expressed in these terms when 100 g of oil is treated with various amounts of clay.

Adsorption from concentrated solutions

When the apparent adsorption of solute is determined over the entire range of concentrations from pure solvent to pure solute, curves such as those of Fig. 11.13 will result. Curves of the shape marked *a* occur when at all concentrations the solute is adsorbed more strongly relative to the solvent. At increasing solute concentrations, the extent of solute adsorption may actually continue to increase; yet the curve showing apparent solute adsorption necessarily returns to point *E*, since in a liquid consisting of pure solute alone there will be no concentration change on addition of adsorbent. In cases where both solvent and solute are adsorbed to nearly the same extent, the S-shaped curves of type *b* are produced. In the range of concentrations from *C* to *D*, solute is more strongly adsorbed than solvent. At point *D*, both are equally well adsorbed, and the apparent adsorption falls to zero. In the range of concentrations from *D* to *E*, solvent is more strongly adsorbed. Consequently, on addition of adsorbent to such solutions, the solute concentration of the liquid increases, and the quantity $V(c_0 - c^*)$ indicates an apparent *negative* solute adsorption.

The true adsorption of the substances may be estimated from apparent adsorption data if some mechanism for the process, such as the applicability of the Freundlich isotherm, separately for each component, is assumed.[3] In this manner, curves such as those of Fig. 11.14 can be computed from the S-shaped apparent adsorption data (note that such data characteristically show a situation analogous to azeotropism in distillation, with relative adsorptivity equal to unity at some liquid concentration). It has been shown, however, that such isotherms are not always applicable, and another approach is to determine the adsorption of a liquid solution by measuring that of the vapor in equilibrium with the liquid.[26,32]

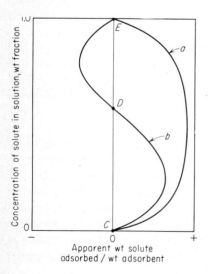

Fig. 11.13 *Apparent adsorption of solute from solutions.*

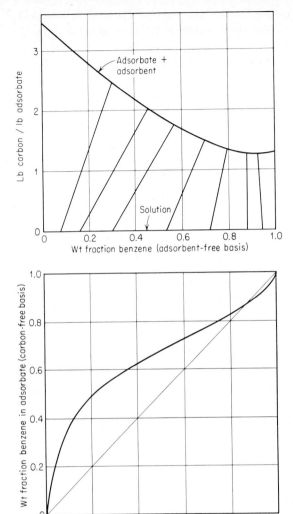

Fig. 11.14 *Calculated adsorption of benzene and ethanol by activated carbon* (*Bartell and Sloan.*[3])

ADSORPTION OPERATIONS

Adsorption is unique in the very diverse nature of its applications. For example, it is applied to such a wide variety of processes as recovery of vapors from dilute mixture with gases, solute recovery and removal of contaminants from solution, and the fractionation of gas and liquid mixtures. The techniques used include both stagewise and continuous-contacting methods, and these are applied to batch, continuous, and semicontinuous operations. Within each of these categories it is possible to recognize operations which are exactly analogous to those already discussed in previous chapters of this book. Thus, when only one component of a fluid mixture (either a gas or a liquid) is strongly adsorbed, the separation of the mixture is analogous for purposes of calculation to gas absorption, where the added insoluble phase is adsorbent in the present case and liquid solvent in the case of absorption. When both components of the fluid (either gas or liquid) are adsorbed strongly, the separation requires a fractionation procedure. The operation is then conveniently considered as being analogous to liquid extraction, where the added insoluble adsorbent corresponds to the use of solvent in extraction. By this means many simplifications in the treatment become possible.

I. STAGEWISE OPERATION

Liquid solutions, where the solute to be removed is adsorbed relatively strongly compared with the remainder of the solution, are treated in batch, semicontinuous, or continuous operations in a manner analogous to the mixer-settler operations of liquid extraction (*contact filtration*). Continuous countercurrent cascades may be simulated or actually realized by use of such techniques as fluidized beds.

Gases are treated for solute removal or for fractionation, usually with fluidized-bed techniques.

Contact filtration of liquids

Typical process applications include:

1. The collection of valuable solutes from dilute solutions, as, for example, the adsorption onto carbon of iodine from brines, after liberation of the element from its salts by oxidation; and the collection of insulin from dilute solutions.

2. The removal of undesirable contaminants from a solution.

Owing to the extremely favorable equilibrium distribution of solute toward the adsorbent which is frequently possible, adsorption becomes a powerful tool for the latter purpose, and most industrial applications of stagewise techniques fall into this category. Adsorption of colored substances from aqueous sugar solutions onto carbon, in order to provide a pure product and to assist the crystallization, is a typical example. Similarly, carbon is sometimes used to adsorb odorous substances from potable water, and grease is adsorbed from dry-cleaning liquids. The colors of petroleum and vegetable oils are lightened by treatment with clay.

Equipment and methods. As pointed out in Chap. 1, each stage requires the intimate contact of two insoluble phases for a time sufficient for a reasonable approach to equilibrium, followed by physical separation of the phases. The equipment used in applying these principles to adsorption is varied, depending upon the process application. That shown in Fig. 11.15 is very typical of many installations operated in a batchwise fashion. The liquid to be processed and the adsorbent are intimately mixed in the treating tank at the desired temperature for the required period of time,

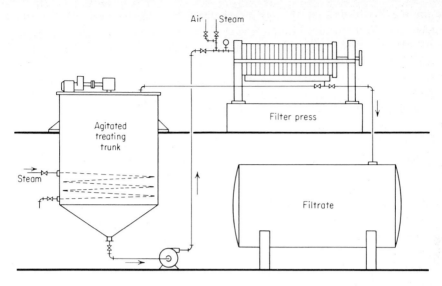

Fig. 11.15   *Contact filtration.   Schematic arrangement, for single-stage batch treatment of liquids.*

following which the thin slurry is filtered to separate the solid adsorbent and accompanying adsorbate from the liquid.   The equipment is readily adaptable to multistage operation by providing additional tanks and filters as necessary.   If the operation is to be made continuous, which is sometimes done in the decolorizing of petroleum lubricating oils, for example, centrifuges or a continuous rotary filter may be substituted for the filter press, or the solid may be allowed to settle out by virtue of its higher density when the mixture is passed through a large tank.

The type of adsorbent used depends upon the solution to be treated.   Aqueous solutions are frequently treated with activated carbon especially prepared for the purpose at hand, whereas organic liquids such as oils are usually treated with inorganic adsorbents such as clays.   Occasionally mixed adsorbents are used.   High selectivity for the solute to be removed is desirable in order to reduce the amount of solid to be added.   In any case, the adsorbent is applied in the form of a very finely ground powder, usually at least fine enough to pass entirely through a 200-mesh screen, and frequently very much finer.

The time required for the adsorbent and liquid to come to substantial equilibrium depends principally upon the concentration and particle size of the solid, the viscosity of the liquid, and the intensity of agitation.   Agitation should be vigorous in order to ensure rapid contact of the adsorbent particles with all the liquid, and the latter will be the more rapid the larger the solid concentration.   The flow regime should be turbulent so that adsorbent particles move relative to the bulk of the liquid, and this is promoted by the presence of baffles in the tank.   Rotational motion accompanied by swirl and vortexing merely carries the particles along with the liquid and does not decrease the required time. Moreover, the air introduced by the vortex frequently has a deleterious effect on the solution owing to the oxidation of sensitive organic substances. The residual concentration of unadsorbed solute still remaining in solution usually varies with time in the manner indicated in Fig. 11.16, falling rapidly at first and approaching the equilibrium value asymptotically. A practical time for agitation is chosen as at point A, where the additional adsorption to be obtained by further contact is insignificant, and this may be of the order of 10 to 30 min. Agitation should be continued during filtration in order to avoid segregation of the fine and coarser particles of the adsorbent.

The highest convenient temperature should be used during the mixing, since the resulting decreased liquid viscosity increases both the rate of diffusion of solute and the ease with which the adsorbent particles may move through the liquid. Usually the equilibrium adsorption is decreased to a small extent at higher temperatures, but this is more than compensated for by the increased rate of approach to equilibrium. Operations are sometimes conducted at the boiling point of the liquid if this temperature will cause no injury to the substances involved. In the clay treatment of petroleum-lubricant fractions the adsorbent-oil mixture may be pumped through a tubular furnace to be heated to as much as 250 to 300°F, and for very heavy oils even to 600 to 700°F. If the adsorbed substance is volatile, however, the equilibrium extent of adsorption will be much more strongly affected by temperature and such material is best handled at ordinary temperatures.

Owing to the large quantity of solution usually treated relative to the amount of adsorption occurring, the temperature rise resulting from release of the heat of adsorption may usually be ignored.

The method of dealing with the spent adsorbent depends upon the particular system under consideration. The filter cake is usually washed to displace the solution held within the pores of the cake, but relatively little adsorbate will be removed in this manner. If the adsorbate is the desired product, it may be desorbed by contact of the solid with a solvent other than that which comprises the original solution, one in which the adsorbate is more soluble. This may be done by washing the cake in the filter or by dispersing the solid into a quantity of the solvent. If the adsorbate is volatile, it may be desorbed by reduction of the partial pressure of the adsorbate over the solid by passage of steam or warm air through the solid. In the case of activated

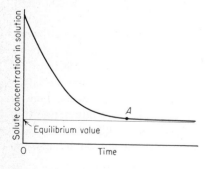

Fig. 11.16 *Approach to equilibrium, batch adsorption.*

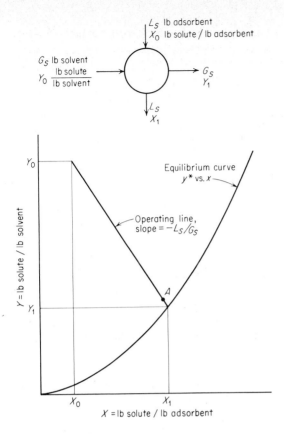

Fig. 11.17 *Single-stage adsorption.*

carbon adsorbents, care must be taken to avoid too high temperatures in using air for this purpose, in order to avoid combustion of the carbon. In the case of most decolorizing operations, the adsorbate is of no value and is difficultly desorbed. The adsorbent may then be revivified by burning off the adsorbate, followed by reactivation. Usually only a limited number of such revivifications is possible before the adsorbent ability is severely reduced, whereupon the solid is discarded.

Single-stage operation. The schematic flow sheet for this type of operation, when done in either batch or continuous fashion, is shown in the upper part of Fig. 11.17. Here the circle represents all the equipment and procedures constituting one stage. The operation is essentially analogous to a single-stage gas absorption, where the solution to be treated corresponds to a "gas" and the solid adsorbent to a "liquid." Since the amount of adsorbent used is ordinarily very small with respect to the amount of solution treated, and since the solute to be removed is adsorbed much more strongly than the other constituents present, the adsorption of the latter may be ignored. Furthermore the adsorbent is insoluble in the solution. Adopting a notation scheme similar to that used for gas absorption, the solution to be treated contains G_S lb unadsorbed substance or solvent, and the adsorbable solute concentration is reduced from Y_0 to Y_1 lb solute/lb solvent. The adsorbent is added to the extent of L_S lb adsorbate-free solid, and the solute adsorbate content increases from X_0 to X_1 lb solute/lb adsorbent. If fresh adsorbent is used, $X_0 = 0$, and in cases of continuous operation G_S and L_S are measured in terms of lb/hr.†

Equating the solute removed from the liquid to that picked up by the solid,

$$G_S(Y_0 - Y_1) = L_S(X_1 - X_0) \tag{11.4}$$

On X, Y coordinates this represents a straight operating line, through points of coordinates (X_0, Y_0) and (X_1, Y_1) of slope $-L_S/G_S$. If the stage is a theoretical or ideal stage, the effluent streams are in equilibrium, so that the point (X_1, Y_1) lies on the equilibrium adsorption isotherm. This is shown on the lower portion of Fig. 11.17. The equilibrium curve should be that obtaining at the final temperature of the operation. If insufficient time of contact is allowed, so that equilibrium is not reached, the final liquid and solid concentrations will correspond to some point such as A (Fig. 11.17), but ordinarily equilibrium is approached very closely.

The use of Eq. (11.4) assumes that the amount of liquid mechanically retained with the solid (but not adsorbed) after filtration or settling is negligible. This is quite satisfactory for most adsorption, since the quantity of solid employed is ordinarily very small with respect to that of the liquid treated. If the operation under consideration is *desorption*, and if again the quantity of liquid retained mechanically by the solid is negligible, Eq. (11.4) applies, but the operating line lies below the equilibrium curve on Fig. 11.17. In this case, however, it is much more likely that the quantity of liquid retained mechanically with the solid will be an appreciable portion of the total liquid used, and the methods of calculation described in Chap. 13 for leaching should be used.

Application of the Freundlich equation. The Freundlich equation can frequently be applied to adsorption of this type, particularly since small adsorbable solute concentrations are usually involved. This may be written in the following form for the concentration units used here,

$$Y^* = mX^n \tag{11.5}$$

and, at the final equilibrium conditions,

$$X_1 = \left(\frac{Y_1}{m}\right)^{1/n} \tag{11.6}$$

Since the adsorbent used ordinarily contains no initial adsorbate and $X_0 = 0$, substitution in Eq. (11.4) yields

$$\frac{L_S}{G_S} = \frac{Y_0 - Y_1}{(Y_1/m)^{1/n}} \tag{11.7}$$

† For the dilute solutions ordinarily used other consistent units may be applied to these terms. Thus, Y may be expressed as lb solute/lb solution (or lb solute/cu ft solution) and G_S as lb (or cu ft, respectively) of solution. When the adsorbed solute is colored matter whose concentration is measured in arbitrary units, the latter may be considered as Y units of color/lb or cu ft solution and the adsorbate concentration on the solid X as units of color/lb adsorbent.

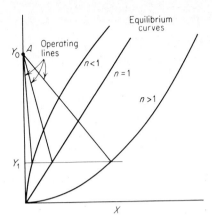

Fig. 11.18 *Single-stage adsorption, Freundlich equilibrium curves.*

This permits analytical calculation of the adsorbent/solution ratio for a given change in solution concentration, Y_0 to Y_1.

Refer to Fig. 11.18, where three typical Freundlich isotherms are shown. The isotherm is straight for $n = 1$, concave upward for $n > 1$, and concave downward for $n < 1$. If in each case the solution concentration is to be reduced from Y_0 to Y_1, the three operating lines radiating from point A apply. The slope of the operating line is in each case directly proportional to the adsorbent/solution ratio. It is generally stated[18] that values of n in the range 2 to 10 represent good, 1 to 2 moderately difficult, and less than 1 poor adsorption characteristics. In the case of the last, impractically large adsorbent dosages may be required for appreciable fractional removal of solute.

Multistage crosscurrent operation. The removal of a given amount of solute may be accomplished with greater economy of adsorbent if the solution is treated with separate small batches of adsorbent rather than in a single batch, with filtration between each stage. This method of operation is sometimes called "split-feed" treatment, and it is usually done in batch fashion, although continuous operation is also possible. Economy is particularly important when activated carbon, a fairly expensive adsorbent, is used. The savings are greater the larger the number of batches used but result at the expense of greater filtration and other handling costs. It is therefore rarely economical to use more than two stages. In rare instances, the adsorption may be irreversible, so that separate adsorbent dosages may be applied without intermediate filtration at considerable savings in operating costs.[17] This is by far the exception rather than the rule, and when applied to ordinary reversible adsorption, it will provide the same end result as if all the adsorbent had been used in a single stage.

A schematic flow sheet and operating diagram for a typical operation of two ideal stages are shown in Fig. 11.19. The same quantity of solution is treated in each stage by amounts of adsorbent L_{S1} and L_{S2} lb in the two stages, respectively, to reduce the solute concentration of the solution from Y_0 to Y_2. The material balances are, for stage 1,

$$G_S(Y_0 - Y_1) = L_{S1}(X_1 - X_0)$$ (11.8)

and for stage 2,

$$G_S(Y_1 - Y_2) = L_{S2}(X_2 - X_0)$$ (11.9)

These provide the operating lines shown on the figure, each of a slope appropriate to the adsorbent quantity used in the corresponding stage. The extension to large numbers of stages is obvious. If the amounts of adsorbent used in each stage are equal, the operating lines on the diagram will be parallel. The least total amount of adsorbent will require unequal dosages in each stage except for the case where the equilibrium isotherm is linear, and in the general case this can be established only by a trial-and-error computation.

Application of the Freundlich equation. When the Freundlich expression [Eq. (11.5)] describes the adsorption isotherm satisfactorily and fresh adsorbent is used in each stage ($X_0 = 0$), the least total amount of adsorbent for a two-stage system can

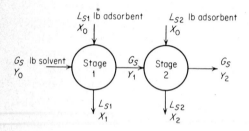

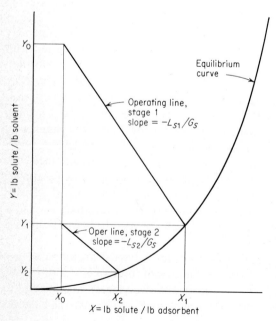

Fig. 11.19 *Two-stage crosscurrent adsorption.*

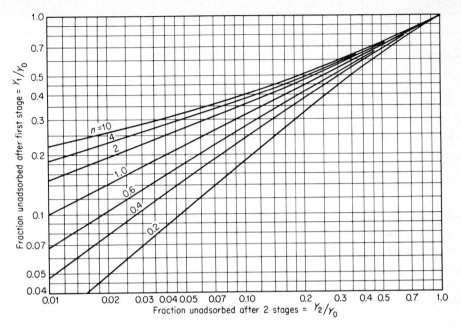

Fig. 11.20 *Solution to Eq.(11.13).   Minimum total adsorbent, two-stage crosscurrent operation.*

be computed directly.[17,42]   Thus, for stage 1,

$$\frac{L_{S1}}{G_S} = \frac{Y_0 - Y_1}{(Y_1/m)^{1/n}} \tag{11.10}$$

and, for stage 2,

$$\frac{L_{S2}}{G_S} = \frac{Y_1 - Y_2}{(Y_2/m)^{1/n}} \tag{11.11}$$

The total amount of adsorbent used is

$$\frac{L_{S1} + L_{S2}}{G_S} = m^{1/n} \left(\frac{Y_0 - Y_1}{Y_1^{1/n}} + \frac{Y_1 - Y_2}{Y_2^{1/n}} \right) \tag{11.12}$$

For minimum total adsorbent, $d[(L_1 + L_2)/G_S]/dY_1$ is set equal to zero, and since for a given case m, n, Y_0, and Y_2 are constants, this reduces to

$$\left(\frac{Y_1}{Y_2} \right)^{1/n} - \frac{1}{n}\frac{Y_0}{Y_1} = 1 - \frac{1}{n} \tag{11.13}$$

Equation (11.13) may be solved for the intermediate concentration Y_1, and the adsorbed quantities calculated by Eqs. (11.10) and (11.11).   Figure 11.20 permits solutions of Eq. (11.13) without trial and error.

Multistage countercurrent operation. Even greater economy of adsorbent can be obtained by countercurrent operation. When batch methods of treating are used, this can only be simulated, for which the general scheme of batch simulation of countercurrent operations shown in Fig. 10.58 for liquid extraction is actually followed. The flow sheet of Fig. 11.21 then becomes the ultimate, steady-state result reached only after a number of cycles. However, truly continuous operation has also been used, as in the simultaneous dissolution of gold and silver from finely ground ore by cyanide solution and adsorption of the dissolved metal upon granular activated carbon in a three-stage operation. Coarse screens between agitated vessels separate the large carbon particles from the pulped ore–liquid mixture.[8]

A solute balance about the N_p stages is

$$G_S(Y_0 - Y_{Np}) = L_S(X_1 - X_{Np+1}) \tag{11.14}$$

which provides the operating line on the figure, through the coordinates of the terminal conditions (X_{Np+1}, Y_{Np}) and (X_1, Y_0) and of slope L_S/G_S. The number of theoretical stages required is found by drawing the usual staircase construction between equilibrium curve and operating line in the manner shown. Alternatively

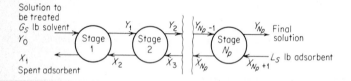

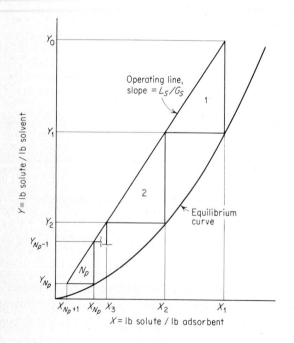

Fig. 11.21 *Countercurrent multistage adsorption.*

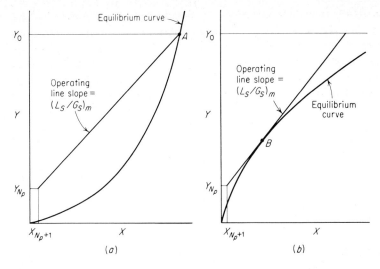

Fig. 11.22 *Operating lines and minimum adsorbent/solvent ratio for infinite stages.*

the adsorbent/solution ratio for a predetermined number of stages may be found by trial-and-error location of the operating line. If the operation is a *desorption* (corresponding to stripping in gas-liquid contact), the operating line falls below the equilibrium curve.

The minimum adsorbent/solvent ratio will be the largest which results in an infinite number of stages for the desired change of concentration. This corresponds to the operating line of largest slope which touches the equilibrium curve within the specified range of concentrations. For cases where the equilibrium isotherm is straight or concave upward, as in Fig. 11.22a, this will cause a *pinch* at the concentrated end of the cascade, as at point A. If the isotherm is concave downward (Fig. 11.22b), the pinch may occur at a point of tangency, as at point B, if Y_0 is sufficiently large. The situations are entirely analogous to those found in gas absorption (Fig. 8.7).

As the number of stages in a cascade is increased, the amount of adsorbent required at first decreases rapidly but approaches the minimum value only asymptotically. In practice, where intermediate filtration of solid from the liquid must be made between stages, it is rarely economical to use more than two stages in a countercurrent cascade.

In small-scale processing, there may be appreciable variation in the amounts of solution to be treated from one batch to the next. Furthermore, long periods of time may pass between batches, so that partially spent adsorbent must be stored between stages. Activated carbon particularly may deteriorate during storage through oxidation, polymerization of the adsorbate, or other chemical change, and in such cases the crosscurrent flow sheet may be more practical.

Application of the Freundlich equation. Trial-and-error calculation for the adsorbent/solvent ratio may be eliminated if the equilibrium curve may be conveniently described algebraically. If the equilibrium curve is linear, the Kremser equations (5.50) to (5.53) and Fig. 5.16 apply. More frequently the Freundlich expression (11.5) is useful, and fresh adsorbent ($X_{Np+1} = 0$) is used in the last stage.[37] For a typical two-stage cascade (Fig. 11.23) a solute material balance for the entire plant is

$$L_S(X_1 - 0) = G_S(Y_0 - Y_2) \tag{11.15}$$

Applying Eq. (11.5) to the effluents from the first ideal stage,

$$X_1 = \left(\frac{Y_1}{m}\right)^{1/n} \tag{11.16}$$

and combining these,

$$\frac{L_S}{G_S} = \frac{Y_0 - Y_2}{(Y_1/m)^{1/n}} \tag{11.17}$$

The operating line for the second ideal stage is shown on the figure and is given by

$$G_S(Y_1 - Y_2) = L_S X_2 = L_S \left(\frac{Y_2}{m}\right)^{1/n} \tag{11.18}$$

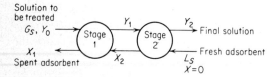

Solution to be treated G_S, Y_0 → Stage 1 → Y_1 → Stage 2 → Y_2 → Final solution

X_1 Spent adsorbent ← X_2 ← Fresh adsorbent L_S $X=0$

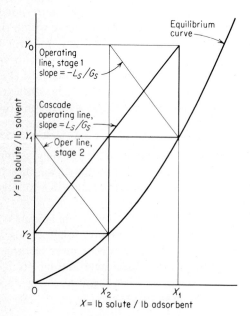

$Y = $ lb solute / lb solvent

Y_0

Operating line, stage 1 slope $= -L_S/G_S$

Cascade operating line, slope $= L_S/G_S$

Y_1

Oper line, stage 2

Y_2

Equilibrium curve

0 X_2 X_1

$X = $ lb solute / lb adsorbent

Fig. 11.23 *Two-stage countercurrent adsorption.*

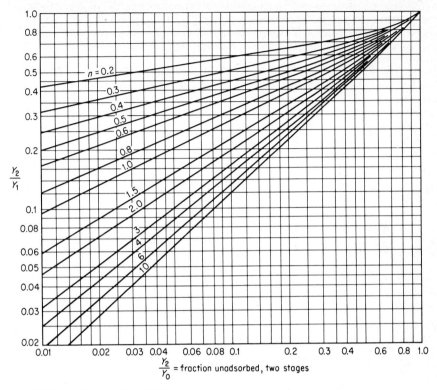

Fig. 11.24 *Solution to Eq. (11.19). Two-stage countercurrent adsorption.*

Eliminating L_S/G_S between Eqs. (11.17) and (11.18), there results

$$\frac{Y_0}{Y_2} - 1 = \left(\frac{Y_1}{Y_2}\right)^{1/n}\left(\frac{Y_1}{Y_2} - 1\right) \tag{11.19}$$

Equation (11.19) may be solved for the intermediate concentration Y_1 for specified terminal concentrations Y_0 and Y_2, and L_S/G_S is then given by Eq. (11.17). Figure 11.24 will assist in the solution of Eq. (11.19). The savings in adsorbent by countercurrent operation over single stage are greater, the greater the value of n.

Illustration 11.2. An aqueous solution containing a valuable solute is colored by small amounts of an impurity. Prior to crystallization, the impurity is to be removed by adsorption on a decolorizing carbon which adsorbs only insignificant amounts of the principal solute. A series of laboratory tests was made by stirring various amounts of the adsorbent into batches of the original solution until equilibrium was established, yielding the following data at constant temperature:

Lb carbon/lb soln	0	0.001	0.004	0.008	0.02	0.04
Equilibrium color	9.6	8.6	6.3	4.3	1.7	0.7

The color intensity was measured on an arbitrary scale, proportional to the concentration of the colored substance. It is desired to reduce the color to 10% of its original value, 9.6. Determine the quantity of fresh carbon required per 1,000 lb of solution (*a*) for a single-stage operation, (*b*) for a two-stage crosscurrent process using the minimum total amount of carbon, and (*c*) for a two-stage countercurrent operation.

Solution. The experimental data must first be converted to a suitable form for plotting the equilibrium isotherm. For this purpose, define Y as units of color per pound of solution and X as units of color adsorbed per pound of carbon. The solutions may be considered as dilute in color, so that operating lines will be straight on X, Y coordinates expressed in this manner. The calculations are made in the manner indicated below.

$\dfrac{\text{Lb carbon}}{\text{Lb soln}}$	$Y^* =$ equilibrium color, units/lb soln	$X =$ adsorbate concn, units/lb carbon
0	9.6	
0.001	8.6	$(9.6 - 8.6)/0.001 = 1{,}000$
0.004	6.3	$(9.6 - 6.3)/0.004 = 825$
0.008	4.3	663
0.02	1.7	395
0.04	0.7	223

The equilibrium data, when plotted on logarithmic coordinates, provide a straight line, so that the Freundlich equation applies (see Fig. 11.25). The slope of the line is $1.66 = n$, and, at $X = 663$, $Y^* = 4.3$. Therefore [Eq. (11.5)]

$$m = \frac{4.3}{663^{1.66}} = 8.91(10^{-5})$$

The Freundlich equation is therefore

$$Y^* = 8.91(10^{-5})X^{1.66}$$

The equilibrium data may also be plotted on arithmetic coordinates (Fig. 11.26).

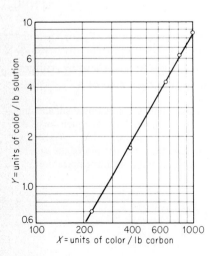

Fig. 11.25 *Equilibrium data, Illustration 11.2.*

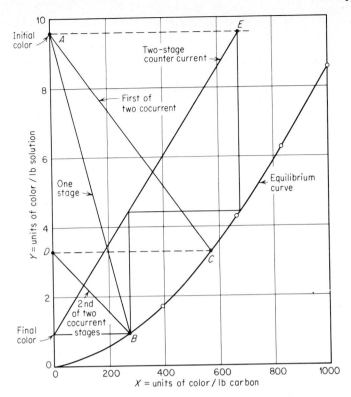

Y = units of color / lb solution

X = units of color / lb carbon

Fig. 11.26 *Solution to Illustration 11.2.*

a. Single-stage operation. $Y_0 = 9.6$ units of color/lb soln,

$$Y_1 = 0.10(9.6) = 0.96 \text{ unit/lb soln}$$

Let $G_s = 1,000$ lb soln. Since fresh carbon is to be used, $X_0 = 0$. On Fig. 11.26, point A representing the initial solution and fresh adsorbent is located, and point B is located on the equilibrium curve at the color concentration of the final solution. At B, $X_1 = 260$. Therefore [Eq. (11.4)]

$$\frac{L_s}{G_s} = \frac{Y_0 - Y_1}{X_1 - X_0} = \frac{9.6 - 0.96}{270 - 0} = 0.032 \text{ lb carbon/lb soln}$$

and

$$L_s = 0.032(1,000) = 32.0 \text{ lb carbon/1,000 lb soln}$$

Alternatively, since the Freundlich equation applies, use Eq. (11.7)

$$\frac{L_s}{G_s} = \frac{Y_0 - Y_1}{(Y_1/m)^{1/n}} = \frac{9.6 - 0.96}{[0.96/8.91(10^{-5})]^{1/1.66}} = 0.032 \text{ lb carbon/lb soln}$$

$$L_s = 0.032(1,000) = 32.0 \text{ lb carbon/1,000 lb soln}$$

b. Two-stage crosscurrent operation. The minimum total amount of carbon may be found on Fig. 11.26 by a trial-and-error procedure. Thus, point C on the equilibrium curve is assumed, the operating lines AC and DB drawn, and the values of L_{S1} and L_{S2} computed by Eqs. (11.8) and (11.9). The position of point C is changed until the sum of L_{S1} and L_{S2} is a minimum. The position of C in Fig. 11.26 is the final value, and its coordinates are ($X_1 = 565$, $Y_1 = 3.30$). $X_2 = 270$ (at B).

Eq. (11.8):
$$L_{S1} = \frac{G(Y_0 - Y_1)}{X_1 - X_0} = \frac{1,000(9.6 - 3.30)}{565 - 0} = 11.14 \text{ lb}$$

Eq. (11.9)
$$L_{S2} = \frac{G(Y_1 - Y_2)}{X_2 - X_0} = \frac{1,000(3.30 - 0.96)}{270 - 0} = 8.67 \text{ lb}$$

$$L_{S1} + L_{S2} = 11.14 + 8.67 = 19.81 \text{ lb carbon/1,000 lb soln}$$

Alternatively, since the Freundlich equation applies, use Fig. 11.20: $Y_2/Y_0 = 0.96/9.6 = 0.10$, $n = 1.66$. From the figure, $Y_1/Y_0 = 0.344$. $Y_1 = 0.344(9.6) = 3.30$.

Eq. (11.10):
$$\frac{L_{S1}}{G_S} = \frac{Y_0 - Y_1}{(Y_1/m)^{1/n}} = \frac{9.6 - 3.30}{[3.30/8.91(10^{-5})]^{1/1.66}}$$
$$= 0.01114 \text{ lb carbon/lb soln into 1st stage}$$

Eq. (11.11):
$$\frac{L_{S2}}{G_S} = \frac{Y_1 - Y_2}{(Y_2/m)^{1/n}} = \frac{3.30 - 0.96}{[0.96/8.91(10^{-5})]^{1/1.66}}$$
$$= 0.00867 \text{ lb carbon/lb soln into 2d stage}$$

Total carbon required $= (0.01114 + 0.00867)1,000 = 19.81 \text{ lb/1,000 lb soln}$

c. Two-stage countercurrent operation. $Y_0 = 9.6$, $Y_2 = 0.96$, $X_{Np+1} = 0$. The operating line is located by trial on Fig. 11.26 until two stages may be drawn between operating line and equilibrium curve, as shown. From the figure at E, $X_1 = 675$.

Eq. (11.14):
$$L_S = \frac{G_S(Y_0 - Y_2)}{X_1 - X_{Np+1}} = \frac{1,000(9.6 - 0.96)}{675 - 0}$$
$$= 12.80 \text{ lb carbon/1,000 lb soln}$$

Alternatively, $Y_2/Y_0 = 0.96/9.6 = 0.10$; $n = 1.66$. From Fig. 11.24, $Y_2/Y_1 = 0.217$, and $Y_1 = Y_2/0.217 = 0.96/0.217 = 4.42$.

Eq. (11.17):
$$\frac{L_S}{G_S} = \frac{Y_0 - Y_2}{(Y_1/m)^{1/n}} = \frac{9.6 - 0.96}{[4.42/8.91(10^{-5})]^{1/1.66}}$$
$$= 0.01280 \text{ lb carbon/lb soln}$$

and
$$L = 0.01280(1,000) = 12.80 \text{ lb carbon/1,000 lb soln}$$

Stage efficiency

The resistance to the attainment of equilibrium during batch operation will be the sum of at least the following resistances: (1) The resistance to mass transfer of the solute through the liquid surrounding each adsorbent particle. This may be minimized by maintaining a high degree of turbulence through intensive agitation. (2) The resistance to diffusion of the solute through the liquid in the pores of the solid, from the outside of the particles to the inner surface where adsorption will occur. The liquid in the pores will be stagnant, uninfluenced by the turbulence in the liquid surrounding the particles, and the solute transfer is by a process of molecular diffusion. The path of the diffusion is relatively long and tortuous, and the rate may be described by an effective diffusivity or a pore-shape factor, characteristic of such "structure-sensitive" diffusion (see Chap. 4). (3) The resistance to adsorption itself. This will exist if there is any finite time for the solute molecules to be adsorbed once they have arrived at the point on the surface where they are finally held. For example, it is conceivable that some orientation of the solute molecules with respect to the surface might be required before actual adsorption would occur. For a given system and type of adsorbent, neither the second nor third of these would be under the control of the operator of the process.

The fairly complex mathematical analysis of these resistances in the unsteady state characteristic of a batch operation has been summarized.[22,41] The internal diffusional resistance of the common adsorbents, i.e., other than certain ion-exchange resins, has not been established. It is known that ordinarily, under high agitation intensities, the mass-transfer resistance of the fluid surrounding the solid particles is negligible and the particle mass-transfer resistance controls.

Under industrial conditions it is usually possible to reach substantial equilibrium between adsorbent and solution within a reasonable time, and stage efficiencies are therefore essentially unity. For the present at least it will be best to establish the necessary time of contact for this experimentally, using actual samples of the adsorbent and solution to be treated, at the same adsorbent/solution ratio as it is planned to use ultimately. The tests could be made on a small scale provided that for both small-scale test and large-scale operation the intensity of agitation is sufficient substantially to eliminate the resistance of the liquid film surrounding the adsorbent particles. Otherwise large-scale tests would be required.

Fluidized and teeter beds

These have been used to a limited extent for recovery of vapors from vapor-gas mixtures,[2,10] for desorption (see drying, Chap. 12), for fractionation of light hydrocarbon vapors with carbon,[11] and a few others. In the case of liquid treating, there have been applications of ion exchange. Applications will unquestionably increase in number.

Consider a bed of granular solids up through which a gas flows, the gas being fairly uniformly distributed over the bottom cross section of the bed. At low gas rates, the gas suffers a pressure drop which may be estimated by Eq. (6.36). As the gas velocity is increased, the pressure drop eventually equals the sum of the weight of the solids per unit area of bed and the friction of the solids at the container walls. If the solids are free flowing, an increment in the gas velocity causes the bed to expand, and the gas pressure drop will equal the weight/area of the bed. Further increase in gas velocity causes further enlargement of the bed, and voidage increases sufficiently for the solid particles to move about locally. This is the condition of a "quiescent fluidized bed." Still further increase in gas velocity further expands the bed, the solid particles move about freely (indeed they are thoroughly circulated throughout the bed), and well-defined bubbles of gas may form and rise through the bed. The bed appears much like a boiling liquid, a distinct interface between the top of the solids and the escaping gas remains evident, and the gas pressure drop is not much different from that of the quiescent fluidized state. This is the condition used for adsorption. Further increase in gas velocity continues to expand the bed, and eventually the solids are carried away with the gas.

Squires[39] has distinguished between *fluidized* beds and *teeter* beds. Fluidized beds are produced by fine powders, usually smaller than 20 mesh and ranging down to 325 mesh, and will retain a great range of particle sizes within the bed, with little particle attrition. They usually operate with superficial gas velocities of the order of 2 ft/sec or less, which may be 10 times that for minimum fluidization. Teeter beds are produced with coarser particles, up to 10 mesh commonly. Gas velocities of from 5 to 10 ft/sec may be used, which may only be twice that for minimum fluidization. There is little gas bubbling, and the size range of particles retained is relatively small. In general, better fluid-solids contacting is obtained in teeter beds, and most adsorption applications are in this category. Solids may also be fluidized by liquids, and these will be ordinarily in the teeter-bed category.

Since the first introduction of these techniques for fluid-solid contact in 1948, with the principal application in the catalysis of gaseous chemical reactions, a very large technology for their design has developed. This is still not in a condition which permits summary for design purposes in the space available here, however, and the works of Leva[31] and Zenz[44,45] should be consulted for such details. The discussion here is limited to the computation of stage requirements and does not include the mechanical design.

Adsorption of a vapor from a gas. Figure 11.27 shows an arrangement typical of that required for adsorption of a vapor from a nonadsorbed gas, in this case drying of air with silica gel.[10] In the upper part of the tower, the gel is contacted countercurrently with the air to be dried on perforated trays in relatively shallow beds, the gel moving from tray to tray through downspouts. In the lower part of the tower, the gel is regenerated by similar contact with hot gas, which desorbs and carries off the moisture. The dried gel is then recirculated by air lift to the top of the tower. In cases where the adsorbed vapor is to be recovered, regeneration might include steam stripping of a carbon adsorbent with distillation or decantation of the condensed water–organic vapor mixture, followed by air drying of the adsorbent before reuse, and obvious changes in the flow sheet would be necessary.

If adsorption is isothermal, the calculations for ideal stages can be made in the same manner as for contact filtration of liquids [Fig. 11.21, Eq. (11.14)], and the same is true for desorption-regeneration. Ordinarily, however, the adsorber will operate adiabatically, and there may be a considerable rise in temperature owing to adsorption (or fall, in the case of desorption). Since the equilibrium then changes with stage number, the calculations are then done stage by stage, much in the manner of gas absorption. The same procedure will apply to any type of stage device and is not limited to fluidized beds. Thus, for the first n stages of the flow sheet of Fig. 11.21, a balance for adsorbable vapor is

$$G_S(Y_0 - Y_n) = L_S(X_1 - X_{n+1}) \tag{11.20}$$

and an enthalpy balance for adiabatic operation is

$$G_S(H_{G0} - H_{Gn}) = L_S(H_{L1} - H_{L,n+1}) \tag{11.21}$$

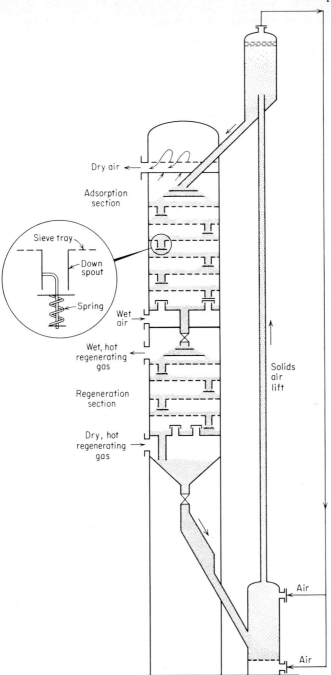

Fig. 11.27 *Fluidized bed, multistage countercurrent adsorber with regeneration. (After Ermenc.[10])*

where H_G = enthalpy of vapor-gas mixture, Btu/lb gas

H_L = enthalpy of solid plus adsorbate, Btu/lb adsorbent.

If enthalpies are referred to solid adsorbent, nonadsorbed gas (component C), and the adsorbate (component A) as a liquid, all at a base temperature t_o, then

$$H_G = C_C(t_G - t_o) + Y[C_A(t_G - t_o) + \lambda_{Ao}] \qquad (11.22)$$

where C_C = gas heat capacity, Btu/(lb)(°F)

C_A = vapor heat capacity, Btu/(lb)(°F)

λ_{Ao} = latent heat of vaporization of A at t_o, Btu/lb

$$H_L = C_B(t_L - t_o) + XC_{AL}(t_L - t_o) + \Delta H_A \qquad (11.23)$$

where C_B = heat capacity of adsorbent (component B), Btu/(lb)(°F)

C_{AL} = heat capacity of liquid A, Btu/(lb)(°F)

ΔH_A = integral heat of adsorption at X and t_o, Btu/lb adsorbent.

Gas and solid leaving an ideal stage are in thermal and concentration equilibrium. Some trial and error is required in the use of these equations with the equilibrium data, of a nature depending on the problem, as shown in Illustration 11.3.

Illustration 11.3. A mixture of nitrogen and acetone vapor, 5 mole % acetone, 1 atm, 30°C (86°F), is to be countercurrently contacted with gas-adsorbent carbon in a fluidized-bed tray tower to reduce the acetone content to 0.01 mole %. Revivified carbon will enter at 40°C (104°F), at the rate 1.5 lb carbon/lb nitrogen, acetone-free initially. Adsorption will be adiabatic, and pressure drop will be ignored. Compute the number of ideal stages required.

Solution. A base temperature $t_o = 86°F$ will be used. Heat capacities are C_A (acetone vapor) = 0.35, C_{AL} (acetone liquid) = 0.54, C_B (carbon) = 0.20, and C_C (nitrogen) = 0.26, all as Btu/(lb)(°F). $\lambda_{Ao} = 237$ Btu/lb. The adsorption equilibria of Fig. 11.5 and heats of adsorption of Illustration 11.1 will be used.

Basis: $G_S = 1$ lb nitrogen, $L_S = 1.5$ lb carbon. Mol wt acetone = 58.1, of nitrogen = 28.

$$Y_0 = \frac{0.05}{0.95}\left(\frac{58.1}{28}\right) = 0.1093 \text{ lb acetone/lb N}_2$$

$$Y_{Np} = \frac{0.0001}{0.9999}\left(\frac{58.1}{28}\right) = 0.000208 \text{ lb acetone/lb N}_2$$

$$X_{Np+1} = 0 \text{ lb acetone/lb carbon}$$

For the entire adsorber, Eq. (11.20) with $n = N_p$:

$$1(0.1093 - 0.000208) = 1.5(X_1 - 0)$$

$$X_1 = 0.0727 \text{ lb acetone/lb carbon}$$

From the data of Illustration 11.1, $\Delta H_A = -1.8$ Btu/lb carbon. Eq. (11.22) for the entering gas ($t_G = t_o = 86°F$): $H_{G0} = 0.1093(237) = 25.9$ Btu/lb N$_2$. Eq. (11.23) for the entering carbon ($t_{L,Np+1} = 104°F$): $H_{L,Np+1} = 0.20(104 - 86) = 3.6$ Btu/lb carbon.

Stage calculations will be made from the bottom upward. To begin, the temperature of the effluent solid is required. This will be obtained by an enthalpy balance about the entire adsorber but requires first an estimate of the effluent-gas temperature. After several trials, assume $t_{G,Np} = 127°F$ (to be checked later).

Eq. (11.22): $H_{G,Np} = 0.26(127 - 86) + 0.000208[0.35(127 - 86) + 237]$

$$= 10.75 \text{ Btu/lb } N_2$$

Eq. (11.21) with $n = N_p$: $1(25.9 - 10.75) = 1.5(H_{L1} - 3.6)$

$$H_{L1} = 14.20 \text{ Btu/lb carbon}$$

Eq. (11.23) for the solid effluent:

$$H_{L1} = 14.20 = 0.20(t_{L1} - 86) + 0.0727(0.54)(t_{L1} - 86) - 1.8$$

$$t_{L1} = 153°F$$

The gas leaving stage 1 is in equilibrium with solid at $X_1 = 0.0727$, $t_{L1} = 153°F$. From Fig. 11.5 (extrapolation and interpolation will be required, for which a cross plot, $\log p^*$ vs. $\log X$, is useful), the equilibrium partial pressure of acetone = 8.0 mm Hg.

$$Y_1 = \frac{8.0}{760 - 8} \frac{58.1}{28} = 0.0221 \text{ lb acetone/lb } N_2$$

Eq. (11.22): $H_{G1} = 0.26(153 - 86) + 0.0221[0.35(153 - 86) + 237]$

$$= 23.15 \text{ Btu/lb } N_2$$

Eq. (11.20) with $n = 1$: $1(0.1093 - 0.0221) = 1.5(0.0727 - X_2)$

$$X_2 = 0.0147 \text{ lb acetone/lb carbon}$$

From Illustration 11.1, $\Delta H_A = -0.12$ Btu/lb carbon.

Eq. (11.21) with $n = 1$: $1(25.9 - 23.15) = 1.5(14.20 - H_{L2})$

$$H_{L2} = 12.37 \text{ Btu/lb carbon}$$

Eq. (11.23): $12.37 = 0.20(t_{L2} - 86) + 0.0147(0.54)(t_{L2} - 86) - 0.12$

$$t_{L2} = 146°F$$

At $X_2 = 0.0147$, $t_2 = 146°F$, the equilibrium partial pressure of acetone = 0.6 mm Hg.

$$Y_2 = \frac{0.6}{760 - 0.6} \frac{58.1}{28} = 0.00164 \text{ lb acetone/lb } N_2$$

In similar fashion, $H_{G2} = 16.02$, $X_3 = 0.001$, $H_{L3} = 7.60$, $t_{L3} = 124°F = t_{G3}$, $Y_3 = 0.000021$, all in the same units as before.

The gas leaving tray 3 is at 124°F (acceptable check with assumed 127°F) and an unnecessarily low acetone concentration. About 2.5 ideal trays are required, and an exact integral number can be obtained with some slight change in the carbon/nitrogen ratio.

There are limited data on mass- and heat-transfer coefficients for fluidized beds[44,45] with which to estimate tray efficiencies after gas velocities and bed depths have been established.

Fractionation of a vapor mixture. For the separation of a vapor mixture consisting of, for example, two adsorbable components for which the adsorbent exhibits a relative adsorptivity, calculations are made in the manner for moving beds to locate operating lines and equilibrium curves [Eqs. (11.31) to (11.43) and Fig. 11.35].

Ideal stages may then be determined by the usual step construction on the lower part of such a figure.

II. CONTINUOUS CONTACT

In these operations the fluid and adsorbent are in contact throughout the entire apparatus, without periodic separation of the phases. The operation may be carried out in strictly continuous, steady-state fashion, characterized by movement of the solid as well as the fluid. Alternatively, owing to the rigidity of the solid adsorbent particles, it is also possible to operate advantageously in semicontinuous fashion, characterized by a moving fluid but stationary solid. This results in unsteady-state conditions, where compositions in the system change with time.

STEADY-STATE–MOVING-BED ADSORBERS

Steady-state conditions require continuous movement of both fluid and adsorbent through the equipment at constant rate, with no change in composition at any point in the system with passage of time. If parallel flow of solid and fluid is used, the net result is at best a condition of equilibrium between the effluent streams, or the equivalent of one theoretical stage. It is the purpose of these applications to develop separations equivalent to many stages, however, and hence only countercurrent operations need be considered. There are applications in treating gases and liquids, for purposes of collecting solute and fractionation, through ordinary adsorption and ion exchange.

Equipment

It is only in relatively recent years that satisfactory large-scale devices for the continuous contacting of a granular solid and a fluid have been developed. These have had to overcome the difficulties of obtaining uniform flow of solid particles and fluid without "channeling" or local irregularities, as well as those of introducing and removing the solid continuously into the vessel to be used.

One such device, developed specifically for fractionation of light hydrocarbon gases with a dense, very hard, active coconut-shell or fruit-pit carbon, is the *Hypersorber*[4,25] (Fig. 11.28), which contains exceptionally interesting devices for the solids-gas-handling problems. Feed gas is introduced more or less centrally. In the "adsorption" section, the more readily adsorbed components are adsorbed upon the descending solid, and the top product consists of poorly adsorbed components. Solid passing to the "rectifying" section below the feed point contains all the constituents of the feed, and in this section a rising stream of gas displaces the more volatile constituents, which pass upward. The adsorbate on the solid leaving this section is then rich in the readily adsorbed constituents. This constitutes the fractionation. In the stripping section, the adsorbate is removed by heating and steaming the solid, part of the desorbed gas is removed as product, and part is returned to the rectifying section as reflux. The solid is recycled to the top by a gas lift.

Figure 11.29 shows the device used for disengaging a product gas stream: the

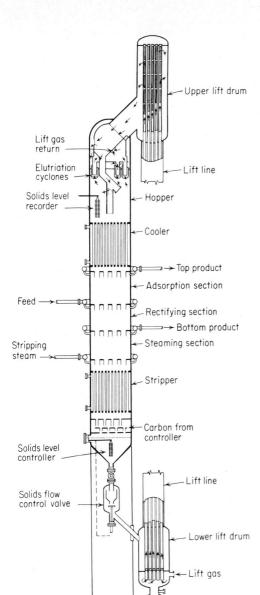

Upper lift drum

Lift gas return

Elutriation cyclones

Solids level recorder

Lift line

Hopper

Cooler

Top product

Adsorption section

Feed

Rectifying section

Bottom product

Steaming section

Stripping steam

Stripper

Carbon from controller

Solids level controller

Lift line

Solids flow control valve

Lower lift drum

Lift gas

Fig. 11.28 *Hypersorber for continuous, counter-current fractionation of a gas into two products. (Union Oil Co. of California.)*

gas collects under the tray and is removed from several points in the tower periphery, while the short pipes carry adsorbent downward through the tray and whatever gas is desired to the upper section. The same device is used for introducing the feed. Figure 11.30 is a schematic representation of the adsorbent flow-controlling device at the bottom of the Hypersorber. The solid must pass through two sets of down-comers, the upper set fixed and the lower set kept in constant reciprocating motion.

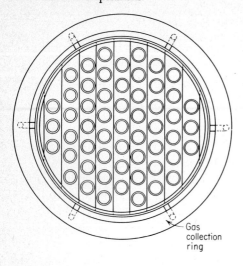

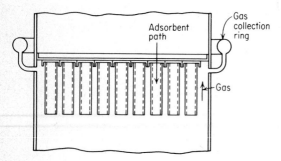

Fig. 11.29 *Device for disengaging solid and gas for Hypersorber.*[4] *(With permission of the American Institute of Chemical Engineers.)*

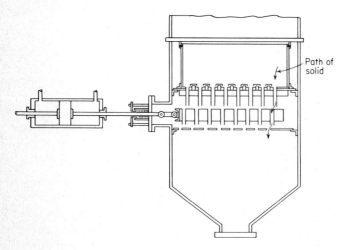

Fig. 11.30 *Adsorbent flow-control device for Hypersorber.*[25] *(With permission of the American Institute of Chemical Engineers.)*

The adsorbent enters the lower set only when they are in juxtaposition with the upper. The reciprocating motion then carries the entrapped solid to openings in the lower plate, through which it is discharged. This device successfully produces a rodlike flow of the compacted solids in the tower.

In the case of liquid treating, far less elaborate devices have been used. Solids may be introduced to the top of the tower by a screw feeder or simply from a bin by gravity flow. Withdrawal of solids at the bottom may be accomplished by several types of devices, e.g., a revolving compartmented valve similar to revolving doors for buildings; it is not generally possible to remove solids entirely free of liquid.[40]

The Higgins contactor,[16,23] developed initially for ion exchange but useful for solids-liquid contacting generally, is unique in the intermittent nature of its operation. Figure 11.31 shows it schematically as arranged for simple solute collection. In Fig. 11.31a, the temporarily stationary upper bed of solids is contacted with liquid flowing downward, so that fluidization does not occur. In the lower bed, the solid is regenerated by an eluting liquid. After several minutes, the liquid flow is stopped, valves are turned as shown in Fig. 11.31b, and the liquid-filled piston pump is moved as shown for a period of several seconds, whereupon solid is moved hydraulically in clockwise fashion. At Fig. 11.31c, with the valves readjusted to their original

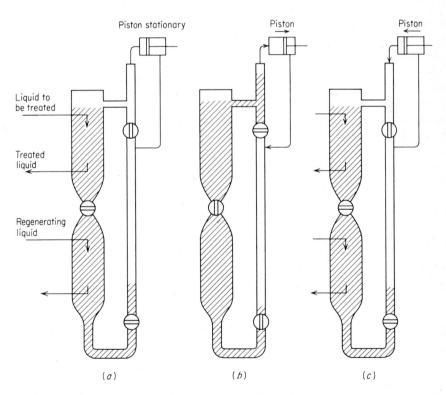

Fig. 11.31 *Higgins contactor, schematic (solids shown shaded).*

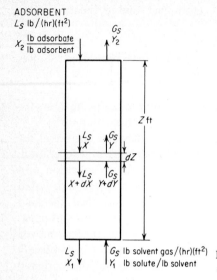

ADSORBENT
L_S lb/(hr)(ft^2)

X_2 lb adsorbate / lb adsorbent

G_S
Y_2

Z ft

L_S X G_S Y

dZ

L_S $X+dX$ G_S $Y+dY$

L_S X_1 G_S lb solvent gas/(hr)(ft^2) Y_1 lb solute/lb solvent

Fig. 11.32 *Continuous countercurrent adsorption of one component.*

position, movement of solid is completed, and liquid flows are started to complete the cycle. Operation, although intermittent and cyclic, is nearly the same as for truly continuous countercurrent operation. Other schemes, for fractionation, for example, are readily arranged.

One component adsorbed

For purposes of computation, the operations are best considered as analogous to gas absorption, with a solid adsorbent replacing the liquid solvent. Refer to Fig. 11.32. The notation used resembles that for gas absorption for a binary gas mixture: G_S and L_S are the superficial mass velocities of solute-free fluid and adsorbate-free solid, respectively, and solute concentrations are expressed as lb solute/lb solute-free substance. A solute balance about the entire tower is

$$G_S(Y_1 - Y_2) = L_S(X_1 - X_2) \tag{11.24}$$

and about the upper part

$$G_S(Y - Y_2) = L_S(X - X_2) \tag{11.25}$$

These establish the operating line on X, Y coordinates, a straight line of slope L_S/G_S joining the terminal conditions (X_1,Y_1) and (X_2,Y_2) (Fig. 11.33). The solute concentrations X and Y at any level in the tower fall upon this line. An equilibrium-distribution curve appropriate to the system and to the prevailing temperature and pressure may also be plotted on the figure as shown. This will fall below the operating line for adsorption and above for desorption. In the same fashion as for absorbers, the minimum solid/fluid ratio is given by the operating line of maximum slope which anywhere touches the equilibrium curve.

The simplifying assumption found useful in gas absorption, that the temperature of the fluid remains substantially constant in adiabatic operations, will be satisfactory only in the case of solute collection from dilute liquid solutions and is unsatisfactory for estimating temperatures in the case of gases. Calculation of the temperature effect when heats of adsorption are large is very complex.[1,38] The present discussion is limited to isothermal operation.

The resistance to mass transfer of solute from the fluid to the adsorbed state on the solid will include that residing in the gas surrounding the solid particles, that corresponding to the diffusion of solute through the gas within the pores of the solid, and possibly an additional resistance at the time of adsorption. During physical adsorption, the last of these will probably be negligible. If the remaining resistances may be characterized by an overall gas mass-transfer coefficient based on a_p, the outside surface of the solid particles, $K_Y a_p$, then the rate of solute transfer over the differential height of adsorber dZ (Fig. 11.32) may be written in the usual manner as

$$L_S\, dX = G_S\, dY = K_Y a_p (Y - Y^*)\, dZ \tag{11.26}$$

where Y^* is the equilibrium composition in the gas corresponding to the adsorbate composition X. The driving force $Y - Y^*$ is then represented by the vertical distance between operating line and equilibrium curve (Fig. 11.33). Rearranging Eq. (11.26) and integrating define the number of transfer units N_{tOG},

$$N_{tOG} = \int_{Y_2}^{Y_1} \frac{dY}{Y - Y^*} = \frac{K_Y a_p\, dZ}{G_S} = \frac{Z}{H_{tOG}} \tag{11.27}$$

where

$$H_{tOG} = \frac{G_S}{K_Y a_p} \tag{11.28}$$

The integral of Eq. (11.27) is ordinarily evaluated graphically and the active height Z determined through knowledge of the height of a transfer unit H_{tOG}, characteristic of the system.

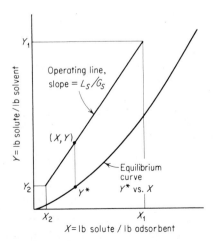

Fig. 11.33 *Continuous countercurrent adsorption of one component.*

The use of an overall coefficient or overall height of a transfer unit implies that the resistance to mass transfer within the pores of the solid particles may be characterized[9] by an individual mass-transfer coefficient $k_S a_p$ or height of a transfer unit H_{tS}, thus,

$$\frac{G_S}{K_Y a_p} = \frac{G_S}{k_Y a_p} + \frac{mG_S}{L_S} \frac{L_S}{k_S a_p} \tag{11.29}$$

or

$$H_{tOG} = H_{tG} + \frac{mG_S}{L_S} H_{tS} \tag{11.30}$$

where $m = dY^*/dX$, the slope of the equilibrium curve.

The resistance within the fluid surrounding the particles H_{tG}, or the corresponding coefficient $k_Y a_p$, may be estimated for moving beds through the correlations available for fixed beds (Table 3.3). Owing to the rigidity of each solid particle and the unsteady-state diffusional conditions existing within each particle as it travels through the adsorber, the use of a mass-transfer coefficient k_S, with an implied linear concentration-difference driving force, is not strictly correct, and Eqs. (11.27) to (11.30) are sound only when the mass-transfer resistance of the fluid surrounding the particles is of controlling size. Ordinarily, however, the diffusional resistance within the particles is of major importance, and for these conditions, which space does not permit consideration of here, the work of Vermeulen[22,41] should be consulted.

Illustration 11.4. Eagleton and Bliss[9] have measured the individual resistances to mass transfer residing in the fluid and within the solid during adsorption of water vapor from air by silica gel, using a fixed-bed semicontinuous method of operation. For low moisture contents of the air, they found that

$$k_Y a_p = 188 G'^{0.55} \text{ lb } H_2O/(hr)(cu \text{ ft})(\Delta Y)$$

and

$$k_S a_p = 217 \text{ lb } H_2O/(hr)(cu \text{ ft})(\Delta X)$$

where G' is the mass velocity of the gas, lb/(hr)(sq ft). Their silica gel had an apparent bed density of 41.9 lb/cu ft, an average particle size of 0.068-in. diameter, and the external surface of the particles was 10.58 sq ft/lb.

It is desired to estimate the height of a continuous countercurrent isothermal adsorber for the drying of air at 80°F, atmospheric pressure, from an initial humidity of 0.005 to a final humidity of 0.0001 lb water/lb dry air. The entering gel will be dry. (*Note:* So-called "dry" silica gel must contain a minimum of about 5% water if it is to retain its adsorptive capacity. Moisture measurements as ordinarily reported do not include this.) A gel rate of 500 lb/(hr)(sq ft) and an air rate of 1,000 lb dry air/(hr)(sq ft) will be used. For the moisture concentrations to be encountered here, the equilibrium adsorption isotherm at 80°F, 1 atm (see Illustration 11.7), may be taken as substantially straight and described by the expression $Y^* = 0.0185X$.

Solution. $Y_1 = 0.005$, $Y_2 = 0.0001$ lb H_2O/lb dry air. $L_S = 500$ lb/(hr)(sq ft), $G_S = 1,000$ lb/(hr)(sq ft), $X_2 = 0$ lb H_2O/lb dry gel.

Eq. (11.24):

$$X_1 = \frac{G_S(Y_1 - Y_2)}{L_S} + X_2 = \frac{1,000(0.005 - 0.0001)}{500}$$

$$= 0.0098 \text{ lb } H_2O/\text{lb dry gel}$$

$$Y_2^* = \text{humidity of air in equilibrium with entering gel} = 0$$

$$Y_1^* = 0.0185 X_1 = 0.0185(0.0098) = 0.0001815 \text{ lb } H_2O/\text{lb dry gel}$$

Since operating line and equilibrium curve will both be straight on X, Y coordinates, the average driving force is the logarithmic average [Eqs. (8.44) to (8.45)].

$$Y_1 - Y_1^* = 0.005 - 0.0001815 = 0.00482$$

$$Y_2 - Y_2^* = 0.0001 - 0 = 0.0001$$

$$\text{Av } \Delta Y = \frac{0.00482 - 0.0001}{\ln (0.00482/0.0001)} = 0.001217$$

$$N_{tOG} = \frac{Y_1 - Y_2}{\Delta Y} = \frac{0.005 - 0.0001}{0.001217} = 4.03$$

If the fixed-bed data are to be used for estimating mass-transfer coefficients for a moving bed of solids, the relative mass velocity of air and solid is appropriate. The linear rate of flow of the solid downward is $500/41.9 = 11.95$ ft/hr, where 41.9 is the apparent density. The density of this substantially dry air at 80°F, 1 atm, is 0.0737 lb/cu ft, and its superficial linear velocity upward is $1,000/0.0737 = 13,590$ ft/hr. The relative linear velocity of air and solid is $13,590 + 11.95 = 13,602$ ft/hr, and the relative mass velocity of the air is $13,602(0.0737) = 1,004$ lb/(hr)(sq ft) $= G'$.

$$H_{tG} = \frac{G_S}{k_Y a_p} = \frac{G_S}{188 G'^{0.55}} = \frac{1,000}{188(1,004)^{0.55}} = 0.118 \text{ ft}$$

$$H_{tS} = \frac{L_S}{k_S a_p} = \frac{500}{217} = 2.30 \text{ ft}$$

$$\frac{mG_S}{L_S} = \frac{0.0185(1,000)}{500} = 0.037$$

Eq. (11.30): $$H_{tOG} = 0.118 + 0.037(2.30) = 0.203 \text{ ft}$$
$$Z = N_{tOG} H_{tOG} = 4.03(0.203) = 0.83 \text{ ft} \quad \textbf{Ans.}$$

Note: The gas-phase mass-transfer coefficient in this case is smaller than that given by item 5, Table 3.3, perhaps because of the very small diameter (0.63 in.) of the bed in which it was measured.

Two components adsorbed; fractionation

When several components of a gas mixture are appreciably adsorbed, fractionation is required for their separation, and a device such as the Hypersorber may be used. This discussion is confined to binary gas mixtures.

For purposes of computation, it is easiest to recall the similarity between the adsorption operation and continuous countercurrent extraction with reflux. Solid adsorbent as the added insoluble phase is analogous to extraction solvent, the adsorbate is analogous to the solvent-free extract, and the fluid stream is similar to the raffinate. Computations may then be made using the methods and equations of Chap. 10 [Eqs. (10.41) to (10.44) and (10.49) to (10.60) with Fig. 10.48]. Some simplification is possible, however, owing to the complete insolubility of adsorbent in the mixture to be separated.

Refer to Fig. 11.34, a schematic representation of the adsorber. Feed enters at the rate of F lb/(hr)(sq ft), containing components A and C. The adsorbate-free adsorbent enters the top of the tower at the rate of B lb/(hr)(sq ft) and flows countercurrent to the gas entering at the bottom at the rate of R_1 lb/(hr)(sq ft). Compositions in the gas stream are expressed as x weight fraction C, the more strongly adsorbed

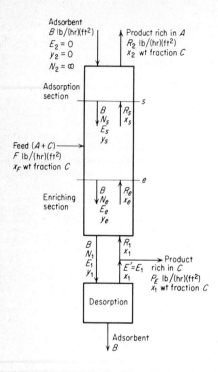

Adsorbent
B lb/(hr)(ft^2)
$E_2 = 0$
$y_2 = 0$
$N_2 = \infty$

Product rich in A
R_2 lb/(hr)(ft^2)
x_2 wt fraction C

Adsorption
section

s

B $\uparrow R_s$
N_s x_s
E_s
y_s

Feed $(A+C)$
F lb/(hr)(ft^2)
x_F wt fraction C

e

Enriching
section

B $\uparrow R_e$
N_e x_e
E_e
y_e

B $\uparrow R_1$
N_1 x_1
E_1
y_1

$E'=E_1$

Product
rich in C
P_E lb/(hr)(ft^2)
x_1 wt fraction C

x_1

Desorption

Adsorbent
B

Fig. 11.34   *Continuous fractionation.*

substance. E represents the weight of adsorbent-free adsorbate $A + C$ upon the solid, lb/(hr)(sq ft), and N the ratio, lb adsorbent/lb adsorbate. At any point in the adsorber, $B \doteq NE$. The adsorbate composition is expressed as y weight fraction component C, on an adsorbent-free basis. Solid leaves the adsorber at the bottom, is stripped of its adsorbate in the desorption section, and the desorbed fluid is split into two streams, the reflux R_1 and the C-rich product P_E. At the top the fluid leaving is the A-rich product, R_2 lb/(hr)(sq ft). The arrangement is very similar to that shown in Fig. 10.47. Calculations are made on a phase diagram of the type shown in the upper part of Fig. 11.8a, with N plotted as ordinate, x and y as abscissa.

Let Δ_E represent the net adsorbent-free flow downward and out of the adsorber. Then $\Delta_E = P_E$, and the coordinates of point Δ_E on the phase diagram are ($N_{\Delta E} = B/P_E$, $y_{\Delta E} = x_1$). At the bottom of the adsorber, $B = N_1 E_1$ and

$$E_1 = E' = P_E + R_1 = \Delta_E + R_1 \tag{11.31}$$

An A-C balance below section e of the enriching section is

$$E_e = P_E + R_e = \Delta_E + R_e \tag{11.32}$$

and, for substance C,

$$E_e y_e = P_E x_1 + R_e x_e = \Delta_E x_1 + R_e x_e \tag{11.33}$$

while for adsorbent it becomes

$$N_e E_e = N_{\Delta E}\, \Delta_E = B \tag{11.34}$$

Δ_E therefore represents the difference $E_e - R_e$ for any level in the enriching section. Equations (11.32) and (11.34) provide a measure of the internal reflux ratio,

$$\frac{R_e}{E_e} = \frac{N_{\Delta E} - N_e}{N_{\Delta E}} = 1 - \frac{N_e}{N_{\Delta E}} \tag{11.35}$$

and at the bottom of the tower the external reflux ratio is

$$\frac{R_1}{P_E} = \frac{R_1}{E_1 - R_1} = \frac{N_{\Delta E} - N_1}{N_1} = \frac{N_{\Delta E}}{N_1} - 1 \tag{11.36}$$

At the top of the adsorber let Δ_R represent the difference between flows of adsorbate and unadsorbed gas, and since $E_2 = 0$, $\Delta_R = -R_2$. The coordinates of Δ_R on the phase diagram are then ($N_{\Delta R} = -B/R_2$, $x_{\Delta R} = x_2$). Material balances above section s are then, for A and C,

$$R_s = E_s + R_2 = E_s - \Delta_R \tag{11.37}$$

for C,

$$R_s x_s = E_s y_s + R_2 x_2 = E_s y_s - \Delta_R x_2 \tag{11.38}$$

and for adsorbent,

$$B = N_s E_s = \Delta_R N_{\Delta R} \tag{11.39}$$

Equations (11.37) and (11.39) provide the internal reflux ratio,

$$\frac{R_s}{E_s} = \frac{N_s - N_{\Delta R}}{-N_{\Delta R}} = 1 - \frac{N_s}{N_{\Delta R}} \tag{11.40}$$

Overall balances about the entire plant are

$$F = R_2 + P_E \tag{11.41}$$

$$F x_F = R_2 x_2 + P_E x_1 \tag{11.42}$$

The definitions of Δ_R and Δ_E, together with Eq. (11.42), provide

$$\Delta_R + F = \Delta_E \tag{11.43}$$

The graphical interpretation of these relations on the phase diagram is the same as that for the corresponding situations in extraction and is shown in detail in Illustration 11.5 below.

If a stage-type device (fluidized beds, for example) is used, the number of ideal stages is readily obtained by the usual step construction on the lower part of a diagram such as Fig. 11.35. For continuous contact,

$$N_{tOG} = \frac{Z}{H_{tOG}} = \int_{p_2}^{p_1} \frac{dp}{p - p^*} = \int_{x_2}^{x_1} \frac{dx}{x - x^*} - \ln\frac{1 + (r - 1)x_1}{1 + (r - 1)x_2} \tag{11.44}$$

where $r = M_A/M_C$ and

$$H_{tOG} = \frac{G}{K_G a_p P_t} \tag{11.45}$$

This may be applied separately to the enriching and adsorption sections. It assumes equimolar counterdiffusion of A and C, which is not strictly the case, but refinement at this time is unwarranted in view of the sparsity of the data.[24] It is also subject to the same limitations considered on page 536.

Illustration 11.5. Determine the number of transfer units and adsorbent circulation rate required to separate a gas containing 60% ethylene C_2H_4 and 40% propane C_3H_8 by volume into products containing 5 and 95% C_2H_4 by volume, isothermally at 25°C and 2.25 atm, using activated carbon as the adsorbent and a reflux ratio of twice the minimum. (*Note:* Hypersorbers customarily operate at reflux ratios closer to the minimum in order to reduce the adsorbent circulation rate. The present value is used in order to make the graphical solution clear.)

Solution. Equilibrium data for this mixture at 25°C and 2.25 atm have been estimated from the data of Lewis et al., *Ind. Eng. Chem.*, **42**, 1319, 1326 (1950), and are plotted in Fig. 11.35. C_3H_8 is the more strongly adsorbed component, and compositions in the gas and adsorbate are expressed as weight fraction C_3H_8. Tie lines have been omitted in the upper part of the plot, and the equilibrium compositions are shown instead in the lower part.

Molecular weights are 28.0 for C_2H_4 and 44.1 for C_3H_8. The feed-gas composition is then $x_F = 0.4(44.1)/[0.4(44.1) + 0.6(28.0)] = 0.512$ wt fraction C_3H_8. Similarly $x_1 = 0.967$, and $x_2 = 0.0763$ wt fraction C_3H_8.

Basis: 100 lb feed gas.

Eqs. (11.41) and (11.42):

$$100 = R_2 + P_E$$
$$100(0.512) = R_2(0.0763) + P_E(0.967)$$

Solving simultaneously, $R_2 = 51.1$ lb, $P_E = 48.9$ lb.

Point F at x_F and point E_1 at x_1 are located on the diagram as shown. From the diagram, N_1 (at point E_1) = 4.57 lb carbon/lb adsorbate. The minimum reflux ratio is found as it is for extraction. In this case, the tie line through point F locates Δ_{Em}, and $\Delta_{Em} = 5.80$.

$$\left(\frac{R_1}{P_E}\right)_m = \frac{5.80}{4.57} - 1 = 0.269 \text{ lb reflux gas/lb product}$$

$$(R_1)_m = 0.269 P_E = 0.269(48.9) = 13.15 \text{ lb}$$

$$(E_1)_m = (R_1)_m + P_E = 13.15 + 48.9 = 62.1 \text{ lb}$$

$$B_m = N_1(E_1)_m = 4.57(62.1) = 284 \text{ lb carbon/100 lb feed}$$

At twice the minimum reflux ratio, $R_1/P_E = 2(0.269) = 0.538$.

Eq. (11.36):

$$0.538 = \frac{N_{\Delta E}}{4.57} - 1$$

$$N_{\Delta E} = 7.03 \text{ lb carbon/lb adsorbate}$$

and point Δ_E is located on the diagram.

$$R_1 = 0.538 P_E = 0.538(48.9) = 26.3 \text{ lb}$$

$$E_1 = R_1 + P_E = 26.3 + 48.9 = 75.2 \text{ lb}$$

$$B = N_1 E_1 = 4.57(75.2) = 344 \text{ lb carbon/100 lb feed}$$

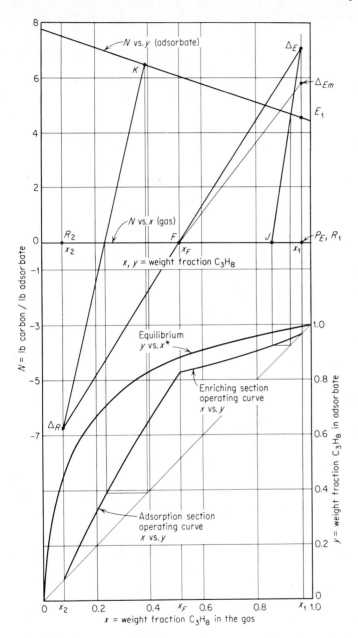

Fig. 11.35 *Solution to Illustration 11.5.*

Point Δ_R may be located by extending line $\Delta_E F$ to intersect the line $x = x_2$. Alternatively, $N_{\Delta_R} = -B/R_2 = -344/51.1 = -6.74$ lb carbon/lb adsorbate. Random lines such as line $\Delta_R K$ are drawn from Δ_R, and the intersections with the equilibrium curves are projected downward in the manner shown to provide the adsorption-section operating curve. Similarly random lines such as line $\Delta_E J$ are drawn from Δ_E, and intersections projected downward to provide the enriching-section operating curve. The horizontal distance between operating and equilibrium curves on the lower diagram is the driving force $x - x^*$ of Eq. (11.44). The following were determined from the diagram:

x	x^*	$\dfrac{1}{x - x^*}$
$x_1 = 0.967$	0.825	7.05
0.90	0.710	5.26
0.80	0.60	5.00
0.70	0.50	5.00
0.60	0.43	5.89
$x_F = 0.512$	0.39	8.20
0.40	0.193	4.83
0.30	0.090	4.76
0.20	0.041	6.29
$x_2 = 0.0763$	0.003	13.65

The third column was plotted as ordinate against the first as abscissa, the area under the curve between x_1 and x_F was 2.65, and that between x_F and x_2 was 2.67. Further, $r = 28.0/44.1 = 0.635$. Applying Eq. (11.44) to the enriching section,

$$N_{tOG} = 2.65 - \ln \frac{1 + (0.635 - 1)0.967}{1 + (0.635 - 1)0.512} = 2.52$$

and to the adsorption section,

$$N_{tOG} = 2.67 - \ln \frac{1 + (0.635 - 1)0.512}{1 + (0.635 - 1)0.0763} = 2.53$$

The total $N_{tOG} = 2.52 + 2.53 = 5.1$.

UNSTEADY STATE—FIXED-BED ADSORBERS

Owing to the inconvenience and relatively high cost of continuously transporting solid particles as required in steady-state operations, it is frequently found more economical to pass the fluid mixture to be treated through a stationary bed of adsorbent. As increasing amounts of fluid are passed through such a bed, the solid adsorbs increasing amounts of solute, and an unsteady state prevails. This technique is very widely used and finds application in such diverse fields as the recovery of valuable solvent vapors from gases, purifying air as with gas masks, dehydration of gases and liquids, decolorizing mineral and vegetable oils, the concentration of valuable solutes from liquid solutions, and many others.

The adsorption wave

Consider the case of a binary solution, either gas or liquid, containing a strongly adsorbed solute at concentration c_0. The fluid is to be passed continuously down through a relatively deep bed of adsorbent initially free of adsorbate. The uppermost layer of solid, in contact with the strong solution entering, at first adsorbs solute rapidly and effectively, and what little solute is left in the solution is substantially all

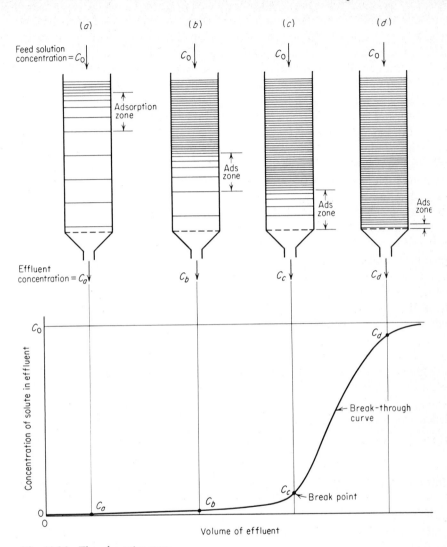

Fig. 11.36 *The adsorption wave.*

removed by the layers of solid in the lower part of the bed. The effluent from the bottom of the bed is practically solute-free as at c_a in the lower part of Fig. 11.36. The distribution of adsorbate in the solid bed is indicated in the sketch in the upper part of this figure at a, where the relative density of the horizontal lines in the bed is meant to indicate the relative concentration of adsorbate. The uppermost layer of the bed is practically saturated, and the bulk of the adsorption takes place over a relatively narrow adsorption zone in which the concentration changes rapidly, as shown. As solution continues to flow, the adsorption zone moves downward as a wave, at a rate ordinarily very much more slowly than the linear velocity of the fluid through the bed. At a later time, as at b in the figure, roughly half of the bed is saturated with solute, but the effluent concentration c_b is still substantially zero. At c in the figure the lower portion of the adsorption zone has just reached the bottom of the bed, and the concentration of solute in the effluent has suddenly risen to an appreciable value c_c for the first time. The system is said to have reached the "breakpoint." The solute concentration in the effluent now rises rapidly as the adsorption zone passes through the bottom of the bed and at d has substantially reached the initial value c_0. The portion of the effluent concentration curve between positions c and d is termed the "breakthrough" curve. If solution continues to flow, little additional adsorption takes place since the bed is for all practical purposes entirely in equilibrium with the feed solution.

If a vapor is being adsorbed adiabatically from a gas mixture in this manner, the evolution of the heat of adsorption causes a temperature wave to flow through the adsorbent bed in a manner somewhat similar to the adsorption wave,[29] and the rise in temperature of the bed at the fluid outlet may sometimes be used as a rough indication of the breakpoint. In the case of adsorption from liquids the temperature rise is usually relatively small.

The shape and time of appearance of the breakthrough curve influence greatly the method of operating a fixed-bed adsorber. The curves generally have an S shape, but they may be steep or relatively flat and in some cases considerably distorted. If the adsorption process were infinitely rapid, the breakthrough curve would be a straight vertical line in the lower part of Fig. 11.36. The actual rate and mechanism of the adsorption process, the nature of the adsorption equilibrium, the fluid velocity, the concentration of solute in the feed, and the length of the adsorber bed·particularly if the solute concentration in the feed is high, all contribute to the shape of the curve produced for any system. The breakpoint is very sharply defined in some cases and in others poorly defined. Generally the breakpoint time decreases with decreased bed height, increased particle size of adsorbent, increased rate of flow of fluid through the bed, and increased initial solute content of the feed. There is a critical minimum bed height below which the solute concentration in the effluent will rise rapidly from the first appearance of effluent. In planning new processes it is best to determine the breakpoint and breakthrough curve for a particular system experimentally under conditions resembling as much as possible those to be encountered in the process.

Adsorption of vapors

One of the most important applications of fixed-bed adsorbers is in the recovery of valuable solvent vapors. Solids saturated with solvents such as alcohol, acetone, carbon disulfide, benzene, and others may be dried by evaporation of the solvent into an air stream, and the solvent vapor may be recovered by passing the resulting vapor-gas mixture through a bed of activated carbon. The very favorable adsorption equilibrium provided by a good grade of carbon for vapors of this sort permits substantially complete vapor recovery, 99 to 99.8 percent, from gas mixtures containing

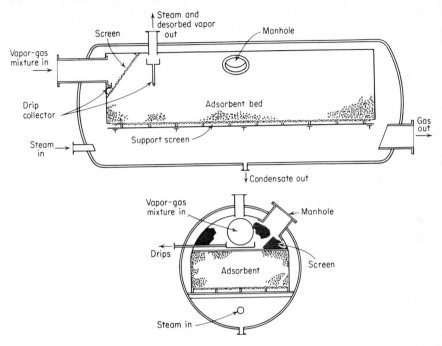

Fig. 11.37 *Adsorber for solvent vapors, schematic.* [*Logan, U.S. Patent* 2,180,712 (1939).]

as little as 0.5 to 0.05 percent of the vapor by volume.[7] Air-vapor mixtures of concentration well below the explosive limits may thus be handled. In most such adsorption plants it is necessary to operate with a small drop in pressure through the bed of adsorbent in order to keep power costs low. Therefore granular rather than powdered adsorbents are used, and bed depths are relatively shallow (12 to 36 in.) and large in cross section. The superficial gas velocity may be in the range 0.8 to 1.8 ft/sec. A typical arrangement of the adsorption vessel is shown in Fig. 11.37.

In a typical operation the air-vapor mixture, if necessary cooled to 90 to 100°F and filtered free of dust particles which might clog the pores of the adsorbent, is admitted to the adsorbent bed. If the breakthrough curve is steep, the effluent air, substantially free of vapor, may be discharged to the atmosphere until the breakpoint is reached, whereupon the influent stream must be diverted to a second adsorber, while the first is regenerated. On the other hand, if the breakthrough curve is flat so that at the breakpoint a substantial portion of the adsorbent remains unsaturated with adsorbate, the gas may be permitted to flow through a second adsorber in series with the first until the carbon in the first is substantially all saturated. The influent mixture is then passed through the second and a third adsorber in series, while the first is regenerated. Such operation is relatively unusual, however, except for liquids.[13]

After gas flow has been diverted from an adsorber, the carbon is usually desorbed by admission of low-pressure steam. This lowers the partial pressure of the vapor in contact with the solid and provides by condensation the necessary heat of desorption. The steam-vapor effluent from the carbon is condensed and the condensed solvent recovered by decantation from the water if it is water-insoluble or by rectification if an aqueous solution results. When desorption is complete, the carbon is saturated with adsorbed water. This moisture is readily displaced by many vapors and evaporated into the air when the air-vapor mixture is readmitted to the carbon, and indeed much of the heat evolved during adsorption of the vapor may be used in desorbing the water, thus maintaining moderate bed temperatures. If the moisture interferes with vapor adsorption, the bed may first be dried by admitting heated air and then cooled by unheated air, prior to reuse for vapor recovery. Figure 11.38 shows a typical

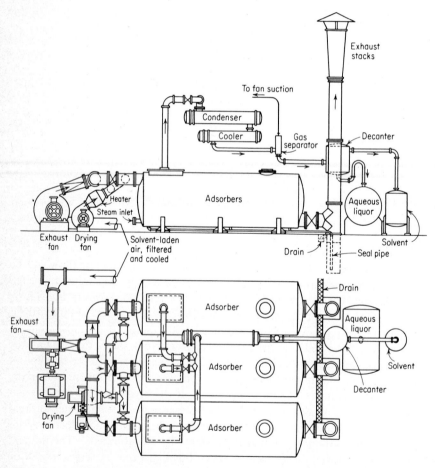

Fig. 11.38 *Solvent-recovery adsorption plant. [After Benson and Courouleau, Chem. Eng. Progr.,* **44,** 466 (1948), *with permission.*]

plant layout arranged for this method of operation. Mantell[33] provides many other operating details.

Moist gases may be dried of their water content by passing them through beds of activated silica gel, alumina, bauxite, or molecular sieves. Especially if the gases are under appreciable pressures, moderately deep beds are used since the pressure drop will still be only a small fraction of the total pressure. Towers containing the adsorbent may be as much as 30 ft tall or more, but in such instances the solid is best supported on trays at intervals of 4 or 5 ft in order to minimize the compression of the bed resulting from pressure drop. After the bed has reached the maximum practical moisture content, the adsorbent may be regenerated, either by application of heat by steam coils embedded in the adsorbent or by admitting heated air or gas. Liquids such as gasoline, kerosene, and transformer oil may also be dehydrated by passage through beds of activated alumina. High-temperature (450°F) steam followed by application of vacuum provided by a steam-jet ejector may be used for regenerating the adsorbent.

Illustration 11.6. A solvent-recovery plant is to recover 800 lb/hr of ethyl acetate vapor from a mixture with air at a concentration of 1.8 lb vapor/1,000 cu ft air at 90°F, 1 atm pressure. The adsorbent will be activated carbon, 6 to 8 mesh (av particle diam 0.0091 ft, apparent density of individual particles 45 lb/cu ft, and apparent density of the packed bed 30 lb/cu ft). The carbon is capable of adsorbing 0.45 lb vapor/lb carbon up to the breakpoint. The adsorption cycle will be set at 3 hr to allow sufficient time for regeneration. Determine the amount of carbon required, choose suitable dimensions for the carbon beds, and estimate the pressure drop.

Solution. In 3 hr the vapor to be adsorbed is $3(800) = 2,400$ lb. The carbon required per bed $= 2,400(1/0.45) = 5,330$ lb. Two beds will be necessary, one adsorbing while the other is being regenerated. Total carbon required is $2(5,330) = 10,660$ lb.

The volume of each bed will be $5,330/30 = 178$ cu ft. If the bed depth is 1.5 ft, the cross section is $178/1.5 = 119$ sq ft, say 7 by 17 ft, and it may be installed horizontally in a suitable vessel such as that shown in Fig. 11.37.

The pressure drop may be estimated by Eq. (6.36). At 90°F, 1 atm, the viscosity of air $= 0.018$ centipoise, or $0.018(2.42) = 0.0436$ lb/(ft)(hr), and the density is $(29/359)(492/550) = 0.0723$ lb/cu ft. One cubic foot of the bed, weighing 30 lb, contains $30/45 = 0.667$ cu ft of solid particles. The fractional void content of the bed (space between particles, but not including pore volume) is $1 - 0.667 = 0.333 = \epsilon$.

The volumetric rate of air flow $= 800(1,000)/1.8 = 445,000$ cu ft/hr, and the superficial mass velocity $= 445,000(0.0723)/119 = 270$ lb/(hr)(sq ft) (linear velocity $= 1.04$ ft/sec). The particle Reynolds number $= Re = d_p G/\mu = 0.0091(270)/0.0436 = 56.3$.

Eq. (6.36) (Chap. 6 notation):
$$\frac{\Delta P}{Z} \frac{g_c' \epsilon^3 d_p \rho_G}{(1 - \epsilon) G'^2} = \frac{150(1 - \epsilon)}{Re} + 1.75$$

$$\frac{\Delta P (4.17)(10^8)(0.333)^3 (0.0091)(0.0723)}{1.5(1 - 0.333)(270)^2} = \frac{150(1 - 0.333)}{56.3} + 1.75$$

$$\Delta P = 25.5 \text{ lb/sq ft, or } 25.5 \frac{12}{62.4} = 4.9 \text{ in. water}$$

Adsorption of liquids; percolation

The dehydration of liquids by stationary beds of adsorbent has already been mentioned. In addition, the colors of petroleum products, such as lubricating oils and transformer oils, and of vegetable oils are commonly reduced by percolation through beds of decolorizing clays; sugar solutions are deashed and decolorized by percolation through bone char; and many other liquid-treating operations use these semibatch methods.

In such service, the bed of adsorbent is commonly called a "filter." It may be installed in a vertical cylindrical vessel fitted with a dished or conical bottom, of diameter ranging up to as much as 15 ft and height up to 30 ft. In the case of decolorizing clays, the beds may contain as much as 50 tons of adsorbent. The granular adsorbent is supported on a screen or blanket, in turn supported by a perforated plate.

The liquid flow is ordinarily downward, either under the force of gravity alone or under pressure from above. At the start of the operation, the adsorbent bed is frequently allowed to "soak" for a time in the first portions of the feed liquid, in order to displace air from the adsorbent particles before the percolation is begun. In decolorizing operations, the concentration of impurity in the initial effluent liquid is usually much smaller than the specifications of the product require, and the break-through curve is frequently rather flat. Consequently it is common practice to allow the effluent liquid to accumulate in a receiving tank below the filter and to blend or composite it until the blended liquid reaches the largest acceptable concentration of impurity. In this way, the largest possible adsorbate concentration may be accumulated upon the solid.

When the solid requires revivification, the flow of liquid is stopped and the liquid in the filter drained. The solid may then be washed in place with an appropriate solvent, e.g., water in the case of sugar-refining filters, naphtha in the case of petroleum products. If necessary the solvent is then removed by admission of steam, following which the solid may be dumped from the filter and reactivated by burning or other suitable procedure, depending upon the nature of the adsorbent.

Elution

Desorption of the adsorbed solute by a solvent is called *elution*. The desorption solvent is the *elutant*, the effluent stream containing the desorbed solute and eluting solvent is the *eluate*. The *elution curve* is a plot of the solute concentration in the eluate against quantity of eluate, as in Fig. 11.39. The initial rise in solute concentration of the eluate, OA in the figure, is found when the void spaces between the adsorbent particles are initially filled with fluid remaining from the adsorption. In the case of liquids, if the bed is drained prior to elution, the elution curve starts at A. If elution is stopped after eluate corresponding to C has been withdrawn, the area under the curve $OABC$ represents the quantity of solute desorbed. For a successful process, this must equal the solute adsorbed during an adsorption cycle, else solute will build up in the bed from one cycle to the next.

Chromatography

Imagine a solution containing two solutes, A and B, which are differently adsorbed at equilibrium, A more strongly. A small quantity of this solution, insufficient to

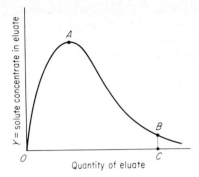

Fig. 11.39 *Elution of a fixed bed.*

saturate all but a small quantity of the adsorbent, is passed through an adsorbent bed, whereupon both solutes are retained in the upper portion of the bed to give rise to adsorbate concentrations as indicated in Fig. 11.40*a*.   A suitable elutant is now passed through the bed, whereupon solute *B* is more readily desorbed than *A*.   At *b*, *c*, and *d* in the figure, the solutes are seen both to be desorbed, only to be readsorbed and redesorbed at lower positions in the bed, but the wave of *B* concentration moves more rapidly downward than that of *A*.†   At *e*, solute *B* has been washed out of the

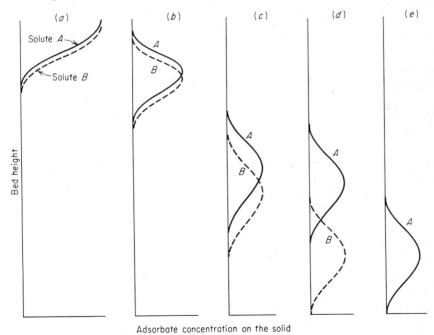

Fig. 11.40 *Chromatographic separation of two solutes.*

† The adsorption bands in some cases have different colors, depending upon the chemical nature of the solutes, and from this arose the terms *chromatographic adsorption* and *chromatography*.

solid, leaving essentially all the A behind. The curves of Fig. 11.40 are idealized, since in reality their shape may change as the concentration waves pass down the column. If the adsorption (or desorption) zone heights are short relative to the height of the bed, and if the selectivity of the adsorbent is sufficiently great, essentially complete separation of the solutes is possible. This technique is the basis of very powerful methods of analysis of mixtures, both gas and liquid, and variants are used for industrial purposes. *Partition chromatography* accomplishes a similar result, using a liquid contained in the pores of a solid as an immobilized solvent for solute separation, rather than adsorption itself.

Rate of adsorption in fixed beds

The design of a fixed-bed adsorber, and the prediction of the length of the adsorption cycle between revivifications, requires knowledge of the percentage approach to saturation at the breakpoint, as shown in Illustration 11.6. This in turn requires the designer to predict the time of the breakpoint and the shape of the breakthrough curve. The unsteady-state circumstances of fixed-bed adsorption and the many factors which influence the adsorption make such computations for the general case very difficult.[22,41] The following simplified treatment due to Michaels[34] is readily used but is limited to isothermal adsorption from dilute feed mixtures and to cases where the equilibrium adsorption isotherm is concave to the solution-concentration axis, where the adsorption zone is constant in height as it travels through the adsorption column, and where the height of the adsorbent bed is large relative to the height of the adsorption zone. Many industrial applications fall within these restrictions. The development here is in terms of adsorption from a gas, but it is equally applicable to treatment of liquids. Nonisothermal cases have also been treated.[29]

Consider the idealized breakthrough curve of Fig. 11.41. This results from the flow of a solvent gas through an adsorbent bed at the rate of G_S lb/(hr)(sq ft), entering with an initial solute concentration Y_0 lb solute/lb solvent gas. The total solute-free effluent after any time is w lb/sq ft of bed cross section. The breakthrough curve is steep, and the solute concentration in the effluent rises rapidly from essentially zero to that in the incoming gas. Some low value Y_B is arbitrarily chosen as the breakpoint concentration, and the adsorbent is considered as essentially exhausted when the effluent concentration has risen to some arbitrarily chosen value Y_E, close to Y_0. We are concerned principally with the quantity of effluent w_B at the breakpoint and the shape of the curve between w_B and w_E. The total effluent accumulated during the appearance of the breakthrough curve is $w_a = w_E - w_B$. The adsorption zone, of constant height Z_a ft, is that part of the bed in which the concentration change from Y_B to Y_E is occurring at any time.

Let θ_a be the time required for the adsorption zone to move its own height down the column, after the zone has been established. Then

$$\theta_a = \frac{w_a}{G_S} \tag{11.46}$$

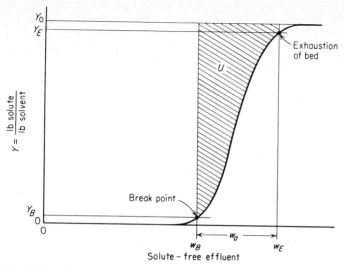

Fig. 11.41 *Idealized breakthrough curve.*

Let θ_E be the time required for the adsorption zone to establish itself and move out of the bed. Then

$$\theta_E = \frac{w_E}{G_S} \tag{11.47}$$

If the height of the adsorbent bed is Z ft, and if θ_F is the time required for the formation of the adsorption zone,

$$Z_a = Z \frac{\theta_a}{\theta_E - \theta_F} \tag{11.48}$$

The quantity of solute removed from the gas in the adsorption zone from the breakpoint to exhaustion is U lb solute/sq ft of bed cross section. This is given by the shaded area of Fig. 11.41, which is

$$U = \int_{w_B}^{w_E} (Y_0 - Y) \, dw \tag{11.49}$$

If, however, all the adsorbent in the zone were saturated with solute, it would contain $Y_0 w_a$ lb solute/sq ft. Consequently at the breakpoint, when the zone is still within the column, the fractional ability of the adsorbent in the zone still to adsorb solute is

$$f = \frac{U}{Y_0 w_a} = \frac{\displaystyle\int_{w_B}^{w_E} (Y_0 - Y) \, dw}{Y_0 w_a} \tag{11.50}$$

If $f = 0$, so that the adsorbent in the zone is essentially saturated, the time of formation of the zone at the top of the bed θ_F should be substantially the same as the time required for the zone to travel a distance equal to its own height, θ_a. On the other hand, if $f = 1.0$, so that the solid in the zone contains essentially no adsorbate, the zone-formation time should be very short, essentially zero. These limiting conditions, at least, are described by

$$\theta_F = (1 - f)\theta_a \tag{11.51}$$

Equations (11.48) and (11.51) provide

$$Z_a = Z \frac{\theta_a}{\theta_E - (1 - f)\theta_a} = Z \frac{w_a}{w_E - (1 - f)w_a} \tag{11.52}$$

The adsorption column, Z ft tall and of unit cross-sectional area, contains $Z\rho_S$ lb adsorbent, where ρ_S is the apparent packed density of the solid in the bed. If this were all in equilibrium with the entering gas and therefore completely saturated at an adsorbate concentration X_T lb adsorbate/lb solid, the adsorbate weight would be $Z\rho_S X_T$ lb. At the breakpoint, the adsorption zone of height Z_a ft is still in the column at the bottom, but the rest of the column, $Z - Z_a$ ft, is substantially saturated. At the breakpoint, therefore, the adsorbed solute is $(Z - Z_a)\rho_S X_T + Z_a\rho_S(1 - f)X_T$ lb. The fractional approach to saturation of the column at the breakpoint is therefore[15]

$$\text{Degree of saturation} = \frac{(Z - Z_a)\rho_S X_T + Z_a\rho_S(1 - f)X_T}{Z\rho_S X_T} = \frac{Z - fZ_a}{Z} \tag{11.53}$$

In the fixed bed of adsorbent, the adsorption zone in reality moves downward through the solid, as we have seen. Imagine instead, however, that the solid moves upward through the column countercurrent to the fluid at sufficient velocity so that the adsorption zone remains stationary within the column, as in Fig. 11.42a. Here the solid leaving at the top of the column is shown in equilibrium with the entering gas, and all solute is shown as having been removed from the effluent gas. This would, of course, require an infinitely tall column, but our concern will be primarily with the concentrations at the levels corresponding to the extremities of the adsorption zone. The operating line over the entire tower is

$$G_S(Y_0 - 0) = L_S(X_T - 0) \tag{11.54}$$

or

$$\frac{L_S}{G_S} = \frac{Y_0}{X_T} \tag{11.55}$$

Since the operating line passes through the origin of Fig. 11.42b, at any level in the column the concentration of solute in the gas Y and of adsorbate upon the solid X are then related by

$$G_S Y = L_S X \tag{11.56}$$

Over the differential height dZ, the ratio of adsorption is

$$G_S \, dY = K_Y a_p (Y - Y^*) \, dZ \tag{11.57}$$

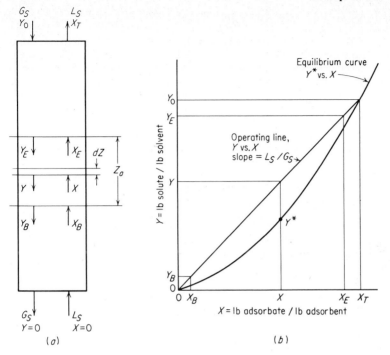

Fig. 11.42 *The adsorption zone.*

For the adsorption zone, therefore,

$$N_{tOG} = \int_{Y_B}^{Y_E} \frac{dY}{Y - Y^*} = \frac{Z_a}{H_{tOG}} = \frac{Z_a}{G_S/K_Y a_p} \qquad (11.58)$$

where N_{tOG} is the overall number of gas transfer units in the adsorption zone. For any value of Z less than Z_a, assuming H_{tOG} remains constant with changing concentrations,

$$\frac{Z \text{ at } Y}{Z_a} = \frac{w - w_B}{w_a} = \frac{\displaystyle\int_{Y_B}^{Y} \frac{dY}{Y - Y^*}}{\displaystyle\int_{Y_B}^{Y_E} \frac{dY}{Y - Y^*}} \qquad (11.59)$$

Equation (11.59) should permit plotting the breakthrough curve by graphical evaluation of the integrals.

In addition to the restrictions outlined at the beginning, the success of this analysis largely hinges upon the constancy of $K_Y a_p$ or H_{tOG} for the concentrations within the adsorption zone. This will, of course, depend upon the relative constancy of the resistances to mass transfer in the fluid and within the pores of the solid. Illustration 11.7 demonstrates the method of using the equations in a typical case.

Illustration 11.7. Air at 80°F, 1 atm, with a humidity of 0.00267 lb water/lb dry air is to be dehumidified by passage through a fixed bed of the silica gel used in Illustration 11.4. The depth of the adsorbent bed is to be 2 ft. The air will be passed through the bed at a superficial mass velocity of 95.5 lb/(hr)(sq ft), and the adsorption will be assumed to be isothermal. The breakpoint will be considered as that time when the effluent air has a humidity of 0.0001 lb water/lb dry air, and the bed will be considered exhausted when the effluent humidity is 0.0024 lb water/lb dry air. Mass-transfer coefficients are given in Illustration 11.4 for this gel. Estimate the time required to reach the breakpoint.

Solution. The equilibrium data are plotted in Fig. 11.43. The gel is initially "dry," and the effluent air initially of so low a humidity as to be substantially dry, so that the operating line passes through the origin of the figure. The operating line is then drawn to intersect the equilibrium curve at $Y_0 = 0.00267$ lb water/lb dry air. $Y_B = 0.0001$, $Y_E = 0.0024$ lb water/lb dry air.

In the accompanying table, column 1 lists values of Y on the operating line between Y_B and Y_E and column 2 the corresponding values of Y^* taken from the equilibrium curve at the same value of X. From these the data of column 3 were computed. A curve (not shown) of column 1 as abscissa, column 3 as ordinate was prepared and integrated graphically between each value of Y in the table and Y_B, to give in column 4 the numbers of transfer units corresponding to each value of Y (thus, for example, the area under the curve from $Y = 0.0012$ to $Y = 0.0001$ equals 4.438). The total number of transfer units corresponding to the adsorption zone is $N_{tOG} = 9.304$, in accordance with Eq. (11.58).

Y, lb H_2O lb dry air (1)	Y^*, lb H_2O lb dry air (2)	$\dfrac{1}{Y - Y^*}$ (3)	$\displaystyle\int_{Y_B}^{Y}\dfrac{dY}{Y - Y^*}$ (4)	$\dfrac{w - w_B}{w_a}$ (5)	$\dfrac{Y}{Y_0}$ (6)
$Y_B = 0.0001$	0.00003	14,300	0	0	0.0374
0.0002	0.00007	7,700	1.100	0.1183	0.0749
0.0004	0.00016	4,160	2.219	0.2365	0.1498
0.0006	0.00027	3,030	2.930	0.314	0.225
0.0008	0.00041	2,560	3.487	0.375	0.300
0.0010	0.00057	2,325	3.976	0.427	0.374
0.0012	0.000765	2,300	4.438	0.477	0.450
0.0014	0.000995	2,470	4.915	0.529	0.525
0.0016	0.00123	2,700	5.432	0.584	0.599
0.0018	0.00148	3,130	6.015	0.646	0.674
0.0020	0.00175	4,000	6.728	0.723	0.750
0.0022	0.00203	5,880	7.716	0.830	0.825
$Y_E = 0.0024$	0.00230	10,000	9.304	1.000	0.899

By dividing each entry in column 4 by 9.304, the values in column 5 were determined in accordance with Eq. (11.59). Column 6 was obtained by dividing each entry in column 1 by $Y_0 = 0.00267$, and column 6 plotted against column 5 provides a dimensionless form of the breakthrough curve between w_B and w_E (Fig. 11.44). Equation (11.53) may be written as

$$f = \frac{\displaystyle\int_{w_B}^{w_E}(Y_0 - Y)\,dw}{Y_0 w_a} = \int_0^{1.0}\left(1 - \frac{Y}{Y_0}\right)d\frac{w - w_B}{w_a}$$

from which it is seen that f equals the entire area above the curve of Fig. 11.44 up to $Y/Y_0 = 1.0$. By graphical integration, $f = 0.530$.

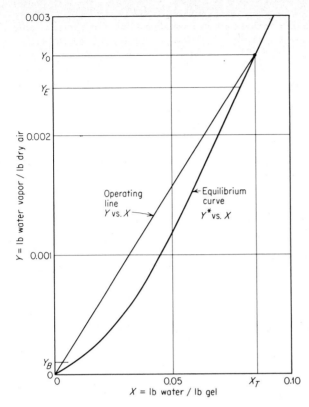

Fig. 11.43 *Solution to Illustration* 11.7.

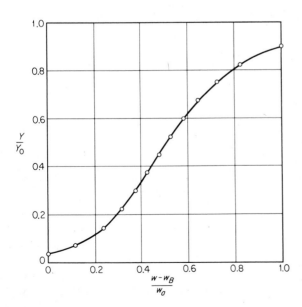

Fig. 11.44 *Calculated breakthrough curve for Illustration* 11.7.

The mass-transfer rates are given in equation form in Illustration 11.4. For a mass velocity of air equal to 95.5 lb/(hr)(sq ft), $k_Y a_p = 188(95.5)^{0.55} = 2{,}310$ lb H_2O/(hr)(cu ft)(ΔY), and $k_S a_p = 217$ lb H_2O/(hr)(cu ft)(ΔX).

From Fig. 11.43, $X_T = 0.0858$ lb water/lb gel.

Eq. (11.55):
$$L_S = \frac{Y_0 G_S}{X_T} = \frac{0.00267(95.5)}{0.0858} = 2.97$$

The average slope of the equilibrium curve is $\Delta Y/\Delta X = 0.0185$, whence $mG_S/L_S = 0.0185(95.5)/2.97 = 0.595$. Equations (11.29) and (11.30):

$$H_{tG} = \frac{G_S}{k_Y a_p} = \frac{95.5}{2{,}310} = 0.0413 \text{ ft} \qquad H_{tS} = \frac{L_S}{k_S a_p} = \frac{2.97}{217} = 0.0137 \text{ ft}$$

$$H_{tOG} = H_{tG} + \frac{mG_S}{L_S} H_{tS} = 0.0413 + 0.595(0.0137) = 0.0495 \text{ ft}$$

Eq. (11.58):
$$Z_a = N_{tOG} H_{tOG} = 9.304(0.0495) = 0.460 \text{ ft}$$

The height of the bed $= Z = 2$ ft. Therefore [Eq. (11.53)]:

$$\text{Degree of bed saturation at breakpoint} = \frac{2 - 0.53(0.460)}{2} = 0.878 \text{ or } 87.8\%$$

The bed contains 2 cu ft gel/sq ft of cross section, and since the bed density is 41.9 lb/cu ft (Illustration 11.4), the weight of the gel $= 2(41.9) = 83.8$ lb/sq ft. At 87.8% of equilibrium with the incoming air, the gel contains $83.8(0.878)(0.0858) = 6.30$ lb water/sq ft cross section. The air introduces $95.5(0.00267) = 0.255$ lb water/(hr)(sq ft), and hence the breakpoint occurs at $6.30/0.255 = 24.7$ hr after air is admitted initially, and $w_B = 24.7(95.5) = 2{,}360$ lb air/sq ft cross section. If the entire bed were in equilibrium with the entering gas, the adsorbed water would be $83.8(0.0858) = 7.18$ lb/sq ft, and hence $U = 7.18 - 6.30 = 0.88$ lb/sq ft $=$ ability of the bed still to adsorb. Therefore $w_A = U/fY_0 = 0.88/0.53(0.00267) = 620$ lb air/sq ft.

The circumstances of this calculation correspond to run $S2$ of Eagleton and Bliss,[9] whose observed breakthrough curve (their fig. 5) agrees excellently with Fig. 11.44. However, they observed that 180 lb air/sq ft flowed through while the effluent humidity rose from $Y/Y_0 = 0.1$ to 0.8, whereas the curve of Fig. 11.44 predicts this amount to be $(0.79 - 0.17)620 = 384$ lb/sq ft. It is noteworthy that better agreement is obtained if the correlation of Table 3.3 is used for the gas-phase mass-transfer coefficient in the above calculations.

ION EXCHANGE

Ion-exchange operations are essentially metathetical chemical reactions between an electrolyte in solution and an insoluble electrolyte with which the solution is contacted. The mechanisms of these reactions and the techniques used to bring them about resemble those of adsorption so closely that for most engineering purposes ion exchange may be simply considered as a special case of adsorption.

Principles of ion exchange[19,27,28,35]

The ion-exchange solids first used were porous, natural or synthetic minerals containing silica, the zeolites, such as the mineral $Na_2O \cdot Al_2O_3 \cdot 4SiO_2 \cdot 2H_2O$, for example. Positively charged ions (cations) of a solution which are capable of diffusing through the pores will exchange with the Na^+ ions of such a mineral, and the latter is therefore called a cation exchanger.   For example,

$$Ca^{++} + Na_2R \rightarrow CaR + 2Na^+$$

where R represents the residual material of the zeolite.   In this manner "hard" water containing Ca^{++} may be softened by contact with the zeolite, the less objectionable Na^+ replacing the Ca^{++} in solution and the latter becoming immobilized in the solid.   The reaction is reversible, and after saturation with Ca^{++} the zeolite may be regenerated by contact with a solution of salt,

$$CaR + 2NaCl \rightarrow Na_2R + CaCl_2$$

Later certain carbonaceous cation exchangers were manufactured by treating substances such as coal with reagents such as fuming sulfuric acid, and the like.   The resulting exchangers can be regenerated to a hydrogen form, HR, by treatment with acid rather than salt.   Thus, hard water containing $Ca(HCO_3)_2$ would contain H_2CO_3 after removal of the Ca^{++} by exchange, and since the carbonic acid is readily removed by degasification procedures, the total solids content of the water may be reduced in this manner.   Early applications of ion exchangers using these principles were largely limited to water-softening problems.

In 1935, synthetic resinous ion exchangers were introduced.   For example, certain synthetic, insoluble polymeric resins containing sulfonic, carboxylic, or phenolic groups can be considered as consisting of an exceedingly large anion and a replaceable or exchangeable cation.   These make exchanges of the following type possible,

$$Na^+ + HR \rightleftharpoons NaR + H^+$$

and different cations will exchange with the resin with different relative ease.   The Na^+ immobilized in the resin may be exchanged with other cations or with H^+, for example, much as one solute may replace another adsorbed upon a conventional adsorbent.   Similarly synthetic, insoluble polymeric resins containing amine groups and anions may be used to exchange anions in solution.   The mechanism of this action is evidently not so simple as in the case of the cation exchangers, but for present purposes it may be considered simply as an ion exchange.   For example,

$$RNH_3OH + Cl^- \rightleftharpoons RNH_3Cl + OH^-$$

$$H^+ + OH^- \rightarrow H_2O$$

where RNH_3 represents the immobile cationic portion of the resin.   Such resins may be regenerated by contact with solutions of sodium carbonate or hydroxide. The synthetic ion-exchange resins are available in a variety of formulations of different exchange abilities, usually in the form of fine, granular solids or beads, 16 to 325 mesh.   The individual beads are frequently nearly perfect spheres.

Techniques and applications

All the operational techniques ordinarily used for adsorption are used also for ion exchange.   Thus we have batch or stagewise treatment of solutions, fluidized- and

fixed-bed operations, and continuous countercurrent operations. Fixed-bed per-
colations are most common. Chromatographic methods have been used for
fractionation of multicomponent ionic mixtures. Applications have been made in
the treatment of ore slurries ("resin-in-pulp") for collection of metal values.

In addition to the water-softening applications mentioned above, the complete
deionization of water may be accomplished by percolation first through a cation
exchanger and then through an anion exchanger. By using a bed formed of an
intimate mixture of equivalent amounts of a strong cationic and a strong anionic
exchange resin, simultaneous removal of all ions at neutrality is possible. For
purposes of regeneration, such mixed-bed resins are separated by hydraulic classification through particle size and density differences for the two resin types, and these
are regenerated separately. The ion exchangers have also been used for treatment
and concentration of dilute waste solutions. Perhaps the most remarkable application of exchange resins has been to the separation of the rare-earth metals, using
chromatographic techniques.

In *ion exclusion*, a resin is presaturated with the same ions as in a solution. It
can then reject ions in such a solution but at the same time absorb nonionic organic
substances such as glycerin, and the like, which may also be in the solution. The
organic matter may then later be washed from the resin in an ion-free state.

Equilibria

The equilibrium distribution of an ion between an exchange solid and a solution can
be described graphically by plotting isotherms in much the same manner used for
ordinary adsorption. Various empirical equations for these isotherms, such as the
Freundlich equation (11.3), have sometimes been applied to them. It is also possible
to apply equations of the mass-action type to the exchange reaction. For example,
for the cationic exchange

$$Na^+ + R^-H^+ \rightleftharpoons R^-Na^+ + H^+$$
$$\text{(soln)} \qquad \text{(solid)} \qquad \text{(solid)} \qquad \text{(soln)}$$

the mass-action-law constant is

$$\alpha = \frac{[R^-Na^+]_{\text{solid}}[H^+]_{\text{soln}}}{[R^-H^+]_{\text{solid}}[Na^+]_{\text{soln}}} = \left[\frac{Na^+}{H^+}\right]_{\text{solid}}\left[\frac{H^+}{Na^+}\right]_{\text{soln}} \tag{11.60}$$

where the square brackets [ ] indicate the use of some suitable equilibrium-
concentration unit. The quantity α is thus seen to be an expression of relative
adsorptivity, in this case of relative adsorptivity of Na^+ to H^+. Since the solution
and the solid remain electrically neutral during the exchange process, we can write

$$\alpha = \frac{X}{X_0 - X}\frac{c_0 - c^*}{c^*} = \frac{X/X_0}{1 - X/X_0}\frac{1 - c^*/c_0}{c^*/c_0} \tag{11.61}$$

where c_0 is in this case the initial concentration of $Na^+ + H^+$ in the solution and
consequently the total of these at any time, c^* the equilibrium Na^+ concentration
after exchange, X the equilibrium concentration of Na^+ in the solid, and X_0 the

concentration if all H^+ were replaced by Na^+, all expressed as equivalents per unit volume or mass.   In the general case for any system, the relative adsorptivity α at a given temperature varies with total cationic concentration c_0 in the solution and also with c.   In some cases, α has been found to be essentially constant with varying c at fixed c_0.

Rate of ion exchange

The rate of ion exchange depends, like ordinary adsorption, upon rates of the following individual processes: (1) diffusion of ions from the bulk of the liquid to the external surface of an exchanger particle; (2) inward diffusion of ions through the solid to the site of exchange; (3) exchange of the ions; (4) outward diffusion of the released ions to the surface of the solid; (5) diffusion of the released ions from the surface of the solid to the bulk of the liquid.   In some instances, the kinetics of the exchange reaction (3) may be controlling, but in others the rate of reaction is apparently very rapid in comparison with the rate of diffusion.   The diffusion rates can be described by appropriate mass-transfer coefficients for equi-equivalent counterdiffusion through the solid and through the liquid, and in some instances at least it appears that the resistance to diffusion in the liquid phase may be controlling.

For cases where the exchange reactions are rapid in comparison with the rates of mass transfer, the methods of design developed for conventional adsorbers may be applied to ion-exchange operations directly.   Some modification of the units of the terms in the various equations may be desirable, owing to the customary use of concentrations expressed as equivalents per unit volume in the cgs system.   The following example illustrates this:

Illustration 11.8. A synthetic ion-exchange resin in bead form is to be used for collecting and concentrating the copper in a dilute waste solution.   The feed contains $CuSO_4$ at a concentration of 20 milligram equivalents (meq) Cu^{++}/liter and is to be treated at the rate of 10,000 gal/hr.   A continuous system is planned: the solution to be treated and regenerated resin will flow countercurrently through a vertical tower, where 99% of the Cu^{++} of the feed will be exchanged; the resin will be regenerated in a second tower by countercurrent contact with 2 N sulfuric acid.   The necessary data are provided by Selke and Bliss, *Chem. Eng. Progr.*, **47**, 529 (1951).

For collection of Cu^{++}. A superficial liquid velocity of 2.2 liters/(hr)(sq cm) will be used for which the mass-transfer rate is 2.0 meq Cu^{++}/(hr)(g resin)(meq Cu^{++}/liter).   The regenerated resin will contain 0.30 meq Cu^{++}/g, and 1.2 times the minimum resin/solution ratio will be used.

For regeneration of the resin. The superficial liquid velocity will be 0.17 liter/(hr)(sq cm), for which the mass-transfer rate is 0.018 meq Cu^{++}/(hr)(g resin)(meq Cu^{++}/liter).   The acid will be utilized to the extent of 70%.

Compute the necessary rates of flow of resin and the amount of resin holdup in each tower.

Solution. Equilibria for the Cu^{++}–H^+ exchange are provided by Selke and Bliss at two concentration levels, 20 and 2,000 meq cation/liter.   These are shown in Fig. 11.45a and b, respectively.

Collection of Cu^{++}. Feed soln = 10,000(3.785) = 37,850 liters/hr. $c_1 = 20$ meq Cu^{++}/liter, $c_2 = 0.01(20) = 0.20$ meq Cu^{++}/liter. Cu^{++} exchanged = 37,850(20 − 0.20) = 750,000 meq/hr.

$X_2 = 0.30$ meq Cu^{++}/g.   The point (c_2, X_2) is plotted on Fig. 11.45a.   For the minimum resin/ solution ratio and an infinitely tall tower, the operating line passes also through point P at $X = 4.9$ on this figure, corresponding to equilibrium with c_1.   The minimum resin rate is then $750,000/(4.9 - 0.30) = 163,000$ g/hr.   For 1.2 times the minimum, the resin rate is 1.2(163,000) = 196,000

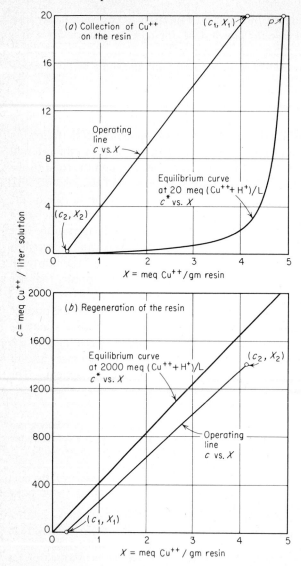

Fig. 11.45 *Solution to Illustration 11.8.*

g/hr, or 430 lb/hr. A copper balance,

$$750,000 = 196,000(X_1 - 0.30)$$

$$X_1 = 4.12 \text{ meq Cu}^{++}/\text{g resin}$$

The point (c_1, X_1) is plotted on Fig. 11.45a, and the operating line may be drawn as a straight line at these low concentrations.

The quantity of resin in the tower may be obtained by application of the rate equation written in a form appropriate to the units of the quantities involved. Adapting Eq. (11.26) to this case, we have

$$V \, dc = \frac{K_L' a_p}{\rho_s} (c - c^*) \, d(SZ\rho_s)$$

where V = liters liquid/hr

c = concn Cu^{++}, meq/liter, in the soln

c^* = concn Cu^{++} in the soln at equilibrium with the resin

$K'_L a_p / \rho_S$ = overall liquid mass-transfer coefficient, meq/(hr)(g resin)(meq/liter)

K'_L = overall liquid mass-transfer coefficient, meq/(hr)(sq cm)(meq/liter)

a_p = surface of resin particles, sq cm/cu cm

ρ_S = packed density of resin, g/cu cm

$SZ\rho_S$ = resin in tower, g

S = cross section of tower, sq cm

Z = height of tower, cm

Rearranging this equation and integrating,

$$SZ\rho_S = \frac{V}{K'_L a_p / \rho_S} \int_{c_2}^{c_1} \frac{dc}{c - c^*}$$

For values of c on the operating line between c_1 and c_2, the corresponding values of c^* from the equilibrium curve at the same value of X are obtained as follows:

c	20	16	12	8	4	2	1	0.2
c^*	2.4	1.9	0.5	0.25	0.10	0.05	0.02	0
$\dfrac{1}{c - c^*}$	0.0568	0.0710	0.0870	0.129	0.256	0.513	1.02	5.0

A curve (not shown) of $1/(c - c^*)$ as ordinate, c as abscissa, is plotted and integrated graphically between the limits c_1 and c_2. The area under the curve is 5.72. (*Note:* This is the number of transfer units N_{tOL}.) Substituting in the integrated equation,

$$\text{Resin holdup} = SZ\rho_S = \frac{37{,}850(5.72)}{2.0} = 108{,}300 \text{ g, or 239 lb}$$

Regeneration of resin. Cu^{++} to be exchanged = 750,000 meq/hr, requiring as many meq H^+/hr. For a 70% utilization of acid, the acid feed must contain $750{,}000/0.70 = 1{,}071{,}000$ meq H^+/hr, or $1{,}071{,}000/2{,}000 = 536$ liters/hr of 2 N acid.

$c_1 = 0$, $c_2 = 750{,}000/536 = 1{,}400$ meq Cu^{++}/liter. $X_1 = 0.30$, $X_2 = 4.12$ meq Cu^{++}/g resin. The points (c_1, X_1) and (c_2, X_2) are plotted on Fig. 11.45b and the operating line drawn. Integration of the rate equation for this case, where both operating and equilibrium lines are straight, provides

$$V(c_2 - c_1) = \frac{K'_L a_p}{\rho_S} (SZ\rho_S)(c^* - c)_m$$

where $(c^* - c)_m$ is the logarithmic average of the driving forces at the extremities of the tower and the other symbols have the same meaning as before.

$c_1^* - c_1 = 120 - 0 = 120$ $c_2^* - c_2 = 1{,}700 - 1{,}400 = 300$ meq Cu^{++}/liter

$$(c^* - c)_m = \frac{300 - 120}{\ln(300/120)} = 196.5 \text{ meq } Cu^{++}/\text{liter}$$

Substituting in the rate equation,

$$750{,}000 = 0.018(SZ\rho_S)(196.5)$$

$$SZ\rho_S = 212{,}000 \text{ g, or 476 lb, resin holdup in regeneration tower}$$

The resin should be water-rinsed before reintroducing it into the adsorption tower. The Cu^{++} in the effluent solution has been concentrated $1,400/20 = 70$ times, equivalent to the evaporation of 9,857 gal of water/hr from the original solution.

NOTATION FOR CHAPTER 11

a_p = external surface of solid particles, sq ft/cu ft of packed volume
B = rate of adsorbent flow in continuous fractionators, lb adsorbate-free solid/(hr)(sq ft)
c = solute concentration in solution, lb/cu ft or, in the case of ion exchange, equivalents/unit volume
C_A = heat capacity of a vapor, Btu/(lb)(°F)
C_{AL} = heat capacity of a liquid, Btu/(lb)(°F)
C_B = heat capacity of adsorbent, Btu/(lb)(°F)
C_G = heat capacity of unadsorbed gas, Btu/(lb)(°F)
d = differential operator
E = rate of flow of adsorbate, lb/(hr)(sq ft)
f = fractional ability of adsorbent zone to adsorb solute, dimensionless
F = feed rate, lb/(hr)(sq ft)
G = total rate of flow of gas, lb moles/(hr)(sq ft)
G' = total rate of flow of gas, lb/(hr)(sq ft)
G_s = solvent in solution, or unadsorbed gas, lb in a batch process or lb/(hr)(sq ft) in a continuous process
$\bar{H}$ = differential heat of adsorption, Btu/lb adsorbate
H_G = enthalpy of gas, Btu/lb solute-free gas
H_L = enthalpy of solid and adsorbed solute, Btu/lb adsorbate-free solid
H_{tG} = height of gas transfer unit, ft
H_{tOG} = overall height of gas transfer unit, ft
H_{tS} = height of solid transfer unit, ft
ΔH_A = integral heat of adsorption, Btu/lb adsorbent, referred to liquid adsorbate
$\Delta H'_A$ = integral heat of adsorption, Btu/lb adsorbent, referred to vapor adsorbate
k = constant
k_Y = gas mass-transfer coefficient, lb/(hr)(sq ft)(lb solute/lb solvent gas)
K_G = overall gas mass-transfer coefficient, lb moles/(hr)(sq ft)(atm)
K_Y = overall gas mass-transfer coefficient, lb/(hr)(sq ft)(lb solute/lb solvent gas)
ln = natural logarithm
log = common logarithm
L_s = adsorbate-free adsorbent, lb in a batch process or lb/(hr)(sq ft) in a continuous process
m = constant
   = in Eqs. (11.29) and (11.30), slope of the equilibrium adsorption isotherm = dY^*/dX, dimensionless
M = molecular weight, lb/lb mole
n = constant
N = adsorbent concentration, lb adsorbate-free adsorbent/lb adsorbate
N_p = number of theoretical stages in a cascade, dimensionless
N_{tOG} = overall number of gas transfer units, dimensionless
p = partial pressure, atm, unless otherwise indicated
P = vapor pressure, atm, unless otherwise indicated
P_E = product rich in the more strongly adsorbed substance, lb/(hr)(sq ft)
P_t = total pressure, atm
r = molecular weight poorly adsorbed gas/molecular weight strongly adsorbed gas, dimensionless
R = rate of flow of gas in a continuous fractionator, lb/(hr)(sq ft)
   = gas constant, (cu ft)(atm)/(lb mole)(°R)
   = nonexchanged portion of an ion exchanger

t_G = gas temperature, °F

t_L = adsorbent temperature, °F

t_o = base temperature for enthalpy computation, °F

T = absolute temperature, °R (°K on Fig. 11.6)

U = solute adsorbed in the adsorption zone, fixed-bed adsorbers, lb/(hr) (sq ft)

V = quantity of solution, cu ft solution/lb adsorbent

w = in a semibatch process, quantity of effluent from fixed-bed adsorber, lb solute-free effluent/sq ft

$w_a = w_E - w_B$

w_B = quantity of effluent from fixed-bed adsorber at the breakpoint, lb solute-free effluent/sq ft

w_E = quantity of effluent from fixed-bed adsorber at bed exhaustion, lb solute-free effluent/sq ft

x = concentration of more strongly adsorbed substance in the fluid, weight fraction

X = adsorbate concentration, lb solute adsorbed/lb adsorbent, or, for ion exchange, equivalents/unit mass or volume

X_T = adsorbate concentration of a fixed-bed adsorber, when in equilibrium with entering fluid, lb solute/lb adsorbent

y = composition of adsorbate, weight fraction more strongly adsorbed substance, adsorbent-free basis

Y = concentration of solute in fluid, lb solute/lb solvent

Y_B = concentration of solute in effluent from fixed-bed adsorber at the breakpoint, lb solute/lb solvent

Y_E = concentration of solute in effluent from fixed-bed adsorber at bed exhaustion, lb solute/lb solvent

Z = active height of adsorber, ft

Z_a = height of adsorption zone in fixed-bed adsorber, ft

α = mass-action-law constant or relative adsorptivity, dimensionless

Δ = difference

θ = time, hr

θ_a = time required for adsorption zone to move a distance Z_a through the fixed bed, hr

θ_E = time required to reach bed exhaustion, hr

θ_F = time of formation of adsorption zone, hr

λ = latent heat of vaporization, Btu/lb

ρ = fluid density, lb/cu ft

ρ_S = apparent packed density of an adsorbent bed, lb solid/cu ft packed space

Subscripts:

e = within the enriching section of a continuous fractionator

F = pertaining to the feed

m = minimum

n = stage n

o = at a base temperature t_o

r = reference subs ance

0 = initial

1 = stage 1; bottom of a continuous-contact adsorber

2 = stage 2; top of a continuous-contact adsorber

Superscript

$*$ = equilibrium

REFERENCES

1. Amundsen, N. R.: *Ind. Eng. Chem.*, **48**, 26 (1956).
2. Anon.: *Chem. Eng.*, **70**, Apr. 15, 92 (1963).
3. Bartell, F. E., and C. K. Sloan: *J. Am. Chem. Soc.*, **51**, 1643 (1929).
4. Berg, C.: *Trans. AIChE.*, **42**, 665 (1946); *Chem. Eng. Progr.*, **47**, 585 (1951).
5. Boer, J. H. de: "The Dynamical Character of Adsorption," Oxford Press, Oxford, 1953.
6. Brunauer, S.: "Adsorption of Gases and Vapors," Princeton University Press, Princeton, N.J., 1943.
7. Courouleau, P. H., and R. E. Benson: *Chem. Eng.*, **55**(3), 112 (1948).
8. Denver Equipment Company: *Deco Trefoil*, Jan.–Feb., 1966, p. 26.
9. Eagleton, L. C., and H. Bliss: *Chem. Eng. Progr.*, **49**, 543 (1953).
10. Ermenc, E. D.: *Chem. Eng.*, **68**, May 27, 87 (1961).
11. Etherington, L. D., R. J. Fritz, E. W. Nicholson, and H. W. Scheeline: *Chem. Eng. Progr.*, **52**, 274 (1956).
12. Etherington, L. D., R. E. D. Haney, W. A. Herbst, and H. W. Scheeline: *AIChE J.*, **2**, 65 (1956).
13. Fornwalt, H. J., and R. A. Hutchins: *Chem. Eng.*, **73**, Apr. 11, 179; May 9, 155 (1966).
14. Goldman, F., and M. Polanyi: *Z. Physik. Chem.*, **132**, 321 (1928).
15. Halle, E. von: personal communication, 1964.
16. Hancher, C. W., and S. H. Jury: *Chem. Eng. Progr. Symp. Ser.*, **55**(24), 87 (1959).
17. Helby, W. A., in J. Alexander (ed.), "Colloid Chemistry," vol. VI, p. 814, Reinhold Publishing Corporation, New York, 1946.
18. Helby, W. A.: *Chem. Eng.*, **59**(10), 153 (1952).
19. Helfferich, F.: "Ion Exchange," McGraw-Hill Book Company, New York, 1962.
20. Henson, T. L., and R. L. Kabel: *AIChE J.*, **12**, 606 (1966).
21. Hersh, C. K.: "Molecular Sieves," Reinhold Publishing Corporation, New York, 1961.
22. Hiester, N. K., T. Vermeulen, and G. Klein: sec. 16 in "The Chemical Engineers' Handbook," 4th ed., McGraw-Hill Book Company, New York, 1963.
23. Higgins, I. R., and J. T. Roberts: *Chem. Eng. Progr. Symp. Ser.*, **50**(14), 87 (1954).
24. Kapfer, W. H., M. Malow, J. Happel, and C. J. Marsel: *AIChE J.*, **2**, 456 (1956).
25. Kehde, H., R. G. Fairfield, J. C. Frank, and L. W. Zahnstecker: *Chem. Eng. Progr.*, **44**, 575 (1948).
26. Kipling, J. J., and D. A. Tester: *J. Chem. Soc.*, **1952**, 4123.
27. Kunin, R.: "Elements of Ion Exchange," Reinhold Publishing Corporation, New York, 1960.
28. Kunin, R.: "Ion Exchange Resins," John Wiley & Sons, Inc., New York, 1958.
29. Leavitt, F. W.: *Chem. Eng. Progr.*, **58**(8), 54 (1962).
30. Lewis, W. K., E. R. Gilliland, B. Chertow, and W. P. Cadogen: *Ind. Eng. Chem.*, **42**, 1319, 1326 (1950).
31. Leva, M.: "Fluidization," McGraw-Hill Book Company, New York, 1959.
32. Lloyd, C. L., and B. L. Harris: *J. Phys. Chem.*, **58**, 899 (1954).
33. Mantell, C. L.: "Adsorption," 2d ed., McGraw-Hill Book Company, New York, 1951.
34. Michaels, A. S.: *Ind. Eng. Chem.*, **44**, 1922 (1952).
35. Nachod, F. C., and J. Schubert: "Ion Exchange Technology," Academic Press Inc., New York, 1956.
36. Othmer, D. F., and F. G. Sawyer: *Ind. Eng. Chem.*, **35**, 1269 (1943).
37. Sanders, M. T.: *Ind. Eng. Chem.*, **20**, 791 (1928).
38. Siegmund, C. W., W. D. Munro, and N. R. Amundsen: *Ind. Eng. Chem.*, **48**, 43 (1956).
39. Squires, A. M.: *Chem. Eng. Progr.*, **58**(4), 66 (1962).
40. Swinton, E. A., D. E. Weiss et al.: *Australian J. Appl. Sci.*, **4**, 316, 510, 519, 530, 543 (1953).
41. Vermeulen, T., in T. B. Drew and J. W. Hoopes (eds.), "Advances in Chemical Engineering," vol. II, p. 147, Academic Press Inc., New York, 1958.

42. Walker, W. H., W. K. Lewis, W. H. McAdams, and E. R. Gilliland: "Principles of Chemical Engineering," 3d ed., p. 511, McGraw-Hill Book Company, New York, 1937.

43. Young, D. M., and A. D. Croswell: "Physical Adsorption of Gases," Butterworth & Co. (Publishers), Ltd., London, 1962.

44. Zenz, F. A.: in A. Acrivos (ed.), "Modern Chemical Engineering," vol. 1, p. 269, Reinhold Publishing Corporation, New York, 1963.

45. Zenz, F. A., and D. F. Othmer: "Fluidization and Fluid-particle Systems," Reinhold Publishing Corporation, New York, 1960.

PROBLEMS

11.1 The equilibrium adsorption of acetone vapor on an activated carbon at 30°C is given by the following data:

G adsorbed/carbon	0	0.1	0.2	0.3	0.35
Partial pressure acetone, mm Hg	0	2	12	42	92

The vapor pressure of acetone at 30°C is 283 mm Hg.

A liter flask contains air and acetone vapor at 1 atm and 30°C, with a relative saturation of the vapor of 35%. Two grams of fresh activated carbon is introduced into the flask, and the flask is sealed. Compute the final vapor concentration at 30°C and the final pressure. Neglect the adsorption of air.

11.2. A solution of washed, raw cane sugar, 48% sucrose by weight, is colored by the presence of small quantities of impurities. It is to be decolorized at 80°C by treatment with an adsorptive carbon in a contact filtration plant. The data for an equilibrium adsorption isotherm were obtained by adding various amounts of the carbon to separate batches of the original solution and observing the equilibrium color reached in each case. The data, with the quantity of carbon expressed on the basis of the sugar content of the solution, are as follows:

Lb carbon/lb dry sugar	0	0.005	0.01	0.015	0.02	0.03
% of color removed	0	47	70	83	90	95

The original solution has a color concentration of 20, measured on an arbitrary scale, and it is desired to reduce the color to 2.5% of its original value.

a. Convert the equilibrium data to $Y^* =$ color units/lb sugar, $X =$ color units/lb carbon. Do they follow the Freundlich equation? If so, what are the equation constants?

b. Calculate the necessary dosage of fresh carbon, per 1,000 lb of solution, for a single-stage process. **Ans.:** 20.4 lb.

c. Calculate the necessary carbon dosages per 1,000 lb of solution for a two-stage crosscurrent treatment, using the minimum total amount of fresh carbon. **Ans.:** 10.54 lb.

d. Calculate the necessary carbon dosage per 1,000 lb of solution for a two-stage countercurrent treatment. **Ans.:** 6.24 lb.

11.3. The sugar refinery of Prob. 11.2 must treat also a raw cane sugar solution, 48 wt % sucrose, of original color 50, based on the same color scale used in Prob. 11.2. The color scale is such that colors are additive, i.e., equal weights of solution of color 20 and color 50 will give a solution of color $(20 + 50)/2 = 35$. The same adsorption isotherm describes the color removal of the darker solution as that of Prob. 11.2. Equal quantities of the dark solution and that of Prob. 11.2 must both be decolorized to a color 0.5.

 a. In a single-stage process, will it be more economical of carbon first to blend the original solutions and to treat the blend, or to treat each separately to color 0.5 and to blend the finished products?

 b. Repeat for a two-stage crosscurrent treatment, fresh carbon in each stage, arranged for the minimum carbon in each case.

 c. Repeat for a countercurrent two-stage treatment.

 d. The following treating scheme was suggested: The light-colored solution is to be treated in a two-stage countercurrent plant to the final desired color. The spent carbon from this operation is to be used to treat an equal weight of the dark solution, and the carbon is then revivified. The residual dark solution is then finished to the desired final color with the necessary amount of fresh carbon. Sketch a flow sheet and an operating diagram (freehand) for the entire process. Determine whether there is any saving of carbon over that for the arrangement of part (*c*).

 e. Determine whether the scheme of Fig. 11.46 offers any economies of carbon.

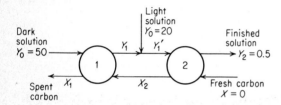

Fig. 11.46   *Flow sheet for Prob. 11.3e.*

11.4. Prove that for crosscurrent two-stage treatment of liquid solutions by contact filtration, when the adsorption isotherm is linear, the least total adsorbent results if the amounts used in each stage are equal.

11.5. For adsorption from dilute liquid solutions in stagewise countercurrent operations, where the Freundlich equation describes the adsorption equilibrium, derive analytical expressions in terms of n, m, Y_0, and Y_{Np} for the minimum adsorbent/solvent ratio when fresh adsorbent is used. Cover both cases of Fig. 11.22.

11.6. Nitrogen dioxide, NO_2, produced by a thermal process for fixation of nitrogen is to be removed from a dilute mixture with air by adsorption on silica gel in a continuous countercurrent adsorber. The gas entering the adsorber at the rate of 1,000 lb/hr contains 1.5% NO_2 by volume, and 90% of the NO_2 is to be removed. Operation is to be isothermal at 25°C, 1 atm. The entering gel will be free of NO_2. The equilibrium adsorption isotherm at this temperature is given by the following data [Foster and Daniels, *Ind. Eng. Chem.*, **43**, 986 (1951)]:

Partial pressure NO_2, mm Hg	0	2	4	6	8	10	12
G NO_2/100 g gel	0	0.4	0.9	1.65	2.60	3.65	4.85

 a. Calculate the minimum weight of gel required per hour.

 b. For twice the minimum gel rate, calculate the number of transfer units required.

 c. A superficial air rate of 300 lb/(hr)(sq ft) is to be used. Assume that the characteristics of the gel are the same as those described in Illustration 11.4. Modify the gas mass-transfer coefficient of Illustration 11.4 so that it will apply to the transfer of NO_2 rather than water. Modify the solid-phase mass-transfer coefficient to apply for NO_2 on the assumption that the transfer in the pores of the solid is by molecular diffusion through the gas filling the pores. The diffusivity of NO_2 in air is estimated to be 0.136 sq cm/sec at 25°C, 1 atm.

Estimate the value of H_{tOG}, and calculate the corresponding height of the adsorber. **Ans.: 9.5 ft.**

11.7. Lewis et al., *J. Am. Chem. Soc.*, **72,** 1157 (1950), report the following for the simultaneous adsorption of acetylene and ethylene from mixtures of the two on silica gel at 1 atm, 25°C (reprinted with permission of the American Chemical Society):

Mole fraction ethylene in adsorbate	Mole fraction ethylene in gas, at equilibrium	Mg moles mixture adsorbed/g adsorbent
0.0686	0.2422	1.622
0.292	0.562	1.397
0.458	0.714	1.298
0.592	0.814	1.193
0.630	0.838	1.170
0.864	0.932	1.078

A gas containing equimolar amounts of acetylene and ethylene is to be fractionated in a continuous countercurrent adsorber, to yield products containing 98 and 2% acetylene by volume. Assume the temperature to remain constant at 25°C and the pressure to be 1 atm. Calculate the number of transfer units and the gel circulation rate per 1,000 cu ft feed gas, using 1.2 times the minimum gel circulation rate. **Ans.:** $N_{tOG} = 15.3$.

11.8. The sulfur content of an oil is to be reduced by percolation through a bed of adsorbent clay. Laboratory tests with the clay and oil in a representative percolation filter show the following instantaneous sulfur contents of the effluent oil as a function of the total oil passing through the filter [adapted from Kaufman, *Chem. Met. Eng.*, **30,** 153 (1924)]:

Bbl oil/ton clay	0	10	20	50	100	200	300	400
% sulfur	0.011	0.020	0.041	0.067	0.0935	0.118	0.126	0.129

Assume that the specific gravity of the oil is unchanged during the percolation. The untreated oil has a sulfur content of 0.134%, and a product containing 0.090% sulfur is desired.

a. If the effluent from the filter is composited, what yield of satisfactory product may be obtained per ton of clay? **Ans.: 240 bbl.**

b. If the effluent from the filter is continually and immediately withdrawn and blended with just sufficient untreated oil to give the desired sulfur content in the blend, what quantity of product may be obtained per ton of clay? **Ans.: 159.4 bbl.**

11.9. A laboratory fixed-bed adsorption column filled with a synthetic sulfonic acid cation-exchange resin in the acid form is to be used to remove Na^+ ions from an aqueous solution of sodium chloride. The bed depth is 33.5 cm, and the solution to be percolated through the bed contains 0.120 meq Na^+/cu cm. At saturation, the resin contains 2.02 meq Na^+/cu cm resin. The solution will be passed through the bed at a superficial linear velocity of 0.31 cm/sec. For this resin, Michaels[34] reports that the overall liquid mass-transfer rate $K'_L a_p = 0.86 v_L^{0.5}$ where v_L is the superficial liquid velocity, cm/sec, and $K'_L a_p$ is expressed as meq Na^+/(sec)(cu cm)(meq/cu cm). The relative adsorptivity of Na^+ with respect to H^+ for this resin is $\alpha = 1.20$, and this is constant for the prevailing concentration level. Define the breakpoint concentration as 5% of the initial solution concentration, and assume that practical bed exhaustion occurs when the effluent concentration is 95% of the initial.   Estimate the volume of effluent at the breakpoint, per unit bed cross section. **Ans.:** 427 cu cm/sq cm.

Note: For these circumstances, Michaels[31] observed that the adsorption-zone height was 23.8 cm, that the breakpoint occurred after 382 ± 10 cu cm effluent/sq cm bed cross section was collected and that the holdup of liquid in the bed was 14.5 ± 2.5 cu cm solution/sq cm bed cross section. Compare the calculated results with these.

CHAPTER TWELVE
DRYING

The term *drying* refers generally to the removal of moisture from a substance. It is so loosely and inconsistently applied that some restriction in its meaning is necessary in the treatment to be given the subject here. For example, a wet solid such as wood, cloth, or paper may be dried by evaporation of the moisture either into a gas stream or without the benefit of the gas to carry away the vapor, but the mechanical removal of such moisture by expression or centrifuging is not ordinarily considered drying. A solution may be "dried" by spraying it in fine droplets into a hot, dry gas, which results in evaporation of the liquid, but evaporation of the solution by boiling in the absence of a gas to carry away the moisture is not ordinarily considered a drying operation. A liquid such as benzene may be "dried" of any small water content by an operation which is really distillation, but the removal of a small amount of acetone by the same process would not usually be called drying. Gases and liquids containing small amounts of water may be dried by adsorption operations, as discussed in Chap. 11. This discussion will be largely limited to the removal of moisture from solids and liquids by evaporation into a gas stream. In practice, the moisture is so frequently water and the gas so frequently air that this combination will provide the basis for most of the discussion. It is important to emphasize, however, that the equipment, techniques, and relationships are equally applicable to other systems as well.

EQUILIBRIUM

The moisture contained in a wet solid or liquid solution exerts a vapor pressure to an extent depending upon the nature of the moisture, the nature of the solid, and the temperature. If then a wet solid is exposed to a continual supply of fresh gas containing a fixed partial pressure of the vapor p, the solid will either lose moisture by evaporation or gain moisture from the gas until the vapor pressure of the moisture of the solid equals p. The solid and the gas are then in equilibrium, and the moisture content of the solid is termed its equilibrium-moisture content at the prevailing conditions.

Insoluble solids

A few typical equilibrium-moisture relationships are shown in Fig. 12.1, where the moisture in each case is water. Here the equilibrium partial pressure p of the water vapor in the gas stream has been divided by the vapor pressure of pure water P to give the relative saturation or relative humidity (see Chap. 7) of the gas, since the curves are then applicable over a modest range of temperatures instead of being useful for one temperature only. Consider the curve for wood. If the wood contained initially a very high moisture content, say 0.35 lb water/lb dry solid, and were exposed to a continual supply of air of 0.6 relative humidity, the wood would lose moisture by evaporation until its equilibrium concentration corresponding to point A on the curve were eventually reached. Further exposure to this air, for even indefinitely long periods, would not bring about additional loss of moisture from the solid.

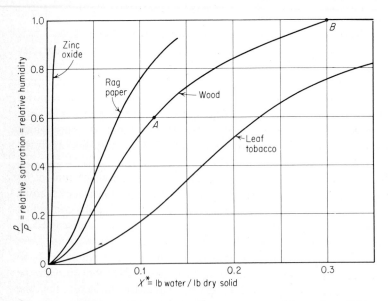

Fig. 12.1 *Equilibrium water content of some common solids at about 25°C. (From "International Critical Tables," vol. 2, pp. 322–325, with permission.)*

The moisture content could, however, be reduced further by exposure of the solid to air of lower relative humidity, but to remove all the moisture would require exposure to perfectly dry air, corresponding to the origin of the curve.   The moisture contained in the wood up to a concentration corresponding to point B in the figure, which exerts a vapor pressure less than that of pure water, may be moisture contained inside the cell walls of the plant structure, moisture in loose chemical combination with the cellulosic material, moisture present as a liquid solution of soluble portions of the solid and as a solid solution, moisture held in small capillaries and crevasses throughout the solid or otherwise adsorbed upon the surface.   Such moisture is called *bound water*.   If exposed to saturated air, the wood may have any moisture content greater than 0.3 lb/lb dry solid (point B), and moisture in excess of that at B, *unbound water*, exerts the vapor pressure of pure water at the prevailing temperature.

The equilibrium moisture for a given species of solid may depend upon the particle size or specific surface, if the moisture is largely physically adsorbed. Different solids have different equilibrium-moisture curves, as shown in the figure. Generally, inorganic solids which are insoluble in the liquid and which show no special adsorptive properties, such as the zinc oxide in the figure, show relatively low equilibrium-moisture contents, while spongy, cellular materials, especially those of vegetable origin such as the tobacco in the figure, generally show large equilibrium moisture contents.   The equilibrium partial pressure for a solid is independent of the nature of the dry gas provided the latter is inert to the solid and is the same in the absence of noncondensable gas also.   The same solids, if wet with liquids other than water, will show different equilibrium curves.   The effect of large changes in temperature may frequently be shown in the form of a reference-substance plot as in Fig. 11.5.[46]   It is seen that the equilibrium moisture is similar in many respects to the adsorption equilibria discussed in Chap. 11.

Hysteresis

Many solids exhibit different equilibrium-moisture characteristics depending upon whether the equilibrium is reached by condensation (adsorption) or evaporation (desorption) of the moisture.   A typical example is shown in Fig. 12.2, and this curve somewhat resembles that of Fig. 11.4.   In drying operations, it is the desorption equilibrium which is of particular interest, and this will always show the larger of the two equilibrium-moisture contents for a given partial pressure of vapor.   The moisture picked up by a dry solid when exposed to moist air, i.e., the adsorption equilibrium, is sometimes called *regain*, and knowledge of this has practical value in the consideration of drying operations.   For example, in the case of Fig. 12.2, it will be of little use to dry the solid to a water content below that corresponding to point A if it is expected to expose the dried material to air of 0.6 relative humidity later.   If it is important that the solid be kept at a lower moisture content, it would have to be packaged or stored immediately out of contact with the air in a moisture-impervious container.

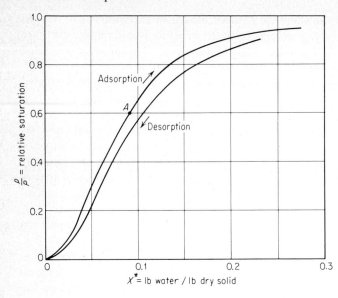

Fig. 12.2 *Equilibrium water content of a sulfite pulp, showing hysteresis.* [*Seborg, Ind. Eng. Chem.* **29,** 160 (1937).]

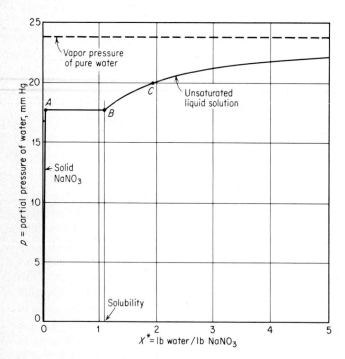

Fig. 12.3 *Equilibrium moisture content of sodium nitrate at 25°C.*

Soluble solids

Solids which are soluble in the liquid in question ordinarily show insignificant equilibrium-moisture contents when exposed to gases whose partial pressure of vapor is less than that of the saturated solution of the solid. Refer to Fig. 12.3, where the characteristics of sodium nitrate–water are shown. A saturated solution of sodium nitrate in water at 25°C exerts a partial pressure of water (*B*) equal to 17.7 mm Hg, and more dilute solutions exert higher partial pressures, as shown by curve *BC*. When exposed to air containing a partial pressure of water less than 17.7 mm Hg, a solution will evaporate, and the residual solid will retain only a negligible amount of adsorbed moisture as shown by the curve from the origin to point *A* and will appear dry. If the solid is exposed to air containing a higher water-vapor content, say 20 mm Hg, moisture will be adsorbed to such an extent that the solid will completely dissolve, or *deliquesce*, to produce the corresponding solution at *C*. Solids of very low solubility, when exposed to ordinary atmospheric air, will not deliquesce since the equilibrium partial pressure of their saturated solutions is greater than that ordinarily found in the air.

Hydrated crystals may show more complicated relationships, such as those of Fig. 12.4 for the system copper sulfate–water at 25°C. Three hydrates are formed in this system, as the figure indicates. The anhydrous salt shows a negligible equilibrium-moisture content, which would in any case consist merely of adsorbed water upon the surface of the crystals. If exposed to air containing a partial pressure of water less than 7.8 and more than 5.6 mm Hg, the salt will take on sufficient water to form the trihydrate, and the crystals will have negligible adsorbed water other than the water

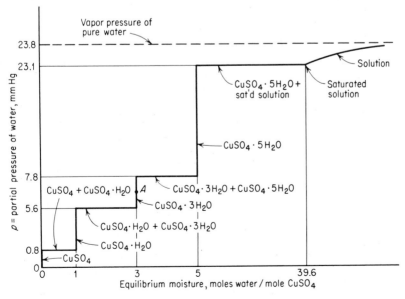

Fig. 12.4 *Equilibrium moisture of copper sulfate at 25°C (not to scale).*

of crystallization. The conditions will correspond to a point such as point *A* on the figure. If the moisture content of the air is then reduced to slightly less than 5.6 mm Hg, the trihydrate will lose moisture (*effloresce*) to form the monohydrate, while at 5.6 mm Hg any proportion of mono- and trihydrate may coexist. Similarly, if the moisture content of the air is increased to slightly more than 7.8 mm Hg, additional moisture will be adsorbed until the pentahydrate is formed. If the moisture content of the air exceeds 23.1 mm Hg, the salt will deliquesce.

Definitions

For convenient reference, certain terms used to describe the moisture content of substances are summarized below.

Moisture content, wet basis. The moisture content of a solid or solution is usually described in terms of weight percent moisture, and unless otherwise qualified this is ordinarily understood to be expressed on the wet basis, i.e., as (lb moisture/lb wet solid)100 = [lb moisture/(lb dry solid + lb moisture)]100 = $100X/(1 + X)$.

Moisture content, dry basis. This is expressed as lb moisture/lb dry solid = X. Percentage moisture, dry basis = $100X$.

Equilibrium moisture X^*. This is the moisture content of a substance when at equilibrium with a given partial pressure of the vapor.

Bound moisture. This refers to the moisture contained by a substance which exerts an equilibrium vapor pressure less than that of the pure liquid at the same temperature.

Unbound moisture. This refers to the moisture contained by a substance which exerts an equilibrium vapor pressure equal to that of the pure liquid at the same temperature.

Free moisture. Free moisture is that moisture contained by a substance in excess of the equilibrium moisture: $X - X^*$. Only free moisture can be evaporated,

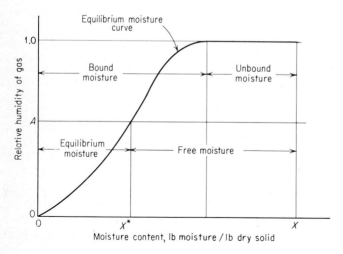

Fig. 12.5 *Types of moisture.*

and the free moisture content of a solid depends upon the vapor concentration in the gas.

These relations are shown graphically in Fig. 12.5 for a solid of moisture content X exposed to a gas of relative humidity A.

Illustration 12.1. A wet solid is to be dried from 80 to 5% moisture, wet basis. Compute the moisture to be evaporated, per 1,000 lb of dried product.

Solution

$$\text{Initial moisture content} = \frac{0.80}{1 - 0.80} = 4.00 \text{ lb water/lb dry solid}$$

$$\text{Final moisture content} = \frac{0.05}{1 - 0.05} = 0.0527 \text{ lb water/lb dry solid}$$

$$\text{Lb dry solid in product} = 1,000(0.95) = 950 \text{ lb}$$
$$\text{Moisture to be evapd} = 950(4 - 0.0527) = 3,750 \text{ lb}$$

DRYING OPERATIONS

Drying operations may be broadly classified according to whether they are batch or continuous. These terms are applied specifically from the point of view of the substance being dried. Thus the operation termed *batch drying* is usually in fact a semibatch process wherein a quantity of the substance to be dried is exposed to a continually flowing stream of air into which the moisture evaporates. In continuous operations, the substance to be dried as well as the gas passes continually through the equipment. No typically stagewise methods are ordinarily used, and all operations involve continuous contact of the gas and the drying substance.

The equipment used for drying may be classified according to any of the following categories:

1. *Method of operation, i.e., batch or continuous.* Batch, or semibatch, equipment is operated intermittently or cyclically under unsteady-state conditions: the drier is charged with the substance, which remains in the equipment until dry, whereupon the drier is emptied and recharged with a fresh batch. Continuous driers are usually operated in steady-state fashion.

2. *Method of supplying the heat necessary for evaporation of the moisture.* In *direct* driers, the heat is supplied entirely by direct contact of the substance with the hot gas into which evaporation takes place. In *indirect* driers, the heat is supplied quite independently of the gas used to carry away the vaporized moisture. For example, heat may be supplied by conduction through a metal wall in contact with the substance, or less frequently by exposure of the substance to infrared radiation or by dielectric heating. In the case of the last, the heat is generated inside the solid by a high-frequency electric field.

3. *Nature of the substance to be dried.* The substance may be a rigid solid such as wood or fiberboard, a flexible material such as cloth or paper, a granular solid such as a mass of crystals, a thick paste or a thin slurry, or a solution. If it is a solid, it may be fragile or sturdy. The physical form of the substance and the diverse methods of handling necessary have perhaps the greatest influence on the type of drier used.

I. BATCH DRYING

Drying in batches is a relatively expensive operation and is consequently limited to small-scale operations, to pilot-plant and development work, and to drying valuable materials whose total cost will be little influenced by added expense in the drying operation.

Direct driers

The construction of such driers depends greatly upon the nature of the substance being dried. *Tray driers*, also called cabinet, compartment, or shelf driers, are used for drying solids which must be supported on trays. This may include pasty materials such as wet filter cakes from filter presses, lumpy solids which must be spread upon trays, and similar materials. A typical device, shown schematically in Fig. 12.6, consists of a cabinet containing removable trays on which the solid to be dried is spread. After loading, the cabinet is closed, and steam-heated air is blown across and between the trays to evaporate the moisture (cross-circulation drying). Inert gas, even superheated steam,[6,16] rather than air may be used if the liquid to be evaporated is combustible: When the solid has reached the desired degree of dryness, the cabinet is opened and the trays replaced with a new batch. Figure 12.7 shows a simple modification, a *truck drier*, where the trays are racked upon trucks

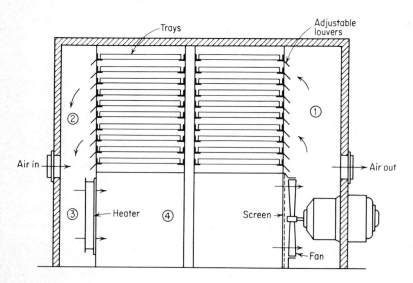

Fig. 12.6 *Typical tray drier.* (*Proctor and Schwartz, Inc.*)

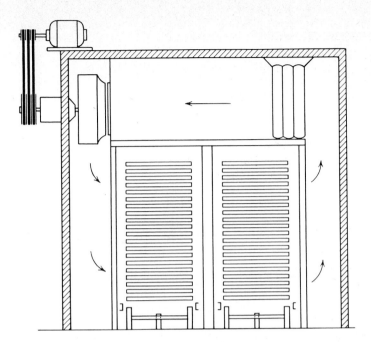

Fig. 12.7 *Two-truck drier.* (*Proctor and Schwartz, Inc.*)

which may be rolled into and out of the cabinet. Since the trucks may be loaded and unloaded outside the drier, considerable time may be saved between drying cycles. Other obvious modifications of the design are also used, depending upon the nature of the drying substance. Thus, skeins of fibers such as rayon may be hung from poles, and wood or boardlike materials may be stacked in piles, the layers separated from each other by spacer blocks.

In the case of granular materials, the solid may be arranged in thin beds supported on screens so that air or other gas may be passed through the beds. This results in very much more rapid drying. A typical device for this purpose, a batch *through-circulation drier*, is shown schematically in Fig. 12.8. Crystalline solids and materials which are naturally granular such as silica gel may be dried in this manner directly. In the case of others, some sort of preliminary treatment to put them into satisfactory form, *preforming*, is necessary. Pastes, for example, those resulting from precipitation of pigments or other solids, may be preformed by (1) extrusion into short, spaghettilike rods, (2) granulation, i.e., forcing them through screens, or (3) by briquetting.[21]

One of the most important difficulties in the use of driers of the type described is the nonuniformity of moisture content found in the finished product taken from various parts of the drier. This is largely the result of inadequate and nonuniform air movement inside the drier. It is important to eliminate stagnant air pockets and to maintain reasonably uniform air humidity and temperature throughout the drier. In order to do this, large volumes of air must be blown over the trays, if possible at

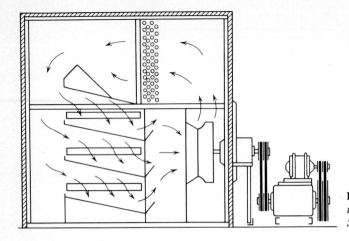

Fig. 12.8 *Through-circula-tion drier. (Proctor and Schwartz, Inc.)*

velocities ranging up to 10 or 20 ft/sec if the solid will not blow from the trays at these air rates. This may be accomplished by blowing large quantities of heated fresh air only once through the drier, but the loss of heat in the discharged air will then usually be prohibitive in cost. Instead, it is the practice to admit only relatively small quantities of fresh air and to recirculate the bulk of it, sometimes as much as 80 to 95 percent.[44] This may be done inside the drier, as shown, for example, in Fig. 12.6, with dampers in the inlet and outlet pipes to regulate the extent of recirculation. The louvers at each tray level may then be adjusted so as to ensure as nearly uniform air velocity over each tray as possible. Alternatively, the heaters and fans may be installed outside the drier, with ductwork and dampers to permit more careful control of the relative amounts of fresh and recirculated air admitted to the drier itself. It is important also that the trays in such driers be filled level to the brim but not overloaded, so that uniform free space for air movement is available between trays.

The recirculation of large quantities of air necessarily raises the humidity of the air in the drier considerably above that of the fresh air. Low percentage humidity and consequently reasonably rapid drying rates are then obtained by using as high a temperature as practicable. The drier must then be thoroughly insulated, not only to conserve heat but also to maintain the inside walls at temperatures above the dew point of the air to prevent condensation of moisture upon the walls. Specially conditioned, low-humidity air is not used except where low-temperature drying is necessary to avoid damage to the product.

Illustration 12.2. The drier of Fig. 12.6 contains trays arranged in a tier of 10, each on racks 4 in. apart, each tray 1.5 in. deep. Each tray is 3 ft wide, and there are 150 sq ft of drying surface. It is desired that the air entering the trays (position 1 on the figure) have a dry-bulb temperature of 200°F and humidity 0.05 lb water/lb dry air. Atmospheric air enters at 80°F, humidity 0.01. The air velocity over the trays at the entrance to the trays is to be 10 ft/sec. At a time when the solid being dried is losing water at a constant rate of 60 lb evaporated/hr, determine the percentage recirculation of air and the conditions of the air in the various parts of the drier.

Solution. At position 1, $Y_1 = 0.05$ lb water/lb dry air, $t_{G1} = 200°F$, and the humid volume (Table 7.1) is $[0.0252 + 0.0405(0.05)](200 + 460) = 17.97$ cu ft/lb dry air.

$$\text{Free area for flow between trays} = \frac{3(4 - 1.5)(11)}{12} = 6.87 \text{ sq ft}$$

$$\text{Rate of air flow to trays} = 10(60)(6.87) = 4,120 \text{ cu ft/min, or } 4,120/17.97$$
$$= 230 \text{ lb dry air/min (at position 1)}$$

The rate of evaporation is $^{60}\!/_{60} = 1.0$ lb water/min, and the humidity at 2 (Fig. 12.6) is therefore $(0.05 + 1)/230 = 0.0544$ lb water/lb dry air. Assuming adiabatic drying, the temperature at 2 may be found on the adiabatic-saturation line (Fig. 7.5), drawn through the conditions at 1, and at $Y_2 = 0.0544$, $t_{G2} = 184°F$.

The condition of the air at 4, and the discharged air, must be the same as at 1. An overall water balance about the drier therefore is

$$G(0.05 - 0.01) = 1.0 \text{ lb water evapd/min}$$
$$G = 25 \text{ lb dry air/min enter and leave}$$

The quantity of air at 3 and 4 (Fig. 12.6) is therefore $230 + 25 = 255$ lb dry air/min, and at position 4 the humid volume must be 17.97 cu ft/lb dry air. The volumetric rate through the fan is therefore $255(17.97) = 4,600$ cu ft/min. The percentage of air recycled is $^{230}\!/_{255}(100) = 90.1\%$.

The enthalpy of the air at 2 (and at 1) is 99.5 Btu/lb dry air (Fig. 7.5, saturated enthalpy at the adiabatic-saturation temperature, $116°F$), and that of the fresh air is 22.4 Btu/lb dry air. Assuming complete mixing, the enthalpy of the air at 3 is, by an enthalpy balance, $[99.5(230) + 22.4(25)]/255 = 92.0$ Btu/lb dry air. Since its humidity is 0.05, its dry bulb temperature (Fig. 7.5) is $173.5°F$. The heater must apply $255(99.5 - 92.0) = 1910$ Btu/min, neglecting heat losses.

The dew-point temperature of the air (Fig. 7.5) at 1, 3, and 4 is $104.5°F$, and at 2 it is $107°F$. The drier should be sufficiently well insulated so that the inside surface will not fall to a temperature of $107°F$.

The general humidity level in the drier may be altered during the drying cycle. This may be especially important in the case of certain solids which warp, shrink, develop surface cracks, or "case-harden" when dried too rapidly. A cake of soap of high moisture content, for example, if exposed to very dry, hot air, will lose moisture by evaporation from the surface so fast that water will not move rapidly enough from the center of the cake to the surface to keep pace with the evaporation. The surface then becomes hard and impervious to moisture (case-hardened), and drying stops even though the average water content of the cake is still very high. In the case of other solids, such as wood, for example, shrinkage at the surface may cause cracks or warping. Such substances should be dried slowly at first with air of high humidity, and drier air may be used only after the bulk of the water has been removed.

Driers of the type described are relatively cheap to build and have low maintenance costs. They are, however, expensive to operate owing to low heat economy and high labor costs. Each time the drier is opened for unloading and loading, the temperature of the interior falls and all the metal parts of the drier must be heated again to the operating temperature when operation is resumed. Steam consumption for heating the air will generally not be less than 2.5 lb steam/lb water evaporated and may be as high as 10, especially for cases where the moisture content of the product is reduced to very low levels.[17] The labor requirement for loading, unloading, and supervision of the drying cycle is high.

Indirect driers

Vacuum shelf driers are tray driers whose cabinets, made of cast-iron or steel plates, are fitted with tightly closing doors so that they may be operated at subatmospheric pressure. No air is blown or recirculated through such driers. The trays containing the solid to be dried rest upon hollow shelves through which warm water or steam is passed to provide the necessary heat for vaporization of moisture. The heat is conducted to the solid through the metal of the shelves and trays. After loading and sealing, the air in the drier is evacuated by a mechanical vacuum pump or steam jet ejector, and distillation of the moisture proceeds. The vapors usually pass to a condenser, where they are liquefied and collected, and only noncondensable gas is removed by the pump. *Agitated pan driers*,[43] which may be used to dry pastes or slurries in small batches, are shallow, circular pans, 3 to 6 ft in diameter and 1 to 2 ft deep, with flat bottoms and vertical sides. The pans are jacketed for admission of steam or hot water for heating. The paste, or slurry, in the pan is stirred and scraped by a set of rotating plows, in order to expose new material to the heated surface. Moisture is evaporated into the atmosphere in the case of atmosphere pan driers, or the pan may be covered and operated under vacuum. *Vacuum rotary driers* are steam-jacketed cylindrical shells, arranged horizontally, in which a slurry, or paste, may be dried in vacuum. The slurry is stirred by a set of rotating agitator blades attached to a central horizontal shaft which passes through the ends of the cylindrical shell. Vaporized moisture passes through an opening in the top to a condenser, and noncondensable gas is removed by a vacuum pump. The dried solid is discharged through a door in the bottom of the drier.

Driers of this category are expensive to build and to operate. Consequently they are used only for valuable materials which must be dried at low temperatures or in the absence of air to prevent damage, such as certain pharmaceutical products, or where the moisture to be removed is an expensive or poisonous organic solvent which must be recovered more or less completely.

Freeze drying. Substances which may not be heated even to moderate temperatures, such as foodstuffs and certain pharmaceuticals, may be dried by this method.[18] The substance to be dried is customarily frozen by exposure to very cold air and placed in a vacuum chamber, where the moisture sublimes and is pumped off by steam-jet ejectors or mechanical vacuum pumps. An alternative method of freezing is by flash vaporization of part of the moisture under vacuum, although foodstuffs which are not rigid in the unfrozen state may be damaged by this procedure. Some foods, beef for example, evidently contain capillary channels, and the water vapor diffuses from the receding ice surface through these channels as drying proceeds.[13] In other cases diffusion through cell walls must occur. In any event, one of the major problems is to supply the heat necessary for sublimation: as the plane of sublimation recedes, heat must be driven through larger thicknesses of dried matter of poor thermal conductivity, requiring increasing temperature differences which may damage the product. Radiant heat is used, and dielectric heat is a possibility although an expensive one. Still an additional method, useful for granular products, is through-circulation drying with air instead of pumping off the water by vacuum pump.

The rate of batch drying

In order to set up drying schedules and to determine the size of equipment, it is necessary to know the time which will be required to dry a substance from one moisture content to another under specified conditions. We shall also wish to estimate the influence that different drying conditions will have upon the time for drying. Our knowledge of the mechanism of drying is so incomplete that it is necessary with few exceptions to rely upon at least some experimental measurements for these purposes. Measurements of the rate of batch drying are relatively simple to make and provide much information not only for batch but also for continuous operation.

Drying tests. The rate of drying may be determined for a sample of a substance by suspending it in a cabinet or duct, in a stream of air, from a balance. The weight of the drying sample may then be measured as a function of time. Certain precautions must be observed if the data are to be of maximum utility. The sample should not be too small. Further, the following conditions should resemble as closely as possible those expected to prevail in contemplated large-scale operation: (1) The sample should be similarly supported in a tray or frame. (2) It should have the same ratio of drying to nondrying surface. (3) It should be subjected to similar conditions of radiant-heat transfer. (4) The air should have the same temperature, humidity, and velocity (both speed and direction with respect to the sample). If possible, several tests should be made on samples of different thicknesses. The dry weight of the sample should also be obtained.

The exposure of the sample to air of constant temperature, humidity, and velocity constitutes drying under *constant drying conditions.*

Rate-of-drying curve. From the data obtained during such a test, a curve of moisture content as a function of time (Fig. 12.9) may be plotted. This will be useful directly in determining the time required for drying larger batches under the same drying conditions. Much information can be obtained if the data are converted to rates of drying, expressed as N lb moisture evaporated/(hr)(sq ft), and plotted against moisture content, as in Fig. 12.10. This may be done by measuring the slopes of tangents drawn to the curve of Fig. 12.9 or by determining from the curve small changes in moisture content ΔX for corresponding small changes in time $\Delta \theta$ and calculating the rate as $N = -L_S \Delta X / A \Delta \theta$. Here L_S is the weight of dry solid, and A is the wet surface over which the gas blows and through which evaporation takes place in the case of cross-air circulation drying. In the case of through-circulation drying, A is the cross section of the bed measured at right angles to the direction of gas flow.

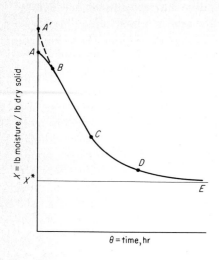

Fig. 12.9 *Batch drying, constant drying conditions.*

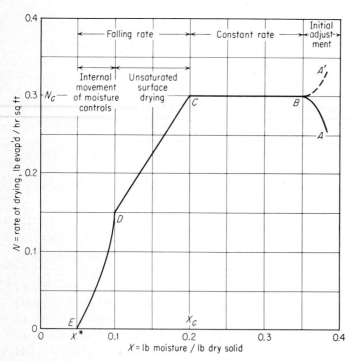

Fig. 12.10 *Typical rate-of-drying curve, constant drying conditions.*

The rate-of-drying curve is sometimes plotted with the ordinate expressed as lb moisture evaporated/(hr)(lb dry solid), which in the present notation is $-dX/d\theta$.

There are usually two major parts to the rate curve of Fig. 12.10, a period of constant rate and one of falling rate, as marked on the figure. While different solids and different conditions of drying will frequently give rise to curves of very different shape in the falling-rate period, the curve shown occurs frequently. Some of the differences which may arise will be considered later, but for the present let us briefly review the reasons generally advanced for the various parts of the curve shown.[12,26,39,41]

If a solid is initially very wet, the surface will be covered with a thin film of liquid, which we shall assume is entirely unbound moisture. When it is exposed to relatively dry air, evaporation will take place from the surface. The rate at which moisture evaporates can be described in terms of a gas mass-transfer coefficient k_Y and the difference in humidity of the gas at the liquid surface Y_s and in the main stream Y. Thus, for cross-circulation drying

$$N_c = k_Y(Y_s - Y) \tag{12.1}$$

The coefficient k_Y may be expected to remain constant as long as the speed and direction of gas flow past the surface do not change. The humidity Y_s is the saturated humidity at the liquid-surface temperature t_s and will therefore depend upon this temperature. Since evaporation of moisture absorbs latent heat, the liquid surface will come to, and remain at, an equilibrium temperature such that the rate of heat flow from the surroundings to the surface exactly equals the rate of heat absorption. Y_s therefore remains constant. Since in addition Y remains unchanged under constant drying conditions, the rate of evaporation must remain constant at the value N_c, as shown on Figs. 12.9 and 12.10 between points B and C. In the beginning, the solid and the liquid surface are usually colder than the ultimate surface temperature t_s, and the evaporation rate will increase while the surface temperature rises to its ultimate value during the period AB on these curves. Alternatively the equilibrium temperature t_s may be lower than the initial value, which will give rise to a curve $A'B$ while the initial adjustment occurs. The initial period is usually so short that it is ordinarily ignored in subsequent analysis of the drying times.

When the average moisture content of the solid has reached a value X_c, the *critical moisture content* (Fig. 12.10), the surface film of moisture has been so reduced by evaporation that further drying causes dry spots to appear upon the surface, and these occupy increasingly larger proportions of the exposed surface as drying proceeds. Since, however, the rate N is computed by means of the constant gross surface A, the value of N must fall even though the rate per unit of wet surface remains constant. This gives rise to the first part of the falling-rate period, the period of *unsaturated surface drying*, from points C to D (Figs. 12.9 and 12.10). Ultimately the original surface film of liquid will have entirely evaporated at an average moisture content for the solid corresponding to point D. This part of the curve may be missing entirely, or it may constitute the whole of the falling-rate period. In the case of some textiles, other explanations for the linear falling-rate period have been necessary.[30]

On further drying, the rate at which moisture may move through the solid, as a result of concentration gradients existing between the deeper parts and the surface, is the controlling step. As the moisture concentration generally is lowered by the drying, the rate of internal movement of moisture decreases. In some cases, evaporation may take place beneath the surface of the solid in a plane or zone which retreats deeper into the solid as drying proceeds. In any event, the rate of drying falls even more rapidly than before, as from D to E (Fig. 12.10). At point E, the moisture content of the solid has fallen to the equilibrium value X^* for the prevailing air humidity, and drying stops.

Time of drying. If it is desired to determine the time of drying a solid under the same conditions for which a drying curve such as Fig. 12.9 has been completely determined, one need merely read the difference in the times corresponding to the initial and final moisture contents from the curve.

Within limits, it is sometimes possible to estimate the appearance of a rate-of-drying curve such as Fig. 12.10 for conditions different from those used in the experiments. In order to determine the time for drying for such a curve, we may proceed as follows: The rate of drying is, by definition,

$$N = \frac{-L_s \, dX}{A \, d\theta} \tag{12.2}$$

Rearranging and integrating over the time interval while the moisture content changes from its initial value X_1 to its final value X_2,

$$\theta = \int_0^\theta d\theta = \frac{L_S}{A} \int_{X_2}^{X_1} \frac{dX}{N} \tag{12.3}$$

1. *The constant-rate period.* If the drying takes place entirely within the constant-rate period so that X_1 and $X_2 > X_c$ and $N = N_c$, Eq. (12.3) becomes

$$\theta = \frac{L_S(X_1 - X_2)}{AN_c} \tag{12.4}$$

2. *The falling-rate period.* If X_1 and X_2 are both less than X_c, so that drying occurs under conditions of changing N, we may proceed as follows:

a. General case. For any shape of falling-rate curve whatsoever, Eq. (12.3) may be integrated graphically by determining the area under a curve of $1/N$ as ordinate, X as abscissa, the data for which may be obtained from the rate-of-drying curve.

b. Special case. N is linear in X, as in the region BC of Fig. 12.10. In this case,

$$N = mX + b \tag{12.5}$$

where m is the slope of the linear portion of the curve and b is a constant. Substitution in Eq. (12.3) provides

$$\theta = \frac{L_S}{A} \int_{X_2}^{X_1} \frac{dX}{mX + b} = \frac{L_S}{mA} \ln \frac{mX_1 + b}{mX_2 + b} \tag{12.6}$$

But since $N_1 = mX_1 + b$, $N_2 = mX_2 + b$, and $m = (N_1 - N_2)/(X_1 - X_2)$, Eq. (12.6) becomes

$$\theta = \frac{L_S(X_1 - X_2)}{A(N_1 - N_2)} \ln \frac{N_1}{N_2} = \frac{L_S(X_1 - X_2)}{AN_m} \tag{12.7}$$

where N_m is the logarithmic average of the rate N_1, at moisture content X_1, and N_2 at X_2.

Frequently the entire falling-rate curve may be taken as a straight line between points C and E (Fig. 12.10). It is often assumed to be so for lack of more detailed data. In this case

$$N = m(X - X^*) = \frac{N_c(X - X^*)}{X_c - X^*} \tag{12.8}$$

and Eq. (12.7) becomes

$$\theta = \frac{L_S(X_c - X^*)}{N_c A} \ln \frac{X_1 - X^*}{X_2 - X^*} \tag{12.9}$$

In any particular drying problem, either or both constant- and falling-rate periods may be involved, depending upon the relative values of X_1, X_2, and X_c. The appropriate equations and limits must then be chosen.

Illustration 12.3. A batch of the solid for which Fig. 12.10 is the drying curve is to be dried from 25 to 6% moisture under conditions identical to those for which the figure applies. The initial weight of the wet solid is 350 lb, and the drying surface is 1 sq ft/8 lb dry weight. Determine the time for drying.

Solution. The total weight of the batch is unimportant. $L_S/A = 8$. At 25% moisture, $X_1 = 0.25/(1 - 0.25) = 0.333$ lb moisture/lb dry solid. At 6% moisture, $X_2 = 0.06/(1 - 0.06) = 0.064$ lb moisture/lb dry solid. Inspection of Fig. 12.10 shows that both constant- and falling-rate periods are involved. The limits of moisture content in the equations for the different periods will be chosen accordingly.

Constant-rate period. From $X_1 = 0.333$ to $X_c = 0.200$. $N_c = 0.30$.

Eq. (12.4):
$$\theta = \frac{L_S(X_1 - X_c)}{AN_c} = \frac{8(0.333 - 0.200)}{1(0.30)} = 3.54 \text{ hr}$$

Falling-rate period. From $X_c = 0.200$ to $X_2 = 0.064$. Use Eq. (12.3). The following table is prepared from the data of Fig. 12.10:

X	N	$\dfrac{1}{N}$
0.20	0.300	3.33
0.18	0.266	3.76
0.16	0.239	4.18
0.14	0.208	4.80
0.12	0.180	5.55
0.10	0.150	6.67
0.09	0.097	10.3
0.08	0.070	14.3
0.07	0.043	23.3
0.064	0.025	40.0

A curve, not shown, is prepared of $1/N$ as ordinate, X as abscissa, and the area under the curve between $X = 0.20$ and $X = 0.064$ is 1.06.

Eq. (12.3):

$$\theta = \tfrac{8}{4}(1.06) = 8.48 \text{ hr}$$

The total drying time is therefore $3.54 + 8.48 = 12.02$ hr

Alternatively, since the drying curve is straight from $X = 0.20$ to $X = 0.10$, Eq. (12.7) may be used in this range of moisture contents,

$$\theta = \frac{L_S(X_c - X_D)}{A(N_c - N_D)} \ln \frac{N_c}{N_D} = \frac{8(0.20 - 0.10)}{1(0.30 - 0.15)} \ln \frac{0.30}{0.15} = 3.70 \text{ hr}$$

Graphical integration in the range $X = 0.1$ to $X = 0.064$ provides, through Eq. (12.3), an additional 4.79 hr, so that the total falling-rate time is $3.70 + 4.79 = 8.49$ hr.

As an approximation, the falling-rate period may be represented by a straight line from C to E (Fig. 12.10). The corresponding falling-rate time is, by Eq. (12.9),

$$\theta = \frac{L_S(X_c - X^*)}{N_c A} \ln \frac{X_c - X^*}{X_2 - X^*} = \frac{8(0.20 - 0.05)}{0.3(1)} \ln \frac{0.20 - 0.05}{0.064 - 0.05} = 9.5 \text{ hr}$$

The mechanisms of batch drying

We now consider the various portions of the rate-of-drying curve in more detail. Our present knowledge permits us to describe the drying process in the constant-rate period reasonably well, but our understanding of the falling-rate periods is very limited.

Cross-circulation drying

The constant-rate period. In this period, where surface evaporation of unbound moisture occurs, it has been shown that the rate of drying is established by a balance of the heat requirements for evaporation and the rate at which heat reaches the surface. Consider the section of a material drying in a stream of gas as shown in Fig. 12.11. The solid of thickness z_S ft is placed on a tray of thickness z_M ft. The whole is immersed in a stream of drying gas at temperature $t_G°$F and humidity Y lb moisture/lb dry gas, flowing at a mass velocity G lb/(hr)(sq ft). The evaporation

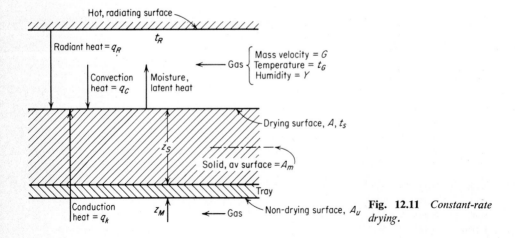

Fig. 12.11 *Constant-rate drying.*

of moisture takes place from the upper surface, A sq ft, which is at a temperature $t_s°F$. The drying surface receives heat from several sources: (1) q_c by convection from the gas stream; (2) q_k by conduction through the solid; (3) q_R by direct radiation from a hot surface at temperature $t_R°F$, as shown, all expressed as Btu/(hr)(sq ft). In accordance with the mechanism discussed earlier, the heat arriving at the surface by these methods is removed by the evaporating moisture, so that the surface temperature remains constant at t_s. The entire mechanism resembles the wet-bulb-thermometer process, complicated by the additional source of heat.

The rate of evaporation and the surface temperature may then be obtained by a heat balance.[38] If q represents the total heat arriving at the surface, then

$$q = q_c + q_R + q_k \tag{12.10}$$

Neglecting the heat required to superheat the evaporated moisture to the gas temperature and considering only the latent heat of vaporization λ_s, then the rate of evaporation N_c and the rate of heat flow are related,

$$N_c \lambda_s = q \tag{12.11}$$

The heat received at the surface by convection is controlled by the appropriate convection heat-transfer coefficient h_c,

$$q_c = h_c(t_G - t_s) \tag{12.12}$$

The heat received by radiation may be estimated by the usual means[23] and can also be expressed as a heat-transfer coefficient h_R,

$$q_R = \varepsilon(1{,}730)(10^{-12})(T_R^4 - T_s^4) = h_R(t_R - t_s) \tag{12.13}$$

$$h_R = \frac{\varepsilon(1{,}730)(10^{-12})(T_R^4 - T_s^4)}{t_R - t_s} \tag{12.14}$$

where ε is the emissivity of the drying surface and T_R and T_s are the absolute temperatures of the radiating and drying surfaces, in degrees Rankine. The heat received by convection and conduction through the solid may be computed by the usual methods for heat transfer through a series of resistances,

$$q_k = U_k(t_G - t_s) \tag{12.15}$$

$$U_k = \frac{1}{(1/h_c)(A/A_u) + (z_M/k_M)(A/A_u) + (z_S/k_S)(A/A_m)} \tag{12.16}$$

where h_c, the convection coefficient for the tray, may ordinarily be taken as the same as that for the drying surface, k_M and k_S are the thermal conductivities of the tray material and the drying solid, and A_u and A_m the nondrying surface and the average area of the drying solid, respectively. A thermal resistance at the junction of the drying solid and the tray material, and an effect of radiation to the tray, may be added to the terms of Eq. (12.16), if desired.

Combining Eqs. (12.1) and (12.10) to (12.15) permits calculation of the rate of drying,

$$N_c = \frac{q}{\lambda_s} = \frac{(h_c + U_k)(t_G - t_s) + h_R(t_R - t_s)}{\lambda_s} = k_Y(Y_s - Y) \qquad (12.17)$$

The surface temperature must be known in order to use the relationship. This may be obtained by consideration of the left-hand portions of Eq. (12.17), which may be rearranged to read

$$\frac{(Y_s - Y)\lambda_s}{h_c/k_Y} = \left(1 + \frac{U_k}{h_c}\right)(t_G - t_s) + \frac{h_R}{h_c}(t_R - t_s) \qquad (12.18)$$

The ratio h_c/k_Y applicable to flow of gases past wet-bulb thermometers [Eqs. (7.27) and (7.28)] may be used for present purposes, and for the system air-water vapor this ratio was shown to be substantially the same as the humid heat of the gas C_s. Since Y_s is the saturated humidity of the gas stream corresponding to t_s when unbound moisture is being evaporated, both these quantities may be found by solving Eq. (12.18) simultaneously with the saturated-humidity curve on a psychrometric chart.

If conduction through the solid and radiation effects is absent, Eq. (12.18) reduces to that for the wet-bulb thermometer [Eq. (7.26)] and the surface temperature is the wet-bulb temperature of the gas. The drying surfaces will also be at the wet-bulb temperature if the solid is dried from all surfaces in the absence of radiation. When pans or trays of drying material are placed one above another, as in Figs. 12.6 and 12.7, most of the solid will receive radiation only from the bottom of the pan immediately above it, and unless gas temperatures are very high, this is not likely to be very important. It is essential therefore not to overemphasize the heat received by radiation in conducting drying tests on single pairs of trays.

For flow of gas parallel to a smooth surface, it should be possible to determine both h_c and k_Y from item 3, Table 3.3. For high Reynolds numbers, in the range usually employed,

$$i_H = \frac{h_c}{C_p G}\,\mathrm{Pr}^{2/3} = j_D = \frac{k_Y}{G_s}\,\mathrm{Sc}^{2/3} = 0.036\,\mathrm{Re}_x^{-0.2} \qquad (12.19)$$

where Re_x is a length Reynolds number xG/μ, x being the length of the drying surface in the direction of gas flow. If the gas is air and the length of the surface is 1 ft, this provides $h_c = 0.0058G^{0.8}$, whereas in a detailed study of drying of sand in trays,[38] h_c was found to be $0.0128G^{0.8}$. Such discrepancies have been assigned to a number of causes: different "calming" lengths ahead of the drying surface,[31] the shape of the leading edge of the drying surface, and the fact that a Reynolds number based on equivalent duct diameter rather than length of surface may be more appropriate.[6] In the absence of more specific data, the following are recommended:

Air flow parallel to surface, $G = 500$ to $6,000$ lb/(hr)(sq ft)(2 to 25 ft/sec)

$$h_c = 0.01G^{0.8} \qquad (12.20)$$

Air flow perpendicular to surface,[28] $G = 800$ *to* $4,000$ $lb/(hr)(sq\ ft)(3$ *to* $15\ ft/sec)$

$$h_c = 0.37G^{0.37} \tag{12.21}$$

The relationships developed in Eqs. (12.17) to (12.21) permit direct estimates of the rate of drying during the constant-rate period, but they should not be considered as complete substitutes for experimental measurements. Perhaps their greatest value is in conjunction with limited experimental data in order to predict the effect of changing the drying conditions.

Effect of Gas Velocity. If radiation and conduction through the solid are negligible, N_c is proportional to $G^{0.8}$ for parallel flow of gas and to $G^{0.37}$ for perpendicular flow. If radiation and conduction are present, the effect of gas rate will be less important.

Effect of Gas Temperature. Increased air temperature increases the quantity $t_G - t_s$ and hence increases N_c. In the absence of radiation effects, and neglecting the variation of λ over moderate temperature ranges, N_c is directly proportional to $t_G - t_s$.

Effect of Gas Humidity. N_c varies directly as $Y_s - Y$, and consequently increasing the humidity lowers the rate of drying. Usually, changes in Y and t_G involve simultaneous changes in t_s and Y_s, and the effects are best estimated by direct application of Eq. (12.17).

Effect of Thickness of Drying Solid. If heat conduction through the solid occurs, Eqs. (12.15) and (12.16) indicate lowered values of N_c with increased solid thickness. However, conduction of heat through edge surfaces of pans and trays may be an important source of heat which can result in increased rate of drying if the edge surface is large. If nondrying surfaces are heat-insulated, or if drying occurs from all surfaces of the solid, N_c is independent of thickness. The *time* for drying between fixed moisture contents within the constant-rate period will then be directly proportional to thickness.

Illustration 12.4. An insoluble crystalline solid wet with water is placed in a 2- by 2-ft rectangular pan, 1 in. deep, made of $\frac{1}{32}$-in.-thick galvanized iron. The pan is placed in an air stream at 150°F, humidity 0.01 lb water/lb dry air, flowing parallel to the upper and lower surfaces at a velocity of 10 ft/sec. The surface of the solid is in direct sight of steam-heated pipes whose surface temperature is 250°F.

a. Make an estimate of the rate of drying at constant rate.

b. Reestimate the rate if the pan were thoroughly heat-insulated and if there were no radiation from the steam pipes.

Solution. a. $Y = 0.01$ lb water/lb dry air, $t_G = 150$°F. The humid volume of the air (Table 7.1) is $[0.0252 + 0.0405(0.01)](150 + 460) = 15.6$ cu ft/lb dry air.

$$\rho_G = \text{density of gas} = \frac{1.01}{15.6} = 0.0647 \text{ lb/cu ft}$$

$$G = 10(3,600)(0.0647) = 2,430 \text{ lb/(hr)(sq ft)}$$

Eq. (12.20): $h_c = 0.01(2430)^{0.8} = 5.10 \text{ Btu/(hr)(sq ft)(°F)}$

Take the emissivity of the solid as $\varepsilon = 0.94$. $t_R = 250°F$, $T_R = 250 + 460 = 710°R$. Tentatively estimate t_s as $100°F$, and $T_s = 100 + 460 = 560°R$.

Eq. (12.14):
$$h_R = \frac{0.94(1,730)(10^{-12})(710^4 - 560^4)}{250 - 100} = 1.70 \text{ Btu/(hr)(sq ft)(°F)}$$

Take $A_m = A = 2(2) = 4$ sq ft. The area of the sides of the pan $= 4(2)(\tfrac{1}{12}) = 0.667$ sq ft, and $A_u = 2(2) + 0.667 = 4.67$ sq ft for bottom and sides (this method of including the heat transfer through the sides is an oversimplification, but adequate for present purposes). Thermal conductivities are $k_M = 26$ for the metal of the pan, and $k_S = 2$ for the wet solid[38] (this value must be carefully chosen: it may bear no simple relation to the conductivities of either the dry solid or the moisture). $z_S = \tfrac{1}{12} = 0.0833$ ft, $z_M = 1/32(12) = 0.0026$ ft.

Eq. (12.16):
$$\frac{1}{U_k} = \frac{1}{5.10}\frac{4}{4.67} + \frac{0.0026}{26}\frac{4}{4.67} + \frac{0.0833}{2}\frac{4}{4}$$
$$U_k = 4.76 \text{ Btu/(hr)(sq ft)(°F)}$$

The humid heat of the air (Table 7.1) is $C_S = 0.24 + 0.45(0.01) = 0.245$, and λ_s at the estimated $100°F$ is 1,037 Btu/lb.

Eq. (12.18):
$$\frac{(Y_s - 0.01)1,037}{0.245} = \left(1 + \frac{4.76}{5.10}\right)(150 - t_s) + \frac{1.70}{5.10}(250 - t_s)$$

This reduces to $Y_s = 0.0991 - 0.000541 t_s$, which must be solved simultaneously with the saturated-humidity curve of the psychrometric chart for air–water vapor. This is most conveniently done graphically, as in Fig. 12.12, by plotting the equation on the pertinent portion of the psychrometric chart (Fig. 7.5). The line marked a on Fig. 12.12 is the above expression, and it intersects the saturated-humidity curve at $Y_s = 0.0445$, $t_s = 101°F$, the surface temperature, which is sufficiently close to the $100°F$ estimated previously to make recalculation unnecessary. At $101°F$, $\lambda_s = 1,036$ Btu/lb.

Eq. (12.17):
$$N_c = \frac{(5.10 + 4.76)(150 - 101) + 1.70(250 - 101)}{1,036}$$
$$= 0.712 \text{ lb water evapd/(hr)(sq ft)}$$

and the evaporation rate is $0.712(4) = 2.848$ lb water/hr.

 b. Where no radiation or conduction of heat through the solid occurs, the drying surface assumes the wet-bulb temperature of the air. For the system air–water at this humidity, the adiabatic-saturation lines of the psychrometric chart serve as wet-bulb lines, and on Fig. 12.12 line b is the

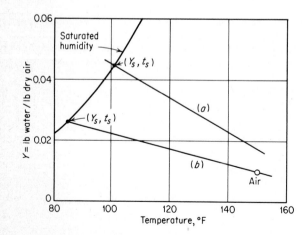

Fig. **12.12** *Solution to Illustration 12.4.*

adiabatic-saturation line through the point representing the air ($t_G = 150°F$, $Y = 0.01$). The line intersects the saturated-humidity curve at the wet-bulb conditions, $t_s = 84.5°F$, $Y_s = 0.026$. At this temperature, $\lambda_s = 1,045$ Btu/lb.

Eq. (12.17): $$N_c = \frac{h_c(t_G - t_s)}{\lambda_s} = \frac{5.10(150 - 84.5)}{1,045} = 0.320 \text{ lb/(hr)(sq ft)}$$

and the evaporation rate is $0.320(4) = 1.280$ lb water/hr.

When the air suffers a considerable change in temperature and humidity in its passage over the solid, as, for example, is indicated in Illustration 12.2, the rate of drying at the leading and trailing edge of the solid will differ and this accounts in part for the nonuniform drying frequently obtained in tray driers. This may be counteracted in part by periodic reversal of the air flow.

Movement of moisture within the solid. When surface evaporation occurs, there must be a movement of moisture from the depths of the solid to the surface. The nature of the movement influences the drying during the falling-rate periods. In order to appreciate the diverse nature of the falling-rate portions of the drying curve which have been observed, let us review very briefly some of the theories advanced to explain moisture movement and the relation of these to the falling-rate curves.

1. *Liquid diffusion.* Diffusion of liquid moisture may result because of concentration gradients between the depths of the solid, where the concentration is high, and the surface, where it is low. These gradients are set up during drying from the surface. This method of moisture transport is probably limited to cases where single-phase solid solutions are formed with the moisture, as in the case of soap, glue, gelatin, and the like; and to certain cases where bound moisture is being dried, as in the drying of the last portions of water from clays, flour, textiles, paper, and wood.[14] The general mechanism of this process is described in Chap. 4. It has been found that the moisture diffusivity usually decreases rapidly with decreased moisture content, so that diffusivities calculated in the manner of Illustration 4.5 are average values over the range of concentrations considered.

During the constant-rate period of drying such solids, the surface-moisture concentration is reduced, but the concentration in the depths of the solid remains high. The resulting high diffusivities permit movement of the moisture to the surface as fast as it can be evaporated, and the rate remains constant. When dry spots appear owing to the projection of portions of the solid into the gas film, a period of unsaturated surface evaporation results. The surface eventually dries to the equilibrium moisture content for the prevailing gas. Further drying occurs at rates which are entirely controlled by the diffusion rates within the solid, since these are slow at low moisture contents. If the initial constant-rate drying is very rapid, the period of unsaturated surface evaporation may not appear, and the diffusion-controlled falling-rate period begins immediately after the constant-rate period is completed,[40] as in Fig. 12.13.

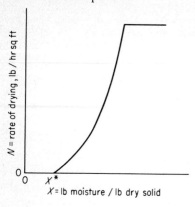

N = rate of drying, lb / hr sq ft

X = lb moisture / lb dry solid

Fig. 12.13 *Diffusion-controlled falling rate.*[40]

For many cases of drying where the diffusion mechanism has satisfactorily explained the rate of drying as a function of average moisture content, the distribution of moisture within the solid at the various stages of drying has not conformed to this mechanism.[14,29] The superficial applicability of the diffusion mechanism is then apparently accidental.

   2. *Capillary movement.*[7,14,29,32,45] Unbound moisture in granular and porous solids such as clays, sand, paint pigments, and the like, moves through the capillaries and interstices of the solids by a mechanism involving surface tension, in the manner that oil moves through a lamp wick. The capillaries extend from small reservoirs of moisture in the solid to the drying surface. As drying proceeds, at first moisture moves by capillarity to the surface sufficiently rapidly to maintain a uniformly wetted surface and the rate of drying is constant. The water is replaced by air entering the solid through relatively few openings and cracks. The surface moisture is eventually drawn to spaces between the granules of the surface, the wetted area at the surface decreases, and the unsaturated-surface drying period follows. The subsurface reservoirs eventually dry up, the liquid surface recedes into the capillaries, evaporation occurs below the surface in a zone or plane which gradually recedes deeper into the solid, and a second falling-rate period results. During this period, diffusion of vapor within the solid will occur from the place of vaporization to the surface.

   In the case of certain pastes dried in pans, the adhesion of the wet cake to the bottom of the pan may not permit ventilation of the subsurface passageways by gas. This may give rise to curves of the sort shown in Fig. 12.14. In this case, the usual constant-rate period prevailed during *a*. When the surface moisture was first depleted, liquid could not be brought to the surface by the tension in the capillaries since no air could enter to replace the liquid, the surface of moisture receded into the capillaries, and the rate fell during *b*. The solid eventually crumpled, admitting air to replace the liquid, whereupon capillary action brought this to the surface and the rate rose again, as at *c*.

   3. *Vapor diffusion.*[32] Especially if heat is supplied to one surface of a solid while drying proceeds from another, the moisture may evaporate beneath the surface and diffuse outward as a vapor. Moisture particles in granular solids, which have been

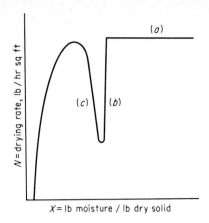

Fig. 12.14 *Effect of adhesion of a drying paste to the pan.* [*After R. C. Ernst, et al.: Ind. Eng. Chem.* **30**, 1119 (1938).]

isolated from the main portion of the moisture flowing through capillaries, may also be evaporated below the surface.

4. *Pressure.* Owing to shrinkage of the outside layers of a solid on drying, moisture may be squeezed to the surface.

Usually we can only speculate as to which of the mechanisms is appropriate to a particular solid and must rely on more or less empirical treatment of the experimental rates of drying.

Unsaturated-surface drying. During such a period the rate of drying N will usually vary linearly with moisture content X. Since the mechanism of evaporation during this period is the same as that in the constant-rate period, the effects of such variables as temperature, humidity, and velocity of the gas and thickness of the solid are the same as for constant-rate drying.

In some cases this period may constitute the whole of the falling-rate drying, giving rise to a curve of the type shown in Fig. 12.15. Equations (12.8) and (12.9)

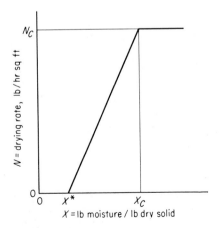

Fig. 12.15 *Linear falling rate.*

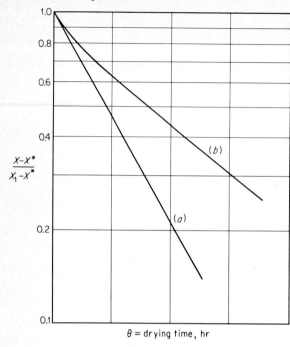

$\theta = $ drying time, hr

Fig. 12.16 *Empirical treatment of falling-rate data.* (a) *N varies linearly with* X; (b) *diffusion-controlled falling rate.*

then apply. Combining Eqs. (12.2), (12.8), and (12.17),

$$-\frac{dX}{d\theta} = \frac{k_Y A(X - X^*)(Y_s - Y)}{L_S(X_c - X^*)} \tag{12.22}$$

Noting that $L_S = z_S A \rho_S$, and letting $k_Y = f(G)$, then

$$-\frac{dX}{d\theta} = \frac{f(G)(X - X^*)(Y_s - Y)}{z_S \rho_S(X_c - X^*)} = \frac{\alpha f(G)(X - X^*)(Y_s - Y)}{z_S} \tag{12.23}$$

where $\alpha = $ const. This expression is sometimes used as an empirical description of the rates of drying for such cases. Alternatively, defining the time θ as that when the moisture content is X, Eq. (12.9) is readily transformed into

$$\ln \frac{X - X^*}{X_1 - X^*} = \frac{-N_c \theta}{\rho_S z_S(X_c - X^*)} \tag{12.24}$$

which suggests that falling-rate data of this nature will plot as a straight line, line *a*, on the semilogarithmic coordinates of Fig. 12.16. If drying tests are made under the same conditions for samples of different thickness, and so that heat is applied to the solid only through the drying surface, the slopes of such lines on this chart should be proportional to $-1/z_S$. The drying time between fixed moisture contents is then directly proportional to the solid thickness.

Internal-diffusion controlling. If a period of drying is developed where internal diffusion of moisture controls the rate, it can be expected that variables which influence the gas coefficients of heat or mass transfer will not influence the rate of drying. The drying rates should be independent of gas velocity, and humidity will be of importance only insofar as it controls the equilibrium-moisture concentration. When a semilogarithmic plot (Fig. 12.16) is prepared from drying data of this type, the curve *b* which results resembles those of Fig. 4.2. For a slab, the curves should be substantially straight at values of the ordinate below 0.6, with slopes proportional to $-1/z_S^2$. The drying time between fixed moisture contents should be proportional to the square of the thickness. Discrepancies may result because the initial moisture distribution is not uniform throughout the solid if a drying period precedes that for which diffusion controls, and because the diffusivity varies with moisture content.

Attempts have been made to describe rates of drying in the falling-rate period by means of overall coefficients of heat and mass transfer,[26] but these have not been too successful owing to the change in the individual resistances to transfer in the solid during the course of the drying.

Critical moisture content. The available data indicate that the average critical moisture content for a given type of solid depends upon the surface-moisture concentration. If drying during the constant-rate period is very rapid, and if the solid is thick, then steep concentration gradients are developed within the solid, and the falling rate begins at high average moisture contents. Generally, the critical moisture content will increase with increased drying rate and thickness of solid. It must usually be measured experimentally.

Through-circulation drying

When a gas passes through a bed of wet, granular solids, both a constant-rate and a falling-rate period of drying may result and the rate-of-drying curves may appear very much like that shown in Fig. 12.10.[21] Consider the case where the bed of solids has an appreciable thickness with respect to the size of the particles, as in Fig. 12.17.[2] The

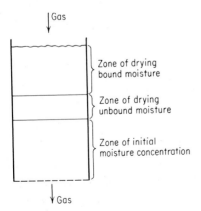

Fig. 12.17 *Through-circulation drying of thick beds of solids.*

evaporation of unbound moisture into the gas occurs in a relatively narrow zone which moves slowly through the bed, and unless the bed is internally heated, the gas leaving this zone is for all practical purposes saturated at the adiabatic-saturation temperature of the entering gas. This is also the surface temperature of the wet particles. The rate of drying is constant as long as the zone is entirely within the bed. When the zone first reaches the end of the bed, the rate of drying begins to fall because the gas no longer leaves in a saturated condition. In other words, a *desorption* wave passes through the bed and the situation is much like that described for elution in fixed beds (Chap. 11). However, the point of view of interest is the moisture content of the solid rather than the concentration changes occurring in the exit gas. In the case of shallow beds composed of large particles, the gas leaves the bed unsaturated from the beginning,[21] but as long as each particle surface remains fully wet, there will still be a constant-rate period. The falling rate then begins when the surface moisture is depleted.

The rate of drying of unbound moisture.[2] Consider a bed of uniform cross section as in Fig. 12.17, fed with a gas of humidity Y_1 at the rate of G_S lb dry gas/(hr)(sq ft bed cross section). The maximum rate of drying N_{max} will occur if the gas leaving the bed is saturated at the adiabatic-saturation temperature, with humidity Y_{as},

$$N_{max} = G_S(Y_{as} - Y_1) \tag{12.25}$$

where N is expressed as lb moisture evaporated/(hr)(sq ft bed cross section). In general, the gas will leave the bed at humidity Y_2, and the instantaneous rate of drying is

$$N = G_S(Y_2 - Y_1) \tag{12.26}$$

For a differential section of the bed where the gas undergoes a change in humidity dY and leaves at a humidity Y, the rate of drying is

$$dN = G_S \, dY = k_Y \, dS(Y_{as} - Y) \tag{12.27}$$

where S is the interfacial surface per square foot of bed cross section. Letting a represent the interfacial surface per unit volume of bed whose thickness is z_S,

$$dS = a \, dz_S \tag{12.28}$$

and Eq. (12.27) becomes

$$\int_{Y_1}^{Y_2} \frac{dY}{Y_{as} - Y} = \int_0^{z_S} \frac{k_Y a \, dz_S}{G_S} \tag{12.29}$$

$$\ln \frac{Y_{as} - Y_1}{Y_{as} - Y_2} = N_{tG} = \frac{k_Y a z_S}{G_S} \tag{12.30}$$

where N_{tG} is the number of gas transfer units in the bed. This equation is the same as Eq. (7.60), developed for a somewhat similar situation. The mean driving force for evaporation is then the logarithmic mean of $Y_{as} - Y_1$ and $Y_{as} - Y_2$, in accordance with Eq. (7.61). Combining Eqs. (12.25), (12.26), and (12.30),

$$\frac{N}{N_{\max}} = \frac{Y_2 - Y_1}{Y_{as} - Y_1} = 1 - \frac{Y_{as} - Y_2}{Y_{as} - Y_1} = 1 - e^{-N_{tG}} = 1 - e^{-k_{Y}az_S/G_S} \quad (12.31)$$

Equation (12.31) provides the rate of drying N if values of $k_Y a$ or N_{tG} can be determined. These have been established for certain special cases as follows:

1. *Particles small* (10 to 200 *mesh, or* 0.08 to 0.0029 *in. diameter*) *with respect to bed depth* (*greater than* 0.45 *in.*); *drying of unbound water from the surface of nonporous particles.*[2] For this case,† the constant rate is given by $N_{\max}$ [Eq. (12.25)]. Equation (12.31) may be used for both constant and falling rates, since at high moisture contents the exponential term becomes negligible. The interfacial surface a varies with moisture content, and it is most convenient to express N_{tG} empirically as

$$N_{tG} = \frac{1.14}{d_p^{0.35}} \left(\frac{d_p G}{\mu} \right)^{0.215} (X \rho_S z_S)^{0.64} \quad (12.32)$$

where d_p is the particle diameter, feet, and ρ_S the apparent density of the bed, lb dry solid/cu ft. Through-drying of such beds in the ordinary equipment may involve a pressure drop for gas flow which is too high for practical purposes, especially if the particles are very small. Drying of such beds is done on continuous rotary filters (crystal-filter driers), however.

2. *Particles large* (⅛ to ¾ *in. diameter*) *in shallow beds* (0.4 to 2.5 *in. thick*); *drying of unbound moisture from porous or nonporous particles.* During the constant-rate period the gas leaves the bed unsaturated, and the constant rate of drying is given by Eq. (12.31). For this purpose, k_Y is given by

$$k_Y = j_D G_S / Sc^{2/3} \quad (12.33)$$

and j_D in turn by item 5, Table 3.3. The interfacial surface may be taken as the surface of the particles. For air drying of water from solids, $Sc = 0.6$. Additional experimental data on a large number of preformed materials are also available.[21] During the falling-rate period, internal resistance to moisture movement may be important, and no general treatment is available. In many cases[21] it is found that semilogarithmic plots of the form of Fig. 12.16 are useful. If the line on this plot is straight, Eqs. (12.8) and (12.9) are applicable.

Drying of bound moisture. Presumably some adaptation of the methods used for adsorption in fixed beds (Chap. 11) could be made to describe this. No experimental confirmation is available, however.

---

† In beds of finely packed solids containing a large percentage of liquid, the liquid is largely forced from between the solid particles by a mechanical process when gas is forced through the bed. See particularly Brownell and Katz, *Chem. Eng. Progr.*, **43**, 537, 601, 703 (1947). Only the last traces of moisture are removed by the drying process considered here.

Illustration 12.5. A cake of a crystalline precipitate is to be dried by drawing air through the cake. The particles of the cake are nonporous, of average diameter 0.008 in., and since they are insoluble in water have negligible equilibrium-moisture content. The cake is 0.7 in. thick, and the apparent density is 85 lb dry solid/cu ft. It is to be dried from 2.5 to 0.1% moisture. The air will enter the cake at the rate of 175 lb dry air/(hr)(sq ft bed cross section), at a dry-bulb temperature of 90°F and 50% humidity. Determine the time for drying.

Solution. $X_1 = 0.025/(1 - 0.025) = 0.0256$ lb water/lb dry solid; $X_2 = 0.001/(1 - 0.001) = 0.001001$ lb water/lb dry solid. From Fig. 7.5, $Y_1 = 0.0158$ lb water/lb dry air; $t_{as} = 75°F$ (the adiabatic-saturation temperature) and $Y_{as} = 0.0190$ lb water/lb dry air. $G_S = 175$ lb dry air/(hr)(sq ft).

$$\text{Approx av } G = 175 + \frac{175(0.0158 + 0.0190)}{2} = 178 \text{ lb/(hr)(sq ft)}$$

Eq. (12.26): $\qquad N_{max} = 175(0.0190 - 0.0158) = 0.56$ lb evapd/(hr)(sq ft)

$$z_S = \frac{0.7}{12} = 0.0583 \text{ ft} \qquad d_p = \frac{0.008}{12} = 0.000665 \text{ ft} \qquad \rho_S = 85 \text{ lb dry solid/cu ft}$$

Viscosity of air at $(75 + 90)/2 = 82.5°F$ is 0.018 centipoise, and $\mu = 0.018(2.42) = 0.0286$ lb/ft hr.

$$\frac{d_p G}{\mu} = \frac{0.000665(178)}{0.0286} = 4.14$$

Eq. (12.32): $\qquad N_{tG} = \frac{1.14(4.14)^{0.215}[X(85)(0.0583)]^{0.64}}{0.000665^{0.35}} = 59.1X^{0.64}$

Eq. (12.31): $\qquad N = 0.56(1 - e^{-59.1X^{0.64}})$

The following table gives values of the rate N, lb evaporated/(hr)(sq ft), for various values of X, lb water/lb dry solid, in accordance with this expression.

X	0.0256	0.02	0.015	0.010	0.008	0.006	0.004	0.002	0.001
N	0.558	0.557	0.550	0.535	0.525	0.500	0.460	0.375	0.279

These provide the rate-of-drying curve of Fig. 12.18. The time of drying is determined by finding the area under a curve of $1/N$ plotted against X, in accordance with Eq. (12.3). The area

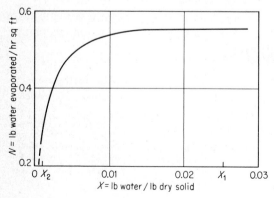

Fig. 12.18 *Solution to Illustration 12.5.*

under this curve (not shown) is 0.0473. Since $L_S/A = \rho_S z_S = 85(0.0583) = 4.95$ lb dry solid/sq ft, the time for drying is, by Eq. (12.3),

$$\theta = 4.95(0.0473) = 0.234 \text{ hr, or 14 min}$$

Illustration 12.6. Wet, porous catalyst pellets in the form of small cylinders, 0.53 in. in diameter and 0.506 in. in height, are to be dried of their water content in a through-circulation drier. The pellets are to be arranged in beds 2 in. deep on screens and are to be dried by air flowing at the rate of 800 lb dry air/(hr)(sq ft bed cross section), entering at 180°F dry-bulb temperature, humidity 0.01 lb water/lb dry air. The apparent density of the bed is 37.9 lb dry solid/cu ft and the particle surface 86 sq ft/cu ft of bed. Estimate the rate of drying, and the humidity and temperature of the air leaving the bed, during the constant-rate period.

Solution. $Y_1 = 0.01$ lb water/lb dry air, and, from Fig. 7.5, $Y_{as} = 0.031$ lb water/lb dry air at the corresponding adiabatic-saturation temperature (90°F). $G_S = 800$ lb dry air/(hr)(sq ft), and the approximate average $G = 800(1.016) = 815$ lb/(hr)(sq ft). The approximate average air viscosity is 0.019 centipoise, or $\mu = 0.019(2.42) = 0.046$ lb/(ft)(hr).

The surface of each particle $= [\pi(0.53)^2(2)/4 + \pi(0.53)(0.506)]/144 = 0.0089$ sq ft. The diameter of a sphere of equal area $= d_p = \sqrt{0.0089/\pi} = 0.0533$ ft. $a = 86$ sq ft/cu ft. $z_S = \frac{2}{12} = 0.1667$ ft.

The Reynolds number for the particles (Re″ of item 5, Table 3.3) $= d_p G/\mu = 0.0533(815)/0.041 = 945$. $\epsilon = $ fraction voids (see Table 3.3) $= 1 - d_p a/6 = 1 - 0.0533(86)/6 = 0.237$. Hence $j_D = 2.06/\epsilon(\text{Re}″)^{0.575} = 0.169$. Sc for air–water vapor $= 0.6$.

Eq. (12.33): $k_Y = 0.169(800)/(0.6)^{2/3} = 190.5$ lb water/(hr)(sq ft)(ΔY)

$$N_{tG} = \frac{k_Y a z_S}{G_S} = \frac{190.5(86)(0.1667)}{800} = 3.41$$

Eq. (12.25): $N_{max} = G_S(Y_{as} - Y_1) = 800(0.031 - 0.01) = 16.8$ lb/(hr)(sq ft)

Eq. (12.31): $$\frac{N}{16.8} = \frac{Y_2 - 0.01}{0.031 - 0.01} = 1 - e^{-3.41}$$

Therefore $N = 16.2$ lb water evapd/(hr)(sq ft) in the constant rate period, and $Y_2 = 0.0303$ lb water/lb dry air for the exit air. The corresponding exit air temperature, from the adiabatic-saturation curve of Fig. 7.5 for the initial air, is 92.5°F.

Since

$$\frac{L_S}{A} = L_S z_S = 37.9(0.1667) = 6.31 \text{ lb dry solid/sq ft}$$

then Eq. (12.2):

$$\frac{-dX}{d\theta} = \frac{NA}{L_S} = \frac{16.2}{6.31} = 2.57 \text{ lb water/(hr)(lb dry solid) during constant rate}$$

These must be considered as estimates only, subject to check by drying-rate tests.

II. CONTINUOUS DRYING

Continuous drying offers the advantages that usually the equipment necessary is small relative to the quantity of product, the operation is readily integrated with continuous chemical manufacture without intermediate storage, the product has a more uniform moisture content, and the cost of drying per unit of product is relatively small. As in the case of batch drying, the nature of the equipment used is greatly dependent upon the type of material to be dried.   Either direct or indirect heating, and sometimes both, may be used.

In many of the direct driers to be described, the solid is moved through a drier while in contact with a moving gas stream.   The gas and solid may flow in parallel or in countercurrent, or the gas may flow across the path of the solid.   If heat is neither supplied within the drier nor lost to the surroundings, operation is adiabatic and the gas will lose sensible heat and cool down as the evaporated moisture absorbs latent heat of vaporization.   By supplying heat within the drier, the gas may be maintained at constant temperature.

In *countercurrent* adiabatic operation, the hottest gas is in contact with the driest solid, and the discharged solid is therefore heated to a temperature which may approach that of the entering gas.   This provides the most rapid drying, since especially in the case of bound moisture the last traces are the most difficult to remove, and this is done more rapidly at high temperatures.   On the other hand, the dry solid may be damaged by being heated to high temperatures in this manner.   In addition, the hot discharged solid will carry away considerable sensible heat, thus lowering the thermal efficiency of the drying operation.

In *parallel* adiabatic operation, the wet solid is contacted with the hottest gas. As long as unbound surface moisture is present, the solid will be heated only to the wet-bulb temperature of the gas, and for this reason even heat-sensitive solids may frequently be dried by fairly hot gas in parallel flow.   For example, a typical flue gas resulting from combustion of a fuel, which may have a humidity of 0.03 lb water vapor/lb dry gas at 800°F, has a wet-bulb temperature of only about 150°F.   In any event, the wet-bulb temperature can never exceed the boiling point of the liquid at the prevailing pressure.   At the outlet of the drier, the gas will have been considerably cooled, and no damage will result to the dry solid.   Parallel flow also permits greater control of the moisture content of the discharged solid, in cases where the solid must not be completely dried, through control of the quantity of gas passing through the drier and consequently its exit temperature and humidity.

Tunnel driers

These direct driers are essentially adaptations of the truck drier to continuous operation.   They consist of relatively long tunnels through which trucks, loaded with trays filled with the drying solid, are moved in contact with a current of gas to evaporate the moisture.   The trucks may be pulled continuously through the drier by a moving chain, to which they are attached.   In a simpler arrangement, the loaded trucks are introduced periodically at one end of the drier, each displacing a truck at the other end.   The time of residence in the drier must be sufficiently great to reduce the moisture content of the solid to the desired value.   For relatively low-temperature operation the gas is usually steam-heated air, while for higher temperatures and especially for products which need not be kept scrupulously clean, flue gas from the combustion of a fuel may be used.   Parallel or countercurrent flow of gas and solid may be used, or in some cases fans placed along the sides of the tunnel blow the gas through the trucks in crossflow.   Operation may be essentially adiabatic, or the gas may be heated

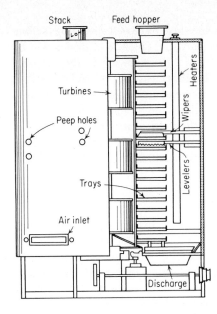

Fig. 12.19 *Turbo-type drier.* *(Wyssmont Co., Inc.)*

by steam coils along its path through the drier, and operation may then be substantially at constant temperature. Part of the gas may be recycled, much as in the case of batch driers, for heat economy. Truck-type tunnel driers may be used for any material which may be dried on trays: crystals, filter cakes, pastes, pottery, and the like.

There are many modifications of the tunnel drier which are essentially the same in principle but different in detailed design owing to the nature of the material being dried. For example, skeins of wet yarn may be suspended from poles or racks which move through the tunnel drier. Hides may be stretched on frames which hang from conveyor chains passing through the drier. Material in continuous sheets, such as cloth, may move through the drier under tension, as in a continuous belt over a series of rollers, or may be hung in festoons from moving racks if it is to be dried in the absence of tension.

Turbo-type driers

Solids which ordinarily may be dried on trays, such as powdery and granular materials, heavy sludges and pastes, beads and crystalline solids, may be continuously dried in a turbo-type drier, a form of direct drier. The simplest of these is shown in Fig. 12.19. The drier is fitted with a series of annular trays arranged in a vertical stack. These rotate slowly (from a fraction to 1 rpm) about a vertical shaft. Each tray is provided with a slot cut into the tray, as well as a leveling rake for spreading the solid. Solid fed in at the top is spread upon the top tray to a uniform thickness, and as the tray revolves, the solid is pushed through the slot by a separate wiper rake, to fall upon the tray beneath. In this way, with overturning and respreading on each tray, the solid progresses to the discharge chute at the bottom of the drier. The drying gas flows upward through the drier, is circulated over the trays by slowly revolving turbine fans, and is reheated by internal heating pipes as shown.   The rate of drying will be faster than that experienced in a tray-equipped tunnel drier, owing to the frequent reloading of the solid on each tray.   Alternative arrangements are possible: external heating of the gas, recirculation of the gas, and arrangements for recovery of evaporated solvents may be provided.   In some installations the solid is carried upon a moving, endless conveyor, which is wound about the vertical axis of the drier in a close-pitched, screw-type spiral.   These driers are regularly built in sizes ranging from 6 to 20 ft in diameter and 6 to 25 ft high.   A few installations as tall as 60 ft have been made.

Through-circulation driers

Granular solids may be arranged in thin beds for through circulation of the gas, and, if necessary, pastes and filter cakes may be preformed into granules, pellets, or noodles as described in the case of batch driers.   In the continuous through-circulation drier of Fig. 12.20,[15] the solid is spread to a depth of 1.5 to 2 in. upon a moving endless conveyor which passes through the drier.   The conveyor is made of perforated plates or woven wire screens in hinged sections in order to avoid failure from repeated flexing of the screen.   Fans blow the heated air through the solid, usually upward through the wet solid, and downward after initial drying has occurred.   In this way, a more uniform moisture concentration throughout the bed is attained.   Much of the gas is usually recycled, and a portion is discarded continuously at each fan position in the drier.   For materials which permit the flow of gas through the bed in the manner shown, drying is much more rapid than for tray-type tunnel driers.

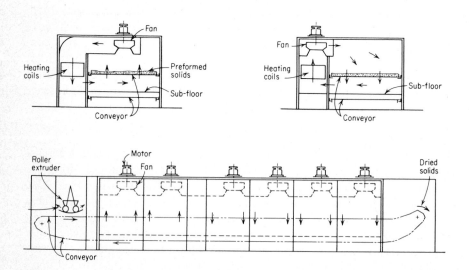

Fig. 12.20 *Continuous through-circulation (single-conveyor) drier with roller extruder.* (*Proctor and Schwartz, Inc.*)

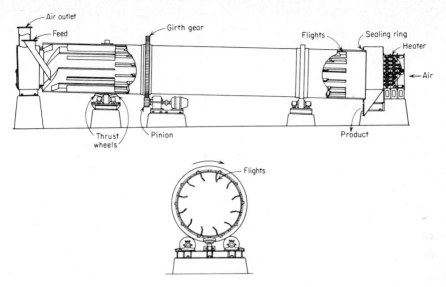

Fig. 12.21   *Ruggles-Coles XW hot-air drier, manufactured by Hardinge Co., Inc.*

Rotary driers

This is a most important group of driers, suitable for handling free-flowing granular materials which may be tumbled about without concern over breakage.   Figure 12.21 shows one form of such a drier, a direct countercurrent hot-air drier.   The solid to be dried is continuously introduced into one end of a rotating cylinder, as shown, while heated air flows into the other.   The cylinder is installed at a small angle to the horizontal, and the solid consequently moves slowly through the device.   Inside the drier, lifting flights extending from the cylinder wall for the full length of the drier lift the solid and shower it down in a moving curtain through the air, thus exposing it thoroughly to the drying action of the gas.   This lifting action also assists in the forward motion of the solid.   At the feed end of the drier, a few short spiral flights assist in imparting the initial forward motion to the solid before the principal flights are reached.   The solid must clearly be one which is neither sticky nor gummy, which might stick to the sides of the drier or tend to "ball" up.   In such cases, recycling of a portion of the dried product may nevertheless permit use of a rotary drier.

The drier may be fed with hot flue gas rather than air, and if the gas leaves the drier at a sufficiently high temperature, discharging it through a stack may provide adequate natural draft to provide sufficient gas for drying.   Ordinarily, however, an exhaust fan is used to pull the gas through the drier, since this provides more complete control of the gas flow.   A dust collector, of the cyclone, filter, or washing type, may be interposed between the fan and the gas exit.   A blower may also be provided at the gas entrance, thus maintaining a pressure close to atmospheric in the drier; this prevents leakage of cool air in at the end housings of the drier, and if the pressure is well balanced, outward leakage will also be minimized.

Rotary driers are made for a variety of operations. The following classification includes the major types.

1. *Direct heat, countercurrent flow.* For materials which may be heated to high temperatures, such as minerals, sand, limestone, clays, etc., hot flue gas may be used as the drying gas. For substances which should not be heated excessively, such as certain crystalline chemical products like ammonium sulfate and cane sugar, heated air may be used. The general arrangement is that shown in Fig. 12.21, and if flue gas is used, the heating coils are replaced by a furnace burning gas, oil, or coal.

2. *Direct heat, parallel flow.* Solids which may be dried with flue gas without

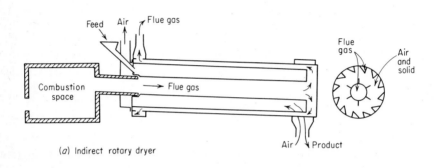

(*a*) Indirect rotary dryer

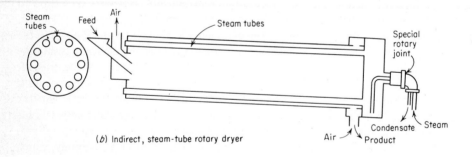

(*b*) Indirect, steam-tube rotary dryer

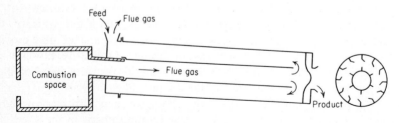

(*c*) Indirect-direct rotary dryer

Fig. 12.22 *Some rotary driers (schematic).*

fear of contamination but which must not be heated to high temperatures for fear of damage, such as gypsum, iron pyrites, and organic material such as peat and alfalfa, should be dried in a parallel-flow drier. The general construction is much like that of Fig. 12.21, except that the gas and solid both enter at the same end of the drier.

3. *Indirect heat, countercurrent flow.* For solids such as white pigments, and the like, which may be heated to high temperatures but which must remain out of contact with flue gas, the indirect drier indicated schematically in Fig. 12.22a may be used. As an alternative construction, the drier may be enclosed in a brick structure and completely surrounded by the hot flue gases. The air flow in such a drier may be kept to a minimum since the heat is supplied by conduction through the shell or central tube, and finely pulverized solids which dust severely may then be handled. For solids which must not be heated to high temperatures and for which indirect heat is desirable such as cattle feed, brewers' grains, feathers, and the like, the steam-tube drier, shown in Fig. 12.22b, may be used. This drier may or may not have lifting flights and may be built with one, two, or more concentric rows of steam-heated tubes. The tubes revolve with the drier, necessitating a special rotary joint where the steam is introduced and the condensate removed. This type of drier is frequently used when recovery of the evaporated liquid is necessary.

4. *Direct-indirect.* These driers, more economical to operate than the direct driers, may be used for solids which may be dried at high temperatures by flue gas, especially when fuel costs are high and when large percentages of moisture must be removed from the solid. A typical schematic arrangement is shown in Fig. 12.22c. In such a drier, the hot gas may enter the center tube at 1200 to 1800°F, cool to 400 to 900°F in its first passage through the drier, and on returning through the annular drying space cool further to 140 to 170°F at discharge. Lignite, coal, and coke may be dried in the inert atmosphere of such a drier at relatively high temperatures without danger of burning or dust explosion.

All these driers are available from various manufacturers in standard sizes, ranging from approximately 3 ft in diameter by 12 ft long to 10 ft in diameter by 100 ft long.

Holdup in rotary driers

The average time of passage, or retention time, of the solid in a drier must equal the required drying time if the solid is to emerge at the desired moisture content. It must be recognized of course that the retention time of individual particles may differ appreciably from the average,[27,37] and this can lead to nonuniformity of product quality. Several agencies bring about the movement of the solid particles through a rotary drier. Flight action is the lifting and dropping of particles by the flights on the drier shell: in the absence of air flow, each time the solid is lifted and dropped, it advances a distance equal to the product of the length of the drop and the slope of the drier. Kiln action is the forward rolling of the particles on top of each other in the bottom of the drier, as in a kiln without flights. The particles also bounce in a forward direction after being dropped from the flight. In addition, the forward motion of the solid is hindered by a counterflowing gas or assisted by parallel flow.

The holdup ϕ_D of solid is defined as the fraction of the drier volume occupied by the solid at any instant, and the average time of retention θ may be computed by dividing the holdup by the volumetric feed rate,

$$\theta = \frac{\phi_D Z \pi d^2/4}{(L_S/\rho_S)(\pi d^2/4)} = \frac{Z \phi_D \rho_S}{L_S} \tag{12.34}$$

where L_S/ρ_S = volumetric feed rate, cu ft/(hr)(sq ft drier cross section)
L_S = rate of flow of dry solids, lb/(hr)(sq ft)
ρ_S = apparent solid density, lb dry solid/cu ft.
Z = length of drier, ft
Although the influence of the character of the solids can be considerable,[12] Friedman and Marshall[11] found that the holdup of a large number of solids under a variety of typical operating conditions could be expressed simply as

$$\phi_D = \phi_{D0} \pm KG \tag{12.35}$$

where ϕ_{D0} = holdup with no gas flow
$\pm KG$ = correction for influence of gas rate, G lb/(hr)(sq ft)
The $+$ sign is used for countercurrent flow of gas and solid, the $-$ sign for parallel flow. Holdup for conditions of no gas flow depends to some extent upon flight design and the nature of the solid, but, under typical conditions and for ϕ_{D0} not exceeding 0.08, their data may be described by

$$\phi_{D0} = \frac{0.0037 L_S}{\rho_S s n^{0.9} d} \tag{12.36}$$

where s = slope of drier, ft/ft
n = rotational speed, rpm
d = drier diameter, ft
The constant K is dependent upon the properties of the solid, and for rough estimates it may be taken as

$$K = \frac{0.0000933}{\rho_S d_p^{1/2}} \tag{12.37}$$

where d_p is the average particle diameter, ft. Holdups in the range 0.05 to 0.15 appear to be best. Higher holdup results in increased kiln action, with consequent poor exposure of the solid to the gas, and an increase in power required for operating the drier.

These empirical relationships are applicable only under conditions of reasonable gas rates which do not cause excessive dusting or blowing of the solid particles from the drier. It is ordinarily desirable to keep dust down to 2 to 5 percent of the feed material as a maximum, and the corresponding permissible gas rates depend greatly upon the nature of the solid. From 200 to 10,000 lb gas/ (hr)(sq ft) is used, depending upon the solid; for most 35-mesh solids (d_p approximately 0.00137 ft), 1,000 lb/(hr)(sq ft) is amply safe.[11] Dusting is less severe for countercurrent than for parallel flow, since then the damp feed acts to some extent as a dust collector, and it is also influenced by design of feed chutes and end breechings. In any case, it is best to depend upon actual tests for final design and to use the equations for initial estimate only.

Driers are most readily built with length/diameter ratios $Z/d = 4$ to 10. For most purposes, the flights extend from the wall of the drier a distance of 8 to 12 percent of the diameter, and their number range from $2d$ to $3d$. They should be able to lift the entire solids holdup, thus minimizing kiln action, which leads to low retention time. Rates of rotation are such as to provide peripheral speeds of 40 to 100 ft/min, and the slopes are usually in the range 0 to 0.08 ft/ft.[11] Negative slopes are sometimes necessary in the case of parallel-flow driers.

Through-circulation rotary driers

Driers of the type indicated in Fig. 12.23 combine the features of the through-circulation and rotary driers. The direct drier shown, the Roto-Louvre,[9] consists of a slowly revolving tapered drum fitted with louvers to support the drying solid and to permit entrance of the hot gas beneath the solid. The hot gas is admitted only to those

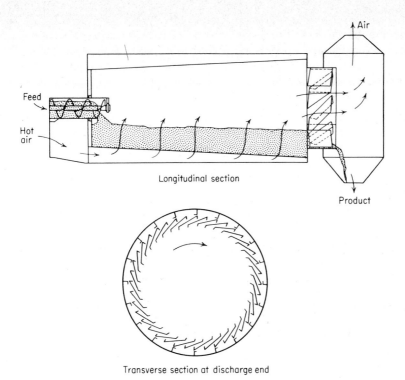

Longitudinal section

Air

Feed

Hot air

Product

Transverse section at discharge end

Fig. 12.23 *Continuous through-circulation rotary drier (Roto-Louvre).* (*Link-Belt Co.*)

louvers which are underneath the bed of solid. There is substantially no showering of the solid through the gas stream, and consequently a minimum of dusting results. The device is satisfactory for both low- and high-temperature drying of the same materials ordinarily treated in a rotary drier.

Drum driers

Fluid and semifluid materials such as solutions, slurries, pastes, and sludges may be dried on an indirect drier, of which Fig. 12.24, a dip-feed drum drier, gives an example. A slowly revolving internally steam-heated metal drum continuously dips into a trough containing the substance to be dried, and a thin film of the substance is retained on the drum surface. The thickness of the film is regulated by a spreader knife, as shown, and as the drum revolves, moisture is evaporated into the surrounding air by heat transferred through the metal of the drum. The dried material is then continuously scraped from the drum surface by a knife. For such a drier, heat transfer rather than diffusion is the controlling factor. The liquid or solution is first heated to its boiling point; moisture is then evolved by boiling at constant temperature if a solute precipitates from a solution at constant concentration, or at increasing temperatures if the concentration change is gradual; and finally the dried solid is heated to approach the temperature of the drum surface. In the case of slurries or pastes of insoluble solids, the temperature remains essentially constant at the solvent boiling point as long as the solid is completely wet and increases only during the last stages of drying. The vapors are frequently collected by a ventilated hood built directly over the drier.

The ability of various slurries, solutions, and pastes to adhere to a heated drum varies considerably, and diverse methods of feeding the drum are resorted to accordingly. Slurries of solids dispersed in liquids are frequently fed to the bottom of the drum on an inclined pan, and the excess nonadherent material is recycled to the feed reservoir. Vegetable glues, and the like, may be pumped against the bottom surface of the drum. The dip-feed arrangement shown in Fig. 12.24 is useful for heavy sludges, while, for materials which stick to the drum only with difficulty, the feed may be spattered on by a rapidly revolving roll. Double-drum driers, consisting of two drums placed close together and revolving in opposite directions, may be fed from above by admitting the feed into the depression between the drums. The entire drum drier may, on occasion, be placed inside a large evacuated chamber for low-temperature evaporation of the moisture.

Cylinder driers are drum driers used for material in continuous sheet form, such as paper and cloth. The wet solid is fed continuously over the revolving drum, or a series of such drums, each internally heated by steam or other heating fluid.

Spray driers

Solutions, slurries, and pastes may be dried by spraying them as fine droplets into a stream of hot gas in a spray drier.[3,20] One such device is shown in Fig. 12.25. The liquid to be dried is atomized and introduced into the large drying chamber, where the droplets are dispersed into a stream of heated air. The particles of liquid evaporate

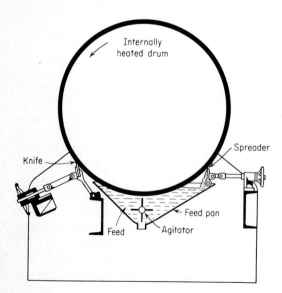

Fig. 12.24 *Dip-feed single-drum drier.* (*Blaw-Knox Co.*)

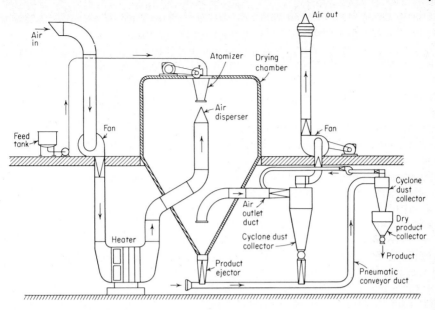

Fig. 12.25 *Spray drier.* (*Nichols Engineering and Research Corp.*)

rapidly and dry before they can be carried to the sides of the chamber, and the bulk of the dried powder which results falls to the conical bottom of the chamber to be removed by a stream of air to the dust collector. The principal portion of the exit gas is also led to a dust collector, as shown, before being discharged. Installations may be very large, as much as 40 ft in diameter and 100 ft high. Arrangements and detailed designs vary considerably, depending upon the manufacturer. Spray driers are used for a wide variety of products, including such diverse materials as organic and inorganic chemicals, pharmaceuticals, food products such as milk, eggs, and soluble coffee, as well as soap and detergent products.

In order to obtain rapid drying, atomization of the feed must provide small particles of high surface/weight ratio, whose diameter is usually in the range 10 to 60 μ. For this purpose, spray nozzles or rapidly rotating disks may be used. Spray nozzles are of two major types: pressure nozzles, in which the liquid is pumped at high pressure and with a rapid circular motion through a small orifice, and two-fluid nozzles, in which a gas such as air or steam at relatively low pressures is used to tear the liquid into droplets. Nozzles are relatively inflexible in their operating characteristics and do not permit even moderate variation in liquid-flow rates without large changes in droplet size. They are also subject to rapid erosion and wear. Rotating disks are therefore favored in the chemical industry. These may be plane, vaned, or cup-shaped, up to 12 to 14 in. in diameter, and may rotate at speeds in the range 3,000 to 12,000 rpm. The liquid or slurry is fed onto the disk near the center and is centrifugally accelerated to the periphery, from which it is thrown in an umbrella-shaped spray. Appreciable variation in liquid properties and feed rates may be satisfactorily handled, and even thick slurries or pastes may be atomized without clogging the device provided they can be pumped to the disk.

The drying gas, either flue gas or air, may enter at the highest practical temperature, 175 to 1400°F, limited only by the heat sensitivity of the product. Since the contact time for product and gas is so short, relatively high temperatures are feasible. The short time of drying requires effective gas-spray mixing, and attempts to improve upon this account in part for the large number of designs of spray chambers. Cool air is sometimes admitted at the drying-chamber walls, in order to prevent sticking of the product to the sides. The effluent gas may convey all the dried product out of the drier, or else only the fines, but in either case the gas must be passed through some type of dust collector such as cyclones or bag filters, and these are sometimes followed by wet scrubbers for the last traces of dust. Recirculation of hot gas to the drier for purposes of heat economy is not practical, since the dust-recovery operation cannot usually be accomplished without appreciable heat loss.

The drops of liquid reach their terminal velocity in the gas stream quickly, within inches of the atomizing device. Evaporation takes place from the surface of the drops, and in the case of many products solid material may accumulate as an impervious shell at the surface. Since heat is nevertheless rapidly being transmitted to the particles from the hot gas, the entrapped liquid portion of the drop vaporizes and expands the still-plastic wall of the drop to 3 to 10 times the original size, eventually exploding a small blowhole in the wall and escaping, to leave a hollow, dried shell of solid as the product. In other cases, the central liquid core diffuses through the shell to the outside, and the reduced internal pressure causes an implosion. In any event, the dried product is frequently in the form of small hollow beads of low bulk density.[8] Some control over the bulk density is usually possible through control of the particle size during atomization or through the temperature of the drying gas (increased gas temperature causes decreased product bulk density by more extensive expansion of the drop contents). For high-density products, the dried beads may be crushed.

Spray drying offers the advantage of extremely rapid drying for heat-sensitive products, a product particle size and density which are controllable within limits, and relatively low operating costs, especially in the case of large-capacity driers. It is rapidly becoming more popular. Although a beginning has been made in the rational design of such driers, incomplete knowledge concerning drop size, drop trajectories, relative velocity of gas and drop, and rates of drying make it necessary to rely largely on experimental tests for spray-drying designs.

Fluidized and spouted beds

Granular solids, fluidized (see Chap. 11) by a drying medium such as hot air, may be dried, and cooled in a similar fluidized bed.[35] Coarse solids, too large for ready fluidization, may be dealt with in a *spouted bed*.[19,22] Here the fluid is introduced centrally into the cone-shaped bottom of the container for the solids instead of uniformly over the cross section; it flows upward through the center of the bed in a column, causing a fountainlike spout of solids at the top. The solids circulate downward around the fluid column. Such a bed has found particular use in the drying of wheat, peas, flax, and the like.[33]

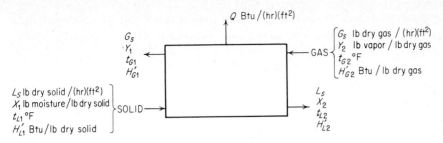

Fig. 12.26 *Material and enthalpy balances, continuous driers.*

Miscellaneous types

Pulverized and granular solids may be dried by suspending and conveying them in a stream of hot gas through a large pipe to a cyclone dust collector, in a system known as flash drying.[1]   Finely divided solids may be dried as they are moved through a screw conveyor, heated by condensing steam or other medium in a jacket surrounding the conveyor.   In such a drier, air need not necessarily be used, and the evaporated moisture may be led directly to a condenser for recovery, particularly if it is non-aqueous.   Continuous drying of pastes, slurries, and solutions on a belt, under vacuum, has also been done.[10]

Material and enthalpy balances

A general flow diagram for a continuous drier, arranged for countercurrent flow, is shown in Fig. 12.26.   Solid enters at the rate L_S lb dry solid/(hr)(sq ft),† is dried from X_1 to X_2 lb moisture/lb dry solid, and undergoes a temperature change t_{L1} to t_{L2}. The gas flows at the rate G_S lb dry gas/(hr)(sq ft) and undergoes a humidity change Y_2 to Y_1 lb moisture/lb dry gas and a temperature change t_{G2} to t_{G1}.   A moisture balance is then

$$L_S X_1 + G_S Y_2 = L_S X_2 + G_S Y_1 \tag{12.38}$$

or

$$L_S(X_1 - X_2) = G_S(Y_1 - Y_2) \tag{12.39}$$

The enthalpy of the wet solid is given by Eq. (11.23),

$$H'_L = C_L(t_L - t_0) + X C_A(t_L - t_0) + \Delta H_A \tag{11.23}$$

where H'_L = enthalpy of wet solid at t_L, referred to solid and liquid at reference temp t_0, Btu/lb dry solid

C_L = heat capacity of dry solid, Btu/(lb)(°F)

C_A = heat capacity of moisture, as a liquid, Btu/(lb)(°F)

ΔH_A = integral heat of wetting (or of adsorption, hydration, or soln) referred to pure liquid and solid, at t_0, Btu/lb dry solid

---

† For purposes of material and enthalpy balances alone, rates of flow of gas and solid may equally well be expressed as lb/hr.

Bound moisture will generally exhibit a heat of wetting (see Chap. 11), although data are largely lacking. The enthalpy of the gas, H'_G Btu/lb dry gas, is given by Eq. (7.13). If the net heat lost from the drier is Q Btu/hr, the enthalpy balance becomes

$$L_S H'_{L1} + G_S H'_{G2} = L_S H'_{L2} + G_S H'_{G1} + Q \tag{12.40}$$

For adiabatic operation, $Q = 0$, and if heat is added within the drier to an extent greater than the heat losses, Q is negative. If the solid is carried on trucks or other support, the sensible heat of the support should also be included in the balance. Obvious changes in the equations may be made for parallel-flow driers.

Illustration 12.7. An uninsulated, hot-air countercurrent rotary drier of the type shown in Fig. 12.21 is to be used to dry ammonium sulfate from 3.5 to 0.2% moisture. The drier is 4 ft in diameter, 22 ft long. Atmospheric air at 75°F, 50% humidity, will be heated by passage over steam coils to 190°F before it enters the drier, and it is desired that it discharge at 90°F. The solid will enter at 75°F, and it is expected to be discharged at 140°F. One ton of product per hour will be delivered.
Estimate the air and the heat requirements for the drier.

Solution. Define rates of flow in terms of lb/hr. $X_2 = 0.2/(100 - 0.2) = 0.0020$; $X_1 = 3.5/(100 - 3.5) = 0.0363$ lb water/lb dry solid. $L_S = 2,000(1 - 0.002) = 1,996$ lb dry solid/hr. The rate of drying is $1,996(0.0363 - 0.0020) = 68.5$ lb water evapd/hr.

At 75°F, 50% humidity, the absolute humidity of the available air is 0.0095 lb water/lb dry air, and this equals Y_2. Since $t_{G2} = 190°F$, and with $t_0 = 32°F$, the enthalpy of the air entering the drier is (Table 7.1)

$$H'_{G2} = [0.24 + 0.45(0.0095)](190 - 32) + 1,075.8(0.0095) = 48.8 \text{ Btu/lb dry air}$$

For the exit air, $t_{G1} = 90°F$.

$$H'_{G1} = (0.24 + 0.45 Y_1)(90 - 32) + 1,075.8 Y_1 = 13.93 + 1,101.3 Y_1$$

The heat capacity of dry ammonium sulfate is $C_L = 0.36$ and that of water 1.0 Btu/(lb)(°F). ΔH_A will be assumed to be negligible for lack of better information. Taking $t_0 = 32°F$ so that enthalpies of gas and solid are consistent, and since $t_{L1} = 75°F$, $t_{L2} = 140°F$, the solid enthalpies, Btu/lb dry solid, are [Eq. (11.23)]

$$H'_{L2} = 0.36(140 - 32) + 0.002(1)(140 - 32) = 39.07$$
$$H'_{L1} = 0.36(75 - 32) + 0.0363(1)(75 - 32) = 17.06$$

The estimated combined natural convection and radiation-heat-transfer coefficient from the drier to the surroundings[23] is 2.0 Btu/(hr)(sq ft)(°F). Taking the mean Δt between drier and surroundings as $[(190 - 75) + (90 - 75)]/2 = 65°F$ and the exposed area as $\pi(4)(22) = 277$ sq ft, the estimated heat loss is

$$Q = 2.0(277)(65) = 36,000 \text{ Btu/hr}$$

Moisture balance [Eq. (12.39)],

$$1,996(0.0363 - 0.0020) = G_S(Y_1 - 0.0095)$$

Enthalpy balance [Eq. (12.40)],

$$1,996(17.06) + G_S(48.8) = 1,996(39.07) + G_S(13.93 + 1,101.3 Y_1) + 36,000$$

Solving simultaneously,

$$G_S = 6,450 \text{ lb dry air/hr} \qquad Y_1 = 0.0203 \text{ lb moisture/lb dry air}$$

The enthalpy of the fresh air (Fig. 7.5) is 21.5 Btu/lb dry air, and hence the heat load for the heater is $6,450(48.8 - 21.5) = 176,000$ Btu/hr.   If 10 psig steam is used, whose latent heat is 952.1 Btu/lb, the steam required is $176,000/952.1 = 185$ lb steam/hr, or $185/68.5 = 2.7$ lb steam/lb water evapd.

Rate of drying for continuous direct-heat driers

Direct-heat driers are best placed in two categories, according to whether high or low temperatures prevail.   For operation at temperatures above the boiling point of the moisture to be evaporated, the humidity of the gas has only a minor influence on the rate of drying, and it is easiest to work directly with the rate of heat transfer.   At temperatures below the boiling point, mass-transfer driving forces are conveniently established.   In any case, it must be emphasized that our imperfect knowledge of the complex drying mechanisms makes experimental testing of the drying necessary. Calculations are useful only for the roughest estimate.

Drying at high temperatures. In a typical situation, three separate zones are distinguished in such driers, recognizable by the variation in temperatures of the gas and solid in the various parts of the drier.[11]   Refer to Fig. 12.27, where typical temperatures are shown schematically by the solid lines for a countercurrent drier.   In zone I, the preheat zone, the solid is heated by the gas until the rate of heat transfer to the solid is balanced by the heat requirements for evaporation of moisture.   Little actual drying will usually occur here.   In zone II, the equilibrium temperature of the solid remains substantially constant while surface and unbound moisture are evaporated.   At point B, the critical moisture of the solid is reached, and, in zone III, unsaturated surface drying and evaporation of bound moisture occur.   Assuming that the heat-transfer coefficients remain essentially constant, the decreased rate of evaporation in zone III results in increased solid temperature, and the discharge temperature of the solid approaches the inlet temperature of the gas.

Zone II represents the major portion for many driers, and it is of interest to consider the temperature-humidity relationship of the gas as it passes through this

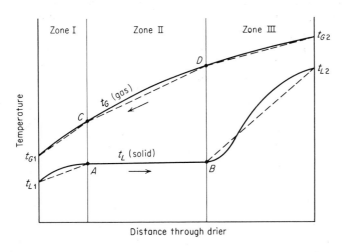

Fig. 12.27 *Temperature gradients in a continuous countercurrent drier.*

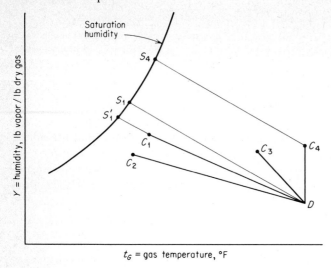

Saturation humidity

S_4

S_1

S_1'

C_1

C_2

C_3

C_4

D

$Y =$ humidity, lb vapor / lb dry gas

$t_G =$ gas temperature, °F

Fig. 12.28 *Temperature-humidity relations in continuous driers.*

section. On the psychrometric chart (Fig. 12.28), point D represents the gas conditions at the corresponding point D of Fig. 12.27. If drying is adiabatic, i.e., without addition to, or loss of heat from, the drier, the adiabatic-saturation line DC_1 will represent the variation of humidity and temperature of the gas as it passes through this section of the drier, and the conditions of the gas leaving this zone (point C, Fig. 12.27) are shown at C_1 on Fig. 12.28. The surface temperature of the solid, which can be estimated by the methods described earlier in the case of batch drying, will vary from that at S_1 (corresponding to point B of Fig. 12.27) to S_1' (corresponding to point A). If radiation and conduction through the solid may be neglected, these are the wet-bulb temperatures corresponding to D and C_1, respectively. For the system air–water, whose wet-bulb and adiabatic-saturation temperatures are the same, these will be both given by an extension of the adiabatic-saturation line DC_1 to the saturation-humidity curve. Heat losses may cause the gas to follow some such path as DC_2. On the other hand, if heat is added to the gas in this section, the path will be represented by a line such as DC_3 and, if the gas is kept at constant temperature, by line DC_4. In the case of the last, the surface temperature of the solid will vary from that at S_1 to that at S_4. For any specific drier, the temperatures and humidities may be computed by means of the moisture and enthalpy balances [Eqs. (12.39) and (12.40)] by application of these to each section separately.

Considering only heat transfer from the gas, and neglecting any indirect heat transfer between the solid and the drier itself, the loss in heat from the gas q_G may be equated to that which is transferred to the solid q and the losses Q. For a differential length of the drier, dZ, this becomes[11]

$$dq_G = dq + dQ \qquad (12.41)$$

Rearranging,

$$dq = dq_G - dQ = U\, dS(t_G - t_L) = Ua(t_G - t_L)\, dZ \qquad (12.42)$$

where U = overall heat-transfer coefficient between gas and solid
$t_G - t_L$ = temperature difference for heat transfer
S = interfacial surface/sq ft drier cross section
a = interfacial surface/cu ft drier volume

Then

$$dq = G_S C_S \, dt'_G = Ua(t_G - t_L) \, dZ \tag{12.43}$$

where dt'_G is the temperature drop experienced by the gas as a result of transfer of heat to the solid only, exclusive of losses, and C_S is the humid heat.

$$dN_{tOG} = \frac{dt'_G}{t_G - t_L} = \frac{Ua \, dZ}{G_S C_S} \tag{12.44}$$

and if the heat-transfer coefficient is constant,

$$N_{tOG} = \frac{\Delta t'_G}{\Delta t_m} = \frac{Z}{H_{tOG}} \tag{12.45}$$

$$H_{tOG} = \frac{G_S C_S}{U_a} \tag{12.46}$$

where N_{tOG} = number of heat-transfer units
H_{tOG} = length of heat-transfer unit
$\Delta t'_G$ = change in gas temperature owing to *heat transfer to solid only*
Δt_m = appropriate average temperature difference between gas and solid
If the temperature profiles in the drier may be idealized as straight lines, such as the broken lines of Fig. 12.27, then *for each zone taken separately* Δt_m is the logarithmic average of the terminal temperature differences and N_{tOG} the corresponding number of transfer units for each zone. In the case of zone III, this simplification will be satisfactory for the evaporation of unsaturated surface moisture, but not for bound moisture, or where internal diffusion of moisture controls the rate of drying.

Tunnel Driers. In drying solids by cross circulation of air over the surface, as in the case of materials on trays or solids in sheet form, the surface temperature in zone II may be estimated through Eq. (12.18). Unless all surfaces are exposed to heat transfer by radiation, this feature of the heat transfer is better ignored, and U in Eq. (12.46) may be taken as $h_c + U_k$. This value will also serve in zone I, and in zone III only for cases of unsaturated surface drying. The quantity a may be computed from the method of loading the drier.

Rotary Driers. The surface of the solid exposed to drying gas cannot be conveniently measured, so the group Ua must be considered together. In countercurrent driers, Ua is influenced by changes in holdup due to changes in gas flow and solid feed rate, but effects of changes in slope or rate of rotation of the drier are small.[11,36]

The effect of gas mass velocity is uncertain.[24]   In the absence of experimental data the group $Uad/G^{0.16}$ may be taken as about 10 for diameters in the range 1 to 2 ft, and about 20 for diameters of from 3 to 10 ft,[25] with the understanding that the character of the solids, since they may offer some of the heat-transfer resistance included in U, may also influence the size of the group.[34]   For economical designs, the exit temperatures of the gas and solid should be chosen so as to provide for 1.5 to 2.5 transfer units in the drier.

Illustration 12.8. A preliminary estimate of the size of a countercurrent direct-heat rotary drier for drying an ore flotation concentrate is to be made.   The solid is to be delivered from a continuous filter and introduced into the drier at 8% moisture, 80°F, and is to be discharged from the drier at 300°F, 0.5% moisture.   There will be 5,000 lb/hr of dried product.   The drying gas is a flue gas analyzing 2.5% CO_2, 14.7% O_2, 76.0% N_2, and 6.8% H_2O by volume.   It will enter the drier at 900°F.   Heat losses will be estimated at 15% of the heat in the entering gas.   The ore concentrate is ground to 200 μ average particle diameter and has a bulk density of 81 lb dry solid/cu ft and a heat capacity 0.2 Btu/(lb)(°F) (dry).   The gas rate ought not to exceed about 500 lb/(hr)(sq ft) to avoid excessive dusting.

Solution. $X_1 = 8/(100 - 8) = 0.0870$; $X_2 = 0.5/(100 - 0.5) = 0.00503$ lb water/lb dry solid. Define L_S and G_S as lb dry material/(hr)(sq ft). $L_S = 5,000(1 - 0.005) = 4,975$ lb dry solid/hr. Water to be evaporated $= 4,975(0.0870 - 0.00503) = 407$ lb/hr.

Basis: 1 mole gas in.   Dry gas $= 1 - 0.068 = 0.932$ mole.

	Moles	lb	Av ht capacity, Btu/(lb mole)(°F), 900–32°F
CO_2	0.025	1.10	10.9
O_2	0.147	4.72	7.15
N_2	0.760	21.3	7.15
Total dry wt		27.1	

Av mol wt dry gas $= 27.1/0.932 = 29.1$ lb/lb mole, nearly the same as air.

$$Y_2 = \frac{0.068(18.02)}{0.932(29.1)} = 0.0452 \text{ lb water/lb dry gas} \qquad t_{G2} = 900°F$$

$$\text{Av ht capacity of dry gas} = \frac{0.025(10.9) + (0.147 + 0.760)(7.15)}{0.932(29.1)}$$

$$= 0.25 \text{ Btu/(lb)(°F)}$$

The exit-gas temperature will be tentatively taken as $t_{G1} = 250°F$.   This is subject to revision after the number of transfer units is computed.   In a manner similar to that above, the average heat capacity of the dry gas, 250 to 32°F, is 0.24 Btu/lb dry gas.

$$\text{Base temperature} = t_0 = 32°F$$

Eq. (7.13):

$$H'_{G2} = [0.25 + 0.47(0.0452)](900 - 32) + 1,075.2(0.0452) = 283.5 \text{ Btu/lb dry gas}$$
$$H'_{G1} = (0.24 + 0.45\,Y_1)(250 - 32) + 1,075.2\,Y_1 = 52.5 + 1,173\,Y_1$$

Take $\Delta H_A = 0$. Eq. (11.23):

$$H'_{L1} = 0.2(80 - 32) + 0.0870(1)(80 - 32) = 13.78 \text{ Btu/lb dry solid}$$
$$H'_{L2} = 0.2(300 - 32) + 0.00503(1)(300 - 32) = 53.6 \text{ Btu/lb dry solid}$$
$$Q = \text{ht loss} = 0.15(283.5)G_S = 42.5G_S \quad \text{Btu/hr}$$

Eq. (12.39): $\qquad\qquad\qquad 407 = G_S(Y_1 - 0.0452)$

Eq. (12.40): $\quad 4{,}975(13.78) + G_S(283.5) = 4{,}975(53.6) + G_S(52.5 + 1{,}173\,Y_1) + 42.5G_S$

Solving simultaneously,

$$G_S = 5{,}170 \text{ lb dry gas/hr} \qquad Y_1 = 0.1238 \text{ lb water/lb dry gas}$$
$$H'_{G1} = 197.6 \text{ Btu/lb dry gas} \qquad Q = 220{,}000 \text{ Btu/hr}$$

Assuming that the psychrometric ratio of the gas is the same as that of air, its wet-bulb temperature is found to be [Eq. (7.26)] about 153°F. The surface of the drying solid particles is subject to radiation from the hot walls of the drier, and the surface of the solid in zone II is then estimated to be 160°F. (*Note:* This should be recalculated after the temperature at point *D*, Fig. 12.27, is known, but in this case any change will have no influence on the overall results.)

For lack of information on the critical moisture content of the solid, which is probably quite low for the conditions found in such a drier, it will be assumed that all moisture is evaporated in zone II at 160°F. Zone I will be taken as a preheat zone for warming the wet solids to 160°F, without drying. Enthalpy of the solid at 160°F, $X = 0.0870$ (point *A*, Fig. 12.27) = $0.2(160 - 32) + 0.0870(1)(160 - 32) = 36.5$ Btu/lb dry solid. Similarly, enthalpy of the solid at 160°F, $X = 0.00503$ (point *B*, Fig. 12.27) = 25.6 Btu/lb dry solid.

Assuming heat losses in the three zones are proportional to the number of transfer units in each zone and to the average temperature difference between the gas and the surrounding air (80°F), the heat losses are apportioned (by a trial-and-error calculation) as 14% in zone I, 65% in zone II, 21% in zone III.

Calculations for zone III. Humid ht of entering gas = $0.25 + 0.47(0.0452) = 0.272$ Btu/(lb dry gas)(°F). A heat balance,

$$5{,}170(0.272)(900 - t_{GD}) = 4{,}975(53.6 - 25.6) + 0.21(220{,}000)$$

$$t_{GD} = \text{gas temp at } D \text{ (Fig. 12.27)} = 768°F$$

The change in gas temperature, exclusive of that due to losses, is

$$\Delta t'_G = \frac{4{,}975(53.6 - 25.6)}{5{,}170(0.272)} = 99°F$$

Av temp difference between gas and solid = av of $768 - 160 = 608°F$ and $900 - 300 = 600°F = 604°F = \Delta t_m$.

$$N_{tOG} = \frac{\Delta t'_G}{\Delta t_m} = \frac{99}{604} = 0.16$$

Calculations for zone I. Humid ht of exit gas = $0.24 + 0.45(0.1238) = 0.294$ Btu/(lb dry gas)(°F). A heat balance,

$$5{,}170(0.294)(t_{GC} - 250) = 4{,}975(36.5 - 13.78) + 0.14(220{,}000)$$

$$t_{GC} = \text{gas temp at } C \text{ (Fig. 12.27)} = 345°F \qquad \Delta t'_G = \frac{4{,}975(36.5 - 13.78)}{5{,}170(0.294)} = 74°F$$

$$\Delta t_m = \text{av of } 345 - 160 = 185°F \text{ and } 250 - 80 = 170°F = 178°F$$

$$N_{tOG} = \frac{\Delta t'_G}{\Delta t_m} = \frac{74}{178} = 0.42$$

Calculations for zone II

$$\text{Av humid ht of gas} = \frac{0.272 + 0.294}{2} = 0.28$$

$$\text{True change in gas temp} = 768 - 345 = 423°F$$

$$\text{Change in temp due to ht loss} = \frac{0.65(220,000)}{5,170(0.28)} = 99°F$$

$$\Delta t_G' \text{ due to ht transfer to solid} = 423 - 99 = 324°F$$

$$\Delta t_m = \frac{(768 - 160) - (345 - 160)}{\ln\,[(768 - 160)/(345 - 160)]} = 360°F$$

$$N_{tOG} = \frac{\Delta t_G'}{\Delta t_m} = \frac{324}{360} = 0.90 \qquad \text{Total } N_{tOG} = 0.16 + 0.42 + 0.90 = 1.48$$

Size of drier. Standard diameters available are 3, 4, 4.5, and 5 ft and larger. The cross-sectional area of the 4-ft diameter drier is $\pi(4^2)/4 = 12.58$ sq ft. Expressing the rates of flow as lb dry material/(hr)(sq ft), $G_S = 5,170/12.58 = 411$, $L_S = 4,975/12.58 = 396$ lb/(hr)(sq ft). This is the only size suitable in view of the permissible gas rate.

Av $G = G_S(1 + Y_{av}) = 411[1 + (0.0452 + 0.1238)/2] = 466$ lb/(hr)(sq ft). For lack of more specific information take $Ua = 20G^{0.16}/d = 20(446)^{0.16}/4 = 13.2$ Btu/(hr)(cu ft)(°F). $H_{tOG} = G_S C_S/Ua = 411(0.28)/13.2 = 8.8$ ft.

$$Z = N_{tOG}H_{tOG} = 1.48(8.8) = 13.0$$

The nearest standard length is 16 ft.

Take the peripheral speed as 65 ft/min, whence the rate of revolution $= n = 65/4\pi = 5.2$ or 5 rpm.

$$d_p = (200\ \mu)(3.28)(10^{-6}) = 0.00065 \text{ ft} \qquad \rho_S = 81 \text{ lb/cu ft}$$

Eq. (12.37):
$$K = \frac{0.0000933}{81(0.00065)^{1/2}} = 0.000045$$

Take the hold-up $\phi_D = 0.05$, and $KG = 0.000045(446) = 0.02$.

Eq. (12.35):
$$\phi_{D0} = \phi_D - KG = 0.05 - 0.02 = 0.03$$

Eq. (12.36):
$$s = \frac{0.0037L_S}{\phi_{D0}\rho_S n^{0.9}d} = \frac{0.0037(396)}{0.03(81)(5)^{0.9}(4)} = 0.0356 \text{ ft/ft, the drier slope}$$

Drying at low temperatures. Continuous driers operating at low temperatures may be divided into zones in the same manner as high-temperature driers. Since the surface moisture will evaporate at a comparatively low temperature in zone II, the preheat zone may generally be ignored and only zones II and III need be considered. Refer to Fig. 12.29, which shows an arrangement for countercurrent flow. In zone II, unbound and surface moisture is evaporated as discussed previously, and the moisture content of the solid falls to the critical value X_c. The rate of drying in this zone would be constant if it were not for the varying conditions of the gas. In zone III, unsaturated-surface drying and evaporation of bound moisture occur, and the gas humidity rises from its initial value Y_2 to Y_c. The latter may be calculated by applying the material-balance relation (12.39) to either zone separately. The

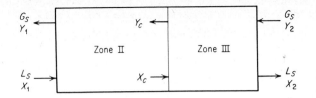

Fig. 12.29 *Continuous low-temper-ature countercurrent drier.*

retention time may be calculated by integration of Eq. (12.3),

$$\theta = \theta_{II} + \theta_{III} = \frac{L_S}{A} \left(\int_{X_c}^{X_1} \frac{dX}{N} + \int_{X_2}^{X_c} \frac{dX}{N} \right) \tag{12.47}$$

where A/L_S is the specific exposed drying surface, sq ft/lb dry solid.

Zone II, $X > X_c$. The rate N is given by Eq. (12.17), which, when substituted in the first part of Eq. (12.47), provides

$$\theta_{II} = \frac{L_S}{A} \frac{1}{k_Y} \int_{X_c}^{X_1} \frac{dX}{Y_s - Y} \tag{12.48}$$

Since $G_S \, dY = L_S \, dX$, Eq. (12.48) becomes

$$\theta_{II} = \frac{G_S}{L_S} \frac{L_S}{A} \frac{1}{k_Y} \int_{Y_c}^{Y_1} \frac{dY}{Y_s - Y} \tag{12.49}$$

Integration of Eq. (12.49) must take into account the variation of Y_s, the humidity of the gas at the solid surface, with Y. If the gas temperature, for example, is held constant in this zone by application of heat, the path of the gas resembles line DC_4 on Fig. 12.28. If furthermore, radiation and conduction effects can be neglected, Y_s for any value of Y on line DC_4 is the saturated humidity at the corresponding wet-bulb temperature. Equation (12.49) may then be integrated graphically.

For the case where Y_s is constant, as for adiabatic drying of water into air, Eq. (12.49) becomes

$$\theta_{II} = \frac{G_S}{L_S} \frac{L_S}{A} \frac{1}{k_Y} \ln \frac{Y_s - Y_c}{Y_s - Y_1} \tag{12.50}$$

Zone III, $X < X_c$. Some simplification is necessary for mathematical treatment. For the case where unsaturated-surface drying occurs and the drying rate is dependent strictly upon the conditions prevailing at any instant, independent of the immediate past history of the drying, Eqs. (12.8) and (12.17) apply. These provide

$$N = \frac{N_c(X - X^*)}{X_c - X^*} = \frac{k_Y(Y_s - Y)(X - X^*)}{X_c - X} \tag{12.51}$$

When this is substituted in the second part of Eq. (12.47), there results

$$\theta_{III} = \frac{L_S}{A} \frac{X_c - X^*}{k_Y} \int_{X_2}^{X_c} \frac{dX}{(Y_s - Y)(X - X^*)} \tag{12.52}$$

This may be evaluated graphically after determining the relationship between X, X^*, Y_s, and Y. For this purpose, the material balance may be written as

$$Y = Y_2 + (X - X_2)\frac{L_S}{G_S} \tag{12.53}$$

The surface humidity Y_s is found in the manner previously described, and X^* is given by the equilibrium-moisture curve for the appropriate Y.

For the special case where the bound moisture is negligible ($X^* = 0$) and Y_s is constant (adiabatic drying), substitution of Eq. (12.53) and its differential $G_S\,dY = L_S\,dX$ in Eq. (12.52) provides

$$\theta_{\text{III}} = \frac{G_S}{L_S}\frac{L_S}{A}\frac{X_c}{k_Y}\int_{Y_2}^{Y_c}\frac{dY}{(Y_s - Y)[(Y - Y_2)G_S/L_S + X_2]} \tag{12.54}$$

$$\theta_{\text{III}} = \frac{G_S}{L_S}\frac{L_S}{A}\frac{X_c}{k_Y}\frac{1}{(Y_s - Y_2)G_S/L_S + X_2}\ln\frac{X_c(Y_s - Y_2)}{X_2(Y_s - Y_c)} \tag{12.55}$$

These methods must not be applied to solids whose internal resistance to movement of moisture is large, where internal diffusion controls the rate of drying, and where casehardening occurs. In these cases, the instantaneous rate of drying under variable conditions is not merely a function of the prevailing conditions but depends upon the immediate past drying history as well. For such solids, the time for drying is best determined experimentally in a carefully planned test which simulates the countercurrent action of the continuous drier.[5]

In applying Eqs. (12.47) to (12.55), it is clear that, should drying take place only above, or only below, the critical moisture content, appropriate changes in the limits of moisture content and gas humidities must be made. In the case of parallel-flow driers, where gas enters at humidity Y_1 and leaves at Y_2, while solid enters at moisture content X_1 and leaves at X_2, Eqs. (12.50) and (12.55) become

$$\theta_{\text{II}} = \frac{G_S}{L_S}\frac{L_S}{A}\frac{1}{k_Y}\int_{Y_1}^{Y_c}\frac{dY}{Y_s - Y} = \frac{G_S}{L_S}\frac{L_S}{A}\frac{1}{k_Y}\ln\frac{Y_s - Y_1}{Y_s - Y_c} \tag{12.56}$$

$$\theta_{\text{III}} = \frac{L_S}{A}\frac{X_c - X^*}{k_Y}\int_{X_2}^{X_c}\frac{dX}{(Y_s - Y)(X - X^*)}$$

$$= \frac{G_S}{L_S}\frac{L_S}{A}\frac{X_c}{k_Y}\frac{1}{(Y_s - Y_c)G_S/L_S - X_2}\ln\frac{X_c(Y_s - Y_2)}{X_2(Y_s - Y_c)} \tag{12.57}$$

Illustration 12.9. Wet rayon skeins, after centrifuging, are to be air-dried from 46 to 8.5% water content in a continuous countercurrent tunnel drier. The skeins are hung on poles which travel through the drier. The air is to enter at 180°F, humidity 0.03 lb water/lb dry air, and is to be discharged at a humidity 0.08. The air temperature is to be kept constant at 180°F by heating coils within the drier. The air rate is to be 1,000 lb/(hr)(sq ft).

The critical moisture content of rayon skeins is 50%, and its percent equilibrium moisture at 180°F can be taken as one-fourth of the percent relative humidity of the air. The rate of drying is then [Simons, Koffolt, and Withrow, *Trans. AIChE*, **39**, 133 (1943)]

$$\frac{-dX}{d\theta} = 0.003G^{1.47}(X - X^*)(Y_W - Y)$$

where Y_W is the saturation humidity of the air at the wet-bulb temperature corresponding to Y.
    Determine the time the rayon should remain in the drier.
    Solution. $X_1 = 0.46/(1 - 0.46) = 0.852$; $X_2 = 0.085/(1 - 0.085) = 0.093$ lb water/lb dry solid.
$Y_1 = 0.08$; $Y_2 = 0.03$ lb water/lb dry air.   A water balance [Eq. (12.39)],

$$\frac{L_s}{G_s} = \frac{0.08 - 0.03}{0.852 - 0.093} = 0.0660 \text{ lb dry solid/lb dry air}$$

    Since the initial moisture content of the rayon is less than the critical, drying takes place entirely
within zone III.   The form of the rate equation is the same as that of Eq. (12.22), where $k_Y A/
L_s(X_c - X^*) = 0.003G^{1.47}$.   Rearranging the rate equation,

$$\theta_{III} = \int_0^\theta d\theta = \frac{1}{0.003G^{1.47}} \int_{X_2}^{X_1} \frac{dX}{(X - X^*)(Y_W - Y)}$$

which is in the form of Eq. (12.52).   On substituting $G = 1,000$, this becomes

$$\theta_{III} = 0.013 \int_{0.093}^{0.852} \frac{dX}{(X - X^*)(Y_W - Y)} \qquad (12.58)$$

Consider that part of the drier where the moisture content of the rayon is $X = 0.4$.

Eq. (12.53): $Y = 0.03 + (0.4 - 0.093)0.066 = 0.0503$ lb water/lb dry gas

At 180°F, $Y = 0.0503$, the wet-bulb temperature is 114°F, and the corresponding saturation humidity
$Y_W = 0.068$ (Fig. 7.5).

Eq. (7.8): $0.0503 = \frac{p}{14.7 - p} \frac{18}{29}$

$$p = \text{partial pressure of water} = 1.10 \text{ psi}$$

The vapor pressure of water at 180°F $= P = 7.51$ psi, and the relative humidity of the air $= (1.10/
7.51)100 = 14.63\%$.   The equilibrium moisture is $14.6/4 = 3.66\%$, and $X^* = 3.66/(100 - 3.66) =
0.038$ lb water/lb dry solid.   Therefore

$$\frac{1}{(X - X^*)(Y_W - Y)} = \frac{1}{(0.4 - 0.038)(0.068 - 0.0503)} = 156$$

In a similar fashion, other values of this quantity are calculated for other values of X, as follows:

X	Y	Y_W	Percent relative humidity	X^*	$\dfrac{1}{(X - X^*)(Y_W - Y)}$
0.852	0.080	0.0950	22.4	0.0594	84
0.80	0.0767	0.0920	21.5	0.0568	88
0.60	0.0635	0.0790	18.17	0.0488	117
0.40	0.0503	0.0680	14.63	0.0380	156
0.20	0.0371	0.0550	11.05	0.0284	325
0.093	0.030	0.0490	9.04	0.0231	755

The integral of Eq. (12.58) is evaluated graphically by determining the area under a curve of the last column of the table plotted as ordinate against the first column as abscissa (not shown). The area = 151.6, whence, by Eq. (12.58),

$$\theta_{III} = 0.013(151.6) = 1.97 \text{ or } 2 \text{ hr} \quad \textbf{Ans.}$$

NOTATIONS FOR CHAPTER 12

a	= interfacial surface of solid, sq ft/cu ft
A	= drying surface, for cross-circulation drying, sq ft
	= cross-sectional area of bed perpendicular to the direction of gas flow, for through-circulation drying, sq ft
A_m	= average cross-sectional area of a drying solid, sq ft
A_u	= nondrying external surface, sq ft
b	= a constant
C_A	= heat capacity of liquid moisture, Btu/(lb)(°F)
C_L	= heat capacity of dry solid, Btu/(lb)(°F)
C_p	= heat capacity at constant pressure, Btu/(lb)(°F)
C_S	= humid heat of a moist gas, Btu/(lb dry gas)(°F)
d	= differential operator
	= diameter of drier, ft
d_p	= diameter of a particle, ft
	= diameter of a sphere of same surface as particle, ft
D	= diffusivity, sq ft/hr
e	= 2.7183
f	= function
G	= mass velocity of gas, lb total gas/(hr)(sq ft)
G_S	= mass velocity of dry gas, lb dry gas/(hr)(sq ft)
h_c	= heat-transfer coefficient, for convection, Btu/(hr)(sq ft)(°F)
h_R	= heat-transfer coefficient, for radiation, Btu/(hr)(sq ft)(°F)
ΔH_A	= integral heat of wetting, Btu/lb dry solid
H'_G	= enthalpy of a moist gas, Btu/lb dry gas
H'_L	= enthalpy of a wet solid, Btu/lb dry solid
H_{toG}	= length of an overall gas transfer unit, ft
j_D	= as defined by Eq. (12.19)
j_H	= as defined by Eq. (12.19)
k_M	= thermal conductivity of tray material, (Btu)(ft)/(hr)(sq ft)(°F)
k_S	= thermal conductivity of the drying solid, (Btu)(ft)/(hr)(sq ft)(°F)
k_Y	= gas-film mass-transfer coefficient, lb evaporated/(hr)(sq ft)(ΔY)
K	= as defined by Eq. (12.37)
L_S	= weight of dry solid in a batch, for batch drying, lb
	= rate of flow of solid, for continuous drying, lb dry solid/(hr)(sq ft)
m	= a constant
n	= rate of revolution, rpm
N	= rate of drying, lb moisture evaporated/(hr)(sq ft solid surface)
N_c	= constant rate of drying, lb/(hr)(sq ft)
N_{tG}	= number of gas transfer units, dimensionless
N_{toG}	= number of overall gas transfer units, dimensionless
p	= partial pressure, atm (unless otherwise specified)
P	= vapor pressure, atm (unless otherwise specified)
Pr	= Prandtl number = $C_p\mu/k$, dimensionless

q = heat received at the drying surface, batch drying, Btu/(hr)(sq ft solid surface)
      = heat received by the solid, continuous drying, Btu/(hr)(sq ft drier cross section)

q_c = heat transferred by convection, Btu/(hr)(sq ft solid surface)

q_G = heat transferred from the gas, Btu/(hr)(sq ft drier cross section)

q_k = heat transferred by conduction, Btu/(hr)(sq ft solid surface)

q_R = heat transferred by radiation, Btu/(hr)(sq ft solid surface)

Q = net heat loss, Btu/(hr)(sq ft drier cross section)

Re_x = Reynolds number $= xG/\mu$, dimensionless

s = slope of a drier, ft/ft

S = interfacial surface, sq ft/sq ft cross section

Sc = Schmidt number $= \mu/\rho D$, dimensionless

t_G = gas temperature, °F

t_L = solid temperature, °F

t_R = temperature of radiator, °F

t_s = temperature of surface, °F

t_0 = reference temperature, °F

T = absolute temperature, °R

U = overall heat-transfer coefficient, Btu/(hr)(sq ft)(°F)

x = length of drying surface in direction of gas flow, ft

X = moisture content of a solid, lb moisture/lb dry solid

X_c = critical moisture content, lb moisture/lb dry solid

X^* = equilibrium moisture content, lb moisture/lb dry solid

Y = humidity of a gas, lb moisture/lb dry gas

z_M = thickness of tray material, ft

z_S = thickness of drying solid, ft

Z = length of drier, ft

α = a constant

Δ = difference

ε = emissivity of drying surface, dimensionless

θ = time, hr

λ_s = latent heat of vaporization at t_s, Btu/lb

μ = viscosity, lb/(ft)(hr)

π = 3.1416

ρ_G = gas density, lb/cu ft

ρ_S = apparent solid density, lb dry solid/cu ft

ϕ_D = holdup of solid in a continuous drier, cu ft solid/cu ft drier

ϕ_{D0} = holdup of solid at no gas flow, cu ft solid/cu ft drier

Subscripts:

as = adiabatic-saturation conditions

c = critical

max   = maximum

m = average

s = surface

W = wet-bulb conditions

I, II, III = pertaining to zones I, II, and III in a continuous drier

REFERENCES

  1. Aldrich, R. S.: *Chem. Eng. Progr.*, **58**(6), 62 (1962).
  2. Allerton, J., L. E. Brownell, and D. L. Katz: *Chem. Eng. Progr.*, **45**, 619 (1949).

3. Belcher, D. W., D. A. Smith, and E. M. Cook: *Chem. Eng.*, **70**, Sept. 30, 83; Oct. 14, 201 (1963).

4. Brier, J. C., and A. S. Foust: *Trans. AIChE*, **35**, 797 (1939).

5. Broughton, D. B., and H. S. Mickley: *Chem. Eng. Progr.*, **49**, 319 (1953).

6. Chu, J. C., S. Finelt, W. Hoerner, and M. Lin: *Ind. Eng. Chem.*, **51**, 275 (1959).

7. Comings, E. W., and T. K. Sherwood: *Ind. Eng. Chem.*, **26**, 1096 (1934).

8. Crosby, E. J., and W. R. Marshall, Jr.: *Chem. Eng. Progr.*, **54**(7), 56 (1958).

9. Erisman, J. L.: *Ind. Eng. Chem.*, **30**, 996 (1938).

10. Fixari, F., W. Conley, and G. K. Viall: *Chem. Eng. Progr.*, **53**(3), 110 (1957).

11. Friedman, S. J., and W. R. Marshall, Jr.: *Chem. Eng. Progr.*, **45**, 482, 573 (1949).

12. Gilliland, E. R., and T. K. Sherwood: *Ind. Eng. Chem.*, **25**, 1134 (1933).

13. Harper, J. C., and A. L. Tappel: "Advances in Food Research," vol. 7, p. 171, Academic Press Inc., New York, 1957.

14. Hougen, O. A., and H. J. McCauley: *Trans. AIChE*, **36**, 183 (1940).

15. Hurxtal, A. O.: *Ind. Eng. Chem.*, **30**, 1004 (1938).

16. Lane, A. M., and S. Stern: *Mech. Eng.*, **78**, 423 (1956).

17. Lapple, W. C., W. E. Clark, and E. C. Dybdal: *Chem. Eng.*, **62**(11), 117 (1955).

18. Loesecke, H. W. von: "Drying and Dehydration of Foods," 2d ed., Reinhold Publishing Corporation, New York, 1955.

19. Malek, M. A., L. A. Madonna, and B. C. Y. Lu: *Ind. Eng. Chem. Process Design Develop.*, **2**, 31 (1963); *Can. J. Chem. Eng.*, **42**, 14 (1964).

20. Marshall, W. R., Jr.: "Atomization and Spray Drying," *Chem. Eng. Progr. Monograph Ser.*, **50**(2) (1954).

21. Marshall, W. R., Jr., and O. A. Hougen: *Trans. AIChE*, **38**, 91 (1942).

22. Mathur, K. B., and P. E. Gishler: *AIChE J.*, **1**, 157 (1955).

23. McAdams, W. H.: "Heat Transmission," 3d ed., McGraw-Hill Book Company, New York, 1954.

24. McCormick, P. Y.: *Chem. Eng. Progr.*, **58**(6), 57 (1962).

25. McCormick, P. Y.: sec. 20, "The Chemical Engineers' Handbook," 4th ed., McGraw-Hill Book Company, New York, 1963.

26. McCready, D. W., and W. L. McCabe: *Trans. AIChE*, **29**, 131 (1933).

27. Miskell, F., and W. R. Marshall, Jr.: *Chem. Eng. Progr.*, **52**(1), 35-J (1956).

28. Molstad, M. C., P. Farevaag, and J. A. Farrell: *Ind. Eng. Chem.*, **30**, 1131 (1938).

29. Newitt, D. M., et al.: *Trans. Inst. Chem. Engrs. (London)*, **27**, 1 (1949); **30**, 28 (1952); **33**, 52, 64 (1955).

30. Nissan, A. H., W. A. Kaye, and J. R. Bell: *AIChE J.*, **5**, 103, 344 (1959).

31. Pasquill, F.: *Proc. Roy. Soc.*, **A182**, 75 (1944).

32. Pearse, J. G., T. R. Oliver, and D. M. Newitt: *Trans. Inst. Chem. Engrs. (London)*, **27**, 1, 9 (1949).

33. Peterson, W. S.: *Can. J. Chem. Eng.*, **40**, 226 (1962).

34. Porter, S. J.: *Trans. Inst. Chem. Engrs. (London)*, **41**, 272 (1963).

35. Quinn, M. F.: *Ind. Eng. Chem.*, **55**(7), 18 (1963).

36. Saeman, W. C.: *Chem. Eng. Progr.*, **58**(6), 49 (1962).

37. Saeman, W. C., and T. R. Mitchell: *Chem. Eng. Progr.*, **50**, 467 (1954).

38. Shepherd, C. B., C. Haddock, and R. C. Brewer: *Ind. Eng. Chem.*, **30**, 389 (1938).

39. Sherwood, T. K.: *Ind. Eng. Chem.*, **21**, 12, 976 (1929); **22**, 132 (1930); **24**, 307 (1932).

40. Sherwood, T. K.: *Trans. AIChE*, **27**, 190 (1931).

41. Sherwood, T. K., and E. W. Comings: *Ind. Eng. Chem.*, **25**, 311 (1933).

42. Spraul, J. R.: *Ind. Eng. Chem.*, **47**, 368 (1955).

43. Uhl, V. C., and W. L. Root: *Chem. Eng. Progr.*, **58**(6), 37 (1962).

44. Victor, V. P.: *Chem. Met. Eng.*, **52**(7), 105 (1945).

45. Wheat, J. A., and MacLeod, D. A.: *Can. J. Chem. Eng.*, **37**, 47 (1959).

46. Whitwell, J. C., and R. K. Toner: *Textile Res. J.*, **17**, 99 (1947).

PROBLEMS

12.1. A plant wishes to dry a certain type of fiberboard in sheets 4 by 6 ft by ½ in. To determine the drying characteristics, a 1- by 1-ft sample of the board, with the edges sealed so that drying took place from the two large faces only, was suspended from a balance in a laboratory cabinet drier and exposed to a current of hot, dry air. The initial moisture content was 75%. The sheet lost weight at the constant rate of 0.8 lb/hr until the moisture content fell to 60%, whereupon the drying rate fell. Measurements of the rate of drying were discontinued, but after a long period of exposure to this air it was established that the equilibrium moisture content was 10%. The dry weight of the sample was 2 lb. All moisture contents are on the wet basis.

Determine the time for drying the large sheets from 75 to 20% moisture under the same drying conditions.

12.2. A sample of a porous, manufactured sheet material of mineral origin was dried from both sides by cross circulation of air in a laboratory drier. The sample was 1 ft square, ¼ in. thick, and the edges were sealed. The air velocity over the surface was 10 ft/sec, its dry-bulb temperature was 125°F, and its wet-bulb temperature 70°F. There were no radiation effects. The solid lost moisture at a constant rate of 0.6 lb water/hr until the critical moisture content, 15% (wet basis), was reached. In the falling-rate period, the rate of evaporation fell linearly with moisture content until the sample was dry. The equilibrium moisture was negligible. The dry weight of the sheet was 4.0 lb.

Estimate the time for drying sheets of this material 2 by 4 ft by ½ in. thick from both sides, from 25 to 2% moisture (wet basis), using air of dry-bulb temperature 150°F, but of the same absolute humidity, at a linear velocity over the sheet of 15 ft/sec. Assume no change in the critical moisture with the changed drying conditions. **Ans.:** 3.95 hr.

12.3. Estimate the rate of drying during the constant-rate period for the conditions existing as the air enters the trays of the drier of Illustration 12.2. The solid being dried is a granular material of thermal conductivity when wet = 1 (Btu)(ft)/(hr)(sq ft)(°F), and it completely fills the trays. The metal of the trays is stainless steel, 16 BWG (0.065 in. thick). Include in the calculations an estimate of the radiation effect from the undersurface of each tray upon the drying surface.

12.4. A laboratory drying test was made on a 1-sq-ft sample of a fibrous boardlike material. The sample was suspended from a balance, its edges were sealed, and drying took place from the two large faces. The air had a dry-bulb temperature of 150°F, wet-bulb temperature 84°F, and its velocity was 5 ft/sec past the sample. The following are the weights recorded at various times during the test:

Time, hr	Wt., lb	Time, hr	Wt., lb	Time, hr	Wt., lb	Time, hr	Wt., lb
0	10.625	2.6	9.570	6.0	8.670	14	8.420
0.1	10.597	3.0	9.412	6.5	8.610	16	8.420
0.2	10.548	3.4	9.273	7.0	8.565		
0.4	10.470	3.8	9.150	7.5	8.535		
0.8	10.305	4.2	9.045	8.0	8.507		
1.0	10.225	4.6	8.944	9.0	8.469		
1.4	10.063	5.0	8.852	10.0	8.448		
1.8	9.900	5.4	8.772	11	8.432		
2.2	9.735	5.8	8.700	12	8.423		

The sample was then dried in an oven at 220°F, and the dry weight was 8.301 lb.

a.   Plot the rate-of-drying curve.

b.   Estimate the time required for drying the same sheets from 20 to 2% moisture (wet basis) using air of the same temperature and humidity, but with a 50% greater air velocity.   Assume the critical moisture remains unchanged.   **Ans.:** 7.25 hr.

12.5.   A pigment material which has been removed wet from a filter press is to be dried by extruding it into small cylinders and subjecting these to through-circulation drying.   The extrusions are ¼ in. in diameter, 2 in. long, and are to be placed on screens to a depth of 2.5 in.   The surface of the particles is estimated to be 90 sq ft/cu ft of bed and the apparent density 65 lb dry solid/cu ft. Air at a mass velocity 700 lb dry air/(hr)(sq ft) will flow through the bed, entering at 250°F, humidity 0.05 lb water/lb dry air.

a.   Estimate the constant rate of drying to be expected.   (*Note:* For long cylinders it is best to take the equivalent diameter as the actual cylinder diameter.)   **Ans.:** 21.7 lb/(hr)(sq ft).

b.   Estimate the constant rate of drying to be expected if the filter cake were to be dried on trays by cross circulation of the air over the surface at the same mass velocity, temperature, and humidity.   Neglect radiation and heat conduction through the solid.   **Ans.:** 0.247 lb/(hr)(sq ft).

12.6.   A louver-type continuous rotary drier (Fig. 12.23) was used to dry wood chips from 40 to 15% moisture [Horgan, *Trans. Inst. Chem. Engrs.*, **6**, 131 (1928)].   The wood entered at 33°F, while the dried product was discharged at 100°F at the rate of 3,162 lb/hr.   The drying medium was the gas resulting from the combustion of fuel, but for purposes of the present calculation it may be assumed to have the characteristics of air.   It entered the drier at 715°F, with a humidity of 0.038 lb water vapor/lb dry gas, at the rate of 275 lb/min (wet).   The gas was discharged at 175°F. The heat capacity of the dry wood may be taken as 0.42 Btu/(lb)(°F), and the heat of wetting may be ignored.   Estimate the heat losses, Btu/hr.

12.7.   A direct-heat parallel-flow rotary drier, 8-ft diameter, 60 ft long, was used to dry chopped alfalfa [see Gutzeit and Spraul, *Chem. Eng. Progr.*, **49**, 380 (1953)].   Over a 5-hr test period, the drier delivered an average of 2,220 lb/hr of dried product at 11% moisture and 145°F, when fed with alfalfa containing 79% moisture at 80°F.   The drying medium was the combustion products resulting from the burning of 13,074 cu ft/hr (80°F, 4 oz gauge pressure) of natural gas (85% methane, 10% ethane, 5% nitrogen by volume) with air at 80°F, 50% humidity.   The gas analyzed 2.9% CO_2, 15.8% O_2, 81.3% N_2 by volume on a dry basis; it entered the drier at 1500°F and left at 195°F. The heat capacity of dry alfalfa is estimated to be 0.37 Btu/(lb)(°F), and the heat of wetting may be neglected.   Compute the volumetric rate of gas flow through the exhaust fan, cu ft/min, and the heat losses, Btu/hr.

12.8.   A direct-heat countercurrent rotary hot-air drier is to be chosen for drying an insoluble crystalline organic solid.   The solid will enter at 70°F, containing 20% water.   It will be dried by air entering at 310°F, 0.01 lb water/lb dry air.   The solid is expected to leave at 250°F, with a moisture content 0.3%.   One thousand pounds per hour of dried product will be delivered.   The specific heat of the dry solid is 0.2 Btu/(lb)(°F), and its average particle size is 0.5 mm.   The superficial air velocity should not exceed 5 ft/sec in any part of the drier.   The drier will be insulated, and heat losses may be neglected for present purposes.   Choose a drier from among the following standard sizes, and specify the amount of air which should be used: 36 in. by 10 ft, 36 in. by 20 ft, 48 in. by 25 ft, 54 in. by 30 ft, 60 in. by 35 ft.   **Ans.:** 48 in. by 25 ft.

12.9.   A manufactured material in the form of sheets 2 by 4 ft by ½ in. is to be continuously dried in an adiabatic countercurrent hot-air tunnel drier at the rate of 100 sheets per hour.   The sheets will be supported on a special conveyor carrying the material in tiers 30 sheets high, and they will be dried from both sides.   The dry weight of each sheet is 25 lb, and the moisture content will be reduced from 50 to 5% water by air entering at 250°F, humidity 0.01 lb water/lb dry air.   Forty pounds dry air will be passed through the drier per pound dry solid.

In a small-scale experiment, when dried with air at constant drying conditions, dry-bulb temperature 200°F, wet-bulb temperature 120°F, and at the same velocity to be used in the large drier, the constant drying rate was 0.25 lb water evaporated/(hr)(sq ft) and the critical moisture content 30%. The equilibrium moisture content was negligible.

   a. Calculate the value of k_Y from the data of the small-scale experiment. **Ans.:** 12.5.

   b. For the large drier, calculate the humidity of the air leaving, and at the point where the solid reaches the critical moisture content.

   c. Estimate the time of drying in the large drier. **Ans.:** 7.3 hr.

   d. How many sheets of material will be in the drier at all times?

   12.10. A continuous countercurrent hot-air tunnel drier is to be designed to dry a filter-press cake of coarse crystals of an inorganic material, insoluble in water. The filter-press cake will be placed on trays 3 by 3 ft by 1 in., 20 trays to a truck, with 2 in. between trays. The tunnel drier will have a cross section 6 ft high by 40 in. wide. The trays have a reinforced screen bottom, so that drying takes place from both top and bottom of each tray. Production is such as to permit introducing one truckload per hour. Each tray contains 65 lb dry solid, which will enter the drier at 75°F, 50% moisture, and will be dried to negligible moisture content. The critical moisture content is 15%, and the equilibrium moisture is negligible. The trucks are steel, each weighing about 300 lb. The air is to enter at 300°F, humidity 0.03 lb water/lb dry air, and the discharged solid is expected to leave at 275°F. The air is to be blown over the trays so that the average velocity at the air entrance is to be 15 ft/sec over the trays. The specific heat of the dry solid is 0.3 Btu/(lb)(°F). The drier is to be well insulated.

   a. Calculate the length of the drier required. **Ans.:** 40 ft.

   b. The entering air is to be prepared by recycling a portion of the discharged air with atmospheric air (75°F, humidity = 0.01 lb water/lb dry air) and heating the mixture to 300°F. Calculate the percentage of discharge air to be recycled and the heat required. Calculate the heat also as Btu/lb water evaporated. **Ans.:** 38.3%; 1530 Btu/lb water.

CHAPTER THIRTEEN
LEACHING

Leaching is the preferential solution of one or more constituents of a solid mixture by contact with a liquid solvent. This unit operation, one of the oldest in the chemical industries, has been given many names, depending to some extent upon the technique used for carrying it out. *Leaching* and *lixiviation* both originally referred to percolation of the liquid through a fixed bed of the solid, but the former term at least is now used to describe the operation generally, by whatever means it may be done. The term *extraction* is also widely used to describe this operation in particular, although it is applied to all the separation operations as well, whether mass-transfer or mechanical methods are involved. *Decoction* refers specifically to the use of the solvent at its boiling temperature. When the soluble material is largely on the surface of an insoluble solid and is merely washed off by the solvent, the operation is sometimes called *elutriation*, or *elution*. This chapter will also consider these washing operations, since they are frequently intimately associated with leaching.

The metallurgical industries are perhaps the largest users of the leaching operation. Most useful minerals occur in mixtures with large proportions of undesirable constituents, and leaching of the valuable material is a separation method which is frequently applied. For example, copper minerals are preferentially dissolved from certain of their ores by leaching with sulfuric acid or ammoniacal solutions, and gold is separated from its ores with the aid of sodium cyanide solutions. Leaching similarly plays an important part in the metallurgical processing of aluminum, cobalt, manganese, nickel, and zinc. Many naturally occurring organic products are separated from their original structure by leaching. For example, sugar is leached from sugar beets with hot water, vegetable oils are recovered from seeds such as soybeans and cottonseed by leaching with organic solvents, tannin is dissolved out of various tree barks by leaching with water, and many pharmaceutical products are similarly recovered from plant roots and leaves. Tea and coffee are prepared both domestically and industrially by leaching operations. In addition, chemical precipitates are frequently washed of their adhering mother liquors by techniques and in equipment quite similar to those used in true leaching operations, as in the washing of caustic soda liquor from precipitated calcium carbonate following the reaction between soda ash and lime.

Preparation of the solid

The success of a leaching and the technique to be used will very frequently depend upon any prior treatment which may be given the solid.

In some instances, small particles of the soluble material are completely surrounded by a matrix of insoluble matter. The solvent must then diffuse into the mass, and the resulting solution must diffuse out, before a separation can result. This is the situation in the case of many metallurgical materials. Crushing and grinding of such solids will greatly accelerate the leaching action, since then the soluble portions are made more accessible to the solvent. A certain copper ore, for example, can be leached effectively by sulfuric acid solutions within 4 to 8 hr if ground to pass through a 60-mesh screen, in 5 days if crushed to ¼-in. granules, and only in 4 to 6 years if 6-in. lumps are used.[29] Since grinding is expensive, the quality of the ore will have much to do with the choice of size to be leached. In the case of certain gold ores, on the other hand, the tiny metallic particles are scattered throughout a matrix of quartzite which is so impervious to the leaching solvent that it is essential to grind the rock to pass through a 100-mesh screen if leaching is to occur at all. When the soluble substance is more or less uniformly distributed throughout the solid or even in solid solution, the leaching action may provide channels for the passage of fresh solvent and fine grinding may not be necessary. Collapse of the insoluble skeleton which remains after solute removal may then present problems, however.

Vegetable and animal bodies are cellular in structure, and the natural products to be leached from these materials are usually found inside the cells. If the cell walls remain intact upon exposure to a suitable solvent, then the leaching action involves osmotic passage of the solute through the cell walls. This may be a slow process. It is, however, impractical and sometimes undesirable to grind the material sufficiently small to release the contents of individual cells. Thus, sugar beets are cut into thin, wedge-shaped slices called "cossettes" before leaching in order to reduce the time required for the solvent water to reach the individual plant cells. The cells are deliberately left intact, however, so that the sugar will pass through the semipermeable cell walls while the undesirable colloidal and albuminous materials largely remain behind. In the case of many pharmaceutical products recovered from plant roots, stems, and leaves, the plant material is frequently dried before treatment, and this does much toward rupturing the cell walls and releasing the solute for direct action by the solvent. Vegetable seeds and beans, such as soybeans, are usually rolled or flaked to give particles in the size range 0.005 to 0.02 in. The cells are, of course, smaller than this, but they are largely ruptured by the flaking process, and the oils are then more readily contacted by the solvent.

When the solute is adsorbed upon the surface of solid particles or merely dissolved in adhering solution, no grinding or crushing is necessary, and the particles may be washed directly.

Temperature of leaching

It is usually desirable to leach at as high a temperature as possible. Higher temperatures result in higher solubility of the solute in the solvent, and consequently higher ultimate concentrations in the leach liquor are possible. The viscosity of the liquid is lower and the diffusivities larger at higher temperatures, and this leads to increased rates of leaching. In the case of some natural products such as sugar beets, however, temperatures which are too high may lead to leaching of excessive amounts of undesirable solutes or chemical deterioration of the solid.

Methods of operation and equipment

Leaching operations are carried out under batch and semibatch (unsteady-state) as well as under completely continuous (steady-state) conditions. In each category, both stagewise and continuous-contact types of equipment are to be found. Two major handling techniques are used: spraying or trickling the liquid over the solid, and immersing the solid completely in the liquid. The choice of equipment to be used in any case depends greatly upon the physical form of the solids and the difficulties and cost of handling them. This has led in many instances to the use of very specialized types of equipment in certain industries.

I. UNSTEADY-STATE OPERATION

The unsteady-state operations include those where the solids and liquids are contacted in purely batchwise fashion and also those where a batch of the solid is contacted with a continually flowing stream of the liquid (semibatch method). Coarse solid particles are usually treated in fixed beds by percolation methods, whereas finely divided solids, which may more readily be kept in suspension, may be dispersed throughout the liquid with the help of some sort of agitator.

In-place leaching

This refers to the percolation leaching of minerals in place at the mine, by circulation of the solvent over and through the ore body. It has been applied to the leaching of low-grade copper ores containing less than 0.5 percent copper, whose value was too low to warrant the expense of mining.[30] It is also regularly used in the removal of salt from deposits below the earth's surface by solution of the salt in water which is pumped down to the deposits.

Heap leaching

Low-grade ores whose mineral values do not warrant the expense of crushing or grinding may be leached in the form of run-of-mine lumps built into huge piles upon impervious ground.   The leach liquor is then pumped over the ore and collected as it drains from the heap.   Copper has been leached from pyritic ores in this manner, in heaps containing as much as 25,000,000 tons of ore, using over 5,000,000 gal of leach liquor per day.   It may require up to 7 or more years to reduce the copper content of such heaps from 2 to 0.3 percent.

Percolation tanks

Solids of intermediate size may be conveniently leached by percolation methods in open tanks.   The construction of these tanks varies greatly, depending upon the nature of the solid and liquid to be handled and the size of the operation, but they are relatively inexpensive.   Small tanks are frequently made of wood, provided that this material is not chemically attacked by the leach liquid.   The solid particles to be leached rest upon a false bottom, which in the simplest construction consists of a grating of wooden strips arranged parallel to each other and sufficiently close to support the solid.   These in turn may rest upon similar strips arranged at right angles, 6 in. or more apart, so that the leach liquor may flow to a collection pipe leading from the bottom of the tank.   For supporting fairly fine particles, the wood grating may be further covered by a coconut matting and a tightly stretched canvas filter cloth, held in place by calking a rope into a groove around the periphery of the false bottom.   Small tanks may also be made entirely of metal, with perforated false bottoms upon which a filter cloth is placed, as in the leaching of pharmaceutical products from plants. Very large percolation tanks (150 by 110 by 18 ft deep) for the leaching of copper ores have been made of reinforced concrete and lined with lead or bituminous mastic. Small tanks may be provided with side doors near the bottom for sluicing away the leached solid, while very large tanks are usually emptied by excavating from the top. Tanks should be filled with solid of as uniform a particle size as practical, since then the percentage of voids will be largest and the pressure drop required for flow of the leaching liquid least.   This also leads to uniformity of the extent of leaching individual solid particles and less difficulty with channeling of the liquid through a limited number of passageways through the solid bed.

The operation of such a tank may follow any of several procedures.   After the tank is filled with solid, a batch of solvent sufficient completely to immerse the solid may be pumped into the tank and the entire mass may be allowed to steep or soak for a prescribed period of time.   During this period the batch of liquid may or may not be circulated over the solid by pumping.   The liquid may then be drained from the solid by withdrawing it through the false bottom of the tank.   This entire operation then represents a single stage.   Repetition of this process will eventually dissolve all the solute.   The only solute then retained is that dissolved in the solution wetting the drained solid.   This may be washed out by filling the tank with fresh solvent and repeating the operation as many times as necessary.   An alternative method is continuously to admit liquid into the tank and continuously to withdraw the resulting solution, with or without recirculation of a portion of the total flow.   Such an operation may be equivalent to many stages.   Since the solution which results is usually more dense than the solvent, convective mixing is reduced by percolation in the downward direction.   Upward flow is sometimes used, nevertheless, in order to avoid clogging of the bed or the filter with fines, but this may result in excessive entrainment of the fines in the overflow liquid.   Still a further modification, less frequently used, is to spray the liquid continuously over the top and allow it to trickle downward through the solid without fully immersing the solid at any time.

Retention of liquid after drainage

Imagine a bed of granular solids whose void space is completely filled with liquid.   When the liquid is allowed to drain under the influence of gravity, with admission of air to the voids from the top of the bed, the rate of liquid flow is at first very rapid.   The rate gradually falls, and after a relatively long period of time no additional drainage occurs.   The bed still contains liquid, however.   The fraction of the void volume still occupied by liquid is termed the *residual saturation S*.   Figure 13.1 shows the variation of S with height of the bed.[6]   In the upper part of the bed the value of S is constant at S_0, and this represents the liquid which remains in the crevasses and small angles between the particles as fillets, held in place by surface tension.   In the lower part of the bed, the liquid is held up in the voids, filling them completely ($S = 1.0$) by capillary action.   The drain height Z_D is defined as the height where the value of S is the average in the range S_0 to unity, as shown in the figure.   The average value of S for the entire bed will be the area between the ordinate axis and the curve of the figure, divided by the bed height Z,

$$S_{\text{av}} = \frac{(Z - Z_D)S_0}{Z} + \frac{Z_D}{Z} \tag{13.1}$$

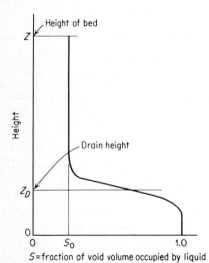

Height of bed

Height

Drain height

Z_D

0

S_0 1.0

S=fraction of void volume occupied by liquid   **Fig. 13.1**   *Drainage of packed beds.*[6]

A large number of measurements of Z_D under a wide variety of conditions showed that, approximately,[6]

$$Z_D = \frac{0.275}{(K/g)^{0.5}(\rho_L/\sigma)} \tag{13.2}$$

where K is the "permeability" of the bed, ρ_L the liquid density, and σ the surface tension of the liquid. The value of S_0 was found to depend upon the group $K\rho_L/g\sigma$, called the *capillary number*, as follows:

$$S_0 = \begin{cases} 0.075 & \dfrac{K\rho_L}{g\sigma} < 0.02 \tag{13.3} \\[2ex] \dfrac{0.0018}{\sqrt{K\rho_L/g\sigma}} & \dfrac{K\rho_L}{g\sigma} \geq 0.02 \tag{13.4} \end{cases}$$

In these expressions it is assumed that drainage has occurred under the action of the force of gravity only and that the contact angle between liquid and solid surfaces is 180°.

The permeability K is the proportionality constant in the flow equation for laminar flow through the bed,

$$G = \frac{K\rho_L \, \Delta P}{\mu_L Z} \tag{13.5}$$

where ΔP is the drop in pressure across the bed and G is the mass velocity of flow based on the entire cross section of the bed. Equation (6.36) describes the flow through beds of granular solids, and for laminar flow only the first term of the right-hand side of this expression is used. If $\Delta P/Z$ from this equation is substituted in Eq. (13.5), with Re replaced by $d_p G/\mu_L$, simplification leads to

$$K = \frac{d_p^2 \epsilon^3 g_c}{150(1 - \epsilon)^2} \tag{13.6}$$

where d_p is the diameter of a sphere of the same surface/volume ratio as the particles of the bed and ϵ is the fractional-void volume. For fibrous material and others whose value of d_p may be difficult to estimate, K may be obtained from Eq. (13.5) after experimental measurement of the pressure drop for laminar flow through the bed.

Illustration 13.1. The sugar remaining in a bed of bone char used for decolorization is leached by flooding the bed with water, following which the bed is drained of the resulting sugar solution. The bed is 10 ft deep, the temperature is 150°F, and the sugar solution which drains has a density 71 lb/cu ft and a surface tension 66 dynes/cm. The bulk density of the char is 60 lb/cu ft and the individual particle density 110 lb/cu ft. The particles have a specific external surface 80 sq ft/lb.

Estimate the weight of solution still retained by the bed after dripping of the solution has stopped. Express this also as lb solution/lb dry bone char.

Solution. The fractional void volume $= \epsilon = 1 - $ (bulk density/particle density) $= 1 - 60/110 = 0.455$ cu ft voids/cu ft bed. The particle surface $= a_p = (80$ sq ft/lb)$60 = 4,800$ sq ft/ cu ft bed.

Eq. (6.37): $\quad d_p = \dfrac{6(1 - \epsilon)}{a_p} = \dfrac{6(1 - 0.455)}{4,800} = 0.000569$ ft

Eq. (13.6): $\quad K = \dfrac{(0.000569)^2(0.455)^3(4.17)(10^8)}{150(1 - 0.455)^2} = 0.285$ cu ft/hr^2

$$\sigma = (66 \text{ dynes/cm})(6.89)(10^{-5}) = 455(10^{-5}) \text{ lb/ft}$$

$$\frac{K\rho_L}{g\sigma} = \frac{0.285(71)}{4.17(10^8)(455)(10^{-5})} = 10.67(10^{-6})$$

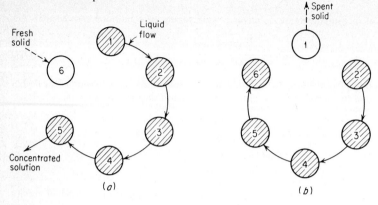

Fig. 13.2   *Countercurrent multiple contact, Shanks system.*

Eq. (13.3): $S_0 = 0.075$

Eq. (13.2): $Z_D = \dfrac{0.275}{[0.285/4.17(10^8)]^{0.5}[71/455(10^{-5})]} = 0.675$ ft

$$Z = 10 \text{ ft}$$

Eq. (13.1): $S_{av} = \dfrac{(10 - 0.675)(0.075)}{10} + \dfrac{0.675}{10} = 0.1375$

$$\frac{\text{Vol of liquid retained}}{\text{Vol of bed}} = 0.1375\epsilon = 0.1375(0.455) = 0.0625 \text{ cu ft/cu ft}$$

$$\text{Wt of liquid in bed} = 0.0625 \frac{\pi(3)^2(10)}{4} 71 = 313 \text{ lb}$$

$$\frac{\text{Wt of liquid}}{\text{Wt of dry solid}} = \frac{0.0625(71)}{1(60)} = 0.073 \text{ lb/lb}$$

Countercurrent multiple contact; the Shanks system

Leaching and washing of the leached solute from the percolation tanks by the cross-current methods described above will inevitably result in weak solutions of the solute. The strongest solution will result if a countercurrent scheme is used, wherein the final withdrawn solution is taken from contact with the freshest solid and the fresh solvent is added to solid from which most of the solute has already been leached or washed. In order to avoid moving the solids physically from tank to tank in such a process, the arrangement of Fig. 13.2, shown schematically for a system of six tanks, is used.   This *Shanks system*,† as it is called, is operated in the following manner:

† Named after James Shanks, who first introduced the system in 1841 into England for the leaching of soda ash from the "black ash" of the Le Blanc process.   It was, however, apparently a German development.

1. Assume at the time of inspecting the system at Fig. 13.2*a* that it has been in operation for some time.   Tank 6 is empty, tanks 1 to 5 are filled with solid, tank 5 most recently and tank 1 for the longest time.   Tanks 1 to 5 are also filled with leach liquid, and the most concentrated is in tank 5 since it is in contact with the freshest solid.   Fresh solvent has just been added to tank 1.

2. Withdraw the concentrated solution from tank 5, transfer the liquid from tank 4 to tank 5, from 3 to 4, from 2 to 3, and from 1 to 2.   Add fresh solid to tank 6.

3. Refer to Fig. 13.2*b*.   Discard the spent solid from tank 1.   Transfer the liquid from tank 5 to tank 6, from 4 to 5, from 3 to 4, and from 2 to 3.   Add fresh solvent to tank 2.   The circumstances are now the same as they were at the start in Fig. 13.2*a*, except that the tank numbers are each advanced by one.

4. Continue the operation in the same manner as before.

The scheme is identical with the batch simulation of a multistage countercurrent operation shown in Fig. 10.58.   After several cycles have been run through in this manner, the concentrations of solution and in the solid in each tank approach very closely the values obtaining in a truly continuous countercurrent multistage leaching. The system can, of course, be operated with any number of tanks, and anywhere from 6 to 16 are common.   They need not be arranged in a circle but are better placed in a row, called an "extraction battery," so that additional tanks may be conveniently added to the system if desired.   The tanks may be placed at progressively decreasing levels, so that liquid may flow from one to the other by gravity with a minimum of pumping.

Such leaching tanks and arrangements are used extensively in the metallurgical industries, for recovery of tannins from tree barks and woods, for leaching sodium nitrate from Chilean nitrate-bearing rock (*caliche*), and in many other processes.

Percolation in closed vessels

When the pressure drop for flow of liquid is too high for gravity flow, closed vessels must be used, and the liquid is pumped through the bed of solid.   Such vessels are sometimes called "diffusers."   Closed tanks are also necessary to prevent evaporation losses when the solvent is very volatile or when temperatures above the normal boiling point of the solvent are desired.   For example, some tannins are leached with water at 250°F, 50-psi pressure, in closed percolation tanks.

Designs vary considerably, depending upon the application.   In the case of leaching of sugar from sugar-beet slices, or cossettes, a diffuser of the type shown in Fig. 13.3 is used.   These are arranged in a battery containing up to 16 vessels, and the beets are leached with hot water in the countercurrent fashion of the Shanks system. Heaters are placed between the diffusers to maintain a solution temperature of 160 to 170°F.   In this manner 95 to 98 percent of the sugar, in beets containing initially about 18 percent, may be leached to form a solution of 12 percent concentration. Countercurrent, continuous equipment is also used in the sugarbeet industry.[13]

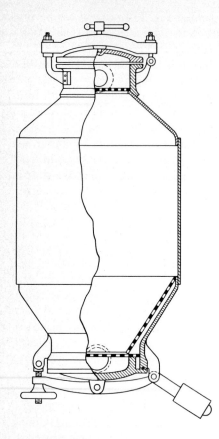

Fig. 13.3   *Sugarbeet diffuser.*[7]   (*Courtesy of the Institution of Chemical Engineers.*)

Filter-press leaching

Finely divided solids, too fine for treatment by percolation in relatively deep percolation tanks, may be filtered and leached in the filter press by pumping the solvent through the press cake.   This is, of course, common practice in the washing of mother liquor from precipitates which have been filtered.

Agitated vessels

Channeling of the solvent in percolation or filter-press leaching of fixed beds, with its consequent slow and incomplete leaching, may be avoided by stirring the liquid and solid in leaching vessels.   For coarse solids, many types of stirred or agitated vessels have been devised.[24]   In such cases, closed cylindrical vessels are arranged vertically (Fig. 13.4a) and are fitted with power-driven paddles or stirrers on vertical shafts, as well as false bottoms for drainage of the leach solution at the end of the operation. In others, the vessels are horizontal, as in Fig. 13.4b, with the stirrer arranged on a horizontal shaft.   In some cases, a horizontal drum is the extraction vessel, and the solid and liquid are tumbled about inside by rotation of the drum on rollers, as in Fig. 13.4c.   These devices are operated in batchwise fashion and provide a single leaching stage. They may be used singly but very frequently also are used in batteries arranged for countercurrent leaching. They have been used extensively in the older European and South American installations for leaching of vegetable oils from seeds, but relatively little in the United States.

Finely divided solids may be suspended in leaching solvents by agitation, and for batch operation a variety of agitated vessels are used. The simplest is the Pachuca tank (Fig. 13.5), which is employed extensively in the metallurgical industries. These tanks may be constructed of wood, metal, or concrete and may be lined with inert metal such as lead, depending upon the nature of the leaching liquid. Agitation is accomplished by an air lift: the bubbles of air rising through the central tube cause the upward flow of liquid and suspended solid in the tube and consequently vertical circulation of the tank contents.[17] The standard mechanical agitators, with turbine-type impellers, for example, may also be used to keep the finely divided solids suspended in the liquid. After the leaching has been accomplished, the agitation is stopped, the solid is allowed to settle in the same or a separate vessel, and the clear, supernatant liquid may be decanted by siphoning over the top of the tank or by withdrawal through discharge pipes placed at an appropriate level in the side of the tank. If the solids are finely divided and settle to a compressible sludge, the amount of solution retained in the settled solids will be considerable. Agitation and settling with several batches of wash solvent may then be necessary to recover the last traces of solute, and this may be done in a countercurrent fashion. Alternatively, the solid may be filtered and washed in the filter.

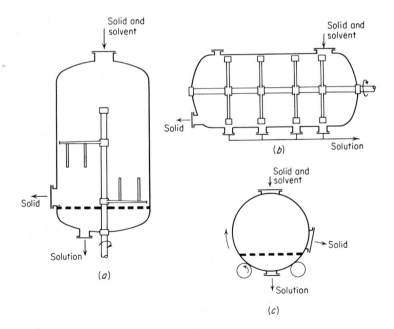

Fig. 13.4 *Agitated batch leaching vessels.*

Batch settling

The settling characteristics of a slurry consisting of a finely divided solid, of uniform density and reasonably uniform particle size, which is dispersed in a liquid are easily followed by observing a sample of the slurry when allowed to stand undisturbed in a vertical cylinder of transparent glass. If the slurry is initially very dilute, the particles will be observed to settle down through the liquid individually, each at a rate dependent upon the particle size, the relative density of solid and liquid, and the viscosity of the liquid, eventually to collect in a pile at the bottom. Ultimately the liquid becomes clear, but at no time until the end is there a sharp line of demarcation between clear liquid and the settling slurry. For more concentrated slurries, of the sort usually encountered in leaching and washing operations, the behavior is different, however. It will usually be observed that the particles settle more slowly owing to mutual interference (hindered settling). Furthermore, except

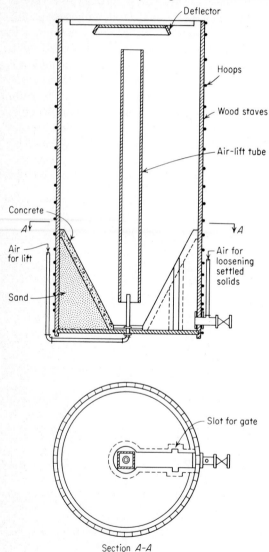

Section *A-A*

Fig. 13.5 *Pachuca tank.*[18]

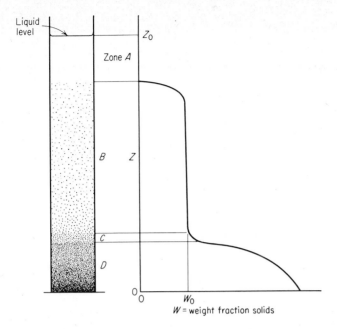

Fig. 13.6 *Batch settling.*

for a few particles of relatively large size which may be present, there is little classification according to size, and the particles largely settle together. As a result there is usually a reasonably sharp line of demarcation between the clear, supernatant liquor in the upper part of the cylinder and the settling mass of solids in the lower part.

Consider the cylinder of Fig. 13.6, initially filled to a height Z_0 with a slurry of uniform concentration w_0 weight fraction solids, in which some settling has already taken place. At the time of observation, there is a zone A of clear liquid at the top. Directly beneath this is zone B, throughout which the solids concentration is reasonably uniform at the initial value w_0, as shown by the accompanying graph.[4] In zone D at the bottom, usually called the "compression zone," the particles accumulating from above have come to rest upon each other, and, owing to their weight, liquid is squeezed out from between the particles. For compressible sludges, this results in increasing solids concentration with depth in this zone, as shown by the curve. Zone C is a transition zone between B and D, and it may not always be clearly defined. As settling continues beyond the time corresponding to that in the figure, the line of demarcation between zones A and B falls and the height of zone D rises, until eventually zone B disappears and only a compression zone containing all the solids remains. This then slowly subsides to some ultimate height.

The rate of settling is usually followed by plotting the height of the line of demarcation between zones A and B against time, as shown by the solid curve of Fig. 13.7. The broken curve represents the position of the upper level of zone D. The top of zone B settles at constant rate (curve of Z vs. time straight) from the beginning until zone B has nearly disappeared and all the solids are in the compression zone. The rate of settling of the compression zone to its ultimate height Z_∞ is then relatively slow and is not constant. In a few cases, two constant-rate settling periods may be observed, with substantially no compression period. The appearance of the curves depends not only upon the type of slurry (nature and particle size of the solid, and nature of the liquid) but also upon the initial height and concentration of the slurry, as well as the extent of flocculation and whether or not any stirring is done during settling.

Flocculation. If the finely divided solid particles are all similarly electrically charged, they repel each other and remain dispersed. If the charge is neutralized by addition, for example, of an electrolyte (flocculating agent) to the mixture, the particles may form aggregates, or flocs. Since the

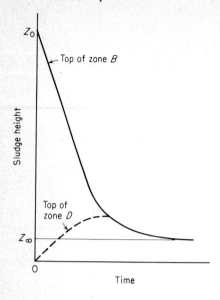

Fig. 13.7 *Rate of settling*.

flocs are of larger size, they settle more rapidly. The slurries and suspensions encountered in chemical operations are usually flocculated.

Stirring. Very slow stirring, so slow that eddy currents are not formed within the liquid, changes the character of the settling profoundly. The floc structure is altered so that the solids concentration in zone B is no longer uniform at the initial value[5] and zone D may not be clearly defined. The ultimate height of the settled slurry may be only a fraction of that obtained without stirring[14]

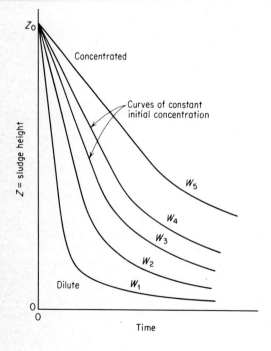

Fig. 13.8 *Batch settling of slurries. Effect of slurry concentration.*

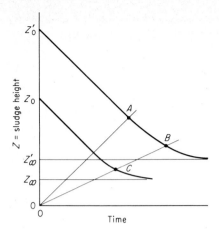

Fig. 13.9 *Batch settling of slurries at different initial heights.*

owing to breakdown of bridged floc structures in the compression zone, and the ultimate concentration of solids in the settled mass is corresponding greater. Generally, however, the zones of constant- and falling-rate settling are still observed, although the rates will be different from those obtained without stirring.[31]

Concentration. The rate of settling decreases with increased initial concentration of the solids owing to the increase of the effective density and viscosity of the medium through which the particles settle. Figure 13.8 illustrates the effect usually to be expected when slurries of increasing concentration of the same substance are settled in columns of the same height. Various attempts have been made to predict the effect of concentration on the settling rate, from knowledge of the curves at one or more concentrations. This has been successful only for slurries which are not compressible.[27]

Height. Refer to Fig. 13.9, which shows settling curves for the same slurry begun at different initial heights. The initial constant settling rate is independent of height, and provided some critical minimum value of Z_0 is exceeded, the ultimate value of Z_∞/Z_0 will apparently also be constant. The constant-settling-rate lines both terminate on a line OA radiating from the origin, and in general any line[31] radiating from the origin such as OB will be cut so that line OC/line $OB = Z_0/Z_0'$. It follows that the time for a slurry to settle to a fixed fractional height Z/Z_0 is proportional to the initial height Z_0. In this way it is possible reasonably well to predict the settling curves for deep tanks from results obtained in small laboratory cylinders. In making such laboratory tests, however, it is important[14] to use cylinders at least 3 ft tall and at least 2 in. in diameter and to maintain all other conditions in the laboratory test identical with those expected to prevail on the large scale.

Percolation vs. agitation

If a solid in the form of large lumps is to be leached, a decision must frequently be made whether to crush it to coarse lumps and leach by percolation or whether to fine-grind it and leach by agitation and settling. No general answer can be given to this problem owing to the diverse leaching characteristics of the various solids and the values of the solute, but among the considerations are the following: Fine grinding is more costly but provides more rapid and possibly more thorough leaching. It suffers the disadvantages that the weight of liquid associated with the settled solid may be as great as the weight of the solid, or more, so that considerable solvent is used in washing the leached solute free of solute and the resulting solution is dilute. Coarsely ground particles, on the other hand, leach more slowly and possibly less thoroughly but on draining may retain relatively little solution, require less washing, and thus provide a more concentrated final solution.

II. STEADY-STATE (CONTINUOUS) OPERATION

Equipment for continuous steady-state operations may be broadly classified into two major categories, according to whether it operates in stagewise or in continuous-contact fashion. Stagewise equipment may sometimes be assembled in multiple units so as to produce multistage effects, whereas continuous-contact equipment may provide the equivalent of many stages in a single device.

Leaching during grinding

As has been pointed out earlier, many solids require grinding in order to make the soluble portions accessible to the leaching solvents, and if continuous wet grinding is practiced, some of the leaching may be accomplished at this time. As much as 50 to 75 percent of the soluble gold may be dissolved by grinding the ore in the presence of cyanide solution, for example. Similarly, castor seeds are ground in an attrition mill with solvent for the castor oil. The liquid and solid flow through a grinding mill in parallel and consequently tend to come to a concentration equilibrium. Such operations are therefore single-stage leachings and are usually supplemented by additional agitation or washing operations, as described later.

Agitated vessels

Finely ground solids which can be readily suspended in liquids by agitation may be continuously leached in any of the many types of agitated tanks or vessels. These must be arranged for continuous flow of liquid and solid into and out of the tank and must be carefully designed so that no accumulation of solid occurs. Owing to the thorough mixing ordinarily obtained these devices are single-stage in their action, the liquid and solid tending to come to equilibrium within the vessel.

Mechanically agitated vessels may be used, for which the turbine-type agitator is probably most generally suitable. Pachuca tanks are frequently used in the metallurgical industries. The Dorr agitator (Fig. 13.10) utilizes both the air-lift principle and mechanical raking of the solids and is extensively used in both the metallurgical and the chemical industry for continuous leaching and washing of finely divided solids. The central hollow shaft of the agitator acts as an air lift and at the same time revolves slowly. The arms attached to the bottom of the shaft rake the settled solids toward the center of the tank bottom, where they are lifted by the air lift through the shaft to the revolving launders attached to the top. The launders then distribute the elevated mixture of liquid and solid over the entire cross section of the tank. The rake arms may be lifted to free them of solids which may settle during a shutdown, and they are also provided with auxiliary air lines to assist in freeing them from settled solid. For unevenly sized solids, operation of the agitator may be so adjusted that coarse particles, which may require longer leaching time, remain in the tank for longer periods of time

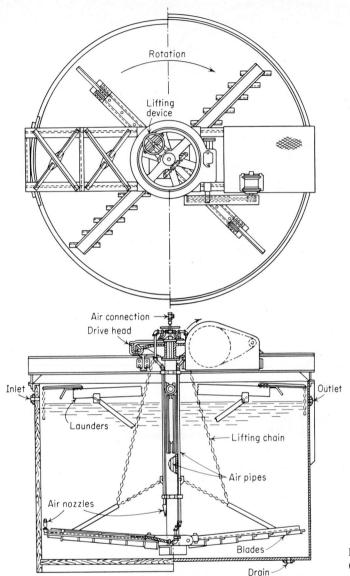

Rotation

Lifting
device

Air connection
Drive head

Inlet

Launders

Outlet

Lifting chain

Air pipes

Air nozzles

Blades

Drain

Fig. 13.10 *Dorr agitator.*
(*The Dorr Co.*)

than the finer. These agitators are regularly built in sizes ranging from 5 to 40 ft in diameter.

The average holding time in an agitated vessel may be calculated by dividing the vessel contents by the rate of flow into the vessel. This may be done separately for solid and liquid, and the holding time for each will be different if the ratio of the amounts of one to the other in the vessel is different from that in the feed. The average holding time of the solid must be sufficient to provide the leaching action

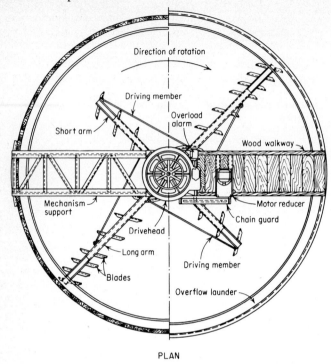

PLAN

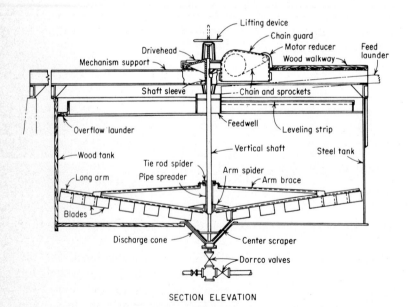

SECTION ELEVATION

Fig. 13.11   *Dorr thickener.*   (*The Dorr Co.*)

required. Individual solid particles, of course, may short-circuit the tank, by which is meant that they may pass through in times much shorter than the calculated average, and this will lead to low stage efficiency. Short circuiting may be eliminated by passing the solid-liquid mixture through a series of smaller agitated vessels, one after the other, the sum of whose average holding time is the necessary leach time. This may be readily accomplished with gravity flow of the slurry by placing the individual tanks in the series at progressively lower levels. Three vessels in series are usually sufficient to reduce short circuiting to a negligible amount. It should be noted that, since liquid and solid pass through these vessels in parallel flow, the entire series is still equivalent to only a single stage.

The effluent from continuous agitators may be sent to a filter for separating liquid from solid, upon which the solid may be washed free of dissolved solids, or to a series of thickeners for countercurrent washing.

Thickeners

Thickeners are mechanical devices designed especially for continuously increasing the ratio of solid to liquid in a dilute suspension of finely sized particles by settling and decanting, producing a clear liquid and a thickened sludge as two separate products. Thickeners may be used prior to any ordinary filter in order to reduce filtering costs. Owing to the fact that both effluents are pumpable and consequently readily transported, however, thickeners are frequently used to wash leached solids and chemical precipitates free of adhering solution in a continuous multistage countercurrent arrangement, and it is in this application that they are of interest here.

A typical single-compartment thickener of the Dorr Company's design is shown in Fig. 13.11. The thin slurry of liquid and suspended solids enters a large settling tank through a feed well at the top center, in such a manner as to avoid mixing of the slurry with the clear liquid at the top of the tank. The solids settle from the liquid which fills the tank, and the settled sludge is gently directed toward the discharge cone at the bottom by four sets of plow blades or rakes. These revolve slowly so as not to disturb the settled solid unduly. The sludge is pumped from the discharge cone by means of a diaphragm pump. The clear, supernatant liquid overflows into a launder built about the upper periphery of the tank. Thickeners are built in sizes ranging from 6 to 325 ft in diameter, for handling granular as well as flocculent solids, and of varying detail design depending upon the size and service. In order to reduce the ground-area requirements, several thickeners operating in parallel, and superimposed as in Fig. 13.12, may be used. Such a device delivers a single sludge product.

The liquid content of the sludge is greatly dependent upon the nature of the solids and liquid and upon the time allowed for settling but in typical cases might be in the range 15 to 75 percent liquid. The less liquid retained, the more efficient will be the leaching or washing process which is being carried on.

Continuous countercurrent decantation

Leaching equipment such as agitators or grinding mills may discharge their effluent into a cascade of thickeners for continuous countercurrent washing of the finely divided solids free of adhering solute.   The same type of cascade may also be used to wash the solids formed during chemical reactions, as in the manufacture of phosphoric acid, by treatment of phosphate rock with sulfuric acid, or of blanc fixe, by reaction of sulfuric acid and barium sulfide, or of lithopone.

A simple arrangement is shown in Fig. 13.13a.   The solids to be leached (or the reagents for a reaction), together with solution from the second thickener, are introduced into the leaching agitators at the left, and the strong solution thus produced is decanted from the solids by the first thickener.   The agitators together with the first thickener then constitute a single stage.   The sludge is passed through the cascade to be washed by the solvent in true countercurrent fashion, and the washed solids are discharged at the right.   There may, of course, be more or fewer than the four stages shown, and the agitators may be replaced by any continuous-leaching device, such as a grinding mill.   Many variations in the flow sheet are regularly made.   For example, the sludge from each stage may be "repulped," or vigorously beaten with the solvent, between stages in order to improve the washing efficiency.   Figure 13.13b shows an arrangement whereby the underflow from the first thickener is agitated with overflow from the third, for the purpose of bringing about the additional leaching possible with dilute solution.   The sludge from the final stage may be filtered, as shown, when the solid is valuable and is to be delivered reasonably dry or when the solute is valuable and solution adhering to the washed solids must be reduced to a minimum.   For successful operation of these plants, very carefully controlled rates of

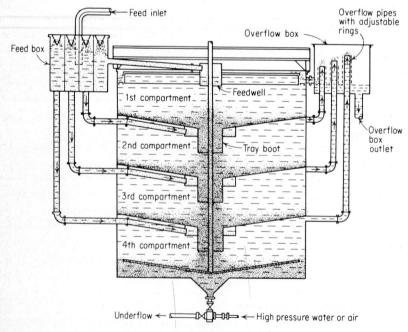

Fig. 13.12 *Dorr balanced-tray thickener.* (*The Dorr Co.*)

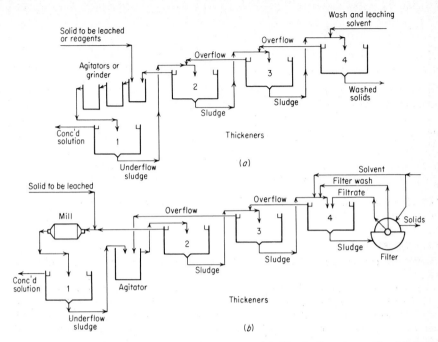

Fig. 13.13   *Continuous countercurrent decantation.   (a) Simple flow sheet; (b) with intermediate agitation and filtration of washed solids.*

flow of both sludges and solution are necessary so as not to disturb the steady-state conditions prevailing.

For small decantation plants, where ground area may be limited, it is possible to obtain a countercurrent cascade of thickeners built in superimposed fashion into a single shell.

Continuous settling

The concentrations existing at the various levels of a continuous thickener under steady-state operation differ considerably from those found in batch settling.   The solid curve of Fig. 13.14 shows typical concentrations during normal operation,[5] and four clearly defined zones are found in the thickener corresponding to the various sections of the curve.   The feed slurry is diluted as it issues from the feed well of the thickener, and the bulk of the liquid passes upward to overflow into the launder about the thickener periphery.   The solid concentration in the top zone is negligible if the overflow is clear.   The solids and the remainder of the feed liquid move downward through the lower three zones and leave in the thickened underflow.   The solids concentration in the settling zone is much lower than that in the feed, owing to the dilution, but rises rapidly in the compression zone immediately below.   In the bottom zone, the action of the rake disturbs arched structures which the settling solids may form, the weight of the solids presses out the liquid, and the concentration rises to the value in the underflow.   If the feed rate to the thickener is increased, the concentration of solids in the settling zone rises and reaches a constant maximum value not related to the feed concentration when the settling capacity of this zone is exceeded.   The excess solids, which cannot

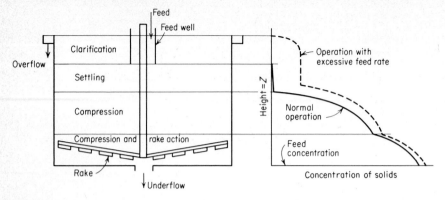

Fig. 13.14   *Continuous thickener characteristics.*[5]   (*Courtesy of Industrial and Engineering Chemistry.*)

settle, overflow with the liquid, as indicated by the broken curve of concentrations in Fig. 13.14 for this condition.

The concentration of solids in the underflow sludge for a given rate and concentration of feed may be increased by reducing the rate of withdrawal of sludge. This increases the depth of the compression zone and increases the detention time of the solids within the thickener, although it is important not to raise the level of the compression zone to such an extent that solids appear in the overflow liquid.

The capacity of continuous thickeners, or their cross-sectional area required for a given solids throughput, can be roughly estimated from batch-settling tests.[8,27] *Initial* settling velocities u for slurries of the solid at various initial uniform concentrations c are determined from the slopes of curves such as those of Fig. 13.8, covering the entire range of solids concentration to be dealt with (it is best to determine these curves for slurries made by suspending a given weight of solids in varying amounts of liquid by adding and subtracting liquid). The flux of solids during settling, $G_S = cu$, is then plotted against c to produce a curve such as that of Fig. 13.15. The tangent of smallest negative slope is then drawn to the curve from point ($G_S = 0$, $c = c_U$), where c_U is the desired underflow concentration, to intersect the ordinate at G_{SL}, the limiting solids flux. The minimum required

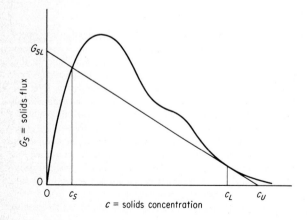

Fig. 13. 5   *Determination of thickener area from flux curve.*

thickener cross section for handling W lb/hr of solids is then

$$A = \frac{W}{G_{SL}} \tag{13.7}$$

Concentration c_L is that at the point of compression and c_S that in the settling zone.

Hydrocyclones

Hydrocyclones, similar to those used for size classification of solids (Fig. 13.16) may also be used as liquid-solid separators in place of thickeners in countercurrent washing of solids in a slurry.

Continuous leaching of coarse solids

Many ingenious devices have been used for moving the solids continuously through a leaching device so that countercurrent action may be obtained.   With the exception of the classifiers, which are used principally in the metallurgical industries, these machines were principally developed for the special solids-handling problems arising in the leaching of sugar beets.and of vegetable seeds such as cottonseed, soybeans, and the like.   Donald[7] has described many of the early devices used for sugar beets. Only the more important of the currently used machines can be described here.

Classifiers

Coarse solids may be leached, or more usually washed free of adhering solution or solute, in some types of machinery ordinarily used in the metallurgical industries

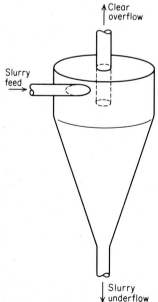

Fig. 13.16   *Hydrocyclone.*

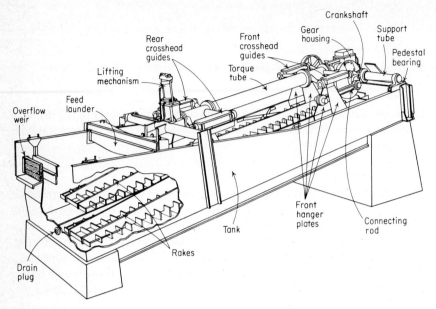

Fig. 13.17 *Single Dorr classifier for washing coarse solids.* (*The Dorr Co.*)

for classification according to particle size.   One such device is shown in Fig. 13.17. The solids are introduced into a tank, which is made with a sloping bottom and which is partly filled with the solvent.   The rakes, which are given a reciprocating and circular lifting motion by the driving mechanism, rake the solids upward along the bottom of the tank and out of the liquid.   In the upper part of the tank the solids are drained and discharged.   The liquid overflows at the deep end of the tank.   The solute concentration in the liquid is reasonably uniform throughout the tank owing to the agitation by the rakes, so that the apparatus produces a single-stage action.   Several classifiers may be placed in a cascade for continuous multistage countercurrent action, however, in which case they may be operated by a single drive mechanism.

Leaching of vegetable seeds

Cottonseeds, soybeans, linseeds (flaxseeds), peanuts, rice bran, castor beans, and many other similar products are regularly leached, or *extracted*, with organic solvents for removing the vegetable oils which they contain.   The seeds must usually be specially prepared for most advantageous leaching, and this may involve dehulling, precooking, adjustment of the moisture (water) content, and rolling or flaking. Sometimes a portion of the oil is first removed mechanically by expelling or expression. Leaching solvents are usually petroleum naphthas, for most oils a fraction corresponding closely to hexane; chlorinated hydrocarbons leave too toxic a residue for the leached meal to be used as an animal feed.   The oil-solvent solution, which usually contains a small amount of finely divided, suspended solids, is called "miscella" and the leached solids "marc." The various leaching devices are usually called "extractors" in this industry.

The *Rotocel*[1,19] is essentially a modification of the Shanks system wherein the leaching tanks are continuously moved, in that way permitting continuous introduction and discharge of the solids. Figure 13.18 is a schematic representation of the device, simplified to show the working principle. A circular rotor, containing 18 cells, each fitted with a hinged screen bottom for supporting the solids, slowly revolves above a stationary compartmented tank. As the rotor revolves, each cell passes in turn under a special device for feeding the prepared seeds and then under a series of sprays by which each is periodically drenched with solvent for leaching. After nearly one revolution, the leached contents of each cell are automatically dumped into one of the lower stationary compartments, from which they are continuously conveyed away. The solvent from each spray percolates downward through the solid and the supporting screen into the appropriate compartment of the lower tank, from which it is continuously pumped to the next spray. The leaching is countercurrent, and the strongest solution is taken from the freshest seeds. A number of ingenious mechanical devices are necessary for maintaining smooth operation, and the entire machine is enclosed in a vaportight housing to prevent escape of solvent vapors.

The *Kennedy* extractor,[26] a modern arrangement of which is indicated schematically in Fig. 13.19, is another stagewise device which has been in use since 1927, originally for leaching tannins from tanbark. It is now used for oilseed and other chemical leaching operations. The solids are leached in a series of tubs and are pushed from one to the next in the cascade by paddles, while the solvent flows in

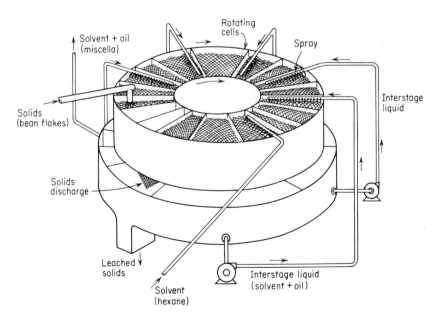

Fig. 13.18 *Schematic arrangement of the Rotocel.*

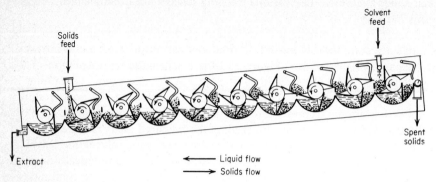

Liquid flow ⟵
Solids flow ⟶

Fig. 13.19 *Kennedy extractor.* (*The Vulcan Copper and Supply Co.*)

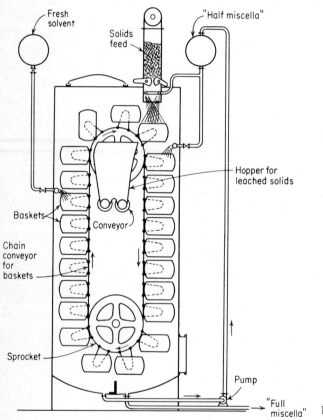

Fig. 13.20 *Bollman extractor.*

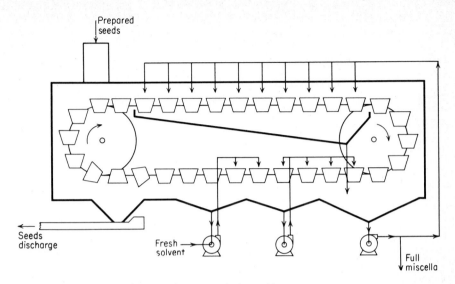

Fig. 13.21 *Continuous horizontal extractor (schematic).*

countercurrent. Perforations in the paddles permit drainage of the solids between stages, and the solids are scraped from each paddle as shown. As many tubs may be placed in a cascade as are required.

The *Bollman* extractor[26] (Fig. 13.20) is one of several basket-type machines. Solids are conveyed in perforated baskets attached to a chain conveyor, down on the right and up on the left in the figure. As they descend, they are leached in parallel flow by a dilute solvent-oil solution ("half miscella") pumped from the bottom of the vessel and sprayed over the baskets at the top. The liquid percolates through the solids from basket to basket, collects at the bottom as the final strong solution of the oil ("full miscella"), and is removed. On the ascent, the solids are leached countercurrently by a spray of fresh solvent to provide the half miscella. A short drainage time is provided before the baskets are dumped at the top. There are many variants of this device, the horizontal arrangement of Fig. 13.21, for example. In still another variation[23] the baskets remain stationary while the filling, leaching, and dumping equipment revolves.

Continuous tilting-pan filters and horizontal filters[9] are also commonly used. Figure 13.22 shows a typical flow-sheet arrangement for a horizontal filter. The filter, in the form of a circular wheel, is divided into a number of sectors and revolves in the horizontal plane. Prepared seeds are slurried with solvent which has already been used for leaching, and the slurry sent to the filter. The first filtrate is passed again through the filter cake to remove finely divided solids (polishing) prior to being discharged as miscella. The principle is much the same as that of the Rotocel. Horizontal moving screen-type belts[28] are also used for conveying the solids during leaching.

The recovery of solvent from both the miscella and the leached seeds or beans is an

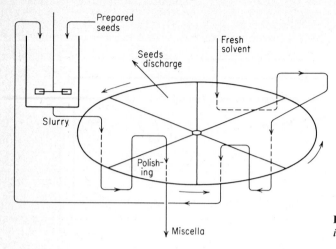

Fig. 13.22   *Flow sheet for hor-izontal-filter leaching.*

essential part of the vegetable-oil leaching process.   In a typical arrangement, the filtered miscella is passed to an evaporator for removal of solvent, sometimes followed by final stripping in a tray column, to produce the solvent-free oil.   The wet seeds are steamed to remove residual solvent and air-cooled.   Vented gas from condensers may be sent to an absorber to be scrubbed with petroleum white oil, and the resulting solvent–white oil solution stripped to recover any solvent.

METHODS OF CALCULATION

It is important to be able to make an estimate of the extent of leaching which may be obtained for a given procedure, i.e., to calculate the amount of soluble substance leached from a solid, knowing the initial solute content of the solid, the number and amount of washings with leaching solvent, the concentration of solute in the leaching solvent, if any, and the method, whether batch or continuous countercurrent.   Alternatively, it may be necessary to compute the number of washings, or number of stages, required to reduce the solute content of the solid to some specified value, knowing the amount and solute concentration of the leaching solvent.

Stage efficiency

Consider a simple batch leaching operation, where the solid is leached with more than enough solvent to dissolve all the soluble solute and where there is no preferential adsorption of either solvent or solute by the solid.   If adequate time of contact of solid and solvent is permitted, all the solute will be dissolved, and the mixture is then a slurry of insoluble solid immersed in a solution of solute in the solvent.   The insoluble phases are then separated physically by settling, filtration, or drainage, and the entire operation constitutes one stage.   If the mechanical separation of liquid and solid were perfect, there would be no solute associated with the solid leaving the operation and complete separation of solute and insoluble solid would be accomplished with a single stage. This would be an ideal stage, of 100 percent stage efficiency. In practice, stage efficiencies are usually much less than this: (1) the solute may be incompletely dissolved because of inadequate contact time; (2) most certainly it will be impractical to make the liquid-solid mechanical separation perfect, and the solids leaving the stage will always retain some liquid and its associated dissolved solute. In cases where solute is adsorbed by the solid, even though equilibrium between the liquid and solid phases is obtained, imperfect settling or draining will result in lowered stage efficiency.

Practical equilibrium

In the general case, it will be easiest to make calculations graphically, as in other mass-transfer operations, and this will require graphical representation of equilibrium conditions. It is simplest to use practical equilibrium conditions which take stage efficiencies into account directly, either entirely or in part, much as was done in the case of gas absorption and distillation. In the simplest cases, we must deal with three-component systems containing pure solvent (A), insoluble carrier solid (B), and soluble solute (C). Computations and graphical representation can be made on triangular coordinates for any ternary system of this sort, and the details of this have been worked out.[10,25] Owing to frequent crowding of the construction into one corner of such a diagram, it is preferable to use a rectangular-coordinate system patterned after that used for fractional adsorption.

The concentration of insoluble solid B in any mixture or slurry will be expressed as N lb B/lb $(A + C)$, whether the solid is wet with liquid solution or not. Solute C compositions will be expressed as weight fractions on a B-free basis: $x = $ wt fraction C in the effluent solution from a stage (B-free basis), and $y = $ wt fraction C in the solid or slurry (B-free basis). The value of y must include all solute C associated with the mixture, including that dissolved in adhering solution as well as undissolved or adsorbed solute. If the solid is dry, as it may be before leaching operations begin, N is the ratio of weights of insoluble to soluble substance, and $y = 1.0$. For pure solvent A, $N = 0$, $x = 0$.

The coordinate system then appears as in Fig. 13.23. Consider first a simple case of a mixture of insoluble solid from which all the solute has been leached, suspended in a solution of the solute in a solvent, as represented by point M_1 on the figure. The concentration of the clear solution is x, and the insoluble solid/solution ratio is N_{M1}. Let the insoluble solid be nonadsorbent. If this mixture is allowed to settle, as in a batch-settling tank, the clear liquid which may be drawn off will be represented by point R_1 and the remaining sludge will consist of the insoluble solid suspended in a small amount of the solution. The composition of the solution in the sludge will be the same as that of the clear liquid withdrawn, so that $y^* = x$. The concentration of solid B in the sludge N_{E1} will depend upon the length of time θ_1 which was allowed for settling, so that point E_1 then represents the slurry. Line E_1R_1 is a vertical tie line joining the points representing the two effluent streams, clear liquid and slurry. If the circumstances described were maintained in an actual leaching, points E_1 and R_1

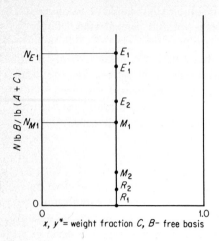

$x, y^* =$ weight fraction C, B– free basis   **Fig. 13.23** *Concentrations in leaching and washing.*

can be taken as the practical conditions of equilibrium for that leaching. Clearly if less time was allowed for settling, say θ_1', the sludge would be less concentrated in insoluble solids and might be represented by point E_1'. There will be some maximum value of N for the sludge, corresponding to its ultimate settled height, in accordance with the description of batch settling given earlier, but usually in practice insufficient time is allowed for this to be attained. Since the concentration of insoluble solid in a sludge settled for a fixed time depends upon the initial concentration in the slurry, a mixture M_2 settled for time θ_1 might result in a sludge corresponding to point E_2. If the solid does not settle to give an absolutely clear solution, if too much solution is withdrawn from the settled sludge so that a small amount of solid is carried with it, or if solid B dissolves to a small extent in the solution, the withdrawn solution would be represented by some point such as R_2, somewhat above the lower axis of the graph. Similar interpretations may be made for compositions obtained when wet solids are filtered or drained of solution rather than settled, or when continuously thickened.

The settling or thickening characteristics of a slurry depend, as shown earlier, upon the viscosity and relative density of the liquid in which the solid is suspended. Since these in turn depend upon the solution composition, it is possible to obtain experimental data showing the variation of compositions of thickened solids with composition of solution and to plot these on the diagram as practical equilibrium conditions. It is evident, however, that in every case they must be obtained under conditions of time, temperature, and concentrations identical with those pertaining in the plant or process for which the calculations are being made. In the case of drained beds of impervious solids, the equilibrium corresponding to the residual saturation after long-time drainage may be estimated by the methods of Illustration 13.1. Data for short-time drainage must be obtained experimentally.

In washing operations where the solute is already dissolved, uniform concentration throughout all the solution is rapidly attained, and reduced stage efficiency is most likely to be entirely the result of incomplete drainage or settling. In leaching an undissolved solute interspersed throughout the solid, on the other hand, lowered stage efficiency may be the result of inadequate time of contact as well as incomplete mechanical separation of liquid and solid. In this case it is possible (but not necessary) to distinguish experimentally between the two effects by making measurements of the amount and composition of liquid retained on the solid after short and after long contact time and to use the latter to establish the equilibrium conditions.

Let us now examine a few of the types of equilibrium curves which may be encountered. Figure 13.24a represents data which might be obtained for cases where solute C is infinitely soluble in solvent A, so that x and y may have values over the entire range from 0 to 1.0. This would occur in the case of the system soybean oil (C)–soybean meal (B)–hexane (A), where the oil and hexane are infinitely soluble. The curve DFE represents the separated solid under conditions actually to be expected in practice, as discussed above. Curve GHJ, the composition of the withdrawn solution, lies above the $N = 0$ axis, and in this case, therefore, either solid B is partly soluble in the solvent or an incompletely settled liquid has been withdrawn. The tie lines such as line FH are not vertical, and this will result (1) if insufficient time of contact with leaching solvent to dissolve all solute is permitted, (2) if preferential adsorption of the solute occurs, or (3) if the solute is soluble in the solid B and distributes unequally between liquid and solid phases at equilibrium. The data may be projected upon a plot of x vs. y, as in the manner of adsorption or liquid-extraction equilibria.

Figure 13.24b represents a case where no adsorption of solute occurs, so that withdrawn solution and solution associated with the solid have the same composition,

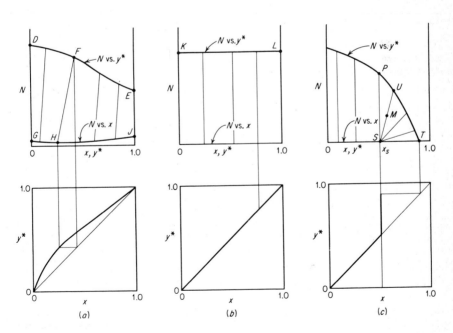

Fig. 13.24 *Typical equilibrium diagrams.*

and the tie lines are vertical. This results in an xy curve in the lower figure identical with the 45° line, and a distribution coefficient m, defined as y^*/x, equals unity. Line KL is horizontal, indicating that the solids are settled or drained to the same extent at all solute concentrations. It is possible to regulate the operation of continuous thickeners so that this will occur, and the conditions are known as "constant under-flow." The solution in this case contains no substance B, either dissolved or sus-pended. Figure 13.24c represents a case where solute C has a limited solubility x_S in solvent A. No clear solution stronger than x_S can be obtained, so that the tie lines joining slurry and saturated solution must converge, as shown. In this case any mixture M to the right of line PS will settle to give a clear saturated solution S and a slurry U whose composition depends on the position of M. Point T represents the composition of pure solid solute after drainage or settling of saturated solution. Since the tie lines to the left of PS are shown vertical, no adsorption occurs, and overflow liquids are clear. It will be appreciated that combinations of these various charac-teristics may appear in a diagram of an actual case.

Single-stage leaching

Consider the single real leaching or washing stage of Fig. 13.25. The circle represents the entire operation, including mixing of solid and leaching solvent and mechanical separation of the resulting insoluble phases by whatever means may be used. Weights of the various streams are expressed as pounds for a batch operation or as lb/hr [or lb/(hr)(sq ft)] for continuous flow. Since for most purposes the solid B is insoluble in the solvent and a clear liquid leach solution is obtained, the B discharged in the leached solids will be taken as the same as that in the solids to be leached. By defini-tion of N,

$$B = N_F F = E_1 N_1 \tag{13.8}$$

A solute (C) balance,

$$F y_F + R_0 x_0 = E_1 y_1 + R_1 x_1 \tag{13.9}$$

A solvent (A) balance,

$$F(1 - y_F) + R_0(1 - x_0) = E_1(1 - y_1) + R_1(1 - x_1) \tag{13.10}$$

and a "solution" (solute + solvent) balance,

$$F + R_0 = E_1 + R_1 = M_1 \tag{13.11}$$

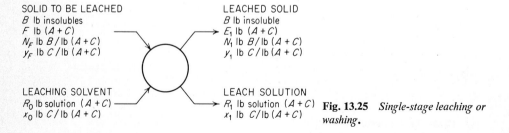

SOLID TO BE LEACHED
B lb insolubles
F lb $(A + C)$
N_F lb B/lb $(A + C)$
y_F lb C/lb $(A + C)$

LEACHED SOLID
B lb insoluble
E_1 lb $(A + C)$
N_1 lb B/lb $(A + C)$
y_1 lb C/lb $(A + C)$

LEACHING SOLVENT
R_0 lb solution $(A + C)$
x_0 lb C/lb $(A + C)$

LEACH SOLUTION
R_1 lb solution $(A + C)$
x_1 lb C/lb $(A + C)$

Fig. 13.25 *Single-stage leaching or washing.*

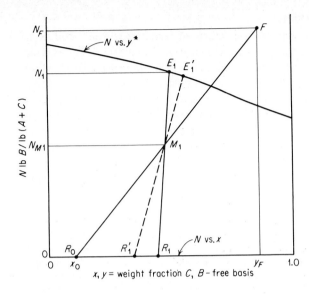

Fig. 13.26 *Single-stage leaching or washing.*

Mixing the solids to be leached and leaching solvent produces a mixture of B-free weight M_1 lb such that

$$N_{M1} = \frac{B}{F + R_0} = \frac{B}{M_1} \qquad (13.12)$$

$$y_{M1} = \frac{y_F F + R_0 x_0}{F + R_0} \qquad (13.13)$$

These relations may be shown on the coordinate system of Fig. 13.26. Point F represents the solids to be leached and R_0 the leaching solvent. Point M_1, representing the overall mixture, must fall on the straight line joining R_0 and F, in accordance with the characteristics of these diagrams described in Chap. 9. Points E_1 and R_1, representing the effluent streams, are located at opposite ends of the tie line through M_1, and their compositions may be read from the diagram. Equation (13.8) permits calculation of the weight of E_1 and Eq. (13.11) that of R_1. Modification to allow for the presence of B in the liquid withdrawn, necessitating an equilibrium diagram of the type shown in Fig. 13.24a, is readily made by analogy with the corresponding problem in liquid extraction.

If the equilibrium data of Fig. 13.26 were obtained experimentally after long contact time of solid and liquid and therefore represent inefficiency of mechanical separation of liquid and solid only, then in a real stage there may be an additional inefficiency owing to short time of contact. The effluent streams may then be represented by points E_1' and R_1' on the figure, and a stage efficiency $(y_F - y_1')/(y_F - y_1)$ may be ascribed to this. In case the equilibrium curve was obtained under conditions of contact time corresponding to the actual leaching, the tie line $E_1 R_1$ will give directly the effluent composition.

Multistage crosscurrent leaching

By contacting the leached solids with a fresh batch of leaching solvent, additional solute may be dissolved or washed away from the insoluble material. The calculations for additional stages are merely repetitions of the procedure for a single stage, with the leached solids from any stage becoming the feed solids to the next. Equations (13.8) to (13.13) apply, with only obvious changes in the subscripts to indicate the additional stages. When the number of stages for reducing the solute content of a solute to some specified value must be determined, it must be recalled that we are dealing with real stages, owing to the use of "practical" equilibrium data, and that therefore the number found must be integral. This may require adjustment by trial of either the amount of solute to be leached or the amount and apportioning of solvent to the stages.

Illustration 13.2. Caustic soda is being made by treatment of slaked lime, $Ca(OH)_2$, with a solution of sodium carbonate. The resulting slurry consists of particles of calcium carbonate, $CaCO_3$, suspended in a 10% solution of sodium hydroxide, NaOH, 0.125 lb suspended solid/lb solution. This is settled, the clear sodium hydroxide solution withdrawn and replaced by an equal weight of water, and the mixture thoroughly agitated. After repetition of this procedure (a total of two fresh-water washes), what fraction of the original NaOH in the slurry remains unrecovered and therefore lost in the sludge? The settling characteristics of the slurry, determined under conditions representing the practice to be followed in the process [Armstrong and Kammermeyer, *Ind. Eng. Chem.*, **34**, 1228 (1942)], show adsorption of the solute on the solid.

x = wt fraction NaOH in clear soln	N = lb $CaCO_3$/lb soln in settled sludge	y^* = wt fraction NaOH in soln of the settled sludge
0.0900	0.495	0.0917
0.0700	0.525	0.0762
0.0473	0.568	0.0608
0.0330	0.600	0.0452
0.0208	0.620	0.0295
0.01187	0.650	0.0204
0.00710	0.659	0.01435
0.00450	0.666	0.01015

Solution. The equilibrium data are plotted in Fig. 13.27. *Basis:* 1 lb solution in the original mixture, containing 0.1 lb NaOH (C) and 0.9 lb H_2O (A). $B = 0.125$ lb $CaCO_3$.

The original mixture corresponds to M_1 with $N_{M1} = 0.125$ lb $CaCO_3$/lb soln, $y_{M1} = 0.10$ lb NaOH/lb soln. M_1 is plotted on the figure, and the tie line through this point is drawn. At point E_1 representing the settled sludge, $N_1 = 0.47$, $y_1 = 0.100$.

Eq. (13.8):
$$E_1 = \frac{B}{N_1} = \frac{0.125}{0.47} = 0.266 \text{ lb soln in sludge}$$

$$1 - 0.266 = 0.734 \text{ lb clear soln withdrawn}$$

Stage 2. $R_0 = 0.734$ lb water added, $x_0 = 0$ lb NaOH/lb soln. Eq. (13.11) adapted to this stage:

$$M_2 = E_1 + R_0 = E_2 + R_2$$

$$M_2 = 0.266 + 0.734 = 1.0 \text{ lb liquid}$$

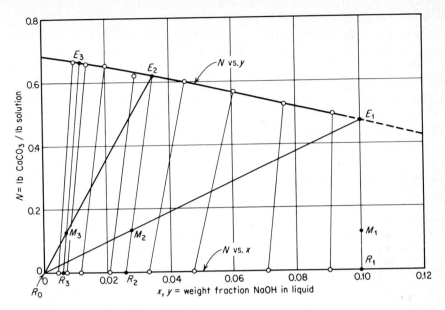

Fig. 13.27 *Solution to Illustration 13.2.*

Eq. (13.12):
$$N_{M2} = \frac{B}{E_1 + R_0} = \frac{B}{M_2} = \frac{0.125}{1.0} = 0.125$$

M_2 is located on line R_0E_1 at this value of N, and the tie line through M_2 is drawn. At E_2, $N_2 = 0.62$, $y_2 = 0.035$.

Eq. (13.8):
$$E_2 = \frac{B}{N_2} = \frac{0.125}{0.62} = 0.202 \text{ lb}$$

$$1 - 0.202 = 0.789 \text{ lb soln withdrawn}$$

Stage 3. $R_0 = 0.798$ lb water added, $x_0 = 0$.

Eq. (13.11):
$$M_3 = E_2 + R_0 = 0.202 + 0.798 = 1.0$$

$$N_{M3} = \frac{B}{M_3} = \frac{0.125}{1} = 0.125$$

Tie line E_3R_3 is located through M_3 as in the case of stage 2, and, at E_3, $N_3 = 0.662$, $y_3 = 0.012$. By Eq. (13.8), $E_3 = B/N_3 = 0.125/0.662 = 0.189$ lb soln in final sludge. $E_3y_3 = 0.189(0.012) = 0.00227$ lb NaOH in sludge, or $(0.00227/0.1)100 = 2.27\%$ of original.

The process permits an appreciable loss and produces three solutions, two of which (R_2 and R_3) are quite dilute. It should be compared with the countercurrent washing operation of Illustration 13.3.

Multistage countercurrent leaching

A general flow sheet for either leaching or washing is shown in Fig. 13.28. Operation must necessarily be continuous for steady-state conditions to prevail, although leaching according to the Shanks system will approach the steady state after a large number

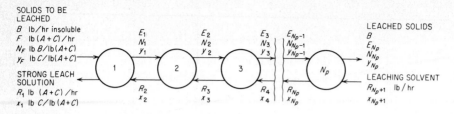

SOLIDS TO BE
LEACHED
B lb/hr insoluble
F lb $(A+C)$/hr
N_F lb B/lb$(A+C)$
y_F lb C/lb$(A+C)$

STRONG LEACH
SOLUTION
R_1 lb $(A+C)$/hr
x_1 lb C/lb $(A+C)$

LEACHED SOLIDS
B
E_{N_p}
N_{N_p}
y_{N_p}

LEACHING SOLVENT
R_{N_p+1} lb/hr
x_{N_p+1}

Fig. 13.28 *Multistage countercurrent leaching or washing.*

of cycles have been worked through. In the flow sheet shown, it is assumed that solid
B is insoluble and is not lost in the clear solution, but the procedure outlined below
is readily modified to take care of cases where this may not be true.†

A solvent balance for the entire plant is

$$F + R_{Np+1} = R_1 + E_{Np} = M \tag{13.14}$$

and a "solution" $(A + C)$ balance,

$$Fy_F + R_{Np+1}x_{Np+1} = R_1x_1 + E_{Np}y_{Np} = My_M \tag{13.15}$$

M represents the hypothetical B-free mixture obtained by mixing solids to be leached
and leaching solvent. Refer to Fig. 13.29, the operating diagram for the plant.
The coordinates of point M are

$$N_M = \frac{B}{F + R_{Np+1}} \tag{13.16}$$

$$y_M = \frac{Fy_F + R_{Np+1}x_{Np+1}}{F + R_{Np+1}} \tag{13.17}$$

Points E_{Np} and R_1, representing the effluents from the cascade, must lie on a line passing through M, and E_{Np} will be on the "practical" equilibrium curve. Equation
(13.14) may be rearranged to read

$$F - R_1 = E_{Np} - R_{Np+1} = \Delta_R \tag{13.18}$$

Similarly, a solution balance about any number of stages, such as the first three, may
be arranged in this form,

$$F - R_1 = E_3 - R_4 = \Delta_R \tag{13.19}$$

Δ_R represents the constant difference in flow $E - R$ (usually a negative quantity)
between each stage. On Fig. 13.29, it can be represented by the intersection of lines
FR_1 and $E_{Np}R_{Np+1}$ extended, in accordance with the characteristics of these coordinates. Since the effluents from each stage are joined by the practical tie line for the

---

† See Illustration 13.4, for example.

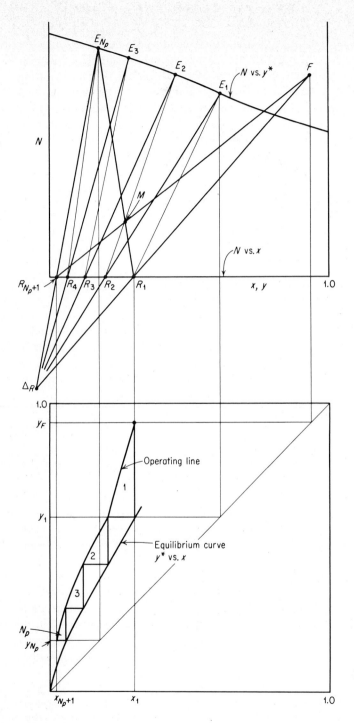

Fig. 13.29 *Multistage countercurrent leaching or washing.*

particular conditions which prevail, E_1 is found at the end of the tie line through R_1. A line from E_1 to Δ_R provides R_2, and so forth. Alternatively the stage constructions may be made on the x, y coordinates in the lower part of the figure after first locating the operating line. This may be done by drawing random lines from point Δ_R and projecting their intersections with the equilibrium diagram to the lower curve in the usual manner. The usual staircase construction then establishes the number of stages. The stages are real rather than ideal, the practical equilibrium data having already taken into account the stage efficiency, and hence there must be an integral number. Especially when the number of stages required is the unknown quantity, some trial-and-error adjustment of the concentrations of the effluents or amount of solvent will be required to obtain an integral number.

If the equilibrium curve of Fig. 13.29 represents inefficiency of mechanical separation of liquid and solid only, and not that resulting from short contact time of solvent and solid, the effect of the latter, if known, may be taken care of by drawing a new equilibrium curve on the x, y coordinates. This should be located between the equilibrium curve shown and the operating line, at a fractional distance from the operating line corresponding to the stage efficiency due to the short contact time, in the manner used earlier in gas absorption and distillation.

In the special case where "constant underflow," or constant value of N for all sludges, pertains, the operating line on the xy diagram is straight and of constant slope R/E. If in addition the practical equilibrium curve on this plot is straight, so that $m = y^*/x = $ const, then Eqs. (5.54) and (5.55) apply. Adapting the former to the present situation,

$$\frac{y_F - y_{Np}}{y_F - mx_{Np+1}} = \frac{(R/mE)^{Np+1} - R/mE}{(R/mE)^{Np+1} - 1} \tag{13.20}$$

Figure 5.16 may be used to solve this rapidly, using $(y_{Np} - mx_{Np+1})/(y_F - mx_{Np+1})$ as ordinate, R/mE as parameter. If in addition the tie lines of the equilibrium diagram are vertical, $m = 1.0$. The form of the equation shown is that which is applicable when the value of F for the feed solids is the same as E, so that R/E is constant for all stages, including the first. It frequently may happen, especially in the case where dry solids comprise the feed, that the ratio R_1/E_1 for stage 1 will be different from that pertaining to the rest of the cascade. In this case Eq. (13.20) or Fig. 5.16 should be applied to that part of the cascade excluding the first stage, by substitution of y_1 for y_F and N_p for $N_p + 1$. In general, the equation or chart may be applied to any part of the cascade where operating line and equilibrium line are both straight, and this may be particularly useful for cases where the solute concentration in the leached solution is very small. Just as in the case of liquid extraction and gas absorption, there is an economic optimum combination of treating solvent/solids ratio, number of stages, and extent of leaching.[3]

Illustration 13.3. Sodium hydroxide, NaOH, is to be made at the rate of 400 lb/hr (dry weight) by reaction of soda ash, Na_2CO_3, with slaked lime, $Ca(OH)_2$, using a flow sheet of the type shown in Fig. 13.13a. The reagents will be used in stoichiometric proportions, and for simplicity it will be assumed that reaction is complete. Pure water is to be used to wash the calcium carbonate, $CaCO_3$, precipitate, and it is desired to produce as overflow from the first thickener a solution containing 10% NaOH. It will be assumed that the settling data of Illustration 13.2 apply.

a. If three thickeners are used, determine the amount of wash water required and the percentage of the hydroxide lost in the discharged sludge.

b. How many thickeners would be required to reduce the loss to at least 0.1% of that made?

Solution. a. Mol wt of $CaCO_3$ (B) = 100, of NaOH (C) = 40. NaOH produced = 400 lb/hr or $400/40$ = 10 lb moles/hr. $CaCO_3$ produced = $10/2$ = 5.0 lb moles/hr or 5.0(100) = 500 lb/hr = B. The water required is that leaving in the strong solution plus that in the final sludge. The amount in the final sludge, according to the settling data, depends upon the NaOH concentration in the final sludge, which is not known. After a trial calculation, it is assumed that the solution in the final sludge will contain 0.01 wt fraction NaOH (y_3 = 0.01), and the settling data indicate N_3 = 0.666 lb $CaCO_3$/lb soln in the final sludge.

$$E = \frac{B}{N_3} = \frac{500}{0.666} = 750 \text{ lb/hr soln lost}$$

$$\text{NaOH lost} = E_3 y_3 = 750(0.01) = 7.50 \text{ lb/hr}$$

$$\text{Water in sludge} = 750 - 7.5 = 742.5 \text{ lb/hr}$$

$$\text{NaOH in overflow} = 400 - 7.5 = 392.5 \text{ lb/hr}$$

$$x_1 = 0.1 \text{ wt fraction NaOH in overflow}$$

$$R_1 = \frac{392.5}{0.1} = 3,925 \text{ lb overflow or strong soln/hr}$$

$$\text{Water in } R_1 = 3,925 - 392.5 = 3,532.5 \text{ lb/hr}$$

$$\text{Fresh water required} = R_{Np+1} = 3,532.5 + 742.5 = 4,275 \text{ lb/hr}$$

For purposes of calculation, it may be imagined that the agitators are not present in the flow sheet and that the first thickener is fed with a dry mixture of the reaction products, $CaCO_3$ and NaOH, together with overflow from the second thickener.

$$F = 400 \text{ lb NaOH/hr} \qquad N_F = \frac{B}{F} = \frac{500}{400} = 1.25 \text{ lb } CaCO_3/\text{lb NaOH}$$

$$y_F = 1.0 \text{ wt fraction NaOH in the dry solid, } CaCO_3\text{-free basis}$$

Plot points R_1, E_3, R_{Np+1}, and F on Fig. 13.30, and locate the difference point Δ_R at the intersection of lines FR_1 and E_3R_{Np+1} extended. The coordinates of point Δ_R are $N_{\Delta R}$ = −0.1419, $y_{\Delta R}$ = −0.00213. (These may be determined analytically, if desired, by simultaneous solution of the equations representing the intersecting lines.) Further computations must be done on an enlarged section of the equilibrium diagram (Fig. 13.31). Point Δ_R is plotted and the stages stepped off in the usual manner. The construction may be projected on to the xy diagram as shown, if desired. Three stages produce a value y_3 = 0.01, so that the assumed value of y_3 is correct. The NaOH lost in the sludge = (7.5/400)100 = 1.87% of that made.

b.
$$\text{NaOH lost} = 0.001(400) = 0.4 \text{ lb/hr}$$

$$\text{Lb } CaCO_3/\text{lb NaOH in final sludge} = \frac{500}{0.4} = 1,250 = \frac{N_{Np}}{y_{Np}}$$

In order to determine the liquid content of the final sludge, convert the equilibrium data for dilute

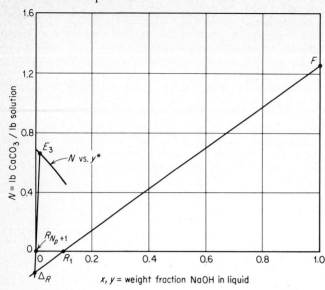

Fig. 13.30 *Solution to Il-lustration 13.3.*

mixtures into the following form:

N	0.659	0.666	0.677	0.679	0.680
y^*	0.01435	0.01015	0.002†	0.001†	0.0005†
N/y^*	45.6	65.6	338	679	1,360

† Estimated values.

By interpolation for $N/y^* = 1,250$, $N_{Np} = 0.680$ lb $CaCO_3$/lb soln, and $y_{Np} = 0.680/1,250 = 0.000544$ wt fraction NaOH in the liquid of the final sludge.

$$E_{Np} = \frac{B}{N_{Np}} = \frac{500}{0.680} = 735 \text{ lb/hr}$$

Water in $E_{Np} = 735 - 0.4 = 734.6$ lb/hr
NaOH in overflow $= 400 - 0.4 = 399.6$ lb/hr

$$R_1 = \frac{399.6}{0.1} = 3,996 \text{ lb/hr}$$

Water in $R_1 = 3,996 - 399.6 = 3,596$ lb/hr
Fresh water $= R_{Np+1} = 3,596 + 734.6 = 4,331$ lb/hr

On the operating diagram (Fig. 13.32) point Δ_R is located in the same way as before, and the stages are constructed in the usual fashion. It becomes impractical to continue graphical construction beyond the fourth stage unless considerable magnification of the chart is made, but computations beyond this point may be made with the help of Fig. 5.16. Beyond the fourth stage, the ratio of overflow to liquid in the sludge becomes substantially constant and equal to $R_{Np+1}/E_{Np} = 4,331/735 = 5.90 = R/E$. This is the initial slope of the operating line on the lower part of Fig. 13.32. The slope of the equilibrium curve at these low concentrations is also substantially constant,

$m = y^*/x = 0.01015/0.00450 = 2.26$, and $R/mE = 5.90/2.26 = 2.61$. $x_{Np+1} = 0$, and $y_4 = 0.007$.
Therefore $(y_{Np} - mx_{Np+1})/(y_4 - mx_{Np+1}) = 0.000544/0.007 = 0.0777$. From Fig. 5.16, an additional 2.3 stages beyond the 4 computed graphically are required.

An additional two stages (six thickeners) would make $y_{Np}/y_4 = 0.099$, or $y_{Np} = 0.099(0.007) = 0.000693$, corresponding to 0.51 lb NaOH lost/hr, while an additional three stages (seven thickeners) would make $y_{Np} = 0.0365(0.007) = 0.000255$, corresponding to 0.187 lb NaOH lost/hr.

It must be emphasized that the cost of these numbers of thickeners probably could not be justified when balanced against the value of the lost NaOH.   The very low NaOH loss was specified in order to demonstrate the computation methods.

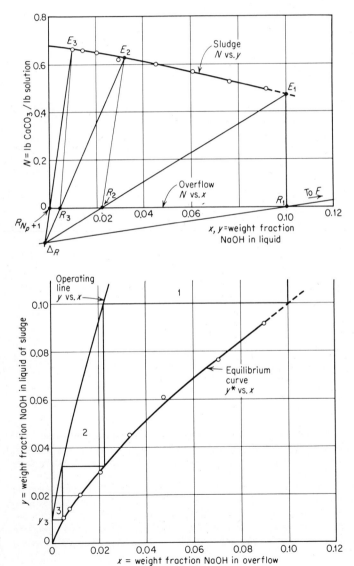

Fig. 13.31 *Solution to Illustration 13.3.*

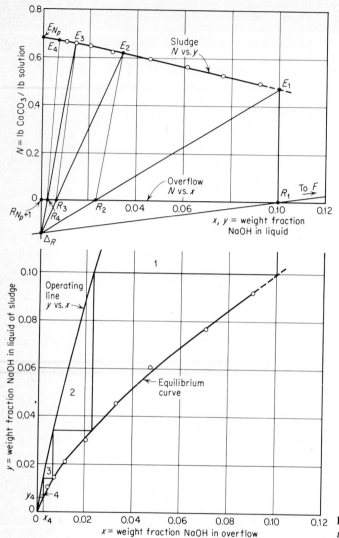

Fig. 13.32 *Solution to Illustration 13.3.*

Illustration 13.4. Flaked soybeans are to be leached with hexane to remove the soybean oil. A 12-in.-thick layer of the flakes (0.009 in. flake thickness) will be fed onto a slowly moving, perforated endless belt which passes under a series of continuously operating sprays.[28] As the solid passes under each spray, it is showered with liquid which percolates through the bed, collects in a trough below the belt, and is recycled by a pump to the spray. The spacing of the sprays is such that the solid is permitted to drain 6 min before it reaches the next spray. The solvent also passes from trough to trough in a direction countercurrent to that of the moving belt, so that a truly continuous countercurrent stagewise operation is maintained with each spraying and draining constituting one stage. Experiments[28] show that the flakes retain solution after 6 min drain time to an extent depending upon the oil content of the solution, as follows:

Wt % oil in soln	0	20	30
Lb soln retained/lb insoluble solid	0.58	0.66	0.70

It will be assumed that the retained solution contains the only oil in the drained flakes.

The soybean flakes enter containing 20% oil and are to be leached to 0.5% oil (on a solvent-free basis). The net forward flow of solvent is to be 1.0 lb hexane introduced as fresh solvent per pound flakes, and the fresh solvent is free of oil. The solvent draining from the flakes is generally free of solid except in the first stage: the rich miscella contains 10% of the insoluble solid in the feed as a suspended solid, which falls through the perforations of the belt during loading. How many stages are required?

Solution. The tie lines are vertical, $x = y^*$. Rearrange the drainage data as follows:

Percent oil in soln $= 100y^*$	$\dfrac{\text{Lb soln retained}}{\text{Lb insoluble solid}} = \dfrac{1}{N}$	N	$\dfrac{\text{Lb oil}}{\text{Lb insoluble solid}} = \dfrac{y^*}{N}$
0	0.58	1.725	0
20	0.66	1.515	0.132
30	0.70	1.429	0.210

Basis: 1 lb flakes introduced.

Soybean feed. $B = 0.8$ lb insoluble; $F = 0.2$ lb oil; $N_F = 0.8/0.2 = 4.0$ lb insoluble solid/lb oil; $y_F = 1.0$ wt fraction oil, solid-free basis.

Solvent. $R_{Np+1} = 1.0$ lb hexane; $x_{Np+1} = 0$ wt fraction oil.

Leached solids. Lb oil/lb insoluble solid $= 0.005/0.995 = 0.00503$. By interpolation in the equilibrium data, $N_{Np} = 1.718$ lb solid/lb soln.

$$\text{Insoluble solid lost to miscella} = 0.8(0.1) = 0.08 \text{ lb}$$

$$\text{Insoluble solid in leached solids} = 0.8(0.9) = 0.72 \text{ lb}$$

$$E_{Np} = \frac{0.72}{1.718} = 0.420 \text{ lb soln retained}$$

$$\text{Lb oil retained} = 0.00503(0.72) = 0.00362 \text{ lb}$$

$$\text{Lb hexane retained} = 0.420 - 0.00362 = 0.416 \text{ lb}$$

$$y_{Np} = \frac{0.00362}{0.420} = 0.0086 \text{ wt fraction oil in retained liquid}$$

Miscella. Hexane $= 1 - 0.416 = 0.584$ lb; oil $= 0.2 - 0.00362 = 0.196$ lb. $R_1 = 0.584 + 0.196 = 0.780$ lb clear miscella; $x_1 = 0.196/0.780 = 0.252$ wt fraction oil in liquid. $N_{R1} = 0.08/0.780 = 0.1027$ lb insoluble solid/lb soln.

The operating diagram is shown in Fig. 13.33. Point R_1 represents the cloudy miscella and is therefore displaced from the axis of the graph at N_{R1}. Point Δ_R is located as usual and the stages determined with the $N = 0$ axis for all stages but the first. Between four and five stages are necessary. Adjustment of the amount of solvent or the amount of unextracted oil, by trial, will provide an integral number.

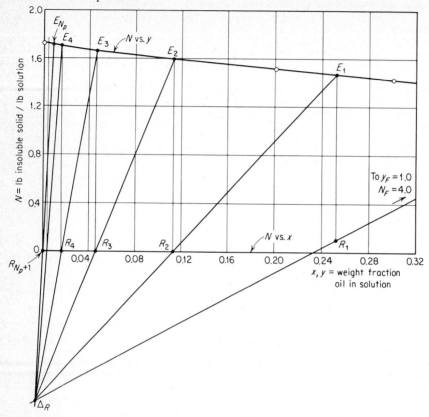

Fig. 13.33 *Solution to Illustration* 13.4.

Rate of Leaching

The many diverse phenomena encountered in the practice of leaching make it impossible to apply a single theory to explain the leaching action. As has been shown, leaching may involve simple washing of the solution from the surface of a solid, or dissolving of a solute from a matrix of insoluble matter, osmosis, and possibly other mechanisms. Our knowledge of these is very limited. The washing of a solution from the surface of impervious solid particles may be expected to be very rapid, requiring only the blending of solution and solvent, and stage efficiencies are then quite likely to be governed entirely by the completeness of the mechanical separation of liquid from solid.

Leaching of a solute from the internal parts of a solid, on the other hand, will be relatively slow. Solids made up of a skeletal structure of insoluble substance, with the pores impregnated with the solute, can be described in terms of a pore-shape factor, as outlined in Chap. 4. The factor is a function of the solid, independent of the nature of the solute and solvent, and is a measure of the complexity of the path through which the solute diffuses. In the case of natural products such as plant materials, the complexity of the structure may make application of these methods difficult. In the case of sugar-beet cossettes,[32] for example, about one-fifth of the cells are ruptured in producing the cossettes, and leaching of sugar from these cells is probably a simple washing process. The remaining cells lose sugar by a diffusion process, and the combination of events produces curves on coordinates such as Fig. 4.2, which deviate considerably from those developed from simple diffusion with constant effective diffusivity or pore-shape factor. Many mechanisms have been considered in an attempt to explain such observations.[2] In another example, wood will show different rates of leaching of an impregnating solute depending upon whether diffusion is in a direction parallel to or across the grain of the wood.[20] If solutes must pass through cell walls by dialysis, it may not be possible to apply the concepts at all. The rates of diffusion of soybean oil from soybean flakes, which do not permit simple interpretation, have been attributed to the presence of several types of structures in the matrix[16] as well as to the presence of a slowly dissolving constituent in the oil.[11,15] Whole seeds cannot be leached; rolling and flaking evidently crushes cell walls and opens up passageways for penetration of the solvent by capillary action.[21,22] The fact that rate of leaching increases with increased surface tension of the solvent-oil solutions and the fact that even for flaked seeds there is a residue of unextractable oil which increases with flake thickness support this view. That the leached oil is composed of several different substances is evident from the different properties of oil obtained after short and long leaching times. A method of dealing with such differently leached substances has been suggested,[12] but these examples serve at least to indicate the complexity of many practical leaching processes. Very little study has been given most of them.

When solids such as those described above are immersed in leaching solvents, it is reasonable to suppose that the resistance to mass transfer within the solid itself is likely to be the controlling resistance and that of the liquid surrounding the solid to be quite minor.[32] In such cases increasing the rate of movement of liquid past the solid surface will not appreciably influence the rate of leaching.

NOTATION FOR CHAPTER 13

a	= a constant
a_p	= surface of particles, sq ft/cu ft of packed space
A	= pure leaching solvent
	= thickener cross section, Eq. (13.7), sq. ft
b	= a constant
B	= insoluble carrier solid, lb (in a batch operation) or lb/hr or lb/(hr)(sq ft)(in a continuous operation)
c	= solids concentration in a slurry, lb/cu ft
c_U	= underflow solids concentration, lb/cu ft
C	= soluble solute
d_p	= diameter of a sphere of same surface/volume ratio as a particle, ft
E	= solvent and solute associated with the leached solids, lb (in a batch operation) or lb/hr or lb/(hr)(sq ft)(in a continuous operation)

F = solute and solvent in solids to be leached, lb (in a batch operation) or lb/hr or lb/(hr)(sq ft)(in a continuous operation)

g = acceleration due to gravity, ft/hr²

g_c = conversion factor, $4.17(10^8)$ lb mass (ft)/(lb force)(hr)²

G = mass velocity, lb/(hr)(sq ft)

G_S = flux of settling solids, lb/(hr)(sq ft)

G_{SL} = limiting solids flux, lb/(hr)(sq ft)

K = permeability, cu ft/hr²

m = slope of equilibrium curve, dy^*/dx, dimensionless

M = solvent and solute content of a slurry or mixture, lb (in a batch operation) or lb/hr or lb/(hr)(sq ft)(in a continuous operation)

N = ratio of weight of insoluble solid to weight of solute and solvent, lb B/lb $(A + C)$

N_p = number of stages, dimensionless

ΔP = pressure drop, lb/sq ft

R = solvent and solute in a leaching solution, lb (in a batch operation) or lb/hr or lb/(hr)(sq ft)(in a continuous operation)

S = residual saturation of a bed of solids, fraction of void volume occupied by liquid, dimensionless

S_0 = residual saturation in the upper part of a packed bed, dimensionless

S_{av} = average residual saturation, dimensionless

u = initial setting rate, ft/hr

w = concentration of insoluble solids in a slurry, weight fraction

W = rate of solids flow, lb/hr

x = concentration of solute in solution, weight fraction, B-free basis

y = concentration of solute in a mixture, weight fraction, B-free basis

y^* = value of y at equilibrium

Z = height of a percolation bed or of a settling solid, ft

Z_D = drain height, ft

Z_0 = initial height of a slurry, ft

Z_∞ = ultimate height of settled solids, ft

ϵ = fractional void volume of a packed bed, dimensionless

θ = time, hr

μ_L = liquid viscosity, lb mass/(ft)(hr)

ρ_L = liquid density, lb mass/cu ft

σ = surface tension, lb force/ft = (dynes/cm)$(6.89)(10^{-5})$

Subscripts:

F = feed; solids to be leached

S = saturated

1, 2, etc. = stage 1, stage 2, etc.

REFERENCES

1. Anderson, E. T., and K. McCubbin: *J. Am. Oil Chemists' Soc.*, **31**, 475 (1954).

2. Bruniche-Olsen, H.: "Solid-Liquid Extraction," NYT Nordisk Forlag Arnold Busch Copenhagen, 1962.

3. Colman, J. E.: *Chem. Eng.*, **70**, Mar. 4, 93 (1963).

4. Comings, E. W.: *Ind. Eng. Chem.*, **32**, 663 (1940).

5. Comings, E. W., C. E. Pruiss, and C. De Bord: *Ind. Eng. Chem.*, **46**, 1164 (1954).

6. Dombrowski, H. S., and L. E. Brownell: *Ind. Eng. Chem.*, **46**, 1267 (1954).

7. Donald, M. B.: *Trans. Inst. Chem. Engrs.* (*London*), **15**, 77 (1937).

8. Fitch, B.: *Ind. Eng. Chem.*, **58**(10), 18 (1966).

9. Gastrock, E. A., et al.: *Ind. Eng. Chem.*, **49**, 921, 930 (1957); *J. Am. Oil Chemists' Soc.*, **32**, 160 (1955).

10. George, W. J.: *Chem. Eng.*, **66**, Feb. 9, 111 (1959).

11. Goss, W. H.: *Oil and Soap*, **23**, 348 (1946).

12. Hassett, N. J.: *Brit. Chem. Eng.*, **3**, 66, 182 (1958).

13. Havighorst, C. R.: *Chem. Eng.*, **71**, Mar. 30, 72 (1964).

14. Kammermeyer, K.: *Ind. Eng. Chem.*, **33**, 1484 (1941).

15. Karnofsky, G.: *J. Am. Oil Chemists' Soc.*, **26**, 564 (1949).

16. King, C. O., D. L. Katz, and J. C. Brier: *Trans. AIChE*, **40**, 533 (1944).

17. Lamont, A. G. W.: *Can. J. Chem. Eng.*, **36**, 153 (1958).

18. Liddell, D. M.: "Handbook of Non-ferrous Metallurgy," 2d ed., McGraw-Hill Book Company, New York, 1945.

19. McCubbins, K., and G. J. Ritz: *Chem. Ind. (London)*, **66**, 354 (1950).

20. Osburn, J. Q., and D. L. Katz: *Trans. AIChE*, **40**, 511 (1944).

21. Othmer, D. F., and J. C. Agarwal: *Chem. Eng. Progr.*, **51**, 372 (1955).

22. Othmer, D. F., and W. A. Jaatinen: *Ind. Eng. Chem.*, **51**, 543 (1959).

23. Price, F. C.: *Chem. Eng.*, **67**, July 25, 84 (1960).

24. Rushton, J. H., and L. H. Maloney: *J. Metals*, **6**, *AIME Trans.*, **200**, 1199 (1954).

25. Sattler-Dornbacher, E.: *Chem.-Ing.-Tech.*, **30**, 14 (1958).

26. Scofield, E. P.: *Chem. Eng.*, **58**(1), 127 (1951).

27. Shannon, P. T., E. M. Tory, et al.: *Ind. Eng. Chem.*, **57**(2), 18 (1965); *Ind. Eng. Chem. Fundamentals*, **2**, 203 (1963); **3**, 184, 250 (1964); **4**, 195, 367 (1965).

28. Smith, C. T.: *J. Am. Oil Chemists' Soc.*, **28**, 274 (1951).

29. Van Arsdale, G. D.: "Hydrometallurgy of Base Metals," McGraw-Hill Book Company, New York, 1953.

30. Weed, R. C.: *Mining Eng.*, **8**, 721 (1956).

31. Work, L. T., and A. S. Kohler: *Ind. Eng. Chem.*, **32**, 1329 (1940).

32. Yang, H. H., and J. C. Brier: *AIChE J.*, **4**, 453 (1958).

PROBLEMS

13.1. A 3-ft-diameter tank fitted with a false bottom and canvas filter is partly filled with 2,000 lb (dry weight) of sea sand wet with seawater. The sand is allowed to drain until it stops dripping, whereupon 1,500 lb fresh water is added and recirculated to reach a uniform salt concentration. The sand is again allowed to drain until dripping stops and is then removed from the tank and dried. Estimate the salt content of the dried sand.

The sand particles have an average particle size $d_p = 0.0013$ ft, a particle density 166 lb/cu ft, and a bulk density 93 lb (dry weight)/cu ft. Seawater contains 3.5% salt; its density is 63.6 lb/cu ft and surface tension 73.6 dynes/cm. The surface tension of water is 72.8 dynes/cm.

13.2. Derive expressions for the coordinates of point $\Delta_R(y_{\Delta R}, N_{\Delta R})$ (Fig. 13.29), and check the results by determining the numerical values in the case of Illustration 13.3a.

13.3. In order to eliminate the solids in the final miscella of Illustration 13.4, it is decided to pass liquid from stage 3 to stage 1, where the liquid will contact fresh solids. The drained liquid from stage 1, containing the suspended solids, will then be passed to stage 2, where it is filtered by passage of the liquid through the bed of solids in this stage. The final miscella is then withdrawn as a clear solution from stage 2. How many stages will then be required for the same solvent/seeds ratio and the same oil concentration in the discharged solids? **Ans.: 6.**

13.4. A mineral containing 20% elemental sulfur is to be leached with hot gas oil, in which the sulfur is soluble to the extent of 10% by weight. The solvent will be repeatedly pumped over the batch of ground mineral, using 1.5 lb fresh solvent/lb mineral. After no further solution of sulfur is obtained, the liquid will be drained and replaced with a fresh batch of 1.5 lb oil/lb original mineral, and the operation repeated. On drainage, the solid materials retain the solution to the extent of one-tenth the weight of undissolved solid (sulfur and gangue). No preferential adsorption takes place.

 a. Calculate the equilibrium data, and plot them in the usual manner.

 b. Determine the amount of sulfur unextracted and the sulfur concentration of the composited leach liquors.

 c. Repeat *b* for the case where a two-stage Shanks system is used, with 3 lb fresh solvent/lb unleached solid. Assume steady state has been reached.

 13.5. Aluminum sulfate, $Al_2(SO_4)_3$, is to be produced by action of sulfuric acid, H_2SO_4, on bauxite in a series of agitators, with a cascade of continuous thickeners to wash the insoluble mud free of aluminum sulfate.

$$Al_2O_3 + 3H_2SO_4 \rightarrow Al_2(SO_4)_3 + 3H_2O$$

The flow sheet is similar to that of Fig. 13.13*a*. The reaction agitators are fed with (1) 25 tons bauxite/day, containing 50% Al_2O_3 and the rest insoluble; (2) the theoretical quantity of aqueous acid containing 60% H_2SO_4; and (3) the overflow from the second thickener. Assume the reaction is complete. The strong product solution is to contain 22% $Al_2(SO_4)_3$, and no more than 2% of the $Al_2(SO_4)_3$ produced is to be lost in the washed mud. The last thickener is to be fed with pure wash water. The underflow from each thickener will contain 4 lb liquid/lb insoluble solid, and the concentration of solubles in the liquid of the underflow for each thickener may be assumed to be the same as that in the overflow. Calculate the number of thickeners required and the amount of wash water required per day. **Ans.:** 3 thickeners.

 (*Note:* In solving this problem, be certain to account for the water in the acid as well as that produced by the reaction. Adapt Fig. 5.16 to all but the first thickener in the cascade.)

 13.6. Barium, occurring naturally as the sulfate, $BaSO_4$, is put in water-soluble form by heating with coal, thus reducing the sulfate to the sulfide, BaS. The resulting reaction mixture, barium "black ash" containing 65% soluble BaS, is to be leached with water. One hundred tons black ash per day is fed to a tube mill, together with the overflow from the second of a cascade of thickeners, and the effluent from the mill is fed to the first thickener. All the barium is dissolved in the mill. The strong solution overflowing from the first thickener is to contain 20% BaS by weight. The thickeners will each deliver a sludge containing 1.5 lb liquid/lb insoluble solid. The solution in the overflow and that in the sludge leaving any thickener may be assumed to have the same BaS concentration. It is desired to keep the BaS lost with the final sludge to at most 2 lb/day.

 a. How many thickeners are required? [Adapt Eq. (5.55) to all except the first thickener.] **Ans.:** 6.

 b. It is decided to pass the final leached sludge to a continuous filter, as in Fig. 13.13*b*, where the liquid content of the filtered solids will be reduced to 15% by weight. The filtrate will be returned to the last thickener, but the filter cake will not be washed. How many thickeners will then be required? **Ans.:** 5.

 13.7. In the manufacture of potassium nitrate, KNO_3, potassium chloride, KCl, is added to a hot, concentrated aqueous solution of sodium nitrate, $NaNO_3$,

$$KCl + NaNO_3 \rightleftharpoons KNO_3 + NaCl$$

Owing to its relatively low solubility, part of the sodium chloride, NaCl, precipitates and is filtered off. A little water is added to the filtrate to prevent further precipitation of NaCl, the mixture is cooled to 20°C, and pure KNO_3 crystallizes. The resulting slurry contains, per 100 lb precipitated KNO_3, 239 lb of a solution analyzing 21.3% KNO_3, 21.6% NaCl, and 57.1% water. The slurry is fed to the first of a cascade of four continuous classifiers, where each 100 lb of crystals is countercurrently washed with 75 lb of a saturated solution of KNO_3, containing 24.0% KNO_3, in order to free them of NaCl. The wet crystals leaving each classifier retain 25% liquid, and the liquid overflows are clear. The washed crystals discharged from the fourth classifier, containing 25% liquid, are sent to a continuous drier. All liquid except that discharged with the washed crystals leaves in the overflow from the first classifier. Equilibrium between solid and liquid is attained in each classifier, and the clear overflows have the same composition as the liquid retained by the crystals. The solubility of KNO_3 in NaCl solutions (KNO_3 is the equilibrium solid phase) at the prevailing temperature is given by the following table:

% NaCl	0	6.9	12.6	17.8	21.6
% KNO₃	24.0	23.3	22.6	22.0	21.3

  a. Plot the equilibrium data [N = lb KNO_3/lb (NaCl + H_2O) for both clear overflow and wet crystals; x and y = lb NaCl/lb (NaCl + H_2O)].

  b. Calculate the percent NaCl content which may be expected on the dried KNO_3 product. **Ans.:** 0.306%.

PART FIVE
THE LESS CONVENTIONAL OPERATIONS

CHAPTER FOURTEEN
THE LESS
CONVENTIONAL
OPERATIONS

The operations considered in this chapter involve, with a few exceptions, solid-fluid contact of various kinds. While some have been applied industrially, they are not commonly used and in most cases their technology is relatively undeveloped. Only a brief, qualitative discussion will be given, to indicate their field of usefulness and some of the problems they entail.

FRACTIONAL CRYSTALLIZATION

The common crystallization process is a solute-recovery operation rather than a fractionation, such as the crystallization of a nonvolatile solid from a solution with a volatile solvent. If it is done by progressively cooling the saturated solution, mass transfer from the bulk solution to the crystal surface and transfer of sensible heat and heat of solution in one fashion or another are involved. In most cases, solute and solvent are insoluble in the solid state, and this gives rise to an equilibrium diagram of the sort shown in Fig. 14.1.

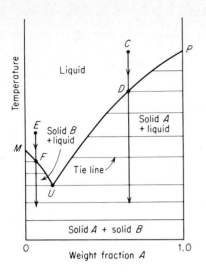

Fig. 14.1 *Binary liquid-solid equilibria, components insoluble in the solid state.*

In Fig. 14.1, M is the melting point of component B, P that of A. Curves MFU and PDU are the solubilities of these components in the liquid solution. A liquid solution C, if cooled, first precipitates pure A at the temperature corresponding to D, and as the temperature is further lowered, additional A crystallizes while the liquid remaining moves along the curve DU toward U. At temperature t_U, the liquid remaining has the eutectic composition at U, and further cooling results in complete solidification of a "eutectic mixture" of A and B, a mass of insoluble crystals which ordinarily cannot be mechanically separated. If the solution is initially at E, the phenomena are much the same except that crystallization begins at F, with pure B solidifying until the liquid remaining reaches the eutectic composition. The diagram is analogous to that for vapor-liquid equilibrium between two components which are completely insoluble in the liquid state.

While in principle a pure component may be recovered up to the point where the eutectic composition is reached, there are practical difficulties. The crystals may mechanically occlude portions of the solution, thus rendering them impure; and complete mechanical separation of crystals from adhering mother liquor is difficult without washing them with some of the pure solvent, which entails some redissolving of the crystals. In any case, the yield of the pure component first precipitated in such a process cannot be larger than that which produces the eutectic composition in the solution remaining. This difficulty is frequently circumvented by boiling or evaporating off the volatile, low-melting component (in Fig. 14.1, component B might be volatile water and A a nonvolatile salt, for example), and if evaporation is carried to dryness, the yield of nonvolatile component can be complete. This is a well-established procedure, the technology of which is highly developed. The rate of crystallization and the phenomenon of nucleation, or initial precipitation of solid, is not fully understood, and will not be considered here. A good review is available.[16]

When, however, the components of a binary mixture have a very low relative

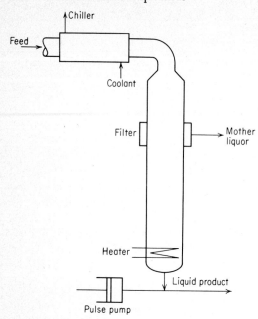

Fig. 14.2 *Continuous, countercurrent crystallizer.*

volatility, boiling or vaporization will not serve. If crystallization is to be used, the problem is then one of making suitably pure crystals by lowering the temperature only. While batch crystallization and washing of the solid has been the general practice in such cases, a recently developed technique uses a continuous, countercurrent operation which conceivably has other applications as well. In the process of separating *p*-xylene from the meta and ortho isomers (boiling point range of the pure components $= 11°F$), the device of Fig. 14.2 is used.[26,29] A feed containing 65 percent *p*-xylene is cooled in a scraper-chiller to a mass consisting of a thick slurry of impure *p*-xylene crystals. The slurry enters the continuous crystallizer, where mother liquor is withdrawn from the side through a suitable filter, and the crystals proceed toward the product outlet. Near the outlet the pure crystals are melted, part of the resulting liquid is withdrawn as product, and part is returned as reflux to wash the crystals countercurrently free of the undesired meta and ortho isomers, which leave with the mother liquor. Movement of the liquid and compaction of the crystals to form a suitable moving bed is accomplished by the pulse pump (see page 430). The device thus accomplishes the purification (product is 98+ percent pure *p*-xylene) and by withdrawing the product as a liquid eliminates the problem of mechanical separation of the crystals.

When the components of the binary mixture are soluble in the solid state (solid-liquid equilibrium diagram resembles the vapor-liquid diagram of Fig. 9.2), or when it is desired to circumvent the yield limit imposed by the eutectic mixture, the following fractionation techniques are possibilities, although they have had as yet only limited application. Rapid extension of their use is anticipated as their technology is developed.

Direct fractional crystallization

When the components of a binary mixture are soluble in the solid state, at least over a range of compositions if not entirely, as well as in the liquid state, separation can be made by a direct countercurrent fractional crystallization. The binary pairs gold-silver and cyclohexane-methylcyclopentane[11] are representative of this type. One can envisage devices of the sort shown in Fig. 14.2 operated in the manner of Fig. 14.3a, although at present no industrial applications are known. Matz[28] has pointed out the applicability of enthalpy-concentration diagrams of the sort shown in Fig. 14.3b to such operations, and the computations for stages would be made in precisely the same manner as shown in Chap. 9 for fractional distillation. Figure 14.3b is representative of the case where the components are completely miscible in both liquid and solid phases. If partial miscibility occurs in the solid, the equilibria are analogous to those for vapor mixtures which condense to form partly soluble liquids.

Zone refining is a batch fractional crystallization which is capable of ultra-purification.[4,22,32] The principle is simple: a zone of liquid is repeatedly passed through a solid ingot of the substance to be purified. This is accomplished by repeatedly moving a high-temperature zone along the ingot which melts the solid, the liquid freezing behind the zone as it moves. Impurities which are more soluble in the liquid phase than in the solid (the usual case) move with the zone and are swept along with the liquid to accumulate at one end of the ingot; impurities which are more soluble in the solid move opposite to the zone, but this is a relatively rare occurrence.

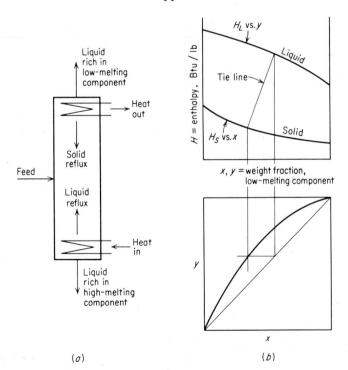

Fig. 14.3 *Direct fractional crystallization.*

Multipassage of the liquid zone then concentrates the impurities at one end of the ingot. The length of the molten zone may approximate one-tenth that of the ingot, and the rate of travel ⅛ to 1.5 in./hr.   The operation is most economically applied to remove trace impurities.   Industrial applications have largely been confined to purification of semiconductors such as silicon and germanium (six passes of a molten zone have reduced the impurities in germanium to 1 part in 10^{10}), but there is no limitation: organic chemicals, pharmaceuticals, even water, have been purified in this manner.   Any of a variety of heating arrangements are possible: heating with a moving flame; induction heating, particularly for metals and semiconductors; or even electric-resistance heating by a number of stationary coils surrounding the ingot which are activated in turn along the ingot.   The operation described above is *zone melting*, but it is equally possible to purify by *zone freezing*, whereby a solid zone is passed through a column of liquid.   Continuous techniques have not yet been developed for either.

Extractive fractional crystallization

Here a solvent which will dissolve both solid components to be separated is used. The solvent may enhance the selectivity (ratio of solutes in liquid/ratio of solutes in solid), or it may be used when melting cannot be done.   An excellent example is the

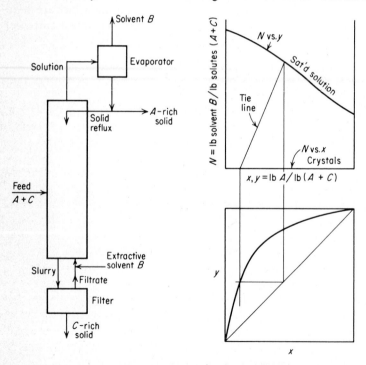

Fig. 14.4 *Continuous, countercurrent, extractive fractional crystallization of a binary solid, A and C, with A more soluble.*

separation of barium and lead nitrates, which form a continuous series of solid solutions, using water as the extractive solvent.[28]   A continuous, countercurrent separation might then follow the scheme of Fig. 14.4a.   The contacting device might be the sort shown in Fig. 14.2, the classifier type of Fig. 13.17, teeter beds (see Chap. 11), a cascade of stages made up of agitator vessels and filters, or the like.   Matz[28] made such a continuous separation in a small, column-type device (using only the section below the feed of Fig. 14.4a), producing $Ba(NO_3)_2$ of 89.8 percent purity from a 50 percent mixture with $Pb(NO_3)_2$, with a remarkably small height equivalent to a theoretical stage.   The minimum reflux ratio and number of stages at a suitable operating reflux ratio may be computed on a diagram similar to that used in liquid extraction and leaching (Fig. 14.4b).[28]   The application of such a diagram to the similar process of washing crystals free of contaminating mother liquor is given in Prob. 13.7.   Batch simulation of continuous, countercurrent separations of this sort have been known for many years, e.g., the separation of rare-earth-metal salts (now replaced by ion-exchange methods), but it is believed that the truly continuous operation has not yet been used commercially.

Adductive fractional crystallization

Here an added substance is used which enters the solid phase.   There are four major types:[10]

1. *Solid solutions.*   Although there are no presently known fractionation processes of this type, a possibility is suggested by Findlay,[10] namely, separation of solutions of hexane and methylcyclopentane by countercurrent contact with solid cyclohexane, which preferentially forms solid solutions with methylcyclopentane.   A complete fractionation process, with feed introduced centrally into a cascade of stages and use of reflux, would be required.

2. *Addition compounds of fixed composition.*   Again there is no industrial example, but several have been suggested.   For example, carbon tetrachloride forms the compound $CCl_4 \cdot p\text{-}C_6H_4(CH_3)_2$ with p-xylene but forms no such compound with the meta or ortho isomers.[9]   Selectivity in this case is excellent for separating the para isomer, and the equivalent of an absorption or extraction section of a complete countercurrent cascade of stages would be all that is necessary.   The limitation on yield imposed by eutectic compositions in the mixture to be separated would disappear.   Separation of the solid product would involve melting and distillation.

3. *Clathrates.*[18]   Here a molecule of twisted or crooked shape, which can crystallize in the form of a cage, is used to entrap a compound in the crystal lattice preferentially, based on shape.   As an example which is used industrially we can cite the separation of p-xylene from a mixture of m- and p-xylenes, using nickel thiocyanate with γ-picoline.[33]   The complex including the metal, the nitrogen base, and the negative radical entraps the para isomer preferentially.   The dry, solid complex may be agitated or ground with the feed to be separated (diluted if necessary with a suitable solvent to form a workable slurry); alternatively a solvent for the complex may be used, and when mixed with the feed to be separated, cooling produces crystals which selectively remove one solute from solution.   Another proposed process is the recovery of water from brines by clathration with hydrocarbon gases such as propane.[21] Ordinarily a cascade of stages is required, to free the crystals of adhering or entrapped solution.   Recovery procedures involve destruction of the clathrate crystal by melting or by vaporization since the clathrate may exhibit a solute vapor pressure.

4. *Adducts.*[12]   These involve crystals whose tunnellike or channellike passageways hold one shape of molecule but exclude another.   For example, urea in the presence of hydrocarbons crystallizes in a structure which can enclose straight-chain hydrocarbons but which accepts only with difficulty highly branched hydrocarbons.   The adduct behaves much like a solid solution, or homogeneous crystal of variable composition.   Frequently an "activator," or polar organic solvent in the case of urea, is also needed.   An industrial example is the adductive dewaxing of oils with urea in the presence of methylene chloride for producing oils of very low pour point.[19]   A fractionation is required for complete solute separation, and the adducts are destroyed by melting to release the solute.

In all these operations, the computations of stages, flow ratios, and the like can be made on phase diagrams plotted with pounds added substance/pounds total solute as ordinate vs. weight fraction of one solute, additive-free basis, as abscissa, with the principles developed in earlier chapters.

SUBLIMATION

Sublimation, a solid-vapor operation, is essentially distillation of a solid.   It is ordinarily done batchwise.   In cases where only one component of a solid mixture is volatile, we have the analog of evaporation of a liquid solution of a nonvolatile solid, and freeze drying (see Chap. 12) is a particular example.   If both components of a binary solid are volatile, fractional sublimation, done batchwise by a simulation of a multistage countercurrent technique, could eventually produce a separation.   Extractive sublimation uses a noncondensing gas to carry the vapors.

One of the principal difficulties in many cases is the inability to apply the required heat rapidly without melting the solid (see page 580) or raising the temperature of the solid to the extent that it is damaged.   Another is the problem of condensing the vapor.   Cold condenser surfaces rapidly accumulate a thick coating of solid, through which heat is very poorly transmitted.   In some cases the condenser can be cleared by periodic heating to melt the accumulated solid; where this is impractical the solid can be knocked off with hammers.   An alternative is to mix the vapors with a cold, inert, noncondensable gas, which causes precipitation of solid in the vapor-gas mixture as snow.   The residual gas will, however, be saturated with the vapor, and when it is cooled for reuse, the vapor condenses as solid upon the cooling surface.   The advantage is that less solid is condensed on the cooling surface than by direct condensation of all the vapor.   Perhaps the most promising development is the possibility of contacting the vapors with solid sublimate in a fluidized bed[6,27] cooled by internal cooling coils or by a cooling jacket about the bed wall.   Evidently the abrasive action of the solids keeps the cooling surface reasonably clear.

FOAM SEPARATIONS

If the solute of a liquid solution is surface-active, it collects at the solution surface when the liquid is exposed to a gas, and there then exists a concentration difference of the solute between the bulk solution and the surface layer. This is accompanied by a lowering of the surface tension of the solvent when the solute is dissolved. If the surface layer is then collected, a certain amount of separation of solute will have been achieved. Foaming the solution by bubbling or sparging a gas into it, followed by collection of the foam and mechanical separation of the liquid and gas of the foam provides a means of accomplishing this.[35] The phenomenon is not one of interphase, i.e., liquid-to-gas, mass transfer, but rather an *intraphase* transfer of solute from the bulk liquid to the surface. The method is particularly effective at low concentrations.

Great interest has developed in this technique for the removal of detergents (which are surface-active) from sewage effluents.[5,15] Solutes which are not surface-active, such as metal ions, can sometimes be complexed with other material to become so and are then amenable to foam collection.[36] Figure 14.5 shows a schematic arrangement for solute collection. The foam-drainage section serves to remove the great part of the liquid from the foam but not the surface layer, thus concentrating the collected solute. For successful operation, the foam must be reasonably stable, which requires that the surface film have a high viscosity, and also be readily destructible at the top of the column. Foam breaking may be accomplished by heating; by

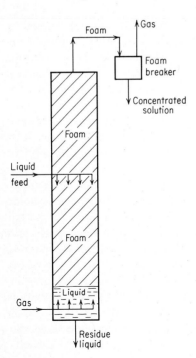

Fig. 14.5 *Solute collection by foaming.*

rupture of the liquid surface mechanically by a sonic whistle or through reduction of the gas pressure, as when the foam flows through an orifice; or by centrifuging.[17] Refluxing part of the liquid reclaimed from the broken foam to the column is possible; this would be important if two solutes of different tendency to collect at the surface were to be separated by *foam fractionation*.

MEMBRANE SEPARATIONS

Separations may be produced by transfer of material between fluids separated by a permeable membrane.   For effective separation, of course, the membrane must be differently permeable to the substances to be separated.   There are various methods whereby this is accomplished.[13,23,34,41]   In some cases the membrane acts somewhat like a mechanical filter, much as a filter paper separates a two-phase solid-liquid mixture, but in the operations considered here the filtration is on a molecular scale. In some cases the components of the solution to be separated diffuse through the passageways of the membrane at different rates by any of a variety of mechanisms (see Chap. 4).   In others the membrane may selectively dissolve a component which can then diffuse through.

Separations of both liquid and gas solutions are possible.   The principal difficulty in most cases is that the rate of passage through the membrane is small and becomes smaller the more selective the membrane.

Dialysis

Dialysis is the separation of solutes of different molecular size in a liquid solution by use of a suitable membrane.   In practice the membrane separates the solution from a quantity of solvent, whereupon solvent and solute of small molecular size pass through relatively easily while passage of large molecules is more difficult.   Practical industrial applications include the separation of sodium hydroxide (small molecules or ions) from hemicellulose (large molecules) in the solutions of the viscose-rayon process using cellophane membranes,[42] separation of sulfuric acid from nickel and copper sulfates in aqueous solutions[41] and from steel-pickling liquors with vinyl-polymer membranes.   In the field of medicine, cellulose membranes are used to dialyze human blood free of poisonous substances in the artificial kidney.

It is possible to make membranes which are highly selective.   For example, early scientific work in this area used membranes of gelatinous copper ferrocyanide precipitated within a porous porcelain support.   Such a membrane will permit passage of water but will prevent passage of ordinary solutes such as sugar or glycerin and even ionic particles such as those of salt solutions.   If a solution is separated from pure solvent by such a membrane, solvent passes through the membrane in the direction solvent to solution, in the direction of concentration drop, and dilutes the solution.   This is known as *osmosis*.   For most practical dialyses such selectivity is not ordinarily required, and the pores of the membrane used in the viscose-rayon process are of the order of 10^{-6} cm in diameter (crystalline solutes have molecular diameters of the order of 10^{-8} cm, and will pass through, along with the solvent).

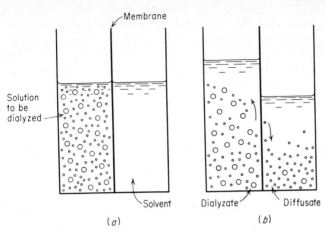

Fig. 14.6 *Batch dialysis.*

Consider the schematic representation of a batch dialysis in Fig. 14.6. The solution to be dialyzed contains large and small solute molecules, represented schematically as shown at *a*, and it is separated initially from a batch of pure solvent by a suitable membrane. The solvent immediately begins to move through the membrane and into the solution by osmosis, and since it ordinarily has a lower specific gravity, a convection current of rising solvent develops on the left of the membrane as at *b* in the figure. If the liquids are not agitated, the solvent spreads out in a layer over the top of the solution and will mix with the solution only very slowly. The solute particles also diffuse through the membrane into the solvent, the smaller ones rapidly but the larger only very slowly. Since the solution formed on the right side of the membrane will generally be more dense than the solvent, it will tend to stratify at the bottom of the vessel, as shown. Owing to the osmotic flow of solvent, the volume of the *dialyzate*, or dialyzed solution, will increase at the expense of the *diffusate*. If the membrane is permeable to both solutes, the solution on either side will eventually come to the same concentrations, and an equilibrium will be established. Because the larger molecules dialyze only very slowly, however, it is possible to make a separation by periodically replacing the diffusate with fresh solvent before equilibrium is established. The concentration of the dialyzate may be kept relatively high, and the rate of dialysis maintained at a reasonable level, by careful withdrawal of the layer of solvent at the top.

Alternatively, a continuous rather than a batch operation may be carried out in the countercurrent manner shown schematically in Fig. 14.7. The solutions flow in such a direction as to take advantage of the tendency toward stratification: the liquid to be dialyzed is introduced at the bottom and withdrawn at the top, while the diffusate flows downward. The membrane is arranged vertically for this reason also.

Typical of the commercial devices is the filter-press type of Fig. 14.8, which uses the principles developed in Fig. 14.7 directly. The membranes are placed between metal frames arranged in a manner reminiscent of the ordinary filter press. A mechanical membrane support built into the frames, not shown in the sketch, may also be used.   Holes in the frames and the membranes form continuous conduits for the liquids when the entire assemblage is pressed tightly together.   Feed solution to be dialyzed is distributed to alternate frames and flows upward past the membranes, and the dialyzate discharges through a channel at the top.   Solvent, in a similar manner, enters the remaining frames and flows downward, and the diffusate leaves through a channel at the bottom.   The liquids flow under the force of gravity, as shown schematically in Fig. 14.7, and are not pumped through the dialyzer.   In the larger units particularly, where many frames may be used, there may be several channels in the frames for introducing feed and solvent, each leading to separate groups of frames.   In this way, more equitable distribution of the flow is obtained.

Reverse osmosis (ultrafiltration)

This operation, not yet commercialized, has possible application in the desalting of brackish water and seawater,[24] for which pilot-plant studies have been made.   The principle is simple: a highly selective membrane is used between pure water and brine. Only the water may pass through, and normally will do so in the direction water to brine (osmosis).   This diffusive flow of solvent can be prevented by a pressure difference in the direction brine to water equal to the equilibrium osmotic pressure (in the case of seawater about 350 psi).   By superimposing a still larger pressure difference, the water flow is reversed to the direction brine to water, and the brine is separated. The expected advantage is the low energy cost for the separation, since latent heat of

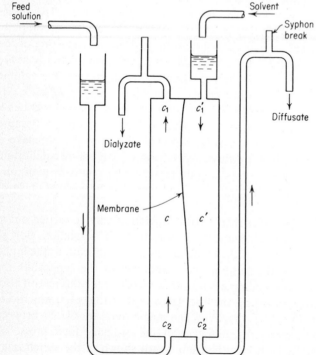

Fig. 14.7   Continuous, counter-current dialysis.

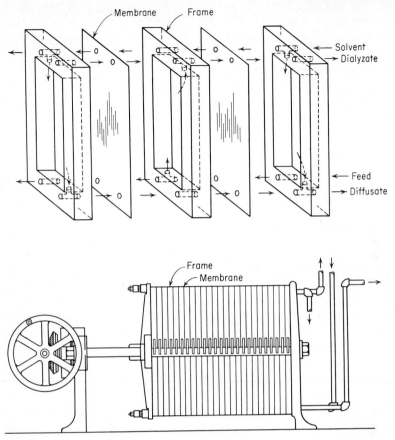

Fig. 14.8 *Filter-press-type dialyzer, Brosites Machine Co. [U.S. Patent 2,399,471 (1946).]*

neither vaporization nor freezing is involved.   The membranes used are usually of either cellulose acetate, especially cast from solution, or other polymeric materials. Among the difficulties are the required membrane strength, membrane life, and the fact that water transfer causes the concentration of salt to increase at the surface of the brine side of the membrane (a sort of polarization effect), thus increasing the osmotic pressure which must be overcome.[38]

Electrodialysis[43]

When electrolytic crystalline substances are to be separated from colloids in solution by dialysis methods, the rate of removal of the ions can be considerably increased by imposing an electromotive force across the membrane, as in Fig. 14.9.   Here the solution to be dialyzed is placed in the central compartment, separated from the anode and cathode compartments by the semipermeable membrane.   The ions then move

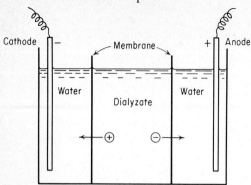

Fig. 14.9   *Electrodialysis.*

through the membrane toward the electrodes much more rapidly than in ordinary dialysis.   In practice two difficulties arise.   The first is due to the electroosmotic transfer of water through the membranes, usually from the anode to the cathode compartments, which not only dilutes the dialyzate but also carries the ions back into the central compartment.   The second is due to the tendency of the membranes to assume an electric charge on each face, positive on that side facing the cathode, negative on the side facing the anode.   The inner face of the membrane nearest the cathode then tends to accumulate hydroxyl ions, which give an alkaline reaction, while the inner face of the membrane nearest the anode tends to give an acid reaction. This may bring about undesirable effects such as coagulation or precipitation of many colloids.   Electrodialysis is nevertheless used extensively in biological-solution separations.

If the membrane nearest the cathode is permeable only to cations but impermeable to anions, and if the other membrane is permeable to anions but not to cations, it is possible to remove the ions from an electrolytic solution efficiently, since the backward flow of ions then ceases.   Membranes are available, made from ion-exchange resins, which are nearly perfectly semipermeable.[13]   Thus, a cation-exchange resin membrane exchanges cations and is permeable to these but will offer considerable resistance to the passage of anions.   Similarly, an anion-exchange resin membrane is preferentially permeable to anions.   Full-scale industrial processes of demineralization by this operation include treatment of brackish water[37] and removal of salts from whey; many others have been proposed.   Equipment is usually arranged with the membranes alternating in stacks of a variety of designs.[8,25,31]

Pervaporation

In this case the membrane is placed between a liquid solution of volatile components to be separated and a vapor phase.   Owing to the different rates of permeation of the liquid components through the membrane, the vapor issuing from the downstream face of the membrane is of different composition from the liquid.   A permanent gas may also be used to carry the vapor away.   The enrichment produced is different from that in ordinary distillation, and solutions which are usually azeotropic are effectively separable.[3,20]   Other separations difficult by distillation, such as that of the xylene isomers, have also been made.[30]   No industrial applications are known.

Gas permeation

Selective permeation through membranes can also be used for separating gas mixtures. In the case of the helium-hydrocarbon mixtures of natural gas, for example, silica or glass is permeable only to the helium, and this could be the basis of separation of helium from the mixture, although the rate is very slow.   Membranes of fluoro-carbons are very selective in this system, although not as completely so as silica, and permit much higher rates.[39]   The process is not yet in commercial use.

Gaseous diffusion

We have seen [Eq. (4.19)] that if a pure gas flows through a diaphragm or barrier containing small holes (whose diameter is of the order of one-tenth the mean free path of the molecules) under conditions of small pressure drop, the rate of flow is inversely proportional to the square root of the molecular weight of the gas and to the drop in pressure across the barrier.   If the gas is a binary mixture of components of different molecular weight, the relative rates of flow of the components through the barrier will be different, and a separation becomes possible.

Since the diffused gas may still not be enriched appreciably in comparison with the feed by one such passage, it may be sent to another barrier or stage; additional stages may then be used for still further enrichment, thus leading to a cascade of stages, as in Fig. 14.10.   Similarly the undiffused gas from any stage may be recycled to the preceding stage for further treatment, and the cascade develops the usual "enriching" and "stripping" sections on either side of the point of introducing the feed.   Since the quantity of gas passing forward toward either product becomes less with each stage, the size of the stage may be progressively reduced in passing from the feed to the products.   Alternatively, instead of very large stages near the center of the cascade, a large number of small units may be operated in parallel, as shown in the figure.   Since, however, all the units operating in parallel bring about identical composition changes, together they affect the enrichment of only one stage, so that the arrangement of Fig. 14.10 is considered as containing only five stages.   It is further characteristic of the gas-diffusion cascade that the gas must be compressed between stages, and the heat developed by the compression must be removed by a cooler, as shown in the figure.

The work of compression, the size and expense of constructing and operating the cascade, and the engineering problems associated with making adequate barriers make gas diffusion useful as a separation method only in cases where other, more conven-tional methods are unusually difficult or impossible.   This may be the case especially in the separation of isotopes of the elements.   The conventional operations described in the earlier chapters of this book depend essentially on differences in the chemical properties of compounds which lead to their unequal distribution between immiscible phases.   Two compounds which differ only because an element in one is replaced by

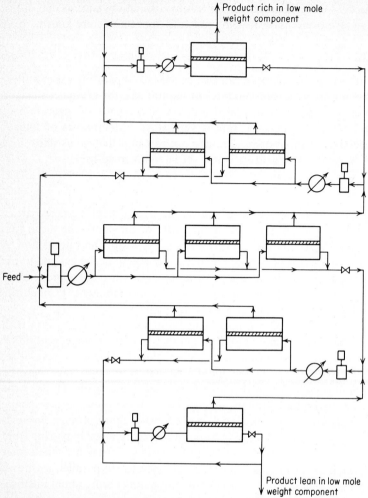

Fig. 14.10 *A five-stage gas-diffusion cascade.*

its isotope in the other will frequently show such small differences in their distribution that the conventional methods become impractical.

Such is the case for separation of the isotopes of uranium, U^{235} and U^{238}, and the gas-diffusion plants for separating the gaseous uranium hexafluorides are examples of the large-scale application of this operation. The compounds $U^{235}F_6$ and $U^{238}F_6$ have molecular weights 349 and 352, respectively, so that the differential enrichment per stage is very small. For a feed made from natural uranium and containing 0.71 percent $U^{235}F_6$ to be separated into products containing 99 and 0.1 percent $U^{235}F_6$, roughly 4,000 stages are used. For each mole of $U^{235}F_6$-rich product withdrawn, some 70,000,000 moles of gas are recycled between the stages, which requires enormous power for pumps and prodigious amounts of cooling water. The requirements for the porous barrier are equally extraordinary: it must contain tremendous numbers of holes of diameters measured in hundredths of microns, be able to withstand a difference in pressure on either side of roughly 1 atm, be chemically indifferent to the gas, and be capable of mass production in quantities that are most conveniently measured in acres.

THERMAL DIFFUSION

If two reservoirs containing a gas mixture are connected by a tube and maintained at different temperatures, it is found that the heavier molecules concentrate in the cooler reservoir, while the lighter molecules concentrate in the warmer.[14]   If the molecules are of equal masses, those of smaller diameter tend to concentrate in the region of higher temperature.   This movement under an imposed temperature gradient is known as thermal diffusion, and the effect can be multiplied by using the apparatus first described by Clusius and Dickel,[7] shown schematically in Fig. 14.11.   Natural convention currents develop in the annular space as shown, owing to the change in gas density with temperature, and these, combined with the tendency to separate by thermal diffusion in the horizontal direction, provide an arrangement which may be equivalent to many stages.   In a well-designed column, the height of a transfer unit may be only a few centimeters.   Even so, a cascade of columns in the general arrangement of Fig. 14.10 would be required for large degrees of separation.   The cold wall of the column would ordinarily be kept at the lowest possible temperature provided by the available cooling water, and a hot-wall temperature of 600 to 900°F would be preferred.[2]   The heat requirements are very large, and the process can be considered practically applicable only to very difficult isotope separations.   For example, commercial-scale separation of the very rare He^3 from He^4 is carried out to provide He^3 for scientific work.

The thermal-diffusion phenomenon is also known to occur in liquid solutions, where it is sometimes called the *Soret effect.*

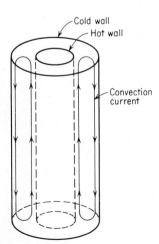

Cold wall
Hot wall
Convection current

Fig. 14.11   *Thermal-diffusion column.*[2]   (*Courtesy of The American Institute of Chemical Engineers.*)

REFERENCES

1. Anon.: *Chem. Eng.*, **71**, Aug. 17, 72 (1964).
2. Benedict, M.: *Chem. Eng. Progr.*, **43**, 41 (1947).
3. Binning, R. C., R. J. Lee, J. Jennings, and E. C. Martin: *Ind. Eng. Chem.*, **53**, 45 (1961).
4. Brooks, M. S., and K. Kennedy: "Ultrapurification of Semiconductor Materials," The Macmillan Company, New York, 1962.
5. Brunner, C. A., and D. G. Stephan: *Ind. Eng. Chem.*, **57**(5), 40 (1965).
6. Ciborowski, J., and S. Wronski: *Chem. Eng. Sci.*, **17**, 481 (1962); *Intern. Chem. Eng.*, **2**, 105 (1962).
7. Clusius, K., and G. Dickel: *Z. Physik. Chem.*, **B44**, 397 (1939).
8. Cohan, H. J.: *Chem. Eng. Progr.*, **57**(2), 72 (1961).
9. Egan, C. J., and R. V. Luthy: *Ind. Eng. Chem.*, **47**, 250 (1955).
10. Findlay, R. A.: in H. M. Schoen (ed.), "New Chemical Engineering Separation Techniques," p. 257, Interscience Publishers, Inc., New York, 1962.
11. Findlay, R. D., and D. L. McKay: *Chem. Eng. Progr. Symp. Ser.*, **55**(25), 163 (1959).
12. Findlay, R. A., and J. A. Weedman: "Separation and Purification by Crystallization," *Advan. Petrol. Chem. Refining*, **1**, 118 (1958).
13. Friedlander, H. Z., and R. N. Rickles: *Chem. Eng.*, **73**, Feb. 28, 111; Mar. 28, 121; Apr. 25, 163; May 23, 153; June 6, 145; June 20, 217 (1966).
14. Grew, K. E., and T. L. Ibbs: "Thermal Diffusion in Gases," Cambridge University Press, London, 1952.
15. Grieves, R. B., C. J. Crandall, and R. K. Wood: *Intern. J. Air Water Pollution*, **8**, 501 (1964).
16. Grove, C. S., R. V. Jelinek, and H. M. Schoen: in T. B. Drew, J. W. Hoopes, Jr., and T. Vermeulen (eds.), "Advances in Chemical Engineering," vol. 3, p. 1, Academic Press Inc., New York, 1962.
17. Haas, P. A., and H. F. Johnson: *AIChE J.*, **11**, 319 (1965).
18. Hagan, M.: "Clathrate Inclusion Compounds," Reinhold Publishing Corporation, New York, 1962.
19. Hoppe, A., and H. Franz: *Petrol. Refiner*, **36**(5), 221 (1957).
20. Kammermeyer, K., and D. H. Hagerbaumer: *AIChE J.*, **1**, 215 (1955).
21. Knox, W. G., M. Hess, G. E. Jones, and H. B. Smith: *Chem. Eng. Progr.*, **57**(2), 66 (1961).
22. Lawson, W. D., and S. Nielsen: in H. M. Schoen (ed.), "New Chemical Engineering Separation Techniques," p. 183, Interscience Publishers, Inc., New York, 1962.
23. Li, N. N., R. B. Long, and E. J. Henley: *Ind. Eng. Chem.*, **57**(3), 18 (1965).
24. Loeb, S., and S. Sourirajan: *UCLA Rept.*, **60–60** (1960); **61–42** (1961).
25. Mason, E. A., and T. A. Kirkham: *Chem. Eng. Progr. Symp. Ser.*, **55**(24), 173 (1959).
26. Marwil, S. J., and S. J. Kolner: *Chem. Eng. Progr.*, **59**(2), 60 (1963).
27. Matz, G.: *Chem.-Ing.-Tech.*, **20**, 319 (1950).
28. Matz, G.: *Wärme*, **68**, 33 (1961); **69**, 127 (1963); Symposium on Zone Melting and Column Crystallization, Karlsruhe, June, 1963, p. 345.
29. McKay, D. L., et al.: *Chem. Eng. Progr.*, **61**(11), 99 (1965); *Ind. Eng. Chem.*, **52**, 197 (1960).
30. Michaels, A. S., R. F. Baddour, H. J. Bixler, and C. Y. Choo: *Ind. Eng. Chem. Process Design Develop.*, **1**, 14 (1962).
31. Mintz, M. S.: *Ind. Eng. Chem.*, **55**(6), 18 (1963).
32. Pfann, W. G.: "Zone Melting," John Wiley & Sons, Inc., New York, 1956.
33. Radzitzky, P. de, and J. Hanotier: *Ind. Eng. Chem. Process Design Develop.*, **1**, 10 (1962).
34. Rickles, R. N.: *Ind. Eng. Chem.*, **58**(6), 19 (1966).
35. Rubin, E., and E. L. Gaden, Jr.: in H. M. Schoen (ed.), "New Chemical Engineering Separation Techniques," p. 319, Interscience Publishers, Inc., New York, 1962.
36. Schnepf, R. W., E. L. Gaden, Jr., E. Y. Microcznik, and E. Schonfeld: *Chem. Eng. Progr.*, **55**(5), 42 (1959).

37. Shaffer, L. H., and M. S. Mintz: in K. S. Spiegler (ed.), "Principles of Desalination," Academic Press Inc., New York, 1966.

38. Sherwood, T. K., P. L. T. Brian, and R. E. Fischer: *Ind. Eng. Chem. Fundamentals*, **4,** 113 (1965).

39. Stern, S. A., T. F. Sinclair, P. J. Garies, N. P. Vahldieck, and P. H. Mohr: *Ind. Eng. Chem.*, **57**(2), 49 (1965).

40. Turwiner, S. B.: "Diffusional Membrane Technology," Reinhold Publishing Corporation, New York, 1962.

41. Turwiner, S. B., and J. R. Smith: "Extractive Metallurgy of Copper and Cobalt," Interscience Publishers, Inc., New York, 1961.

42. Volrath, H. B.: *Chem. Met. Eng.*, **43,** 303 (1936).

43. Wilson, J. R.: "Demineralization by Electrodialysis," Butterworth Scientific Publications, London, 1960.

INDEX

INDEX